WORKS OF KĀLIDĀSA

WORKS OF KĀLIDĀSA

—— *THREE PLAYS* ——

◆ Abhijñāna Śākuntalam
◆ Vikramorvaśiyam ◆ Mālavikāgnimitram

Edited with an Exhaustive Introduction, Translation and Critical and Explanatory Notes by

C.R. DEVADHAR

VOLUME I

MOTILAL BANARSIDASS PUBLISHERS
PRIVATE LIMITED ● DELHI

10th Reprint: Delhi, 2015
First Edition: Delhi, 1996

ISBN: 978-81-208-0026-6 (Vol. I)

MOTILAL BANARSIDASS
41 U.A. Bungalow Road, Jawahar Nagar, Delhi 110 007
8 Mahalaxmi Chamber, 22 Bhulabhai Desai Road, Mumbai 400 026
203 Royapettah High Road, Mylapore, Chennai 600 004
236, 9th Main III Block, Jayanagar, Bangaluru 560 011
8 Camac Street, Kolkata 700 017
Ashok Rajpath, Patna 800 004
Chowk, Varanasi 221 001

Printed in India

by RP Jain at NAB Printing Unit,
A-44, Naraina Industrial Area, Phase I, New Delhi–110028
and published by JP Jain for Motilal Banarsidass Publishers (P) Ltd,
41 U.A. Bungalow Road, Jawahar Nagar, Delhi-110007

PUBLISHER'S NOTE

The best productions of the Indian drama are nearly a dozen in number, and date from a period from about the beginning of the fifth to the end of the eighth century A.D., embracing something like four hundred years. These plays are the compositions of the great dramatists Kālidāsa and Bhavabhūti, or have come down under the names of the royal patrons Śūdraka and Śrīharṣa, to whom their real authors attributed them.

The greatest of all is Kālidāsa, already known to us as the author of several of the best Kāvyas. Three of his plays have been preserved, *Abhijñāna Śākuntalam*, *Vikramorvaśīyam* and *Mālavikāgnimitram.* The richness of creative fancy which he displays in these, and his skill in the expression of tender feeling, assign him a unique place among the dramatists of the world. The harmony of the poetic sentiment is nowhere disturbed by anything violent or terrifying. Every passion is softened without being enfeebled. The ardour of love never goes beyond aesthetic bounds; it never maddens to wild jealousy or hate. The torments of sorrow are toned down to a profound and touching melancholy.

We have collected in this volume, the representatives of the romantic drama of India, *Abhijñāna Śākuntalam* and *Vikramorvaśīyam*, dealing with the love-adventures of two famous kings of ancient epic legend. *Mālavikāgnimitra*, on the other hand, is a story of contemporary love and fancy.

CONTENTS

अभिज्ञानशाकुन्तलम्

ABHIJÑĀNA-ŚĀKUNTALA

OF

KĀLIDĀSA

INTRODUCTION

Kālidāsa, his date, life and works.

Howsoever overlaid with fantasies or encrusted with a mass of isolated events separated in time and place, a widely circulated literary tradition contains within itself a germ of historical truth and can be set aside on pain of doing serious harm to that truth. Thus it is with king Vikramāditya of Ujjain, the liberal patron of learning and arts, of whom the great poet Kālidāsa was a contemporary. This tradition forms the starting point and the basis of the numerous theories regarding the age of Kālidāsa. Of these two rival theories may here be stated as those deserving of consideration. According to one held by most European scholars, the Vikramāditya of the tradition is no other than the Gupta king Candragupta II who assumed the title of Vikramāditya and succeeded his father Samudragupta 375 A.D. and made Ujjain his capital. Vincent Smith in his early history of India (P. 304, foot-note) expresses the view that the earlier works of Kālidāsa were composed before 413 A. D. during the regime of Candragupta and his later works were written under Kumārgupta I (413 A. D. to 455 A. D.) and that possibly his literary career extended even into the reign of Skandagupta (453 A. D. to 480 A. D.).

Some are inclined to suggest from the reference to the conquest of the Huns by Raghu in his Digvijaya, that Kālidāsa must have lived after the victory of Skandagupta over the Huns half a century later than the date suggested. But the evidence has no probative value. "There is nothing to indicate any reference to reality in this account of the exploits of a king of long ago, and if Kālidāsa had lived in the reign of Skandagupta when the fortune of the royal house was evidently tottering to a fall, it would be difficult to understand the calm contentment with the established order which marks all his works."

The other view held by many Indian scholars puts Kālidāsa in the first century before our era, and makes him a contemporary and a protege of King Vikramāditya the founder of the Saṁvat Era—57 B.C. That there is nothing implausible in the assumption is clear when on the strong testimony of Patañjali's Mahābhāṣya it has been possible to put back the beginnings of court poetry in general by a few centuries of the Christian Era. And "Epigraphy not merely confirms the evidence of the Mahābhāṣya that artificial poetry originated before the commencement of our era, but shows that that poetry continued to be cultivated throughout the succeeding centuries." Already in the days of Kaniṣka (78 A.D.) Aśvaghoṣa wrote his Buddhacarita in the artificial style and called it a Mahākāvya.

In connexion with this writer it is interesting to observe that there is a striking resemblance between his poetry and the poetry of Kālidāsa. Not only is there a close parallelism between a few isolated passages and descriptions, but between ideas and expressions fairly distributed over the poem. As Prof. R. N. Apte has observed these close resemblances warrant the conclusion that "one of the poets is using the other." It must be remembered that Aśvaghoṣa is a philosopher first and a poet afterwards; while Kālidāsa is an original poet. The probability, therefore, is that Aśvaghoṣa is the borrower and Kālidāsa his original. Cowell's theory of Kālidāsa's indebtedness to Aśvaghoṣa rests upon the view that Kālidāsa belongs to the Gupta period. The hollowness of this view, has, however, been shown by Prof. Shembavnekar in an article on 'the Date of Kālidāsa' contributed to "the Journal of the University of Bombay" (Vol. I, Part VI, pp. 232-246) who points out that the Gupta theory is based on the assumption that Chandragupta II was the first monarch who bore the name Vikramāditya, whereas on the testimony of the Rajput Chronicles and the Kathāsaritsāgara the first king to bear that appellation was King Vikramāditya of the Paramāra dynasty, the hero of countless legends, the ruler of Ujjayinī in Kālidāsa's day. It is held by many that the title 'Vikramorvaśīya' is chosen by the poet in order to glorify and immortalize his patron's name. According to Kathāsaritsāgara the father of Vikramāditya was Mahendrāditya. It is curious to note that the word Mahendra as an epithet of Indra is repeated by the poet no less than fourteen times in the play and in one place it is particularly significant to find the names of the father and son linked up : (दिष्ट्या महेंद्रोपकार्यापैन विक्रममहिम्ना वर्धते भवान् ।) It is possible, as Prof. Shembavnekar suggests, that the play was written at the time of the intended retirement of Mahendra from active life, and the coronation of Vikrama as king (Kathāsaritsāgara XVIII. 59-60). The last act of the play, therefore, where prince Āyus is installed as the young king is but a poetic reflex of the actual course of events of the times.

There is nothing in the arguments adduced by European scholars which is repugnant to this theory that Kālidāsa lived in the 1st century before our era at the court of King Vikrama of Ujjayinī who founded the Saṁvat era. Prof. Keith's view that the conclusive evidence displayed in the works preserved to us of elaborate training in all the learning available to a Brahmin student of the Gupta era from the science of politics to astrology and the Kāmasūtra....everything points to his flourishing in the time of Gupta glory" is only a dogmatic assertion. With regard to the astronomical terms, such as the names of the signs of the Solar Zodiac which are supposed to be of Greek origin and on which European critics lay so much emphasis, it has already been proved by scholars like S. P. Pandit, R. N. Apte, that there is nothing to show that they were unknown to the people of India a few centuries before the Christian Era. While the occurrence of un-Pāṇinian expressions and grammatical forms such as पातयां प्रथममास;प्रभ्रंशयां यो नहुषं चकार, दाश्वान् कामयान, in Kālidāsa can be satisfactorily explained only on the assumption that he belonged to a time when the Pāṇinian grammar had not obtained a complete vogue.

The foregoing discussion is enough to justify the truth and the vitality of the age-long tradition that the poet belongs to the days of the glorious King Vikramāditya of Ujjayinī—the founder of the Saṁvat era (57 B. C.).

With regard to the external details of the poet's life, we know next to nothing; the numerous legends told about him are but empty figments, and only bear testimony to the greatness and extreme popularity of the poet in the land of his birth. "The truly great stand upon no middle ledge; they are either famous or unknown." But Kālidāsa is both famous and unknown. We look in vain in his works for knowledge about the facts of his life. The impression that we gather about him from them is that of a man, deeply learned in literature and philosophy and other traditional lore of the times, and more deeply learned in the book of nature. Ujjayinī was the city of his heart and he is delighted to sing of her glories and of the romantic loves of her maidens. He sings of this Gem of Avantī, rich with the storied legends of Udayana and the consecrated past, this radiant bit of heaven, with her flower-sweet balconies, and black-eyed maidens; of the dread shrine of Śiva, Mahākāla, of her rich gardens and lotus-lakes that send their fugitive sweetness through the dark; and his fondness for the city is so evident in his loving and lingering description of her varied charms that one might legitimately conclude that the poet must have spent at least a part of his life in this city. Further he was a widely-travelled man and was a keen observer of nature—not only of her sublime and wild aspects, but also of her mild and minute manifestations. "Rarely has a man walked our earth who observed the phenomena of living nature as accurately as he, though his accuracy was of course that of a poet, not that of the scientist."

He was essentially an eclectic in his religion and philosophy for if the Kumārasaṁbhava is distinctly Śivaistic, the Raghuvaṁśa is no less distinctly Viṣṇuite in tendency ; while Vedāntic monism or Sāṁkhya dualism, or the active devotion of Yoga equally engaged his regard ; so that, as Ryder says, "Kālidāsa moved among the jarring sects with sympathy for all, fanaticism for none." A pleasing trait of his personality is his modesty which Coleridge recognises as a sure sign of great genius. Above all, his writings are coloured with the suffusion of a charmed equanimity and give the impression of a man who walked the earth with a serene and god-like tread, with mind and senses keenly responsive to every form of beauty, and accepting life and the good things it offers in a spirit of sublime acquiescence.

Of his seven works which have come down to us, three are dramas, two epics, one a lyrical piece and one a descriptive poem. It is possible to fix the chronology of his dramas, the Mālavikāgnimitra being the composition of his salad days, the Vikramorvaśīya coming next, and the Śākuntala composed when he was in the prime of his manhood. There can be no reasonable doubt that the Ṛtusaṁhāra was a juvenile piece ; while with regard to the two epics Raghuvaṁśa and Kumārasaṁbhava, opinions differ, for whereas the introductory stanzas of the Raghu suggest that it was written before Kumāra, the abrupt and undignified ending of it suggests that the hand that wrote it was cold before it was finished ; but then we have to remember the tradition that in its original form it consisted of twenty-five cantos, of which only nineteen have come down to us. In general it would be only reasonable to assume that the great works on which his fame chiefly rests—the Śākuntala, the Raghuvaṁśa, the Kumārasaṁbhava and the Meghadūta—belong to a period of his life when his genius had attained to the fullest maturity of its powers.

The Story of Śākuntala in the Mahābhārata.

We shall now proceed to give the original story in full in order to realise how wonderfully baser metal is transmuted into gold by passing through the crucible of the poet's imagination.

Once upon a time that strong-armed king accompanied by a large army entered a thick wood: There he chased various beasts and killed them by the hundred. Then pursuing a deer, he came to a beautiful hermitage on the banks of the river Mālinī. He left his army on the skirt of that tranquil resort, and laying aside the insignia of royalty, entered the place alone, and sought the sage Kaṇva ; but finding no one there he cried aloud " Who is there ? " until the forest resounded with his cry. Hearing his voice, a beautiful maiden, dressed in hermit's garb came out and hailed him with words of welcome. On being asked his purpose he told her that he had come to pay reverence to the holy saint Kaṇva. Did she know where he had gone ?

Śakuntalā said, " My blessed father is gone to gather fruits in the forest. Please wai awhile : you shall see him when he returns."

Then, in the absence of the sage, the king seeing this lovely maiden of the fair hips and charming smiles, shining in her radiant beauty and youth, and her penance and self-restraint, said to her, " Who are you ? Whose are you lovely maid ? Why have you come to the forest ? You stole my heart at the first glance. I wish to know more of you. Lovely maid answer me."

Thus asked the maiden smiling said in her sweet voice, "O Duṣyanta, I am the daughter of the sage Kaṇva, the high-souled, austere, and self possessed saint."

Duṣyanta said, "But he is chaste, gentle maid, pure and holy in the world's regard. Even virtue may swerve from its course, but he would never swerve from his hard vow. How were you born his daughter, for you are so fair? I am filled with doubt about this. Pray answer me."

She then told him the story of her birth as she had heard it from the saint. Once, Indra, afraid of the austerities of the sage Viśvāmitra, sent the nymph Menakā to tempt him. She went to the sage and made reverence to him, and while she was sportively moving about the hermitage her garment was carried away by the wind; the sage was disturbed and called her to him. They stayed together for a long time and a daughter was born of the union. Menakā deserted her on the banks of the Mālinī and returned to Indra's court. The child was cared for by Śakuntas (birds) and hence was called Śakuntalā. The saint found her there and reared her up as his foster-child.

Then Duṣyanta said, "So you are a princess, auspicious maiden; be my loving bride. Tell me what I may do for you. Let the whole of my realm be yours today; be mine by rites of Gāndharva marriage; become my wife, sweet maid."

Śakuntalā answered, "Promise me truly what I ask you in secret. If the son that will be born to me becomes king after you, then, O Duṣyanta, I will marry you."

So be it," the king said without thinking and added "O my bride of the charming smile, I will take you to my city." He, then, married her duly according to the Gāndharva rite and dwelt with her. Then on the day of parting, he comforted her and repeatedly promised her that he would send a large army to bring his sweet smiling bride to his capital.

Having thus promised her, the king returned to his capital, his mind filled with thoughts of the sage Kaṇva, and wondering what he might do on hearing the news. Sometime after he had left, Kaṇva came back to the hermitage, and Śakuntalā durst not approach him for shame. But the great saint knew it through his divine vision and he was pleased and said, "Dear child, that you lived secretly with a man, forgetting me, is as I see it, not against the law; for the Gāndharva form of marriage is declared to be the best for a Kṣatriya, when both love one another, and no consecration by holy chants is deemed necessary. Duṣyanta is the best among the men, noble and law-abiding; and since you have found a loving husband, you shall give birth to a noble son, mighty in the world."

Śakuntalā then begged of the sage to think kindly of Duṣyanta, her husband.

She gave birth to a boy of unmeasured powers in the hermitage; his hands were marked with the quoit, and he quickly grew to be a splendid boy. When he was only six years old he rode on the back of lions, tigers and bears near about the hermitage and tamed them and sported with them; so that they gave him the name 'Sarvadamana' the 'All-tamer.' Then seeing the child and his more than human deeds, Kaṇva said that it was time the child was consecrated as Yuvaraja and calling to him his pupils he bade them take Śakuntalā and her boy to her husband's home. For people do not like a married woman to stay long among her relatives, as it is against the law, and destroys their character and reputation.

They then set out with Śakuntalā and her son for Hastināpura, and drawing near the king who instantly recognised her, they led her into his presence. She bowed to him and said, " This is your son, O king, install him as Yuvarāja, even as you promised before, when we met."

Hearing those words, the king, although he remembered everything, said, " I know not whose you are, you vile hermit-woman ; I do not remember to have wedded you for duty, pleasure or wealth. Stay or leave as you choose ; do what you like."

Having heard those words Śakuntalā was nigh fainting for shame and grief and stood motionless like a pillar. Her eyes became red with grief and anger ; her lips quivered, and she looked obliquely at the king seeming to consume him with her glances. Concealing her feelings and controlling her anger she held in check the magic power that her penance had given her. She thought for a while and looked at her husband in rage and grief, and said passionately to him, " How do you say " I do not know " like any ordinary person when you know everything, O king ? "

" I do not remember the son born of you, O Śakuntalā. Women are ever such liars. Who will believe your words ? Are you not ashamed to talk to me such incredible things ? Go, you vile hermit-woman."

Śakuntalā made answer, "King, remember truth is the highest divinity ; do not break your promise. But if you cling to a lie and believe not your own self, I must go away. There is no union with a man like you. Even without you my son shall protect the foursquare earth adorned with the lofty mountains."

So saying, Śakuntalā started, when a bodiless voice spoke to Duṣyanta, " Take your child, Duṣyanta, do not scorn your wife Śakuntalā. You are indeed the father of her boy. Śakuntalā tells the truth." Having heard thus, the king joyfully said to his chaplain and ministers : " Hear these words of the angels. For if I were to receive my son, solely relying on her words, he would be suspected by the people, he would not be pure."

Then he received the boy and lovingly embraced him. He then honoured his wife and comforting her, said, "Our marriage was a secret one ; so to save your reputation, I hesitated thus, my Queen ; for the people would have thought that it was a woman's passion that brought you to me. I gladly forgive you the harsh words which in an excess of passion you spoke to me, because you love me." Then Duṣyanta gave the name 'Bharata' to Śakuntalā's son, and made him crown prince (Yuvarāja).

The changes introduced by the poet.

Such is the story in its original form set forth with a considerable concision of all extraneous elements. Into the dry bones of this bare and unromantic tale, the poet has breathed the life of poetry and lifted it from a story of sordid passion into one of the most moving and ideal of loves. Into this matrix of the old the poet's dramatic imagination has fitted in such new elements, transforming, adding and reshaping it as to sublimate it into the very essence of poetry.

The fatal flaw in the original story is the rejection of Śakuntalā by Duṣyanta for reasons which are anything but convincing. They give him the character of a rake who would fain hide the folly of his youth, and degrade his love into lust, rank and disgusting—a mere diversion in the enforced separation from his harem-love. Thus the Duṣyanta of the epic is decidedly contemptible.

So the first great change which the poet introduces into the story is the curse of Durvāsas which clouds the king's memory—a supernatural element whose influence is of a compulsive kind and we feel it has removed the king's capacity or responsibility for dealing with the situation; so that what is base and unconscionable betrayal of trustful innocence becomes only a tragic error involving no conscious breach of right—but on the other hand accompanied by a full conviction of right. We thus feel that "Men fight blindly in the dark 'themselves the authors of their proper woe,' and the power that works through them makes them the instrument of a design not their own" This influence of the supernatural thus saves the king from moral responsibility in his repudiation of Śakuntalā. But the recognition-ring which Duṣyanta gave to Śakuntalā might have saved the situation; so the play of chance which has such an appreciable influence at the most critical point in the action. It is just an accident that Śakuntalā drops her ring in the holy water at Śakrāvatāra, before that fatal moment of her encounter with the king. The curse, however, is so modified as to exert its baneful influence for a time only until the king sees the ring—so miraculously recovered from the maw of a carp which a fisherman opened. Here perhaps—in the matter of the curse and its modification which to the Indian mind are matters of frequent occurrence—a foreigner will have to exercise what Coleridge happily describes as "that willing suspension of disbelief which constitutes poetic faith": although it must be remembered that "the poet has so delicately managed the matter as not to shock even a Modern and Western reader with a feeling of strong improbability."

Śakuntalā is certainly charming in the epic; she is direct in her simplicity and fearful innocence. So also is the king's proposal of marriage a direct one—he is not troubled by those doubts by which a lover's heart is assailed. Straightway they go to the job, Śakuntalā feels no qualms in telling the king the story of her birth; and like practically minded parents who arrange the dowries and the destinies of their children, she bargains with the king for the destiny of her offspring and only after she has secured the promise does she yield to his importunities. How drab, how prosaic is this tale of the wooing and winning of the bride! And how wonderfully has the poet transfused it into the very quintessence of romance and poetry! Their meeting, the story of her birth, the rapid growth of a mutual passion, the ecstasy of his adoration, the rapturous confession of their mutual love, and the final winning—how the minds of both are followed through passion, doubt, despair to exaltation and intense love. And yet "the ardour of love is not allowed to go beyond aesthetic bounds." The story of Śakuntalā's birth is most skilfully woven into the conversation of the king with her two friends, and the promise as to Śakuntalā's future destiny comes spontaneously from the king and is not extracted from him as the condition of their union. And both these have been managed with absolute delicacy and grace, Śakuntalā with a maiden's exquisite modesty and shyness playing the part of an interested listener.

Thirdly Śakuntalā leaves her forest-home for the palace before her son is born; and lastly the final union takes place after a long period of suffering and remorse.

Besides these changes, the poet has added largely from his imagination some very beautiful scenes and characters. As Ryder points out "only acts one and five, with a part of Act VII rest upon the ancient text, while acts two, three, four and six with most of seven, are a creation of the poet." It is obvious that a drama cannot be successfully written with such a meagre number of characters as in the epic—Duṣyanta, Śakuntalā and Kaṇva with the small boy somewhere in the background. To these Kālidāsa has added from the hermitage, the palace and the street, and finally from the "Elysian region which is represented with vague precision in the last act."

And yet it is interesting to note how minutely the poet has utilised his sources, how many are the epic suggestions which he has incorporated into his play. These it is worth listing together "to show how keen is the eye of genius." A careful student will not fail to notice for instance that the king lays aside the insignia of royal office, that Śakuntalā appears in a bark dress, and the name Śakuntalā itself is used in a very beautiful and effective way in the recognition scene in Act VII. Kaṇva's power of divination which saved the heroine from telling herself of her union with the king, the marks of imperial birth on the hand of the child, his rough play with the wild animals which earned him his nick-name "All-tamer" these and many others have not only been preserved but utilised with very great skill and delicacy.

Construction and analysis of the plot.

As Tagore remarks there are two unions in Śākuntala and the central motif of the play is the progress from the earlier union of the first three acts with its youthful beauty and romance through an interval of separation and intense and speechless agony to the ultimate union in the Elysian regions of eternal bliss described in the last act. The play, therefore, naturally falls into three divisions each having a distinct atmosphere of its own—the first four acts constituting the first division, the fifth and sixth the second, and the seventh act the last.

For the first four acts the scene is laid in the hermitage. The poet has already in the prelude intimated that it was the time of pleasant summer, and even within the precincts of the sacred grove every tree and plant is touched by its magic fingers so that "the wild-wood bloom outglows the garden flowers." No poet had a richer and fuller sense of sensuous loveliness or a more masterly command of the resources of suggestive incidents, imagery and pictorial phrasing such as would reveal that loveliness in words. Thus along with the exquisite peace of the place, the king feels what the throbbing of his arm has intimated to him, the presence of "Beauty that takes all peace away."

Then come the maidens on the scene, with the lovely Śakuntalā in the centre, delicate as a jasmine blossom, who waters her leafy sisters and takes delight in that duty : whose dawning youth is slyly suggested by her friend remarking that it was youth that had given her bosom its lovely swell. The Kesara tree is beckoning to her with his leafy fingers as if he means to speak to her and as she approaches him she looks a lovely vine that twines about him ; her breath-taking beauty is observed by the king who remarks how " youth with all its magic charm blossoms within her blood." How lovely was the season for the union of 'the moonlight of the forest', " all flowers now, all youth, and like a bridegroom newly dressed the mango takes and holds her to his breast."

Thus as Tagore has remarked the poet " has fully painted all the blandishments, playfulness and fluttering of the intoxicating sense of youth, the struggle between deep bashfulness and strong self-expression." Nature is not something outside of man with a life-spirit and purpose of its own ; but it is a background for reflecting human emotion. This which is felicitously described as " atmospheric subjectivity " is one feature of Kālidāsa's nature poetry.

How skilfully is the king introduced to the heroine ; the bee has left the jasmine and is trying to settle on Śakuntalā's face ; she calls for help and her friend playfully suggests that she had better call on Duṣyanta, the king, whose duty it was to protect the hermitage. This gives Duṣyanta, who so long had been eagerly watching them, his cue. He enters, and Śakuntalā feels a strange flutter in her heart at sight of him. She had not known Cupid before ; and hence 'her heart was bare of armour ; she could not distrust either the sentiment of love or the character of her lover ; but there was no need to arm herself against the sentiment or to distrust the lover's character. For in the subsequent conversation between her friends and the king, it has been very artistically revealed that he was in every way worthy of her, and her friends too feel that if father Kaṇva were present he would do honour to the guest and offer him the one possession he prized most. Duṣyanta's doubts regarding her birth are stilled when urged by him Śakuntalā's friends narrate to him how she was the daughter of Viśvāmitra and Menakā and is being reared not for the religious life but for marriage with some one worthy of her. Śakuntalā in feigned anger rises to leave when Priyaṁvadā detains her saying she had promised her the watering of two trees and she could not leave before she had paid her debt ; at which the king most gallantly gives her the ring to redeem her debt. This is the fatal ring which failed Śakuntalā just at the critical moment, and whose recovery restored the king's memory. The ring episode has indeed been very skilfully woven into the texture of the play and forms a sort of an organic filament in the whole fabric.

Their conversation is disturbed by the alarm of the elephant, which very beautifully signalises the storming of the peaceful and serene forest-retreat by the importunate forces of love and the outside world.

Act II shows how the king now pines for love, which allows him no rest at night and deprives him of all his zest for the pleasures of hunting. He recounts his feelings to his unsympathetic friend, the Vidūṣaka, and gratefully receives the request of the young hermit to protect the hermitage against the attacks of the demons. Then comes a messenger from the palace requesting the king's presence at a festival there, and this gives the king the opportunity to dismiss all his retinue and the Vidūṣaka, assuring him, to prevent a scandal, that his remarks about Śakuntalā were not made in earnest

The third Act intimates to us in its introductory scene the love-stricken condition of Śakuntalā. The king has already driven off the powers of evil, and dismissed by the hermits, now seeks his love who spends those hours of midday heat with her friends on the vine-wreathed banks of the Mālinī. There she is discovered reclining on a bed of lotus-leaves, writing at her friend's suggestion a love-missive to the king. How careful is the poet to show that Śakuntalā in her maiden shame has not revealed her passion even to the friends of her bosom for long; it is only now when importuned by them that she talks of the desperate state to which she has been driven by love. Then follows a scene of ideal passion which is enshrined in syllables of imperishable fire; Śakuntalā has composed a song which breathes of the keen anguish that fills her heart, and the king who has overheard all comes on the scene and assures them of his deep devotion for the fair Śakuntalā. With rare skill, the poet makes Śakuntalā jealously remark that they should not tax the great king's courtesy—is he not separated from the fair eyes that long await his return to the palace? Upon which comes the confession of his passionate love for her. But they have heard that kings are prodigal of their love to many, Anasūyā remarks—whereupon the king assures them that in spite of many a wife in the palace courts, henceforth this dear friend of theirs shall be the chief glory of his throne. The friends now make excuses and leave and the lovers are left to themselves. How gracefully, how delicately is the love-scene drawn; "a kiss unkissed is the climax beyond which the affair does not pass." As already remarked the poet does not allow love to go beyond aesthetic bounds. The scene is ended by the arrival of Gautamī who comes to take away Śakuntalā to the hermitage.

The fourth act is full of the shadows of the coming doom. Anasūyā expresses her fears that surrounded by the bright ladies with their courtly ways, the king may not remember Śakuntalā or the hermitage. Priyaṁvadā, however, assures her that persons so noble are not changeable; what troubles her on the other hand is to know what Father Kaṇva will say when he knows of the union. Then comes the dread Durvāsas to the Āśrama. Poor Śakuntalā is far too deeply burdened to notice him. Care has already come and nested in her bosom; then like a knife on the innocent lamb falls the fierce imprecation of the choleric sage, which, however, is modified through the intercession of the agitated Priyaṃvadā. He graciously grants that although Śakuntalā shall be clean razed from her husbands memory, yet at the sight of the recognition ring the spell shall break. Happily the king has given Śakuntalā his signet-ring that the friends feel will save her; they decide to tell no one of the incident; for poor Śakuntalā ought not to be troubled; who would sprinkle boiling water on the jasmine flower and scald it?

The next scene opens in the tearful glimmer of the languid dawn, where in a very suggestive stanza a pupil of Kaṇva compares with the simultaneous rise and fall of heaven's brightest luminaries, the strange mutations of human life. Kaṇva by now has returned, and a divine voice has informed him of the marriage of Śakuntalā and her approaching maternity. He decides to send her under the escort of his trusty pupils and Gautamī to the king. And now follows the scene of leaving-taking which is drenched through and through in the heavy dew of long and living sorrow at the severence from a Paradise of love, innocence and vital memories— a Paradise which for ever vanishes from the picture. Hard of heart must he be who can read the act without mist in his eyes or catch in his voice! What tender leave-taking of the trees and plants, of the deer and peacock of the Vanajyotsnā, of the doe that is slow by the weight of her young, of the fawn, her foster-child, that would fain prevent her going and catches the end of her garment, and lastly of the friends of her girlhood and her father. What lingering farewell! Who can tear the fond parent from his beloved child! How the truth of the Prākṛt verse comes home to us चुम्बिज्जई सअहुत्तं अवरुन्धिज्जई सहस्सहुत्तम्मि ....पिओ जणो णत्थि पुनरुत्तं ॥ चुम्ब्यते शतकृत्वोऽवरुध्यते सहस्रकृत्वः। ...प्रियो जनो नास्ति पुनरुक्तम् ॥ With a mind galled and bleeding Śakuntalā finds herself between two worlds the one now lost to her, and the other dark and uncertain. The friends are already filled with apprehensions and tell Śakuntalā to show the ring in case the king is slow to recognise her, and with her father's words of consolation and advice in her ears, and with a heart heavy with grief she bids fare-well to the forest-world.

Here the lyrical element of the play reaches its climax. It is a most luminous picture of a great experience of life passed through the recreative process of expression and its pathos is profound and almost lacerating. And here again nature not only echoes the feelings of the persons and even the progress of their thought—but actively partakes of man's joys and sorrows and gives a foreboding of the approaching catastrophe.

We now come to the second division of the play. "In passing from the Fourth Act to the fifth we suddenly enter a new atmosphere"—as Tagore remarks, "from the ideal world of the hermitage we go forth to the royal court with its hard hearts, crooked ways of love-making, difficulties of union." Now the poet momentarily draws aside the curtain from the king's love affairs; we hear a woman's voice singing in an impassioned strain: it is a taunt to the king for his forgetting of Haṁsapadikā, on account of queen Vasumatī. Tagore describes it as "a small rent in the veil through which we can get an idea of the royal sin". Of course, he is judging from present day standards, imputing moral obliquity to Duṣyanta when nothing of the kind is ever intended. What he calls "the tear-strained song of a stricken-heart" is nothing more than a part of the give and take between the king and the women of the harem. It gives us a rude shock without doubt. The beauteous dream of the hermitage has already vanished. The two hermits who are escorting Śakuntalā at once feel that they have entered an altogether new world, "a house lapped in flames of fire," peopled with folk "who are unclean and manacled and fettered as slaves." By such touches as these does the poet prepare us for the crisis, for which he has now secured an effective setting.

Haṁsapadikā's song has caused a strange disturbance in Duṣyanta's soul, as if it sought something it could not find—the shadow of something dearly loved in a former and forgotten birth. And in this mood, with a heart, filled with a longing like sweet pain, he comes to face Śakuntalā and the hermits. What a fine and moving irony is there in that sweet song which tells of the effect of music, and of beauty.

The repudiation scene is one of the most masterly scenes in the whole range of literature, and we clearly feel how the avalanche is loosed and is coming inch by inch until gathering force it hurtles down with a tremendous force and crashes upon the dear head of the devoted Śakuntalā. The king denies having had anything to do with Śakuntalā, he does not recognize her when her veil is removed ; and by a most fatal chance the ring of recognition has already been lost. Thus when direct evidence (प्रत्यक्ष प्रमाण) fails the poor Śakuntalā makes the pathetic attempt of reviving his memory by verbal testimony (शाब्द प्रमाण) The irony of the king's remark श्रोतव्यं इदानीं संवृत्तम् cuts like a sharp knife, when everything fails her, with a mind torn between the pangs of despised love and the anguish of remorse, she bewails that in the innocence of her heart she should have given her honour to a man whose mouth drops honey, but whose heart is filled with poison! Śāraṅgarava has a few spars with the king, and roundly abuṣing both Duṣyanta and Śakuntalā, bids them leave. "With rare poetic insight Kālidāsa has declined to restore Śakuntalā to Kaṇva's hermitage. It was impossible for her to live in harmony with that hermitage in the way she had done before..A mighty silence was now needed, worthy of the mighty grief of the mourner."

The fifth Act with its painful and tense tragedy has strained our nerves to the utmost, and we stand in need of relief. So with a rare judgment the poet gives us at the beginning of the sixth act, a scene drawn almost raw from life, but one which is of vital importance to the play. For it describes the recovery of the ring from the maw of a carp which a fisherman had opened, and in the main act the poet describes how the king recognizes the wrong unwittingly done and of his heart-wrenching agony at loss of his beloved wife. He seeks to console himself with a portrait he had himself drawn of his love, when the jealous queen Vasumati is reported to be coming to him; but her presence would have been altogether out of place in a scene of severe penitence and tenderness, and the poet very skilfully avoids it by making the thoughtful queen give precedence to affairs of state. The minister obtains from the king the decision of a law-point involving the right of inheritance—an episode which only deepens the King's regret by reminding him of his childlessness.

The screams of the Vidūṣaka, who has been roughly handled by Mātali, awaken the king from his despair. This is necessary as Mātali explains "for bringing the king back to the realization that there are duties superior to private feeling." Indra requires his help in quelling the demons—the brood of Kālanemi.

We come to the last division of the play ; and from the gross and stifling atmosphere of the court and the capital, we escape into a divine and rarified atmosphere. What a contrast does it present with Kaṇva's hermitage. "We have there a hermit's daughter in the exuberance of youth, her two companions running over with playfulness..the bee intoxicated with perfume.." From this Eden of bliss, Śakuntalā, one of Eve's daughter, is exiled in disgrace. "But far different was the aspect of the other hermitage where Śakuntalā the mother of Bharata and the incarnation of goodness took refuge.... There a single boy fills the loving bosom of the entire forest-world ; he absorbs all the liveliness of the trees, creepers, flowers and foliage". Now as before when he was about to enter Kaṇva's Āśrama, the arm of the king throbs presaging his approaching fortune. He hears the matrons chiding the unruly boy and finds him dragging at the tousselled mane of a lion's cub. The anagnorisis is the most skilfully and delicately managed of scenes. "What fire is in the child !" the king remarks. His heart goes out to him ; then as he stretches his hand, the marks of imperial birth are revealed. And then as the matrons say to him "Is not the Śākuntala lovely"—the most wonderful and effective use of word-play ever met with in literature—the child begins to look about for his mother Śakuntalā. When at last, in despair they call him to help them with the unruly boy, they are amazed at the "Speaking likeness" between him and the child, and tell him that the child belonged to Puru's line, that he had a heavenly nymph for mother who was cruelly abandoned by her heartless husband—a very beautiful instance of the use of irony in Kālidāsa—yet all this is not enough for the king. It is only when he touches the magic amulet, and is told by the matrons that none but his father or mother can touch it with impunity, that he realises that his dearest hope has come true Then comes Śakuntalā on the scene who may be described in the words of Bhavabhūti as करुणस्य मूर्तिरथवा शरीरिणी विरहव्यथैव– "Pathos incarnate or the very pain of severence embodied ·" the heart of the loving wife is full of understanding, of forgiveness; she blames only her fate which had been fixed for her by some former transgression of hers, and under the auspices of the divine pair Śakuntalā and her boy are united to Duṣyanta; and even if "there is one Paradise lost" yet there is "another Paradise regained."

Śākuntala, its inner meaning :

Starting with Goethe's words that the Śākuntala "blends together the young year's blossoms and the fruits of its decline, that it combines heaven and earth in one, Dr. Tagore remarks that the Śākuntala according to Goethe "contains the history of a development—the development of flower into fruit, of earth into heaven, of matter into spirit." The drama "was meant for translating the whole subject from one world to another—to elevate love from the sphere of physical beauty to the eternal heaven of moral beauty." "One sudden gust of youthful impulse had in a moment given her up to Duṣyanta, but that was not the true the full winning of her; the best means of winning is by devotion, by *Tapasya*. Therefore, the poet has made the two lovers undergo a long and austere *tapasya* that they may gain each other truly, eternally." "In this drama Kalidāsa has extinguished the volcanic fire of tumultuous passion by means of the tears of the penitent heart."

Here is a poet's interpretation of a poet, and howsoever beautiful it may be, it should not blind us to its central defect —it regards the first union of the lovers as a moral lapse. There is nothing to show that the poet ever regards the lovers as sinners, nor do any of the characters in the stage so regard it. On the other hand, every one commends the union and blesses it. Love is a beautiful passion of the soul, and youth a stuff that will not endure ; do not, therefore, despise love ; cherish it, and cherish the noble, and generous impulses of youth. Ah ! but youth and love are not all ; the gods are jealous ; " like flies to wanton boys are we to the gods, they kill us for their sport." This tragic circumstance of our being is illustrated in the drama. Śakuntalā is happy and apparently secure ; but suddenly a total reverse of fortune comes upon her —the calamity descending on her from the clouds with lighting swiftness. It makes us feel that man is blind and helpless, the plaything of an inscrutable power.

Character.

As already remarked, the poet has added to the meagre number of characters in the epic tale very largely from the grove, the city and the heavenly regions. It is remarkable that with great insight the poet gives but little part to the conventional Vidūṣaka in this play than in the others ; he has absolutely very little place in so serious a play. In the Mālavikā, he plays a principal part and arranges all the intrigues ; in the Vikramorvasiya, although he plays secondary role, yet his presence contributes greatly to the humour of the play and also to the complication of the plot. In the Śākuntala, however, he sinks into utter insignificance. Yes, he knows the love-affair in the grove ; but addlepatted that he is, he believes what the king says at the moment, viz. that his love for Śakuntalā was all a joke—and never again speaks to the king about it. Here is irony—a literary expedient which Kālidāsa has very skilfully used in the play. Had he been present at the repudiation he would have spoken, and the tragedy averted. He is very cleverly dismissed on other business in Act II, as his presence would have spoilt the beautiful love idyll.

The two companions of Śakuntalā are drawn with delicate taste. How well are they differentiated, Anasūyā grave and sensible, Priyaṁvadā playful, vivacious, and yet both are equally devoted to Śakuntalā ; so also are the two pupils Śārańgarava and Śāradvata skilfully distinguished—one proud and haughty, not afraid to rebuke the king severely, and the other more reserved and calm. Kaṇva, the loving hermit, and the motherly Gautamī, too, both brimful of affection for Śakuntalā are excellent creations. While the divine pair Mārica and Aditi are wonderfully contrasted with them with their solemn majesty, and with their unwearied contemplation of the world, intervening to set it right whenever necessary with disinterested zeal. " The small boy in the last act " as Ryder remarks "has magically become an individual in Kālidāsa's hands."

The fisherman and the policemen are drawn with no less skill in the opening scene of Act VI. They are drawn ' raw from life " ; their unjust, overbearing conduct to the fisherman representing the spirit of those in office generally, who are made giddy by power.

Very grave injustice is done to Duṣyanta by representing him as a bee that ever seeks fresh honey. The fact that he had many wives in his harem, and therefore, as is natural, there are intrigues in the palace to win him and oust the rival from his affection does not necessarily show moral depravity when it is remembered that polygamy was so common in those days and is current to this day in India. Dhanamitra, the seafaring merchant was a rich man; " he must have many wives," Duṣyanta remarks. This shows that polygamy was quite an accepted fact in those days. Kālidāsa has taken very great pains to save him "from his epic shabbiness." He is a worthy hero, the ornament of the Purus, full of noble impulses, and careful to see that there is nothing in his conduct that is against the law. He is very brave and exerts himself nobly in the interest of his subjects. He is commended on all hands, by the hermits, by Kaṇva, by Mārica, the divine father of creation, and by the officers in the palace—and this is no mere flattery of the king. With scrupulous care does Kālidāsa show that he would not entertain any immoral thought about women. We have only to think of the apprehensions that filled his heart when he realised that Śakuntalā had already captured it. His intuition was infallible ; no unworthy thought would receive quarter in his mind. And it turns out that what he feared "as fire was the jewel of his desire." He relies upon the genial sense of youth. To him "love is an unerring light, and joy its own security." His later rejection of Śakuntalā also is not due to the fact that he despises her, but his fear that in accepting her whom he does not remember to have married, he would have committed an egregious sin.

And what words, will adequately describe the noblest and the loveliest of poetic creations the sweet Śakuntalā? She "dominates the whole play. She is actually on the stage in five of the acts, and her spirit pervades the other two, the second and the sixth." "So noble a union of sweetness with strength is one of the miracles of art." Bred in the hermitage, amid the plants and trees, there is an innate simplicity and purity in her character. She yields to the impulse of love, and yet with a maiden's modesty would rather suffer in silence than speak of her passion. There is struggle in her soul "between deep bashfulness and strong self-expression." She is trustful ; that gives her strength in her distress—the rigid, tearless endurance of the blows of circumstance. She is forgiving, and kind to her husband, in spite of the cruellest breach of her confidence.

Her character grows under our very eyes—from the sweet, loving girl she has been developed into "the model of a devoted wife, with her reserve, endurance of sorrow, and a life of rigid spiritual discipline." She has passed through great experiences of life—love, friendship, motherhood, most cruel humiliation and suspicion, and finally reunion with her husband. Like a flower meshed with the grey dew to the end she appears as a vision of sweetness, purity and strength.

The Title of the play.

Like the ornaments of Vasantsenā in the Mṛcchakatika, the signet ring has been used as a dominant motif in the play. In the first act Duṣyanta offers it to Śakuntalā's friend to redeem the debt she owes her ; and in the fourth act, after the curse of Durvāsas, when Anasūyā goes to appease his anger and he modifies his curse by saying that the spell shall break at the sight of some token of recognition. Priyaṃvadā tells us how the king at time of parting put the ring, engraved with his own name, in Śakuntalā's finger to remember him by ; and that will save Śakuntalā. Here Kālidāsa has most skilfully employed dramatic irony ; the well-meaning friends, with the desire to spare the feelings of Śakuntalā decide not to speak to any one of the episode of the curse, although towards the end of act IV they merely drop a hint by saying to Śakuntalā that should the king be slow to recognize her, she should show him the ring. Supposing they had explained, the tragedy of Śakuntalā's cruel rejection would well have been averted. "Our deeds are ours their ends none of our own." We know how the fatal ring fails Śakuntalā at the most critical moment in the court scene in the fifth act ; and in the opening scene of act VI we hear of its miraculous recovery from the maw of a carp-fish opened by the fisherman. At its sight, memory is revived, and Duṣyanta is now consumed with remorse. He reviles the ring ; but the Vidūṣaka consoles the king by pointing to the ring as one that shows that incredible meetings do take place. Finally in the seventh act when Śakuntalā sees the ring, the king tells her how at the sight of the ring his memory returned. He offers to put it on her finger, but Śakuntalā would not trust it; she would rather have the king wear it.

Thus it will be seen that this episode of the ring whose loss prevents the immediate recognition of Śakuntalā is very effectively conceived and woven into the texture of the play. Aptly, therefore, is the play given the name "Abhijñāna-Śākuntala."

Kālidāsa repeats himself.

If we compare the three plays of Kālidāsa, it will be seen how many incidents are repeated in the three plays; but in the Śākuntala these incidents are handled with far more perfect art. Thus the pretty idea of the king concealing himself and listening to the confidential talk of Śakuntalā and her friends is found in Act III of the Mālavikāgnimitra. When leaving Śakuntalā makes the pretext that her foot is pricked by a sharp blade of grass, and casts a stolen glance at the king; even so does Urvaśī in the Vikramorvaśīya pretend that her garment is caught in the branches to delay her going. Both express their love by letters. While Āyus has a peacock to play with, Bharata is given a clay peacock to induce him to give up his rough play with the lion's cub. The love-intrigues in the harem which figure so largely in the Vikramorsīya and Mālavikagnimitra are simply hinted at in the Śākuntala. Haṁsapadikā sings her song hinting at the king's inconstancy and queen Vasumatī in a jealous fit snatches the box of paint-brushes from Caturikā, the maid, who was taking them to the king. However, these are never brought on the stage. With true poetic insight Kālidāsa has avoided the temptation of bringing any other woman into competition with Śakuntalā.

Śākuntala, its recensions.

There is no wonder that several recensions of the play should have become current in India. Of these four are generally distinguished from one another, the Bengālī, Devanāgarī, Kāśmirī, and south Indian ; but in point of fact we need take into account only two recensions the longer one being the Bengālī, with 221 stanzas with the commentaries of Śankara and Candraśekhara, and the Devanágarī with 194 stanzas with Rāghavabhatta's commentary ; the Kāśmirī gives an introductory scene to act VII, but is no more than a combined version of these two, while the south Indian with the commentary of Kāṭayavema, closely follows the Devanāgarī. The text represented by Sir William Jone's translation as also that of Ryder is the Bengālī, and Ryder remarks "I find it hard to believe that any lesser artist could pad such a masterpiece and pad it all over, without making the fraud apparent on almost every page. The briefer version, on the other hand might easily grow out of the longer, either as an acting text, or as a schoolbook." This is also the view of Bollensen. Pischel lays stress on the more correct Prākrit of the Bengālī, but, as Keith points out, this argument from the Prākrit is not conclusive, for it may be due to the superior knowledge of the copyists in Bengal from whom the Bengālī version ultimately issued. Nothing conclusive can be said in regard to which of these recensions gives Kālidāsa's text correctly. However, the erotic passages in Act III in the Bengālī recensions are out of taste and mar the delicacy of the love-scene and as Weber points out, some of the Devanāgarī readings are distinctly better, and some of the Bengālī stanzas are mere repetitions of others found in both the versions. We are, therefore, inclined to give priority to the Devanāgarī text.

The law of inheritance.

From the VI act of the Śākuntala we get some idea of the law of inheritance prevailing in the days of Kālidāsa. The prime minister, the noble Piśuna, sends the following report of a case which he refers to the king for decision :—" A seafaring merchant named Dhanamitra has been lost in shipwreck. He dies childless, and his immense property becomes by law forfeited to the king". Now the king's reply is "As he had great riches, he must have several wives. Let inquiry be made. There may be a wife who is with child." And when he is told that one of his wives—the daughter of a merchant from Sāketa is soon to become a mother, the king decides that the child shall receive the inheritance. The unborn child has a title to his father's property.

From this passage it is clear that in the days of Kālidāsa a widow was not entitled to inherit her husband's propery. The king directs an inquiry to be made, not whether there are widows of the merchant but whether there is a child in the womb which is entitled to its father's estate. The prime minister had simply inquired if there was a living child, and not whether a child was conceived, and thus a very nice point of law has been raised. This shows the poet's acquaintance with the laws prevailing in his time, and it follows, therefore, that in his days a widow was not entitled to her husband's property, though the right of the unborn child was admitted.

The widow's right to inherit as Prof. R. N. Apte shows, was gradually recognized. " Manu, Āpastamba and Vasīṣṭha do not recognise her as heir. Narada makes provision for her maintenance. .Bṛhaspati seems to admit her right for the first time. .Śaṅkha, Likhita and Yajñavalkya also admit her right. If this is the gradual development of the right of a widow, and this right is not recognized in the case before Duṣyanta, we may place Śākuntala before Bṛhaspati and after Manu or Āpastamba." So Prof. R. N. Apte concludes, that as the probable date of Bṛhaspati is the 1st century A.D. Kālidāsa must be placed before this date—a conclusion which accords well with the date of Kālidāsa already suggested.

The law of theft.

The opening scene of the VI act is a scene of rollicking humour in Kālidāsa. The fisherman is handcuffed and led by two guards and the officer; for they find the king's signet-ring in his possession. The punishment for theft is death and already the fingers of one of the guards are itching to kill this cutpurse. Thus, it would appear, that for theft of a gem there was capital punishment in Kālidāsa's days. So also in the Vikramorvaśīya the vulture who has carried away the Saṅgamanīya jewel is spoken of as आत्मनो वधमाहर्ता विहगतस्करः। "The winged thief that courts his own death."

Prof. Apte observes: "Tracing the law of theft from the times of Manu down to those of Yājñavalkya we find the punishment for theft of a gem has gradually been reduced from death to fine". Manu and Āpastamba say that such an offender shall suffer capital punishment. Bṛhaspati recommends that a fine shall be imposed equal to the value of the property stolen, or double the amount, or the thief shall be executed to prevent the repetition of the offence. Yājñavalkya does not give any hard and fast rules, and says that capital punishment may be inflicted, but all circumstances of time, place, age and health of the offender should be taken into consideration in giving the punishment. Here again there is a gradual tendency to lighten the punishment from death in the times of Manu and Āpastamba to an option between fine and death according to circumstances in the days of Bṛhaspati. "It appears therefore, that the law of our poet's days had not reached this stage of which the representative is the smṛti of Bṛhaspati."

TEXT WITH TRANSLATION

अथ

अभिज्ञानशाकुन्तलम् ।

या सृष्टिः स्रष्टुराद्या वहति विधिहुतं या हविर्या च होत्री
ये द्वे कालं विधत्तः श्रुतिविषयगुणा या स्थिता व्याप्य विश्वम् ।
यामाहुः सर्वबीजप्रकृतिरिति यया प्राणिनः प्राणवन्तः
प्रत्यक्षाभिः प्रपन्नस्तनुभिरवतु वस्ताभिरष्टाभिरीशः ॥ १ ॥

(नान्द्यन्ते)

सूत्रधारः—(नेपथ्याभिमुखमवलोक्य ।) आर्ये, यदि नेपथ्यविधानमवसितम्, इतस्तावदागम्यताम् ।

(प्रविश्य)

नटी—अज्जउत्त, इयं म्हि । आणवेदु अज्जो को णिओओ अणुचिट्ठीअदु त्ति । आर्यपुत्र, इयमस्मि । आज्ञापयत्वार्यः को नियोगोऽनुष्ठीयतामिति ।

सूत्रधारः—आर्ये, अभिरूपभूयिष्ठा परिषदियम् । अद्य खलु कालिदासग्रथितवस्तुना नवेनाभिज्ञानशाकुन्तलाख्येन नाटकेनोपस्थातव्यमस्माभिः । तत्प्रतिपात्रमाधीयतां यत्नः ।

नटी—सुविहिदप्पओअदाए अज्जस्स ण किं पि परिहाइस्सदि ।
सुविहितप्रयोगतयार्यस्य न किमपि परिहास्यते ।

सूत्रधारः—आर्ये, कथयामि ते भूतार्थम् ।

आ परितोषाद्विदुषां न साधु मन्ये प्रयोगविज्ञानम् ।
बलवदपि शिक्षितानामात्मन्यप्रत्ययं चेतः ॥ २ ॥

ABHIJÑĀNAŚĀKUNTALA

That which is the first creation of the Creator; that which bears the offering made according to due rites; that which is the offerer; those two which make time; that which pervades all space, having for its quality what is perceived by the ear; that which is the womb of all seeds; that by which all living beings breathe; endowed with these eight visible forms, may the supreme Lord protect you! (1)

(*At the end of the benediction*)

THE STAGE-DIRECTOR (*Looking towards the dressing-room*). My lady, if you have finished with your dressing, pray, come here.

(*Entering*)

AN ACTRESS. Here I am, my lord; let my lord direct what I am to do.

STAGE-DIRECTOR. My lady, this audience is for the most part composed of learned men. To-day, we are indeed to entertain them with a new play, composed by Kālidāsa; so please bestow great care on every part.

ACTRESS. As your arrangements are well-made, nothing will be wanting.

STAGE-DIRECTOR. My lady, I will tell you the truth:

Until the wise are satisfied, I cannot feel that my knowledge of acting is sound; the mind of even the best-trained (persons) is loth to trust itself. (2)

नटी—अज्ज, एवं णेदम्। अणन्तरकरणिज्जं दाव अज्जो आणवेदु। आर्य, एवमेतत्। अनन्तरकरणीयं तावदार्य आज्ञापयतु।

सूत्रधारः—किमन्यदस्याः परिषदः श्रुतिप्रसादनतः। तदिममेव तावदचिरप्रवृत्तमुपभोगक्षमं ग्रीष्मसमयमधिकृत्य गीयताम्। संप्रति हि

सुभगसलिलावगाहाः पाटलसंसर्गसुरभिवनवाताः।
प्रच्छायसुलभनिद्रा दिवसाः परिणामरमणीयाः॥ ३॥

नटी—तह। तथा। (इति गायति।)

ईसीसिचुम्बिआइं भमरेहिं सुउमारकेसरसिहाइं।
ओदंसयन्ति दअमाणा पमदाओ सिरीसकुसुमाइं॥ ४॥

ईषदीषच्चुम्बितानि भ्रमरैः सुकुमारकेसरशिखानि।
अवतंसयन्ति दयमानाः प्रमदाः शिरीषकुसुमानि॥ ४॥

सूत्रधारः—आर्ये, साधु गीतम्। अहो रागबद्धचित्तवृत्तिरालिखित इव सर्वतो रङ्गः। तदिदानीं कतमत्प्रकरणमाश्रित्यैनमाराधयामः।

नटी—णं अज्जमिस्सेहिं पढमं एव्व आणत्तं अहिण्णाणसउन्दलं णाम अपुव्वं णाडअं पओएण अधिकरीअदुत्ति। नन्वार्यमिश्रैः प्रथममेवाज्ञप्तमभिज्ञानशाकुन्तलं नामापूर्वं नाटकं प्रयोगेणाधिक्रियतामिति।

सूत्रधारः—आर्ये, सम्यगनुबोधितोऽस्मि। अस्मिन्क्षणे विस्मृतं खलु मया। कुतः।

तवास्मि गीतरागेण हारिणा प्रसभं हृतः।
एष राजेव दुष्यन्तः सारङ्गेणातिरंहसा॥ ५॥

(निष्क्रान्तौ।)

इति प्रस्तावना।

ACTRESS. So it is. Let my lord now command what is to be done next.

STAGE-DIRECTOR. What other than to please the ears of this audience? Therefore, sing about this very summer-season, (so) enjoyable, which has just begun. For now,

> Come the days so delightful towards their close, when a plunge in water is so grateful; when the fresh-breeze is fragrant from contact with the Pāṭala flower; and when sleep is easily induced in deep shady places. (3)

ACTRESS. Right. (*Sings.*)

> Tender-hearted ladies make ear-ornaments of the Śirīṣa-blossoms with delicate filament-points, that are very gently kissed by bees. (4)

STAGE-DIRECTOR. Well-sung, my lady. The theatre on all sides has its mental activity arrested by your melody and sits as if painted in a picture. So now what play shall we give to entertain them?

ACTRESS. Why, the noble audience has already given the command that a new play called Abhijñāna-Śākuntala should be staged.

STAGE-DIRECTOR. My lady, well have you reminded me. For the moment I had quite forgotten. For,

> I was forcibly carried away by the charming melody of your song like king Duṣyanta here by the very fleet deer. (5)

(*Exeunt.*)

Here ends the Prologue

(ततः प्रविशति मृगानुसारी सशरचापहस्तो राजा रथेन सूतश्च ।)

सूतः—(राजानं मृगं चावलोक्य ।) आयुष्मन्,

कृष्णसारे ददच्चक्षुस्त्वयि चाधिज्यकार्मुके ।
मृगानुसारिणं साक्षात्पश्यामीव पिनाकिनम् ॥ ६ ॥

राजा—सूत, दूरममुना सारङ्गेण वयमाकृष्टाः । अयं पुनरिदानीमपि

ग्रीवाभङ्गाभिरामं मुहुरनुपतति स्यन्दने बद्धदृष्टिः
पश्चार्धेन प्रविष्टः शरपतनभयाद्भूयसा पूर्वकायम् ।
दर्भैरर्धावलीढैः श्रमविवृतमुखभ्रंशिभिः कीर्णवर्त्मा
पश्योदग्रप्लुतत्वाद्वियति बहुतरं स्तोकमुर्व्यां प्रयाति ॥ ७ ॥

(सविस्मयम् ।) कथमनुपतत एव मे प्रयत्नप्रेक्षणीयः संवृत्तः ।

सूतः—आयुष्मन्, उद्घातिनी भूमिरिति मया रश्मिसंयमनाद्रथस्य मन्दीकृतो वेगः । तेन मृग एष विप्रकृष्टान्तरः संवृत्तः । संप्रति समदेशवर्तिनस्ते न दुरासदो भविष्यति ।

राजा—तेन हि मुच्यन्तामभीशवः ।

सूतः—यदाज्ञापयत्यायुष्मान् । (रथवेगं निरूप्य) आयुष्मन्, पश्य पश्य ।

मुक्तेषु रश्मिषु निरायतपूर्वकाया
निष्कम्पचामरशिखा निभृतोर्ध्वकर्णाः ।

(Then enter king in a chariot, pursuing an antelope, bow and arrow in hand and his charioteer.)

CHARIOTEER *(Looking at the king and the antelope)*. O long-lived one,

When I cast my eye on that black antelope and on you with your braced bow, I see (before me) as it were the Pināka-wielder in person, chasing a deer. (6)

KING. Charioteer, the antelope has given us a long chase. Even now he from time to time,

Looking back gracefully by the bending of his neck, at the car which follows him; now, through fear of a descending shaft, by his haunches drawing himself mostly into the fore-part of his body, strewing his track with grass, half-chewed, which drops from his mouth, kept open from exhaustion, mark, how by reason of his lofty boundings, he moves much more through the air, and but lightly skims the ground. (7)

(Wonderingly). How now the deer is scarce discernible to me though I have been pursuing him?

CHARIOTEER. Long-lived one, seeing that the ground was uneven, I pulled up the reins and slackened the speed of the chariot. But now that you are on level ground, you will not find it difficult to overtake him.

KING. Well, then, loosen the reins.

CHARIOTEER. As the long-lived one commands.

(Exhibiting by gesticulation the speed of the car). Long-lived one! look! look!

the reins being loosed, the chariot-horses run along as if impatient of the speed of the deer,

आत्मोद्धतैरपि रजोभिरलङ्घनीया
धावन्त्यमी मृगजवाक्षमयेव रथ्याः ॥ ८ ॥

राजा—(सस्मितम् ।) सत्यम् । अतीत्य हरितो हरींश्च वर्तन्ते वाजिनः । तथा हि

यदालोके सूक्ष्मं व्रजति सहसा तद्विपुलतां
यदर्धे विच्छिन्नं भवति कृतसंधानमिव तत् ।
प्रकृत्या यद्वक्रं तदपि समरेखं नयनयो-
र्न मे दूरे किंचित्क्षणमपि न पार्श्वे रथजवात् ॥ ९ ॥

सूत, पश्यैनं व्यापाद्यमानम् । (इति शरसंधानं नाटयति ।)

(नेपथ्ये ।)

भो भो राजन्, आश्रममृगोऽयं न हन्तव्यो न हन्तव्यः ।

सूतः—(आकर्ण्यावलोक्य च ।) आयुष्मन्, अस्य खलु ते बाणपथवर्तिनः कृष्णसारस्यान्तरे तपस्विन उपस्थिताः ।

राजा—(ससंभ्रमम् ।) तेन हि प्रगृह्यन्तां वाजिनः ।

सूतः—तथा । (इति रथं स्थापयति ।)

(ततः प्रविशत्यात्मना तृतीयो वैखानसः ।)

वैखानसः—(हस्तमुद्यम्य ।) राजन्, आश्रममृगोऽयं न हन्तव्यो न हन्तव्यः ।

न खलु न खलु बाणः सन्निपात्योऽयमस्मिन्
मृदुनि मृगशरीरे पुष्पराशाविवाग्निः ।
क्व बत हरिणकानां जीवितं चातिलोलं
क्व च निशितनिपाताः वज्रसाराः शरास्ते ॥ १० ॥

with the fore-part of their bodies well stretched out, with the chowrie-crests motionless, with ears erect and steady, not to be overtaken even by the dust that they themselves raise. (8)

KING (*With joy*). Truly, the horses are outstripping the horses of the sun and those of Indra.

For,

Objects which to my sight appeared minute suddenly become large; what was really divided, seems united; and what was in truth bent appears straight to my eyes. So swift the motion of the chariot, that nothing even for a moment seems either near or distant. (9)

CHARIOTEER. Behold him as I kill him. (*Acts fixing an arrow in his bowstring.*)

(*Behind the scenes*)

O king, that is a deer of the hermitage : he must not be slain, he must not be slain.

CHARIOTEER (*Listening and looking*). Long-lived one, here have hermits advanced between you and the antelope that presents a fair mark for your arrows.

KING (*Hastily*). Well, then, rein in the horses.

CHARIOTEER. Very well. (*Stops the chariot.*)

(*Then enter a hermit with two others.*)

HERMIT (*Raising his hand*). This is a deer of the hermitage; this must not be slain, this must not be slain.

Not indeed, not indeed, must this arrow be allowed to fall upon this tender body of the deer, like fire upon a heap of flowers. Compared with thy sharp-falling adamantine shafts, how weak must be the very frail existence of fawns! (10)

तत्साधुकृतसंधानं प्रतिसंहर सायकम् ।
आर्तत्राणाय वः शस्त्रं न प्रहर्तुमनागसि ॥ ११ ॥

राजा—एष प्रतिसंहृतः । (इति यथोक्तं करोति ।)

वैखानसः—सदृशमेतत्पुरुवंशप्रदीपस्य भवतः ।

जन्म यस्य पुरोर्वंशे युक्तरूपमिदं तव ।
पुत्रमेवंगुणोपेतं चक्रवर्तिनमाप्नुहि ॥ १२ ॥

इतरौ—(बाहू उद्यम्य ।) सर्वथा चक्रवर्तिनं पुत्रमाप्नुहि ।

राजा—(सप्रणामम् ।) प्रतिगृहीतम् ।

वैखानसः—राजन्, समिदाहरणाय प्रस्थिता वयम् । एष खलु कण्वस्य कुलपतेरनुमालिनीतीरमाश्रमो दृश्यते । न चेदन्यकार्यातिपातः, तत्प्रविश्य प्रतिगृह्यतामातिथेयः सत्कारः । अपि च ।

रम्यास्तपोधनानां प्रतिहतविघ्नाः क्रियाः समवलोक्य ।
ज्ञास्यसि कियद्भुजो मे रक्षति मौर्वीकिणाङ्क इति ॥ १३ ॥

राजा—अपि संनिहितोऽत्र कुलपतिः ।

वैखानसः—इदानीमेव दुहितरं शकुन्तलामतिथिसत्काराय नियुज्य दैवमस्याः प्रतिकूलं शमयितुं सोमतीर्थं गतः ।

राजा—भवतु । तामेव द्रक्ष्यामि । सा खलु विदितभक्तिर्मां महर्षेः कथयिष्यति ।

वैखानसः—साधयामस्तावत् । (इति सशिष्यो निष्क्रान्तः ।)

राजा—सूत, चोदयाश्वान् । पुण्याश्रमदर्शनेन तावदात्मानं पुनीमहे ।

Replace, therefore, thy well-aimed arrow. Thy weapon is designed for the relief of the distressed, not for the destruction of the guiltless. (11)

KING. Well, it is replaced. (*Does as said.*)

HERMIT. This is worthy of thee—the light of the race of Puru.

This is exceedingly worthy of thee, who art descended from Puru. Mayest thou have a son, adorned with like virtues, sovereign of the world. (12)

OTHERS (***Raising their hands***). Oh, by all means, mayest thou have a son, the sovereign of the world!

KING (*Bowing*). It is accepted.

HERMIT. King, we have set out to collect wood for solemn rites. And this, on the bank of the Mālinī, is, in truth, the religious domicile of the great sage Kaṇva. If no other duty is interfered with, then enter and accept the rights of hospitality. And, moreover,

Beholding the pleasing rites of those whose wealth is their piety, performed without any hindrances, thou wilt know how much thy arm marked with the scar of the bow-string defends. (13)

KING. Is the patriarch of the family at home?

HERMIT. Just now, charging his daughter Śakuntalā to perform the rights of hospitality, he is gone to Somatīrtha, in hopes of deprecating her adverse fate.

KING. Well, I will see her; and she, having observed my devotion, will report it to the venerable sage.

HERMIT. Well, we will now depart. (*Exit with his pupils.*)

KING. Charioteer, drive on the horses. By visit-

सूतः—यदाज्ञापयत्यायुष्मान्। (इति भूयो रथवेगं निरूपयति।)

राजाः—(समन्तादवलोक्य।) सूत, अकथितोऽपि ज्ञायत एव यथायमाभोगस्तपोवनस्येति।

सूतः—कथमिव।

राजा—किं न पश्यति भवान्। इह हि

नीवाराः शुकगर्भकोटरमुखभ्रष्टास्तरूणामधः
प्रस्निग्धाः क्वचिदिङ्गुदीफलभिदः सूच्यन्त एवोपलाः।
विश्वासोपगमादभिन्नगतयः शब्दं सहन्ते मृगा-
स्तोयाधारपथाश्च वल्कलशिखानिष्यन्दरेखाङ्किताः ॥१४॥

अपि च।

कुल्यांभोभिः पवनचपलैः शाखिनो धौतमूला
भिन्नो रागः किसलयरुचामाज्यधूमोद्गमेन।
एते चार्वागुपवनभुवि च्छिन्नदर्भाङ्कुरायां
नष्टाशङ्का हरिणशिशवो मन्दमन्दं चरन्ति ॥ १५ ॥

सूतः—सर्वमुपपन्नम्।

राजा—(स्तोकमन्तरं गत्वा।) तपोवननिवासिनामुपरोधो मा भूत्। अत्रैव रथं स्थापय। यावदवतरामि।

सूतः—धृताः प्रग्रहाः। अवतरत्वायुष्मान्।

ing the abode of holiness, we shall purify ourselves.

CHARIOTEER. As the long-lived one commands.

(*Again gesticulates swift movement of the chariot.*)

KING (*Looking around*). Charioteer, even without being told, it may be known indeed that these are the precincts of the sacred grove.

CHARIOTEER. How indeed?

KING. Don't you see? For here,

Under (yonder) trees are the grains of wild rice fallen from the openings of the hollow-trunks filled with parrots; in other places are seen the polished stones which have bruised the fruit of the Ingudī; and the fawns, too, from having acquired confidence bear the sound (of our approach) without varying their course; and the paths of the reservoirs are marked with lines by the drippings from the fringes of bark-garments. (14)

Moreover,

The roots of yon trees are bathed in the waters of canals which quiver as the wind plays upon them; the glowing lustre of the fresh leaves is partially obscured by the smoke that rises from (oblations of) clarified butter; and here in front, these young fawns are leisurely grazing without fear on the garden-lawns where the sprouts of Darbha-grass have been cut away. (15)

CHARIOTEER. All is indeed true.

KING (*Going a little way*). Let the dwellers of the sacred grove be not disturbed. Stop the chariot just here, that I may descend.

CHARIOTEER. The reins are held in. Let the long-

राजा—(अवतीर्यात्मानमवलोक्य च ।) सूत, विनीतवेषेण प्रवेष्टव्यानि तपोवनानि नाम । इदं तावद्गृह्यताम् । (इति सूतस्याभरणानि धनुश्चोपनीय ।) सूत, यावदाश्रमवासिनः प्रत्यवेक्ष्याहमुपावर्ते तावदार्द्रपृष्ठाः क्रियन्तां वाजिनः ।

सूतः—तथा । (इति निष्क्रान्तः ।)

राजा—(परिक्रम्यावलोक्य च ।) इदमाश्रमद्वारम् । यावत्प्रविशामि । (प्रविश्य । निमित्तं सूचयन् ।)

शान्तमिदमाश्रमपदं स्फुरति च बाहुः कुतः फलमिहास्य ।
अथवा भवितव्यानां द्वाराणि भवन्ति सर्वत्र ॥ १६ ॥

(नेपथ्ये ।)

इदो इदो सहीओ । इत इतः सख्यौ ।

राजा—(कर्णं दत्वा ।) अये, दक्षिणेन वृक्षवाटिकामालाप इव श्रूयते । यावदत्रे गच्छामि । (परिक्रम्यावलोक्य च ।) अये, एतास्तपस्विकन्यकाः स्वप्रमाणानुरूपैः सेचनघटैर्बालपादपेभ्यः पयो दातुमित एवाभिवर्तन्ते । (निपुणं निरूप्य ।) अहो, मधुरमासां दर्शनम् ।

शुद्धान्तदुर्लभमिदं वपुराश्रमवासिनो यदि जनस्य ।
दूरीकृताः खलु गुणैरुद्यानलता वनलताभिः ॥ १७ ॥

यावदिमां छायामाश्रित्य प्रतिपालयामि । (इति विलोकयन्स्थितः ।)

lived one descend.

KING (*Having descended, and looking at himself*) Charioteer, sacred groves must indeed be entered in humble habiliments ; therefore take these. (*Giving his ornaments and bow to the charioteer*). Charioteer, by the time I return after visiting the inmates of this holy sanctuary, let the horses be washed and refreshed.

CHARIOTEER. Very well. (*Exit.*)

KING (*Walking round and looking*). This is the entrance to the hermitage. Let me enter. (*Entering and acting as if he perceived an omen*).

> Tranquil is this hermitage, and yet my arm throbs ; whence can there rise the fruit of this in such a place ? But yet the gates of predestined events are in all places open. (16)

(*Behind the scenes*)

Come hither, my friends, come hither.

KING (*Listening*). Ha ! I seem to hear voices to the right of the grove of trees. So I will proceed. (*Walking about and observing*). There are some damsels belonging to the hermits' family coming in this direction, to water the young plants from water-pots of different sizes proportioned to their strength. (*Eyeing them closely*). How lovely they look ;

> If such the beauty of maids, who dwell in woodland retreats, the like of which is not easily to be found in the recesses of a palace, then indeed are the garden-plants well surpassed in merit by the woodland creepers. (17)

So I will stand in this shade and await (them).

(*He stands gazing at them.*)

[ततः प्रविशति यथोक्तव्यापारा सह सखीभ्यां शकुन्तला ।]

शकुन्तला—इदो इदो सहीओ । इत इतः सख्यौ ।

अनसूया—हला सउन्दले, तुवत्तो वि तादकस्सवस्स अस्समरुक्खआ पिअदरत्ति तक्केमि । जेण णोमालिआकुसुमपेलवा वि तुमं एदाणं आलवालपूरणे णिउत्ता । हला शकुन्तले, त्वत्तोऽपि तातकाश्यपस्याश्रमवृक्षकाः प्रियतरा इति तर्कयामि । येन नवमालिकाकुसुमपेलवा त्वमप्येतेषामालवालपूरणे नियुक्ता ।

शकुन्तला—ण केअलं तादणिओओ एव्व । अत्थि मे सोदरसिणेहो वि एदेसु । (इति वृक्षसेचनं रूपयति ।) न केवलं तातनियोग एव । अस्ति मे सोदरस्नेहोऽप्येतेषु ।

राजा—कथमियं सा कण्वदुहिता । असाधुदर्शी खलु तत्रभवान्काश्यपः, य इमामाश्रमधर्मे नियुङ्क्ते ।

इदं किलाव्याजमनोहरं वपु-
स्तपःक्षमं साधयितुं य इच्छति ।
ध्रुवं स नीलोत्पलपत्रधारया
शमीलतां छेत्तुमृषिर्व्यवस्यति ॥ १८ ॥

भवतु । पादपान्तरित एव विश्वस्तां तावदेनां पश्यामि । (इति तथा करोति ।)

शकुन्तला—सहि अणसूए, अदिपिणद्धेण वक्कलेण पिअंवदाए णिअन्तिदम्हि । सिढिलेहि दाव णं । सखि अनसूये, अतिपिनद्धेन वल्कलेन प्रियंवदया नियन्त्रितास्मि । शिथिलय तावदेतत् ।

अनसूया—तह । (इति शिथिलयति ।) तथा ।

प्रियंवदा—(सहासम् ।) **एत्थ पओहरवित्थारइत्तअं अत्तणो जोव्वणं उवालह । मं किं उवालम्भेसि ।** अत्र पयोधरविस्तारयितृ आत्मनो यौवनमुपालभस्व । मां किमुपालभसे ।

(*Then enter Śakuntalā occupied in the manner described and her two friends.*)

ŚAKUNTALĀ. Come hither, my friends, come hither.

ANASŪYĀ. Friend Śakuntalā, I think the trees in the hermitage are dearer to father Kāśyapa than your own self, since he has appointed even you, who are soft like a Navamālikā flower, to fill their basins.

ŚAKUNTALĀ. It is not only in obedience to our father, but I really feel the affection of a sister for them.

(*Acts watering the plant.*)

KING. How ! Is this Kaṇava's daughter ? Truly the venerable Kāśyapa has but little discrimination, since he has allotted her the duties of the hermitage.

> The sage who would make this artlessly-charming form capable of enduring penance would attempt, I suppose, to cleave the Śamī tree with the edge of the blue lotus-leaf. (18)

Well, concealed by the trees even as I am, I will gaze on her without diminishing her confidence. (*Does so.*)

ŚAKUNTALĀ. Friend Anasūyā, I feel quite tied down by the bark-garment which Priyaṁvadā has too tightly fastened. Pray loosen it.

ANASŪYĀ. Very well. (*Loosens it.*)

PRIYAṀVADĀ (*Laughing*). In this, you better revile your youthful prime which gives your bosom such a swell ; why do you blame me.

राजा—सम्यगियमाह ।

इदमुपहितसूक्ष्मग्रन्थिना स्कन्धदेशे
स्तनयुगपरिणाहाच्छादिना वल्कलेन ।
वपुरभिनवमस्याः पुष्यति स्वां न शोभां
कुसुममिव पिनद्धं पाण्डुपत्त्रोदरेण ॥ १९ ॥

अथवा काममननुरूपमस्या वपुषो वल्कलं न पुनरलंकारश्रियं न पुष्यति । कुतः ।

सरसिजमनुविद्धं शैवलेनापि रम्यं
मलिनमपि हिमांशोर्लक्ष्म लक्ष्मीं तनोति ।
इयमधिकमनोज्ञा वल्कलेनापि तन्वी
किमिव हि मधुराणां मण्डनं नाकृतीनाम् ॥ २० ॥

शकुन्तला—(अग्रतोऽवलोक्य ।) एसो वादेरिदपल्लवङ्गलीहिं तुवरेदि विअ मं केसररुक्खओ । जाव णं संभावेमि । (इति परिक्रामति ।) एष वातेरितपल्लवाङ्गुलीभिस्त्वरयतीव मां केसरवृक्षकः । यावदेनं संभावयामि ।

प्रियंवदा—हला सउन्दले एत्थ एव्व दाव मुहुत्तअं चिट्ठ । हला शकुन्तले, अत्रैव तावन्मुहूर्तं तिष्ठ ।

शकुन्तला—किंणिमित्तं । किंनिमित्तम् ।

प्रियंवदा—जाव तुए उवगदाए लदासणाधो विअ अअं केसररुक्खओ पडिभादि । यावत्त्वयोपगतया लतासनाथ इवायं केसरवृक्षकः प्रतिभाति ।

शकुन्तला—अदो क्खु पिअंवदा सि तुमं । अतः खलु प्रियंवदासि त्वम् ।

राजा—प्रियमपि तथ्यमाह शकुन्तलां प्रियंवदा । अस्याः खलु

अधरः किसलयरागः कोमलविटपानुकारिणौ बाहू ।
कुसुममिव लोभनीयं यौवनमङ्गेषु संनद्धम् ॥ २१ ॥

KING. She speaks well.

This her youthful body, by reason of the bark garment tied with delicate knots upon the shoulder, and covering the expanse of her twin breasts, does not exhibit its own charms, like a flower enfolded by a pale leaf. (19)

Or rather, granted that the bark-garment suits but ill her figure, yet it really does possess the charm of an ornament. For,

The lotus, though moss may overlay it, is, nevertheless, beautiful ; the spot on the moon, for all its darkness, heightens the charm of the moon ; this slender (maiden) is more lovely even in her dress of bark : for what indeed is not an embellishment of sweet forms ? (20)

ŚAKUNTALĀ (*Looking before her*). This Kesara-tree, with its fingers of leaves, which the gale gently agitates, bids me hasten as it were (towards it). I will just attend to it. (*Moves about.*)

PRIYAṀVADĀ. Friend Śakuntalā, just stand where you are for a moment.

ŚAKUNTALĀ. Why ?

PRIYAṀVADĀ. For, with you standing near it, the Kesara appears as though possessed of a creeper.

ŚAKUNTALĀ. Hence indeed are you properly named Priyaṁvadā.

KING. Though agreeable, still it is the truth which Priyaṁvadā says to Śakuntalā.

Truly, her lower lip glows like a tender leaf, her arms resemble flexible stalks. And youth, bewitching like a blossom, shines in all her lineaments. (21)

अनसूया—हला सउन्दले, इअं सअंवरवहू सहआरस्स तुए किद्णामहेआ वणजोसिणित्ति णोमालिआ। णं विसुमरिदा सि। हला शकुन्तले, इयं स्वयंवरवधूः सहकारस्य त्वया कृतनामधेया वनज्योत्स्नेति नवमालिका। एनां विस्मृतवत्यसि।

शकुन्तला—तदा अत्ताणं वि विसुमरिस्सं। (लतामुपेत्यावलोक्य च सहर्षम्।) हला, रमणीए क्खु काले इमस्स लदापाअवमिधुणस्स वइअरो संवुत्तो। णवकुसुमजोव्वणा वणजोसिणी, बद्धपल्लवदाए उवभोअक्खमो सहआरो। (इति पश्यन्ती तिष्ठति।) तदात्मानमपि विस्मरिष्यामि। हला, रमणीये खलु काल एतस्य लतापादपमिथुनस्य व्यतिकरः संवृत्तः। नवकुसुमयौवना वनज्योत्स्ना, स्निग्धपल्लवतयोपभोगक्षमः सहकारः।

प्रियंवदा—(सस्मितम्।) अणसूए, जाणासि किंणिमित्तं सउन्दला वणजोसिणीं अदिमेत्तं पेक्खदित्ति। अनसूये, जानासि किंनिमित्तं शकुन्तला वनज्योत्स्नामतिमात्रं पश्यतीति।

अनसूया—ण क्खु विभावेमि। कहेहि। न खलु विभावयामि। कथय।

प्रियंवदा—जधा वणजोसिणी अणुरूवेण पाअवेण संगदा अवि णाम एव्वं अहं वि अत्तणो अणुरूवं वरं लहेअंति। यथा वनज्योत्स्नानुरूपेण पादपेन संगता, अपि नामैवमहमप्यात्मनोऽनुरूपं वरं लभेयेति।

शकुन्तला—एसो णूणं तुह अत्तगदो मणोरधो। (इति कलशमावर्जयति।) एष नूनं तवात्मगतो मनोरथः।

राजा—अपि नाम कुलपतेरियमसवर्णक्षेत्रसंभवा स्यात्। अथवा कृतं संदेहेन।

असंशयं क्षत्रपरिग्रहक्षमा
　　यदार्यमस्यामभिलाषि मे मनः।
सतां हि संदेहपदेषु वस्तुषु
　　प्रमाणमन्तःकरणप्रवृत्तयः॥ २२॥

तथापि तत्त्वत एनामुपलप्स्ये।

Anasūyā. Oh, Śakuntalā ! Here is the Navamālikā, named by you the Light of the Grove, the self-elected bride of the mango tree. Have you forgotten her ?

ŚAKUNTALĀ. Then I shall forget even my own self !

(*Approaching the creeper and looking at it*). Friend, at a charming season, indeed, has the union between the pair—the creeper and the tree—taken place. Vanajyotsnā shows her youth in her fresh blossoms ; and the Sahakāra his readiness to enjoy, in his sprouting young leaves.

PRIYAṀVADĀ (*Smiling*). Do you know, my Anasūyā, why Śakuntalā is gazing so intently at Vanajyotsnā ?

ANASŪYĀ. No, I cannot guess. Pray, tell me.

PRIYAṀVADĀ. "As the Vanajyotsnā is united to a suitable tree, thus, may I, too, hope for a bridegroom to my mind."

ŚAKUNTALĀ. This is, indeed what you want for yourself.

(*She tips her water-pot.*)

KING. May I hope that she is the daughter of the patriarch by a wife of a different caste ? But have done with doubt.

Surely, she cannot but be fit to be wedded to a Kṣatriya, since my noble soul has longing towards her : for in matters beset with doubts, the promptings of the heart are to the good an authoritative guide. (22)

Nevertheless, I will ascertain the truth about her.

शकुन्तला—(ससंभ्रमम् ।) अम्मो । सलिलसेअसंभमुग्गदो णोमालिअं उज्झिअ वअणं मे महुअरो अहिवट्टइ । (इति भ्रमरबाधां रूपयति ।) अम्मो । सलिलसेकसंभ्रमोद्गतो नवमालिकामुज्झित्वा वदनं मे मधुकरोऽभिवर्तते ।

राजा—(सस्पृहं विलोक्य ।)

यतो यतः षट्चरणोऽभिवर्तते
ततस्ततः प्रेरितलोललोचना ।
विवर्तितभ्रूरियमद्य शिक्षते
भयादकामापि हि दृष्टिविभ्रमम् ॥ २३ ॥

अपि च । (सासूयमिव ।)

चलापाङ्गां दृष्टिं स्पृशसि बहुशो वेपथुमतीं
रहस्याख्यायीव स्वनसि मृदु कर्णान्तिकचरः ।
करौ व्याधुन्वत्याः पिबसि रतिसर्वस्वमधरं
वयं तत्त्वान्वेषान्मधुकर हतास्त्वं खलु कृती ॥ २४ ॥

शकुन्तला—ण एसो धिट्ठो विरमदि । अण्णदो गमिस्सं । (पदान्तरे स्थित्वा सदृष्टिक्षेपम् ।) कधं इदो वि आअच्छदि । हला, परित्ताअध मं इमिणा दुव्विणीदेण दुट्ठमहुअरेण अहिहूअमाणं । न एष धृष्टो विरमति । अन्यतो गमिष्यामि । कथमितोऽप्यागच्छति । हला, परित्रायेथां मामनेन दुर्विनीतेन दुष्टमधुकरेणाभिभूयमानाम् ।

उभे—(सस्मितम् ।) काओ अम्हे परित्तादुं । दुस्सन्दं अक्कन्द । राअरक्खिदव्वाइं तवोवणाइं णाम । के आवां परित्रातुम् । दुष्यन्तमाक्रन्द । राजरक्षितव्यानि तपोवनानि नाम ।

राजा—अवसरोऽयमात्मानं प्रकाशयितुम् । न भेतव्यं (इत्यर्धोक्ते । स्वगतम् ।) राजभावस्त्वभिज्ञातो भवेत् । भवतु । एवं तावदभिधास्ये ।

शकुन्तला—(पदान्तरे स्थित्वा । सदृष्टिक्षेपम् ।) कधं इदोवि मं अणुसरदि । कथमितोऽपि मामनुसरति ।

ŚAKUNTALĀ (*Excitedly*). Ah! Rising through the disturbance caused by the sprinkling of water, a bee has left the Navamālikā and is fluttering round my face.

(*She shows herself annoyed by the bee.*)

KING (*Looking longingly*).

In whichever direction the bee turns, in that direction she turns her rolling eyes. Arching her brows, she is learning to day coquettish play of her eyes through fright (only) and not from love. (23)

Moreover, (*A bit jealously*).

Frequently dost thou touch her throbbing eye with its outer corner trembling; approaching her ear, thou murmurest softly, as if thou wert whispering a secret of love; and while she waves her hands, thou sippest her lower lip which contains all the treasure of delight; whilst we, O bee, through search after truth are disappointed, thou hast gained thy wish! (24)

ŚAKUNTALĀ. This importunate bee does not stop. I will remove to another place. (*Stepping aside, and looking about her*). How, now! He is coming this way too! Save me, friends, save me from this ill-mannered bee which hath quite baffled me.

BOTH (*Smiling*). What power have we to deliver you? Call upon Duṣyanta. Indeed holy groves are to be protected by the king.

KING. A good opportunity this to discover myself; fear not (*When half through these words to himself*). But my royal character will be known to them. Well, I will speak thus.

ŚAKUNTALĀ (*Stepping aside and looking about*). How even here he follows me!

राजा—(सत्वरमुपसृत्य ।) आः ।

कः पौरवे वसुमतीं शासति शासितरि दुर्विनीतानाम् ।
अयमाचरत्यविनयं मुग्धासु तपस्विकन्यासु ॥ २५ ॥

(सर्वा राजानं दृष्ट्वा किंचिदिव संभ्रान्ताः ।)

अनसूया—अज्ज, ण क्खु किंपि अच्चाहिदं। इअं णो पिअसही महुअरेण अहिहूअमाणा कादरीभूदा । (इति शकुन्तलां दर्शयति ।) आर्य, न खलु किमप्यत्याहितम् । इयं नः प्रियसखी मधुकरेणाभिभूयमाना कातरीभूता ।

राजा—(शकुन्तलाभिमुखो भूत्वा ।) अपि तपो वर्धते ।

(शकुन्तला साध्वसादवचना तिष्ठति ।)

अनसूया—दाणिं अदिधिविसेसलाहेण । हला सउन्दले, गच्छ उडअं। फलमिस्सं अग्घं उवहर। इदं पादोदअं भविस्सदि। इदानीमतिथिविशेषलाभेन । हला शकुन्तले, गच्छोटजम् । फलमिश्रमर्घमुपहर । इदं पादोदकं भविष्यति ।

राजा—भवतीनां सूनृतयैव गिरा कृतमातिथ्यम् ।

प्रियंवदा—तेण हि इमस्सिं पच्छाअसीदलाए सत्तवण्णवेदिआए मुहुत्तअं उवविसिअ परिस्समविणोदं करेदु अज्जो। तेन ह्यस्यां प्रच्छायशीतलायां सप्तपर्णवेदिकायां मुहूर्तमुपविश्य परिश्रमविनोदं करोत्वार्यः।

राजा—नूनं यूयमप्यनेन कर्मणा परिश्रान्ताः ।

अनसूया—हला सउन्दले, उइदं णो पज्जुवासणं अदिधीणं। एत्थ उवविसम्ह। (इति सर्वा उपविशन्ति ।) हला शकुन्तले, उचितं नः पर्युपासनमतिथीनाम् । अत्रोपविशामः ।

शकुन्तला—(आत्मगतम् ।) किं णु क्खु इमं पेक्खिअ तवोवणविरोहिणो विआरस्स गमणीअम्हि संवुत्ता। किं नु खल्विमं प्रेक्ष्य तपोवनविरोधिनो विकारस्य गमनीयास्मि संवृत्ता ।

राजा—(सर्वा विलोक्य ।) अहो समवयोरूपरमणीयं भवतीनां सौहार्दम् ।

KING (*Quickly advancing.*)

While a descendent of Puru, a chastiser of the ill-behaved, governs the world, who is this that is so rude to these artless hermit-girls ? (25)

(*All are slightly confused at sight of the king.*)

ANASŪYĀ. It is nothing very dreadful, gentle sir ; but this our dear friend was teased and frightened by a bee. (*Indicates Śakuntalā.*)

KING (*Turning to Śakuntalā*). I trust your devotion prospers.

(*Śakuntalā stands speechless through embarrassment.*)

ANASŪYĀ. Now through the arrival of a distinguished guest. Go to the cottage, Śakuntalā, and fetch an offering mixed with fruits. This will serve as water for the feet.

KING. The rites of hospitality have been performed by your sweet and sincere words.

PRIYAMVADĀ. Then, sir, pray sit down for a while on the raised-seat under the Saptaparṇa tree which is cool and deeply shady, and beguile your fatigue.

KING. You, too, must all be fatigued by this work.

ANASŪYĀ. Friend Śakuntalā, it is proper for us to wait upon our guests. Let us be seated here. (*All sit down.*)

ŚAKUNTALĀ (*To herself*). How is it, that at the sight of this person, I feel an emotion scarce consistent with a grove devoted to piety ?

KING (*Looking at them all*). How delightful is our friendship with the (charming) equality of your ges and of your beauty.

प्रियंवदा—(जनान्तिकम्।) **अणसूए, को णु क्खु एसो चउरगम्भीराकिदी महुरं आलवन्तो पहाववन्तो विअ लक्खीअदि।** अनसूये, को नु खल्वेष चतुरगम्भीराकृतिर्मधुरमालपन्प्रभाववानिव लक्ष्यते।

अनसूया—सहि, मम वि अत्थि कोदूहलं। पुच्छिस्सं दाव णं। (प्रकाशम्।) **अज्जस्स महुरालावजणिदो वीसम्भो मं मन्तावेदि। कदमो अज्जेण राएसिणो वंसो अलंकरीअदि, कदमो वा विरहपज्जुस्सुअजणो किदो देसो, किंणिमित्तं वा सुउमारदरो वि तवोवणगमणपरिस्समस्स अत्ता पदं उवणीदो।** सखि, ममाप्यस्ति कौतूहलम्। पृच्छामि तावदेनम्। आर्यस्य मधुरालापजनितो विश्रम्भो मां मन्त्रयते। कतम आर्येण राजर्षेर्वंशोऽलंक्रियते, कतमो वा विरहपर्युत्सुकजनः कृतो देशः, किंनिमित्तं वा सुकुमारतरोऽपि तपोवनगमनपरिश्रमस्यात्मा पदमुपनीतः।

शकुन्तला—(आत्मगतम्) **हिअअ, मा उत्तम्म। एसा तुए चिन्तिदाइं अणसूआ मन्तेदि।** हृदय, मोत्ताम्य। एषा त्वया चिन्तितान्यनसूया मन्त्रयते।

राजा—(आत्मगतम्।) **कथमिदानीमात्मानं निवेदयामि, कथं वात्मापहारं करोमि। भवतु। एवं तावदेनां वक्ष्ये।** (प्रकाशम्।) **भवति, यः पौरवेण राज्ञा धर्माधिकारे नियुक्तः सोऽहमविघ्नक्रियोपलम्भाय धर्मारण्यमिदमायातः।**

अनसूया—सणाधा दाणिं धम्मआरिणो। सनाथा इदानीं धर्मचारिणः।

(शकुन्तला शृङ्गारलज्जां रूपयति।)

सख्यौ—(उभयोराकारं विदित्वा। जनान्तिकम्।) **हला सउन्दले, जइ एत्थ अज्ज तादो संणिहिदो भवे।** हला शकुन्तले, यद्यत्राद्य तातः संनिहितो भवेत्।

शकुन्तला—तदो किं भवे। ततः किं भवेत्।

सख्यौ—इमं जीविदसव्वस्सेण वि अदिधिविसेसं किदत्थं करिस्सदि। इमं जीवितसर्वस्वेनाप्यतिथिविशेषं कृतार्थं करिष्यति।

PRIYAMVADĀ (*Aside*). Who can this be, my Anasūyā, who combines liveliness with dignity in his mien, and seems to be endowed with majesty while speaking to us sweetly?

ANASŪYĀ. Friend, I am curious, too. I shall just ask him. (*Aloud*). Your sweet speech gives me the confidence to speak to you. What house of royal sages is embellished by your honour? And what country has its people grieving at your absence? On what account has your person, though very delicate, been submitted to the weary journey into our pious grove?

ŚAKUNTALĀ (*Aside*). O my heart! be not uneasy. This Anasūyā speaks your very thoughts.

KING (*To himself*). How shall I reveal, or how shall I disguise myself now? Well, I will speak to her thus. (*Aloud*). Lady, I am the person appointed by the king, the descendent of Puru, to supervise religious rites, and have arrived at this grove of piety to ascertain whether the religious rites suffer no obstruction.

ANASŪYĀ. Then the people engaged in acts of piety have now found some one to take care of them.

(*Śakuntalā acts amorous bashfulness.*)

THE TWO FRIENDS (*Observing the demeanour of the two, aside*). Śakuntalā, dear, if only father were here today—

ŚAKUNTALĀ (*With anger*). What would happen then?

THE TWO FRIENDS. He would make this distinguished guest happy, even if it took the most valuable possession of his life.

शकुन्तला—तुह्मे अवेध। किं पि हिएअ कदुअ मन्तेध। ण वो वअणं सुणिस्सं। युवामपेतम्। किमपि हृदये कृत्वा मन्त्रयेथे। न युवयोर्वचनं श्रोष्यामि।

राजा—वयमपि तावद्भवत्योः सखीगतं किमपि पृच्छामः।

सख्यौ—अज्ज, अणुग्गहो विअ इअं अब्भत्थणा। आर्य, अनुग्रह इवेयमभ्यर्थना।

राजा—भगवान्काश्यपः शाश्वते ब्रह्मणि स्थित इति प्रकाशम्। इयं च वः सखी तदात्मजेति कथमेतत्।

अनसूया—सुणादु अज्जो। अत्थि को वि कोसिओत्ति गोत्तणामहेओ महाप्पहावो राएसी। श्रृणोत्वार्यः। अस्ति कोऽपि कौशिक इति गोत्रनामधेयो महाप्रभावो राजर्षिः।

राजा—अस्ति। श्रूयते।

अनसूया—तं णो पिअसहीए पहवं अवगच्छ। उज्झिदाए सरीरसंवड्ढणादीहिं तादकस्सवो से पिदा। तमावयोः प्रियसख्याः प्रभवमवगच्छ। उज्झितायाः शरीरसंवर्धनादिभिस्तातकाश्यपोऽस्याः पिता।

राजा—उज्झितशब्देन जनितं मे कौतूहलम्। आ मूलाच्छ्रोतुमिच्छामि।

अनसूया—सुणादु अज्जो। गोदमीतीरे पुरा किल तस्स राएसिणो उग्गे तवसि वट्टमाणस्स किंपि जादसङ्केहिं देवेहिं मेणआ णाम अच्छरा पेसिदा णिअमविग्घकारिणी। श्रृणोत्वार्यः। गौतमीतीरे पुरा किल तस्य राजर्षेरुग्रे तपसि वर्तमानस्य किमपि जातशङ्कैर्देवैर्मेनका नामाप्सराः प्रेषिता नियमविघ्नकारिणी।

राजा—अस्त्येतदन्यसमाधिभीरुत्वं देवानाम्।

अनसूया—तदो वसन्तोदारसमए से उम्मादइत्तअं रूवं पेक्खिअ—(इत्यर्धोक्ते लज्जया विरमति) ततो वसन्तोदारसमये तस्या उन्मादयितृ रूपं प्रेक्ष्य—

राजा—परस्तादवगम्यत एव। सर्वथाप्सरःसंभवैषा।

अनसूया—अह इं। अथ किम्।

ŚAKUNTALĀ. Go to! you form some (absurd) notion in your mind and speak. I will not listen to you.

KING. We, too, would like to ask something about your friend.

THE TWO FRIENDS. Sir, your request is as a favour to us.

KING. The revered Kāśyapa lives in the constant practice of continence; how then can this friend of yours be, as it is said, his daughter?

ANASŪYĀ. Listen, sir. There is a certain royal sage of great majesty whose family name is Kauśika.

KING. Ah, yes, I have heard (of him).

ANASŪYĀ. Know him to be the source of our dear friend's being; but father Kāśyapa is her father, through his having taken care of her person and such like acts when she was abandoned.

KING. The word 'abandoned' has wakened my curiosity. I would like to hear from the beginning.

ANASŪYĀ. Listen, sir. Formerly, while the royal sage was leading a life of stern austerities on the banks of the Gautamī, the gods, becoming somehow alarmed, sent the nymph Menakā to disturb him.

KING. Yes, there is this jealousy of the gods towards the austerities of others.

ANASŪYĀ. Then at the advent of spring, having beheld her intoxicating beauty—(*She stops through bashfulness when this is half said.*)

KING. What followed is quite plain. So, she is sprung from a nymph.

ANASŪYĀ. Exactly so.

राजा—उपपद्यते।

मानुषीषु कथं वा स्यादस्य रूपस्य संभवः।
न प्रभातरलं ज्योतिरुदेति वसुधातलात्॥ २६॥

(शकुन्तलाधोमुखी तिष्ठति।)

राजा—(आत्मगतम्।) लब्धावकाशो मे मनोरथः। किंतु सख्याः परिहासोदाहृतां वरप्रार्थनां श्रुत्वा धृतद्वैधीभावकातरं मे मनः।

प्रियंवदा—(सस्मितं शकुन्तलां विलोक्य नायकाभिमुखी भूत्वा।) पुणो वि वत्तुकामो विअ अज्जो। पुनरपि वक्तुकाम इवार्यः।

(शकुन्तला सखीमङ्गुल्यातर्जयति।)

राजा—सम्यगुपलक्षितं भवत्या। अस्ति नः सच्चरितश्रवणलोभादन्यदपि प्रष्टव्यम्।

प्रियंवदा—अलं विआरिअ। अणिअन्तणाणुओओ तवस्सिअणो णाम। अलं विचार्य। अनियन्त्रणानुयोगस्तपस्विजनो नाम।

राजा— इति सखीं ते ज्ञातुमिच्छामि।

वैखानसं किमनया व्रतमाप्रदाना-
द्व्यापाररोधि मदनस्य निषेवितव्यम्।
अत्यन्तमात्मसदृशेक्षणवल्लभाभि-
राहो निवत्स्यति समं हरिणाङ्गनाभिः॥ २७॥

प्रियंवदा—अज्ज, धम्मचरणे वि परवसो अअं जणो। गुरुणो उण से अणुरूववरप्पदाणे संकप्पो। आर्य, धर्मचरणेऽपि परवशोऽयं जनः। गुरोः पुनरस्या अनुरूपवरप्रदाने संकल्पः।

राजा—(आत्मगतं सहर्षम्।) न दुरवापेयं खलु प्रार्थना।

भव हृदय साभिलाषं संप्रति संदेहनिर्णयो जातः।
आशङ्कसे यदग्निं तदिदं स्पर्शक्षमं रत्नम्॥ २८॥

KING. That is, as it should be.

Or how could any woman give birth to such a lovely form? The light that sparkles with tremulous beams does not rise from the surface of the earth. (26)

(Śakuntalā hangs her head.)

KING *(To himself)*. My desire has found scope. Nevertheless having heard of her desire for a husband, mentioned in pleasantry by her friend, my heart is filled with suspense and anxiety.

PRIYAṀVADĀ *(Looking with a smile at Śakuntalā and turning to the hero)*. Sir, it seems as if you had more to say.

(Śakuntalā threatens her friend with her finger.)

KING. You have rightly observed. From an eagerness to know more of a virtuous life, I have another question to ask.

PRIYAṀVADĀ. Do not hesitate. For hermits may indeed be questioned without any reserve.

KING. I wish to know your friend.

Is this monastic vow, so opposed to the ways of love, to be observed by her till her marriage only, or is she destined to reside for life along with the female deer, her favourites from having eyes like her own? (27)

PRIYAṀVADĀ. Sir, even in the practice of religious duties this person is dependent on another. But it is her father's intention to give her to a suitable bridegroom.

KING *(To himself, with joy)*. This desire indeed is not difficult to obtain.

My heart, be hopeful; for now all doubt is done; what you dreaded as fire, the same is a

शकुन्तला—(सरोषमिव ।) **अणसूए, गमिस्सं अहं ।** अनसूये, गमिष्याम्यहम् ।

अनसूया—किंणिमित्तं । किंनिमित्तम् ।

शकुन्तला—इमं असंबद्धप्पलाविणिं पिअंवदं अज्जाए गोदमीए णिवेदइस्सं । इमामसंबद्धप्रलापिनीं प्रियंवदामार्यायै गौतम्यै निवेदयिष्यामि ।

अनसूया—सहि, ण जुत्तं अकिदसक्कारं अदिधिविसेसं विसज्जिअ सच्छन्ददो गमणं । सखि, न युक्तमकृतसत्कारमतिथिविशेषं विसृज्य स्वच्छन्दतो गमनम् ।

(शकुन्तला न किंचिदुक्त्वा प्रस्थितैव)

राजा—(ग्रहीतुमिच्छन्निगृह्यात्मानम् । आत्मगतम् ।) **अहो चेष्टाप्रतिरूपिका कामिजनमनोवृत्तिः । अहं हि**

> **अनुयास्यन्मुनितनयां सहसा विनयेन वारितप्रसरः ।**
> **स्थानादनुच्चलन्नपि गत्वेव पुनः प्रतिनिवृत्तः ॥ २९ ॥**

प्रियंवदा—(शकुन्तलां निरुध्य ।) **हला, ण दे जुत्तं गन्तुं ।** हला, न ते युक्तं गन्तुम् ।

शकुन्तला—(सभ्रूभङ्गम्) **किं णिमित्तं ।** किंनिमित्तम् ।

प्रियंवदा—रुक्खसेअणे दुवे धारेसि मे । एहि दाव । अत्ताणं मोचिअ तदो गमिस्ससि । (इति बलादेनां निवर्तयति) वृक्षसेचने द्वे धारयसि मे । एहि तावत् । आत्मानं मोचयित्वा ततो गमिष्यसि ।

राजा—भद्रे, वृक्षसेचनादेव परिश्रान्तामत्रभवतीं लक्षये । तथा ह्यस्याः

> **स्रस्तांसावतिमात्रलोहिततलौ बाहू घटोत्क्षेपणा-**
> **दद्यापि स्तनवेपथुं जनयति श्वासः प्रमाणाधिकः ।**

gem capable of being touched. (28)

ŚAKUNTALĀ (*Feigning anger*). Anasūyā, I am going.

ANASŪYĀ. What for?

ŚAKUNTALĀ. I am going to tell the venerable Gautamī how impertinently Priyaṁvadā has been prattling.

ANASŪYĀ. It is not proper, my friend, for you to leave at will, before the rites of hospitality are done to an honoured guest.

(*Śakuntalā has already started without saying anything.*)

KING (*Wishing to detain her, then checking himself, aside*). Ah! the state of a lover's mind is an exact reflection of bodily movement; for

Thinking of following the hermit's daughter, all at once I have been held back from advancing by decorum; although not moving from my place it seems as if I had gone and turned back again. (29)

PRIYAṀVADĀ (*Detaining Śakuntalā*). Dear, it is not proper for you to leave.

ŚAKUNTALĀ (*Knitting her eyebrows*). Why not?

PRIYAṀVADĀ. You owe me the watering of two trees. Come then, you will pay your debt and then you can leave.

(*She forces her to turn back.*)

KING. Good lady, it is only by watering trees that the lady, I imagine, is wearied. For,

Her shoulders droop, and the palms of her hands are excessively reddened by lifting up the watering-jar; even now her breathing which is heavier than usual causes a heaving of her breasts; on her face a collection of the drops of sweat has broken out, impeding (the

बद्धं कर्णशिरीषरोधि वदने घर्माम्भसां जालकं
बन्धे स्रंसिनि चैकहस्तयमिताः पर्याकुला मूर्धजाः ॥ ३० ॥

तदहमेनामनृणां करोमि । (इत्यङ्गुलीययं दातुमिच्छति ।)

(उभे नाममुद्राक्षराण्यनुवाच्य परस्परमवलोकयतः ।)

राजा—अलमस्मानन्यथा संभाव्य । राज्ञः परिग्रहोऽयमिति राजपुरुषं मामवगच्छथ ।

प्रियंवदा—तेण हि णारिहदि एदं अङ्गुलीअअं अङ्गुलीविओअं । अज्जस्स वअणेण अणिरिणा दाणिं एसा । (किंचिद्विहस्य ।) हला सउन्दले, मोइदासि अणुअम्पिणा अज्जेण, अधवा महाराएण । गच्छ दाणिं । तेन हि नार्हत्येतदङ्गुलीयकमङ्गुलीवियोगम् । आर्यस्य वचनेनानृणेदानीमेषा । हला शकुन्तले, मोचितास्यनुकम्पिनार्येण, अथवा महाराजेन । गच्छेदानीम् ।

शकुन्तला—(आत्मगतम् ।) जइ अत्तणो पहविस्सं । (प्रकाशम् ।) का तुमं विसज्जिदव्वस्स रुन्धिदव्वस्स वा । यद्यात्मनः प्रभविष्यामि । का त्वं विसर्जितव्यस्य रोद्धव्यस्य वा ।

राजा—(शकुन्तलां विलोक्य, आत्मगतम् ।) किं नु खलु यथा वयमस्यामेवमियमप्यस्मान्प्रति स्यात् । अथवा लब्धावकाशा मे प्रार्थना । कुतः ।

वाचं न मिश्रयति यद्यपि मद्वचोभिः
कर्णं ददात्यभिमुखं मयि भाषमाणे ।
कामं न तिष्ठति मदाननसंमुखीयं
भूयिष्ठमन्यविषया न तु दृष्टिरस्याः ॥ ३१ ॥

(नेपथ्ये ।)

भो भोस्तपस्विनः, संनिहितास्तपोवनसत्त्वरक्षायै भवत । प्रत्यासन्नः किल मृगयाविहारी पार्थिवो दुष्यन्तः ।

play of) the Śirīsa flower in her ear; and the braid getting loose, her dishevelled hair are held together with one hand. (30)

So I will pay back her debt. (*Desires to give a ring.*)

(*Both reading the letters of the name on the seal look at each other.*)

KING. Do not take me to be different (from what I am); this is a present from the king; so, know me to be the king's officer.

PRIYAṀVADĀ. Then indeed this ring does not deserve to be separated from your finger. Your word has already remitted her debt. (*Smiling a little*). Well, Śakuntalā, you are set free by the kind gentleman—or rather by the king himself. So you can go.

ŚAKUNTALĀ (*To herself*). If I have power over myself! (*Aloud*). Who are you to send me away or hold me back?

KING (*Looking at Śakuntalā; to himself*). Is it possible that she feels towards me as I do towards her? Or rather there is ground for hope. For

Although she mingles not her speech with mine, yet when I speak she turns her ear directly opposite to me. Granted that she does not stand with her face turned towards mine, nevertheless, her eyes for the most part are not turned to any other object. (31)

(*Behind the scenes*). Ye hermits, keep close at hand to defend the creatures in the pious grove. For they say king Duṣyanta is diverting himself with the chase in the neighbourhood.

तुरगखुरहतस्तथा हि रेणु-
विटपविषक्तजलार्द्रवल्कलेषु ।
पतति परिणतारुणप्रकाशः
शलभसमूह इवाश्रमद्रुमेषु ॥ ३२ ॥

अपि च ।

तीव्राघातप्रतिहततरुः स्कन्धलग्नैकदन्तः
पादाकृष्टव्रततिवलयासङ्गसंजातपाशः ।
मूर्तो विघ्नस्तपस इव नो भिन्नसारङ्गयूथो
धर्मारण्यं प्रविशति गजः स्यन्दनालोकभीतः ॥ ३३ ॥

(सर्वाः कर्णं दत्वा किंचिदिव संभ्रान्ताः ।)

राजा—(आत्मगतम् ।) अहो धिक् । पौरा अस्मदन्वेषिणस्तपोवनमुपरुन्धन्ति । भवतु । प्रतिगमिष्यामस्तावत् ।

सख्यौ—अज्ज, इमिणा आरण्णअवुत्तन्तेण पज्जाउलम्ह । अणुजाणाहि णो उडअगमणस्स । आर्य, अनेनारण्यकवृत्तान्तेन पर्याकुलाः स्मः । अनुजानीहि न उटजगमनाय ।

राजा—(ससंभ्रमम् ।) गच्छन्तु भवत्यः । वयमप्याश्रमपीडा यथा न भवति तथा प्रयतिष्यामहे ।

(सर्वे उत्तिष्ठन्ति ।)

सख्यौ—अज्ज, असंभाविदअदिहिसक्कारं भूओ वि पेक्खणणिमित्तं लज्जेमो अज्जं विण्णविदुं । आर्य, असंभावितातिथिसत्कारं भूयोऽपि प्रेक्षणनिमित्तं लज्जावहे आर्यं विज्ञापयितुम् ।

राजा—मा मैवम् । दर्शनेनैव भवतीनां पुरस्कृतोऽस्मि ।

शकुन्तला—अणसूए अहिणवकुससूईए परिक्खदं मे चलणं । कुरवअसाहापरिलग्गं च वक्कलं । दाव परिपालेध मं जाव णं मोआवेमि ।

The dust raised by the hoofs of his horses, red as the evening twilight, falls like a locust-swarm on the trees of the hermitage having bark-garments, moist with water, suspended on the boughs. (32)

Moreover,

An elephant, alarmed at the appearance of a car, enters the pious grove, scaring the herd of deer, with fetters formed by the clinging of Vratati coils dragged along by his feet ; having one of his tusks fixed in a tree-trunk, struck by a cruel blow, a very interruption incarnate of our penance. (33).

(*All listen and are a little bewildered.*)

KING (*To himself*). Alas ! my officers are disturbing the holy grove in their search for me. Well I must go back.

THE TWO FRIENDS. Noble sir, this alarm of the wild (elephant) has greatly frightened us. Give us leave to return to the cottage.

KING (*excitedly*). Yes, you go ; and it shall be my care that no disturbance happens in your hermitage.

(*All rise.*)

THE TWO FRIENDS. Noble sir, we are ashamed to request that you will give us the pleasure of seeing you once again, since you have not now been received with the hospitality due to a guest.

KING. Nay, not so ; I feel honoured by the mere sight of you.

ŚAKUNTALĀ. Anasūyā, my foot is cut by the point of a fresh Kuśa-blade ; and my bark-dress is caught on a Kurabaka twig. Wait for me while I loosen it.

अनसूये, अभिनवकुशसूच्या परिक्षतं मे चरणम्। कुरबकशाखापरिलग्नं च वल्कलम्। तावत् परिपालयतं मां यावदेतन्मोचयामि।

(इति राजानमवलोकयन्ती सव्याजं विलम्ब्य सह सखीभ्यां निष्क्रान्ता।)

राजा—मन्दौत्सुक्योऽस्मि नगरगमनं प्रति। यावदनुयात्रिकान्समेत्य नातिदूरे तपोवनस्य निवेशयेयम्। न खलु शक्नोमि शकुन्तलाव्यापारादात्मानं निवर्तयितुम्। मम हि

गच्छति पुरः शरीरं धावति पश्चादसंस्तुतं चेतः।
चीनांशुकमिव केतोः प्रतिवातं नीयमानस्य॥ ३४॥

(इति निष्क्रान्ताः सर्वे।)

इति प्रथमोऽङ्कः।

(*She casts a glance at the king alone and delaying under pretexts goes out with the two friends.*)

KING. I am not very eager now to return to the city. Meanwhile I will join my followers and encamp at no great distance from the holy grove. I cannot, in truth, divert my mind from occupying itself with (thoughts about) Śakuntalā ;

for my

Body moves onward, but my heart, (as if) unrelated (with the former) runs back, like the silken cloth of a banner borne against the wind. (34).

(*Exeunt Omnes.*)

Here Ends Act One.

द्वितीयोऽङ्कः ।

(ततः प्रविशति विषण्णो विदूषकः ।)

विदूषकः—(निःश्वस्य ।) भो दिट्ठं । एदस्स मिअआसीलस्स रण्णो वअस्सभावेण णिव्विण्णो म्हि । अअं मिओ अअं वराहो अअं सद्दूलो त्ति मज्झण्णे वि गिम्हविरलपाअवच्छाआसु वणराईसु आहिण्डीअदि अडवीदो अडविं । पत्तसंकरकसाआइं कडुआइं गिरिणईजलाइं पीअन्ति । अणिअदवेलं सुल्लमंसभूइट्ठो आहारो अण्हीअदि । तुरगाणुधावणकण्डिदसंधिणो रत्तिम्मि वि णिकामं सइदव्वं णत्थि । तदो महन्ते एव्व पच्चूसे दासीएपुत्तेहिं सउणिलुद्धएहिं वणग्गहणकोलाहलेण पडिबोधिदोम्हि । एत्तिएण दाणिं पि पीडा ण णिक्कमदि । तदो गण्डस्स उवरि पिण्डिआ संवुत्ता । हिओ किल अम्हेसु ओहीणेसु तत्तहोदो मिआणुसारेण अस्समपदं पविट्ठस्स तावसकण्णआ सउन्दला णाम मम अधण्णदाए दंसिदा । संपदं णअरगमणस्स मणं कहं वि ण करेदि । अज्ज वि से तं एव्व चिन्तअन्तस्स अच्छीसु पभादं आसि । का गदी । जाव णं किदाचारपरिक्कमं पेक्खामि । (इति परिक्रम्यावलोक्य च ।) एसो बाणासणहत्थाहिं जवणीहिं वणपुप्फमालाधारिणीहिं परिखुदो इदो एव्व आअच्छदि पिअवअस्सो । होदु । अङ्गभङ्गविअलो विअ भविअ चिट्ठिस्सं । जइ एव्वं वि णाम विस्समं लहेअं । (इति दण्डकाष्ठमवलम्ब्य स्थितः) भो दृष्टम् । एतस्य मृगयाशीलस्य राज्ञो वयस्यभावेन निर्विण्णोऽस्मि । अयं मृगोऽयं वराहोऽयं शार्दूल इति मध्याह्नेऽपि ग्रीष्मविरलपादपच्छायासु वनराजीष्वाहिण्ड्यतेऽटवीतोऽटवीम् । पत्रसंकरकषायाणि कटूनि गिरिनदीजलानि पीयन्ते । अनियतवेलं शूल्यमांसभूयिष्ठ आहारो भुज्यते । तुरगानुधावनकण्डितसंधे रात्रावपि निकामं शयितव्यं नास्ति । ततो महत्येव प्रत्यूषे दास्याः पुत्रैः शकुनिलुब्धकैर्वनग्रहणकोलाहलेन प्रतिबोधितोऽस्मि । इयतेदानीमपि पीडा न निष्क्रामति । ततो गण्डस्योपरि पिण्डिका संवृत्ता । ह्यः किलास्मास्ववहीनेषु तत्रभवतो मृगानुसारेणाश्रमपदं प्रविष्टस्य तापसकन्यका

ACT II.

(*Then Enter Vidūṣaka dejected.*)

VIDŪṢAKA (*Sighing*). Oh my fate! I am tired of being friends with this king who is so addicted to the chase. 'Here's a deer,' 'There's a boar,' 'Yonder's a tiger,' thus, even at mid-day, we wander about from forest to forest, amid rows of woods with summer-thinned tree-shades. We drink hot, stinking waters of mountain-torrents, astringent from the mixture of leaves. At irregular hours, we get our meal (consisting) chiefly of meat roasted on spits. And even in the night, I cannot have enough sleep, as my joints are all dislocated by riding on horseback (after the chase). Then at the very earliest dawn, the sons of slave-girls—the fowlers, wake me up with the din of taking the forest. And yet even with all this, my troubles do not end; (for) then there is a (new) pimple growing on the old boil. For, indeed, yesterday, while we were left behind, his Majesty had entered the grounds of the religious domicile, when as my ill-luck would have it, a hermit's daughter named Śakuntalā was presented to his view. And now he has not even a thought of going back to the city. Even to-day, while he was thinking only of her, the (light of) dawn broke upon his eyes. What help! Well, I will see him when he will have performed his usual toilet. (*Walking round and observing*). Ah, here comes my dear friend in this very direction, surrounded by Yavana-girls holding bows in their hands, and wearing garlands of wild-flowers; well, then, I will stand as if crippled by paralysis of my limbs, if even thus I may know (some) respite. (*Stands leaning on a staff.*)

शकुन्तला नाम ममाधन्यतया दर्शिता । सांप्रतं नगरगमनस्य मनः कथमपि न करोति । अद्यापि तस्य तामेव चिन्तयतोऽक्ष्णोः प्रभातमासीत् । का गतिः । यावत्तं कृताचारपरिक्रमं पश्यामि । एष बाणासनहस्ताभिर्यवनीभिर्वनपुष्पमालाधारिणीभिः परिवृत इत एवागच्छति प्रियवयस्यः । भवतु । अङ्गभङ्गविकल इव भूत्वा स्थास्यामि । यद्येवमपि नाम विश्रमं लभेय ।

(ततः प्रविशति यथानिर्दिष्टपरिवारो राजा ।)

राजा—

कामं प्रिया न सुलभा मनस्तु तद्भावदर्शनाश्वासि ।
अकृतार्थेऽपि मनसिजे रतिमुभयप्रार्थना कुरुते ॥ १ ॥

(स्मितं कृत्वा ।) **एवमात्माभिप्रायसंभावितेष्टजनचित्तवृत्तिः प्रार्थयिता विडम्ब्यते । तद्यथा**

स्निग्धं वीक्षितमन्यतोऽपि नयने यत्प्रेरयन्त्या तया
यातं यच्च नितम्बयोर्गुरुतया मन्दं विलासादिव ।
मा गा इत्युपरुद्धया यदपि सा सासूयमुक्ता सखी
सर्वं तत्किल मत्परायणमहो कामी स्वतां पश्यति ॥ २ ॥

विदूषकः—(तथा स्थित एव ।) **भो वअस्स, ण मे हत्थपाआ पसरन्ति । ता वाआमेत्तएण जीआवइस्सं ।** भो वयस्य, न मे हस्तपादं प्रसरति । तद्वाङ्मात्रेण जापयिष्यामि ।

राजा—कुतोऽयं गात्रोपघातः ।

विदूषकः—कुदो किल सअं अच्छीइं आउलीकरिअ अस्सुकारणं पुच्छसि । कुतः किल स्वयमक्षीण्याकुलीकृत्याश्रुकारणं पृच्छसि ।

राजा—न खल्ववगच्छामि । भिन्नार्थमभिधीयताम् ।

विदूषकः—भो वअस्स, जं वेदसो खुज्जलीलं विडम्बेदि तं किं अत्तणो पहावेण । णं णईवेअस्स । वयस्य, यद्वेतसः कुब्जलीलां विडम्बयति, तत्किमात्मनः प्रभावेण । ननु नदिवेगस्य ।

(*Enter king with attendants as described.*)

KING. True, my darling is not easily attainable; yet my heart assumes confidence from observing the manner in which she seems affected. Even though our love has not hitherto prospered, yet our mutual longing causes delight. (1)

(*Smiling*). Thus is the lover beguiled, who judges of the state of his beloved's feeling by his own desires. It is thus

The tender look she cast, even while she directed her eyes elsewhere; her slow movement caused by the heaviness of her hips, as if for grace's sake; the angry words she spoke to her friend who detained her saying 'Do not go;'—all this was, no doubt, on my account! Ah! how does a lover discover his own (everywhere)! (2)

VIDŪṢAKA (*Still in the same position*). O friend, my hands are incapable of movement; therefore, by words merely I will wish you victory.

KING. Whence this palsy of limbs?

VIDŪṢAKA. How, indeed, having yourself troubled my eyes, you ask what makes them weep?

KING. Indeed, I know not what you mean; speak intelligibly.

VIDŪṢAKA. Well, my friend, when the reed imitates the character of the Kubja plant, is it by its own act, or by the force of the stream?

राजा—नदीवेगस्तत्र कारणम् ।

विदूषकः—मम वि भवं । ममापि भवान् ।

राजा—कथमिव ।

विदूषकः—एव्वं राअकज्जाणि उज्झिअ एदारिसे आउलप्पदेसे वणचरवुत्तिणा तुए होदव्वं । जं सच्चं पच्चहं सावदाणुसरणेहिं संखोहिअसंधिबन्धाणं मम गत्ताणं अणीसो म्हि संवुत्तो । त्ता पसादइस्सं विसज्जिदुं मं एक्काहं वि दाव विस्समिदुं । एवं राजकार्याण्युज्झित्वैतादृश आकुलप्रदेशे वनचरवृत्तिना त्वया भवितव्यम् । यत्सत्यं प्रत्यहं श्वापदानुसरणैः संक्षोभितसंधिबन्धानां मम गात्राणामनीशोऽस्मि संवृत्तः । तत्प्रसादयिष्यामि विसर्जितुं मामेकाहमपि तावद्विश्रमितुम् ।

राजा—(स्वगतम् ।) अयं चैवमाह । ममापि काश्यपसुतामनुस्मृत्य मृगयाविक्लवं चेतः । कुतः ।

न नमयितुमधिज्यमस्मि शक्तो
धनुरिदमाहितसायकं मृगेषु ।
सहवसतिमुपेत्य यैः प्रियायाः
कृत इव मुग्धविलोकितोपदेशः ॥ ३ ॥

विदूषकः—(राज्ञो मुखं विलोक्य ।) अत्तभवं किं वि हिअए करिअ मन्तेदि । अरण्णे मए रुदिअं आसि । अत्रभवान्किमपि हृदये कृत्वा मन्त्रयते । अरण्ये मया रुदितमासीत् ।

राजा—(सस्मितम् ।) किमन्यत् । अनतिक्रमणीयं मे सुहृद्वाक्यमिति स्थितोऽस्मि ।

विदूषकः—चिरं जीअ । (इति गन्तुमिच्छति) चिरं जीव ।

राजा—वयस्य, तिष्ठ । सावशेषं मे वचः ।

विदूषकः—आणवेदु भवं । आज्ञापयतु भवान् ।

राजा—विश्रान्तेन भवता ममाप्यनायासे कर्मणि सहायेन भवितव्यम् ।

विदूषकः—किं मोदअखण्डिआए । तेण हि अअं सुगहीदो खणो । किं मोदकखण्डिकायाम् । तेन ह्ययं सुगृहीतः क्षणः ।

KING. The force of the stream is the cause of it.

VIDŪṢAKA. So are you, of my (troubles).

KING. How indeed?

VIDŪṢAKA. That you should leave the affairs of your empire, and live like a forester in a wild and unfrequented region like this! So that, truth to say, I am become no longer master of my own limbs whose joints are all shaken up by my daily running after wild animals. I, therefore, entreat you to favour me with your permission to repose but a single day.

KING (*To himself*). He says this; and I, too, when I think of Kaṇva's daughter, have little relish for hunting. For

> I am not able to bend this strung bow, with the arrow fixed upon it, against the fawns, who, abiding with my darling, have taught her those beautiful glances! (3)

VIDŪṢAKA (*Looking at the king's face*). You have something in your mind and have been deliberating. Mine is a cry in the wilderness.

KING (*Smilingly*). What else? I ought not to disregard a friend's advice; and so I stand here.

VIDŪṢAKA. May you live long! (*Desires to leave.*)

KING. Stay, friend, I have not done.

VIDŪṢAKA. Let the king command.

KING. When you have taken repose, I, too, shall want your assistance in another business, that will cause you no fatigue.

VIDŪṢAKA. Eating a few sweetmeats? Well, then, I accept the engagement.

राजा—यत्र वक्ष्यामि। कः कोऽत्र भोः।

(प्रविश्य।)

दौवारिकः—[प्रणम्य।] आणवेदु भट्टा। आज्ञापयतु भर्ता।

राजा—रैवतक, सेनापतिस्तावदाहूयताम्।

दौवारिकः—तह। (इति निष्क्रम्य सेनापतिना सह पुनः प्रविश्य।) एसो अण्णावअणुक्कण्ठो भट्टा इदो दिण्णदिट्ठी एव्व चिट्ठदि। उवसप्पदु अज्जो। तथा। एष आज्ञावचनोत्कण्ठो भर्तेतो दत्तदृष्टिरेव तिष्ठति। उपसर्पत्वार्यः।

सेनापतिः—(राजानमवलोक्य।) दृष्टदोषापि स्वामिनि मृगया केवलं गुण एव संवृत्ता। तथा हि देवः

अनवरतधनुर्ज्यास्फालनक्रूरपूर्वं
रविकिरणसहिष्णु क्लेशलेशैरभिन्नम्।
अपचितमपि गात्रं व्यायतत्वादलक्ष्यं
गिरिचर इव नागः प्राणसारं बिभर्ति॥ ४॥

(उपेत्य।) जयतु स्वामी। गृहीतश्वापदमरण्यम्। किमिति स्थीयते।

राजा—मन्दोत्साहः कृतोऽस्मि मृगयापवादिना माठव्येन।

सेनापतिः—(जनान्तिकम्।) सखे, स्थिरप्रतिबन्धो भव। अहं तावत्स्वामिनश्चित्तवृत्तिमनुवर्तिष्ये। (प्रकाशम्।) प्रलपत्येष वैधेयः। ननु प्रभुरेव निदर्शनम्।

मेदश्छेदकृशोदरं लघु भवत्युत्थानयोग्यं वपुः
सत्त्वानामपि लक्ष्यते विकृतिमच्चित्तं भयक्रोधयोः।

KING. I will tell you where. Hola ! Who is there ?

(*Entering*) DOOR-KEEPER. Let my sovereign command me.

KING. Raivataka, bid the General attend.

DOOR-KEEPER. I obey--(*He goes out and returns with the General*). There is his Majesty eager to give (some) command, looking in this very direction ; sir, you will draw near.

GENERAL (*Looking at the king*). Though reckoned a vice, hunting has proved only an advantage in our King. Thus his Majesty

> Like a mountain-roving elephant possesses a body, whose forepart is hardened by the ceaseless friction of the bow-string, which is capable of enduring the sun's rays, and is not affected by the slightest fatigue ; though reduced in bulk yet is not marked (as such) by reason of its muscular development, and is all life and vitality. (4)

(*Approaching*). May our monarch ever be victorious. The forest has its beasts of prey tracked ; why then delay ?

KING. My ardour has been all damped by Māṭhavya who has been preaching against hunting.

GENERAL (*Aside*). Friend, be firm in your opposition. I will humour the king for a while. (*Aloud*). This fool talks nonsense. Why, our king himself is an example. Consider, your Majesty ;

> The (hunter's) body, with the waist attenuated by the removal of fat becomes light and fit

उत्कर्षः स च धन्विना यदिषवः सिध्यन्ति लक्ष्ये चले
मिथ्यैव व्यसनं वदन्ति मृगयामीदृग्विनोदः कुतः ॥ ५ ॥

विदूषकः—(सरोषम्) अवेहि रे उच्छाहहेतुअ । अत्तभवं पकिदिं आपण्णो । तुमं दाव अडवीदो अडवीं आहिण्डन्तो णरणासिआलोलुवस्स जिण्णरिच्छस्स कस्स वि मुहे पडिस्ससि । अपेहि रे उत्साहहेतुक । अत्रभवान्प्राकृतिमापन्नः । त्वं तावदटवीतोऽटवीमाहिण्डमानो नरनासिकालोलुपस्य जीर्णऋक्षस्य कस्यापि मुखे पतिष्यसि ।

राजा—भद्र सेनापते, आश्रमसंनिकृष्टे स्थिताः स्मः । अतस्ते वचो नाभिनन्दामि । अद्य तावत्

गाहन्तां महिषा निपानसलिलं शृङ्गैर्मुहुस्ताडितं
छायाबद्धकदम्बकं मृगकुलं रोमन्थमभ्यस्यतु ।
विश्रब्धं क्रियतां वराहततिभिर्मुस्ताक्षतिः पल्वले
विश्रामं लभतामिदं च शिथिलज्याबन्धमस्मद्धनुः ॥ ६ ॥

सेनापतिः—यत्प्रभविष्णवे रोचते ।

राजा—तेन हि निवर्तय पूर्वगतान्वनग्राहिणः । यथा न मे सैनिकास्तपोवनमुपरुन्धन्ति तथा निषेद्धव्याः । पश्य ।

शमप्रधानेषु तपोवनेषु
गूढं हि दाहात्मकमस्ति तेजः ।
स्पर्शानुकूला इव सूर्यकान्ता-
स्तदन्यतेजोऽभिभवाद्वमन्ति ॥ ७ ॥

for exertion ; besides, the spirit of even the beasts is observed to be affected with various emotions, through fear and anger ; and that is the glory of the archers, when their arrows hit the mark as it flies ; falsely indeed do they call hunting a vice ; no recreation, surely, can be compared with it. (5)

VIDŪṢAKA (*Angrily*). Away, you inciter. His Majesty has come to his senses ; but you chasing from forest to forest, will surely fall into the jaws of some old bear greedy after a man's nose !

KING. Good General, we are staying in the vicinity of a hermitage. I cannot, therefore, approve your words. So for to-day,

Let the buffaloes plunge into the waters of tanks struck repeatedly with their horns ; let the deer herding together underneath the shade chew the cud ; let herds of boar, undisturbed, bruise the Mustā grass in the pool ; and let this my bow, take repose with a slackened string. (6)

GENERAL. As it pleases your Majesty.

KING. Well, then recall the forest-beaters that have already left ; and forbid my soldiers to vex this hallowed grove. Remember,

Holy men, pre-eminent in the virtue of quietism, conceal within their bosom a scorching flame, which, like sun-crystals which are grateful to the touch, they emit when assailed by some foreign lustre. (7)

सेनापतिः—यदाज्ञापयति स्वामी ।

विदूषकः—गच्छ भो दासीएपुत्त । धंसदु दे उच्छाहवुत्तन्तो
गच्छ भो दास्याःपुत्र । ध्वंसतां त उत्साहवृत्तान्तः ।

(निष्क्रान्तः सेनापतिः ।)

राजा—(परिजनं विलोक्य ।) अपनयन्तु भवत्यो मृगयावेषम् । रैवतक, त्वमपि स्वं नियोगमशून्यं कुरु ।

परिजनः—जं देवो आणवेदि । (इति निष्क्रान्तः ।) यद्देव आज्ञापयति ।

विदूषकः—किदं भवदा णिम्मच्छिअं । संपदं एदस्सिं पादवच्छाआए विरइदलदाविदाणदंसणीआए आसणे णिसीददु भवं जाव अहं वि सुहासीणो होमि । कृतं भवता निर्मक्षिकम् । सांप्रतमेतस्यां पादपच्छायायां विरचितलतावितानदर्शनीयायामासने निषीदतु भवान्, यावदहमपि सुखासीनो भवामि ।

राजा—गच्छाग्रतः ।

विदूषकः—एदु भवं । एतु भवान् ।

(इत्युभौ परिक्रम्योपविष्टौ ।)

राजा—माठव्य, अनवाप्तचक्षुःफलोऽसि । येन त्वया दर्शनीयं न दृष्टम् ।

विदूषकः—णं भवं अग्गदो मे वट्टदि । ननु भावनग्रतो मे वर्तते ।

राजा—सर्वः कान्तमात्मीयं पश्यति । तामाश्रमललामभूतां शकुन्तलामधिकृत्य ब्रवीमि ।

विदूषकः—(स्वगतम्) होदु । से अवसरं ण दाइस्सं । (प्रकाशम्) भो वअस्स, ते तावसकण्णआ अब्भत्थणीआ दीसदि । भवतु । अस्यावसरं न दास्ये । भो वयस्य, ते तापसकन्यकाभ्यर्थनीया दृश्यते ।

राजा—सखे, न परिहार्ये वस्तुनि पौरवाणां मनः प्रवर्तते ।

GENERAL. As your Majesty commands.

VIDŪṢAKA. Get away, you son of a slave-girl! You have talked in vain about exertion (in the chase.)

(*Exit General.*)

KING (*Looking to his attendants*). Put off your hunting apparel; and thou, Raivataka, return to thy post of duty.

ATTENDANTS. As our lord bids. (*Exit.*)

VIDŪṢAKA. So you have now cleared the stage. Now be seated on this stone-slab, over which the trees spread their beautiful, canopy of shade; so that I, too, will sit at mine ease.

KING. Lead the way.

VIDŪṢAKA. Come along, sir.

(*They walk about and sit down.*)

KING. Māthavya, you have not obtained the fruit of your eyes, since you have not beheld the fairest of all objects.

VIDŪṢAKA. Why, you are there in front of me.

KING. Every one thinks his own as beautiful; but I am speaking in reference to that same Śakuntalā, who is the ornament of the hermitage.

VIDŪṢAKA (*Aside*). Well, I will give him no chance. (*Aloud*). Well, my friend, it appears she is a hermit's daughter whom you love.

KING. Friend, the thoughts of Puru's descendants will never dwell on any forbidden object.

सुरयुवतिसंभवं किल मुनेरपत्यं तदुज्झिताधिगतम् ।
अर्कस्योपरि शिथिलं च्युतमिव नवमालिकाकुसुमम् ॥ ८ ॥

विदूषकः—(विहस्य)—जह कस्स वि पिण्डखज्जूरेहिं उव्वेजिदस्स तिन्तिणीए अहिलासो भवे, तह इत्थिआरदणपरिभाविणो भवदो इअं अब्भत्थणा । यथा कस्यापि पिण्डखर्जूरैरुद्वेजितस्य तिन्तिण्यामभिलाषो भवेत्, तथा स्त्रीरत्नपरिभाविनो भवत इयमभ्यर्थना ।

राजा—न तावदेनां पश्यसि येनैममवादीः ।

विदूषकः—तं क्खु रमणिज्जं जं भवदो वि विम्हअं उप्पादेदि । तत्खलु रमणीयं यद्भवतोऽपि विस्मयमुत्पादयति ।

राजा—वयस्य, किं बहुना ।

चित्रे निवेश्य परिकल्पितसत्त्वयोगा
रूपोच्चयेन मनसा विधिना कृता नु ।
स्त्रीरत्नसृष्टिरपरा प्रतिभाति सा मे
धातुर्विभुत्वमनुचिन्त्य वपुश्च तस्याः ॥ ९ ॥

विदूषकः—जइ एव्वं पच्चादेसो दाणिं रूववदीणं । यद्येवं प्रत्यादेश इदानीं रूपवतीनाम् ।

राजा—इदं च मे मनसि वर्तते ।

अनाघ्रातं पुष्पं किसलयमलूनं कररुहै-
रनाविद्धं रत्नं मधु नवमनास्वादितरसम् ।
अखण्डं पुण्यानां फलमिव च तद्रूपमनघं
न जाने भोक्तारं कमिह समुपस्थास्यति विधिः ॥ १० ॥

Sprung from a nymph of heaven, so it is said, this sage's child was found by him when she deserted her; like a Navamallikā flower loosened and flung upon the Sun-plant. (8)

VIDŪṢAKA (*Laughing*). This desire of yours, who scorn the bright gems of women in your palace, is like the fancy of a man who has lost his relish for dates, and longs for the (sour) tamarind.

KING. You have not seen her; and, therefore, you speak thus.

VIDŪṢAKA. That indeed must be charming, which excites even your admiration.

KING. Friend, what need is there of many words?

Was she delineated in a picture and then endowed with life? Or was she moulded in the Creator's mind from an assemblage (selection) of all lovely forms? When I meditate on the power of the creator, and on her lineaments, she appears to me like a matchless creation of the loveliest of women. (9)

VIDŪṢAKA. If that is so, she must render all other handsome women contemptible.

KING. This, moreover, is in my thought:

This immaculate beauty is like a flower not yet smelt, a delicate shoot not torn by the nails; an unperforated diamond; or fresh honey whose sweetness is yet untasted; or the full reward of meritorious deeds. I know not whom Destiny will approach as the enjoyer here (of this form). (10)

विदूषकः—तेण हि लहु परित्ताअदु णं भवं । मा कस्स वि तवस्सिणो इङ्गुदीतेल्लचिक्कणसीसस्स हत्थे पडिस्सदि । तेन हि लघु परित्रायतामेनां भवान् । मा कस्यापि तपस्विन इङ्गुदीतैलमिश्रचिक्कण-शीर्षस्य हस्ते पतिष्यति ।

राजा—परवती खलु तत्रभवती । न च संनिहितोऽत्र गुरुजनः ।

विदूषकः—अध भवन्तं अन्तरेण कीदिसो से दिट्ठिराओ । अथ भवन्तमन्तरेण कीदृशस्तस्या दृष्टिरागः ।

राजा—निसर्गादेवाप्रगल्भस्तपस्विकन्याजनः । तथापि तु

अभिमुखे मयि संहृतमीक्षितं
हसितमन्यनिमित्तकृतोदयम् ।
विनयवारितवृत्तिरतस्तया
न विवृतो मदनो न च संवृतः ॥ ११ ॥

विदूषकः—णं क्खु दिट्ठमेत्तस्स तुह अङ्कं आरोहदि । ननु खलु दृष्टमात्रस्य तवाङ्कमारोहति ।

राजा—मिथःप्रस्थाने पुनः शालीनतयापि काममाविष्कृतो भावस्तत्रभवत्या । तथा हि ।

दर्भाङ्कुरेण चरणः क्षत इत्यकाण्डे
तन्वी स्थिता कतिचिदेव पदानि गत्वा ।
आसीद्विवृत्तवदना च विमोचयन्ती
शाखासु वल्कलमसक्तमपि द्रुमाणाम् ॥ १२ ॥

विदूषकः—तेण हि गहीदपाधेओ होहि । किदं तुए उववणं तवोवणं त्ति पेक्खामि । तेन हि गृहीतपाथेयो भव । कृतं त्वयोपवनं तपो-वनमिति पश्यामि ।

VIDŪṢAKA. Let your Highness make haste, then, to rescue her, lest she should fall into the hands of some hermit whose head shines with the oil of Ingudi.

KING. She is not her own mistress; and her father is not here.

VIDŪṢAKA. Well, what kind of feeling did her eyes betray towards your Honour?

KING. The daughters in a hermit's family are naturally (so) reserved; yet,

> She averted her eyes, when I stood facing her and she smiled (as it were) from some other cause (than love); hence love, whose course was checked by modesty was neither fully displayed (by her) nor yet wholly concealed. (11)

VIDŪṢAKA. Surely you did not expect her to climb into your lap the moment she saw you!

KING. But, at our mutual parting, she did betray her feeling towards me, though with modesty.

> For when the slim (girl) had proceeded but a few steps, she stopped all of a sudden, saying, "My foot is hurt by the points of the Kuśa grass;" and then she turned back her face (towards me), whilst (pretending to be occupied with) disentangling her bark-dress from the branches of the shrubs in which it had not really been caught. (12)

VIDŪṢAKA. Well, then, provide yourself with a stock of provender; you have made a pleasure-garden of the penance-grove, I find.

राजा—सखे, तपस्विभिः कैश्चित्परिज्ञातोऽस्मि। चिन्तय तावत्केनापदेशेन सकृदप्याश्रमे वसामः।

विदूषकः—को अवरो अवदेसो। णं तुमं राआ। णीवारच्छट्ठभाअं अम्हाणं उपहरन्तु त्ति। कोऽपरोऽपदेशः। ननु त्वं राजा। नीवारषष्ठभागमस्माकमुपहरन्त्विति।

राजा—मूर्ख, अन्यद्भागधेयमेतेषां रक्षणे निपतति, यद्रत्नराशीनपि विहायाभिनन्द्यम्। पश्य।

यदुत्तिष्ठति वर्णेभ्यो नृपाणां क्षयि तत्फलम्।
तपःषड्भागमक्षय्यं ददत्यारण्यका हि नः॥ १३॥

(नेपथ्ये।)

हन्त, सिद्धार्थौ स्वः।

राजा—(कर्णं दत्त्वा।) अये, धीरप्रशान्तस्वरैस्तपस्विभिर्भवितव्यम्।

(प्रविश्य।)

दौवारिकः—जेदु भट्टा। एदे दुवे इसिकुमारआ पडिहारभूमिं उवट्ठिदा। जयतु भर्ता। एतौ द्वौ ऋषिकुमारौ प्रतीहारभूमिमुपस्थितौ।

राजा—तेन ह्यविलम्बितं प्रवेशय तौ।

दौवारिकः—एसो पवेसेमि। (इति निष्क्रम्य ऋषिकुमाराभ्यां सह प्रविश्य।) इदो इदो भवन्ता। एष प्रवेशयामि। इत इतो भवन्तौ।

(उभौ राजानं विलोकयतः।)

प्रथमः—अहो दीप्तिमतोऽपि विश्वसनीयतास्य वपुषः। अथवोपपन्नमेतदृषिभ्यो नातिभिन्ने राजनि। कुतः।

KING. Friend, a few hermits have recognized me; find out, therefore, some pretext for our entering into that religious domicile once again.

VIDŪṢAKA. What (need of any) other pretext? Are you not the king? (You can enter saying) "Bring us our sixth part of your grain."

KING. Fool, these hermits pay quite a different tribute, which is welcomed more than heaps of jewels; see,

> The wealth of princes, collected from the (four) classes (of their subjects) is perishable; but these hermits give us a sixth part of (the fruits of their) piety which is imperishable. (13)

(*Behind the scenes.*)

O joy! We have now attained the object of our desire.

KING (*Listening*). Oh! These must be hermits (to judge) by their grave and (yet) calm voices.

(*Entering*) DOOR-KEEPER. May the king be victorious! Here are two hermit-boys arrived at the door.

KING. Well, then, introduce them without delay.

DOOR-KEEPER. Well, I will bring them. (*He goes out and then returns with the young hermits.*) This way, sir, this way.

(*Both look at the king.*)

FIRST. Oh! A majestic presence, and yet what confidence it inspires! Or this is quite proper in a king who is very little inferior to a sage. For

अध्याक्रान्ता वसतिरमुनाप्याश्रमे सर्वभोग्ये
रक्षायोगादयमपि तपः प्रत्यहं संचिनोति ।
अस्यापि द्यां स्पृशति वशिनश्चारणद्वन्द्वगीतः
पुण्यः शब्दो मुनिरिति मुहुः केवलं राजपूर्वः ॥ १४ ॥

द्वितीयः—गौतम, अयं स बलभित्सखो दुष्यन्तः ।

प्रथमः—अथ किम् ।

द्वितीयः—तेन हि

नैतच्चित्रं यदयमुदधिश्यामसीमां धरित्री-
मेकः कृत्स्नां नगरपरिघप्रांशुबाहुर्भुनक्ति ।
आशंसन्ते सुरसमितयो बद्धवैरा हि दैत्यै-
रस्याधिज्ये धनुषि विजयं पौरुहूते च वज्रे ॥ १५ ॥

उभौ—(उपगम्य ।) विजयस्व राजन् ।

राजा—(आसनादुत्थाय ।) अभिवादये भवन्तौ ।

उभौ—स्वस्ति भवते ।

(इति फलान्युपहरतः ।)

राजा—(सप्रणामं परिगृह्य ।) आज्ञापयितुमिच्छामि ।

उभौ—विदितो भवानाश्रमसदामिहस्थः । तेन भवन्तं प्रार्थयन्ते ।

राजा—किमाज्ञापयन्ति ।

उभौ—तत्रभवतः कण्वस्य महर्षेरसांनिध्याद्रक्षांसि न इष्टिविघ्नमुत्पादयन्ति । तत्कतिपयरात्रं सारथिद्वितीयेन भवता सनाथीक्रियतामाश्रम इति ।

He, too, now abides in that stage of life which is open to the enjoyment of everyone; and through his exertions for (our) safety he has been accumulating the merit of penance from day to day; and the sacred title of Muni preceded by the (word) Rāja of this king, too, who has conquered his passions, frequently ascends to heaven, being chanted by pairs of bards. (14)

SECOND. Gautama, so this is Duṣyanta, the friend of Indra.

FIRST. Yes, it is.

SECOND. Then, indeed,

It is not wonderful that he whose arm is long as the bar of a city (gate) alone protects the whole earth bounded by the dark (green) ocean. For the Gods, rooted in their enmity with the demons, rely for victory in battles on his braced bow and Indra's thunder-bolt. (15)

BOTH (*Advancing*). O king, be victorious!

KING (*Rising from his seat*). I salute you.

BOTH. Blessings on you! (*They offer fruit.*)

KING (*Receiving it with a bow*). I desire (to know) your command.

BOTH. Your Highness is known by the dwellers of the hermitage to be staying here; and they, therefore, implore your Highness—

KING. What is their command?

BOTH. In the absence of his Reverence, the great sage Kaṇva, some evil demons are disturbing our sacrificial

राजा—अनुगृहीतोऽस्मि।

विदूषकः—(अपवार्य।) एसा दाणिं अणुऊला ते अब्भत्थणा। एषेदानीमनुकूला तेऽभ्यर्थना।

राजा—(स्मितं कृत्वा।) रैवतक, मद्वचनादुच्यतां सारथिः सबाणासनं रथमुपस्थापयेति।

दौवारिकः—जं देवो आणवेदि। (इति निष्क्रान्तः।) यद्देव आज्ञापयति।

उभौ—(सहर्षम्।)

अनुकारिणि पूर्वेषां युक्तरूपमिदं त्वयि।
आपन्नाभयसत्रेषु दीक्षिताः खलु पौरवाः॥१६॥

राजा—(सप्रमाणम्।) गच्छतां पुरौ भवन्तौ। अहमप्यनुपदमागत एव।

उभौ—विजयस्व। (इति निष्क्रान्तौ।)

राजा—माठव्य, अप्यस्ति शकुन्तलादर्शने कुतूहलम्।

विदूषकः—पढमं सपरीवाहं आसि। दाणिं रक्खसवुत्तन्तेण बिन्दूवि णावसेसिदो। प्रथमं सपरीवाहमासीत् इदानीं राक्षसवृत्तान्तेन बिन्दुरपि नावशेषितः।

राजा—मा भैषीः। ननु मत्समीपे वर्तिष्यसे।

विदूषकः—एस रक्खसादो रक्खिदो म्हि। एष राक्षसाद्रक्षितोऽस्मि।

(प्रविश्य।)

दौवारिकः—सज्जो रधो भट्टिणो विजअप्पत्थाणं अवेक्खदि। एस उण णअरादो देवीणं आणत्तिहरओ करभओ आअदो। सज्जो रथो भर्तुर्विजयप्रस्थानमपेक्षते। एष पुनर्नगराद्देवीनामाज्ञप्तिहरः करभक आगतः।

राजा—(सादरम्।) किमम्बाभिः प्रेषितः।

दौवारिकः—अह इं। अथ किम्।

राजा—ननु प्रवेश्यताम्।

rites. Deign, therefore, accompanied by your charioteer to be master of the hermitage, for a few nights.

KING. I am highly favoured.

VIDŪṢAKA (*Aside*). Here is now a request favourable to you!

KING (*Smiling*). Raivataka, say to the charioteer in my name, "Bring my car and my bow."

DOOR-KEEPER. As your Majesty commands. (*Exit.*)

BOTH. (*With joy*).

This well becomes you, who emulate your ancestors; truly the descendants of Puru are the officiating priests in the sacrifices of delivering from fear the distressed. (16)

KING (*Bowing*). Go first, sirs; I too will follow instantly.

BOTH. Be ever victorious. (*Exeunt.*)

KING. Māṭhavya, have you any curiosity to see Śakuntalā?

VIDŪṢAKA. At first it was full to overflowing; but now by this talk of the demons, not even a drop is left.

KING. Oh, fear nothing: you will be with me.

VIDŪṢAKA. I am protected from the demons.

(*Entering*) DOOR-KEEPER. The car is ready, and awaits my Lord's advance to victory; but here is Karabhaka, just arrived from the city, bearing a message from the Queen-mother.

KING. (*Respectfully*). What, sent by my mother?

DOOR-KEEPER. Yes.

KING. Well, bring him to me.

दौवारिकः—तह। (इति निष्क्रम्य करभकेण सह प्रविश्य।) एसो भट्टा। उवसप्प। तथा। एष भर्ता। उपसर्प।

करभकः—जेदु भट्टा। देवी आणवेदि। आआमिणि चउत्थदिअहे पुत्तपिण्डपालणो णाम उववासो भविस्सदि। तहिं दीहाउणा अवस्सं संभाविदव्वा त्ति। जयतु भर्ता। देव्याज्ञापयति। आगामिनि चतुर्थदिवसे पुत्रपिण्डपालनो नाम उपवासो भविष्यति। तत्र दीर्घायुषावश्यं संभावनीयेति।

राजा—इतस्तपस्विकार्यम्। इतो गुरुजनाज्ञा। द्वयमनतिक्रमणीयम्। किमत्र प्रतिविधेयम्।

विदूषकः—तिसङ्कु विअ अन्तराले चिट्ठ। त्रिशङ्कुरिवान्तराले तिष्ठ।

राजा—सत्यमाकुलीभूतोऽस्मि।

कृत्ययोर्भिन्नदेशत्वाद्द्वैधीभवति मे मनः।
पुरः प्रतिहतं शैले स्रोतः स्रोतोवहो यथा॥ १७॥

(विचिन्त्य।) सखे, त्वमम्बया पुत्र इति प्रतिगृहीतः। अतो भवानितः प्रतिनिवृत्य तपस्विकार्यव्यग्रमानसं मामावेद्य तत्रभवतीनां पुत्रकृत्यमनुष्ठातुमर्हति।

विदूषकः—णं क्खु मं रक्खोभीरुअं गणेसि। ननु खलु मां रक्षोभीरुकं गणयसि।

राजा—(सस्मितम्) कथमेतद्भवति संभाव्यते।

विदूषकः—जह राआणुएण गन्तव्वं तह गच्छामि। यथा राजानुजेन गन्तव्यं तथा गच्छामि।

राजा—ननु तपोवनोपरोधः परिहरणीय इति सर्वानानुयात्रिकांस्त्वयैव सह प्रस्थापयामि।

DOOR-KEEPER. Yes. (*Goes out and returns with Karabhaka.*) Here is his Majesty. Advance.

KARABHAKA. Victory to your Majesty. The royal mother sends this command : On the fourth day from to-day, falls the fast named "Putra-pinda-pālana ;" and on that occasion the long-lived one ought not fail to honour us with his presence.

KING. On one hand is a commission from holy hermits ; on the other, a command from my revered parent : neither may be neglected ; what is the remedy ?

VIDŪSAKA. Stay suspended (between them both) like Triṣanku.

KING. In truth I am (greatly) perplexed.

My mind is distracted by the difference of the two places where the two duties have to be performed, as the stream of a river is split in two by rocks lying before it. (17)

(*Musing*). You have been treated by the Queen-mother as a son. Do you, therefore, return from hence and tell her how my mind is intent on this commission of the hermits, and have the goodness to perform yourself the offices of a son.

VIDŪṢAKA. But you will not really suppose that I was afraid of the demons.

KING (*Smilingly*). How is this possible in your Honour ?

VIDŪṢAKA. But I would go, as befits a younger brother of the king.

KING. Surely, I will dispatch my whole train to attend you, for the pious grove must not be disturbed.

विदूषकः—तेण हि जुवराओ म्हि दाणिं संवुत्तो। तेन हि युवराजोऽस्मीदानीं संवृत्तः।

राजा—(आत्मगतम् ।) चपलोऽयं बटुः। कदाचिदस्मत्प्रार्थनामन्तःपुरेभ्यः कथयेत्। भवतु। एनमेवं वक्ष्ये। (विदूषकं हस्ते गृहीत्वा। प्रकाशम् ।) वयस्य, ऋषिगौरवादाश्रमं गच्छामि। न खलु सत्यमेव तापसकन्यकायां ममाभिलाषः। पश्य।

क्व वयं क्व परोक्षमन्मथो
मृगशावैः सममेधितो जनः।
परिहासविजल्पितं सखे
परमार्थेन न गृह्यतां वचः॥ १८॥

(इति निष्क्रान्ताः सर्वे ।)

इति द्वितीयोऽङ्कः।

VIDŪṢAKA (*Proudly*). Then indeed I am the young prince.

KING. (*To himself*). The fellow is a chatterbox. He might disclose my present pursuit to the ladies in the palace. Good, then ; I will say this to him. (*He takes Vidūṣaka by the hand. Aloud*). Friend, I shall enter the hermitage (only) through respect for the sages. Do not think that I have any real inclination for the hermit-girl Śakuntalā. Just think :

Where are we, and where a person bred with the fawns, and a stranger to love ! O friend ! let not the light words spoken in jest be taken in earnest. (18)

VIDŪṢAKA. Yes, to be sure.

(*All go out.*)

End of act II.

तृतीयोऽङ्कः ।

(ततः प्रविशति कुशानादाय यजमानशिष्यः ।)

शिष्यः—अहो, महानुभावः पार्थिवो दुष्यन्तः । प्रविष्टमात्र एवाश्रमं तत्रभवति राजनि निरुपप्लवानि नः कर्माणि संवृत्तानि ।

का कथा बाणसंधाने ज्याशब्देनैव दूरतः ।
हुंकारेणेव धनुषः स हि विघ्नानपोहति ॥ १ ॥

यावदिमान्वेदिसंस्तरणार्थं दर्भानृत्विग्भ्य उपनयामि (परिक्रम्यावलोक्य च । आकाशे ।) प्रियंवदे, कस्येदमुशीरानुलेपनं मृणालवन्ति च नलिनीपत्राणि नीयन्ते । (श्रुतिमभिनीय ।) किं ब्रवीषि । आतपलङ्घनाद्बलवदस्वस्था शकुन्तला । तस्याः शरीरनिर्वापणायेति । तर्हि त्वरितं गम्यताम् । सा खलु भगवतः कण्वस्य कुलपतेरुच्छ्वसितम् । अहमपि तावद्वैतानिकं शान्त्युदकमस्यै गौतमीहस्ते विसर्जयिष्यामि । (इति निष्क्रान्तः ।)

विष्कम्भकः ।

(ततः प्रविशति कामयमानावस्थो राजा ।)

राजा—(निःश्वस्य ।)

जाने तपसो वीर्यं सा बाला परवतीति मे विदितम् ।
न च निम्नादिव सलिलं निवर्तते मे ततो हृदयम् ॥ २ ॥

ACT III.

(Then enter the sacrificer's pupil bearing Kuśa-grass.)

PUPIL. How great is the power of king Duṣyanta! Since his Highness had no sooner entered the hermitage than we could continue our holy rites undisturbed.

> Why talk of aiming the shaft? For by the mere sound of the bow-string from afar, as if by the angry murmur of his bow, he disperses (at once) our obstacles. (1)

Now, then, I shall deliver to the priests this Kuśa-grass to be scattered round the altar. (*Moving about and observing; in the air*). Ah! Priyaṁvadā, for whom are you carrying this Uśīra ointment and these lotus-leaves with stalks? (*Acting as if he has heard*). What say you? "That Śakuntalā is extremely disordered from injury caused by the Sun's heat, and these are for cooling her body." Well, then, go quickly; for she is the very life-breath of the venerable Kaṇva, the head of our society. I, too, will send to Gautamī for her some healing water consecrated in the sacrificial rites.

(*Exit.*)

Here ends the prelude.

(*Enter Duṣyanta, expressing the distraction of a lover.*)

KING. (*With a sigh*).

> I know the power of penance: and I am further aware that the maiden is not her own mistress; and yet my heart can no more turn back from her, than water can from a slope. (2)

भगवन्कुसुमायुध, त्वया चन्द्रमसा च विश्वसनीयाभ्यामति-
संधीयते कामिजनसार्थः । कुतः ।

तव कुसुमशरत्वं शीतरश्मित्वमिन्दो-
र्द्वयमिदमयथार्थं दृश्यते मद्विधेषु ।
विसृजति हिमगर्भैरग्निमिन्दुर्मयूखै-
स्त्वमपि कुसुमबाणान्वज्रसारीकरोषि ॥ ३ ॥

(मदनबाधां निरूप्य । सासूयम् ।) भगवन्मन्मथ । कुतस्ते कुसुमायुधस्य शरतैक्ष्ण्यमेतत् । (स्मृत्वा ।) आं ज्ञातम् ।

अद्यापि नूनं हरकोपवह्नि-
स्त्वयि ज्वलत्यौर्व इवाम्बुराशौ ।
त्वमन्यथा मन्मथ मद्विधानां
भस्मावशेषः कथमेवमुष्णः ॥ ४ ॥

अथवा—

अनिशमपि मकरकेतुर्मनसो रुजमावहन्नभिमतो मे ।
यदि मदिरायतनयनां तामधिकृत्य प्रहरतीति ॥ ५ ॥

(सखेदं परिक्रम्य ।) क्व नु खलु संस्थिते कर्मणि सदस्यैरनुज्ञातः श्रमक्लान्तमात्मानं विनोदयामि । (निःश्वस्य ।) किं नु खलु मे प्रियादर्शनादृते शरणमन्यत् । यावदेनामन्विष्यामि । (सूर्यमवलोक्य ।) इमामुग्रातपां वेलां प्रायेण लतावलयवत्सु मालिनीतीरेषु ससखीजना शकुन्तला गमयति । तत्रैव तावद्गच्छामि ।

O divine flower-armed god, by you and by the Moon, though each of you seems worthy of confidence, the whole company of lovers is (cruelly) deceived. For

> Your having flowery shafts and the Moon's having cool beams—both these are observed to be untrue for such as me. For the Moon sheds fire (on them) with her dewy rays; and you make your flowery-darts hard as adamant. (3)

(*Acting as if he is afflicted by love; angrily*). Whence this sharpness of yours who are flower-armed? (*Remembering*). Ah, I know.

> Verily the fire of Hara's wrath even now burns in you like the submarine fire in the ocean; how else could you, O agitator of the soul, who were consumed to ashes, be so scorching to such as me? (4)

Nevertheless,

> This God, who bears a fish on his banner, and who is incessantly giving pain to my mind, will give me real delight, if he strikes me because of her whose eyes are large and bewitching. (5)

(*Moving about in anguish*).

Where indeed can I recreate my afflicted soul, being permitted by those who took part (in the sacrifice) at the conclusion of the rite? (*Sighing*). What else, indeed, can bring me relief but a sight of my beloved? So I will find her out. (*Looking at the sun.*) Śakuntalā and her friends are probably passing this intensely hot noon on the creeper-wreathed banks of the Mālini. So I will advance thither.

(परिक्रम्य स्पर्शं रूपयित्वा ।) अहो प्रवातसुभगोऽयमुद्देशः ।

शक्यमरविन्दसुरभिः कणवाही मालिनीतरङ्गाणाम् ।
अङ्गैरनङ्गतप्तैरविरलमालिङ्गितुं पवनः ॥ ६ ॥

(परिक्रम्यावलोक्य च ।) अस्मिन्वेतसपरिक्षिप्ते लतामण्डपे संनिहितया तया भवितव्यम् । तथा हि । (अधो विलोक्य ।)

अभ्युन्नता पुरस्तादवगाढा जघनगौरवात्पश्चात् ।
द्वारेऽस्य पाण्डुसिकते पदपङ्क्तिर्दृश्यतेऽभिनवा ॥ ७ ॥

यावद्विटपान्तरेणावलोकयामि । (परिक्रम्य तथा कृत्वा सहर्षम् ।) अये, लब्धं नेत्रनिर्वाणम् । एषा मे मनोरथप्रियतमा सकुसुमास्तरणं शिलापट्टमधिशयाना सखीभ्यामन्वास्यते । भवतु । श्रोष्याम्यासां विश्रम्भकथितानि । (इति विलोकयन्स्थितः ।)

(ततः प्रविशति यथोक्तव्यापारा सहसखीभ्यां शकुन्तला ।)

सख्यौ—(उपवीज्य सस्नेहम् ।) हला सउन्दले, अवि सुहेदि दे णलिणीपत्तवादो । हला शकुन्तले, अपि सुखयति ते नलिनीपत्रवातः ।

शकुन्तला—किं वीअअन्ति मं सहीओ । किं वीजयतो मां सख्यौ ।

(सख्यौ विषादं नाटयित्वा परस्परमवलोकयतः ।)

राजा—बलवदस्वस्थशरीरा शकुन्तला दृश्यते । (सवितर्कम् ।) तत्किमयमातपदोषः स्यात् । उत यथा मे मनसि वर्तते । (साभिलाषं निर्वर्ण्य ।) अथवा कृतं संदेहेन ।

(*Moving about and gesticulating that he feels touch*).

Ah ! this is a pleasant spot, with the fresh breeze blowing !

> It is possible to embrace closely, with my limbs which are inflamed by the bodiless god, the breeze fragrant with the lotuses and wafting the spray from the waves of the Mālinī. (6)

(*Moving about and observing*). She must be somewhere in this bower of creepers encircled by reeds. For, (*looking down*).

> On the white sand at its door is discerned a fresh line of footsteps, raised in front, and depressed behind by the weight of her hips. (7)

So I will look through the branches. (*Walking and doing so, with joy*). Ah ! my eyes have been fully gratified. The darling of my thoughts, reposing on a flat stone-slab strewn with flowers, is attended by her two friends. Well, I will hear what they say to each other in all confidence. (*He stands gazing.*)

(*Enter Śakuntalā as described with her two friends.*)

FRIENDS (*Fanning affectionately*). Dear Śakuntalā, is the breeze from the lotus leaves refreshing to you ?

ŚAKUNTALĀ. What ? Are my friends fanning me ?

(*The two friends look sorrowfully at one another.*)

KING. Śakuntalā appears to be seriously indisposed. (*Guessing*). Is it the fault of the heat, or is it what my heart suggests ? (*Looking longingly*). Or, I need have no doubt.

स्तनन्यस्तोशीरं शिथिलितमृणालैकवलयं
प्रियायाः साबाधं किमपि कमनीयं वपुरिदम् ।
समस्तापः कामं मनसिजनिदाघप्रसरयो-
र्न तु ग्रीष्मस्यैवं सुभगमपराद्धं युवतिषु ॥ ८ ॥

प्रियंवदा—(जनान्तिकम्) अणसूए, तस्स राएसिणो पढमदंसणादो आरहिअ पज्जुस्सुआ विअ सउन्दला । किंणु क्खु से तण्णिमित्तो अअं आतङ्को भवे । अनसूये तस्य राजर्षेः प्रथमदर्शनादारभ्य पर्युत्सुकेव शकुन्तला । किं नु खलु तस्यास्तन्निमित्तोऽयमातङ्को भवेत् ।

अनसूया—सहि, ममवि ईदिसी आसङ्का हिअअस्स । होदु । पुच्छिस्सं दाव णं । (प्रकाशम्) सहि, पुच्छिदव्वासि किंपि । बलवं क्खु दे संदावो । सखि, ममापीदृश्याशङ्का हृदयस्य । भवतु । प्रक्ष्यामि तावदेनाम् । सखि, प्रष्टव्यासि किमपि । बलवान्खलु ते संतापः ।

शकुन्तला—(पूर्वार्धेन शयनादुत्थाय ।) हला, किं वत्तुकामासि । हला, किं वक्तुकामासि ।

अनसूया—हला सउन्दले, अणब्भन्तरा क्खु अम्हे मदणगदस्स वुत्तन्तस्स । किंदु जादिसी इतिहासणिबन्धेसु कामअमाणाणं अवत्था सुणीअदि तादिसीं दे पेक्खामि । कहेहि किंणिमित्तं दे संदावो । विआरं क्खु परमत्थदो अजाणिअ अणारम्भो पडिआरस्स । हला शकुन्तले, अनभ्यन्तरे खल्वावां मदनगतस्य वृत्तान्तस्य । किंतु यादृशीतिहासनिबन्धेषु कामयमानानामवस्था श्रूयते तादृशीं तव पश्यामि । कथय किंनिमित्तं ते संतापः । विकारं खलु परमार्थतोऽज्ञात्वानारम्भः प्रतीकारस्य ।

राजा—अनसूयामप्यनुगतो मदीयस्तर्कः ।

शकुन्तला—(आत्मगतम् ।) बलिअं क्खु मे अहिणिवेसो । दाणिं वि सहसा एदाणं ण सक्कणोमि णिवेदिदुं । बलवान्खलु मेऽभिनिवेशः इदानीमपि सहसैतयोर्न शक्नोमि निवेदयितुम् ।

प्रियंवदा—सहि सउन्दले, सुट्ठु एसा भणादि । किं अत्तणो आतङ्कं उवेक्खसि । अणुदिअहं क्खु परिहीअसि अङ्गेहिं । केवलं लावण्णमई छाआ तुमं ण मुञ्चदि । सखि शकुन्तले, सुष्ठ्वेषा भणति ।

The Uśīra salve has been applied to her bosom, and her only bracelet of lotus-stalks is hanging loose ; thus this form of my beloved (thus) disordered is yet exquisitely beautiful. True it is that love and the influence of summer inflame (us) equally : still the disorder brought about by the hot weather does not affect maidens in such a charming manner. (8)

PRIYAṀVADĀ (*Aside*). Anasūyā, Śakuntalā appears to have been greatly affected since she first saw the pious monarch. May it be that this her malady is due to him ?

ANASŪYĀ. Friend, the same suspicion has risen in my mind. Well. I will just ask her. (*Aloud*). My dear, I must ask you something. You are, indeed, greatly troubled.

ŚAKUNTALĀ (*Rising from her bed with the upper half.*) My dear, what would you ask ?

ANASŪYĀ. Śakuntalā, dear, we are indeed perfectly ignorant about matters relating to love. But I suspect your case to be like that of love-sick persons described in legendary tales. Tell us what causes your illness. For without knowing the exact nature of a disorder, there can be no application of the remedy.

KING. Anasūyā too has guessed my thoughts.

ŚAKUNTALĀ (*To herself*). Great indeed is my attachment ; even now I am unable to disclose it to them all at once.

PRIYAṀVADĀ. She speaks the truth, dear Śakuntalā. Why do you neglect your malady ? Your

किमात्मन आतङ्कमुपेक्षसे। अनुदिवसं खलु परिहीयसेऽङ्गैः । केवलं लावण्यमयी छाया त्वां न मुञ्चति।

राजा—अवितथमाह प्रियंवदा। तथा हि।

क्षामक्षामकपोलमाननमुरः काठिन्यमुक्तस्तनं
मध्यः क्लान्ततरः प्रकाममविनतावंसौ छविः पाण्डुरा।
शोच्या च प्रियदर्शना च मदनक्लिष्टेयमालक्ष्यते
पत्राणामिव शोषणेन मरुता स्पृष्टा लता माधवी ॥ ९ ॥

शकुन्तला—सहि, कस्स वा अण्णस्स कहइस्सं। आआसइ-त्तिआ दाणिं वो भविस्सं। सखि, कस्य वान्यस्य कथयिष्यामि। आयासयित्री-दानीं वां भविष्यामि।

उभे—अदो एव्व क्खु णिब्बन्धो। सिणिद्धजणसंविभत्तं हि दुक्खं सज्झवेदणं होदि। अत एव खलु निर्बन्धः। स्निग्धजनसंविभक्तं हि दुःखं सह्यवेदनं भवति।

राजा—

पृष्टा जनेन समदुःखसुखेन बाला
नेयं न वक्ष्यति मनोगतमाधिहेतुम्।
दृष्टो विवृत्य बहुशोऽप्यनया सतृष्ण-
मत्रान्तरे श्रवणकातरतां गतोऽस्मि ॥ १० ॥

शकुन्तला—सहि, जदो पहुदि मम दंसणपहं आअदो सो तवोवणरक्खिदा राएसी, (इत्यर्धोक्तेन लज्जां नाटयति।) सखि, यतः प्रभृति मम दर्शनपथमागतः स तपोवनरक्षिता राजर्षिः—

उभे—कधेदु पिअसही। कथयतु प्रियसखी।

शकुन्तला—तदो आरहिअ तग्गदेण अहिलासेण एतदवत्थम्हि संवुत्ता। तत आरभ्य तद्गतेनाभिलाषेणैतदवस्थास्मि संवृत्ता।

राजा—(सहर्षम्।) श्रुतं श्रोतव्यम्।

limbs are wasting away every day, though your exquisite beauty has not forsaken you.

KING. Priyaṁvadā speaks the truth. For indeed

Her face has its cheeks excessively emaciated, her bosom has lost the firmness of its breasts; her waist is more slender (than before); her shoulders are very much drooping; her complexion is wan; thus tormented by love, she appears both deplorable and charming, like the Mādhavī creeper when touched by the wind that dries up its leaves. (9)

ŚAKUNTALĀ. Friend, to whom else shall I relate? But I shall now be the occasion of your sorrow.

BOTH. For that very reason are we (so) importunate. For grief shared with affectionate friends becomes bearable pain.

KING.

Being questioned by the persons who share her sorrows as well as joys, she cannot fail to disclose the cause of her malady now hidden in her breast. Although she turned round again and again and looked upon me with longing, nevertheless, at the present moment I am filled with nervous fear to hear her (answer). (10)

ŚAKUNTALĀ. Friend, from the very instant the pious king who guards our hallowed forest met my eye— (*She breaks off and looks abashed.*)

BOTH. Speak on, beloved friend.

ŚAKUNTALĀ. From that instant, my love for him has reduced me to this plight.

KING. (*With joy*). I have heard what is worth hearing.

स्मर एव तापहेतुर्निर्वापयिता स एव मे जातः ।
दिवस इवाभ्रश्यामस्तपात्यये जीवलोकस्य ॥ ११ ॥

शकुन्तला—तं जइ वो अणुमदं ता तह वट्टह जह तस्स राएसिणो अणुकम्पणिज्जा होमि । अण्णहा अवस्सं सिञ्चध मे तिलोदअं। तद्यदि वामनुमतं तदा तथा वर्तेथां यथा तस्य राजर्षेरनुकम्पनीया भवामि। अन्यथावश्यं सिञ्चतं मे तिलोदकम् ।

राजा—संशयच्छेदि वचनम् ।

प्रियंवदा—(जनान्तिकम् ।) अणसूये, दूरगअवम्महा अक्खमा इअं कालहरणस्स । जस्सिं बद्धभावा एसा सो ललामभूदो पोरवाणं। ता जुत्तं से अहिलासो अहिणन्दिदुं। अनसूये, दूरगतमन्मथाक्षमेयं कालहरणस्य । यस्मिन्बद्धभावैषा स ललामभूतः पौरवाणाम् । तद्युक्तमस्या अभिलाषोऽभिनन्दितुम् ।

अनसूया—तह जह भणसि । तथा यथा भणसि ।

प्रियंवदा—(प्रकाशम् ।) सहि, दिट्ठिआ अणुरूवो दे अहिणिवेसो । साअरं उज्झिअ कहिं वा महाणई ओदरइ । को दाणिं सहआरं अन्तरेण अदिमुत्तलदं पल्लविदं सहेदि । सखि, दिष्टयानुरूपस्तेऽभिनिवेशः । सागरमुज्झित्वा कुत्र वा महानद्यवतरति । क इदानीं सहकारमन्तरेणातिमुक्तलतां पल्लवितां सहते ।

राजा—किमत्र चित्रं यदि विशाखे शशाङ्कलेखामनुवर्तेते ।

अनसूया—को उण उवाओ भवे जेण अविलम्बिअं णिहुअं अ सहीए मणोरमं संपादेम्ह । कः पुनरुपायो भवेद्येनाविलम्बितं निभृतं च सख्या मनोरथं संपादयावः ।

प्रियंवदा—णिहुअंत्ति चिन्तणिज्जं भवे । सिग्घंत्ति सुअरं । निभृतमिति चिन्तनीयं भवेत् । शीघ्रमिति सुकरम् ।

अनसूया—कहं विअ । कथमिव ।

प्रियंवदा—णं सो राएसी इमस्सिं सिणिद्धदिट्ठीए सूइदाहिलासो इमाइं दिअहाइं पजाअरकिसो लक्खीअदि । ननु स राजर्षिरेतस्यां स्निग्धदृष्ट्या सूचिताभिलाष एतान्दिवसान्प्रजागरकृशो लक्ष्यते ।

It was, indeed, love that caused my fever, and it is love alone that (now) allays it ; as, at the end of summer, a day, grown black with clouds, relieves the living world from the heat which itself had caused. (11)

ŚAKUNTALĀ. Then if you approve (of it) so contrive that the good king takes pity on me. Otherwise most certainly (you will) sprinkle for me water with sesasum-seed.

KING. Her words end all doubt.

PRIYAṀVADĀ (*Aside*). Anasūyā, she is far gone in love and cannot endure any delay. He on whom she has fixed her affection is the ornament of the Pauravas; it is, therefore, proper that her love finds our approval.

ANASŪYĀ. Just as you say.

PRIYAṀVADĀ (*Aloud*). My dear, fortunately your affection is placed on one worthy of yourself. Or rather where could a great river flow if not into the sea ? What other tree except the Mango can support the Atimukta creeper with new sprouts ?

KING. What wonder if the two Viśākhā stars follow the crescent-moon ?

ANASŪYĀ. But by what expedient can we accomplish the desire of our friend quickly and secretly ?

PRIYAṀVADĀ. Your "secretly" will have to be thought about ; the "quickly" is not hard.

ANASŪYĀ. How do you mean ?

PRIYAṀVADĀ. Why, the good king who has shown himself to be enamoured of her by his tender glances has been observed, during these days, to be wasting through sleeplessness.

राजा—सत्यमित्थंभूत एवास्मि । तथाहि ।

इदमशिशिरैरन्तस्तापाद्विवर्णमणीकृतं
निशि निशि भुजन्यस्तापाङ्गप्रसारिभिरश्रुभिः ।
अनभिलुलितज्याघाताङ्कं मुहुर्मणिबन्धना-
त्कनकवलयं स्रस्तं स्रस्तं मया प्रतिसार्यते ॥ १२ ॥

प्रियंवदा—(विचिन्त्य ।) **हला, मअणलेहो से करीअदु । इमं देवदासेसावदेसेण सुमणोगोविदं करिअ से हत्थअं पावइस्सं ।** हला, मदनलेखोऽस्य क्रियताम् । इमं देवताशेषापदेशेन सुमनोगोपितं कृत्वा तस्य हस्तं प्रापयिष्यामि ।

अनसूया—**रोअइ मे सुउमारो पओओ । किं वा सउन्दला भणादि ।** रोचते मे सुकुमारः प्रयोगः । किं वा शकुन्तला भणति ।

शकुन्तला—**सहीणिओओवि विकप्पीअदि ।** सखीनियोगोऽपि विकल्प्यते ।

प्रियंवदा—**तेण हि अत्तणो उवण्णासपुव्वं चिन्तेहि दाव किंपि ललिअपदबन्धणं ।** तेन ह्यात्मन उपन्यासपूर्वं चिन्तय तावत् किमपि ललितपदबन्धनम् ।

शकुन्तला—**हला, चिन्तेमि अहं । अवहीरणभीरुअं पुणो वेवइ मे हिअअं ।** हला, चिन्तयाम्यहम् । अवधीरणभीरु पुनर्वेपते मे हृदयम् ।

राजा—(सहर्षम् ।)

अयं स ते तिष्ठति संगमोत्सुको
विशङ्कसे भीरु यतोऽवधीरणाम् ।
लभेत वा प्रार्थयिता न वा श्रियं
श्रिया दुरापः कथमीप्सितो भवेत् ॥ १३ ॥

सख्यौ—**अत्तगुणावमाणिणि, को दाणिं सरीरणिव्वावत्तिअं सारदिअं जोसिणिं पडन्तेण वारेदि ।** आत्मगुणावमानिनि, क इदानीं शरीरनिर्वापयित्रीं शारदीं ज्योत्स्नां पटान्तेन वारयति ।

KING. True it is that I have become just so. For

This golden bracelet, which has its gems sullied by tears which are hot from internal pain, and nightly flow from the corner of my eye that rests upon my arm, slipping every now and then from the wrist without touching the scars made by the friction of the bow-string, is constantly being pushed back by me. (12)

PRIYAṀVADĀ (*Reflecting*). Well, she should write him a love-letter. And I will hide it in flowers and deliver it into his hands under the pretext of their being the remains of an offering presented to some deity.

ANASŪYĀ. A pretty plan and I like it ; but what says Śakuntalā to this ?

ŚAKUNTALĀ. What ? How may I doubt my friend's injunction ?

PRIYAṀVADĀ. Well, then, think of some pretty composition in verse beginning with an allusion to yourself.

ŚAKUNTALĀ. Friend, I will think out ; but then my heart flutters for fear he will despise me.

KING (*With joy*).

Here stands the man eager for union with you from whom, O timid one, you are apprehensive of a refusal. The seeker may or may not find fortune ; but could fortune, seeking, fail to find ? (13)

FRIENDS. O scorner of your own merits, who now would ward off with the edge of his garments the moonlight of autumn which can allay the fever of his body ?

शकुन्तला—(सस्मितम् ।) **णिओइदा दाणिं म्हि ।** (इत्युपविष्टा चिन्तयति ।) नियोजितेदानीमस्मि ।

राजा—स्थाने खलु विस्मृतनिमेषेण चक्षुषा प्रियामवलोकयामि । यतः

उन्नमितैकभ्रूलतमाननमस्याः पदानि रचयन्त्याः ।
कण्टकितेन प्रथयति मय्यनुरागं कपोलेन ॥ १४ ॥

शकुन्तला—हला, चिन्तिदं मए गीदवत्थु । ण क्खु सण्णिहिदाणि उण लेहणसाहणाणि । हला, चिन्तितं मया गीतवस्तु । न खलु संनिहितानि पुनर्लेखनसाधनानि ।

प्रियंवदा—इमस्सिं सुओदरसुउमारे णलिणीपत्ते णहेहिं णिक्खित्तवण्णं करेहि । एतस्मिञ्छुकोदरसुकुमारे नलिनीपत्रे नखैर्निक्षिप्तवर्णं कुरु ।

शकुन्तला—(यथोक्तं रूपयित्वा ।) **हला, सुणुह दाणिं संगदत्थं ण वेत्ति ।** हला शृणुतमिदानीं संगतार्थं न वेति ।

उभे—अवहिद म्ह । अवहिते स्वः ।

शकुन्तला—(वाचयति ।)

तुज्झ ण आणे हिअअं मम उण कामो दिवावि रत्तिंपि ।
णिग्घिण तवेइ बलिअं तुइ वुत्तमणोरहाइं अङ्गाइं ॥ १५ ॥

तव न जाने हृदयं मम पुनः कामो दिवापि रात्रावपि ।
निर्घृण तपति बलीयस्त्वयि वृत्तमनोरथान्यङ्गानि ॥

राजा—(सहसोपसृत्य ।)

तपति तनुगात्रि मदनस्त्वामनिशं मां पुनर्दहत्येव ।
ग्लपयति यथा शशाङ्कं न तथा हि कुमुद्वतीं दिवसः ॥ १६ ॥

सख्यौ—(सहर्षम् ।) **साअदं अविलम्बिणो मणोरधस्स ।** स्वागतमविलम्बिनो मनोरथस्य ।

ŚAKUNTALĀ (*Smilingly*). So now I have been directed.

(*She sits up and meditates.*)

KING. It is only proper that I should gaze at my darling with eyes that forget to wink! For

As she is composing words (for her song),
her face, with one creeper-like eye-brow lifted,
reveals her passion for me by her thrilling
cheeks. (14)

ŚAKUNTALĀ. Well, I have thought out a little song. But we haven't any writing-materials.

PRIYAṀVADĀ. Here on this lotus-leaf smooth as a parrot's breast, do you engrave the letters with your nails.

ŚAKUNTALĀ (*Acting as said*). Friends, listen (and say) if it makes sense.

BOTH. We are attentive.

ŚAKUNTALĀ (*Reads*).

Thy heart I know not: but Love, O cruel
one, fiercely inflames both by day and by night
my limbs, whose desires are centred on thee. (15)

KING (*Hastily Advancing*).

Thee, O slender maid, Love only inflames
incessantly, but me he quite consumes: for the
day does not cause the lotus to fade so much
as it does the Moon. (16)

FRIENDS (*With joy*). Welcome to (the object of your) desire which presents itself without delay.

(शकुन्तलाभ्युत्थातुमिच्छति)

राजा—अलमलमायासेन ।

संदष्टकुसुमशयनान्याशुक्लान्तबिसभङ्गसुरभीणि ।
गुरुपरितापानि न ते गात्राण्युपचारमर्हन्ति ॥ १७ ॥

अनसूया—इदो सिलातलेक्कदेसं अलंकरेदु वअस्सो । इत शिलातलैकदेशमलंकरोतु वयस्यः ।

(राजोपविशति । शकुन्तला सलज्जा तिष्ठति ।)

प्रियंवदा—दुवेणं पि वो अण्णोण्णाणुराओ पच्चक्खो । सहीसिणेहो मं पुणरुत्तवादिणीं करेदि । द्वयोरपि युवयोरन्योन्यानुरागः प्रत्यक्षः सखीस्नेहो मां पुनरुक्तवादिनीं करोति ।

राजा—भद्रे, नैतत्परिहार्यम् । विवक्षितं ह्यनुक्तमनुतापं जनयति ।

प्रियंवदा—आवण्णस्स विसअणिवासिणो जणस्स अत्तिहरेण रण्णा होदव्वं त्ति एसो वो धम्मो । आपन्नस्य विषयनिवासिनो जनस्यार्तिहरेण राज्ञा भवितव्यमित्येष युष्माकं धर्मः ।

राजा— नास्मात्परम् ।

प्रियंवदा—तेण हि इअं णो पिअसही तुमं उद्दिसिअ इमं अवत्थन्तरं भअवदा मअणेण आरोविदा । ता अरुहसि अब्भुववत्तीए जीविदं से अवलम्बिदुं । तेन हीयमावयोः प्रियसखी त्वामुद्दिश्येदमवस्थान्तरं भगवता मदनेनारोपिता । तदर्हस्यभ्युपपत्त्या जीवितं तस्याः अवलम्बितुम् ।

राजा—भद्रे, साधारणोऽयं प्रणयः । सर्वथानुगृहीतोऽस्मि ।

शकुन्तला—(प्रियंवदामवलोक्य ।) **हला, किं अन्तेउरविरहपज्जुस्सुअस्स राएसिणो उवरोहेण ।** हला, किमन्तःपुरविरहपर्युत्सुकस्य राजर्षेरुपरोधेन ।

(*Śakuntalā expresses an inclination to rise.*)

KING. Give yourself no pain.

Your limbs, which closely press the couch of flowers, and bear the fragrance of pieces of lotus-stalks which have quickly faded, being grievously inflamed, must not be fatigued by ceremony. (*Lit.* do not deserve to perform the customary salutation). (17)

ANASŪYĀ. Let our friend favour a part of this stone-slab here (by sitting upon it).

(*The king sits; Śakuntalā feels bashful.*)

PRIYAṀVADĀ. Your mutual love is (quite) evident. But affection for my friend prompts me to speak something superfluous.

KING. Excellent damsel, that ought not to be suppressed. For to leave unsaid what was intended to be said produces subsequent regret.

PRIYAṀVADĀ. A king ought to remove the sufferings of the distressed people living in his kingdom—such is your duty.

KING. No other than this.

PRIYAṀVADĀ. Then (understand that) this our dear friend has been brought to this altered condition by the divinity Love on your account. It is, therefore, proper that you favour her and preserve her life.

KING. Excellent damsel, our passion is reciprocal. I feel favoured in every way.

ŚAKUNTALĀ (*Looking at Priyaṁvadā*). Why should you detain the pious king who must be afflicted by separation from his royal-consorts?

राजा—

इदमनन्यपरायणमन्यथा
हृदयसंनिहिते हृदयं मम ।
यदि समर्थयसे मदिरेक्षणे
मदनबाणहतोऽस्मि हतः पुनः ॥ १८ ॥

अनसूया—वअस्स, बहुवल्लहा राआणो सुणीअन्ति । जह णो पिअसही बन्धुअणसोआणिज्जा ण होई तह णिव्वत्तेहि । वयस्य, बहुवल्लभा राजानः श्रूयन्ते । यथा नौ प्रियसखी बन्धुजनशोचनीया न भवति तथा निर्वर्तय ।

राजा—भद्रे, किं बहुना ।

परिग्रहबहुत्वेऽपि द्वे प्रतिष्ठे कुलस्य मे ।
समुद्रवसना चोर्वी सखी च युवयोरियम् ॥ १९ ॥

उभे—णिव्वुद म्ह । निर्वृते स्वः ।

प्रियंवदा—(सदृष्टिक्षेपम् ।) **अणसूए, जह एसो इदोदिण्णदिट्ठी उत्सुओ मिअपोदओ मादरं अण्णेसदि । एहि । संजोएम णं ।** (इत्युभे प्रस्थिते ।) अनसूये, यथैष इतोदत्तदृष्टिरुत्सुको मृगपोतको मातरमन्विष्यति । एहि । संयोजयाव एनम् ।

शकुन्तला—हला, असरण म्हि । अण्णदरा वो आअच्छदु । हला, अशरणास्मि । अन्यतरा युवयोरागच्छतु ।

उभे—पुहवीए जो सरणं सो तुह समीवे वट्टइ । (इति निष्क्रान्ते ।) पृथिव्या यः शरणं स तव समीपे वर्तते ।

शकुन्तला—कहं गदाओ एव्व । कथं गते एव ।

राजा—अलमावेगेन । नन्वयमाराधयिता जनस्तव समीपे वर्तते ।

KING.

Thou, with bewitching eyes, that art near my heart, if this heart of mine, which is devoted to no other, thou judgest to be otherwise, then I who was slain by Love's arrow, am slain once again ! (18).

ANASŪYĀ. Friend, kings are said to have many favourite consorts. You must, therefore, act in such a way that our dear friend may not become a cause of grief to her kinsmen.

KING. Good damsel, what need is there of many words ?

Let there be ever so many wives of mine,
there will be but two chief glories of my race—
the sea-clad Earth, and this friend of yours. (19)

BOTH. We are content.

PRIYAṀVADĀ (*Casting a glance*). Anasūyā, there is the eager young antelope turning his eyes in this direction and seeking his mother ; so come, let us help him to join his mother.

(*Both start.*)

ŚAKUNTALĀ. Dear, I am in such a helpless state. Let one of you come back.

BOTH. The protector of the Earth is with you ! (*Exeunt.*)

ŚAKUNTALĀ. How ! they are already gone !

KING. Do not be anxious. Is not this person, your adorer, near you ?

किं शीतलैः क्लमविनोदिभिरार्द्रवातान्
संचारयामि नलिनीदलतालवृन्तैः ।
अङ्के निधाय करभोरु यथासुखं ते
संवाहयामि चरणावुत पद्मताम्रौ ॥ २० ॥

शकुन्तला—ण माणणीएसु अत्ताणं अवराहइस्सं । (इत्युत्थाय गन्तुमिच्छति ।) न माननीयेष्वात्मानमपराधयिष्ये ।

राजा—सुन्दरि, अपरिनिर्वाणो दिवसः । इयं च ते शरीरावस्था ।

उत्सृज्य कुसुमशयनं नलिनीदलकल्पितस्तनावरणम् ।
कथमातपे गमिष्यसि परिबाधापेलवैरङ्गैः ॥ २१ ॥

(इति बलादेनां निवर्तयति ।)

शकुन्तला—पोरव, रक्ख अविणअं । मअणसंतत्तावि ण हु अत्तणो पहवामि । पौरव, रक्षाविनयम् । मदनसंतप्तापि न खल्वात्मनः प्रभवामि ।

राजा—भीरु, अलं गुरुजनभयेन । दृष्ट्वा ते विदितधर्मा तत्रभवान्नात्र दोषं ग्रहीष्यति कुलपतिः । अपि च ।

गान्धर्वेण विवाहेन बह्व्यो राजर्षिकन्यकाः ।
श्रूयन्ते परिणीतास्ताः पितृभिश्चाभिनन्दिताः ॥ २२ ॥

शकुन्तला—मुञ्च दाव मं । भूओ वि सहीजणं अणुमाणइस्सं । मुञ्च तावन्माम् । भूयोऽपि सखीजनमनुमानयिष्ये ।

राजा—भवतु । मोक्ष्यामि ।

शकुन्तला—कदा । कदा ।

Shall I set in motion moist breezes by means of fans of cool lotus-leaves to dissipate your languor, or shall I, O round-thighed (maiden), lay those feet red as lotuses in my lap and press them so as to relieve your pain? (20)

ŚAKUNTALĀ. I will not offend against those whom I am bound to respect.

(*Rises up and desires to leave.*)

KING. The day is not yet cool, beautiful one, and such is your condition.

Leaving the couch of flowers where lotus-leaves formed the covering of your bosom, how will you go in the sun, with your limbs rendered so languid by suffering? (21)

(*He forcibly draws her back.*)

ŚAKUNTALĀ. O descendant of Puru, keep within the bounds of modesty. For although I am inflamed by Love, yet I have not the power of disposing of myself.

KING. Timid one, do not fear your elders. For the revered Father of your society, who knows the law, will not take exception to it when he sees it. Moreover

Many daughters of royal sages are heard to have been married by the ceremony called Gāndharva, and (even) their fathers have approved them. (22)

ŚAKUNTALĀ. Leave me awhile; I will again take counsel with my friends.

KING. Yes, I will leave you.

ŚAKUNTALĀ. When?

राजा—

अपरिक्षतकोमलस्य याव-
त्कुसुमस्येव नवस्य षट्पदेन ।
अधरस्य पिपासता मया ते
सदयं सुन्दरि गृह्यते रसोऽस्य ॥ २३ ॥

(इति मुखमस्याः समुन्नमयितुमिच्छति । शकुन्तला परिहरति नाट्येन ।)

(नेपथ्ये ।)

चक्कवाकवहुए, आमन्तेहि सहअरं । उवट्ठिदा रअणी । चक्रवाकवधूः आमन्त्रयस्व सहचरम् । उपस्थिता रजनी ।

शकुन्तला — (ससंभ्रमम् ।) **पोरव, असंसअं मम सरीरवुत्तन्तोवलम्भस्स अज्जा गोदमी इदो एव्व आअच्छदि । जाव विडवन्तरिदो होहि ।** पौरव, असंशयं मम शरीरवृत्तान्तोपलम्भायार्या गौतमीत एवागच्छति । यावद्विटपान्तरितो भव ।

राजा—तथा । (इत्यात्मानमावृत्य तिष्ठति ।)

(ततः प्रविशति पात्रहस्ता गौतमी सख्यौ च ।)

सख्यौ—इदो इदो अज्जा गोतमी । इत इत आर्या गौतमी ।

गौतमी—(शकुन्तलामुपेत्य ।) **जादे, अवि लहुसंदाबाइं दे अङ्गाइं ।** जाते, अपि लघुसंतापानि तेऽङ्गानि ।

शकुन्तला—अज्जे, अत्थि मे विसेसो । आर्ये, अस्ति मे विशेषः ।

गौतमी—इमिणा दब्भोदएण णिराबाधं एव्व दे सरीरं भविस्सदि । (शिरसि शकुन्तलामभ्युक्ष्य) **वच्छे, परिणदो दिअहो । एहि । उडजं एव्व गच्छम्ह ।** अनेन दर्भोदकेन निराबाधमेव ते शरीरं भविष्यति । वत्से, परिणतो दिवसः । एहि । उटजमेव गच्छामः ।

(इति प्रस्थिताः ।)

शकुन्तला—(आत्मगतम् ।) **हिअअ, पढमं एव्व सुहोवणदे मणोरहे कादरभावं ण मुञ्चसि । साणुसअविहडिअस्स महं दे संपदं संदाबो ।** (पदान्तरे स्थित्वा । प्रकाशम् ।) **लादावलअ संदा-**

KING.

When the nectar of your lower lip, O fair one, is gently stolen by me thirsting (for it), as by the bee the honey of the fresh and untouched flower. (23)

(*Desires to raise her face. Śakuntalā gesticulates as if she repels him. Behind the Scenes*)

O female Cakrawāka, bid farewell to thy mate : (for) the night approaches.

ŚAKUNTALĀ (*Hurriedly*). Paurava, surely this is mother Gautamī come to inquire after my health. Hide yourself, therefore, behind the branches.

KING. I will do so. (*Remains in hiding; enter Gautami with a vessel in her hand, and friends.*)

FRIENDS. This way, venerable Gautamī, this way.

GAUTAMĪ (*Approaching Śakuntalā*). Child, is the fever of your body a little abated?

ŚAKUNTALĀ. Venerable mother, there is a change for the better in me.

GAUTAMĪ. With this water mixed with Kuśa-grass, your body will assuredly be relieved of pain. (*Sprinkling water on Śakuntalā's head*) Child, the day is departing ; come let us both go to the cottage.

(*They start*).

ŚAKUNTALĀ (*To herself*). O my heart, even before, when the object of your desire came of itself so readily, you did not find courage (to accept it) ; why then this anguish now when separated and (consequently) filled with repentence? (*Taking a step and standing still; aloud*), O bower of creepers that removed my suffering,

वहारअ, आमन्तेमि तुमं भूओ वि परिमोअस्स। (इति दुःखेन निष्क्रान्ता शकुन्तला सहेतराभिः।) हृदय, प्रथममेव सुखोपनते मनोरथे कातरभावं न मुञ्चसि। सानुशयविघटितस्य कथं ते सांप्रतं संतापः। लतावलय संतापहारक, आमंत्रये त्वां भूयोऽपि परिभोगाय।

राजा—(पूर्वस्थानमुपेत्य। सनिःश्वासम्।) **अहो विघ्नवत्यः प्रार्थितार्थसिद्धयः। मया हि**

मुहुरङ्गुलिसंवृताधरोष्ठं
प्रतिषेधाक्षरविक्लवाभिरामम्।
मुखमंसविवर्ति पक्ष्मलाक्ष्याः
कथमप्युन्नमितं न चुम्बितं तु ॥ २४ ॥

क्व नु खलु संप्रति गच्छामि। अथवा। इहैव प्रियापरिभुक्तमुक्ते लतावलये मुहुर्तं स्थास्यामि। (सर्वतोऽवलोक्य)

तस्याः पुष्पमयी शरीरलुलिता शय्या शिलायामियं
क्लान्तो मन्मथलेख एष नलिनीपत्रे नखैरर्पितः।
हस्ताद्भ्रष्टमिदं बिसाभरणमित्यासज्यमानेक्षणो
निर्गन्तुं सहसा न वेतसगृहाच्छक्नोमि शून्यादपि ॥ २५ ॥

(आकाशे।)

राजन्,

सायंतने सवनकर्मणि संप्रवृत्ते
वेदीं हुताशनवतीं परितः प्रकीर्णाः।
छायाश्चरन्ति बहुधा भयमादधानाः
संध्यापयोदकपिशाः पिशिताशनानाम् ॥ २६ ॥

राजा—अयमयमागच्छामि। (इति निष्क्रान्तः।)

इति तृतीयोऽङ्कः।

I bid you farewell (hoping) to be once more happy (under your shade). (*Śakuntalā departs in pain, with others.*

THE KING. (*Returning to the former spot; heaving a sigh*). How the accomplishment of one's wishes is beset with obstacles!

For the face of that (maiden) with soft eye-lashes, which had the lower lip repeatedly covered by her fingers, which looked beautiful as it stammered words of denial and which was turned on one side, was somehow raised by me but not kissed! (24)

Where, indeed, shall I go now? Or rather, I will remain for a little while in this bower of creepers where my beloved lay, but which is now deserted by her.

(*Looking all around*).

Here lies on the stone-slab her flowery couch crushed by her form; here is the faded love-missive committed to the lotus-leaf with her nails; and here the bracelet of lotus-stalk dropped down from her arm—as I fix my eyes on these (objects) I have no power to tear myself away from this reedy bower, even though deserted by her. (25)

(*In the air*). O king!

As the evening sacrifice is commenced, the shadows of the flesh-eating demons, brown as evening clouds, and scattered around the blazing altar, are flitting about and creating terror in a variety of ways. (26)

KING. Here I am coming. (*Exit.*)

End of Act III.

चतुर्थोऽङ्कः ।

(ततः प्रविशतः कुसुमावचयं नाटयन्त्यौ सख्यौ ।)

अनसूया—हला पिअंवदे, जइ वि गन्धव्वेण विवाहविहिणा णिव्वुत्तकल्लाणा सउन्दला अणुरूवभत्तुगामिणी संवुत्तेत्ति णिव्वुदं मे हिअअं, तह वि एत्तिअं चिन्तणिज्जं । हला प्रियंवदे, यद्यपि गान्धर्वेण विवाहविधिना निर्वृत्तकल्याणा शकुन्तलानुरूपभर्तृगामिनी संवृत्तेति निर्वृतं मे हृदयम्, तथाप्येतावच्चिन्तनीयम् ।

प्रियंवदा—कहं विअ । कथमिव ।

अनसूया—अज्ज सो राएसी इट्ठिं परिसमाविअ इसीहिं विसज्जिदो अत्तणो णअरं पविसिअ अन्तेउरसमागदो इदोगदं वुत्तन्तं सुमरदि वा ण वेत्ति । अद्य स राजर्षिरिष्टिं परिसमाप्य ऋषिभिर्विसर्जित आत्मनो नगरं प्रविश्यान्तःपुरसमागत इतोगतं वृत्तान्तं स्मरति वा न वेति ।

प्रियंवदा—वीसद्धा होहि । ण तादिसा आकिदिविसेसा गुणविरोहिणो होन्ति । किंदु तादो दाणिं इमं वुत्तन्तं सुणिअ ण आणे किं पडिवज्जिस्सदि त्ति । विस्रब्धा भव । न तादृशा आकृतिविशेषा गुणविरोधिनी भवन्ति । किंतु तात इदानीमिमं वृत्तान्तं श्रुत्वा न जाने किं प्रतिपत्स्यत इति ।

अनसूया—जइ अहं देक्खामि, तह तस्स अणुमदं भवे । यथाहं पश्यामि, तथा तस्यानुमतं भवेत् ।

प्रियंवदा—कहं विअ । कथमिव ।

अनसूया—गुणवदे कण्णआ पडिवादणिज्जेत्ति अअं दाव पढमो संकप्पो । तं जइ देव्वं एव्व संपादेदि, णं अप्पआसेण किदत्थो गुरुअणो । गुणवते कन्यका प्रतिपादनीयेत्ययं तावत्प्रथमः संकल्पः । तं यदि दैवमेव संपादयति नन्वप्रयासेन कृतार्थो गुरुजनः ।

प्रियंवदा—(पुष्पभाजनं विलोक्य ।) **सहि, अवइदाइं बलिकम्मपज्जत्ताइं कुसुमाइं ।** सखि, अवचितानि बलिकर्मपर्याप्तानि कुसुमानि ।

ACT IV

(*Then enter the two friends, acting the gathering of flowers.*)

ANASŪYĀ. O my Priyaṁvadā, although my heart is comforted by the thought that Śakuntalā has her nuptials celebrated according to the Gāndharva form and has now been united to a husband worthy of her, yet there is still some cause for uneasiness.

PRIYAṀVADĀ. How do you mean?

ANASŪYĀ. Whether the pious king, who is dismissed to-day by the hermits at the completion of the sacrifice, will remember things here, when after entering his capital he will be surrounded by his ladies in the recesses of the palace.

PRIYAṀVADĀ. You need have no anxiety (about that). Such distinguished forms as these can never be opposed to virtue. But I cannot tell now what reply the father will make when he shall have heard what has passed.

ANASŪYĀ. As I see it, he will approve.

PRIYAṀVADĀ. Why do you think so?

ANASŪYĀ. One can desire nothing better than that one's daughter is married to a virtuous husband; and if fate brings this about of itself, then indeed the father has his desire accomplished without effort.

PRIYAṀVADĀ (*Looking at the flower-basket*). My friend, we have gathered flowers enough for the offering.

अनसूया—णं पिअसहीए सउन्दलाए सोहग्गदेवआ अच्चणीआ। ननु प्रियसख्याः शकुन्तलायाः सौभाग्यदेवतार्चनीया।

प्रियंवदा—जुज्जदि। युज्यते।

(इति तदेव कर्मारभेते।)

(नेपथ्ये।)

अयमहं भोः।

अनसूया—(कर्णं दत्त्वा।) **सहि, अदिधीणं विअ णिवेदिदं।** सखि, अतिथीनामिव निवेदितम्।

प्रियंवदा—णं उडजसंणिहिदा सउन्दला। (आत्मगतम्।) **अज्ज उण हिअएण असंणिहिदा।** ननूटजसंनिहिता शकुन्तला। अद्य पुनर्हृदयेनासंनिहिता।

अनसूया—होदु। अलं एत्तिएहिं कुसुमेहिं। भवतु। अलमेतावद्भिः कुसुमैः।

(इति प्रस्थिते।)

(नेपथ्ये।)

आः अतिथिपरिभाविनी,

विचिन्तयन्ती यमनन्यमानसा
तपोधनं वेत्सि न मामुपस्थितम्।
स्मरिष्यति त्वां न स बोधितोऽपि स-
न्कथां प्रमत्तः प्रथमं कृतामिव ॥ १ ॥

प्रियंवदा—हद्धी हद्धी। अप्पिअं एव्व संवुत्तं। कस्सिं पि पूआरुहे अवरद्धा सुण्णहिअआ सउन्दला। (पुरोऽवलोक्य।) **ण हु जास्सिं कस्सिं पि। एसो दुव्वासो सुलहकोवो महेसी। तह सविअ वेअबलुप्फुल्लाए दुव्वाराए गईए पडिणिवुत्तो। को अण्णो हुदवहादो दहिदुं पहविस्सदि।** हा धिक् हा धिक्। अप्रियमेव संवृत्तम्। कस्मिन्नपि पूजार्हेऽपराद्धा शून्यहृदया शकुन्तला। न खलु यस्मिन्कस्मिन्नपि। एष दुर्वासाः सुलभकोपो महर्षिः। तथा शप्त्वा वेगबलोत्फुल्लया दुर्वारया गत्या प्रतिनिवृत्तः। कोऽन्यो हुतवहाद्दग्धुं प्रभविष्यति।

ANASŪYĀ. But surely the deity that watches over the fortune of our dear friend Śakuntalā will have to be honoured (by us).

PRIYAṀVADĀ. Very well. (*They act doing the same.*)

(*Behind the scenes*)

It is I—Hola!

ANASŪYĀ (*Listening*). My dear, it sounds like some guest announcing himself.

PRIYAṀVADĀ. Well, Śakuntalā is near the cottage. (*To herself*). But not near with her heart to day.

ANASŪYĀ. Well, these flowers will do.

(*They start away.*)

(*Behind the scenes*). Ah, thou that art disrespectful to a guest,

> He on whom thou art meditating with a mind that is regardless of everything else, while thou perceivest not me, rich in penance, to have arrived, will not remember thee, though reminded, like a drunken man the words previously spoken. (1)

PRIYAṀVADĀ. Alas! alas! a very unpleasant thing has indeed occurred. Sakuntalā has, through absence of mind, offended some one deserving reverence. (*Looking ahead*). Not, indeed, any ordinary person! This is the great sage Durvāsas, so quick-tempered. After uttering such an imprecation he is striding away with a step bounding and irresistible through its impetuosity. Who besides fire has power to consume?

अनसूया—गच्छ । पादेसु पणमिअ णिवत्तेहि णं, जाव अहं अग्घोदअं उवकप्पेमि । गच्छ । पादयोः प्रणम्य निवर्तयैनं, यावदहमर्घोदकमुपकल्पयामि ।

प्रियंवदा—तह । (इति निष्क्रान्ता ।) तथा ।

अनसूया—(पदान्तरे स्खलितं निरूप्य ।) **अम्मो । आवेअक्खलिदाए गईए पब्भट्ठं मे अग्गहत्थादो पुप्फभाअणं ।** (इति पुष्पोच्चयं रूपयति ।) अहो । आवेगस्खलितया गत्या प्रभ्रष्टं ममाग्रहस्तात्पुष्पभाजनम् ।

(प्रविश्य ।)

प्रियंवदा—सहि, पकिदिवक्को सो कस्स अणुणअं पडिगेण्हदि । किं पि उण साणुक्कोसो किदो । सखि, प्रकृतिवक्रः स कस्यानुनयं प्रतिगृह्णाति । किमपि पुनः सानुक्रोशः कृतः ।

अनसूया—(सस्मितम् ।) **तस्सिं बहु एदं पि । कहेहि ।** तस्मिन्बह्वेतदपि । कथय ।

प्रियंवदा—जदा णिवत्तिदुं ण इच्छदि तदा विण्णविदो मए । भअवं, पढमं त्ति पेक्खिअ अविण्णादतवप्पहावस्स दुहिदुजणस्स भअवदा एक्को अवराहो मरिसिदव्वोत्ति । यदा निवर्तितुं नेच्छति तदा विज्ञापितो मया । भगवन्, प्रथम इति प्रेक्ष्याविज्ञाततपःप्रभावस्य दुहितृजनस्य भगवतैकोऽपराधो मर्षितव्य इति ।

अनसूया—तदो तदो । ततस्ततः ।

प्रियंवदा—तदो मे वअणं अण्णहाभविदुं णारिहदि । किंदु अहिण्णाणाभरणदंसणेण सावो णिवत्तिस्सदि त्ति मन्तअन्तो सअं अन्तरिहिदो । ततो मे वचनमन्यथाभवितुं नार्हति । किंत्वभिज्ञानाभरणदर्शनेन शापो निवर्तिष्यत इति मन्त्रयन्स्वयमन्तर्हितः ।

ANASŪYĀ. Go, fall at his feet, and bring him back, whilst I prepare a propitiatory offering and water.

PRIYAMVADĀ. I will. (*Exit.*)

ANASŪYĀ (*Showing that she stumbles at the next step*). As I stumbled in my excitement, the flower-baskets fell out from my hands.

(*She acts the gathering up of the flowers.*)

(*Entering*) PRIVAMVADĀ. Whose entreaties would this ill-tempered person accept? However, I softened him a little.

ANASŪYĀ (*Smiling*). Even that is a good deal for him: tell me.

PRIYAMVADĀ. When he would not return, I prayed to him: "Holy sir, considering it is the first time, this one offence of the daughter, who did not recognize the potency of penance, should be forgiven her by your reverence."

ANASŪYĀ. And then—

PRIYAMVADĀ. And then saying, "My word must not be recalled: but the curse shall be lifted at the sight of the ornament (given her) for a token," he vanished from sight.

अनसूया—सक्कं दाणिं अस्ससिदुं । अत्थि तेण राएसिणा संपत्थिदेण सणामहेअङ्किअं अङ्गुलीअअं सुमरणीअंत्ति सअं पिणद्धं । तस्सिं साहीणोबाआ सउन्दला भविस्सदि । शक्यमिदानीमाश्वसितुम् । अस्ति तेन राजर्षिणा संप्रस्थितेन स्वनामधेयाङ्कितमङ्गुलीयकं स्मरणीयमिति स्वयं पिनद्धम् । तस्मिन्स्वाधीनोपाया शकुन्तला भविष्यति ।

प्रियंवदा—सहि, एहि । देवकज्जं दाव णिव्वत्तेम्ह । सखि, एहि । देवकार्यं तावन्निर्वर्तयावः ।

(इति परिक्रामतः ।)

प्रियंवदा—(विलोक्य ।)**अणसूए, पेक्ख दाव । वामहत्थोवहिदवअणा आलिहिदा विअ पिअसही । भत्तुगदाए चिन्ताए अत्ताणं पि ण एसा विभावेदि । किं उण आअन्तुअं ।** अनसूये, पश्य तावत् । वामहस्तोपहितवदनालिखितेव प्रियसखी । भर्तृगतया चिन्तयात्मानमपि नैषा विभावयति । किं पुनरागन्तुकम् ।

अनसूया—पिअंवदे, दुवेणं एव्व णं णो मुहे एसो वुत्तन्तो चिट्ठदु । रक्खिदव्वा क्खु पकिदिपेलवा पिअसही । प्रियंवदे, द्वयोरेव ननु नौ मुख एष वृत्तान्तस्तिष्ठतु । रक्षितव्या खलु प्रकृतिपेलवा प्रियसखी ।

प्रियंवदा—को णाम उण्होदएण णोमालिअं सिञ्चेदि । को नामोष्णोदकेन नवमालिकां सिञ्चति ।

(इत्युभे निष्क्रान्ते ।)

विष्कम्भः ।

(ततः प्रवशति सुप्तोत्थितः शिष्यः ।)

शिष्यः—वेलोपलक्षणार्थमादिष्टोऽस्मि तत्रभवता प्रवासादुपावृत्तेन काश्यपेन । प्रकाशं निर्गतस्तावदवलोकयामि कियदवशिष्टं रजन्या इति । (परिक्रम्यावलोक्य च ।) **हन्त प्रभातम् । तथा हि**

यात्येकतोऽस्तशिखरं पतिरोषधीना-
माविष्कृतारुणपुरःसर एकतोऽर्कः ।

ANASŪYĀ. We can now feel confident : at his departure the good king himself put a ring, engraved with his own name, (on her finger) as a souvenir. In that Śakuntalā will be possessed of a remedy in her own power.

PRIYAṀVADĀ. Come, dear, let us worship the gods.

(*They walk about.*)

PRIYAṀVADĀ (*Gazing*). See, my Anasūyā, there is the dear girl, with her face resting on her left hand, looking like a painted picture. With her mind so intent on her husband, she is not conscious of even her own self, much less of a stranger.

ANASŪYĀ. Priyaṁvadā, let this incident remain in the mouth of us two only ; we must spare the dear girl, who is naturally (so) delicate.

PRIYAṀVADĀ. Who would sprinkle the jasmine with boiling water ?

(*Both go out.*)

End of the introductory scene.

(*Then enter a pupil of Kaṇva, just risen from sleep*).

PUPIL. I am bidden by the venerable Kāśyapa, who is returned from his pilgrimage, to find out what time it is. I will go into the open air and see how much of the night remains. (*Walking about and observing.*) See ! It is the break of day. For

On one side, the lord of herbs is sinking to the summit of the western mount, while on the other the Sun heralded by Aruṇa has just become visible. By the contemporaneous rise

तेजोद्वयस्य युगपद्व्यसनोदयाभ्यां
लोको नियम्यत इवात्मदशान्तरेषु ॥ १ ॥

अपि च ।

अन्तर्हिते शशिनि सैव कुमुद्वती मे
दृष्टिं न नन्दयति संस्मरणीयशोभा ।
इष्टप्रवासजनितान्यबलाजनस्य
दुःखानि नूनमतिमात्रसुदुःसहानि ॥ २ ॥

अनसूया—(प्रविश्यापटीक्षेपेण ।)—एवं णाम विसअपरम्मुहस्स वि जणस्स ण एदं ण विदिअं जधा तेण रण्णा सउन्दलाए अणज्जं आअरिदं । एवं नाम विषयपराङ्मुखस्यापि जनस्य नैतन्न विदितं यथा तेन राज्ञा शकुन्तलायामनार्यमाचरितम् ।

शिष्यः—यावदुपस्थितां होमवेलां गुरवे निवेदयामि । (इति निष्क्रान्तः ।)

अनसूया—पडिबुद्धा वि किं करिस्सं । ण मे उइदेसु वि णिअकरणिज्जेसु हत्थपाआ पसरन्ति । कामो दाणिं सकामो होदु । जेण असच्चसंधे जणे सुद्धहिअआ सही पदं कारिदा । अहवा दुव्वाससावो एसो विआरेदि । अण्णहा कहं सो राएसी तारिसाणि मन्तिअ एत्तिअस्स कालस्स लेहमेत्तं पि ण विसज्जेदि । ता इदो अहिण्णाणं अङ्गुलीअअं से विसज्जेम । दुक्खसीले तवस्सिजणे को अब्भत्थीअदु । णं सहीगामी दोसो त्ति ववसिदा वि ण पारेमि पवासपडिणिउत्तस्स तादकस्सवस्स दुस्सन्तपरिणीदं आवण्णसत्तं सउन्दलं णिवेदिदुं । इत्थंगए अम्हेहि किं करणिज्जं । प्रतिबुद्धापि किं करिष्ये । न म उचितेष्वपि निजकार्येषु हस्तपादं प्रसरति । काम इदानीं सकामो भवतु । येनासत्यसंधे जने शुद्धहृदया सखी पदं कारिता । अथवा दुर्वासःशाप एष विकारयति । अन्यथा कथं स राजर्षिस्तादृशानि मन्त्रयित्वैतावत्कालस्य लेखमात्रमपि न विसर्जयति । तदितोऽभिज्ञानमङ्गुलीयकं तस्य विसर्जयावः । दुःखशीले तपस्विजने कोऽभ्यर्थ्यताम् । ननु सखीगामी दोष इति

and fall of these twin lights of heaven, people are as it were instructed regarding the vicissitudes of their life. (1)

And again,

When the Moon is hidden, the same night-lotus no longer pleases the eye, its beauty being now only a matter of remembrance. Surely the sorrows of a tender girl produced by the absence of the loved one are beyond all measure very hard to bear. (2)

ANASŪYĀ (*Entering with a hurried toss of the curtain*). However withdrawn from all worldly concerns this person (I) may be, yet it is not unknown to her that Śakuntalā has been treated shamefully by the king.

PUPIL. I will just tell the preceptor that the hour of sacrifice is come. (*Exit*)

ANASŪYĀ. Although wide-awake, what shall I do? My hands and feet move not readily to the usual occupations of the morning. Let Love now enjoy his triumph, who persuaded the pure-minded girl to repose confidence in that perfidious man. Or does the imprecation of Durvāsas cause the change? How else could the good king say such (sweet) things and then not send so much as a letter for such a (long) time? Therefore, we must send him from here the ring he has left as a token. And who, among the ascetics inured to hardship, should be implored? And because the blame lies with my friend, I cannot, although I have made up my mind, summon up courage to tell father Kāśyapa who has returned from his pilgrimage that Śakuntalā

व्यवसितापि न पारयामि प्रवासप्रतिनिवृत्तस्य तातकाश्यपस्य दुष्यन्तपरिणीतामापन्नसत्त्वां शकुन्तलां निवेदयितुम् । इत्थंगतेऽस्माभिः किं करणीयम् ।

प्रियंवदा—(प्रविश्य सहर्षम् ।) **सहि, तुवर तुवर सउन्दलाए पत्थाणकोदुअं णिव्वत्तिदुं ।** सखि, त्वरस्व त्वरस्व शकुन्तलायाः प्रस्थानकौतुकं निर्वर्तयितुम् ।

अनसूया—**सहि, कहं एदं ।** सखि, कथमेतत् ।

प्रियंवदा—**सुणाहि दाणिं । सुहसइदपुच्छिआ सउन्दलासआसं गदम्हि । तदो जाव एणं लज्जावणदमुहिं परिस्सजिअ सअं तादकस्सवेण एव्वं अहिणन्दिदं । दिट्ठिआ धूमाउलिददिट्ठिणो वि जअमाणस्स पाअए एव्व आहुदी पडिदा । वच्छे, सुसिस्सपरिदिण्णा विज्जा विअ असोअणिज्जा संवुत्ता । अज्ज एव्व इसिरक्खिदं तुमं भत्तुणो सआसं विसज्जेमि त्ति ।** शृणु इदानीम् । सुखशयितपृच्छिका शकुन्तलासकाशं गतास्मि । ततो यादवेनां लज्जावनतमुखीं परिष्वज्य स्वयं तातकाश्यपेनैवमभिनन्दितम् । दिष्ट्या धूमाकुलितदृष्टेरपि यजमानस्य पावक एवाहुतिः पतिता । वत्से, सुशिष्यपरिदत्ता विद्येवाशोचनीया संवृत्ता । अद्यैव ऋषिरक्षितां त्वां भर्तुः सकाशं विसर्जयामीति ।

अनसूया—**अह केण सूइदो तादकस्सवस्स वुत्तन्तो ।** अथ केन सूचितस्तातकाश्यपस्य वृत्तान्तः ।

प्रियंवदा—**अग्गिसरणं पविट्ठस्स सरीरं विणा छन्दोमईए वाणिआए ।** अग्निशरणं प्रविष्टस्य शरीरं विना छन्दोमय्या वाण्या ।

अनसूया—(सविस्मयं) **कहेहि ।** कथय ।

प्रियंवदा—(संस्कृतमाश्रित्य ।)

दुष्यन्तेनाहितं तेजो दधानां भूतये भुवः ।
अवेहि तनयां ब्रह्मन्नग्निगर्भां शमीमिव ॥ ३ ॥

अनसूया—(प्रियंवदामाश्लिष्य ।) **सहि, पिअं मे । किंदु अज्ज एव्व सउन्दला णीअदित्ति उक्कण्ठासाधारणं परितोसं अणुहोमि ।** सखि, प्रियं मे । किंत्वद्यैव शकुन्तला नीयत इत्युत्कण्ठासाधारणं परितोष-मनुभवामि ।

is married to Duṣyanta and is pregnant. What shall we do then under the circumstances?

PRIYAMVADĀ (*Entering; with joy*). Hasten, my dear, hasten to perform the festive solemnities at Śakuntalā's departure.

ANASŪYĀ. How is this, my dear?

PRIYAMVADĀ. Hear me. I just went to Śakuntalā to inquire if she had slept well. And then father Kāśyapa having of his own accord embraced her, while she hung her head in shame, congratulated her thus: "O joy! the offering of the sacrificer fell straight into the fire, albeit his sight was impeded by the smoke. My child, like knowledge imparted to an excellent pupil, thou art not to be sorrowed for. This very day I will send thee to thy husband escorted by hermits."

ANASŪYĀ. But who told father Kāśyapa what had passed?

PRIYAMVADĀ. An incorporeal metrical speech, when he had entered the fire-sanctuary.

ANASŪYĀ (*Astonished*). Tell me.

PRIYAMVADĀ. (*Speaking in Sanskrit*).

Know, Brāhmaṇa, that your daughter bears, for earth's prosperity, the glorious seed implanted by Duṣyanta, as the Śamī tree is pregnant with fire. (3)

ANASŪYĀ (*Hugging Priyamvadā*). I am so glad, my dear; and yet my joy is mingled with sorrow when I think that Śakuntalā is going to be taken away only to-day.

प्रियंवदा—सहि, अम्हे दाव उक्कण्ठं विणोदइस्सामो । सा वस्सिणी णिव्वुदा होदु । सखि, आवां तावदुत्कण्ठां विनोदयिष्यावः । सा तपस्विनी निर्वृता भवतु ।

अनसूया—तेण हि एदस्सिं चूदसाहावलम्बिदे णारिएरसमुग्गए एतण्णिमित्तं एव्व कालन्तरक्खमा णिक्खित्ता मए केसरमालिआ । ता इमं हत्थसंणिहिदं करेहि । जाव अहंपि से मिअलोअणं तित्थमित्तिअं दुव्वाकिसलआणित्ति मङ्गलसमालम्भणाणि विरएमि । तेन ह्येतस्मिंश्चूतशाखावलम्बिते नारिकेलसमुद्गक एतन्निमित्तमेव कालान्तरक्षमा निक्षिप्ता मया केसरमालिका । तदिमां हस्तसंनिहितां कुरु । यावदहमपि तस्यै मृगरोचनां तीर्थमृत्तिकां दूर्वाकिसलयानीति मङ्गलसमालम्भनानि विरचयामि ।

प्रियंवदा—तह करीअदु । तथा क्रियताम् ।

(अनसूया निष्क्रान्ता । प्रियंवदा नाट्येन सुमनसो गृह्णाति ।)

(नेपथ्ये ।)

गौतमि, आदिश्यन्तां शार्ङ्गरवमिश्राः शकुन्तलानयनाय ।

प्रियंवदा—(कर्णं दत्त्वा ।) **अणसूए, तुवर तुवर । एदे क्खु हत्थिआउरगामिणो इसीओ सद्दावीअन्ति ।** अनसूये, त्वरस्व त्वरस्व । एते खलु हास्तिनापुरगामिन ऋषय शब्दाय्यन्ते ।

(प्रविश्य समालम्भनहस्ता ।)

अनसूया—सहि, एहि । गच्छम्ह । सखि, एहि । गच्छावः ।

(इति परिक्रामतः ।)

प्रियंवदा—(विलोक्य ।) **एसा सुज्जोदय एव्व सिहामज्जिदा पडिच्छिदणीवारहत्थाहिं सोत्थिवाअणकाहिं तावसीहिं अहिणन्दीअमाणा सउन्दला चिट्ठइ । उवसप्पम्ह णं ।** एषा सूर्योदय एव शिखामज्जिता प्रतिष्ठितनीवारहस्ताभिः स्वस्तिवाचनिकाभिस्तापसीभिरभिनन्द्यमाना शकुन्तला तिष्ठति । उपसर्पाव एताम् ।

(इत्युपसर्पतः ।)

PRIYAṀVADĀ. Well, my dear, we will dissipate all anxiety. Only let the poor-girl be made happy.

ANASŪYĀ. Well, then, in this cocoa-nut casket, hanging on the branch of the mango-tree I have put a Keśara-garland which is capable of keeping fresh for a time, with this very object. Therefore take it in your hand : while I prepare for her auspicious decorations such as yellow orpiment, holy earth and Durvā sprouts.

PRIYAṀVADĀ. Be it so done.

(*Exit Anasūyā. Priyaṁvadā acts the gathering of flowers. Behind the Scenes.*)

Gautamī, bid the worthy Śārṅgarava and others escort Śakuntalā.

PRIYAṀVADĀ (*Listening*). Hurry, Anasūyā, hurry. They are calling the hermits who are to go to Hastināpura.

(*Entering, with the decorations in her hand*).

Anasūyā Come, dear, let us go. (*They walk round.*)

PRIYAṀVADĀ (*Observing*). There stands our Śakuntalā, after bathing overhead at earliest sunrise, while the hermit-women, who are congratulating her have the hallowed grains in their hands, and are invoking blessings on her. Let us advance to her. (*They advance.*)

(ततः प्रविशति यथोद्दिष्टव्यापारासनस्था शकुन्तला ।)

तापसीनामन्यतमा—(शकुन्तलां प्रति ।) **जादे, भत्तुणो बहुमाणसूअअं महादेईसद्दं लहेहि ।** जाते, भर्तुर्बहुमानसूचकं महादेवीशब्दं लभस्व ।

द्वितीया—वच्छे, वीरप्पसविणी होहि । वत्से, वीरप्रसविनी भव ।

तृतीया—वच्छे, भत्तुणो बहुमदा होहि । वत्से, भर्तुर्बहुमता भव ।

(इत्याशिषो दत्त्वा गौतमीवर्जं निष्क्रान्ताः ।)

सख्यौ—(उपसृत्य ।) **सहि सुहमज्जणं दे होदु ।** सखि, सुखमज्जनं ते भवतु ।

शकुन्तला—साअदं मे सहीणं । इदो णिसीदह । स्वागतं मे सख्योः । इतो निषीदतम् ।

उभे—(मङ्गलपात्राण्यादाय । उपविश्य ।) **हला, सज्जा होहि । जाव मङ्गलसमालम्भणं विरएम ।** हला, सज्जा भव । यावन्मङ्गलसमालम्भनं विरचयावः ।

शकुन्तला—एदं पि बहु मन्तव्वं । दुल्लहं दाणिं मे सहीमण्डणं भविस्सदि त्ति । (इति बाष्पं विसृजति ।) एतदपि बहु मन्तव्यम् । दुर्लभमिदानीं मे सखीमण्डनं भविष्यतीति ।

उभे—सहि, उइअं ण दे मङ्गलकाले रोइदुं । (इत्यश्रूणि प्रमृज्य नाट्येन प्रसाधयतः ।) सखि, उचितं न ते मङ्गलकाले रोदितुम् ।

प्रियंवदा—आहरणोइदं रूवं अस्समसुलहेहिं पसाहणेहिं विप्पआरीअदि । आभरणोचितं रूपमाश्रमसुलभैः प्रसाधनैर्विप्रकार्यते ।

(प्रविश्योपायनहस्तौ ।)

ऋषिकुमारकौ—इदमलंकरणम् । अलंक्रियतामत्रभवती ।

(सर्वा विलोक्य विस्मिताः ।)

गौतमी—वच्छ णारअ, कुदो एदं । वत्स नारद, कुत एतत् ।

प्रथमः—तातकाश्यपप्रभावात् ।

गौतमी—किं माणसी सिद्धी । किं मानसी सिद्धिः ।

(*Enter Śakuntalā seated, and engaged as described.*)

ONE OF THE HERMIT-WOMEN. (*To Śakuntalā*). My child, mayst thou receive the title of 'Great Queen' showing how well thy husband honours thee!

SECOND. Child, mayest thou be delivered of a hero!

THIRD. Child, mayest thou be highly esteemed by thy husband!

(*Having blessed her thus, exeunt all except Gautamī.*)

FRIENDS (*Approaching*). Friend, may it prove to thee a happy ablution!

ŚAKUNTALĀ. My friends, are welcome : sit here.

BOTH (*Taking up the vessels containing the auspicious materials, and seating themselves*). Get ready, dear, while we put on (you) the auspicious decorations.

SAKUNTALĀ. Even this ought to be highly valued : adornment at the hands of my friends will be ever so rare to me. (*She sheds tears.*)

BOTH. You ought not to weep, dear, at this happy time. (*Wiping off her tears, they act adorning her*).

PRIYAṀVADĀ. Your beauty which deserves (richer) ornaments is disfigured by such decorations as we could procure in the hermitage.

(*Entering with presents in hand.*)

TWO HERMIT-LADS. Here are ornaments. Let her ladyship put them on.

(*All are amazed on seeing them.*)

GAUTAMĪ. Child Nārada, whence come these things?

FIRST. From the holy power cf father Kāśyapa.

GAUTAMĪ. A creation of his mind?

द्वितीयः—न खलु। श्रूयताम् । तत्रभवता वयमाज्ञप्ताः शकुन्तलाहेतोर्वनस्पतिभ्यः कुसुमान्याहरतेति । तत इदानीं

क्षौमं केनचिदिन्दुपाण्डु तरुणा माङ्गल्यमाविष्कृतं
निष्ठ्यूतश्चरणोपभोगसुलभो लाक्षारसः केनचित् ।
अन्येभ्यो वनदेवताकरतलैरापर्वभागोत्थितै-
र्दत्तान्याभरणानि तत्किसलयोद्भेदप्रतिद्वन्द्विभिः ॥ ४ ॥

प्रियंवदा—हला, इमाए अब्भुववत्तीए सूइआ दे भत्तुणो गेहे अणुहोदव्वा राअलच्छित्ति । हला, अनयाभ्युपपत्त्या सूचिता ते भर्तुर्गेहेऽनुभवितव्या राजलक्ष्मीरीति ।

(शकुन्तला व्रीडां रूपयति ।)

प्रथमः—गौतम, एह्येहि । अभिषेकोत्तीर्णाय काश्यपाय वनस्पतिसेवां निवेदयावः ।

द्वितीयः—तथा ।

(इति निष्क्रान्तौ ।)

सख्यौ—अए, अणुवजुत्तभूसणो अअं जणो । चित्तकम्मपरिअएण अङ्गेसु दे आहरणविणिओअं करेम्ह । अये, अनुपयुक्तभूषणोऽयं जनः । चित्रकर्मपरिचयेनाङ्गेषु ते आभरणविनियोगं कुर्वः ।

शकुन्तला—जाणे वो णेउणं । जाने वां नैपुणम् ।

(उभे नाट्येनालंकुरुतः ।)

(ततः प्रविशति स्नानोत्तीर्णः काश्यपः ।)

काश्यपः—

यास्यत्यद्य शकुन्तलेति हृदयं संस्पृष्टमुत्कण्ठया
कण्ठः स्तम्भितबाष्पवृत्तिकलुषश्चिन्ताजडं दर्शनम् ।
वैक्लव्यं मम तावदीदृशमपि स्नेहादरण्यौकसः
पीड्यन्ते गृहिणः कथं न तनयाविश्लेषदुःखैर्नवैः ॥ ५ ॥

SECOND. Not, indeed. Listen. The venerable (sage) gave us his order "Bring hither flowers for Śakuntalā from the trees." And then

by a certain tree was exhibited an auspicious silken garment white as the moon; another distilled the lac-dye so excellent to stain her feet; and from others were presented ornaments by fairy-hands extending as far as the wrist that rivalled the first sproutings of delicate leaves of those trees. (4)

PRIYAṀVADĀ. This favour is a presage of the royal fortune which you are to enjoy in your husband's home.

(*Śakuntalā looks bashful.*)

FIRST. Come, my Gautama, come. We shall tell father Kāśyapa (who must have) returned from bathing, of the service done by the trees.

SECOND. All right (*Exeunt.*)

FRIENDS. My dear, we are never used to ornaments; but our acquaintance with the art of painting will help us to adjust these ornaments on your limbs.

ŚAKUNTALĀ. I know how clever you are. (*Both act adorning her.*)

(*Enter Kāśyapa returning after bathing.*)

This day will Śakuntalā depart: at such (a thought) my heart is smitten with anguish; my voice is choked by suppressing the flow of tears; and my senses paralysed by anxious thought. If such, through affection, is the affliction even of me a hermit, O with what pangs must they who are fathers of families be afflicted at the first parting with their daughters? (5)

(इति परिक्रामति)

सख्यौ—हला सउन्दले अवसिदमण्डणासि । परिधेहि संपदं खोमजुअलं । हला शकुन्तले, अवसितमण्डनासि । परिधत्स्व सांप्रतं क्षौमयुगलम् ।

(शकुन्तलोत्थाय परिधत्ते ।)

गौतमी—जादे, एसो दे आणन्दपरिवाहिणा चक्खुणा परिस्सजन्तो विअ गुरू उवट्ठिदो । आआरं दाव पडिवज्जस्स । जाते, एष त आनन्दपरिवाहिणा चक्षुषा परिष्वजमान इव गुरुरुपस्थितः । आचारं तावत्प्रतिपद्यस्व ।

शकुन्तला—(सव्रीडम् ।) **ताद, वन्दामि ।** तात वन्दे ।

काश्यपः—वत्से,

ययोतेरिव शर्मिष्ठा भर्तुर्बहुमता भव ।
सुतं त्वमपि सम्राजं सेव पूरुमवाप्नुहि ॥ ६ ॥

गौतमी—भअवं, वरो क्खु एसो ण आसिसा । भगवन्, वर खल्वेषो नाशीः ।

काश्यपः—वत्से, इतः सद्योहुताग्नीन्प्रदक्षिणीकुरुष्व ।

[सर्वे परिक्रामन्ति ।]

काश्यपः—(ऋक्छन्दसाशास्ते ।)

अमी वेदिं परितः क्लृप्तधिष्ण्याः
समिद्वन्तः प्रान्तसंस्तीर्णदर्भाः ।
अपघ्नन्तो दुरितं हव्यगन्धै-
र्वैतानास्त्वां वह्नयः पावयन्तु ॥ ७ ॥

प्रतिष्ठस्वेदानीम् । (सदृष्टिक्षेपम् ।) **क्व ते शार्ङ्गरवमिश्राः ।**

(प्रविश्य ।)

शिष्यः—भगवन्, इमे स्मः ।

काश्यपः—भगिन्यास्ते मार्गमादेशय ।

(*Walks about.*)

FRIENDS. Dear Śakuntalā, your decoration is completed. Now put on the pair of silken garments.

(*Śakuntalā rises and puts them on.*)

GAUTAMĪ. My child, here comes your father, whose eyes overflow with tears of joy, as if (already) embracing you. Just, therefore, do him the customary reverence.

ŚAKUNTALĀ (*Bashfully*). Father, I salute you.

KĀŚYAPA. My child,

> Mayest thou be cherished by thy husband, as Śarmiṣṭhā was cherished by Yayāti. And mayest thou bear a son, as she did Puru, who shall be the sovereign of the world. (6)

GAUTAMĪ. Holy sir, this is indeed a boon, not a mere benediction.

KĀŚYAPA. My child, this way go round the fires in which the offerings have just been thrown.

(*All walk about.*)

KĀŚYAPA. (*Pronounces a blessing in the metre of the Rgveda*).

> Let these sacrificial fires, whose places are fixed round the altar, fed with holy wood, having the Darbha grass strewn around their margins, removing sin by the perfume of the oblations, purify thee. (7)

Now set out (on thy journey.) (*Looking round*). Where are Śārṇgarava and others?

(*Entering*) PUPIL. Holy sire, here we are.

KĀŚYAPA. Show thy sister her way.

शार्ङ्गरवः—इत इतो भवती।

(सर्वे परिक्रामन्ति।)

काश्यपः—भो भोः संनिहितास्तपोवनतरवः,

पातुं न प्रथमं व्यवस्यति जलं युष्मास्वपीतेषु या
नादत्ते प्रियमण्डनापि भवतां स्नेहेन या पल्लवम्।
आद्ये वः कुसुमप्रसूतिसमये यस्या भवत्युत्सवः
सेयं याति शकुन्तला पतिगृहं सर्वैरनुज्ञायताम्॥ ८॥

(कोकिलरवं सूचयित्वा)

अनुमतगमना शकुन्तला
तरुभिरियं वनवासबन्धुभिः।
परभृतविरुतं कलं यथा
प्रतिवचनीकृतमेभिरीदृशम्॥ ९॥

(आकाशे।)

रम्यान्तरः कमलिनीहरितैः सरोभि-
श्छायाद्रुमैर्नियमितार्कमयूखतापः।
भूयात्कुशेशयरजोमृदुरेणुरस्याः
शान्तानुकुलपवनश्च शिवश्च पन्थाः॥ १०॥

(सर्वे सविस्मयमाकर्णयन्ति।)

गौतमी—जादे, णादिजणसिणिद्धाहिं अणुण्णादगमणासि तवोवणदेवदाहिं। पणम भअवदीणं। जाते, ज्ञातिजनस्निग्धाभिरनुज्ञातगमनासि तपोवनदेवताभिः। प्रणम भगवतीभ्यः।

शकुन्तला—(सप्रणामं परिक्रम्य। जनान्तिकम्।) **हला पिअंवदे, णं अज्जउत्तदंसणुस्सुआए वि अस्समपदं परिच्चअन्तीए दुक्खेण मे चलणा पुरदो पवट्टन्ति।** हला प्रियंवदे, नन्वार्यपुत्रदर्शनोत्सुकाया अप्याश्रमपदं परित्यजन्त्या दुःखेन मे चरणौ पुरतः प्रवर्तेते।

ŚĀRNGARAVA. This way, this way, lady.

(*They all walk about.*)

KĀŚYAPA. Ye neighbouring trees of the pious grove !

She who would not drink water first, before you were watered ; she who cropped not through affection for you one of your fresh leaves, though she is so fond of ornaments : she whose chief delight was in the season of the first appearance of your bloom ; even that same Śakuntalā is going to the palace of her wedded lord. Let all give their consent. (8)

(*Acting as if he heard the note of a Koil.*)

Śakuntalā is given leave to depart by the trees, the companions of her forest—life; since a song to this effect, a sweet Koil-song was employed as an answer by them. (9)

(*In the air*)

May her path, pleasant at intervals with lakes that are green with lotus-beds, where the heat of the sun's rays is mitigated by shady-trees, where the dust is soft as the pollen from the lotuses, be cheered by gentle and pleasant breezes and be (altogether) prosperous. (10)

(*All listen with wonderment.*)

GAUTAMĪ. Child, the deities of the holy forest, who are dear to thee as thy own kinsfolk, have given thee leave to depart. Pay reverence to the holy ones.

ŚAKUNTALĀ (*She walks round bowing ; aside*). Priyaṁvadā, dear, long as I may to see my husband, yet in leaving this hermitage, my feet can hardly move forward.

प्रियंवदा—ण केवलं तवोवणविरहकादरा सही एव्व । तुए उवट्ठिदविओअस्स तवोवणस्स वि दाव समवत्था दीसइ । न केवलं तपोवनविरहकातरा सख्येव । त्वयोपस्थितवियोगस्य तपोवनस्यापि तावत्समवस्था दृश्यते ।

उग्गलिअदब्भकवला मिआ परिच्चत्तणच्चणा मोरा ।
ओसरिअपण्डुपत्ता मुअन्ति अस्सू विअ लदाओ ॥ ११ ॥

उद्गलितदर्भकवला मृग्यः परित्यक्तनर्तना मयूराः ।
अपसृतपाण्डुपत्रा मुञ्चन्त्यश्रूणीव लताः ॥

शकुन्तला—(स्मृत्वा ।) **ताद, लदाबहिणिअं वणजोसिणिं दाव आमन्तइस्सं ।** तात, लताभगिनीं वनज्योत्स्नां तावदामन्त्रयिष्ये ।

काश्यपः—अवैमि ते तस्यां सोदर्यस्नेहम् । इयं तावद्दक्षिणेन ।

शकुन्तला—(लतामुपेत्य ।) **वणजोसिणी, चूदसंगता वि मं पच्चालिङ्ग इदोगदाहिं साहाबाहाहिं । अज्जप्पहुदि दूरपरिवत्तिणी दे खु भविस्सं ।** वनज्योत्स्ने, चूतसंगतापि मां प्रत्यालिङ्गेतोगताभिः शाखाबाहाभिः । अद्यप्रभृति दूरपरिवर्तिनी ते खलु भविष्यामि ।

काश्यपः—

संकल्पितं प्रथममेव मया तवार्थे
भर्तारमात्मसदृशं सुकृतैर्गता त्वम् ।
चूतेन संश्रितवती नवमालिकेय-
मस्यामहं त्वयि च संप्रति वीतचिन्तः ॥ १२ ॥

इतः पन्थानं प्रतिपद्यस्व ।

शकुन्तला—(सख्यौ प्रति ।) **हला, एसा दुवेणं वो हत्थे णिक्खेवो ।** हला, एषा द्वयोर्युवयोर्हस्ते निक्षेपः ।

सख्यौ—अअं जणो कस्स हत्थे समप्पिदो । (इति बाष्पं विहरतः ।) अयं जनः कस्य हस्ते समर्पितः ।

PRIYAṀVADĀ. My friend is not the only one to feel distressed at this separation from the pious grove. One may observe the same condition even of the grove now when the time of your departure approaches.

> The deer let fall the morsels of Darbha-grass, the peacocks stop their dancing, and the creepers, whose pale leaves fall (to the ground), appear to shed tears. (11)

ŚAKUNTALĀ (*Remembering*). Father, I will just say good-bye to Vanajyotsnā, my sister among the creepers.

KĀŚYAPA. I know thou lovest her as thy sister. Here she is now to the right.

ŚAKUNTALĀ (*Approaching the creeper*). O Vanajyotsnā, although wedded to the mango-tree, yet embrace me, too, with your arms, these branches, which are turned in this direction. I shall be far away from you after this day.

KĀŚYAPA.

> Thy merits have gained thee a husband equal to thyself, who had already been originally determined upon by me for thee; this Navamālikā has resorted to the mango-tree, so that now my solicitude for thee and for her is at an end. (12)

From here, proceed on thy journey.

ŚAKUNTALĀ (*To her friends*). Friends, this (creeper) is a deposit in your hands.

FRIENDS. (But) into whose hands shall we be left? (*they shed tears.*)

काश्यपः—अनसूये, अलं रुदित्वा। ननु भवतीभ्यामेव स्थिरीकर्तव्या शकुन्तला।

(सर्वे परिक्रामन्ति।)

शकुन्तला—ताद, एसा उडजपज्जन्तचारिणी गब्भमन्थरा मिअवहू जदा अणघप्पसवा होइ तदा मे कंपि पिअणिवेदइत्तअं विसज्जइस्सह। तात एषोटजपर्यंतचारिणी गर्भमन्थरा मृगवधूर्यदानघप्रसवा भवति तदा मह्यं कमपि प्रियनिवेदयितृकं विसर्जयिष्यथ।

काश्यपः—नेदं विस्मरिष्यामः।

शकुन्तला—(गतिभङ्गं रूपयित्वा।) को णु क्खु एसो णिवसणे मे सज्जइ। (इति परावर्तते।) को नु खल्वेष निवसने मे सज्जते।

काश्यपः—वत्से,

यस्य त्वया व्रणविरोपणमिङ्गुदीनां
तैलं न्यषिच्यत मुखे कुशसूचिविद्धे।
श्यामाकमुष्टिपरिवर्धितको जहाति
सोऽयं न पुत्रकृतकः पदवीं मृगस्ते॥ १३॥

शकुन्तला—वच्छ, किं सहवासपरिच्चाइणिं मं अणुसरसि। अचिरप्पसूदाए जणणीए विणा वड्ढिदो एव्व। दाणिं पि मए विरहिदं तुमं तादो चिन्तइस्सदि। णिवत्तेहि दाव। (इति रुदती प्रस्थिता।) वत्स, किं सहवासपरित्यागिनीं मामनुसरसि। अचिरप्रसूतया जनन्या विना वर्धित एव। इदानीमपि मया विरहितं त्वां तातश्चिन्तयिष्यति। निवर्तस्व तावत्।

काश्यपः—

उत्पक्ष्मणोर्नयनयोरुपरुद्धवृत्तिं
बाष्पं कुरु स्थिरतया विरतानुबन्धम्।

KĀŚYAPA. Anasūyā, enough of weeping! It is you, surely, who must cheer Śakuntalā.

(*All walk round.*)

ŚAKUNTALĀ. Father, when yon female antelope grazing about near the hut, who now moves slowly from the weight of her young, shall be safely delivered of it, then you will send me some one to announce the happy event.

KĀŚYAPA. I shall not forget it.

ŚAKUNTALĀ (*Showing her movement is obstructed.*) Ah! who is it that clings to my dress?

(*She turns round.*)

KĀŚYAPA. My darling,

It is thy adopted child, the (little) fawn whose mouth, when the sharp points of Kuśa grass wounded it, was sprinkled by thee with the healing oil of Ingudī, who has been tenderly reared by thee with handfuls of Śyāmāka grains; and who now will not leave thy footsteps. (13)

ŚAKUNTALĀ. My child, why should you follow me who must leave your company? You were indeed brought up by me when bereft of your mother shortly after she was delivered of you; now also, when separated from me, will father attend you with anxious care; go back then. (*She walks on weeping.*)

KĀŚYAPA.

Be firm and check the rising tears, that obstruct the free action of thy eyes, with their upturned eyelashes. For here on this path

अस्मिन्नलक्षितनतोन्नतभूमिभागे
मार्गे पदानि खलु ते विषमीभवन्ति ॥ १४ ॥

शार्ङ्गरवः—भगवन्, ओदकान्तं स्निग्धो जनोऽनुगन्तव्य इति श्रूयते। तदिदं सरस्तीरम्। अत्र संदिश्य प्रतिगन्तुमर्हसि।

काश्यपः—तेन हीमां क्षीरवृक्षच्छायामाश्रयामः।

(सर्वे परिक्रम्य स्थिताः।)

काश्यपः—(आत्मगतम्।) किं नु खलु तत्रभवतो दुष्यन्तस्य युक्तरूपमस्माभिः संदेष्टव्यम्। (इति चिन्तयति।)

शकुन्तला—(जनान्तिकम्।) हला, पेक्ख। णलिणीपत्तन्तरिदं वि सहअरं अदेक्खन्ती आदुरा चक्कवाई आरडदि दुक्करं अहं करेमि त्ति। हला, पश्य नलिनीपत्रान्तरितमपि सहचरमपश्यन्त्यातुरा चक्रवाक्यारौति दुष्करमहं करोमीति।

अनसूया—सहि, मा एव्वं मन्तेहि। सखि, मैवं मन्त्रयस्व।

एसा वि पिएण विणा गमेइ रअणिं विसाअदीहअरं।
गरुअं पि विरहदुक्खं आसाबन्धो सहावेदि ॥ १५ ॥

एषापि प्रियेण विना गमयति रजनीं विषाददीर्घतराम्।
गुर्वपि विरहदुःखमाशाबन्धः साहयति ॥

काश्यपः—शार्ङ्गरव, इति त्वया मद्वचनात्स राजा शकुन्तलां पुरस्कृत्य वक्तव्यः।

शार्ङ्गरवः—आज्ञापयतु भवान्।

काश्यपः—

अस्मान्साधु विचिन्त्य संयमधनानुच्चैः कुलं चात्मन-
स्त्वय्यस्याः कथमप्यबान्धवकृतां स्नेहप्रवृत्तिं च ताम्।

where the undulations of ground are not discernible, they footsteps must needs be unequal. (14)

ŚĀRṄGARAVA. It is a sacred rule, holy father, that one should accompany a loved person as far as the water's brink. Give us your message here, and be pleased to return.

KĀŚYAPA. Let us, then rest in the shade of this Kṣīra-tree.

(*All walk around and stop.*)

KĀŚYAPA (*To himself*). What message should be sent by me that would be most appropriate for the noble Duṣyanta ? (*He reflects.*)

ŚAKUNTALĀ (*Aside*). Look, friend, the female Cakravāka, not perceiving her dear mate when only hidden behind lotus-leaves is crying in her anguish 'How hard is my lot !'

ANASŪYĀ. Friend, do not say so.

Even she, without her beloved, passes away the night made too long by grief. The bond of hope makes the pain of severence, however keen, supportable. (15)

KĀŚYAPA. Śārṅgarava, when you present Śakuntalā to the king, address him thus in my name.

ŚĀRṄGARAVA. Give your commands, holy father.

KĀŚYAPA.

Having well considered us as rich in devotion, thy own exalted birth and the free flow of affection of this (girl) towards thee, which arose in her without any interference of her kindred,

सामान्यप्रतिपत्तिपूर्वकमियं दारेषु दृश्या त्वया
भाग्यायत्तमतःपरं न खलु तद्वाच्यं वधूबन्धुभिः ॥ १६ ॥

शार्ङ्गरवः—गृहीतः संदेशः ।

काश्यपः—वत्से, त्वमिदानीमनुशासनीयासि । वनौकसोऽपि सन्तो लौकिकज्ञा वयम् ।

शार्ङ्गरवः—न खलु धीमतां कश्चिदविषयो नाम ।

काश्यपः—सा त्वमितः पतिकुलं प्राप्य

शुश्रूषस्व गुरून्कुरु प्रियसखीवृत्तिं सपत्नीजने
भर्तुर्विप्रकृतापि रोषणतया मा स्म प्रतीपं गमः ।
भूयिष्ठं भव दक्षिणा परिजने भाग्येष्वनुत्सेकिनी
यान्त्येवं गृहिणीपदं युवतयो वामाः कुलस्याधयः ॥ १७ ॥

कथं वा गौतमी मन्यते ।

गौतमी—एत्तिओ वहूजणस्स उवदेसो । जादे, एदं क्खु सव्वं ओधारेहि । एतावान्वधूजनस्योपदेशः । जाते, एतत्खलु सर्वमवधारय ।

काश्यपः—वत्से, परिष्वजस्व मां सखीजनं च ।

शकुन्तला—ताद, इदो एव्व किं पिअंवदामिस्साओ सहीओ णिवत्तिस्सन्ति । तात, इत एव किं प्रियंवदामिश्राः सख्यो निवर्तिष्यन्ते ।

look on her among thy wives with the same respect (kindness) which they experience: more than that depends upon the will of heaven, and should, not indeed, be demanded by the bride's kinsfolk. (16)

ŚĀRṄGARAVA. I have (well) comprehended your message.

KĀŚYAPA. My child, I must now give thee my advice. Though I live in the forest, yet well do I know the ways of the world.

ŚĀRṄGARAVA. Nothing, indeed, to the wise is out of reach.

KĀŚYAPA. When thou wilt have gone from here to thy husband's home,

Pay respectful attention to thy elders; treat thy rivals as thy dear friends; should thy husband wrong thee, let not thy resentment lead thee to disobedience. Be ever courteous towards thy servants; not puffed with pride in thy fortune. By such behaviour, young women become honoured wives; but perverse wives are the bane of a family. (17)

But what does Gautamī say?

GAUTAMĪ. This is the advice to be given to a young bride. My child, be sure to remember it all.

KĀŚYAPA. Come, my child, embrace me and thy friends.

ŚAKUNTALĀ. O my father, must my friends turn back from here?

काश्यपः—इमे अपि प्रदेये। न युक्तमनयोस्तत्र गन्तुम्। त्वया सह गौतमी यास्यति।

शकुन्तला—(पितरमाश्लिष्य।) **कहं दाणिं तादस्स अङ्कादो परिब्भट्ठा मलअतडुम्मूलिआ चन्दणलदा विअ दसन्तरे जीविअं धारइस्सं।** कथमिदानीं तातस्याङ्कात्परिभ्रष्टा मलयतटोन्मूलिता चन्दनलतेव देशान्तरे जीवितं धारयिष्ये।

काश्यपः—वत्से, किमेवं कातरासि।

अभिजनवतो भर्तुः श्लाघ्ये स्थिता गृहिणीपदे
विभवगुरुभिः कृत्यैस्तस्य प्रतिक्षणमाकुला।
तनयमचिरात्प्राचीवार्कं प्रसूय च पावनं
मम विरहजां न त्वं वत्से शुचं गणयिष्यसि॥ १८॥

(शकुन्तला पितुः पादयोः पतति।)

काश्यपः—यदिच्छामि ते तदस्तु।

शकुन्तला—(सख्यावुपेत्य।) **हला, दुवे वि मं समं एव्व परिस्सजह।** हला, द्वे अपि मां सममेव परिष्वजेथाम्।

सख्यौ—(तथा कृत्वा।) **सहि, जइ णाम सो राआ पच्चहिण्णाणमन्थरो भवे तदो से इमं अत्तणामहेअङ्किअं अङ्गुलीअअं दंसेहि।** सखि, यदि नाम स राजा प्रत्यभिज्ञानमन्थरो भवेत्ततस्तस्येदमात्मनामधेयाङ्कितमङ्गुलीयकं दर्शय।

शकुन्तला—इमिणा संदेहेण वो आकम्पिदम्हि। अनेन संदेहेन वामाकम्पितास्मि।

सख्यौ—मा भाआहि। अदिसिणेहो पावसङ्की। मा भैषीः। अतिस्नेहः पापशङ्की।

KĀŚYAPA. These, too, are to be given away in marriage. It would not be proper for them to go there, but Gautamī will accompany thee.

ŚAKUNTALĀ (*Embracing her father*). Removed from the lap of my father, like a young sandal tree, rent from the slopes of the Malaya, how shall I exist in a strange soil?

KĀŚYAPA. My child, why shouldst thou be so anxious?

When thou shalt be occupying the honoured position of the consort of a nobly-born husband; engrossed every moment in his affairs important through his greatness; and when before long thou wilt have given birth to a child that will purify (his race) as the East brings forth the Sun, then wilt thou think but lightly of this affliction caused by severence from me. (18)

(*Śakuntalā falls at the feet of her father.*)

KĀŚYAPA. My darling, mayest thou have all that I desire for thee!

ŚAKUNTALĀ (*Advancing to her friends*). Come, friends; embrace me, both of you together.

FRIENDS (*So doing*). Friend, should the king be slow to recognize you, show him this ring on which his own name is engraved.

ŚAKUNTALĀ. My heart flutters at the apprehension which you have raised.

FRIENDS. Do not be afraid. Excessive love is apt to suspect evil.

शार्ङ्गरवः—युगान्तरमारूढः सविता । त्वरतामत्रभवती ।

शकुन्तला—(आश्रमाभिमुखी स्थित्वा ।) **ताद, कदा णु भूओ तवोवणं पेक्खिस्सं** । तात, कदा नु भूयस्तपोवनं प्रेक्षिष्ये ।

काश्यपः—श्रूयताम् ।

भूत्वा चिराय चतुरन्तमहीसपत्नी
दौष्यन्तमप्रतिरथं तनयं निवेश्य ।
भर्त्रा तदर्पितकुटुम्बभरेण सार्धं
शान्ते करिष्यसि पदं पुनराश्रमेऽस्मिन् ॥ १९ ॥

गौतमी—जादे, परिहीअदि गमणवेला । णिवत्तेहि पिदरं । अहवा चिरेण वि पुणो पुणो एसा एव्वं मन्तइस्सदि । णिवत्तदु भवं । जाते, परिहीयते गमनवेला । निवर्तय पितरम् । अथवा चिरेणापि पुनः पुनरेषैवं मन्त्रयिष्यते । निवर्ततां भवान् ।

काश्यपः—वत्से, उपरुध्यते तपोऽनुष्ठानम् ।

शकुन्तला—(भूयः पितरमाश्लिष्य ।) **तवच्चरणपीडिदं तादसरीरं । ता मा अदिमेत्तं मम किदे उक्कण्ठिदुम्** । तपश्चरणपीडितं तातशरीरम् । तन्मातिमात्रं मम कृत उत्कण्ठितुम् ।

काश्यपः—(सनिःश्वासम् ।)

शममेष्यति मम शोकः कथं नु वत्से त्वया रचितपूर्वम् ।
उटजद्वारविरूढं नीवारबलिं विलोकयतः ॥ २० ॥

गच्छ । शिवास्ते पन्थानः सन्तु ।

(निष्क्रान्ता शकुन्तला सहयायिनश्च ।)

सख्यौ—(शकुन्तलां विलोक्य ।) **हद्धी हद्धी । अन्तरिहिदा सउन्दला वणराईए** । हा धिक्, हा धिक् । अन्तर्हिता शकुन्तला वनराज्या ।

ŚĀRṄGARAVA. The Sun has ascended to another quarter of the heavens. Let the worthy lady hasten.

ŚAKUNTALĀ (*Turning her face towards the hermitage*). Father, when shall I behold this pious grove again?

KĀŚYAPA. Listen.

When thou shalt long have been a co-wife of the Earth bounded by the four cardinal-points, and settled in marriage in Duṣyanta's son by thee, a matchless warrior ; then with thy husband who shall have transferred the burden of family-cares to him, thou shalt again set foot in this peaceful hermitage. (19)

GAUTAMĪ. My child, the (proper) hour of our journey is slipping by. Suffer thy father to return. Or since ever so long she will go on talking again and again in the same strain, let the holy father return.

KĀŚYAPA. Sweet child, the practice of devotions is interrupted.

ŚAKUNTALĀ (*Embracing her father again*). Father's body is already worn out by his devotion. Do not, therefore, grieve for me beyond measure.

KĀŚYAPA (*Sighing*). How, my child, will my grief cease, as I look at the hallowed rice-grains formerly offered by thee, germinating at the door of my cottage? (20)

Go, may thy journey prosper.

(*Exeunt Śakuntalā and her escort.*)

FRIENDS (*Gazing after Śakuntalā*). Alas! Alas! Śakuntalā is hidden by the thick trees.

काश्यपः—(सनिःश्वासम् ।) **अनसूये, गतवती वां सहधर्मचारिणी । निगृह्य शोकमनुगच्छतं मां प्रस्थितम् ।**

उभे—**ताद, सउन्दलाविरहिदं सुण्णं विअ तवोवणं कहं पविसामो ।** तात, शकुन्तलाविरहितं शून्यमिव तपोवनं कथं प्रविशावः ।

काश्यपः—**स्नेहप्रवृत्तिरेवंदर्शिनी ।** (सविमर्शं परिक्रम्य ।) **हन्त भोः, शकुन्तलां पतिकुलं विसृज्य लब्धमिदानीं स्वास्थ्यम् । कुतः**

अर्थो हि कन्या परकीय एव
तामद्य संप्रेष्य परिग्रहीतुः ।
जातो ममायं विशदः प्रकामं
प्रत्यर्पितन्यास इवान्तरात्मा ॥ २१ ॥

(इति निष्क्रान्ताः सर्वे ।)

चतुर्थोऽङ्कः ।

KĀSYAPA (*Sighing*). Anasūyā, your companion is (at length) departed. Check your grief and follow me who am leaving.

BOTH. Father, how shall we enter the pious grove which without Śakuntalā seems a perfect vacuity?

KĀŚYAPA. So your love interprets. (*He walks round meditating*). Ah, dismissing Śakuntalā to her husband's home, I have regained my natural serenity of mind. For

> In truth a daughter is another's property; and having to-day sent her to her lord, I find my soul has become quite clear as if after restoring a deposit. (21)

(*Exeunt All.*)

Here ends Act IV

पञ्चमोऽङ्कः ।

(ततः प्रविशत्यासनस्थो राजा विदूषकश्च ।)

विदूषकः—(कर्णं दत्त्वा ।) **भो वअस्स, संगीदसालन्तरे अवधाणं देहि । कलविसुद्धाए गीदीए सरसंजोओ सुणीअदि । जाणे तत्तहोदी हंसवदिआ वण्णपरिअअं करेदि त्ति ।** भो वयस्य, संगीतशालान्तरेऽवधानं देहि । कलविशुद्धाया गीतेः स्वरसंयोगः श्रूयते । जाने तत्रभवती हंसपदिका वर्णपरिचयं करोतीति ।

राजा—तूष्णीं भव । यावदाकर्णयामि ।

(आकाशे गीयते ।)

अहिणवमहुलोलुवो तुमं
तह परिचुम्बिअ चूअमञ्जरिं ।
कमलवसइमेत्तणिव्वुदो
महुअर विम्हरिओ सि णं कहं ॥ १ ॥

अभिनवमधुलोलुपस्त्वं तथा परिचुम्ब्य चूतमञ्जरीम् ।
कमलवसतिमात्रनिर्वृतो मधुकर विस्मृतोऽस्येनां कथम् ॥

राजा—अहो रागपरिवाहिनी गीतिः ।

विदूषकः—किं दाव गीदीए अवगदो अक्खरत्थो । किं तावद्गीत्या अवगतोऽक्षरार्थः ।

राजा—(स्मितं कृत्वा ।) **सकृत्कृतप्रणयोऽयं जनः । तदस्या देवीं वसुमतीमन्तरेण महदुपालम्भं गतोऽस्मि । सखे माठव्य, मद्वचनादुच्यतां हंसपदिका । निपुणमुपालब्धोऽस्मीति ।**

ACT V

(*Enter king seated and the Vidūṣaka.*)

VIDŪṢAKA (*Listening.*) O friend, turn your attention to the interior of the Music-hall. One hears harmonious notes blended in a sweet and clear song. I believe the lady Haṁsapadikā is practising singing.

KING. Be quiet, that I may listen.

(*A song is sung in the air.*)

O bee, how comes it that you who eagerly long for fresh-honey, after having kissed the mango-blossom in that way, should have forgotten it, being now satisfied with mere dwelling in the lotus ! (1)

KING. O, what an impassioned song ?

VIDŪṢAKA. But, do you understand the meaning of the words of the song ?

KING (*Smiling*). I was once in love with her, and am now reproved on account of the queen Vasumatī. Friend Māṭhavya inform Haṁsapadikā in my name that I am well reproved.

विदूषकः—जं भवं आणवेदि । (उत्थाय ।) भो वअस्स, गहीदस्स ताए परकीएहिं हत्थेहिं सिहण्डए ताडीअमाणस्स अच्छराए वीदराअस्स विअ णत्थि दाणिं मे मोक्खो । यद्भवानाज्ञापयति । भो वयस्य, गृहीतस्य तया परकीयैर्हस्तैः शिखण्डके ताड्यमानस्याप्सरसा वीतरागस्येव नास्तीदानीं मे मोक्षः ।

राजा—गच्छ । नागरिकवृत्त्या संज्ञापयैनाम् ।

विदूषकः—का गई । (इति निष्क्रान्तः ।) का गतिः ।

राजा—(आत्मगतम् ।) किं नु खलु गीतार्थमाकर्ण्येष्टजनविरहादृतेऽपि बलवदुत्कण्ठितोऽस्मि । अथवा ।

रम्याणि वीक्ष्य मधुरांश्च निशम्य शब्दा-
न्पर्युत्सुकीभवति यत्सुखितोऽपि जन्तुः ।
तच्चेतसा स्मरति नूनमबोधपूर्वं
भावस्थिराणि जननान्तरसौहृदानि ॥२॥

(इति पर्याकुलस्तिष्ठति ।)

(ततः प्रविशति कञ्चुकी ।)

कञ्चुकी—अहो नु खल्वीदृशीमवस्थां प्रतिपन्नोऽस्मि ।

आचार इत्यवहितेन मया गृहीता
या वेत्रयष्टिरवरोधगृहेषु राज्ञः ।
काले गते बहुतिथे मम सैव जाता
प्रस्थानविक्लवगतेरवलम्बनार्था ॥ ३ ॥

भोः, कामं धर्मकार्यमनतिपात्यं देवस्य । तथापीदानीमेव धर्मासनादुत्थिताय पुनरुपरोधकारि कण्वशिष्यागमनमस्मै नोत्सहे निवेदितुम् । अथवाविश्रमोऽयं लोकतन्त्राधिकारः । कुतः ।

VIDŪṢAKA. As your Majesty, commands. (*Rising*). But now there will be no liberation for me when seized by her with the hands of others by the crest-lock and belaboured, any more than for a sage whose passions are spent, if seized by a nymph.

KING. Go, tell her in a courtly style.

VIDŪṢAKA. What help ! (*He goes out.*)

KING (*To himself*). Why am I filled with such deep sadness when I am in fact not separated from any real object of my affection, on hearing the meaning of the song? Or,

> When even a happy being is filled with wistful longings on seeing beautiful forms and listening to sweet sounds, then surely without being conscious of it, he remembers in his mind the friendships of a former birth deeply-rooted there in the form of impressions. (2)

(*He remains deeply troubled.*)

(*Then enter a chamberlain.*)

CHAMBERLAIN. Alas ! To such a state am I reduced !

> This staff which I assumed as a matter of form for the discharge of my duties in the inner apartment of my king, has, now when much time has elapsed since then, become the support to aid my faltering steps. (3)

Ah, surely the king cannot neglect a religious duty. And yet I have not the heart to announce to him, who has just risen from his tribunal the arrival of Kaṇva's pupils which will again detain him. But, this office of supporting the world will not allow any repose. For

भानुः सकृद्युक्ततुरङ्ग एव
रात्रिंदिवं गन्धवहः प्रयाति ।
शेषः सदैवाहितभूमिभारः
षष्ठांशवृत्तेरपि धर्म एषः ॥ ४ ॥

यावन्नियोगमनुतिष्ठामि । (परिक्रम्यावलोक्य च ।) एष देवः

प्रजाः प्रजाः स्वा इव तन्त्रयित्वा
निषेवते श्रान्तमना विविक्तम् ।
यूथानि संचार्य रविप्रतप्तः
शीतं दिवा स्थानमिव द्विपेन्द्रः ॥ ५ ॥

(उपगम्य ।) जयतु जयतु देवः । एते खलु हिमगिरेरुपत्यकारण्यवासिनः काश्यपसंदेशमादाय सस्त्रीकास्तपस्विनः संप्राप्ताः । श्रुत्वा देवः प्रमाणम् ।

राजा—(सादरम् ।) किं काश्यपसंदेशहारिणः ।

कञ्चुकी—अथ किम् ।

राजा—तेन हि मद्वचनाद्विज्ञाप्यतामुपाध्यायः सोमरातः । अमूनाश्रमवासिनः श्रौतेन विधिना सत्कृत्य स्वयमेव प्रवेशयितुमर्हतीति । अहमप्यत्र तपस्विदर्शनोचिते प्रदेशे स्थितः प्रतिपालयामि ।

कञ्चुकी—यदाज्ञापयति देवः । (इति निष्क्रान्तः ।)

राजा—(उत्थाय ।) वेत्रवति, अग्निशरणमार्गमादेशय ।

The Sun has yoked his steeds but once, the gale breathes by night and by day : Śeṣa continually sustains the weight of the Earth ; this also is the duty of him whose subsistence arises from a sixth part (of his people's income). (4)

Let me then attend to my duty. (*Walking about and observing*). Here is his Majesty

Attending to his people as to his own children, he now, being wearied in mind, seeks seclusion ; as an elephant, the chief of his herds, after having taken them round, and being heated by the Sun, repairs to a cool place during (the oppresive heat of) the day. (5)

(*Advancing*) Victory, victory to your Majesty ! Here are hermits with some women, come from their abode in the forest at the foot of the snowy mountains, and they bring a message from Kāśyapa. Having heard, your Majesty will command.

KING (*Respectfully.*) Do they bring a message from Kāśyapa ?

CHAMBERLAIN. It is even so.

KING. Well then, order the priest Somarāta, in my name : It is proper that you should give them a reception in the form appointed by the scriptures, and bring them (into the palace). I, too, shall await (them) here in this place fit for the reception of hermits.

CHAMBERLAIN. As your Majesty commands. (*exit.*)

KING. (*Rising*). Vetravati, lead the way to the fire-sanctuary.

प्रतीहारी—इदो इदो देवो । इत इतो देवः ।

राजा—(परिक्रामति । अधिकारखेदं निरूप्य ।) सर्वः प्रार्थितमर्थमधिगम्य सुखी संपद्यते जन्तुः । राज्ञां तु चरितार्थता दुःखोत्तरैव ।

औत्सुक्यमात्रमवसादयति प्रतिष्ठा
क्लिश्नाति लब्धपरिपालनवृत्तिरेव ।
नातिश्रमापनयनाय यथा श्रमाय
राज्यं स्वहस्तधृतदण्डमिवातपत्रम् ॥ ६ ॥

(नेपथ्ये ।)

वैतालिकौ—विजयतां देवः ।

प्रथमः—

स्वसुखनिरभिलाषः खिद्यसे लोकहेतोः
प्रतिदिनमथवा ते वृत्तिरेवंविधैव ।
अनुभवति हि मूर्ध्ना पादपस्तीव्रमुष्णं
शमयति परितापं छायया संश्रितानाम् ॥ ७ ॥

द्वितीयः—

नियमयसि विमार्गप्रस्थितानात्तदण्डः
प्रशमयसि विवादं कल्पसे रक्षणाय ।
अतनुषु विभवेषु ज्ञातयः सन्तु नाम
त्वयि तु परिसमाप्तं बन्धुकृत्यं प्रजानाम् ॥ ८ ॥

राजा—एते क्लान्तमनसः पुनर्नवीकृताः स्मः । (इति परिक्रामति ।)

PORTRESS. This way, your Majesty, this way.

KING. (*Moves about ; betraying the cares of office*). Every one is happy on attaining his desire ; but to kings, the attainment of their desire is only followed by pain.

The attainment of one's ambition destroys only all eager longing ; but the task of retaining what has been secured gives extreme pain. A kingdom, like an umbrella, of which a man carries the staff in his own hand, does not so much remove fatigue as it causes fatigue. (6)

(*Behind the Scenes*)

TWO BARDS. May the king be victorious !

FIRST.

Thou seekest not thy own happiness, but for the people thou dost toil from day to day. Or thus is thy very nature made. For the Tree bears on his head the fierce heat (of day) while his shade allays the fever of those who seek shelter under him. (7)

SECOND.

Wielding the rod of justice, thou bringest to order all those who have set out on bad courses ; thou biddest contention cease ; and thou preservest thy people. One may have, in truth, a number of kinsmen, when wealth abounds ; but in thee the duty of your subjects' kinsmen towards them finds perfection. (8)

KING. Now, wearied in mind that I was, I feel refreshed. (*Walks round.*)

प्रतीहारी—अहिणवसम्मज्जणससिरीओ सण्णिहिदहोमधेणू-अग्गिसरणालिन्दो । आरुहदु देवो । अभिनवसंमार्जनसश्रीकः संनिहित-होमधेनुरग्निशरणालिन्दः । आरोहतु देवः ।

राजा—(आरुह्य परिजनांसावलम्बी तिष्ठति ।) वेत्रवति, किमुद्दिश्य भगवता काश्यपेन मत्सकाशमृषयः प्रेषिताः स्युः ।

किं तावद्व्रतिनामुपोढतपसां विघ्नैस्तपो दूषितं
धर्मारण्यचरेषु केनचिदुत प्राणिष्वसच्चेष्टितम् ।
आहोस्वित्प्रसवो ममापचरितैर्विष्टम्भितो वीरुधा-
मित्यारूढबहुप्रतर्कमपरिच्छेदाकुलं मे मनः ॥ ९ ॥

प्रतीहारी—सुचरिदणन्दिणो इसीओ देवं सभाजइदुं आअदे त्ति तक्केमि । सुचरितनन्दिन ऋषयो देवं सभाजयितुमागता इति तर्कयामि ।

(ततः प्रविशन्ति गौतमीसहिताः शकुन्तलां पुरस्कृत्य मुनयः ।)

[पुरश्चैषां कञ्चुकी पुरोहितश्च ।]

कञ्चुकी—इत इतो भवन्तः ।

शार्ङ्गरवः—शारद्वत,

महाभागः कामं नरपतिरभिन्नस्थितिरसौ
न कश्चिद्वर्णानामपथमपकृष्टोऽपि भजते ।
तथापीदं शश्वत्परिचितविविक्तेन मनसा
जनाकीर्णं मन्ये हुतवहपरीतं गृहमिव ॥ १० ॥

PORTRESS. Here is the terrace of the fire sanctuary, which being newly-swept looks beautiful, and near it is the cow that yields the milk for sacrifice. Let the king ascend.

KING. (*Ascends and stands leaning on the shoulder of an attendant*). Vetravati, with what object has the revered Kāśyapa sent these sages to me?

May it be that the penance of those who have commenced a vow and stored up religious merit, has been defiled by obstacles? Or has any harm been inflicted by any one on the animals who graze in the hallowed forest? Or my sins have checked the flowering of the plants? Thus my mind which is assailed by many doubts, is perplexed on account of its inability to decide. (9)

PORTRESS. I imagine the pious men have come to pay homage to their king with whose pious rule they are pleased.

(*Then enter sages accompanied by Gautamī, leading Śakuntalā before them; and in front of them the chamberlain and the chaplain.*)

CHAMBERLAIN. This way, this way, sirs.

ŚĀRṄGARAVA. Śāradvata,

Granted that this glorious king does not swerve from rectitude; and that none of all the grades, not even the lowliest, seeks the path of wrong: nevertheless my mind having ever been accustomed to solitude, I consider this (place) thronged with men to be like a house all lapped about with flame. (10)

शारद्वतः—स्थाने भवान्पुरप्रवेशादित्थंभूतः संवृत्तः । अहमपि

अभ्यक्तमिव स्नातः शुचिरशुचिमिव प्रबुद्ध इव सुप्तम् ।
बद्धमिव स्वैरगतिर्जनमिह सुखसङ्गिनमवैमि ॥ ११ ॥

शकुन्तला—(निमित्तं सूचयित्वा ।) अम्महे, किं मे वामेदरं णअणं विप्फुरदि । अहो, किं मे वामेतरन्नयनं विस्फुरति ।

गौतमी—जादे पडिहदं अमङ्गलं । सुहाइं दे भत्तुकुलदेवदावो वितरन्दु । (इति परिक्रामति ।) जाते, प्रतिहतममङ्गलम् । सुखानि ते भर्तृकुलदेवता वितरन्तु ।

पुरोहितः—(राजानं निर्दिश्य ।) भो भोस्तपस्विनः असावत्रभवान्वर्णाश्रमाणां रक्षिता प्रागेव मुक्तासनो वः प्रतिपालयति । पश्यतैनम् ।

शार्ङ्गरवः—भो महाब्राह्मण, काममेतदभिनन्दनीयम् । तथापि वयमत्र मध्यस्थाः । कुतः ।

भवन्ति नम्रास्तरवः फलागमै-
र्नवाम्बुभिर्भूरिविलम्बिनो घनाः ।
अनुद्धताः सत्पुरुषाः समृद्धिभिः
स्वभाव एवैष परोपकारिणाम् ॥ १२ ॥

प्रतीहारी—देव, पसण्णमुहवण्णा दीसन्ति । जाणामि वीसद्धकज्जा इसीओ । देव, प्रसन्नमुखवर्णा दृश्यन्ते । जानामि विश्रब्धकार्या ऋषयः ।

राजा—(शकुन्तलां दृष्ट्वा ।) अथात्रभवती

Śāradvata. Rightly have you become thus on entering this city. I, too,

> Look on these people here devoted to worldly joys as a man (just) bathed on a man smeared with oil, as the pure on the impure, as the waking on the sleeping, or as the free man on the captive. (11)

Śakuntalā (*Indicating an omen*). Oh, why does my right eye throb ?

Gautamī. May the evil be averted, my sweet child ! May thy husband's household gods confer happiness upon thee !

(*She walks round.*)

Chaplain. (*Indicating the king*). There, holy men, is he the protector of the four orders and classes, who having already quitted the seat (of justice) is awaiting you. Behold him.

Śārṅgarava. O great Brahmin, this is surely commendable ; yet we do not think much of it ; for

> These become bent down by the abundance of their fruit ; clouds hang low when they teem with fresh rain ; good men are never elated by riches ; this is the very nature of the benefactors of others. (12)

Portress. O king, the holy men appear to have placid looks ; so I think they come on an errand about which they feel confident.

King. (*Beholding Śakuntalā*).

> Who is she, shrouded in the veil, the loveliness of whose person is not fully revealed,

काऽस्विदवगुण्ठनवती नातिपरिस्फुटशरीरलावण्या ।
मध्ये तपोधनानां किसलयमिव पाण्डुपत्राणाम् ॥ १३ ॥

प्रतीहारी—देव, कुदूहलगब्भोपहिदो ण मे तक्को पसरदि । णं दंसणीआ उण से आकिदी लक्खीअदि । देव, कुतूहलगर्भोपहितो न मे तर्कः प्रसरति । ननु दर्शनीया पुनरस्या आकृतिर्लक्ष्यते ।

राजा—भवतु । अनिर्वर्णनीयं परकलत्रम् ।

शकुन्तला—(हस्तमुरसि कृत्वा । आत्मगतम्) हिअअ, किं एव्वं वेवसि । अज्जउत्तस्स भावं ओधारिअ धीरं दाव होहि । हृदय, किमेवं वेपसे । आर्यपुत्रस्य भावमवधार्य धीरं तावद्भव ।

पुरोहितः—(पुरो गत्वा ।) एते विधिवदर्चितास्तपस्विनः । अस्ति कश्चिदेषामुपाध्यायसंदेशः । तं देवः श्रोतुमर्हति ।

राजा—अवहितोऽस्मि ।

ऋषयः—(हस्तानुद्यम्य) विजयस्व राजन् ।

राजा—सर्वानभिवादये ।

ऋषयः—इष्टेन युज्यस्व ।

राजा—अपि निर्विघ्नतपसो मुनयः ।

ऋषयः—

कुतो धर्मक्रियाविघ्नः सतां रक्षितरि त्वयि ।
तमस्तपति घर्मांशौ कथमाविर्भविष्यति ॥ १४ ॥

राजा—अर्थवान्खलु मे राजशब्दः । अथ भगवांल्लोकानुग्रहाय कुशली काश्यपः ।

ऋषयः—स्वाधीनकुशलाः सिद्धिमन्तः । स भवन्तमनामयप्रश्नपूर्वकमिदमाह ।

looking in the midst of hermits like a fresh bud among yellow leaves? (13)

PORTRESS. Your Majesty, my reason, though impelled by curiosity, does not work; but she appears to have a lovely figure.

KING. Enough! One ought not to gaze upon another's wife.

ŚAKUNTALĀ (*Laying her hand on her bosom; to herself*). My heart, why dost thou palpitate so? Call to mind the love of thy lord and be firm.

CHAPLAIN (*Going forward*). The holy men have been duly honoured. They have some message from their preceptor. Let the king deign to hear it.

KING. I am attentive.

SAGES (*Raising their hands*). Victory to you, O king.

KING. I salute you all.

SAGES. May you attain your desires!

KING. Has the devotion of the hermits been uninterrupted?

SAGES. How could the pious rites be disturbed when thou art the preserver of the good? How, when the bright Sun blazes, should darkness make its appearance? (14)

KING. My royal title, indeed, is not an empty one. Is the holy Kāśyapa now all well, to bless the world?

SAGES. They who possess miraculous powers can command welfare. He first asks after your health and then addresses you in these words—

राजा—किमाज्ञापयति भगवान् ।

शार्ङ्गरवः—यन्मिथः समयादिमां मदीयां दुहितरं भवानुपायंस्त तन्मया प्रीतिमता युवयोरनुज्ञातम् । कुतः ।

त्वमर्हतां प्राग्रसरः स्मृतोऽसि नः
शकुन्तला मूर्तिमती च सत्क्रिया ।
समानयंस्तुल्यगुणं वधूवरं
चिरस्य वाच्यं न गतः प्रजापतिः ॥ १५ ॥

तदिदानीमापन्नसत्त्वा प्रतिगृह्यतां सहधर्मचरणायेति ।

गौतमी—अज्ज, किंपि वत्तुकामम्हि । ण मे वअणावसरो अत्थि । कहंत्ति । आर्य, किमपि वक्तुकामास्मि । न मे वचनावसरोस्ति । कथमिति ।

णावेक्खिओ गुरुअणो इमीअ ण तुए वि पुच्छिदो बन्धू ।
एक्कक्कमेव्व चरिए भणामि किं एक्कमेक्कस्स ॥ १६ ॥

नापेक्षितो गुरुजनोऽनया न त्वयापि पृष्टो बन्धुः ।
एकैकमेव चरिते भणामि किमेकैकम् ।

शकुन्तला—(आत्मगतम् ।) किं णु क्खु अज्जउत्तो भणादि । किं नु खल्वार्यपुत्रो भणति ।

राजा—किमिदमुपन्यस्तम् ।

शकुन्तला—(आत्मगतम् ।) पावओ क्खु एसो वअणोवण्णासो । पावकः खल्वेष वचनोपन्यासः ।

शार्ङ्गरवः—कथमिदं नाम । भवन्त एव सुतरां लोकवृत्तान्तनिष्णाताः ।

सतीमपि ज्ञातिकुलैकसंश्रयां
जनोऽन्यथा भर्तृमतीं विशङ्कते ।

KING. What does the holy one command?

ŚĀRṄGARAVA. By reciprocal agreement hast thou married this daughter of mine which I have with pleasure approved. For

Thou art known, to us as the best of worthy men; while my Śakuntalā is virtue itself in human form; Brahman, who has now united a bride and bridegroom of equal merit, has after a long time incurred no censure. (15)

Therefore, now receive her, who is quick with child, that she may perform, in conjunction with thee, the duties prescribed by religion.

GAUTAMĪ. Noble sir, I wish to say something. And (yet) there is no occasion for my words. (If you ask) how so?

Her elderly relatives were not regarded by her, nor were kinsmen consulted by thee. The affair being transacted solely by mutual (consent), what may one say to either? (16)

ŚAKUNTALĀ (*To herself*). What will my lord say now?

KING. What is (all) this brought before me?

ŚAKUNTALĀ (*To herself*). Like fire indeed are these words he has uttered.

ŚĀRṄGARAVA. How, indeed, is this? You yourself know the world's ways well enough.

People suspect a married woman, living wholly in her kinsmen's family, although chaste, to be otherwise. Therefore, her kinsmen desire

अतः समीपे परिणेतुरिष्यते
तदप्रियापि प्रमदा स्वबन्धुभिः ॥ १७ ॥

राजा—किं चात्रभवती मया परिणीतपूर्वा ।

शाकुन्तला—(सविषादम् । आत्मगतम् ।) हिअअ, संपदं दे आसङ्का । हृदय, सांप्रतं त आशङ्का ।

शार्ङ्गरवः—

किं कृतकार्यद्वेषाद्धर्मं प्रति विमुखतोचिता राज्ञः ।

राजा—कुतोऽयमसत्कल्पनाप्रश्नः ।

शार्ङ्गरवः—

मूर्च्छन्त्यमी विकाराः प्रायेणैश्वर्यमत्तेषु ॥ १८ ॥

राजा—विशेषेणाधिक्षिप्तोऽस्मि ।

गौतमी—जादे, मुहुत्तअं मा लज्ज । अवणइस्सं दाव दे ओउण्ठणं । तदो तुमं भट्टा अहिजाणिस्सदि । (इति यथोक्तं करोति ।) जाते, मुहूर्तं मा लज्जस्व । अपनेष्यामि तावत्तेऽवगुण्ठनम् । ततस्त्वां भर्ताभिज्ञास्यति ।

राजा—(शकुन्तलां निर्वर्ण्य । आत्मगतम् ।)

इदमुपनतमेवं रूपमक्लिष्टकान्ति
प्रथमपरिगृहीतं स्यान्न वेत्यव्यवस्यन् ।
भ्रमर इव विभाते कुन्दमन्तस्तुषारं
न खलु च परिभोक्तुं नैव शक्नोमि हातुम् ॥ १९ ॥

(इति विचारयन् स्थितः ।)

प्रतीहारी—अहो धम्मावेक्खिदा भट्टिणो । इदिसं णाम सुहोवणदं रूवं देक्खिअ को अण्णो विआरेदि । अहो धर्मापेक्षिता भर्तुः । ईदृशं नाम सुखोपनतं रूपं दृष्ट्वा कोऽन्यो विचारयति ।

a young woman to be with her husband even though he love her not. (17)

KING. And, was this lady married to me before?

ŚAKUNTALĀ (*Sorrowfully; to herself*). O my heart, thy fears are justified!

ŚĀRṄGARAVA.

Does it become a king to depart from the rules of justice, merely because of his aversion to a deed done?

KING. What means this accusation based upon a false assumption?

ŚĀRṄGARAVA.

Such fickleness of disposition mostly takes effect in those whom power intoxicates. (18)

KING. I am reproved with too great severity.

GAUTAMĪ. Child, forget thy shame for a while. I will just remove the veil, so that thy husband will then recognize thee. (*Does as said.*)

KING. (*Observing Śakuntalā; to himself.*)

While I am doubtful whether this unblemished beauty which is thus brought near to me may or may not have been formerly married by me, verily I neither can enjoy nor forsake her like a bee at the close of night, the Kunda flower filled with dew. (19)

(*Keeps reflecting.*)

PORTRESS. How greatly is virtue honoured by our lord! Would any other man hesitate when he saw such beauty presenting herself with ease?

शार्ङ्गरवः—भो राजन्, किमिति जोषमास्यते ।

राजा—भोस्तपोधनाः, चिन्तयन्नपि न खलु स्वीकरणमत्रभवत्याः स्मरामि । तत्कथमिमामभिव्यक्तसत्त्वलक्षणां प्रत्यात्मानं क्षेत्रिणमाशङ्कमानः प्रतिपत्स्ये ।

शकुन्तला—(अपवार्य ।) अज्जस्स परिणए एव्व संदेहो । कुदो दाणिं मे दूराहिरोहिणी आसा । आर्यस्य परिणय एव संदेहः । कुत इदानीं मे दूराधिरोहिण्याशा ।

शार्ङ्गरवः—मा तावत्

कृताभिमर्शामनुमन्यमानः
सुतां त्वया नाम मुनिर्विमान्यः ।
मुष्टं प्रतिग्राहयता स्वमर्थं
पात्रीकृतो दस्युरिवासि येन ॥ २० ॥

शारद्वतः—शार्ङ्गरव, विरम त्वमिदानीम् । शकुन्तले, वक्तव्यमुक्तमस्माभिः । सोऽयमत्रभवानेवमाह । दीयतामस्मै प्रत्ययप्रतिवचनम् ।

शकुन्तला—(अपवार्य ।) इमं अवत्थन्तरं गदे तारिसे अणुराए किं वा सुमराविदेण । अत्ता दाणिं मे सोअणीओ त्ति ववसिदं एदं । (प्रकाशम् ।) अज्जउत्त, (इत्यर्धोक्ते ।) संसइदे दाणिं परिणए ण एसो समुदाआरो । पोरव, ण जुत्तं णाम दे तह पुरा अस्समपदे सहावुत्ताणहिअअं इमं जणं समअपुव्वं पतारिअ ईदिसेहिं अक्खरेहिं पच्चाचक्खिदुं । इदमवस्थान्तरं गते तादृशेऽनुरागे किं वा स्मारितेन । आत्मेदानीं मे शोचनीय इति व्यवसितमेतत् । आर्यपुत्र । संशयित इदानीं परिणये नैष समुदाचारः । पौरव, न युक्तं नाम ते तथा पुराश्रमपदे स्वभावोत्तानहृदयमिमं जनं समयपूर्वं प्रतार्येदृशैरक्षरैः प्रत्याख्यातुम् ।

राजा—(कर्णौ पिधाय ।) शान्तं पापम् ।

ŚĀRṄGARAVA. Why do you sit silent, O king?

KING. Ye holy men! I do not remember, much as I think of it, to have taken this lady in marriage. How then shall I receive her, bearing evident signs of pregnancy, when I have doubts about being her husband?

ŚAKUNTALĀ (*Aside*). My lord even casts doubt on our marriage. Where is now my high-soaring hope?

ŚĀRṄGARAVA. Do not indeed——

Would you insult the sage who approved his daughter who had been seduced by you; and who allowing his stolen property to be kept by you has deemed you worthy of the gift; as one would a robber by allowing him to retain one's stolen goods? (20)

ŚĀRADVATA. Rest you, now, my Śārṅgarava. Śakuntalā, we have now said what was for us to say. His Honour has spoken thus. Let a convincing reply be given him.

ŚAKUNTALĀ (*Aside*). When such (great) affection has suffered this change, of what use will it be to recall his remembrance (of me)? It is settled now that I should deplore my own self. (*Aloud*). My noble Lord!—(*When half said*)—This is not the proper form of address, now that the very marriage is called in question. O, Son of Puru, it is not becoming in you that having formerly in the hermitage beguiled in that way this person (myself) naturally open-hearted, after making an agreement, you should reject me with such words.

KING. (*Stopping his ears*). Be the sin removed from my soul!

व्यपदेशमाविलयितुं किमीहसे जनमिमं च पातयितुम् ।
कूलंकषेव सिन्धुः प्रसन्नमम्भस्तटतरुं च ॥ २१ ॥

शकुन्तला—होदु । जइ परमत्थदो परपरिग्गहसङ्किणा तुए एव्वं पउत्तं ता अहिण्णाणेण इमिणा तुह आसङ्कं अवणइस्सं। भवतु । यदि परमार्थतः परपरिग्रहशङ्किना त्वयैवं प्रवृत्तं तदभिज्ञानेनानेन तवाशङ्कामपनेष्यामि ।

राजा—उदारः कल्पः ।

शकुन्तला—(मुद्रास्थानं परामृश्य) हद्धी । अङ्गुलीअअसुण्णा मे अङ्गुली। (इति सविषादं गौतमीमवेक्षते ।) हा धिक् । अङ्गुलीयकशून्या मेऽङ्गुलिः ।

गौतमी—णूणं दे सक्कावदारब्भन्तरे सचीतित्थसलिलं वन्दमाणाए पब्भट्टं अङ्गुलीअअं । नूनं ते शक्रावताराभ्यन्तरे शचीतीर्थसलिलं वन्दमानायाः प्रभ्रष्टमङ्गुलीयकम् ।

राजा—(सस्मितम् ।) इदं तत्प्रत्युत्पन्नमति स्त्रैणमिति यदुच्यते ।

शकुन्तला—एत्थ दाव विहिणा दंसिदं पहुत्तणं । अवरं दे कहिस्सं। अत्र तावद्विधिना दर्शितं प्रभुत्वम् । अपरं ते कथयिष्यामि ।

राजा—श्रोतव्यमिदानीं संवृत्तम् ।

शकुन्तला—णं एक्कस्सिं दिअहे णोमालिआमण्डवे णलिणीपत्तभाअणगदं उदअं तुह हत्थे संणिहिदं आसि। नन्वेकस्मिन्दिवसे नवमालिकामण्डपे नलिनीपत्रभाजनगतमुदकं तव हस्ते संनिहितमासीत् ।

राजा—श्रृणुमस्तावत् ।

शकुन्तला—तक्खणं सो मे पुत्तकिदओ दीहापङ्गो णाम मिअपोदओ उवट्ठिओ । तुए अअं दाव पढमं पिअउ त्ति अणुअम्पिणा उवच्छन्दिदो उअएण। ण उण दे अपरिचआदो हत्थब्भासं उगवदो । पच्छा तस्सिं एव्व मए गहिदे सलिले णेण किदो पणओ। तदा तुमं इत्थं पहसिदो सि । सव्वो सगन्धेसु विस्ससदि। दुवेवि एत्थ आरण्णआ त्ति । तत्क्षणे स मे पुत्रकृतको दीर्घापाङ्गो नाम मृगपोतक उपस्थितः। त्वयायं तावत्प्रथमं पिबत्वित्यनुकम्पिनोपच्छन्दित उदकेन।

Why seek you to sully your family, and drag me down, as a stream, that eats away the bank, sullies its clear water and drags down the trees on its banks? (21)

ŚAKUNTALĀ. Well, if you act thus because you really think me to be another's wife, I will remove your doubts by this token of recognition.

KING. A capital suggestion.

ŚAKUNTALĀ (*Touching the place of the ring*). Alas! My finger is without the ring! (*She looks sadly at Gautamī.*)

GAUTAMĪ. The ring must have in all probability dropped (From thy finger) as thou worshippedst the Śacītīrtha at Śakrāvatāra.

KING (*Smiling*). This is an instance of the proverb "Women are ready-witted."

ŚAKUNTALĀ. Here now destiny has shown its power. I will tell you something else.

KING. Now it has come to something to be heard!

ŚAKUNTALĀ. One day, in the Navamālikā bower, you had in your hand water in a vase of lotus-leaves.

KING. Well, I am listening.

ŚAKUNTALĀ. At that moment the fawn Dīrghāpānga, my foster-child, came up. Then you took pity on him saying "Let him drink first", and coaxed him to drink; but as he did not know you, he would not come to drink water from your hand. But later, when I held the very same water, he liked it. Then you said in jest: "Every one trusts his own kindred. You are both foresters alike."

न पुनस्तेऽपरिचयाद्धस्ताभ्याशमुपगतः । पश्चात्तस्मिन्नेव मया गृहीते सलिलेऽनेन कृतः प्रणयः । तदा त्वमित्थं प्रहसितोऽसि । सर्वः सगन्धेषु विश्वसिति । द्वावप्यत्रारण्यकाविति ।

राजा—एवमादिभिरात्मकार्यनिर्वर्तिनीनामनृतमयवाङ्मधुभिराकृष्यन्ते विषयिणः ।

गौतमी—महाभाअ, ण अरुहसि एव्वं मन्तिदुं । तवोवणसंवड्ढिदो अणभिण्णो अअं जणो कइदवस्स । महाभाग, नार्हस्येवं मन्त्रयितुम् । तपोवनसंवर्धितोऽनभिज्ञोयं जनः कैतवस्य ।

राजा—तापसवृद्धे,

स्त्रीणामशिक्षितपटुत्वममानुषीषु
संदृश्यते किमुत याः प्रतिबोधवत्यः ।
प्रागन्तरिक्षगमनात्स्वमपत्यजात-
मन्यैर्द्विजैः परभृताः खलु पोषयन्ति ॥ २२ ॥

शकुन्तला—(सरोषम् ।) अणज्ज, अत्तणो हिअआणुमाणेण पेक्खसि । को दाणिं अण्णो धम्मकञ्चुअप्पवेसिणो तिणच्छण्णकूवोवमस्स तव अणुकिदिं पडिवदिस्सदि । अनार्य, आत्मनो हृदयानुमानेन पश्यसि । क इदानीमन्यो धर्मकञ्चुकप्रवेशिनस्तृणच्छन्नकूपोपमस्य तवानुकृतिं प्रतिपत्स्यते ।

राजा—(आत्मगतम् ।) संदिग्धबुद्धिं मां कुर्वन्नकैतव इवास्याः कोपो लक्ष्यते । तथा ह्यनया

मय्येव विस्मरणदारुणचित्तवृत्तौ
वृत्तं रहः प्रणयमप्रतिपद्यमाने ।
भेदाद्भ्रुवोः कुटिलयोरतिलोहिताक्ष्या
भग्नं शरासनमिवातिरुषा स्मरस्य ॥ २३ ॥

(प्रकाशम् ।) भद्रे, प्रथितं दुष्यन्तस्य चरितम् । तथापीदं न लक्षये ।

शकुन्तला—सुट्ठु दाव अत्त सच्छन्दचारिणी किदम्हि जा अहं इमस्स पुरुवंसप्पच्चएण मुहमहुणो हिअअट्ठिअविसस्स हत्थब्भासं

KING. By such honeyed falsehoods are voluptuaries ensnared by (women) who seek to compass their own ends.

GAUTAMĪ. Worthy sir, forbear to speak thus. She was bred in the sacred grove, and she does not know guile.

KING. Old hermit-woman,

> The female's untaught cunning may be observed even in those that are not of the human race; far more in those who are endowed with reason. The female cuckoos, it is well-known, allow their young ones to be reared by other birds, before they can soar in the sky. (22)

ŚAKUNTALĀ (*Angrily*). Wicked man, you measure (all this) by your own heart. What other man would act like you, who wearing the garb of virtue, resemble a grass-concealed well?

KING. (*To himself*). Throwing my mind in doubt, her anger seems to be unfeigned. For

> When I, whose mental attitude was harsh (towards her) from the absence of all recollection, would not admit our secret love, it seemed that she, whose eyes were flashing red, bending her curved eyebrows, fiercely snapped Love's bow. (23)

(*Aloud*). Good woman, Duṣyanta's conduct is well known; yet this is not found (in it).

ŚAKUNTALĀ. Well have I been made (to appear) a wanton woman, who trusting Puru's race put myself in the hands of one who had honey in his mouth, but

उवगदा । (इति पटान्तेन मुखमावृत्य रोदिति ।) सुष्ठु तावदत्र स्वच्छन्दचारिणी कृतास्मि याहमस्य पुरुवंशप्रत्ययेन मुखमधोर्हृदयस्थितविषस्य हस्ताभ्याशमुपगता ।

शार्ङ्गरवः—इत्थमामकृतत्मप्रतिहतं चापलं दहति ।

अतः परीक्ष्य कर्तव्यं विशेषात्संगतं रहः ।
अज्ञातहृदयेष्वेवं वैरीभवति सौहृदम् ॥ २४ ॥

राजा—अयि भोः, किमत्रभवतीप्रत्ययादेवास्मान्संभृतदोषैः क्षिणुथ ।

शार्ङ्गरवः—(सासूयम् ।) श्रुतं भवद्भिरधरोत्तरम् ।

आ जन्मनः शाठ्यमशिक्षितो य-
स्तस्याप्रमाणं वचनं जनस्य ।
परातिसंधानमधीयते यै-
र्विद्येति ते सन्तु किलाप्तवाचः ॥ २५ ॥

राजा—भोः सत्यवादिन्, अभ्युपगतं तावदस्माभिरेवम् । किं पुनरिमामतिसंधाय लभ्यते ।

शार्ङ्गरवः—विनिपातः ।

राजा—विनिपातः पौरवैः प्रार्थ्यत इति न श्रद्धेयम् ।

शारद्वतः—शार्ङ्गरव, किमुत्तरेण । अनुष्ठितो गुरोः संदेशः । प्रतिनिवर्तामहे वयम् । (राजानं प्रति ।)

तदेषा भवतः कान्ता त्यज वैनां गृहाण वा ।
उपपन्ना हि दारेषु प्रभुता सर्वतोमुखी ॥ २६ ॥

गौतमि, गच्छाग्रतः ।

(इति प्रस्थिताः ।)

poison in his heart! (*She covers her face with the end of her garment and weeps.*)

ŚĀRṄGARAVA. Thus does one's own levity, if not bridled, breed poignant remorse.

Therefore, a union, especially, a secret one, ought to be formed with great circumspection; with those who know not each other's heart, love thus turns to hate. (24)

KING. O sir, would you rely on her, and reproach me with accumulated faults?

ŚĀRṄGARAVA (*Scornfully*). Have you heard (such a) perversion!

The words of one who from birth has never learnt deceit are to receive no credit; while they, forsooth, who make the deception of others their study, calling it a science, are to be considered as worthy of trust! (25)

KING. Now, truth-teller, we admit it for a moment; but what would be gained by deceiving her?

ŚĀRṄGARAVA. Damnation!

KING. It is unthinkable that damnation would be sought by Puru's line.

ŚĀRADVATA. Śārṅgarava, what avails you answer? We have executed the commands of our preceptor, and we now return. (*To the king*).

Here then is your wife, (whether you) desert her or acknowledge her. For the authority over wives is admitted to be absolute. (26). Gautamī, lead the way.

(*They start.*)

शकुन्तला—कहं इमिणा किदवेण विप्पलद्ध म्हि । तुम्हे वि मं परिच्चअध । (इत्यनुप्रतिष्ठते ।) कथमनेन कितवेन विप्रलब्धास्मि । यूयमपि मां परित्यजथ ।

गौतमी—(स्थित्वा) वच्छ सङ्गरव, अनुगच्छदि इअं क्खु णो करुणपरिदेविणी सउन्दला । पच्चादेसपरुसे भत्तरि किं वा मे पुत्तिआ करेदु । वत्स शार्ङ्गरव, अनुगच्छतीयं खलु नः करुणपरिदेविनी शकुन्तला । प्रत्यादेशपरुषे भर्तरि किं वा मे पुत्रिका करोतु ।

शार्ङ्गरवः—(सरोषं निवृत्य ।) किं पुरोभागिनि, स्वातंत्र्यमवलम्बसे ।

(शकुन्तला भीता वेपते ।)

शार्ङ्गरवः—शकुन्तले,

यदि यथा वदति क्षितिपस्तथा
त्वमसि किं पितुरुत्कुलया त्वया ।
अथ तु वेत्सि शुचि व्रतमात्मनः
पतिकुले तव दास्यमपि क्षमम् ॥ २७ ॥

तिष्ठ । साधयामो वयम् ।

राजा—भोस्तपस्विन् , किमत्रभवतीं विप्रलभसे । कुतः

कुमुदान्येव शशाङ्कः सविता बोधयति पङ्कजान्येव ।
वशिनां हि परपरिग्रहसंश्लेषपराङ्मुखी वृत्तिः ॥ २८ ॥

शार्ङ्गरवः—यदा तु पूर्ववृत्तमन्यसङ्गाद्विस्मृतो भवांस्तदा कथमधर्मभीरुः ।

राजा—भवन्तमेवात्र गुरुलाघवं पृच्छामि ।

ŚAKUNTALĀ. How have I been deceived by the perfidious man! But will you, too, leave me?

(*She starts to follow.*)

GAUTAMĪ (*Stopping*). Śārṅgarava, my son, Śakuntalā is indeed, following us, lamenting piteously; or what can my poor child do, when her husband is so ruthless in rejecting her?

ŚĀRṄGARAVA (*Turning back in anger*). Well, wanton girl, would you affect independence?

(*Śakuntalā trembles in fear.*)

ŚĀRṄGARAVA. Śakuntalā,

If you are what the king makes you out to be, what has father to do with you—a disgrace to your family? But if you know your (marriage) vow to be pure, it will become you to wait even as a handmaid in the mansion of your lord. (27)

STAY. We must return.

KING. O hermit, why deceive the lady? For

The Moon opens the night-lotuses only and the Sun the day-lotuses. The feelings of those who are self-controlled ever recoil from any connection with the wife of another. (28)

ŚĀRṄGARAVA. But when you have forgotten a former engagement on account of union with another (wife) how are you (to be regarded as) one who fears to offend virtue?

KING. I would ask your reverence which is the greater and which the lesser evil:

मूढः स्यामहमेषा वा वदेन्मिथ्येति संशये
दारत्यागी भवाम्याहो परस्त्रीस्पर्शपांसुलः ॥ २९ ॥

पुरोहितः—(विचार्य) यदि तावदेवं क्रियताम् ।

राजा—अनुशास्तु मां भवान् ।

पुरोहितः—अत्रभवती तावदाप्रसवादस्मद्गृहे तिष्ठतु । कुत इदमुच्यत इति चेत् । त्वं साधुभिरुद्दिष्टः प्रथममेव चक्रवर्तिनं पुत्रं जनयिष्यसीति । स चेन्मुनिदौहित्रस्तल्लक्षणोपपन्नो भविष्यति, अभिनन्द्य शुद्धान्तमेनां प्रवेशयिष्यसि । विपर्यये तु पितुरस्याः समीपनयनमवस्थितमेव ।

राजा—यथा गुरुभ्यो रोचते ।

पुरोहितः—वत्से, अनुगच्छ माम् ।

शकुन्तला—भअवदि वसुहे, देहि मे विवरं । भगवति वसुधे, देहि मे विवरम् । (इति रुदती प्रस्थिता । निष्क्रान्ता सह पुरोधसा, तपस्विभिश्च)

(राजा शापव्यवहितस्मृतिः शकुन्तलागतमेव चिन्तयति ।)

(नेपथ्ये ।)

आश्चर्यम् ।

राजा—(आकर्ण्य) किं नु खलु स्यात् ।

(प्रविश्य ।)

पुरोहितः—(सविस्मयम् ।) देव, अद्भुत खलु संवृत्तम् ।

राजा—किमिव ।

In a doubt as to whether I be infatuated or she speak falsely, shall I forsake my own wife, or defile myself by having intercourse with the wife of another? (29)

CHAPLAIN (*Deliberating*). Well, then, if this were done—

KING. Let the venerable one instruct me.

CHAPLAIN. Let the lady dwell till her delivery in my house. If you ask why I say this, (my answer is) you have been told by the sages that at the very first you will beget a son who will bear the mark of a discus (on his hand). If then the son of the hermit's daughter bears that mark, then greet her and introduce her to the female apartments. But if the reverse happens, it is evident enough that she must be taken to her father.

KING. As it pleases my worthy teacher.

CHAPLAIN. Daughter, follow me.

ŚAKUNTALĀ. Divine Earth, open (to receive me).

(*She is in tears as she starts; exit with the Chaplain and the hermits; the king, whose memory is still clouded by the curse, ponders on something regarding Śakuntalā herself*).

(*Behind the Scenes*).

A miracle!

KING. (*Listening*). What could it be?

(*Entering*) Chaplain (*in amazement*). Your Majesty, a wonderful thing has happened!

KING. What is it?

पुरोहितः—देव, परावृत्तेषु कण्वशिष्येषु

सा निन्दन्ती स्वानि भाग्यानि बाला
बाहूत्क्षेपं क्रन्दितुं च प्रवृत्ता ।

राजा—किं च ।

पुरोहितः—

स्त्रीसंस्थानं चाप्सरस्तीर्थमारा-
दुक्षिप्यैनां ज्योतिरेकं जगाम ॥ ३० ॥

(सर्वे विस्मयं रूपयन्ति ।)

राजा—भगवन् प्रागपि सोऽस्माभिरर्थः प्रत्यादिष्ट एव । किं वृथा तर्केणान्विष्यते । विश्राम्यतु भवान् ।

पुरोहितः—(विलोक्य ।) विजयस्व । (इति निष्क्रान्तः ।)

राजा—वेत्रवति, पर्याकुलोऽस्मि । शयनभूमिमार्गमादेशय ।

प्रतीहारी—इदो इदो देवो । (इति प्रस्थितः ।) इत इतो देवः ।

राजा—

कामं प्रत्यादिष्टां स्मरामि न परिग्रहं मुनेस्तनयाम् ।
बलवत्तु दूयमानं प्रत्याययतीव मां हृदयम् ॥ ३१ ॥

(इति निष्क्रान्ताः सर्वे ।)

पञ्चमोऽङ्कः ।

CHAPLAIN. Your Majesty, when Kaṇva's pupils had departed,

The young girl, blaming her fortunes, threw up her arms and started weeping—

KING. What then?

CHAPLAIN.

When a body of light, in a female shape, snatched her up from afar, and went to Apsaras-tīrtha. (30)

(*All betray astonishment.*)

KING. Revered sir, we have already dismissed that object from us. What need to reason more on it? Please rest you, sir.

CHAPLAIN (*Observing*). Victory to your Majesty! (*Goes out.*)

KING. Vetravati, I am troubled. Lead the way to the bed-chamber.

PORTRESS. This way, your Majesty, this way.

(*Starts.*)

KING.

True I do not recollect this daughter of the sage (now) repudiated to be my wife; nevertheless my heart being powerfully agitated almost persuades me to believe (her story). (31)

(*Exeunt Omnes.*)

End of Act V

षष्ठोऽङ्कः ।

(ततः प्रविशति नागरिकः श्यालः पश्चाद्बद्धपुरुषमादाय रक्षिणौ च ।)

रक्षिणौ—(ताडयित्वा ।) **अले कुम्भिलआ, कहेहि कहिं तुए एशे मणिबन्धणुक्किण्णणामहेए लाअकीए अङ्गुलीअए शमाशादिए ।** अरे कुम्भिलक, कथय कुत्र त्वयैतन्मणिबन्धनोत्कीर्णनामधेयं राजकीयमङ्गुलीयकं समासादितम् ।

पुरुषः—(भीतिनाटितकेन ।) **पशीदन्तु भावमिश्शे । हगे ण ईदिशकम्मकाली ।** प्रसीदन्तु भावमिश्राः । अहं नेदृशकर्मकारी ।

प्रथमः—**किं खु शोहणे बम्हणेत्ति कलिअ लण्णा पडिग्गहे दिण्णे ।** किं खलु शोभनो ब्राह्मण इति कृत्वा राज्ञा प्रतिग्रहो दत्तः ।

पुरुषः—**शुणध दाणिं । हगे शक्कावदालब्भन्तलवाशी धीवले ।** शृणुतेदानीम् । अहं शक्रावताराभ्यन्तरवासी धीवरः ।

द्वितीयः—**पाडच्चला, किं अम्हेहिं जादी पुच्छिदा ।** पाटच्चर, किमस्माभिर्जातिः पृष्टा ।

श्यालः—**सूअअ, कहेदु सव्वं अणुक्कमेण । मा णं अन्तरा पडिबन्धह ।** सूचक, कथयतु सर्वमनुक्रमेण । मैनमन्तरे प्रतिबन्धय ।

उभौ—**जं आवुत्ते आणवेदि । कहेहि ।** यदावुत्त आज्ञापयति । कथय ।

पुरुषः—**अहके जालुग्गालादीहिं मच्छबन्धणोवाएहिं कुडुम्बभलणं कलेमि ।** अहं जालोद्गालादिभिर्मत्स्यबन्धनोपायैः कुटुम्बभरणं करोमि ।

श्यालः—(विहस्य ।) **विसुद्धो दाणि आजीवो ।** विशुद्ध इदानीमाजीवः ।

पुरुषः—

शहजे किल जे विणिन्दिए ण हु दे कम्म विवज्जणीअए ।
पशुमालणकम्मदालुणे अणुकम्पामिदु एव्व शोत्तिए ॥ १ ॥

ACT VI

(*Enter the King's brother-in-law (as) the chief of the city-police with two policemen leading a man with his hands bound behind his back.*)

THE TWO POLICEMEN (*Striking*). Now, thief, tell us where you found this royal ring the setting of which is engraven with his name.

THE MAN (*With a gesticulation of fear*). Be pleased, your honours. I would never do such an act.

FIRST. Was it, then, a present given by the king, thinking you were an illustrious Brahmin?

THE MAN. Hear me, now. I am a fisherman dwelling at Śakrāvatāra.

SECOND. Thief, we did not ask about your caste.

ŚYĀLA. Let him tell the story in order, Sūcaka. Do not interrupt him in the middle.

BOTH. As the brother-in-law commands. Speak.

MAN. I support my family with things you catch fish with—nets and hooks and such like.

ŚYĀLA (*Smiling*). A virtuous way of gaining a livelihood!

MASTER. Do not say that, master.

The occupation in which one was born, as
they say, how low soever, must not be forsaken.
The same learned Brahmin who is cruel in the
act of killing animals (for the sacrifice), is
yet soft with pity. (1)

सहजं किल यद्विनिन्दितं न खलु तत्कर्म विवर्जनीयम् ।
पशुमारणकर्मदारुणोऽनुकम्पामृदुरेव श्रोत्रियः ॥

श्यालः—तदो तदो । ततस्ततः ।

पुरुषः—एक्कश्शिं दिअशे खण्डशो लोहिअमच्छे मए कप्पिदे जाव तश्श उदलब्भन्तले एदं लदणभाशुलं अङ्गुलीअअं देक्खिजं । पच्छा अहके शे विक्कआअ दंशअन्ते गहिदे भावमिश्शेहिं । मालेह वा मुञ्चेह वा । अअं शे आअमवुत्तन्ते । एकस्मिन्दिवसे खण्डशो रोहितमत्स्यो मया कल्पितो यावत् तस्योदराभ्यन्तर इदं रत्नभासुरमङ्गुलीयं दृष्टम् । पश्चादहं तस्य विक्रयाय दर्शयन्गृहीतो भावमिश्रैः । मारयत वा मुञ्चत वा । अयमस्यागमवृत्तान्तः ।

श्यालः—जाणुअ, विस्सगन्धी गोहादी मच्छबन्धो एव्व णिस्संसअं । अङ्गुलीअअदंसणं से विमरिसिदव्वं । राउलं एव्व गच्छामो । जानुक, विस्रगन्धी गोधादी मत्स्यबन्ध एव निःसंशयम् । अङ्गुलीयकदर्शनमस्य विमर्शयितव्यम् । राजकुलमेव गच्छामः ।

रक्षिणौ—तह । गच्छ अले गण्ठिभेदअ । तथा । गच्छ अरे ग्रन्थिभेदक ।

(सर्वे परिक्रामन्ति ।)

श्यालः—सूअअ, इमं पुरदुआरे अप्पमत्ता पडिवालह । जाव इमं अङ्गुलीअअं जहागमणं भट्टिणो णिवेदिअ तदो सासणं पडिच्छिअ णिक्कमामि । सूचक, इमं पुरद्वारेऽप्रमत्तौ प्रतिपालयतम् । यावदिदमङ्गुलीयकं यथागमनं भर्तुर्निवेद्य ततः शासनं प्रतीक्ष्य निष्क्रमामि ।

उभौ—पविशदु आवुत्ते शामिपशादश्श । प्रविशत्वावुत्तः स्वामिप्रसादाय ।

(इति निष्क्रान्तः श्यालः ।)

प्रथमः—जाणुअ, चिलाअदि क्खु आवुत्ते । जानुक, चिरायते खल्वावुत्तः ।

द्वितीयः—णं अवशलोवशप्पणीआ लाआणो । नन्ववसरोपसर्पणीया राजानः ।

प्रथमः—जाणुअ, फुलन्ति मे हत्था इमश्श वज्झश्श शुमणो पिणद्धुं । (इति पुरुषं निर्दिशति ।) जानुक, स्फुरतो मम हस्तावस्य वध्यस्य सुमनसः पिनद्धुम् ।

ŚYĀLA. Go on, go on.

MAN. Well, one day I was cutting open a carp when in its maw I saw this ring, flashing with its gem. When later I offered it for sale, I was apprehended by your honours. Now kill me or leave me alone. (But) that is the way I got it.

ŚYĀLA. O Jānuka, he is doubtless a fisherman, stinking as he does of raw flesh—this eater of alligators. But the finding of the ring by him requires to be considered. Let us proceed to the palace itself.

THE TWO POLICEMEN. Just so; move on, you cutpurse.

(*All walk round.*)

ŚYĀLA. Sūcaka guard him carefully at the city-gate, while I tell the king how this ring was found, and receiving his commands, come out.

BOTH. Let the master enter to receive the king's favour.

(*Exit Śyāla.*)

FIRST. Jānuka, the chief is indeed taking too long a time.

SECOND. Well, kings can only be approached at their leisure.

FIRST. Jānuka, how my hands tingle to fasten flowers about the head of this victim! (*He points to the man.*)

पुरुषः—ण अलुहदि भावे अकालणमालणे भविदुं । नार्हति भावोऽकारणमारणो भवितुम् ।

द्वितीयः—(विलोक्य ।) **एशे अम्हाणं शामी पत्तहत्थे लाअशाशणं पडिच्छिअ इदोमुहे देक्खीअदि । गिद्धबली भविश्शशि । शुणो मुहं वा देक्खिश्शशि ।** एष नौ स्वामी पत्रहस्तो राजशासनं प्रतीक्ष्येतोमुखो दृश्यते । गृध्रबलिर्भविष्यसि, शुनो मुखं वा द्रक्ष्यसि ।

(प्रविश्य ।)

श्यालः—सूअअ, मुञ्चेदु एसो जालोअजीवी । उववण्णो क्खु अङ्गुलीअस्स आअमो । सूचक, मुच्यतामेष जालोपजीवी । उपपन्नः खल्वङ्गुलीयस्यागमः ।

सूचकः—जह आवुत्ते भणादि । यथावुत्तो भणति ।

द्वितीयः—एशे जमशदणं पविशिअ पडिणिवुत्ते । (इति पुरुषं परिमुक्तबन्धनं करोति ।) एष यमसदनं प्रविश्य प्रतिनिवृत्तः ।

पुरुषः—(श्यालं प्रणम्य ।) **भट्टा, अह कीलिशे मे आजीवे ।** भर्तः, अथ कीदृशो मे आजीवः ।

श्यालः—एसो भट्टिणा अङ्गुलीअअमुल्लसम्मिदो पसादो वि दाविदो । (इति पुरुषायार्थं प्रयच्छति ।) एष भर्त्राङ्गुलीयकमूल्यसमितः प्रसादोऽपि दापितः ।

पुरुषः—(सप्रणामं प्रतिगृह्य ।) **भट्टा, अणुग्गहीदम्हि ।** भर्तः, अनुगृहीतोऽस्मि ।

सूचकः—एशे णाम अणुग्गहिदे जे शूलादो अवदालिअ हत्थिक्खन्धे पडिट्ठाविदे । एष नामानुगृहीतो यच्छूलादवतार्य हस्तिस्कन्धे प्रतिष्ठापितः ।

जानुकः—आवुत्त, पालिदोशिअं कहेदि तेण अङ्गुलीअएण भट्टिणो शम्मदेण होदव्वं । आवुत्त, पारितोषिकं कथयति तेनाङ्गुलीयकेन भर्तुः संमतेन भवितव्यम् ।

MAN. You would not kill a man without reason, master.

SECOND (*Observing*). There is our chief, letter in hand, who is coming towards us after receiving the king's command. You will either be food for vultures or will see the face of a dog.

(*Entering*) ŚYĀLA. Sūcaka, let the fisherman be discharged. This finding of the ring is indeed explained.

SŪCAKA. As the chief says.

SECOND. Here he returns, after having entered the abode of the God of death.

(*Unbinds the prisoner.*)

MAN (*Bowing to Śyāla*). Master, how do you think is my profession ?

ŚYĀLA. And the king has further given him a sum of money equal to the full value of the ring. (*Offers the man money.*)

MAN (*Accepting with a bow*). I am favoured by my master.

SŪCAKA. He has, indeed, been favoured, who after being taken down from the stake, has been set on the withers of an elephant.

JĀNUKA. My chief, the reward shows that the ring must be highly prized by the king.

श्यालः—ण तस्सिं महारुहं रदणं भट्टिणो बहुमदं त्ति तक्केमि। तस्स दंसणेण भट्टिणो अभिमदो जणो सुमराविदो। मुहुत्तअं पकिदिगम्भीरो वि पज्जुसुअणअणो आसि। न तस्मिन्महार्हं रत्नं भर्तुर्बहुमतमिति तर्कयामि। तस्य दर्शनेन भर्तुरभिमतो जनः स्मारितः। मुहूर्तं प्रकृतिगम्भीरोऽपि पर्युत्सुकनयन आसीत्।

सूचकः—शेविदं णाम आवुत्तेण। सेवितं नामावुत्तेन।

जानुकः—णं भणाहि। इमश्श कए मच्छिआभत्तुणो त्ति। (इति पुरुषमसूयया पश्यति।) ननु भण। अस्य कृते मात्स्यिकभर्तुरिति।

पुरुषः—भट्टालके, इदो अद्धं तुम्हाणं शुमणोमुल्लं होदु। भट्टारक, इतोऽर्धं युष्माकं सुमनोमूल्यं भवतु।

जानुकः—एत्तके जुज्जई। एतावद्युज्यते।

श्यालः—धीवर, महत्तरो तुमं पिअवअस्सओ दाणिं मे संवुत्तो। कादम्बरीसक्खिअं अम्हाणं पढमसोहिदं इच्छीअदि। ता सोण्डिआपणं एव्व गच्छामो। धीवर, महत्तरस्त्वं प्रियवयस्यक इदानीं मे संवृत्तः। कादम्बरीसाक्षिकमस्माकं प्रथमसौहृदमिष्यते। तच्छौण्डिकापणमेव गच्छामः। (इति निष्क्रान्ताः सर्वे।)

प्रवेशकः।

(ततः प्रविशत्याकाशयानेन सानुमती नामाप्सराः।)

सानुमती—णिव्वत्तिदं मए पज्जाअणिव्वत्तणिज्जं अच्छरातित्थसण्णिज्झं जाव साहुजणस्स अभिसेअकालो त्ति। संपदं इमस्स राएसिणो उदन्तं पच्चक्खीकरिस्सं। णं मेणआसंबन्धेण सरीरभूदा मे सउन्दला। ताए अ दुहिदुणिमित्तं आदिट्ठपुव्वम्हि। (समन्तादवलोक्य।) **किं णु क्खु उदुच्छवे वि णिरुच्छवारम्भं विअ राअउलं दीसइ। अत्थि मे विहवो पणिधाणेण सव्वं परिण्णादुं। किंदु सहीए आदरो मए माणइदव्वो। होदु। इमाणं एव्व उज्जाणपालिआणं तिरक्खरिणीपडिच्छण्णा पस्सवत्तिणी**

ŚYĀLA. I do not think that the costly gem in it was prized by the king; but, at its sight, the king remembered somebody he loves; and although naturally firm, he became for a moment agitated in mind.

SŪCAKA. Our master has given (the king) extreme pleasure.

JĀNUKA. Rather say, for the sake of this chief of fishermen. (*Eyes the man enviously*).

MAN. Let half of this be the price of your flower, master.

JĀNUKA. That is right.

ŚYĀLA. Fisherman, now you are the biggest and the best friend I have got. It is desirable that we pledge our first friendship over (some) wine. So let us get along to a wine-shop.

(*They all go out.*)

End of the introductory scene.

(*Then enter in an aerial car a nymph named Sānumatī.*)

SĀNUMATĪ. Attendance at Apsaras-tīrtha which is to be performed by turns, during the time the pious people have their ablutions, has been performed by me. I will now see with my own eyes what the good king is doing. Śakuntalā has, indeed, now become a part of myself, through my relation with Menakā. And she has already sent me on this commission on her daughter's account. (*Looking about*). How even at the festival of the season, no preparations for a celebration

भविअ उवलहिस्सं। (इति नाट्येनावतीर्य स्थिता ।) निर्वर्तितं मया पर्यायनिर्वर्तनीयमप्सरस्तीर्थसांनिध्यं यावत्साधुजनस्याभिषेककाल इति । सांप्रतमस्य राजर्षेरुदन्तं प्रत्यक्षीकरिष्यामि । ननु मेनकासंबन्धेन शरीरभूता मे शकुन्तला । तथा च दुहितृनिमित्तमादिष्टपूर्वास्मि । किं नु खलु ऋतूत्सवेऽपि निरुत्सवारम्भमिव राजकुलं दृश्यते । अस्ति मे विभवः प्रणिधानेन सर्वं परिज्ञातुम् । किं तु सख्या आदरो मया मानयितव्यः । भवतु । अनयोरेवोद्यानपालिकयोस्तिरस्करिणीप्रतिच्छन्ना पार्श्ववर्तिनी भूत्वोपलप्स्ये ।

(ततः प्रविशति चूताङ्कुरमवलोयन्ती चेटी । अपरा च पृष्ठतस्तस्याः ।)

प्रथमा—

आतम्महरिअपण्डुर वसन्तमासस्स जीअसव्वस्स ।
दिट्ठो सि चूदकोरअ उदुमङ्गल तुमं पसाएमि ॥ २ ॥

आताम्रहरितपाण्डुर वसन्तमासस्य जीवसर्वस्व ।
दृष्टोऽसि चूतकोरक ऋतुमङ्गल त्वां प्रसादयामि ॥

द्वितीया—परहुदिए, किं एआइणी मन्तेसि । परभृतिके, किमेकाकिनी मन्त्रयसे ।

प्रथमा—महुअरिए, चूदकलिअं देक्खिअ उम्मत्तिआ परहुदिआ होदि । मधुकरिके, चूतकलिकां दृष्ट्वोन्मत्ता परभृतिका भवति ।

द्वितीया—(सहर्षं त्वरयोपगम्य ।) **कहं उवट्ठिदो महुमासो ।** कथमुपस्थितो मधुमासः ।

प्रथमा—महुअरिए, तव दाणिं कालो एसो मदविब्भमगीदाण । मधुकरिके, तवेदानीं काल एष मदविभ्रमगीतानाम् ।

द्वितीया—सहि, अवलम्ब मं । जाव अग्गपादट्ठिआ भविअ चूदकलिअं गेण्हिअ कामदेवच्चणं करेमि । सखी, अवलम्बस्व मां यावदग्रपादस्थिता भूत्वा चूतकलिकां गृहीत्वा कामदेवार्चनं करोमि ।

प्रथमा—जइ मम वि क्खु अद्धं अच्चणफलस्स । यदि ममापि खल्वर्धमर्चनफलस्य ।

are to be seen at the palace? I might learn everything by exerting my supernatural power. But respect must be shown to (the desire of) my friend. I will make myself invisible through my supernatural powers and standing near these girls who take care of the garden, will find out.

(*She acts descending, and stops*).

(*Then enter a maid gazing at the mango-blossom, and another behind her.*)

FIRST.

O mango-blossom, a little pink and green and pale, the very essence of the life of spring, thou art seen by me, and I beg thee to favour (me), thou blesssing of the season. (2)

SECOND. Parabhṛtikā, what are you talking about to yourself?

FIRST. Madhukarikā, when a female kokil sees the mango-blossom, she goes crazy with delight.

SECOND (*Hastily advancing; with joy*). What, is the spring really come?

FIRST. Madhukarikā, this is the time for your wild and graceful songs.

SECOND. Hold me, dear, while I stand tip-toe and take the mango-blossom to worship God Kāma.

FIRST. If mine would be half the reward of the worship.

द्वितीया—अकहिदे वि एदं संपज्जइ जदो एक्कं एव्व णो जीविदं दुधा ट्ठिदं सरीरं । (सखीमवलम्ब्य स्थिता चूताङ्कुरं गृह्णाति ।) अए, अप्पडिबुद्धो वि चूदप्पसवो एत्थ बन्धणभङ्गसुरभी होदि । अकथितेऽप्येतत्संपद्यते यत एकमेव नौ जीवितं द्विधा स्थितं शरीरम् । अये, अप्रतिबुद्धोऽपि चूतप्रसवोऽत्र बन्धनभङ्गसुरभिर्भवति ।

(कपोतहस्तकं कृत्वा ।)

तुं सि मए चूदङ्कुर दिण्णो कामस्स गहिदधणुअस्स ।
पहिअजणजुवइलक्खो पञ्चब्भहिओ सरो होहि ॥ ३ ॥

त्वमसि मया चूताङ्कुर दत्तः कामाय गृहीतधनुषे ।
पथिकजनयुवतिलक्ष्यः पञ्चाभ्यधिकः शरो भव ॥

(इति चूताङ्कुरं क्षिपति ।)

(प्रविश्यापटीक्षेपेण कुपितः)

कञ्चुकी—मा तावत् । अनात्मज्ञे, देवेन प्रतिषिद्धे वसन्तोत्सवे त्वमाम्रकलिकाभङ्गं किमारभसे ।

उभे—(भीते) पसीददु अज्जो । अग्गहीदत्थाओ अम्हे । प्रसीदत्वार्यः । अगृहीतार्थे आवाम् ।

कञ्चुकी—न किल श्रुतं युवाभ्यां यद्वासन्तिकैस्तरुभिरपि देवस्य शासनं प्रमाणीकृतं तदाश्रयिभिः पत्रिभिश्च । तथाहि

चूतानां चिरनिर्गतापि कलिका बध्नाति न स्वं रजः
संनद्धं यदपि स्थितं कुरबकं तत्कोरकावस्थया ।
कण्ठेषु स्खलितं गतेऽपि शिशिरे पुंस्कोकिलानां रुतं
शङ्के संहरति स्मरोऽपि चकितस्तूणार्धकृष्टं शरम् ॥ ४ ॥

उभे—णत्थि संदेहो । महाप्पहावो राएसी । नास्ति संदेहः । महाप्रभावो राजर्षिः ।

SECOND. That goes without saying, dear; for our life is but one, though our bodies stand apart. (*Stands leaning on her friend and takes the mango-blossom*). Ah, the mango-blossom though not opened, is yet fragrant as its stalk is cut. (*Joining her hands together*).

> O mango-sprout, thou art offered by me to God Kāma, who has taken up his bow. Be an arrow more splendid than (his) five, having for thy marks the girls whose lovers are journeying. (3)

(*She throws down the mango-sprout.*)

(*Entering with a hurried toss of the curtain; angrily*)

CHAMBERLAIN. Don't, thoughtless girl; the king having forbidden the spring-festival, how have you started breaking off mango-buds?

BOTH (*frightened*). Please, sir, we did not know about it.

CHAMBERLAIN. You knew it not! When the king's command is obeyed even by the vernal trees, and the birds that dwell in them! Thus

> The mango-buds, which have long appeared do not yet form their own pollen; the Kurabaka (flower) also though all-ready to bloom, remains in the state of a bud; the voice of the male-cuckoos, though the cold season is gone, falters in the throat; while I suspect even Smara, being awed, replaces the shaft half-drawn from his quiver. (4)

BOTH. There is no doubt of it. The pious king possesses great power.

प्रथमा—अज्ज कदि दिअहाइं अम्हाणं मित्तावसुणा रट्ठिएण भट्टिणो पाअमूलं पेसिदाणं। इत्थं अ णो पमदवणस्स पालणकम्म समप्पिदं । ता आअन्तुअदाए अस्सुदपुव्वो अम्हेहिं एसो वुत्तन्तो । आर्य, कति दिवसान्यावयोर्मित्रावसुना राष्ट्रीयेण भर्तुः पादमूलं प्रेषितयोः । इत्थं च नौ प्रमदवनस्य पालनकर्म समर्पितम् । तदागन्तुकतया-श्रुतपूर्व आवाभ्यामेष वृत्तान्तः ।

कञ्चुकी—भवतु। न पुनरेवं प्रवर्तितव्यम्।

उभे—अज्ज, कोदूहलं णो। जदि इमिणा जणेण सोदव्वं कहेदु भवं किंणिमित्तं भट्टिणा वसन्तुस्सवो पडिसिद्धो । आर्य, कौतूहलं नौ । यद्यनेन जनेन श्रोतव्यं कथयतु भवान् किंनिमित्तं भर्त्रा वसन्तोत्सवः प्रतिषिद्धः ।

सानुमती—उस्सवप्पिआ क्खु मणुस्सा । गुरुणा कारणेण होदव्वं । उत्सवप्रियाः खलु मनुष्याः । गुरुणा कारणेन भवितव्यम् ।

कञ्चुकी—बहुलीभूतमेतत्किं न कथ्यते । किमत्रभवत्योः कर्ण-पथं नायातं शकुन्तलाप्रत्यादेशकौलीनम्।

उभे—सुदं रट्ठिअमुहादो जाव अङ्गुलीअअदंसणं। श्रुतं राष्ट्रीय मुखाद्यावदङ्गुलीयकदर्शनम् ।

कञ्चुकी—तेन ह्यल्पं कथयितव्यम् । यदैव खलु स्वाङ्गुलीयक-दर्शनादनुस्मृतं देवेन सत्यमूढपूर्वा मे तत्रभवती रहसि शकु-न्तला मोहात्प्रत्यादिष्टेति । तदाप्रभृत्येव पश्चात्तापमुपगतो देवः । तथाहि ।

रम्यं द्वेष्टि यथापुरा प्रकृतिभिर्न प्रत्यहं सेव्यते
शय्याप्रान्तविवर्तनैर्विगमयत्युन्निद्र एव क्षपाः ।
दाक्षिण्येन ददाति वाचमुचितामन्तःपुरेभ्यो यदा
गोत्रेषु स्खलितस्तदा भवति च व्रीडाविलक्षश्चिरम् ॥ ५ ॥

सानुमती—पिअं मे। प्रियं मे ।

FIRST. Noble sir, but a few days ago, we were sent to the feet of his Majesty, by Mitrāvasu, the king's brother-in-law, and were entrusted with the duty of keeping the pleasure-garden ; thus being strangers, we have heard nothing of this affair.

CHAMBERLAIN. Well, you must not do so again.

BOTH. Sir, we are curious. If we may know, pray tell us what induced our sovereign to forbid the spring festival ?

SĀNUMATĪ. Men are, indeed, fond of festivals ; there must be some weighty reason.

CHAMBERLAIN. Why should I not tell it, when it is generally known ? Have not your ladyships heard the scandal concerning Śakuntalā's rejection ?

BOTH. We have heard it from the mouth of the king's brother-in-law up to the point of the recovery of the ring.

CHAMBERLAIN. Then, I have a little to add. When at the sight of his own ring the king remembered that he had indeed secretly married the lady Śakuntalā, and had rejected her under a delusion, from that time the king was struck with remorse. Thus

> He abhors everything pleasurable ; he is not daily waited upon by his ministers as in former times ; spends sleepless nights in tossing about on the edge of his bed and when by courtesy he addresses suitable words to the ladies of his palace, he blunders in their names and becomes for a long while abashed with shame. (5)

SĀNUMATĪ. This is very pleasing to me.

कञ्चुकी—अस्मात्प्रभवतो वैमनस्यादुत्सवः प्रत्याख्यातः ।

उभे—जुज्जइ । युज्यते ।

(नेपथ्ये ।)

एदु एदु भवं । एतु एतु भवान् ।

कञ्चुकी—(कर्णं दत्त्वा ।) अये, इत एवाभिवर्तते देवः । स्वकर्मानुष्ठीयताम् ।

उभे—तह । (इति निष्क्रान्ते) तथा ।

(ततः प्रविशति पश्चात्तापसदृशवेषो राजा विदूषकः प्रतीहारी च ।)

कञ्चुकी—(राजानमवलोक्य ।) अहो सर्वास्ववस्थासु रमणीयत्वमाकृतिविशेषाणाम् । एवमुत्सुकोऽपि प्रियदर्शनो देवः । तथाहि ।

प्रत्यादिष्टविशेषमण्डनविधिर्वामप्रकोष्ठार्पितं
बिभ्रत्काञ्चनमेकमेव वलयं श्वासोपरक्ताधरः ।
चिन्ताजागरणप्रताम्रनयनस्तेजोगुणादात्मनः
संस्कारोल्लिखितो महामणिरिव क्षीणोऽपि नालक्ष्यते ॥ ६॥

सानुमती—(राजानं दृष्ट्वा ।) ठाणे क्खु पच्चादेसविमाणिदा वि इमस्स किदे सउन्दला किलम्मदि । स्थाने खलु प्रत्यादेशविमानिताप्यस्य कृते शकुन्तला क्लाम्यति

राजा—(ध्यानमन्दं परिक्रम्य)।

प्रथमं सारङ्गाक्ष्या प्रियया प्रतिबोध्यमानमपि सुप्तम् ।
अनुशयदुःखायेदं हतहृदयं संप्रति विबुद्धम् ॥ ७ ॥

CHAMBERLAIN. By reason of this deep mental derangement the festival has been forbidden.

BOTH. It is proper.

(*Behind the scenes*).

Let your Majesty come.

CHAMBERLAIN (*Listening*). Ah, his Majesty is coming here. Attend to your duties.

BOTH. All right. (*Exeunt.*)

(*Enter the king in a dress indicative of remorse; the Vidūṣaka and a portress.*)

CHAMBERLAIN (*Observing the king*). How charming are noble forms under all conditions ! Thus his Majesty has a pleasing appearance even in his affliction. For

Rejecting special modes of decoration, he wears but one golden bracelet fastened on the left fore-arm ; his lip is faded by sighs ; his eyes are very red from sleeplessness caused by thought (of Śakuntalā). Yet through the excellence of his own lustre, though he has grown emaciate he is scarcely observed to be so, even like a magnificent diamond ground away on the polishing-stone. (6)

SĀNUMATĪ (*Looking at the king*). No wonder Śakuntalā languishes for him even though he dishonoured her by his repudiation of her.

KING. (*Walking round slowly in meditation*).

This my blighted heart which previously slept even when it was wakened from sleep by my fawn-eyed beloved is now broad awake to feel the anguish of remorse. (7)

सानुमती—णं ईदिसाणि तवस्सिणीए भाअहेआणि । नन्वीदृशानि तपस्विन्या भागधेयानि ।

विदूषकः—(अपवार्य ।) लङ्घिदो एसो भूओ वि सउन्दलावाहिणा । ण आणे कहं चिकिच्छिदव्वो भविस्सदि त्ति ।

कञ्चुकी—(उपगम्य ।) जयतु जयतु देवः । महाराज, प्रत्यवेक्षिताः प्रमदवनभूमयः । यथाकाममध्यास्तां विनोदस्थानानि महाराजः ।

राजा—वेत्रवति, मद्वचनादमात्यमार्यपिशुनं ब्रूहि । चिरप्रबोधान्न संभावितमस्माभिरद्य धर्मासनमध्यासितुम् । यत्प्रत्यवेक्षितं पौरकार्यमार्येण तत्पत्रमारोप्य दीयतामिति ।

प्रतीहारी—जं देवो आणवेदि । (इति निष्क्रान्ता ।) यद्देव आज्ञापयति ।

राजा—वातायन, त्वमपि स्वं नियोगमशून्यं कुरु ।

कञ्चुकी—यदाज्ञापयति देवः । (इति निष्क्रान्तः ।)

विदूषकः—किदं भवदा णिम्मच्छिअं । संपदं सिसिरातवच्छेअरमणीए इमस्सिं पमदवणुद्देसे अत्ताणं रमइस्ससि । कृतं भवता निर्मक्षिकम् । सांप्रतं शिशिरातपच्छेदरमणीयेऽस्मिन्प्रमदवनोद्देश आत्मानं रमयिष्यसि ।

राजा—वयस्य, रन्ध्रोपनिपातिनोऽनर्था इति यदुच्यते तदव्यभिचारि वचः । कुतः ।

मुनिसुताप्रणयस्मृतिरोधिना
मम च मुक्तमिदं तमसा मनः ।
मनसिजेन सखे प्रहरिष्यता
धनुषि चूतशरश्च निवेशितः ॥ ८ ॥

विदूषकः—चिट्ठ दाव । इमिणा दण्डकट्ठेण कन्दप्पवाणं णासइस्सामि । (इति दण्डकाष्ठमुद्यम्य चूताङ्कुरं पातयितुमिच्छति ।) तिष्ठ तावत् । अनेन दण्डकाष्ठेन कन्दर्पबाणं नाशयिष्यामि ।

SĀNUMATĪ. Such is also the fate of the poor girl.

VIDŪṢAKA (*Aside*). He is again seized by his Śakuntalā sickness ; and I hardly know a remedy for his illness.

CHAMBERLAIN (*Advancing*). Victory to your Majesty! The grounds of the pleasure-park have been inspected. Your Majesty may visit its pleasure-spots at will.

KING. Vetravati, tell the minister, the noble Piśuna, in my name, that owing to long sleeplessness, it was not possible for me to sit in the tribunal to-day. Whatever business of the citizens the worthy sir may have investigated, should be written down and dispatched to me.

PORTRESS. As your Majesty commands. (*Exit.*)

KING. And you, Vātāyana, attend to your business.

CHAMBERLAIN. As my king commands. (*Exit.*)

VIDŪṢAKA. You have not left a fly in this place. Now you will amuse yourself in this part of the pleasure-park which is cool and delightful by the mitigation of heat.

KING. Friend, the proverb 'Misfortunes rush through the weak spot' is an infallible one. For

> No sooner does the darkness that clouded the remembrance of my love for the sage's daughter, lift from my mind, than the God of Love, preparing to strike, puts the shaft of mango blossom to his bow. (8)

VIDŪṢAKA. Wait a bit, while I destroy Love's arrow with my stick. (***He raises his stick and desires to strike down the mango-shoot.***)

राजा—(सस्मितम् ।) भवतु । दृष्टं ब्रह्मवर्चसम् । सखे, क्वोपविष्टः प्रियायाः किंचिदनुकारिणीषु लतासु दृष्टिं विलोभयामि ।

विदूषकः—णं आसण्णपरिआरिआ चदुरिआ भवदा संदिट्ठा । माहवीमण्डवे इमं वेलं अदिवाहिस्सं । तहिं मे चित्तफलअगदं सहत्थलिहिदं तत्तहोदीए सउन्दलाए पडिकिदिं आणेहित्ति । नन्वासन्नपरिचारिका चतुरिका भवता संदिष्टा । माधवीमण्डप इमां वेलामतिवाहयिष्ये । तत्र मे चित्रफलकगतां स्वहस्तलिखितां तत्रभवत्याः शाकुन्तलायाः प्रतिकृतिमानयेति ।

राजा—ईदृशं हृदयविनोदस्थानम् । तत्तमेव मार्गमादेशय ।

विदूषकः—इदो इदो भवं । इत इतो भवान् ।

(उभौ परिक्रामतः । सानुमत्यनुगच्छति ।)

विदूषकः—एसो मणिसिलापट्टअसणाहो माहवीमण्डवो उवहाररमणिज्जदाए णिस्संसअं साअदेण विअ णो पडिच्छदि । ता पविसिअ णिसीददु भवं । एष मणिशिलापट्टकसनाथो माधवीमण्डप उपहाररमणीयतया निःसंशयं स्वागतेनेव नौ प्रतीच्छति । तत्प्रविश्य निषीदतु भवान् ।

(उभौ प्रवेशं कृत्वोपविष्टौ ।)

सानुमती—लदासंस्सिदा देक्खिस्सं दाव सहीए पडिकिदिं । तदो से भत्तुणो बहुमुहं अणुराअं णिवेदइस्सं । (इति तथा कृत्वा स्थिता ।) लतासंश्रिता द्रक्ष्यामि तावत्सख्याः प्रतिकृतिम् । ततोऽस्या भर्तुर्बहुमुखमनुरागं निवेदयिष्यामि ।

राजा—सखे, सर्वमिदानीं स्मरामि शकुन्तलायाः प्रथमवृत्तान्तम् । कथितवानस्मि भवते च । स भवान्प्रत्यादेशवेलायां मत्समीपगतो नासीत् । पूर्वमपि न त्वया कदाचित्संकीर्तितं तत्रभवत्या नाम । कच्चिदहमिव विस्मृतवानसि त्वम् ।

विदूषकः—ण विसुमरामि । किंतु सव्वं कहिअ अवसाणे उण तुए परिहासविअप्पओ एसो ण भूदत्थोत्ति आचक्खिदं । मए वि मिप्पिण्डबुद्धिणा तह एव्व गहीदं । अहवा भविदव्वदा

KING (*Smiling*). Enough ! I have seen a Brahmin's power. Now, friend, where shall I sit and recreate my sight with the slender shrubs which bear a faint resemblance to my beloved ?

VIDŪṢAKA. Well, have you not told Caturikā, your attendant, that you would be spending this hour in the Mādhavī bower, and that she should bring you there the picture of the lady Śakuntalā which you yourself painted on a tablet ?

KING. Will such a place divert me ? Well, lead the way to the same place.

VIDŪṢAKA. This way, your Majesty, this way.

(*Both walk round ; Sānumatī follows them.*)

VIDŪṢAKA. This Mādhavī bower furnished with a marble slab with its lovely flower-offerings appears to bid us welcome. Let your Honour enter and sit.

(*Both enter and seat themselves.*)

SĀNUMATĪ. Concealed behind the creepers I will just see the dear girl's picture. Then I shall be able to tell her how sincere her husband's love is.

(*Does so, and pauses.*)

KING. Friend, I now remember all the previous affair with Śakuntalā. And I have spoken to you (about it.) You, however, were not present near me at the time I disavowed her. Nor did you ever before mention her ladyship's name. Had you forgotten her even as I did ?

VIDŪṢAKA. No, I did not forget. But after telling the whole story, you said at the end that it was all a joke and that there was no truth in it. And I who

क्खु बलवदी । न विस्मरामि । किंतु सर्वं कथयित्वावसाने पुनस्त्वया परिहासविजल्प एष न भूतार्थ इत्याख्यातम् । मयापि मृत्पिण्डबुद्धिना तथैव गृहीतम् । अथवा भवितव्यता खलु बलवती ।

सानुमती—एव्वं णेदं । एवमेवैतत् ।

राजा—(ध्यात्वा ।) **सखे, त्रायस्व माम्** ।

विदूषकः—भो, किं एदं । अणुववण्णं क्खु ईदिसं तुइ । कदा वि सप्पुरिसा सोअपत्तप्पाणो ण होन्ति । णं पवादे वि णिक्कम्पा गिरीओ । भोः, किमेतत् । अनुपपन्नं खल्वीदृशं त्वयि । कदापि सत्पुरुषा शोकपात्रात्मानो न भवन्ति । ननु प्रवातेऽपि निष्कम्पा गिरयः ।

राजा—वयस्य, निराकरणविक्लवायाः प्रियायाः समवस्थामनुस्मृत्य बलवदशरणोऽस्मि । सा हि

इतः प्रत्यादेशात्स्वजनमनुगन्तुं व्यवसिता
मुहुस्तिष्ठेत्युच्चैर्वदति गुरुशिष्ये गुरुसमे ।
पुनर्दृष्टिं बाष्पप्रसरकलुषामर्पितवती
मयि क्रूरे यत्तत्सविषमिव शल्यं दहति माम् ॥ ९ ॥

सानुमती—अम्महे । ईदिसी सकज्जपरदा । इमस्स संदावेण अहं रमामि । अहो । ईदृशी स्वकार्यपरता । अस्य संतापेनाहं रमे ।

विदूषकः—भो, अत्थि मे तक्को । केण वि तत्तहोदी आआसचारिणा णीदेत्ति । भोः, अस्ति मे तर्कः । केनापि तत्रभवत्याकाशचारिणा नीतेति ।

राजा—कः पतिदेवतामन्यः परामर्ष्टुमुत्सहेत । मेनका किल सख्यास्ते जन्मप्रतिष्ठेति श्रुतवानस्मि । तत्सहचारिणीभिः सखी ते हृतेति मे हृदयमाशङ्कते ।

सानुमती—संमोहो क्खु विम्हअणिज्जो ण पडिबोहो । संमोहः खलु विस्मयनीयो न प्रतिबोधः ।

विदूषकः—जइ एव्वं अत्थि क्खु समाअमो कालेण तत्तहोदीए । यद्येवमस्ति खलु समागमः कालेन तत्रभवत्या ।

have no more intelligence than a lump of clay believed it. Or rather fate is powerful.

SĀNUMATĪ. It is even so.

KING (*Meditating*). Friend, help me!

VIDŪṢAKA. Oh, what is it? This is indeed unbecoming in you. Never do great men give themselves up to grief; the mountains are calm even in a tempest.

KING. When I remember my beloved's condition who was greatly affected by my desertion I feel quite forlorn.

When I rejected her from here, she made an attempt to follow her kinsfolk; and when her father's pupil, revered as her father himself, repeatedly cried "stay" in a loud voice, then once more she fixed on me, who had become inexorable, a glance bedimmed with gushing tears; (the idea of) it all burns me like an envenomed shaft. (9)

SĀNUMATĪ. Dear me! Such is one's regard for one's own interest that I delight in his pain.

VIDŪṢAKA. O I have a guess that her ladyship was carried away by some heavenly being.

KING. Who else would dare to touch rudely a wife to whom her husband is a divinity? I have heard that Menakā gave birth to your friend. And her companions have, I imagine, carried her away.

SĀNUMATĪ. His delusion is, to be wondered at, not the awakening from it.

VIDŪṢAKA. If that is so, you will meet her again after a time.

राजा—कथमिव।

विदूषकः—ण क्खु मादापिदरा भत्तुविओअदुक्खिदं दुहिदरं देक्खिदुं पारेन्ति। न खलु मातापितरौ भर्तृवियोगदुःखितां दुहितरं द्रष्टुं पारयतः।

राजा—वयस्य,

स्वप्नो नु माया नु मतिभ्रमो नु
क्लिष्टं नु तावत्फलमेव पुण्यम्।
असंनिवृत्त्यै तदतीतमव
मनोरथा नाम तटप्रपाताः॥ १०॥

विदूषकः—मा एव्वं। णं अङ्गुलीअअं एव्व णिदंसणं अवस्संभावी अचिन्तणिज्जो समाअमो होदि त्ति। मैवम्। नन्वङ्गुलीयकमेव निदर्शनमवश्यंभाव्यचिन्तनीयः समागमो भवतीति।

राजा—(अङ्गुलीयकं विलोक्य।) अये, इदं तावदसुलभस्थानभ्रंशि शोचनीयम्।

तव सुचरितमङ्गुलीय नूनं
प्रतनु ममेव विभाव्यते फलेन।
अरुणनखमनोहरासु तस्या-
श्च्युतमसि लब्धपदं यदङ्गुलीषु॥ ११॥

सानुमती—जइ अण्णहत्थगदं भवे सच्चं एव्व सोअणिज्जं भवे। यद्यन्यहस्तगतं भवेत्सत्यमेव शोचनीयं भवेत्।

विदूषकः—भो, इअं णाममुद्दा केण उग्घदेण तत्तहोदीए हत्थसंसग्गं पाविदा। भोः, इयं नाममुद्रा केनोद्धातेन तत्रभवत्या हस्तसंसर्गं प्रापिता।

सानुमती—मम वि कोदूहलेण आआरिदो एसो। ममापि कौतूहलेनाकारित एषः।

राजा—श्रूयताम्। स्वनगराय प्रस्थितं मां प्रिया सबाष्पमाह। कियच्चिरेणार्यपुत्रः प्रतिपत्तिं दास्यतीति।

विदूषकः—तदो तदो। ततस्ततः।

KING. How so?

VIDŪṢAKA. No father and mother can (long) endure to see their daughter separated from her husband.

KING. Friend,

> Was it a dream? or an illusion? or the infatuation of my mind? Or was it that my merit having borne me that much fruit, was exhausted? It is gone, never to return: these my hopes are like falls from a precipice. (10)

VIDŪṢAKA. Do not speak thus. Is not the ring itself a proof that there may be an unexpected meeting with that which must necessarily happen?

KING. (*Looking at the ring*). This, indeed, which has fallen from a station hard to gain, deserves my pity.

> Verily, O ring, thy merit like mine is proved to be but slight from (thy) reward; since after finding a place on her lovely pink-nailed fingers thou hast suffered a fall. (11)

SĀNUMATĪ. Had it found a way to any other hand, its lot would have been truly deplorable.

VIDŪṢAKA. With what object was the ring placed in her ladyship's hand?

SĀNUMATĪ. He, too, seems to be impelled by the curiosity I feel.

KING. Listen: when I started for the capital, my darling wept and said: After how long will my lord send me news?

VIDŪṢAKA. Well, what then?

राजा—पश्चादिमां मुद्रां तदङ्गुलौ निवेशयता मया प्रत्यभिहिता ।

एकैकमत्र दिवसे दिवसे मदीयं
नामाक्षरं गणय गच्छसि यावदन्तम् ।
तावत्प्रिये मद्वरोधगृहप्रवेशं
नेता जनस्तव समीपमुपैष्यतीति ॥ १२ ॥

तच्च दारुणात्मना मया मोहान्नानुष्ठितम् ।

सानुमती—रमणीओ क्खु अवही विहिणा विसंवादिदो । रमणीयः खल्ववधिर्विधिना विसंवादितः ।

विदूषकः—कहं धीवलकप्पिअस्स लोहिअमच्छस्स उदलब्भन्तले आसि । कथं धीवरकल्पितस्य रोहितमत्स्यस्योदराभ्यन्तर आसीत् ।

राजा—शचीतीर्थे वन्दमानायाः सख्यास्ते हस्ताद्गङ्गास्रोतसि परिभ्रष्टम् ।

विदूषकः—जुज्जइ । युज्यते ।

सानुमती—अदो एव्व तवस्सिणीए सउन्दलाए अधम्मभीरुणो इमस्स राएसिणो परिणए संदेहो आसि । अहवा ईदिसो अणुराओ अहिण्णाणं अवेक्खदि । कहं विअ एदं । अत एव तपस्विन्याः शकुतलाया अधर्मभीरोरस्य राजर्षेः परिणये संदेह आसीत् । अथवेदृशोऽनुरागोऽभिज्ञानमपेक्षते । कथमिवैतत् ।

राजा—उपालप्स्ये तावदिदमङ्गुलीयकम् ।

विदूषकः—(आत्मगतम् ।) गहीदो णेण पन्था उम्मत्तआणं । गृहीतोऽनेन पन्था उन्मत्तानाम् ।

राजा—

कथं नु तं बन्धुरकोमलाङ्गुलिं
करं विहायासि निमग्नमम्भसि ।

अथवा ।

अचेतनं नाम गुणं न लक्षये-
न्मयैव कस्मादवधीरिता प्रिया ॥ १३ ॥

KING. Then, fixing this ring on her finger, I said :

> Count one by one every day the letters of my name on this (ring) ; as soon as you reach the end, my darling, the messenger who is to lead you to the entrance of the inner apartment, will come into your presence. (12)

And hard-hearted that I am, I failed to carry it out in my madness.

SĀNUMATĪ. A charming interval, indeed, which was, however, marred by fate.

VIDŪṢAKA. How did it get inside the maw of the carp cut up by the fisherman ?

KING. While your friend was worshipping Śacītīrtha, it must have slipped from her hand into the stream of the Ganges.

VIDŪṢAKA. It is explained.

SĀNUMATĪ. It was hence that the king, who is afraid of doing anything unrighteous, doubted his marriage with poor Śakuntalā. And yet such love does not require a token. How could it be ?

KING. Well, I will now reproach the ring.

VIDŪṢAKA (*To himself*). (So) he is (again) going the the way of madmen !

KING.

> How couldst thou leave that hand with its slender delicate fingers and fall into the water ? Or a lifeless thing may well not appreciate excellence. But how could I scorn my beloved ? (13)

विदूषकः—(आत्मगतम् ।) **कहं बुभुक्खाए खादिदव्वो म्हि** कथं बुभुक्षया खादितव्योऽस्मि ।

राजा—अकारणपरित्यक्ते अनुशयतप्तहृदयस्तावदनुकम्प्यतामयं जनः पुनर्दर्शनेन ।

(प्रविश्यापटीक्षेपेण चित्रफलकहस्ता ।)

चतुरिका—इअं चित्तगदा भट्टिणी । (इति चित्रफलकं दर्शयति ।) इयं चित्रगता भट्टिनी ।

विदूषकः—साहु वअस्स, महुरावत्थाणदंसणिज्जो भावाणुप्पवेसो । क्खलदि विअ मे दिट्ठी णिण्णुण्णअप्पदेसेसु । साधु वयस्य, मधुरावस्थानदर्शनीयो भावानुप्रवेशः । स्खलतीव मे दृष्टिर्निम्नोन्नतप्रदेशेषु ।

सानुमती—अम्मो एसा राएसिणो णिउणदा । जाणे सही अग्गदो मे वट्टदित्ति । अहो एषा राजर्षेनिपुणता । जाने सख्यग्रतो मे वर्तत इति ।

राजा—

यद्यत्साधु न चित्रे स्यात्क्रियते तत्तदन्यथा ।
तथापि तस्या लावण्यं रेखया किंचिदन्वितम् ॥ १४ ॥

सानुमती—सरिसं एदं पच्छादावगुरुणो सिणेहस्स अणवलेवस्स अ । सदृशमेतत्पश्चात्तापगुरोः स्नेहस्यानवलेपस्य च ।

विदूषकः—भो, दाणिं तिण्णि तत्थहोदीओ दीसन्ति । सव्वाओ अ दंसणीआओ । कदमा इत्थ तत्तहोदी सउन्दला । भोः, इदानीं तिस्रस्तत्रभवत्यो दृश्यन्ते । सर्वाश्च दर्शनीयाः । कतमात्र तत्रभवती शकुन्तला ।

सानुमती—अणभिण्णो क्खु ईदिसस्स रूवस्स मोहदिट्ठी अअं जणो । अनभिज्ञः खल्वीदृशस्य रूपस्य मोघदृष्टिरयं जनः ।

राजा—त्वं तावत्कतमां तर्कयसि ।

विदूषकः—तक्केमि जा एसा सिढिलकेसबन्धणुव्वन्तकुसुमेण केसन्तेण उब्भिण्णसेअबिन्दुणा वअणेण विसेसदो ओसरीआहिं बाहाहिं अवसेअसिणिद्धतरुणपल्लवस्स चूअपाअवस्स पासे ईसिपरिस्सन्ता विअ आलिहिदा सा सउन्दला । इदराओ सहीओत्ति ।

VIDŪṢAKA (*To himself*). How ? must I be devoured by hunger ?

KING. O (My darling) abandoned without reason, let me, whose heart is stung with remorse, be once more blessed with a sight of thee ?

(*Entering with a toss of the curtain, tablet in hand*).

CATURIKĀ. Here is our lady in the picture. (*She shows the tablet.*)

VIDŪṢAKA. Excellent, my friend ! How beautifully are the feelings represented in this lovely posture ! mine eyes stumble as it were over its uneven parts.

SĀNUMATĪ. What great skill the virtuous king possesses ! My friend seems to stand before my eyes.

KING.

Whatever is not well executed in the picture may be (retouched and) improved; and yet (even then) her loveliness will be possessed by the picture in some measure only. (14)

SĀNUMATĪ. This is befitting an affection increased by remorse, and absence of conceit.

VIDŪṢAKA. There are to be seen three ladies now, and all are beautiful. Which one is the lady Śakuntalā ?

SĀNUMATĪ. What use are his eyes to this man who is ignorant of such beauty ?

KING. Which one do you think ?

VIDŪṢAKA. I think that she who is represented as if a little fatigued by the side of the mango-tree whose young leaves are glistening after her watering, with

तर्कयामि यैषा शिथिलकेशबन्धनोद्वान्तकुसुमेन केशान्तेनोद्भिन्नस्वेदबिन्दुना वदनेन विशेषतोऽपसृताभ्यां बाहुभ्यामवसेकस्निग्धतरुणपल्लवस्य चूतपादपस्य पार्श्वे ईषत्परिश्रान्तेवालिखिता सा शकुन्तला। इतरे सख्याविति।

राजा—निपुणो भवान्। अस्त्यत्र मे भावचिह्नम्।

स्विन्नाङ्गुलिविनिवेशो रेखाप्रान्तेषु दृश्यते मलिनः।
अश्रु च कपोलपतितं दृश्यमिदं वर्तिकोच्छ्वासात्॥ १५॥

चतुरिके, अर्धलिखितमेतद्विनोदस्थानम्। गच्छ। वर्तिकां तावदानय।

चतुरिका—अज्ज माठव्व, अवलम्ब चित्तफलअं जाव आअच्छामि। आर्य माठव्य, अवलम्बस्व चित्रफलकं यावदागच्छामि।

राजा—अहमेवैतदवलम्बे। (इति यथोक्तं करोति।)

(निष्क्रान्ता चेटी।)

राजा—अहं हि

साक्षात्प्रियामुपगतामपहाय पूर्वं
चित्रार्पितां पुनरिमां बहु मन्यमानः।
स्रोतोवहां पथि निकामजलामतीत्य
जातः सखे प्रणयवान्मृगतृष्णिकायाम्॥ १६॥

विदूषकः—(आत्मगतम्।) **एसो अत्तभवं णदिं अदिक्कमिअ मिअतिण्हिआं संकन्तो।** (प्रकाशम्।) **भो, अवरं किं एत्थ लिहिदव्वं।** एषोऽत्रभवान्नदीमतिक्रम्य मृगतृष्णिकां संक्रान्तः। भोः, अपरं किमत्र लिखितव्यम्।

सानुमती—जो जो पदेसो सहीए मे अहिरूवो तं तं आलिहिदुकामो भवे। यो यः प्रदेशः सख्या मेऽभिरूपस्तं तमालिखितुकामो भवेत्।

राजा—श्रूयताम्।

arms drooping in a peculiar manner ; with a face on which drops of perspiration have broken out ; with locks of her hair the flowers of which have dropped down from the loosened braid ; that is Śakuntalā. The others are her friends.

KING. You are clever. Here are proofs of my love.

At the edges of the drawing is seen the soiled impression of my perspiring fingers ; and here is to be observed this tear that fell from my cheek from the swelling of the paint. (15)

CATURIKĀ, this source of my consolation is but half finished. Therefore, go, get me a brush.

CATURIKĀ. Worthy Māṭhavya, hold the picture-tablet till I get back.

KING. I will myself hold it. (*Does as said.*)

(*Exit maid.*)

KING. I, now,

Having first rejected my darling who had approached me in person, and now again and again doing homage to her drawn in this picture, have become, O friend, possessed of a longing for the mirage, after passing by a river on my way having plenty of water. (16)

VIDŪṢAKA (*To himself*). Here is his honour, having passed by a river, gone to a mirage. (*Aloud*). Oh what else is to be painted here ?

SĀNUMATĪ. He may be desirous of painting every spot that the dear girl loved.

KING. Listen —

कार्या सैकतलीनहंसमिथुना स्रोतोवहा मालिनी
पादास्तामभितो निषण्णहरिणा गौरीगुरोः पावनाः ।
शाखालम्बितवल्कलस्य च तरोर्निर्मातुमिच्छाम्यधः
शृङ्गे कृष्णमृगस्य वामनयनं कण्डूयमानां मृगीम् ॥ १७ ॥

विदूषकः—(आत्मगतम् ।) जह अहं देक्खामि पूरिदव्वं णेण चित्तफलअं लम्बकुच्चाणं तावसाणं कदम्बेहिं । यथाहं पश्यामि पूरितव्यमनेन चित्रफलकं लम्बकूर्चानां तापसानां कदम्बैः ।

राजा—वयस्य, अन्यच्च शकुन्तलायाः प्रसाधनमभिप्रेतं विस्मृतमस्माभिः ।

विदूषकः—किं विअ । किमिव ।

सानुमती—वणवासस्स सो उमारस्स अ जं सरिसं भविस्सदि । वनवासस्य सौकुमार्यस्य च यत्सदृशं भविष्यति ।

राजा—

कृतं न कर्णार्पितबन्धनं सखे
शिरीषमागण्डविलम्बिकेसरम् ।
न वा शरच्चन्द्रमरीचिकोमलं
मृणालसूत्रं रचितं स्तनान्तरे ॥ १८ ॥

विदूषकः—भो, किं णु तत्तहोदी रत्तकुवलअपल्लवसोहिणा अग्गहत्थेण मुहं आवारिअ चइदचइदा विअ ठिआ । (सावधानं निरूप्य दृष्ट्वा ।) आ, एसो दासीए पुत्तो कुसुमरसपाडच्चरो तत्तहोदीए वअणं अहिलङ्घदि महुअरो । भोः, किं नु तत्रभवती रक्तकुवलयपल्लवशोभिनाग्रहस्तेन मुखमावार्य चकितचकितेव स्थिता । आः, एष दास्याः पुत्रः कुसुमरसपटच्चरस्तत्रभवत्या वदनमभिलङ्घति मधुकरः ।

राजा— ननु वार्यतामेष धृष्टः ।

The stream of Mālinī ought to be drawn with a pair of swans resting on its sands; and on both its sides must appear the sacred hills at the base of the Himālayan ranges, where the deer are squatting; and I wish to draw, underneath a tree that bears some bark-garments suspended from its boughs, a doe that rubs her left eye on the horn of a black antelope. (17)

VIDŪṢAKA (*To himself*). As I imagine, he will fill up the picture with multitudes of long-bearded hermits.

KING. Friend, I have forgotten to draw another of Śakuntalā's ornament which I had intended to draw.

VIDŪṢAKA. What is it?

SĀNUMATĪ. Such as becomes her forest life and her delicacy.

KING.

A Śirīṣa-flower with its stalk fastened over her ear, and its filaments waving over her cheek, has been omitted, O friend; nor has a necklace of lotus fibres, soft like the rays of the moon of autumn, been drawn between her breasts. (18)

VIDŪṢAKA. But why does the lady stand, as if she is very much frightened, covering her face with the palm of her hand glowing like the petal of a red-lotus? (*Looking closely*). Ah! Here is this bee, this son of a slave, this thief who robs the flowers of their honey, attacking her ladyship's face.

KING. Drive off this impudent (bee).

विदूषकः—भवं एव्व अविणीदाणं सासिदा इमस्स वारणे पहविस्सदि । भवानेवाविनीतानां शासितास्य वारणे प्रभविष्यति ।

राजा—युज्यते । अयि भोः, कुसुमलताप्रियातिथे, किमत्र परिपतनखेदमनुभवसि ।

एषा कुसुमनिषण्णा तृषितापि सती भवन्तमनुरक्ता ।
प्रतिपालयति मधुकरी न खलु मधु विना त्वया पिबति ॥ १९ ॥

सानुमती—अज्ज अभिजादं क्खु एसो वारिदो । अद्याभिजातं खल्वेष वारितः ।

विदूषकः—पडिसिद्धा वि वामा एसा जादी । प्रतिषिद्धापि वामैषा जातिः ।

राजा—एवं भोः, न मे शासने तिष्ठसि । श्रूयतां तर्हि संप्रति ।

अक्लिष्टबालतरुपल्लवलोभनीयं
पीतं मया सदयमेव रतोत्सवेषु ।
बिम्बाधरं स्पृशसि चेद्भ्रमरप्रियाया-
स्त्वां कारयामि कमलोदरबन्धनस्थम् ॥ २० ॥

विदूषकः—एव्वं तिक्खदण्डस्स किं ण भाइस्सदि । (प्रहस्य । आत्मगतम् ।) एदो दाव उम्मत्तो । अहं पि एदस्स सङ्गेण ईदिसवण्णो विअ संवुत्तो । (प्रकाशम् ।) भो, चित्तं क्खु एदं । एवं तीक्ष्णदण्डस्य किं न भेष्यति । एष तावदुन्मत्तः । अहमप्येतस्य सङ्गेनेदृशवर्ण इव संवृत्तः । भोः, चित्रं खल्वेतत् ।

राजा—कथं चित्रम् ।

सानुमती—अहं पि दाणिं अणवगदत्था, किं उण जहालिहिदाणुभावी एसो । अहमपीदानीमनवगतार्था, किं पुनर्यथालिखितानुभाव्येषः ।

राजा— वयस्य, किमिदमनुष्ठितं पौरोभाग्यम् ।

VIDŪṢAKA. Your honour alone, that punishes all offenders, has the power to drive him off.

KING. True. O welcome guest of flowering-plants, why undergo the trouble of hovering round here?

There, perched on a flower, is the female bee
who loves thee, and though athirst, is waiting
for thee still, nor without thee will she taste
its honey. (19)

SĀNUMATĪ. For once now is he kept off quite in a courteous manner.

VIDŪṢAKA. This kind is perverse, however it may be warned off.

KING. Thus, then, thou wilt not obey my command. Well then listen;

Shouldst thou touch, O bee, the bimba-lip of
my darling, sweet as a virgin leaf on a tree, the
lip from which I drank delight in love-feasts,
then I will make thee imprisoned in the hollow
of a lotus. (20)

VIDŪṢAKA. How should he not be afraid of one who gives so severe a punishment? (*Laughing, to himself*). As for him, he is quite crazy, and I too am just as bad, from keeping him company! (*Aloud*). O, it is only a picture.

KING. How? A picture?

SĀNUMATĪ. I, too, did not realise the fact; how much less he who is experiencing what he has painted!

KING. Friend, why have you done such a wicked thing?

दर्शनसुखमनुभवतः साक्षादिव तन्मयेन हृदयेन ।
स्मृतिकारिणा त्वया मे पुनरपि चित्रीकृता कान्ता ॥ २१ ॥

(इति बाष्पं विहरति ।)

सानुमती—पुव्वावरविरोही अपुव्वो एसो विरहमग्गो । पूर्वापरविरोध्यपूर्व एष विरहमार्गः ।

राजा—वयस्य, कथमेवमविश्रान्तदुःखमनुभवामि ।

प्रजागरात्खिलीभूतस्तस्याः स्वप्ने समागमः ।
बाष्पस्तु न ददात्येनां द्रष्टुं चित्रगतामपि ॥ २२ ॥

सानुमती—सव्वहा पमज्जिदं तुए पच्चादेसदुक्खं सउन्दलाए । सर्वथा प्रमार्जितं त्वया प्रत्यादेशदुःखं शकुन्तलायाः ।

(प्रविश्य ।)

चतुरिका—जेदु जेदु भट्टा । वट्टिआकरण्डअं गेण्हिअ इदोमुहं पत्थिदम्हि । जयतु जयतु भर्ता । वर्तिकाकरण्डकं गृहीत्वेतोमुखं प्रस्थितास्मि ।

राजा—किं च ।

चतुरिका—सो मे हत्थादो अन्तरा तरलिआदुदीआए देवीए वसुमदीए अहं अज्जउत्तस्स उवणइस्सं त्ति सबलक्कारं गहीदो । स मे हस्तादन्तरा तरलिकाद्वितीयया देव्या वसुमत्याहमेवार्यपुत्रस्योपनेष्यामीति सबलात्कारं गृहीतः ।

विदूषकः—दिट्ठिआ तुमं मुक्का । दिष्ट्या त्वं मुक्ता ।

चतुरिका—जाव देवीए विडवलग्गं उत्तरीअं तरलिआ मोचेदि ताव मए णिव्वाहिदो अत्ता । यावद्देव्या विटपलग्नमुत्तरीयं तरलिका मोचयति तावन्मया निर्वाहित आत्मा ।

While I was enjoying the rapture of beholding her as if she stood before my eyes, with my heart completely wrapped up in her, you have, by reviving my memory, again transformed my darling into a picture. (21).

(*Sheds tears.*)

SĀNUMATĪ. Quite without a precedent is this way of (one in a state of) separation, involving as it does an inconsistency between what preceded and what followed.

KING. Friend, why do I thus experience unremitting grief?

Union with her is prevented by my sleeplessness; and my tears will not suffer me to view her even in this picture. (22).

SĀNUMATĪ. You have completely atoned for the pain you caused Śakuntalā by repudiating her.

(*Entering*) CATURIKĀ. Victory victory, to your Majesty! I had started in this direction with the box of paint-brushes——

KING. Well?

CATURIKĀ. When on the way it was forcibly snatched from my hand by queen Vasumatī who was accompanied by Taralikā; (the queen) saying "I will take it to my lord myself."

VIDŪṢAKA. Fortunately you were let off.

CATURIKĀ. While Taralikā was disengaging the queen's upper garment which had been caught by the branch of a shrub, I took myself off.

राजा—वयस्य, उपस्थिता देवी बहुमानगर्विता च भवानिमां प्रतिकृतिं रक्षतु ।

विदूषकः—अत्ताणं त्ति भणाहि । (चित्रफलकमादायोत्थाय च ।) **जइ भवं अन्तेउरकालकूडादो मुञ्चीअदि तदो मं मेहप्पडिच्छन्दे पासादे सद्दावेहि ।** (इति द्रुतपदं निष्क्रान्तः ।) आत्मानमिति भण । यदि भवानन्तःपुरकालकूटान्मोक्ष्यते तदा मां मेघप्रतिच्छन्दे प्रासादे शब्दापय ।

सानुमती—अण्णसंकन्तहिअओ वि पढमसंभावणं अवेक्खदि । सिढिलसोहदो दाणिं एसो । अन्यसंक्रान्तहृदयोऽपि प्रथमसंभावनामपेक्षते । शिथिलसौहार्द इदानीमेषः ।

(प्रविश्य पत्रहस्ता ।)

प्रतीहारी—जेदु जेदु देवो । जयतु जयतु देवः ।

राजा—वेत्रवति, न खल्वन्तरा दृष्टा त्वया देवी ।

प्रतीहारी—अह इं । पत्तहत्थं मं देक्खिअ पडिणिउत्ता । अथ किम् । पत्रहस्तां मां प्रेक्ष्य प्रतिनिवृत्ता ।

राजा—कार्यज्ञा कार्योपरोधं मे परिहरति ।

प्रतीहारी—देव, अमच्चो विण्णवेदि । अत्थजादस्स गणणाबहुलदाए एक्कं एव्व पोरकज्जं अवेक्खिदं तं देवो पत्तारूढं पच्चक्खीकरेदु त्ति । देव, अमात्यो विज्ञापयति । अर्थजातस्य गणनाबहुलतयैकमेव पौरकार्यमवेक्षितं तद्देवः पत्रारूढं प्रत्यक्षीकरोत्विति ।

राजा—इतः पत्रिकां दर्शय ।

(प्रतीहार्युपनयति ।)

राजा—(अनुवाच्य ।) **कथम् । समुद्रव्यवहारी सार्थवाहो धनमित्रो नाम नौव्यसने विपन्नः । अनपत्यश्च किल तपस्वी । राज-**

KING. Friend, the queen is come, and she is rendered arrogant by (my) great attentions to her. Do you take care of this picture.

VIDŪṢAKA. Say " yourself." (*Taking the picture-board and rising*). If your honour is freed from the bane of the inner apartments then call me in the Meghapraticchanda palace.

(*Goes out with hurried steps.*)

SĀNUMATĪ. Although his heart is transferred to another he yet cares for his first love. His love has very much lost its ardour now.

(*Entering, letter in hand*) PORTRESS. Victory to your Majesty.

KING. Vetravati, did not you meet the queen on the way ?

PORTRESS. Yes, I did. But she turned back when she saw me carrying a letter in my hand.

KING. She knows (the importance of state) business, and avoids interrupting my duty.

PORTRESS. Your Majesty, the minister requests : On account of the heavy work of counting the various items of revenue, only one citizen's suit has been attended to ; let your Majesty consider the same which is committed to writing.

KING. Give me the letter.

(*The portress brings it.*)

KING. (*Reading*). How ! The merchant Dhanamitra who had (extensive) commerce at sea had been lost in a

गामी तस्यार्थसंचय इत्येतदमात्येन लिखितम् । (सविषादम् ।) कष्टं खल्वनपत्यता । बहुधनत्वाद्बहुपत्नीकेन तत्रभवता भवितव्यम् । विचार्यतां यदि काचिदापन्नसत्त्वा तस्य भार्यासु स्यात् ।

प्रतीहारी—देव, दाणिं एव्व साकेदअस्स सेट्ठिणो दुहिआ णिव्वुत्तपुंसवणा जाआ से सुणिअदि । देव, इदानीमेव साकेतस्य श्रेष्ठिनो दुहिता निर्वृत्तपुंसवना जायास्य श्रूयते ।

राजा—ननु गर्भः पित्र्यं रिक्थमर्हति । गच्छ एवममात्यं ब्रूहि ।

प्रतीहारी—जं देवो आणवेदि । (इति प्रस्थिता) यद्देव आज्ञापयति ।

राजा—एहि तावत् ।

प्रतीहारी—इअम्हि । इयमस्मि ।

राजा—किमनेन संततिरस्ति नास्तीति ।

येन येन वियुज्यन्ते प्रजाः स्निग्धेन बन्धुना ।
स स पापादृते तासां दुष्यन्त इति घुष्यताम् ॥ २३ ॥

प्रतीहारी—एव्वं णाम घोसइदव्वं । (निष्क्रम्य । पुनः प्रविश्य ।) काले पवुट्ठं विअ अहिणन्दिदं देवस्स सासणम् । एवं नाम घोषयितव्यम् । काले प्रवृष्टमिवाभिनन्दितं देवस्य शासनम् ।

राजा—(दीर्घमुष्णं च निःश्वस्य ।) एवं भोः संततिच्छेदनिरवलम्बानां कुलानां मूलपुरुषावसाने संपदः परमुपतिष्ठन्ति । ममाप्यन्ते पुरुवंशश्रियः एष वृत्तान्तः ।

shipwreck. And they say that the poor man had no child. All his accumulated wealth reverts to the king; thus the minister writes. (*Sorrowfully*). It is indeed dreadful to be childless. He had great riches, he must have wedded several wives; let an inquiry be made whether any one among his wives is with child.

PORTRESS. Your Majesty, it is reported that his wife, the daughter of a merchant from Sāketa, has even now gone through the Puṁsavana ceremony.

KING. Surely the child in the womb has a title to its father's property. Go, say so to the minister.

PORTRESS. As your Majesty commands.

(*Starts to leave.*)

KING. Come for a while.

PORTRESS. I am here.

KING. What does it matter whether he has or has not left offspring?

> Let it be proclaimed that whatever dearly loved kinsman any one of my subjects may lose, Duṣyanta will supply the place of that kinsman to them, the wicked excepted. (23)

PORTRESS. Thus surely it shall be proclaimed (*Going out and returning*). The royal decree was welcomed (by the people) like a timely shower.

KING. (*Heaving a deep and hot sigh*). O, thus it is that the wealth of families which are bereft of support through the failure of progeny passes on the death of the representative of the progenitor, to a stranger. When I die, such will be the fate of the wealth of Puru's line.

प्रतीहारी—पडिहदं अमङ्गलम् । प्रतिहतममङ्गलम् ।

राजा—धिङ्मामुपस्थितश्रेयोऽवमानिनम् ।

सानुमती—असंसअं सहिं एव्व हिअए करिअ णिन्दिदो णेण अप्पा । असंशयं सखीमेव हृदये कृत्वा निन्दितोऽनेनात्मा ।

राजा—

संरोपितेऽप्यात्मनि धर्मपत्नी
त्यक्ता मया नाम कुलप्रतिष्ठा ।
कल्पिष्यमाणा महते फलाय
वसुंधरा काल इवोप्तबीजा ॥ २४ ॥

सानुमती—अपरिच्छिण्णा दाणिं दे संददी भविस्सदि । अपरिच्छिन्नेदानीं ते संततिर्भविष्यति ।

चतुरिका—(जनान्तिकम् ।) अए इमिणा सत्थवाहवुत्तन्तेण दिउणुव्वेओ भट्टा । णं अस्सासिदुं मेहप्पडिच्छन्दादो अज्जं माढव्वं गेण्हिअ आअच्छ । अयि, अनेन सार्थवाहवृत्तान्तेन द्विगुणोद्वेगो भर्ता । एनमाश्वासयितुं मेघप्रतिच्छन्दादार्यं माठव्यं गृहीत्वागच्छ ।

प्रतीहारी—सुट्ठु भणासि । (इति निष्क्रान्ता ।) सुष्ठु भणसि ।

राजा—अहो दुष्यन्तस्य संशयमारूढाः पिण्डभाजः । कुतः ।

अस्मात्परं बत यथाश्रुति संभृतानि
को नः कुले निवपनानि नियच्छतीति ।
नूनं प्रसूतिविकलेन मया प्रसिक्तं
धौताश्रुशेषमुदकं पितरः पिबन्ति ॥ २५ ॥

(इति मोहमुपगतः ।)

चतुरिका—(ससंभ्रममवलोक्य ।) समस्ससदु भट्टा । समाश्वसितु भर्ता

PORTRESS. Heaven avert the calamity !

KING. Fie on me who despised the happiness that had offered itself.

SĀNUMATĪ. Surely he has the dear girl in mind when he thus reproaches himself.

KING.

> Verily my lawful wife, the glory of my family was forsaken by me, although my own self was implanted (in her) like the earth sown with seed at the right season, when she promises the richest fruit. (24)

SĀNUMATĪ. Now your line will never be interrupted.

CATURIKĀ (*Aside*). The merchant's story has doubled our lord's remorse. Go to the Meghapraticchanda palace and fetch the noble Māṭhavya to comfort him.

PORTRESS. A good idea. (*Exit.*)

KING. Ah me ! Duṣyanta's ancestors, who claim a share in the funeral offering, are brought to a critical situation. For,

> Thinking "who indeed after this (man) in our family will offer us the libations prepared according to scriptural precept ?" my ancestors verily drink such of the water offered by me, who am destitute of progeny, as remains to them after washing their tears. (25)

(*Faints.*)

CATURIKĀ (*Looking about in haste*). Take heart, my lord.

सानुमती—हद्धी हद्धी। सदि क्खु दीवे ववधाणदोसेण एसो अन्धआरदोसं अणुहोदि। अहं दाणिं एव्व णिव्वुदं करोमि। अहवा सुदं मए सउन्दलं समस्सासअन्तीए महेन्दजणणीए मुहादो जण्णभाओस्सुआ देवा एव्व तह अणुचिट्ठिस्सन्ति जह अइरेण धम्मपदिणिं भट्टा अहिणन्दिस्सदित्ति। ता जुत्तं एदं कालं पडिपालिदुं। जाव इमिणा वुत्तन्तेण पिअसहिं समस्सासेमि। (इत्युद्भ्रान्तकेन निष्क्रान्ता।) हा धिक् हा धिक्। सति खलु दीपे व्यवधानदोषेणैषोऽन्धकारदोषमनुभवति। अहमिदानीमेव निर्वृत्तं करोमि। अथवा श्रुतं मया शकुन्तलां समाश्वासयन्त्या महेन्द्रजनन्या मुखाद्यज्ञभागोत्सुका देवा एव तथानुष्ठास्यन्ति यथाऽचिरेण धर्मपत्नीं भर्ताभिनन्दिष्यतीति। तद्युक्तमेतं कालं प्रतिपालयितुम्। यावदनेन वृत्तान्तेन प्रियसखीं समाश्वासयामि।

(नेपथ्ये।)

अब्बम्हण्णं अब्बम्हण्णं। अब्रह्मण्यम्, अब्रह्मण्यम्।

राजा—(प्रत्यागतप्राणः कर्णं दत्त्वा।) **अये, माढव्यस्येवार्तस्वरः। कः कोऽत्र भोः।**

(प्रविश्य।)

प्रतीहारी—(ससंभ्रमम्।) **परित्ताअदु देवो संसअगदं वअस्सं।** परित्रायतां देवः संशयगतं वयस्यम्।

राजा—केनात्तगन्धो माणवकः।

प्रतीहारी—अदिट्ठरूवेण केण वि सत्तेण अदिक्कमिअ मेहप्पडिच्छन्दस्स पासादस्स अग्गभूमिं आरोविदो। अदृष्टरूपेण केनापि सत्त्वेनातिक्रम्य मेघप्रतिच्छन्दस्य प्रासादस्याग्रभूमिमारोपितः।

राजा—(उत्थाय।) **मा तावत्। ममापि सत्त्वैरभिभूयन्ते गृहाः। अथवा।**

अहन्यहन्यात्मन एव ताव-
ज्ज्ञातुं प्रमादस्खलितं न शक्यम्।
प्रजासु कः केन पथा प्रयाती-
त्यशेषतो वेदितुमस्ति शक्तिः॥ २६॥

(नेपथ्ये।)

भो वअस्स, अविहा अविहा। भो वयस्य, अविहा अविहा।

SĀNUMATĪ. Alas, alas! Though the light is there he is suffering the evil effects of darkness by reason of the intervening screen. I can make him happy even now. But I have heard from the mouth of the mother of the great Indra as she was consoling Śakuntalā, that the Gods themselves, longing for their portions of the sacrifice, will so devise it that before long the husband will welcome his true wife. It is, therefore, proper to wait for this period. In the meanwhile, I will comfort the dear girl with the news. (*Exit by flying through the sky.*)

(*Behind the scenes*)

Help, help!

KING (*Coming to himself and listening*). Ah, that sounds like the distressed cry of Māṭhavya. Who is there, ho!

(*Entering*) PORTRESS (*Confusedly*). Let your Majesty save your friend who is fallen into danger.

KING. Who has humbled Māṇavaka?

PORTRESS. Some invisible spirit, who having overpowered him took him to the top-most floor of the Meghapraticchanda palace.

KING. (*Rising*). This must not be. How, even my house is infested by evil spirits! Or,

> Even when the mischiefs occasioned by one's own negligence from day to day are scarcely known, how then can one have the power to know fully what path each of my subjects is treading? (26)

(*Behind the scenes.*)

O friend, alas! alas!

राजा—(गतिभेदेन परिक्रामन् ।) **सखे, न भेतव्यं न भेतव्यम् ।**

(नेपथ्ये ।)

(पुनस्तदेव पठित्वा ।) **कहं ण भाइस्सं । एस मं को वि पच्छावणदसिरोहरं इक्खुं विअ तिण्हभङ्गं करेदि ।** कथं न भेष्यामि । एष मां कोऽपि पश्चादवनतशिरोधरमिक्षुमिव त्रिभङ्गं करोति ।

राजा—(सदृष्टिक्षेपम् ।) **धनुस्तावत् ।**

(प्रविश्य शार्ङ्गहस्ता ।)

यवनी—**भट्टा, एदं हत्थावावसहिदं सरासणं ।** भर्तः, एतद्धस्तावापसहितं शरासनम् ।

(राजा सशरं धनुरादत्ते ।)

(नेपथ्ये ।)

एष त्वामभिनवकण्ठशोणितार्थी
शार्दूलः पशुमिव हन्मि चेष्टमानम् ।
आर्तानां भयमपनेतुमात्तधन्वा
दुष्यन्तस्तव शरणं भवत्विदानीम् ॥ २७ ॥

राजा—(सरोषम् ।) **कथं मामेवोद्दिशति । तिष्ठ कुणपाशन, त्वमिदानीं न भविष्यसि ।** (शार्ङ्गमारोप्य ।) **वेत्रवति, सोपानमार्गमादेशय ।**

प्रतीहारी—**इदो इदो देवो ।** इत इतो देवः ।

(सर्वे सत्वरमुपसर्पन्ति ।)

राजा—(समन्ताद्विलोक्य ।) **शून्यं खल्विदम् ।**

(नेपथ्ये ।)

अविहा अविहा । अहं अत्तभवन्तं पेक्खामि । तुमं मं ण पेक्खसि । बिडालग्गहीदो मूसओ विअ णिरासो म्हि जीविदे संवुत्तो । अविहा अविहा । अहमत्रभवन्तं पश्यामि । त्वं मां न पश्यसि । विडालगृहीतो मूषिक इव निराशोऽस्मि जीविते संवृत्तः ।

राजा—**भोस्तिरस्करिणीगर्वित, मदीयं शस्त्रं त्वां द्रक्ष्यति । एष तमिषुं संदधे,**

यो हनिष्यति वध्यं त्वां रक्ष्यं रक्षति च द्विजम् ।
हंसो हि क्षीरमादत्ते तन्मिश्रा वर्जयत्यपः ॥ २८ ॥

KING. (*Moving round with an altered gait*). Fear not, my friend, fear not. (*Behind the scenes.*)

(*After repeating the same*). Fear not? There is some one trying to break me into pieces violently like a sugarcane having bent back my neck.

KING. (*Looking about*). Hola! my bow—

(*Entering, bow is hand*) YAVANI. My lord, here is the bow with the arm-guard.

(*The King takes the bow and arrows.*)

(*Behind the scenes*) Now, thirsting for the fresh blood from the neck, I will slay thee struggling as a tiger (slays) a beast. Let Duṣyanta now, who takes his bow to remove the fear of the oppressed, be thy protector. (27)

KING. (*Angrily*). How, he even refers to me! Stay, carrion-eater; you shall die now. (*Stringing his bow*). Vetravati, show the way to the stairs.

PORTRESS. This way, this way, your Majesty.

(*All advance in haste.*)

KING (*Looking around*). There is, indeed, no one here.

(*Behind the scenes.*)

Alas! Alas! I see your honour, but you see me not. I despair of my life like a mouse caught by a cat.

KING. You, who pride yourself on your power which renders you invisible, my weapon will see you; here I will fix an arrow,

Which will slay you that deserve death and save the Brahmin who deserves to be saved. The swan drinks up the milk and leaves the water which has been mingled with it. (28)

(इत्यस्त्रं संधत्ते ।)

(ततः प्रविशति विदूषकमुत्सृज्य मातलिः ।)

मातलिः—

कृताः शरव्यं हरिणा तवासुराः
शरासनं तेषु विकृष्यतामिदम् ।
प्रसादसौम्यानि सतां सुहृज्जने
पतन्ति चक्षूंषि न दारुणाः शराः ॥ २९ ॥

राजा—(अस्त्रमुपसंहरन् ।) अये मातलिः । स्वागतं महेन्द्रसारथये ।

(प्रविश्य ।)

विदूषकः—अहं जेण इट्ठिपसुमारं मारिदो सो इमिणा साअदेण अहिणन्दीअदि । अहं येनेष्टिपशुमारं मारितः सोऽनेन स्वागतेनाभिनन्द्यते ।

मातलिः—(सस्मितम् ।) आयुष्मन्, श्रूयतां यदस्मि हरिणा भवत्सकाशं प्रेषितः ।

राजा—अवहितोऽस्मि ।

मातलिः—अस्ति कालनेमिप्रसूतिर्दुर्जयो नाम दानवगणः ।

राजा—अस्ति । श्रुतपूर्वं मया नारदात् ।

मातलिः—

सख्युस्ते स किल शतक्रतोरजय्य-
स्तस्य त्वं रणशिरसि स्मृतो निहन्ता ।
उच्छेत्तुं प्रभवति यन्न सप्तसप्ति-
स्तन्नैशं तिमिरमपाकरोति चन्द्रः ॥ ३० ॥

स भवानात्तशस्त्र एव इदानीं तमैन्द्ररथमारुह्य विजयाय प्रतिष्ठताम् ।

राजा—अनुगृहीतोऽहमनया मघवतः संभावनया । अथ माठव्यं प्रति भवता किमेवं प्रत्युक्तम् ।

(*Aims his arrow.*)

(*Then enter Mātali leaving the Vidūṣaka.*)

MĀTALI.

The demons are made by Indra thy mark; against them let thy bow be drawn. The good cast not cruel shafts, but eyes soft with kindness on their friends. (29)

KING. (*Withdrawing his arrow*). Ah, Mātali! Welcome to the charioteer of the great Indra.

(*Entering*) VIDŪṢAKA. What, he by whom I was being butchered like a sacrificial animal, is greeted by him with a welcome!

MĀTALI (*Smiling*). Hear, long-lived one, on what errand I am dispatched to you by Indra.

KING. I am attentive.

MĀTALI. There is a host of demons, called Durjaya —the brood of Kālanemi.

KING. Yes; I have heard so from Nārada.

MĀTALI. Thy friend Indra, it is said, is unable to quell them; but that thou wouldst smite them in the front of battle. That nocturnal darkness, which the Sun is not able to dispel, is scattered by the Moon. (30)

Therefore, grasping thy weapon thus, mount the car of Indra, and set forth for victory.

KING. I am grateful for the honour which Indra shows me. But why did you act thus towards Māṭhavya?

मातलिः—तदपि कथ्यते । किंचिन्निमित्तादपि मनःसंतापादायुष्मान्मया विक्लवो दृष्टः । पश्चात्कोपयितुमायुष्मन्तं तथा कृतवानस्मि । कुतः ।

ज्वलति चलितेन्धनोऽग्निर्विप्रकृतः पन्नगः फणां कुरुते ।
प्रायः स्वं महिमानं क्षोभात्प्रतिपद्यते हि जनः ॥ ३१ ॥

राजा—(जनान्तिकम् ।) वयस्य, अनतिक्रमणीया दिवस्पतेराज्ञा । तदत्र परिगतार्थं कृत्वा मद्वचनादमात्यपिशुनं ब्रूहि ।

त्वन्मतिः केवला तावत्परिपालयतु प्रजाः ।
अधिज्यमिदमन्यस्मिन्कर्मणि व्यापृतं धनुः ॥ ३२ ॥

इति ।

विदूषकः—जं भवं आणवेदि । (इति निष्क्रान्तः ।) यद्भवानाज्ञापयति ।

मातलिः—आयुष्मान्रथमारोहतु ।

(राजा रथाधिरोहणं नाटयति ।)

(इति निष्क्रान्ताः सर्वे ।)

षष्ठोऽङ्कः ।

MĀTALI. I will tell that. I perceived that by some inner sorrow caused by one thing or another, the long-lived one was distressed. Thereafter I acted thus to provoke the wrath of the long-lived one. For

> The fire blazes when the fuel is stirred ; the serpent, when provoked, expands its hood ; for a man generally regains his proper greatness, under some provocation. (31)

KING. (*Aside*). Friend, inviolable is the command of heaven's lord. So acquaint the minister Piśuna with the matter and tell him in my name—

> Let thy wisdom alone secure my people from harm, (while) this braced bow has a different employment. (32)

VIDŪṢAKA. As your Honour commands. (*Exit.*)

MĀTALI. Let the long-lived one mount the chariot. (*The king acts mounting the chariot.*)

Exeunt Omnes

End of Act VI

सप्तमोऽङ्कः ।

(ततः प्रविशत्याकाशयानेन रथाधिरूढो राजा मातलिश्च ।)

राजा—मातले, अनुष्ठितनिदेशोऽपि मघवतः सत्क्रियाविशेषादनुपयुक्तमिवात्मानं समर्थये ।

मातलिः—(सस्मितम् ।) आयुष्मन्, उभयमप्यपरितोषं समर्थये ।

प्रथमोपकृतं मरुत्वतः
प्रतिपत्त्या लघु मन्यते भवान् ।
गणयत्यवदानविस्मितो
भवतः सोऽपि न सत्क्रियागुणान् ॥ १ ॥

राजा—मातले, मा, मैवम् । स खलु मनोरथानामप्यभूमिर्विसर्जनावसरसत्कारः । मम हि दिवौकसां समक्षमर्धासनोपवेशितस्य

अन्तर्गतप्रार्थनमन्तिकस्थं
जयन्तमुद्वीक्ष्य कृतस्मितेन ।
आमृष्टवक्षोहरिचन्दनाङ्का
मन्दारमाला हरिणा पिनद्धा ॥ २ ॥

मातलिः—किमिव नामायुष्मानमरेश्वरान्नार्हति । पश्य ।

ACT VII

(Then enter king seated in a chariot that flies through the air, and Mātali.)

KING. Mātali, although I have executed the mission which Indra gave me, yet considering the special welcome he accorded me, I think myself to have been of very little service to him.

MĀTALI (*Smiling*). Long-lived one, I think neither of you is satisfied.

> Your Highness considers the prior benefit (conferred by you) on Indra as trifling (in comparison) with the honour (done by him to you); while he reckons as of little account the special honours (bestowed) on your Highness, being filled with wonder at your heroic achievement. (1)

KING. Mātali, no, say not so; for the honour done me at parting surpassed my warmest expectations. For making me sit on half of his throne before the eyes of the gods,

> And smiling to see Jayanta, who stood near him, filled with an inward longing (for the same honour), a wreath of Mandāra flowers, marked with the yellow-sandal from its rubbing on his breast, was by Indra placed about my neck. (2)

MĀTALI. But what does not the long-lived one deserve from the king of the gods? See

सुखपरस्य हरेरुभयैः कृतं
त्रिदिवमुद्धृतदानवकण्टकम् ।
तव शरैरधुना नतपर्वभिः
पुरुषकेसरिणश्च पुरा नखैः ॥ ३ ॥

राजा—अत्र खलु शतक्रतोरेव महिमा स्तुत्यः ।

सिध्यन्ति कर्मसु महत्स्वपि यन्नियोज्याः
संभावनागुणमवेहि तमीश्वराणाम् ।
किंवाभविष्यदरुणस्तमसां विभेत्ता
तं चेत्सहस्रकिरणो धुरि नाकरिष्यत् ॥ ४ ॥

मातलिः—सदृशमेवैतत् । (स्तोकमन्तरमतीत्य ।) आयुष्मन्, इतः पश्य नाकपृष्ठप्रतिष्ठितस्य सौभाग्यमात्मयशसः ।

विच्छित्तिशेषैः सुरसुन्दरीणां
वर्णैरमी कल्पलतांशुकेषु ।
विचिन्त्य गीतक्षममर्थजातं
दिवौकसस्त्वच्चरितं लिखन्ति ॥ ५ ॥

राजा—मातले, असुरसंप्रहारोत्सुकेन पूर्वेद्युर्दिवमधिरोहता न लक्षितः स्वर्गमार्गः । कतरस्मिन्मरुतां पथि वर्तामहे ।

मातलिः—

त्रिस्रोतसं वहति यो गगनप्रतिष्ठां
ज्योतींषि वर्तयति च प्रविभक्तरश्मिः ।

The heaven of ease-loving Indra has been made free from the thorns of Danu's race by two (means) : now by your smooth-jointed shafts, and formerly by the claws of the man-lion. (3)

KING. In the present case, really, the greatness of Indra alone deserves praise.

That servants succeed even in great enterprises—know that to be the effect of the honour shown to them by their masters. Could Aruṇa dispel the shades of night if the thousand-rayed one had not placed him in front (of his chariot ?) (4)

MĀTALI. That is quite worthy (of you). (*Going a little distance*). Long-lived one, see the full exaltation of your glory, which (now) rides on the back of heaven !

With the residue of colours used by nymphs of heaven to adorn their persons, these dwellers of heaven are writing your exploits on vestments of the heavenly trees, thinking out verses suitable for singing. (5)

KING. Mātali, In my eagerness for battle with the demons, I did not observe the way to heaven, while ascending the sky the other day. In what path of the winds are we now journeying ?

MĀTALI.

They call this the way of the wind Parivaha, which is freed from all darkness by being the second step of Viṣṇu, and which bears the

तस्य द्वितीयहरिविक्रमनिस्तमस्कं
वायोरिमं परिवहस्य वदन्ति मार्गम् ॥ ६ ॥

राजा—मातले, अतः खलु सबाह्यान्तःकरणो ममान्तरात्मा प्रसीदति। (रथाङ्गमवलोक्य।) मेघपदवीमवतीर्णौ स्वः।

मातलिः—कथमवगम्यते।

राजा—

अयमरविवरेभ्यश्चातकैर्निष्पतद्भि-
र्हरिभिरचिरभासां तेजसा चानुलिप्तैः।
गतमुपरि घनानां वारिगर्भोदराणां
पिशुनयति रथस्ते सीकरक्लिन्ननेमिः ॥ ७ ॥

मातलिः—क्षणादायुष्मान्स्वाधिकारभूमौ वर्तिष्यते।

राजा—(अधोऽवलोक्य।) वेगावतरणादाश्चर्यदर्शनः संलक्ष्यते मनुष्यलोकः। तथाहि।

शैलानामवरोहतीव शिखरादुन्मज्जतां मेदिनी
पर्णाभ्यन्तरलीनतां विजहति स्कन्धोदयात्पादपाः।
संतानैस्तनुभावनष्टसलिला व्यक्तिं भजन्त्यापगाः
केनाप्युत्क्षिपतेव पश्य भुवनं मत्पार्श्वमानीयते ॥ ८ ॥

मातलिः—साधु दृष्टम्। (सबहुमानमवलोक्य।) अहो, उदाररमणीया पृथिवी।

triple-streamed river flowing through the sky, and causes the luminaries to roll in a circle diffusing their beams. (6)

KING. Mātali, that is why my inner self, with the internal and external senses, feels a pleasurable repose. (*Looking at the wheel of the chariot*). We have descended to the region of the clouds.

MĀTALI. How is that perceived?

KING.

This your chariot, with the rims of its wheels bedewed with spray indicates by the Cātakas flying through the interstices of its spokes, and by the horses lapped in lightning-flashes that we are now moving over clouds pregnant with showers. (7)

MĀTALI. In a moment, the long-lived one will be in the land under his rule.

KING. (*Looking down*). Through our quick descent, the world of men appears a wonderful sight. For

The earth appears to descend from the summits of mountains that emerge upwards; the trees no longer appear to be enveloped in their foliage, as their trunks heave in sight; the rivers whose waters were lost to view from their narrowness become visible from the expansion (of their waters). Behold the earth is being brought near me as if by some one throwing it upwards. (8)

MĀTALI. Well-observed. (*Looking with reverence*). How grand, how noble is the earth!

राजा—मातले, कतमोऽयं पूर्वापरसमुद्रावगाढः कनकरसनिस्यन्दी सांध्य इव मेघपरिघः सानुमानालोक्यते ।

मातलिः—आयुष्मन्, एष खलु हेमकूटो नाम किंपुरुषपर्वतस्तपःसंसिद्धिक्षेत्रम् । पश्य ।

स्वायंभुवान्मरीचेर्यः प्रबभूव प्रजापतिः ।
सुरासुरगुरुः सोऽत्र सपत्नीकस्तपस्यति ॥ ९ ॥

राजा—तेन ह्यनतिक्रमणीयानि श्रेयांसि । प्रदक्षिणीकृत्य भगवन्तं गन्तुमिच्छामि ।

मातलिः—प्रथमः कल्पः ।

(नाट्येनावतीर्णौ ।)

राजा—(सविस्मयम् ।)

उपोढशब्दा न रथाङ्गनेमयः
प्रवर्तमानं न च दृश्यते रजः ।
अभूतलस्पर्शतया निरुन्धत-
स्तवावतीर्णोऽपि रथो न लक्ष्यते ॥ १० ॥

मातलिः—एतावानेव शतक्रतोरायुष्मतश्च विशेषः ।

राजा—मातले, कतमस्मिन्प्रदेशे मारीचाश्रमः ।

मातलिः—(हस्तेन दर्शयति ।)

वल्मीकाग्रनिमग्नमूर्तिरुरसा संदष्टसर्पत्वचा
कण्ठे जीर्णलताप्रतानवलयेनात्यर्थसंपीडितः ।

KING. Mātali, what mountain is seen yonder, that dives into the eastern and western sea, dripping with liquid gold, like a bank of evening cloud?

MĀTALI. Long-lived one, this is the mountain Hema-Kūṭa of the Kiṁpuruṣas—a place where the powers of penance are fully attained. See,

> That Prajāpati who sprang from Mārīci, the son of the self-existent, father of the gods and demons, practises penance here along with his wife. (9)

KING. Well then (opportunities for obtaining) blessings must not be neglected. It is my desire to proceed after walking humbly round the holy sage.

MĀTALI. An excellent idea.

(*Gesticulate descending.*)

KING. (*Wonderingly*).

> The rims of the chariot-wheels produce no sound; nor does dust appear to be raised; and the chariot, as you rein-in (the steeds), is scarcely marked to have descended to the earth, when it has really done so, on account of its not touching the surface of the earth. (10)

MĀTALI. That is all the difference between Indra and the long-lived one.

KING. Mātali, where is the holy retreat of Mārīca?

MĀTALI (*Pointing with his hand*).

> There where stands yonder sage, facing the Sun's orb, inmovable as a pollard half buried in an ant-hill, with his breast closely encircled by the

अंसव्यापि शकुन्तनीडनिचितं बिभ्रज्जटामण्डलं
यत्र स्थाणुरिवाचलो मुनिरसावभ्यर्कबिम्बं स्थितः ॥ ११ ॥

राजा—नमस्ते कष्टतपसे ।

मातलिः—(संयतप्रग्रहं रथं कृत्वा ।) महाराज, एतावदितिपरिवर्धितमन्दारवृक्षं प्रजापतेराश्रमं प्रविष्टौ स्वः ।

राजा—स्वर्गादधिकतरं निर्वृतिस्थानम् । अमृतह्रदमिवावगाढोऽस्मि ।

मातलिः—(रथं स्थापयित्वा ।) अवतरत्वायुष्मान् ।

राजा—(अवतीर्य ।) मातले, भवान्कथमिदानीम् ।

मातलिः—संयन्त्रितो मया रथः । वयमप्यवतरामः । (तथा कृत्वा ।) इत आयुष्मन् । (परिक्रम्य ।) दृश्यन्तामत्रभवतामृषीणां तपोवनभूमयः ।

राजा—ननु विस्मयादवलोकयामि ।

प्राणानामनिलेन वृत्तिरुचिता सत्कल्पवृक्षे वने
तोये काञ्चनपद्मरेणुकपिशे धर्माभिषेकक्रिया ।
ध्यानं रत्नशिलातलेषु विबुधस्त्रीसंनिधौ संयमो
यत्काङ्क्षन्ति तपोभिरन्यमुनयस्तस्मिंस्तपस्यन्त्यमी ॥ १२ ॥

मातलिः—उत्सर्पिणी खलु महतां प्रार्थना । (परिक्रम्य आकाशे ।) अये वृद्धशाकल्य, किमनुतिष्ठति भगवान्मारीचः । किं

slough of a serpent; his neck is heavily squeezed by a coil of the tendrils of old creepers; and he has a mass of matted hair that covers his shoulders and is filled with the nests of birds. (11)

KING. Bow to thee of such austere devotion.

MĀTALI (*Drawing in the reins of the chariot*). O king, here now we have entered the sanctuary of the Prajāpati, in which the Mandāra-trees are reared by Aditi.

KING. It is place more delightful than heaven; I seem plunged in a pool of nectar.

MĀTALI (*Stopping the chariot*). Let the long-lived one descend.

KING. (*Descending*). But what of you, now Mātali?

MĀTALI. I have stopped the chariot. I too will alight. (*Doing so*). This way, long-lived one. (*Walking round*). Behold the holy retreat of the revered sage.

KING. Indeed I am looking on with amazement.

Here in this forest of Kalpa-trees, they draw from air life's necessary sustenance; in waters yellow with the golden dust of the lotus, they perform ablutions for religious vows; on jewelled slabs, they meditate; and restrain their passions in the midst of celestial nymphs: they practise penance in a place which other sages by their austerities seek to win. (12)

MĀTALI. Verily the aspirations of the great ever mount upwards. (*Walking about; in the air*). O Vṛddhaśākalya how is the holy Mārīca occupied? What do you say? Being questioned by Aditi respecting the

ब्रवीषि। दाक्षायण्या पतिव्रताधर्ममधिकृत्य पृष्टस्तस्यै महर्षिपत्नी-सहितायै कथयतीति।

राजा—(कर्णं दत्त्वा।) अये, प्रतिपाल्यावसराः खलु मुनयः।

मातलिः—(राजानमवलोक्य।) अस्मिन्नशोकवृक्षमूले तावदास्तामायुष्मान्, यावत्त्वामिन्द्रगुरवे निवेदयितुमन्तरान्वेषी भवामि।

राजा—यथा भवान्मन्यते। (इति स्थितः।)

मातलिः—आयुष्मन्, साधयाम्यहम्। (इति निष्क्रान्तः।)

राजा—(निमित्तं सूचयित्वा।)

मनोरथाय नाशंसे किं बाहो स्पन्दसे वृथा।
पूर्वावधीरितं श्रेयो दुःखं हि परिवर्तते॥ १३॥

(नेपथ्ये।)

मा क्खु चावलं करेहि। कहं गदो एव्व अत्तणो पकिदिं। मा खलु चापलं कुरु। कथं गत एवात्मनः प्रकृतिम्।

राजा—(कर्णं दत्त्वा।) अभूमिरियमविनयस्य। को नु खल्वेष निषिध्यते। (शब्दानुसारेणावलोक्य। सविस्मयम्।) अये, को नु खल्वयमनुबध्यमानस्तपस्विनीभ्यामबालसत्वो बालः।

अर्धपीतस्तनं मातुरामर्दक्लिष्टकेसरम्।
प्रक्रीडितुं सिंहशिशुं बलात्कारेण कर्षति॥ १४॥

(ततः प्रविशति यथानिर्दिष्टकर्मा तपस्विनीभ्यां बालः।)

बालः—जिम्भ सिङ्घ, दन्ताइं दे गणइस्सं। जृम्भस्व सिंह, दन्तांस्ते गणयिष्ये।

duties of a faithful wife, he is explaining them to her in company with the wives of the great sages?

KING (*Listening*). Ah! We must await the leisure of saints.

MĀTALI (*Looking at the king*). Let the long-lived one rest at the foot of the Aśoka tree; in the meanwhile I will wait for an opportune moment to announce your arrival to the father of Indra.

KING. As your Honour thinks. (*Stands.*)

MĀTALI. Long-lived one, I will depart. (*Exit.*)

KING (*Indicating an omen*).

I do not hope to obtain my desire; why, O my arm, dost thou vainly throb? Happiness that was scorned before, surely turns into pain. (13).

(*Behind the scenes*)

Do not be so wild. What! Gone already to your own nature!

KING (*Listening*). This is no place, surely, for any rudeness. Who can be thus rebuked? (*Looking in the direction of the sound; in surprise*). Who is this child, closely attended by two female-ascetics—a child that possesses not the strength of a mere child?

He forcibly drags towards him, for sport, a lion's whelp that has but half-sucked its mother's dug, and has its mane ruffled by pulling. (14)

(*Enter a boy acting as described, and two female ascetics.*)

BOY. Open thy mouth, lion, that I may count thy teeth.

प्रथमा—अविणीद, किं णो अपच्चणिव्विसेसाणि सत्ताणि विप्पअरेसि। हन्त, वड्ढइ दे संरम्भो। ठाणे क्खु इसिजणेण सव्वद-मणो त्ति किदणामहेओ सि। अविनीत, किं नोऽपत्यनिर्विशेषाणि सत्त्वानि विप्रकरोषि। हन्त, वर्धते तव संरम्भः। स्थाने खलु ऋषिजनेन सर्वदमन इति कृतनामधेयोऽसि।

राजा—किं नु खलु बालेऽस्मिन्नौरस इव पुत्रे स्निह्यति मे मनः। नूनमनपत्यता मां वत्सलयति।

द्वितीया—एसा क्खु केसरिणी तुमं लङ्घेदि जइ से पुत्तअं ण मुञ्चेसि। एषा खलु केसरिणी त्वां लङ्घयिष्यति यदि तस्याः पुत्रकं न मुञ्चसि।

बालः—(सस्मितम्।) **अम्हहे, बलिअं क्खु भीदो म्हि।** (इत्यधरं दर्शयति।) अहो, बलीयः खलु भीतोऽस्मि।

राजा—

महतस्तेजसो बीजं बालोऽयं प्रतिभाति मे।
स्फुलिङ्गावस्थया वह्निरेधापेक्षा इव स्थितः॥ १५॥

प्रथमा—वच्छ, एदं बालमिइन्दअं मुञ्च। अवरं दे कीलणअं दाइस्सं। वत्स, एनं बालमृगेन्द्रं मुञ्च। अपरं ते क्रीडनकं दास्यामि।

बालः—कहिं। देहि णं। (इति हस्तं प्रसारयति।) कुत्र। देह्येतत्।

राजा—कथं चक्रवर्तिलक्षणमप्यनेन धार्यते। तथा ह्यस्य

प्रलोभ्यवस्तुप्रणयप्रसारितो
विभाति जालग्रथिताङ्गुलिः करः।
अलक्ष्यपत्रान्तरमिद्धरागया
नवोषसा भिन्नमिवैकपङ्कजम्॥ १६॥

द्वितीया—सुव्वदे, ण सक्को एसो वाआमेत्तेण विरमाविदुं। गच्छ तुमं। ममकेरए उडए मक्कण्डेअस्स इसिकुमारअस्स वण्ण-चित्तिदो मित्तिआमोरओ चिट्ठदि। तं से उवहर। सुव्रते, न शक्य एष वाचामात्रेण विरमयितुम्। गच्छ त्वम्। मदीय उटजे मार्कण्डेयस्यर्षि-कुमारस्य वर्णचित्रितो मृत्तिकामयूरस्तिष्ठति। तमस्योपहर।

प्रथमा—तह। (इति निष्क्रान्ता) तथा।

FIRST. Naughty boy, why dost thou torment the animals whom we cherish as if they were our own offspring? Ha! thou art getting more wild. Aptly have the sages named thee Sarvadamana.

KING. Ah, what means it that my heart inclines to this boy as if he were my own son? No doubt my childlessness makes me soft-hearted.

SECOND. This lioness will surely attack thee, if thou release not her whelp.

BOY (*Smiling*). Oh, I am indeed dreadfully scared! (*Pouts his under-lip.*)

KING. This boy appears to me to be the germ
of heroic valour and looks like fire in a tiny
spark waiting only for fuel (to blaze up). (15)

FIRST. Child, set at liberty this little lion; and I will give thee another plaything.

BOY. Where is it? Give it me. (*Extends his hands.*)

KING. How, he bears the marks of universal royalty! Thus his

Hand extended in eagerness to grasp the
coveted object, with fingers connected by a
web, appears like a single lotus, the interspaces
of whose petals are not visible, blown open by
the early dawn with its glow enkindled. (16)

SECOND. Suvratā, it is not possible to stop him by mere words. Go; in my cottage you will find a painted clay peacock that belongs to the hermit-boy Mārkaṇḍeya. Give that to him.

FIRST. As you say. (*Exit.*)

बालः—इमिणा एव्व दाव कीलिस्सं । (इति तापसीं विलोक्य हसति ।) अनेनैव तावत्क्रीडिष्यामि ।

राजा—स्पृहयामि खलु दुर्ललितायास्मै ।

आलक्ष्यदन्तमुकुलाननिमित्तहासै-
रव्यक्तवर्णरमणीयवचःप्रवृत्तीन् ।
अङ्काश्रयप्रणयिनस्तनयान्वहन्तो
धन्यास्तदङ्गरजसा मलिनीभवन्ति ॥ १७ ॥

तापसी—होदु । ण मं अअं गणेदि । (पार्श्वमवलोकयति ।) को एत्थ इसिकुमाराणं । (राजानमवलोक्य ।) भद्दमुह, एहि दाव । मोएहि इमिणा दुम्मोअहत्थग्गाहेण डिम्भलीलाए बाहीअमाणं बालमिइन्दअं । भवतु । न मामयं गणयति । कोऽत्र ऋषिकुमाराणाम् । भद्रमुख, एहि तावत् । मोचयानेन दुर्मोकहस्तग्रहेण डिम्भलील्या बाध्यमानं बालमृगेन्द्रम् ।

राजा—(उपगम्य । सस्मितम् ।) अयि भो महर्षिपुत्र ।

एवमाश्रमविरुद्धवृत्तिना
संयमः किमिति जन्मतस्त्वया ।
सत्त्वसंश्रयसुखोऽपि दूष्यते
कृष्णसर्पशिशुनेव चन्दनम् ॥ १८ ॥

तापसी—भद्दमुह, ण क्खु अअं इसिकुमारओ । भद्रमुख, न खल्वयं ऋषिकुमारः ।

राजा—आकारसदृशं चेष्टितमेवास्य कथयति । स्थानप्रत्ययात्तु वयमेवंतर्किणः । (यथाभ्यर्थितमनुतिष्ठन्बालस्पर्शमुपलभ्य । आत्मगतम् ।)

अनेन कस्यापि कुलाङ्कुरेण
स्पृष्टस्य गात्रेषु सुखं ममैवम् ।
कां निर्वृतिं चेतसि तस्य कुर्या-
द्यस्यायमङ्कात्कृतिनः प्ररूढः ॥ १९ ॥

BOY. In the meanwhile, I will play with this. (*Looks at the hermit-woman and laughs.*)

KING. How my heart goes out to this unmanagable child!

> Blessed are they who, carrying their sons that fondly seek their laps, with bud-like teeth that slightly appear in their causeless smiles, lisping their charming inarticulate prattle, are soiled by the dust of their limbs. (17)

HERMIT-WOMAN. Well, he does not mind me. (*Looks back*). Which one of the hermit-boys is here? (*Looking at the king*). Come, gentle sir, and free this lion-cub being tormented in childish sport by this child from whose grasp it is difficult to disengage it.

KING. (*Approaching; smilingly*). O son of some great sage,

> Why is it, that by thee acting in a way opposed to the hermitage is befouled, from thy very birth that virtue of forbearance which delights in the protection of animals like the sandal tree by the black-serpent's brood? (18)

HERMIT-WOMAN. But, good sir, he is not the son of a sage.

KING. His actions, indeed, which are conformable to his appearance bespeak it. But I took that view from the evidence of the place. (*Acting as requested, and feeling the boy's touch, to himself*).

> If it gives me such delight to touch the limbs of the child who is the scion of some stranger's family, what rapture will arise in the heart of that happy man from whose body he sprang? (19)

तापसी—(उभौ निर्वर्ण्य ।) **अच्छरिअं अच्छरिअं** । आश्चर्यमाश्चर्यम् ।

राजा—आर्ये, किमिव ।

तापसी—इमस्स बालअस्स दे वि संवादिणी आकिदी त्ति विम्हाविदम्हि । अपरिइदस्य वि दे अप्पडिलोमो संवुत्तो त्ति । अस्य बालकस्य तेऽपि संवादिन्याकृतिरिति विस्मापितास्मि । अपरिचितस्यापि तेऽप्रतिलोमः संवृत्त इति ।

राजा—(बालकमुपलालयन् ।) **नचेन्मुनिकुमारोऽयम्, अथ कोऽस्य व्यपदेशः ।**

तापसी—पुरुवंसो । पुरुवंशः ।

राजा—(आत्मगतम् ।) **कथमेकान्वयो मम । अतः खलु मदनुकारिणमेनमत्रभवती मन्यते । अस्त्येतत्पौरवाणामन्त्यं कुलव्रतम् ।**

भवनेषु रसाधिकेषु पूर्वं
क्षितिरक्षार्थमुशन्ति ये निवासम् ।
नियतैकयतिव्रतानि पश्चा-
त्तरुमूलानि गृहीभवन्ति तेषाम् ॥ २० ॥

(प्रकाशम् ।) **न पुनरात्मगत्या मानुषाणामेष विषयः ।**

तापसी—जह भद्दमुहो भणादि । अच्छरासंबन्धेण इमस्स जणणी एत्थ देवगुरुणो तवोवणे पसूदा । यथा भद्रमुखो भणति । अप्सरःसंबन्धेनास्य जनन्यत्र देवगुरोस्तपोवने प्रसूता ।

राजा—(अपवार्य ।) **हन्त, द्वितीयमिदमाशाजननम् ।** (प्रकाशम् ।) **अथ सा तत्रभवती किमाख्यस्य राजर्षेः पत्नी ।**

तापसी—को तस्स धम्मदारपरिच्चाइणो णाम संकीतिदुं चिन्तिस्सदि । कस्तस्य धर्मदारपरित्यागिनो नाम संकीर्तयितुं चिन्तयिष्यति ।

HERMIT-WOMAN (*gazing at both*). Oh wonderful !

KING. What is it, holy woman ?

HERMIT-WOMAN. I am astonished to mark the resemblance between your form and the child's. And although he had no (former) acquaintance with you, yet he did not take any dislike to you.

KING (*Fondling the child*). If he is not the son of a hermit, what is his family ?

HERMIT-WOMAN. The family of Puru.

KING. (*To himself*). How, he belongs to the same family as mine ? That is how the lady thinks he resembles me. For this is the last family-vow of the descendants of Puru.

> To them who dwell at first in palaces which abound in all the pleasures of sense, for protecting the world, the roots of trees where the one vow of asceticism is rigidly observed serve as homes afterwards. (20)

(*Aloud*) But the place is inaccessible to mortals by their own power.

HERMIT-WOMAN. As the good sir says. But in consequence of her relationship to a nymph, his mother brought him forth in the pious grove of the father of the gods.

KING (*To himself*). Ah, this is a second ground of hope. (*Aloud*). What is the name of the virtuous monarch who claims the noble lady for his wife ?

HERMIT-WOMAN. Who, indeed, would think of speaking his name who rejected his lawful wife ?

राजा— (स्वगतम् ।) **इयं खलु कथा मामेव लक्ष्यीकरोति । यदि तावदस्य शिशोर्मातरं नामतः पृच्छामि । अथवानार्यः परदारव्यवहारः ।**

(प्रविश्य मृण्मयूरहस्ता ।)

तापसी—सव्वदमण, सउन्दलावण्णं पेक्ख । सर्वदमन, शकुन्तलावण्यं प्रेक्षस्व ।

बालः—(सदृष्टिक्षेपम् ।) **कहिं वा मे अज्जू** । कुत्र वा मम माता ।

उभे—णामसारिस्सेण वञ्चिदो माउवच्छलो । नामसादृश्येन वञ्चितो मातृवत्सलः ।

द्वितीया—वच्छ, इमस्स मित्तिआमोरअस्स रम्मत्तणं देक्खत्ति भणिदो सि । वत्स, अस्य मृत्तिकामयूरस्य रम्यत्वं पश्येति भणितोऽसि ।

राजा—(आत्मगतम् ।) **किंवा शकुन्तलेत्यस्य मातुराख्या । सन्ति पुनर्नामधेयसादृश्यानि । अपि नाम मृगतृष्णिकेव नाममात्रप्रस्तावो मे विषादाय कल्पते ।**

बालः—अज्जुए, रोअदि मे एसो भद्दमोरओ । (इति क्रीडनकमादत्ते ।) मातः, रोचते म एष भद्रमयूरः ।

प्रथमा—(विलोक्य सोद्वेगम् ।) **अम्हहे, रक्खाकरण्डअं से मणिबन्धे ण दीसदि** । अहो, रक्षाकरण्डकमस्य मणिबन्धे न दृश्यते ।

राजा—अलमलमावेगेन । नन्विदमस्य सिंहशावविमर्दात्परिभ्रष्टम् । (इत्यादातुमिच्छति ।)

उभे—मा क्खु एदं अवलम्बअ । कहं गहिदं णेण (इति विस्मयादुरोनिहितहस्ते परस्परमवलोकयतः ।) मा खल्विदमवलम्ब्य । कथं गृहीतमनेन ।

राजा—किमर्थं प्रतिषिद्धा स्मः ।

KING. (*To himself*). This story, really, points at me alone. Suppose I ask the name of the child's mother. But it is against good manners to inquire concerning the wife of another man.

(*Entering with the clay peacock in her hand*). HERMIT-WOMAN. Sarvadamana, look at the bird's beauty—the Śakunta-loveliness.

BOY (*Looking about*). Where is my mamma ?

BOTH. Tenderly loving his mother, how he is deceived by the similarity (of the sound) to her name !

SECOND. Dear boy, thou wast asked to see how pretty the clay-peacock was.

KING. (*To himself*). What, his mother's name is Śakuntalā ! But names are alike. Will it be that the mention of a mere name, like some mirage, would in the end lead to bitter disappointment ?

BOY. Mother, I like this fine peacock. (*Takes up the plaything.*)

FIRST (*Looking ; with alarm*). Oh, the amulet is not on his wrist !

KING. Don't get alarmed. It was dropped while he was struggling with the lion's cub. (*Desires to pick it up.*)

BOTH. Don't take it. How he has already picked it up !

(*They lay their hands on their bosom and gaze with surprise at each other.*)

KING. Why was I forbidden ?

प्रथमा—सुणादु महाराओ । एसा अवराजिदा णाम ओसही इमस्स जादकम्मसमए भअवदा मारीएण दिण्णा । एदं किल मादापिदरो अप्पाणं च वज्जिअ अवरो भूमिपडिदं ण गेण्हादि । शृणोतु महाराजः । एषापराजिता नामौषधिरस्य जातकर्मसमये भगवता मारीचेन दत्ता । एतां किल मातापितरावात्मानं च वर्जयित्वापरो भूमिपतितां न गृह्णाति ।

राजा—अथ गृह्णाति ।

प्रथमा—तदो तं सप्पो भविअ दंसइ । ततस्तं सर्पो भूत्वा दशति ।

राजा—भवतीभ्यां कदाचिदस्याः प्रत्यक्षीकृता विक्रिया ।

उभे—अणेअसो । अनेकशः ।

राजा—(सहर्षम् । आत्मगतम् ।) **कथमिव संपूर्णमपि मे मनोरथं नाभिनन्दामि ।** (इति बालं परिष्वजते ।)

द्वितीया—सुव्वदे, एहि । इमं वुत्तन्तं णिअमव्वावुडाए सउन्दलाए णिवेदेम्ह । सुव्रते, एहि । इम वृत्तान्तं नियमव्यापृतायै शकुन्तलायै निवेदयावः ।

(इति निष्क्रान्ते ।)

बालः—मुञ्च मं । जाव अज्जुए सआसं गमिस्सं । मुञ्च माम् । यावन्मातुः साकाशं गमिष्यामि ।

राजा—पुत्रक, मया सहैव मातरमभिनन्दिष्यसि ।

बालः—मम क्खु तादो दुस्सन्दो । ण तुमं । मम खलु तातो दुष्यन्तः । न त्वम् ।

राजा—(सस्मितम् ।) **एष विवाद एव प्रत्याययति ।**

(ततः प्रविशत्येकवेणीधरा शकुन्तला ।)

शकुन्तला—विआरकाले वि पकिदित्थं सव्वदमणस्स ओसहिं सुणिअ ण मे आसा आसि अत्तणो भाअहेएसु । अहवा जह साणुमदीए आचक्खिदं तह संभावीअदि एदं । विकारकालेऽपि प्रकृतिस्थां सर्वदमनस्यौषधिं श्रुत्वा न म आशासीदात्मनो भागधेयेषु । अथवा यथा सानुमत्याख्यातं तथा संभाव्यत एतत् ।

राजा—(शकुन्तलां विलोक्य ।) **अये, सेयमत्रभवती शकुन्तला । यैषा**

वसने परिधूसरे वसाना
नियमक्षाममुखी धृतैकवेणिः ।

FIRST. Listen, your Majesty. This is the herb Aparājitā given at his birth-rites by the holy Mārīca. They say, that in case it fell to the earth no one but the parents or the boy himself may touch it.

KING. And supposing he takes it?

FIRST. It becomes a serpent and bites him.

KING. Did you ever see it thus transformed?

BOTH. Several times.

KING. (*With joy; to himself*). Why then do I not welcome my hope fulfilled at last? (*Embraces the boy.*)

SECOND. Suvratā, come let us carry the news to Śakuntalā who is engaged in the observance of her vows. (*Exeunt.*)

BOY. Leave me that I might go to my mother.

KING. My child, thou shalt go with me to greet thy mother.

BOY. My father is Duṣyanta, not you.

KING. (*Smiling*). Even this contradiction convinces me.

(*Enter Śakuntalā wearing her hair twisted into a single braid.*)

ŚAKUNTALĀ. Hearing that Sarvadamana's amulet remained in its natural form, even when there was an occasion when it ought to have changed its form, I could scarcely trust my fortunes. Or perhaps as Sānumatī told me, this is possible.

KING. (*Looking at Śakuntalā*). Ah, here is the lady Śakuntalā. She who,

Wearing two dark-grey garments, having a face worn by her vows, and wearing a single

अतिनिष्करुणस्य शुद्धशीला
मम दीर्घं विरहव्रतं बिभर्ति ॥ २१ ॥

शकुन्तला—(पश्चात्तापविवर्णं राजानं दृष्ट्वा ।) ण क्खु अज्जउत्तो विअ । तदो को एसो दाणिं किदरक्खामङ्गलं दारअं मे गत्तसंसग्गेण दूसेदि । न खल्वार्यपुत्र इव । ततः क एष इदानीं कृतरक्षामङ्गलं दारकं मे गात्रसंसर्गेण दूषयति ।

बालः—(मातरमुपेत्य ।) अज्जुए, एसो कोवि पुरिसो मं पुत्तेत्ति आलिङ्गदि । मातः, एष कोऽपि पुरुषो मां पुत्र इत्यालिङ्गति ।

राजा—प्रिये, क्रौर्यमपि मे त्वयि प्रयुक्तमनुकूलपरिणामं संवृत्तम् । यदाहमिदानीं त्वया प्रत्यभिज्ञातमात्मानं पश्यामि ।

शकुन्तला—(आत्मगतम्) हिअअ, समस्सस समस्सस । परिच्चत्तमच्छरेण अणुअम्पिअम्हि देव्वेण । अज्जउत्तो क्खु एसो । हृदय, समाश्वसिहि ससाश्वसिहि । परित्यक्तमत्सरेणानुकम्पितास्मि दैवेन । आर्यपुत्रः खल्वेषः ।

राजा—प्रिये,

स्मृतिभिन्नमोहतमसो दिष्ट्या प्रमुखे स्थितासि मे सुमुखि ।
उपरागान्ते शशिनः समुपगता रोहिणी योगम् ॥ २२ ॥

शकुन्तला—जेदु जेदु अज्जउत्तो । (इत्यर्धोक्ते बाष्पकण्ठी विरमति ।) जयतु जयत्वार्यपुत्रः ।

राजा—सुन्दरि,

बाष्पेण प्रतिषिद्धेऽपि जयशब्दे जितं मया ।
यत्ते दृष्टमसंस्कारं पाटलोष्ठपुटं मुखम् ॥ २३ ॥

बालः—अज्जुए, को एसो । मातः, क एषः ।

शकुन्तला—वच्छ, दे भाअहेआइं पुच्छेहि । वत्स, ते भागधेयानि पृच्छ ।

braid of hair, and pure in her conduct, is undergoing a long vow of separation from me who have been exceedingly cruel to her. (21)

ŚAKUNTALĀ (*Observing the king pale with remorse*). Certainly he does not look like my husband. Who then could he be that sullies with the contact of his body my child protected by an auspicious amulet?

BOY (*Advancing to his mother*). Mother, who is this man who calls me son and embraces me?

KING. Oh my beloved, even the cruelty I showed to you has come to have a happy conclusion, since I find that you have recognized me.

ŚAKUNTALĀ (*To herself*). Be comforted, my heart; fate, no longer envious, has taken pity on me. This is indeed my husband.

KING. Darling,

By the kindness of heaven, O lovely faced one, thou standest again before me, the darkness of whose delusion has been dispelled by recollection. The star Rohiṇī at the end of an eclipse rejoins her (beloved) Moon. (22)

ŚAKUNTALĀ. Victory to my noble lord! (*Tears choke her voice when this is half-said.*)

KING. Lovely one,

Though the word victory be suppressed by thy tears, yet have I gained victory since I see thy unadorned face with its red lips. (23)

BOY. Mother, who is he?

ŚAKUNTALĀ. Ask thy fate, my child.

राजा—(शकुन्तलायाः पादयोः प्रणिपत्य ।)

> **सुतनु हृदयात्प्रत्यादेशव्यलीकमपैतु ते**
> **किमपि मनसः संमोहो मे तदा बलवानभूत् ।**
> **प्रबलतमसामेवंप्रायाः शुभेषु प्रवृत्तयः**
> **स्रजमपि शिरस्यन्धः क्षिप्तां धुनोत्यहिशङ्कया ॥ २४ ॥**

शकुन्तला—**उट्ठेदु अज्जउत्तो । णूणं मे सुअरिअप्पडिबन्धअं पुराकिदं तेसु दिअहेसु परिणाममुहं आसि जेण साणुक्कोसो वि अज्जउत्तो मइ विरसो संवुत्तो ।** उत्तिष्ठत्वार्यपुत्रः । नूनं मे सुचरितप्रतिबन्धकं पुराकृतं तेषु दिवसेषु परिणाममुखमासीद्येन सानुक्रोशोऽप्यार्यपुत्रो मयि विरसः संवृत्तः ।

(राजोत्तिष्ठति ।)

शकुन्तला—**अह कहं अज्जउत्तेण सुमरिदो दुक्खभाई अअं जणो ।** अथ कथमार्यपुत्रेण स्मृतो दुःखभाग्ययं जनः ।

राजा—**उद्धृतविषादशल्यः कथयिष्यामि ।**

> **मोहान्मया सुतनु पूर्वमुपेक्षितस्ते**
> **यो बाष्पबिन्दुरधरं परिबाधमानः ।**
> **तं तावदाकुटिलपक्ष्मविलग्नमद्य**
> **बाष्पं प्रमृज्य विगतानुशयो भवेयम् ॥ २५ ॥**

(इति यथोक्तमनुतिष्ठति ।)

शकुन्तला—(नाममुद्रां दृष्ट्वा ।) **अज्जउत्त, एदं तं अङ्गुलीअअं ।** आर्यपुत्र, एतत्तदङ्गुलीयकम् ।

राजा—**अस्मादङ्गुलीयोपलम्भात्खलु स्मृतिरुपलब्धा ।**

शकुन्तला—**विसमं किदं णेण जं तदा अज्जउत्तस्स पच्चाअकाले दुल्लहं आसि ।** विषमं कृतमनेन यत्तदार्यपुत्रस्य प्रत्ययकाले दुर्लभमासीत् ।

KING (*Falling at Śakuntalā's feet*).

O fair one let the unpleasantness caused by my desertion of thee depart from thy heart ; for at that time a violent frenzy somehow overpowered my soul. Such, for the most part, is the attitude towards good of those in whose minds the darkness of illusion prevails. A blind man shakes off even a wreath of flowers thrown over his head, mistaking it for a snake. (24)

ŚAKUNTALĀ. Rise, my husband ; surely some (evil) deed of mine in a former existence coming in the way (of the action) of my virtue, was in those days approaching fruition ; since my husband, who is so kind at heart became unfeeling towards me. (*The king rises.*) Śakuntalā. But how did my husband remember this unfortunate woman ?

KING. I will tell thee when I shall have plucked the dart of sorrow.

Fair one, the anguish of my heart shall cease by wiping off the tears that now cling to thy slightly curved eye-lashes—the tears which formerly paining thy under-lip were neglected by me through mental delusion. (25)

(*Does as said.*)

ŚAKUNTALĀ (*Seeing the signet-ring*). My husband, this is the ring.

KING. It was the recovery of this ring that restored my memory.

ŚAKUNTALĀ. It has acted wickedly, since it was not found at the time of convincing my husband.

राजा—तेन ह्यृतुसमवायचिह्नं प्रतिपद्यतां लता कुसुमम् ।

शाकुन्तला—ण से विस्ससामि । अज्जउत्तो एव्वं णं धारेदु । नास्या विश्वसिमि । आर्यपुत्र एवैतद्धारयतु ।

(ततः प्रविशति मातलिः ।)

मातलिः—दिष्ट्या धर्मपत्नीसमागमेन पुत्रमुखदर्शनेन चायुष्मान् वर्धते ।

राजा—अभूत्संपादितस्वादुफलो मे मनोरथः । मातले, न खलु विदितोऽयमाखण्डलेन वृत्तान्तः स्यात् ।

मातलिः—(सस्मितम् ।) किमीश्वराणां परोक्षम् । एत्वायुष्मान् । भगवान्मारीचस्ते दर्शनं वितरति ।

राजा—शकुन्तले, अवलम्ब्यतां पुत्रः । त्वां पुरस्कृत्य भगवन्तं द्रष्टुमिच्छामि ।

शकुन्तला—हिरिआमि अज्जउत्तेण सह गुरुसमीवं गन्तुं । जिह्रेम्यार्यपुत्रेण सह गुरुसमीपं गन्तुम् ।

राजा—अप्याचरितव्यमभ्युदयकालेषु । एह्येहि ।

(सर्वे परिक्रामन्ति ।)

(ततः प्रविशत्यदित्या सार्धमासनस्थो मारीचः ।)

मारीचः—(राजानमवलोक्य ।) दाक्षायणि,

पुत्रस्य ते रणशिरस्ययमग्रयायी
दुष्यन्त इत्यभिहितो भुवनस्य भर्ता ।
चापेन यस्य विनिवर्तितकर्म जातं
तत्कोटिमत्कुलिशमाभरणं मघोनः ॥ २६ ॥

अदितिः—संभावणीआणुभावा से आकिदि । संभावनीयानुभावास्याकृतिः ।

KING. Then let the creeper receive her flower as a sign of her union with spring.

ŚAKUNTALĀ. I do not trust it. Let my husband alone wear it.

(*Then enter Mātali.*)

MĀTALI. I congratulate the long-lived one on reunion with his lawful wife, and on seeing the face of his son.

KING. My desire has come to attain a sweet fruit. Mātali, was not this event really known to Indra?

MĀTALI (*Smiling*). What is unknown to the Gods? Come, long-lived one. The divine Mārīca gives you an audience.

KING. Śakuntalā, take our son by the hand; I wish to see the holy one, leading thee into his presence.

ŚAKUNTALĀ. I am ashamed to go before my elders with my husband.

KING. But that is the custom on (such) happy occasions. Come, come.

(*All walk round.*)

(*Then enter seated Mārīca and Aditi.*)

MĀRĪCA (*Looking at the king*). Aditi,

This is he that marches foremost in the front of thy son's battles, named Duṣyanta, the ruler of the earth, through whose bow that edged thunder-bolt of Indra, all its work being accomplished, has become (a mere) ornament. (26)

ADITI. His greatness may be inferred from his appearance.

मातलिः—आयुष्मन्, एतौ पुत्रप्रीतिपिशुनेन चक्षुषा दिवौकसां पितरावायुष्मन्तमवलोकयतः। तावुपसर्प।

राजा—मातले एतौ

प्राहुर्द्वादशधा स्थितस्य मुनयो यत्तेजसः कारणं
भर्तारं भुवनत्रयस्य सुषुवे यद्यज्ञभागेश्वरम्।
यस्मिन्नात्मभवः परोऽपि पुरुषश्चक्रे भवायास्पदं
द्वन्द्वं दक्षमरीचिसंभवमिदं तत्स्रष्टुरेकान्तरम्॥ २७॥

मातलिः—अथ किम्।

राजा—(उपगम्य।) उभाभ्यामपि वासवानुयोज्यो दुष्यन्तः प्रणमति।

मारीचः—वत्स, चिरं जीव। पृथिवीं पालय।

अदितिः—वच्छ अप्पडिरहो होहि। वत्स अप्रतिरथो भव।

शकुन्तला—दारअसहिदा वो पादवन्दणं करेमि। दारकसहिता वां पादवन्दनं करोमि।

मारीचः—वत्से,

आखण्डलसमो भर्ता जयन्तप्रतिमः सुतः।
आशीरन्या न ते योग्या पौलोमीसदृशी भव॥ २८॥

अदितिः—जादे, भत्तुणो अभिमदा होहि। अवस्सं दीहाऊ वच्छओ उहअकुलणन्दणो होदु। उवविसह। जाते, भर्तुरभिमता भव। अवश्यं दीर्घायुर्वत्स उभयकुलनन्दनो भवतु। उपविशत।

(सर्वे प्रजापतिमभित उपविशन्ति।)

मारीचः—(एकैकं निर्दिशन्।)

दिष्ट्या शकुन्तला साध्वी सदपत्यमिदं भवान्।
श्रद्धा वित्तं विधिश्चेति त्रितयं तत्समागतम्॥ २९॥

MĀTALI. Long-lived one, these parents of the gods are gazing upon you with an eye that betrays parental affection. Approach them.

KING. Mātali,

Are those the pair, sprung from Dakṣa and Mārīci, at one remove from the Creator, whom sages pronounce the fountain of glory apparent in the twelve forms (of the sun) ; who begot the lord of the triple world, the lord of the (gods who are the) sharers of every sacrifice, the pair whom Viṣṇu, who is higher than the self-existent himself, chose as the source of his birth ? (27)

MĀTALI. Yes, quite so.

KING. (*Approaching*). Duṣyanta, Indra's servant, bows to you both.

MĀRĪCA. Child, mayest thou live long ! Protect the earth.

ADITI. Be thou a matchless hero.

ŚAKUNTALĀ. I salute your feet along with my son.

MĀRĪCA. Like Indra is thy husband ; and like Jayanta thy son ; no other blessing would be suitable to thee. Mayest thou be like Paulomī ! (28)

ADITI. Child, be thou highly honoured by thy husband. May thy child be long-lived and unfailingly be the joy of both the families. Sit down.

(*All sit down around Prajāpati.*)

MĀRĪCA (*Pointing to each of them by turns*).

The virtuous Śakuntalā, her noble child and your Honour—here fortunately are combined faith, fortune, and action. (29)

राजा—भगवन्, प्रागभिप्रेतसिद्धिः। पश्चाद्दर्शनम्। अतोऽपूर्वः खलु वोऽनुग्रहः। कुतः।

उदेति पूर्वं कुसुमं ततः फलं
घनोदयः प्राक्तदनन्तरं पयः।
निमित्तनैमित्तिकयोरयं क्रम-
स्तव प्रसादस्य पुरस्तु संपदः॥ ३०॥

मातलिः—एवं विधातारः प्रसीदन्ति।

राजा—भगवन्, इमामाज्ञाकरीं वो गान्धर्वेण विवाहविधिनोपयम्य कस्यचित्कालस्य बन्धुभिरानीतां स्मृतिशैथिल्यात्प्रत्यादिशन्नपराद्धोऽस्मि तत्रभवतो युष्मत्सगोत्रस्य कण्वस्य। पश्चादङ्गुलीयकदर्शनादूढपूर्वां तद्दुहितरमवगतोऽहम्। तच्चित्रमिव मे प्रतिभाति।

यथा गजो नेति समक्षरूपे
तस्मिन्नपक्रामति संशयः स्यात्।
पदानि दृष्ट्वा तु भवत्प्रतीति-
स्तथाविधो मे मनसो विकारः॥ ३१॥

मारीचः—वत्स, अलमात्मापराधशङ्कया। संमोहोऽपि त्वय्यनुपपन्नः। श्रूयताम्।

राजा—अवहितोऽस्मि।

मारीचः—यदैवाप्सरस्तीर्थावतरणात्प्रत्यक्षवैक्लव्यां शकुन्तलामादाय मेनका दाक्षायणीमुपगता तदैव ध्यानादवगतोऽस्मि दुर्वाससः

KING. Holy one, First came the fulfilment of my desires, and afterwards, the sight of you; thus the favour you showed me is without parallel. For

> First appears the flower, then the fruit ; first the clouds and then come the showers ; such is the regular course of cause and effect ; but fortunes came before your grace. (30)

MĀTALI. That is how the creators of all beings show favour.

KING. Holy sir, I married this your hand-maid by the Gāndharva ceremony and when after a time she was brought to me by her kindred, my memory failing me, I rejected her and thus committed a grievous offence against the venerable Kaṇva who is kin to you. But afterwards on seeing the ring, I perceived that I had married his daughter. This strikes me as very wonderful.

> As if a man were to say 'This is not an elephant' when its form was before his eyes ; and when it has marched past him, were to doubt (what animal it could be) ; but conviction were to take place on seeing its foot-prints ; of such a kind has been the change that had come over my mind. (31)

MĀRĪCA. Cease, my son to charge thyself with an offence ; nor is infatuation explicable in thee. Listen.

KING. I am all attention.

MĀRĪCA. Even when Menakā took Śakuntalā whose distress was so evident, from the steps of the Apsarastirtha, and brought her to Aditi, at that very time I

शापादियं तपस्विनी सहधर्मचारिणी त्वया प्रत्यादिष्टा नान्यथेति। स चायमङ्गुलीयकदर्शनावसानः।

राजा—(सोच्छ्वासम्।) एष वचनीयान्मुक्तोऽस्मि।

शाकुन्तला—(स्वगतम्।) दिट्ठिआ अकारणपच्चादेसी ण अज्जउत्तो। ण हु सत्तं अत्ताणं सुमरेमि। अहवा पत्तो मए स हि सावो विरहसुण्णहिअआए ण विदिदो। अदो सहीहिं संदिट्ठम्हि भत्तुणो अङ्गुलीअअं दंसइदव्वं त्ति। दिष्ट्याकारणप्रत्यादेशी नार्यपुत्रः। न खलु शप्तमात्मानं स्मरामि। अथवा प्राप्तो मया स हि शापो विरहशून्यहृदयया न विदितः। अतः सखीभ्यां संदिष्टास्मि भर्तुरङ्गुलीयकं दर्शयितव्यमिति।

मारीचः—वत्से, चरितार्थासि। सहधर्मचारिणं प्रति न त्वया मन्युः कार्यः। पश्य।

शापादसि प्रतिहता स्मृतिरोधरूक्षे
भर्तर्यपेततमसि प्रभुता तवैव।
छाया न मूर्च्छति मलोपहतप्रसादे
शुद्धे तु दर्पणतले सुलभावकाशा॥ ३२॥

राजा—यथाह भगवान्।

मारीचः—वत्स, कच्चिदभिनन्दितस्त्वया विधिवदस्माभिरनुष्ठितजातकर्मा पुत्र एष शाकुन्तलेयः।

राजा—भगवन्, अत्र खलु मे वंशप्रतिष्ठा। बालं हस्तेन गृह्णाति।

मारीचः—तथा भाविनमेनं चक्रवर्तिनमवगच्छतु भवान्। पश्य।

रथेनानुद्घातस्तिमितगतिना तीर्णजलधिः
पुरा सप्तद्वीपां जयति वसुधामप्रतिरथः।

perceived through my powers of contemplation that this thy poor dutiful wife was repudiated by thee in consequence of Durvāsas' curse, and through no other cause; that curse was to terminate at the sight of the ring.

KING. (*With a sigh*). So I am free from blame.

ŚAKUNTALĀ (*To herself*). Happy am I that my husband did not repudiate me without cause. But, indeed I don't remember I was cursed. Or I did not know I was cursed as I was absent-minded through separation; for my friends advised me to show the ring to my husband.

MĀRĪCA. Thou knowest, my daughter, the whole truth and must not give way to anger against thy rightful husband. Remember

> Thou wast rejected in consequence of the curse, thy husband being cruel to thee through the obstruction of his memory; but now when his mind is freed from darkness, thou alone wilt rule him. As an image has no effect on a mirror whose surface is sullied with dirt, but on a clean one finds an easy access. (32)

MĀRĪCA. Child, have you greeted this son whom Śakuntalā bore (to you) whose birth-rites have been duly performed by us?

KING. Holy one, in him is the hope of my family.

MĀRĪCA. Know that he will be a universal monarch in days to come.

> First, a matchless warrior, he will cross the ocean in a chariot whose motion would be steady and free from jolts and conquer the earth consisting of her seven islands; here

इहायं सत्त्वानां प्रसभदमनात्सर्वदमनः
पुनर्यास्यत्याख्यां भरत इति लोकस्य भरणात् ॥ ३३ ॥

राजा—भगवता कृतसंस्कारे सर्वमस्मिन्वयमाशास्महे ।

अदितिः—भअवं, इमाए दुहिदुमणोरहसंपत्तीए कण्णो वि दाव सुदवित्थारो करीअदु । दुहिदुवच्छला मेणआ इह एव्व उपचरन्ती चिट्ठदि । भगवन् अनया दुहितृमनोरथसंपत्त्या कण्वोऽपि तावच्छ्रुतविस्तारः क्रियताम् । दुहितृवत्सला मेनाकेहैवोपचरन्ती तिष्ठति ।

शकुन्तला—(आत्मगतम् ।) मणोरहो क्खु मे भणिदो भअवदीए । मनोरथः खलु मे भणितो भगवत्या ।

मारीचः—तपःप्रभावात्प्रत्यक्षं सर्वमेव तत्रभवतः ।

राजाः—अतः खलु मम नातिक्रुद्धो मुनिः ।

मारीचः—तथाप्यसौ प्रियमस्माभिः प्रष्टव्यः । कः कोऽत्र भोः ।

(प्रविश्य ।)

शिष्यः—भगवन् , अयमस्मि ।

मारीचः—गालव, इदानीमेव विहायसा गत्वा मम वचनात्तत्रभवते कण्वाय प्रियमावेदय । यथा पुत्रवती शकुन्तला तच्छापनिवृत्तौ स्मृतिमता दुष्यन्तेन प्रतिगृहीतेति ।

शिष्यः—यदाज्ञापयति भगवान् । (इति निष्क्रान्तः ।)

मारीचः—वत्स, त्वमपि स्वापत्यदारसहितः सख्युराखण्डलस्य रथमारुह्य ते राजधानीं प्रतिष्ठस्व ।

राजा—यदाज्ञापयति भगवान् ।

he is called Sarvadamana, because he forcibly tames all animals ; but (later) he shall acquire the name of Bharata, because he shall sustain the world. (33)

KING. I anticipate all (this) from him for whom the purificatory-rites were performed by the holy one.

ADITI. Holy one, let Kaṇva also be apprised of all the circumstances of the attainment by his daughter of all that her heart desired. Menakā, who is (so) fond of her daughter, is here in attendance upon me.

ŚAKUNTALĀ (*To herself*). The holy one has, indeed, given expression to my heart's desire.

MĀRĪCA. But the holy one knows the whole matter through the power of his devotions.

KING. Hence it is that the sage was not very much angry with me.

MĀRĪCA. Nevertheless, he must be questioned by me about this happy event. Ho, who is there ?

(*Entering*) Pupil. Holy one, here I am.

MĀRĪCA. Gālava, fly through the air at once, and inform the holy Kaṇva of the happy event, in my name : That Śakuntalā with her son is accepted by Duṣyanta when his memory revived on the termination of her curse.

PUPIL. As the holy one commands. (*Exit.*)

MĀRĪCA. My son, thou too now ascend the chariot of thy friend Indra along with this wife and child, and set out for thy capital.

KING. As the holy one commands.

मारीचः—अपि च ।

तव भवतु बिडौजाः प्राज्यवृष्टिः प्रजासु
त्वमपि विततयज्ञः वज्रिणं प्रीणयस्व ।
युगशतपरिवर्तानेवमन्योन्यकृत्यै-
र्नयतमुभयलोकानुग्रहश्लाघनीयैः ॥ ३४ ॥

राजा—भगवन्, यथाशक्ति श्रेयसे यतिष्ये ।

मारीचः—वत्स, किं ते भूयः प्रियमुपकरोमि ।

राजा—अतः परमपि प्रियमस्ति । यदिह भगवान्प्रियं कर्तुमिच्छति तर्हीदमस्तु । (भरतवाक्यम् ।)

प्रवर्ततां प्रकृतीहिताय पार्थिवः
सरस्वती श्रुतमहतां महीयताम् ।
ममापि च क्षपयत नीललोहितः
पुनर्भवं परिगतशक्तिरात्मभूः ॥ ३५ ॥

(इति निष्क्रान्ताः सर्वे)

सप्तमोऽङ्कः ।

समाप्तमिदमभिज्ञानशाकुन्तलं नाम नाटकम् ॥

MĀRĪCA. Moreover,

May Indra send copious rain for (the benefit of) thy subjects; and mayest thou with frequent sacrifices please him. Thus pass periods of hundreds of ages with reciprocal friendly offices laudable on account of the benefits conferred on both the worlds. (34)

KING. Holy one, I shall strive, as far as I can, to attain (that) felicity.

MĀRĪCA. My son, what other favours can I bestow on thee?

KING. Can there be any favour greater still than this? As (however) the holy one desires to bestow a favour then let this be (fulfilled). (*Epilogue*).

May the king apply himself to the attainment of the happiness of his subjects. May the speech of those who stand high in their knowledge of the Veda be honoured, and may the self-existent Siva whose energy is immanent in all things put an end to my rebirth. (35)

(*Exeunt Omnes.*)

End of Act VII

Here ends the drama Abhijnāna-Śākuntala.

NOTES

ACT I

P. 1. From the Nāṭyaśāstra we learn that before the commencement of a drama, an elaborate series of preliminaries (पूर्वरङ्ग) had to be performed, consisting chiefly of the प्रत्याहार which would announce the beginning of the performance, the अवतरण, when the musicians enter and take their places, the आरम्भ when the chorus try their voices, and the आश्रवण when the musicians try their instruments, and so on up to Nāndi. All these preliminaries are performed by the सूत्रधार, who then leaves the stage and his place is immediately taken by another similar person called स्थापक who introduces the play to the audience. This elaborate practice, was however given up later on, and we find that the सूत्रधार alone performed both the functions of the preliminaries and of the prologue. Cf. पूर्वरङ्गं विधायादौ सूत्रधारे विनिर्गते । प्रविश्य तद्वदपरः काव्यमास्थापयेन्नटः ॥ ...सूचयेद्वस्तु बीजं वा मुखं पात्रमथापि वा ॥ दशरूपक० III. 2–3.

I. 1. This benedictory stanza praises god Śiva and invokes his blessing and protection. He manifests himself through his eight different forms, for the support of this universe. These eight visible forms corresponded to the eight different manifestations of god Śiva called Rudras, viz. रुद्र, भव, सर्व, ईशान, पशुपति, भीम, उग्र and महादेव. " Brahmā assigned to them their respective stations: water, the sun, earth, fire, air, ether, the officiating Brāhmana, and the moon; these are termed their visible forms (तनवः) "—विष्णुपुराण. Cf. अष्टाभियस्य कृत्स्नं जगदपि तनुभिर्बिभ्रतो नाभि-

मानः । माल० I. 1. Also कुमा० V. 26. विदितं वो यथा स्वार्था न मे काश्चित् प्रवृत्तयः । ननु मूर्तिभिरष्टाभिरित्थंभूतोऽस्मि सूचितः ॥ Also कलितान्योन्यसामर्थ्यैः पृथिव्यादिभिरात्मभिः । येनेदं ध्रियते विश्वं धुर्यैर्यानमिवाध्वनि ॥ ibid. V. 76. या स्रष्टुः आद्या सृष्टिः—Which was the first creation of the Creator i. e. water. According to the Paurāṇic conception of the creation of the universe, water was created first. Cf. अप एव ससर्जादौ तासु वीर्यमवासृजत् । तदण्डमभवद्धैमं सहस्रांशुसमप्रभम् ॥ मनु० I. या विधिहुतं हविः वहति–Which carries the oblations (to the various gods), offered with due rites. Agni does the duty of delivering the offerings to the various gods. He is thus a carrier of oblations–a veritable portman. The significance of the adjective विधिहुत is best understood when it is known that the offerings not so given are not delivered unto the gods, but are reduced to ashes. (अविधिहुतं भस्मीभवति). ये द्वे कालं विधत्तः–The two, who make time viz. the sun and the moon. The Time or Kāla is infinite, but then the divisions of Time and its reckoning are possible because of the two luminaries. The day and night, the fortnight, the month, the seasons, the year etc, into which Time could thus be divided, are to be calculated by the sun and the moon, and therefore, they make (विधत्तः) Time. श्रुति...गुणा –श्रुतेः विषयः (शब्दः) गुणः यस्याः सा–Characterised by the object of hearing viz. the sound. आकाश or ether, invisible as it is, has its characteristic गुण of conveying sound from the place of origin to the sense of hearing. Cf. अथात्मनः शब्दगुणं गुणज्ञः पदं विमानेन विगाहमानः । रघु० XVIII. सर्वबीजप्रकृतिः–The source of all seeds viz. the Earth, प्रकृति is the उत्पत्तिस्थान or the source. Cf. इयं भूमिर्हि भूतानां शाश्वती योनिरुच्यते ॥ मनु० IX. 37. Note the other reading सर्वभूतप्रकृतिः, which is also good. यया प्राणिनः प्राणवन्तः–By which, the living beings are endowed with प्राण i. e. vital breaths. Beings have life in them because of these five vital breaths in the body. They are:—प्राण, अपान, व्यान, उदान and समान. प्राण is the all-in-all of a living being, the essence of life, as is illustrated by the Upanisadic parable in the form of the dialogue between the various senses and Prāṇa, in the छांदोग्योपनिषद्. प्रपन्नः– उपेतः, Endowed with, i. e. manifested in those eight visible forms. ' Known i. e. inferred to exist. The existence of ईश is inferred from his eight forms (अष्टाभिः तनुभिः) which are directly perceived (प्रत्यक्षाभिः)'—Ray. Note the other reading, प्रसन्नः 'Pleased'. With this reading, the meaning would be 'May god Śiva, pleased, protect you with his eight manifested forms.'

नान्द्यन्ते. At the end of the Nāndi or benediction. The verse, explained above, constitutes the नान्दी, which is defined thus–आशीर्नमस्क्रियारूपः श्लोकः काव्यार्थसूचकः i. e. 'a verse or verses of the form of a salutation or a benediction and suggestive of the story of the drama. It is called नान्दी, because by the praise which it contains and is a source of delight to the gods. Cf. नन्दन्ति देवता यस्यां तस्मान्नान्दीति कीर्तिता। Its another characteristic of suggesting the Kāvyārtha has led commentators into ingenious attempts to find out far-fetched fantastic allusions to the elements or the various characters in the drama. Thus the expression या सृष्टिः etc. refers to that paragon of beauty, शकुन्तला, who has been described as अपरा स्त्रीरत्नसृष्टिः in the II Act, or in the terms of the Meghaduta, may be described as सृष्टिराद्येव धातुः। while the expression ये द्वे etc. refers to the two friends of शकुन्तला.

सूत्रधारः–The principal stage–manager who arranges the cast of characters, instructs them in their different roles, and is thus responsible for the successful performance of the drama–" The threads of which he holds in his hands, as it were." According to मातृगुप्ताचार्य he must have the following accomplishments:–

चतुरातोद्यनिष्णातोऽनेकभाषासमावृतः । नानाभाषणतत्त्वज्ञो नीतिशास्त्रार्थतत्त्ववित् ॥ नानागतिप्रचारज्ञो रसभावविशारदः । नाट्यप्रयोगनिपुणो नानाशिल्पकलान्वितः ॥ छन्दोविधानतत्त्वज्ञः सर्वशास्त्रविचक्षणः । तत्तद्गीतानुगलयकलातालावधारणः ॥ अवधानप्रयोक्ता च योक्तॄणामुपदेशकः । एवंगुणगणोपेतः सूत्रधारोऽभिधीयते ॥

नेपथ्याभिमुखम्–Towards the tiring or the dressing room. The word नेपथ्य means 'the Dress or Costume' (Cf. विरलनेपथ्ययोः

पात्रयोः प्रवेशोऽस्तु । माल० I), or the dressing room, the space where the actors attire themselves, which is always behind the curtain. नेपथ्यविधानम्–Arrangements in the tiring room or the dressing. अवसितम्–finished, P. P. of √अव+सो. नियोग –Task, duty assigned. अभिरूपभूयिष्ठा–अभिरूपाः भूयिष्ठाः यस्यां सा or आभिरूपैः भूयिष्ठा–Mostly consisting of wise men. आभिरूप means here 'Learned, enlightened'. परिषद्–An assembly, audience. कालिदास...वस्तु–कालिदासेन ग्रथितं वस्तु यस्य तत्–The story of which has been woven into the plot (of this drama) by Kālidāsa. अभिज्ञानशकुन्तलाख्ये–called the 'Token–Śakuntalā' or 'Ring–(recognised) Śakuntalā.' The word is thus explained:–अभिज्ञानेन स्मृता शकुन्तला–अभिज्ञानशकुन्तला, a compound of the शाकपार्थिव type, where we get the elision of the second member, and which has to be supplied while dissolving the compound. अभिज्ञानशकुन्तलां आधिकृत्य कृतं (नाटकं)–अभिज्ञानशकुन्तलं ; अभि...न्तलं आख्या यस्य तद्–अभिज्ञानशकुन्तलाख्यम् । उपस्थातव्यम्–Pot. pass. part. of उप + स्था 'To wait upon, to serve'. प्रतिपात्रम्–पात्रे पात्रे–For every part or character. आधीयतां यत्नः–Care should be taken, effort should be made. सुविहितप्रयोगतया–on account of the fact that the performance (प्रयोग) has been well-arranged. न किमपि परिहास्यते. Nothing will be found to be amiss or wanting. If the Sūtradhāra is overcareful in his eagerness to see that nothing goes wrong, his wife Natī is in a self-complacent mood and wants to compliment her husband on his efficient management. भूतार्थः–सत्यार्थः–the truth, the true state of the case. Cf. कः श्रद्धास्यति भूतार्थं सर्वो मां तुलयिष्यति । मृच्छ० III.

I. 2. प्रयोगविज्ञानम्–the profound knowledge of acting. बलवत्–Adv. greatly. Lit. mightily ; to be construed with शिक्षितानाम् । आत्मनि अप्रत्ययम्–diffident in itself, wanting in one's own confidence. The सूत्रधार means that it is no good flattering oneself with the thought of one's own proficiency, which must stand the test of public criticism, which alone proves the inherent merit, if there is any. It is for this reason, that even the wisest men tremble in their shoes with feelings of diffidence, when they have to face the general public.

P. 2. अनन्तरकरणीयं–what has to be done next i. e. immediately (अनन्तरं). श्रुतिप्रसादनतः–श्रवणेन्द्रियतर्पणात्–besides pleasing the ears (of the audience); the Abl. governed by अन्य acc. to the सूत्र-अन्यारादितरर्ते । पा० II. 3. 29. उपभोगक्षमं–Fit to be enjoyed, suited to the enjoyment of pleasures. आधिकृत्य–Lit. 'Having placed over; having made the prominent object'; about, with reference to.

I. 3. सुभगसलिलावगाहाः (दिवसाः)–सुभगः सलिले अवगाहः येषु ते–On which a plunge (अवगाह) in water is so delightful. पाटल...वाताः–पाटलानां संसर्गेण सुरभयः वनवाताः येषु–When the forest-breezes are (rendered) fragrant by their contact with the trumpet flowers. The flower has a red hue and possesses sweet fragrance. प्रच्छायसुलभनिद्राः–प्रच्छाये सुलभा निद्रा येषु–When slumber is easily induced in a thick shady-place. प्रच्छायं–प्रकृष्टा छाया यत्र तत् स्थानं or प्रकृष्टा छाया–प्रच्छायम् । परि...णीयाः–परिणामे रमणीयाः–Charming at the close. परिणाम–Lit. means 'Ripening, development,' here it means 'evening, the close of the day.' Cf. प्रचण्डसूर्यः स्पृहणीयचन्द्रमाः सदावगाहक्षमवारिसंचयः । दिनान्तरम्योऽभ्युपशान्तमन्मथो निदाघकालोऽयमुपागतः प्रिये ॥ ऋतु० I ।

I. 4. ईषद्...चुम्बितानि–Very gently kissed (by the bees). They sip the honey very softly without harming the flower. सुकुमार......शिखानि–सुकुमाराः केसराणां शिखाः (अग्रभागाः) येषु तानि (शिरीषकुसुमानि)–With tender tips of the filaments, अवतंसयन्ति–A denominative verbal form from अवतंस meaning 'an ear-ornament.' दयमानाः–Compassionate, tender-hearted; a present Part. from... दय् I. A. 'To take pity on.' प्रमदा–A youthful lady. Note that the verse is a Prākrit song, a द्विपदी or a couplet, having thirty मात्राs in each line. It is being sung by the नटी, 'to the tunes of the सारङ्ग melody, which has proved highly captivating.' राग...वृत्तिः–रागेण बद्धा चित्तवृत्तिर्यस्य सः–With all its mental activity arrested by the melody (of the song). The Com. राघवभट्ट solves the compound thus–रागे बद्धा चित्तवृत्तिर्यस्य सः– 'Having all mental activity fixed on the melody.' आलिखितः–Painted, drawn in a picture. रङ्गः–The audience, the assembly. प्रकरणम्–A topic, a subject of representation ; a play in general. The word is usually used with reference to a particular type of a drama, like the मृच्छकटिक, or मालतीमाधव, which has a fictitious plot. आर्यमिश्रैः–'By your reverence, your respectable self.' It should however be taken as an epithet of the audience meaning the noble men in the audience.' Cf. यावदिदानीं आर्यमिश्रान् विज्ञापयामि ॥ विक्र० I. मिश्र is a honorific title, (usually affixed to the names of great men and scholars, e. g. वसिष्ठमिश्रः, मण्डनमिश्रः). अनुबोधितः–Reminded.

I. 5. हारिणा–(i) With reference to गीतरागेण–'ravishing, captivating' (ii) With reference to सारङ्गेण–'luring, drawing away' (into the forest). प्रसभं–forcibly. अतिरंहसा–अतिशयितं रंहः यस्य सः तेन–Having a great speed (रंहस्). सारङ्गेण–By the antelope or the spotted deer; " by the सारङ्ग melody of the song (गीतरागेण)." Prof. Ranade's सुशिक्षितांचें संगीत P. 4.

Here ends the प्रस्तावना or the Prologue called also आमुख, which generally consists of an introductory dialogue between the सूत्रधार and नटी or one of the actors. After giving an account of the author and his qualifications, it introduces the incidents of the drama. Cf. सूत्रधारो नटीं ब्रूते मार्षं वाथ विदूषकम् । स्वकार्यं प्रस्तुताक्षेपि चित्रोक्त्या यत्तदामुखम् । प्रस्तावना वा ॥ दश. III. 8. Also नटी विदूषको वापि पारिपार्श्वक एव वा । सूत्रधारेण सहिताः संलापं यत्र कुर्वते ॥ चित्रैर्वाक्यैः स्वकार्योत्थैः प्रस्तुताक्षेपिभिर्मिथः । आमुखं तत्तु विज्ञेयं नाम्ना प्रस्तावनापि वा ॥ Of the प्रस्तावना there are three varieties, according to दशरूपक (or five according to साहित्यदर्पण) of which प्रयोगातिशय or particular presentation is one in which a character is introduced by a remark of the stage–manager. एषोऽयमित्युपक्षेपात् सूत्रधारप्रयोगतः । पात्रप्रवेशो यत्रैष प्रयोगातिशयो मतः ॥ ३ ॥ Thus the प्रस्तावना of our drama also is of the प्रयोगातिशय type. आयुष्मन्–A respectable mode of addressing kings. Cf. 'आयुष्मन्' इति वाच्यस्तु रथी सूतेन सर्वदा '–Com.

I. 6. अधिज्यकार्मुके (त्वयि)–Having a strung bow, अधिज्यं कार्मुकं यस्य सः तस्मिन् । The word आधिज्य means 'having the string up'; ज्यामधिगतं or अधिरूढा ज्या यत्र तद् (पिनाकिन् is an epithet of god Siva armed as he is with his bow called पिनाक. मृगानुसारिणम् The expression has a reference to the following mythological episode. ' Śiva, not having been invited to दक्ष's celebrated horse-sacrifice, was so indignant, that with his wife, he suddenly presented himself, confounded the sacrifice, dispersed and mutilated the gods, and chasing यज्ञ, ' the lord of sacrifice', who fled in the form of a fleet deer, overtook and decapitated him. ' Cf. तत्प्रसुप्तभुजगेन्द्रभीषणं वीक्ष्य दाशरथिराददे धनुः । विद्रुतक्रतुमृगानुसारिणं येन बाणमसृजद्वृषध्वजः ॥ रघु० XI. 44.

I. 7. The verse gives a fine description of the pursued antelope. ग्रीवा......रामं–To be construed with बद्धदृष्टिः–In a charming manner because of the bending. of the neck (ग्रीवा). अनुपतति–Loc. Sing. of अनुपतत्–a Pres. Part. of ✓ अनु + पत्–' to rush behind, to pursue.' Cf. कथमनुपतत एव प्रयत्नप्रेक्षणीयः संवृत्तः ।. बद्धदृष्टिः,–With his eyes fixed (upon the chariot). Note V. L. दत्तदृष्टिः, which, with the word मुहुः suggesting frequent interruption in the steadfast look, is to be preferred. For बद्धदृष्टि, compare– स्यन्दनाबद्धदृष्टिषु । रघु० I. 40. पश्चार्धेन–by hinder half (of the body) अपरः अर्धः पश्चाधः । Cf. वार्तिक ' अपरस्यार्धे पश्चभावो वक्तव्यः । पूर्वकायम्–पूर्वं कायस्य–The fore-part of the body. श्रम...भ्रंशिभिः (दर्भैः)–dropping from his mouth forced open (विवृत) through exhaustion. कीर्णवर्त्मा–कीर्णं वर्त्म यस्य सः–whose path was strewn (with grass). उदग्रप्लुतत्वात्. By reason of his lofty bounds (प्लुत) in the air. स्तोकम्–अल्पम्–Very little. उर्व्याम्–Loc. Sing. of उर्वी 'the earth'. The poet means that because of his high boundings, he appears to be traversing the distance mostly through the air, and very little on the earth, which he has to touch while taking leaps one after another. प्रयत्नप्रेक्षणीयः–To be seen with effort. उद्घातिनी–Bumpy, giving shocks, causing jolting (of the chariot). The reading उत्खातिनी–would mean 'Having ups and downs, uneven.' विप्रकृष्टान्तरः–विप्रकृष्टं अन्तरं यस्य सः–Separated by a long interval or distance.

I. 8. निरायतपूर्वकायाः-नितरां आयतः पूर्वकायः येषाम्-the fore-part of whose bodies has been fully stretched out. निष्कम्पचामरशिखाः-निष्कम्पाः चामराणां शिखा येषाम्-With the (decorative) chowrie-crests (between the two ears) standing motionless. The great speed taken by the horses had made them stiff and unmoving. Cf. चित्रारम्भविनिश्चलं हयशिरस्यायामवच्चामरम् । विक्र॰ I. 4. निभृतोर्ध्वकर्णाः-With their ears erect (ऊर्ध्व) and steady (निभृत).

P. 8. आत्मोद्धतैः Raised (उद्धत) by themselves. Pischel reads-स्वेषामपि प्रसरतां रजसामलङ्घ्याः ।. मृग...मया मृगजवस्य अक्षमया-Out of impatience. or intolerant jealousy of the deer's speed. For this line Pischel reads-धावन्ति वर्त्मनि तरन्ति नु वाजिनस्ते । " These horses, they gallop on the road, no, (I should say) they swim along. " हरितः-Acc. plu. of हरित् a bay horse of the sun. हरिः-A horse of Indra.

I. 9. This verse gives a realistic description of the king's experience in a fast-moving chariot—an experience, the like of which every one gets while going in a train. अर्धे विच्छिन्न cut in half; Note V. L. अद्धा विच्छिन्नं ' really (अद्धा) disconnected कृतसंधानम्-कृतं संधानं यस्य तत् which is joined. समरेखम्-समा रेखा यस्य तद्-Straight. बाणपथवर्तिनः-standing within the range (पथ) of the arrow. V. L. बाणपातवर्तिनः which is not good.

I. 10. संनिपात्यः-which should be allowed to descend upon. पुष्पराशौ V. L. तूलराशौ. The reading पुष्पराशौ-is to be preferred. क्व...क्व-implies great incongruity between the two viz. the frail tender life of the deer and the hard-hitting arrows. अतिलोलम्-Extremely frail. निशितनिपाताः-निशितः निपातः येषाम्-coming down with piercing sharpness. वज्रसाराः-वज्रस्य इव सारः येषाम् ते-Having the strength (सार) of a thunderbolt.

I. 11. आर्तत्राणाय-For the protection (त्राण) of the distressed (आर्त) अनागसि-Loc. Sing. of अनागस्-' One who has not offended, harmless, innocent.

युक्तरूपम्-अतिशयेन युक्तं-युक्तरूपम् । 'प्रशंसायां रूपम् प्रत्ययः' highly befitting. अनुमालिनीतीरम्=मालिनीनदीतीरे; 'विभक्त्यर्थेऽव्ययीभावः। On the bank of the Mālini river. अन्य...पात-अन्यकार्यस्य अतिपातः-A transgression of other (more important) duty, आतिथेयः-अतिथिषु साधुः-good for guests, cf. पथ्यतिथिवसतिस्वपतेर्ढञ्। पा॰ सू॰

I. 13. प्रतिहतविघ्नाः-The disturbance from which has been removed. मौर्वीकिणाङ्कः (भुजः)-मौर्व्याः किणः अङ्कं यस्य सः-Having a mark of the bow-string (मौर्वी). दैवं प्रतिकूलं शमयितुम्-Herein we get the first inkling of the tragic situation in V Act. सोमतीर्थम्-modern प्रभास, acc. to some, a holy place in the Kathiawar, near the temple of Somnāth. Others, however, locate it near Pānipat, 'between कुरुक्षेत्र and गंगाह्रद, a holy place near कुरुक्षेत्र.' P. 12 आभोगः-Premises, precincts.

I. 14. शुक...भ्रष्टाः-शुकाः गर्भे येषाम्-तादृशानां कोटराणां मुखेभ्यः भ्रष्टाः-dropped down from the mouths of the hollowtrunks with parrots inside. इङ्गुदीफलभिदः-used in crushing the Ingudi fruit. This fruit was commonly used by the ascetics for extracting oil, which was used for lamps and also for toilet. अभिन्नगतयः without breaking their (slow) gait into a run. They are not disturbed by the noise of the chariot, because of the sence of security created in them by the affectionate behaviour of the sages. तोयाधारपथाः-The paths leading to the reservoirs of water. वल्कल...ङ्किताः-वल्कलानां शिखाभ्यः यः निष्यदः, तस्य याः रेखाः, ,ताभिः अङ्किताः (°पथाः)-Marked by the lines of dripping water from the fringes (शिखाः) of the barkgarments.

I. 15. कुल्यांभोभिः-by the waters of canals (कुल्या). धौतमूलाः-with their roots washed (धौत). किसलयरुचां रागः भिन्नः-The red tint of sprouts is diversified. The smoke has partially obscured the red lustre. अर्वाक्-अग्रतः-In front, near. छिन्नदर्भाङ्कुरायां, where the stalks of Darbha grass have been mown (by the grazing fawns). नष्टाशङ्काः-Free from timidity (आशङ्का). This fine verse has been rejected by annotators like Ray, on the ground that it does not suit the context, and gives a repetition of the features already noted in the preceding verse. The latter describes, however, the तपोवनाभोग, or the precincts of the forest-grove. May we not suppose that the king has moved on further in his chariot, and has now come nearer the hermitage, though not actually in it, and that in this verse he describes the features of the vicinity of the hermitage ? The verse has this justification and should not be rejected.

उपरोधः-Disturbance. The hermits are sure to be disturbed in their daily routine by the unusual advent of the king in his chariot. प्रग्रहाः-Reins. P. 14. विनीतवेषेण-In a dress of a humble ordinary gentleman ; दुष्यन्त would not like to enter as a king in state having a gaudy attire, but as an ordinary gentleman. Note his regard for the feelings of ascetics. आर्द्रपृष्ठाः-Lit. ' wet-backed ' i. e. watered and refreshed. निमित्तं-An omen ; it is the throbbing of the right arm, which, in the case of man, indicates union with a beautiful woman.

I. 16. The king means that a tranquil hermitage is certainly the last place where such romantic omens prove effective ; and yet, who knows, how fate will work to find out openings for predestined events. They are to be had everywhere. भवितव्यानाम्— of things or events that are to happen दक्षिणेन वृक्षवाटिकां-To the right of the grove of trees. दक्षिणेन governs the accusative as also the genitive. Cf. एनपा द्वितीया । एनपेति योगविभागात् षष्ठ्यपि । दक्षिणेन ग्रामं ग्रामस्य वा । स्वप्रमाणानुरूपैः-Suited to their own size or stature (प्रमाण) ; or better still ' suited to their strength ' Cf. पयोघटैराश्रमबालवृक्षान् संवर्धयन्ती स्वबलानुरूपैः । रघु० XIV. 78. पयो दातुम्-Cf. the Marathi idiom पाणी देणें.

I. 17. The king gives expression to his feelings of wonder and admiration in a figurative manner. He never expected such beauty of form to reside in forests, their proper resort being the secluded harem in the city, where alone, like creepers in a garden, beauty is developed and nourished. If, therefore, such forms are met with in the woodland retreats, then it clearly signifies a defeat of the garden-creepers by the forest ones, untended and uncared for by human beings, as they are. शुद्धान्तः-Harem. दूरीकृताः-Surpassed, excelled. The figure is निदर्शना, which is defined as अभवन्वस्तुसंबन्ध उपमापरिकल्पकः ।

P. 16. नव...पेलवा-Delicate (पेलवा) like a Jasmine flower. आलवालं-A basin. सोदरस्नेहः-A sisterly affection असाधुदर्शी-one who sees not aright; wanting in discrimination.

I. 18. The king explains why कण्व, according to him, lacks discretion. अव्याजमनोहरं-Artlessly (अव्याजं) beautiful. तपःक्षमं-Fit to undergo penance. शमीलता-The शमी tree, which is very tough, and which is supposed to conceal fire within. Cf. शमीमिवाभ्यन्तरलीनपावकाम्। रघु० III. 9. This verse is a fine example of निदर्शना. अतिपिनद्धेन-fastened too tightly. पिनद्ध P. P. of √अपि+नह् पयोधरविस्तारयितृ-which swells the bosom.

P. 18. I. 19. The king means that the bark-garment is not a fitting apparel for such a lovely form whose charms are definitely marred by it. उप...ग्रन्थिना-secured with delicate knots (ग्रन्थि). स्तन...च्छादिना-covering the fully developed orbs of her two breasts. अभिनवं-Fresh, in her prime of youth. स्वां शोभां न पुष्यति-does not develop the fulness of its own charms. पाण्डु...दरेण पिनद्धं-Enveloped by a calyx (उदर) of pale (पाण्डु) leaves. अथवा-The particle introduces the other alternative, or पक्षान्तर. काम...पुष्यति-In the preceding verse, he has given it as his opinion that she does not look charming with the bark-garment on. He changes his mind, and reverts to the other alternative. 'Although the bark-garment is certainly not a suitable apparel for such a form, I cannot say that in her case it does not heighten her physical charm; indeed she does look beautiful even with a bark-garment.'

I. 20. शैवलेन अनुविद्धम्-Intertwined or overspread with moss (शैवल, Cf. Mar शेवाळें). लक्ष्मन् n.-the speck or spot. लक्ष्मीं तनोति-

Increases the glory. मनोज्ञा–Lovely, charming, Lit. मनो जानाति सा–One who knows the mind; a clever, attractive woman. मण्डनम्–Decoration, ornament, embellishment. This is a fine illustration of अर्थान्तरन्यास, wherein we get a generalisation based upon particular instances or vice versa. वाते...लीभिः-वातेन ईरिताः पल्लवाः एव अङ्गुल्यः–ताभिः–With his sprout–like fingers moved by the breeze, संभावयामि–I shall honour him (by granting his request). The suggestion, in this sentence, is that of a loving friend beckoning her to come near and do him a good turn. Cf. इदं चैकदेशविवर्ति रूपकम्। तेन केसरवृक्षस्य वयस्यत्वमपि रूपितं भवति। तेनायमर्थः। यथा कश्चन सखाऽत्यन्तमुत्कण्ठितोऽङ्गुलीचालनेन मित्रं त्वरयति तद्वदिति। Com. लतासनाथः–In the company (सनाथ) of a creeper. शकुन्तला is imagined to be a creeper, and the two together thus present the sight of a pretty couple. This idea lends greater charm if we believe that दुष्यन्त is standing just behind the केसर tree all along, and was associated with the tree in beckoning her to him and grant him his request. प्रियंवदा–one who talks sweet.

I. 21. शकुन्तला was likened to a creeper, and the idea has caught the king's fancy. He, therefore, tries to analyse her charms to see in what respects they agree with the creeper's charms. किसलयरागः-किसलयस्य इव रागः यस्य सः—Having the red glow of a tender sprout (किसलय). कोमल...कारिणौ–Resembling tender twigs (विटप). लोभनीयं–Alluring, covetable, bewitching. अङ्गेषु संनद्धम्–Pervades her limbs, is fully developed in all parts of the body; 'is arrayed in the limbs'–Ray. अत्राङ्गेष्विति बहुवचनेन वदने कान्तिमत्ता नयनयोस्तरलता कण्ठे कम्बुत्रिरेखावत्त्वं वक्षसि स्तनोज्जृम्भणं नाभौ गभीरता नितम्बे मध्यनिम्नत्वमुभयभागे चतुरस्रत्वं जघनजङ्घाजानुमण्डलोरुदेशानां मांसलत्वं गतौ सविलासत्वमित्यादि ध्वनितम्।

P. 20. स्वयंवरवधूः-स्वयं वृणीते इति स्वयंवरा–सा च वधूश्च–who has elected herself to be the (bride of the Mango tree), self-elected. कृतनामधेया–Named. कृतं नामधेयं यस्याः सा। Cf. मिथुनं परिकल्पितं त्वया सहकारः फलिनी च नन्विमौ। अविधाय विवाहसत्क्रियामनयोर्गम्यत इत्यसांप्रतम्॥ रघु० VIII. 61. व्यतिकरः–Union, blending, intertwining, intermingling.

अपि नाम–would that! How I wish that! एष नूनं...मनोरथाः–The joke of प्रियंवदा has really gone home, and hence such a reply. For we cannot believe that Śakuntalā had no such romantic thoughts of love and union. Her appreciation of the pretty couple of the सहकार and वनजोत्स्ना clearly indicates how in her mind youthful charm is associated with the pleasure of union. असवर्ण...भवा–असवर्णे क्षेत्रे संभवः यस्याः सा–Born of a wife belonging to a caste not his own; sprung from a wife dissimilar in caste. If शकुन्तला were कण्व's daughter born from a Brahmin wife, दुष्यन्त, a क्षत्रिय, cannot marry her as she is ineligible as क्षत्रिय's wife. If, on the other hand, she is his daughter sprung from a wife the क्षत्रिय class–a custom sanctioned in those days–then दुष्यन्त had no legal or religious difficulty in marrying her. Cf. मनु॰ III. 13. शूद्रैव भार्या शूद्रस्य सा च स्वा च विशः स्मृते । ते च स्वा चैव राज्ञश्च ताश्च स्वा चाग्रजन्मनः ॥

I. 22. क्षत्र...क्षमा–क्षत्रस्य परिग्रहः (कलत्रत्वेन अङ्गीकारः)–तस्य क्षमा (योग्या)–Fit to be accepted as a wife by a क्षत्रिय. आर्यं मनः–My noble heart, my honourable soul. अभिलाषि–filled with a longing. सतां हि etc. The meaning is 'That I was conscious of a sudden liking for her is a clean proof of the fact that she is eligible for me a क्षत्रिय; since such a feeling of sympathy could only arise towards a legitimate object. The inner voice or the secret prompting of the heart is always decisive, in the case of men of a higher and nobler mind.' तत्वतः–In reality, in her true nature. उपलप्स्ये-ज्ञास्ये–I shall ascertain. P. 22 सलिल...द्रुतः–dislodged by the disturbance caused in the sprinkling of water.

I. 23. प्रेरितलोलल्लोचना–प्रेरिते लोले लोचने यया– Directing her tremulous eyes. विवर्तितभ्रूः–who has bent or curved her eye-brows (through fear). अकामा–uninfluenced by love. The poet means that the coquettish movements of the eyes are due to the inspiration of amorous feelings. In the case of शकुन्तला, that was impossible. It appears, however, that she is taking lessons in that art, which she has very soon to exhibit. दृष्टिविभ्रमः–The playful movements of the eyes.

I. 24. The king is jealous of the bee and addresses this verse to him who is taking so much liberty with her. The bee is represented as an aggressive lover, having no scruples, and paying little heed to the delicate sentiments of his beloved. Such a type has succeeded, however, while he, a cool calculating rational lover is left in the lurch to witness their amours taking place before his very eyes. चलापाङ्गां (दृष्टिं)–चलः अपाङ्गः (प्रान्तभागः) यस्याः सा ताम्–With its tremulous outer corner. वेपथुमतीम्–Trembling, possessed of a tremor (वेपथुः) रहस्याख्यायीव etc. Cf. कर्णे लोलः कथयितुमभूदाननस्पर्शलोभात् । मेघ॰ II. रतिसर्वस्वं–(the lip) which has the all-in-all of amorous pleasure. याधुन्वत्याः (अस्याः) of her who is waving (her hand). Pres. Part. of √ वि + आ + धु–तत्वान्वेषात्–In our attempt to ascertain the truth viz. the real character of शकुन्तला. Cf. तथापि तत्त्वत एनामुपलप्स्ये । हताः–Undone, ruined, frustrated (in our desires). कृती–कृतं यस्यास्तीति–One who has done i. e. accomplished his purpose; successful. धृष्टः–P. P. of √धृष्–Impudent, presumptuous. The Prākrit is धिट्ठो, corresponding to the Marathi धीट. दुर्विनीत–ill-trained, ill-behaved. अभिभूयमानाम्–Being assailed or overpowered. के आवां परित्रातुं–' who are we to protect? We are as weak and helpless as you are'. Apparently they make slight of the fright of शकुन्तला caused by a mere bee.

P. 24. I. 25. पौरवे शासात (सति)–Loc. Absolute construction. While a descendant of Puru is governing.' Note how he refers to himself in an indirect manner. कोऽयमविनयं आचरति–'Who is this that practises rudeness.' The king tries to show that he had just come on the scene, having casually heard of Śakuntalā's cry, and that he knew nothing of the bee episode. किंचिदिव संभ्रान्ताः–They are slightly confused, because the king entered as an ordinary humble man. अत्याहितं–A great calamity or danger. अपि तपो वर्धते–'Does your piety thrive?' This was a regular form of salutation on meeting a Brahmin. साध्वसात्–Through nervous excitement. अवचना–Without speaking a word. Note that throughout the whole interview, she has not exchanged one single word with the king. इदानीं...लोभेन–When Śakuntalā gave no reply to the king's question, she has filled in the gap by coming forward to answer the king's question. " Yes ; now indeed, does Tapas prosper by the acquisition of a distinguished guest. " Observe how Anasūyā, elderly and senior amongst the three, directs the interview on their side. अर्घ or अर्घ्यम्–A respectful offering to a guest of rice, Dūrvā grass, flowers, fruit etc. with water in a small boat-shaped vessel. ' The rites of hospitality were enforced amongst the Hindus by very stringent regulations. The observance of them ranked as one of the five great sacraments (महायज्ञ) under the title of नृयज्ञ or मनुष्ययज्ञ, the man-sacrament.' Brahmā, Prajāpati, Indra, Fire, the Vasus and the Sun were supposed to be present in the person of a guest and to partake of the food that was given to him. If a guest departed disappointed from any house, his sins were to be transferred to the house-holder, and all the merits of the house-holder were to be transferred to him. " Monier Williams. इदं (पादोदकं) This water (brought by us for watering the trees). सूनृतया गिरा–By your kind yet sincere language ; complimentary and friendly words without flattery. (प्रियं सत्यं च वचनम्). सप्तपर्णवेदिकायाम्–On the raised-seat under the सप्तपर्ण tree. It is quite an ancient custom to construct platforms or raised-seats (Cf. Mar. पार) round the trunk of big trees. परिश्रमविनोदः–Removal of fatigue. पर्युपासनम्-Lit. sitting by the side, waiting upon. तपोवनविरोधिनः विकारस्य गमनीया–Susceptible to an emotion which is out of place in this forest-grove devoted to piety. A particular attraction she has felt for the king at his first sight and impulse the like of which she never felt for any man in the hermitage so far. This is the first awakening of love, which has unnerved and excited her a little. Innocent as she is, however, she is not able to explain her feeling. सम...रमणीयं–Pleasing because of equal age and beauty of form. सौहार्दम्–Friendship; abstract, noun from सुहृद्. P. 26. चतुरगम्भीराकृतिः–Possessed of a form, smart (चतुर) and dignified. प्रभाववान्–Possessed of majestic glory (प्रभाव). Pischel reads this sentence differently thus:—को णु क्खु एसो दुरवगावगंभीराकिदी महुरं आलवंतो पहुत्तदक्खिण्णं वित्थारेदि । विरह...जनः (देशः)–विरहेण पर्युत्सुकाःजनाः यत्र–The people in which are left in anxiety on account of your separation. °परिश्रमस्य आत्मा पदं उपनीतः–' You have exposed yourself to the hardship of the journey, etc. ' मा उत्ताम्य–' Be not impatient. ' त्वया चिन्तितानि–She too was very eager to know these details about the king. She, however, kept silent, lest her emotion should be detected. आत्मापहारः–conceal-ment of (my) identity. पौरवेण राज्ञा may as well refer to his father as to himself. He would like, however, to introduce himself as king Dusyanta's official, appointed to supervise the penance–forests and guard them from disturbances. In case he is found out to be the king, it is open to him to say, that in speaking thus about himself he has not spoken a lie because had not his father entrusted him with the sacred duty of looking after the sages ? सनाथाः–Possessed of a lord and protector (नाथ). A very clever suggestion is made by अनसूया in this her remark—सनाथा इदानीं धर्मचारिणः । शकुन्तला devoted to the observance of piety, has now found one who could be a नाथ–also meaning ' husband ' to her. This शकुन्तला fully understands, and hence the stage–remark शकुन्तला शृङ्गारलज्जां निरूपयति । आकारं विदित्वा–Understanding the gestures of both who appeared to be enamoured of each other. आकार–means ' the outward appearance, accompanied with various gestures, which indicates the inner state of mind. जीवितसर्वस्वेन–With the all-in-all, the most valuable treasure of his life, i. e. Śakuntalā. Cf. सा भगवतः कण्वस्य कुलपतेरुच्छ्वसितम् । Act III. Anasūyā suggests that their mutual love is apparent ; and if only father काश्यप had been here, this guest would have been made happy with the gift of शकुन्तला.

P. 28. युवां अपेतम्–' Get off with you ! ' As a girl would say in Marathi. चला चालत्या व्हा ! सखीगतं–About or relating to (गतं) your friend. Cf. आत्मगतम् ।. शाश्वते ब्रह्मणि–In perpetual celibacy (ब्रह्मणि = ब्रह्मचर्ये). तदात्मजा–तस्य (कण्वस्य) आत्मजा–His own daughter ; born of himself. गोत्रनामधेयः–गोत्रेण नामधेयं यस्य सः–Having a family name of कौशिक. i. e. The famous royal sage विश्वामित्र. किमपि जातशङ्कैः–Frightened, for what reason we cannot tell (किमपि). अन्यसमाधिभीरुत्वं The dread of the devotion (समाधि) of others. वसन्तोदारसमये–' During the charming (उदार) Spring–time. Prākrit expression वसंतोदारसमए may also be translated as वसन्तावतारसमये–' During the season of the advent of spring'. उन्मादयितृ–Maddening, exhilerating.

P. 30 I. 26. मानुषीषु–Amongst mortal females. प्रभातरलं ज्योतिः–The tremulously radiant–flash i. e. lightning. लब्धावकाशः–लब्धः अवकाशः येन–Which has found scope (अवकाश). He has ascertained now that she is eligible, and therefore he feels he could entertain a desire for her hand. धृत...कातरं–धृतः द्वैधीभावः–तेन कातरम्–Nervous or anxious because of the suspense. The king refers to what प्रियंवदा said before, viz. अपि नामैवमहमप्यात्मनोऽनुरूपं वरं लभेयेति ।, and he apprehends the possibility of her marriage having been not only contemplated but perhaps fixed up already. Hence, says he, his mind is in suspense. वक्तुकामः–वक्तुं कामः यस्य सः–With a desire to speak. This was more or less intended to tease Śakuntalā, and hence the stage-remark ' शकुन्तला सखीमङ्गुल्या तर्जयति । सच्चरित...लोभात्–' out of a keen desire to hear the life of the pious people.' Really speaking, the king only wanted to know whether Śakuntalā was likely to be married, and if so, to whom. अनि...योगः–न विद्यते नियन्त्रणा यस्य–तादृशः अनुयोगः यस्य सः (तपस्विजनः)–To whom a question (अनुयोग) may be asked without any restraint or reserve (नियंत्रणा).

I. 27. वैखानसं–Relating to a विखानस or hermit. तेन कृतं प्रोक्तं वा व्रतं वैखानसं, तत्तु नियतारण्यवासरूपम् । 'A vow which is performed by him or enjoined on him is called वैखानस, and that consists in always living in the woods.' आप्रदानात्–प्रदानपर्यन्तम् i. e. आविवाहात्–Up to the period of her marriage. मदनस्य

व्यापाररोधि कामक्रियानिवारकम्–Prohibiting indulgence in the ways of love. अत्यन्तम्–For all time, for ever. आत्म...वल्लभाभिः (हरिणाङ्गनाभिः)–dear (वल्लभा) to her because of their eyes like her own (आत्मसदृश). आत्मसदृशे ईक्षणे यासां ताः °क्षणाः–अत एव वल्लभाः–ताभिः । It may be optionally resolved into आत्मसदृशेक्षणवल्लभा: आभिः । In that case it would mean 'with these (female deer), of whom she is a favourite for having eyes like their own. आहो–A particle of doubt, is used पक्षान्तरे or विकल्पे i. e. antithetically, in stating an opposite alternative. परवशः–dependent on another, under the control of another i. e. the sage कण्व. संकल्पः–Intention, thought. दुःखापा–Difficult to obtain. दुःखेन अवाप्तुं शक्या । प्रार्थना Desire, longing (for शकुन्तला).

I. 28 स्पर्शक्षमं–That bears a touch, fit to be touched. He means the lustre of this gem–like शकुन्तला first dazzled his eyes, and made him suspect that she was beyond his reach and like fire must remain untouched by human hands. It transpires now that he can reasonably covet her hand, which if touched will not only not burn him, but will prove a veritable Kohinoor in his possession.

P. 32 असंबद्धप्रलापिनी–Prattling nonsense or absurdly (असंबद्ध). She refers to the action of प्रियंवदा in volunteering information regarding her marriage etc. स्वच्छन्दतः–At (your) sweet will. ग्रहीतु...त्मानम्–V. L. उत्थाय जिघृक्षुरिव इच्छां निगृह्य–'Rising up as if desirous of holding her (and then) restraining his intention.' चेष्टाप्रतिरूपिका प्रतिगतं रूपं अस्यां सा प्रतिरूपा–प्रतिरूपा एव प्रतिरूपिका–A reflector, a counter–part. चेष्टा प्रतिरूपिका यस्याः सा–रूपिका (कामि...वृत्तिः) Having a physical action (चेष्टा) for its counter–part; presenting itself as reflected in a physical action. As the stage-direction informs us, when शकुन्तला left the place, the king almost felt impelled by an inward powerful impulse, to go after her and bring her back. That would have looked highly improper and absurd, if not actually indecent. He has therefore restrained himself, and in his cooler moment, reviews what happened a few seconds before. The mental inclination of a lover is found reflected in a physical action. ' The desire to restrain शकुन्तला was so powerful that I feel what I desired has been actually translated in physical action (चेष्टा).'

I. 29. अनुयास्यन्–Future Part. of √अनु + या–' About to or on the point of following.' वारितप्रसर :–वारितः प्रसरः यस्य सः–Whose movement was checked. वृक्षसेचने–' Two waterings of trees. ' ' You owe me the labour, according to our agreement, of watering two more shrubs.' The delicate शकुन्तला, on a former occasion, could not complete the watering of a certain number of trees, fixed for each one of them. प्रियंवदा, therefore, helped her, on the understanding that शकुन्तला was to pay back, on demand, this debt of labour. Very cleverly therefore, प्रियंवदा has thought of that, with a view to detain her on this pretext, when even Anasūyā's reasoning of propriety failed to stop her. आत्मानं मोचयित्वा–Releasing yourself (from this debt).

I. 30. अति...तलौ (बाहू)–With the palms (तलौ) excessively red (लोहित). प्रमाणाधिकः–स्वाभाविकमानादधिकः–More than usual or natural; abnormal P. 34. बद्धम्–formed. जालकम्–Lit. A net-work, a collection. Cf. तस्य कर्कशविहारसंभवं स्वेदमाननविलग्नजालकम् । रघु० IX. 68. बन्धे स्रंसिनि–The knot (binding the hair) getting loose. पर्याकुल–Dishevelled. अनृणा–Free from debt.–(अविद्यमानं ऋणं यस्याः सा). परिग्रहः–V. L. प्रतिग्रहः–A gift. राजपुरुषं...गच्छथ–He means that the ring should not be taken as evidence for his identity as दुष्यन्त. It is a gift he has received in his capacity as a राजपुरुष, which would thus have a two–fold meaning. राजपुरुष–(i) राज्ञः पुरुषः–A King's official. (ii) राजा चासौ पुरुषश्च–A royal person, which दुष्यन्त is, while the ring he obtained was a gift from his kingly father. अथवा महाराजेन shows clearly that the king has not succeeded in deceiving प्रियंवदा at least. यद्यात्मनः...प्रभविष्यामि–She means that the king's company has so much hypnotised her that she has no power left over her body to move away. Cf. भवतु कोपिष्यामि यद्यात्मनः प्रभवामि। उत्तर० I. विस्रष्टव्यस्य रोद्धव्यस्य वा–(To decide) what should be allowed to go and what should be restrained.

I. 31. कर्णं ददाति— i. e. अवहिता, तत्परा अस्ति–is very attentive. Cf. Mar. कान देते. अन्यविषया–अन्यः विषयः यस्याः सा–Having a different object (to observe).

P. 36. I. 32. विटप...वल्कलेषु (० द्रुमेषु)–विटेपेषु विषक्तानि जलार्द्राणि वल्कलानि येषां तेषु। (The trees) on the branches of which were suspended (विषक्त) the bark garments wet with water. परि...प्रकाशः (रेणुः)–Shining (प्रकाश) like the twilight glow. अरुण्य is the glow either of sun–rise or sun–set, more usually the former.

I. 33. स्कन्ध...दन्तः–स्कन्धे लग्नः एकदन्तः यस्य–One of whose tusks was fixed in a tree–trunk. The Bengali Mss. read–तीव्राघातादभिमुखतरुस्कन्धभग्नैकदन्तः। ' with a violent blow, having broken one tusk against the trunk of a tree standing in his way. ' पादा...पाशः–पादेन आकृष्टानि व्रततिवलयानि–तेषां आसङ्गेन संजातः पाशः यस्य सः–with fetters formed by the clinging (आसङ्ग) of creeper–coils dragged along by his feet. आरण्यकवृत्तान्तेन–By this forest incident viz. of the wild–elephant. असंभा...सत्कारं–To whom the due (rites of) hospitality were not profferred. पुरस्कृतः–सत्कृतः—Hospitably entertained; received. कुशसूचिः–The needle–like point of the Kuśa grass. परिपालयत–wait. सव्याजम्–With some pretext (व्याज) For lingering. Cf. अहो लता विटपे ममैकावली लग्ना। विक्र० I.

P. 38 मन्दौत्सुक्यः–मन्दं औत्सुक्यं यस्य सः–Whose eagerness (to return) has slackened ; grown indifferent. अनुयात्रिक–A follower. निवेशयामि–Causal of √ नि + विश्–meaning ' to enter, to take up a station, to encamp ' as an army. शकुन्तला०व्यापारात्–From busying or occupying myself with thoughts regarding शकुन्तला.

I. 34. असंस्तुतं–अपरिचितं–Unacquainted, unrelated. He means, the connection between the mind and the body is severed as it were, both going in diverse ways and not working in harmony. The word also means अवश i. e. not under the control (of the body); V. L. असंस्थितं meaning ‘ restless, unstable. ’ चीनांशुकं–A silken cloth from China. Even in those days, there was great export of silk from China. प्रतिवातं–Against the wind–current.

ACT II

P. 40. भो दिष्टम्–'Oh my (evil) destiny, my fate!' Some translate दिट्ठं by दृष्टं, to mean almost the same thing, दृष्ट and अदृष्ट being two kinds of fate, one referring to its visible working, and the other to its secret or invisible working. निर्विण्णः–Tired, disgusted. वयस्यभावः–Friendship. शार्दूलः–A tiger. आहिण्ड्यते–Pres. Passive, III sing. of √आ + हिण्ड्–'to wander about'. पत्रसंकरकषायाणि–Astringent (कषाय) from the mixture (संकर) of leaves. कटूनि–Pungent, bad-smelling. अनियतवेलम्–न नियता वेला यस्मिन् कर्मणि यथा तथा–At irregular hours. शूल्यमांसभूयिष्ठः–mostly consisting of roast-meat, i. e. meat cooked or roasted on spits. शूल्य is explained as शूले संस्कृतम्। तुरगा...सन्धेः–with my joints bruised or dislocated (कण्डित) by having to ride in pursuit on horse-back. निकामं शयितव्यम्–enough sleep, comfortable lying down (in bed). महति प्रत्यूषे–At the very earliest (महति) dawn. Cf. Mar. मोठ्या पहांटेस. दास्याः पुत्रैः–is the same as दासीपुत्रैः, being one compound. The genitive in this compound is used in reviling and abusing (आक्रोशे). शकुनिलुब्धकः–Bird-hunter, a fowler. वनग्रहणं–Beating the forest; surrounding and taking possession of a wood for the purpose of hunting the animals it contains. इयता–एतावता–'with this much'. गण्डस्य...संवृत्ता–Note this Sanskrit idiom. It means 'A small boil or a pimple (पिण्डिका or पिटका) has grown on the (old) boil (गण्ड).' पिण्डिका or according to some पिटका means 'a pustule, a pimple, a small boil.' Cf. 'To add misery to misfortune.' अवहीनेषु–पश्चात् पतितेषु–Left behind; dropped behind. अधन्यतया–Through ill–luck or misfortune. मनः न करोति–Does not form or fix up his mind. अक्ष्णोः प्रभातमासीत्–i. e. जाग्रतः एव or दृशोः उन्मीलतोः सतोः रजनी निर्गता। The day dawned on his eyes (wide awake). कृता...क्रमं–कृतः आचारप्राप्तः परिक्रमः येन सः–who has finished the usual or customary routine (of the morning duties). V. L. °परिकर्माणम्–परिकर्म–Toilet, decoration after bath! बाणासनं–शरासनं–A bow. यवनी–A native woman of यवन or Arabia.

The word is also applied to the Greek or Ionian maiden. Wilson remarks that Tartarian or Bactrian women may be intended. The business of these attendants was to act as the bearers of the king's bow and arrows, and during war-time, she gives weapons to the king. अङ्गभङ्गविकलः—Crippled by palsy or paralysis of the limbs.

P. 42. II. 1. तद्भाव...श्वासि – Deriving encouragement from the observance of her gestures. V. L. °दर्शनायासि—' Exerting to observe her (favourable) gestures' is not so good, as it implies that the favourable indication in the form of gestures may not exist, in which case, whatever he says later on—' स्मितं कृत्वा...स्वतां पश्यति, has no proper justification, based as these remarks are on the assumption of the existence of the favourable gestures. अकृतार्थे मनसिजे—Even if love has not achieved its object viz. union with the beloved. उभयप्रार्थना—Longing for both, love felt by both. रतिं कुरुते–gives delight ; Cf. अनातुरोत्कण्ठितयोः प्रसिध्यता समागमेनापि रतिर्न मां प्रति । परस्परप्राप्तिनिराशयोर्वरं शरीरनाशोऽपि समानुरागयोः ॥ माल० III. 15. आत्मा...वृत्तिः (प्रार्थयिता)—आत्मनः आभिप्रायेण संभाविता इष्टजनस्य चित्तवृत्तिः येन सः—Who judges of the state of feeling of his beloved one, by his own desires (अभिप्राय). विडम्ब्यते—Is deluded (to find that he was wandering in a fool's paradise.)

II. 2. स्निग्धं—Adverb going with वीक्षितं—Tenderly, softly, full of love. विलासादिव—As if through dalliance. It is one of the Bhāvās caused by love and is thus explained:—विलासोऽङ्गे विकारो यः प्रियाप्तावासनादिषु । मा गाः–' Do not go. ' गाः–Aorist form √ इ, with the augment dropped because of the particle मा. उपरुद्धया–V. L. अवरुद्धया. By her who was obstructed. सासूयम्–Angrily, disdainfully. मत्परायणम्–अहमेव परं अयनं यस्य तत् । Chiefly meant for me. He means that all these gestures like the soft look, the graceful slow gait, the disdainful remark were all intended for me, to convey to me her inner feeling. अहो–denotes wonder (आश्चर्यं). कामी स्वतां पश्यति–How a lover sees himself everywhere. In every movement of his beloved, he tries to discover the influence of his own love. न प्रसरति–Do not move i. e. are paralysed. वाङ्मात्रेण–By words merely (and not by the usual Anjali, or the joining of two hands and raising them to the forehead). जाप्यसे–Causal, Pass. II sing. of √ जि. स्वयं...पृच्छसि. विदूषक–speaks by a turn of the speech, probably quoting some proverb. The Com. शंकर explains it thus:—यथा कोऽपि कस्यचिन्नयनयोरङ्गुल्यादिकं प्रवेश्य पृच्छति, 'भवतश्चक्षुषोरश्रु कथमायाति तथा त्वमपि पृच्छसि। भिन्नार्थम्–स्फुटार्थम्–Distinctly, clearly ; V. L. वेतसः—Reed ; कुब्जलीलाम्–The gait or character of the hunch-backed, कुब्ज means 'hump-backed (cf. Mar. कुबडा); it is also a name for a crooked aquatic plant, also called वारि° or जलकुब्ज. ' To appreciate विदूषक's pleasantry in comparing himself to an upright reed, accidentally transformed into a crooked plant, we must bear in mind that his natural form was that of a lame hump-backed man. '–Monier Williams. विडम्बयाति–Imitates, copies. P. 44. आकुलप्रदेशे–In a wild region. Some read in addition अमानुषसंचारे–' Unfrequented. ' यत्सत्यं–To tell you the truth, to speak the truth. सन्धिबन्धः–' The tendon or ligament binding the joints together. ' अनीशः–अप्रभुः–Not a master, i. e. one who has lost all control. प्रसादयिष्यामि–Causal, Future I sing. of √ प्र + सद्. It means ' I beg of you to favour me. ' मृगयाविक्लवं–Disinclined or averse to hunting.

II. 3. आहितसायकम्–आहितः सायकः यस्मिन्–With an arrow (सायक) fixed upon it मुग्धविलोकित–A lovely glance. अरण्ये...सीत्–(It means:) I have cried in wilderness (where nobody listens or replies) ; a kind of a proverbial phrase. Cf. तदलमधुनारण्यरुदितैः। अमरु० 76. अनतिक्रमणीयं–which cannot be set aside or disregarded सावशेषम्–अवशेषेण सहितं–With a remnant, with something left (unspoken yet). अनायासे (कर्मणि)–न विद्यते आयासः यस्मिन्–Where no physical exertion is involved, which would give no physical trouble. मोदकखण्डिका–Bits of sweet–meats. V. L. मोदकखादिकायाम्–' In eating sweet-meats. ' सुगृहीतः क्षणः–I have pledged my word, I accept the invitation. ' The phrase has origin in a formula ; used in connection with the श्राद्ध ceremony. A Brahmin is duly invited to attend the ceremony, and he uses this expression, when he accepts the invitation. गृहीत्वामुकसंज्ञस्यामुकगोत्रस्य चामुके । श्राद्धे तु वैश्वदेवार्थं करणीयः क्षणस्त्वया ॥ इत्येवं श्राद्धकृद् ब्रूयात् तं प्राप्नोतु भवानिति । स वदेत् प्राप्नवानीतीतरस्तं प्रति द्विजः ॥ Cited by Pandit from शौनक° 16.—' The person who addresses in the words of the formula (the श्राद्धकृत्) is said to give the क्षण, and the Brahmin to whom it is addressed) to take the क्षण, in the language of ignorant priests. Hence because the word क्षण is so often used in the formula, so has come, in the common parlance of Brahmanas, who subsist mostly upon, occasional dinners at Śrāddhas, and to which class our विदूषक belonged, to signify ' an engagement at Srāddha, which, when once begun, must be carried out, on pain of incurring sin. ' It may be observed that Vidūṣaka's way of expressing his obligation to accomplish what he has undertaken is perfectly in keeping with his character. ' क्षण घेणें ' is still used in Marathi in the sense of ' pledging one's self for the performance of a thing'– Pandit.

P. 46. आज्ञावचनोत्कण्ठः–eager (to speak out) words of command. दृष्टदोषा–दृष्टाः दोषाः यस्यां सा (मृगया) । Found fault with, observed to have evil effects. मृगया is looked as one of the ten vices which a king has to avoid. Cf. पानमक्षाः स्त्रियश्चैव मृगया च यथाक्रमम् । एतत्कष्टतमं विद्याच्चतुष्कं कामजे गणे ॥ मनु° VII. 50.

II. 4. अनवरत...पूर्वं (गात्रं)–अनवरतं धनुर्ज्यायाः आस्फालनं तेन क्रूरः पूर्वः (पूर्वभागः) यस्य तत्–The fore-part of which was tough because of the incessant friction (आस्फालन) of the bow-string. सहिष्णु–capable of enduring. Read क्लेशलेशैः–By the slightest fatigue. The reading स्वेद° is possibly a misreading of खेद in the Mss. अपचितम्–Reduced in bulk व्यायतत्वात्–कृतव्यायामत्वात्–दृढत्वात्–Because of the muscular development; व्यायाम–coming from the same root means this. प्राणसारं (गात्रं)–which is all life and energy. प्राणः सारः स्थिरांशः यत्र तत्–with vatality alone left behind. अपवादिन्–one who speaks ill. or censures. स्थिरप्रतिबन्धः–Persisting in opposition, persevering in throwing obstacles in the way. वैधेयः–मूर्खः–A fool, blockhead.

निदर्शनम्–Illustration, example. Cf. हिमसेकविपतिरत्र मे नलिनी पूर्वनिदर्शनं मता ।

II. 5. मेद...दरं–मेदसः छेदेन कृशं उदरं यस्य तद्–With the waist attenuated by the cutting down of fat. उत्थानं–Activity, exertion. सत्वानाम्–जन्तूनां सिंहादीनाम्–of creatures. भयक्रोधयोः विकृतिमत् चित्तं–Their minds undergoing various changes (विकृति) or affected by various emotions under the influence of fear and anger. P. 48. उत्कर्षः Excellence, glory. चले लक्ष्ये सिध्यन्ति. Succeed in hitting a moving target. (लक्ष्यं). Men practising shooting will realise how difficult it is to shoot a moving target and what delight it gives when they succeed in doing so. उत्साहहेतुक–' one who incites or encourages one to action viz. hunting. ' प्रकृतिमापन्न–Has come back to his normal, healthy state of the mind, (hunting mood being looked upon as an aberration). प्रकृति is the natural quiescent state of the soul, as opposed to विकृति, explained above. जीर्णऋक्षस्य–of an old bear Cf. भल्लूका मनुष्याणां नासिकां गृह्णन्ति । दशकुमार०

II. 6. निपानं...आहावः–A reservoir or trough near a well. छाया...म्बकं–छायायां बद्धः कदम्बकः येन–Forming a group in the shade. रोमन्थः–भुक्तस्य पुनः पुनराकृष्य or उद्गीर्य चर्वणम्–Ruminating, chewing the cud. वराहततिभिः–By the herd (तति) of the boars. V. L. वराहपतिभिः ।. मुस्ताक्षतिः–Destroying or uprooting (क्षति) of the मुस्ता grass. ' मुस्ता–is a sort of fragrant grass, eaten by swine and hence are they called ' मुस्ताद. ' शिथिल...बन्धम्–शिथिलः ज्यायाः बन्धः यस्मिन्–With the bow-string loosened.

II. 7. शमप्रधानेषु–शमः प्रधानः येषाम् ते । °प्रधानाः तेषु–By whom self-control or exemption from all passion and feeling is regarded as the summum bonum or everything. स्पर्शानुकूल–agreeable to the touch. सूर्यकान्तः–The sun-gem, a shining stone, a sun-crystal. It is supposed to emit lustre, when touched by the sun's rays. Its properties thus resemble those of a glass lens. It is also called सूर्यमणि or दीप्तोपल ; and corresponding to it, there is the चन्द्रकान्त or चन्द्रमणि which is believed to be oozing drops of water when the moon's rays fall on it. Cf. यदचेतनोऽपि पादैः स्पृष्टः प्रज्वलति सवितुरतिकान्तः ।

तत्तेजस्वी पुरुषः परकृतनिकृतिं कथं सहते ॥ भर्तृ॰ ii. 30. अन्य...भवात् Through the opposition of other forces or lustre (तेजस्). वमन्ति–Emit. The root वम् ' to vomit ' is one of those objectionable ones which should not be used in good poetry, unless in a secondary or figurative sense. Cf. निष्ठ्यूतोद्गीर्णवान्तानि गौणवृत्तिव्यपाश्रयम्। अतिसुन्दरमन्यत्र ग्राम्यकक्षां विगाहते ॥ काव्या॰ I. The Bengali reading is— स्पर्शानुकूला अपि सूर्यकान्तास्ते ह्यन्यतेजोऽभिभवाद्दहन्ति। He means that the sages, though outwardly calm and quiet, and given to the subduing of passions, have a latent destructive energy with them; and if they are provoked by wanton insults, will not fail to destroy those who molest them.

50. ध्वंसतां...वृत्तान्तः–Let all your agreement to (provoke the king) to action prove futile. स्वं...अशून्यं कुरु–Fulfil your office or post of duty i. e. Stand at the door. निर्मक्षिकम्–मक्षिकाणां अभावः clear of the flies i. e. free from all people. विरचित...नीयायाम् (छायायां) pleasant with the canopy of creepers formed above. अनवाप्त...फलः–न अवाप्तं चक्षुषः फलं येन सः–Who has not obtained the fruit i. e. the benefit of the eyes. दर्शनीयं–A worthy object of sight, V. L. द्रष्टव्यानां परं. The best of things worthy to be seen! He means that unless and until शकुन्तला is observed by him, he may consider his eyes to have been created in vain. Cf. यदृच्छया त्वं सकृदप्यवन्ध्ययोः। पथि स्थिता सुन्दरि यस्य नेत्रयोः। विक्र॰ I. ननु... वर्तते. विदूषक retorts saying that he has observed the most handsome person in दुष्यन्त and thus has obtained the reward of his eyes. आश्रमललामभूता–who serves as an embellishment of the hermitage. ललाम-अलंकारः ornament, decoration अवसरं न दास्ये I shall give him no opportunity (अवसरं) (to speak about शकुन्तला). ते तापसकन्यका...दृश्यते. He means that a hermit's daughter can never be a proper object of his love–a fact which it seems he has overlooked in his ardour for शकुन्तला. परिहार्य–Fit to be avoided.

II. 8. किल ' So goes the report, so I hear ' (किलेति ऐतीह्ये). तदु...गतम् तया आदौ उज्झितं पश्चात् (मुनिना) अधिगतम् Found by the sage after having been deserted by her i. e. by the celestial nymph मेनका. अर्कस्योपरि On the sun-plant. It is a large vigorous plant with medicinal sap and rind (Mar. रुई). शिथिलं-वृन्तात् च्युतं- severed from the stem. नवमालिका is a tender delicate plant, which as a creeper requires some other tree for support. Note the correspondence of words in the first line with those in the second. सुरयुवति with नवमालिका, मुनि with अर्क, अपत्य with कुसुम, उज्झित with शिथिल, and अधिगत with च्युत. पिण्डखर्जूरैः उद्वेजितः वैमनस्यं प्रापितः Disgusted or tired of eating the dates; तिन्तिणी or V. L. तिन्तिडिका Tamarind. Mar. चिंच. स्त्रीरत्नपरिभाविन् slighting the jewels amongst women.

II. 9. The king imagines that in creating शकुन्तला, either of these two methods must have been used by the Creator. चित्रे... योगा–Having first of all painted a faultless figure on the canvas, he breathed the principle of life in it. परि...योगा–परिकल्पितः सत्वेन योगः यस्याः–Who was endowed with life (सत्व). सत्वयोग–A combination of the various properties of being and life. रूपो...नु–Or may it be that having collected into one ideal model all excellent forms, she was created by mind (without the touch of hands). रूपोच्चयेन–चन्द्राद्युपमानवस्तुसमुच्चयेन–By a collection of all exquisite forms, or models of beauty like the moon etc, for the creation of one ideal perfect Beauty. मनसा (करणेन) कृता–Formed by means of the mind. अत एव करस्पर्शाद्यभावात्तादृशं कान्तिमत्त्वमेतादृग्लक्षणत्वादिकमिति भावः। Com. राघव०. Cf. मन्ये च मातङ्गजातिस्पर्शदोषभयादस्पृशतेयमुत्पादिता प्रजापतिना; अन्यथा कथमियमक्लिष्टता लावण्यस्य। न हि करतलस्पर्शक्लेशितानामीदृशी भवति कान्तिः। कादं० I. विधिना–By the Creator. अपरा स्त्रीरत्नसृष्टिः–A matchless or extra-ordinary (अपरा) creation of the loveliest of women. अपरा–is also interpreted to mean 'last'; the idea would be that by creating शकुन्तला, the Creator has said the last word in the matter. विभुत्वं–Omnipotence. प्रत्यादेशः–The eclipser, the supplanter; one who throws into the back-ground. Cf. प्रत्यादिश्यन्त इव मे दृष्टलक्ष्यभिदः शराः। रघु० I. उर्वशी प्रत्यादेशो रूपगर्वितायाः श्रियः। विक्र० I.

II. 10. The verse gives beautiful Rūpakas or metaphors for the beautiful form of शकुन्तला. कररुहैः–By the nails. अलूनं-शाखावस्थितं -Not cut, unplucked. लून–P. P. of √ लू ' to cut'. अनाविद्धं असमुत्कीर्ण-Unperforated, not pierced (by a diamond pin) Cf. मणौ वज्रसमुत्कीर्णे सूत्रस्येवास्ति मे गतिः । रघु० 1. 3. अना...रसम्–(Honey) whose flavour is yet untasted. पुण्यानां अखण्डं फलं–Unimpaired or complete and perfect reward of the meritorious actions (done in former life.) He means the beauty of शकुन्तला represents a full and perfect development of all the merits of her former birth. अनघं–Faultless इह i. e. अस्मिन् रूपविषये–With reference to this form.

P. 54 इङ्गुदी...शीर्षस्य. इङ्गुदीतैलेन चिक्कणं शीर्षं यस्य–whose head is greasy (चिक्कण) with the Ingudī oil (applied to the head). तपस्विनः–of some hermit ; ' of some wretched rustic'–M. Williams. दृष्टिरागः or चक्षूरागः means ' love as betrayed or displayed by the eyes. ' भवन्तमन्तरेण–About you, with reference to (अन्तरेण) you. अन्तरेण governs the Accusative. अप्रगल्भः–Not bold, shy, modest, reserved.

II. 11. अन्य...दयम् (हसितं)–अन्येन निमित्तेन कृतः उदयः यस्य तत्–(feigned to be) raised from some other cause (than love). As a matter of fact, says the king, love's influence was the cause of her smile. विनय...वृत्तिः (मदनः)–विनयेन वारिता वृत्तिः यस्य सः–Love which was checked in its manifestation by modesty. न विवृतः न च संवृतः–(Love) was neither fully manifested (विवृतः) nor was it fully concealed (संवृतः). Note how cleverly has the poet delineated love's manifestation in a typically Indian girl. न खलु... आरोहति–विदूषक means that it is just the way in which girls normally would behave under the influence of love. Surely he i. e. दुष्यन्त never expected that at his very first sight, she will come straightway and sit in his lap ! मिथःप्रस्थाने–At our mutual departure, when both of us took leave of one another and departed. शालीनतया–Through modesty (शालीनता). Cf. सखे, कुतूहलवानपि निसर्गशालिनः स्त्रीजनः । माल० IV. The word शालीन is generally explained as शालाप्रवेशमर्हतीति–one who is fit to enter an apartment of a house i. e. well-behaved, shy.

II. 12. अकाण्डे–अकस्मात्–Suddenly. विवृत्तवदना–Having turned her face back (towards me). The verse has a reference to Act I. अनसूये, अभिनवकुशसूच्या परिक्षतं मे चरणम् । कुरबकशाखापरिलग्नं च वल्कलम् । तावत् परिपालयतं मां यावदेतन्मोचयामि । and the stage-remark इति राजानमवलोकयन्ती सव्याजं विलम्ब्य सह सखीभ्यां निष्क्रान्ता । गृहीतपाथेयः–गृहीतं पाथेयं येन सः–One who has supplied himself with the provisions of the journey. पाथेय–a stock of provender. विदूषक means that the king will have now to stay for a longer time. He should, therefore, make provision for this lengthened stay. Note how विदूषक is anxious mainly about the provision. उपवनं–A pleasure-garden. A place of piety has been turned into a pleasure-resort by the king. P. 56 अपदेशः–Pretext, excuse. नीवारषष्ठभागं–The sixth portion of the produce of the forest-grain. A king was entitled to receive as tax, a sixth part of liquids, flowers, roots, fruit, grass etc. But from a Brahmin, learned in the Vedas, he was not to receive anything although dying of want. Cf. मनु० vii. 131–133. भागधेयः–यं–Share, tribute. भाग एव भागधेयः । Cf. भागरूपनामभ्यो धेयः ।. वर्णेभ्यः–From the four classes of people viz. ब्राह्मण, क्षत्रिय, वैश्य and शूद्र. क्षयि–Perishable अक्षय्यं–अविनाशि, Impossible to perish. Cf. क्षय्यजय्यौ शक्यार्थे ।. सिद्धार्थौ–who have accomplished their object viz. the king's interview. दीप्तिमतः–Resplendent, possessed of majestic lustre. He means that the king's form, although endowed with kingly glory, does not repel but inspires confidence in the minds of those who approach him. Cf. भीमकान्तैर्नृपगुणैः स बभूवोपजीविनाम् । अधृष्यश्चाभिगम्यश्च यादोरत्नैरिवार्णवः ॥ रघु० I. उपपन्नं–योग्यम्. Proper. ऋषिभ्यः नातिभिन्न–Who is not much different (in character) from the sages. V. L. ऋषिकल्पे–' Resembling a ऋषि, but with a degree of inferiority.'

P. 58. II. 14. सर्वभोग्ये आश्रमे–गार्हस्थ्ये–In the order (of house-holder) which is open to every one for enjoyment.

अध्याक्रान्ता-Taken up, accepted. Like the sage the king also abides in an आश्रम. रक्षायोगात्- By reason of (योगात्) the protection he offers to the subjects. This is a form of penance which he observes. चारणद्वन्द्वगीतः-गन्धर्वमिथुनगीतः-Sung by a pair of Gandharvas, or celestial-choristers. 'These beings were the musicians or minstrels of Indra's heaven, just as the Apsarasas were the dancers and actresses; and their business was to amuse the inhabitants of Svarga by singing the praises of gods, saints and heroes.'—M. W. राजपूर्वः-Preceded by the word राजन्. He is therefore राजमुनि a राजर्षि. Cf. दशपूर्वरथं यमाख्यया दशकण्ठारिगुरुं विदुर्बुधाः । रघु० XI. बलभित्सखः-The friend of बलभिद् i. e. Indra who crushes armies with his thunderbolt.

II. 15. उदधि......सीमां-उदधिभिः श्यामाः सीमाः यस्याः सा- With its boundaries darkened by the oceans. नगर...बाहुः-नगरस्य परिघः इव प्रांशू बाहू यस्य सः-Having long arms like the iron-bar of a city (gate). परिघ-अर्गल-The iron-bar to secure a gate. 'In a city-gate it was both massive and long (स्त्यान and दीर्घ), and therefore an object of comparison highly significant of muscular strength. It should be borne in mind that length and vigour of arm were prime requisites in the ancient hero, whose fame depended on his skill and power in managing a bow. Hence the appropriateness of such epithets as महाबाहु and प्रांशुबाहु.' M. W. आशंसन्ते-expect, long for (victory). सुरसमितयः-Groups of Gods. दैत्यैः बद्धवैराः-In constant enmity with the demons. V. L. समितिषु सुराः सक्तवैराः etc. where समितिषु would mean 'in battles.' Another reading is सुरयुवतयः बद्धवैराः etc. of the Com. राघवभट्ट, who remarks thus 'सुरयुवतयः इति युवतिग्रहणं तासामतिभीरुत्वा-द्वन्दीदुःखाद्यनुभवात् स्त्रीत्वेन युद्धाभिमानाद्यभावाच्च । पौरुहूते वज्रे-On the thunderbolt of पुरुहूत i. e. Indra (lit. invoked by many पुरुभिः बहुभिः हूतः). आश्रमसद्-आश्रमवासिन्-The inhabitant of the hermitage. Note the construction of this sentence, where विदित is used with the genitive. कतिपयरात्रं-for a few nights. The demons caused trouble during night.

P. 60. II. 16. पूर्वेषां–Of (your) predecessors. आप...त्रेषु–आपद्गतानां भयत्राणे–In the sacrifices (सत्रेषु) viz. giving security to the distressed. दीक्षिताः–consecrated, initiated. सपरिवाहम्–परिवाहेण सहितं–overflowing, flooded. Cf. पुरोत्पीडे तडागस्य परीवाहः प्रतिक्रिया । उत्तर॰ III. मा भैषीः–Aorist II sing. of √ भी 'to fear,' with the augment अ dropped, because of the prohibitive particle मा. एष राक्षसात् etc. V. L. एष तव चक्ररक्षीभूतोऽस्मि । 'Here I will guard the wheel of your chariot.' विजयप्रस्थानं–A march unto victory. आज्ञाप्तिहरः–Bearing a message of command.

P. 62. पुत्रपिण्डपालनः–(The ceremony of) cherishing the body of a son ; this ceremony seems to be akin to the birth-day ceremony and on this occasion, as the commentator काटयमेव observes, various presents are to be given to the son, in the form of sweet-meats, clothes etc. The V. L. प्रवृत्तपारणो मे उपवासो भविष्यति । 'My fast will be coming to an end (on the fourth day)' is not so satisfactory as our reading, which mentioning the definite ceremony, proves the importance of the king's presence for it. संभावयितव्या–Should be honoured by (your) presence. त्रिशङ्कुरिव–Like त्रिशङ्कु–' a just and a pious prince who aspired to celebrate a great sacrifice, hoping thereby to ascend the heaven in his mortal body. He first requested the sage वसिष्ठ to officiate for him ; but being refused, he then applied to the sage's hundred sons, by whom he was cursed and degraded to the condition of a Cāndāla. In this pitiable state, he had recourse to विश्वामित्र, who undertook to conduct the sacrifice and invited all the gods to be present; they however, refused to attend. Upon this, the enraged विश्वामित्र transported त्रिशङ्कु to the skies, whither he had no sooner arrived than he was hurled down again, head foremost, by Indra and the gods; but being arrested in his downward course by विश्वामित्र, remained suspended, between heaven and earth, forming a constellation in the southern hemisphere.'—M. W. अन्तराले–between the two.

II. 17. भिन्नदेशत्वात्–On occount of a difference or divergence in place (देश) शैले प्रतिहतं–Driven back, made to recoil by a hill

(शैल) in front (पुरः). स्रोतोवहः Gen. Sing of स्रोतोवह् 'a river.' तपोवनापरोध: Disturbance to the penance grove. Very cleverly has दुष्यन्त done away with his retinue which was a source of disturbance to him also. चपल: Restive, fickle, lacking control over his tongue. बटुः 'A lad, chap.'

II. 18. परोक्षमन्मथः To whom the (ways of) love are foreign, one who has had no experience of love. मृगशाव: A young one of a deer, a fawn. एधित: वर्धित: Bred up. He means, the association of such young creatures as fawns has left her thoroughly innocent of the working of love. परिहासविजल्पितं (which amounted to) mere prattling in joke हास्यभाषितं । परमार्थेन न गृह्यताम् should not be taken in earnest i. e. as representing the true state of things (परमार्थ).

ACT III.

P. 66. महानुभावः-महान् अनुभावः यस्य सः । Of great prowess. निरुपप्लवानि-free from obstacles; some have निरुपद्रवाणि which gives the same meaning. उपप्लव an obstruction. Cf. जीवन्पुनः शश्वदुपप्लवेभ्यः प्रजाः प्रजानाथ पितेव पासि ॥ रघु० II. 48.

III. 1. का कथा what talk, or mention; what account i. e. where is the need of fitting the arrow to the bow when the mere twanging of the bow is enough to expel the demons who impede their rites, in the same way as the roar (हुंकार) of some fierce animal suffices to scare away those who hear it. Cf. वसुधाधरकन्दराभिसर्पी प्रतिशब्दोऽपि हरेर्भिनत्ति नागान् ॥ विक्रमो० I. अपोहति from अप+ऊह्-dispels, removes. ऋत्विज्-ऋतौ यजतीति formed with the affix क्विन् of which nothing remains; one sacrificing at prescribed times, also means a priest who officiates at a sacrifice. आकाशे-this is an example of आकाशभाषितम्-a speech addressed to some person off the stage, the actor at the time fixing his eyes in the air; the answer which is supposed to be given is also आकाशभाषितम् and is not heard by the audience-the actor on the stage pretending to hear it (श्रुतिमभिनीय) repeats the imaginary reply with the words किं ब्रवीषि. Cf. किं ब्रवीष्येवमित्यादि विना पात्रं ब्रवीति यत् । श्रुत्वेवानुक्तमप्येकस्तत्स्यादाकाशभाषितम् ॥ दशरू०. उशीर is a kind of fragrant grass called वाळा in Marathi. आतपलङ्घनात्-from injury caused by the heat. लङ्घ् to leap over also signifies as here "to inflict some injury." निर्वापणाय-for cooling, from निर्वप् to extinguish; after this Monier Williams gives प्रियंवदे यत्नात् उपचर्य्यताम् । Let her be nursed with care'. उच्छ्वसितम्-life-breath—as precious to him as his own life. वैतानिक-वितानसम्बन्धि pertaining to a sacrifice (वितान). शान्त्युदकं-शान्त्यर्थं उदकम् । water which has the power to allay fever, to soothe and comfort. विष्कम्भः an introductory monologue or dialogue so called from its compressing (वि+स्कम्भ्) into a short space an account of those secondary incidents of the story which are not enacted before the audience, but a knowledge of which is essential for comprehending the action of the play. Cf. वृत्तवर्तिष्यमाणानां कथांशानां निदर्शकः । संक्षिप्तार्थस्तु विष्कम्भः ।. It is two-fold-शुद्ध when in Sanskṛit by a middling character or characters (मध्यपात्र) and मिश्र when in mixed Sankrit and Prākrit by characters belonging to the middling or lower rank (नीचमध्यमैः). It may come at the beginning of any act, even the first, immediately after the प्रस्तावना. When, however, the characters are exclusively of an inferior class, and speak Prākrit only, it is called a प्रवेशक, which can come at the beginning of any act except the first. कामयमानावस्थः–others give समदनावस्थः । कामयानावस्थः । The form कामयानः is used by Kālidāsa elsewhere : राजयक्ष्मपरिहानिरायथौ कामयानसमवस्थया तुलाम् ॥ कामयते विषयान् इच्छति इति कामयानः । Although the regular form is कामयमान, yet this form can be defended on the ground that the rule prescribing the augment म् (मुमागम) is not universal.

III. 2. V. L. अलमस्मि ततो हृदयं तथापि नेदं निवर्तयितुम् । etc. I am not able to turn my heart from her. The reading we have chosen is न च निम्नादिव सलिलं निवर्तते मे ततो हृदयम् । This reading is supported by the commentators.

P. 68. विश्वसनीयाभ्याम्—Because the one has only flowers for his arrows and the other has cool rays that distil nectar. Stanza 3. अयथार्थम्–is explained as विपरीतक्रियम् having a contrary effect. The five arrows of Cupid are अरविन्दमशोकं च चूतं च नवमालिका । नीलोत्पलं च पञ्चैते पञ्चबाणस्य सायकाः । Some substitute other flowers in the list; while sometimes other kinds of arrows are mentioned : उन्मादनस्तापनश्च शोषणः स्तम्भनस्तथा । संमोहनश्च कामस्य पञ्च बाणाः प्रकीर्तिताः ॥ In erotic poetry, the cooling rays of the moon or the cooling objects such as sandal or Southern breeze etc. are often spoken of as having a heating effect. Cf. in this connection Urvśaī's love-song in act II–नन्दनवनवाता अपि भवन्ति अत्युष्णाः शरीरे । or the king's remark towards the end of Act III. पादास्त एव शशिनः सुखयन्ति गात्रम् । etc.

III. 4. The story of the burning of Kāmadeva from a scorching flame issuing from the third eye of Śiva is well–known and given fully by our poet in the Kumāra, Canto III. For the idea. Cf. कर्पूर इव दग्धोऽपि शक्तिमान्यो जने जने। नमोऽस्त्ववार्यवीर्याय तस्मै मकरकेतवे ॥ बालरामायण–act III. और्वः Submarine fire also called वाडव; according to the legend given in the Harivaṁśa और्व is the son of the sage उर्व who had gained great power by his austerities, and who was requested by the gods to beget children to perpetuate his race. He consented but warned them that his offspring would consume the world. So from his thigh he created a devouring fire which would have consumed the world, had not Brahma assigned to it the ocean as its habitation and the waters as its food–उर्वस्य मुनेरपत्यं पुमान् और्वः।

III. 4. मकरकेतुः The God of love so called because of the मकर or sea–monster, subdued by him, painted on his banner (केतु). यदि मदिरायत etc. anything, even affliction and restlessness are welcome to him if they are caused by Śakuntalā or have a reference to her. After this Stanza the following is given by some editions:–भगवन् कन्दर्प। एवमुपालब्धस्य ते न मां प्रत्यनुक्रोशः। वृथैव सकल्पशतै-रजस्रमनङ्ग नीतोऽसि मया विवृद्धिम्। आकृष्य चापं श्रवणोपकण्ठे मय्येव युक्तस्तव बाणमाक्षः ॥–The passage, however, is not supported by many of the Devanāgarī Mss. although it is found in a few, and in all Bengalī Mss. संस्थिते कर्मणि–after the sacrificial rites are concluded, finished. सदस्यैः–सदसि साधवः सदस्याः। तैः उपद्रष्टृभिः। The superintending priests or simply those who took part in the rites. P. 70. after तत्रैव तावद् गच्छामि, some read अनया बालपादपवीथ्या सुतनुर चिरं गतेति तर्कयामि। कुतः–सम्मीलन्ति न तावद् बन्धनकोषास्तयावचितपुष्पाः। क्षीर–स्निग्धा-श्यामी दृश्यन्ते किसलयच्छेदाः ॥ This is a beautiful example of अनुमाना-लंकार which is frequently used by भास and कालिदास but it is not supported by all Devanāgarī Mss. प्रवातः–प्रकृष्टः वातः।

III. 6. शक्यम् etc. used impersonally. पवनः आलिङ्गितुं शक्यम् is equal to पवनस्य आलिङ्गनं शक्यम्–where the act of embracing (आलिङ्गनं) implied in the infinitive goes with the predicate शक्यम्–

hence the neu. Cf. एवं हि प्रणयवती सा शक्यमुपेक्षितुं कुपिता । मालव० III. 22 or शक्यं श्वमांसादिभिरपि क्षुत् प्रतिहन्तुम् ।. The full significance of the stānza which is here implied is clearly brought out in the following from भवभूती's मालति०. तामीषत्प्रचलविलोचनां नताङ्गीमालिङ्गन् पवन मम स्पृशाङ्गमङ्गम् ॥ I. 41.

III. 7. Here again is an instance of अनुमानालंकार. The idea is also found in विक्रमो० IV. पश्चान्नता गुरुनितम्बतया ततोऽस्या दृश्येत चारुपदपङ्क्तिरलक्तकाङ्का ॥. नेत्रनिर्वाणम् = The full bliss of my eyes. निर्वाण lit. 'What is blown out' refers to the state of release, to the Vedāntic idea that each who seems a separate whole fuses all the skirts of self and again remerges in the Absolute. That is the highest happiness, the "Summum Bonum." Cf. प्रसक्ते निर्वाणे हृदय परितापं वहसि किम् ॥ मालवि० III. 1. सुखयति Denom. from सुख in the sense of giving comfort.

P. 72. III. 8. स्तनन्यस्तोशीरं and शिथिलित...वलयं are to be taken adjectivally with वपुः. एकवलयम्–implies the extreme tenderness of the wearer; a single lotus-bracelet was all she could bear, so weak she had grown. किमपि indescribably—hence, exquisitely. प्रसरः–action,influence. There is figure व्यतिरेक as मनसिज and निदाघ are compared and then the superiority of मनसिज over निदाघ is pointed out in the last line. सुभगं अपराद्धं=affecting a person in such a charming manner. पर्युत्सुका–greatly affected by love. Cf. पर्युत्सुकां कथयसि प्रियदर्शनां तामार्तं न पश्यसि पुरूरवसं तदर्थे ॥ विक्रमो० II. 16. आतङ्कः–anguish, malady, painful condition. अनभ्यन्तरे –not acquainted with, perfectly ignorant about; lit. not inside. Cf. अहो प्रयोगाभ्यन्तरः प्राश्निकः । मालविका० II. प्रतीकारस्य or प्रतिकारस्य–both forms are correct. प्रतिकारः = प्रतिकरणम् from प्रतिकृ + the affix घञ्. The ending vowel of a preposition when following by a word formed with the affix घञ् and not denoting 'man' is optionally lengthened–उपसर्गस्य घञ्यमनुष्ये बहुलम् । So we have परिवाहः or परीवाहः परिपाकः or परीपाकः. अनसूयामपि अनुगतः–Some read अनुसूययापि अवगतः । which we have followed in the translation–but which through mistake was not printed in the text. The former means, "my guess has also occurred to Anasūyā." अभिनिवेशः–firm attachment.

परिहीयसे अङ्गैः–mark the idiom thou art abandoned by thy limbs–hence thou art wasting away. लावण्यमयी छाया–your exquisite beauty–छाया here means कान्तिः complexion, your lovely complexion. P. 74. अवितथम्–thus derived : विगतं तथा सत्यं यस्मात् तत् वितथम्, न वितथमवितथम् ।

III. 9. क्षामक्षाम० अतिकृश–the repetition implies excess. It may also imply the idea of becoming gradually more and more emaciate. काठिन्यमुक्त–the Bengali has युक्त–but that is not correct because the loss of firmness is a sign of weakness. शोषणेन means शोषकेण–that dries up.

III. 10. समदुःखसुखेन–Cf. समदुःखसुखः सखीजनः । रघु० VII. 65. Cf. also समदुःखः पिबतीव मां नयनाभ्याम् । विक्रमो०. I. बाला properly a girl sixteen years of age. अत्रान्तरे is अस्मिन् अवसरे ।. स्निग्धवीक्षित is one of the four ways by which a maiden encourages the advances of her lover. According to भरत they are लेखप्रस्थापन, स्निग्धवीक्षित, मृदुभाषित and दूतीसंप्रेषण. Now he was encouraged by Śakuntalā by स्निग्धवीक्षित because she again and again turned round and looked longingly at the king. But now that she is actually going to confess what she felt, the king's mind is in an agonising suspense. मम दर्शनपथमागतः Came across the path of my sight–quite a common idea ; Cf. यदृच्छया त्वं सकृदप्यवन्ध्ययोः पथि स्थिता सुन्दरि यस्य नेत्रयोः । विक्रमो० I. 9.

P. 76. III. 11. निर्वापयिता lit. the extinguisher ; hence allaying the fever. तपात्यये at the end of Summer ग्रीष्मान्ते. अभ्रश्यामः–Some read अर्धश्यामः partially-dark, half-obscured which is not quite good. The days are very sultry when the clouds come ; but these clouds allay the heat by their grateful showers. Thus we have in रत्नावली–तपति प्रावृषि नितरामभ्यर्णजलागमो दिवसः ॥. तिलोदकम्–Water with sesamum seed–she means that her friends will have to celebrate her funeral obsequies–for these, such water is poured out. दूरगतमन्मथा Cf. दूरारूढः प्रणयः असहनः । विक्रमो० IV. किमत्र चित्रं... विशाखे etc. the two friends of शकुन्तला are here compared to the two stars in the constellation विशाखा and शकुन्तला herself who has grown so emaciated to शशाङ्कलेखा. Cf. the remark of रम्भा in विक्रमो० Act I. एष चित्रलेखाद्वितीयां प्रियसखीमुर्वशीं गृहीत्वा विशाखासमीपगत इव भगवांश्चन्द्र उपस्थितो राजर्षिः ॥. The union of the moon with the constellation of विशाखा is described as particularly charming by our poet ; so also with चित्रा as in हिमनिर्मुक्तयोर्योगे चित्राचन्द्रमसोरिव ॥ रघु० I. 46. because in summer the चित्रा and विशाखा shine very brightly. एतान् दिवसान्–According to " कालाध्वनोरत्यन्तसंयोगे " we have the accu. indicating that the king did not sleep even for a moment.

P. 78. III. 12. This gives a picture of the king as pensively he rests his head upon the palm of his hand sideways, so that the tears which trickle down from the corner of his eye (अपाङ्गप्रवर्तिभिरश्रुभिः) soil the gems in the golden bracelet which constantly slips down from his wrist (मणिबन्धनात्) and is not prevented from slipping down because the callosities on the forearm are not sufficiently prominent. This is a favourite idea with Kālidāsa Cf. कनकवलयभ्रंशरिक्तप्रकोष्ठः । मेघ० २. मणिबन्धन is " the wrist " so called because it is a place round which jewels are bound. देवताशेषापदेशेन–The remains of an offering of flowers presented to some deity. It was usual to offer these in the way mentioned. आत्मनः उपन्यासपूर्व–preceded by a reference or allusion to yourself. ललितपदबन्धनम्–Cf. ललितार्थबन्धम् in विक्रमो० II. 14.

III. 13. श्रीः Lakṣmi or fortune ; when she herself seeks a man, how could she fail ? A man seeking fortune may or may not find her. Similarly the suitor may or may not win the beautiful maiden he loves–but if he is loved by her, how can she have any difficulty in gaining him ? Cf. the same idea in कुमार० V. 45 न रत्नमन्विष्यति मृग्यते हि तत्। आत्मगुणावमानिनी one who undervalues, scorns her own virtues or merits. क इदानीं etc. This is characteristic of Kālidāsa's style. An apt parallel to the situation in question which constitutes an illustration or (निदर्शनम्) and gives the figure of speech निदर्शना or ललितं according to some rhetoricians.

P. 80. नियोजिता so now I am directed by you–I do this by your orders—so that you will be responsible for the consequences विस्मृतनिमेषेण–which has forgotten winking–very expressive of an earnest longing gaze. Cf. पपौ निमेषालसपक्ष्मपङ्क्तिरुपोषिताभ्यामिव लोचनाभ्याम् ॥ रघु० II. 19.

III. 14. उन्नमित०=उन्नमिता एका भ्रूलता यस्य तत् । कण्टकितेन having the hair erect like thorns, the same as पुलकित–the hair starting up erect on the body is a sign of exquisite delight or some pleasurable emotion. Cf. उद्यत्कठोरपुलकाङ्कितकण्टकाग्रैर्यत् खिद्यते तव पदं ननु सा व्यथा मे ॥ अलंकारसर्वस्व. Cf. also स्पृष्टः सरोमविक्रियमङ्कुरितं मनसिजेनेव ॥ कण्टकाः संजाताः अस्य । कण्टक+इत (चू). गीतवस्तु–the subject-matter of the song. निक्षिप्तवर्ण–निक्षिप्ताः वर्णाः यस्य तत् । the syllables of which are transcribed. संगतार्थम्–well–connected in sense.

III. 15. रत्तिंमि–better read रत्तिम्पि which gives रात्रिमपि–which is better than रात्रावपि, for the accusative implies the ceaselessness of her torments by the rule कालाध्वनोरत्यन्तसंयोगे द्वितीया । वृत्तमनोरथानि–Monier Williams reads वृत्तमनोरथायाः । I whose desires are centred on thee.

III. 16. Here is a beautiful दृष्टान्त ; naturally therefore, there is बिम्बप्रतिबिम्बभाव–the king and शकुन्तला aud मदन are compared respectively to शशाङ्क ; कुमुद्वती and दिवसः He means that he is affected by love far more violently than Śakuntalā herself. So in विक्रमो० the king says पर्युत्सुकां कथयसि प्रियदर्शनां तां आर्तं नं पश्यसि पुरूरवसं तदर्थे । She is filled with anxious longing but he is distracted on her account. अविलम्बिनः मनोरथस्य 'the desire of the heart, which does not delay' refers to Duṣyanta by लक्षणा–Cf. अत्यायतं नयनयोर्मम जीवितमेतदायाति ॥ मालविका. III. 7. where the king refers to मालविका as his very life जीवितम् ।

P. 82. III. 17. संदष्ट from संदंश् to press the teeth closely together, bite, hence "press closely, come in close contact". Cf. संदष्टवस्त्रेष्वबलानितम्बेषु० रघु. XVI. 16. Cf. also the word संदंशः which means "a pair of tongs". आशु० आशुक्रान्ताः ये बिसभङ्गाः तैः

सुरभीणि । उपचारम्–is the usual salutation, आचार; she need not give up her recumbent posture and rise to receive him. पुनरुक्तवादिनी–She was going to tell him how her dear friend was affected by love on his account; but their love for one another was too evident; her words, therefore, were superfluous–i. e. simple repetition of what was already well-known; Cf. प्रहर्षचिन्हानुमितं प्रियायै शशंस वाचा पुनरुक्तयेव । पुनरुक्त lit. what is said again, repeated, has further acquired the sense of "what is superfluous," or "unnecessary," and hence at times simply 'additional.' Cf. अभिव्यक्तायां चन्द्रिकायां किं दीपिकापौनरुक्त्येन । विक्रमो॰ III. मुक्तावलीविरचनापुनरुक्तमस्रैः ॥ विक्रमो॰ V. विषयनिवासिनो जनस्य–engaged in the affairs of life as M. Williams translates it; but the proper meaning is those living within his territory—hence his subjects. आर्तिः distress. अवस्थान्तरम् आरोपिता reduced to this altered condition; अन्या अवस्था अवस्थान्तरम् ।—an alteration from her normal healthy condition. अभ्युपपत्त्या–By favouring her; Cf. रतिमभ्युपपद्यमातुरां मधुरात्मानमदर्शयत्पुरः ॥ कुमार॰ IV. 25 साधारणोऽयं प्रणयः–Cf. विक्रमो॰ II. 16 साधारणोऽयमुभयोः प्रणयः ॥ किं... उपरोधेन ।–Mark this sly remark of Śakuntalā; "Tax not his courtesy too much–for he must be eager to join the bright ladies at his court".

III. 18. अनन्य॰ न अन्यत् परायणं यस्य–which has nothing else as its highest object, which is devoted to no other. हृदयसन्निहिते O thou that abidest in my heart. मदिरेक्षणे–माद्यति अनेन इति मदिरा–is properly wine–hence by लक्षणा–intoxicating like wine; मदिरे ईक्षणे यस्याः–Having eyes intoxicating like wine–hence fascinating or bewitching eyes; an epithet of common occurrence–and thus defined सौष्ठवेनापरित्यक्ता स्मेरापाङ्गमनोहरा । वेपमानान्तरा दृष्टिर्मदिरा परिकीर्तिता ॥. He was already killed by love's shaft; and this her unkind remark, therefore, slays him again. बहुवल्लभा etc. kings are prodigal to many of their love–hence this request with which Cf. चित्रलेखा's request to पुरूरवस् in act III. of विक्रमो॰. For निर्वर्तय some read निर्वाहय.

III. 19. How naturally in the ardour of his love does the king give this promise—not as in the original Mahābhārata story–is there a bargaining for her future. प्रतिष्ठे–प्रतिष्ठा–a cause of stability–but here cause of renown, " chief glory. " समुद्रवसना–V. L. समुद्ररशना–the sea girdled, the sea-girt earth. संयोजयावः–lit. let us cause it to join its mother–lead it to its mother; obviously this is a mere pretext. They want to leave the lovers to themselves–Cf. निर्यातश्शनकैरलीकवचनोपन्यासमालीजनः । अमरु; also बकुलावलिके एष बालाशोकवृक्षस्य पवल्लानि हरिणो लङ्घितुमागच्छति । एहि निवारयावः एनम् । माल० IV. आराधयिता–your adorer, worshipper of a deity, hence implying adoration as well as service.

P. 86. III. 20. करभोरु–करभ is the part of the hand between the wrist and the fingers; it is better however to understand करभ to mean by लक्षणा a part of करभ an elephant; i. e. the trunk of an elephant, so that the thighs are rounded and tapering like the trunk of an elephant. करभ इव ऊरू यस्याः सा । the affix ऊ (ङ्) is applied to ऊरु when it is the second member of a compound, and resemblance is implied. Cf. कुमार० I. 36. or द्विरदनासोरूः of भट्टि० IV. 17. न माननीयेषु etc. I will not make myself in fault with those who are worthy of respect i. e. with father Kaṇva and the elders. अपरिनिर्वाणः Lit. quite extinguished–not yet cool; it was still very hot.

III. 21. परिबाधापेलवैः–'incapable of bearing hardships.' M. W.; but the proper meaning is " rendered languid through suffering. कोमलैः is substituted for पेलवैः in the Bengali. रक्ष अविनयम्–some read रक्ष विनयम्. न आत्मनः प्रभवामि–she was not mistress of herself विदितधर्मा–who knows the law. धर्म because धर्मन् at the end of a बहुव्रीहि compound.

III. 22. गान्धर्वेण etc. the गान्धर्व is one of the *eight forms of* marriage which are ब्राम्हो दैवस्तथैवार्षः प्राजापत्यस्तथाऽऽसुरः । गान्धर्वो राक्षसश्चैव पैशाचश्चाष्टमोऽधमः॥. गान्धर्व is thus defined इच्छयान्योन्यसंयोगः कन्यायाश्च वरस्य च । गान्धर्वः स तु विज्ञेयो मैथुन्यः कामसंभवः ॥ मनु० III 32. It is the marriage of a maiden and a young man at their sweet will concluded without any ceremony and without the consent of the elders

अनुमानयिष्ये–from the causal of अनुमन् to cause or induce to assent –hence take counsel with, to ask the consent of.

P. 88. III. 23. अपरिक्षत etc. a flower untouched, uninjured and fresh. The reference here is to the दन्तक्षतं which is often spoken of in Sanskrit erotic poetry–Cf. दन्तक्षतं कपोले वध्वाः वेदना सपत्नीनाम् । अधरस्य पिपासता etc. पिपासता–पान्तु इच्छता. Desid. from पा to drink. Cf. पिबसि रतिसर्वस्वमधरम् । Act I. 24. Mark how in his depiction of love-passages Kālidāsa does not go beyond aesthetic bounds– "A kiss unkissed is all beyond which the affair does not pass." चक्रवाकवधूः–How delicately and cleverly are the lovers warned ! The Cakrawākas are models of constancy and connubial affection. They keep together during the day, but are doomed to pass the night apart. There are frequent allusions to the habits of these birds in Sanskrit literature. Cf. सरसि नलिनीपत्रेणापि त्वमावृतविग्रहां ननु सहचरीं दूरे मत्वा विरौषि समुत्सुकः ॥ विक्रमो॰ IV. 20. दूरीभूते मयि सहचरे चक्रवाकीमिवैकाम् । मेघ॰. शशिनं पुनरेति शर्वरी दयिता द्वंद्वचरं पतत्रिणम् । रघु॰ VIII. 56. शरीरवृत्तान्तोपलम्भाय–to inquire after my health, ascertain the state of my bodily health. लघु॰ लघुः संतापः येषां तानि Whose fever is abated. अस्ति मे विशेषः is idiomatic–there is a change for the better in me. सानुशयविघटितस्य–is contrasted with सुखोपनत–the desire of her heart came so readily and brought with it सुख happiness (सुखेन सह उपनत) but the separation comes and brings अनुशय repentance, or regret with it. लतावलय etc. A double entendre is intended, one meant for गौतमी, and the other for the king.

P. 90. III. 24. The first two lines are to be construed adjectivally with मुखं in the third line-.अङ्गुलिभिः संवृतः अधरोष्ठः यस्य तत् । प्रतिषेधा॰– प्रतिषेधस्य यानि अक्षराणि तेषु विक्लवं अत एव अभिरामम्–looking beautiful as it simply stammered forth, could not utter distinctly the words of prohibition. अंसे विवर्तते इति अंसविवर्ति । पक्ष्मल is पक्ष्म + the affix ल (च्) having soft, beautiful eyelashes. परिभुक्तमुक्ते-आदौ परिभुक्तः पश्चात् मुक्तः तस्मिन् । शरीरलुलिता–crushed by her body. आसज्यमानं ईक्षणं यस्य–whose eyes are rivetted or fixed. III. 25. सायंतन

-belonging to the evening–तन is applied in this sense to adverbs of time. Cf. चिरंतन, प्राक्तन. परितः governs the accusative अभितः परितः–समयानिकषाहाप्रतियोगेऽपि । सवनकर्म–sacrificial rite, sacrifice. As the demons were stalking about, their shadows, dark-brown like evening-clouds, fell on the altar where the sacred fire was kindled. पिशिताशनानाम्–the eaters of raw flesh (पिशित raw flesh + अशन). अयमयं etc.–Observe the use of अयं " this one " with the verb in the first person. Some read however अयमहमागच्छामि ।

ACT IV

92. कुसुमावचयम्–according to पाणिनि III. 3–40 हस्तादाने चेरस्तेये। The root चि takes the affix घ (ञ्) when the sense is "taking something with the hand" except when the thing is stolen. Thus the proper form is अवचाय because घ (ञ्) causes Vrddhi in the root-vowel. However the rule implies that the thing so taken is quite within reach; and so the commentator defends the form अवचय by supposing that the flowers were not quite within the reach of the girls. The defence, however, is evidently very weak. This is rather a case of poetic license. निर्वृत्तकल्याणा–निर्वृत्त p. p. of निर् + वृत्–effected, accomplished. कल्याणम् is happiness, good–fortune; here used in the sense of marriage on which so much of man's happiness depends; "having her nuptials celebrated." निर्वृतम्–Happy, comforted–p. p. of निस् + वृ. आकृतिविशेषाः etc.–Distinguished excellent forms; आकृतीनां विशेषाः or आकृतिविशेषो येषां ते–Whose distinction lies in their noble form. This prepossession in favour of beautiful, excellent persons is pretty commonly expressed by Sanskrit poets–the outward form is an index to inward worth. Cf. न ह्याकृतिः सुसदृशं विजहाति वृत्तम्। मृच्छ० IX. 16 यत्राकृतिस्तत्र गुणा वसन्ति।. घोणोन्नतं मुखमपाङ्गविशालनेत्रं नैतद्धि कारणमकारणदूषणानाम्॥ मृच्छ० किं प्रतिपत्स्यते–किं अभिधास्यति–What he would say, what reply he would make; or किं अवधारयिष्यति–what he would think. प्रथमः संकल्पः–The first desire of his heart, hence the best desire as in प्रथमः कल्पः—than which he can wish nothing better.

P. 94. सौभाग्यदेवता–The deity that presides over her fortune and welfare; the tutelary deity. निवेदितम्–निवेदनम् नपूंसके भावे क्तः। The p. p. is used as an abstract noun and is neuter. अतिथीनां–the plural to show respect; some honoured guest announcing himself. Some read अदिधिणा (अतिथिना) but that is not the Devnāgarī reading. हृदयेनासन्निहिता–With her heart, she is not near, her heart is far away with Dusyanta. अतिथिपरिभाविनि–One who slights, scorns, or is disrespectful to a guest. No punishment was thought too severe for one who violated the rites of hospitality.

IV. 1. अनन्यमानसा–अविद्यमानं अन्यत् यस्य तद् अनन्यं च तत् मानसं यस्याः सा ।. One whose mind is regardless of everything else, thinking of him to the exclusion of all other objects. बोधितोऽपि–the full significance of this word comes home to us in the fifth act where Śakuntalā tries to revive the king's memory by reporting to him of some of the incidents of their privacy. वेगबलोत्फुल्लया गत्या उत्फुल्ल from उद्+स्फुल् to leap–hence bounding through its impetuosity. The other reading is वेअचहुलुप्फुल्लदुव्वाराए = वेगचटुलोत्फुल्लदुर्वारया–with a step (गत्या) tremulous, bounding and difficult to be checked through its impetuosity. Some have अविरलपादतुवराए = अविरलपादत्वरया–but it is too tame a description of the choleric saint bounding away in anger कोऽन्यो हुतवहात् etc.–a fine दृष्टान्त. The wrath of a Brahmin is frequently compared to fire.

P. 96. आवेगस्खलितया गत्या–owing to her steps stumbling through her excitement. अग्रहस्तात्–a very puzzling compound explained thus: अग्रश्चासौ हस्तश्च–where one is अवयव and the other अवयवी ; but these are not identical while in a कर्मधारय such as नीलोत्पलं–नीलं च तत् उत्पलम् च–both the members of the compound refer to one and the same object. The defence, however, is that both अग्र and हस्त may be regarded as identical on account of the relation of the part and the whole between them ; and thus the compound is a कर्मधारय. Some however explain–हस्तस्य–अग्रम्–हस्ताग्रम् and account for the पूर्वनिपात of अग्र by putting the compound in the आहिताग्न्यादि class, but this rule of पूर्वनिपात applies to बहुव्रीहि compounds, hence the first explanation is better. Here is an ill omen; the poet is preparing the ground for the tense feeling of this and the tragedy of the next act. अन्यथाभवितुं must not be falsified, hence must not be recalled शापो निवर्तिष्यते–curse and its modification are altogether so common in the Paurāṇic tales.

P. 98. आश्वसितुम्–it is possible to take cheer or comfort–feel confident. स्वाधीनोपाया–She will be possessed of a resource or remedy in her own power. द्वयोरेव ननु नौ मुखे etc. mark the tragic irony ; with the best of intentions the friends resolve on a course of action which only helps on the tragedy. Had they revealed the incident, Śakuntalā would have been more careful about the ring and perhaps the tragedy may have been averted. विष्कम्भः Really speaking this is मिश्रविष्कम्भ with its Sanskrit and Prākrit. But perhaps the characters are all middling मध्य, while मिश्र– requires मध्य and नीच characters. प्रकाशं-विवृतप्रदेशम्–Open spot, open air. हन्त–Here shows surprise.

IV. 1. अस्त–It is believed that there are two mountains the अस्ताचल in the West and the उदयाचल in the East–and the rising and setting of the sun and the moon depends upon their going behind the अस्ताचल and coming from behind the उदयाचल. पतिरोषधीनाम्–One of the names of the moon is ओषधीपतिः। ओषधी is explained as फलपाकान्ता a plant which dies after the ripening of its fruit, hence any medicinal plant. These are supposed to thrive under the influence of the moon hence the moon is ओषधीपतिः. Really speaking the सोम plant is described in the Veda as the king of plants ; but when later सोम became the appellation of the moon,—the latter too received the epithet ओषधीपतिः. Even the lord of medicinal herbs which revive and help to live–dies–such is the beautiful suggestion. आविष्कृतारुण etc. V. L. आविष्कृतोऽरुणपुरः etc. But this requires us to suppose that आविष्कृतः is used in an active sense–आवीर्भूतः अरुणः पुरःसरः यस्य एतादृशः अर्कः एकतः दृश्यते। We have to supply this word दृश्यते. अरुण the herald of the sun is the dawn personified ; according to the Purānās अरुण is the son of कश्यप and विनता and the elder brother of गरुड. His mother is said to have prematurely broken the egg which was to be hatched for a thousand years, and so the child was born thighless: later on he became the charioteer of the sun ; hence the latter is called अनूरुसारथिः. लोको नियम्यते इव– people are guided as it were ; restrained or governed i. e. people are taught the lesson that when even the highest suffer rise and fall how can mortals escape it. The stanza beautifully suggests the reverse of fortune which is to come over Śakuntalā. The दशान्तराणि–the various vicissitudes of life are alluded to in the well-known verse नीचैर्गच्छत्युपरि च दशा चक्रनेमिक्रमेण ।–मेघदूत० ।

IV. 2. संस्मरणीयशोभा–Whose beauty is now a matter of remembrance. The poet here beautifully refers to the condition of the heroine in the absence of दुष्यन्त. The last two lines give a generalisation, and so the figure is अर्थान्तरन्यास. अपटीक्षेप–A hurried toss of the curtain–a stage-direction indicating the sudden entrance of a character who is flurried through joy or sorrow etc. एवं नाम–etc. the passage is very corrupt and variously read. She is referring to herself by the word जनस्य–विषयपराङ्मुख–she was पराङ्मुख averse to, withdrawn from all विषय worldly concerns ; one unacquainted with them अनार्य–as a noun–ungentlemanly conduct–what is unworthy of an आर्य. उचितेषु–The usual duties, from " usual " the word came to mean "proper". कामः इदानीं etc. Cf. अलब्धफलनीरसान्मम विधाय तस्मिञ्जने । समागममनोरथान् भवतु पञ्चबाणः कृती ॥ विक्रमो० II. 11. शुद्धहृदया–V. L. शून्यहृदया । पदं कारिता–caused to have dealings with, repose confidence in. Cf. हञ्जे पश्य पश्य । कारितैवैतस्मिन् बकुलावलिकया पदं मालविका । मालवि० III. 14. 3. also धर्मेणापि पदं शर्वे कारिते पार्वतीं प्रति । पूर्वापराधभीतस्य कामस्योच्छ्वसितं मनः ॥ कुमार० VI. 14. एतावत्कालस्य the genitive irregularly for the accusative. दुःखशीले–they are inured to hardships–hence either it would not be proper to trouble them any more–or they would not be able to sympathise with Śakuntalā and her friends as they are rendered callous to sufferings. Or, who are hard to please, bad-tempered and hence cannot be easily induced. व्यवसिताऽपि–although I am resolved, have made up my mind. आपन्नसत्त्वा–आपन्नः सत्त्वः (गर्भः) अनया । A pregnant woman.

P. 102. प्रस्थानकौतुकम्–कौतुक festive solemnities auspicious ceremonies that attend the departure. Cf. अथ तस्य विवाहकौतुकं ललितं

बिभ्रत एव पार्थिवः । रघु० VIII. 1 ; where कौतुक is explained as मङ्गलम्- or as हस्तसूत्र. "कौतुकं मङ्गले हर्षे हस्तसूत्रे कुतूहले-इति शाश्वतः । In the स्वप्न. III we have both कौतुक and मङ्गल combined-अद्यैव कौतुकमङ्गलं कर्तव्यमत्यस्माकं भट्टीनी भणति ।-where the reference is to the auspicious ceremony of the tying of the nuptial thread सुखशयन-पृच्छिका-रात्रौ तव सुखशयनं जातं इति या पृच्छति सा । सुखशयन + पृच्छ् + the affix ण्वुल् (अक) + आ. There is also the form सौखशायनिक- Raghu X. 14. धूमाकुलितस्य etc. Both the comparisons are very appropriate in the mouth of Kaṇva. सुशिष्यपरिदत्ता-a common idea. Cf. the Nirukta passage विद्या ह वै ब्राह्मणमाजगाम । गोपाय मां शेवधिस्तेऽहमस्मि । etc. अग्निशरणं the fire sanctuary-the house (शरणं=गृहं) where the sacred fire is kept. Cf. later अग्निशरणालिन्द in Act V.

IV. 3. भूतये भुवः for earth's prosperity, suggesting that the child would be सार्वभौम. अग्निगर्भां शमीमिव ।-for the idea Cf. शमीमिवाभ्यन्तरलीनपावकाम् । रघु० III. 9. Agni who bore the seed of Śiva at the request of the gods felt a consuming fire spreading through his body-so he entered the Śami tree ; when the gods discovered him there, they assigned the tree to him as his permanent abode; the story is told in the अनुशासनपर्व chap. 35. उत्कण्ठासाधारणम्- mingled or mixed with anxiety. Cf. वीज्यते स हि संसुप्तः श्वाससाधारणानिलैः । कुमार० II. 42.

P. 104. तपस्विनी-the poor girl, the helpless one ; one deserving pity. समुद्गकः A small box or casket. मृगरोचना- yellow ointment, the concrete bile of deer used as such. समालंभनानि- Here decorations ; properly समालम्भनं is besmearing the body with ointments-समालंभो विलेपने इत्यमरः । शार्ङ्गरवमिश्राः-मिश्र At the end of a compound has the sense of पूज्य respectable-as also the additional sense " and others " हस्तिनापुर- So called because it was founded by हस्तिन् the great grandson of भरत ; thus it is an anachronism to call दुष्यन्त's capital by that name. शिखामज्जिता- meaning with her hair (शिखा) combed or cleansed. प्रातिष्ठित- Consecrated or hallowed-or placed in i. e. carrying, having in their hands. स्वस्तिवाचनिकाभिः-invoking blessings on her, wishing to pronounce blessing on her. स्वस्तिवाचनाय हिताभिः । स्वस्तिवाचन

also means a present given to Brahmins for blessings from him–but that sense is not appropriate here.

P. 106. गौतमीवर्जम्–गौतमीं वर्जयित्वा an instance of the gerund in अम् (णमुल्); leaving Gautami, except Gautami. आभरणोचितं etc. आभरण and प्रसाधन are contrasted–the former meaning rich costly ornaments from the root आ + भृ implying opulence–the latter simple decorations such as garlands etc. मानसी सिद्धिः a creation of his mind–created through the superhuman power (सिद्धि) acquired through Yaugic practices.

P. 108. IV. 4. क्षौमम्–क्षुमायाः विकारः–क्षुमा is flax or silk. माङ्गल्यम्–auspicious–it is explained as मङ्गले साधुः but the form would be मङ्गल्यम् ।; so it may be explained thus मङ्गल्यं एव माङ्गल्यं–by applying the affix अ (ण्) स्वार्थे i. e. without any change of meaning. निष्ठ्यूतः distilled–lit. vomited: but it is not अश्लील when used by लक्षणा in a secondary sense (गौणवृत्तिव्यपाश्रयात् अतिसुन्दरमन्यत्र ग्राम्यकक्षां विगाहते ।) लाक्षारसः "A red dye prepared from an insect analogous to the cochineal insect" आपर्व° पर्वभागं मर्यादीकृत्य–as far as the wrists. किसलय° किसलयोद्भेदाः उद्भिद्यमानपल्लवाः तत्प्रतिद्वंद्विभिः–तत्प्रतिस्पर्धिभिः ।–The hands of the fairies were as red as the fresh sprouts of trees. अणुवजुत्त–V. L. अणुवहुत्त=अनुपभुक्त° The girls were taught the art of painting or perhaps they would put the ornaments on her person even as they have seen them in pictures.

IV. 5. संस्पृष्टम्–not simply touched, but smitten powerfully, affected. स्तम्भित etc. स्तम्भिता या बाष्पस्य वृत्तिः प्रवृत्तिः तया कलुषः स्वरभङ्गवान् ।. दर्शनम् lit. the sight, the sense of vision–better तत्तदिन्द्रियजं ज्ञानम् । hence he felt all his senses paralysed. अरण्यौकसः–अरण्यं ओकः यस्य–Cf. दिवौकस्, वनौकस्. The argument employed is what is called कैमुतिकन्याय–a fortiori and the figure of speech is अर्थापत्तिः–आनन्दपरिवाहिणा–आनन्दस्य परिवाहः अस्यास्तीति–overflowing with joy–with tears of joy.

IV. 6. ययाति was an ancient king the father of पुरु from whom Duṣyanta himself derived his descent. He had two wives देवयानी and शर्मिष्ठा the daughter of वृषपर्वन्. शर्मिष्ठा by her superior charms won the heart of ययाति. She like शकुन्तला had married ययाति by the गांधर्व form–the simile is thus appropriately chosen. प्रदक्षिणीकुरुष्व is a च्वि form. प्रगतो दक्षिणं प्रदक्षिणं । अव्ययीभावः । अप्रदक्षिणं प्रदक्षिणं संपद्यमानं करोति प्रदक्षिणीकरोति ।. Cf. प्रदक्षिणीकृत्य हुतं हुताशम् । रघु॰ II. 71. walking round an object worthy of one's veneration keeping it to one's right. ऋक्छन्दसा–the metre is त्रिष्टुप् which is so common in Rgveda; it consists of 11 syllables to a पाद and is irregular in arrangements.

IV. 7. क्लृप्तानि धिष्ण्यानि येषां–whose places are fixed round the altar. प्रान्त॰ the दर्भ grass was strewn round their margins to give additional sanctity. हव्यगन्धैः etc. for this virtue of the smell Cf. पुनानं पवनोध्दूतैर्धूमैराहुतिगन्धिभिः । रघु. 1. 53. घ्रात्वा हविर्गन्धि रजोविमुक्तः समश्नुते मे लघिमानमात्मा ॥ रघु. XIII. 37. भगिन्याः the genitive is to be taken objectively; show thy sister her way.

P. 112. IV. 8-9 अपीतेषु–when you were not watered–lit. before you have had your fill of water–or when you have not drunk. This describes how dearly this daughter of the forest loved her brothers and sisters–the trees; they were her वनवासबन्धु–the friends or kinsfoik that surrounded her in forest-life. Cf. उत्तर॰ III. 8. यत्र द्रुमा अपि मृगा अपि बन्धवो मे ।. परभृत–परे or परैः भृत–the koil, so called because the female is supposed to leave her eggs in the nest of a crow which unknowingly hatches them. Cf. प्रागन्तरिक्षगमनात्स्वमपत्यजातमन्यैर्द्विजैः परभृताः खलु पोषयन्ति । Act. V. 22. Cf. for a similar idea उदीरयामासुरिवोन्मदानामालोकशब्दं वयसां विरावैः ॥ रघु॰ II. 9.

IV. 10. The four lines beautifully describe her path. रम्यान्तरः–रम्यं अन्तरं यस्य । "Having its intervening spaces delightful or charming," छायाद्रुमैः–छायाप्रधानैः द्रुमैः–मध्यम॰ तत्पुरुष. कुशेशय॰–with the dust (रेणुः) soft like the pollen (रजः) of lotuses. कुशे जले शेते इति । कुश + शी + the affix अ (च्) according to अधिकरणे शेते । पाणिनि॰ III. 2. 15. It is an अलुक् समास. There is some difficulty with regard to the construction. If the आशंसा is to be taken as repeated with each attribute—thus अस्याः पन्थाः रम्यान्तरः भूयात्–नियमितार्कमयूखतापः भूयात् and so on as the commentators do, then the च would have to be repeated every time and not twice only. This shows therefore that there is समुच्चय of two आशंसाs only–may her path–described as above–be शान्तानुकूलपवनः and शिवः। So that the first three lines give the उद्देश्य only and the last line the विधेय. शान्तानुकूल॰ Cf. पवनस्यानुकूलत्वात् प्रार्थनासिद्धिशंसिनः॥ रघु॰ I. 42. because such a wind is a good augury for the future fulfilment of the desired object. शिवश्च पन्थाः।–a phrase commonly used as a parting benediction; the usual phrase is शिवास्ते पन्थनः सन्तु।. जातिजनास्निग्धाभिः–Dear to these (स्निग्ध) as thy own kinsfolk–the same idea as expressed by वनवासबन्धुभिः–। of Stz. 9. P. 114. समवस्था = समावस्था–the same condition. Cf. रघु॰ VIII. 41.

IV. 11. उद्गलित॰–उद्गलिताः दर्भाणां कवलाः यासां ताः। उद्गलित means the same as उद्गीर्ण of the Bengali–ejected from the mouth, dropped from the mouth. Cf. with this रघु॰ XIV 69. which expresses the same sentiment नृत्यं मयूराः कुसुमानि वृक्षाः दर्भानुपात्तान् विजहुर्हरिण्यः। तस्याः प्रपन्ने समदुःखभावमत्यन्तमासिद्रुदितं वनेऽपि॥ सोदर्यस्नेहम् sisterly affection समाने उदरे शयितः सोदर्यः–she looked upon her as her sister. Cf. लताभगिनीं शाखाबाहाभिः–बाहा is the same as बाहुः–the feminine form as M. W. observes is more appropriately joined with शाखा.

IV. 12. वीतचिन्तः–वीता चिन्ता यस्य। Mark how Kaṇva not only has no resentment that Śakuntalā should have not consulted him but that he had in mind दुष्यन्त as the husband who was in every way worthy of Śakuntalā.

P. 116. स्थिरीकर्तव्या–rendered firm, hence cheered. उटजपर्यन्तचारिणी–grazing about the hut–in the neighbourhood (पर्यन्त) of the hut, अनघप्रसवा–अनघः प्रसवः यस्याः सा। Will have happily brought forth, safely delivered of her young. Cf. अनघप्रसूतिः in इतो भविष्यत्यनघप्रसूतेरपत्यसंस्कारमयो विधिस्ते॥ रघु॰ XIV. 75. प्रियनिवेदयितृ-

कम्–the same as प्रियनिवेदयितारम्–One who conveys the good tidings.

IV. 13. व्रणविरोपणम्–qualifies तैलं–that which heals a wound–causes a scar to cicatrize–hence healing oil. व्रणं विरोपयतीति । from the causal of विरुह् + the affix अन (ल्युट्) in the sense of the agent. परिवर्धितकः–the affix क used in the sense of अनुकम्पा–or in endearment. अनुकम्पया परिवर्धितः–tenderly reared. पुत्रकृतकाः–कृत्रिमः पुत्रः । Adopted son.

IV. 14. The first two lines should be thus construed उत्पक्ष्मणोः नयनयोः उपरुद्धवृत्तिं बाष्पं स्थिरतया विरतानुबन्धं कुरु ।. firmly make the tears cease to rise or cling continuously in thy eyes with their upturned eye-lashes–obstructing their action. विरतः अनुबन्धः यस्य–whose continuity i. e. continuous flow has stopped. उत्पक्ष्मणोर्नयनयोः this is to be connected with वृत्ति in the compound उपरुद्धवृत्तिम्–which is rather loose–the action (वृत्ति) of the eyes is impeded by the rising tears. अलक्षिताः नतोन्नताः भूमिभागाः यस्य तस्मिन् qualifies मार्गे–विषमीभवन्ति–become unequal, are liable to trip or stumble.

P. 118. ओदकान्तं–आ + उदकान्तम् । as far as the water's brink. श्रूयते–It is enjoined by श्रुति i. e. scripture–it is a scriptural rule. क्षीरवृक्ष lit. milk–tree–a kind of fig–tree which yields a milky juice and is large enough to afford abundant shade. युक्तरूपम्–Cf. युक्तरूपमिदं तव Act I. 12 ; II. 16. रूप is here a प्रत्यय, the word is not a compound. नलिनीपत्रान्तरितमपि–Precisely the same sentiment is to be found in the विक्रमोर्वशीय–सरसि नलिनीपत्रेणापि त्वमावृतविग्रहां ननु सहचरीं दूरे मत्वा विरौषि समुत्सुकः । A few lines before this passage the cry is compared to the sound कः कः–it is possible that the harsh expression दुष्करं करोमि may refer to this peculiar cry. " Hard is the lot I suffer " " Hard is my lot."

IV. 15. विषाददीर्घतरां–Cf. अविनोददीर्घयामा कथं नु रात्रिर्गमयितव्या ॥ विक्रमो॰ III. 4. आशाबन्धः साहयति–causal–the bond of hope causes, helps us to bear. Cf. the parallel passage in मेघ॰ 12. आशाबन्धः कुसुमसदृशं प्रायशो ह्यङ्गनानां सद्यःपाति प्रणयि हृदयं विप्रयोगे रुणद्धि ॥

IV. 16. संयमधनान्–thinking well of us who are rich in self-control. विचिन्त्य–He asks दुष्यन्त to think of three circumstances–think of him who was self-controlled–implying by it that he was worthy of respect ; think of his own family–implying that he would acquit himself well and worthily ; and her love for him which was spontaneous–implying, therefore, that he should be very kind to her. सामान्यप्रतिपत्तिपूर्वकम्–प्रतिपात्ति is respect ; साधारणगौरव पुरःसरम्–the word पूर्व at the end of a compound often denotes the manner in which anything is done–so the meaning is सामान्यप्रतिपत्त्या–with equal respect. दारेषु–the word is mas. plu. लौकिकज्ञाः–Acquainted with worldly affairs. न खलु धीमतां–This is a generalisation–which supports the previous remark of काश्यप–the figure would be thus अर्थान्तरन्यास. Such generalisations are in the characteristic manner of कालिदास and भास.

IV. 17. गुरून् not only father or father-in-law, but elders ; any male relation that is entitled to respect. प्रियसखीवृत्तिं–acting the part of a dear friend towards them treating them as dear friends. सपत्नी०–समानः पतिः यासां ताः । according to पत्युर्नो यज्ञसंयोगे । पा० V. I. 33. the word पति takes the augment न् before the fem. affix ई when participation in a sacrifice is meant–hence पत्नी is one who is entitled to join her husband in the performance of religious rites. भाग्येषु अनुत्सेकिनी–Cf. अनुत्सेको लक्ष्म्याम् भर्तृहरि II. 54. वामाः–Perverse, those of an opposite character. प्रतीपदर्शिनी वामा । अमरः । प्रदेये–" the प्र implies that the thing is given once for all and cannot be taken back. " P. 122. मलयतटो०–How very appropriate the simile ; the sandal-tree transplanted from its native–soil—the slopes of Malaya, may not thrive in another place ; that is the image for Śakūntala leaving her forest–home.

IV. 18. अभिजनवतः possessed of a noble birth, nobly-born. विभवगुरुभिः Important from his dignity or greatness ; so that every moment she will be fully occupied with them. प्राची–is often poetically represented as the mother of the sun and the moon. प्रत्यभिज्ञानमन्थरः slow to recognize. Mark that the incident of the curse was kept a secret by the friends. But they are careful enough to warn Śakuntalā about the ring, who unfortunately could not understand the full significance of the warning. अतिस्नेहः पापशङ्की–Cf. प्रेम पश्यति भयान्यपदेऽपि । किराता॰ IX. 70. Love sees causes of alarm although without foundation. P. 124. युगान्तरं–युग is according to some equal to a प्रहर " a division of the day comprising one eighth of the sun's diurnal revolution, or three hours ; according to others हस्तचतुष्टयम्–a space of four cubits.

IV. 19. चतुरन्तमहीसपत्नी–the earth bounded by the four (quarters), the entire earth. चत्वारः अन्ताः यस्याः सा । दौष्यन्ति–दुष्यन्तस्य अपत्यं पुमान् । अप्रतिरथम्=अप्रतिराथिकम्–रथ by लक्षणा means a रथिक warrior who fights from a chariot ; having no rival, having no antagonist. निवेश्य–Having caused to marry, having settled in marriage. Cf. तान्निवेश्य चतुरोऽपि तत्र सः । रघु॰ XI. 57. अहमपि तव सूनावायुषि न्यस्तराज्यः । विचरितमृगयूथान्याश्रयिष्ये वनानि । अहवा चिरेण वि पुणो etc. How beautifully the same thought is expressed in the प्राकृत verse, vide intro. XX. मा उत्कण्ठितुं–gives the sense of मा उत्कण्ठस्व the infinitive is thus combined with मा and idiomatically used in the sense of the imperative. This use of the infinitive is rare ; but in भास it is common enough.

IV. 20. उटजद्वारविरूढं etc. " बलि or गृहबलि is a particular kind of offering identical with the भूतयज्ञ–i. e. a sacrifice for all creatures, but especially in honour of those demigods and spiritual beings called गृहदेवताः household deities–which are supposed to hover round and protect house-holds–(मनु॰ III. 80). This offering was made by throwing up into the air (मनु॰ III. 90) in some part of the house generally at the door (मनु॰ III. 88) the remains of the morning and evening meal of rice or grain." M. W. The reference here, however, is not necessarily to the भूतयज्ञ ; as Kaṇva speaks of the germination of the seeds, it must be uncooked grains scattered about the threshold. Generally this is consumed by crows, dogs or insects; hence बलिभुज्–बलिपुष्ट

as the names of a crow, or a crane; such of the grains as escaped being devoured by them would be likely to germinate about the threshold. Cf. यासां बलिः सपदि मद्गृहदेहलीनां हंसैश्च सारसगणैश्च विलुप्तपूर्वः । तास्वेव संप्रति विरूढतृणाङ्कुरासु बीजाञ्जलिः पतति कीटमुखावलीढः ॥. मृच्छ० I.

P. 126. सहधर्मचारिणी–Rather unusual–"friend in religious duties;" it means a wife. स्नेहप्रवृत्ति० etc. the course of affection views it thus—thus your love interprets. हन्त–is an exclamation of joy. स्वास्थ्यं—natural serenity of mind–I feel as if a load of anxiety is taken off my mind.

IV. 21. परिग्रहीतुः–परिग्रहीतृ is the husband and परिग्रह is the wife. Lit. one who accepts; while a wife is one who is accepted. विशदः–Serene, clear, tranquil. प्रकामं=अत्यर्थम्–the Bengali reading is जातोऽस्मि सम्यग्विशदान्तरात्मा । चिरस्यनिक्षेपमिवार्पयित्वा ॥ A deposit is a source of very great anxiety because it is another's property held in trust. Cf. सुखमर्थो भवेद् दातुं सुखं प्राणाः सुखं तपः । सुखामन्यद्भवेत्सर्वं दुःखं न्यासस्य रक्षणम् ॥ स्वप्न० I. 10.

ACT V

कलविशुद्ध–Soft and clear. कल is generally explained as अव्यक्त-मधुर, sweet and indistinct. स्वरसंयोग:–A combination of harmonious sounds. The blending of harmonious notes required by a particular Rāga or melody. वर्णपरिचय–Acquaintance with the Varnās; practice in singing. The word वर्ण means 'The order or arrangement of a subject in a song (गीतकम्).' Cf. उपात्तवर्णे चरिते पिनाकिनः....। कुमार॰ V. 56. Where मल्लिनाथ quotes हलायुध– 'गीतक्रमे स्तुतौ वेदे वर्णशब्दः प्रयुज्यते।. It may also mean 'a musical mode.' Cf. गीतिषु चत्वारो वर्णा भवन्ति। यदाह भरतः–स्थायी तथैव संचारी तथा रोहावरोहिणौ। वर्णाश्चत्वार एवैते कथिताः सर्वगीतिषु। Com. शंकर.

V. 1. अभि......लोलुपः–Eagerly longing (लोलुप) for fresh honey. तथा परिचुम्ब्य–Having kissed in such a manner i. e. so ardently. कमल... निर्वृतः–कमले वसतिः एव-कमलवसतिमात्रं-तेन निर्वृतः–Being altogether contented or satisfied by merely dwelling (may be, without enjoyment) in the lotus. विस्मृतः–Past Passive Participle used actively. The song of हंसपदिका, as the king remarks, has a veiled reproof for the king, who after a brief period of amours with her, left her in favour of his Queen. The king has been represented by her as the bee who flies from flower to flower in his eager search for fresh honey. चूतमञ्जरी is her own self who has been the victim of his momentary passion (Cf. परिचुम्ब्य), while the lotus, his usual resort in the evening after the day's wandering is over, represents the Queen वसुमती. Observe how skilfully the poet prepares the audience to face the tragic catastrophe of the repudiation of शकुन्तला, that is soon to follow. रागपरिवाहिणी–Impassioned, overflowing with feeling or passion. Cf. प्रथमं सपरिवाहमासीत्। Act II. अक्षरार्थः–The meaning of words, (lit. of the letters.). (सकृत्) कृतप्रणयः–कृतः प्रणयः येन सः–Who made love. (to her). If अयं जनः–this person is taken to refer to हंसपदिका, then it would mean 'who was once loved' (कृतः प्रणयः यस्याः सः). उपालम्भं गतः–Become an object of taunt or censure. परकीयैः हस्तैः-By the hands of others i. e. through her servants. शिखण्डके-(seized) by the tuft of hair. Mar शेण्डी. अप्सरसा (गृहीतस्य) वीतरागस्य-Like a sage who was free from passions, but who has been ensnared by a celestial nymph. This reference ordinarily ought to suggest to the king the name of शकुन्तला, who owes her birth to such an incident. The hint falls flat, however, since it rouses no such recollection. मोक्षः-(i) Escape; (ii) liberation of the soul from further transmigration. नागरिकवृत्त्या-In a polite or courtly manner. नागरिक 'a city-bred man, who has developed politeness of manners. It also implies 'insincerity, as a man shows exaggerated attention to his first mistress, while he is courting some one else. '—M. W. इष्टजनविरहादृतेऽपि Even without (ऋते) the separation from a beloved person. Note how cleverly the poet suggests by the expression that the curse of the sage Durvāsas has proved effective in obliterating all trace of शकुन्तला from the mind of दुष्यन्त.

V. 2. पर्युत्सुकीभवति—Becomes filled with ardent longing. सुखितः-Happy in every respect अबोधपूर्वं (स्मरति)-without any definite knowledge of the particular details of the object of recollections. Cf. विषयविशेषज्ञानाभावपूर्वम् । Com. राघव० भावस्थिराणि-Which remains clinging (to the soul) in the forms of impressions भावैः वासनाभिः स्थिराणि ।. जननान्तरसौहृदानि-Friendships of the other i. e. former births. The doctrine of पुनर्जन्म or the transmigration of the soul is an essential dogma of the Hindu religion, according to which, the soul migrates from one body to another, taking with it, in the form of impression, all associations of its former life, and its deeds, good or bad. The present condition of every person derives its character from the virtues or vices of his previous life, while very often vague recollections of occurrences and associations do cross his mind dimly, without his being aware of them in a definite form. Our present ties of friendship could also be thus traced to the former associations of intimacy existing between the two souls. Kālidāsa refers to these ideas very often. Cf. उन्मनाः प्रथमजन्मचेष्टितान्यस्मरन्नपि बभूव राघवः । रघु० XI. 22. फलानुमेयाः

प्रारम्भाः संस्काराः प्राक्तना इव ॥ रघु० I. 20. मनो हि जन्मान्तरसंगतिज्ञम् । रघु० VII. 15. कंचुकिन् or a chamberlain is an attendant in the royal harem, an old man, a Brahmin endowed with numerous good qualities. He is to enter the stage as a decrepit old man, tottering with age and lamenting his hard lot in the harem. आचार इति– Thinking it to be customary, or a matter of form. अवरोधगृहेषु– in the harem or the inner apartments. वेत्रयष्टिः–A cane staff with a gold or silver knob, used as a symbol or badge of office. बहुतिथे–बहूनां पूरणः बहुतिथः ।. The affix तिथ (तिथुक्) indicates measure or length of time. Cf. बहुपूगगणसंघस्य तिथुक् ।. प्रस्थानविक्लवगतेः– प्रस्थाने विक्लवा गतिर्यस्य–With a faltering or tottering step while walking. V. L. वृद्धस्य विक्लवगतेः । अवलम्बनार्था–अवलम्बनाय इयम्– (Become indispensable) for support. अनतिपात्यम्–Which ought not to be neglected or set aside. Cf. न चेदन्यकार्यातिपातः etc. Act I. धर्मासनं–The seat or judgment where the king sits to hear the grievances or complaint of the people and administer justice. अविश्रमः–न विद्यते विश्रमः यस्य सः–Knowing no rest or repose. लोकतन्त्राधिकारः–The office (आधिकार) of governing (तन्त्र) the people–Cf. प्रजाः प्रजाः स्वा इव तन्त्रयित्वा । V. 5.

V. 4. युक्ततुरङ्गः–युक्ताः तुरङ्गाः येन सः । who has yoked the horses (to his chariot) once for all, (सकृत्) and he knows no rest, but drives on eternally. रात्रिंदिवम्–रात्रौ च दिवा च–day and night. गन्धवहः–Lit. the carrier of fragrance; the wind. आहितभूमिभारः– आहितः भूमेः भारः येन सः–who has placed (on his head) the burden of the earth. शेषः–' i. e. अनन्त, a mythological serpent, the personification of eternity (अनन्तता) and king of the Nāgas or snakes who inhabit the lowermost of the seven Pātālas or infernal regions. His body formed the couch of विष्णु, reposing on the waters of Chaos, whilst his thousand heads were the god's canopy. He is also said to uphold the world on one of his heads. He has become incarnate at various times, especially in the god बलराम, the elder brother of कृष्ण'. M. W. षष्ठांशवृत्तिः–षष्ठांशेन वृत्तिः यस्य सः–The king who lives on the tribute given by the people viz. one-sixth of the produce.

V. 5. स्वाः प्रजाः इव–Like his own children. तंत्रयित्वा–Having ruled or governed. √तंत्र्–has also the sense of 'Maintaining or supporting (as a family)'. श्रान्तमनाः–with a wearied mind. V. L. शान्तमनाः–'with a peaceful or composed mind' is not so good. विविक्त–A secluded or solitary place. यूथानि संचार्य–Having led or conducted the herds (यूथ); Lit. 'Having caused to move about or graze.' दिवा–i. e. मध्याह्न–At mid-day. उपत्यका–अद्रेरासन्ना भूमिः the slope of the mountain, a lowland at the foot of the mountain. सस्त्रीकाः–with (two) women (accompanying). श्रौतेन विधिना–According to the form prescribed by the scriptures (श्रुति). चरितार्थता–The state of having obtained everything desired by them (i.e. kings). दुःखोत्तरा–खेदसंवलिता–V. L. दुःखान्तरैव 'painful, encompassed with trouble or worry.' He means that the interval between the desire and its attainment, accompanied as it is with keen effort to win the object and its phases of hope and disappointment, is indeed a very lively period in man's life. This is however denied to a king who has everything at his disposal, and has nothing to wish for. This very condition, however, is positively painful to him.

V. 6. प्रतिष्ठा–The high position, the (royal) glory, the dignity –सर्वोत्कृष्टं गौरवम्।. M. W. Understands it in the sense of 'the attainment of the object of ambition' agreeing with प्रार्थितार्थाधिगम or चरितार्थता. अवसादयति–satisfies. अवसाययति—V. L. Terminates, finishes; he means that the dignity of a king, by which he gets everything the moment he desires it, destroys even the eagerness or the anxious longing (औत्सुक्यं) for that object, because it is so easily attainable. Cf. अन्यजनस्य तु यत्किंचिद्विषयिणी समुत्पन्नोत्कण्ठा तथैव तिष्ठति तत्तद्विषयालाभात्। राज्ञस्तु–फललाभादुत्कण्ठापरिपूर्तिः। राघव० लब्ध... वृत्तिः—The duty or the (King's) function of preserving whatever he has obtained. नातिश्रमापनयनाय–' Not so much conducive to the removal of fatigue–' The king's position, because of its accompanying worries of preserving his kingdom intact, is not calculated to give him any physical or mental relief. 'Uneasy lies the head that wears a crown.' यथा श्रमाय–As it is (positively) for causing fatigue or exhaustion (by its cares and anxieties). Note the other reading–नातिश्रमापनयनाय न च श्रमाय. ' Is not for the removal of great fatigue and not for fatigue i.e. royalty does lead to fatigue. ' स्वहस्त...दण्डम्–स्वहस्ते धृतः दण्डः यस्य तत्—The handle of which is held in one's own hand आतपत्रम्–A parasol, umbrella. ' The Indian parasol or छत्र, from the shelter it affords, has been chosen as one of the insignia of royalty. It is very heavy and being fixed on a long pole, greatly fatigues the person holding it. It is always borne by a servant; but here the king is figuratively made to bear it himself, so that he cannot give shelter to himself and others, without undergoing great personal fatigue.' M. W. वैतालिकः–A herald, bard, a panegyrist. ' He was a kind of a herald or crier whose duty was to announce, in measured verse, the fixed periods, into which the king's day was divided. '

V. 7. स्वसुखनिरभिलाषः–स्वसुखे निर्गतः अभिलाषः यस्य सः– Having no desire for personal happiness indifferent to your own ease. खिद्यसे–(you) exert, toil. A fine illustration of दृष्टान्त.

V. 8. नियमयसि–(You) restrain, curb, punish. आत्तदण्डः–आत्तः दण्डः येन सः–Who has assumed the sceptre, the symbol of punishment and justice. विवादः–Dispute, quarrel. कल्पसे–You are fit for or adequate to (the protection). अतनुषु विभवेषु–In great (अतनु) prosperity, in affluent circumstances. नाम–in the sense of प्राकाश्ये ' as it is well known. ' त्वयि परिसमाप्तं–In you is perfected, is fully comprehended. ' बन्धुकृत्यं–The duty of a kinsman. He means that the king stands as the chief kinsman to his subjects, the so–called relatives being with man only during his prosperous time. Compare the king's declaration at the end of the VI Act–येन येन वियुज्यन्ते प्रजाः स्निग्धेन बन्धुना । स स पापादृते तासां दुष्यन्त इति घुष्यताम् ॥ Cf. also प्रजानां विनयाधानाद्रक्षणाद्भरणादपि । स पिता पितरस्तसां केवलं जन्महेतवः ॥ रघु॰ 1. 24. नवीकृतः–Refreshed. आभि...सश्रीकः–अभिनवेन संमार्जनेन सश्रीकः (श्रिया सहितः) Beautiful after its recent purification by the sprinkling of water. अग्नि...लिन्दः–A terrace (अलिन्द) of the fire–sanctuary.

V. 9. व्रतिन्–An ascetic, a hermit. उपोढतपस्–उपोढं तपः यस्य सः–who has accumulated or hoarded (a store of) penitential merit. दूषितं–marred, frustrated. For this idea, compare आपाद्यते न व्ययमन्तरायैः कच्चिन्महर्षेस्त्रिविधं तप स्तत्। रघु० V. 5. असत्–wrong, harm, injury. आहोस्वित्–used in introducing generally a third alternative. अपचरितं–A misdeed, a sinful action वीरुधां प्रसवः–The flowering or the blossoming of creepers. विष्टम्भितः–Paralysed, checked. The line (आहोस्वित् etc.) has a reference to the belief that the king's sins are visited on his subjects in the form of various calamities. Cf. न राजापचारमन्तरेण प्रजास्वकालमृत्युश्चरति। उत्तर० II. Also. राज्ञोऽपचारात् पृथिवी स्वल्पसस्या भवेत्किल। अल्पायुषः प्रजाः सर्वा दरिद्रा व्याधिपीडिताः ॥ Quoted by राघ० आरूढ...तर्क (मनः) आरूढाः (संजाताः) बहवः प्रतर्काः यस्मिन् तत्–In which various conjectures had arisen. अपरिच्छेदाकुलं–Perplexed with an inability to decide. अपरिच्छेदः–want of decision. सभाजयितुं–To congratulate, to greet. Cf. स्नेहात् सभाजयितुमेत्य दिनान्यमूनि। उत्तर० I.

V. 10. Kanva's pupil शार्ङ्गरव feels extremely out of sorts, when he finds himself in the midst of the swarming multitudes of the palace, and he tries to discover the causes thereof. महाभागः–eminent in virtues. अभिन्नस्थितिः–न भिन्ना स्थितिः येन सः–who has not broken away from the right path, not swerved from rectitude. He means that this uneasy feeling of his cannot certainly be attributed to the unrighteous policy of the king's behaviour, which is absolutely correct. अपकृष्टोऽपि–Even the lowest (of the four classes—वर्णानां). अपथं–The wrong path. The word is always neuter. हुतवहपरीतं–enveloped in the flames of fire. इदं–i. e. पुरोवर्ति नृपाङ्गणं–This royal court before my eyes. He explains his feelings. Accustomed as he was to seclusion, the crowd of the palace has made him restless, and he feels something out of the way has happened; the palace is as it were on fire and hence the throng of people.

V. 11. The other pupil शारद्वत has a similar experience. He feels, he is in an atmosphere of sin, impurity, uncleanliness of mind and body, of moral depravity. अभ्यक्तं–Anointed with oil. He is regarded as unclean until he has bathed. Cf. तैलाभ्यङ्गे चिताधूमे मैथुने क्षौरकर्मणि । तावद्भवति चाण्डालो यावत् स्नानं समाचरेत् ॥ –Kale. प्रबुद्ध इव सुप्तम्–Men who rise early in the morning have generally the tendency to look down upon those who get up late after sun-rise. सुखसंगिनम्–Addicted to pleasures. It is this fond attachment to or thirst for material pleasures that characterises the city people and that gives him this feeling of sin and impurity. While शार्ङ्गरव has taken a horror of the city-life and would like to run away far from the madding crowd, शारद्वत only pities them for their insatiable thirst for happiness which involves them in sin. निमित्तं–The bad omen viz. the throbbing of the right eye, which is most inauspicious and evil-foreboding in the case of woman. Cf. अङ्गविस्फुरणं नृणां दक्षिणं सर्वकामदं । तदेव शस्यते सद्भिर्नारीणामप्रदक्षिणम् ॥ Cf. जुगूह तस्याः पथि लक्ष्मणो यत् सव्येतरेण स्फुरता तदक्ष्णा । आख्यातमस्यै गुरु भावि दुःखमत्यन्तलुप्तप्रियदर्शनेन ॥ रघु० XIV. 49, where सीता too had a similar omen before she was cast away by लक्ष्मण. प्रतिहतं etc.–The sentence is commonly used to express the speaker's desire that the evil be averted. Cf. Mar. इडा पिडा टळो, अमंगळ पळो. वितरन्तु–May give. वर्णाश्रमाणां रक्षिता–The protector of the four classes (वर्ण) and the four orders or stages of human life viz. ब्रह्मचर्य, गार्हस्थ्य, वानप्रस्थ and संन्यास. महाब्राह्मण–There is a tinge of sarcasm in this expression, which we do get when the word महत् is prefixed to such words as ब्राह्मण,, वैद्य, implying निन्दा or censure which amounts to the absence of the real qualities. शार्ङ्गरव is slightly provoked by the Purohita's flowery description of the king as the protector of the Varnas and Āśramas and as one who favours them, as it were, with an interview. मध्यस्थाः–Unconcerned, indifferent. He means he has nothing to ask of the king, no suit to urge, no petition to present. This benevolent trait in the king is therefore more to the advantage of the पुरोहित than of him.

V. 11. फलागमैः –better than V. L. फलोद्गमैः. दूरविलम्बिनः–Hanging far (too low). दूरं विलम्बन्ते इत्येवंशीलाः । V. L. भूरिविलंबिनः.

अनुद्धताः–Not elated, not puffed up. प्रसन्नमुखवर्णाः–प्रसन्नः मुखवर्णः येषाम् ते–Having a serene, pleased facial expression. विश्रब्धकार्याः–Having a quiet and easy business, (Lit. which inspires confidence).

V. 12. का स्वित्–' who possibly '. स्वित्–a particle of question and doubt. स्विदिति वितर्के । अवगुण्ठनवति–Possessed of a veil (अवगुण्ठन)–It shows that ladies of high family used the veil in ancient days. नाति...लावण्या–न अतिपरिस्फुटं शरीरस्य लावण्यं यस्याः सा–whose loveliness of the body is not fully displayed (being obscured by the veil). कुतूहलगर्भोपहितः–कुतूहलेन गर्भे (मध्ये) उपहितः–Full of curiosity, being hindered (by the veil etc.). अनिर्वर्णनीयम्-अदर्शनीयम्–ought not to be gazed at. भावमवधार्य–Having reflected i. e. called to mind, the (intensity of) the feeling.

V. 14. तपति घर्मांशौ–Loc. Abs. when the sun is blazing. Cf. सूर्ये तपत्यावरणाय दृष्टेः कल्पेत लोकस्य कथं तमिस्रा । रघु० V. अर्थवान्–Full of significance. Cf. यथा प्रल्हादनाच्चन्द्रः प्रतापात्तपनो यथा । तथैव सोऽभूदन्वर्थो राजा प्रकृतिरञ्जनात् ॥. रघु० IV. 12. लोकानुग्रहाय–For the welfare of the world. The sage's health is conducive to the world's welfare. स्वाधीनकुशलाः-who have prosperity in their power. अनामयप्रश्नपूर्वकम्–अनामयप्रश्नः पूर्वं यस्मिन् तत्–preceded by the question of health (अनामय–Lit. Absence of disease). Cf. ब्राह्मणं कुशलं पृच्छेत् क्षत्रं पृच्छेदनामयम् । मनु० II. 127. मिथः समयात्–By mutual agreement (समय). उपायंस्त–Aorist III. Sing. of √उप+यम् 'to marry'.

V. 15. अर्हतां प्राग्रसरः–The chief of the respectable (अर्हत्). नःस्मृतोऽसि–is esteemed by us. मूर्तिमती सत्क्रिया–Virtue incarnate or in person. समानयन्–Bringing together, uniting. तुल्यगुणं–तुल्याः गुणाः यस्य तत्–(The two) of equal merit. वधूवरं–वधूश्च वरश्च (एतयोः समाहारः) तत्–वधूवरं–a समाहारद्वन्द्व compound. चिरस्य–After a long time. वाच्यं न गतः–Has not been exposed to censure, has incurred no blame. He means that so long every marriage was a union of two incompatibles, there being some flaw either in the bride or in the bride-groom. No couple was found to be a happy one in all respects. In the present union, however, the creator has succeeded in bringing two suitable persons together–an event which has saved him from blame for the first time after such a long period. आपन्नसत्वा–गर्भवती–Quick with child. Cf. आपन्नसत्वा स्याद् गुर्विण्यन्तर्वत्नी च गर्भिणी । अमर० सहधर्मचरणाय–For the joint discharge of religious obligations. A wife has to take part in all religious rites that the husband performs. The rites here may be certain संस्कारs to be done conjointly for the child before and after birth. किमपि etc. गौतमी's speech conveys a veiled censure for the king's action in secretly marrying शकुन्तला, without consulting her who was almost a mother to her. न मे...सरोऽस्ति–'There is no occasion for me to put in a word on behalf of शकुन्तला, when on a former occasion neither you nor she herself thought it fit to consult me.'

V. 16. न अपेक्षितः–Not referred to. एकैकं एव चरिते–when the affair was transacted quite privately (एकैकं–Lit one with the other, and no third person was there) भणामि किमेकैक्कं–what can I say to any one of you i. e. either to शकुन्तला or to you also. V. L. भणदु एक्क एक्कस्स = भणतु एकः एकस्य । 'what has each one to say to the other.' वचनोपन्यासः–The import of the speech लोकनिष्णाताः–well versed or fully acquainted with the ways of the world.

V. 17. ज्ञाति...संश्रयां–ज्ञातिकुलं (एव) एकः संश्रयः यस्याः सा–who solely resides in the family of her kinsmen ज्ञाति–relatives of the family of birth–अन्यथा विशङ्कते–suspect (her) to be otherwise i. e. unchaste. प्रियाप्रिया वा–Liked or disliked (by him) ; V. L. तदप्रियापि ' although disliked by him. सांप्रतं–Correct, proper, justified.

V. 18. कृतकार्यद्वेषात्–' Through dislike of a thing done !' He means that the king seems to be repenting of his sojourn in the hermitage that led to a marriage with शकुन्तला, and hence has he turned his face away (विमुखता) from Duty viz. the acceptance of his lawful wife. उचिता राज्ञः–Is it befitting a King ? V..L. कृतकार्यद्वेषो धर्मं प्राति विमुखता कृतावज्ञा । कृतावज्ञा–a wilful disregard. असत्कल्पनः प्रश्नः–A question based upon a fabrication of false-hood. ' The very assumption of marriage is a great fraud being falsely invented. What of this question based upon this false-hood ?' मूर्छन्ति–Take effect, grow strong. ऐश्वर्यमत्त–Intoxicated with sovereignty. विशेषेण अधिक्षिप्तोऽस्मि–The अधिक्षेप or censure though worded in general terms is especially aimed at me. I am the especial target of this censorious remark viz. ऐश्वर्यमत्त. It may also mean ' I am greatly censured or rebuked. '

V. 19. एवं उपनतं–Thus presented to me (without any effort on my part). अयत्नप्राप्तम्। Or एवं–i. e. in a pregnant condition ' to correspond with अन्तस्तुषारं । अक्लिष्टकान्ति (रूपं)–Of unblemished loveliness. प्रथमपरिगृहीतं–Accepted (in marriage) before अव्यवस्यन्° Unable to decide (√वि + अव + सो). V. L. व्यवस्यन्–' Deliberating, trying to decide.' अन्तस्तुषारं–अन्तर्गतः तुषारः यस्य तत्–' With the dew-drop inside.' The dew-drop covers the honey and keeps off the bee by its cold. The king also has to keep his hands off शकुन्तला, because she is now pregnant. विभाते–Cf. अत्र विभात इत्युक्तेस्तदनन्तरं रविकिरणैर्हिमे नीते मकरन्दभोगोऽत्रश्यः। एवमिहाप्यभिज्ञानदर्शनेन शापे गते तत्स्वीकारोऽत्रश्य इति द्योतयन्त्योपमया रतेः स्थायित्वदाढर्यं ध्वनितम्। धर्मापेक्षिता–consideration or regard for virtue. जोषम्–Silent. अभि...लक्षणां–अभिव्यक्तानि सत्वस्य (गर्भस्य) लक्षणानि यस्याः–Whose signs of pregnancy are clearly manifested. क्षेत्रिणमाशङ्कमानः–Suspecting myself (with regard to her) to be only a क्षेत्रिन्. क्षेत्रिन् the owner of the field, as opposed to बीजिन् i. e. one who sows the seed in the field, The figurative language was used in the law-books to refer to woman as क्षेत्र ' Field ', while the man who begets children from her was called बीजिन्–in cases where the husband differed from procreator of the child, there arose the controversy as regards the child's ownership, and the position of the क्षेत्रिन् who claimed the child simply because he happened to be the legal husband of the woman, was greatly deprecated. The king, in this case, therefore, has his own scruples about the similar relation he would bear to the child and hence he hesitates to accept her. Cf. भर्तुः पुत्रं विजानन्ति श्रुतिद्वैधं तु भर्तरि। आहुरुत्पादकं केचिदपरे क्षेत्रिणं विदुः।...बीजस्य चैव योन्याश्च

बीजमुत्कृष्टमुच्यते । सर्वभूतप्रसूतिर्हि बीजलक्षणलक्षिता ॥ मनु० IX. 32 ff. दूराधिरोहिणी. High–soaring.

V. 20. मा तावत्–May be taken with विमान्यः in the verse. 'May not the sage be insulted by you ?–Why, yes, he must be insulted etc.' Cf. मा तावदिति श्लोकेन संबध्यते ।...नामेति क्रोधे । मा विमान्यः न विमाननीयः । अपि तु विमाननीय एव । राघव० It may also be taken separately; 'enough, no more of this vow.' In that case the first line will have sarcastic twist, meaning 'The sage forsooth deserved to be thus disrespected by you, since he consented to your dastardly outrage on the modesty of his own daughter etc." The second interpretation is certainly preferable. कृताभिमर्शा–कृतः अभिमर्शः बलाद्धर्षणं यस्याः सा–Who was seduced or ravished. मुष्टं...येन–Construe :–येन (मुनिना) स्वं मुष्टं (अपि त्वां) प्रतिग्राहयता दस्युः इव त्वं पात्रीकृतः असि । The sage's action could be thus compared to that of a man who, finding his treasure robbed, invites the robber, and honourably makes him a gift of that very stolen treasure. पत्ययप्रतिवचनम्–A convincing reply; a reply calculated to produce conviction. शोचनीयः–To be sorrowed for. V. L शोधनीयः 'I myself am now to be cleared (justified) by myself; I have to vindicate the purity of my conduct." संशयिते–In doubt. समुदाचारः–Mode of address. स्वभावोत्तानहृदयं–स्वभावतः उत्तान हृदयं यस्य–तम्–(This person) who by nature is open-hearted. उत्तान–unreserved, frank. समयपूर्वम्–After a formal agreement (समय).

V. 21. व्यपदेश–व्यपदिश्यते अनेन सः—कुलं नाम वा । The designation, the litle or the name (of the family). The family is of शकुन्तला and not of the king, as is clear from the simile of the river making its own waters turbid. पातयितुम्–To bring down, to ruin. कूलंकषा–कूलं कषतीति सा तटसंघर्षिणी–Scratching the banks. उदारः कल्पः–A capital idea, a good proposal. शक्रावताराभ्यन्तरे–Within the शक्रावतार. शक्र is an epithet of Indra, and शक्रावतार is, therefore, some sacred place of pilgrimage where he descended upon the earth. अवतार–means also a descent into the river, a landing–place of stony steps (Mar. घाट). शचीतीर्थं–A holy bathing place, sacred to शची, wife of Indra. इदं तत् etc.–The king thinks the reply of गौतमी to be the work of a quick flash of imagination, and a masterly example of woman's instinctive ready wit. प्रत्युत्पन्नमति–प्रत्युत्पन्ना मतिः यस्य तत्–Ready-witted. स्त्रैणम्–स्त्रीणां समूहः–i. e. स्त्रीजातिः–Womanhood. प्रभुत्वम्–Power, sovereignty. श्रोतव्यमिदानीं संवृत्तम्–What was to be seen (द्रष्टव्य) just a minute before, has now turned into what has to be heard (श्रोतव्य). Evidence of the eyes has changed into that of hearing.' Note the tone of contempt and mockery in the words of the king, who feels now fully convinced that he is tried to be duped by this pack of scoundrels in the garb of ascetics, who want to force this pregnant woman into the seclusion of his harem, and father the illegitimate child on him. शृणुमस्तावत्–'Let us hear; (go on).' Clearly indicating that he is not going to believe a single word of what she will say. पुत्रकृतकः–Adopted as a child. पुत्रश्चासौ कृतकश्च–Lit. 'made a son.' स मृगपोतकः–The fawn, (mentioned in IV. यस्य त्वया etc.). उपच्छन्दितः उदकेन–प्रलोभितः, जलपानाय प्रेरितः–Was coaxed or enticed to drink water. √उपछन्द्–To conciliate privately by flattering or coaxing language.' Cf. तस्मादुपच्छन्दयति प्रयोज्यं मयि त्वया न प्रतिरोधरौक्ष्यम्। रघु० V. 58. हस्ताभ्यासं–हस्तसमीपं–Near your hand; M. W. understands the word to mean 'Lit. the use of the hand. i. e. stroking with the hand, caressing,' with उपगम्, 'to approach for fondling, to allow to be caressed, to entrust one's self into any one's hands." प्रणयः कृतः–Showed a favourable disposition; evinced his desire. प्रहसितः–Laughed in a joke. सगन्ध–सदृश°–or संबन्धिजनः–Relative, kith and kin. आत्मकार्यनिर्वर्तिनी–'Accustomed to accomplish one's own purpose.' M. W. takes it to mean 'Turning (voluptuaries) away form their own duty.' अनृतमयवाङ्मधु–The honey of false words. कैतवस्य अनभिज्ञः–Unfamiliar or unacqainted with roguery. तापसवृद्धा–वृद्धा तापसी–वृद्धतापसी–or as we have it तापसवृद्धा according to पाणिनि० II. 2. 38., although the former form would be more usual. Note the king's harsh and jeering tone in the use of this expression with reference to गौतमी.

V. 22. अशिक्षितपटुत्वं–Untaught cleverness or inborn cunning. Cf. स्त्रियो हि नाम खल्वेता निसर्गादेव पण्डिताः । पुरुषाणां तु पाण्डित्यं शास्त्रेणैवोपदिश्यते ॥ मृच्छ० IV. अमानुषीषु–Among non-human species of creatures, i. e. in lower creatures. किमुत–'How much more'. प्रतिबोधवत्यः–ज्ञानिन्यः चैतन्यभाजः–gifted with intellect, endowed with reason. प्राक् 'Before', governs ablative. परभृता–A female cuckoo. In this verse, the king has unconsciously alluded to the story of शकुन्तला's birth, by the use of words which have a double meaning. i. e. अमानुषीषु–may refer to the celestial nymph, मेनका, the mother of शकुन्तला. प्रागन्तरिक्षगमनात्–would refer to her flight to heaven, after the birth of शकुन्तला, her अपत्यजात which is left in the care of a द्विज i. e. the Brahmin sage, कण्व. The expression that refers to her mother, is परभृता i. e. 'fed by others, a courtezan,' which in reality the Apsarasas are. All these invidious suggestions must have been read by शकुन्तला, who was exasperated to find that the king knowingly refers in this to her own story heard in that very आश्रम, and still repudiates her having full well recognised her; that he goes to the indecent length of almost abusing her own mother by calling her a harlot (परभृता), and further he reaches a climax in insulting her by suggesting, even शकुन्तला, who too is no better than a परभृता, has come down here, in imitation of her mother's conduct, to father her own prospective offspring on him. It is here that she feels convinced of the fact that the king is a liar and a scoundrel, and hence in her next sentence, she bursts out in a temper to call him an अनार्य. हृदयानुमानेन–By the measure of your own heart, by an inference drawn in comformity with the (wicked and villainous feelings and impulses of) your own heart. धर्मकञ्चुकप्रवेशिनः–Putting on (Lit. entering into or hiding himself underneath) the cloak or garb of virtue. तृणच्छन्नकूपोपम–Resembling a well covered or concealed underneath the grass, calculated to entrap innocent and unsuspecting creatures. अनुकृतिं प्रतिपत्स्यते–will act in imitation of yo ur conduct; will be so low and degraded as to act like you. संदिग्धबुद्धिं कुर्वन्–Making me doubt my own judgment. अकैतवः–Unfeigned, genuine. The following passage is read by Ray, before संदिग्धबुद्धिं etc. वनवासादविभ्रमः पुनरत्रभवत्याः कोपो लक्ष्यते। तथाहि-न तिर्यगवलोकितं भवति चक्षुरालोहितं वचोऽपि परुषाक्षरं न च पदेषु संसज्यते। हिमार्त इव वेपते सकल एष बिम्बाधरः स्वभावविपते भ्रवौ युगपदेव भेदं गते ॥.

V. 23. विस्मरण...वृत्तौ–विस्मरणेन दारुणा चित्तवृत्तिर्यस्य सः तस्मिन्–(on me) who exhibited a dreadful state of mind by my loss of memory. वृत्तं रहः प्रणयं–(An affair of) love that happened in secret (रहः). भ्रुवोः भेदात्–By the knitting lit. by the parting of her eye-brows. अतिरुषा–Through excessive anger. स्मरस्य शरासनं मय्येव भग्नम् इव–'It seemed as if the bow of Cupid was snapped asunder even against me.' The two curved eye-brows with the bridge of the nose in between present the appearance of a bow in their normal attitude, and have often been imagined to be Cupid's bow, while the glances are likeness to arrows discharged from it. Cf. तस्याः शलाकाञ्जननिर्मितेव कान्तिर्भ्रुवो-रायतलेखयोर्या। तां वीक्ष्य लीलाचतुरामनङ्गः स्वचापसौन्दर्यमदं मुमोच ॥ कुमा० I. 47. Now, when these brows were parted from each other, being knit in a frown, they appeared like two pieces of a bow broken in the centre. Note also the double entendre in the word स्मर, which means 'recollection,' as well as 'the God of love.' इदं–this i. e. wicked treacherous conduct. स्वच्छन्दचारिणी–a self-willed woman, wanton, one who acts on the impulse of the moment. मुखमधोः–मुखे मधु यस्य-सः–तस्य–Who has honey on his lips. Cf. मधु तिष्ठति वाचि योषितां हृदि हालाहलमेव केवलम्। also मधुतिष्ठति जिह्वाग्रे हृदये तु हलाहलम् ॥ आत्मकृतं–Self-committed (without consulting any one else). अप्रतिहतं–When not checked or counter-acted. चापलं–A hasty action, a rash act. दहति Brings on repentance, leads to remorse.

V. 24. The first line is variously interpreted thus:–(i) राघव०–अतः कारणात् संगतं मैत्र्यं परीक्ष्य कर्तव्यम्। रह एकान्ते संगतं विशेषात् परीक्ष्य कर्तव्यमित्यनुषज्यते। Therefore a union, especially (when) in private, ought to be formed with great circumspection, after having made proper inquiry, and investigating each other's characters and circumstances.' (ii) Ray–' Hence secret union has to be made after having specially (विशेषात्) tested (each other).' अज्ञात...सौहृदम्–' Thus does friendship become enmity, between those who know not each other's hearts.' A fitting advice indeed to those who play with love indiscreetly. It is not, as Kale suggests, a stricture on love-marriage. संभृतदोषैः Accumulated accusations. V. L. संयुतदोषाक्षरैः–सम्यक् न त्वीषत् युतः संपृक्तः न तु स्पृष्टः दोषो येषु तान्यक्षराणि येषु वचनेषु तैर्वचनैरिति विशेष्यमुन्नेयम्।–With words full of accusation. अधिक्षिपथ–Reproach. V. L. क्षिणुथ–Harm, injure. सासूयम्–Sarcastically, ironically. अधरोत्तरम्–अधरं (हीनं) च तदुत्तरं च–निकृष्टप्राधान्यम्–' Ascendancy of the low, placing that at the top which ought to be at the bottom.' The word occurs in the Manusmriti, where it means ' a confused and contradictory statement. Cf. अदेश्यं यश्च दिशति निर्दिश्यापह्नुते च यः । यश्चाधरोत्तरानर्थान् विगतान्नावबुध्यते ॥ मनु० VIII. 53. It would mean here ' Inversion of the proper order of things, something made topsyturvy, a perversion of things.' The sentence may therefore mean, being addressed to all the people assembled in the sacrificial hall, " Have you heard of such a perversion ? " M. W. understands the sentence as addressed to the king, with reference to the ironical statement in the succeeding verse. Hence the meaning may be ' you have been taught upside down or backwards.' In other words, ' The usual definition of the fourth प्रमाण viz. शब्द as आप्तवाक्य, you would make it अनाप्तवाक्य, the words of an improper person.' Ray takes the expression to mean ' a preposterous suggestion,' remarking that शार्ङ्गरव wants the audience to note how the undeserving दुष्यन्त appears deserving and the deserving शकुन्तला as undeserving. The Com. राघवभट्ट takes it to mean ' a base answer.'

V. 25. परातिसन्धानम्–The deceiving of others. विद्येति–As a fine (honourable) art. He probably refers to the king's study of works like कौटिल्य's अर्थशास्त्र, dealing with politics, wherein the

विजिगीषु is taught to employ even questionable methods to gain his ends. आप्तवाचः-आप्तस्य इव वाक् येषां ते-Whose words are (as authoritative) as those of an आप्त. आप्त is defined as one who is trustworthy and who speaks the truth and is thus reliable. आप्तस्तु श्रद्धेयवचनः यथार्थवक्ता. ते सन्तु...वाचः—Let them, forsooth, be considered as men worthy of belief!' Note the ironical tone of शार्ङ्गरव. He exposes the perversity of the situation, where innocent people are being branded as liars, while professional cheats have the high honour of authoritative worthies. विनिपातः-Ruin, destruction, down-fall. Com. शंकर takes it to mean नरकगमन. किमुत्तरेण-'What is the use of replying, no use bandying words.'

V. 26. तदेषा...कान्ता-Saying this, after all argumentation, शारद्वत has proved that he is not going to believe the king. He has faith in शकुन्तला whom he looks upon as the king's lawful wife. The Bengālī Mss. read पत्नी instead of कान्ता. सर्वतोमुखी-सर्वतः मुखानि यस्याः सा-All-sided, in all respects, of every kind, unlimited. Lit. Facing all directions. करुणपरिदेविनी-Wailing or lamenting piteously. प्रत्यादेशपरुष-Harsh or cruel by his rejection of her. पुरोभागिनि-Voc. of पुरोभागिनी-a wanton, perverse person.' The word पुरोभागिन्-first means 'one who takes the first share or more than his proper share' (पुरो भागः यस्य सः) i. e. a grasping character. Cf. मा मां पुरोभागिनीति समर्थयसि । विक्र० III. Hence secondarily it means 'a censorious, malevolent person.' It has also the sense of 'one who is given to the habit of finding faults with others.' Cf. दोषैकदृक् पुरोभागी । अमर० Even this sense holds good here. शार्ङ्गरव wanting to suggest that शकुन्तला could easily call her own husband a rascal (कितव), while she has absolutely no sense of her wifely duty to abide with him in any circumstances. स्वातन्त्र्यमवलम्बसे-A wife has no independence or initiative of her own in her husband's house. Cf. पिता रक्षति कौमारे भर्ता रक्षति यौवने । पुत्रस्तु स्थाविरे भावे न स्त्री स्वातन्त्र्यमर्हति ॥ मनु० IX. 3.

V. 27. उत्कुला-उत्क्रान्ता कुलात् or उत्क्रान्तं कुलं यया सा-Fallen from the family. व्रतं-चारित्रं marriage-vow, conduct. क्षमम्-योग्यम्-Fit, proper. M. W. takes it to mean 'supportable.' किं...विप्रलभसे–Why do you deceive her into the belief that she will be retained by me in my house-hold as my wife, if she persists in staying on here!

V. 28. कुमुदान्येव etc. Cf. विकसति हि पतङ्गस्योदये पुण्डरीकम्। उत्तर० पर...मुखी परस्य परिग्रहः तस्य आश्लेषः तस्मात् पराङ्मुखी–Recoiling or turning away with abhorrence from the embrace of another's wife. गुरुलाघवम्–गुरु च लघु च–तस्य भावः। An abstract noun from गुरुलघु, a द्वंद्व compound, the वृद्धि taking place in the second member of the compound instead of the first. It means 'the greater and the less, the heavier and the lighter (sin).' The king wants to know from the Purohita, which of the two courses, viz. rejection of a lawful wife, or acceptance of another's wife as one's own wife, would involve less sin.

V. 29. मूढः–Infatuated. परस्त्री...पांसुलः–Defiled (पांसुल Lit. soiled with dust) by contact with another's wife. आदिष्टपूर्वः–पूर्वं आदिष्टः–Already informed. V. L. उद्दिष्टः–Declared. चक्रवर्तिन्–A Universal monarch, a sovereign ruler–Lit. One who stands at the head of the circle (चक्र) of princes round–about. M. W. takes it to mean 'one who has the mark of the चक्र (or discus) in his hand.' When the lines of the right hand formed themselves into a circle, this was the mark of the future hero and emperor. The word also means 'one whose empire extends to the horizon (चक्र) or from sea to sea.' मुनिदौहित्रः–मुनिदुहितुः अपत्यं पुमान्–The son of the sage's daughter. Note the argumentative style of Purohita's speech, who is more expected to be well–versed in Nyāya and Vedānta than in Kāvya. विवरं–Entrance, admission. She means, she wishes no longer to live in the land of the living. Cf. तथा विश्वंभरे देवि मामन्तर्धातुमर्हसि। रघु० XV. 81. शापव्यवहितस्मृतिः–Whose memory was obscured by the curse.

V. 30. बाहुत्क्षेपं–बाहू उत्क्षिप्य–An instance of णमुल् gerund. Throwing up her arms.' स्त्रीसंस्थानं–स्त्रियाः इव संस्थानं (आकारः,

अंवयवविन्यासः) यस्य तत्–Having the shape or form of a woman. आरात्– 'Near,' governs accusative.

V. 31. Construe:-कामं प्रत्यादिष्टां मुनेस्तनयां परिग्रहं न स्मरामि। I admit (कामं) I do not remember the repudiated sage's daughter to be my wife (परिग्रह). दूयमानं–Being troubled, being agitated. मां प्रत्याययतीव–Forces me as it were to believe her.

ACT VI

प्रवेशकः–See note on विष्कम्भक, Act III, IV. M. W. places this Praveśaka, not at the beginning of the VI Act as is done by almost all the editors, but between the two Acts V and VI. Cf. अथ पञ्चमषष्ठाङ्कमध्ये प्रवेशकः । M. W.'s edition, P. 217. नागरिकः–Superintendent of the city-police; नगरे नियुक्तः or नगराधिकारी । श्याल=राष्ट्रीय, is the (King's) brother-in-law, acting as the Police Superintendent, a character often introduced in the plays. Cf. मृच्छ० राजश्याल or राष्ट्रियश्याल. कुंभीलक–or V. L. कुंभीरक means 'a thief.' Cf. लोप्त्रेण गृहीतस्य कुम्भीलकस्यास्ति वा प्रतिवचनम् । विक्र० II. also अहो कुम्भीलकैः परिहरणीया चन्द्रिका । माल० IV. मणि...धेयं–मणिबंधने उत्कीर्णं नामधेयं यस्य–The setting of which is engraven with his name. 'मणिबन्धन usually meaning a 'wrist' (cf. III) has here the sense of the 'setting or the collet of the Jewel which formed the Mudrā or the seal of the ring. मणिः खच्यते यस्मिन्–इति मणिबन्धनः ।. The name might have been engraven on the stone itself or on the gold in which it was set. उत्कीर्ण–Engraven, excavated, inscribed. V. L. महामणिभासुले उक्किण्णणामाक्खले । Note the dialect spoken by the Policemen. It conforms to the characteristics of the Māgadhī, and is to be distinguished from the language of the श्याल or the other Prakrit–speaking characters, who give us the शौरसेनी dialect. प्रतिग्रहः–A present, gift. पाटच्चरः–A thief, a robber; explained as पाटयन् चरति–one who moves about by breaking open the walls. प्रतिबध्नीतम्–from √प्रति + बन्ध् to interrupt. जालोद्गालादिभिः–With fishing nets (जाल) and hooks (उद्गाल). मत्स्यबन्धनोपायैः–With contrivances to catch fish. विशुद्धः–'very pure'; said, of course, ironically; The निषाद or the fisherman's caste was looked upon as the lowest cf. मनु० x. 46–48. आजीवः–Profession.

VI. 1. सहजं–Lit. born along with (the person), कुलक्रमागतम् । किल–As the saying goes, as they say; he refers possibly to the popular quotations from the भगवद्गीता like स्वधर्मे निधनं श्रेयः परधर्मो

भयावहः । II 35 or better still, सहजं कर्म कौन्तेय सदोषमपि न त्यजेत् ॥ XVIII. 48. विनिन्दितं-censured, found fault with. The sense of अपि is understood after this word. श्रोत्रियः-A learned Brāhmaṇa, one well-versed in sacred learning. Cf. जन्मना ब्राह्मणो ज्ञेयः संस्कारैर्द्विज उच्यते । विद्यया याति विप्रत्वं त्रिभिः श्रोत्रिय उच्यते ॥ पशु...श्रोत्रियः-He means that even a learned Brahmin, although soft-hearted and tender with pity (for creatures in general) has to be cruel or dreadful in his slaughter of the sacrificial animal–a thing which ordinarily is an object of public censure. रोहितः-'Lit. 'Red–fish' is a kind of carp, found in lakes and ponds in the neighbourhood of the Ganges. It grows to the length of three feet, is very voracious, and its flesh, though coarse, is eaten. Its back is olive-coloured, its belly of a beautiful golden hue, its fins and eyes red'-M. W. कल्पितः-Cut. विस्रगन्धि-विस्रस्य-आममांसस्य-गन्ध अस्ति यस्मिन्-Smelling of raw meat (विस्र). गोधादी-An eater of गोधा i. e an alligator. Some read the Prakrit गोहादी as गोघाती i. e. a cow-killer ; and as cow-killing is looked upon as a heinous crime, the word is applied as a reproachful epithet to any rogue or low person. Thus in मृच्छ०, the चाण्डाल is called गोह or गोघ्न '. M. W. मत्स्यबन्धः-A fish-catcher, a fisherman. विमर्शयितव्यम्-Ought to be investigated or closely inquired into. ग्रन्थिभेदक-Lit. 'knot-cutter or knot-breaker', a cut-purse. V. L. गण्डभेदक which means the same thing. Read प्रतीष्य for प्रतीक्ष्य-Having received'. आवुत्तः-Brother-in-law. 'आवुत्तो भगिनीपतिः' अमर० अवसरोपसर्पणीयाः-That could be approached (only) at the proper time. सुमनसः पिनद्धुम्-to bind flowers into a wreath round the head of the victim. It is evident from works like the मालतीमाधव and the मृच्छकटिक, that a person about to be executed or offered as a victim to a deity like Śiva or Durgā had a wreath of flowers bound round the head. शुनो मुखं द्रक्ष्यसि-'will see the face of a dog'. The two policemen have no doubt about the fact that the fisherman guilty of such a criminal theft of the royal ring will receive capital punishment, and that he is soon to be executed. After the execution is carried out, his body will be thrown out, to be preyed upon by vultures or by dogs. If any doubt exists, it is only in regard to his later disposal by the vultures or by the dogs. 'Dr. Boethlingk has adopted an emendation, शिशुणो मुहं i. e. शिशोर्मुखं, and translated, 'or thou wilt see the face of (thy) child (once more).' There is, however, no authority for such an emendation. According to Ray, this refers to execution in which the condemned man is buried upto the neck under ground and dogs are then let loose to tear him up. The victim can see (द्रक्ष्यसि) the dogs coming because he is not dead yet.' जालोपजीवी–who maintains himself by means of a fishing-net. उपपन्नः–Justified, confirmed, found true. अङ्गु...संमितः–commensurate with the ring's value. दापितः–P. P. of the causal of √दा–'caused to be given, bestowed through me.' एष नाम etc. V. L. एष नामानुग्रहः etc.–'such indeed is the favour.' शूल–'A stake for impaling criminals.' हस्तिस्कन्धे प्रतिष्ठापितः–Mounted or seated on an elephant i. e. elevated to a high dignity, was given a great honour. Elephants, as we know, were used in triumphal processions. संमत–Highly favoured or prized. V. L. बहुमतेन. Read पर्युत्सुकमनाः instead of पर्युत्सुकनयनः। 'Excited in mind.' The V. L. पज्जस्सुणअणो=पर्यश्रुनयनः–'With tearful eyes' is also very good. मात्स्यिकभर्तुः (कृते)–For the sake of this chief of the fishermen. The Prakrit word can be translated by मत्स्यिकाभर्तुः–'For the sake of the husband of the female fish'–said rather in vulgar joke and smacks of contemptuous envy. V. L. मच्छसत्तुणो=मत्स्यशत्रोः–'For the enemy of the fish. सुमनोमूल्यम्–Of the value of a flower i. e. as insignificant as a flower; compare the Marathi idiom, फूल नाहीं फुलाची पांकळी M. W. looks upon this utterance, as an ironical remark with reference to their earlier comment on his profession—विशुद्ध इदानीमाजीवः। In fact he has taunted them before by his remark भर्तः, अथ कीदृशो म आजीवः। महत्तरः–Bigger, greater. The Mar. word म्हातारा owes its origin to this comparative form of महत्. कादम्बरीसाक्षिकं–कादम्बरी साक्षिणी यस्मिन् तद्–With liquor (कादंबरी) for its (i. e. friendship's) witness. कादम्बरी–Wine distilled from कदम्ब flowers. शौण्डिकापणम्–The liquorshop. Lit. the shop of a wine-seller (शौण्डिक). P. 168. पर्यायनिर्वर्तनीयम्–Which is to be carried out in turns (पर्याय), or rotation. For similar duty assigned to the celestial nymphs, Cf. अप्सरोवारपर्यायेणेह भगवतः सूर्यस्य पादमूलोपस्थानं वर्तते इति बलवत् खल्वर्वश्यामुत्कण्ठितास्मि । वि० III. उदन्तः–News, incident, circumstances. शरीरभूता–A veritable body, my own self. निरुत्सवारम्भं–निर्गतः उत्सवारम्भाः यस्मात्–Bereft of preparations (आरम्भ) to celebrate the the festival (of spring). 'The वसन्तोत्सव or 'the vernal festival' in celebration of the return of spring and said to be in honour of the god Krishna. Originally his son Kāma-deva, the god of love, must have been the object of worship in his festival. It is identified with the Holi or Dolā-yātrā, the Saturnalia, or rather, Carnival of the Hindus, when people of all conditions take liberties with each other, especially by scattering red powder and coloured water on the clothes of persons passing in the street as described in the Ratnāvalī Act I, where syringe and waterpipes are used by the crowd. Flowers and especially the opening blossoms of the mango, would naturally be much used for decorations at this festival, and as offerings to the god of love. It was formerly held on the full moon of the month of Caitra, or about the beginning of April, but now on the full moon of Phālguna, or about the beginning of March.' M. W. प्रणिधानम्–deep mental concentration; profound meditation. विभवः–power. आदरः–Eagerness, keen desire (that I should see the king's condition with my own eyes). तिरस्करिणीप्रतिच्छन्ना–covered by a magic veil. तिरस्करिणी is a magic art known to the divine beings, who employ it for the purpose of making themselves invisible to the mortals. Cf. Com. राघव० who explains this expression thus :- अन्तर्धानविद्यया परिच्छन्ना ।

VI. 2. जीवसर्वस्व–The essence or the all-in-all of life. V. L. जीवितसर्वम् ।. चूतकोरकः–The mango-blossom. ऋतुमङ्गल–The auspicious thing that opens the season. प्रसादयामि–causal of √प्र + सद्–I entreat you to favour (me). परभृतिका–A female cuckoo. मधुकरिका–A female bee. These are also the names of the two garden-maids, and significant as they are, they fit in with the atmosphere of spring which the poet has created and where the cuckoo is prominent with her sweet warbling and the bee by its humming and hovering over the fresh mango blossoms. मदविभ्रमगीतानाम्-Of songs of love and intoxication. अप्रतिबुद्धः-not fully bloomed. बन्धनभङ्गसुरभिः-fragrant after the cutting of the stalk (बन्धन). कपोतहस्तकं-The word कपोत, originally meaning 'a dove or a pigeon,' is technically applied to 'a mode of joining the hands together, in an humble entreaty, respectful representation, or fear.' Cf. सर्वपार्श्वसमाश्लेषात् कपोतः सर्व (सप) शीर्षकः। भीतौ विज्ञापने चैव विनये च प्रयुज्यते ॥. Com. शंकर.

VI. 3. गृहीतधनुषे-The compound correctly should be गृहीतधन्वने. To (the God-of-Love) who has taken up the bow, (now that spring has set in, and he is supplied with his shafts viz. the mango-blossoms). पथिक...लक्ष्यः-पथिकजनानां युवतयः लक्ष्यं यस्य सः-Having young women whose husbands have gone abroad, as the target. पञ्चाभ्यधिकः-The best of the five. पंचसु अभ्यधिकः।. अनात्मज्ञा-आत्मानं न जानाति सा-One who knows not her own self i. e. a silly thoughtless person. अगृहीतार्था-अगृहीतनिषेधवस्तुस्वरूपा-unacquainted with the incident (of prohibition). वासन्तिक-Belonging to the season वसन्त, i. e blossoming in spring. प्रमाणीकृतं-'Looked upon or admitted as authority, received as a rule.'

VI. 4. चूतानां etc. Cf. ईषद्बद्धरजःकणाग्रकपिशा चूते नवा मञ्जरी। विक्र० II. 7. संनद्धम्-Fully developed and therefore ready to blossom. Cf. यौवनमङ्गेषु संनद्धम्। Act I. रुतं-The warbling. संहरति-withdraws. महाप्रभावः राजर्षिः-The king was believed to have power to direct or prohibit the advent of any season. Cf. मुनयोऽपि व्याहरन्ति राजा कालस्य कारणमिति। तत्किमहं जलदसमयं न प्रत्यादिशामि। विक्र० IV. कति दिवसानि-a few days; to be construed with the predicate गतानि. आगन्तुकता-The condition of being a stranger (आगन्तुक) उत्सवप्रियाः-fond of festivals. बहुलीभूतम्-Spread far and wide; known to all, become notorious. कर्णपथः-The range or the path of ears. कौलीनम्-लोकवादः-A scandal, an evil report; derived from कुल 'a family', and may signify 'report relating to family or private matters,' family scandal. कुल also means 'a group of people' and therefore, what is talked in a group is also very often nothing else but a scandal. (कुले जनसमूहे भवम्).

VI. 5. रम्यं–(everything) delighting or pleasurable. यथा पुरा–As before. शय्याप्रान्तविवर्तनैः–Rolling or tossing about on the edge of the bed. उन्निद्रः–उद्गता निद्रा यस्य सः–Whose sleep has fled away, sleepless. क्षपा–A night. दाक्षिण्यं–courtesy, politeness. It has also the sense of 'outward politeness lacking in the sincerity of love'. Cf. निषिञ्चन् माधवीमेतां लतां कौन्दीं च नर्तयन् । स्नेहदाक्षिण्ययोर्योगात् कामीव प्रतिभाति मे ॥ विक्र० गोत्रेषु स्खलितः–blundering in the (proper) names. Due to his absence of mind, he calls the particular lady by the name uppermost in his mind ; viz. that of शकुन्तला. This is a common idea with Kālidāsa. Cf. स्मरसि स्मर मेखलागुणैरुत गोत्रस्खलितेषु बन्धनम् ॥ कुमार० III. 8. also आर्य, यन्निमित्तं भर्ता उत्कण्ठितस्तस्याः स्त्रिया नामधेयेन भर्त्रा देवी आलपिता ॥ विक्र० II. पुरुषोत्तमेति भणितव्ये पुरूरवसीति निर्गता वाणी ॥ ibid. III. व्रीडाविलक्षः–Embarrassed by a feeling of inward shame. प्रभवतः–Abl. of प्रभवत्–Arising, overpowering, वैमनस्यम्–Abstract noun from विमनस्–विषण्णं मनः यस्य सः । Dejection, mental depression. सर्वास्ववस्थासु etc. Compare अहो सर्वास्ववस्थासु चारुता शोभां पुष्यति । माल० II.

VI. 6. प्रत्यादिष्टवि...विधिः–प्रत्यादिष्टः विशेषमण्डनस्य विधिः येन सः–Who has scorned all special forms of decoration. बिभ्रत्–Pres. Part. of √भृ–to wear. वामप्रकोष्ठार्पित–Placed on or fastened upon the left fore-arm (प्रकोष्ठ). Read श्वासापरक्ताधरः–श्वासैः अपरक्तः अधरः यस्य सः–Whose lower lip became discoloured i. e. bloodless on account of (hot) sighs. संस्कारोल्लिखितः–Rubbed or ground on a polishing stone. The word संस्कार refers to the act of polishing as also the polishing stone. The poet means that the king, although attenuated in form, does not appear to be such because of his magnificent majestic lustre, as is the case of a gem, which when polished loses its portion and yet shines brighter by its innate lustre ; similar idea, Cf. अपचितमपि गात्रं व्यायतत्वादलक्ष्यम् । Act II. क्लाम्यति–Pines. स्थाने खलु–etc. Sānumatī means that the king is so charming that there is no wonder that शकुन्तला should pine for him, although insulted by his rejection of her. Any woman would feel the loss of such a lovely husband.

VI. 7. हतहृदयम्-This wretched or accursed heart हत. When so prefixed has this sense. Cf. कुर्यामुपेक्षां हतजीवितेऽस्मिन् । रघु० XIV. अनुशयः—Remorse, repentance नन्वीदृशानि etc.–' Such is her lot, poor pitiable girl ! ' Sānumati observes how unfortunate was the life of शकुन्तला who was repudiated when she had gone to her husband in person, while now when he remembers everything, she is far away from him, deeply merged in grief. लङ्घितः- Attacked, seized, overpowered. Cf. आतपलङ्घनाद् बलवदस्वस्थशरीरा शकुन्तला । Act III. चिकित्सितव्यः-who should be treated after a diagnosis of his disease. चिकित्सा is diagnosis and cure. प्रत्यवेक्षिताः- Thoroughly examined or inspected. This has to be done to ensure close privacy for the king as also to see that no danger to his life comes from an assassin or a hostile person. पत्रमारोप्य- Putting (it) on paper, committing that to writing. The king was always the final authority to give judgment in cases which the minister would investigate. शिशिरा...रमणीय-शिशिरस्य च आतपस्य च छेदेन रमणीयः-Lovely because of the absence of (excessive) cold and heat. Cf नाप्यत्यन्तं शिशिरं नाप्यातपः । Com. राघव०. Ray takes it to mean ' lovely in the interval (छेद) between winter and summer, i. e. spring. रन्ध्रोपनिपातिनः-Rushing through the (first) hole (रन्ध्र) they can find ; the word रन्ध्र meaning ' a hole ' signifies ' a weak point in man. ' Cf. छिद्रेष्वनर्था बहुलीभवन्ति । or the English idiom, ' Misfortunes never come single. ' अव्याभिचारि-न व्याभिचरते तत्-which never fails, which is invariably true, having no exception.

VI. 8. Note the use of च-च which signifies simultaneous occurrence. मुनि...रोधिना (तमसा)-which obstructed the memory of my love for the sage's daughter. प्रहरिष्यता-Wishing to strike, desirous of striking, a Future Part. from √प्र+हृ. Compare for a similar sentiment, अये परावृत्तभागधेयानां दुःखं दुःखानुबन्धि ।. अयमेकपदे तया वियोगः प्रियया चोपनतः सुदुःसहो मे । नववारिधरोदयादहोभिर्भवितव्यं च

निरातपत्वरम्यैः ॥ विक्र० IV. 3. अनेन दण्डकाष्ठेन etc.–This reminds us of Śudraka's विदूषक or मैत्रेय in the मृच्छकटिक, who too is ever ready to help his friend with his crooked stick. V. L. कन्दर्पव्याधिम् । ब्रह्मवर्चसम्–ब्रह्मणः वर्चः–The Brahmanic lustre; said ironically in view of his ridiculous attempt to destroy the arrows of love. (वेलां) अतिवाहयिष्ये–I shall pass (my) time. चित्रफलकं–picture tablet. मणिशिलापट्टकसनाथः–furnished with a jewelled marble slab. उपहारः–An offering of flowers. प्रतिकृतिः–A portrait, a picture. परिहासः...भूतार्थः–Note the dramatic irony of these remarks. The very words which he had said to विदूषक to stop him from babbling his affair with शकुन्तला to the inmates of his harem, are being returned to him by विदूषक, in such a tragic manner. मृत्पिण्डबुद्धिः–मृदां पिण्डः इव बुद्धिः यस्य सः–Having intellect like a lump of clay, 'where understanding is as dense and lacking in receptivity, as a clod of earth;' clod-pated, block–head Cf. प्रभवति शुचिर्बिम्बोद्ग्राहे मणिर्न मृदां चयः । उत्तर० II. सखे त्रायस्व माम्–The acute pang of remorseful meditation on शकुन्तला has become unbearable to him. शोकपात्रात्मानः–शोकस्य पात्रं आत्मा येषाम् ते–Whose hearts have become receptacles (पात्र) of grief, who have given themselves up to grief. V. L. शोकवक्तव्याः–yields no sense. Ray incorrectly translates सोअवत्तव्वा as शोकवास्तव्याः–' Abode of grief.' प्रवातेऽपि etc. Cf द्रुमसानुमतां किमन्तरं यदि वायौ द्वितयेऽपि ते चलाः । रघु० VIII. 90. समवस्था–has the same sense as अवस्था, 'plight, miserable condition.'

VI. 9. व्यवसिता–Tried (to follow), made an attempt (only). मुहुस्तिष्ठति etc. refers to the words of शार्ङ्गरव, 'किं पुरोभागिनि, स्वातन्त्र्यमवलम्बसे ।' बाष्पप्रसरकलुषां–Bedimmed with the flow of tears. स्वकार्यपरता–' Devotion to one's own cause, absorption in one's own object.' Sānumatī means that her eagerness to accomplish her purpose for which she came, viz. to witness the king's condition after Śakuntalā's rejection, has so much affected her, that she feels actually delighted to observe the king's tragic plight and his outbursts of grief. पतिदेवता–पतिः (एव) देवता यस्याः

सा-'To whom her husband is a god, a chaste, faithful wife.' M. W. translates it with an Englishman's outlook, thus "The idol or the goddess of her husband" or as we should say, 'a wife idolised by her husband.' परिमार्ष्टुम्- To touch, to hold, to outrage the modesty of. जन्मप्रतिष्ठा-जन्मस्थानम् The source of birth. सख्याः ते- of your friend i. e. of शकुन्तला. विदूषक, the king's friend, is being spoken of by the king as his wife's friend. Cf. जाने संख्यास्तव मयि मनः संभृतस्नेहमस्मात् । etc. संमोह...प्रतिबोधः-Sānumatī means that it is indeed a great wonder that this king should have been under such a delusion as to forget everything about Śakuntalā; that he remembers her now, the cloud of forgetfulness being lifted off his mind, is nothing to be wondered at. न पारयतः- Are not able.

VI. 10. The blissful period in the hermitage in the company of Śakuntalā was so uncommonly delightful that it appears, when recalled to the mind, to be a dream (स्वप्न) as it were. But it cannot be such a vision, since I am sure, I was not under the influence of sleep. Was it magic (माया) practised on me by a juggler ? But it cannot be that, either, since there was not the slightest tinge of unreality in the whole experience, followed by the tragic repudiation of the real Śakuntalā. In the same manner, the idea that it was perhaps some mental delusion or hallucination, has to be dismissed. If then real, it was so short-lived, possibly because the store of my merit which gave me this much reward (तावदेव फलं यस्य-तावत्फलं), was meagre and got exhausted (क्लिष्टं), by this much experience, as a result of it. Cf. अखंडं पुण्यानां फलमिव च तद्रूपमनघम् ॥ Act II. In this strain does the king argue about the nature and the causes of his love's period with Śakuntalā. माया-Magic, illusion; used in the Vedānta philosophy to signify 'The imagining of something which does not actually exist, super-imposition of one thing upon another.' असंनिवृत्त्यै-For the purpose of never returning, never to come back. मनोरथानामतटप्रपाताः-All the fondest hopes of meeting Śakuntalā once again are veritable crumblings of the river banks (तट) or like falls from a steep precipice, i. e. are to be ruthlessly frustrated and crushed. M. W. reads मनोरथानामतटप्रप्रातः–' And so (it–तद्) has become the steep precipice (अतट) of my heart's fondest hopes. Ray reads–तदतीतमेते । मनोरथानामतटप्रपाताः । एते, according to him, refers to the four possibilities, like स्वप्न etc. while the last line means, ' These are the precipices for my wishes (मनोरथानि) to drop from. ' The reading and the interpretation given above is supported by the com. राघवभट्ट, who remarks:—अतः परमेते त्वयोच्यमाना मया वाशस्यमाना मनोरथाः । नामेत्यलीके । अलीका मनोरथा इत्यर्थः । ते तटप्रपाता इति भिन्नरूपकम् । यथा वर्षासमये गङ्गादेस्तटा ओघेन पीड्यमाना अहमहमिकया पतन्ति । एकः पतति तदुपर्यन्यस्तदुपरीतरः । एवं मनोरथानामेके विलीयन्तेऽन्य उत्पद्यन्ते तेऽपि विलीयन्ते तदितरे उत्पद्यन्ते इत्यर्थः । निदर्शनम्– Example, illustration. असुलभ°.. भ्रंशि–असुलभात् स्थानात् भ्रश्यति तद्– which slipped away from a place which was ordinarily beyond reach or inaccessible. शोचनीयम्–Fit to be lamented.

VI. 11. सुचरितं–good action, merit. फलेन विभाव्यते–Is to be inferred by its result (फलं). अरुण......मनोहरासु (अङ्गुलीषु)–(The fingers) charming with its rosy nails (अरुण). लब्धपदं–लब्धं पदं येन तद्–which obtained a place.उद्घातः–Reference, allusion; or occasion. विदूषक all innocently wants to know what occasion was there for the king to give her the ring. निवेशयता–(By me) who was putting (the ring on her finger).

VI. 12. मद्...प्रवेशं नेता–who will lead you to the entrance of my inner apartment. The ring had the king's name दुष्यन्त engraved on it, and it will not, therefore, take more than three days for the king's servant to come to the hermitage to take away Śakuntalā. अवधिः–Period, interval (of expectation), the appointment of a period. विसंवादितः–made to fail in keeping up the promise, frustrated. शचीतीर्थं वन्दमानायाः–etc.–And these were the very words said by गौतमी in explanation of the loss of the ring, that were jeered at by the king. ईदृशः...वैतत्–' How could it be explained that such (deep) love stands in the expectation of a token-ring, for the beloved to be recognised by her lover. '

VI. 13. बन्धुर...ङ्गुलिं (करं)–बन्धुराः कोमलाश्च अङ्गुल्यः यस्य तम् With its lovely (बन्धुर) delicate fingers. अचेतनं etc. He means that the ring is after all an inanimate object, and is not likely to use any discretion and appreciate excellence (गुणं). He was, however, more to blame since he, endowed with चेतना, rejected her when she had come to him of her own accord. अनुशय...हृदया– Whose heart is scorched with remorse (अनुशय). इयं चित्रगता भट्टिनी– The entrance of चतुरिका with the picture of शकुन्तला just at a time when the king is craving for her sight, is very opportune. मधुरा.. प्रवेशः–The representation (अनुप्रवेश) of the various feelings (of fear, bewilderment, curiosity etc.) is very charming because of the lovely posture (अवस्थान) Cf. Com. राघव० मधुरं सुन्दरं यदवस्थान-माकृतिस्तया दर्शनीयो भावस्यानुप्रवेशोऽभ्यन्तरीकरणम् । सुन्दराकारतया भावाविर्भावो रम्यतर इत्यर्थः । M. Williams translates it thus: 'The presence of the prevailing sentiment (love–रति) is delightful by its sweet abiding in every part.' स्खलतीव...प्रदेशेषु–My sight stumbles, as it were, over the uneven parts of the body, Lit. on the depressions and prominences. 'The relief or appearance of projection and depression in the picture is so well managed that my eye is deceived, and seems to follow the inequalities of surface.' M. W.

VI. 14. चित्रे साधु न स्यात्–May not be well drawn in a picture, falls short of the real because of the painter's lack of skill. तदन्यथा क्रियते–Is improved upon, having been retouched. M. W. translates it thus, ' whatever is not well (executed) in the picture, all that is wrongly portrayed). तथापि–In spite of (all the retouching that is done to the picture). तस्या......न्वितम्–Her loveliness is exhibited in the picture, in a slight measure i. e. very faintly. He means that with all his effort and skill that he could bring to bear on this painting, he has failed in bringing out her natural loveliness which could be imitated very faintly. रेखा-लेखनं, The sketch, the delineation. राघवभट्ट quotes the following to define रेखा–शिरोनेत्रकरादीनामङ्गानां मेलने सति । कार्यस्थितिर्यतो नेत्रहरा रेखा प्रकीर्तिता ॥. अनवलेपः–Absence of conceit. For the remarks of

विदूषक viz. इदानीं तिस्रः etc. compare, वि० विदूषकः—कथं नैषा उर्वशी। तस्यास्तत्रभवत्या अभिमता सहचरी। which shows how विदूषक has no eye for beauty. मोघदृष्टिः–Having eyes in vain, possessed of sight, which serves no purpose. Some read मोहदृष्टिः–' dull–sighted.' उद्वान्त-कुसुमेन—the flowers from which have been thrown out (lit. vomited). विशेषतः अपसृताभ्यां–drooping down very much. अव...... पल्लवस्य–With its fresh foliage glistening with the sprinkling of water. भावचिह्नम्–A sign of love, an indication of passion.

VI. 15. स्विन्ना...वेशः–The impression (विनिवेश) of the perspiring fingers. रेखाप्रान्तेषु–On the edges of the picture. कपोलपतितं अश्रु–A tear-drop fallen on the cheek (of Śakuntalā in the picture). As he was drawing her portrait, the overpowering grief filled his eyes with tears, one of which dropped down on the picture. वर्तिका–A painting brush, a pencil. वर्तिकोच्छ्वासात्–By the swelling (in colour) caused by the brush with which the drop was tried to be removed. V. L. वर्णि (र्ण) कोच्छ्वासात्–from the coming out or puff of the paint; cf. रङ्गस्य उत्फुल्लत्वात्।.

VI. 16. बहुमन्यमानः–Thinking much, showing so much regard. स्रोतोवहा—A river. निकामजला—Having plenty of water. प्रणयवान्—full of love or desire. मृगतृष्णिका मृगाणां तृष्णा अस्यां–सा मृगतृष्णा—सैव मृगतृष्णिका—Mirage. This is a fine illustration of निदर्शना. अभिरूपः–favourite.

VI. 17. The picture was only half-drawn, and these details have to be supplied to make the picture complete. सैकत...मिथुना–With couples of swans resting unnoticed on the sandy bank (सैकत). निषण्णहरिणाः–With the deer sitting or reclining. गौरीगुरोः पादाः–The sloping hills of the mountain Himālaya, lit. the father of Gauri or Pārvati. तामभितः–On both the sides of the river. शाखा...वल्कलस्य शाखासु आलम्बितानि वल्कलानि यस्य–तस्य (तरोः). On whose branches are suspended the bark-garments. वामनयनं कण्डूयमानां–Scratching or rubbing her left eye. Note how the king wants to create an atmosphere of love in the picture. The river Mālini with the mountain by its side, the pairs of swans and last of all, the picture of the female deer rubbing her left eye on the horn of her mate, the black antelope will certainly lend a peculiar charm to this picture of Śakuntalā. लम्बकूर्च–Having long beard. प्रसाधनम्–Decoration.

VI. 18. कर्णार्पितबन्धनं (शिरीषं)–कर्णे अर्पितं बन्धनं यस्य तत् With its stalk (बन्धनं) placed on the ear आगण्ड...केसरम्–आगण्डं (गण्डपर्यन्तं) विलम्बिनः केसराः यस्य तत्–With its filaments hanging down up to the cheeks. शर...कोमलं– (The lotus-fibre) soft like the ray of the autumnal moon. स्तनान्तरे–Between the two breasts, in the midst of her bosom. Cf. अन्योन्यमुत्पीडयदुत्पलाक्ष्याः स्तनद्वयं चारु तथा प्रवृद्धम् । मध्ये यथा श्याममुखस्य तस्य मृणालसूत्रान्तरमप्यलभ्यम् ॥ कुमार० I 40. चकितचकितेन–As if greatly frightened or scared. ननु...धृष्टः–Cf. न एष धृष्टो विरमति । Act I. अविनीतानां शासिता–The chastiser of the impudent. विदूषक reminds him, as it were, of his own words (कः पौरवे वसुमतीं शासति शासितरि दुर्विनीतानाम् । Act I.) said by him while introducing himself to the girls. कुसुमलताप्रिय–dear unto the flowering creepers. परिपतनम्–Flying or hovering about.

VI. 19. प्रतिपालयति–Waits (for you). अभिजातं–Politely, nobly, in a courteous manner. वामा–Wanton, perverse.

VI. 20. अक्लिष्ट...नीयः–अक्लिष्टः यः बालः तरुपल्लवः, तदिव लोभनीयः–Alluring or enticing like an unfaded fresh sprout of a tree. Cf. अधरः किसलयरागः etc. Act I. रतोत्सवेषु–During love's festivals or love's banquets. कमलोदरबन्धनस्थं कारयामि–I shall get you thrown in the prison of the hollow of a lotus. A culprit guilty of molesting a woman is punished usually by imprisonment ; and the same punishment will therefore be meted out to the bee as well, both in his capacity of a king and as her husband. In the first Act (Cf. चलापाङ्गां दृष्टिं etc.), the king's position was different. Both of them, were on equal footing, although later, as a king he steps in to ward off his successful rival. एवं तीक्ष्णदण्डस्य–' Of you, giving such a severe punishment '–said, of course, ironically. एष उन्मत्तः...संवृत्तः–विदूषक now realises that he too like the mad king, had transformed himself into the atmosphere of the picture, where the whole scene, he felt, was actually being enacted before his eyes. अनवगतार्था-one who had not understood the thing, viz. that it was a picture. V. L. अनवगतार्था-would mean, 'I too realised it just now.' पौरोभाग्यम्-पुरोभागी दुष्टः-तस्य कर्म पौरोभाग्यम्-Mischief, a wanton, ill-natured act.

VI. 21. तन्मयेन हृदयेन-With a heart fully absorbed (in the picture). चित्रीकृता-Was turned into a picture. He means, he had rescued her from the lifeless picture, by the power of his mental absorption, and made her live and move before his eyes; by reminding him that it is a picture, विदूषक has again turned her into the picture पूर्वापरविरोधी-Involving a contradiction between what preceded (पूर्व) and what followed (अपर). She means that his actions before (i. e. when he did not remember her and consequently most cruelly discarded her) bear a strange contrast to his moping attitude of grief and bereavement. He was stern like steel, before, and soft like wax now. The Com. राघव takes it differently thus:- पूर्वं चित्रस्य चित्रत्वेन ज्ञानं पुनस्तस्योन्मादावस्थायां सत्यत्वेन ज्ञानं पुनरपि चित्रत्वेन ज्ञानमिति पूर्वापरविरोधः।

VI. 22. खिलीभूतः—prevented, barred. द्रष्टुं न ददाति—Do not allow me to see (her in a picture). Note the idiom, which is very much like the Marathi expression, पाहूं देत नाहीं. The tears obstructing the lover's view of his beloved drawn in a picture, is a favourite idea of कालिदास. Cf. त्वामालिख्य प्रणयकुपितां धातुरागैः शिलायां... अस्त्रैस्तावन्मुहुरुपचितैर्दृष्टिरालुप्यते मे। मे० II. मत्संभोगः कथमुपनमेत् स्वप्नजोऽपीति निद्रामाकाङ्क्षन्तीं नयनसलिलोत्पीडरुद्धावकाशाम्॥ मे० II. हृदयमिषुभिः कामस्यान्तः सशल्यमिदं सदा। कथमुपलभे निद्रां स्वप्ने समागमकारिणीम्। न च सुवदनामालेख्येऽपि प्रियामसमाप्य तां मम नयनोरुद्बाष्पत्वं सखे न भविष्यति॥ विक्र० II. 10. प्रमार्जितं-Wiped away, fully atoned for. अन्तरा-On the way, midway. आत्मा निर्वाहितः-I took myself off. I made my escape. Lit. my own self was carried off (by me). बहुमानगर्विता-Puffed up or elated with vanity, because of the great attention (बहुमान) I show to her. आत्मानं (रक्षतु) इति भण-विदूषक is afraid of his own safety more than that of the picture. अन्तःपुरकालकूटात्– From the bane or the deadly poison (कालकूट) of the harem, (which is full of bitter jealousy and hatred). V. L. अन्तपुरकूट-वागुरातः–' From the noose of perfidy of the harem. ' प्रथमसंभावनाम-पेक्षते–Respects or shows his regard to his first love. It is read as one sentence by some. Cf. अन्यसंक्रान्तप्रेमाणो नागरा अधिकं दक्षिणा भवन्ति ॥ विक्र० III. अर्थजातं– The various items of revenue ; Ray ' several receipts. ' विपन्नः–died. तपस्वी–Poor man ! बहुधनत्वात् बहु-पत्नीकः–Polygamy, especially among the rich, was the rule of the day. He had as it were a right to marry many wives, because he had ample wealth ! साकेतस्य श्रेष्ठी–A merchant from Sāketa i. e. Ayodhyā. पुंसवनं–' The rite performed on the quickening of the foetus' with a view to secure the birth of a male child. It is second of the 16 संस्कारs, coming next after the गर्भाधान ceremony, and performed generally in the third or fourth month after conception. Cf. व्यक्ते गर्भे तृतीये तु मासे पुंसवनं भवेत् । गर्भेऽव्यक्ते तृतीये तु चतुर्थे मासि वा भवेत् ॥ शौनक० The ceremony consists in placing यव grain and two माष grains (representing the male organs of generation on the right palm of the lady, who is to swallow them, along with some cream, to the accompaniment of the sacred Mantrās. रिक्थं–Property, wealth.

VI. 23. पापादृते–(i) except it be a sinful relation ; for instance, that of a husband to a widow. (ii) The wicked excepted ; i. e. if the man is a sinner and a culprit, and therefore deserves no patronage from the king. सन्तति...लम्बाना– (Of families) that are supportless by the lapse of progeny (that would have maintained the continuity). मूलपुरुषवसाने At the end i. e. the death (अवसान) of the representative of the race or the original stock. मूलपूरुष would properly mean the original proginitor but here it means ' the stock-man, the eldest surviving son. ' राघव and M. W. read ममाप्यन्ते पुरुवंशश्रीरकाल इवोप्तबीजा भूरेवंवृत्ता । उपस्थित–...मानिनम्–उपस्थितं श्रेयः अवमन्यते सः–तम् Who despised the bliss that waited on him.

VI. 24. आत्मनि संरोपितेऽपि–' Although myself was implanted (in her womb), she was sown with myself, i. e. she bearing my second self in her womb.' This refers to the belief that a child is an incarnation or a reproduction of one's own self. Cf. अङ्गादङ्गात् संभवसि हृदयादभिजायते । आत्मा वै पुत्रनामासि स जीव शरदः शतम् ॥. Also पतिर्जायां प्रविशति गर्भो भूत्वेह मातरम् । जायायास्तद्धि जायात्वं यदस्यां जायते पुनः ॥ मनु०. कुलप्रतिष्ठा–The stability of the family. काले–At the proper season; if अकाले–is read, then it has to be construed with त्यक्ता, meaning 'forsaken at a wrong time, when just the harvest was ready.' अपरिच्छिन्ना–' Uninterrupted.' She knows that he has a son from Śakuntalā संशयमारूढाः–' Have reached a critical state, (when they have become apprehensive as regards offerings to them in future, after me.').

VI. 25. यथाश्रुति संभृतानि–prepared in accordance with the scriptural texts. निवपनानि–Libations. नियच्छति–Offers. V. L. करिष्यति । प्रसूतिविकल–destitute of progeny, deficient in offspring. धौताश्रुशेषं–Remaining after being used for washing the tears (caused by this galling thought), मोहमुपगतः–This shows how keen was the king's anxiety, caused by an implicit faith in the prevailing notion of the Srāddha ceremony and its efficacy. व्यवधानदोषेण–By the fault of the intervening curtain that obscures the view. She means, the king has a son, but because of his ignorance of this fact, he bewails his childless condition, like a man groping in the darkness, the light being obscured by the screen. Read निर्वृतं–Happy, satisfied. यज्ञ...त्सुकाः–Eager to have their share of oblations in a sacrifice. The kings used to perform great sacrifices in celebration of joyful occasions like marriage etc. and Indra as also the other inferior gods were invited to partake of portions intended for them. महेन्द्रजननी The mother of Indra viz. अदिति, who was the wife of कश्यप. आत्तगंधः–आत्तः गन्धः–गर्वः–यस्य सः–Who has his pride removed, humbled, insulted. Cf. पक्षच्छिदा गोत्रभिदात्तगन्धाः । रघु० XIII. 7. सत्वं–An evil spirit, (भूत). गृहाः–गृह is used in Masc. Plural to denote, 'a house, or a wife.'

VI. 26. प्रमादस्खलितं–'blunder through carelessness, a false step through heedlessness. वेदितुमस्ति शक्तिः–A question asked, with a peculiar change in the tone which is suggestive of the reply. This is called a प्रश्नकाकु. शक्तिरस्ति किम् ? नास्तित्यर्थः । अविहा or अविधा– (आक्रोशे) used in calling for assistance. पश्चादवनतशिरोधरं–पश्चात् अवनता शिरोधरा यस्य सः–तम्–Whose neck is bent backwards. V. L. पच्चवणदसिरोहरं = प्रत्यवनतशिरोधरं, which means the same thing. तीक्ष्णभङ्ग–who is being cut violently (तीक्ष्ण) into pieces. V. L. तिण्णभङ्गं = त्रिभङ्गं–cut into three pieces. हस्तावाप–A protection for the hand or fore-arm, a leather band, a handguard.

VI. 27. चेष्टमानम्–Struggling (to escape). शरणं–Refuge, protector. Cf. शरणं गृहरक्षित्रोः । अमर०. कुणपाशनः–कुणपं–शवं–अश्नाति यः–An eater of dead bodies, a carrion-eater.

VI. 28. हंसो हि–A royal swan or a flamingo is supposed to have the power of separating milk from water ; hence we have the हंसक्षीरन्याय. Cf. न त्वस्य दुग्धजलभेदविधौ प्रसिद्धां वैदग्ध्यकीर्तिमपहर्तुमसौ समर्थः ॥ नीति० 18. नीरक्षीरविवेके हंसालस्यं त्वमेव तनुषे चेत् etc. । भा० वि० I. 13. मातलिः–is the name of Indra's charioteer.

VI. 29. शरण्यम्–A mark, a target. हरिणा–By Hari i. e. Indra. प्रसाद etc. Construe सुहृज्जने सतां प्रसादसौम्यानि चक्षुंषि पतन्ति, न दारुणाः शराः (पतान्ति) । प्रसादसौम्यानि–Softened with kindly favour. इष्टिपशुमारम्–A णमुल् gerund used with the उपमान viz. इष्टिपशु– 'Beaten like a sacrificial animal.' Cf. कर्मकर्त्रोर्णमुलि... । का० प्र० X. 89. कालनेमिः–' Son of the demon हिरण्यकशिपु. He had hundred arms and as many heads. These दैत्यs were sometimes called दानवs, from their mother दनु who, as well as दिति, was one of the wives of कश्यप and daughters of दक्ष.' M. W. नारदः– A celebrated divine sage, usually reckoned among the ten प्रजापतिs, first created by ब्रह्मा. He acts as a kind of messenger of the gods.

VI. 30. सः–i. e. The host of demons, called दुर्जयः–अजय्यः– जेतुं अशक्यः–Invincible, unconquerable. Cf. क्षय्यजय्यौ शक्यार्थे ।. It should be distinguished from अजेयः–जेतुं अयोग्यः । शतक्रतुः–An epithet of Indra, meaning 'one who has performed hundred sacrifices (क्रतु).' He is so called because the rank which he occupies is unattainable excepting through a hundred अश्वमेधs or 'horse-sacrifices'. Cf. तथा विदुर्मां मुनयः शतक्रतुं द्वितीयगामी न हि शब्द एष नः ॥ रघु० III. 49. रणशिरसि–In the fore-front (शिरसि) of the battle, at the head of the fight. Read प्रयुक्तम्–Acted, behaved. किंचिन्निमित्त–किंचिद् निमित्तं यस्य सः–Having some reason, (which I did not know).

VI. 31. चलितेन्धनः–चलितं इन्धनं यस्य सः–With its fuel stirred. विप्रकृतः–provoked, molested. फणां कुरुते–expands its hood. V. L. फणं. क्षोभात्–Through provocation. V. L. कोपात्. दिवस्पतिः–The lord of the heaven, i. e. Indra. परिगतार्थं कृत्वा–Having acquainted (the minister) of this circumstance.

VI. 32. केवला–Single, unaided (by my bow). व्यापृतं–Employed, engaged.

ACT VII

P. 210. आकाशयान–The aerial path. यान–also means a 'conveyance'. अनुष्ठितनिदेशः–अनुष्ठितः निदेशः येन सः । ब० । One who has executed or carried out the orders given to him. सत्क्रियाविशेषात्–Because of the high mark of respect or extraordinary honour. अनुपयुक्तम्–i. e. अयोग्यम्. Unworthy, not deserving. The word मघवतः can be construed with both अनुष्ठित° and सत्क्रिया°. Mark the modesty of the king. He is illustrating the saying अनुत्सेकः खलु विक्रमालङ्कारः । उभयमपि–etc. But both are dissatisfied with what they have done. The king feels that the respect shown to him was out of all proportion to the services rendered while Indra feels that he could not adequately reward the king for his timely and generous services.

VII. 1. प्रथमोपकृतं–The previous obligations: i. e, the signal service you rendered to the leader of gods. प्रतिपत्तिः–Honour. अवदानविस्मितः Amazed at (your) heroic deed. अवदानम्–A valorous deed. A feat. मनोरथानामभूमिः etc. the king did expect that he would be honoured by Indra for the great feat of arms achieved by him in vanquishing the demons. And so he was so to say anticipating some reception. But what actually took place far exceeded his imagination and so he says that the reception was beyond even the pale of imagination or expectation. By even the most powerful stretch of my imagination I could not have hoped for the honour I received. अभूमिः–अविषयः–Beyond reach. विसर्जन–Dismissing. Bidding farewell.अर्द्धासनोपवेशित°–etc. Seated on half of the throne of Indra.–Sharing the throne with Indra. This was supposed to be a very high mark of honour for the mortals and many even in the Durbar of Indra craved for it. Cf. अर्द्धासनं गोत्रभिदोऽधितष्ठौ । रघु०

VII. 2. अन्तर्गतप्रार्थनम्–Etc. जयन्त, The son of Indra, who was standing close by, was inwardly–in the heart of his hearts–longing for that garland. Indra knew that and hence जयन्तमुद्वीक्ष्य Etc. He simply cast a glance at his son and smiled. आपृष्ट–Rubbed. हरिचन्दनाङ्क–Marked by the yellow sandal. पिनद्धा–Fastened.

VII. 3. सुखपरस्य–Etc. This explains why Indra often used to take the aid of his mortal friends to oust out the demons. There is of course the other reading सुरसखस्य which absolves him from this draw-back. त्रिदिवं–The heaven. उभयैः–The word उभय is generally used in the singular: here it is a peculiar use उद्धृत॰ Etc. With the thorns in the form of demons extracted. नतपर्वभिः–नतानि पर्वाणि येषाम्–तैः। By the flat–jointed (arrows) or smooth–jointed: पुरुषकेसरिणः–The reference here is to the fourth, Man–lion incarnation of Viṣṇu. The king is compared to this particular Avatāra of Viṣṇu in that both freed the heaven from the tyranny of the demons. The arrows of दुष्यन्त are on a par with the claws of Nara–Siṅha with which he tore to pieces the demon Hiraṇya–Kaśipu father of Prahlāda.

VII. 4. सिध्यन्ति–Etc. But the king would not admit any such idea. The servants succeed in mighty enterprises only because they have the moral support of their masters. Their ability is only like reflected light. सम्भावनागुणम्—The quality of 'Thinking well of' or honouring giving patronage. धुरि–रथाग्रे–or पुरोभागे–in the forefront–अरुण or Dawn by himself could never have been able to dispel the darkness but for the patronage it receives at the hands of the sun. Cf. also–वज्रिण एव वीर्यमेतद्विजयन्ते द्विषतो यदस्य पक्ष्याः। विक्रमो॰ नाकपृष्ठगत Etc. The glory of the king had already reached the heaven; and the celestial bards were already busy composing panegyrics about his wonderful feat of arms. सौभाग्यम्–सुभगस्य भावः। Sublimity–beauty or grandeur.

VII. 5. दिवौकसः–द्यौः ओकः येषाम् ते। बहु॰। The denizens of heaven. विच्छित्तिशेष–The remnants or residues of the paints. विच्छित्ति–lit. means 'cutting off.' But it has also the sense of

'Paint' or rogue. कल्पलतांशुकेषु–on garments in the form of the leaves of the desire–yielding tree. The vestments or tapestry. The writing material was provided by the कल्पलता । गीतक्षममर्थजातम् Materials–verses–capable of being sung, or set to music. The V. L. अर्थबन्ध would mean–'पद्s.' They choose only melodious expressions which could be sung. On his way to the heavens, the king was not in a mood to indulge in sight-seeing. And so on his way back he wants to visit all the different charming spots. पूर्वेद्युः–पूर्वस्मिन् दिने । on a previous day. मरुतां पथि–In the course of the wind. "According to Hindu mythology, the heavenly region is divided into seven Paths of Courses, with a particular वायु or wind assigned for each. The first of these seven vāyu–mārgas or vāyu–pathas is identical with the bhuvar–loka, or atmospheric region, extending from the bhur–loka, or terrestrial region, [comprising the earth, and the adhō–lōka, called Pātāla] upwards to the sun. The wind assigned to this Mārga is called āvaha, and its office is to bear along the atmosphere, clouds, meteors lightning, etc. The other six make up the swar-loka or heavenly region with which Swarga is often identified in the following order:—The 2nd Mārga is that of the sun; and its wind, called pravaha or pravāha, causes the sun to revolve; 3rd that of the moon, its wind saṁvaha or saṁvāha impels the moon; 4th that of the nakaṣtra, or lunar constellations; its wind, udvaha, causes the revolution of these asterisms; 5th that of the graha, or planets; its wind vivaha bears along the seven planets 6th that of the Saptarsi or seven stars of the Great Bear; its wind parivaha bears along these luminaries, as well as the swar-ganga, or heavenly Gangas [saptarshi–chakram swar-gangam shashthah parivahas tatha : not as Dr. Boehtlingk suggests gaptarshi–chakram swarga-gah, etc.] : it appears from the next verse that this was the Mārga in which Indra's car was at the moment moving; 7th that of dhruva, or the polar star, the pivot or axis of the whole planetary system, to which, according to the Visṇu–Purāṇa [pp. 230, 240, Wilson], 'all the celestial luminaries are bound by aerial cords, and are made to travel in their proper orbits, being kept in their places by their respective bands of air. According to the Bramhānda–purāṇa, from which, as quoted by Katavema, the above account is taken, the wind of the 7th Mārga, causing the revolution of the polar-star, is paravāha [or paravaha]."

VII. 6. त्रिस्रोतसम्–त्रीणि स्रोतांसि यस्याः सा त्रिस्रोताः । The triple streamed river–i. e. the Ganges. Cf गङ्गां त्रिपथगां नदीम् । It has three courses (1) Flowing through the Heaven and identical with the Milky way and named Mandākinı. (2) The second is on the Earth named भागीरथी and (3) third is in the Pātāla, the residence of Daityas and Nāgās–and named भोगावती. गगनप्रतिष्ठाम्–गगनस्थाम्. Located in Heaven. It is possible to interpret it as गगनस्य प्रतिष्ठाम् the glory of Heaven. प्रविभक्तरश्मिः–प्रविभक्ता रश्मयः अर्थाद्वायुरूपा एव यत्र कर्माणि । duly distributing their rays. वर्तयति–परिभ्रमति–Revolves. ज्योतीषि–The luminaries. द्वितीयहरिविक्रम्–etc. The reference is to the Dwarf, or वामन incarnation of Viṣṇu. The story is told thus: A particular demon named बलि had become all powerful and reigned over all the three worlds. To relieve Indra of the oppression of बलि. Viṣṇu went to him in the form of a dwarf. बलि was performing a sacrifice and he had declared that he would give इच्छादान to all the suitors. But here was a curious demand of only 'three steps' which was granted immediately. But then, the dwarf assumed gigantic dimensions and pervaded the whole of the Earth only with his one step. The second pervaded the entire heavenly region. And now he asked बलि for room for the third step. But बलि knew now who the suitor was and in his great joy he offered the Lord his head for the third step. Viṣṇu pressed him down to the nether regions, but being pleased with his devotion, he gave him the Sovereignty of Pātāla and himself remained as his doorkeeper in the form of the dwarf. Thus, the region was rendered absolutely pure–it was in fact consecrated by the second step of Viṣṇu.

विक्रमः-Treading of step. It is for this that Viṣṇu is named as 'त्रिविक्रम' त्रिपाद्. निस्तमस्कं-Com. पापरहितं शोकरहितं च। The third, and fouth lines are read differently—

तस्य व्यपेतरजसः प्रवहस्य वायोर्मार्गो द्वितीयहरिविक्रमपूत एषः ॥

The only difficulty is regarding the name of the wind. According to this reading, the region or Path would belong to the second course and not to the sixth.

सबाह्यान्तःकरणः-With internal as also the external senses. The sense-organ, according to the Sāṁkhya system are divided into two classes-Internal or external. अन्तरिन्द्रिय and बाह्येन्द्रिय. The latter are again subdivided into two-ज्ञानेन्द्रियs and कर्मेन्द्रियs, each having five subdivisions. The Internal organs are three-मनस्, बुद्धि and अहंकार-Individuality or self-consciousness. चित्त-the heart or the organ of feeling, sometimes is added to the list. For the expression Cf. also. त्वद्दर्शनादेव प्रसन्नबाह्यान्तःकरणोन्तरात्मा । वि० IV. मेघपदवी-The path of clouds. But this means that the chariot has descended with the speed of lightning-traversing the four intervening मार्गs within no time. The Bengāli reading 'प्रवहस्य' in the preceding stanza for परिवहस्य removes this difficulty as the transition in that case would be from one मार्ग to the other.

VII. 7. अरविवरेभ्यः Through the interstices of spokes. चातकैः etc. The चातक birds, it appears, could conveniently fly through the interstices of spokes of the chariot. The चातकs are classical rain-birds. हरिभिः-Names of Indra's horses. Cp. I. Act. अचिरभासां etc. अचिरा भा यासां ताः । विद्युताम् इत्यर्थः । The horses were shining because of the flashes of lightning. अनुलिप्तैः-परीतैः or रञ्जितैः Tinged with, covered with. गतम्—गमनम् । पिशुनयति—Indicates. नेमिः-The rim. शीकरक्लिन्न-Bedewed with drops (of water). वारिगर्भाणि उदराणि येषां ते वारिगर्भोदराः । स्वाधिकारभूमौ-In the land within (your) jurisdiction-which is under (your) control. आश्चर्यदर्शनः-आश्चर्यं दर्शनं यस्य सः । curious to behold.

VII. 8. The king is now giving the description of the earth as he sees from a great height. It is an aerial pen-picture. उन्मज्जताम्–Rising upwards. Shooting up. At first when the king was at a great distance from the earth, the earth and the mountains appeared to be on the same level. But as the king began to descend down rapidly, the earth appeared also to have slipped down from the mountain-tops. स्कन्धोदयः–Because of the rise (i. e. coming into sight) of the trunks. पर्णाभ्यन्तरलीनता–The state of being enveloped in foliage. The trees had worn so to say the veil in the form of thick foliage and so could not be distinguished from a great height. सन्तानात्–From expansion or continuity. व्यक्ति–Manifestation. आपगाः अपां समूहः–आपः । आपेन गच्छन्ति इति आपगाः । Rivers. उत्क्षिपता–By one throwing up. The earth appeared as if it were being thrown upwards by somebody. पूर्वापरसमुद्रावगाढा–Plunging, merging in the eastern and western Seas. Cf. पूर्वापरौ तोयनिधी वगाह्य । कुमार०. सन्ध्यायां भवः सान्ध्यः । Evening cloud. परिघः–A bar. हेमकूट–Or ' the golden-peaked ' one of the sacred mountains among the Himālaya chain. It is adjacent to Kailāsa and inhabited by किंपुरुषs or the servants of कुबेर. किंपुरुषाः–कुत्सिताः पुरुषाः । तत्पुरुष. । These are so called because they are said to have the body of a man and the head of a horse. They are also called किन्नरs or अश्वमुखs.

VII. 9. स्वायम्भुवात्–स्वयं भवतीति स्वयम्भूः । स्वयम्भुवः अपत्यं स्वायम्भुवः । –From the sun of the self-existent one. Kāṣyapa is the *son* of मरीचि (and so called मारीच) and the grandson of ब्रह्मन्. He is called प्रजापति–or the lord of creation, but he is not one of the seven original प्रजापतिs nor of the ten mentioned by मनु. He is here said to be one of the प्रजापतिs, who were Brahmā's sons, created by him to supply the universe with inhabitants. He married the thirteen daughters of दक्ष but the eldest one अदिति was his favourite with whom he is practising penance here. तपस्यति like नमस्यति is a denominative from तपस्. अनतिक्रमणीयानि श्रेयांसि–The fortunes or blessings (which can be acquired by paying homage to these revered ascetics) cannot be passed by. In the first act also he just has the same feeling 'पुण्याश्रमदर्शनेन तावदात्मानं पुनीमहे' where he meets Śakuntalā for the first time. Now also, his reunion with her is due to his reverence for these ascetics. प्रथमः कल्पः–A noble resolve, or a fine or capital idea. Cf. उदारः कल्पः ।

VII. 10. उपोढ–P. P. from उप+वह्. Commenced. निरुन्धतः–of thee–checking the speed. The chariot glided down on the earth without making any sound whatsoever. This is the difference between the car of Indra and that of mortal kings.

VII. 11. We get a very vivid description of the sage who is much absorbed in his austerities that he has lost all regard for his body–which is covered over with an anthill. उरसा– The instr. is इत्थंभूतलक्षणे–showing अचलत्व. संदष्ट–closely sticking or encircled by. लताप्रतान–लतासंतान circles of creepers–coils. अंसव्यापि–covering the shoulders. निचितम्–filled with. अभ्यर्कबिम्बम्–We can take it as an अव्ययीभाव or as two separate words. कष्टतपसे–कष्टं तपः यस्य सः । तस्मै । of severe austerities. भवान् कथमिदानीम्–what about you ? What do you intend to do ?

VII. 12. वृत्तिः–sustenance. उचिता–योग्या i. e. Proper, suitable, habitual. सत्कल्प० विद्यमानकल्पवृक्षे । Even when there were desire–yielding trees. कपिश–Brown. संयमः–self–control. The sages already possessed the things which are eagerly sought by others. उत्सर्पिणी–Soaring high, lofty. दाक्षायणी–The daughter of दक्ष–Aditi. प्रतिपाल्यावसराः etc.–The saints must be seen at their leisure: i. e. we must wait till an opportune moment to see the saints–i. e. should not visit them at an odd hour or when they are otherwise engaged. Cf. अवसरोपसर्पणीयाः राजानः ।–The king, therefore, is conscious that others also have their own engagements. There is the reading प्रतिपाल्यावसरः खलु प्रस्तावः—The subject matter deserves some waiting (on our part): i. e. The sage would take some time before he would finish his discourse on the पतिव्रताधर्म–and so it would be better on the part of the king to see him after a while. अन्तरान्वेषी-Seeking an opportune moment. निमित्तं-An omen.

VII. 13. मनोरथाय—मनोरथमाप्तुं-To obtain (my) desire-viz. Śakuntalā. i. e. I cherish absolutely no hopes of obtaining her. पूर्वावधीरितम्-Slighted-spurned before. दुःखं हि परिवर्तते-(1) Misery alone surrounds me or (2) The bliss is turned into misery. चापलं-Naughtiness, wilfulness-Cf. The sense in चपलोऽयं बटुः in II. अनुबध्यमानः-Being closely followed by, from अनु+बन्ध्- 'flying after', closely following'.

VII. 14. आमर्द-Rough-handling. Hard pulling. अपत्यनिर्विशेष-Not different from (our) children. Just like (our) children. औरसः-one of the 12 kinds of sons, enumerated by Manu. उरसः जातः औरसः। अनपत्यता Etc. The king is here generalising a great truth. Generally those who have no children crave eagerly for them. They then shower all their affections on the children of other people. Childlessness is a sort of a gap in life which these men try to fill up with small children belonging to strangers even. वत्सलयति-Denominative from वत्सल. अधरं दर्शयति-A very fine touch of child-psychology. The child wants to ridicule the woman who tried to scare it. अधरदर्शन is sign of contempt.

VII. 15. एधापेक्षः-waiting (only) for fuel. महतः तेजसोबीजम्-(The boy) so to say (possesses) the germ of mighty energy (or spirit). The child is the father of man and so the king could judge from the undaunted spirit displayed by the boy that he is destined to be an eminent personality. The child is not to be easily outwitted. It is not prepared to give up the thing in hand for something which is simply a promise. It stretches out its hand to get the toy-when the king gets an opportunity to notice the lines on its hand.

VII. 16. प्रलोभ्यवस्तु०-Desired or coveted object. प्रणय-longing, eagerness or craving. जालग्रथिताङ्गुलिः-जालेषु ग्रथिताः अङ्गुलयः यस्य

(The hand) whose fingers were united together by a web. ‘ webbed hand ’ is indicative of great valour. अलक्ष्यपत्रान्तरम्– etc. The hand is compared to a lotus–whose petals cannot be (distinctly) seen–(because of their closeness). इद्धरागया–इद्धः दीप्तः or समृद्धः रागः–लौहित्यम् यस्याः सा तथा । if we take it as an adjective to उषसा, otherwise इद्धो रागो यया–उषस्–which made the lotus red. The redness of the lotus and the hand are to be compared. एकपङ्कजम्–A solitary or single lotus दुर्ललित–दुर्लभं ललितं–इप्सित–यस्य । Unmanageable, difficult to be coaxed or naughty. Cf. विक्रम° where the king applies the adjective to his eye–उपवनलतासु चक्षुर्न बध्नाति धृति तद्रूपालोकदुर्ललितम् ।

VII. 17. Here we get a fine picture of those who are blessed with children. आलक्ष्य°–slightly perceptible. अनिमित्तहासैः–By their innocent smiles : lit. for no reason. अव्यक्त–indistinct. °प्रणयिनः–longing. दुर्मोचहस्तग्राहेण–By the grasp of his hand which is very difficult to loosen.

VII. 18. सत्त्वसंश्रयसुखः (संयमः)–(Forbearance) that takes delight in giving protection to (all) animals. V. L. जन्मनः–of thy father.–Lit. of the source, used for जन्मनः हेतोः. Cf. the word ‘ कारण ’ which is also used in this way. न कारणत्स्वाद्भिभिदे कुमारः । etc. The simile in the second line is not, however, quite a happy one. स्थानप्रत्ययात्– owing to the reliance in the place.–Circumstantial evidence. The whole incident–viz दुष्यन्त’s seeing the boy–is psychologically very interesting. He experiences a sort of paternal feeling for the boy, but he dare not express it even to himself. He says it only in a round about way. रूपसंवादिना–‘ Resembling the form.’ अप्रतिलोमः– Not averse. Not untractable. प्रतिलोम–Lit. ‘ against the course or direction of hair. ’ व्यपदेशः Family, pedigree. Cf. व्यपदेशमाविल- यितुं etc.

VII. 20. रसाधिकेषु–Abounding in pleasures of senses. V. L. सुधासितेषु–white due to chunam. उशन्ति from वश् to wish. नियतैकयतिव्रतानि–नियतं एकं यतिव्रतं येषु–Where the vows of asceticism alone (are practised). It was a common practice with ancient Indian kings to retire into forest and lead the life of a hermit after they had reigned for a sufficiently long period–entrusting the whole responsibility to their sons. आत्मगत्या–By their own means. विषयः–प्रदेशः । The difficulty is that no mortal could of his own accord, reside in a place like this–viz. the part of heaven. Hence the query. सम्बन्ध–Relationship. अनार्यः परदार॰ etc. to indulge in a gossip regarding the wife of another is ungentlemanly; Cf. अनिर्वर्णनीयं परकलत्रम् ।. The king was anxious to know the name of the mother of the boy. But his sense of propriety does not allow him to put a blunt question. Now he knows the name–and once more there is reason for him to hope–that after all the boy might he his own son.' नाममात्रप्रस्तावः—mere mention of the name, अंतिका–ज्येष्ठा भगिनी = धात्री । Elder sister. रक्षाकरण्डकम्–The amulet or the talisman. करण्डक also means a herb. This might have been a sort of a locket worn on the wrist. This picking up of the रक्षाबन्ध is the last and convincing incident. Now there remains no doubt whatsoever in the mind of दुष्यन्त–after he is acquainted with the history of the amulet by the two ladies. जातकर्म–The natal ceremony. It is the fourth of the twelve Saṁskāras or purificatory rites described by Manu and the first after the child's birth. It is performed by giving the child honey and clarified butter out of a golden spoon, before separating the navel string. विक्रिया–The change–transformation; विवादः contradiction, dispute. This contradiction is convincing. एकवेणीधरा–The single braid is a sign of mourning. A Hindu woman is supposed not to comb her hair in the absence of her husband. Cf. Megh. V. 90. न मे आशा etc. Śakuntalā had given up all hopes of reunion with दुष्यन्त. Hence, she cherishes no hope even when she learns the रक्षाबन्ध incident. The news is too good to be true for her; प्रकृति–Natural state. विकार–Change. अथवा–etc. सानुमती, it appears, had however prepared the ground.

VII. 21. वसने etc. This shows her absolute indifference to outwardly appearance. ॰क्षाम–Emaciated. अतिनिष्करुणस्य–etc. She is observing this 'vow of separation' for me–who was so harsh to her. अनुकूलपरिणामम्–Taking a favourable turn, ending favourably. Śakuntalā at present is in a 'tight corner' so to say. She could not recognise the king in whom remorse had wrought a complete change. Then she had great misgivings regarding her fortune. She, therefore, thinks twice before accepting even facts.

VII. 22. मोहतमस्–Darkness in the form of delusion. उपराग–Eclipse. रोहिणी was the forth of the twenty seven daughters of Dakṣa and most beloved spouse of the Moon.

VII. 23. असंस्कार०–Unadorned. i. e. without any संस्कार i. e. toilet. वत्स etc. Śakuntalā, instead of giving a direct reply, asks the boy to consult his destiny. This is the height of pathos. The king also could not contain himself any longer and so he begs her unconditional, sincere apology–and not content with mere words, even falls prostrate at her feet.

VII. 24. व्यलीक–Grief. Unpleasantness. प्रबलतमसाम्–Those who are completely under the sway of delusion. एवंप्रायाः–प्रायेण एवम् । सुप्सुप् ।. Mostly such, such for the most part. पादयोः पतति–Some commentators make the king fall down at her feet before repeating the stanzas, which would mean that the king repeats the verse falling prostrate at the feet of Sakuntalā and she also listens patiently and then asks him to rise up. But this would be very unnatural. सुचरितप्रतिबन्धकम्–Opposed to virtuous conduct: परिणाममुखम्–Drawing towards its issue, on the point of becoming mature, about to ripen. Sakuntalā is after all a Hindu lady and rather than blame her husband for having repudiated her, she blames her own fate!

VII. 25. पूर्वम्–Formerly, i. e. at the time of repudiating her. आकुटिल–Curved. आ = ईषत् । अनुशय–remorse. बाष्पबिन्दुः–The tear-drop. विषमं कृतम्–It acted adversely. तेन हि etc. the king wants to see the ring once more in its proper place. So he says 'let the creeper bear the fruit as the mark of the union (or advent) of the season (of spring). Here the ring is the fruit, शकुन्तला the creeper and दुष्यन्त–the Vernal Season. But Śakuntalā had enough of the ring. She is not prepared to trust it again !

VII. 26. पुत्रस्य ते i. e. इन्द्रस्य । His bow having accomplished all the work, the thunderbolt of Indra is merely an embellishment for him. विनिवर्तित–Turned away from–resting from its work. अनुभाव–Prowess. °पिशुन indicative of.

VII. 27. द्वादशधा स्थितस्य तेजसः etc. This refers to the solar light: There are supposed to be twelve आदित्यs for twelve months and are described as the sons of अदिति and कश्यप. The gods Viṣṇu and Indra are reckoned amongst their sons : According to the commentator द्वादशधा–refers to the twelve digits of the sun. यज्ञभागेश्वरम्–The lord of a share in (every) sacrifice, or यज्ञभागाः–Gods–those who enjoy a share in sacrifices तेषामीश्वरः–इन्द्रः Indra also is said to be their son. आत्मभुवः परः–Higher even than the self-existent (Brahman). V. L. आत्मभवः–The self-existent one. This seems to be better: i. e. though there was no necessity for him to be born, still he chose this couple as his father and mother. परः पुरुषः The Highest Being. पुरुष–पुरि शेते इति ।–That which sleeps or abides in the body. नियोज्यः—The servant, वासव-नियोज्य–The king wants to imply that he is but an humble servant of their son.

VII. 28. पौलोमी–शची । The Wife of Indra.

VII. 29. श्रद्धा–Piety or faith.—Represents Śakuntalā. वित्तम्–Wealth = अपत्यम्–The offspring. विधिः–The Precept, or practice, (represents दुष्यन्त). Cf. the same idea in श्रद्धेव साक्षाद्विधिनोपपन्ना । Raghu II. 16.

VII. 30. निमित्त–The cause. नैमित्तिक–The effect: The cause must always precede the effect. But here the order was reversed. And hence the favour is अपूर्व–unprecedented. विधातारः–Creators, ordainers. आज्ञाकरी–Hand-maid, servant. This also is a विनयोक्ति. Cf.–वासवानुयोज्यः दुष्यन्त etc. कस्यचित्

कालस्य–After some time. युष्मत्सगोत्रस्य–of the some गोत्र as you समानं गोत्रं अस्य इति सगोत्रः । But कश्यप was the originator of the race; we have, therefore, to take it as simply 'of your Gotra' i. e. your descendent. दुष्यन्त is all along feeling uneasy for his repudiation of शकुन्तला. Especially the fact that he spurned her when she went to him of her own accord and later on began to pine for her–is inexplicable to him. So at last he asks the sage to enlighten him on this point. प्रत्यक्षवैक्लव्याम्–(1) whose distress was personally witnessed by her (i. e. by मेनका) or (2) who has clear marks of distress (on her face). अवसानः–Terminating with. This removal of misunderstanding was of course very essenrial. Otherwise the memory of it would have haunted them both throughout their life. वचनीय–Blame; चरितार्था–कृतार्था ।

VII. 32. छाया–The image or reflection. न मूर्च्छति–has no effect. Cf. न पादपोन्मूलनशक्ति रंहः शिलोच्चये मूर्च्छति मारुतस्य । Raghu II. 34. सुलभावकाशा–It finds easy access to...Cf. The idea in उत्तर० प्रभवति शुचिर्बिम्बोद्ग्राहे मणिर्न मृदां चयः ।

वंशप्रतिष्ठा–The stability or performance of (my) family. तया भाविनम्–Destined to be like that.

VII. 33. अनुद्घात–Absence of uneven ground. Cf. ययौ अनुद्घातसुखेन–Raghu. II. 72. पुरा जयति–will conquer. पुरा used with the present tense has the sense of Future. Cf. आलोके ते निपतति पुरा । etc. मेघ० सप्तद्वीपाम्–According to Hindu mythology, the Earth consisted of seven islands; the one inhabited by human beings was called जम्बूद्वीप. भरत so named because of his being the universal supporter. This same भरत was the ancestor of the Kauravas and Pāṇḍavas. आशास्महे–' we expect '–is better than we invoke (all blessings). The news has got to be communicated to कण्व and so an aerial messenger is dispatched.

VII. 34. प्राज्यवृष्टिः–प्राज्या (abundant) वृष्टिः यस्य । very liberal in sending down showers. वितत°–stretched out. Spread over. विस्तृत. °यज्ञः–with long-spread sacrifices. प्रणियस्व–V. L. प्रीणयालम् ।

°परिवर्त–Cycles, revolutions. In this way by reciprocal friendly acts, pass the time etc. Cf. Bhag. देवान् भावयतानेन ते देवा भावयंतु वः। परस्परं भावयंतः श्रेयः परमवाप्स्यथ ॥ III. 11. उभय° The two worlds. Cf. also Raghu. I. 26. भरतवाक्यम्–The (formal) closing stanza of the drama containing blessings to all and put in the mouth of some venerable person entitled to give such blessing; it is named in honour of भरत the founder of the science of dramaturgy and music. He is also supposed to be the author of नाट्यशास्त्र and is said to have superintended the exhibition of the drama Laxmi-Swayaṃvara of Saraswatī–in Indra's Heaven.

VII. 35. सरस्वती–The Muse of Learning and Speech. श्रुतमहताम्–great on account of their knowledge of veda. महीयताम्–Be honoured. i. e. Let those, who are masters of learning be properly respected. नीललोहितः–An epithet of Śiva; blue and red. This is variously explained: वामभागे नीलः दक्षिणभागे लोहितः । or नीलः कण्ठे लोहितश्च केशेषु । and so on. परिगतशक्तिः (i) परिगता प्राप्ता शक्तिः–पार्वती–येन सः । 'The wives of the deities were supposed to personify their energy or active powers.' or (2) It might refer to the eight Śaktis of Śiva. or (3) शक्ति–Majesty–prowess in general. So exemption from further transmigration is the Summum bonum–which the writer asks for. The play begins and also ends with a prayer to Śiva–who had a large temple in Ujjayinī–The city of Vikramāditya and the abode of the poet. 'Both actors and spectators would probably repeat the prayer after the speaker and appropriate it to themselves.' (M. W.).

METRICAL TABLE

Metrical Table.

Number of Syllables	Name of the Metre	Where employed	Total	Measure.
8	अनुष्टुप्	I. 5, 6, 11, 12, 26 ; II. 13, 16, 17; III. 1, 19, 22 ; IV. 3, 6 ; V. 14, 24, 26, 29 ; VI. 14, 22, 23, 28. 32 ; VII. 9, 13, 14, 15, 23, 28, 29.	29	पञ्चमं लघु सर्वत्र सप्तमं द्विचतुर्थयोः । गुरु षष्ठं च पादानां चतुर्णां स्यादनुष्टुभि ॥
11	त्रिष्टुप्	IV. 7.	1	A Vedic metre consisting of four quarters of 11 syllables, where great liberty is allowed in the matter of rhythm.
,,	इन्द्रवज्रा	IV. 21 ; V. 4.	2	स्यादिन्द्रवज्रा यदि तौ जगौ गः ।
,,	उपजाति	II. 7 ; III. 4 ; V. 5, 20, 25 ; VI. 10, 24, 26 ; VII. 2, 5, 19, 31.	12	स्यादिन्द्रवज्रा यदि तौ जगौ गः । उपेन्द्रवज्रा प्रथमे लघौ सा । } इत्यनयोरुपजातिः ।
,,	शालिनी	V. 30.	1	मात्तौ गौ चेच्छालिनी वेदलोकैः ।

11	रथोद्धता	VII. 18.	1	रात्परैर्नरलगौ रथोद्धता ।
12	द्रुतविलम्बित	II. 11; III. 18; V. 27; VI. 8; VII. 3.	5	द्रुतविलम्बितमाह नभौ भरौ ।
,,	वंशस्थ or वंशस्थविल	I. 18, 22, 23; III. 13; IV. 1; V. 12, 15, 17; VI. 13, 18, 29; VII. 10, 16, 30.	14	जतौ तु वंशस्थमुदीरितं जरौ ।
13	प्रहर्षिणी	VI. 27, 30.	2	त्र्याशाभिर्मनजरगाः प्रहर्षिणीयम् ।
,,	रुचिरा	VII. 35.	1	जभौ सजौ गिति रुचिरा चतुर्ग्रहैः ।
14	वसन्ततिलका	I. 8, 27, 31; II. 9, 12; III. 10, 20, 26; IV. 1, 2, 10, 12, 13, 14, 19; V. 2, 3, 6, 22, 23; VI. 12, 16, 20, 25; VII. 4, 6, 17, 25, 26, 32.	30	उक्ता वसन्ततिलका तभजा जगौ गः ।
15	मालिनी	I. 10, 19, 20; II. 4; III. 3; V. 7, 8, 19; VII. 7, 34.	10	ननमयययुतेयं मालिनी भोगिलोकैः ।
17	मन्दाक्रान्ता	I. 15, 33; II. 14, 15.	4	मन्दाक्रान्ताम्बुधिरसनगैर्मो भनौ तौ गयुग्मम् ।

Continued on next page

17	शिखरिणी	I. 9, 24; II. 10; III. 8; V. 10; VI. 9; VII. 33.	7	रसै रुद्रैश्छिन्ना यमनसभला गः शिखरिणी ।
,,	हरिणी	III. 12; IV. 18; VII. 24.	3	नसमरसला गः षड्वेदैर्हयैर्हरिणी मता ।
19	शार्दूलविक्रीडित	I. 14, 30; II. 2, 5, 6; III. 9, 25; IV. 4, 5, 8, 16, 17; V. 9; VI. 4, 5, 6, 17; VII. 8, 11, 12, 27;	21	सूर्याश्वैर्यदि मः सजौ सततगाः शार्दूलविक्रीडितम् ।
21	स्रग्धरा	I. 1, 7.	2	म्रभ्नर्यानां त्रयेण त्रिमुनियतियुता स्रग्धरा कीर्तितेयम् ।
10/11	वैतालीय or वियोगिनी	II. 18; VI. 1; VII. 1.	3	विषमे ससजा गुरुः समे सभरा लोऽथ गुरुर्वियोगिनी ।
11/12	अपरवक्त्र	IV. 9; V. 1.	2	अयुजि ननरला गुरुः समे तदपरवक्त्रमिदं नजौ जरौ ।
,,	औपच्छन्दसिक	III. 23, 24; VII. 20, 21.	4	पर्यन्ते यौं तथैव (वैतालीये इव) शेषमौपच्छन्दसिकं सुधीभिरुक्तम् ।
12/13	पुष्पिताग्रा	I. 32; II. 3; VI. 11.	3	अयुजि नयुगरेफतो यकारो युजि तु नजौ जरगाश्च पुष्पिताग्रा ।
	आर्या	I. 2, 3, 13, 16, 17, 21, 25, 28, 29, 34; II. 1, 8; III. 2, 5, 6, 7, 11, 14, 16, 17,	39	यस्याः प्रथमे पादे द्वादश मात्रास्तथा तृतीयेऽपि । अष्टादश द्वितीये चतुर्थके पञ्चदश सार्या ॥

	21 ; IV. 11, 15, 20 ; V. 11, 13, 16, 18, 21, 28, 31 ; VI. 2, 3, 7, 15, 19, 21, 31 ; VII. 22.		
गीति	I. 4 ; III. 15.	2	आर्यापूर्वार्धसमं द्वितीयमपि भवति यत्र हंसगते । छन्दोविदस्तदानीं गीतिंताममृतवाणि भाषन्ते ॥

विक्रमोर्वशीयम्

VIKRAMORVAŚĪYA

OF

KĀLIDĀSA

INTRODUCTION

Kalidasa, His Date, Life and Works.

Howsoever overlaid with fantasies or encrusted with a mass of isolated events separated in time and place, a widely circulated literary tradition contains within itself a germ of historical truth and can be set aside on pain of doing serious harm to that truth. Thus it is with king Vikramaditya of Ujjain, the liberal patron of learning and arts, of whom the great poet Kalidasa was a contemporary. This tradition forms the starting point and the basis of the numerous theories regarding the age of Kalidasa. Of these two rival theories may here be stated as those deserving of consideration. According to one held by most European scholars, the Vikramaditya of the tradition is no other than the Gupta king Candragupta II who assumed the title of Vikramaditya and succeeded his father Samudragupta 375 A. D. and made Ujjain his capital. Vincent Smith in his early history of India (P. 304, foot-note) expresses the view that the earlier works of Kalidasa were composed before 413 A. D. during the regime of Candragupta and his later works were written under Kumaragupta I (413 A. D. to 455 A.D.) and that possibly his literary career extended even into the reign of Skandagupta (453 A. D. 480 A. D.).

Some are inclined to suggest from the reference to the conquest of the Huns by Raghu in his Digvijaya, that Kalidasa must have lived after the victory of Skandagupta over the Huns half a century later than the date suggested. But the evidence has no probative value. " There is nothing to indicate any reference to reality in this account of the exploits of a king of long ago; and if Kalidasa had lived in the reign of Skandagupta when the fortune of the royal house was evidently tottering to a fall, it would be difficult to understand the calm contentment with the established order which marks all his works."

The other view held by many Indian scholars puts Kalidasa in the first century before our era, and makes him a contemporary and a protege of King Vikramaditya, the founder of the Samvat Era-57 B. C. That there is nothing implausible in the assumption is clear when on the strong testimony of Patanjali's Mahabhashya it has been possible to put back the beginning of court poetry in general by a few centuries of the Christian Era. And "Epigraphy not merely confirms the evidence of the Mahabhashya that artificial poetry originated before the commencement of our era, but shows that that poetry continued to be cultivated throughout the succeeding centuries." Already in the days of Kanishka (78 A. D.) Ashvaghosha wrote his Buddhacarita in the artificial style and called it a Mahakavya.

In connexion with this writer it is interesting to observe that there is a striking resemblance between his poetry and the poetry of Kalidasa. Not only is there a close parallelism between a few isolated passages and descriptions, but between ideas and expressions fairly distributed over the poem. As Prof. R. N. Apte has observed these close resemblances warrant the conclusion that "one of the poets is using the other." It must be remembered that Ashvaghosha is a philosopher first and a poet afterwards; while Kalidasa is an original poet The probability, therefore, is that Ashvaghosha is the borrower and Kalidasa his original. Cowell's theory of Kalidasa's indebtedness to Ashvaghosha rests upon the view that Kalidasa belongs to Gupta period. The hollowness of this view, has, however, been shown by Prof. Shembavnekar in an article on 'the Date of Kalidasa' contributed to "the Journal of the University of Bombay" (Vol. I. Part VI. P. 232-246) who points out that the Gupta theory is based on the assumption that Candragupta II was the first monarch who bore the name Vikramaditya, whereas on the testimony of the Rajput Chronicles and the Kathasaritsagara the first king to bear that appellation was King Vikramaditya of the Paramara dynasty, the hero of countless legends, the ruler of Ujjayini in Kalidasa's day. It is held by many that the title 'Vikramorvashiya' is chosen by the poet in order to glorify and immortalize his patron's name. According to Kathasaritsagara the father of Vikramaditya was Mahendraditya. It is curious to note that the word Mahendra as an epithet of Indra is repeated by the poet no less than fourteen times in the play and in one place it is particularly significant to find the names of the father and son linked up: (दिष्टया महेंद्रोपकारपर्याप्तेन विक्रममहिम्ना वर्धसे भवान्।) It is possible as Prof. Shembavnekar suggests, that the play was written at the time of the intended retirement of Mahendra from active life, and the coronation of Vikrama as king (Kathasaritsagara XVIII. 59-60). The last act of the play, therefore, where prince Ayus is installed as the young king is but a poetic reflex of the actual course of events of the times

There is nothing in the arguments adduced by European scholars which is repugnant to this theory that

Kalidasa lived in the 1st century before our era at the court of King Vikrama of Ujjayini who founded the Samvat era. Prof. Keith's view that 'the conclusive evidence displayed in the work preserved to us of elaborate training in all the learning available to a Brahmin student of the Gupta era from the science of politics to astrology and the Kamasutra....everything points to his flourishing in the time of Gupta glory" is only a dogmatic assertion. With regard to the astronomical terms, such as the names of the signs of the Solar Zodiac which are supposed to be of Greek origin and on which European critics lay so much emphasis, it has already been proved by scholars like S. P. Pandit, R. N. Apte, that there is nothing to show that they were unknown to the people of India a few centuries before the Christian Era. While the occurrence of un-Paninian expressions and grammatical forms such as पातयां प्रथममास; प्रभ्रंशयां यो नहुषं चकार, दाश्वान्. कामयान, in Kalidasa can be satisfactorily explained only on the assumption that he belonged to a time when the Paninian grammar had not obtained a complete vogue.

The foregoing discussion is enough to justify the truth and the the vitality of the age-long tradition that the poet belongs to the days of the glorious King Vikramaditya of Ujjayini–the founder of the Samvat era (57 B. C.)

With regard to the external details of the poet's life, we know next to nothing; the numerous legends told about him are but empty figments, and only bear testimony to the greatness and extreme popularity of the poet in the land of his birth. "The truly great stand upon no middle ledge; they are either famous or unknown."

But Kalidasa is both famous and unknown. We look in vain in his works for knowledge about the facts of his life. The impression that we gather about him from them is that of a man, deeply learned in literature and philosophy and other traditional lore of the times, and more deeply learned in the book of nature. Ujjayini was the city of his heart and he is delighted to sing of her glories and of the romantic loves of her maidens. He sings of this Gem of Avanti, rich with the storied legends of Udayana and the consecrated past, this radiant bit of heaven, with her flower-sweet balconies, and black-eyed maidens; of the dread shrine of Shiva, Mahakala, of her rich gardens and lotus-lakes that send their fugitive sweetness through the dark; and his fondness for the city is so evident in his loving and lingering description of her varied charms that one might legitimately conclude that the poet must have spent at least a part of his life in this city. Further he was a widely-travelled man and was a keen observer of nature—not only of her sublime and wild aspects, but also of her mild and minute manifestations. "Rarely has a man walked our earth who observed the phenomena of living nature as accurately as he, though his accuracy was of course that of a poet, not that of the scientist."

He was essentially an eclectic in his religion and philosophy: for if the Kumarasambhava is distinctly Shivaistic, the Raghuvamsa is no less distinctly Vishnuite in tendency; while Vedantic monism or Samkhya dualism, or the active devotion of Yoga equally engaged his regard; so that, as Ryder says, "Kalidasa moved among the jarring sects with sympathy for all, fanaticism for none." A pleasing trait of his personality is his modesty which Coleridge recognises as a sure sign of great genius. Above all, his writings are coloured with the suffusion of a charmed equanimity and give the impression of a man who walked the earth with a serene and god-like tread, with mind and senses keenly responsive to every form of beauty, and accepting life and the good things it offers in a spirit of sublime acquiescence.

Of his seven works which have come down to us, three are dramas, two epics, one a lyrical piece and one a descriptive poem. It is possible to fix the chronology of his dramas, the Malavikagnimitra being the composition of his salad days, the Vikramorvashiya coming next, and the Shakuntala composed when he was in the prime of his manhood. There can be no reasonable doubt that the Rtusamhara was a juvenile piece; while with regard to the two epics Raghuvamsha and Kumarasambhava, opinions differ, for whereas the introductory stanzas of the Raghu suggest that it was written before Kumara, the abrupt and undignified ending of it suggests that the hand that wrote it was cold before it was finished; but then we have to remember the tradition that in its original form it consisted of twenty-five cantos, of which only nineteen have come down to us. In general it would be only reasonable to assume that the great works on which his fame chiefly rests—the Shakuntala, the Raghuvamsha, the Kumarasambhava and the Meghaduta—belong to a period of his life when his genius had attained to the fullest maturity of its powers.

Vikramorvashiya: its Sources.

The romance of Pururavas and Urvashi, which Kalidasa has dramatized in the Vikramorvashiya, is one of the most ancient and popular stories that we have in the literature of India. For we find it recorded in the form of a dialogue in the Rigveda, which is regarded as the oldest literary monument of Indo-European civilization. And although, in the course of its transmigration of thousands of years in Indian literature, it has undergone several changes in single points of detail, it has remained almost the same in all its essential features—so profound has been its hold upon the Indian mind.

Let us here consider the oldest and the most poetic form of this beautiful romance--the one that has been preserved to us in the Rigveda (X. 95).

King Pururavas, a mortal, and the Apsaras Urvashi find themselves irresistibly in mutual love. Urvashi consents to live with Pururarvas on earth as his wife, but only on the definite agreement, that she should never behold him divested of his apparel. This agreement (समय) is the central point of the whole story and at the same time the rock on which the matrimony must sometime be wrecked. After the loving couple have lived together for a period of four years, giving themselves up entirely to the enjoyment of conjugal happiness, the Gandharvas, who have a more ancient claim upon Urvashi and who do not wish her to stay away from themselves any more, come one night to the residence of Pururavas and produce a sound as of the bleating of lambs. Urvashi fancies that her pet lambs are being stolen away by some one and calls upon Pururavas to rescue them. As soon as Pururavas jumps out of his bed in order to pursue the supposed thief, the Gandharvas send forth a flash of lightning, and in its light Urvashi sees Pururavas stark naked. The compact is broken and Urvashi ruthlessly abandons Pururavas, whom she has loved loyally and sincerely so long, and vanishes forthwith.

Full of despair and frantic with grief, Pururavas wanders about here and there in search of her, until at last he meets her accidently. He implores her to come back to him, dwelling, in plaintive numbers, upon the memories of past happiness in her company and pleading with her by her duty as a wife and even by a threat of suicide. She, however, cold and relentless, rejects his entreaties, saying that she is hard to catch like the wind (दुरापना वात इवाहमस्मि । St. 2). With scant ceremony she asks him to go back to his house as it is impossible that he should have her again (परेहि अस्तंनहि मूरमापः । St. 13), and advises him against laying violent hands upon his life for the sake of a woman. "For" says she, "with woman there can be no lasting friendship: hearts of wolves are the hearts of women!" Though at last she yields to compassion and comforts him with the hopes of a distant future happiness, the story remains, as indeed it is bound to, a tragedy—the tragedy of love between human and divine.

We find this very romance of Pururavas and Urvashi narrated with more or less variation in details, in the following and several other texts:

(i) शतपथब्राह्मण, 11, 5.

(ii) वेदार्थदीपिका, (a commentary on the सर्वानुक्रमणी of the Rigveda by षड्गुरुशिष्य), introductory remarks on Rigiveda X. 95.

(iii) हरिवंश, X. 26 ff.

(iv) विष्णुपुराण, IV. 6.

(v) भागवत, IX 14.

(vi) मत्स्यपुराण, XXIV.

Some of these texts (*e. g.* वेदार्थदीपिका, विष्णुपुराण, भागवत) give us, as it were the previous history of the romance. Mitra and Varuna had received consecration for a certain sacrifice and were consequently bound to observe *Brahmacarya.* But then the Apsaras Urvashi appeared there on the scene, and was rather guilty of a human weakness towards the two Gods. Enraged there at, they cursed and banished her from heaven to live in the world of mortals to expiate her sin. And then she fell in love with Pururavas.

In many of these texts again (*e.* g. शतपथब्राह्मण, हरिवंश, विष्णुपुराण, भागवत), the original story suffers a very important change in that its tragic character is entirely given up, and we are told that Urvashi, taking pity upon Pururavas, allowed him to visit her once a year, or that Pururavas performed a certain sacrifice, and as a consequence of that the Gods allowed Urvashi to live with him to the end of his life, or that, finally, as a result of the same sacred rite Pururavas was exalted to the position of the Gandharvas and remained there never again to be separated from Urvashi.

Such is then the beautiful romance that Kalidasa has dramatized in the Vikramorvashiya. Considerations of art have of course led him to make several deviations from, and modifications in, the original story. In the first place one will not fail to notice, that in consonance with a tendency which had already set in as early as the time of the शतपथब्राह्मण, and in obedience to a very important rule of Indian dramatic technique, according to which a tragedy is strictly forbidden on the stage, Kalidasa had to change the original tragic story into one of blissful union between the hero and the heroine. Other important changes introduced by him in the original story are: (i) The abduction of Urvashi by the demon Keshin and her deliverance by Pururavas; (ii) The episode of the love-letter, the enragement of the Queen and her final reconciliation; (iii) The episode of the heavenly drama, the curse pronounced upon Urvashi by the sage Bharata and its modification by Indra; (iv) Urvashi's flight from Pururavas in a spasm of jealousy, her metamorphosis into a creeper and her subsequent recovery through the power of the gem of reunion; (v) The incident of the loss of the gem and the restoration to Pururavas of his son Ayus, occasioned by its discovery; and (vi) The final removal of Urvashi's curse even in its modified form. The bungling clown (विदूषक), the artful Nipunika, the whole paraphernalia of the royal court, the celestial friends of Urvashi, the venerable Cyavana, the old Tapasi, the sage Narada all these owe their existence entirely to the inventive genius of Kalidasa. In short he has done all that was necessary in the interests of dramatic art to turn the ancient tragic story into a noble drama of intensely human interest.*

The Vikramorvashiya: its Recensions.

The immense popularity which this drama has enjoyed in India has given rise to numerous divergences in the transmission of its text. These divergences are of such a fundamental character, that we can easily distinguish between two recensions: The northern Recension repesented by Bengali and Nagari Mss., and the Southern Recension represented by most of the South Indian Mss. The former is commented upon by Ranganatha, who wrote his विक्रमोर्वशीप्रकाशिका in 1712 (Ca. 1656 or 1790 A. D., according as we take it to be the Samvat or the Shaka era), while the latter by Katayavema, the Minister of the Reddi Prince Kumaragiri of Kondavidu (Ca. 1400 A. D.). Katayavema calls his commentary कुमारगिरिराजीय after the name of his King and patron. In the Northern Recension the play is called विक्रमोर्वशी and is spoken of as a त्रोटक. In the Southern Recension, however, it is called विक्रमोर्वशीय and is designated as a नाटक. (On the meaning of the word त्रोटक *vide* "Technical Names.")

On comparing the two recensions we find, that generally speaking the Northern Recension shows a marked

---

* The version of the story of Pururavas and Urvashi as found in the Matsya Purana shows a good many affinities to the drama of Kalidasa. As. however, the age of the Puranas in general is unsettled and as their texts have been tampered with by later writers, one cannot say for certain that Kalidasa used the Matsya Purana in writing the present play. On the contrary it is quite possible, that the version of the story as contained in the Matsya Purana is a Pauranic adaptation of the drama of Kalidasa.

tendency towards amplifying the matter contained in the southern Recension. This is the case especially with several prose passages which appear in a terse form in the Southern Recension, while in the Northern we find them swollen and amplified by means of the addition of words which scarcely improve the sense. In regard to metrical portions the Northern Recension shows considerable deviations from the Southern Recension. Thus in the Northern Recension we find the following four stanzas in excess of those appearing in the Southern Recension :

(1) After श्रूयते in I. 2.6

मत्तानां कुसुमरसेन षट्पदानां शब्दोऽयं परभृतनाद एष धीरः ।
आकाशे सुरगणसेविते समंतात् किं नार्यः कलमधराक्षरं प्रगीताः ॥

(2) After तथाहि in I. 5.4

मन्दारकुसुमदाम्ना गुरुरस्याः सूच्यते हृदयकम्पः ।
मुहुरुच्छ्वसता मध्ये परिणाहवतोः पयोधरयोः ॥

(3) After मार्गस्य in IV. 29.5

अभिनवकुसुमस्तबकिततरुवरस्य परिसरे
मदकलकोकिलकूजितमधुपझंकारमनोहरे ।
नन्दनविपिने निजकरिणीविरहानलेन संतप्तो
विचरति गजाधिपतिरैरावतनामा ॥

(4) After. V. 24.

सर्वस्तरतु दुर्गाणि सर्वो भद्राणि पश्यतु ।
सर्वः कामानवाप्नोतु सर्वः सर्वत्र नन्दतु ॥

In addition to these stray stanzas we find in the Northern Recension in act IV, thirty-one stanzas in Maharashtri and Apabhramsha (six in Maharashtri, and twenty-five in Apabhramsha) in various metres, as also directions in prose as to the way in which they are to be sung to the accompaniment of music and danoe. In the Southern Recension, however, we have nothing corresponding to these.

The existence of these Maharashtri and Apabhramsha stanzas in the Northern Recension alone raises a very important problem in the textual criticism of the Vikramorvashiya. It is a problem that has not yet been solved finally. Most of the scholars (S. P. Pandit, Th. Bloch, H. Jacobi etc.) think that the stanzas in question are spurious. Mr. Pandit (Ed. Vikramorvashiya, Introd. p. 8 f.), for instance, gives the following reasons :

(1) Throughout his commentary on the fourth Act, Katayavema observes complete silence about these stanzas, showing thus that he was not aware of their existence.

(2) Many of these stanzas are obviously to be recited by the King. But then it is unwarrantable to put Prakrit stanzas in the mouth of the King, who, being an उत्तमपात्र must not speak in Prakrit.

(3) In several cases these stanzas are superfluous, since they only repeat the sense of Sanskrit verses preceding or following them.

(4) Many of them, though obviously forming part of the King's soliloquy, are full of indirect description, vague allusions and references in the third person to some one in the situation of the king rather than to himself.

(5) But the strongest reason for holding these stanzas as spurious is that not only are they superfluous to the action of the play, but several of them also seriously

interfere with the free and natural flow of the sentiments expressed in the Sanskrit stanzas.

Sten Konow (Das Indische Drama, p. 64.) urges against the genuineness of these stanzas the further consideration that in none of the many later imitations of this very Act (*e. g.* Malatimadhava, Act IX; Balaramayana, Act V; Prasannaraghava, Act VI; Mahanataka, Act IV, etc.) do we come across any Apabhramsha stanzas.

It must however be confessed, that all these considerations have no probative value at all, and, for aught we know. these stanzas may have come from the pen of Kalidasa. If it is true, then we must say that from the very first they were never intended to be recited by the King at all, but that they were to be sung, from time to time by some one behind the scenes to the accompaniment of music and dance, in order just to create the proper atmosphere that was so very necessary for heightening the effect of the mournful lamentations of the King plunged in grief for the loss of his beloved.

Development of the Plot.

We shall now consider how very skilfully the poet has developed the story. In the first act which is a sort of induction setting forth the circumstances in which the germ of the love finds soil, the two lovers are fond of each other and we at once see the end in the beginning—for we know that such a reciprocity of passion must lead to union. Yet there are several obstacles to be got over —several problems to be solved; and these problems are not thrust on the reader but they come as natural issues of the story, though often the reader is taken by surprise by these issues. Thus at the end of the first act we are sure that the lovers will meet and have their desire. But as soon as we proceed to the second act and listen to the dialogue between Nipunika and Manavaka our interest deepens; for now we begin to realize the problems raised by the love of the King for the nymph of heaven—one of them being how the chief Queen, the sole wardress of the King's heart, will receive this reckless errantry of her husband. Here again there is considerable ironic humour in the King's dearest friend being tricked by the artful maid into betraying the secret of the King's passion and with breathless interest we await the issue.

There are also other complications in the story. Urvashi to assure her doubting lover of her feelings towards him, writes her love message on a *bhurja* leaf and throws it towards the King before revealing herself. Secondly when the two meet and are feasting on the presence of each other, there is announced the mandate of heaven's lord that Urvashi was to be back to *swarga* to dance to the tune of her master's humour. In the meanwhile the addle-pated companion of the King has carelessly dropped the missive of love and it falls into the hands of the Queen. Armed with this documentary evidence of her husband's breach of his avowals of fidelity, the already incensed Queen confronts that delinquent; and he has no recourse save to yield, to confess, and sue for pardon. The Queen leaves him all in a tantrum only to be afterwards reconciled to the superior rival in her husband's love, which she does apparently with a good grace in the third act.

Thus in the second act we see that there are two difficulties to be solved: How was the celestial damsel, if their union was to be permanent, to be free to act her own will and follow the lead of her heart, and secondly how was the King to pacify the irate Queen, the rival of his love.

The third act resolves these complications. The Queen, who conforms to the Hindu ideal of a wife, is weighed down by the enormity of her crime in insulting her husband and gives him freedom to indulge his vagaries; while the curse which is pronounced by Urvashi's preceptor in heaven for her unconsious substitution of her lover's name in the rehearsal of her part in the drama, Lakshmi-swayamvara, which was represented by herself and her aery companions before heaven's lord, is a blessing in disguise; for thereby she could find joy in her lover's embraces till she was with child by him.

The end of the third act has a finality about it, and the reader is likely to suppose that the drama comes to a close with the union of Pururavas and Urvashi. He thinks that no thread now remains to connect the sequel with the story so far as he has followed it. But this will be only a hasty conclusion. We know that the union of the lovers is but the memory of a sweet dream, for it is conditioned by what lovers at that stage of their love would regard as an accident of their union—the birth of a child; and the poet has to see that the beloved is not torn from the embraces of her lover by anything save their own desires. Secondly the connection appears still more organic if we look to the character of Pururavas of which more anon.

The fourth act, which is unique in several respects finds that Urvashi has left her mortal lover in a spasm of jealousy and while wandering in the dull stupor of her own distress has entered on proscribed grounds and immediately been transformed into a jasmine creeper. The King, all woe-begone, with his frail reason snapped by the shock of his sudden misery, wanders in search of her and at last finds the jewel by whose touch she is brought back to herself, and together they enter the city of Pratishthana to enjoy each other's company.

In the fifth act we learn that Urvashi has a son, and that her term of life with him comes to a close; the revelation of this fact is skilfully managed by the short episode of the vulture pouncing upon the Sangamaniya jewel and carrying it away. The vulture was killed by an arrow on which was incised the name of आयुस्, the son of Pururavas. Then while the lovers are lamenting the perversity of fate and while the king is resolving to take to sack-cloth and ashes, there enters Narada on the stage and announces the pleasure of Indra that Urvashi was his to the end of his life and the action of the drama comes to a close.

Thus from act to act our expectation is ever upward—our interest never flags. In every act we feel that we are on the verge of a catastrophe and find it skilfully averted; and what at first sight looks a simple story opens up so many complications which are still natural.

The Vikramorvashiya: Time Analysis.

The only indication of time that we get in the first Act is that its action commences in the early morning, as is evident from the following words of Pururavas: सूर्योपस्थानात्प्रतिनिवृत्तं पुरूरवसं मामुपेत्य कथ्यतां कुतो भवत्यः परित्रातव्या इति ।

(I. 3. 8). He is returning just after paying his morning visit to the sphere of the Sun.

We have absolutely no means of determining the interval of time that passes between Act I and II. The incidents of the second act commence on a morning in early spring and close slightly after midday. That the spring has only recently set in can be gathered from the following passages among others: II. 6. 6. (विदूषकः । प्रेक्षतां भवान् वसन्तावतारसूचकं अत्याभिरामत्वं प्रमदवनस्य ।); II. 7. अग्रे स्त्रीनखपाटलं e e.); II, 6 (इदमसुलभवस्तु etc.) and II. 19. 24 (भगवन् वसन्तप्रिय मलयानिल ।) alluding to the Malaya breeze.

That the action of the second Act commences in the morning and ends slightly after midday is shown by the following passages :

II. 1. 5 (विदूषकः । एष कार्यासनादुत्थित इत एवागच्छति वयस्यः ।). The King is just returning from the council hall. It must, therefore, be at least 10 A. M. int he morning, as Mr. Pandit suggests (Notes p. 38).

II. 2. 15. (विदूषकः । तत्र पंचविधस्याभ्यवहारस्य उपनतसंभारस्य योजनां etc.) This shows that preparations for the midday meal are going on apace in the kitchen.

II. 17. 7. (राजा । कथमर्धं गतं दिवसस्य ।) II. stanza 22 which describes the moon.

The dialogue between the pupils of Bharata, which takes place in the first scene of the third Act shows, by a remark occurring towards its end, that the evening is approching. Witness III. 1. 45 (पल्लवः । कथाप्रसंगेन अपराद्धा अभिषेकवेला । The अभिषेक is here of course the evening. *Vide* III. 1. 5. रमणीयःखलु दिवसावसानवृत्तान्तो राजवेश्मनि ।) and III. stanza 2 (उत्कीर्णा इव etc). It is the first or second day in the dark fortnight since the moon has not yet risen. See III. 5.9. (विदूषकः । भोः प्रत्यासन्नेन चन्द्रोदयेन भवितव्यम् ।) And when the moon rises, her orb is not full and complete but with a slight portion of it broken off. See III. 6. 1 (विदूषकः । ही ही । भो एष खण्डमोदकसश्रीक उदितो राजा द्विजातीनाम् ।) We learn from a remark of चित्रलेखा towards the end of the third Act (III. 17. 6.) that the spring is drawing to a close and that the summer is close at hand (वसन्तानन्तरे उष्णसमये भगवान् सूर्यो मयोपचरितव्यः ।) It would appear from this, that the action of the second and the third Act takes place within the space of two months covered by the spring season.

From a remark of चित्रलेखा in the first scene of the fourth Act (IV. o. 45), we learn that the rainy season has just set in (अनेन पुनर्निर्वृतानामपि उत्कण्ठाकारिणा मेघोदयेन अनर्थाधीनो भविष्यति ।). The second Scene of the fourth Act further contains numerous references to the rainy season. From this it becomes clear, that only two months covered by the summer season separate the third from the fourth Act.

Several years elapse between Act IV and V. Ayus, the son of Pururavas and Urvashi, who is introduced to us in the fifth Act, is already a grown up-lad, capable of bearing on his body the heavy coat of mail (कवचधरः संवृत्तः । V. 12. 16) and thoroughly educated in the different arts and sciences (गृहीतविद्यः । *ibid*). This becomes still more clear from the King's remark at V. 12. 16. (अयि वत्स उषितं त्वया पूर्वस्मिन्नाश्रमे । द्वितीयमध्यासितुं तव समयः ।). Ayus has already passed through the first Ashrama (*viz.* ब्रह्मचर्य) and is now of an age to enter upon the second (*viz.* गृहस्थाश्रम).

To sum up the whole thing we can say, that the interval between the first and the second Act is not definitcly indicated. The incidents described in the second, third and fourth Acts transpire within the space of four months covered by spring and summer. The interval between the fourth and the fifth Act is several years.

Characters.

PURURAVAS.

Pururavas, the hero of the present play, is the type technically known as धीरोदात्त दक्षिण *i. e.* Valiant, dignified, and considerato in his loves. According to writers on dramaturgy, a hero of this type possesses several qualities such as nobility of heart, patience, modesty, aversion to self-flattery, self-possession and extreme courteousness towards the fair sex. To any careful reader of our play it cannot but strike that Pururavas possesses all these qualities and many more besides, and thus answers in every respect to the conception of the धीरोदात्त hero.

Let us now, see how some of the more important of these qualities are evidenced in the play in connection with the character of Pururavas, by making reference to a couple of striking incidents.

His high sense of chivalry and courtesy towards the fair sex is shown by his impatience to learn the details of the misfortune that has befallen the Apsarases, the readiness with which he volunteers his services in order to deliver Urvashi and Citralekha from the power of the demon and the anxious concern that he feels for Urvashi's recovery from her swoon. He is extremely gentle and polite in his address to the Apsarases as also to his Queen. He is ever solicitous not to hurt the feelings of the Queen and seizes the first opportunity that he gets to make truce with her.

Next to his chivalry and courtesy his humility and aversion to self-flattery claim our attention. Although he himself has overpowered and crushed the demon Keshin by the might of his arm, he gives the credit for it entirely to the all-saving prowess of Indra (त्रिलोकरक्षी महिमा हि वज्रिणः ।) I. 5; see also I. 15.

His self-possession is in evidence when in the second Act Urvashi is called away to heaven immediately after he meets her. With wonderful self-restraint he gives her permission to depart, though not without much reluctance (cf. II. 18.10 नास्मि भवत्योरीश्वरनियोगप्रत्यर्थी । स्मर्तव्यस्त्वयं जनः ।).

We can continue the examination of the play in the same way and find ample evidence in it for many more admirable qualities in the character of Pururavas. But all the same we cannot fail to notice an important weakness in him *viz.* his sensuousness. From the very first Pururavas strikes us as extremely sensuous and the nymph so airy "so pure a thing, so free from mortal touch." In the whole of the play we miss very much indeed the virility or the sani y or the judgment of a Dushyanta in our hero. He scarcely does anything save bewail his state and grow sentimental. He longs for the sight of her face, the touch of her hand, the pressure of her limbs; in all this he is so morbid, and this is a trait in his character which ultimately develops into madness in Act IV. Thus with true psychological insight the poet has from the very beginning prepared us for the abnormal state of mind in which the hero comes on the stage in Act IV.

We see, then, that although Pururavas answers remakably well to the description of the conventional hero in Indian drama, his character reveals on further scrutiny certain repelling features such as his sensuousness, his morbid sentimentality and the earthly character of his passion for Urvashi. Not so, however, the case with Urvashi, the heroine of our play. She is perfectly free from the earthly part—the grossness of that passion. She finds that she could scarcely live in the stifling atmosphere of Indra's court. Her attendance on him was the forced homage of an unwilling vassal. It was only when she saw Pururavas that she awakened to life. Love is the element of her being. And she is only too jealous of her love; for she considers no sacrifice too great when it is made for the sake of love. She will not look upon her son's face, for ever so many years, for fear that their union will cease to be. Some will say hard things about her on that account; but they scarcely understand the intensity of that all-consuming passion. And besides she has chosen between two evils; if she were to disclose that a son was born to them she had instantly to forego both son and lover; if on the other hand she kept that fact concealed, she could enjoy her lover's company, while her son was brought up and educated in the severe discipline of the *Ashrama*. Kalidasa has thus given us in Urvashi altogether a rare and lovable type of womanhood, for woman is at her best when she loves and deems no sacrifice too great but she may go in for *it*.

URVASHI.

The only other character in the play that invites our attention is the Vidushaka, the boon companion of the King. He does not of

VIDUSHAKA.

course help the King in attaining to the fulfilment of his passion for Urvashi. If at all, he only serves to make matters worse for the King by falling an easy prey to the trickery of Nipunika and divulging the secret of the King's love for Urvashi; by dropping down Urvashi's love-letter, and thus supplying the already suspecting Queen with a written proof of the King's infidelity; and by uttering all sorts of foolish things calculated to expose the King in her eyes. He creates a good deal of humour by making constant references, in time and out of time, to the dainties of the table of which, it would seem, he is a *connoisseur*. He is so occupied all along with thoughts about food and drink, that almost each and everything he sees about himself has no meaning and reality to him except in terms of these. The rising orb of the waning Moon appeals to him simply because he can liken it in his mind to a round mass of sweetmeat with its apex broken off. (Vide III 6. 2. ही ही । भो एष खण्डमोदकसश्रीक उदितो राजा द्विजातीनाम् ।). Paradise with all its pleasures and attraction fails to charm him since, as he says, the pleasures of the table are denied to the denizens thereof (See. III. 17. 11. किं वा स्वर्गे स्मर्तव्यम् । न वा अश्यते न वा पीयते ।)

We thus see that the Vidushaka does not stand in any vital relationship with the action of the play. He could well have been dispensed with by the poet, had it not been for the fact that his appearance on the stage and the humorous remarks that he makes from time to time serve to offer to the reader or the spectator a much-needed relaxation in the midst of the sentimental effusions of the love-lorn King.

Some Technical Names.

SUTRADHARA:—

He is the principal stage-manager who arranges the cast of characters, instructs them and takes a prominent part in the Prastavana. मातृगुप्ताचार्य describes him in these terms :—

चतुरातोद्यनिष्णातोऽनेकभाषासमावृतः ।
नानाभाषणतत्त्वज्ञो नीतिशास्त्रार्थतत्त्ववित् ॥
नानागतिप्रचारज्ञो रसभावविशारदः ।
नाट्यप्रयोगनिपुणो नानाशिल्पकलान्वितः ॥
छन्दोविधानतत्त्वज्ञः सर्वशास्त्रविचक्षणः ।
तत्तद्गीतानुगलयकलातालावधारणः ॥
अवधानप्रयोक्ता च योक्तृणामुपदेशकः ।
एवंगुणगणोपेतः सूत्रधारोऽभिधीयते ॥

PRASTAVANA OR STHAPANA :—

We are told in Natyashastra that before the commencement of a drama, an elaborate series of preliminary rites (पूर्वरङ्ग) had to be gone through, of which नान्दी formed the concluding rite. These were performed by the सूत्रधार who then left the stage and his place was taken by another similar person called स्थापक who then introduced the play to the audience.

पूर्वरङ्गं विधायादौ सूत्रधारे विनिर्गते ।
प्रविश्य तद्वदपरः काव्यमास्थापयेन्नटः ॥

Later on, with the reformation of the stage, these preliminaries were considerably shortened, and the Sutradhara alone performed both the functions of the पूर्वरङ्ग and of the prologue.

This prologue or प्रस्तावना (आमुखं) or स्थापना, as it is called in some plays of the Bhasa group, is an introductory dialogue between the सूत्रधार and the नटी or one of the actors. After giving an account of the author and his qualifications it introduces the incidents of the drama : cf.

सूत्रधारो नटीं ब्रूते मार्षं वाथ विदूषकम् ।
स्वकार्यं प्रस्तुताक्षेपि चित्रोक्त्या यत्तदामुखम् ॥

Of the many varieties of this prologue we are concerned with the प्रयोगातिशय " particular presentation " in which a character is introduced by a remark of the stage-manager:—

यदि प्रयोग एकस्मिन् प्रयोगोऽन्यः प्रयुज्यते ।
तेन पात्रप्रवेशश्चेत् प्रयोगातिशयो मतः ॥

VISHAMBHAKA

It is an explanatory scene, so called from its concisely compressing (वि+स्कम्भ्) into a short space those subordinate parts of the story, not enacted before the audience, but a knowledge of which is quite essential to the comprehending of the action of the play. cf.

वृत्तवर्तिष्यमाणानां कथांशानां निदर्शकः ।
संक्षिप्तार्थस्तु विष्कम्भो मध्यपात्रप्रयोजितः ॥

It is a monologue, or a dialogue, and in the latter case it is performed by two persons or more, of the same or different classes, according as it is शुद्ध or संकीर्ण (मिश्र).

एकानेककृतः शुद्धः संकीर्णो नीचमध्यमैः ॥

It may occur at the beginning of any of the acts, even the first, just after the प्रस्तावना.

PRAVESHAKA

This also is an explanatory scene serving the same purpose as the विष्कम्भक, only with this difference that the characters taking part in this scene are exclusively of the inferior class who speak the Prakrit dialect. It must come between two acts; thus unlike the विष्कम्भक, its existence in Act I is not possible. cf.

तद्वदेवानुदात्तोक्त्या नीचपात्रप्रयोजितः ।
प्रवेशोऽङ्कद्वयस्यान्तः शेषार्थस्योपसूचकः ॥

TROTAKA

The Trotaka, which is one of the eighteen Uparupakas, is a drama having five, seven, eight or nine acts. It deals with the doings of Gods and men and the Vidushaka makes his appearance in every Act. cf.

सप्ताष्टनवपंचाङ्कं दिव्यमानुषसंश्रयम् ।
त्रोटकं नाम तत्प्राहुः प्रत्यङ्कं सविदूषकम् ॥

The rule that the Vidushaka should be presented in every act of a Trotaka is not, however, strictly observed. For example, in the Vikramorvashiya which is regarded as a Trotaka, the Vidushaka appears only in Acts II, III and V. Besides the Vikramorvashiya, there is also mentioned as a Trotaka a seven act play called स्तम्भित-रम्भम्, which, unfortunately, has not come down to us.

TEXT WITH TRANSLATION

॥ श्रीः ॥

विक्रमोर्वशीयम् ।

प्रथमोऽङ्कः ।

वेदान्तेषु यमाहुरेकपुरुषं व्याप्य स्थितं रोदसी
यस्मिन्नीश्वर इत्यनन्यविषयः शब्दो यथार्थाक्षरः ।
अन्तर्यश्च मुमुक्षुभिर्नियमितप्राणादिभिर्मृग्यते
स स्थाणुः स्थिरभक्तियोगसुलभो निःश्रेयसायास्तु वः ॥ १ ॥

[नान्द्यन्ते]

सूत्रधारः— [नेपथ्याभिमुखमवलोक्य] मारिष इतस्तावत् ।

[प्रविश्य पारिपार्श्वकः]

पारिपार्श्वकः—भाव अयमस्मि ।

सूत्रधारः—मारिष बहुशस्तु परिषदा पूर्वेषां कवीनां दृष्टः प्रयोगबन्धः । सोऽहमद्य विक्रमोर्वशीयं नामापूर्वं नाटकं प्रयोक्ष्ये । तदुच्यतां पात्रवर्गः स्वेषु स्वेषु पाठेष्वसंमूढैर्भवितव्यमिति ।

पारिपार्श्वकः—यदाज्ञापयति भावः ।

[इति निष्क्रान्तः]

सूत्रधारः—यावदिदानीमार्यमिश्रान् विज्ञापयामि ।

[प्रणिपत्य ।]

प्रणयिषु वा दाक्षिण्यादथवा सद्वस्तुपुरुषबहुमानात् ।
शृणुत मनोभिरवहितैः क्रियामिमां कालिदासस्य ॥ २ ॥

VIKRAMORVASĪYA

PROLOGUE

ACT I.

May the Eternal One who is attainable by firm faith and meditation; who is hailed as the Supreme Spirit in the Vedanta, who pervades and is present in the whole of heaven and earth; to whom alone the name of Lord, not signifying any other being, is properly applied; and who is sought within themselves by those desirous of salvation by restraining the vital breaths Prana and others, bestow upon you the highest bliss. [1]

(*At the end of the benediction*)

THE MANAGER—Ho! Marisha, come hither.

(*Entering*)

ACTOR—Here I am, sir.

THE MANAGER—Marisha, many a time has this assembly witnessed the compositions of former bards. I, therefore, propose to stage one not hitherto exhibited, the play of Vikrama and Urvashi. Speak to the actors, therefore, to attend carefully to their respective parts.

ACTOR—As you desire, sir. (*Exit*)

THE MANAGER—I have now to make (this) request to the noble audience. (*Bowing*).

Listen to this work of Kalidasa with attentive minds, in consideration of either your regard towards (us), your humble servants, or your respect for the excellent hero of this play. [2]

नेपथ्ये। **परित्ताअदु परित्ताअदु जो सुर-पक्ख-वादी जस्स वा अम्बर-अले गदी अत्थि।** परित्रायतां परित्रायतां यः सुरपक्षपाती यस्य वा अम्बरतले गतिरस्ति।

सूत्रधारः--[कर्णं दत्त्वा] **अये किं नु खलु मद्विज्ञापनानन्तरं कुररीणामिव आकाशे शब्दः श्रूयते।** [विचिन्त्य] **भवतु। ज्ञातम्।**

ऊरूद्भवा नरसखस्य मुनेः सुरस्त्री
कैलासनाथमुपसृत्य निवर्तमाना।
बन्दीकृता विबुधशत्रुभिरर्धमार्गे
क्रन्दत्यतः शरणमप्सरसां गणोऽयम्॥ ३॥

[इति निष्क्रान्तः]

प्रस्तावना।

[ततः प्रविशन्ति अप्सरसः।]

सर्वाः—**परित्ताअदु परित्ताअदु जो सुर-पक्ख-वादी जस्स वा अम्बर-अले गदी अत्थि।** परित्रायतां परित्रायतां यः सुरपक्षपाती यस्य वा अम्बरतले गतिरस्ति।

[ततः प्रविशति राजा रथेन सूतश्च।]

राजा--**अलमलमाक्रन्दितेन। सूर्योपस्थानात् प्रतिनिवृत्तं पुरूरवसं मामुपेत्य कथ्यतां कुतो भवत्यः परित्रातव्या इति।**

रम्भा—**असुरावलेवादो।** असुरावलेपात्।

राजा--**किं पुनरसुरावलेपेन भवतीनामपराद्धम्।**

मेनका—**सुणादु महाराओ। जा तवो-विसेस-परिसङ्किदस्स सुउमारं पहरणं महिन्दस्स। पच्चादेसो रूव-गव्विदाए सिरीए। अलंकारो सग्गस्स। सा णो पिअसही**

(*Behind the Scenes*)

Help ! Help ! Whoso is a friend to the gods, or has power to move in the space of heaven.

The Manager–(*Listening*). What sounds are these in the air, as of the female ospreys, that break in upon my words ! (*Reflecting*) Ah ! I know.

The celestial nymph, sprung from the thigh of the sage, the friend of Nara, is, while returning after her attendance upon the Lord of Kailasa, taken prisoner on the way by the enemies of the gods ; that is why this group of Apsarasas is crying for protection. [3]

(*Exit*)

END OF THE PROLOGUE.

(*Enter the nymphs of heaven*).

ALL—Help ! Help ! Whoso is a friend to the gods or has power to move in the space of heaven.

(*Enter King in his Chariot and the Charioteer*)

KING—Cease your cries. Come to me, Pururavas, returned from my attendance upon the Sun, and tell me against what do the ladies seek help.

RAMBHA—Against a demon's violence.

KING—What wrong have the ladies suffered through the demon's violence ?

उव्वसी कुबेर-भवणादो पडिणिवट्टमाणा समावत्तिदिट्ठेण हिरण्णउरवासिणा केसिणा दाणवेण चित्तलेहादुदीआ
१८ **अद्धपहं जेव्व बन्दिग्गाहं गहिदा।** श्रृणोतु महाराजः । या तपोविशेषपरिशङ्कितस्य सुकुमारं प्रहरणं महेन्द्रस्य । प्रत्यादेशो रूपगर्विताया: श्रियः । अलङ्कारः स्वर्गस्य । सा नः प्रियसखी उर्वशी
२१ कुबेरभवनात् प्रतिनिवर्तमाना समापत्तिदृष्टेन हिरण्यपुरवासिना केशिना दानवेन चित्रलेखाद्वितीया अर्धपथ एव बन्दिग्राहं गृहीता ।

राजा—अपि ज्ञायते कतमेन दिग्भागेन गतः स जाल्म इति।

२४ **सहजन्या—पुव्वुत्तरेण** । पूर्वोत्तरेण ।

राजा—तेन हि विमुच्यतां विषादः। यतिष्ये वः सखी-प्रत्यानयनाय।

२७ **रम्भा—सरिसं खु सोमादो एक्कन्दरस्स।** सदृशं खलु सोमादेकान्तरस्य ।

राजा—क्व पुनर्मां भवत्यः प्रतिपालयिष्यन्ति।

३० **सर्वाः—इमस्सिं हेमकूड-सिहरे।** एतस्मिन् हेमकूटशिखरे ।

राजा—सूत वैशानीं दिशं प्रति चोदयाश्वानाशुगमनाय।

सूतः—यदाज्ञापयत्यायुष्मान् [इति यथोक्तं करोति ।]

३३ **राजा—**[रथवेगं निरूपयन्] **साधु साधु। अनेन रथवेगेन पूर्वप्रस्थितं वैनतेयमप्यासादयेयं किं पुनस्तमपकारिणं मघोनः । तथा हि**

अग्रे यान्ति रथस्य रेणुवदमी चूर्णीभवन्तो घना
श्चक्रभ्रान्तिररान्तरेषु जनयत्यन्यामिवारावलीम् ।
चित्रन्यस्तमिवाचलं हयशिरस्यायामवच्चामरं
यष्टयग्रे च समं स्थितो ध्वजपटः प्रान्ते च वेगानिलात् ॥४॥

[निष्क्रान्तो रथेन राजा सूतश्च]

MENAKA—Listen, your majesty: our dear friend Urvashi, the delicate weapon of the great Indra when he is frightened by the excellence of Tapas, who shames proud Shri's loveliness, who is heaven's ornament, was, while on her way from Kubera's mansion, taken captive, along with Chitralekha, by the demon Keshin of Hiranyapura, who came upon us all of a sudden.

KING—Know ye what direction the wretch took?

SAHAJANYA—The North-East.

KING—Well then, banish your fears. I shall endeavour to restore you your friends.

RAMBHA—That is worthy of the descendant of the Moon only one degree removed.

KING—Where will you await my return?

ALL—Here, on the peak of yonder Hemakuta.

KING—Charioteer, urge the horses on to the North-East that we may speedily go.

CHARIOTEER—As my lord commands. (*Does as bidden*).

KING—(*Looking at the speed of his Chariot*). Well, with this speed, I may overtake Vainateya even if he has the start of me; what then of this offender of Lord Indra. For,

These heavy clouds, being pulverized, are rising before the chariot like dust; the revolution of the wheels is creating as it were another set of spokes within the spokes; the long streamer is standing on the heads of the horses as motionless as in a picture; and by the wind (produced by) the great speed, the banner-cloth spreads out evenly between the top-point of the flag-staff and its own end. [4]

रम्भा—हला जह-णिद्दिट्ठं पदेसं संकमामो। हला यथा निर्दिष्टं प्रदेशं संक्रामामः।

शेषाः—तह। तथा। [इति सर्वाः शैलावतरणं नाटयित्वा स्थिताः]

रम्भा—अवि णाम सो राएसी समुद्धरे णो हिअअ-सल्लं। अपि नाम स राजर्षिः समुद्धरेद् नो हृदयशल्यम्।

मेनका—मा दे संसओ होदु। उवट्ठिदसंपराओ महिन्दो मज्झिम-लोआदो सबहुमाणं आणाविअ तं एव्व विअअ-सेणा-मुहे णिओजेदि। मा ते संशयो भवतु। उपस्थित-संपरायो महेन्द्रो मध्यमलोकात् सबहुमानमानाय्य तमेव विजयसेना-मुखे नियोजयति।

रम्भा—सव्वहा इह विअई भोदु। सर्वथा इह विजयी भवतु।

सहजन्या—[क्षणमात्रं स्थित्वा] **हला समस्ससध। समस्ससध। एसो उच्चलिद-हरिण-केदणो तस्स राएसिणो सोमदत्तो रहो दीसदि। ण खु सो अकिदत्थो णिवत्तिस्सदि।** हला समाश्वसित समाश्वसित। एष उच्चलितहरिणकेतनस्तस्य राजर्षेः सोमदत्तो रथो दृश्यते। न खलु सोऽकृतार्थो निवर्तिष्यते। [सर्वा उच्चक्षुषो विलोकयन्ति।]

[ततः प्रविशति राजा सूतश्च। चित्रलेखावलम्बितहस्ता भयनिमीलिताक्षी चोर्वशी।]

चित्रलेखा—समस्ससदु समस्ससदु पिअ-सही। समाश्वसितु समाश्वसितु प्रियसखी।

राजा—सुन्दरि समाश्वसिहि समाश्वसिहि।

(*Exit King with Chariot and the Charioteer.*)

RAMBHA—Now, friends, let us proceed to the place pointed out.

OTHERS—As you say. (*All gesticulate descending to the mountain-peak and making a halt.*)

RAMBHA—Will the royal sage be able to extract this dart from our hearts?

MENAKA—You make no doubt of that. For even the great Indra, when hostilities are imminent, honours him and bringing him from the world of mortals, appoints him to the command of his conquering hosts.

RAMBHA—May he succeed in every way in the present case.

SAHAJANYA—Friends, take heart, take heart. Here is to be seen his chariot, Somadatta, with its deer-emblazoned banner dancing in the wind. Surely he will not return before accomplishing his object.

(*All look with eyes upturned.*)

(*Enter King, Charioteer, and Urvashi with eyes shut in fear and supported on Chitralekha's arm.*)

CHITRALEKHA—Take cheer, take cheer, my dear friend!

गतं भयं भीरु सुरारिसंभवं
त्रिलोकरक्षी महिमा हि वज्रिणः ।
तदेतदुन्मीलय चक्षुरायतं
महोत्पलं प्रत्युषसीव पद्मिनी ॥ ५ ॥

चित्रलेखा—अम्हहे कहं ऊससिद-मेत्त-जीविदा अज्जवि
सण्णं ण पडिवज्जदि । अहो कथमुच्छ्वसितमात्रजीविता अद्यापि
३ संज्ञां न प्रतिपद्यते ।

राजा—बलवदत्रभवती परित्रस्ता । तथा हि

मुञ्चति न तावदस्याः कम्पं कुसुमसमबन्धनं हृदयम् ।
पश्य हरिचन्दनेन स्तनमध्योच्छ्वासिना कथितम् ॥६ ॥

चित्रलेखा—हला पज्जवत्थावेहि अत्ताणं । अणच्छरा
विअ मे पडिहासि । सखि पर्यवस्थापय आत्मानम् । अनप्सरा
३ इव मे प्रतिभासि ।

राजा—अयि प्रकृतिमापद्यते ते सखी । पश्य

आविर्भूते शशिनि तमसा मुच्यमानेव रात्रि-
र्नैशस्यार्चिर्हुतभुजइव च्छिन्नभूयिष्ठधूमा ।
मोहेनान्तर्वरतनुरियं लक्ष्यते मुक्तकल्पा
गङ्गा रोधःपतनकलुषा गृह्णतीव प्रसादम् ॥ ७ ॥

चित्रलेखा—सहि वीसद्धा होहि । पराभूदा खु तिदस-
परिपन्थिणो हदासा । सखि विश्रब्धा भव । पराभूताः खलु
३ त्रिदशपरिपन्थिनो हताशाः ।

उर्वशी—[चक्षुषी उन्मील्य] किं पहाव-दंसिणा महिन्देण ।
किं प्रभावदर्शिना महेन्द्रेण ।

६ चित्रलेखा—ण महिन्देण । महिन्द-सरिसाणुभावेण

KING—Fair nymph, cheer up, cheer up.

Gone, timid one, is the fear caused by the demons; for, indeed, the three worlds rest secure in Indra's greatness. Open those big eyes, even as the lotus-plant at dawn its big lotuses. [5]

CHITRALEKHA—Alas! How does she not recover consciousness yet, in whom her breath alone is what is left of life?

KING—Greatly is her ladyship troubled. For,

Behold, her heart (fluttering) like a flower on its stem does not yet forego its tremor, which is indicated by the sandal-smearings rising up between her two breasts. [6]

CHITRALEKHA—Friend, do compose yourself. Meseems you scarcely look a nymph of heaven.

(*Urvashi recovers herself*).

KING—Lady, your dear friend is coming to herself.

Look, The fair one seems well-nigh relieved of her mental stupor like the night freed from darkness when the Moon appears, or like the flame of evening fire from which the smoke has been mostly removed, or like the Ganges regaining her clearness after her waters have been soiled, by the crumbling in of her banks. [7]

CHITRALEKHA—Friend, have no fear. Vanquished are those wretches, the foes of heaven.

URVASHI—(*Opening her eyes*) By the great Indra who sees through his divine power?

इमिणा राएसिणा । न महेन्द्रेण । महेन्द्रसदृशानुभावेन अनेन राजर्षिणा ।

९ उर्वशी--[राजानं विलोक्य । आत्मगतम्] उवकिदं खु दाणवेहिं । उपकृतं खलु दानवैः ।

राजा--[प्रकृतिस्थामुर्वशीं निर्वर्ण्य । स्वगतम्] स्थाने खलु
१२ नारायणमृषिं विलोभयन्त्यस्तदूरुसंभवामिमां दृष्ट्वा व्रीडिताः सर्वा अप्सरस इति । अथ वा नेयं तपस्विनः सृष्टिर्भवितुमर्हति । तथा हि

अस्याः सर्गविधौ प्रजापतिरभूच्चन्द्रो नु कान्तप्रभः
शृङ्गारैकरसः स्वयं नु मदनो मासो नु पुष्पाकरः ।
वेदाभ्यासजडः कथं नु विषयव्यावृत्तकौतूहलो
निर्मातुं प्रभवेन्मनोहरमिदं रूपं पुराणो मुनिः ॥८॥

उर्वशी--हला सो सही-जणो कहिं खु भवे । हला स सखीजनः क्व खलु भवेत् ।

३ चित्रलेखा--महाराओ अभअ-दाई जाणादि । महाराजः अभयदायी जानाति ।

राजा--[उर्वशीमवलोकयन्] महति विषादे वर्तते । पश्यतु भवती

यदृच्छया त्वं सकृदप्यवन्ध्ययोः
पथि स्थिता सुन्दरि यस्य नेत्रयोः ।
त्वया विना सोपि समुत्सुको भवेत्
सखीजनस्ते किमुतार्द्रसौहृदः ॥ ९ ॥

उर्वशी--[अपवार्य] अहिजादं खु से वअणं । अहवा चन्दादो अमिअं ति किं एत्थ अच्छरिअं [प्रकाशम्]
३ अहो एत्थ णं पेक्खिदुं तुवरदि मे हिअअं । अभिजातं

CHITRALEKHA—Not by Mahendra ; but by this roval sage who in his prowess is the equal of Mahendra.

URVASHI—(*Looking at the King, to herself*) Then have the demons obliged me !

KING—(*Looking at Urvashi who has regained consciousness, to himself*) How very proper that the nymphs of heaven while endeavouring to entice the sage Narayana were put to shame as they saw her spring from his thigh. Or rather, she cannot be the creation of a poor ascetic ! For,

Was the moon of lovely brightness her creator ?
Or Madana himself who joys in love and love alone ?
Or the vernal month ? For how could an aged anchorite who has grown dull through the study of the Vedas, and who has withdrawn himself from all worldly pleasures, fashion such a lovely form ? [8]

URVASHI—Where are our friends, my dear ?

CHITRALEKHA—The King,our protector, knows.

KING—They are greatly distressed. Look dear lady,

Even he, O fair one, within the path of whose fruitful eyes you but once moved, will feel a yearning in your absence : what then of your friends, ever full of love (for you) ? [9]

खल्वस्य वचनम् । अथवा चन्द्रादमृतमिति किमत्राश्चर्यम् । अत एवैनं प्रेक्षितुं त्वरते मे हृदयम् ।

राजा—[हस्तेन दर्शयन्]

एताः सुतनु मुखं ते सख्यः पश्यन्ति हेमकूटगताः ।
प्रत्यागतप्रसादं चन्द्रमिवोपप्लवान्मुक्तम् ॥ १० ॥

चित्रलेखा—**हला पेक्ख** । हला पश्य ।

उर्वशी—[राजानं सस्पृहं पश्यन्ती] **सम-दुक्खो पिबइ व्व मं णयणेहिं** । समदुःखः पिबतीव मां नयनाभ्याम् ।

चित्रलेखा—[साकूतम्] **अयि को** । अयि कः ।

उर्वशी—**सहि-अणो** । सखीजनः ।

रम्भा—[सहर्षम्] **एसो चित्तलेहा-दुदिअं उव्वसिं गेण्हिअ विसाहा-समीव-गदो विअ चन्दो उवट्ठिदो राएसी** । एष चित्रलेखाद्वितीयामुर्वशीं गृहीत्वा विशाखासमीपगत इव चन्द्रः उपस्थितो राजर्षिः ।

मेनका—[निर्वर्ण्य] **दुवे वि णो पिआणि उवणदाणि । इअं पच्चाणीदा सही अअं च अपरिक्खदो महाराओ त्ति ।** द्वे अप्यस्माकं प्रिये उपनते । इयं प्रत्यानीता सखी अयं चापरिक्षतो महाराज इति ।

सहजन्या—**सुट्ठु भणासि । दुज्जआ खु दाणवा ।** सुष्ठु भणसि । दुर्जयाः खलु दानवाः ।

राजा—**सूत इदं तच्छैलशिखरम् । अवतार्यतां रथः ।**

सूतः—**यदाज्ञापयत्यायुष्मान्** [इति यथोक्तं करोति]

राजा—[चक्रोद्घातं रूपयित्वा । आत्मगतम्] **हन्त दत्तफलो मे विषमावतारः ।**

URVASHI—(*Aside*) How noble his words ! Or what wonder that nectar (should flow) from the moon ! (*aloud*) That is why my heart is eager to meet them.

KING—(*Pointing by his hand*).

These your friends are watching your face—O fair one—from Hemakuta, like the Moon emerging from an eclipse and regaining its brightness. [10]

CHITRALEKHA—Dear friend, look.

URVASHI—(*Longingly looking at the King*) Equal in suffering, seems to drink me up with (thirsty) eyes

CHITRALEKHA—(*Significantly*) Who, my dear ?

URVASHI—This group of my friends.

RAMBHA—Here comes the royal sage taking Urvashi and Chitralekha with him, as if he were the Moon attended by the Vishakha (stars).

MENAKA—(*Looking closely*) We joy in both the things—here is our friend restored to us, while his majesty is unhurt.

SAHAJANYA—You speak the truth ; for the demons are hard to quell.

KING—Charioteer, here is the peak of the mountain. Bring the chariot down.

CHARIOTEER—As my lord commands. (*Does as bidden.*)

KIKG—(*Gesticulating jolting of the wheel, to himself*). Ah, not vain my descent on this uneven ground :

यदयं रथसंक्षोभादंसेनांसो रथोपमश्रोण्याः ।
स्पृष्टः सरोमविक्रियमङ्कुरितं मनसिजेनेव ॥ ११ ॥

उर्वशी—[सव्रीडम्] हला किं वि परदो ओसर । सखि किमपि परतोऽपसर ।

३ चित्रलेखा—[सस्मितम्] णाहं सक्का । नाहं शक्ता ।

रम्भा—एध संभावेम्ह रासिं । [सर्वा उपसर्पन्ति] एत संभावयामो राजर्षिम् ।

६ राजा—सूत स्थापय तावद् रथम् ।

यावत् पुनरियं सुभ्रूरुत्सुकाभिः समुत्सुका ।
सखीभिर्याति संपर्कं लताभिः श्रीरिवार्तवी ॥ १२ ॥

[सूतस्तथा करोति ।]

सर्वाः—दिट्ठिआ महाराओ विअएण वड्ढदि । दिष्ट्या
३ महाराजो विजयेन वर्धते ।

राजा—भवत्यश्च सखीसमागमेन ।

उर्वशी—[चित्रलेखादत्तहस्ता रथादवतीर्य] हला एध पीडिदं
६ मं परिस्सजध । ण खु मे आसा आसि भूओवि सही-
अणं पेक्खिस्सं ति । हला एत पीडितं मां परिष्वजध्वम् ।
न खलु मम आशासीद् भूयोऽपि सखीजनं द्रक्ष्यामीति ।

९ सत्वरं परिष्वजन्ते ।

रम्भा—सव्वहा महाराओ कप्प-सदाइं पुहविं पालअन्तो होदु । सर्वथा महाराजः कल्पशतानि पृथ्वीं पालयिता भवतु ।

१२ सूतः—आयुष्मन् पूर्वस्यां दिशि महता रथवेगेनोपदर्शितः शब्दः ।

अयं च गगनात् कोपि तप्तचामीकराङ्गदः ।
अवरोहति शैलाग्रं तडित्वानिव तोयदः ॥ १३ ॥

That my shoulder should have rubbed the shoulder of that lovely damsel in the joltings of the chariot, so as to thrill me (with joy) looks as if love hath sprouted (within). [11]

URVASHI—(*Bashfully*). Well friend, will you move a bit.

CHITRALEKHA—I cannot.

RAMBHA—Come along—let us honour the royal sage.

(*All approach*).

KING—Charioteer, stop the chariot,

So that like the beauty of spring coming to the plants, she—this fair one—may hasten to meet her eager companions. [12]

(*The charioteer does as bidden*)

ALL—We congratulate your majesty upon your victory.

KING—And your ladyships too (are to be congratulated) upon the recovery of your friend.

URVASHI—(*Helped by Chitralekha with her arm, alighting from the chariot*). Friends come press me closely. Little did I hope to meet my friends again.

(*They quickly embrace*).

RAMBHA—May the King protect the earth a hundred *Kalpas* !

CHARIOTEER—My lord, from the East is indicated the sound of a rushing chariot.

And here is some one descending to the peak of the mountain from the sky—his armlet gleaming like heated gold, like a cloud (adorned by) lightning. [13]

(*The Nymphs look*).

2

[पश्यन्त्यप्सरसः ।]

सर्वाः—**अम्मो चित्तरहो ।** अहो चित्ररथः ।

[ततः प्रविशति चित्ररथः ।]

चित्ररथः—[राजानं दृष्ट्वा सबहुमानम्] **दिष्ट्या महेन्द्रोपकारपर्याप्तेन विक्रममहिम्ना वर्धते भवान् ।**

राजा—**अये गन्धर्वराजः** [रथादवतीर्य] **स्वागतं प्रियसुहृदे** [परस्परं हस्तौ स्पृशतः]

चित्ररथः—**वयस्य केशिना हृतामुर्वशीं नारदादुपश्रुत्य प्रत्याहरणार्थमस्याः शतक्रतुना गन्धर्वसेना समादिष्टा । ततो वयमन्तरा चारणेभ्यस्त्वदीयं जयोदाहरणं श्रुत्वा त्वामिहस्थमुपागताः । स भवानिमां पुरस्कृत्य सहास्माभिर्मघवन्तं द्रष्टुमर्हति । महत् खलु तत्रभवतो मघोनः प्रियमनुष्ठितं भवता । पश्य**

पुरा नारायणेनेयमतिसृष्टा मरुत्वते ।
दैत्यहस्तादपाच्छिद्य सुहृदा संप्रति त्वया ॥ १४ ॥

राजा—मा मैवम् ।

ननु वज्रिण एव वीर्यमेतद्
विजयन्ते द्विषतो यदस्य पक्ष्याः ।
वसुधाधरकन्दराभिसर्पी
प्रतिशब्दोपि हरेर्भिनत्ति नागान् ॥ १५ ॥

चित्ररथः—युक्तमेतत् । अनुत्सेकः खलु विक्रमालंकारः ।

राजा—सखे नायमवसरो मम शतक्रतुं द्रष्टुम् । त्वमेवात्रभवतीं प्रभोरन्तिकं प्रापय ।

चित्ररथः—यथा भवान् मन्यते । इत इतो भवत्यः ।

[अप्सरसः प्रस्थिताः ।]

ALL—Behold ! it is Chitraratha.

(*Then enter Chitraratha*).

CHITRARATHA—(*Looking at the King respectfully*). I congratulate you on the greatness of your prowess which sufficeth to confer obligations on the great Indra.

KING—Ah, the King of the Gandharvas. (*Alighting from his chariot*). Welcome, my dear friend.

(*They touch each other's hands*).

CHITRARATHA—Friend, having heard from Narada that Urvashi was abducted by Keshin, Indra ordered the army of the Gandharvas to her rescue. So on our way we heard your panegyrics sung by the bards and now come to wait upon you here. It behoves you therefore, to meet Indra with us, taking her with you. Great is the service you have rendered to Indra. See,

Formerly she was presented to Indra by Narayana—and now is she being presented by you, his friend, by rescuing her from the demon's violence. [14]

KING—Do not think thus.

It is, indeed, Indra's might that enables his friends to conquer his foes: the very echo of the lion's roar, as through the rocky caves it spreads (and deepens) appals the mighty elephants. [15]

CHITRARATHA—That is proper. Humility is ever found the ornament of valour.

KING—Friend, I do not think this a proper occasion for me to see Lord Indra. Do you, therefore, take this nymph to my Lord.

CHITRARATHA—As my friend thinks. This way, ladies, this way.

उर्वशी—[जनान्तिकम्] **हला चित्तलेहे उवआरिणं पि राएसिं ण सक्कुणोमि आमन्तेदुं। ता तुमं मे मुहं होहि।** हला चित्रलेखे उपकारिणमपि राजर्षिं न शक्नोमि आमन्त्रयितुम्। तत् त्वं मम मुखं भव।

चित्रलेखा—[राजानमुपेत्य] **वअस्स उव्वसी विण्णवेदि महाराएण अब्भणुण्णादा इच्छामि पिअ-सहिं विअ महाराअस्स कित्तिं महिन्द-लोअं णेदुं ति।** वयस्य उर्वशी विज्ञापयति महाराजेन अभ्यनुज्ञाता इच्छामि प्रियसखीमिव महाराजस्य कीर्तिं महेन्द्रलोकं नेतुमिति।

राजा—गम्यतां पुनर्दर्शनाय।

[सर्वाः सगन्धर्वा आकाशोत्पतनं रूपयन्ति।]

उर्वशी—[उत्पतनभङ्गं रूपयित्वा] **अम्हहे लदा-विडवे मे एआवली लग्गा।** [परिवृत्य] **चित्तलेहे मोआवेहि दाव णं।** अहो लताविटपे ममैकावली लग्ना। चित्रलेखे मोचय तावदेनाम्।

चित्रलेखा—[सस्मितम्] **दिढं खु लग्गा। दुम्मोआ विअ मे पडिहादि। होदु जदिस्सं दाव।** दृढं खलु लग्ना। दुर्मोचनीयेव प्रतिभाति। भवतु यतिष्ये तावत्।

उर्वशी—सुमरेहि दाव एदं अत्तणो वअणं। स्मर तावदेतदात्मनो वचनम्।

[चित्रलेखा मोचनं नाटयति।]

राजा—[स्वगतम्]

प्रियमाचरितं लते त्वया मे
गमनेऽस्याः क्षणविघ्नमाचरन्त्या।
यदियं पुनरप्यपाङ्गनेत्रा
परिवृत्तार्धमुखी मयाद्य दृष्टा ॥ १६ ॥

(*The nymphs set out*).

URVASHI—(*Aside*). Friend Chitralekha, I cannot bid adieu to this royal sage even though he is my benefactor. Do you, therefore, speak for me.

CHITRALEKHA—(*Approaching the King*). Friend, Urvashi requests leave of my Lord to take with her to heaven, as a dearly cherished friend, your fame.

KING—Adieu, till we meet again!

(*All gesticulate flying up into the heavens*).

URVASHI—(*Showing as if she is impeded in her flight*). Oh, this my necklace has got entangled in the thicket of creepers. (*Turning round*). Chitralekha, do extricate it.

CHITRALEKHA—(*Smiling*). Seems too deeply entangled to be set free. Well, I will try.

URVASHI—Be mindful of your words.

(*Chitralekha acts as if she is extricating it*).

KING—(*To himself*). A kind turn you have done me, O plant, by causing a moment's obstacle in her way. For thus I could behold her once again, with her sidelong glances and her half-averted face. [16]

सूतः—आयुष्मन् ।

अदः सुरेन्द्रस्य कृतापराधान्
प्रक्षिप्य दैत्यान् लवणाम्बुराशौ ।
वायव्यमस्त्रं शरधिं पुनस्ते
महोरगः श्वभ्रमिव प्रविष्टम् ॥ १७ ॥

राजा—तेन ह्युपश्लेषय रथं यावदारोहामि ।

[रथमुपश्लेषयति । राजा नाटयेन रथमारूढः ।
उर्वशी राजानं विलोक्य सनिःश्वासं सह सख्या निष्क्रान्ता चित्ररथश्च ।]

राजा—[उर्वशीमार्गोन्मुखः] अहो नु खलु दुर्लभाभिनिवेशी मदनः ।

एषा मनो मे प्रसभं शरीरात्
पितुः पदं मध्यममुत्पतन्ती ।
सुराङ्गना कर्षति खण्डिताग्रात्
सूत्रं मृणालादिव राजहंसी ॥ १८ ॥

[इति निष्क्रान्ताः सर्वे]

विक्रमोर्वशीये नाटके प्रथमोऽङ्कः समाप्तः ॥

CHARIOTEER—Royal sir,

Having hurled deep in the salt ocean the demon foes that offended against the King of the Gods, this Vayavya shaft now comes to rest in your quiver as comes the snake to its (wonted) covert. [17]

KING—Well then bring close to us the chariot, so that we might ascend.

(*The charioteer drives the chariot close to the King. The King acts ascending it. Urvashi sighingly looks at the King and departs with her friends and Chitraratha*).

KING—(*Looking after her*) What unattainable object doth Love attach one to !

This nymph of heaven bears off my heart forcibly out of my body, as through the mid-region of her sire she flies ; so flies the swan with a fibre from the lotus-stalk, the end of which is broken. [18]

[*Exeunt Omnes*].

HERE ENDS ACT ONE.

द्वितीयोऽङ्कः ।

[ततः प्रविशति विदूषकः ।]

विदूषकः—ही ही भो णिमन्तणोवाअणेण बम्हणो विअ राअरहस्सेण फुट्टमाणो ण सक्कुणोमि आइण्णे अत्तणो जीहं रक्खिदुं । ता जाव तत्तभवं वअस्सो कज्जासणादो उट्ठेदि दाव इमस्सिं विरल-जण-संवादे विमाणुच्छङ्ग-परिसरे चिट्ठिस्सं । [परिक्रम्य स्थितः]

ही ही भो निमन्त्रणोपायनेन ब्राह्मण इव राजरहस्येन स्फोटमानो न शक्नोमि आकीर्णे आत्मनो जिह्वां रक्षितुम्। तथावत् तत्रभवान् वयस्यः कार्यासनादुत्तिष्ठति तावदेतस्मिन् विरल-जनसंपाते विमानोत्सङ्गपरिसरे स्थास्यामि।

[प्रविश्य ।] चेटी—आणत्तम्हि देवीए कासि-राअ-पुत्तीए हञ्जे णिउणए जदो-पहुदि भअवदो अक्कस्स उवत्थाणं करिअ पडिणिवुत्तो अज्जउत्तो तदो आरहिअ सुण्ण-हिअओ विअ लक्खीअदि । ता तस्स पिअ-वअस्सादो अज्ज-माणवआदो जाणाहि दाव से उक्कण्ठा-कालणं ति । कहं खु मए बम्ह-बन्धू अदिसंधेओ । अहवा विरल-तण-लग्गं विअ अवस्साअसलिलं चिरं तस्सिं रहस्सं ण चिट्ठदि । जाव णं अण्णेसामि [परिक्रम्य अवलोक्य च] एसो आलिहिदो वाणरो विअ किं पि तुण्हिं-भूदो अज्जमाणवओ चिट्ठदि । जाव णं उवसप्पामि [उपसृत्य] अज्ज वन्दामि । आज्ञप्तास्मि देव्या काशीराजपुत्र्या हञ्जे निपुणिके यतःप्रभृति भगवतः अर्कस्योपस्थानं कृत्वा प्रतिनिवृत्त आर्यपुत्रस्तत आरभ्य शून्यहृदय

ACT. II.

(*Enter Vidushaka*).

VIDUSHAKA—Bursting as I am with the King's secret like a Brahmin with the presents he has had at some invitation, I shall not be able to set guard upon my tongue when in company. So I will bide here in the precincts of this Vimanaotsanga palace, but sparsely attended by people, until my friend comes forth from the council chamber.

(*Walks about and stands apart*).
(*Enter Nipunika, an attendant*).

NIPUNIKA—My Queen, the daughter of the King of Kashi, has bidden me: Girl Nipunika, since my Lord returned after his attendance upon the Sun, he looks absent-minded.

इव लक्ष्यते । तत् तस्य प्रियवयस्यादार्यमाणवकाज्जानीहि तावदस्योत्कण्ठाकारणमिति । कथं खलु मया ब्रह्मबन्धुरतिसंधेयः । अथवा विरलतृणलग्नमिव अवश्यायसलिलं चिरं तस्मिन् रहस्यं न तिष्ठति । यावदेनमन्विष्यामि । एष आलिखितो वानर इव किमपि तूष्णींभूतः आर्यमाणवकस्तिष्ठति । यावदेनमुपसर्पामि । आर्य वन्दे ।

विदूषकः—सत्थि भोदीए । [आत्मगतम्] **इमं दुट्ठ-चेडिअं पेक्खिअ तं राअरहस्सं हिअअं भिन्दिअ णिक्कमदि ।** [प्रकाशम्] **णिउणिए संगीद-वावारं उज्झिअ कहिं पत्थिदा सि ।** स्वस्ति भवत्यै । इमां दुष्टचेटिकां दृष्ट्वा तद् राजरहस्यं हृदयं भित्वा निष्क्रामति । निपुणिके संगीतव्यापारमुज्झित्वा क्व प्रस्थितासि ।

निपुणिका—देवीए वअणेण अज्जं एव्व पेक्खिदुं । देव्या वचनेन आर्यमेव द्रष्टुम् ।

विदूषकः—किं तत्तहोदी आणवेदि । किं तत्रभवत्याज्ञापयति ।

निपुणिका—देवी भणादि सदा वि अज्जो मह पक्खवादी ण मं अणुइद-वेअणा-दुक्खिदं उवेक्खदि त्ति । देवी भणति सदाप्यार्यो मयि पक्षपाती न मामनुचितवेदनादुःखितामुपेक्षत इति ।

विदूषकः—[सवितर्कम्] **किं वा वअस्सेण तत्तभोदीए पडिऊलं आचरिदं ।** किं वा वयस्येन तत्रभवत्याः प्रतिकूलमाचरितम् ।

निपुणिका—अज्ज जं-णिमित्तं भट्टा उक्कण्ठिदो ताए इत्थिआए णामधेएण भट्टिणा देवी आलविदा । आर्य यन्निमित्तं भर्ता उत्कण्ठितस्तस्याः स्त्रिया नामधेयेन भर्त्रा देवी आलपिता ।

विदूषकः—[स्वगतम्] **कहं सअं एव्व तत्तभवदा रहस्स-भेदो किदो । किं दाणिं अहं जीहा-जन्तणेण दुक्खं**

Do you, therefore, know the cause of his anxiety from his dear friend, the noble Manavaka. But how may I trick that fool of a Brahmin? Or rather a secret can rest no longer in his breast, than morning dew upon the point of a thin grass-blade. I will, therefore, find him out. (*Walking about and looking*). There is he sitting silent owing to some cause or other, the very picture of a monkey. So I will go to him. (*Approaching*). Arya Manavaka, I salute you.

VIDUSHAKA—Prosperity attend you! (*Apart*). How the King's secret is bursting out of my heart at the sight of this wicked girl! (*Aloud*) Well, Nipunika, where are you going leaving your practice of music?

NIPUNIKA—Just to see you, at the Queen's bidding.

VIDUSHAKA—What are the commands of Her Majesty?

NIPUNIKA—The Queen says that you have been ever a friend of hers, and therefore will not be indifferent to her in her present anxiety which is due to some unusual distress.

VIDUSHAKA—(*Guessing*). May it be that my friend has done anything to offend her?

NIPUNIKA—Noble Sir, the King addressed the Queen by the name of the very woman who has been the source of his anxiety.

अणुहवामि । [प्रकाशम्] **किं आमन्तिदा तत्तहोदी उव्वसी त्ति । ताए दंसणेण उम्मादिदो तत्तभवं ण केवलं तत्तभोर्दि मं पि विणोद-विमुहो दढं पीडेदि ।** कथ स्वयमेव तत्रभवता रहस्यभेदः कृतः । किमिदानीमहं जिह्वायन्त्रणेन दुःखमनुभवामि । किमामन्त्रिता तत्रभवती उर्वशीति । तस्या दर्शनेन उन्मादितस्तत्रभवान् न केवलं तत्रभवतीं मामपि विनोदविमुखो दृढं पीडयति ।

निपुणिका—[आत्मगतम्] **किदं मए भेदणं भट्टिणो रहस्स-दुग्गस्स** [प्रकाशम्] **अज्ज किं दाव देवीए णिवेदेमि ।** कृतं मया भेदनं भर्तू रहस्यदुर्गस्य । आर्य किं तावद् देव्यै निवेदयामि ।

विदूषकः—**णिउणिए विण्णवेहिं तत्तभोर्दि । जदामि दाव मिअतिण्हिआदो णिवत्तेदुं वअस्सं तदो देवीए मुहं पेक्खिस्सं ति ।** निपुणिके विज्ञापय तत्रभवतीम् । यते तावद् मृगतृष्णिकाया निवर्तयितुं वयस्यं ततो देव्या मुखं द्रक्ष्यामीति ।

निपुणिका—**जं अज्जो आणवेदि ।** यदार्य आज्ञापयति ।

[इति निष्क्रान्ता ।]

[नेपथ्ये वैतालिकः ।] **जयतु देवः ।**

आ लोकान्तात् प्रतिहततमोवृत्तिरासां प्रजानां
तुल्योद्योगस्तव दिनकृतश्चाधिकारो मतो नः ।
तिष्ठत्येष क्षणमधिपतिर्ज्योतिषां व्योममध्ये
षष्ठे भागे त्वमपि दिवसस्यात्मनश्छन्दवर्ती ॥ १ ॥

विदूषकः—[कर्णं दत्वा] **एसो कज्जासणादो उट्ठिदो इदो एव्व आअच्छदि वअस्सो जाव से पासवत्ती होमि ।**

[इति निष्क्रान्तः ।]

एष कार्यासनादुत्थित इत एव आगच्छति वयस्यः । यावदस्य पार्श्ववर्ती भवामि ।

VIDUSHAKA—(*To himself*). How has His Majesty let out the secret himself! What need that I should suffer by putting restraint upon my tongue? (*Aloud*). What. did he call the Queen-Urvashi? Ever since he saw her he has been out of his senses, and has annoyed not only Her Majesty but me also by setting his face against all recreations.

NIPUNIKA—(*To herself*). Here have I made a breach in the fortress of the royal secret. (*Aloud*). Noble sir, what may I say to the Queen?

VIDUSHAKA—Say to Her Grace: 'I shall endeavour to wean His Majesty from this (chase of the) mirage. and then will I see the Queen's face

NIPUNIKA—As the noble sir says. [*Exit*].

(*Behind the scenes a bard*).

Glory to the King!

Your power and that of the Sun appear to us to do similar work—for you suppress the evil tendencies of your subjects all over the world as the Sun drives away darkness beyond its confines (for the benefit of the people); the Lord of luminaries rests for a moment in the middle of the sky, and you too follow your own inclination in the sixth part of the day. [1]

VIDUSHAKA—(*Listening*). My friend has left the council-chamber and is coming in this very direction · so I will join him. [*Exit*]

END OF THE INTRODUCTORY SCENE.

प्रवेशकः ।

[ततः प्रविशति उत्कण्ठितो राजा विदूषकश्च ।]

राजा—

आ दर्शनात् प्रविष्टा सा मे सुरलोकसुन्दरी हृदयम् ।
बाणेन मकरकेतोः कृतमार्गमवन्ध्यपातेन ॥ १ ॥

विदूषकः—[आत्मगतम्] **संपीडिदा खु दाव तवस्सिणी कासिराअउत्ती ।** संपीडिता खलु तावत् तपस्विनी काशीराजपुत्री ।

राजा—अपि रक्ष्यते रहस्यनिक्षेपः ।

विदूषकः—[सविषादमात्मगतम्] **हद्धी हद्धी अहिसंधिदो म्हि दासीए । अण्णधा ण वअस्सो एव्वं पुच्छदि ।** हा धिक् हा धिक् अभिसंहितोऽस्मि दास्या । अन्यथा न वयस्य एवं पृच्छति ।

राजा—[साशङ्कम्] **किं भवांस्तूष्णीमास्ते ।**

विदूषकः—एव्वं मए णिअन्तिदा जीहा जं भवदो वि सहसा पडिवअणं ण देमि । एवं मया नियन्त्रिता जिह्वा यद् भवतोपि सहसा प्रतिवचनं न ददामि ।

राजा—युक्तम् । अथ केदानीमात्मानं विनोदयेयम् ।

विदूषकः—महाणसं गच्छम्ह । महानसं गच्छावः ।

राजा—किं तत्र ।

विदूषकः—तहिं पञ्च-विहस्स अब्भवहारस्स उवणद-संभारस्स जोअणं पेक्खमाणेहिं सक्कं उक्कण्ठा विणोदेदुं। तत्र पञ्चविधस्य अभ्यवहारस्य उपनतसंभारस्य योजनां प्रेक्षमाणाभ्यां शक्यमुत्कण्ठा विनोदयितुम् ।

राजा—[सस्मितम्] **तत्रेप्सितसंनिधानाद् भवान् रंस्यते। मया खलु दुर्लभप्रार्थनः कथमात्मा विनोदयितव्यः।**

(Enter King in a love-lorn condition and the Vidushaka)

KING—Ever since I saw her, that celestial one has enthroned herseslf in my heart to which access was given to her by the unerring shafts of Love. [2]

VIDUSHAKA—(*To himself*). Surely the poor (Queen) daughter of the King of Kashi must have been deeply annoyed.

KING—I hope you keep the secret entrusted to you.

VIDUSHAKA—(*Ruefully-to himself*). Alas ! Alas ! I am excellently tripped up by that wench. How else would my friend ask such a question ?

KING—(*Alarmed*). How ! you are silent ?

VIDUSHAKA—I have so (effectively) restrained my tongue, that I cannot answer off-hand even your inquiries.

KING—Well done. Where shall I divert myself ?

VIDUSHAKA—We shall proceed to the kitchen.

KING—What for ?

VIDUSHAKA—There the very sight of the preparation of the five kinds of dishes with all their materials put together will be sufficient to dissipate all distressing thoughts.

KING—(*Smilingly*). There you will surely find much diversion, because what you covet will be at hand. But with my heart longing for an unattainable object, how may I find diversion ?

विदूषकः—णं भवं तत्तहोदीए उव्वसीए दंसण-पहं गदो। ननु भवांस्तत्रभवत्या उर्वश्या दर्शनपथं गतः।

राजा—ततः किम्।

विदूषकः—ण खु सा दुल्लह त्ति समत्थेमि। न खलु सा दुर्लभेति समर्थये।

राजा—पक्षपातोयमवधार्यताम्।

विदूषकः—एत्तिअं मन्तअन्तेण भवदा वड्ढिदं मे कोदूहलं। किं तत्तभोदी उव्वसी अदुदिआ रूवेण अहं विअ विरूवदाए। एतावद् मन्त्रयमाणेन भवता वर्धितं मे कौतूहलम्। किं तत्रभवत्युर्वशी अद्वितीया रूपेण अहमिव विरूपतया।

राजा—माणवक प्रत्यवयवमशक्यवर्णनां नामवेहि। समासतः श्रूयताम्।

विदूषकः—अवहिदो म्हि। अवहितोस्मि।

राजा—

आभरणस्याभरणं प्रसाधनविधेः प्रसाधनविशेषः।
उपमानस्यापि सखे प्रत्युपमानं वपुस्तस्याः॥ ३॥

विदूषकः—अदो खु भवदा दिव्व-रसाहिलासिणा चादअव्वदं गहिदं। अतः खलु भवता दिव्यरसाभिलाषिणा चातकव्रतं गृहीतम्।

राजा—विविक्तादृते नान्यदुत्सुकस्य शरणमस्ति। तद् भवान् प्रमदवनमार्गमादेशयतु।

विदूषकः—[आत्मगतम्] **का गदी** [प्रकाशम्] **इदो इदो भवं** [परिक्रम्य] **एदेण पमद-वण-चोदिदेण विअ पच्चुग्गदो भवं आअन्तुओ दक्खिण-मारुदेण।** का गतिः। इत इतो भवान्। एतेन प्रमदवनचोदितेनेव प्रत्युद्गतो भवानागन्तुको दक्षिणमारुतेन।

VIDUSHAKA—Has the lady Urvashi seen my friend?

KING—What then?

VIDUSHAKA—Why, then, I should think her not quite unattainable.

KING—Remember, this is your partiality for me.

VIDUSHAKA—What Your Highness says only adds to my curiosity. What! Is she without a peer in beauty as I in deformity?

KING—Manavaka, I assure you, words cannot paint the loveliness of each part of her body; so hear her (described) in brief.

VIDUSHAKA—I am all attention.

KING—Her form is the ornament of ornaments,
an excellent decoration of decorations, and, my friend,
a standard of comparison to the (accepted) standards. [3]

VIDUSHAKA—That is why you have taken the vow of the *Chataka*, yearning as you do for heavenly drink.

KING—To one smarting under love's pain, there is no other solace than solitude. Do you, therefore, lead the way to the Pramadavana.

VIDUSHAKA—(*To himself*). What help! (*Aloud*). This way, this way, my Lord. (*Walking about*). This southern breeze, as if deputed by the Pramadavana advances to greet you, its guest.

राजा—[विलोक्य] उपपन्नं विशेषणमस्य वायोः। अयं हि

निषिञ्चन् माधवीमेतां लतां कौन्दीं च नर्तयन् ।
स्नेहदाक्षिण्ययोर्योगात् कामीव प्रतिभाति मे ॥ ४ ॥

विदूषकः—ईरिसो एव्व दे अहिणिवेसो होदु [परिक्रामितकेन] एदं पमदवण-दुवारं । पविसदु भवं । ईदृश
३ एव तवाभिनिवेशो भवतु । एतत् प्रमदवनद्वारम् । प्रविशतु भवान् ।

राजा—प्रविशाग्रतः ।

उभौ प्रविशतः ।

६ राजा—[अग्रतो विलोक्य] वयस्य मया न साधु समर्थितमापत्प्रतीकारः किल प्रमदवनोद्यानप्रवेश इति ।

विविक्षुर्यदहं तूर्णमुद्यानं तापशान्तये ।
स्रोतोजवोह्यमानस्य प्रतीपतरणं हि तत् ॥ ५ ॥

विदूषकः—कहं विअ । कथमिव ।

राजा—

इदमसुलभवस्तुप्रार्थनादुर्निवारं
प्रथममपि मनो मे पञ्चबाणः क्षिणोति ।
किमुत मलयवातोन्मूलितापाण्डुपत्रै-
रुपवनसहकारैर्दर्शितेष्वङ्कुरेषु ॥ ६ ॥

विदूषकः—अलं परिदेविदेण । अइरेण दे इच्छिअसंपादइत्तओ अणङ्गो एव्व सुहदो भविस्सदि । अलं
३ परिदेवितेन । अचिरेण तव इष्टसंपादयिता अनङ्ग एव सुखदो भविष्यति ।

राजा—प्रतिगृहीतं ब्राह्मणवचनम् ।

परिक्रामतः ।

६ विदूषकः—पेक्खदु भवं वसन्तोदारसूअअं अहिरामत्तणं पमदवणस्स । पश्यतु भवान् वसन्तावतारसूचकमभिरामत्वं प्रमदवनस्य ।

KING—(*Looking*). This is but a proper epithet for this breeze. For,

Impregnating this Madhavi creeper and making the Kaundi dance, he appears to me like a lover, as he combines in himself love (to one) and kindness (to the other). [4]

VIDUSHAKA—Let your love also be such and no other. (*Walking*) . Here is the entrance to the Pramadavana ; please you to enter.

KING—Go ahead.

(*Both enter*).

KING—(*Looking ahead*). Well, my friend, I was not right when I imagined that to enter this Pramadavana garden would yield relief to my affliction.

For the thought of entering this garden so quickly to dispel my anguish is (as vain as) the swimming against the current by one who is borne backwards by the stream. [5]

VIDUSHAKA—How so ?

KING—Already the five-arrowed god has pierced my heart which is difficult to be withdrawn from its desire for the unattainable : what then when the mango-trees of the garden, whose pallid leaves have been blown away by the Malaya breeze, are showing fresh sprouts ? [6]

VIDUSHAKA—Away with your lamentations ! Before long this very Love will be agreeable to you by yielding you the object of your desire.

KING—I accept these words of a Brahmin.

(*They pace about*).

VIDUSHAKA—Let my friend notice the beauty of this garden (Pramadavana) heralding the advent of spring.

राजा—ननु प्रतिपादपमेवावलोकयामि । अत्र हि

अग्रे स्त्रीनखपाटलं कुरबकं श्यामं द्वयोर्भागयो-
र्बालाशोकमुपोढरागसुभगं भेदोन्मुखं तिष्ठति ।
ईषद्बद्धरजःकणाग्रकपिशा चूते नवा मञ्जरी
मुग्धत्वस्य च यौवनस्य च सखे मध्ये मधुश्रीः स्थिता ॥७॥

विदूषकः—एसो मणि सिला-पट्टअ-सणाहो अदिमुत्त-
लदामण्डवो भमर-संघट्ट-पडिदेहिं कुसुमेहिं सअं विअ
३ किदोवआरो भवन्तं पडिच्छदि । अणुगेण्हीअदु दाव
एसो । एष मणिशिलापट्टकसनाथः अतिमुक्तलतामण्डपो भ्रमरसंघट्टप-
तितैः कुसुमैः स्वयमिव कृतोपचारो भवन्तं प्रतीच्छति । तदनुगृ-
६ ह्यतां तावदेषः ।

राजा—यथा भवते रोचते । [परिक्रम्योपविष्टौ]

विदूषकः—इह सुहासीणो भवं ललिद-लदा-विलोहोअ-
९ माणणअणो उव्वसी-गदं उक्कण्ठं विणोदेदु । इह सुखा-
सीनो भवान् ललितलताविलोभ्यमाननयनः उर्वशीगतामुत्कण्ठां
विनोदयतु ।

१२ राजा—[निःश्वस्य]

मम कुसुमितास्वपि सखे नोपवनलतासु नम्रविटपासु ।
चक्षुर्बध्नाति धृतिं तद्रूपालोकदुर्ललितम् ॥ ८ ॥

तदुपायश्चिन्त्यतां यथा सफलप्रार्थनो भवेयम् ।

विदूषकः—[विहस्य] भो अहल्ला-कामुअस्स महिन्दस्स
वेज्जो उव्वसीपज्जुस्सुअस्स भवदो अहं वि दुवे एत्थ
३ उम्मत्तआ । भोः अहल्याकामुकस्य महेन्द्रस्य वैद्य उर्वशीपर्युत्सुकस्य
भवतोहमपि द्वावत्रोन्मत्तौ ।

राजा—मा मैवम् । अतिस्नेहः खलु कार्यदर्शी ।

६ विदूषकः—एसो चिन्तेमि । मा उण परिदेविदेण मम

KING—Well! I mark it on every tree. For,

Here is the *Kurabaka* flower red at the tip like a woman's nails, and black at the sides; the young *Ashoka* bud charming owing to increased redness, is ready to burst (into flower); the new blossom of the mango is yellow at the ends as the pollen is yet imperfectly formed; (thus) the Beauty of spring stands, my friend, between childhood and youth. [7]

VIDUSHAKA—The Jasmine-bower yonder, with its slab of marble, seems itself to present you with flowers which have been dropped down by the bees coming into contact with them, and offers you welcome. Please you to favour it.

KING—As you please.

(*They walk about and seat themselves*).

VIDUSHAKA—Now, seated comfortably in this place, you may dissipate your longing for Urvashi with your eyes captivated by these lovely creepers.

KING—(*Sighing*). My eye, grown fastidious by looking on her charms, does not find any pleasure in these garden-plants with their branches bent, although they have now flowered. [8]

So, think of an expedient to secure me the object of my wishes.

VIDUSHAKA—(*Laughing*). Well, the physician to the great Indra who was enamoured of Ahalya, and I to you pining for Urvashi, both are madmen in this affair.

KING—Nay, do not say so. Genuine affection ever counsels wisely.

VIDUSHAKA—Well, I will turn the matter over in my mind; but then you must not disturb my meditation by your sighs.

समाधिं भञ्जिस्ससि [चिन्तां रूपयति] एष चिन्तयामि । मा पुनः परिदेवितेन मम समाधिं भङ्क्ष्यसि ।

राजा—[निमित्तं सूचयित्वा आत्मगतम् ।]

न सुलभा सकलेन्दुमुखी च सा
किमपि चेदमनङ्गविचेष्टितम् ।
अभिमुखोष्विव काङ्क्षितसिद्धिषु
व्रजति निर्वृतिमेकपदे मनः ॥ ९ ॥

[जाताशस्तिष्ठति । ततः प्रविशत्याकाशयानेन उर्वशी चित्रलेखा च ।]

चित्रलेखा—हला कहिं अणिद्दिट्ठकालणं गच्छीअदि । हला क्व अनिर्दिष्टकारणं गम्यते ।

उर्वशी—सहि तदा हेमऊड-सिहरे लदा-विडवेण खण-विग्घिदाआसगमणं मं ओहसिअ किं दाणिं पुच्छसि । सखि तदा हेमकूटशिखरे लताविटपेन क्षणविघ्निताकाशगमनां मामुपहस्य किमिदानीं पृच्छसि ।

चित्रलेखा—किं तस्स राएसिणो पुरूरवस्स सआसं पत्थिदा सि । किं तस्य राजर्षेः पुरूरवसः सकाशं प्रस्थितासि ।

उर्वशी—अअं मे अवहत्थिद-लज्जो ववसाओ । अयं मम अपहस्तितलज्जो व्यवसायः ।

चित्रलेखा—को उण सहीए पुढमं पेसिदो । कः पुनः सख्या प्रथमं प्रेषितः ।

उर्वशी—हिअअं । हृदयम् ।

चित्रलेखा—सअं एव्व साहु संपधारीअदु दाव । स्वयमेव साधु संप्रधार्यतां तावत् ।

उर्वशी—मअणो खु मं णिओएदि । किं एत्थ संपधा-

(*Vidushaka acts as if he is meditating*).

KING—(*Showing that he has perceived an omen, to himself*).

The damsel with her face lovely as the full-orbed moon, is far beyond my reach; and yet here is this act of Love for some reason or another; for, all of a sudden, my mind feels relief as it would when the fulfilment of its desire was nigh [9].

(*Feels hope revived within him. Enter Urvashi and Chitralekha in the air*).

CHITRALEKHA—Tell me, dear girl, whither we are going for some unknown purpose.

URVASHI—How can you ask me such a question, friend, having chaffed me at that time on the peak of the *Hemakuta*, where owing to the branch of some plant I felt a moment's obstacle in my flight in the sky?

CHITRALEKHA—Are you going to meet the royal sage, Pururavas?

URVASHI—Yes, such my venture, and I have thrown to the winds all shame about it.

CHITRALEKHA—And, pray, whom hath my friend sent ahead?

URVASHI—Well, my heart.

CHITRALEKHA—Think well, beforehand, yourself.

URVASHI—Love leads me on: what is there to be considered?

रीअदि । मदनः खलु मां नियोजयति । किमत्र संप्रधार्यते ।

चित्रलेखा--अदो वरं णत्थि मे उत्तरं । अतः परं नास्ति ममोत्तरम् ।

उर्वशी--तेण हि आदिसीअदु मग्गो जह गच्छन्तीणं अन्तराओ ण भवे । तेन हि आदिश्यतां मार्गो यथा गच्छन्त्योरन्तरायो न भवेत् ।

चित्रलेखा--सहि वीसद्धा होहि । णं भअवदा देवगुरुणा अवराइदं णाम सिहा-बन्धण-विज्जं उवदिसन्तेण तिदस—पडिवक्खस्स अलङ्घणिज्जा कदम्ह। सखि विश्रब्धा भव । ननु भगवता देवगुरुणा अपराजितां नाम शिखाबन्धनविद्यामुपदिशता त्रिदशप्रतिपक्षस्य अलङ्घनीये कृते स्वः ।

उर्वशी--अहो विसुमरिदं मे हिअअं । अहो विस्मृतं मम हृदयम् ।

[सिद्धमार्गमासाद्य ।]

चित्रलेखा--एदं भअवदीए भाईरहीए जउँणा-संगम-विसेस-पावणेसु सलिलेसु ओलोअन्तस्स विअ अत्ताणअं पइट्ठाणस्स सिहाभरण-भूदं राएसिणो भवणं उवट्ठिदम्ह । एतद् भगवत्या भागीरथ्या यमुनासंगमविशेषपावनेषु सलिलेष्ववलोकयत इव आत्मानं प्रतिष्ठानस्य शिखाभरणभूतं राजर्षेर्भवनमुपस्थिते स्वः ।

उर्वशी—[विलोक्य] णं वत्तव्वं ठाणन्तर-गदो सग्गो त्ति । [विचार्य] हला कहिं णु खु सो आवण्णाणुकम्पी भवे । ननु वक्तव्यं स्थानान्तरगतः स्वर्ग इति । हला क्व नु खलु स आपन्नानुकम्पी भवेत् ।

चित्रलेखा—एदस्सिं णन्दण-वणेक्कदेसे विअ पमद-वणे ओदरिअ जाणिस्सामो । एतस्मिन् नन्दनवनैकदेश इव प्रमदवने अवतीर्य ज्ञास्यावः ।

CHITRALEKHA—Well then, I make no further question.

URVASHI—Advise me, then, which way we should proceed, so that we may not meet with any impediment on our way.

CHITRALEKHA—Have no fear, dear girl. Have not we two been made inviolable of the enemy of the gods by the revered preceptor of the immortals by imparting to us the mystic art of tying up the hair called the *Aparajita* ?

URVASHI—How could I be so forgetful!
(*Coming to the path of the Siddhas*).

CHITRALEKHA—Here have we come to the palace of the royal sage, the crest-borne gem of Pratisthana, which appears as it were to look at its own reflection in the waters of the divine Ganges, rendered particularly holy by her confluence with the Yamuna.

URVASHI—*(Looking).* Rather it should be said that the heavens have been transferred to another place! *(Reflecting).* But friend, where shall we find him—that pitying friend of the helpless?

CHITRALEKHA—Let us first alight in this Pramadavana which looks like a part of the garden of heaven, and we shall find out.

[उभे अवतरतः ।]

चित्रलेखा—[दृष्ट्वा सहर्षम्] **हला एसो खु पढमोदिदो विअ चन्दो कोमुदिं विअ तुमं पडिच्छदि ।** सखि एष खलु प्रथमोदित इव चन्द्रः कौमुदीमिव त्वां प्रतीक्षते ।

उर्वशी—[विलोक्य] **हला दाणिं पुढम-दंसणादो सविसेसं पिअदंसणो महाराओ पडिहादि ।** सखि इदानीं प्रथमदर्शनात् सविशेषं प्रियदर्शनो महाराजः प्रतिभाति ।

चित्रलेखा—जुज्जदि । ता एहि उवसप्पम्ह । युज्यते । तदेहि उपसर्पावः ।

उर्वशी—तिरक्खरिणी-पडिच्छण्णा पासगदा से भविअ सुणिस्सं दाव । पास-पडिवत्तिणा वअस्सेण सह विअणे किं पि मन्तअन्तो चिट्ठदि । तिरस्करिणीप्रतिच्छन्ना पार्श्वगता अस्य भूत्वा श्रोष्यामि तावत् । पार्श्वपरिवर्तिना वयस्येन सह विजने किमपि मन्त्रयमाणस्तिष्ठति ।

चित्रलेखा—जह दे रोअदि । [यथोक्तमनुतिष्ठतः ।] यथा ते रोचते ।

विदूषकः—भो चिन्तिदो मए दुल्लह-प्पणइणी-समाअमोवाओ । भोः चिन्तितो मया दुर्लभप्रणयिनीसमागमोपायः ।

[राजा तूष्णीमास्ते ।]

उर्वशी—का णु खु एसा इत्थिआ इमिणा पत्थीअमाणा अत्ताणअं विकत्थेदि । का नु खल्वेषा स्त्री अनेन प्रार्थ्यमाना आत्मानं विकत्थते ।

चित्रलेखा—किं उण माणुस्सअं विडम्बीअदि । किं पुनर्मानुष्यं विडम्ब्यते ।

(*Both alight*).

CHITRALEKHA—(*Looking with joy*). Friend, here is he expecting you, like the newly-risen moon expecting moonlight.

URVASHI—(*Observing*) My dear, does not he look more graceful now than when first he met my gaze ?

CHITRALEKHA—Quite so; well then, come along, let us approach.

URVASHI—Let me for a while remain hidden by the power of the *tiraskarini* charm, and approaching him, listen. He seems to be talking something to his friend who is near, in this solitary place.

CHITRALEKHA—As you like it.

(*They do, as said*).

VIDUSHAKA—Well, friend, I have thought out a plan for securing you an interview with the person you love, although she is inaccessible.

(*The King remains silent*).

URVASHI—What woman thinks much of herself (that she should hold out) even when made love to, by him ?

CHITRALEKHA—But why do you act the part of a mortal ?

उर्वशी—भयामि सहसा पभावादो विण्णादुं । बिभेमि सहसा प्रभावाद् विज्ञातुम् ।

विदूषकः—णं भणामि चिन्तिदो उवाओ त्ति । ननु भणामि चिन्तित उपाय इति ।

राजा—तेन हि कथ्यताम् ।

विदूषकः—सिविण-समाअम-आरिणिं णिद्दं सेवदु भवं । अहवा तत्थभोदीए उव्वसीए पडिकिदिं आलिहिअ ओलोअन्तो चिट्ठ । स्वप्नसमागमकारिणीं निद्रां सेवतां भवान् । अथवा तत्रभवत्या उर्वश्याः प्रतिकृतिमालिख्य अवलोकयंस्तिष्ठ ।

उर्वशी—[सहर्षम्] हीण-सत्त हिअअ समस्सस समस्सस । हीनसत्त्व हृदय समाश्वसिहि समाश्वसिहि ।

राजा—उभयमप्यनुपपन्नम् ।

हृदयमिषुभिः कामस्यान्तः सशल्यमिदं सदा
कथमुपलभे निद्रां स्वप्ने समागमकारिणीम् ।
न च सुवदनामालेख्येपि प्रियामसमाप्य तां
मम नयनयोरुद्बाष्पत्वं सखे न भविष्यति ॥ १० ॥

चित्रलेखा—सुदं तुए । श्रुतं त्वया ।

उर्वशी—सुदं । ण उण पज्जत्तं हिअअस्स । श्रुतम् । न पुनः पर्याप्तं हृदयस्य ।

विदूषकः--एत्तिओ मे मदि-विहवो । एतावान् मम मतिविभवः ।

राजा—[सनिःश्वासम्]

नितान्तकठिनां रुजं मम न वेद सा मानसीं
प्रभावविदितानुरागमवमन्यते वापि माम् ।
अलब्धफलनीरसान् मम विधाय तस्मिञ्जने
समागममनोरथान् भवतु पञ्चबाणः कृती ॥ ११ ॥

URVASHI—But I fear too soon to know through my power.

VIDUSHAKA—Well, I say, I have hit upon a plan.

KING—Well then, tell me.

VIDUSHAKA—Let Your Majesty enjoy a nap, which will effect your union in dreams; or delineate a likeness of the lady Urvashi and remain gazing upon the picture.

URVASHI—(*With joy*). Be of good cheer, my timid heart.

KING—Both are impracticable, (I fear).

For the shafts of love are ever rankling inside my breast · how then can I enjoy sleep which in dreams might effect our union ? And even before I have completed the picture of the beloved one with the lovely face, tears would surely not fail to start in my eyes. [11]

CHITRALEKHA—Have you heard ?

URVASHI—Yes I have; but that scarcely sufficeth to comfort my heart.

VIDUSHAKA—Well, my ingenuity extends only so far.

KING—(*Sighing*).

Perhaps she does not know the very keen anguish of my heart; or knowing my love through her supernatural power, she but despises me. Let the God of the five shafts feel happy by making my desires of union with that person void of any pleasure on account of their fruitlessness. [11]

चित्रलेखा—सुदं तुए । श्रुतं त्वया ।

उर्वशी—हद्धी हद्धी । मं एव्वं अवगच्छदि । असमत्थम्हि अग्गदो भविअ से पडिवअणस्स । पहाव-णिम्मिदेण भुज्ज-वत्तेण संपादिदुत्तरा होदुं इच्छामि । हा धिक् हा धिक् । मामेवमवगच्छति । असमर्थास्मि अग्रतो भूत्वा अस्य प्रतिवचनस्य । प्रभावनिर्मितेन भूर्जपत्रेण संपादितोत्तरा भवितुमिच्छामि ।

चित्रलेखा—अणुमदं मे । अनुमतं मम ।

[उर्वशी ससंभ्रमं गृहीत्वा यथोक्तं करोति ।]

विदूषकः—[दृष्ट्वा] **अविहा अविहा । भो किं णु खु एदं भुअङ्ग-णिम्मोअं विअ संमुहे णो णिवडिदं ।** अविहा अविहा । भोः किं नु खल्वेतद् भुजङ्गनिर्मोक इव संमुखे आवयोः निपतितम् ।

राजा—[विभाव्य] **भूर्जपत्रगतोयमक्षरविन्यासः ।**

विदूषकः—ण खु अदिट्ठाए तत्तहोदीए उव्वसीए भवदो परिदेविदं सुणिअ समाणाणुराअ-सूअआइं अक्खराइं विसज्जिआइं होन्ति । न खल्वदृष्टया तत्रभवत्या उर्वश्या भवतः परिदेवितं श्रुत्वा समानानुरागसूचकान्यक्षराणि विसृष्टानि भवन्ति ।

राजा—नास्त्यगतिर्मनोरथानाम् [गृहीत्वा अनुवाच्य । सहर्षम् ।] **सखे प्रसन्नस्ते तर्कः ।**

विदूषकः—भवं दाणिं पसीददु । एत्थ लिहिदं सुणिदुं इच्छामि । भवान् इदानीं प्रसीदतु । अत्र लिखितं श्रोतुमिच्छामि ।

उर्वशी—साहु अज्ज णाअरिओ सि । साधु आर्य नागरिकोसि ।

राजा—श्रूयताम् । [वाचयति]

सामिअ संभाविआ जह अहं तुए अमुणिआ ।
तह अणुरत्तस्स जइ णाम तुह उवरि ॥ १२ ॥

CHITRALEKHA—Have you heard?

URVASHI—Alas! Alas! He takes me to be thus! I cannot confront him and give him answer; so I desire to make answer to him by means of a Bhurja leaf which I will produce through my power.

CHITRALEKHA—I agree.

(Urvashi takes it in haste and does as said).

VIDUSHAKA—(*Seeing*). Holla! What is here, in front of us, that looks like the slough of a snake?

KING—(*Looking closely*). This is some letter written upon a Bhurja-leaf.

VIDUSHAKA—May it be that the lady Urvashi, unperceived, has overheard, your lamentation and has sent this letter indicating therein her equal love for you?

KING—There is nothing to which desires do not soar. *(Takes and reads it; with joy).* Very happy was your guess, my friend.

VIDUSHAKA—Please to favour me; for I desire to hear what may be written on it.

URVASHI—Well said, sir; you have proved yourself a town-gallant.

KING—Listen. (*Reads*).

" Lord, if I am indeed, what in your ignorance, you make me out to be, towards you who love me, how

णं मे लुलिअ-पारिजाअ-सअणिज्जअम्मि होन्ति ।
णन्दण-वण-वाआ वि अच्चुण्हआ सरीरए ॥ १३ ॥

स्वामिन् संभाविता यथाहं त्वया अज्ञाता ।
तथानुरक्तस्य यदि नाम तवोपरि ॥ १२ ॥
ननु मम लुलितपारिजातशयनीये भवन्ति ।
नन्दनवनवाता अप्यत्युष्णकाः शरीरके ॥ १४ ॥

उर्वशी—किं णु खु संपदं भणिस्सदि । किं नु खलु सांप्रतं भणिष्यति ।

३ चित्रलेखा—णं भणिदं एव्व कमल-णालाअमाणेहिं अङ्गेहिं । ननु भणितमेव कमलनालायमानैरङ्गैः ।

विदूषकः—दिट्ठिआ मए विअ बुभुक्खिदेण सोत्थि-
६ वाअणं उवलद्धं भवदा समासासणं । दिष्ट्या मयेव बुभुक्षितेन स्वस्तिवाचनमुपलब्धं भवता समाश्वासनम् ।

राजा—समाश्वासनमिति किमुच्यते ।

तुल्यानुरागपिशुनं ललितार्थबन्धं
पत्रे निवेशितमुदाहरणं प्रियायाः ।
उत्पक्ष्मणो मम सखे मदिरेक्षणाया-
स्तस्याः समागतमिवाननमाननेन ॥ १४ ॥

उर्वशी—एत्थ णो सम-विभाआ पीदी । अत्र आवयोः समविभागा प्रीतिः ।

३ राजा—वयस्य अङ्गुलीस्वेदेन दूष्येरन्नक्षराणि । धार्यतामयं प्रियायाः स्वहस्तः ।

विदूषकः—[गृहीत्वा] किं दाणिं तत्तभोदी उव्वसी भवदो
६ मणोरहाणं कुसुमं दंसिअ फले विसंवददि । किमिदानीं तत्रभवत्युर्वशी भवतो मनोरथानां कुसुमं दर्शयित्वा फले विसंवदति ।

is it that even the heavenly breezes are felt to be so hot to my body even while reclining on a bed of crushed *Parijata* flowers? [12—13]

URVASHI—What, indeed, would he say now?

CHITRALEKHA—Has not he already said, with his limbs acting the part of the lotus-stalk?

VIDUSHAKA—Fortunately now my friend has as much cause for comfort as I should have if I receive a present (*just*) when I feel hungry.

KING—How say you! cause for comfort?

This song of the beloved one, indicative of equal love, and charming in its import, which is put on this leaf, is, as it were, the face of her, with its upturned eyelashes and its bewitching eyes, coming close to my face. [14]

URVASHI—Ours, then, is a case of reciprocal love.

KING—Friend, the sweat of my fingers might soil the characters; do you, therefore, hold this my beloved's autograph.

VIDUSHAKA—(*Holding*). Will the lady Urvashi, now when she has shown you the blossom of your desires, fail to show you the fruit thereof?

उर्वशी—हला जाव उवगमण-कादरं हिअअं पज्जवत्थावेमि दाव तुमं से अत्ताणं दंसिअ जं मे खमं तं भणाहि। हला यावदुपगमनकातरं हृदयं पर्यवस्थापयामि तावत् त्वमस्मै आत्मानं दर्शयित्वा यन्मम क्षमं तद् भण ।

चित्रलेखा—[तिरस्करिणीमपनीय राजानमुपेत्य] जेदु जेदु महाराओ । जयतु जयतु महाराजः ।

राजा—[सहर्षम्] स्वागतं भवत्यै । भद्रे

न तथा नन्दयसि मां सख्या विरहिता तया ।
संगमे पूर्वदृष्टेव यमुना गङ्गया विना ॥ १५ ॥

चित्रलेखा—णं पढमं मेह-राई दीसदि पच्छा विज्जुल्लदा। ननु प्रथमं मेघराजिर्दृश्यते पश्चाद् विद्युल्लता ।

विदूषकः—[अपवार्य] कहं ण एसा उव्वसी । ताए तत्तहोदीए अहिमदा सहअरी । कथं नैषा उर्वशी । तस्यास्तत्रभवत्या अभिमता सहचरी ।

चित्रलेखा—उव्वसी महाराअं सिरसा पणमिअ विण्णवेदि । उर्वशी महाराजं शिरसा प्रणम्य विज्ञापयति ।

राजा—किमाज्ञापयति ।

चित्रलेखा—मह सुरारि-संभवे दुज्जादे महाराओ एव्व सरणं आसि । सा अहं तुह दंसण-समुत्थेण मअणेण बलिअं बाहीअमाणा भूओ वि महाराएण अणुकम्पणीअ त्ति । मम सुरारिसंभवे दुर्जाते महाराज एव शरणमासीत् । साहं तव दर्शनसमुत्थेन मदनेन बलवद् बाध्यमाना भूयोऽपि महाराजेन अनुकम्पनीयेति ।

राजा—भद्रमुखि

पर्युत्सुकां कथयसि प्रियदर्शनां ता-
मार्तं न पश्यसि पुरूरवसं तदर्थे ।

URVASHI—Well, friend, while I compose my heart which has grown faint at the prospect of meeting him, do you disclose yourself and say what is proper about me.

CHITRALEKHA—(*Removing the Tiraskarini and approaching the King*). Glory, Glory, to our Lord!

KING—(*With joy*). Welcome, dear Lady. Fair lady,

In the absence of that dear friend of yours, you give me no more joy than does the Yamuna, first seen at the confluence, in the absence of the Ganges. [15]

CHITRALEKHA—Well, the clouds come first, and then the lightening.

VIDUSHAKA—(*Aside*). How! This is not the lady Urvashi; but the dear friend of Her Ladyship!

CHITRALEKHA—Urvashi bows down her head before the King, and makes the request—

KING—What are her commands?

CHITRALEKHA—That in her (former) peril caused by the enemy of the gods, Your Majesty gave her protection; she, therefore, prays that on this occasion, too, when fiercely assailed by love that has arisen at your sight, Your Majesty should take compassion on her.

KING—Dear Lady,

You tell me that the fair one is pining in love, but you do not see how Pururavas is afflicted on her account. Alike is our request to the God of love; hot iron deserves to be welded with hot iron. [16]

साधारणोयमुभयोः प्रणयः स्मरस्य
तप्तेन तप्तमयसा घटनाय योग्यम् ॥ १६ ॥

चित्रलेखा—[उर्वशीमुपेत्य] हला एहि । तुवत्तो वि णिद्दअदरं मअणं देक्खिअ पिअदमस्स दे दूदि म्हि संवुत्ता । सखि एहि । त्वत्तोपि निर्दयतरं मदनं दृष्ट्वा प्रियतमस्य ते दूत्यस्मि संवृत्ता ।

उर्वशी—[तिरस्करिणीमपनीय] अम्महे लहुअं तुए उज्झिद म्हि । अहो लघु त्वया उज्झितास्मि ।

चित्रलेखा—इदो मुहुत्तादो जाणिस्सं का कं उज्झिस्सदि त्ति । आआरं दाव पडिवज्ज । इतो मुहूर्तात् ज्ञास्यामि का कामुज्झिष्यतीति । आचारं तावत् प्रतिपद्यस्व ।

उर्वशी—[सव्रीडम्] जेदु जेदु महाराओ । जयतु जयतु महाराजः ।

राजा—सुन्दरि

मया नाम जितं यस्य त्वयायं समुदीर्यते ।
जयशब्दः सहस्राक्षादगतः पुरुषान्तरम् ॥ १७ ॥

[हस्ते गृहीत्वा एनामुपवेशयति ।]

विदूषकः—भोदि रण्णो पिअ-वअस्सो बम्हणो किं ण वन्दीअदि । भवति राज्ञः प्रियवयस्यो ब्राह्मणः किं न वन्द्यते ।

[उर्वशी सस्मितं प्रणमति ।]

विदूषकः—सत्थि भोदीए । स्वस्ति भवत्यै ।

देवदूतः—[नेपथ्ये] चित्रलेखे त्वरयोर्वशीम् ।

मुनिना भरतेन यः प्रयोगो
भवतीष्वष्टरसाश्रयो नियुक्तः ।
ललिताभिनयं तमद्य भर्ता
मरुतां द्रष्टुमनाः सलोकपालः ॥ १८ ॥

CHITRALEKHA—(*Approaching Urvashi*). Come, friend; seeing that Love afflicts him more relentlessly than he does you, I have become the messenger of your beloved.

URVASHI—(*Removing the Tiraskarini*). Ah, how suddenly have you deserted me!

CHITRALEKHA—I will soon see who deserts whom. But now offer your salutation.

URVASHI—(*Bashfully*). Victory to the King!

KING—Fair Lady,

Surely have I triumphed, since the word 'victory' which from your lips has never hailed any other person save the thousand-eyed Indra, has now been used by you for (greeting) me. [17]

(*Takes her by the hand and leads her to a seat*).

VIDUSHAKA—Fair lady, here is the dear friend of the King, a Brahmin, who remains unsaluted.

(*Urvashi bows to him smiling*).

VIDUSHAKA—Prosperity attend you!

(*Behind the scenes a messenger of the Gods*)—

Chitralekha, hasten Urvashi.

The Lord of the Gods, together with the guardians of the quarters, desires to witness to-day the play, (so) gracefully acted, which the sage Bharata has taught you, and which contains (all) the eight poetic flavours. [18].

[सर्वे कर्ण ददति । उर्वशी विषादं नाटयति]

चित्रलेखा—सुदं पिअ-सहीए देव-दूदस्स वअणं । अणुमाणीअदु महाराओ । श्रुतं प्रियसख्या देवदूतस्य वचनम् । अनुमान्यतां महाराजः ।

उर्वशी—णत्थि मे वाआ । नास्ति मे वाक् ।

चित्रलेखा—महाराअ पर-वसो अअं जणो । ता महा-राएण अब्भणुण्णादा इच्छदि देवेसु अणवरद्धं अत्ताणअं कादुं । महाराज परवशोऽयं जनः । तद् महाराजेनाभ्यनुज्ञाता इच्छति देवेष्वनपराद्धमात्मानं कर्तुम्

राजा—[कथंचिद् वाचं व्यवस्थाप्य] **नास्मि भवत्योरीश्वर-नियोगप्रत्यर्थी । स्मर्तव्यस्त्वयं जनः ।**

[उर्वशी वियोगदुःखं रूपयन्ती सह सख्या निष्क्रान्ता ।]

राजा—[सनिःश्वासम्] **सखे वैयर्थ्यमिव चक्षुषः संप्रति ।**

विदूषकः—[पत्रं दर्शयितुकामः] **णं पत्तं** [इत्यर्धोक्ते आत्मगतम् ।] **हद्धी हद्धी उव्वसो-दंसण-विम्हिदेण मए तं भुज्ज-वत्तअं पब्भट्ठं पि हत्थादो पमादेण ण विण्णादं ।** नन्वेतत्-हा धिक् हा धिक् । उर्वशीदर्शनविस्मितेन मया तद् भूर्जपत्रं प्रभ्रष्टमपि हस्तात् प्रमादेन न विज्ञातम् ।

राजा—भद्र किमसि वक्तुकाम इव ।

विदूषकः—मा भवं अण्णाइं मुज्झदु । दढं खु तुए बद्ध-भावा उव्वसी । ण सा इदो-गदं अणुराअं सिढिलेदि । मा भवानज्ञानि मुह्यतु । दृढं खलु त्वयि बद्धभावा उर्वशी । न सा इतोगतमनुरागं शिथिलयति ।

(*All Listen; Urvashi gesticulates disappointment*).

CHITRALEKHA—Has my dear friend heard the message of the Gods' messenger? So take your leave of my Lord.

URVASHI—I cannot speak.

CHITRALEKHA—My Lord, this person is subservient to another's will; hence by My Lord's leave she desires not to offend the Gods.

KING—(*Composing his speech with great difficulty*). I do not wish to interrupt the task which your Lords assign you. Only do not forget me.

(*Urvashi gesticulates sorrow at the parting, and departs with her companion*).

KING—(*Sighingly*). In vain, indeed, are we now gifted with sight.

VIDUSHAKA—(*Desiring to show the letter*) Why, this—(*When half through the words—to himself*). Why, bless me, I was so fascinated by the presence of Urvashi, that I did not mark that the Bhurja-leaf slipped unconsciously out of my hands.

KING—Friend, you were about to say something.

VIDUSHAKA—Let not my friend yield to despair. Urvashi is firmly attached to you; she will not relax her attachment towards you.

२४ राजा—ममाप्येतदाशंसि मनः । तया खलु प्रस्थाने

अनीशया शरीरस्य हृदयं स्ववशं मयि ।
स्तनकम्पक्रियालक्ष्यैर्न्यस्तं निःश्वसितैरिव ॥ १९ ॥

विदूषकः—[आत्मगतम्] वेवदि मे हिअअं इमं वेलं तत्तभवदा तस्स भुज्ज-वत्तस्स णाम गेण्हिदव्वं भविस्सदि
३ त्ति । वेपते मे हृदयमिमां वेलां तत्रभवता तस्य भूर्जपत्रस्य नाम ग्रहीतव्यं भविष्यतीति ।

राजा—केनेदानीं दृष्टिं विलोभयामि । [स्मृत्वा] आ उप-
६ नयतु भवान् भूर्जपत्रम् ।

विदूषकः—[विषादं नाटयति ।] हन्त ण दीसदि । गदं उव्वसीए मग्गेण । हन्त न दृश्यते । गतमुर्वश्या मार्गेण ।

९ राजा—सर्वत्र प्रमादी वैधेयः । ननु विचिनोतु भवान् ।

विदूषकः—[उत्थाय] णं इदो भवे इदो भवे [इति विचेतव्यं नाटयति] नन्वितो भवेदितो भवेत् ।

१२ [ततः प्रविशति काशीराजपुत्री सपरिवारा देवी ।]

देवी—हञ्जे णिउणिए सच्चं तुए भणिदं इमं लदा-गेहं पविसन्तो अज्ज-माणवअ-सहाओ अज्जउत्तो दिट्ठो त्ति ।
१५ हञ्जे निपुणिके सत्यं त्वया भणितमिदं लतागेहं प्रविशन्नार्यमाणवकसहाय आर्यपुत्रो दृष्ट इति ।

निपुणिका—किं अण्णहा भट्टिणी मए विण्णविद-पुव्वा ।
१८ किमन्यथा भट्टिनी मया विज्ञापितपूर्वा ।

देवी—तेण हि लदन्तरिदा सुणिस्सं दाव से वीसद्धा-मन्तिदाणि । जं तुए कहिदं तं सच्चं ण व त्ति । तेन
२१ हि लतान्तरिता श्रोष्यामि तावदस्य विश्रब्धामन्त्रितानि । यत् त्वया कथितं तत् सत्यं न वेति ।

KING—My mind, too, is filled with the same hope. For at the time of departing, she,

Not mistress of her own person, seemed to lodge her heart in mine, free as she was to dispose of it, through her sighs indicated by the panting of her bosom. [19]

VIDUSHAKA—(*To himself*). How my heart trembles lest my friend should now mention that Bhurja-leaf !

KING—What shall now console my eyes ? (*Remembering*). Well, friend, give me the Bhurja-leaf.

VIDUSHAKA—(*Gesticulates despair*). Dear me, it is not to be seen--has gone after Urvashi.

KING—A blundering fool, everywhere ! Will you not search for it ?

VIDUSHAKA—(*Rising*). May be, it is here, may be, it is there.

(*Gesticulates searching it*).

(*Enter Queen, the daughter of the King of Kasi, together with her retinue*).

QUEEN—Girl Nipunika, did you tell me the truth when you said you saw my noble Lord entering this arbour with the noble Manavaka ?

NIPUNIKA—Have I ever told a falsehood to my mistress ?

QUEEN—Well, then, screening myself behind the creepers, I will just hear his confidential talk--whether what you told me is right or not.

निपुणिका--जं भट्टिणी आणवेदि्। यद् भट्टिनी आज्ञापयति।

देवी--[परिक्रम्य] **हञ्जे णिउणिए किं एदं जिण्ण-चीरं विअ इदोमुहं दक्खिण-मारुदेण आणीअदि्**। हञ्जे निपुणिके किमेतज्जीर्णचीरमिव इतोमुखं दक्षिणमारुतेन आनीयते।

निपुणिका--[विभाव्य] **भट्टिणि पडिवत्तण-विभाविदक्खरं भुज्ज-वत्तं खु एदं। हन्त भट्टिणीए एव्व णेउर-कोडीए लग्गं।** [गृहीत्वा] **कहं। वाईअदु।** भट्टिनि परिवर्तनविभावितक्षरं भूर्जपत्रं खल्वेतत्। हन्त भर्त्र्या एव नूपुरकोट्या लग्नम्। कथम्। वाच्यताम्।

देवी--अणुवाएहि दाव णं। जदि अविरुद्धं तदो सुणिस्सं। अनुवाचय तावदेतत्। यदि अविरुद्धं ततः श्रोष्यामि।

निपुणिका--[तथा कृत्वा] **भट्टिणि तं एव्व कोलीणं विअ पडिहादि। भट्टारअं उद्दिसिअ उव्वसीए कव्व-बन्धो त्ति तक्केमि। अज्जमाणवअ-पमादेण अम्हाणं हत्थं गदो त्ति।** भट्टिनि तदेव कौलीनमिव प्रतिभाति। भर्तारमुद्दिश्य उर्वश्या काव्यबन्ध इति तर्कयामि। आर्यमाणवकप्रमादेन आवयोर्हस्तं गत इति।

देवी—तेण हि से गहिदत्था होमि। तेन ह्यस्य गृहीतार्था भवामि।

[निपुणिका राज्ञा पूर्ववाचितं वाचयति।]

देवी—एत्थ इमिणा एव्व उवाअणेण अच्छरा-कामुअं पेक्खामि। [इति परिजनसहिता लतागृहं परिक्रामति।] अत्र अनेनैव उपायनेन अप्सरःकामुकं पश्यामि।

विदूषकः—भो वअस्स किं एदं पमद-वण-समीव-गद-कीलापव्वद-पज्जन्ते दीसदि। भो वयस्य किमेतत् प्रमदवनसमीपगतक्रीडापर्वतपर्यन्ते दृश्यते।

NIPUNIKA—As the mistress commands.

QUEEN—(*Moving about*). Girl Nipunika what could this be that is driven along towards us by the southern breeze—looking like a tattered shred of a garment?

NIPUNIKA—(*Looking closely*). Mistress, this is surely a Bhurja-leaf on which are to be seen some characters when it is turned round (by the wind). Why, it has clung to the end of my mistress' anklet. How! Shall I read (it)?

QUEEN—Read it to yourself. If there is nothing objectionable, I will hear it.

NIPUNIKA—(*Doing as bidden*). Mistress, it is that same (story)-what looks like a scandal. It seems to me to be some song of Urvashi addressed to my Lord. It has fallen into our hands by the heedlessness of the noble Manavaka.

QUEEN-Well then, I should like to know its contents. (*Nipunika reads what was formerly read out by the King*).

QUEEN—Well, I will see this nymph-enamoured person here, with this very present.

(*She goes round the arbour along with her retinue*).

VIDUSHAKA—Well, friend, what do you see yonder at the edge of the pleasure-mound near the Pramadavana?

राजा—[उत्थाय] भगवन् वसन्तप्रिय दक्षिणवायो ।

वासार्थं हर संभृतं सुरभिणा पौष्पं रजो वीरुधां
किं मिथ्या भवतो हृतेन दयितास्नेहस्वहस्तेन मे ।
जानीते हि मनोविनोदनफलैरेवंविधैर्धारितं
कामार्तं जनमङ्गनां प्रति भवानालक्षितप्रार्थनः ॥२०॥

निपुणिका—भट्टिणि एदस्स एव्व अण्णेसणा वट्टदि । भट्टिनि एतस्यैवान्वेषणा वर्तते ।

देवी—पेक्खामि । पश्यामि ।

विदूषकः—भो मिलाअमाण-केसरच्छविणा मोर-पिच्छेण विप्पलद्धो म्हि । भो म्लायमानकेसरच्छविना मयूरपिच्छेन विप्रलब्धोऽस्मि ।

राजा—सर्वथा हतोऽस्मि ।

देवी—[उपेत्य] अज्जउत्त अलं आवेएण । एदं तं भुज्जवत्तं । आर्यपुत्र अलमावेगेन । एतत् तद् भूर्जपत्रम् ।

राजा—[ससंभ्रमम्] अये देवी । स्वागतं देव्यै ।

विदूषकः—[अपवार्य] दुरागदं दाणिं संवुत्तं । दुरागतमिदानीं संवृत्तम् ।

राजा—[जनान्तिकम्] सखे किमत्र प्रतिविधेयम् ।

विदूषकः—लोत्तेण गहिदस्स कुम्भीलअस्स अत्थि वा पडिवअणं । लोत्रेण गृहीतस्य कुम्भीरकस्य अस्ति वा प्रतिवचनम् ।

राजा—देवि नेदं मया मृग्यते । स खलु परसमन्वेषणार्थमारम्भोयम् ।

देवी—जुज्जदि अत्तणो सोहग्गं पच्छादेदुं । युज्यत आत्मनः सौभाग्यं प्रच्छादयितुम् ।

KING—(*Rising*). Noble breeze of the south, the friend of spring,

You may remove from the plants the flowery-pollen produced by spring for (scattering). perfume; but why vainly rob me of those characters written through love by my beloved with her own hand? For surely you, who are known to have loved Anjana, know that a love-afflicted person lives on such means intended to solace his heart. [20]

NIPUNIKA—Mistress, they are searching this very thing.

QUEEN—I see.

VIDUSHAKA—O, I was deceived by a peacock-feather of the colour of a faded Kesara flower.

KING—So I am ruined everyway!

QUEEN—(*Approaching*). Noble Lord do not grieve. Here is the Bhurja-leaf.

KING—(*Confusedly*) Oh, the Queen. Welcome, Queen.

VIDUSHAKA—(But) now it is the reverse of welcome.

KING—(*Aside*). Friend, how to meet the present (situation)?

VIDUSHAKA—How can a thief answer for himself, when caught with a portion of the stolen article on his person?

KING—Queen, this was not the object of my search; but I was searching some other object.

QUEEN—It is but proper to conceal one's good fortune.

विदूषकः—भोदि तुवरेहि से भोअणं जं पित्तोवसमणसमत्थं होदि। भवति त्वरयास्य भोजनं यत् पित्तोपशमनसमर्थं भवति।

देवी—णिउणिए सोहणं खु बम्हणेण आसासिदो वअस्सो। निपुणिके शोभनं खलु ब्राह्मणेन आश्वासितो वयस्यः।

विदूषकः—भोदि णं पेक्ख आसासिदो पिसाओ वि भोअणेण। भवति ननु पश्य आश्वासितः पिशाचोपि भोजनेन।

राजा—मूर्ख बलादपराधिनं मामापादयसि।

देवी—णत्थि भवदो अवराहो। अहं एव्व एत्थ अवरद्धा। जा पडिऊल-दंसणा भविअ अग्गदो दे चिट्ठामि। इदो अहं गमिस्सं। [कोपं नाटयित्वा प्रस्थिता।] नास्ति भवतोपराधः। अहमेवात्र अपराद्धा। या प्रतिकूलदर्शना भूत्वा अग्रतस्ते तिष्ठामि। इतोऽहं गमिष्यामि।

राजा—

अपराधी नामाहं प्रसीद रम्भोरु विरम संरम्भात्।
सेव्यो जनश्च कुपितः कथं नु दासो निरपराधः ॥२१॥

[इति पादयोः पतति।]

देवी—[आत्मगतम्] मा खु लहु-हिअआ अहं अणुणअं बहु मण्णे। किं दु अदक्खिण्ण-किदस्स पच्छादावस्स भाएमि। [राजानमपहाय सपरिवारा निष्क्रान्ता।] मा खलु लघुहृदयाहमनुनयं बहु मन्ये। किं तु अदाक्षिण्यकृतात् पश्चात्तापाद् बिभेमि

विदूषकः—पाउस-णदी विअ अप्पसण्णा गदा देवी। उट्ठेहि। प्रावृण्नदीव अप्रसन्ना गता देवी। उत्तिष्ठ।

राजा—[उत्थाय] वयस्य नेदमनुपपन्नम्। पश्य

प्रियवचनशतोपि योषितां
दयितजनानुनयो रसादृते।

VIDUSHAKA—Madam, quickly get ready his dinner, which will be an effectual remedy for his bile.

QUEEN—Nipunika, how well has the Brahmin consoled his friend !

VIDUSHAKA—Madam, don't you see even a ghost is laid by dinner.

KING—Blockhead, how falsely you represent me as guilty !

QUEEN—It is not your fault. It is I that am at fault, since I stand before you even when my presence is disagreeable. I will go from hence.

(*Gesticulates anger and starts to go*).

KING—I confess my guilt; be pleased, O fair one, curb your resentment ; for when the master is angry it cannot be but that the servant is at fault. [21]

(*Prostrates himself at her feet*).

QUEEN—(*To himself*). I am not so light-hearted as to take his importunities seriously. But I am afraid of the remorse that would be caused by my incivility

(*Leaves the King, and departs along with her retinue*).

VIDUSHAKA—Like a turbid river in the rains, Her Majesty has gone off in (high) dudgeon. Rise

KING—(*Rising*). Friend, this is not unreasonable.

The solicitations of a favoured person although full of hundreds of flattering compliments will not

प्रविशति हृदयं न तद्विदां
मणिरिव कृत्रिमरागयोजितः ॥ २२ ॥

विदूषकः—अणुऊलं एत्थभवदो एदं । ण हु अक्खिदुक्खिदो अहिमुहे दीव-सिहं सहेदि । अनुकूलमत्रभवत एतत् । न खल्वक्षिदुःखितः अभिमुखे दीपशिखां सहते ।

राजा—मा मैवम् । उर्वशीगतमनसोपि मे स एव देव्यां बहुमानः । किं तु प्रणिपातलङ्घनादहमस्यां धैर्यमवलम्बिष्ये ।

विदूषकः—चिट्ठदु दाव भवदो धीरदा । बुभुक्खिदस्स बम्हणस्स जीविदं अवलम्बदु भवं । समओ खु ण्हाण-भोअणं सेविदुं । तिष्ठतु तावद् भवतो धीरता । बुभुक्षितस्य ब्राह्मणस्य जीवितमवलम्बतां भवान् । समयः खलु स्नानभोजनं सेवितुम् ।

राजा—[ऊर्ध्वमवलोक्य] गतमर्धं दिवसस्य ।

उष्णालुः शिशिरे निषीदति तरोर्मूलालवाले शिखी
निर्भिद्योपरि कर्णिकारमुकुलान्यालीयते षट्पदः ।
तप्तं वारि विहाय तीरनलिनीं कारण्डवः सेवते
क्रीडावेश्मनि चैष पञ्जरशुकः क्लान्तो जलं याचते ॥२३॥

[इति निष्क्रान्ताः सर्वे ।]

इति द्वितीयोऽङ्कः ।

---

touch a woman's heart in the absence of (real) love; just as a gem artificially coloured finds little favour with those who are the connoisseurs (of that art). [22]

VIDUSHAKA—This is quite agreeable to you. For a person whose eyes are dazzled will not bear the lamp-flame in his face.

KING—Do not think thus. Although my heart is given to Urvashi, yet I retain my former regard for the Queen. Only I will face her courageously now, since she has so disdained my prostrations.

VIDUSHAKA—Talk not of your courage. But please to sustain the life of a famished Brahmin It is indeed (high) time to bathe and eat.

KING—(*Looking upwards*). Half the day is over.

Exhausted by the heat the peacock now rests in the cool basin round the root of (yonder) tree; the bees lie snugly inside the Karnikara buds, having forced them open at the top, the water-fowl leaves the heated water and lurks in the lotus-plant on the brink; while the drooping parrot in its cage in the pleasure-house calls for water [23]

(*Exeunt Omnes*)

HERE ENDS THE SECOND ACT

तृतीयोऽङ्कः ।

[ततः प्रविशतो भरतशिष्यौ ।]

प्रथमः—सखे पल्लव महेन्द्रसदनं गच्छतोपाध्यायेन त्वमासनं प्रतिग्राहितः । अग्निशरणसंरक्षणाय स्थापितोहम् । अतः खलु पृच्छामि । अपि गुरोः प्रयोगेण दिव्या परिषदाराधिता ।

द्वितीयः—गालव ण आणे आराहिदा ण वेत्ति । तस्सिं उण सरस्सई-किद-कव्व-बन्धे लच्छी-सअंवरे तेसु तेसु रसन्तरेसु तम्मआ आसि । किं तु—गालव न जाने आराधिता न वेति । तस्मिन् पुनः सरस्वतीकृतकाव्यबन्धे लक्ष्मीस्वयंवरे तेषु तेषु रसान्तरेषु तन्मयी आसीत् । किं तु—

प्रथमः—सदोषावकाश इव ते वाक्यशेषः ।

द्वितीयः—आम । तर्हिं उव्वसीए वअणं पमाद-क्खलिदं आसि । आम् । तस्मिन्नुर्वश्या वचनं प्रमादस्खलितमासीत् ।

प्रथमः—कथमिव ।

द्वितीयः—लच्छी-भूमिआए वट्टमाणा उव्वसी वारुणी-भूमिआए वट्टमाणाए मेणआए पुच्छिदा । सहि समाअदा एदे तेलोक्कसुपुरिसा सकेसवा लोअ-वाला । कदमस्सिं दे भावाहिणिवेसो त्ति । लक्ष्मीभूमिकायां वर्तमाना उर्वशी वारुणीभूमिकायां वर्तमानया मेनकया पृष्टा । सखि समागता एते त्रैलोक्यसुपुरुषाः सकेशवा लोकपालाः । कतमस्मिंस्ते भावाभिनिवेश इति ।

प्रथमः—ततस्ततः ।

द्वितीयः—तदो ताए पुरिसोत्तमे त्ति भणिदव्वे पुरूरवे

ACT III

(*Enter two disciples of Bharata*).

FIRST—Friend Pallava, you were asked to carry the seat by our preceptor when he had gone to Indra's palace, while I was left behind to keep watch over the holy fire. That is why I ask: Was the assembly of the Immortals pleased with the performance of our master?

SECOND—I do not know whether it was pleased or not. But then it quite lost itself in the various emotions of that play of Lakshmisvayamvara composed by Sarasvati. But—

FIRST—The rest of your sentence seems to imply that there is something wrong.

SECOND—Yes, for Urvashi stumbled in her part.

FIRST—How was it?

SECOND—Urvashi who played the part of Lakshmi was questioned by Menaka who played Varuni's part: Friend here are assembled the best men in the three worlds—the guardians of the spheres together with Keshava To whom inclines your heart?

FIRST—What then?

SECOND—Her reply should have been 'to Purushotta-

त्ति णिग्गदा वाणी । ततस्तया पुरुषोत्तम इति भणितव्ये पुरूरवसीति निर्गता वाणी ।

प्रथमः—भवितव्यतानुविधायीनीन्द्रियाणि । न खलु तामभिक्रुद्धो गुरुः ।

द्वितीयः—सा खु सत्ता उवज्झाएण । महिन्देण उण अणुगहिदा । सा खलु शप्ता उपाध्यायेन । महेन्द्रेण पुनरनुगृहीता ।

प्रथमः—कथमिव ।

द्वितीयः—जेण मम उवदेसो तुए लङ्घिदो तेण ण दे दिव्वं ठाणं हविस्सदि त्ति उवज्झाअस्स सावो । महिन्देण उण पेक्खणावसाणे लज्जावणद-मुही भणिदा जस्सिं बद्धभावा सि तस्स मे रण-सहाअस्स राएसिणो पिअं एत्थ करणिज्जं। सा तुमं जहा-कामं पुरूरवसं उवचिट्ठ जाव सो तुह दिट्ठसंताणो भोदि त्ति। येन ममोपदेशस्त्वया लङ्घितस्तेन न ते दिव्यं स्थानं भविष्यतीति उपाध्यायस्य शापः । महेन्द्रेण पुनः प्रेक्षणावसाने लज्जावनतमुखी भणिता यस्मिन् बद्धभावासि तस्य मे रणसहायस्य राजर्षेः प्रियमत्र करणीयम् । सा त्वं यथाकामं पुरूरवसमुपतिष्ठस्व यावत् स त्वयि दृष्टसंतानो भवेदिति ।

प्रथमः—सदृशं पुरुषान्तरविदो महेन्द्रस्य ।

द्वितीयः—[सूर्यमवलोक्य] कधा-पसङ्गेण अम्हेहिं अवरद्धा अहिसेअ-वेला क्खु उवज्झाअस्स । ता एहि से पास-परिवत्तिणो होम । कथाप्रसङ्गेन अस्माभिरपराद्धा अभिषेकवेला खलूपाध्यायस्य । तदेह्यस्य पार्श्वपरिवर्तिनौ भवावः ।

[इति निष्क्रान्तौ ।]

मिश्रविष्कम्भकः ॥

ma,' but instead, the words 'to Pururavas' escaped her lips.

FIRST—The senses are but the slaves of destiny. Was not our preceptor highly displeased with her

SECOND—Yes, he denounced a curse upon her, but she found favour with Mahendra.

FIRST—How so ?

SECOND—'Since you have forgotten my instruction, you shall lose your divine place;' that was the curse of the preceptor; Mahendra, however, at the end of the performance said to her as she stood with her face bowed in shame, "The royal sage on whom you have set your heart, my ally in battles, is entitled to my favour. Do you, then, as you desire, remain with Pururavas till he beholds the child you will bear him."

FIRST—This was like Mahendra who knows other men's hearts.

SECOND—(*Looking at the Sun*). In the course of the talk, we have indeed passed over our preceptor's time of bathing. Come, then, let us approach him. (*Exeunt*)

END OF THE INTRODUCTORY SCENE

[ततः प्रविशति कञ्चुकी ।]

कञ्चुकी—

सर्वः कल्ये वयसि यतते लब्धुमर्थान् कुटुम्बी
पश्चात्पुत्रैरपहृतभरः कल्पते विश्रमाय ।
अस्माकं तु प्रतिदिनमियं सादयन्ती शरीरं
सेवाकारा परिणतिरहो स्त्रीषु कष्टोऽधिकारः ॥ १ ॥

[परिक्रम्य ।] आदिष्टोऽस्मि सनियमया काशीराजपुत्र्या व्रत
संपादनार्थं मया मानमुत्सृज्य निपुणिकामुखेन पूर्वं
२ याचितो महाराजः । तदेव मद्वचनाद् विज्ञापयेति ।
यावदिदानीमवसितसंध्याजाप्यं महाराजं पश्यामि ।
[परिक्रम्य अवलोक्य च] रमणीयः खलु दिवसावसानवृ-
६ त्तान्तो राजवेश्मनि । इह हि

उत्कीर्णा इव वासयष्टिषु निशानिद्रालसा बर्हिणो
धूपैर्जालविनिःसृतैर्वलभयः संदिग्धपारावताः ।
आचारप्रयतः सपुष्पबलिषु स्थानेषु चार्चिष्मतीः
संध्यामङ्गलदीपिका विभजते शुद्धान्तवृद्धो जनः ॥२॥

[नेपथ्याभिमुखं दृष्ट्वा] अये इत एव प्रस्थितो देवः ।

परिजनवनिताकरार्पिताभिः
परिवृत एव विभाति दीपिकाभिः ।
गिरिरिव गतिमानपक्षलोपा-
दनुतटपुष्पितकर्णिकारयष्टिः ॥ ३ ॥

यावदेनमवलोकनमार्गे स्थितः प्रतिपालयामि ।

[ततः प्रविशति यथानिर्दिष्टो राजा विदूषकश्च ।]

३ **राजा**—[आत्मगतम्]

(Then Enter a Chamberlain)

CHAMBERLAIN—As long as life is vigorous, a married man strives to acquire wealth, and afterwards relieved by his sons of the burden (of family cares) he takes rest; but to persons like us old age is a veritable servitude that saps the body every day! Alas, for the duty of watching over women! [1]

(Walking about), I have been told by the daughter of the King of Kashi who has engaged herself in a vow, that for the fulfilment of that vow she having laid aside all sense of pride, has already requested His Majesty's presence through Nipunika. I have been now asked to make the same request on her behalf. So I will see my Lord who has now finished his evening prayer.

(Walking about and observing). The scene at the palace at the close of the day is certainly so delightful For here,

The peacocks drowsing at the approach of night look like sculptured (figures) on their perches; the pigeons on the terrace-tops are scarcely disting shable from the incense that flows through the lattices: and the old matrons of the inner apartment ready to perform the customary acts (of the hour) are distributing in places adorned with flower-offerings the auspicious lights of evening that are burning brightly. [2]

(Looking towards the curtain)–Ah My Lord is coming hither.

Surrounded by the torches borne in their hands by the female attendants, he looks like a mountain moving because its wings are unclipt, that has the tall, thin, Karnikara trees in full blossom on both its sides. [3]

I shall, therefore, keeping him within sight, wait for him.

(Enter King as described and Vidushaka).

KING—*(To himself)*.

कार्यान्तरितोत्कण्ठं दिनं मया नीतमनतिकृच्छ्रेण ।
अविनोददीर्घयामा कथं नु रात्रिर्गमयितव्या ॥ ४ ॥

कञ्चुकी—[उपगम्य] जयतु जयतु देवः । देवी विज्ञापयति मणिहर्म्यपृष्ठे सुदर्शनश्चन्द्रः । तत्र संनिहितेन देवेन प्रतिपालयितुमिच्छामि यावद् रोहिणीसंयोग इति ।

राजा—आर्य लातव्य विज्ञाप्यतां देवी यस्ते छन्द इति ।

कञ्चुकी—यदाज्ञापयति देवः ।

[इति निष्क्रान्तः]

राजा—वयस्य किं परमार्थत एव देव्या व्रतनिमित्तोऽयमारम्भः स्यात् ।

विदूषकः—भो तक्केमि जाद-पच्छादावा तत्तभोदी वदावदेसेण भवदो पणिपाद-लङ्घणं पमज्जिदु-काम त्ति ।
भोः तर्कयामि जातपश्चात्तापा तत्रभवती व्रतापदेशेन भवतः प्रणिपातलङ्घनं प्रमार्ष्टुकामेति ।

राजा—उपपन्नं भवानाह । तथा हि

अवधूतप्रणिपाताः पश्चात्संतप्यमानमनसोऽपि ।
निभृतैर्व्यपत्रपन्ते दयितानुनयैर्मनस्विन्यः ॥ ५ ॥

तदादेशय मणिहर्म्यपृष्ठमार्गम् ।

विदूषकः—इदो इदो भवं । इमिणा गङ्गा-तरङ्ग-सस्सिरीएण फलिहमणि-सोवाणेण आरोहदु भवं पदोसावसररमणिज्जं मणिहम्मिअं । इत इतो भवान् । एतेन गङ्गातरङ्गसश्रीकेण स्फटिकमणिसोपानेन आरोहतु भवान् प्रदोषावसररमणीयं मणिहर्म्यम् ।

राजा—आरोहाग्रतः ।

[सर्वे सोपानारोहणं रूपयन्ति ।]

विदूषकः—[विलोक्य] भो पच्चासण्णेण चन्दोदएण

I could pass the day without much difficulty as the cares of state drowned all anxious thoughts of love; but how am I to pass the night which, on account of the absence of any diversion, will be (drearily) long in its watches? [4]

CHAMBERLAIN—(*Approaching.*) Glory to our Lord! Her Majesty requests: "The terrace of the crystal pavilion affords a glorious view of the Moon; so in the presence of My Lord I desire to wait there till the Moon enters the asterism Rohini."

KING—Noble Latavya, say to the Queen, "(Do) as it pleases you."

CHAMBERLAIN—As Your Majesty commands.

(*Exit*).

KING—Friend, do you think it is really on account of a vow that the Queen undertakes these proceedings?

VIDUSHAKA—Well, my view is that her ladyship, stung with remorse, wishes to efface the indignity with which she treated your prostration, under the pretext of her (present) vow.

KING—You speak the truth; for,

Proud women having slighted the prostrations of their lord, are subsequently filled with repentance; yet with all this they are secretly ashamed of doing any acts conciliating their beloved ones. [5]

VIDUSHAKA—This way, this way, sir. Here, up the flight of crystal steps gleaming (white) like the waves of the Ganges, do you, sir, ascend the crystal palace which looks so lovely at eventide.

KING—Do you ascend first.

(*All act ascending the flight of steps*).

होदव्वं । जह तिमिर--रेईअमाणं पुव्व-दिसा-मुहं आ-
लोअ-सुहअं दीसदि । भोः प्रत्यासन्नेन चन्द्रोदयेन भवितव्यम् ।
१२ यथा तिमिररिच्यमानं पूर्वदिशामुखमालोकसुभगं दृश्यते ।

राजा--सम्यगाह भवान् ।

उदयगूढशशाङ्कमरीचिभिस्तमसि दूरमितः प्रतिसारिते ।
अलकसंयमनादिव लोचने हरति मे हरिवाहनदिङ्मुखम् ॥६॥

विदूषकः--ही ही । भो एसो खण्ड-मोदअ-स्सिरीओ
उदिदो राआ दुआदीणं । ही ही । भोः एष खण्डमोदकसश्रीक
उदितो राजा द्विजातीनाम् ।

राजा—[सस्मितम्] सर्वमौदरिकस्य अभ्यवहार्यमेव
विषयः [प्राञ्जलिः प्रणिपत्य] भगवन्क्षपानाथ

रविमावसते सतां क्रियायै सुधया तर्पयते सुरान् पितृंश्च ।
तमसां निशि मूर्च्छतां निहन्त्रे हरचूडानिहितात्मने नमस्ते ॥७॥

[उत्तिष्ठति]

विदूषकः—भो बम्हणसंकामिदक्खरेण दे पिदामहेण
३ अब्भणुण्णादो आसण-ट्ठिदो होहि जाव अहं पि सुहा-
सीणो होमि । भोः ब्राह्मणसंक्रामिताक्षरेण ते पितामहेन अभ्यनुज्ञातः
आसनस्थितो भव यावदहमपि सुखासीनो भवामि ।

६ राजा—[विदूषकवचनं परिगृह्य उपविष्टः । परिजनं विलोक्य]
अभिव्यक्तायां चन्द्रिकायां किं दीपिकापौनरुक्त्येन ।
विश्राम्यन्तु भवत्यः ।

परिजनः—जं देवो आणवेदि । यद् देव आज्ञापयति ।

[इति निष्क्रान्तः ।]

VIDUSHAKA—O, the Moon is just about to rise since the Eastern horizon, relieved of darkness is so lovely to view.

KING—You spoke the truth.

For, now that the (evening) gloom retires before the rays of the Moon that is hid behind the rising mountain, the face of the East captivates my eyes as though her (masses of) hair are pound up. [6]

VIDUSHAKA—Ha! Ha! Yonder riseth the King of the twice-born, looking like a broken ball of sweets!

KING—(*Smiling*). A gourmet thinks of nothing else but food everywhere.

(*Bowing with folded hands*) Divine Lord of the Night

Bow to you who dwell in the sun to enable the righteous to perform the religious rites; who regale the gods and the Manes with ambrosia; who destroy darkness prevailing at night, and who have placed yourself in the crest of Hara. [7]

(*Rises*)

VIDUSHAKA—Sir, through this Brahmin to whom he communicates his words, your grand-sire bids you sit, that I too, may repose myself.

KING—(*Saying 'yes sits; looking at the attendants*). When the Moon shines splendidly, why the superfluous light of lamps ? Rest ye.

ATTENDANTS—As Your Majesty commands.

(*Exeunt*)

राजा—[चन्द्रमसमवलोक्य] वयस्य परं मुहूर्तादागमनं देव्याः । तद् विविक्ते कथयिष्यामि त्वामवस्थाम् ।

विदूषकः—णं दीसदि एव्व सा । किं दु तारिसं अणुराअं पेक्खिअ सक्कं आसा-बन्धेण अत्ताणं धारेदुं । ननु दृश्यत एव सा किं तु तादृशमनुरागं दृष्ट्वा शक्यमाशाबन्धेन आत्मानं धारयितुम् ।

राजा—एवमेतत् । बलवान् पुनर्मम मनसोभितापः ।

नद्या इव प्रवाहो विषमशिलासंकटस्खलितवेगः ।
विघ्नितसमागमसुखो मनसिशयः शतगुणोभवति ॥८॥

विदूषकः—जहा परिहीयमाणेहिं अङ्गेहिं अहिअं सोहसि तहा अदूरे पिअ-समागमं ते पेक्खामि । यथा परिहीयमानैरङ्गैरधिकं शोभसे तथा अदूरे प्रियासमागमं ते पश्यामि ।

राजा—[निमित्तं सूचयित्वा] वयस्य

वचोभिराशाजननैर्भवानिव गुरुव्यथम् ।
अयं मां स्पन्दितैर्बाहुराश्वासयति दक्षिणः ॥ ९ ॥

विदूषकः—ण हु अण्णहा बम्हणस्स वअणं । न खलु अन्यथा ब्राह्मणस्य वचनम् ।

[राजा सप्रत्याशस्तिष्ठति]

[प्रविश्य आकाशयानेन अभिसारिकावेषा उर्वशी चित्रलेखा च ।]

उर्वशी—[आत्मानं विलोक्य] हला चित्तलेहे अवि रोअदि दे अअं मे अप्पाभरण-भूसिदो णीलंसुअ-परिग्गहो अहिसारिआ-वेसो । हला चित्रलेखे अपि रोचते तेऽयं मे अल्पाभरणभूषितो नीलांशुकपरिग्रहोऽभिसारिकावेषः ।

चित्रलेखा—णत्थि मे वाआ-विहवो पसंसिदुं । इदं तु

KING—(*Looking at the Moon*). Friend, the Queen will be coming after a while; so now, in this solitude I will describe to you my condition.

VIDUSHAKA—Why, that is so manifest. But it is possible to keep up your spirits with hope considering the intensity of Urvashi's love for you.

KING—That is true; and yet severe is the agony of my heart.

My fond desire becomes more fervid as (fresh) impediments obstruct the pleasure of union, as the current of a river, checked by uneven rocks, splits itself into hundred streams. [8]

VIDUSHAKA—Since even with limbs attenuated you look more handsome, therefore, I argue that your meeting with the beloved is not far distant.

KING—(*Showing that he perceives an omen.*) Friend my right arm by its pulsations soothes me that am heavily suffering, like you with hope-inspiring words. [9]

VIDUSHAKA—Surely the words of a Brahmin will never be falsified

(*The King is filled with hope revived*).

(*Enter in the air Urvashi dressed as an Abhisarika and Chitralekha*).

URVASHI—(*Looking at herself*). Now dear Chitralekha, what say you to these blue robes of an Abhisarika thus scantily trimmed with ornaments?

चिन्तेमि । अवि णाम अहं पुरूरवा भवेअं त्ति । नास्ति मे वाग्विभवः प्रशंसितुम् । इदं तु चिन्तयामि । अपि नामाहं पुरूरवा भवेयमिति ।

उर्वशी—सहि मदणो खु तुमं आणवेदि ! सिग्घं णेहि मं तस्स सुहअस्स वसदिं । सखि मदनः खलु त्वामाज्ञापयति । शीघ्रं नय मां तस्य सुभगस्य वसतिम् ।

चित्रलेखा—णं एदं परिवत्तिदं विअ केलास-सिहरं पिअदमस्स दे भवणं उवगद म्ह । नन्वेतत् परिवर्तितमिव कैलासशिखरं प्रियतमस्य ते भवनमुपगते स्वः ।

उर्वशी—तेण हि पहावदो जाणाहि दाव कहिं सो मम हिअअचोरो किं वा अणुचिट्ठदि त्ति । तेन हि प्रभावात् जानीहि तावत् क्व स मम हृदयचोरः किं वानुतिष्ठतीति ।

चित्रलेखा—[ध्यात्वा । आत्मगतम्] **भोदु कीलिस्सं दाव एदाए ।** [प्रकाशम्] **हला एसो मणोरह-लद्ध-पिआ-समाअम-सुहं अणुहवन्तो उवहोअ-क्खमे ओआसे चिट्ठदि ।** भवतु क्रीडिष्यामि तावदेतया । हला एष मनोरथलब्धप्रियासमागमसुखमनुभवन्नुपभोगक्षमेऽवकाशे तिष्ठति ।

[उर्वशी विषादं नाटयति ।]

चित्रलेखा—मुद्धे का उण अण्णा चिन्ता पिआ-समाअमस्स । मुग्धे का पुनरन्या चिन्ता प्रियासमागमस्य ।

उर्वशी—[सोच्छ्वासम्] **अदक्खिणं संदेहदि मे हिअअं ।** अदक्षिणं संदिग्धे मे हृदयम् ।

चित्रलेखा—[विलोक्य] **एसो मणि-हम्मिअ-गदो वअस्स मेत्त-सहाओ राएसी । ता एहि उवसप्पाम णं ।** एष मणिहर्म्यगतो वयस्यमात्रसहायो राजर्षिः । तदेहि । उपसर्पाव एनम् ।

उभे अवतरतः ।

राजा—वयस्य रजन्या सह विजृम्भते मदनबाधा ।

CHITRALEKHA—Words fail me to describe it. But this is what is in my mind Would that I were Pururavas!

URVASHI—Dear, Love himself bids you-take me quick to that loved one's dwelling.

CHITRALEKHA—Here we come to your lover s palace which looks like the summit of Kailasa changed into another form

URVAS —Know, then, through your power where he is, that thief who - has stolen my heart, and what employs him.

CHITRALEKHA—(*Contemplating to herself*). Well, I shall chaff her a bit. (*Aloud*) Friend, here he is in a place fit for enjoyment, happy in the company of his beloved whom he has obtained according to his wishes.

(*Urvashi expresses despair*).

CHITRALEKHA—Child, but why any other thought about the company of the beloved?

URVASHI—(*Sighing*). My unkind heart becomes suspicious.

CHITRALEKHA—Here is the royal sage with his friend as his only attendant in the crystal palace. So come let us advance towards him.

(*They descend*).

KING—Friend, how do the torments of Love increase with the night!

उर्वशी--अणिब्भिण्णत्थेण इमिणा वअणेण आकम्पिदं मे हिअअं । अन्तरिदा एव्व सुणाम से सेरालावं जाव णो संसअ-च्छेदो होदि । अनिर्भिन्नार्थेन अनेन वचनेन आकम्पितं मम हृदयम् । अन्तरिते एव शृणुवः अस्य स्वैरालापं यावदावयोः संशयच्छेदो भवति ।

चित्रलेखा--जं दे रोअदि । यत् ते रोचते ।

विदूषकः--णं इमे अमिअ-गब्भा सेवीअन्तु चन्द-पादा । नन्वेते अमृतगर्भाः सेव्यन्तां चन्द्रपादाः ।

राजा--वयस्य एवमादिभिरनुपक्रम्योयमातङ्कः । पश्य ।

कुसुमशयनं न प्रत्यग्रं न चन्द्रमरीचयो
न च मलयजं सर्वाङ्गीणं न वा मणियष्टयः ।
मनसिजरुजं सा वा दिव्या समालगपोहितुम्-

उर्वशी--का वा अवरा । का वापरा ।

राजा--

रहसि लघयेदारब्धा वा तदाश्रयिणी कथा ॥ १० ॥

उर्वशी--हिअअ दाणिं मं उज्झिअ इदो संकन्तेण तुए फलं उवलद्धं । हृदय इदानीं मामुज्झित्वा इतः संक्रान्तेन त्वया फलमुपलब्धम् ।

विदूषकः--आम । हंपि जदा मिट्ठ-हरिणी-मंस-भोअणं ण लहे तदा णं पत्थअन्तो संकित्तअन्तो आसासेमि । आम् । अहमपि यदा मिष्टहरिणीमांसभोजनं न लभे तदा एतत प्रार्थयमानः संकीर्तयन्नाश्वसिमि ।

राजा--संपद्यत इदं भवतः ।

विदूषकः--भवं पि तं अचिरेण पाविस्सदि । भवानपि तामचिरेण प्राप्स्यति ।

URVASHI—My heart is all in a flutter at these dubious words; let us, therefore, remain invisible and overhear his unreserved utterances till doubt be all dispersed.

CHITRALEKHA—Just as you please.

VIDUSHAKA—You should enjoy the rays of the Moon that are charged with ambrosia.

KING—Friend, small is the power of such remedies to mitigate this malady. Mark,

Neither fresh flower-beds, nor the rays of the Moon, nor sandal-smearing all over the body nor jewel-necklaces will allay the pangs of Love; she alone - that woman divine can do it——

URVASHI—And who else?

KING—Or secret converse regarding her can mitigate (the suffering). [10]

URVASHI—My heart, now have you reaped the fruit of having gone over to him after deserting me.

VIDUSHAKA—Quite so. I too, when I do not get a dinner of dainty venison, but feel a desire for it, take comfort in speaking about it.

KING—But you get that.

VIDUSHAKA—And you too will get her in a short time.

राजा--सखे एवं मन्ये-

चित्रलेखा--सुणु असंतुट्ठे सुणु । शृणु असंतुष्टे शृणु ।

विदूषकः--कहं विअ । कथमिव ।

राजा-

अयं तस्या रथक्षोभादंसेनांसो निपीडितः ।
एकः कृती शरीरेऽस्मिन् शेषमङ्गं भुवो भरः ॥ ११ ॥

चित्रलेखा—किं दाणिं विलम्बीअदि। किमिदानीं विलम्ब्यते।

उर्वशी—[सहसोपसृत्य] हला अग्गदो वि मम गदाए उदासीणो विअ महाराओ । हला अग्रतोपि मम गताया उदासीन इव महाराजः ।

चित्रलेखा—[सस्मितम्] अदितुवरिदे अणुक्खित्त-तिरक्खरिणीआ सि । अतित्वरिते अनुत्क्षिप्ततिरस्करिणीकासि ।

[नेपथ्ये ।] इदो इदो भट्टिणी । इत इतो भर्त्री ।

[सर्वे कर्णं ददति ।]

[उर्वशी सह सख्या विपण्णा ।]

विदूषकः—अविहा अविहा उवट्ठिदा देवी । ता वाअंजमो होहि । अविहा अविहा उपस्थिता देवी । तद् वाचंयमो भव ।

राजा—भवानपि संवृताकारमास्ताम् ।

उर्वशी—हला किं एत्थ करणिज्जं । हला किमत्र करणीयम् ।

चित्रलेखा—अलं आवेएण । अन्तरिदा वयं । उववासणिअमवेसा राएसि-महिसी दीसदि । ता ण एसा चिरं चिट्ठिस्सदि । अलमावेगेन । अन्तर्हिते आवाम् । उपवासनियमवेषा राजर्षिमहिषी दृश्यते । तन्नैषा इह चिरं स्थास्यति ।

[ततः प्रविशति औपहारिकहस्तपरिजना देवी ।]

देवी--[परिक्रम्य अवलोक्य च] हञ्जे णिउणिए एसो रोहिणी-संजोएण अहिअं सोहदि भअवं मिअ-लञ्छणो।

KING—Friend, I think that——

CHITRALEKHA—Hear, unsatisfied that you are, hear.

VIDUSHAKA—What ?

KING—This shoulder that was pressed by hers owing to the jolting of the chariot is the only limb that exists with reason; the rest is a mere burden to the earth. [11]

CHITRALEKHA—Why do you delay now ?

URVASHI—(*Suddenly advancing*) Friend, although I stand in his presence, he deigns not to regard me !

CHITRALEKHA—(*Smiling*). O impatient one, you have not put off the Tiraskarini.

(*Behind the Scenes*).

This way, mistress, this way,

(*All Listen*).

(*Urvashi and her friend feel despair*).

VIDUSHAKA—Holla, the Queen is here: you had better be mute.

KING—You, too, should conceal the expression of your face

URVASHI—What may we do now, dear ?

CHITRALEKHA—Don't you worry. We are invisible. The Queen of the royal sage wears a dress befitting the observance of a fast: she will, therefore, not tarry here long.

(*Enter Queen with attendants carrying materials of worship*).

QUEEN—(*Walking about and seeing*). Girl Nipunika

हञ्जे निपुणिके एष रोहिणीसंयोगेन अधिकं शोभते भगवान् मृगलाञ्छनः ।

चेटी—णं देवी-सहिदो भट्टा विसेस-रमणिज्जो [परिक्रामति] ननु देवीसहितो भर्ता विशेषरमणीयः ।

विदूषकः—[दृष्ट्वा] भो ण जाणामि सोत्थि-वाअणं देइ त्ति आदु भवदो वद-व्ववदेसेण मुक्क-रोसा पणि-पाद-लङ्घणं पमज्जिदुकामा त्ति अज्ज मे अक्खीणं सुह-दंसणा देवी । भो न जानामि स्वस्तिवायनं ददातीति अथवा भवतो व्रतव्यपदेशेन मुक्तरोषा प्रणिपातलङ्घनं प्रमार्ष्टुकामेति अद्य ममाक्ष्णोः शुभदर्शना देवी ।

राजा—[सस्मितम्] उभयमपि घटते । तथापि भवता यत् पश्चादभिहितं तन्मां प्रति भाति । यदत्रभवती

सितांशुका मङ्गलमात्रभूषणा
पवित्रदूर्वाङ्कुरलाञ्छितालका ।
व्रतापदेशोज्झितगर्ववृत्तिना
मयि प्रसन्ना वपुषैव लक्ष्यते ॥ १२ ॥

देवी—[उपगम्य] जदु जेदु अज्जउत्तो । जयतु जयतु आर्यपुत्रः ।

परिजनः—जेदु जेदु भट्टा । जयतु जयतु भर्ता ।

विदूषकः—सत्थि भोदीए । स्वस्ति भवत्यै ।

राजा—स्वागतं देव्यै [तां हस्तेन गृहीत्वा उपवेशयति]

उर्वशी—हला इअं ठाणे देवी-सद्देण उवअरीअदि । ण किं पि परिहीअदि सचीए ओजस्सिदाए । हला इयं स्थाने देवीशब्देनोपचर्यते । न किमपि परिहीयते शच्या ओजस्वितया ।

this union with the constellation of Rohini yields new brilliance to the divine Moon.

ATTENDANT—Does not His Majesty in the company of the Queen look so beautiful?

VIDUSHAKA—I do not know whether because she is to offer a present, or because using the occasion of the vow to lay aside her anger she (in fact) wishes to obliterate the recollection of her contemptuous treatment of your prostration–but Her Majesty to my eyes looks very charming to-day.

KING—(*Looking*). Both are likely; but what you said last appears to my mind to be the truth; her ladyship,

> Clad in white garments, wearing only (a few) auspicious ornaments, and with the tresses of her hair marked by the sprouts of holy Durva grass, appears to be reconciled to me by her very bodily appearance which has dismissed its haughty bearing under the pretext of a vow. [12]

QUEEN—(*Approaching*) Glory to my noble Lord!

ATTENDANTS—Glory to our Lord!

VIDUSHAKA—Prosperity attend your Ladyship!

KING—Queen, welcome. (*Takes her by the hand and leads her to a seat*).

URVASHI—Friend, how properly is she called "Devi"; for she does not fall short of Shachi in dignity.

चित्रलेखा—साहु असूआ-परम्मुहं मन्तिदं । साधु असूयापराङ्मुखं मन्त्रितम् ।

देवी—अज्जउत्तं पुरो करिअ को वि वद-विसेसो मए संपादणीओ । ता मुहुत्त उवरोहो सहीअदु । आर्यपुत्रं पुरस्कृत्य कोपि व्रतविशेषो मया संपादनीयः । तद् मुहूर्तमुपरोधः सह्यताम् ।

राजा—मा मैवम् । अनुग्रहः खलु नोपरोधः ।

विदूषकः—ईरिसो सोत्थि-वाअणवन्तो उवरोहो बहुसो होदु । ईदृशः स्वस्तिवायनवानुपरोधो बहुशो भवतु ।

राजा—किंनामधेयमेतद् देव्या व्रतम् ।

[देवी निपुणिकामवेक्षते ।]

निपुणिका—भट्टा पिआणुप्पसादणं णाम । भर्तः प्रियानुप्रसादनं नाम ।

राजा—[देवीं विलोक्य] **यद्येवम्**

अनेन कल्याणि मृणालकोमलं
व्रतेन गात्रं ग्लपयस्यकारणम् ।
प्रसादमाकाङ्क्षति यस्तवोत्सुकः
स किं त्वया दासजनः प्रसाद्यते ॥ १३ ॥

उर्वशी—महन्तो खु से इमस्सि बहु-माणो । महान् खल्वस्य एतस्यां बहुमानः ।

चित्रलेखा—अइ मुद्धे अण्ण-संकन्त-प्पेम्माणो णाअरिआ अधिअं दक्खिणा होन्ति । अयि मुग्धे अन्यसंक्रान्तप्रेमाणो नागरिका अधिकं दक्षिणा भवन्ति ।

देवी—[सस्मितम्] **णं इमस्स वद-परिग्गहस्स अअं पहावो जं एत्तिअं मन्ताविदो अज्जउत्तो ।** नन्वेतस्य व्रतपरिग्रहस्य अयं प्रभावः यदेतावद् मन्त्रित आर्यपुत्रः ।

CHITRALEKHA—Good, you speak without envy.

QUEEN—I have to fulfil a certain vow with my noble Lord's help: bear with the moment's inconvenience it may cause.

KING—Do not speak thus. It is, indeed, a favour and no inconvenience.

VIDUSHAKA—Would that such inconvenience often befall, that I might each time receive presents!

KING—What is the name of the Queen's vow?

(*Queen looks at Nipunika*).

NIPUNIKA—My Lord, the conciliation of the beloved.

KING—(*Looking to the Queen*). If that is so,

Then it is needless, O fair one, to wear this form, delicate as the lotus-stem, with this vow. How, do you propitiate this slave of yours who eagerly seeks your favour! (13)

URVASHI—Great indeed is his regard for her.

CHITRALEKHA—You simple one, these citizens when they transfer their affections to other women, become, indeed, very courteous (to their wives).

QUEEN—(*Smiling*). Such the effect of the vow that My Lord is made to speak thus.

विदूषकः—विरमदु भवं । ण जुत्तं सुहासिदं पच्चाचरिदुं । विरमतु भवान् । न युक्तं सुभाषितं प्रत्याचरितुम् ।

देवी—दारिआओ उवणेध ओवहारिअं जाव मणिहम्मिअ-गदे चन्द-पादे अच्चेमि । दारिका उपनयत औपहारिकं यावद् मणिहर्म्यगतांश्चन्द्रपादानर्चामि ।

परिजनः—एसो गन्ध-कुसुमादिउवहारो । एष गन्धकुसुमाद्युपहारः ।

देवी—[नाट्येन गन्धपुष्पादिभिश्चन्द्रपादानभ्यर्च्य] **हञ्जे इमे ओवहारिअ-मोदए अज्ज-माणवअं लम्भावेहि ।** हञ्जे एतानौपहारिकमोदकानार्यमाणवकं लम्भय ।

परिजनः—जं देवी आणवेदि । अज्ज-माणवअ एदं दाव दे । यद् देवी आज्ञापयति । आर्यमाणवक एतत् तावत् ते ।

विदूषकः—[मोदकशरावं गृहीत्वा] **सोत्थि भोदीए । बहुफलो दे उववासो होदु ।** स्वस्ति भवत्यै । बहुफलस्तवोपवासो भवतु ।

देवी—अज्जउत्त इदो दाव । आर्यपुत्र इतस्तावत् ।

राजा—अयमस्मि ।

देवी—[राज्ञः पूंजामभिनीय प्राञ्जलिः प्रणिपत्य] **एसा अहं देवदामिहुणं रोहिणी-मिअ-लञ्छणं सक्खी-करिअ अज्ज-उत्तं अणुप्पसादेमि । अज्ज-प्पहुदि जं इत्थिअं अज्जउत्तो पत्थेदि जा अज्जउत्तस्स समाअमप्पणइणी ताए मए पीदि-बन्धेण वत्तिदव्वं त्ति ।** एषाहं दवतामिथुनं रोहिणीमृगलाञ्छनं साक्षीकृत्य आर्यपुत्रमनुप्रसादयामि । अद्यप्रभृति यां स्त्रियमार्यपुत्रः प्रार्थयते या आर्यपुत्रस्य समागमप्रणयिनी तया मया प्रीतिबन्धेन वर्तितव्यमिति ।

VIDUSHAKA—Forbear, my friend. You ought not to oppose auspicious words.

QUEEN—Girls, bring to me the materials of worship, that I may worship the rays of the Moon that have streamed into this crystal palace.

ATTENDANT—Here are materials of worship—sandal, flowers and others.

QUEEN—(*Acting worshipping the rays of the Moon with sandal, flowers etc.*). Girl, offer these sweets used in the worship to the noble Manavaka.

ATTENDANT—As the Queen commands. Noble Manavaka, this is for you.

VIDUSHAKA—(*Taking the platter of the Sweets*). Prosperity attend your Ladyship! May your fast bear manifold fruits!

QUEEN—My Lord, please to come here.

KING—Here I come.

QUEEN—(*Acting worshipping the King, and bowing with folded hands*). In the presence of these twin divinities—Rohini and the Moon—I now conciliate my noble Lord: henceforth whatever woman attracts my Lord's regard, or desires union with him, will be treated by me with kind complacency.

उर्वशी—अम्हहे ण आणे किं-परं से वअणं ति। मम उण वीसास-विसदं हिअअं संवुत्तं। अहो न जाने किंपरमस्या वचनमिति। मम पुनर्विश्वासविशदं हृदयं संवृत्तम्।

चित्रलेखा—सहि महाणुहावाए पदिव्वदाए अब्भणुण्णादो अणन्तराओ दे पिअ-समाअमो हविस्सदि। सखि महानुभावया पतिव्रतया अभ्यनुज्ञातः अनन्तरायस्ते प्रियसमागमो भविष्यति।

विदूषकः—[अपवार्य] **छिन्न-हत्थो मच्छे पलाइदे णिव्विण्णो धीवरो भणादि धम्मो मे हविस्सदि त्ति।** [प्रकाशम्] **भोदि किं तारिसो पिओ तत्तभवं।** छिन्नहस्तो मत्स्ये पलायिते निर्विण्णो धीवरो भणति धर्मो मे भविष्यतीति। भवति किं तादृशः प्रियस्तत्रभवान्।

देवी—मूढ अहं खु अत्तणो सुहावसाणेण अज्जउत्तं णिव्वुदसरीरं कादुं इच्छामि। एत्तिएण चिन्तेहि दाव पिओ ण व त्ति। मूढ अहं खलु आत्मनः सुखावसानेन आर्यपुत्रं निर्वृतशरीरं कर्तुमिच्छामि। एतावता चिन्तय तावत् प्रियो न वेति।

राजा—

दातुं वा प्रभवसि मामन्यस्मै कर्तुमेव वा दासम्।
नाहं पुनस्तथा त्वं यथा हि मां शङ्कसे भीरु ॥ १४ ॥

देवी—होहि वा मा वा। जधा-णिद्दिट्ठं संपादिदं पिआणुप्पसादणं वदं। दारिआओ एध गच्छम्ह। [प्रस्थिता देवी] भव वा मा वा। यथानिर्दिष्टं संपादितं प्रियानुप्रसादनं व्रतम्। दारिका एत गच्छामः।

राजा—प्रिये न खलु प्रसादितोऽस्मि यदि संप्रति विहाय गम्यते।

URVASHI—Well, I am scarce able to divine her purport, yet mightily do these words assuage the apprehensions of my heart.

CHITRALEKHA—Friend, nothing will anymore impede your union with your love, now that it is assented to by this lady of such an exalted spirit, who is such a devoted wife.

VIDUSHAKA—(*Aside*). When the fish has broken loose from his hand the fisherman in despair says 'A meritorious deed would be recorded in my favour. (*Aloud*). What! Is His Majesty dear to you in that manner?

QUEEN—Fool, desiring to promote my Lord's happiness I have resigned my own. Think from this whether he was dear to me or not.

KING—Yours the power to give me away or make me a slave to yourself. But I am indeed not what you—O timid one—doubt me to be. [14]

QUEEN—You may be so or may not be so. I have accomplished the vow 'conciliation of the loved one' as prescribed. Girls, now, come along. (*Queen starts to go*).

KING—My dear. I am indeed not pleased it you leave me now and go.

देवी—अज्जउत्त अलङ्घिद-पुव्वो मए णिअमो । आर्यपुत्र अलङ्घितपूर्वो मया नियमः ।

[निष्क्रान्ता सपरिवारा देवी]

उर्वशी—हला पिअ-कलत्तो राएसी । ण उण हिअअं णिवत्तेदुं सक्कुणोमि । हला प्रियकलत्रो राजर्षिः । न पुनर्हृदयं निवर्तयितुं शक्नोमि ।

चित्रलेखा—किं उण तुए णिरासाए णिवत्तीअदि । किं पुनस्त्वया निराशया निवर्त्यते ।

राजा—[आसनमुपेत्य] **वयस्य न खलु दूरं गता देवी ।**

विदूषकः—भण वीसद्धं जं सि वत्तु-कामो । असज्झो त्ति वेज्जेण आदुरो विअ सेरं मुत्तो भवं तत्तहोदीए । भण विश्रब्धं यदसि वक्तुकामः । असाध्य इति वैद्येनातुर इव स्वैरं मुक्तो भवांस्तत्रभवत्या ।

राजा—अपि नामोर्वशी—

उर्वशी—अज्ज किदत्था भवे । अद्य कृतार्था भवेत् ।

राजा—

गूढा नूपुरशब्दमात्रमपि मे कान्तं श्रुतौ पातयेत्
पश्चादेत्य शनैः कराम्बुजवृते कुर्वीत वा लोचने ।
हर्म्येऽस्मिन्नवतीर्य साध्वसवशान्मन्दायमाना बला-
दानीयेत पदात् पदं चतुरया सख्या ममोपान्तिकम् ॥१५॥

उर्वशी—हला इमं दाव से मणोरहं संपादइस्सं । [पृष्ठतो गत्वा राज्ञो नयने संवृणोति] हला इमं तावदस्य मनोरथं संपादयिष्यामि ।

[चित्रलेखा विदूषकं संज्ञापयति ।]

राजा—[स्पर्शं रूपयित्वा] **सखे नारायणोरुसंभवा सेयं वरोरूः ।**

QUEEN—My noble Lord, never before have I broken a sacred rule.

(Exit Queen with retinue).

URVASHI—Friend, the royal sage is fond of his wife. and yet I am not able to reclaim my heart.

CHITRALEKHA—But why should you despair and withdraw?

KING—*(Approching his seat)*. Friend, the Queen indeed has not gone far.

VIDUSHAKA—You may say whatever you wish, safely enough. You are fairly given over by her ladyship, like a sick man in despair by his physician.

KING—Would that Urvashi—

URVASHI—Find her happiness to day!

KING—Herself concealed let fall the sweet music of her anklets in mine ear! Or that with her lotus-hands, as lightly she stole behind me, she veiled my eyes! Or descending to this palace and yet delaying to come through fear she were brought to me, step after step, with (welcome) violence by some clever friend! [15]

URVASHI—Friend, let me grant him his desire.

(Going behind him, covers the King's eyes).

(Chitralekha makes a sign to the Vidushaka).

KING—*(Showing that he feels the touch)*. Friend, this is that fair lady sprung from the lap of the sage Narayana

विदूषकः—कहं भवं अवगच्छदि । कथं भवानवगच्छति ।

राजा—किमत्र ज्ञेयम् ।

अङ्गमनङ्गक्लिष्टं सुखयेदन्या न मे करस्पर्शात् ।
नोच्छ्वसिति तपनकिरणैश्चन्द्रस्येवांशुभिः कुमुदम् ॥१६॥

उर्वशी— [हस्तावपनीय उत्तिष्ठति। किंचिदुपसृत्य:] जेदु जेदु महाराओ । जयतु जयतु महाराजः ।

राजा—सुन्दरि स्वागतम् [एकासने उपवेशयति]

चित्रलेखा—अवि सुहं वअस्सस्स । अपि सुखं वयस्यस्य ।

राजा—नन्वेतदुपस्थितम् ।

उर्वशी—हला देवीए दिण्णो महाराओ । तदो से पणअवदी विअ सरीर-संपक्कं गद म्हि । मा खु मं पुरोभाइणिं समत्थेहि । हला देव्या दत्तो महाराजः । ततोऽस्य प्रणयवतीव शरीरसंपर्कं गतास्मि । मा खलु मां पुरोभागिनीं समर्थयस्व ।

विदूषकः—कहं इह ज्जेव तुम्हाणं अत्थमिदो सुज्जो । कथमिहैव युवयोरस्तमितः सूर्यः ।

राजा—[उर्वशीमवलोक्य]

देव्या दत्त इति यदि व्यापारं व्रजसि मे शरीरेऽस्मिन् ।
प्रथमं कस्यानुमते चोरितमेतत् त्वया हृदयम् ॥ १७ ॥

चित्रलेखा—वअस्स णिरुत्तरा एसा । संपदं मह विण्णप्पं सुणीअदु । वयस्य निरुत्तरैषा । साम्प्रतं मम विज्ञाप्यं श्रूयताम् ।

राजा—अवहितोऽस्मि ।

चित्रलेखा—वसन्ताणन्तरे उण्ह-समए भअवं सुज्जो मए उवअरिदव्वो । ता जहा इअं मे पिअ-सही सग्गस्स ण उक्कण्ठेदि तहा वअस्सेण कादव्वं । वसन्तानन्तरे उष्णसमये भगवान् सूर्यो मयोपचरितव्यः । तद् यथेयं मे प्रियसखी स्वर्गस्य नोत्कण्ठते तथा वयस्येन कर्तव्यम् ।

VIDUSHAKA—How do you know?

KING—What is there to be known!

None else would give such delight to the body, afflicted by love, through the touch of her hand. The Kumuda wakes not at the touch of the solar ray as at the touch of moonbeams. [16]

URVASHI—(*Removing her hands and rising—slightly approaching*). Glory to the King!

KING—Welcome, fair one.

(*Makes her share his seat*).

CHITRALEKHA—I hope my friend feels happiness.

KING—Why it just comes to me.

URVASHI—Friend the Queen has given (me) His Majesty. So I approach his person-like his loving wife. You will not regard me as officious—will you?

VIDUSHAKA—How, has the Sun set to you even here?

KING—(*Looking at Urvashi*).

If you approach my person, because the Queen has presented me to you, who was it that first granted you permission to rob me of my heart? [17]

CHITRALEKHA—Friend, she can proffer no reply. Now listen to my prayer.

KING—I am all attention.

CHITRALEKHA—After spring, in summer, I have to wait upon the divine Sun. See to it, therefore, that you behave in such a manner that my dear friend does not long for heaven.

विदूषकः—किं वा सग्गे सुमरिदव्वं। ण वा अण्हीअदि ण वा पीअदि । केवलं अणिमिसेहिं णअणेहिं मीणा विडम्बीअन्ति । किं वा स्वर्गे स्मर्तव्यम् । न वा अश्यते न वा पीयते । केवलमनिमिषैर्नयनैर्मीना विडम्ब्यन्ते ।

राजा—भद्र

अनिर्देश्यसुखः स्वर्गः कस्तं विस्मारयिष्यति ।
अनन्यनारीसामान्यो दासस्त्वस्याः पुरूरवाः ॥ १८ ॥

चित्रलेखा—अणुगहिद म्हि । हला उव्वसि अकादरा भविअ विसज्जेहि मं । अनुगृहीतास्मि । हला उर्वशि अकातरा भूत्वा विसर्जय माम् ।

उर्वशी—[चित्रलेखां परिष्वज्य] **सहि मा खु मं विसुमरेहि ।** सखि मा खलु मां विस्मर ।

चित्रलेखा—[सस्मितम्] **वअस्सेण संगदा तुमं एव्व एदं मए जाचिदव्वा।** वयस्येन संगता त्वमेव एतद् मया याचितव्या ।

विदूषकः— दिट्ठिआ मणोरह- संपत्तीए वड्ढदि भवं। दिष्ट्या मनोरथसंपत्त्या वर्धते भवान् ।

राजा—इयं तावद् वृद्धिर्मम । पश्य ।

सामन्तमौलिमणिरञ्जितशासनाङ्क-
मेकातपत्त्रमवनेर्न तथा प्रभुत्वम् ।
अस्याः सखे चरणयोरहमद्य कान्त-
माज्ञाकरत्वमधिगम्य यथा कृतार्थः ॥ १९ ॥

उर्वशी—णत्थि मे विहवो अदो पिअदरं मन्तिदुं । नास्ति मे विभवः अतः प्रियतरं मन्त्रयितुम् ।

राजा—[उर्वशीं हस्तेनावलम्ब्य] **अहो विरुद्धसंवर्धन ईप्सितलाभो नाम ।**

VIDUSHAKA—What is there to remember of heaven? They neither eat nor drink in that place; but they only mock the fish by not closing their eyes even for a twinkle.

KING—Fair lady,

The heaven is a place of joy ineffable; who can efface its memory? But Pururavas will be a slave unto no other woman than her. [18]

CHITRALEKHA—I am beholden to you. Friend Urvashi, summon up courage and bid me adieu.

URVASHI—(*Embracing Chitralekha*). Friend, you will not forget me?

CHITRALEKHA—(*Smiling*). That I should rather beg of you now that you are united to my friend.

(*Bowing to the King, departs*).

VIDUSHAKA—I congratulate you on the accomplishment of your desire.

KING—It is true, I reach the height of joy. See, I do not feel so blest by the sovereignty of the earth in which none holds the royal umbrella save myself and in which the royal edicts are illumined by the light of the jewels in the crests of the feudatories, as I do by obtaining the fair position of a slave to her feet! [19]

URVASHI—I have no words to give expression to sentiments dearer than these.

KING—(*Holding Urvashi by the hand*). How wonderful is the accomplishment of one's wishes, giving rise to contraries!

पादास्त एव शशिनः सुखयन्ति गात्रं
बाणास्त एव मदनस्य मनोऽनुकूलाः ।
संरम्भरूक्षमिव सुन्दरि यद्यदासीत्
त्वत्संगमेन मम तत्तदिवानुनीतम् ॥ २० ॥

उर्वशी—अवरद्धम्हि चिर-कारिआ अज्जउत्तस्स ।
अपराद्धास्मि चिरकारिका आर्यपुत्रस्य ।

राजा—मा मैवम् ।

यदेवोपनतं दुःखात् सुखं तद् रसवत्तरम् ।
निर्वाणाय तरुच्छाया तप्तस्य हि विशेषतः ॥ २१ ॥

विदूषकः—भो सेविदा पदोस-रमणीआ चन्द-वादा ।
समओ खु दे वास-घर-पवेसस्स । भोः सेविताः प्रदोपर-
३ मणीयाश्चन्द्रपादाः । समयः खलु ते वासगृहप्रवेशस्य ।

राजा—तेन हि सख्यास्ते मार्गमादेशय ।

विदूषकः—इदो इदो भवदी । [इति निष्क्रामन्ति] इत इतो
६ भवती ।

राजा—सुन्दरि इयमिदानीमभ्यर्थना ।

उर्वशी—कहं विअ । कथमिव ।

९ राजा—

अनधिगतमनोरथस्य पूर्वं
शतगुणितेव गता मम त्रियामा ।
यदि तु तव समागमे तथैव
प्रसरति सुभ्रु ततः कृती भवेयम् ॥ २२ ॥

[इति निष्क्रान्ताः सर्वे]

तृतीयोऽङ्कः समाप्तः ॥

Those very moon-beams soothe my body, those very shafts of love are now agreeable to my mind; whatever, O fair one, was harsh (as if) through anger seems now to be reconciled to me through your union. [20]

URVASHI—I have wronged my Lord by causing delay.

KING—No, not so.

The joy that follows grief gains richer zest; the traveller who has been scorched by the fierce day can better tell how sweet is the shelter of the tree. [21]

VIDUSHAKA—Well, sir, we have enjoyed the moon-light so lovely at night. It is high time now for you to retire to the inner apartment.

KING—Well then show your friend the way.

VIDUSHAKA—This way, this way, your ladyship. (*They leave*).

KING—Beloved. this is my request now.

URVASHI—What is it?

KING—Dearest, before the fruition of my most cherished desires a hundredfold were my nights prolonged! If that were the case now that we are together, I would be happy indeed. [22]

(*Exeunt Omnes.*)

END OF ACT III.

चतुर्थोऽङ्कः ।

[ततः प्रविशति विमनस्का चित्रलेखा सहजन्या च ।]

सहजन्या—[चित्रलेखां विलोक्य] **सहि मिलाअमाण-सद-वत्तस्स विअ दे मुहस्स छाआ हिअअस्स अस्सत्थदं सूएदि। ता कहेहि णिव्वेद-कारणं। सम-दुक्खा भविदुं इच्छामि ।** सखि म्लायमानशतपत्रस्येव ते मुखस्य च्छाया हृदयस्य अस्वस्थतां सूचयति । तत् कथय निर्वेदकारणम् । समदुःखा भवितुमिच्छामि ।

चित्रलेखा—अच्छरा-वार-पज्जाएण इह भअवदो सुज्जस्स पाद-मूलोवट्ठाणं वट्टदि त्ति बलिअं खु उव्वसीए उक्कण्ठिद म्हि । अप्सरोवारपर्यायेण इह भगवतः सूर्यस्य पादमूलोपस्थानं वर्तत इति बलवत् खलूर्वश्यामुत्कण्ठितास्मि ।

सहजन्या— जाणे वो अण्णोण्ण-सिणेहं । तदो तदो । जाने युवयोरन्योन्यस्नेहम् । ततस्ततः ।

चित्रलेखा—तदो इमाइं दिवसाइं को णु खु वुत्तन्तो त्ति पणिधाण-ट्ठिदाए मए अच्चाहिदं उवलद्धं। तत एतेषु दिवसेषु को नु खलु वृत्तान्त इति प्रणिधानस्थितया मया अत्याहितमुपलब्धम् ।

सहजन्या—[सावेगम्] **कीरिसं विअ ।** कीदृशमिव ।

चित्रलेखा—उव्वसी किल तं रदि-सहाअं राएसिं अमच्चेसु णिवेसिद-रज्ज-धुरं गेण्हिअ गन्धमादण-वणं विहरिदुं गदा । उर्वशी किल तं रतिसहायं राजर्षिममात्येषु निवेशितराज्यधुरं गृहीत्वा गन्धमादनवनं विहर्तुं गता ।

Act IV

(*Enter Chitralekha dejected in mind and Sahajanya).*

SAHAJANYA—(*Looking at Chitralekha*) Your face, looking like a faded lotus-flower, speaks the sadness of your heart. Tell me, then, the cause of your distress. I wish to share half your grief.

CHITRALEKHA—By the turn of service incumbent upon the nymphs, I was engaged in attending upon the Sun, and, therefore, I felt a deep longing for Urvashi.

SAHAJANYA–I know your mutual love. Well what then?

CHITRALEKHA—Then desiring to know how it was with her during all these days I put myself in contemplation and discerned a calamity.

SAHAJANYA—(*Feelingly*). Of what sort?

CHITRALEKHA—Urvashi took with her the King, her companion in her pleasures, who had put the yoke of the kingdom upon his ministers, and went to disport in the Gandhamadana Groves.

सहजन्या—सो णाम संभोओ जो तारिसेसु पदेसेसु। तदो तदो। स नाम संभोगो यस्तादृशेषु प्रदेशेषु। ततस्ततः।

चित्रलेखा—तहिं खु मन्दाइणीए पुलिणेसु गदा सिअदा-पव्वद-केलीहिं कीलमाणा विज्जाहर-दारिआ उदयवदी णाम तेण राएसिणा णिज्झाइद त्ति कुविदा उव्वसी। तत्र खलु मन्दाकिन्याः पुलिनेषु गता सिकतापर्वतकेलीभिः क्रीडन्ती विद्याधरदारिका उदयवती नाम तेन राजर्षिणा निध्यातेति कुपिता उर्वशी।

सहजन्या—होदव्वं। दूरारूढो क्खु पणओ असहणो। तदो तदो। भवितव्यम्। दूरारूढः खलु प्रणयः असहनः। ततस्ततः।

चित्रलेखा—तदो भट्टिणो अणुणअं अपडिवज्जमाणा गुरु-साव-संमूढ-हिअआ इत्थिआ-जण-परिहरणिज्जं कुमार-वणं पविट्ठा। पवेसाणन्तरं च काणणोवन्त-वत्ति-लदाभावेण परिणदं से रूवं। ततो भर्तुरनुनयमप्रतिपद्यमाना गुरुशाप-संमूढहृदया स्त्रीजनपरिहरणीयं कुमारवनं प्रविष्टा। प्रवेशानन्तरं च काननोपान्तवर्तिलताभावेन परिणतमस्या रूपम्।

सहजन्या—णत्थि विहिणो अलङ्घणिज्जं। तस्स अणुराअस्स अअं णाम एक्क-वदे ईरिसो अणत्थो। अह किमवत्थो सो राएसी। नास्ति विधेरलङ्घनीयम्। तस्यानुरागस्य अयं नाम एकपद ईदृशोनर्थः। अथ किमवस्थः स राजर्षिः।

चित्रलेखा—तस्सिं एव्व काणणे पिअदमं विचिण्णन्तो अहोरत्ते अदिवाहेदि। इमिणा उण णिव्वुदाणं पि उक्कण्ठा-कारिणा मेहोदएण अणत्थाहीणो हविस्सदि। तस्मिन्नेव कानने प्रियतमां विचिन्वन्नहोरात्रानतिवाहयति। एतेन पुनर्निर्वृतानामपि उत्कण्ठाकारिणा मेघोदयेन अनर्थाधीनो भविष्यति।

सहजन्या—सहि तारिसा आकिदि-विसेसा चिरं दुक्ख-भाइणो ण होन्ति। अवस्सं किं पि अणुग्गह-णिमित्तं

SAHAJANYA—That is indeed enjoyment as is obtained in such places. What then?

CHITRALEKHA—There, the royal sage looked intently at Udayavati, a Vidyadhara damsel playing with (making) mountains of sand on the banks of the Mandakini, and that angered Urvashi.

SAHAJANYA—That is possible; for intense love is so intolerant. What next?

CHITRALEKHA—Then not accepting the apologies of her husband and with her mind darkened by the curse the preceptor had denounced her with, she entered the grove sacred to Kumara, which is forbidden to women. And after she had entered it, she was transformed into a creeper on the skirt of the grove.

SAHAJANYA—There is nothing that fate may not assail. Alas! that such dire calamity should have all of a sudden befallen such affection! And, pray, what is the condition of the royal sage?

CHITRALEKHA—He is in that same forest passing days and nights in searching her.

SAHAJANYA—Friend, but such excellent forms do not undergo misery for long. Surely there will befall some

भूओ वि समाअम-कारणं हविस्सदि । ता एहि उद-उम्मुहस्स भअवदो सुज्जस्स उवट्ठाणं करेम्ह । सखि

५२ तादृशा आकृतिविशेषाश्चिरं दुःखभागिनो न भवन्ति । अवश्यं किमपि अनुग्रहनिमित्तं भूयोपि समागमकारणं भविष्यति । तदेहि उदयोन्मुखस्य भगवतः सूर्यस्य उपस्थानं कुर्वः ।

'५५ [इति निष्क्रान्ते ।]

प्रवेशकः ॥

[ततः प्रविशति उन्मत्तवेषो राजा ।]

५८ राजा—आः दुरात्मन् रक्षस्तिष्ठ तिष्ठ । क्व मे प्रियतमामादाय गच्छसि । हन्त शैलशिखराद् गगनमुत्पत्य बाणर्मामभिवर्षति । [विभाव्य]

नवजलधरः संनद्धोऽयं न दृप्तनिशाचरः
सुरधनुरिदं दूराकृष्टं न नाम शरासनम् ।
अयमपि पटुर्धारासारो न बाणपरंपरा
कनकनिकषस्निग्धा विद्युत् प्रिया न ममोर्वशी ॥१॥

[विचिन्त्य] । क्व नु खलु रम्भोरूर्गता स्यात्

तिष्ठेत् कोपवशात् प्रभावपिहिता दीर्घं न सा कुप्यति
स्वर्गायोत्पतिता भवेन्मयि पुनर्भावार्द्रमस्या मनः ।
तां हर्तुं विबुधद्विषोऽपि न च मे शक्ताः पुरोवर्तिनीं
सा चात्यन्तमदर्शनं नयनयोर्यातेति कोऽयं विधिः ॥२॥

[दिशोऽवलोक्य । सनिःश्वासम् ।] अये पराधृत्तभागधेयानां दुःखं दुःखानुबन्धि । कुतः ।

अयमेकपदे तया वियोगः प्रियया चोपनतः सुदुःसहो मे ।
नववारिधरोदयादहोभिर्भवितव्यं च निरातपत्वरम्यैः ॥३॥

event making for reunion caused by some favourable circumstances. So come along, let us worship the divine Sun, that is just about to rise. (*Exeunt*).

END OF THE INTRODUCTORY SCENE.

(*Enter King dressed as an insane person*).

KING—Hold, you wicked fiend, hold Where are you going, taking my beloved ? Ha, from the mountain-peak up-flying he rains showers of arrows on me. (*Looking closely*).

This is a fresh cloud ready to shower, and not a haughty fiend girt in armour. This here is the heavens rainbow striding a vast length and not a (warrior's) bow stretched out; and this a pelting shower of rain that is so sharp and not a volley of arrows; while this is only a flash of lightning gleaming like a streak of gold on the touch-stone, and not my beloved Urvashi. [1]

(*Reflecting*)—Where can the fair one have gone ?

Has she through her power remained invisible in anger ? But she will not be angry long. Has she flown up to the heavens ? But her heart yearns in ever fresh love for me. While even the foes of the immortals cannot wrest her, while in my presence. And yet she is quite invisible to mine eyes ! What fate is this ? [2]

(*Looking into space, sighing*). Ah ! How one upon another calamities whelm those whom once misfortune has assailed ! For,

While all of a sudden I have suffered severance from my beloved which is unbearably painful, here the fresh clouds appear making the days so genial by mitigating their intense heat. [3]

[विहस्य] मुधैव खलु मनसः परितापवृद्धिरुपेक्ष्यते ।
यथा मुनयोऽपि व्याहरन्ति राजा कालस्य कारणमिति ।
२ तत् किमहं जलदसमयं न प्रत्यादिशामि । अथ वा
प्रावृषेण्यैरेव लिङ्गैर्मम राजोपचारः संप्रति । कथमिव ।

विद्युल्लेखाकनकरुचिरं श्रीवितानं ममाभ्रं
व्याधूयन्ते निचुलतरुभिर्मञ्जरीचामराणि ।
घर्मच्छेदात् पटुतरगिरो बन्दिनो नीलकण्ठा
धारासारोपनयनपरा नैगमाश्चाम्बुवाहाः ॥ ४ ॥

भवतु । किमेवं परिच्छदश्लाघया । यावदस्मिन् कानने
तां प्रियामन्वेषयामि [विलोक्य] हन्त व्यवसितस्य मे
३ संदीपनमिव संवृत्तम् कुतः

आरक्तराजिभिरियं कुसुमैर्नवकन्दली सलिलगर्भैः ।
कोपादन्तर्बाष्पे स्मरयति मां लोचने तस्याः ॥ ५ ॥

इतो गतेति कथं नु तत्रभवती मया सूचयितव्या ।

पद्भ्यां स्पृशेद् वसुमतीं यदि सा सुगात्री
मेघाभिवृष्टसिकतासु वनस्थलीषु ।
पश्चान्नता गुरुनितम्बतया ततोऽस्या
दृश्येत चारुपदपङ्क्तिरलक्तकाङ्का ॥ ६ ॥

[परिक्रम्य अवलोक्य च सहर्षम् ।] उपलब्धमुपलक्षणं येन
तस्याः कोपनाया मार्गोऽनुमीयते ।

हृतोष्ठरागैर्नयनोदबिन्दुभि-
र्निमग्ननाभेर्निपतद्भिरङ्कितम् ।
च्युतं रुषा भिन्नगतेरसंशयं
शुकोदरश्याममिदं स्तनांशुकम् ॥ ७ ॥

(*Laughing*). Or, in vain do I bear all these troubles of my mind. For even the wise say that the King is the lord of time. Why should I not countermand the rainy season? Or rather the signs of the rainy season are the only insignia that are doing me royal honour.

> Here the clouds spread my splendid canopy, shot with the gold of lightning streaks; The Nichula trees wave their (tufted) blossoms as *chowries*; the peacocks growing clamorous, now that summer is gone, are my bards; while the clouds are the (rich) merchants that proffer me tribute of rain-showers. [4]

But let it be. Why should I laud my paraphernalia? So I will search that love of mine in this forest.

(*Looking*).—Dear me? As I set about it here is something that aggravates (my troubles). For,

> This fresh Kandali plant with its flowers streaked with red veins, and with water inside them painfully reminds me of her eyes with the tears starting inside them through anger. [5]

How am I to know that her ladyship has gone hence

> If she were to touch the earth with her feet here in these woodland spots whose sandy soil is showered over by the clouds, then would I trace her lovely footprints marked with the Alaktaka dye, pressed deep in the soil at the back owing to the heaviness of her hips. [6]

(*Walking about and looking with joy*).—Here have I found a sign by which I can infer the way, the irate one has gone

> Here is the scarf covering her breasts, dark-green like a parrot's belly, which assuredly must have slipped down as in anger she stumbled on, and marked by the tears of that fair one with a deep navel—tears which falling first upon her lips carried with them their red paint. [7]

[विभाव्य ।] कथम् । सेन्द्रगोपं नवशाद्वलमिदम् । कुतो नु खलु निर्जने वने प्रियाप्रवृत्तिरवगमयितव्या [दृष्ट्वा] अये आसारोच्छ्वसितशैलेयस्थलीपाषाणमारूढः

आलोकयति पयोदान् प्रबलपुरोवातनर्तितशिखण्डः ।
केकागर्भेण शिखी दूरोन्नमितेन कण्ठेन ॥ ८ ॥

[उपेत्य ।] यावदेनं पृच्छामि ।

नीलकण्ठ ममोत्कण्ठा वनेऽस्मिन् वनिता त्वया ।
दीर्घापाङ्गा सितापाङ्ग दृष्टा दृष्टिक्षमा भवेत् ॥ ९ ॥

कथमदत्त्वा प्रतिवचनं नर्तितुं प्रवृत्तः । किं नु खलु हर्षकारणमस्य । [विचिन्त्य] भवतु । विदितमेतत् ।

मृदुपवनविभिन्नो मत्प्रियाया विनाशाद्
घनरुचिरकलापो निःसपत्नोऽस्य जातः ।
रतिविगलितबन्धे केशहस्ते सुकेश्याः
सति कुसुमसनाथे किं करोत्येष बर्ही ॥ १० ॥

भवतु । परव्यसननिर्वृतं न खल्वेनं पृच्छामि [परिक्रम्य] इयमातपान्तसंक्षुभितमदा जम्बूविटपमध्यास्ते परभृता । विहंगमेषु पण्डिता जातिरेषा । यावदेनामभ्यर्थये । भवति

त्वां कामिनो मदनदूतिमुदाहरन्ति
मानावभङ्गनिपुणं त्वममोघमस्त्रम् ।
तामानय प्रियतमां मम वा समीपं
मां वा नयाशु कलभाषिणि यत्र कान्ता ॥ ११ ॥

[आकाशे ।] किमाह भवती । कथं त्वामेवमनुरक्तं विहाय गतेति । शृणोतु भवती ।

(*Looking closely*).—How, this is fresh sward with the Indragopa insects! Where indeed can I get the intelligence of my love in this lonesome wild?

(*Seeing*).—Ah, here, perched on a stone in the rocky soil, bright-looking on account of rain-showers, is a peacock,

That looks (proudly) at the clouds with neck out-stretched and clamorous with rapture, his crest waved by the breezes blowing in his face. [8]

(*Approching*).—So I will inquire of him.

O blue-necked peacock, with eyes white in the corners, have you seen my love-lorn lady of broad big eyes in this forest? For her charms deserve your gaze. [9]

How he deigns no answer but simply treads a measure. What could have exhilarated him? (*Reflecting*) Well I have it.

Owing to the disappearance of my love, his beautiful, thick plumage, divided by the gentle breeze, is now without a rival; but where would be his boast, before the excellent tresses of her hair decked with flowers, when loosened in amorous sport? [10]

Let be.—I shall not ask him, who seems to be happy in another's .misfortune. (*Walking about*). Here is a Koil sitting on the Jambu tree, her passions inflamed at the end of summer. She is a wise bird among the winged flook. So I will request her.

They call you the lover's messenger of love—the unfailing missile able to break down pride; do you, O sweet-tongued, bring my dearest to me, or lead me to where she is. [11]

What do you say? 'How did she leave you when you were so devoted to her?' Hear,

कुपिता न तु कोपकारणं सकृदप्यात्मगतं स्मराम्यहम् ।
प्रभुता रमणेषु योषितां न हि भावस्खलितान्यपेक्षते ॥१२॥

कथं कथाच्छेदकारिणी स्वकार्य एव सक्ता ।

महदपि परदुःखं शीतलं सम्यगाहुः
प्रणयमगणयित्वा यन्ममापद्गतस्य ।
अधरमिव मदान्धा पातुमेषा प्रवृत्ता
फलमभिमुखपाकं राजजम्बूद्रुमस्य ॥ १३ ॥

एवंगतेऽपि प्रियेव मे मञ्जुस्वनेति न कोपोऽस्याम् ।
इतो वयम्- [परिक्रामितकेन। कर्णं दत्त्वा] अये दक्षिणेन
२ प्रियाचरणनिक्षेपशंसी नूपुररवः । यावदत्र गच्छामि ।
[परिक्रम्य] अहो धिक् धिक् ।

मेघश्यामा दिशो दृष्ट्वा मानसोत्सुकचेतसाम् ।
कूजितं राजहंसानां नेदं नूपुरशिञ्जितम् ॥ १४ ॥

भवतु । यावदेते मानसोत्सुकाः पतत्त्रिणः सरसो नोत्प-
तन्ति तावदेतेभ्यः प्रियाप्रवृत्तिरवगमयितव्या । [उपेत्य]
२ भो भो जलविहंगमराज

पश्चात् सरः प्रति गमिष्यसि मानसं तत्
पाथेयमुत्सृज बिसं ग्रहणाय भूयः ।
मां तावदुद्धर शुचो दयिताप्रवृत्त्या
स्वार्थात् सतां गुरुतरा प्रणयिक्रियैव ॥ १५ ॥

यथोन्मुखो विलोकयति मानसोत्सुकेन मया न लक्षिते-
त्येवं वचनमाह ।

Angry I find her, but I do not remember to have even for once given her any cause for offence. The fond tyranny that women exercise over those who love them does not require any deviation from love for them to get angry. [12]

How now ! She seems to mind her own business and not heed our conversation.

It is well said that howsoever great another's woe, a stranger will not be in the least affected by it Thus she disregards my request and lo ! speeds to yon excellent Jambu tree to drink the (luscious) juice of its now ripe fruit, as one intoxicated (by the draught of love) to sip the honey of (roseate) lips. [13]

Although it is thus, yet I scarcely feel angry with her as she has the sweet voice of my love. Hence we— (*Going about and listening*). Ah ! from the South I hear the jingle of anklets indicating the tread of my Love's feet. So I will proceed thither (*Moving about*). Oh, fie !

This is not the chime of tinkling anklets, but the cooing of swans who, seeing the space darkened with clouds, are filled inwardly with a longing to go to the Manasa lake. [14]

Well, while these birds, filled as they are with a (passionate) yearning for the Manasa lake, are not flown from the lake, let me get from them news about my Love. (*Approaching*). You, prince of aquatic birds,

After a while, you will begin your journey to the Manasa lake ; forego the provender of lotus-stem; you will have that again. Do you first redeem me from despair by imparting some tidings of my beloved ; for the good regard it worthier to render kindly offices to the suppliants than be mindful of their own business. [15]

Since he looks up he seems to say that in his longing for the Manasa, he has not marked her.

यदि हंस गता न ते नतभ्रूः
सरसो रोधसि दर्शनं प्रिया मे ।
मदखेलपदं कथं नु तस्याः
सकलं चोर गतं त्वया गृहीतम् ॥ १६ ॥

अतश्च—

हंस प्रयच्छ मे कान्तां गतिरस्यास्त्वया हृता ।
विभावितैकदेशेन देयं यदभियुज्यते ॥ १७ ॥

[विहस्य] । एष चोरानुशासी राजेति भयादुत्पतितः । [परिक्रम्य] अयमिदानीं प्रियासहायश्चक्रवाकः । तावदेनं पृच्छामि ।

रथाङ्गनामन् वियुतो रथाङ्गश्रोणिबिम्बया ।
अयं त्वां पृच्छति रथी मनोरथशतैर्वृतः ॥ १८ ॥

कथं कः क इत्याह । मा तावत् । न खलु विदितोऽहमस्य ।

सूर्याचन्द्रमसौ यस्य मातामहपितामहौ ।
स्वयं वृतः पतिर्द्वाभ्यामुर्वश्या च भुवा च यः ॥१९॥

कथं तूष्णीं स्थितः । भवतु । उपालप्स्ये तावदेनम् ।

सरसि नलिनीपत्रेणापि त्वमावृतविग्रहां
ननु सहचरीं दूरे मत्वा विरौषि समुत्सुकः ।
इति च भवतो जायास्नेहात् पृथक्स्थितिभीरुता
मयि च विधुरे भावः कान्ताप्रवृत्तिपराङ्मुखः ॥२०॥

सर्वथा मदीयानां भाग्यविपर्ययाणामयं प्रभावः । यावदन्यमवकाशमवगाहे । [पद्मान्तरे स्थित्वा] भवतु न तावद् गच्छामि ।

Well, O swan, if you have not seen my love with her arched eye-brows, on the bank of the lake, how could you, O thief, have wholly taken her gait, elegant through youthful pride? [16]

Therefore,

O swan, give me my Love; you have stolen her gait. He who is proved guilty as regards a part should restore the whole of what is claimed. [17]

(*Laughing*).—He has flown up fearing that a King the chastiser of thieves, is here (*Walking about*). Here is the Chakrawaka with his mate. So I will ask him.

O Chakrawaka, this warrior, here severed from his broad-hipped Love and filled with a hundred longings, asks you. [18]

How does he say "Who?" Who? That will not do It seems he knows me not.

The Sun and the Moon are my grandsires on both sides; while I am the self-chosen Lord of Urvashi and the Earth. [19]

How, he keeps quiet! Well, I will remonstrate with him.

If by so much as a lotus-leaf thy mate is screened from sight in the lake, thou wilt pour out thy plaints, all yearning for her, thinking her to be far-removed. Thus art thou apprehensive of thy mate's separation through thy fondness for her. Why, then, friend, dost thou seem so averse to giving me news about my Love, even when I am so distressed? [20]

In every respect my fortune has been so perverse to me. So I will go to another region. (*Stopping after a step*). Well, I will not go

इदं रुणद्धि मां पद्ममन्तःकूजितषट्पदम् ।
मया दष्टाधरं तस्याः ससीत्कारमिवाननम् ॥ २१ ॥

भवतु। अस्मिन्नेव कमलाध्यासिनि मधुकरे प्रणयित्वं करिष्ये । इतो गतस्यानुशयो मा भूदिति ।

मधुकर मदिराक्ष्याः शंस तस्याः प्रवृत्ति
[विभाव्य ।]

वरतनुरथवासौ नैव दृष्टा त्वया मे ।
यदि सुरभिमपास्यस्तन्मुखोच्छ्वासगन्धं
तव रतिरभविष्यत् पुण्डरीके किमस्मिन् ॥ २२ ॥

साधयामस्तावत् [परिक्रामितकेन] एष नीपस्कन्धनिषण्णहस्तः करिणीसहायो नागराजस्तिष्ठति । अस्मात् प्रियोदन्तमुपलप्स्ये [विलोक्य] भवतु न त्वरा कार्या।

अयमचिरोद्गतपल्लवमुपनीतं प्रियकरेणुहस्तेन ।
अभिलषतु तावदासवसुरभिरसं सल्लकीभङ्गम् ॥ २३ ॥

[क्षणमात्रं स्थित्वा।] हन्त कृताह्निकः संवृत्तः। भवतु पृच्छामि।

मदकल युवतिशशिकला गजयूथप यूथिकाशबलकेशी।
स्थिरयौवना स्थिता ते दूरालोके सुखालोका ॥ २४ ॥

[सहर्षम् ।] अनेन स्निग्धमन्द्रेण गर्जितेन प्रियोपलम्भशंसिना समाश्वासितोऽस्मि। साधर्म्याच्च त्वयि मे भूयसी प्रीतिः।

मामाहुः पृथिवीभृतामधिपतिं नागाधिराजो भवान्
अव्युच्छिन्नपृथुप्रवृत्ति भवतो दानं ममाप्यर्थिषु ।
स्त्रीरत्नेषु ममोर्वशी प्रियतमा यूथे तवेयं वशा
सर्वं मामनु ते प्रियाविरहजां त्वं तु व्यथां मानुभूः ॥२५॥

This lotus, here, amidst whose petals the bees are sweetly murmuring, arrests me; it is thus like my beloved's face, murmuring protest at my somewhat rudely sipping its lower lip. [21]

Well then, I shall woo this honey-sipper sitting on the lotus lest I should regret when I go hence.

Bee, give me the intelligence of that fair one with bewitching eyes.

(*Looking closely*).

Or rather, you have not seen that fair Love of mine; for had you tasted the fragrance of her delicious breath, you would certainly have scorned the lotus. [22]

I will leave, then. (*Walking about*). Here is the Lord of elephants with his mate, resting his trunk on the stem of a Nipa tree. I will get news of the dear one from him. (*Looking*). Let him be. I should not be in a hurry.

Let him eat the bough of the Sallaki with its newly-appearing shoots and its rich fragrant juice offered to him by his dear mate. [23]

(*Waiting for a moment*). Well, now he has had his meal; so I will ask him.

Lord of elephants, charming with the pride of youth, have you beheld (even) afar off that beautiful one, blooming with eternal youth, like the crescent Moon among (the stars of) women, her hair decked with the Yuthika flowers? [24]

(*With joy*). I am (mightily) consoled by this kind and gentle roar conveying some intimation of my Love. And great is my love for you because of our likeness.

For while they call me the lord of kings, you are the lord of elephants; your bounty sheds the frontal ichor profusely without break, while my wealth is lavishly showered on the needy; Urvashi is my Love among the jewels of womankind, and this gentle one your mate in the herd; thus everything of yours accords with mine. May you, however, never know the pangs of severance from your beloved. [25]

सुखमास्तां भवान् । साधयामस्तावत् । [पार्श्वतो दृष्टिं दत्त्वा] अये सुरभिकन्दरो नाम विशेषरमणीयः सानुमानालोक्यते । प्रियश्चायमप्सरसाम् । अपि नाम सुतनुरस्योपत्यकायामुपलभ्येत । [परिक्रम्य अवलोक्य च] कथमन्धकारः । भवतु । विद्युत्प्रकाशेनावलोकयामि । हन्त मदीयैर्दुरितपरिणामैर्मेघोऽपि शतह्रदाशून्यः संवृत्तः । तथापि शिलोच्चयमेतमपृष्ट्वा न निवर्तिष्ये ।

अपि वनान्तरमल्पकुचान्तरा श्रयति पर्वत पर्वसु संनता ।
इदमनङ्गपरिग्रहमङ्गना पृथुनितम्ब नितम्बवती तव ॥२६॥

कथं तूष्णीमास्ते । शङ्के विप्रकृष्टो न शृणोतीति । समीपेऽस्य गत्वा पुनरेनं पृच्छामि [परिक्रम्य]

सर्वक्षितिभृतां नाथ दृष्टा सर्वाङ्गसुन्दरी ।
रामा रम्ये वनान्तेऽस्मिन् मया विरहिता त्वया ॥२७॥

[आकर्ण्य । सहर्षम् ।] कथं यथाक्रमं दृष्टेत्याह । भवानपि अतः प्रियतरं शृणोतु । क्व तर्हि मम प्रियतमा । [नेपथ्ये तदेवाकर्ण्य ।] हा धिक् । ममैवायं कन्दरमुखविसर्पी प्रतिशब्दः । [विषादं रूपयित्वा] श्रान्तोऽस्मि । अस्यास्तावद् गिरिनद्यास्तीरे स्थितस्तरङ्गवातमासेविष्ये । इमां नवाम्बुकलुषामपि स्रोतोवहां पश्यतो मे रमते मनः ।

तरङ्गभ्रूभङ्गा क्षुभितविहगश्रेणिरसना
विकर्षन्ती फेनं वसनमिव संरम्भशिथिलम् ।
यथाविद्धं याति स्खलितमभिसंधाय बहुशो
नदीभावेनेयं ध्रुवमसहना सा परिणता ॥ २८ ॥

May you rest in peace. I will go. (*Looking at his side*). Here is the mountain 'Surabhikandara,' particularly lovely and a loved resort of the nymphs. May it be that the fair one is to be found on it ledges? (*Moving about and observing*). Oh, how is it dark? Well, I will see with the flash of lightning. What a (sad) result of my sins that even the clouds are bereft of lightning! Still I will not return without making inquiry of this mountain.

> Does she, of close breasts, and full in the joints, and plump in the hips, resort the interior of this forest, sacred to love, O large-sided mountain? [26]

How is he silent? I am afraid he does not hear me being at a distance. I will approach him and ask him again. (*Walking about*).

> O Lord of mountains, have you seen that lovely woman, beautiful in all limbs, in this charming forest, severed from me? [27]

(*Listening; with joy*). How, in the same order, he said 'I have seen'! May you, too, hear sweeter words than these. Where, then, is my beloved? (*Hearing the same words from behind the scenes*). Ah, bless me! This is only my voice reverberating from the mouth of the cave. (*Showing despair*). I am tired. So reposing on the bank of this mountain-stream I shall enjoy the breezes from its waves. My mind is charmed as I look upon this stream although it is turbid with fresh water.

> The rippling wave is her arching brow: the fluttering line of birds her girdle; drawing along its foam, which is as it were her garment loosened through anger, it flows meanderingly, avoiding the many obstacles in the way, like my beloved who stumbles along as she remembers my faults; so surely that irascible one has been transformed into this river. [28]

भवतु । याचिष्ये तावदेनाम् । [अञ्जलिं कृत्वा]

त्वयि निबद्धरतेः प्रियवादिनः
प्रणयभङ्गपराङ्मुखचेतसः ।
कमपराधलवं मम पश्यसि
त्यजसि मानिनि दासजनं यतः ॥ २९ ॥

अथ वा परमार्थसरिदेवैषा । न खलूर्वशी पुरूरवसम-
पहाय समुद्राभिसारिणी भविष्यति । भवतु । अनिर्वे-
३ दप्राप्याणि श्रेयांसि । यावदमुमेव प्रदेशं गच्छामि यत्र
मे नयनयोः सुनयना तिरोभूता । [परिक्रम्य अवलोक्य]
हन्त दृष्टमुपलक्षणं तस्या मार्गस्य ।

रक्तकदम्बः सोऽयं प्रियया घर्मान्तशंसि यस्यैकम् ।
कुसुममसमग्रकेसरविषममपि कृतं शिखाभरणम् ॥३०॥

[विलोक्य ।] इमं तावत् प्रियाप्रवृत्तिनिमित्तं सारङ्गमासी-
नमभ्यर्थये ।

कृष्णसारच्छविर्योऽसौ दृश्यते काननश्रिया ।
वनशोभावलोकाय कटाक्ष इव पातितः ॥ ३१ ॥

[विलोक्य ।] किं नु खलु मामवधीरयन्निव अन्यतोमुखः
संवृत्तः । [दृष्ट्वा ।]

अस्यान्तिकमायान्ती शिशुना स्तनपायिना मृगी रुद्धा ।
तामयमनन्यदृष्टिर्भुग्नग्रीवो विलोकयति ॥ ३२ ॥

हंहो यूथपते

अपि दृष्टवानसि मम प्रियां वने
कथयामि ते तदुपलक्षणं शृणु ।
पृथुलोचना सहचरी यथैव ते
सुभगं तथैव खलु सापि वीक्षते ॥ ३३ ॥

Well, I will implore her. (*Folding his hands*).

I am devoted to you, ever speak agreeably to you and have a heart that has never deviated from love so what fault, even the slightest, have I committed that you fly from me so wholly yours? [29]

Or, rather this is really a stream; for surely Urvashi will not quit her Pururavas for the Ocean. So let it be. Fortune crowns those who yield not to despair. So I will go to the place where the fair-eyed one was lost to me. (*Walking about and observing*). Ah, now I see this indication as to the way she took.

Here is the Raktakadamba tree, one of whose flowers, uneven on account of its filaments being incompletely formed and suggesting the end of summer, was used by her to deck her hair. [30]

(*Observing*). I will now request the antelope squatting yonder to give me some intelligence of my love.

That one, seen yonder, of black and variegated hue, looks as if it is a glance cast by the sylvan deity to observe the beauty of the forest [31]

(*Seeing*). How, disregarding me, he has turned his face in another direction? (*Seeing*).

A doe approaching him was obstructed by her suckling fawn. So with a bent neck he is intently looking at her. [32]

O Lord of the herd,

Have you seen my beloved in this forest? I will give you her marks, listen. Even as your broad-eyed mate looks charmingly even so does she cast beautiful glances. [33]

कथमनादृत्य मद्वचनं कलत्राभिमुखं स्थितः । उपपद्यते ।
परिभवास्पदं दशाविपर्ययः । इतो वयम्–[परिक्रामितकेन
३ अवलोक्य] शिलाभेदान्तरगतं किमेतदालोक्यते ।

प्रभालेपी नायं हरिहतमृगस्यामिषलवः
स्फुलिङ्गः स्यादग्नेर्गगनमभिवृष्टं पुनरिदम् ।

[विभाव्य ।]

अये रक्ताशोकस्तबकसमरागो मणिरयं
यमुद्धर्तुं पूषा व्यवसित इवालम्बितकरः ॥ ३४ ॥

हरति मे मनः । आदास्ये तावदेनम् । अथवा

मन्दारपुष्पैरधिवासितायां यस्याः शिखायामयमर्पणीयः ।
सैव प्रिया संप्रति दुर्लभा मे किमेनमस्रोपहतं करोमि ॥३५॥

[नेपथ्ये ।] वत्स गृह्यतां गृह्यताम् ।

संगमनीय इति मणिः शैलसुताचरणरागयोनिरयम् ।
आवहति धार्यमाणः संगममचिरात् प्रियजनेन ॥ ३६ ॥

राजा—[कर्णं दत्त्वा] को नु खलु मामेवमनुशास्ति ।
[दिशोवलोक्य ।] अये अनुकम्पते मां कश्चिन्मृगचारी मुनि-
३ र्भगवान् । भगवन् अनुगृहीतोऽस्म्यहमुपदेशात् भवतः ।
[मणिमादाय] हंहो संगमनीय

तया वियुक्तस्य विलग्नमध्यया
भविष्यसि त्वं यदि संगमाय मे ।
ततः करिष्यामि भवन्तमात्मनः
शिखामणिं बालमिवेन्दुमीश्वरः ॥ ३७ ॥

[परिक्रम्य अवलोक्य च ।] अये किं नु खलु कुसुमरहितामपि
लतामिमां पश्यतो मे रतिरुपलब्धा । अथवा स्थाने
३ मनोरमा ममेयम् । इयं हि

How, heedless of what I said he turns towards nis mate! But that is proper; for a reverse of fortune subjects one to insults; so from here–I–(*Walking and looking*). What is this to be seen in the rift of the rock?

This could not be a piece of the flesh of deer killed by a lion, since it is covered with lustre; nor is it a spark of fire for the sky has (just) rained.

(*Looking closely*);

Ah, this is some gem gleaming like a bunch of Ashoka blossoms, and the sun seems to endeavour to clutch at it by stretching forth his rays. [34]

How it captivates my heart! I will have it. Or rather my beloved whose hair fragrant with Mandara flowers should be adorned by this (gem) is now lost to me; why should I then soil it with my tears? [35]

(*Behind the Scenes*). Child, take it, do take it. It is the Samgamaniya jewel, sprung from the dye applied to Gauri's feet; when borne, it brings about, within a short time, union with the loved one. [36]

KING—Who is this that instructs me thus? (*Looking in space*). Some holy ascetic living the life of a deer feels compassion for me. Revered sir, I am obliged to you for this advice. (*Taking the gem*). O gem of union,

If severed as I am from her of slender waist, you unite me to her, then surely I will make you my crest-gem, even as Ishvara his crescent-moon. [37]

(*Walking about and observing*). How is it that my mind is charmed even by looking at this creeper, albeit bereft of flowers? Or rather, it is proper it should charm my mind. This is

तन्वी मेघजलार्द्रपल्लवतया धौताधरेवाश्रुभिः
शून्येवाभरणैः स्वकालविरहाद् विश्रान्तपुष्पोद्गमा ।
चिन्तामौनमिवास्थिता मधुलिहां शब्दैर्विना लक्ष्यते
चण्डी मामवधूय पादपतितं जातानुतापेव सा ॥३८॥

यावदस्याः प्रियानुकारिण्याः परिष्वङ्गप्रणयी भवामि ।
३ [इति लतामालिङ्गति । ततः प्रविशति तत्स्थान एवोर्वशी]

राजा—[निमीलिताक्ष एव स्पर्शं रूपयित्वा] अये उर्वशीगात्र-
संपर्कादिव निर्वृतं मे शरीरम् । तथापि न पुनरस्ति
६ विश्वासः । कुतः ।

समर्थये यत् प्रथमं प्रियां प्रति
क्षणेन तन्मे परिवर्तते ऽन्यथा ।
अतो विनिद्रे सहसा विलोचने
करोमि न स्पर्शविभावितप्रियः ॥ ३९ ॥

[शनैश्चक्षुरुन्मील्य ।] कथं सत्यमेव प्रियतमा ।

उर्वशी—[बाष्पं विसृज्य] जेदु जेदु महाराओ । जयतु
३ जयतु महाराजः ।

राजा—

त्वद्वियोगोद्भवे तन्वि मया तमसि मज्जता ।
दिष्ट्या प्रत्युपलब्धासि चेतनेव गतासुना ॥ ४० ॥

उर्वशी—अब्भन्तर-करणाए मए पच्चक्खी-किद-वुत्तन्तो
खु महाराओ । अभ्यन्तरकरणया मया प्रत्यक्षीकृतवृत्तान्तः खलु
३ महाराजः ।

That slender one, and the tender leaves wetted by the clouds her lower lip washed by her tears; not decked with blossom, as it is past its time of flowering, it is she with her ornaments cast aside ; since the bees are not humming to it, she has been silent in anxious thoughts. So it is that irascible one, who having spurned me fallen at her feet, now seems to be stung with remorse. [38]

I will therefore, press this likeness of my beloved to my heart. (*Embraces the creeper*).

(*Enter Urvashi at that very place*).

KING—(*With eyes yet closed, showing that he perceives touch*). Ah, how the fever of my body is allayed as at the touch of Urvashi's person ? Still my mind misgives me, For,

Whatever I fancy as belonging to my love turns to be otherwise a moment after. So will I not open my eyes all of a sudden, (though) I recongnize my Lo-- through touch. [39]

(*Slowly opening his eyes*) How ! my Love forsooth !

URVASHI—(*Shedding tears*). Glory to my Lord !

KING—O slender one, while I was sinking in the darkness caused by your loss, I have fortunately recovered you, as a person dead might recover life.[40]

URVASHI—With my senses lying hidden in me, I witnessed the plight of my Lord.

राजा—अभ्यन्तरकरणयेति न खलु ते वचनार्थमवैमि ।

उर्वशी—कहइस्सं । इमं दाव पसीददु महाराओ जं मए कोववसं गदाए एदं अवत्थन्तरं पाविदो महाराओ ।
कथयिष्यामि । एतत् तावत् प्रसीदतु महाराजो यन्मया कोपवशं गतया एतदवस्थान्तरं प्रापितो महाराजः ।

राजा—कल्याणि न तावदहं प्रसादयितव्यः । त्वद्दर्शनादेव प्रसन्नः सबाह्यान्तःकरणो ममान्तरात्मा । कथय कथमियन्तं कालमवस्थिता मया विना भवती ।

उर्वशी—सुणादु महाराओ । भअवदा कुमारेण सासदं कुमारवदं गेण्हिअ अकलुसो णाम गन्धमादण-कच्छो अज्झासिदो किदो अ एस विही । शृणोतु महाराजः । भगवता कुमारेण शाश्वतं कुमारव्रतं गृहीत्वा अकलुषो नाम गन्धमादनकच्छोध्यासितः कृतश्चैष विधिः ।

राजा—क इव ।

उर्वशी—जा इमं पदेसं इत्थिआ पविसदि सा लदाभावेण परिणमिस्सदि । गोरी-चरण-संभवं मणिं विणा तदो ण मुच्चिस्सदि त्ति । साहं गुरु-साव-संमूढ-हिअआ देवदा-समअं विसुमरिअ अगहिदाणुणआ कुमारवणं पविट्ठा । पवेसाणन्तरं एव्व वासन्ती लदा संवुत्ता ।
या एतं प्रदेशं स्त्री प्रवेक्ष्यति सा लताभावेन परिणंस्यति । गौरीचरणसंभवं मणिं विना ततो न मोक्ष्यत इति । साहं गुरुशापसंमूढहृदया देवतासमयं विस्मृत्य अगृहीतानुनया कुमारवनं प्रविष्टा । प्रवेशानन्तरमेव वासन्ती लता संवृत्ता ।

KING—I really do not understand what you mean by " the senses lying hidden."

URVASHI—I will explain. But let my Lord forgive that yielding to anger I wrought so sad a change in my Lord.

KING—Fair one, you have not to beg my forgiveness For your very sight has brought gratification to my soul together with the external and internal senses. Tell me, how you could live without me so long.

URVASHI—Let my Lord hear. The warrior God, vowing eternal celibacy, dwelt in the region bordering on the Gandhamadana, called Akalusha ; and he made this rule.

KING—What is it ?

UARVASHI—Whatever woman entered this region, would be transformed into a creeper ; and she would not be restored to her form in the absence of the gem sprung from the feet of Gauri. So, as my memory was oblitera-ted by the curse of the preceptor, I forgot the rule pres-cribed by the deity, and not accepting your entreaties, entered the forest sacred to Kumara. And the moment I became a Vasanti creeper.

२७ राजा—सर्वमुपपन्नम् ।

रतिखेदसुप्तमपि मां शयने या मन्यसे प्रवासगतम् ।
सा त्वं प्रिये सहेथाः कथं मदीयं चिरविप्रयोगम् ॥४१॥

इदं तद् यथाकथितं त्वत्संगमनिमित्तं मुनेरुपलभ्य मा॰
प्रभावादासादिता त्वमस्माभिः । [मणिं दर्शयति]

३ उर्वशी—अम्मो संगमणीआ । अदो खु महाराएण आ-
लिङ्गिदमेत्तव्व पकिदित्थ म्हि संवुत्ता [मणिमादाय
मूर्धनि वहति] अहो संगमनीयः । अतः खलु महाराजेन आलि-
६ ङ्गितमात्रैव प्रकृतिस्थास्मि संवृत्ता ।

राजा—एवमेव सुन्दरि क्षणमात्रं स्थीयताम् ।

स्फुरता विच्छुरितमिदं रागेण मणेर्ललाटनिहितस्य ।
श्रियमुद्वहति मुखं ते बालातपरक्तकमलस्य ॥ ४२ ॥

उर्वशी—महन्तो खु कालो तुह पइट्ठाणादो णिग्गदस्स ।
असूअन्ति मं पकिदीओ । ता एहि णिवुत्तम्ह । महान्
३ खलु कालस्तव प्रतिष्ठानात् निर्गतस्य । असूयन्ति मय्यं प्रकृतयः ।
तदेहि निवर्तावहे ।

राजा—यदाज्ञापयति भवती ।

६ उर्वशी—कहं महाराओ गन्तुं इच्छदि । कथं महाराजो
गन्तुमिच्छति ।

राजा—

अचिरप्रभाविलसितैः पताकिना
सुरकार्मुकाभिनवचित्रशोभिना ।
गमितेन खेलगमन विमानतां
नय मां नवेन वसतिं पयोमुखा ॥ ४३ ॥

[इति निष्क्रान्ताः सर्वे ।]

विक्रमोर्वशीये चतुर्थोऽङ्कः समाप्तः ॥

KING—Everything is explained.

You who would regard me as gone away on a journey, when I would be merely sleeping, overcome by fatigue of love-dalliance, how could you (otherwise) bear long severance from me? (41)

Here then having learnt from the sage, as already narrated, this gem to be the cause of my reunion with you, through the power of this gem I recovered you. (*Shows the gem*)

URVASHI—Oh, the gem of union! that is why I was restored to myself the moment my Lord embraced me. (*Takes the gem and holds it on her head*).

KING—Hold yourself, O fair one, hold a moment thus.

Irradiated by the glow of this gem placed upon your brow, your face looks as splendid as a lotus red-gleaming in the morning light. (42)

URVASHI—It is a long time that you left Pratishthana; surely the subjects must have been incensed against me. So come, let us return.

KING—As you command, Lady.

URVASHI—How will it please my Lord to travel?

KING—Take me, O stately of gait, to my place on a cloud turned into an aerial car, with the flashes of the evanescent lightning for its banner and the bow of Indra for the fresh paintings that beautify it. [43]

(*Exeunt Omnes*)

END OF ACT IV

पञ्चमोऽङ्कः ।

[ततः प्रविशति परितुष्टो विदूषकः ।]

विदूषकः—दिट्ठिआ चिरस्स कालस्स उव्वसी-सहाओ णन्दण-वण-प्पमुहेसु देवदा-रण्णेसु विहरिअ पडिणिवुत्तो पिअ-वअस्सो । दाणिं ससक्कारोवआरेहिं पकिदीहिं अणुरज्जन्तो रज्जं करेदि । असंताणत्तणं वज्जिअ ण किं वि से हीणं । अज्ज तिहि-विसेसो त्ति भअवदीणं गङ्गा-जउँणाणं संगमे देवीहिं सह किदाहिसेओ संपदं उवआरिअं पविट्ठो । ता जाव तत्तभवदो अलंकरीअमाणस्स अणुलेवण-मल्ले अग्ग-भागी होमि [इति परिक्रामति] दिष्ट्या चिरस्य कालस्य उर्वशीसहायो नन्दनवनप्रमुखेषु देवतारण्येषु विहृत्य प्रतिनिवृत्तः प्रियवयस्यः । इदानीं ससत्कारोपचारैः प्रकृतिभिरनुरज्यमानो राज्यं करोति । असंतानत्वं वर्जयित्वा न किमपि अस्य हीनम् । अद्य तिथिविशेष इति भगवत्योर्गङ्गायमुनयोः संगमे देवीभिः सह कृताभिषेकः सांप्रतमुपकार्यां प्रविष्टः । तद् यावत् तत्रभवतः अलंक्रियमाणस्य अनुलेपनमाल्ये अग्रभागी भवामि ।

[नेपथ्ये ।] हद्धी हद्धी । दुऊलुत्तरच्छदे ताल-वेण्टाधारे णिक्खिविअ णीअमाणो मए भट्टिणो अब्भन्तर-विलासिणी-मोलि-रअण-जोग्गो मणी आमिस-सङ्किणा गिद्धेण अक्खित्तो । हा धिक् हा धिक् । दुकूलोत्तरच्छदे तालवृन्ताधारे निक्षिप्य नीयमानो मया भर्तुरभ्यन्तरविलासिनीमौलिरत्नयोग्यो मणिरामिषशङ्किना गृध्रेणाक्षिप्तः ।

विदूषकः—[कर्णं दत्त्वा] अच्चाहिदं । परं बहु-मदो क्खु

ACT V.

(*Enter Vidushaka who seems satisfied*).

VIDUSHAKA—Fourtunately, my dear friend has now come back, after spending a long time enjoying with Urvashi in the gardens of the gods, Nandanavana and others. Now he rules, well pleased with his subjects who treat him with honour and respect. With the exception of his childless state, there is nothing wanting to make his happiness complete. To-day being an auspicious day, he has bathed at the confluence of the Ganges and the Yamuna along with his queens and has just now entered his tent. So while he adorns himself let me partake of the first portion of the flowers and perfumes. (*Walks about*)

(*Behind the scenes*)

Alas! Alas! Here has a hawk borne away the ruby, taking it for a piece of flesh, the ruby which well would adorn the crown of our Lord's dearest Queen, when I was taking it along in a silk-covered box of palm-leaf.

VIDUSHAKA—(*Listening*). What a mischance! That was the crest-gem of reunion highly prized by my friend.

सो वअस्सस्स संगमणीओ णाम चूडा-मणी। अदो खु असमत्त-णेवच्छो तत्तभवं आसणादो उट्ठिअ इदो एव्व आअच्छदि। जाव णं उवसप्पामि। अत्याहितम्। परं बहुमतः खलु स वयस्यस्य संगमनीयो नाम चूडामणिः। अतः खलु असमाप्तनेपथ्यस्तत्रभवानासनादुत्थाय इत एवागच्छति। यावदेनमुपसर्पामि।

[ततः प्रविशति सावेगपरिजनो राजा।]

राजा—

आत्मनो वधमाहर्ता क्वासौ विहगतस्करः।
येन तत्प्रथमं स्तेयं गोप्तुरेव गृहे कृतम् ॥ १ ॥

किराती—एसो एसो क्खु मुह-कोडि-लग्ग-हेम-सुत्तेण मणिणा आलिहन्तो विअ आआसं पडिब्भमदि। एष एष खलु मुखकोटिलग्नहेमसूत्रेण मणिना आलिखन्निव आकाशं परिभ्रमति।

राजा—पश्याम्येनम्।

असौ मुखालम्बितहेमसूत्रं बिभ्रन्मणिं मण्डलचारशीघ्रः।
अलातचक्रप्रतिमं विहंगस्तद्रागरेखावलयं तनोति ॥२॥

किं नु खलु कर्तव्यम्।

विदूषकः—[उपेत्य] अलं एत्थ घिणाए। अवराही सासणीओ। अलमत्र घृणया। अपराधी शासनीयः।

राजा—सम्यगाह भवान्। धनुर्धनुस्तावत्।

[निष्क्रान्ता धनुर्ग्राहिणी यवनी।]

राजा—वयस्य न दृश्यते विहंगः।

विदूषकः—इदो दक्खिणन्तेण अवगदो सासणीओ कुणवभोअणो। इतो दक्षिणान्तेन अपगतः शासनीयः कुणपभोजनः।

That is why, before finishing his attire, my friend leaves his seat and comes here. So I will approach him

(Then enter King with attendants in flurry).

KING—Where is the winged thief that courts his own death and presumes to violate for the first time the dwelling of his own protector? (1)

A forest-woman—There is he hovering in the sky, and scratching it, as it were, with the gem, the golden thread whereof he holds in his beak.

KING—Yes I see him.

As quick he flies in swift circles, with the gem the golden chain of which is in his beak, the bird seems to be hemmed in a fiery ring, by the circle of its flashing lustre. (2)

What indeed, is to be done?

VIDUSAKA—Banish compassion in the present case. A culprit deserves to be punished.

KING—You counsel wisely. A bow, a bow.

(Exit a Yavani—a bow-bearer to the King)

KING—Friend, the bird is not to be seen,

VIDUSAKA—He has flown away in the south. this carrion-feeder that ought to be punished.

१ राजा—[परिवृत्य अवलोक्य] हन्त इदानीम् ।

प्रभापल्लवितेनासौ करोति मणिना खगः ।
अशोकस्तबकेनेव दिङ्मुखस्यावतंसकम् ॥ ३ ॥

[प्रविश्य चापहस्ता यवनी ।]

यवनी—भट्टा एदं हत्थावाव-सहिदं सरासणं । भर्तः
२ एतद्धस्तावापसहितं शरासनम् ।

राजा—किमिदानीं धनुषा । बाणपथमतीतः क्रव्य-
भोजनः । तथा हि ।

आभाति मणिविशेषो दूरमिदानीं पतत्रिणा नीतः ।
नक्तमिव लोहिताङ्गः परुषघनच्छेदसंयुक्तः ॥ ४ ॥

[कञ्चुकिनं विलोक्य ।] लातव्य मद्वचनादुच्यतां नागरिकः
सायं निवासवृक्षाग्रया विचीयतां विहगदस्युरिति ।
२ कञ्चुकी—यदाज्ञापयति देवः ।

[इति निष्क्रान्तः]

विदूषकः—उवविसदु भवं संपदं । कहिं गदो रअण-
६ कुम्भीलओ भवदो सासणादो मुच्चिस्सदि । उपविशतु
भवान् सांप्रतम् । क गतो रत्नकुम्भीरको भवतः शासनाद् मोक्ष्यते ।

राजा—[विदूषकेण सहोपविश्य ।]

रत्नमिति न मम तस्मिन् मणौ प्रियत्वं विहंगमाक्षिप्ते ।
प्रियया तेनास्मि सखे संगमनीयेन संगमितः ॥ ५ ॥

विदूषकः—णं परिगदत्थो म्हि किदो भवदा । ननु परि-
गतार्थोऽस्मि कृतो भवता ।

[ततः प्रविशति शरं मणिमादाय कञ्चुकी ।]

कञ्चुकी—जयतु देवः ।

KING—(*Turning and looking*) Now I see.

With the gem looking large owing to its flashing lustre the bird seems to adorn the face of the quarter as with an ear-ornament made of a bunch of Asoka flowers. [3]

(*Enter a Yavani, with a bow in her hand*)

YAVANI—My Lord, here is a bow with an arm-guard.

King—What use is the bow, now? The vulture has flown beyond the arrow's reach. For

That excellent gem, as it is carried further by the bird looks like Mars clinging to a strip of a thick cloudlet. [4]

(*Looking towards the chamberlain*) Latavya, say to the prefect in my name, 'Do you track this thief of a bird at night to his tree of perch.

CHAMBERLAIN—As my lord commands.

VIDUSHAKA—Rest you my friend now. Wheresoever gone, this thief of the gem cannot escape your punishment.

KING—(*Sitting along with the Vidushaka*).

Merely as a gem I have very little regard for the precious stone snatched by the bird; but to this gem of union, I owe reunion with my love. [5]

VIDUSHAKA—Well, you have already told me so.

(*Enter Chamberlain bringing with him the gem and an arrow*).

CHAMBERLAIN—Victory to my Lord !

अनेन निर्भिन्नतनुः स वध्यो
रोषेण ते मार्गणतां गतेन।
प्राप्यापराधोचितमन्तरिक्षात्
समौलिरत्नः पतितः पतत्री ॥ ६ ॥

[सर्वे विस्मयं रूपयन्ति ।]

कञ्चुकी—अद्भिः प्रक्षालितो मणिः कस्मै प्रदीयताम् ।

३ राजा—किराति अग्निशुद्धमेनं कृत्वा पेटकं प्रवेशय ।

किराती—जं भट्टा आणवेदि [इति मणिं गृहीत्वा निष्क्रान्ता।]
यद् भर्ता आज्ञापयति ।

६ राजा—लातव्य अपि जानीते भवान् कस्यायं बाण इति ।

कञ्चुकी—नामाङ्कितो दृश्यते न तु मे वर्णविचारक्षमा दृष्टिः।

राजा—तेन ह्युपनय शरम् ।

९ [कञ्चुकी तथा करोति ।]

[राजा नामाक्षराण्यनुवाच्य । सापत्यतां रूपयति ।]

कञ्चुकी--यावन्नियोगमशून्यं करोमि ।

१२ [इति निष्क्रान्तः

विदूषकः--किं भवं विआरेदि । किं भवान् विचारयति ।

राजा--शृणु तावत् प्रहर्तुर्नामाक्षराणि [वाचयति]

उर्वशीसंभवस्यायमैलसूनोर्धनुर्भृतः
कुमारस्यायुषो बाणः प्रहर्तुर्द्विषदायुषाम् ॥ ७ ॥

विदूषकः—[सपरितोषम्] दिट्ठिआ संताणेण वड्ढदि
भवं । दिष्ट्या संतानेन वर्धते भवान् ।

३ राजा—सखे कथमेतत् ।अन्यत्र नैमिषेयसत्त्रादवियुक्तो-
ऽहमुर्वश्या । न च मया गर्भव्यक्तिरालक्षिता । कुत एव
प्रसूतिः । किं तु

Pierced by your anger turned into an arrow, the bird that deserved death, having thus met adequate punishment, has fallen from the sky together with the crest-gem. [6]

(*All express wonder*).

CHAMBERLAIN—To whom shall this gem, cleaned with water, be given?

KING—Ho, forester, purify it in fire and keep it in its box.

Forestwoman—As my Lord commands.

(*Takes the gem and departs*).

KING—Latavya know you to whom the shaft belongs?

CHAMBERLAIN—There is some name inscribed upon it, but my eye-sight cannot distinguish the characters.

KING—Well, then, bring the arrow to me.

(*The Chamberlain does as bidden; the King reads the letters of the name and he is a father.*)

CHAMBERLAIN—In the meanwhile, I will attend to my business.

(*Exit*).

VIDUSHAKA—What are you thinking?

KING—Hear the name of the striker.

" The arrow of Ayus, the archer who strikes at the life of his enemies, the son of Urvashi and Pururavas." [7]

VIDUSHAKA—(*With satisfaction*). I congratulate you upon your having a son.

KING—Friend, how is this? I have never been away from Urvashi, but for the interval of the sacrifice performed in the Naimisha forest. And I never marked that she was carrying. Whence then this child? But.

आविलपयोधराग्रं लवलीदलपाण्डुराननच्छायम् ।
तानि दिनानि वपुरभूत् केवलमलसेक्षणं तस्याः ॥ ८ ॥

विदूषकः--मा भवं सव्वं माणुसी-धम्मं दिव्वासु संभावेदु । पहावणिगूढाइं ताणं चरिदाइं । मा भवान् सर्वं मानुषीधर्मं दिव्यासु संभावयतु । प्रभावनिगूढानि तासां चरितानि ।

राजा--अस्तु तावदेवं यथा भवानाह । पुत्रसंवरणे किमिव कारणं तत्रभवत्याः ।

विदूषकः--को देवदा-रहस्साइं तक्कइस्सदि । को देवता-रहस्यानि तर्कयिष्यति ।

[प्रविश्य कञ्चुकी ।]

कञ्चुकी--जयतु जयतु देवः । देव च्यवनाश्रमात् कुमारं गृहीत्वा तापसी संप्राप्ता देवं द्रष्टुमिच्छति ।

राजा--उभयमपि अविलम्बितं प्रवेशय ।

कञ्चुकी--यदाज्ञापयति देवः ।

[इति निष्क्रम्य चापहस्तेन कुमारेण तापस्या च सह प्रविष्टः ।]

कञ्चुकी--इत इतो भगवती । [सर्वे परिक्रामन्ति ।]

विदूषकः--[विलोक्य] किं ण खु सो एसो तत्तभवं खत्तिअ-कुमारओ जस्स णामङ्किदो गिद्ध-लक्ख-वेधी अद्ध-णाराओ । तह बहुअरं भवन्तं अणुकरेदि । किं न खलु स एष तत्रभवान् क्षत्रियकुमारको यस्य नामाङ्कितो गृध्रलक्षवेधी अर्धनाराचः । तथा बहुतरं भवन्तमनुकरोति ।

राजा-- स्यादेवम् । अतः खलु

बाष्पायते निपतिता मम दृष्टिरस्मिन्
वात्सल्यबन्धि हृदयं मनसः प्रसादः ।

During those days, her breasts had their nipples darkened, and her cheeks grew pale as the Lavali leaf, and her eyes were full of lassitude. [8]

VIDUSHAKA—You must not suppose that the heavenly nymphs betray the qualities of mortals. They can keep their doings hidden through their power.

KING—It may be as you say. But why should she have concealed her son?

VIDUSHAKA—Who can fathom the mystery of the celestial beings?

(*Enter chamberlain*).

CHAMBERLAIN—Glory to our Lord! a hermit-woman has come from the religious domicile of the sage Chyavana, with a boy, and desires to see Your Majesty.

KING—Usher both of them without delay.

CHAMBERLAIN—As my Lord commands.

(*Departs, and then enters leading the boy with a bow in his hand, and the hermit woman*).

CHAMBERLAIN—This way, madam, this way.

(*All move about*)

VIDUSHAKA—(*Observing*). Could this be the Kshatriya lad, to whom belongs the arrow that hit the vulture? To be sure, he looks your image to a great extent.

KING—That is possible. And hence?

My eyes are dimmed with tears as they rest on him, my heart is filled with tenderness, and my mind

संजातवेपथुभिरुज्झितधैर्यवृत्ति-
रिच्छामि चैनमदयं परिरब्धुमङ्गैः ॥ ९ ॥

कञ्चुकी—भगवति एवं स्थीयताम् ।

[तापसीकुमारौ स्थितौ ।]

राजा—अम्ब अभिवादये ।

३ तापसी—महा-भाअ सोम-वंस-वित्थारइत्तओ होहि ।
[आत्मगतम्] अम्हो अणाचक्खिदोवि विण्णादो इमस्स
राएसिणो आउसो अ ओरसो संबन्धो । [प्रकाशम्]
६ जाद पणम दे गुरुं । महाभाग सोमवंशविस्तारयिता भव । अहो
अनाख्यातोपि विज्ञातः अस्य राजर्षेरायुपश्चौरसः संबन्धः । जात प्रणम
ते गुरुम् ।

९ [कुमारश्चापगर्भमञ्जलिं करोति ।]

राजा—आयुष्मान् भव ।

कुमारः—[आत्मगतम्]

यदि हार्दमिदं श्रुत्वा पिता ममायं सुतोऽहमस्येति ।
उत्सङ्गवर्धितानां गुरुषु भवेत् कीदृशः स्नेहः ॥ १० ॥

राजा—भगवति किमागमनप्रयोजनम् ।

तापसी—सुणादु महाराओ । एसो दीहाऊ आऊ जाद-
३ मेत्तो एव्व उव्वसीए किंवि णिमित्तं अवेक्खिअ मम
हत्थे णासी-किदो । जं खत्तिअ-कुमारअस्स जाद-कम्मादि
विहाणं तं से भअवदा चवणेण असेसं अणुचिट्ठिदं ।
६ गहिद-विज्जो धणुव्वेदे अहिविणीदो । शृणोतु महाराजः ।
एष दीर्घायुरायुर्जातमात्र एव उर्वश्या किमपि निमित्तमपेक्ष्य मम
हस्ते न्यासीकृतः । यत् क्षत्रियकुमारस्य जातकर्मादि विधानं तदस्य

becomes serene. Seized by a tremor, and my equanimity gone, I desire to clasp him close with my limbs. [9]

CHAMBERLAIN—Revered lady, here pause.

(*The hermit woman and the boy stand*).

KING—Hail, holy dame!

HERMIT-WOMAN—Fortunate one, may you continue the line of Soma. (*To herself*) Ah, without being told, one may tell that the royal sage and Ayus are bound by ties of blood. (*Aloud*) Boy, pay your homage to your father.

(*Joins his hands in reverence, still holding the bow in them*).

KING—May your years be many!

BOY—(*To himself*). If such my love on hearing that he is my father and I his son, how great must be the love of those who grew up fondled in the laps by their fathers? [10]

KING--Revered lady, what brings you here?

HERMIT-WOMAN—Let my lord hear. This long-lived child was for some cause confided to my care by Urvashi, the moment he was born. The rites of birth and other rites proper to the warrior-lad have been duly performed by the sage Chyavana. After having learned the sciences, he has been trained to archery.

भगवता च्यवनेन अशेषमनुष्ठितम् । गृहीतविद्यो धनुर्वेदेऽभिविनीतः ।

राजा—सनाथः खलु संवृत्तः ।

तापसी—अज्ज पुप्फ-समिदत्थं इसि-कुमारएहिं सह-गदेण इमिणा अस्सम-विरुद्धं आअरिदं । अद्य पुष्पसमिदर्थमृषिकुमारकैः सह गतेन अनेन आश्रमविरुद्धमाचरितम् ।

विदूषकः—[सावेगम्] किं विअ । किमिव ।

तापसी—गहिदामिसो किल गिद्धो पादव-सिहरे णिलीअमाणो अणेण लक्खी-किदो बाणस्स । गृहीतामिषः किल गृध्रः पादपशिखरे निलीयमानोऽनेन लक्ष्यीकृतो बाणस्य

[विदूषको राजानमवलोकयति ।]

राजा—ततस्ततः ।

तापसी—तदो उवलद्ध-उत्तन्तेण भअवदा चवणेण अहं समादिट्ठा । णिज्जादेहि हत्थ-णासंति । ता इच्छामि देविं उव्वसिं पेक्खिदुं । तत उपलब्धवृत्तान्तेन भगवता च्यवनेन अहं समादिष्टा । निर्यातय हस्तन्यासमिति । तदिच्छामि देवीमुर्वशीं प्रेक्षितुम् ।

राजा—तेन हि आसनमनुगृह्णातु भगवती ।

(तापसी उपनीत आसने उपविशति ।)

राजा—लातव्य आहूयतामुर्वशी ।

कञ्चुकी—यदाज्ञापयति देवः ।

[इति निष्क्रान्तः]

राजा—[कुमारमवलोक्य] एह्येहि वत्स ।

सर्वाङ्गीणः स्पर्शः सुतस्य किल तेन मामुपगतेन ।
आह्लादयस्व तावच्चन्द्रकरश्चन्द्रकान्तमिव ॥ ११ ॥

KING—So he had a protector indeed.

HERMIT-WOMAN–Today while he had gone out to fetch flowers and wood with the boys of the ascetics, he acted in a way to violate (the sanctity of,) the hermitage.

VIDUSHAKA—(*Hurriedly*) How ?

HERMIT-WOMAN—They say that he aimed an arrow at a vulture that carried a bit of flesh and was perched on a tree-top.

(*Vidushaka looks at the King*).

KING—What next ?

HERMIT-WOMAN—Then the revered Chyavana who learnt about it, bade me return your deposit. So I wish to see Queen Urvashi.

KING—Well, please, holy dame, take a seat.

(*The Hermit-Woman occupies a seat brought for her*).

KING—Latavya, call Urvashi.

CHAMBERLAIN—As my Lord commands.

(*Exit*).

KING—(*Looking at the prince*). Come, child, come.

The touch of a son's person, they say shoots ecstasy through the whole body: therefore come and gladden me, as the moon's ray, the moonstone. [11]

तापसी—जाद आणन्देहि पितरं । जात आनन्दय पितरम् ।

[कुमारः राजानमुपगम्य पादग्रहणं करोति ।]

३ राजा—[कुमारं परिष्वज्य पादपीठे चोपवेश्य] वत्स इतस्तव पितुः प्रियसखं ब्राह्मणमशङ्कितो वन्दस्व ।

विदूषकः—किं ति सङ्किस्सदि । अस्सम-वास-परिचिदो एव्व साहामिओ । किमिति शङ्किष्यते । आश्रमवासपरिचित एव शाखामृगः ।

कुमारः—[सस्मितम्] तात वन्दे ।

९ विदूषकः—सत्थि भवदो । स्वस्ति भवते ।

[ततः प्रविशति उर्वशी कञ्चुकी च ।]

कञ्चुकी—इत इतो देवी ।

१२ उर्वशी—[कुमारमवलोक्य] को णु खु एसो स-बाणासणो पादपीठे सअं महाराएण संजमीअमाण-सिहण्डओ चिट्ठदि [तापसीं दृष्ट्वा] अम्मो सच्चवदी-सूइदो मे पुत्तओ

१५ आऊ । महन्तो खु संवुत्तो । [परिक्रामति] को नु खल्वेष सबाणासनः पादपीठे स्वयं महाराजेन संयम्यमानशिखण्डकस्तिष्ठति । अहो सत्यवतीसूचितो मम पुत्रक आयुः । महान् खलु संवृत्तः ।

१८ राजाः—[उर्वशीं दृष्ट्वा]

इयं ते जननी प्राप्ता त्वदालोकनतत्परा ।
स्नेहप्रस्रवनिर्भिन्नमुद्वहन्ती स्तनांशुकम् ॥ १२ ॥

तापसी—जाद एहि पच्चुग्गच्छ मादरं । जात एहि प्रत्युद्गच्छ मातरम् ।

[कुमार उर्वशीं प्रत्युद्गच्छति ।]

उर्वशी—अम्ब पाद-पणामं करेमि । अम्ब पादप्रणामं करोमि ।

HERMIT-WOMAN—Child, gladden your father.

(The prince approaches the King and touches his feet).

KING—*(Embracing the prince and placing him on the foot-stool).* Child, here is this Brahmin, your father's dear friend. Bow to him without fear.

VIDUSHKA—Why should he fear ? He has been familiar enough with monkeys during his stay in the hermitage.

PRINCE—Father, I bow.

VIDUSHAKA—Fortune attend thee.

(Enter Urvashi and the Chamberlain).

CHAMBERLAIN—This way, Queen, this way.

URVASHI—*(Looking at the prince).* Who is this, armed with the bow and seated on footstool, whose crest-knot is being tied by my Lord himself ? *(Looking at the hermit-woman).* Oh, it must be my son Ayus, as Satyavati's presence makes clear. *(Walks about).*

KING—*(Seeing Urvashi).*

Here comes your mother boy, her gaze .intently fixed upon you; and her breast-scarf all wetted with the milk distilled through a mother's love. [12]

HERMIT-WOMAN—Child, come, meet your mother.

(The prince goes to meet Urvashi).

URVASHI—Mother, I reverence your feet.

तापसी—वच्छे भत्तुणो बहु-मदा होहि। वत्से भर्तुर्बहुमता भव ।

कुमारः—अम्ब अभिवादये ।

उर्वशी—[कुमारमुन्नमितमुखं परिष्वज्य] **वच्छ पिदरं आराधइत्तओ होहि।** [राजानमुपेत्य] **जेदु जेदु महाराओ ।** वत्स पितरमाराधयिता भव । जयतु जयतु महाराजः ।

राजा—स्वागतं पुत्रवत्यै । इत आस्यताम् [अर्धासनं ददाति]

[उर्वशी उपविशति ।]

तापसी—एसो गहिद-विज्जो आऊ संपदं कवअ-हरो संवुत्तो । एदस्स दे भत्तुणो समक्खं णिज्जादिदो हत्थणिक्खेवो । ता विसज्जेदुं इच्छामि । उवरुज्झइ मे अस्समधम्मो । एष गृहीतविद्य आयुः सांप्रतं कवचहरः संवृत्तः । तदेतस्य ते भर्तुः समक्षं निर्यातितो हस्तनिक्षेपः । तद् विसर्जयितुमिच्छामि । उपरुध्यते ममाश्रमधर्मः ।

उर्वशी—चिरस्स अज्जं देक्खिअ अहिअदरं अवितिण्हम्हि । ण सक्कुणोमि विसज्जिदुं । अण्णय्यं उवरोहिदुं । गच्छदु अज्जा पुणो-दंसणाअ । चिरस्यार्यां दृष्ट्वा अधिकतरमवितृष्णास्मि । न शक्नोमि विस्रष्टुम् । अन्याय्यमुपरोद्धुम् । गच्छत्वार्या पुनर्दर्शनाय ।

राजा—अम्ब भगवते च्यवनाय मां प्रणिपातय ।

तापसी—एव्वं भोदु । एवं भवतु ।

कुमारः—आर्ये सत्यं यदि निवर्तसे मामपि आश्रमं नेतुमर्हसि ।

राजा—अयि वत्स उषितं त्वया पूर्वस्मिन्नाश्रमे । द्वितीयमध्यासितुं तव समयः ।

HERMIT-WOMAN—Child, ever may you retain your Lord's highest regard!

PRINCE—Mother, accept my salutations.

URVASHI—(*Embracing the prince, whose face is upturned*). Child, may you ever please your father. (*Approaching the King*). Glory to my Lord!

KING—To the matron, honour! Please to sit here. (*Gives her half his seat*).

(*Urvashi sits; all take their proper seats*)

HERMIT-WOMAN—This Ayus, who has been taught the sciences, is now old enough to wear the armour. So I have returned this deposit in the presence of your husband. So I wish to take my leave of you. For, my duties in the hermitage suffer.

URVASHI—Having seen you after such a long time, I feel particularly eager (to see you). I am not able to give you leave to go. But it would be on the other hand unjust to detain you. So may you go now to meet again.

KING—Mother, bear my reverence to the holy Chyavana.

HERMIT-WOMAN—It would be so.

PRINCE—Noble lady, if you are really going, will you not take me to the hermitage?

KING—Well, child, you have already lived the life of a student. It is now time you enter the second order (the life of a householder)

तापसी—जाद गुरुणो वअणं अणुचिट्ठ । जात गुरोर्वचनमनुतिष्ठ ।

कुमार—तेन हि

यः सुप्तवान् मदङ्के शिखण्डकण्डूयनोपलब्धसुखः ।
तं मे जातकलापं प्रेषय मणिकण्ठकं शिखिनम् ॥ १३ ॥

तापसी—[विहस्य] एव्वं करेमि । सत्थि भोदु तुम्हाणं । एवं करोमि । स्वस्ति भवतु युष्मभ्यम् ।

३ [इति निष्क्रान्ता ।

राजा—कल्याणि

अद्याहं पुत्रिणामग्र्यः सत्पुत्रेणामुना तव ।
पौलोमीसंभवेनेव जयन्तेन पुरंदरः ॥ १४ ॥

[उर्वशी स्मृत्वा रोदिति ।]

विदूषकः—किं णु खु तत्तहोदी एक्क-पदे अस्सु-मुही
३ संवुत्ता । किं नु खलु तत्रभवती एकपदेऽश्रुमुखी संवृत्ता ।

राजा—[सावेगम्]

किं सुन्दरि प्ररुदितासि ममोपपन्ने
वंशस्थितेरधिगमान्महति प्रमोदे ।
पीनोन्नतस्तनविसर्पिभिरानयन्तो
मुक्तावलीविरचनापुनरुक्तिमस्रैः ॥ १५ ॥

[बाष्पमस्याः प्रमार्ष्टि ।]

उर्वशी—सुणादु महाराओ पढमं उण पुत्त-दंसणेण
३ विसुमरिद म्हि । दाणिं महिन्द-संकित्तणेण समओ मह हिअअं आआसेदि । शृणोतु महाराजः प्रथमं पुनः पुत्रदर्शनेन विस्मृतास्मि । इदानीं महेन्द्रसंकीर्तनेन समयो मम हृदयमायासयति ।

HERMIT-WOMAN—Child, follow the bidding of your father.

PRINCE—Well then.

Send me the peacock Manikanthaka when he will have grown his plumage. the peacock that feeling happy at my scratching him about the crest would go to sleep in my lap. [13]

HERMIT-WOMAN—(*Smiling*). That I will do. Peace unto all. (*Exit*).

KING—Fair one,

By this excellent son of yours, I think myself the first among fathers like Indra by Jayanta, the son of Paulomi. [14]

(*Urvashi remembers and weeps*).

VIDUSHAKA—How all of a sudden the face of my lady is veiled with tea s ?

KING—(*Hurriedly*).

When great joy has come to me through the perpetuation of my race why should you, my dearest, weep, thus rendering superfluous the pearl-string by your tears that roll upon your heaving breast? [15]

(*Wipes away her tears*).

URVASHI—Listen, my Lord. I forgot awhile at the sight of this boy; but now the name of the great Indra brings to my mind the decree that pains my heart.

६ राजा। कथ्यतां समयः।

उर्वशी--अहं पुरा महाराअ-गहिद-हिअआ महिन्देण आणत्ता-अहं पुरा महाराजगृहीतहृदया मन्हेन्द्रेण आज्ञापिता-

९ राजा--किमिति।

उर्वशी--जदा एसो मम पिअ-सहो राएसी तुइ समु-
प्पण्णस्स वंस-करस्स मुहं पेक्खिस्सदि तदा तुए भूओ
७२ वि मम समीवं आअन्तव्वं ति। तदो मए महाराअ-
विओअ-भीरुदाए जादमेत्तो एव्व विज्जागम-णिमित्तं
भअवदो चवणस्स अस्सम-पदे अज्जाए सच्चवदीए हत्थे
७५ अप्पआसं णिक्खित्तो। अज्ज पिदुणो आराहण-समत्थो
संवुत्तो त्ति कलअन्तीए णिज्जादिदो मे दीहाऊ। ता
एत्तिओ मे महाराएण संवासो। यदैष मम प्रियसखो राज-
७८ र्षिस्त्वयि समुत्पन्नस्य वंशकरस्य मुखं प्रेक्षिष्यते तदा त्वया भूयोपि
मम समीपमागन्तव्यमिति। ततो मया महाराजवियोगभीरुतया
जातमात्र एव विद्यागमनिर्मित्तं भगवतश्च्यवनस्याश्रमपदे आर्यायाः
२७ सत्यवत्या हस्ते अप्रकाशं निक्षिप्तः अद्य पितुरारीधनसमर्थः संवृत्त इति
कलयन्त्या निर्यातितो मे दीर्घायु। तदेतावान् मे महाराजेन संवासः।

[सर्वे विषादं रूपयन्ति ।

२४ राजा—[सनिःश्वासम्] अहो सुखप्रत्यर्थिता दैवस्य।

आश्वासितस्य मम नाम सुतोपलब्ध्या
सद्यस्त्वया सह कृशोदरि विप्रयोगः।
व्यावर्तितातपरुजः प्रथमाभ्रवृष्ट्या
वृक्षस्य वैद्युत इवाग्निरुपस्थितोऽयम् ॥ १६ ॥

विदूषकः—अअं सो अत्थो अणत्थाणुबन्धो संवुत्तो संपदं

KING—Tell me what decree.

URVASHI—Formerly when my heart was lost to my Lord, I was bidden by the great Indra—

KING—What was it ?

URVASHI—"When this my dear friend, the royal sage, sees the face of a son that you will bear him, who will perpetuate his family, then will you again come back to me." So afraid of severance from my Lord, I secretly put him, the moment he was born, in charge of the holy dame Satyavati in the hermitage of the sage Chyavana, that he may be initiated into the sciences. Thinking that this day he is of an age when he might give joy to his father, she has brought him back—this my long-lived boy. So my stay with my dear Lord extends no further.

(*All gesticulate sorrow*).

KING—(*Sighing*). How hostile to man's happiness is fate !

Scarce have I known the blessing of a son, when my fair one is snatched away from me, as though the blasting lightning should fall on a tree just when it revives from languishment in the blaze of heat, as the young rain descends upon it. [16

VIDUSHAKA—So this is how good fortune is followed by a series of misfortunes. I should think now that my

तक्केमि तत्तभवदा वक्कलं गेण्हिअ तवो-वणं गन्दव्वं ति। अयं सोऽर्थः अनर्थानुबन्धः संवृत्तः। सांप्रतं तर्कयामि तत्रभवता वल्कलं गृहीत्वा तपोवनं गन्तव्यमिति।

उर्वशी—मं पि मन्द-भाइणिं किद-विणअस्स पुत्तस्स लाभाणन्तरं सग्गारोहणेण अवसिद-कज्जं महाराओ समत्थेदि। मामपि मन्दभागिनीं कृतविनयस्य पुत्रस्य लाभानन्तरं स्वर्गारोहणेन अवसितकार्यां महाराजः समर्थयते।

राजा—मा मैवम्

न हि सुलभवियोगा कर्तुमात्मप्रियाणि
प्रभवति परवत्ता शासने तिष्ठ भर्तुः।
अहमपि तव सूनावायुषि न्यस्तराज्यो
विचरितमृगयूथान्याश्रयिष्ये वनानि ॥ १७ ॥

कुमारः—नार्हति तातः पुंगवधारितायां धुरि दम्यं नियोजयितुम्।

राजा—अयि वत्स

शमयति गजानन्यान् गन्धद्विपः कलभोऽपि सन्
भवति सुतरां वेगोदग्रं भुजंगशिशोर्विषम्।
भुवमधिपतिर्बालावस्थोऽप्यलं परिरक्षितुं
न खलु वयसा जात्यैवायं स्वकार्यसहो भरः ॥ १८ ॥

लातव्य मद्वचनादमात्यपरिषदं ब्रूहि संभ्रियतामायुषो राज्याभिषेक इति।

कञ्चुकी—यदाज्ञापयति देवः। [इति दुःखितो निष्क्रान्तः]

[सर्वे दृष्टिप्रविघातं रूपयन्ति।]

राजा—[आकाशमवलोक्य] किं नु खलु निरभ्रे विद्युत्संपातः।

friend should wear barks and himself to some holy forest retreat.

URVASHI—Will the King regard me—unfortunate that I am—as one who has done her task, when I shall be gone to Svarga, now that I have got back my child who has finished his education!

KING—No, not so.

It is dependence, which, making severance only too natural, does not allow a person to have his own way. Do you obey your Lord. For me, I will resign my throne to your son Ayus and retire into the forest where herds of deer freely move [17]

PRINCE—It is scarcely meet that father should put an inexperienced bull to a yoke borne by a veteran.

KING—Ah, child

Even the cub of an excellent elephant soon subdues other elephants; the infant snake produces deadliest poison; a king even in his childhood is endowed with power to protect the earth. It is nature, therefore, and not age that gives each this fitness to bear his responsibility. [18]

Latavya, bid, in my name, our ministers to prepare for the coronation of Ayus.

CHAMBERLAIN—As my lord commands.

(*Departs in sadness*).

(*All show as if their eyes are dazed*).

KING—(*Looking to the sky*). How, a lightning-flash in a fair sky!

६ उर्वशी—[विलोक्य] अम्मो भअवं णारदो । अहो भगवान् नारदः ।

राजा—अये भगवान् नारदः । य एष

गोरोचनानिकषपिङ्गजटाकलापः
संलक्ष्यते शशिकलामलवीतसूत्रः ।
मुक्तागुणातिशयसंभृतमण्डनश्री-
र्हेमप्ररोह इव जङ्गमकल्पवृक्षः ॥ १० ॥

अर्घ्यमस्मै ।

उर्वशी—[यथाक्रमादाय] इअं भअवदे अरिहणा । इयं
२ भगवतेऽर्हणा ।

[ततः प्रविशति नारदः ।]

नारदः—विजयतां मध्यमलोकपालः ।

राजा—[उर्वशीहस्तादर्घ्यमादाय आवर्ज्य] भगवन्नभिवादये ।

उर्वशी—भअवं पणमामि । भगवन् प्रणमामि ।

नारदः—अविरहितौ दंपती भूयास्ताम् ।

१ राजा—[आत्मगतम्] अपि नामैवं स्यात् [प्रकाशम् ।
कुमारमाश्लिष्य] वत्स भगवन्तमभिवादयस्व ।

कुमारः—भगवन्नौर्वशेय आयुः प्रणमति ।

नारदः—आयुष्मानेधि ।

राजा—अयं विष्टरोऽनुगृह्यताम् ।

[नारदस्तथोपविष्टः ।

सर्वे नारदमनूपविशन्ति ।]

नारदः—राजन् श्रूयतां महेन्द्रसंदेशः ।

राजा—अवहितोऽस्मि ।

URVASHI—(*Observing*). Ah, it is Narada.

KING—Ah, the holy Narada! Who with his matted hair bright yellow like a streak of Gorochana on a touchstone, his sacred thread pure as the crescent of the moon looks like a moving tree of heaven profusely adorned with wreaths of excellent pearls, and growing shoots of gold. [19]

Bring materials of worship for him.

URVASHI—(*Bringing what is asked for*). Here is offering for the holy sage.

(*Enter Narada*)

NARADA—Hail to the Lord of this middle sphere!

KING—(*Taking the offering from Urvashi and presenting it*). Reverence to the sage!

URVASHI—My homage to the holy one.

NARADA—Never be wife and husband disunited!

KING—(*To himself*) Oh, might this be! (*Aloud, embracing the prince*) Child, pay your adoration to the holy sage.

PRINCE—Holy sir, here is Ayus, the son of Urvashi, paying his homage.

NARADA—May your days be many!

KING—Please to honour this seat.

(*Narada takes his seat. Others occupy their seats after Narada.*)

NARADA—King, listen to the message of the great Indra.

KING—I am all attention.

नारदः--प्रभावदर्शी मघवा वनगमनाय कृतबुद्धिं भवन्तमनुशास्ति

राजा--किमाज्ञापयति ।

नारदः--त्रिकालदर्शिभिर्मुनिभिरादिष्टः सुरासुरसंगरो भावी । भवांश्च सांयुगीनः सहायो नः । तेन त्वया न शस्त्रं संन्यस्तव्यम् । इयं चोर्वशी यावदायुस्तव सहधर्मचारिणी भवत्विति ।

उर्वशी--[अपवार्य] अम्महे सल्लं मे हिअआदो अवणीदं विअ । अहो शल्यं मे हृदयादपनीतमिव ।

राजा--परवानस्मि देवेश्वरेण ।

नारदः--युक्तम् ।

त्वत्कार्यं वासवः कुर्यात् त्वं च तस्येष्टमाचरेः ।
सूर्यः समेधयत्यग्निमग्निः सूर्यं च तेजसा ॥ २० ॥

[आकाशमवलोक्य ।] रम्भे उपनीयतां स्वयं महेन्द्रेण संभृतः कुमारस्यायुषो यौवराज्याभिषेकः ।

[प्रविश्य यथोक्तहस्ता अप्सरसः ।]

अप्सरसः--भअवं इमे अभिसेअ-संभारा । भगवन्नेतेऽभिषेकसंभाराः ।

नारदः--उपवेश्यतामायुष्मान् भद्रपीठे ।

रम्भा--इदो वच्छ [कुमारमुपवेशयति] इतो वत्स ।

नारदः--[कुमारस्य शिरसि कलशमावर्ज्य] रम्भे निर्वर्त्यतां शेषो विधिः ।

रम्भा--[यथोक्तं निर्वर्त्य] वच्छ पणम भअवन्तं मादापिदरे अ । वत्स प्रणम भगवन्तं मातापितरौ च ।

NARADA—Indra, who knows through his divine power, bids you who have made up your mind to retire to the forest—

KING—What are his commands?

NARADA—Sages, who can see the past, the future, and the present, have foretold hostilities between gods and demons. You are our worthy ally in the wars. Therefore, do not relinquish your arms; and this Urvashi shall be your wife as long as you live.

URVASHI—(*Aside*). A barbed arrow has been extracted from my bosom!

KING—I am subservient to the will of the King of the Gods.

NARADA—It is wisely said.

> Indra will work your good, and you too will act according to his wishes; the Sun sustains Fire with light, and Fire too with light nourishes the Sun. [20]

(*Looking to the sky*). Rambha, bring the materials for the coronation of prince Ayus as Yuvaraja, which great Indra himself has prepared.

(*Enter nymphs carrying in their hands the materials mentioned*).

NYMPHS—Holy sir, here are the materials of coronation.

NARADA—Let the prince be seated on the holy throne.

RAMBHA—Come here, child. (*Leads the prince to the seat*).

NARADA—(*Pouring water from the ewer on the head of the prince*). Rambha, complete the rite.

RAMBHA—(*Doing as bidden*) Child, pay you adoration to the holy sage and to your parents.

[कुमारः यथाक्रमं प्रणमति ।]

नारदः—स्वस्ति भवते।

राजा—कुलधुरंधरो भव ।

उर्वशी—पिदुणो आराधइत्तओ होहि। पितुराराधयिता भव।

[नेपथ्ये वैतालिकौ ।]

प्रथमः—विजयतां युवराजः ।

अमरमुनिरिवात्रिर्ब्रह्मणोऽत्रेरिवेन्दु-
बुंध इव शिशिरांशोर्बोधनस्येव देवः ।
भव पितुरनुरूपस्त्वं गुणैर्लोककान्तै-
रतिशयिनि समाप्ता वंश एवाशिषस्ते ॥ २१ ॥

द्वितीयः—

तव पितरि पुरस्तादुन्नतानां स्थितेऽस्मिन्
स्थितिमति च विभक्ता त्वय्यनाकम्प्यधैर्ये ।
अधिकतरमिदानीं राजते राज्यलक्ष्मी-
र्हिमवति जलधौ च व्यस्ततोयेव गङ्गा ॥ २२ ॥

अप्सरसः—[उर्वशीमुपेत्य] दिट्ठिआ पुत्तस्स जुव-राअ-सिराए भत्तुणो अविरहेण वड्ढसि। दिष्ट्या पुत्रस्य युवराजश्रिया भर्तुरविरहेण वर्धसे ।

उर्वशी—साहारणो एसो अब्भुदओ। [कुमारं हस्ते गृहीत्वा] एहि वच्छ जेट्ठ-मादरं अभिवन्देहि। साधारण एषोऽभ्युदयः। एहि वत्स ज्येष्ठमातरमभिवन्दस्व ।

[कुमारः प्रतिष्ठते ।]

राजा--तिष्ठ। सममेव तत्रभवत्याः समीपं यास्यामस्तावत्।

(The prince bows in due order)

NARADA—Blessing on you.

KING—Be you the foremost of your family.

URVASHI—Be obedient to your father.

(Behind the scenes, bards)

FIRST BARD—Glory to the young King.

Like the Divine sage Atri of Brahman, or the Moon of Atri, or Budha of the moon, and our King of Budha, so do you be worthy of your father by your qualities which are dear to the people. For in your most exalted family all blessings have indeed reached their highest pitch. [21]

SECOND BARD—

Now royal glory shines more bright divided as it is between your father, the foremost of the exalted, and yourself whose fortitude is unshakable and who are so upright, like the Ganges whose waters are divided between the Himalaya and the Ocean. [22]

NYMPHS—(*Approaching Urvashi*) We congratulate you upon your son's coronation as Yuvaraja and upon your union, without fear of separation, with your husband.

URVASHI—This happiness is common to us all. (*Holding the prince by the hand*). Come, child, pay your reverence to your elder mother.

(The prince starts).

KING—Wait. We shall all go together to her ladyship.

१ नारदः—

आयुषो यौवराज्यश्रीः स्मारयत्यात्मजस्य ते ।
अभिषिक्तं महासेनं सैनापत्ये मरुत्वता ॥ २३ ॥

राजा—एवमनुगृहीतो भगवता कथं न योग्यो भविष्यति ।

नारदः—किं ते भूयः पाकशासनः प्रियं करोतु ।

३ राजा—यदि मे मघवा प्रसन्नः किमतः परमिच्छामि । तथापीदमस्तु ।

[भरतवाक्यम् ।]

परस्परविरोधिन्योरेकसंश्रयदुर्लभम् ।
संगतं श्रीसरस्वत्योर्भूतयेऽस्तु सदा सताम् ॥ २४ ॥

[इति निष्क्रान्ताः सर्वे ।]

॥ इति विक्रमोर्वशीये नाटके पञ्चमोऽङ्कः ॥

॥ समाप्तमिदं विक्रमोर्वशीयं नाटकम् ॥

NARADA—This installation as Yuvaraja of your son Ayus reminds me of the coronation of Mahasena by Indra, as chief of the heavenly host. [23]

KING—When so favoured by the holy sage, how could he fail to prove worthy ?

NARADA—What further favour would you ask of Indra ?

KING—If Lord Indra is pleased with me, what more can I desire ? Still let this be my prayer.

(*Benediction*).

May learning and wealth, that oppose each other, unite in one common abode, which is ever so rare, to bring prosperity to the good. [24]

(*Exeunt Omnes*).

END.

Appendix—A.

श्लोकसूची ।

Appendix B—Metrical Table.

Number of syllables per quarter.	Name of the Metre.	Where employed.	Total	Measure.
8	अनुष्टुप्	I. 12,13, 14;II4, 5, 15,17,19;III.9,II,18, 21; IV.9,14,17, 18, 19,21,27,31,40;V.1, 3,7,12,14,20,23,24.	29	पञ्चमं लघु सर्वत्र सप्तमं द्विचतुर्थयोः । गुरु षष्ठं च पादानां चतुर्णां स्यादनुष्टुभि ॥
11	उपजाति	I.17,18;IV 35; V. 2, 6.	5	स्यादिन्द्रवज्रा यदि तौ जगौ गः । उपेन्द्रवज्रा प्रथमे लघौ सा । (इत्यनयोरुपजातिः ।)
12	द्रुतविलम्बित	II. 9;III.6;IV 26,29.	4	द्रुतविलम्बितमाह नभौ भरौ ।
12	वंशस्थ	I. 5, 9; III. 12, 13; IV. 7, 37, 39.	7	जतौ तु वंशस्थमुदीरितं जरौ ।
13	मञ्जुभाषिणी	IV. 33, 43.	2	सजसा जगौ च यदि मञ्जुभाषिणी ।
14	वसंततिलका	I. 3;II,14,16;III. 19 20;IV.6, 11,15;V.9 15, 16, 19.	12	ज्ञेया वसंततिलका तभजा जगौ गः ।
15	मालिनी	II. 6, IV; 10,13,22; V. 17, 21, 22.	7	ननमयययुतेयं मालिनी भोगिलोकैः ।

(Continued on next page)

17	पृथ्वी	II. 11.	1	जसौ जसयला वसुग्रहयतिश्च पृथ्वी गुरुः ।
17	मन्दाक्रान्ता	I.7;II.1;III.1;IV.4.	4	मन्दाक्रान्ताम्बुधिरसनगैर्मो भनौ तौ गयुग्मम् ।
17	शिखरिणी	IV. 28, 34.	2	रसै रुद्रैश्छिन्ना यमनसभला गः शिखरिणी ।
17	हरिणी	II.10;III.10;IV.20; V. 18.	5	नसमरसला गः षड्वेदैर्हयैर्हरिणी मता ।
19	शार्दूलविक्रीडित	I.1,4,8;II.7,20,23; III.2,15;IV.2,25,38.	11	सूर्याश्वैर्यदि मः सजौ सततगाः शार्दूलविक्रीडितम् ।
10/11	वैतालीय (वियोगिनी)	IV. 12.	1	विषमे ससजा गुरुः समे सभरा लोऽथ गुरुर्वियोगिनी ।
11/12	अपरवक्त्र	II. 22.	1	अयुजि ननरला गुरुः समे तदपर- वक्त्रमिदं नजौ जरौ ।
11/12	औपच्छन्दसिक	I.15,16;II,18;III.7; IV. 3, 16.	6	पर्यन्ते यौ तथैव शेषमौपच्छन्दसिकं सुधीभिरुक्तम् ।
12/13	पुष्पिताग्रा	III. 3, 22.	2	अयुजि नयुगरेफतो यकारो युजि तु नजौ जरगाश्च पुष्पिताग्रा ।
	आर्या	I.2,6.10,11;II.2,3, 8,21;III.4,5,8,14, 16,17;IV.5,8,23,24, 30,32,36,41,42;V.4, 5, 8, 10, 11, 13.	29	यस्याः पादे प्रथमे द्वादश मात्रास्तथा तृतीयेऽपि । अष्टादश द्वितीये चतुर्थके पञ्चदश सार्या ॥

N. B.—Verses 12 and 13 of act II are Prakrit Gathas.

Appendix C.

Text of Act IV according to the Northern Recension.

पिअ-सहि-विओअ-विमणा सहि हंसी वाउला समुल्लवइ।
सूर-कर-फंस-विअसिअ-तामरसे सरवरूसङ्गे ॥ 1 ॥

प्रियसखीवियोगविमनाः सखी हंसी व्याकुला समुल्लपति ।
सूर्यकरस्पर्शविकसिततामरसे सरोवरोत्सङ्गे ॥ 1 ॥

[इति चित्रलेखासहजन्ययोः प्रावेशिक्याक्षिप्तिका । ततः प्रविशति विमनस्का चित्रलेखा सहजन्या च । चित्रलेखाप्रवेशान्तरे द्विपदिकया दिशोऽवलोक्य ।]

सहअरि-दुक्खालिद्धअं। सरवरअम्मि सिणिद्धअं ॥
वाहोवग्गिअ-णअणअं। तम्मइ हंसी-जुअलअं ॥ 2 ॥

सहचरीदुःखालीढं सरोवरे स्निग्धम् ।
बाष्पाववल्गितनयनं ताम्यति हंसीयुगलम् ॥ 2 ॥

सहजन्या—[चित्रलेखां विलोक्य] सहि मिलाअमाण-सदवत्तस्स विअ दे मुहस्स छाआ हिअअस्स अस्सत्थदं सूएदि। ता कहेहि णिव्वेद-कारणं। सम-दुक्खा भविदुं इच्छामि।

सखि म्लायमानशतपत्रस्येव ते मुखस्य छाया हृदयस्य अस्वस्थतां सूचयति । तत् कथय निर्वेदकारणम् । समदुःखा भवितुमिच्छामि ।

चित्रलेखा—अच्छरा-वार-पज्जाएण इह भअवदो सुज्जस्स पादमूलोवट्ठाणं वट्टदि त्ति बलिअं खु उव्वसीए

उक्कण्ठिद म्हि । अप्सरोवारपर्यायेण इह भगवतः सूर्यस्य पादमूलोपस्थानं वर्तत इति बलवत् खलूर्वश्यामुत्कण्ठितास्मि ।

सहजन्या—जाणे वो अण्णोण्ण-सिणेहं । तदो तदो । जाने युवयोरन्योन्यस्नेहम् । ततस्ततः ।

चित्रलेखा—तदो इमाइं दिवसाइं को णु खु वुत्तन्तो त्ति पणिधाणट्ठिदाए मए अच्चाहिदं उवलद्धं । तत एतेषु दिवसेषु को नु खलु वृत्तान्त इति प्रणिधानस्थितया मया अत्याहितमुपलब्धम् ।

सहजन्या—[सावेगम्] **कीरिसं विअ ।** कीदृशमिव ।

चित्रलेखा—उव्वसी किल तं रदि-सहाअं राएसिं अमच्चेसु णिवेसिद-रज्ज-धुरं गेण्हिअ गन्धमादण-वणं विहरिदुं गदा । उर्वशी किल तं रतिसहायं राजर्षिममात्येषु निवेशितराज्यधुरं गृहीत्वा गन्धमादनवनं विहर्तुं गता ।

सहजन्या—सो णाम संभोओ जो तारिसेसु पदेसेसु । तदो तदो । स नाम संभोगो यस्तादृशेषु प्रदेशेषु । ततस्ततः ।

चित्रलेखा—तहिं खु मन्दाइणीए पुलिणेसु गदा सिअदापव्वदकेलीहिं कीलमाणा विज्जाधर-दारिआ उदयवदी णाम तेण राएसिणा णिज्झाइद त्ति कुविदा उव्वसी । तत्र खलु मन्दाकिन्याः पुलिनेषु गता सिकतापर्वतकेलीभिः क्रीडन्ती विद्याधरदारिका उदयवती नाम तेन राजर्षिणा निध्यातेति कुपिता उर्वशी ।

सहजन्या—होदव्वं । दूरारूढो खु पणओ असहणो । तदो तदो । भवितव्यम् । दूरारूढः खलु प्रणयः असहनः । ततस्ततः ।

चित्रलेखा—तदो भट्टिणो अणुणअं अपडिवज्जमाणा गुरुसाव-संमूढ-हिअआ इत्थिआ-जण-परिहरणिज्जं कुमार-वणं पइट्ठा । पवेसाणन्तरं च काणणोवन्तवत्तिलदाभा-

वेण परिणदं से रूवं । ततो भर्तुरनुनयमप्रतिपद्यमाना गुरुशापसंमूढहृदया स्त्रीजनपरिहरणीयं कुमारवनं प्रविष्टा । प्रवेशानन्तरं च काननोपान्तवर्तिलताभावेन परिणतमस्या रूपम् ।

सहजन्या—णत्थि विहिणो अलङ्घणिज्जं । तस्स अणुराअस्स अअं णाम एक्कवदे ईरिसो अणत्थो । अह किमवत्थो सो राएसी । नास्ति विधेरलङ्घनीयम् । तस्यानुरागस्य अयं नाम एकपद ईदृशोनर्थः । अथ किमवस्थः स राजर्षिः ।

चित्रलेखा—तस्सिं एव्व काणणे पिअदमं विचिण्णन्तो अहोरत्ते अदिवाहेदि । इमिणा उण णिव्वुदाणं पि उक्कण्ठाकारिणा मेहोदएण अणत्थाहीणो हविस्सदि । तस्मिन्नेव कानने प्रियतमां विचिन्वन्नहोरात्रानतिवाहयति । एतेन पुनर्निर्वृतानामपि उत्कण्ठाकारिणा मेघादयेन अनर्थाधीनो भविष्यति ।

[अनन्तरे जम्भालिका ।]

सहअरि-दुक्खालिद्धअं सरवरअम्मि सिणिद्धअं ।
अविरल-बाह-जलोल्लअं तम्मइ हंसी-जुअलअं ॥3॥

सहचरीदुःखालीढं सरोवरे स्निग्धम् ।
अविरलबाष्पजलार्द्रं ताम्यति हंसीयुगलम् ॥ 3 ॥

सहजन्या—सहि तारिसा आकिदि-विसेसा चिरं दुक्खभाइणो ण होन्ति । अवस्सं किंपि अणुग्गह-णिमित्तं भूओ वि समाअम-कारणं हविस्सदि । ता एहि उदअम्मुहस्स भअवदो सुज्जस्स उवट्ठाणं करेम्ह । सखि तादृशा आकृतिविशेषाश्चिरं दुःखभागिनो न भवन्ति । अवश्यं किमपि अनुग्रहनिमित्तं भूयोपि समागमकारणं भविष्यति । तदेहि उदयोन्मुखस्य भगवतः सूर्यस्य उपस्थानं कुर्वः ।

[अनन्तरे खण्डधारा ।]

चिन्ता-दुम्मिअ-माणसिआ। सहअरि-दंसण-लालसिआ॥
विअसिअ-कमल-मणोहरए। विहरइ हंसी सरवरए ॥4॥

चिन्तादूनमानसिका । सहचरीदर्शनलालसिका ॥
विकसितकमलमनोहरे । विहरति हंसी सरोवरे ॥ 4 ॥

[इति निष्क्रान्ते ।]

प्रवेशकः ॥

गहणं गइन्द-णाहो पिअ-विरहुम्माअ-पअलिअ-विआरो।
विसइ तरु-कुसुम-किसलअ-भूसिअ-णिअ-देह-पब्भारो ॥5॥

गहनं गजेन्द्रनाथः प्रियाविरहोन्मादप्रकटितविकारः ।
विशति तरुकुसुमकिसलयभूषितनिजदेहप्राग्भारः ॥ 5 ॥

[इति पुरूरवसः प्रावेशिकी आक्षिप्तिका। ततः प्रविशति उन्मत्तवेषो राजा।]

राजा—आः दुरात्मन् रक्षस्तिष्ठ तिष्ठ । क्व मे प्रियतमामादाय गच्छसि । हन्त शैलशिखराद् गगनमुत्पत्य बाणैर्मामभिवर्षति । [लोष्टं गृहीत्वा हन्तुं धावन्। अनन्तरे द्विपदिकया दिशोऽवलोक्य ।]

हिअआहिअ-पिअ-दुक्खओ। सरवरए धुद-पक्खओ ॥
वाहोवग्गिअ-णअणओ । तम्मइ हंस-जुआणओ ॥ 6 ॥

हृदयाहितप्रियादुःखः । सरोवरे धुतपक्षः ॥
बाष्पाववल्गितनयनः। ताम्यति हंसयुवा ॥ 6 ॥

[पुनर्विभाव्य ।]

नवजलधरः संनद्धोऽयं न दृप्तनिशाचरः
सुरधनुरिदं दूराकृष्टं न नाम शरासनम् ।
अयमपि पटुर्धारासारो न बाणपरंपरा
कनकनिकषस्निग्धा विद्युत् प्रिया न ममोर्वशी ॥१॥

[इति मूर्छितः पतति । द्विपदिकया उत्थाय निःश्वस्य ।]

मइँ जाणिअ मिअ-लोअणि णिसअरु को इ हरेइ ।
जाव ण णव-तलि-सामलो धाराहरु वरिसेइ ॥ 7 ॥

मया ज्ञातं मृगलोचनीं निशाचरः कोपि हरति ।
यावन्नु नवतडिच्छयामलो धाराधरो वर्षति ॥ 7 ॥

विचिन्त्य । क्व नु खलु रम्भोरुर्गता स्यात् ।

तिष्ठेत् कोपवशात् प्रभावपिहिता दीर्घं न सा कुप्यति
स्वर्गायोत्पतिता भवेन्मयि पुनर्भावार्द्रमस्या मनः ।
तां हर्तुं विबुधद्विषोऽपि न च मे शक्ताः पुरोवर्तिनीं
सा चात्यन्तमदर्शनं नयनयोर्यातेति कोऽयं विधिः ॥२॥

इति द्विपदिकया दिशोऽवलोक्य । सनिःश्वासम् । सास्रम् । अये परावृत्तभागधेयानां दुःखं दुःखानुबन्धि । कुतः ।

अयमेकपदे तया वियोगः प्रियया चोपनतः सुदुःसहो मे ।
नववारिधरोदयादहोभिर्भवितव्यं च निरातपत्वरम्यैः ॥३॥

[अनन्तरे चर्चरी ।]

जलहर संहरु एहु, को पइँ आढत्तओ
अविरल-धारासार-दिसा-मुह-कन्तओ ।
ए मइँ पुहवि भमन्तेँ जइ पिअ पेक्खीहि
तव्वे जं जु करीहिसि तंतु सहीहिमि ॥ 8 ॥

जलधर संहरैतत्, कस्त्वामाज्ञापितवान्
अविरलधारासारदिङ्मुखक्रान्तम् ।
ए मया पृथ्वीं भ्रमता यदि प्रिया प्रेक्षिष्यते
तदा यद्यत् करिष्यसि तत्तत् सहिष्ये ॥ 8 ॥

[विहस्य ।] मुधैव खलु मनसः परितापवृद्धिरुपेक्ष्यते । यथा मुनयोऽपि व्याहरन्ति राजा कालस्य कारणमिति । तत् किमहं जलदसमयं न प्रत्यादिशामि ।

[अनन्तरे चर्चरी ।]

गन्धुम्माइअ-महुअरवरगीएहिं
वज्जन्तेहिं परहुअरव-तूरेहिं ।
पसरिअ-पवणुव्वेल्लिर-पल्लव-णिअरु
सुललिअ-विविह-पआरेँ णच्चइ कप्प-अरु ॥9॥

गन्धोन्मादितमधुकरवरगीतै-
र्वाद्यमानैः परभृतरवतूर्यैः ।
प्रसृतपवनोद्वेल्लनशीलपल्लवनिकरः
सुललितविविधप्रकारेण नृत्यति कल्पतरुः ॥ 9 ॥

[इति नर्तित्वा ।] अथवा प्रावृषेण्यैरेव लिङ्गैर्मम राजोपचारः संप्रति । कथमिव ।

विद्युल्लेखाकनकरुचिरं श्रीवितानं ममाभ्रं
व्याधूयन्ते निचुलतरुभिर्मञ्जरीचामराणि ।
घर्मच्छेदात् पटुतरगिरो बन्दिनो नीलकण्ठा
धारासारोपनयनपरा नैगमाश्चाम्बुवाहाः ॥ ४ ॥

भवतु । किमेवं परिच्छदश्लाघया । यावदस्मिन् कानने तां प्रियामन्वेषयामि [पुनश्चर्चरीपाठस्यान्ते भिन्नकः ।]

दइआ-रहिओ अहिअं दुहिओ विरहाणुगओ परिमन्थरओ ॥
गिरि-काणणए कुसुमुज्जलए गज-जूह-वई बहु झीण-गई ॥10॥

दयितारहितोधिकं दुःखितो विरहानुगतः परिमन्थरः ॥
गिरिकानने कुसुमोज्ज्वले गजयूथपतिर्बहु क्षीणगतिः ॥ 10 ॥

[विलोक्य ।] हन्त व्यवसितस्य मे संदीपनमिव संवृत्तम् । कुतः ।

आरक्तराजिभिरियं कुसुमैर्नवकन्दली सलिलगर्भैः ।
कोपादन्तर्बाष्पे स्मरयति मां लोचने तस्याः ॥ ६ ॥

इतो गतेति कथं नु तत्रभवती मया सूचयितव्या ।

पद्भ्यां स्पृशेद् वसुमतीं यदि सा सुगात्री
मेघाभिवृष्टसिकतासु वनस्थलीषु ।
पश्चान्नता गुरुनितम्बतया ततोऽस्या
दृश्येत चारुपदपङ्क्तिरलक्तकाङ्का ॥ ६ ॥

[द्विपदिकया परिक्रम्य अवलोक्य च सहर्षम् ।] उपलब्धमुपलक्षणं येन तस्याः कोपनाया मार्गोऽनुमीयते ।

इतोष्ठरागैर्नयनोदबिन्दुभिर्निमग्ननाभेर्निपतद्भिरङ्कितम् ।
च्युतं रुषा भिन्नगतेरसंशयं शुकोदरश्याममिदं स्तनांशुकम् ॥७

[विभाव्य ।] कथम् । सेन्द्रगोपं नवशाद्वलमिदम् । कुतो नु खलु निर्जने वने प्रियाप्रवृत्तिरवगमयितव्या । [दृष्ट्वा] अये आसारोच्छ्वसितशैलेयस्थलीपाषाणमारूढः

आलोकयति पयोदान् प्रबलपुरोवातनर्तितशिखण्डः ।
केकागर्भेण शिखी दूरोन्नमितेन कण्ठेन ॥ ८ ॥

[उपेत्य ।] यावदेनं पृच्छामि । [अनन्तरे खण्डकः ।]

संपत्त-विसूरणओ । तुरिअं पर-वारणओ ॥
पिअदम-दंसण-लालसओ गअ-वरु विम्हिअ-माणसओ ॥11॥

[तेना खण्डकान्ते चर्चरी ।]

बंहिण पइँ अब्भत्थेमि आअक्खहि मं ता ।
एत्थु रण्णेँ भमन्तेँ जइ पइँ दिट्ठी सा महु कन्ता ॥
णिसम्महि मिअङ्क-सरिसेँ वअणेँ हंस-गईं ।
एँ चिण्हेँ जाणिहिसि आअक्खिउ तुज्झु मईं ॥ 12 ॥

संप्राप्तविसूरणः त्वरितं परवारणः ॥
प्रियतमादर्शनलालसः गजवरो विस्मितमानसः ॥ 11 ॥

बर्हिण त्वामभ्यर्थये आचक्ष्व मे तत् ।
अत्र अरण्ये भ्रमता यदि त्वया दृष्टा सा मम कान्ता ॥
निशामय मृगाङ्कसदृशवदनेन हंसगत्या ।
अनेन चिह्नेन ज्ञास्यस्याख्यातं तव मया ॥ १२ ॥

[चर्चरिकया उपविश्य अञ्जलिं बद्ध्वा ।]

नीलकण्ठ ममोत्कण्ठा वनेऽस्मिन् वनिता त्वया ।
दीर्घापाङ्गा सितापाङ्ग दृष्टा दृष्टिक्षमा भवेत् ॥ ९ ॥

[चर्चरिकया अवलोक्य ।] कथमदत्त्वा प्रतिवचनं नर्तितुं प्रवृत्तः । किं नु खलु हर्षकारणमस्य । [विचिन्त्य] भवतु ! विदितमेतत् ।

मृदुपवनविभिन्नो मत्प्रियाया विनाशाद्
घनरुचिरकलापो निःसपत्नोऽस्य जातः ।
रतिविगलितबन्धे केशहस्ते सुकेश्याः
सति कुसुमसनाथे किं करोत्येष बर्ही ॥ १० ॥

भवतु । परव्यसननिर्वृत्तं न खल्वेनं पृच्छामि [अनन्तरे खुरकः]

विज्जज्झर-काणण-लीनओ ।
दुक्ख-विणिग्गअ-बाहुप्पीडओ ॥
दूरोसारिअ-हिअआणन्दओ ।
अम्बर-माणे भमइ गइन्दओ ॥ 13 ॥

[खुरकान्ते चर्चरी ।] हेले हेले

परहुअ महुर-पलाविणि कन्ति ।
णन्दण-वण सच्छन्द भमन्ति ॥
जइ पइँ पिअअम सा महु दिट्ठी ।
ता आअक्खहि महु परपुट्ठि ॥ 14 ॥

विद्याधरकाननलीनो दुःखविनिर्गतबाष्पोत्पीडः ।।
दूरोत्सारितहृदयानन्दः भ्रमरमानेन भ्रमति गजेन्द्रः ॥13॥
परभृते मधुरप्रलापिनि कान्ते नन्दनवने स्वच्छन्दं भ्रमन्ति ।।
यदि त्वया प्रियतमा सा मम दृष्टा तदाचक्ष्व मम परपुष्टे ॥14॥

[एतदेव नर्तित्वा । वलन्तिकया उपसृत्य जानुभ्यां स्थित्वा]

इयमातपान्तसंधुक्षितमदा जम्बूविटपमध्यास्ते परभृता । विहंगमेषु पण्डिता जातिरेषा । यावदेनामभ्यर्थये । भवति

त्वां कामिनो मदनदूतिमुदाहरन्ति
मानावभङ्गनिपुणं त्वममोघमस्त्रम् ।
तामानय प्रियतमां मम वा समीपं
मां वा नयाशु कलभाषिणि यत्र कान्ता ॥ ११ ॥

[वामकेन किंचिद् वलित्वा । आकाशे ।] किमाह भवती । कथं त्वामेवमनुरक्तं विहाय गतेति । शृणोतु भवती ।

कुपिता न तु कोपकारणं
सकृदप्यात्मगतं स्मराम्यहम् ।
प्रभुता रमणेषु योषितां
न हि भावस्खलितान्यपेक्षते ॥ १२ ॥

कथं कथाच्छेदकारिणी स्वकार्ये एव सक्ता ।

महदपि परदुःखं शीतलं सम्यगाहुः
प्रणयमगणयित्वा यन्ममापद्गतस्य ।
अधरमिव मदान्धा पातुमेषा प्रवृत्ता
फलमभिमुखपाकं राजजम्बूद्रुमस्य ॥ १३ ॥

एवंगतेऽपि प्रियेव मे मञ्जुस्वनेति न कोपोऽस्याम् । इतो वयम्—[द्विपदिकया परिक्रामितकेन कर्णं दत्त्वा] अये

दक्षिणेन मं प्रियाचरणनिक्षेपशंसी नूपुररवः । यावदत्र गच्छामि ।

[परिक्रम्य ।]

पिअअम-विरह-किलामिअ-वअणओ ।
अविरल-बाह-जलाउल-णअणओ ॥
दूसह-दुक्ख-विसंठुल-गमणओ ।
पसरिअ-उरु-ताव-दीविअ-अङ्गओ ॥
अहिअं दुम्मिअ-माणसओ ।
काणणं भमइ गइन्दओ ॥ 15 ॥

प्रियतमाविरहक्लान्तवदनः अविरलबाष्पजलाकुलनयनः ॥
दुःसहदुःखविसंष्ठुलगमनः प्रसृतगुरुतापदीप्ताङ्गः ॥
अधिकं दूनमानसः काननं भ्रमति गजेन्द्रः ॥ 15 ॥

[इति ककुभेन षड्पमङ्गाः । अनन्तरे द्विपदिकया दिशोऽवलोक्य ।]

पिअ-करिणी-विच्छोइअओ गुरु-सोआणल-दीविअओ ।
बाह जलाउल-लोअणओ करि-वरु भमइ समाउलओ ॥16॥

प्रियकरिणीवियुक्तो गुरुशोकानलदीप्तः ।
बाष्पजलाकुललोचनः करिवरो भ्रमति समाकुलः ॥ 16 ॥

अहो धिक् धिक् ।

मेघश्यामा दिशो दृष्ट्वा मानसोत्सुकचेतसाम् ।
कूजितं राजहंसानां नेदं नूपुरशिञ्जितम् ॥ १४ ॥

भवतु । यावदेते मानसोत्सुकाः पतत्रिणः सरसो नोत्पतन्ति तावदेतेभ्यः प्रियाप्रवृत्तिरवगमयितव्या । [वलन्तिकया उपेत्य] भो भो जलविहंगमराज

पश्चात् सरः प्रति गमिष्यसि मानसं तत्
पाथेयमुत्सृज बिसं ग्रहणाय भूयः ।

मां तावदुत्तर शुचो दयितामवृत्त्या
स्वार्थात् सतां गुरुतरा प्रणयिक्रियैव ॥ १५ ॥

यथोन्मुखो विलोकयति मानसोत्सुकेन मया न लक्षिते-त्येवं वचनमाह [उपविश्य चर्चरी]

रेरे हंसा किं गोप्पइ
रेरे हंस किं गोप्यते ।

[इति नर्तित्वोत्थाय ।]

यदि हंस गता न ते नतभ्रूः
सरसो रोधसि दर्शनं प्रिया मे ॥
मदखेलपदं कथं नु तस्याः
सकलं चोर गतं त्वया गृहीतम् ॥ १६ ॥

गइ-अणुसारें मइँ लक्खिअउ ॥
गत्यनुसारेण मया लक्ष्यते ॥

[चर्चरिकया उपसृत्य अञ्जलिं बद्ध्वा] भवतु

हंस प्रयच्छ मे कान्तां गतिरस्यास्त्वया हृता
विभावितैकदेशेन देयं यदभियुज्यते ॥ १७ ॥

[पुनश्चर्चरी ।]

कइँ पइँ सिक्खिअउ ए गइलालस ।
सा पइँ दिट्ठी जहण-भरालस ॥ 17 ॥

कुतस्त्वया शिक्षिता एषा गतिलालसा ।
सा त्वया दृष्टा जघनभरालसा ॥ 17 ॥

[पुनश्चर्चरी । इह प्रवेशकस्यादि पठित्वा द्विपदिकया निसृत्य विसृत्य ।]
एष चोरानुगामी राजेति भयादुत्पतितः [परिक्रम्य]
अयमिदानीं प्रियासहायश्चक्रवाकः । तावदेनं पृच्छामि ।
[अनन्तरे कुटिलिका ।]

मम्मर-रणिअ-मणोहरए ।
[मल्लघटी ।] कुसुमिअ-तरु-वर पल्लवए ।
[चर्चरी ।] दइआ-विरहुम्माइअओ ।
काणणं भमइ गइन्दओ ॥ 18 ॥

मर्मररणितमनोहरे ।
कुसुमिततरुवरपल्लवे ।
दयिताविरहोन्मादितः ।
काननं भ्रमति गजेन्द्रः ॥ 18 ॥

[द्विलयान्ते चर्चरी ।] गोरोअण-वण्णा चक्का भण्णइ मइँ ।
महु-वासर कीलन्ती घणिअ ण दिट्ठी पइँ ॥19॥

गोरोचनवर्णे चक्र भण्यते मया ।
मधुवासरे क्रीडन्ती धन्या न दृष्टा त्वया ॥ 19 ॥

[चर्चरिकया उपसृत्य जानुभ्यां स्थित्वा ।]

रथाङ्गनामन् वियुतो रथाङ्गश्रोणिबिम्बया ।
अयं त्वां पृच्छति रथी मनोरथशतैर्वृतः ॥ १८ ॥

कथं कः क इत्याह । मा तावत् । न खलु विदितोऽहमस्य ।

सूर्याचन्द्रमसौ यस्य मातामहपितामहौ ।
स्वयं वृतः पतिर्द्वाभ्यामुर्वश्या च भुवा च यः ॥१९॥

कथम् तूष्णीं स्थितः । भवतु । उपालप्स्ये तावदेनम् ।

सरसि नलिनीपत्रेणापि त्वमावृतविग्रहां
ननु सहचरीं दूरे मत्वा विरौषि समुत्सुकः ।
इति च भवतो जायास्नेहात् पृथक्स्थितिभीरुता
मयि च विधुरे भावः कान्ताप्रवृत्तिपराङ्मुखः ॥२०॥

सर्वथा मदीयानां भाग्यविपर्ययाणामयं प्रभावः । याव-
दन्यमवकाशमवगाहे [पदान्तरे स्थित्वा] भवतु न तावद्
गच्छामि [द्विपदिकया परिक्रम्य अवलोक्य च]

इदं रुणद्धि मां पद्ममन्तःकूजितषट्पदम् ।
मया हृताधरं तस्याः ससीत्कारमिवाननम् ॥ २१ ॥

भवतु । अस्मिन्नेव कमलाभ्यासिनि मधुकरे प्रणयित्वं करिष्ये । इतो गतस्यानुशयो मा भूदिति [अस्यान्तरे अर्धद्विचतुरस्रकः]

एक्केक्कम-वड्ढिअ-गुरुअर-पेम्म-रसे ।
सरे हंस-जुआणओ कीलइ काम-रसें ॥ 20 ॥

एकैकवर्धितगुरुतरप्रेमरसे ।
सरसि हंसयुवा क्रीडति कामरसेन ॥ 20 ॥

[चतुरस्रकेण उपेत्य अञ्जलिं बद्ध्वा ।]

मधुकर मदिराक्ष्याः शंस तस्याः प्रवृत्तिं-

[विभाव्य ।]

वरतनुरथवासौ नैव दृष्टा त्वया मे ।
यदि सुरभिमवाप्स्यस्तन्मुखोच्छ्वासगन्धं
तव रतिरभविष्यत् पुण्डरीके किमस्मिन् ॥ २२ ॥

साधयामस्तावत् [द्विपदिकया परिक्रामितकेन] एष नीपस्कन्धनिषण्णहस्तः करिणीसहायो नागराजस्तिष्ठति । अस्मात् प्रियोदन्तमुपलप्स्ये [कुटिलिकया]

करिणी-विरह-संताविअओ ॥

[मल्लघटी ।]

काणणे गन्धुद्धअ-महुअरओ ॥ 21 ॥

करिणीविरहसंतापितः
कानने गन्धोद्धतमधुकरः ॥ 21 ॥

[अतोऽन्तरे विलोक्य ।] भवतु न त्वरा कार्या ।

अयमचिरोद्गतपल्लवमुपनीतं प्रियकरेणुहस्तेन ।
अभिलषतु तावदासवसुरभिरसं सल्लकीभङ्गम् ॥ २३ ॥

[क्षणमात्रं स्थित्वा । सानन्दम् अवलोक्य] हन्त कृताह्निकः संवृत्तः । भवतु पृच्छामि ।

हउँ पइँ पुच्छिमि अक्खहि गअ-वरु
ललिअ-पहारेँ णासिअ-तरु-वरु ।
दूर-विणिज्जिअ-ससहर-कन्ती
दिट्ठी पिअ पइँ संमुह जन्ती ॥ 22 ॥

अहं त्वां पृच्छामि आचक्ष्व गजवर
ललितप्रहारेण नाशिततरुवर ।
दूरविनिर्जितशशधरकान्तिः
दृष्टा प्रिया त्वया संमुखं यान्ती ॥ 22 ॥

[तदन्तरं पुनः उपसृत्य ।]

मदकल युवतिशशिकला
गजयूथप यूथिकाशबलकेशी ।
स्थिरयौवना स्थिता ते
दूरालोके सुखालोका ॥ २४ ॥

[सहर्षम् ।] अनेन स्निग्धमन्द्रेण गर्जितेन प्रियोपलम्भशंसिना समाश्वासितोऽस्मि। साधर्म्याच्च त्वयि मे भूयसी प्रीतिः।

मामाहुः पृथिवीभृतामधिपतिं नागाधिराजो भवान्
अव्युच्छिन्नपृथुप्रवृत्ति भवतो दानं ममाप्यर्थिषु ।
स्त्रीरत्नेषु ममोर्वशी प्रियतमा यूथे तवेयं वशा
सर्वं मामनु ते प्रियाविरहजां त्वं तु व्यथां मानुभूः ॥२५॥

सुखमास्तां भवान् । साधयामस्तावत् [पार्श्वतो दृष्टिं दत्त्वा] अये सुरभिकन्दरो नाम विशेषरमणीयः सानु-

मानालोक्यते । प्रियश्चायमप्सरसाम् । अपि नाम सुत-
नुरस्योपत्यकायामुपलभ्येत [परिक्रम्य अवलोक्य च] कथ-
मन्धकारः । भवतु । विद्युत्प्रकाशेनावलोकयामि ' हन्त
मदीयैर्दुरितपरिणामैर्मेघोऽपि शतह्रदाशून्यः संवृत्तः ।
तथापि शिलोच्चयमेतमपृष्ट्वा न निवर्तिष्ये [अनन्तरे खण्डिका]

पसरिअ-खर-खुर दारिअ-मेइणिओ वण-गहणे अविआल्लु ।
परिसक्कइ पेच्छहु लीणो णिअ-कज्जुज्जुअ कोलु ॥ 23 ॥

प्रसृतखरखुरदारितमेदिनीको वनगहनेऽविचलः ।
परिष्वक्क्ते पश्यत लीना निजकार्योद्युक्तः कोलः ॥ 23 ॥

अपि वनान्तरमल्पकुचान्तरा श्रयति पर्वत पर्वसु संनता ।
इदमनङ्गपरिग्रहमङ्गना पृथुनितम्ब नितम्बवती तव ॥२६॥

कथं तूष्णीमास्ते । शङ्के विप्रकृष्टो न शृणोतीति । समी-
पेऽस्य गत्वा पुनरेनं पृच्छामि [अनन्तरे चर्चरी]

फलिह-सिला-अल-णिम्मल-णिज्झरु ।
बहु-विह-कुसुमे विरइअ-सेहरु ॥
किण्णर-महुरुग्गीअ-मणोहरु ।
देक्खावहि महु पिअअम महिहरु ॥ 24 ॥

स्फटिकशिलातलनिर्मलनिर्झर ।
बहुविधकुसुमैर्विरचितशेखर ॥
किंनरमधुरोद्गीतमनोहर ।
दर्शय मम प्रियतमां महीधर ॥ 24 ॥

[इति परिक्रम्य अञ्जलिं बद्ध्वा ।]

सर्वक्षितिभृतां नाथ दृष्टा सर्वाङ्गसुन्दरी ।
रामा रम्ये वनान्तेऽस्मिन् मया विरहिता त्वया ॥२७॥

[आकर्ण्य । सहर्षम् ।] कथं यथाक्रमं इत्येत्याह । भवानपि अतः प्रियतरं गृणोतु । क तर्हि मम प्रियतमा [नेपथ्ये तदेवाकर्ण्य] हा धिक् । ममैवायं कन्दरमुखविसर्पो प्रतिशब्दः । [विषादं रूपयित्वा] श्रान्तोऽस्मि । अस्यास्तावद् गिरिनद्यास्तीरे स्थितस्तरङ्गवातमासेविष्ये । इमां नवाम्बुकलुषामपि स्रोतोवहां पश्यतो मे रमते मनः ।

तरङ्गभ्रूभङ्गा क्षुभितविहगश्रेणिरसना
विकर्षन्ती फेनं वसनमिव संरम्भशिथिलम् ।
यथाविद्धं याति स्खलितमभिसंधाय बहुशो
नदीभावेनेयं ध्रुवमसहना सा परिणता ॥ २८ ॥

भवतु । याचिष्ये तावदेनाम् [अनन्तरे कुटिलिका]

पसिअ पिअअम सुन्दरि एणए ।
खुहिअकरुण-विहङ्गमए णए ॥
सुर-सरि-तीर-समूसुअएणए ।
अलि-उल-झङ्कारिअए णए ॥ 25 ॥

[कुटिलिकान्तरे चर्चरी ।]

पुव्व-दिसा-पवणाहअ-कल्लोलुग्गअ-बाहओ
मेहअअङ्क णच्चइ सललिअ जलणिहि-णाहओ ।
हंस-रहङ्ग-कुङ्कुम-सङ्ख-कआभरणु
करि-मअराउल-कसण-कमल-कआवरणु ॥
वेला-सलिलुव्वेल्लिअ-हत्थ-दिण्ण-तालु
ओत्थरइ दस दिस रुन्धेविणु णव-मेहजालु ॥26॥

प्रसीद प्रियतमे सुन्दरि एनया ।
क्षुभितकरुणविहंगमे नत्या ॥

सुरसरिन्नीरसमुत्सुकेनके ।
अलिकुलझङ्कारिते नदि ॥ 25 ॥

पूर्वदिक्पवनाहतकल्लोलोद्गतबाहुः
मेघाङ्गेन नृत्यति सललितं जलनिधिनाथः ।

हंसरथाङ्गकुङ्कुमशङ्खकृताभरणः
करिमकराकुलकृष्णकमलकृतावरणः ॥
वेलासलिलोद्वेल्लितदत्तहस्ततालः
अवस्तृणाति दश दिशो रुद्ध्वा नवमेघकालः ॥ 26 ॥

[इत्युपसृत्य अञ्जलिं कृत्वा ।]

त्वयि निबद्धरतेः प्रियवादिनः
प्रणयभङ्गपराङ्मुखचेतसः ।
कमपराधलवं मम पश्यसि
त्यजसि मानिनि दासजनं यतः ॥ २९ ॥

अथवा परमार्थसरिदेवैषा । न खलूर्वशी पुरूरवसमपहाय समुद्राभिसारिणी भविष्यति । भवतु । अनिर्वेदप्राप्याणि श्रेयांसि । यावदमुमेव प्रदेशं गच्छामि यत्र मे नयनयोः सुनयना तिरोभूता । [परिक्रम्य अवलोक्य] हन्त दृष्टमुपलक्षणं तस्या मार्गस्य ।

रक्तकदम्बः सोयं प्रियया घर्मान्तशंसि यस्यैकम् ।
कुसुममसमग्रकेसर-विषममपि कृतं शिखाभरणम् ॥३०॥

[विलोक्य] । इमं तावत् प्रियाप्रवृत्तिनिमित्तं सारङ्गमासी-नमभ्यर्थये ।

अभिनवकुसुमस्तबकिततरुवरस्य परिसरे
मदकलकोकिलकूजितरवझङ्कारमनोहरे ।

नन्दनविपिने निजकरिणीविरहानलेन संतप्तो
विचरति गजाधिपतिरैरावतनामा ॥ 27 ॥

[गलितकः । जानुभ्यां स्थित्वा ।]

कृष्णशारच्छविर्योऽसौ दृश्यते काननश्रिया ।
वनशोभावलोकाय कटाक्ष इव पातितः ॥ ३१ ॥

[विलोक्य] । किं नु खलु मामवधीरयन्निव अन्यतोमुखः संवृत्तः । [दृष्ट्वा ।]

अस्यान्तिकमायान्ती शिशुना स्तनपायिना मृगी रुद्धा ।
तामयमनन्यदृष्टिर्भुग्नग्रीवो विलोकयति ॥ ३२ ॥

[इति नर्तित्वा चर्चरी ।]

सुर-सुन्दरि जहण-भरालस पीणुत्तुङ्ग-घण-त्थणि
थिर-जोव्वण तणुअ-सरीहि हंस-गइ ।
गअणुज्जल-काणणे मिअ-लोअणि भमन्तें दिट्ठा पइँ
तह विरह-समुद्दन्तरे उत्तारहि मइँ ॥ 28 ॥

सुरसुन्दरी जघनभरालसा पीनोत्तुङ्गघनस्तनी
स्थिरयौवना तनुशरीरा हंसगतिः ।
गगनोज्ज्वलकानने मृगलोचना भ्रमता दृष्टा त्वया
तर्हि विरहसमुद्रान्तरादुत्तारय माम् ॥ 28

[उपसृत्य अञ्जलिं बद्ध्वा ।] हंहो यूथपते

अपि दृष्टवानसि मम प्रियां वने
कथयामि ते तदुपलक्षणं शृणु ।
पृथुलोचना सहचरी यथैव ते
सुभगं तथैव खलु सापि वीक्षते ॥ ३३ ॥

कथमनादृत्य मद्वचनं कलत्राभिमुखः स्थितः । उपपद्यते ।

परिभवास्पदं दशाविपर्ययः । इतो वयम्-[परिक्रामितकेन अवलोक्य] शिलाभेदान्तरगतं किमेतदालोक्यते ।

प्रभालेपी नायं हरिहतमृगस्यामिषलवः
स्फुलिङ्गः स्यादग्नेर्गगनमभिवृष्टं पुनरिदम् ।

[विभाव्य ।]

अये रक्ताशोकस्तबकसमरागो मणिरयं
यमुद्धर्तुं पूषा व्यवसित इवालम्बितकरः ॥ ३४ ।

हरति मे मनः । आद्रास्ये तावदेनम् ।

पणइणि-बद्धासाइअओ वाहाउल-णिअ-णअणओ
गअ-वइ गहणे दूहिअओ भमइ क्खामिअ-वअणओ ॥29॥

प्रणयिनीबद्धाशाको बाष्पाकुलनिजनयनः ।
गजपतिर्गहने दुःखितः भ्रमति क्षामितवदनः ॥ 29 ॥

[द्विपदिकया उपसृत्य । ग्रहणं नाटयति ।] अथवा
मन्दारपुष्पैरधिवासितायां यस्याः शिखायामयमर्पणीयः ।
सव प्रिया संप्रति दुर्लभा मे किमेनमस्रोपहतं करोमि ॥३५॥

[नेपथ्ये ।] वत्स गृह्यतां गृह्यताम् ।

संगमनीय इति मणिः शैलसुताचरणरागयोनिरयम् ।
आवहति धार्यमाणः संगममचिरात् प्रियजनेन ॥ ३६ ॥

राजा—[कर्णं दत्त्वा] को नु खलु मामेवमनुशास्ति ।
[दिशोऽवलोक्य ।] अये अनुकम्पते मां कश्चिन्मृगचारी मुनिर्भगवान् । भगवन् अनुगृहीतोऽस्म्यहमुपदेशाद् भवतः ।
[मणिमादाय] हंहो संगमनीय

तया वियुक्तस्य विलग्नमध्यया
भविष्यसि त्वं यदि संगमाय मे ।

ततः करिष्यामि भवन्तमात्मनः
शिखामणिं बालमिवेन्दुमीश्वरः ॥ ३७ ॥

[परिक्रम्य अवलोक्य च ।] अये किं नु खलु कुसुमरहितामपि लतामिमां पश्यतो मे रतिरुपलब्धा । अथवा स्थाने मनोरमा ममेयम । इयं हि

तन्वी मेघजलार्द्रपल्लवतया धौताधरेवाश्रुभिः
शून्येवाभरणैः स्वकालविरहाद् विश्रान्तपुष्पोद्गमा।
चिन्तामौनमिवास्थिता मधुलिहां शब्दैर्विना लक्ष्यते
चण्डी मामवधूय पादपतितं जातानुतापेव सा ॥ ३८ ॥

यावदस्याः प्रियानुकारिण्याः परिष्वङ्गप्रणयी भवामि ।

लए पेक्खु विणु हिअएँ भमामि ।
अइ विहि-जोएँ पुणि तहिं पाविमि ॥
ता रण्णेँ विणुकरमि णिब्भन्ती ।
पुणु णइ मेल्लइ ताह कअन्ती ॥ 30 ॥

लते प्रेक्षस्व विना हृदयेन भ्रमामि
यदि विधियोगेन पुनस्तां प्राप्नोमि ।
तदरण्येन विनाकरोमि निर्भ्रान्ति
पुनर्न वियोजयति तस्याः कृतान्तः ॥30॥

[इति चर्चरिकया उपसृत्य लतामालिङ्गति ।]

[ततः प्रविशति तत्स्थान एवोर्वशी ।]

राजा—[निमीलिताक्ष एव स्पर्शं रूपयित्वा ।] अये उर्वशीगात्रसंपर्कादिव निर्वृतं मे शरीरम् । तथापि न पुनरस्ति विश्वासः । कुतः ।

समर्थये यत् प्रथमं प्रियां प्रति
क्षणेन तन्मे परिवर्ततेऽन्यथा ।

अतो विनिद्रे सहसा विलोचने
करोमि न स्पर्शविभावितप्रियः ॥ ३९ ॥

[शनैश्चक्षुरुन्मील्य ।] कथं सत्यमेव प्रियतमा । [इति मूर्छितः पतति ।]

उर्वशी--[बाष्पं विसृज्य] जेदु जेदु महाराओ । जयतु जयतु महाराजः ।

राजा—

त्वद्वियोगोद्भवे तन्वि मया तमसि मज्जता ।
दिष्टया प्रत्युपलब्धासि चेतनेव गतासुना ॥ ४० ॥

उर्वशी—अब्भन्तर-करणाए मए पच्चक्खी-किद-वुत्तन्तो खु महाराओ । अभ्यन्तरकरणया मया प्रत्यक्षीकृतवृत्तान्तः खलु महाराजः ।

राजा—अभ्भन्तरकरणयेति न खलु ते वचनार्थमवैमि ।

उर्वशी—कहइस्सं । इमं दाव पसीददु महाराओ जं मए कोववसं गदाए एदं अवत्थन्तरं पाविदो महाराओ । कथयिष्यामि । एतत् तावत् प्रसीदतु महाराजो यन्मया कोपवशं गतया एतदवस्थान्तरं प्रापितो महाराजः ।

राजा—कल्याणि न तावदहं प्रसादयितव्यः । त्वद्दर्शनादेव प्रसन्नः सबाह्यान्तःकरणो ममान्तरात्मा । कथय कथमियन्तं कालमवस्थिता मया विना भवती ।
[अनन्तरे चर्चरी ।]

मोरो परहुअ हंस रहङ्गम
अलि गअ पव्वअ सरिअ कुरङ्गम ।
तुज्झह कारणेँ रण्णे भमन्ते
को ण हु पुच्छिउ मइँ रोअन्ते ॥ 31 ॥

मयूरः परभृतो हंसो रथाङ्गः ।
अलिर्गजः पर्वतः सरित् कुरङ्गमः ॥
तव कारणेनारण्ये भ्रमता ।
को न खलु पृष्टो मया रुदता ॥ 31 ॥

उर्वशी—एव्वं अन्तक्करण-पच्चक्खी-किद-वुत्तन्तो महाराओ ।
एवमन्तःकरणप्रत्यक्षीकृतवृत्तान्तो महाराजः ।

राजा—प्रिये अन्तःकरणमिति न खल्ववगच्छामि ।

उर्वशी—सुणादु महाराओ । भअवदा कुमारेण सासदं कुमारवदं गेण्हिअ अकलुसो णाम गन्धमादण-कच्छो अज्झासिदो किदो अ एस विही । श्रृणोतु महाराजः । भगवता कुमारेण शाश्वतं कुमारव्रतं गृहीत्वा अकलुषो नाम गन्धमादनकच्छोध्यासितः कृतश्चैष विधिः ।

राजा—क इव ।

उर्वशी—जा इमं पदेसं इत्थिआ पविसदि सा लदा-भावेण परिणमिस्सदि । गोरी-चरण-संभवं मणिं विणा तदो ण मुच्चिस्सदि त्ति । साहं गुरु-साव-संमूढ-हिअआ देवदा-समअं विसुमरिअ अगहिदाणुणआ कुमार-वणं पविट्ठा । पवेसाणन्तरं एव्व वासन्ती लदा संवुत्ता । या एतं प्रदेशं स्त्री प्रविशति सा लताभावेन परिणंस्यति । गोरीचरणसंभवं मणिं विना ततो न मोक्ष्यत इति । साहं गुरुशापसंमूढहृदया देवतासमयं विस्मृत्य अगृहीतानुनया कुमारवनं प्रविष्टा । प्रवेशानन्तरमेव वासन्ती लता संवृत्ता ।

राजा—सर्वमुपपन्नम् ।

रतिखेदसुप्तमपि मां शयने या मन्यसे प्रवासगतम् ।
सा त्वं प्रिये सहेथाः कथं मदीयं चिरवियोगम् ॥४१॥

इदं तद् यथाकथितं त्वत्संगमनिमित्तं मुनेरुपलभ्य मणिप्रभावादासादिता त्वमस्माभिः । [मणिं दर्शयति ।]

उर्वशी—अम्मो संगमणीओ । अदो खु महाराएण आलिङ्गिदमेत्तव्व पकिदित्थ म्हि संवुत्ता [मणिमादाय मूर्धनि वहति ।] अहो संगमनीयः । अतः खलु महाराजेन आलिङ्गितमात्रैव प्रकृतिस्थास्मि संवृत्ता ।

राजा—एवमेव सुन्दरि क्षणमात्रं स्थीयताम् ।

स्फुरता विच्छुरितमिदं रागेण मणेर्ललाटनिहितस्य ॥
श्रियमुद्वहति मुखं ते बालातपरक्तकमलस्य ॥ ४२ ॥

उर्वशी—महन्तो खु कालो तुह पइट्ठाणादो णिग्गदस्स । असुअन्ति मं पकिदीओ । ता एहि णिवुत्तम्ह । महान् खलु कालस्तव प्रतिष्ठानाद् निर्गतस्य । असूयन्ति मां प्रकृतयः । तदेहि निवर्तावहे ।

राजा—यदाज्ञापयति भवती ।

उर्वशी—कहं महाराओ गन्तुं इच्छदि । कथं महाराजो गन्तुमिच्छति ।

राजा—

अचिरप्रभाविलसितैः पताकिना
सुरकार्मुकाभिनवचित्रशोभिना ।
गमितेन खेलगमने विमानतां
नय मां नवेन वसतिं पयोमुचा ॥ ४३ ॥

[चर्चरी ।]

पाविअ-सहअरि-संगमओ पुलअ-पसाहिअ-अङ्गअओ ।
सेच्छा-पत्त-विमाणओ विहरइ हंस-जुआणओ ॥ 32 ॥

प्राप्तसहचरीसंगमः पुलकप्रसाधिताङ्गकः ।
स्वेच्छाप्राप्तविमानो विहरति हंसयुवाः ॥ 32 ॥

[इति खण्डधारया निष्क्रान्तौ]

विक्रमोर्वशीये चतुर्थोङ्कः समाप्तः ॥

NOTES

ACT 1.

The prologue.

[The play is introduced with the Prastavana or prologue which opens with the usual benedictory stanza called Nandi, after which the Sutradhara or manager makes his appearance on the stage. He then calls his assistant and tells him that as he is going to stage the new play of Kalidasa called विक्रमोर्वशीय, the actors should be advised to attend carefully to their respective parts. The Sutradhara then requests the audience to hear and witness attentively the play of Kalidasa about to be staged. Just then the screams of heavenly nymphs crying for help are heard from behind the scenes. The Sutradhara concludes that the heavenly nymphs must be screaming and crying for help as their friend Urvashi has been abducted by the demons. Thereafter he makes his exit.]

In consonance with the time-honoured practice of Indian writers, Kalidasa opens his play with a benedictory stanza (the so-called नान्दी), invoking the grace of Shiva. According to the science of Indian Dramaturgy, an elaborate series of preliminaries (called the पूर्वरङ्ग) had to be performed before the actual commencement of a drama The last of these preliminaries was called the नान्दी, which consisted of a stanza or stanzas in glorification of some deity. The नान्दी was regarded as the most important part of the पूर्वरङ्ग, so that although in the course of time the other preliminaries were conveniently omitted in practice, the नान्दी was always attended to and religiously carried out (cf. Bharata: यद्यप्यंगानि भूयांसि पूर्वरंगस्य नाटके । तथाप्यवश्यं कर्तव्या नान्दी विघ्नप्रशान्तये ।). The two other plays of Kalidasa open with similar benedictory stanzas in praise of Shiva. The Raghuvamsha too opens with a salutation to Shiva. In the Meghaduta and Kumarasambhava also, we come across several appreciative references to the same deity. All this would make it seem probable that Kalidasa was a votary of Shiva. But it must not be forgotten that although Kalidasa had a particularly soft corner in his heart for Shiva, he was still by no means a bigot in his religious views. If we read Raghuvamsha X and Kumarasambhava II, we find that his admiration for Vishnu and Brahmadeva was as great as for Shiva. Altogether he was a man thoroughly catholic in his religious persuasions and by no means a bigoted fanatic. Vide Introduction p. V–VI.

I. 1. Construe: यं वेदान्तेषु रोदसी व्याप्य स्थितम् एकपुरुषम् आहुः । यस्मिन् ईश्वरः इति अनन्यविषयः शब्दः यथार्थाक्षरः (भवति) । यः च नियमितप्राणादिभिः मुमुक्षुभिः अन्तः मृग्यते । सः स्थिरभक्तियोगसुलभः स्थाणुः वः निःश्रेयसाय अस्तु । वेदान्तेषु—In the Upanishads. The Upanishads are called वेदान्त, because they form the concluding portion of each Veda, which consists of four parts, संहिता, ब्राह्मण, आरण्यक and उपनिषद्. Chronologically, too, the Upanishads are the last compositions in the literature coming under each Veda. Doctrinally again they represent the culminating phase of Vedic thought. एकपुरुषम् — The Supreme Spirit, or Being, which is the one without a second (एकमेवाद्वितीयम्) as the Upanishads put it. रोदसी व्याप्य स्थितम् — who completely pervades the two worlds viz. heaven and earth.

For this use of the root स्था along with the absolutive form of another root cf. Shakuntala I. 1 श्रुतिविषयगुणा या स्थिता व्याप्य विश्वम्। cf. also the Purushasukta (Rigveda X. 90), stanza 1: स भूमिं विश्वतो वृत्वा अत्यतिष्ठत् दशाङ्गुलम् । ईश्वरः The Lord or Ruler. The word is derived from the root ईश् (II. A.) to rule + the suffix वर, which we find also in such words as नश्वर, इत्वर, मत्वर etc. अनन्यविषयः—न विद्यते अन्यः विषयः (वाच्यत्वेन यस्य सः। not signifying anything else, exclusively applicable to Him alone and none else. Other gods are called ईश्वर only by sufferance and courtesy, but Shiva alone is called ईश्वर with the fullest justification, as he possesses all the qualities signified and implied by that epithet. यथार्थाक्षरः—यथार्थानि (अर्थम् अनतिक्रान्तानि) अक्षराणि यस्य सः (शब्दः) literally true, significant to the letter. cf. II. 17 *infra*: जयशब्दः सहस्राक्षादागतः पुरुषान्तरम्, where अगतः पुरुषान्तरम्=अनन्यविषयः। नियमितप्राणादिभिः मुमुक्षुभिः—by spiritual aspirants (literally, those who are desirous of salvation) who have restrained the five vital airs, प्राण, and others. In Yogic physiology the vital functions of the body are analysed into the five vital breaths or airs प्राण, अपान, व्यान, उदान and समान, and the spiritual aspirant is recommended to hold these under control and to regulate their movements while practising abstract contemplation. मुमुक्षु is a desiderative adjective from the root मुच्, used in the sense of a substantive. अन्तः within i.e. in the mind or heart (हृदये, मनसि वा). स्थिरभक्तियोगसुलभः—This compound may be variously explained: (1) स्थिरः भक्तियोगः येषां ते स्थिरभक्तियोगाः, तैः सुलभः। (2) स्थिरौ भक्तियोगौ येषां ते स्थिरभक्तियोगाः, तैः सुलभः। (3) स्थिरेण भक्तियोगेन सुलभः। (4) स्थिरा भक्तिः, योगः (ध्यानं) च ताभ्यां सुलभः। भक्तियोग means the same as भक्तिमार्ग – the path or way of devotion. योग

by itself means abstract meditation. स्थाणुः from the root स्था. It literally means that which stands, that which is stationary. Hence, immovable, eternal, abiding. As an epithet of Shiva it means the Eternal One. निःश्रेयसाय अस्तु—May he conduce to your highest good i.e. salvation. निःश्रेयसम् means that which has nothing superior to it, hence the highest welfare or spiritual well-being in the form of मोक्ष. निर्गतं (i.e. अविद्यमानं) श्रेयः यस्मात् तत् निःश्रेयसम् or according to the सिद्धान्तकौमुदी, निश्चितं श्रेयः निःश्रेयसम् । The final अ in this word is laid down by Panini V. 4. 77.

I.1.1. नान्द्यन्ते—At the end of the benedictory stanza. नान्दी is defined as आशीर्नमस्क्रियारूपः श्लोकः काव्यार्थसूचकः *i. e.* a stanza of the form of a salutation or benediction which is suggestive of the story of the drama. It is called नान्दी because it is a source of delight to the gods. cf. नन्दन्ति देवता यस्यां तस्मान्नान्दीति कीर्तिता. The commentators काटयवेम and others take special pains to show how the नान्दी stanza of our play hints indirectly at the subject-matter. एकपुरुष refers to Pururavas, the hero of the play; व्याप्य स्थितं रोदसी hints at his world-wide reputation. The second line of the stanza suggests that Pururavas alone deserves the title ईश्वर, on account of his unique prowess. The words अन्तः मृग्यते in the third line are supposed to hint at the fact of Urvashi having of her own accord decided to seek his company. The commentators proceed in the same strain to show that the remaining expressions in the stanza are suggestive more or less indirectly of the subject-matter of the play. But it must be said that such attempts on the part of the commentators are purely fantastic, and one wonders if the author of the play ever intended the नान्दी stanza to express such a deeper meaning as the commentators try to read into it.

I. 1. 2. नेपथ्याभिमुखम्—In the direction of the tiring or green room. The word नेपथ्य means here जवनिकान्तर्भूमिः वेषपरिग्रहस्थलम्—the space behind the scenes. where the actors dress themselves and do their toilet. मारिष—This is a term of polite address used by the Sutradhara in addressing his assistant. cf. भावो मान्यः समुद्दिष्टः किंचिदूनस्तु मारिषः। and also सूत्रधारं वदेद् भाव इति वै पारिपार्श्वकः। सूत्रधारो मारिषेति पारिपार्श्वकमादिशेत्।

I. 1. 3. पारिपार्श्वकः (or according to काटवेम, पारिपार्श्विकः) —the assistant of the Sutradhara. The word is derived from परिपार्श्व + the suffix अण् (in the sense of तत्र भवः) + क (स्वार्थे) परिपार्श्वे भवः पारिपार्श्वः। स एव पारिपार्श्वकः। If, however we adopt the form पारिपार्श्विक, we shall have to derive it from परिपार्श्व+ठक्(इक). Vide Panini IV. 4. 29. and सिद्धान्तकौमुदी. He is characterized as follows by भरत in his नाट्यशास्त्र- सूत्रधारस्य पार्श्वे यः प्रवदन् कुरुतेऽर्थनाम्। काव्यार्थसूचनालापं स भवेत् पारिपार्श्वकः

I. 1. 4. भाव—Exalted sir. When an inferior person addresses his superior, he uses the word भाव; cf. the quotations given above under मारिष. I. 1. 6. प्रयोगबंध dramatic composition, play. प्रयुज्यते इति प्रयोगः, तस्य बंधः The singular is used here for the plural. We have a variant reading : दृष्टप्रयोगाः प्रबंधाः। Here प्रबंध would mean a dramatic composition and प्रयोग would mean theatrical representation. The Nirnayasagara Ed. reads परिचयेषा पूर्वेषां कवीनां दृष्टरसप्रबंधा. In this case रसप्रबंध would mean a dramatic composition abounding in emotional flavour. रसप्रधानः प्रबंध रसप्रबंधः। All these readings are good in their own way and it is difficult to say which is the best परिषद्—Assembly *i. e.* the audience or spectators. पूर्वेषां कवीनाम् We know from the मालविकाग्निमित्र, that भास, सौमिल्ल, कविपुत्र etc., were among the predecessors of Kalidasa. सोऽहं......प्रयोक्ष्ये । This is virtually equal to तस्मादहं......प्रयोक्ष्ये 'Therefore shall I exhibit on the stage. 'Therefore' *i. e.* because the audience have many a time witnessed the plays of former poets. विक्रमोर्वशीयम्—The title of our play is explained in two ways: (1) विक्रमं (पुरूरवसं) च उर्वशीं च अधिकृत्य कृतं नाटकम् (काटयवेम). Here विक्रम is taken as a name of पुरूरवस् (विक्रमशब्दः पुरूरवसः संज्ञा इति संप्रदायः । काटयवेम), although there is no authority for taking the word in that sense, beyond the संप्रदाय (tradition or convention) referred to by काटयवेम. The form is explained on the analogy of such formations as किरातार्जुनीयम्, राघवपाण्डवीयम् etc. Vide Panini IV. 3. 38 (2) विक्रमेण (पराक्रमेण) लब्धा या उर्वशी ताम् अधिकृत्य कृतं नाटकम् । on the analogy of अभिज्ञानशाकुन्तलम्. In the former case the title would mean 'The drama of Pururavas and Urvashi,' while in the latter case it would mean 'The drama of Urvashi won by valour.' The latter way of explaining the title is open to the objection that the rescue of Urvashi by Pururavas, although it starts the action of the play, is by no means its central theme so as to justify its giving the name to the play after itself. Whatever the way in which we explain the title of the play, the hidden allusion to the patron of the poet is unmistakable. cf. I. 13. 5 (विक्रममहिम्ना वर्धते भवान्) and I. 15. 1 (अनुत्सेकः खलु विक्रमालंकारः), where also there is a similar secret allusion to the patron of the poet. अपूर्वम्—न विद्यते पूर्वं यस्य तत् । which has not been staged here-to-fore. For नाटके we get in the Northern Recension the reading त्रोटक. त्रोटक is only a variety of नाटक. For the technical meaning of the term, see Introduction, Technical Names, *p*. XXVI. I. 1. 11. आर्यमिश्रान्—the noble audience. The word आर्य in itself means noble or honourable. मिश्र is simply an honorific addition. cf. Ranganatha : पूज्ये मिश्रवचनं नित्य-बहुवचनान्तम् ।

I. 2. प्रणयिषु-प्रणयः विद्यते यस्य सः प्रणयी । प्रणय means an humble request, a petition, प्रणयिन् means a servant, a supplicant. दाक्षिण्य courtesy, regard, generosity of dis-position. सद्वस्तुपुरुषबहुमानात्-वस्तुनः पुरुषः वस्तुपुरुषः । सन् (शोभनः) वस्तुपुरुषः सद्वस्तुपुरुषः । तस्मिन् बहुमानः । वस्तु means इतिवृत्त or the plot of the play. वस्तुपुरुष means कथानायक. क्रिया-work, dramatic composition.

I. 2. 1. नेपथ्ये-Behind the scenes. Here नेपथ्य means curtain or scene. पक्षपातिन् – a friend, one who is favou-rably disposed, a sympathiser. गतिः unimpeded move-ment. अंबरतले – Through the sky – along the surface of the sky. I. 2.6. कुररी an osprey–what is called *Titavi* in Marathi. It is a bird often found in the vicinity of rivers and lakes and is only too well-known for its shrill and yet plaintive tone. cf. रघुवंश XIV. सा मुक्तकण्ठं व्यसना-तिभाराच्चक्रन्द विग्ना कुररीव भूयः ।; also मालतीमाधव V.20 नादस्ताव-द्विकलकुररीकूजितस्निग्धतारः । After I. 2.6, the Nirnayasagara Ed. gives an additional stanza: मत्तानां कुसुमरसेन षट्पदाना शब्दोऽयं परभृतनाद एष धीरः । आकाशे सुरगणसेविते समन्तात् किं नार्यः कलमधुराक्षरं प्रगीताः । Vide Introduction. p. XII. Rang-anatha comments upon it. Katayavema passes over it in silence. The stanza contains three guesses put forward by the Sutradhara in the process of identifying the mournful sounds, which he has only recently heard. It is only after these probable guesses that he comes to the definite knowledge that the sounds in question are the wailings of the Apsarases. That the stanza is an interpolation is quite evident from the improbability of the Sutradhara indulging in three guesses one after another especially when he has heard a shrill and plaintive cry (as of an osprey) indicative of some one in distress. Further the wording of the stanza is very faulty, especially because in the first two lines, the particle किं has got to be supplied. I. 3. Construe: नरसखस्य मुनेः ऊरूद्भवा सुरस्त्री कैलासनाथमुपसृत्य निवर्तमाना विबुधशत्रुभिः अर्धमार्गे बंदीकृता, अतः अयम् अप्सरसां गणः शरणं क्रन्दति । सुरस्त्री means not "The wife of a god," but "A divine or heavenly woman or a nymph". cf. सुरांगना used in this very sense in I. 18. ऊरूद्भवा—ऊरुः उद्भवः (source) यस्याः or ऊरोः उद्भवः (birth, springing into existence) यस्याः । नरसखस्य—of the friend of Nara. नरस्य सखा नरसखः, according to राजाहःसखिभ्यः टच् । Panini V. 4. 91. नरसख means नारायण. नर and नारायण were two great sages of yore, who used to practise penance together and were great friends of each other. In later mythology नर came to be identified with Arjuna and नारायण with कृष्ण or विष्णु. नर and नारायण figure amongst the ऋषिs or poets of the Rig-veda. In regard to the sage नारायण, it is said that while he was practising austere penance, Indra, alarmed at his penance, sent a band of Apsarases to him in order to entice and seduce him. The Apsarases came to him and tried their best to allure him by their seductive charms. नारायण, however, was not to be lured away by these, and he put them all to shame by producing from his thigh (ऊरु) a damsel of surpassing beauty, whom he sent as a present to Indra. cf. I. 14. *infra*. This damsel was none else but

उर्वशी, and she is therefore called here नरसखस्य मुनेः कल्पस्त्रता. cf. I. 7. 12. *infra.* कैलासनाथ—Kubera and not Shiva as Ranganatha wrongly takes it. cf. I. 3. 21. below, where it is expressly said. कुबेरभवनात् प्रतिनिवर्तमाना । उपस्थाय=सेवित्वा having approached him *i. e.* having paid him a visit in order to wait upon him. बंदीकृता (predicate) was taken prisoner; a च्वि formation from बन्दि m. a prisoner or captive. अर्धमार्गे while half on her way. मार्गस्य अर्धम् अर्धमार्गः। विबुधशत्रुभिः by the enemies of the gods *i. e.* the demons. अप्सरसां गणः Band or company of Apsarases. The Apsarases are so called because they are believed to have sprung from the water of the ocean when it was churned by the gods and demons (अप् water+सरस् from सृ to move, to start). शरणं क्रन्दति cries for help or protection. This reading is to be preferred to करुणं क्रन्दति, since it directly tells us what it was that the Apsarases were crying for-करुणं क्रन्दति would mean "Cries in a piteous manner" and would be therefore very vague and uncertain.

I. 3, 2. प्रस्तावना—The prelude or prologue. It is also called आमुख or Introduction. The प्रस्तावना is of several kinds. The one that we have here in our play is called प्रयोगातिशय, since the Sutradhara introduces the Apsarases with the words अप्सरसां गणोऽयम्. For details, vide Introduction, under Technical Names, *p.* XXV.

THE MAIN SCENE.

The first Act is easily divisible into six scenes as follows:—

(1) FIRST SCENE IN THE SKY.

The Apsarases रंभा, मेनका and सहजन्या who are crying for help against the violenee done to them by the demon Keshin in kidnapping उर्वशी along with चित्रलेखा, accidentally meet पुरूरवस् and inform him of the nature of the outrage. Pururavas at once sets out in pursuit of the demon.

(2) **SECOND SCENE** : ON A PEAK OF THE HEMAKUTA MOUNTAIN:

The Apsarases in the meanwhile descend from the sky on to a peak of the Hemakuta Mountain and rest there for sometime awaiting the King's return, speculating about the chances of his success in rescuing Urvashi from the demon when they see in the distance the returning chariot of the King in the sky.

(3) **THIRD SCENE** : IN THE SKY, NEAR THE PEAK OF THE HEMAKUTA; THE KING MOVING IN HIS CHARIOT.

The King makes his appearance in his chariot along with उर्वशी and चित्रलेखा. The King and चित्रलेखा try to comfort and cheer up उर्वशी, who has fainted away on account of the outrage done to her. After some time उर्वशी regains her consciousness and learns from her friend चित्रलेखा that she must thank King Pururavas for their deliverance from the demon. The King and Urvashi exchange mutual glances and straightway fall in love with one another.

(4) **FOURTH SCENE** : PEAK OF THE HEMAKUTA.

रंभा, मेनका and सहजन्या are very much delighted to see the King return triumphant and unhurt along with उर्वशी and चित्रलेखा.

(5) **FIFTH SCENE** : IN THE SKY AND THEN ON THE GROUND; THE KING'S CHARIOT STILL IN MOTION.

At the command of the King, his charioteer lands the chariot on the peak of the Hemakuta and drives over the uneven regions of the mountain to where the Apsarases are waiting for the King.

(6) SIXTH SCENE : ON THE PEAK OF THE HEMAKUTA.

While the Apsarases and the King are rejoicing at the rescue of उर्वशी and are congratulating one another, चित्ररथ, the chief of the Gandharvas, who was sent by Indra with an army to rescue Urvashi on learning about her abduction by Keshin from Narada, descends upon the peak of Hemakuta, having learnt on his way about the deliverance of Urvashi by Pururavas. He offers his congratulations to the King and requests him to see Indra. The King, however, declines the request, whereupon चित्ररथ leaves with the Apsarases. Urvashi departs slowly, with a parting glance at Pururavas. The latter also makes his exit in a sad and depressed manner.

I. 3. 8 सूर्योपस्थानात् प्रतिनिवृत्तम्—Just returned from (*i. e.* after performing) attendance upon the Sun. उपस्थान—Attendance upon, service. It appears to have been the practice of King Pururavas to pay visits to the Sun—his great grand-father on the mother's side—from time to time and to wait upon him. King Pururavas, although a mortal, had access to heaven and his assistance was called upon even by Indra whenever a war with the demons arose; cf. I. 4. 7. and V. 19. 20*ff. infra.* The reason why he mentions his own name and speaks of himself as having just returned after waiting upon the Sun, is to inspire confidence in the minds of the frightened Apsarases. They already know the fame and the might of Pururavas arms. cf. I. 4. 7–9 and I. 4. 15 below. I. 3. 11—अवलेप violence, outrage. I. 3. 12 किं पुनः......अपराद्धम् । 'But say in what way (किम्=केन प्रकारेण) have your ladyships suffered from the demon's violence ?' Pururavas wants to know the exact nature of the outrage committed by the demon or demons, before he can dart off in his pursuit of the same. किं....अपराद्धम् is an impersonal construction, meaning कः अपराधः कृतः । I. 3. 19. तपोविशेषपरिशंकितस्य सुकुमारं प्रहरणं महेन्द्रस्य—Indra, the lord of the gods, is always represented in classical mythology as being jealous or intolerant of an excess of penance practised by any one on earth. He at once sends down a band of nymphs in order to entice the person practising penance into vice and immorality. This is a trait in Indra's character often referred to in the works of Kalidasa. cf. Shakuntala I. अस्ति एतद् अन्यसमाधिभीरुत्वं देवानाम् । and Raghuvamsha VIII. 79 भरतः किल दुश्चरं तपः तृणबिन्दोः परिशंकितः पुरा । प्रजिघाय समाधिभेदिनीं हरिरस्मै हरिणीं सुरांगनाम् । सुकुमारं प्रहरणम्—a weapon delicate enough in appearance but dangerous in its consequences. Indra's usual weapon is his वज्र or bolt. But is is extremely hard, while उर्वशी is a very tender weapon in the armoury of Indra. प्रत्यादेशः 'One that obscures or eclipses, puts to shame or throws into shade,' 'Obscurer.' श्रियः—of Laxmi the goddess of wealth and beauty. I. 3. 21. समापत्तिदृष्टेन—seen by accident or chance *i. e.* seen all of a sudden, unexpectedly. cf. मालविका III.19.32 समापत्तिदृष्टेन देव्याः परिजनेन संकथा ।; also Raghu. VII. 23 and Kumara VII. 75. चित्रलेखाद्वितीया—Having चित्रलेखा for her second *i. e.* together with चित्रलेखा. अर्धपथे एव । cf. अर्धमार्गे above (I. 3). पथः अर्धम् अर्धपथः । पथिन् (m) path, becomes पथ at the end of a compound according to Panini V. 4. 74 (ऋक्पूरब्धूःपथामानक्षे)—बन्दिग्राहं गृहीता । 'Was taken captive.' बन्दिग्राहं is a gerundial formation from बन्दि (m. captive) and the root ग्रह to seize + the suffix णमुल् (अम्), according to Panini III, 4. 45-46 (उपमाने कर्मणि च । कषादिषु यथाविध्यनुप्रयोगः।) The meaning is the same as बन्दीकृता (stanza 3 above). बन्दिमिव गृहीत्वा गृहीता—बन्दिग्राहं गृहीता । I. 3. 23. जाल्मः Villain, wretch, miscreant. I. 3. 24 पूर्वोत्तरेण In the North-eastern direction. पूर्वस्याः उत्तरस्याः च दिशः अन्तरालभूतः दिग्विभागः पूर्वोत्तरः। Vide Panini II. 2. 26. I. 3. 25 विषादः Distress, fear. I. 3. 27 सदृशं—Worthy of, becoming=उचितं,योग्यम्। सोमादेकान्तरस्य—Removed from Soma (the Moon) only by one degree. Pururavas was the son of Budha and the grandson of Soma (the Moon). Cf. III. 7. 2. and V. 21 below. एकः बुधः अन्तरं व्यवधानं यस्य सः एकान्तरः। The Nirnayasagara Ed. reads सोमवंशसंभवस्य, which is evidently secondary since it simplifies the sense of सोमादेकान्तरस्य. Moreover our reading is supported by काटयवेम.

I. 3. 31. ऐशानी दिक् The direction presided over by ईशान *i. e.* Shiva, the North-east. Cf. पूर्वोत्तर above, I. 3. 24. I. 3. 32 आयुष्मन् literally "Oh long-lived one!" The word is used much in the sense of "My lord, my dear sir." I. 3. 33. The stage direction रथवेगं निरूपयन् (gesticulating speed of the chariot) is used because actual speed such as is described in the following stanza is impossible on the stage, and has therefore only to be gesticulated. वैनतेय—विनतायाः अपत्यं पुमान् वैनतेयः The son of Vinata, wife of Kashyapa, *i. e.* Garuda, who is regarded as the king of birds and is perhaps the fastest member of its class. आसादयेयम्—I shall approach *i. e.* overtake. पूर्वप्रस्थितम् started in advance of me *i. e.* having the start of me. अपकारिणं मघोनः The offender against Maghavan *i. e.* Indra. This refers to the demon Keshin who had kidnapped Urvashi and thus offended against Indra.

I. 4. construe: अमी चूर्णीभवन्तो घनाः रेणुवत् रथस्य अग्रे यान्ति । चक्रभ्रान्तिः अरान्तरेषु अन्याम् अरावलिं जनयतीव । वेगानिलात् हयशिरसि आयामवत् चामरं चित्रन्यस्तमिव अचलं (भाति or दृश्यते)

(वेगानिलात्) ध्वजपटःयष्ट्यग्रे च प्रान्ते च समं स्थितः । चूर्णीभवन्तो घनाः The heavy clouds (घन as an adjective means, solid or heavy) that are being reduced to powder under the ponderous tread of the horses. रेणुवत् like the particles of dust. रथस्य अग्रे यान्ति rise or are rising before the chariot. चक्रभ्रान्तिः=चक्रयोः भ्रमणम्-the rapid revolutions of the wheels. अरान्तरेषु in the intervals of the spokes. अर m. means the spoke of a wheel. अन्तर n. means space between or interval. अरान्तराणि means, therefore, the interstices between the spokes. अन्याम् अरावलिं जनयतीव-produces as it were another series or set of spokes. Any one who has observed a revolving wheel will remember that the space between the spokes becomes less and less as the rapidity of the revolutions increases, so that at last the number of spokes appears to be doubled or trebled. Hence it is said here that another series of intermediate spokes is produced as it were, by the revolutions of the wheels. आयामवत् चामरम्-The long (tall) chowries (fixed on the heads of the horses as ornaments). The singular चामरं is used for the plural. चामर means a mass of the bushy tail of the चमर deer, used as an ornamental fan, a chowri. हयशिरसि (singular) is used for the plural हयशिरःसु चित्रन्यस्तमिवाचलम् 'Motionless as if they were painted in a picture.' The idea is that on account of the wind produced by the high speed of the horses, their tall ornamental chowries were held erect and motionless. Cf. शाकुंतल I. 8 निष्कंपचामरशिखा निभृतोर्ध्वकर्णाः । ध्वजपटः the banner-cloth. समं स्थितः stands straight, even, level, without a single fold upon it. यष्ट्यग्रे च प्रान्ते च between the top of the flagstaff (यष्टि) and its own skirt (प्रान्त). But for the powerful wind produced by the high speed, the banner-cloth would have fallen down parallel to the flag-staff. Here, however, it is held in an out-stretched and horizontal position on account of the wind produced by the high speed. We get a various reading रेणुपदवीं for रेणुवदमी in the first line. Ranganath explains it as follows: रेणुपदवीं यान्ति–रेणुमार्गम् अनुसरन्ति । जलगुरवोपि जलदाः चक्रधारया पिष्टीकृताः मत्स्यंदनाग्रतः पांसुवद् उत्सर्पन्ति । रेणुपदवीं यान्ति means "Behave like particles of dust" (रेणुवद् आचरन्ति, रेणुत्वं यान्ति वा ।) Kalidasa is very fond of giving realistic descriptions of rapidly moving objects. Cf. शाकुन्तल I.7 (the high speed of a deer), I.8 and 9 (the speed of a chariot), VII.8 (an aerial car making a rapid descent to the ground). I. 4.2. यथानिर्दिष्टं प्रदेशं– To the spot pointed out (by us to the King) i.e. the हेमकूटशिखर. I. 4.4. The nymphs were all this while in the air and hence the stage-direction that they gesticulate descending to the mountain-peak.

I. 4.7. उपस्थितसंपरायः "Whenever hostilities are imminent." उपस्थितः (approached) संपरायः (युद्धं) यस्य । Like Pururavas, Dushyanta also was called upon to help the Gods in their hostilities against the demons. Cf. Shakuntala II. 15, VI 29, 30. विजयसेनामुखे—"At the head of his victorious or conquering forces."

I. 4.14. उच्चलितहरिणकेतनः । "Having its deer-emblazoned flag proudly lifted on high." केतन (*n*) means "A flag." हरिणकेतन "A flag having the figure of a deer upon its cloth." The flag is proudly lifted up उच्चलित or उल्लसित (v. l.), because the king is returning victorious.

I. 5. भीरु. "Oh timid one," त्रिलोकरक्षी महिमा हि वज्रिणः । Mark the humility of the King in attributing the deliverance of Urvashi to the all-saving prowess of Indra. Vide I. 15 below. चक्षुः आयतम्–"Large eye." Singular again for the dual. प्रत्युषस् (n). "Morning", "Dawn", "Day-break." पद्मिनी "Lotus plant". The Nirnayasagara Ed. reads "निशावसाने नलिनीव पङ्कजम् ।" This reading has the advantage that निशावसाने exactly corresponds to गतं भयं सुरारिसंभवम्. The night is to the lotus plant what the demon's violence is to Urvashi. But then, as Mr. Pandit points out, पंकजम् by itself does not match well with चक्षुरायतम्. As each of the two readings has one point of advantage, it is not possible to decide which is the better.

I. 5.1. उच्छ्वसितमात्रजीविता—"Whose vital activity (जीवित) consists only in her hard breathing" "Alive only because she is breathing out." उच्छ्वसित means "Breathing or respiration." Ranganath reads: उच्छ्वसितमात्रसंभावितजीविता "Who is supposed or believed to be living only on account of her hard breathing." संज्ञा "Consciousness". संज्ञां प्रतिपद्—"To recover consciousness, to come to one's self."

I. 5.4. बलवत् Adverb, "Powerfully", "Exceedingly", Cf. शाकुन्तल I. 2 बलवदपि शिक्षितानाम् । and *ibid* III बलवदस्वस्थशरीरा शकुन्तला । The Northern Recension adds here the stanza मन्दारकुसुमदाम्ना etc., which we have given in our Introduction p. XII. It contains almost the same idea as that of stanza 6.

I. 6. Construe : पश्य । अस्याः कुसुमसमबन्धनं हृदयं (कर्तृ) स्तनमध्योच्छ्वासिना हरिचन्दनेन कथितं (सूचितम्) कम्पं (कर्म) न तावद् (अद्यापि) मुञ्चति ।

कुसुमसमबन्धनं हृदयम् "Her heart tender like a flower." This is the subject and कम्प (tremor) is the object

कुसुमसमं बन्धनं यस्य—"Whose stem is delicate like that of a flower." बन्धन seems to mean here "Structure, construction." "Whose structure is as delicate as that of a flower." Cf. Meghaduta I 9. "कुसुमसदृशम्.....अंगनानाम्...... हृदयम् ।" हरिचन्दन (*n*) "Yellow sandal." Here "Paste or smearing of yellow sandle." स्तनमध्योच्छ्वासिना "Heaving up and down between her breasts." The Nirnayasagara Ed. reads this stanza as follows :—

मुञ्चति न तावदस्या भयकम्पः कुसुमकोमलं हृदयम् ।
सिचयान्तेन कथंचित् स्तनमध्योच्छ्वासिना कथितः ॥

Although the expression कुसुमकोमलं is more direct than कुसुमसमबन्धनं, the word कथंचित् spoils the whole sense and so the reading has to be rejected.

I. 6. 1. पर्यवस्थापय—"Compose yourself."

अनप्सरा इव मम प्रतिभासि—"You strike me as if you were not a nymph, although you are really one" चित्रलेखा means to say that in being so much overpowered by fear Urvashi behaves like a human being rather than like an Apsaras, who in her nature must be above fear.

प्रत्यागच्छति — "Comes to herself, regains consciousness."

I. 6. 4. प्रकृतिम् आपद्—"To recover consciousness."

I. 7. Construe : शशिनि आविर्भूते तमसा मुच्यमाना रात्रिः इव, नैशस्य हुतभुजः छिन्नभूयिष्ठधूमा अर्चिः इव,: रोधःपतनकलुषा प्रसादं गृह्णती गंगा इव, इयं वरतनुःअन्तः मोहेन मुक्तकल्पा (सती) लक्ष्यते ।

नैशस्य हुतभुजः अर्चिः इव "Like the flame of a nocturnal fire." छिन्नभूयिष्ठधूमा—छिन्नः भूयिष्ठः (बहुलः) धूमः यस्याः सा । "From which the smoke has been mostly removed or or from which most of the smoke has been removed." रोधःपतनकलुषा—"Turbid on account of the tumbling in of the banks." प्रसादं गृह्णती—"Regaining her natural clearness or purity." अन्तः (=हृदये) मोहेन मुक्तकल्पा "Almost relieved of her mental stupor." The suffix कल्प has the sense of "Almost, for the most part." Cf. Panini V. 3. 67. ईषदसमाप्तौ कल्पब्देश्यदेशीयरः। Thus : ईषदूना मुक्ता=मुक्तकल्पा *i. e.* मुक्तप्राया. We get a v. l. मुच्यमाना which conveys the same sense as मुक्तकल्पा.

I. 7. 1. विश्रब्धा "Of good cheer, cheerful." हताशाः "Wretched, vile, accursed." त्रिदशपरिपन्थिनः "The opponents or enemies of the Gods." त्रिदश literally "The thrice ten" is a name of the Gods collectively. Mallinatha on Kumar III. 1. explains the word as : त्रिः आवृत्ताः दश परिमाणम् एषाम् इति त्रिदशाः "Whose number is thrice ten."

I. 7. 4. किं प्रभावदर्शिना महेन्द्रेण। Mark the naturalness and extreme innocence of Urvashi's question. As soon as she hears that the demons have been defeated, she most naturally thinks that Indra and none else must have been the cause of their overthrow. प्रभावदर्शिना महेन्द्रेण "By the great Indra who saw (the whole thing *i. e.* the outrage committed by the demons) by means of his divine power (प्रभाव)." प्रभावेण द्रष्टुं शीलम् अस्य इति प्रभावदर्शी ।

I. 7. 9. उपकृतं खलु दानवैः—Urvashi thinks that in committing an outrage upon her, the demons have obliged her, for how could she otherwise have had the privilege of seeing the King, and coming in such intimate contact with him?

I. 7. 11. प्रकृतिस्था "Completely recovered," "Come to herself." स्थाने खलु etc. Vide notes on अनुत्सेका नरसरवस्य etc. above p. 7.

I. 8. कान्तप्रभः "Of lovely light." सर्गविधौ—निर्माणकर्मणि "In creating." प्रजापतिः अभूत् "Acted the part of the creator" नु expresses the sense of guess or conjecture.

(Cf. नु: वितर्के). शृंगारैकरसः मदनः ": Cupid, who excels in the graces of love, or who joys or revels in love and love alone." शृंगारः एकः एव रसः यस्य। पुष्पाकरः मासः "The month which is a repertory of flowers *i. e.* the vernal season-spring." पुष्पोद्गमवस्थानरूपः वसन्तः। पुराणो मुनिः "The ancient ascetic, the ascetic of yore" referring to the sage नारायण, who is supposed to have produced Urvashi from his thigh. वेदाभ्यासजडः "Made blunt or dull by his constant lucubrations over the Vedas." विषयव्यावृत्तकौतूहलः "Whose curiosity has been weaned away from the pleasures of the senses." विषयेभ्यः व्यावृत्तं कौतूहलं यस्य सः। The idea is : Urvashi, being a damsel of surpassing beauty, presupposes a creator equally beautiful and charming, so in her case either the Moon or the Vernal season or the God of love himself must have been the creator, and *definitely not* that old sage नारायण, who has lost all zest for sensual pleasures on account of his constant application to the study of Vedas. Cf. मालतीमाधव I. 21. तस्याः सखे नियतमिन्दुसुधामृणालज्योत्स्नादि कारणमभूत् मदनश्च वेधाः ॥

I. 8. 3. अभयदायी—"Who has given us protection from danger." अभय (*n*) means "Security or protection."

I. 9. Construe : हे सुन्दरि, त्वं यस्य अवन्ध्ययोः नेत्रयोः पथि यदृच्छया सकृदपि स्थिता, सः अपि त्वया विना समुत्सुकः भवेत्। आर्द्रसौहृदः ते सखीजनः किमुत। यदृच्छया "By chance, accidentally" अवन्ध्य—"Firuitful, fortunate, lucky:" it is the opposite of वन्ध्य "barren" (Cf. वांझ in Marathi and Gujarati.) नेत्रयोः पथि स्थिता "Stood within the Sange of the eyes." समुत्सुकः "Full of deep longing." आर्द्रसौहृदः—आर्द्रं सौहृदं यस्य. "Whose affection for you is ever fresh." सौहृद (*n*) "Friendship or affection" from सुहृद् "A friend."

I. 9.1. अभिजातम्—"Noble, dignified." वचनम्—"Speech, manner of address." चन्द्राद् अमृतम्—The Moon is believed to be a repository of nectar or ambrosia. मे हृदयं त्वरते—"My heart hastens or grows impatient."

I. 10. उपप्लवात् मुक्तम् —"Released from eclipse." प्रत्यागतप्रसादम्–प्रत्यागतः प्रसादः यं सः प्रत्यागतप्रसादः। "Who has regained his clearness."

I. 10.1. Chitralekha wants to direct Urvashi's attention to Rambha and Sahajanya who are standing on the summit of Hemakuta. Urvashi obviously understands her meaning, but all the same she continues looking at the King with steadfast gaze and says "समदुःखः पिबतीव मां नयनाभ्याम् ।" These words apply to the friends of Urvashi as well as to the king. Urvashi does this in order to draw the attention of चित्रलेखा to her own feelings as regards the King, and she succeeds in calling her friend's attention to that fact. For in I.10.4 चित्रलेखा asks her "अयि कः" Showing thereby that she has become aware of Urvashi's state of mind.

I. 10.7. विशाखासमीपगतः (to be construed with चन्द्रः) "Standing in the vicinity of the constellation विशाखा." विशाखा is the sixteenth lunar mansion consisting of two stars. Pururavas who is accompanied by उर्वशी and चित्रलेखा is compared to the Moon accompanied by the two stars of the विशाखा constellation. Cf. शाकुन्तल III. "किमत्र चित्रं यदि विशाखे शशांकलेखामनुवर्तेते ।"

I. 10.12. प्रत्यानीता—"Brought back or restored to us."

I. 10.15. Sahajanya means that the demons are really so powerful that there is every reason why they should rejoice at the victory and safe return of the King.

I. 10. 18. चक्रोद्घातं रूपयित्वा—"Acting as if he received a jolting of the chariot-wheels." विषमावतार: "Descent upon an uneven (rugged) surface." सत्फल:—सत् फलं येन—"Not vain, not futile." हन्त is a particle expressing joy. I. 11. Construe: यद् रथसंक्षोभाद् अयं (मम) अंस: रथोपमश्रोण्या: अंसेन सरोमविक्रियं स्पृष्ट: (तत्) मनसिजेन अंकुरितमिव । रथसंक्षोभ—"Jolting of the chariot". रथोपमश्रोणी seems to be elliptical for रथचक्रोपमश्रोणी "Whose hips are round like the wheel of a chariot", "Fair, beautiful." Cf. IV. 18. रथांगश्रोणिबिंबया. सरोमविक्रियम्—रोमविक्रियया (रोमांचेन) सहितं यथा स्यात् तथा—"So as to cause horripilation on the body." We have to supply तत् before अंकुरितं मनसिजेनेव । The construction is : यद् अयं अंस:......स्पृष्ट:, तत् मनसिजेन अंकुरितमिव । "That my shoulder was touched by hers so as to cause horripilation upon the body seems like the sprouting of love." The fact is that at the thrilling touch of Urvashi's shoulder, Pururavas felt a horripilation upon his body. This horripilation is fancied by the poet to be the sprouting of the future tree of love. Cf. for this representation of the emergence of love as the sprouting of the tree of love, मालविकाग्निमित्र IV. 1. The Nirnayasagara Ed. reads : " यदिदं रथसंक्षोभादंगेनागं रथोपश्रोण्या: । स्पृष्टं सरोमविक्रिय-मंकुरितं मनसिजेनेव ॥ Katayavema reads : अंकुरितमनोभवेनेव for अंकुरितं मनसिजेनेव. In this case अंकुरितमनोभवेन would be an adjective qualifying अंसेन. This reading gives a simpler grammatical construction.

I. 11.2. किमपि परत: अपसर "Move a little further" Urvashi says this because she feels rather ashamed that her shoulder should have brushed against that of Pururavas.

I. 11.5. संभावयाम:—"Let us honour or greet or pay our congratulations to."

I. 12. यावत् "So that." सुभ्रूः "Having beautiful eye-brows", "Fair". सखीभिः संपर्कं याति—"May join her friends." आर्तवी श्रीः "Vernal beauty" आर्तवी (ऋतोः इयम् आर्तवी) "Of the season (viz. Spring)" i. e. "Vernal".

I. 12.7. पीडितम् used adverbially—"Hard, powerfully, closely."

I. 12.10. कल्पशतानि "For hundreds of Kalpas." कल्प is a fabulous period of time equal to 1000 Yugas or 432 millions of human years. पृथिवीं पालयिता भवतु—One would naturally expect here पृथिव्याः पालयिता; but that is prohibited by Panini II. 3. 69. न लोकाव्ययनिष्ठाखलर्थतृनाम् ।

I. 13.3-4. महेन्द्रोपकारपर्याप्त—"Sufficient to oblige the great Indra", "Capable of laying the great Indra under obligations." विक्रममहिमा—"The greatness or excess of valour."

परस्परं हस्तौ स्पृशतः "Touch each other's hands." Touching or shaking or holding by the hand was a mode of greeting among Hindus of ancient times. Mr. Pandit gives the following quotation from the भागवत पुराण X. 65.5: समुपेत्याथ गोपालान् हास्यहस्तग्रहादिभिः । विश्रान्तं सुखमासीनं पप्रच्छुः पर्युपागताः ॥ which mentions the practice of हस्तग्रह.

I. 13.10. अन्तरा "In the mean-while." चारण "A bard, minstrel or panegyrist." जयोदाहरणम्—"A panegyric in verse beginning with some such word as जयति, ornamented with alliterations and containing all the eight cases of Nominal Declension." To give the reader an idea of what a जयोदाहरण is like, we quote in full the following stanza from the रामरक्षा of बुधकौशिक—रामो दाशरथिः सदा विजयते, रामं रमेशं भजे । रामेणाभिहता निशाचरचमू रामाय तस्मै नमः ॥ रामान्नास्ति परायणं परतरं रामस्य दासोऽस्म्यहम् । रामे चित्तलयः सदा भवतु मे, भो राम मामुद्धर ॥ Cf. Raghu. IV 78.

where Mallinatha explains the word as follows: जय-स्यापकः प्रबन्धविशेषः I. 14. पुरा नारायणेनेयम् etc. vide Notes on I. 3 above. मरुत्वते=इन्द्राय. मरुत्वान् is a title of Indra. मरुत् means a god in general, and मरुत्वत् means "Lord of the Gods". i. e. Indra. In the Rgveda, the मरुत्s are the storm-Gods, and Indra is their lord; hence he is called मरुत्वान्.

I. 15. भिनत्ति—"Shatters or puts to flight." Mark again the modesty of the King. Cf. I. 5 above, and Notes *ad. loc.*

I. 15.1. अनुत्सेकः खलु विक्रमालंकारः अनुत्सेकः means "Humility, modesty, freedom from pride or vanity." विक्रमालंकार "The ornament of valour." In choosing the word विक्रम alone of all those that express the idea of valour (e. g. वीर्य, शौर्य, पराक्रम, etc.) the poet no doubt wants to make a hidden allusion to the name of his patron. the illustrious विक्रमादित्य. Cf. also I. 13.4. and Note on the title of the play, under I. 1.4 above. For the idea Cf. नीतिशतक 82. शौर्यस्य वाक्संयमः (विभूषणम्)

I. 15.9. त्वं मे मुखं भव ॥ "Be you my mouth" i. e. "Speak for me or on my behalf."

I. 15.13. इच्छामि प्रियसखीमिव महाराजस्य कीर्तिं महेन्द्रलोकं नेतुम् This is a round-about way of asking for the permission of Pururavas to depart "I wish to take your fame to the world of Indra" means "I wish to have your permission to go away."

I. 15.15 गम्यतां पुनर्दर्शनाय Mr. Pandit compares the French expression "*au revoir*.

I. 15.17. उत्पतनभङ्गं रूपयित्वा—"Acting as if her flight (उत्पतन) was suddenly obstructed. अहो लताविटपे मे एकावली लग्ना। We have a very parallel situation in Shakuntala Act I, where while Shakuntala is about to leave Dushyanta, her foot is pricked by a thorn and her bark-garment becomes entangled in the branches of a tree. This is of course intended by the poet to enable the heroine to cast a parting glance at the hero. एकावली "A single string of pearls."

I. 15.20. दृढं खलु लग्ना । दुर्मोचनीया इव मे प्रतिभाति ॥ Chitralekha says this smilingly (सस्मितम्). She of course intends to convey the idea that Urvashi has fallen desperately in love with Pururavas.

I. 15. 23. स्मर तावद् आत्मनः वचनम् ॥ "Remember these words of yours," referring to भवतु, यतिष्ये तावत् ॥ Urvashi asks Chitralekha not to forget her promise (expressed in the words "भवतु, यतिष्ये तावत् ।") to help her in her love for Pururavas. Cf. II. 9.6–7. below.

I. 16. अपांगनेत्रा—According to V. S. Apte this expression means "Having her eyes turned towards their corners." अपांगयोः प्रेरिते नेत्रे यया सा ॥ अपांग *m.* means "The corner of the eye." The expression would therefore ultimately mean "Casting side-glances." Ranganatha takes अपांग in the sense of Cupid (the bodiless). अपांगनेत्रा means then, मदनजनकनेत्रा "Having love-darting eyes." पुनरपि अद्य "Once again for the last time, this day."

I. 17. सुरेन्द्रस्य कृतापराधान् is an irregular expression having the sense: कृतसुरेन्द्रापराधान् ॥ We come across many such instances in Kalidasa's works. Cf. Raghu. VI. 20 ततो नृपाणां श्रुतवृत्तवंशा—ततः श्रुतनृपवृत्तवंशा ॥ Mallinatha observes: सापेक्षत्वेऽपि गमकत्वात् समासः ॥ वायव्यम् अस्त्रम्—"A missile weapon (shaft) presided over by the deity वायु." The idea is that the missile weapon is to be hurled against the enemy with a मन्त्र or incantation addressed to the God वायु.

I. 17. 1. उपश्लेषय "Bring here."

I. 17. 4. दुर्लभाभिनिवेशी ॥ दुर्लभे (वस्तुनि) अभिनिविशते इति दुर्लभाभिनिवेशी ॥ "Bent upon the unattainable" *i. e.* "Causing one to long for an unattainable object."

I. 18. पितुः मध्यमं पदम् "The middle footstep of her father" *i. e.* the sky. We have seen above that the sage नारायण was the father of Urvashi. In latter mythology this नारायण was indentified with विष्णु. Here पितुः मध्यमं पदम् means विष्णोः मध्यमं पदम् ॥ "The middle footstep of Vishnu." In the Rgveda विष्णु appears as a personification of the sun who is said to traverse the whole world in three steps. These three steps refer to the three stages of the sun in his daily march from the East to the West. The first step corresponds to the rise of the sun on the eastern horizon; the second to the zenith position of the sun at midday; and the third to his setting behind the western horizon. Thus the second or middle step of विष्णु means the sky. In classical Mythology also the sky is regarded as the second (or middle) of the three steps that विष्णु took in the वामनावतार. The sky is, therefore, often called विष्णुपद in sanskrit. Cf. Raghuvansha XIII. 1. अथात्मनः शब्दगुणं गुणज्ञः पदं विमानेन विगाहमानः ॥ एषा सुरांगना—"This heavenly damsel". सूत्रम्—"The fibre or filament in a lotus-stalk".

ACT II.

[The Second Act opens with an introductory scene-technically called प्रवेशक, followed by the main scene.

Introductory Scene : Precincts of the विमानोत्संग palace of the King.

Vidushaka, the boon companion of Pururavas, has learnt from the latter about his amour for Urvashi.

The King has however charged him to keep the matter to himself. Vidushaka is carrying on a heroic flight with his extremely communicative nature. Nipunika, the maid-servant of the Queen makes her entry and in the course of a soliloquy tells us that the Queen (काशिराजपुत्री *alias* औशीनरी) has noticed a great change in Pururavas, ever since his return from his सूर्योपस्थान and that she is considerably worried over it. At the Queen's instance, Nipunika wants to know from Vidushaka what the matter is with the King. She approaches him and by using a very ingenious trick succeeds in screwing out of him the secret of the King's passion for Urvashi. A bard announces the hour of midday, which is the time for the King to leave his council-chamber for bath, meal, etc.

THE MAIN SCENE.

The main scene in Act II contains as many as 7 sub-scenes, as shown below:—

1. **FIRST SCENE** : THE PALACE.

The King enters with his friend Vidushaka. The King is suffering severely from the pangs of love for Urvashi.

2. **SECOND SCENE** THE PRAMADAVANA

To divert his mind the King goes to the प्रमदवन. He however finds that the beauty of the प्रमदवन instead of offering any relaxation to his mind, only augments his love-longing.

3. **THIRD SCENE** : THE अतिमुक्तलतामण्डप IN THE प्रमदवन.

The King and Vidushaka while wandering in the प्रमदवन reach the अतिमुक्तलतामण्डप, enter it and take their seats within. At the request of the King, Vidushaka begins to meditate and think out some means of bringing about a meeting between the king and Urvashi. The king has a good omen and his mind is filled with hope.

4. **FOURTH SCENE** : IN THE SKY.

Urvashi and Chitralekha, moving in the air, reach the region where the King's palace is situated. They move on in the air to the region of the प्रमदवन.

5. **FIFTH SCENE** : THE अतिमुक्तलतामण्डप AGAIN.

They get down from the sky and see the King in the garden with his friend. Urvashi approaches the King unseen in order to overhear his talk with his friend. From what she hears, she is convinced of the King's deep love for her. The King blames Urvashi for her indifference to him, whereupon Urvashi writes on a Bhurja-patra (birch leaf) two stanzas expressing her deep love for Pururavas and drops it before the King. The King is overjoyed to read Urvashi's protestation of love for him. He hands over the love-letter to Vidushaka for safe-keeping. In the meanwhile Chitralekha goes to the King and communicates to him the prayer of Urvashi that the King should take pity on her and accept her love. The King only too willingly gives his consent to the proposal. Urvashi also now reveals herself to the King and greets him with victory. The King receives her and seats her by his side. Just then a देवदूत announces that Urvashi and Chitralekha must return to heaven immediately, as their presence is required there in connection with the staging of a drama composed by the sage Bharata. Urvashi being helpless leaves the King most reluctantly. The King now wants some consolation and asks his friend for the love-letter. But Vidushaka has in the meanwhile dropped it and allowed it to be blown away by the wind. He begins to look for it here and there.

(6) **SIXTH SCENE** : BACKSIDE OF THE अतिमुक्तलतामण्डप.

Enter Queen and Nipunika. The Queen, who has learnt from Nipunika that the King has gone to the अतिमुक्तलतामण्डप along with Vidushaka wants to over-hear him and to see if she can get any confirmation for the report brought by Nipunika about the King's amour for Urvashi. As she is about to hide herself behind a bush she sees a scroll of birch-leaf blown along by the wind, which at last clings to her anklet. On further scrutiny it proves to be a love-letter from Urvashi to the King. The Queen takes hold of the letter with a view to confronting the King with that irrefutable proof of his illicit love.

(7) **SEVENTH SCENE** : THE अतिमुक्तलतामण्डप ONCE AGAIN.

Vidushaka is still looking for the love-letter but to no purpose, and the King is grievously disappointed. Just then the Queen enters, with the birch-leaf in her hand. The King is able to give only a lame excuse by saying that it is altogether a different birch-leaf that has been missing and for which he has been looking and not the one the Queen has brought with her. But this does not satisfy the Queen. Vidushaka tries to defend the King but only makes matters worse. The King begs the Queen's pardon for his crime-in-love, which he can no longer deny, and prostrates at her feet. The Queen however leaves him in a rage in utter disregard of his prostration. The King is stung with a sense of humiliation at the scant ceremony with which the Queen has treated his apology, though he still continues to hold her in loving regard.—The midday hour having now approached, the King repairs to the palace for his bath, meal etc.

II. o. 8. आकीर्णे "In the midst of a crowd", "When in company with others." आकीर्णे=जनसंपाते. (Katayavema) कार्यासन "The seat, sitting on which he settles disputes and dispenses justice;" "Council hall;" "The seat of judgement." विरलजनसंपाते-विरल: जनसंपात: यत्र । "Which is but slightly frequented by people." विमानोत्संगपरिसरे—"In the precincts of the palace called विमानोत्संग" Katayavema reads विमानप्रतिच्छन्द as the name of the palace. Ranganatha reads देवच्छन्द as its name. In the Shakuntala the palace of Dushyanta is called मेघप्रतिच्छन्द. Whatever the reading that we adopt, this much is certain that it is the name of a palace.

II. o. 21. देव्या काशिराजपुत्र्या *i. e.* Aushinari, the queen of Pururavas. ब्रह्मबन्धु: "An unworthy, wicked, vile Brahmin." It is used as a contemptuous term. ब्रह्मबन्धुरधिक्षेपे–Amarakosha. It is to be explained as: ब्रह्म (ब्राह्मणजातिरेव) बन्धु: अस्य । जात्या एव ब्राह्मण:, न तु कर्मणा आचारेण वा ।

आलिखित: वानर: इव "The very picture of a monkey." The विदूषक is usually an ugly, deformed man and so निपुणिका calls him "The very picture of a monkey." Cf. V. 11. 6. below. किमपि तूष्णीं भूत: "Sitting silent for some reason or another."

आर्यमाणवक: The noble, Manavaka. माणवक is the name of the Vidushaka. He is of a short stature and hence gets the appropriate name माणवक– a dwarf, manikin. क्षुद्रो मानव:–माणवक: ।

II. o. 32. संगीतव्यापारम् "Your practice of music." Nipunika was not a mere attendant upon the Queen, but was also an accomplished woman.

II. o. 39: मयि पक्षपाती "Favourably disposed towards me, a friend of mine." अनुचितवेदनादुःखिताम्—अनुचितया वेदनया दुःखिताम् "Distressed or afflicted by an unusual suffering." It must not be forgotten by the reader that the Queen's message delivered by Nipunika to the विदूषक is nothing but an invention of her own brain.

II o. 45. आलपिता "Was addressed." नामधेयेन. The suffix धेय is added to नाम without any additional sense. Thus नामधेय means the same thing as नाम.

II. o. 51. जिह्वायन्त्रणेन By restraining my tongue."

II. o. 61. मृगतृष्णिका Mirage. Here the mirage is of course the attainment of Urvashi.

II. o. 64. वैतालिकः—"Bard, minstrel." विविधेन तालेन गायतीति वैतालिकः The duty of the वैतालिक was to announce to the King the different periods of the day, by means of suitable descriptive songs in praise of the King. The भावप्रकाश describes the वैतालिक as follows :—

तत्तत्प्रहरकयोग्यै रागैस्तत्कालवाचिभिः श्लोकैः ।
सरभसमेव विनालं गायन् वैतालिको भवति ॥

II. 1 आ लोकान्तात् etc. applies to the Sun as well as to the King. आ लोकान्तात् प्रजानां प्रतिहततमोवृत्तिः (i) "Driving to away the darkness oppressing the people, beyond the confines of the world." (ii) "Suppressing the criminal tendencies of the subjects all over the wide world." तमोवृत्ति means (i) तमोव्यापार "The obscuring and oppressing activity of darkness." (ii) तमोगुण. "Criminal or evil tendencies of the people." दिवसस्य षष्ठे भागे "In the sixth part or division of the day." According to works on politics (अर्थशास्त्र). a king is recommended to divide the day (*i. e.* from morning to evening) into eight parts, each part being thus equal to one hour and a half. Different duties are assigned to these divisions of the day. The sixth division commences at about 1–30 P. M. and lasts till 3 P.M. The King is recommended to pass this period of time according to his will *i. e.* he is not required to do any particular or set duty, but is allowed to spend that time according to his pleasure आत्मन: छन्दवर्ती तिष्ठत्येव etc. does not refer to the time of the day when the king rises from his judgment seat. It is said only in a general way to bring out the comparison between the Sun and the King. The King has to pass a very busy day in the midst of various engagements and gets rest only in the sixth part of the day. So too the Sun stands and rests for a moment when he comes to the zenith-position, and then again commences his rapid course westwards.

प्रवेशक:—For the technical meaning of this term, see Introduction, Technical Names. p. XXVI

II. 2. Construe : मकरकेतो: अवन्ध्यपातेन बाणेन कृतमार्गे मे हृदयं सा सुरलोकसुन्दरी आ दर्शनात् प्रविष्टा (अस्ति) । मकरकेतु "The dolphin-bannered God" i. e. "Cupid" whose banner is adorned with the figure of a fish (मकर). अवन्ध्यपातेन (Scil. बाणेन) "Infallible, unerring, unmissing (अवन्ध्य) in its aim" कृतमार्गम्—कृत: मार्ग: यस्मिन् तत् कृतमार्गम् । "Access to which was given" "A breach in which was effected."

II. 2-3. तपस्विनी "Poor, miserable". A term of commiseration. संपीडिता "Sorely afflicted or pained at heart." Vidushaka has already promised निपुणिका, that he would try his best to dissuade the King from running after the mirage. Now from the speech of the King he sees that he has fallen over head and ears in love with Urvashi, and therefore commiserates the Queen in the words संपीडिता etc....

II. 2.3. रहस्यनिक्षेपः=निक्षिप्तं रहस्यम् "The secret entrusted to you."

II. 2.6. अभिसंहितोस्मि "I have been outwitted or overreached". दास्या "By that wench, slave girl."

II. 2.10. सहसा "Off-hand, without due consideration." Mark the presence of mind shown by the Vidushaka in answering the question of the King.

II. 2.17. पंचविधस्य अभ्यवहारस्य। Katayavema gives the following as the five varieties of articles of food. (1) भक्ष्य Things to be thoroughly chewed before they are eaten, such as bread; (2) भोज्य Things to be eaten without much chewing, such as boiled rice; (3) लेह्य Things to be licked, such as liquid condiments and soups; (4) चोष्य Things to be sucked, such as mango-pickles; (5) पेय Things to be drunk, such as milk, etc. Or the expression might refer to some five specific food-preparations, corresponding perhaps to Marathi पंच पक्वान्न. उपनतसंभारस्य "Having all the requisite articles or materials brought together." योजनाम् "Preparation". शक्यम् उत्कण्ठा विनोदयितुम्। This is a contamination of two constructions: शक्यम् उत्कण्ठां विनोदयितुम् and शक्या उत्कण्ठा विनोदयितुम्। Ranganatha justifies this irregular construction by citing a precedent for it from no less an authority than the महाभाष्यकारः—शक्यं श्वमांसादिभिरपि क्षुत् प्रतिहन्तुम् इति महाभाष्यकारप्रयोगाद् उत्कण्ठा विनोदयितुं शक्यम् इति साधु॥ Cf. also मालविकाग्निमित्र III. 23. एवं हि प्रणयवती सा शक्यमुपेक्षितुं कुपिता॥ विनोदय् means to remove, drive away, beguile.

II. 2.20. दुर्लभप्रार्थनः "Desiring or longing for an object difficult to be had." दुर्लभं प्रार्थनं यस्य or दुर्लभवस्तुविषयिका प्रार्थना यस्य सः। विनोदयितव्यः Here विनोदय् means to divert, amuse, entertain, please.

II. 2.20 ननु भवान् etc. The Vidushaka means to say "If Urvashi has but once seen you, she cannot help falling in love with you and making a voluntary offer of herself to you, so handsome and lovable you are."

II. 2.24. पक्षपातोयमवधार्यताम् "If you choose to pay such a compliment to me, though, as I very well know, I am unworthy of it, it is your affection for (पक्षपात:-partiality) me that is responsible for it."

II. 2.28. अहमिव विरूपतया । As remarked above the Vidushaka in the Sanskrit Drama is always represented as an ugly and deformed person. Cf. विकृताङ्गवचोवेषहास्यकारी विदूषकः quoted by रंगनाथ.

II. 3. आभरणस्याभरणम् । Cf. Kumara. I.42. कण्ठस्य तस्याः स्तनबन्धुरस्य मुक्ताकलापस्य च निस्तलस्य । अन्योन्यशोभाजननाद् बभूव साधारणो भूषणभूष्यभावः ॥

II 3. 2. दिव्यरसाभिलाषिणा चातकव्रतं गृहीतम् । चातकव्रतम् means 'The vow of the Chataka bird", which, it is said, does not drink water lying on the ground, however thirsty it may be, but always looks up towards the sky and cries aloud piteously until at last rain-drops fall into its mouth. Cf. नीतिशतक 121: सूक्ष्मा एव पतंति चातकमुखे द्वित्राः पयोबिन्दवः । also नीतिशतक 51 रे रे चातक सावधानमनसा etc. दिव्यरसाभिलाषिणा is used here in a double sense. With the Chataka it means "Longing for heavenly water, water coming directly from the clouds" With the King it means "Longing for heavenly love *i.e.* the love of a heavenly nymph". रस means both water and love.

II. 3.4. उत्सुक "Love-sick, love-lorn". विविक्तम् "Solitude" प्रमदवन The name of the pleasure garden attached to the King's palace. Literally "The garden of pleasure".

II. 3.6. का गतिः "What escape (*is there*) from the King's command? I must obey it against my will." चोदित "Deputed, sent forward". आगन्तुकः "A guest". भवान् दक्षिणमारुतेन प्रत्युद्गतः "Your Honour is being received with respect by the southern wind (i.e. the Malaya breeze). Cf. मालविकाग्निमित्र III. वसन्तः किल एताभिः पवनचलिताभिः पल्लवांगुलीभिः त्वरयतीव भवन्तम्, एतत् प्रमदवनं प्रविशेति । प्रति + उद् + गम् means "To rise and go forward to meet or receive a guest".

II. 3.11. The King understands the expression दक्षिण-मारुतेन used above by the Vidushaka in a second sense also, besides that in which it was used by the Vidushaka. He says "This cool breeze here, is fit to be called दक्षिण-मारुत, not only because it proceeds from the south, but also because it is generous or considerate, solicitous to oblige, attentive to ladies" as is shown in the following stanza. दक्षिण means "Southern" and also " Solicitous to oblige, attentive to ladies" The epithet दक्षिण is usually applied to lovers (दक्षिणाः कामिनः) who even when they really love one lady, do not fail to please others also by their kindness and solicitous attention. Cf. अनेकासु नायिकासु अवैषम्येण स्नेहानुवर्ती दक्षिणो नायकः (प्रतापरुद्रीय).

II 4. In this stanza the King compares the Malaya breeze to a lover (कामी). Like a lover, who, while really loving one lady, is solicitous to oblige others also, the Malaya breeze too, while impregenating the माधवी creeper with honey-drops (निषिञ्चन्) and thus showing its genuine love (स्नेह) for the same, makes the कौन्दी creeper dance and thus shows its kindness and solicitous attention (दाक्षिण्य) to it. The माधवी is a creeper flowering in spring. It is otherwise called वासन्ती. मधु means " Spring " or the " Vernal season " and so the creeper that flowers in spring comes to be called माधवी (or वासन्ती) "The spring creeper". कौन्दी (Also called माघी) Is a creeper flowering two months before the माधवी, in the month of Magha: By the time that Malaya breeze sets in, the कौन्दी creeper is no longer in flowers, having outlived its day. So the best attention that the Malaya breeze can show unto it is to make it dance. In this stanza the माधवी creeper is compared (suggestively though) to a young sweet-heart and the कौन्दी to an elderly sweet-heart who has already passed the pink of youthful loveliness and perfection.

II. 4. 2-3. ईदृश एव ते अभिनिवेशः भवतु । अभिनिवेश means "Determination". The Vidushaka means to say that the King must henceforth behave himself just like the Malaya breeze, i.e. while he may love Urvashi, he must not be indifferent to Queen औशीनरी, but must do his best to please and placate her. It will appear in the sequel, that the King in fact acts up to this advice of the Vidushaka. Cf. II. 22 4-5; III 4. 4.

II. 4. 6-7. मया न साधु समर्थितम् " I was not right in imagining that etc." आपत्प्रतीकारः "A remedy against distress or affliction."

II. 6. असुलभवस्तुप्रार्थनादुर्निवारम् । असुलभवस्तुप्रार्थनायाः (Ablative) दुःखेन निवार्यते इति । "Very difficult to be withdrawn from its longing for an unattainable object." प्रथममपि "Even as it is, even already." पंचबाणः-The five-arrowed or five-armed God" i. e. Cupid, who is supposed to be armed with the five arrows mentioned in the following stanza:—अरविंदमशोकं च चूतं च नवमल्लिका । नीलोत्पलं च पंचैते पंचबाणस्य सायकाः ॥ किमुत etc. Because the sight of the mango-trees with their fresh tender sprouts and the touch of the gentle Malaya breeze are very potent excitants of the passion of love and immensely intensify the torments of the already suffering, miserable victim of Love.

II. 6. 3. अचिरेण हृदयसंतापयिता etc. Cf. Shakuntla III. स्मर एव तापहेतुर्निर्वापयिता स एव मे जातः । and III. 20 below.

II. 6. 4. प्रतिगृहीतं ब्राह्मणवचनम् Referring to the belief that the words of a Brahmin are bound to be fulfilled although they might have been uttered casually and off-hand Cf. मालविकाग्निमित्र III. विदूषकः । प्रहरिष्यति तत्रभवती (Scil मालविका) त्वामपराद्धम् ॥ राजा । प्रतिगृहीतं वचः सिद्धिदर्शिनो ब्राह्मणस्य ॥

II. 7. उपोढरागसुलभम् । उपोढेन (प्राप्तेन, प्रवृद्धेन वा) रागेण सुभगम् ॥ भेदोन्मुखम् । " Ready to burst or bloom or open ". ईषद्बद्धरजःकणाग्रकपिशा । ईषद्बद्धैः रजःकणैः अग्रे (अग्रभागे) कपिशा । कपिश– " Yellow " मुग्धत्वस्य च यौवनस्य च मध्ये, " On the borderland between childhood and youth ".

II. 7. 4. मणिशिलापट्टकसनाथः " Furnished with a marble (मणिशिला crystal) seat " or " Furnished with a jewelled stone-seat. " कृतोपचारः । कृतः उपचारः येन । " Honouring (you)". प्रतीच्छति " Recevies " (you) ". The hovering bees dash against the delicate अतिमुक्तक flowers & cause them to fall down. The poet fancies that the अतिमुक्तक bower is as it were receiving the King with honour by making an offering of flowers.

II. 8. कुसुमित is derived from कुसुम + thetermination इतच् (इत) according to Panini V 2-36 तदस्य संजातं तारकादिभ्य इतच् ॥ कुसुमानि संजातानि अस्याःसा कुसुमिता (लता) । धृति बन्ध् " To take delight in " दुर्ललित " Fastidious, hard to please by anything else. "

II. 8. 3. अहल्याकामुकस्य महेन्द्रस्य वैद्यः " The physician to the great Indra who had fallen in love with अहल्या. " Who the physician to Indra is cannot be ascertained Perhaps the reference is not to any particular physician of Indra but only in a general way to any physician in the service of Indra whom the latter must have consulted in his wasting love-malady caused by his unfulfilled passion for Ahalya. According to the Ramayana, Ahalya was the first woman to be created by Brahma. She was given in marriage to गौतम. Indra however became enamoured of her and seduced her by assuming the form of Gautama. When Gautama came to know of this, he expelled Ahalya from his hermitage and caused her to become a stone and to remain in that condition until she should be touched by the feet of Dasharathi Rama.

उन्मत्तौ–" Mad, helpless " " At our wit's end. '

II. 8. 5. We read मा मा एवम् before अतिस्नेहः खलु कार्यदर्शी, following four of Mr. Pandit's eight Mss. We think the words are absolutely necessary to connect the preceding speech of the Vidushaka with the following remark of the King. Cf. मालविकाग्निमित्र IV. 6. कार्यसिद्धिपथः सूक्ष्मः स्नेहेनाप्युपलभ्यते

II. 8. 9. ॥ निमित्तं सूचयित्वा Katayavema observes निमित्तं दक्षिणाक्षिस्पन्दनम् । " " An omen i.e. the palpitation or throbbing of the right eye." Cf. also III. 9. च...च । Such a construction shows the contrast or incompatibility between the two things described. इदम् अनंगविचेष्टितम् । Referring to the omen which he has had just now. " This (omen) inspired or produced by Cupid, " किमपि "Unaccountable" अभिमुखीष्विव etc. These two lines describe the condition of his mind immediately after the perception of the good omen.

II. 9. 6. तदा हेमकूटशिखरे etc. Cf. I. 15. 17–22. above.

II. 9. 11. अपहस्तितलज्जः व्यवसायः–" An undertaking or adventure in which I have cast aside all sense of shame."

अपहस्तित=निरस्त, परित्यक्त, दूरीकृत अपहस्तित is the past passive participle from the denominative अपहस्तय् "To take hands off a thing" hence "To abandon, give up, cast away."

II. 9. 16. संप्रधार्यतां तावत् "Think well beforehand (तावत्) whether you are right in going to him" (तावत्) first of all, beforehand.

II. 9. 18. Urvashi means to say that if she were going of her own accord then it would have been proper for her to consider whether it was right to do so. But she is going to Pururavas at the command of Madana (Cupid) and so it is not her business to consider the propriety or otherwise of what she is doing,

अपराजिता नाम शिखाबन्धनविद्या–"The mysterious lore of tying the hair, called अपराजिता 'The invincible'." It seems the preceptor of the Gods–बृहस्पति had taught the Apsarases this mysterious lore of tying the hair to the accompaniment of certain magic charms whereby they could make themselves inaccessible to the demons, the enemies of the Gods.

II. 9. 29. अहो विस्मृतं मे हृदयम्। This shows that Urvashi was so deeply engrossed with thoughts about Pururavas, that she forgot the fact that she was under the influence of the mysterious lore अपराजिता. Well indeed has Prof. Ryder said about her: "She is too much of a woman to be a nymph."

सिद्धमार्गम् आसाद्य। "Coming down to the path of the Siddhas." सिद्धs are semi-divine beings possessed of supernatural powers and capable of flying in the sky at a short distance from the surface of the earth. सिद्धमार्गम् आसाद्य, then, means that the Apsarases come down and move across the sky at a short distance from the surface of the ea th.

II. 9. 34. प्रतिष्ठान—Modern Allahabad was the capital of Pururavas. It stood at the confluence of the Ganges and the Jamna, Cf. विष्णुपुराण–राज्यं स कारयामास प्रयागे पृथिवीपतिः । उत्तरे जाह्नवीतीरे प्रतिष्ठाने महायशाः ॥ शिखामरणभूत " Being as it were the crest-ornament (of प्रतिष्ठान)."

II. 9. 40. आपन्नानुकम्पी " Friend of the distressed " आपन्नान् नुकम्पते इति । This refers to her recent deliverance by Pururavas from the power of the demon Keshin.

II. 9. 47. प्रतीक्षते " Is waiting for you, is expecting you."

II. 9. 55. तिरस्करिणीप्रतिच्छन्ना । " Hidden or concealed by means of the तिरस्करिणी विद्या". तिरस्करिणी is a magic lore by means of which a person can make himself invisible at will. तावत् " For a while, just for some time." विजने " In a retired, solitary place."

II. 9. 62. तूष्णीमास्ते–because his mind is too much occupied with thoughts about Urvashi, to allow him to hear attentively the words of the विदूषक.

II. 9. 65. आत्मानं विकत्थते । " Boasts of herself," "Remains stubborn and indifferent in her pride or haughtiness."

II. 9. 66–67. किं पुनः मानुष्यं विडम्ब्यते " But why do you act the part of a human being?" " You are not a human being, but an Apsaras. So you can, by consulting your supernatural powers, easily find out who is the subject of the King's thoughts. Why do you behave like a poor, miserable, helpless mortal?" विडम्बय् " To imitate, to act like."

II. 9. 68. But to this Urvashi says that she is afraid of knowing by means of her supernatural powers something that is most unpalatable to her. For, who knows, the King might be entertaining thoughts about some other damsel than herself? And if it were true, what a great shock would that revelation bring to her? Here again we see that Urvashi is too much of a woman to be a nymph.

II. 9. 78. हीनसत्व हृदय "Oh timid heart." सत्त्व (n) means "Courage."

II. 10. न च etc. Construe : हे सखे तां सुवदनां प्रियाम् आलेख्ये असमाप्यापि मम नयनयोः उद्बाष्पत्वं न भविष्यति इति न i. e. भविष्यत्येव ।

असमाप्यापि "Even before finishing" (*her likeness in the painting*). उद्बाष्पत्वम् "Being flooded with tears." The construction is ungrammatical, for the gerund (असमाप्य) must have the same subject as the principal verb (भविष्यति). Here, however, अहम् is the subject of असमाप्य and उद्बाष्पत्वं is the subject of भविष्यति. The correct construction would be: तां सुवदनां प्रियाम् आलेख्ये असमापितवतोऽपि मम etc. or तां सुवदनां प्रियाम् आलेख्ये असमाप्यापि अहम् उद्बाष्पनयनः न भविष्यामि (इति) न ॥ For a similar idea Cf. शाकुंतल VI. 22. प्रजागरात्खिलीभूतः तस्याः स्वप्ने समागमः । बाष्पस्तु न ददात्येनां द्रष्टुं चित्रगतामपि॥ Also मेघदूत II. 45. (त्वामालिख्य etc.) मालतीमाधव I. 35.

II. 11. प्रभाव means divine, supernatural power. अलब्धफलनीरसान्–अलब्धफलाश्च ते नीरसाश्च अलब्धफलनीरसाः तान् "Vain, because of their failing to get their object." भवतु पंचबाणः कृती. The King means to say that he is quite powerless before the all-conquering shafts of Cupid, and that if Cupid wants to regard himself as triumphant by frustrating the desires of the King, he should by all means do so and glory himself in having killed a poor victim. For the King is sure to die, if his desires are frustrated. तस्मिन् जने = उर्वश्याम् "In regard to Urvashi" कृती "Victorious," "Blessed."

II. 11. 6. प्रभावनिर्मितेन "Produced by means of divine power," because no natural one was at hand.

II. 11. 9. अविधा or अविदा An interjection showing surprise and fear at the sight of something never seen before. अविधेत्याक्रोशे (कात्यवेम); अविदेत्यदृष्टाश्रुतप्राप्तौ(रंगनाथ)

II. 11. 13. अक्षरविन्यासः "A writing", literally "Arrangement of letters".

II. 11. 14. अक्षराणि विसृष्टानि भवन्ति—"Letters may have been sent (to you). " अक्षराणि "Syllables. letters."

II. 11.18. नास्ति अगतिः मनोरथानाम् Cf. Kumara. V. 64. मनोरथानामगतिर्न विद्यते। "There is nothing inaccessible or too high for desires." अनुवाच्य "Reading to himself." Cf. II. 19.33. and V. 6.10. प्रसन्न "Happy, felicitous, correct."

II. 11.21. भवानिदानीं प्रसीदतु। The Vidushaka makes a pun upon the word प्रसन्न used by the King in II 11. 18. He means to say, "The guess has shown itself to be प्रसन्न i.e. correct; now be yourself प्रसन्न i.e. pleased to read out the contents of the letter."

II. 11.22. नागरिक—"Belonging to the town, urban, clever, ingenious" as opposed to जानपद "Rustic."

II. 12–13. Construe : हे स्वामिन्, यदि नाम अज्ञाता अहं यथा त्वया संभाविता तथा अनुरक्तस्य तव उपरि (स्याम्) (तर्हि) ननु मे लुलितपारिजातशयनीये शरीरके नंदनवनवाता अपि अत्युष्णा भवन्ति। अज्ञाता—"Being unknown to you", "Whose heart or feelings or sufferings are unkown to you". In stanza 11, Pururavas has made a serious allegation against Urvashi, viz. that Urvashi is indifferent to him although she very well knows how he is pining for her. To this allegation Urvashi replies in this stanza: "If I am really indifferent to you as you imagine me to be, then how is it, that even when I lie upon a bed strewn over with Parijata flowers, my body exposed to the delightful breezes of the Nandanavana, I roll about restlessly and do not find even a moment's relief from the oppressive pangs of love ?" She means to say that the King does not really know the state of her mind; hence she speaks of herself as अज्ञाता. If, on the other hand, the King knew that she is constantly pining for him, he would never make such an allegation against her. लुलितपारिजातशयनीये (Scil. शरीरके) । लुलितं पारिजातस्य शयनीयं येन तस्मिन् । Compare with this, the love-letter written by Shakuntala in Shakuntala III. 15.

तव न जाने हृदयं मम पुनः कामो दिवापि रात्रावपि ।
निर्घृण तपति बलीयस्त्वयि वृत्तमनोरथाया अंगानि ॥

II. 13.1. किं नु खलु सांप्रतं भणिष्यति । That is " Will he say that he loves me or will he say that he does not love me ?"

II. 13.4. कमलनालायमानैः अंगैः । "By means of his limbs that have become thin and flaccid like a lotus-stalk", on account of his deep yearning for you. Chitralekha means to say that it is not at all necessary that the King should say verbally that he loves Urvashi. His emaciated body itself bears eloquent testimony to his love for Urvashi.

II. स्वस्तिवाचनम्—"मंगलार्थकस्वस्तिपदस्य वाचनं पठनं स्वस्तिवाचनम् । पुण्याहवाचनमित्यर्थः । 'स्वस्ति भवन्तो ब्रुवन्तु' इति यजमानः प्रार्थयते, ततो ब्राह्मणाः 'आयुष्मते स्वस्ति' इति उक्त्वा "स्वस्ति न इन्द्र" इत्यादीन् मन्त्रान् पठन्ति । तेन पुण्याहवाचनकर्मणः स्वस्तिवाचनमिति नामधेयम् ॥" Raddi Shastri. स्वस्तिवाचन is the same as पुण्याहवाचन. It is a rite performed immediately before any solemn observance, in which the Brahmins sprinkle water over the Yajamana and invoke blessings on him by means of मन्त्रs from the scriptures. The Brahmins receive, in return for their services, sweet-meats, presents etc. Hence the importance of the स्वस्तिवाचन to the विदूषक. स्वस्तिवाचन literally means "Invocation of good fortune" by means of the repetition of sacred mantras. Mr. Pandit, however, thinks that the Sanskrit equivalent of the original Prakrit सोत्थिवाअण is स्वस्ति-उपायन and not स्वस्तिवाचन. स्वस्ति-उपायन would mean "A present offered to a Brahmin in order to secure his good wishes and blessings at the end of any religious ceremony." समाश्वासनम् "Consolation, encouragement."

II. 14. Construe : हे सखे, पत्रे निवेशितं तुल्यानुरागपिशुनं ललितार्थबन्धं प्रियायाः उदाहरणम्, उत्पक्ष्मणः मम आननेन तस्याः मदिरेक्षणायाः आननं समागतमिव। तुल्यानुरागपिशुनम्=तुल्यप्रेमसूचकम्— "Indicating a love as great as that of mine for her." ललितार्थबन्धम्. "Full of charming meaning." ललितः अर्थबन्धः यस्मिन् तत्। उदाहरणम्—" Utterance, expression;" more correctly here "Song, piece of poetry.,' पत्रे निवेशितम् "Committed to writing on the Bhurja leaf." मदिरेक्षणा "Having bewitching (मदिर = मादक) eyes." उपिक्ष्मणो मम "Of me (who am looking at it) with upturned or raised up eyelashes," i. e. "Of me (who am looking at it) with staring eyes." V. I. उत्पक्ष्मलं-Agreeing with तस्याः आननम्-means the same thing : Vide Translation. तस्याः आननं मम आननेन समागतमिव। "Her face has as it were come into contact with mine." The King means that his reading the letter of Urvashi is not simply a consolation to him but that it is as if her face came into contact with his own. For the words coming from her mouth and committed to writing on the Bhurja leaf, are devoured by the King with his eager eyes.

II. 14. 1. अत्र आवयोः प्रीतिः समविभागा—"Here i. e. now, is our love of equal shares" i. e. "Now it is proved beyond doubt that we love each other equally."

II. 14. 3. अंगुलीस्वेदेन। स्वेद—Perspiration is one of the eight involuntary manifestations of inner love. (सात्त्विकभावs as they are called). अयं प्रियायाः स्वहस्तः "This autograph of my beloved."

II. 14. 6–7. The Vidushaka thinks that the King has asked him to preserve the autograph of Urvashi, as a written evidence of her avowal of love that could be used against her in case she denies her having ever made such an avowal. Therefore he asks the King whether it is possible that Urvashi will ever disappoint him, having made such a confession of her love. The King of course wanted the Vidushaka to preserve that letter simply as a valuable hand-writing and memorial of Urvashi विसंवद्—"To fail to fulfil any promise, to disagree, to fail to produce an expected result."

II. 14. 11. Mark how human Urvashi is in her attitude towards the King. She is afraid of placing herself directly into his presence all of a sudden. So she first sends चित्रलेखा as her agent.

II. 14. 13. तिरस्करिणीम् अपनीय—"Casting aside the veil of invisibily"—"Withdrawing or removing the influence of the तिरस्करिणी spell."

II. 15. संगमे पूर्वदृष्टेव etc. "Like the Yamuna first seen in confluence with the Ganga, but then afterwards seen without the Ganga" as a person proceeds upstream along the river-bank; i.e. The Yamuna by herself is not so charming as she is when united with the Ganga.

II. 12. सुरारिसंभवे दुर्जाते—Referring to her encounter with the demon Keshin. दुर्जात (n) " Misfortune, calamity ".

II. 15. 15. भद्रमुखि " Oh sweet-faced one ! ", i. e. " My good lady ".

II. 16. प्रियदर्शना " Fair one ". तदर्थे आर्त—" Afflicted on her account, pining for her ". प्रणय: " Prayer, solicitation, humble request ". स्मरस्य = स्मरं प्रति " Unto the God of love ". घटन (n) " Joining together ". Mr. Pandit translates the third line as follows : " This prayer proceeding from love is common to us both. " But it is unwarrantable to take स्मरस्य प्रणय: in the sense of स्मरनिमित्तक: प्रणय: । We therefore propose to take स्मरस्य in the sense of स्मरं प्रति and translate : " This is our common prayer unto the God of love ". The prayer that two lovers make unto the god of love is, of course, that they should be united before long.

II. 16. 3. त्वत्तोऽपि निर्दयतरम्—" Even more merciless (to him) than to you."

II. 16. 6. लघु " Lightly, only too readily, willingly." त्वया उज्झितास्मि । Because चित्रलेखा has now become the messenger of Pururavas, she has as it were given up Urvashi.

II. 16. 9. आचारं तावत् प्रतिपद्यस्व.—" Observe first the formality (आचारं)," (of greeting the King appropriately).

II. 17. जयशब्द: सहस्राक्षाद् अगत: पुरुषान्तरम्–" The word " Victory " which proceeding from your mouth, does not greet any other being save the thousand-eyed God (Indra)." Cf. यस्मिन्नीश्वर इत्यनन्यविषय: शब्दो यथार्थाक्षर: I. 1–above.

II. 18. मुनिना भरतेन—The sage Bharata who is regarded as the founder of the drama and the originator of the histrionic art. He is credited with the authorship of that famous work on dramaturgy the भारतीयनाटयशास्त्र. अष्ट-रसाश्रयः प्रयोगः "The drama viz. लक्ष्मीस्वयंवर which forms the substratum for the display and development of the eight रसs or emotional flavours." The eight रसs which were to be exhibited in the drama in question, are enumerated in the following stanza: शृंगारहास्यकरुणवीररौद्रभयानकाः। बीभत्साद्भुतसंज्ञौ चेत्यष्टौ नाटये रसाः स्मृताः। काव्यप्रकाश, IV. 29. The लक्ष्मीस्वयंवर appears to have been a wonderful play that afforded scope for the development of all the eight रसs. नियुक्तः "Has been assigned" (to your ladyships). ललिताभिनयम् "Abounding in beautiful acting" i. e. "Which calls into play a good deal of very fine acting." सलोकपालः "Together with the लोकपालs i. e.(guardians of the eight quarters of the world." द्रष्टुमनाः "Is desirous of witnessing."

II. 18. 4. अनुमान्यतां महाराजः "Secure the assent of His Majesty" to your departure i. e. "Take your leave of His Majesty."

II. 18. 8. अयं जनः "This humble lady here." इच्छति देवेषु अनपराद्धम् आत्मानं कर्तुम् "Wishes to avoid offending against the Gods," "Wishes to make herself blameless towards the Gods." i.e. "Wishes to go at once and thus avoid offending them by disobeying their commands."

II. 18. 13. वैयर्थ्यमिव चक्षुषः "My eyes are useless as it were," since Urvashi has gone away. Singular for the dual.

II. 18. 22. मा भवान् अंगानि मुंचतु "Do not drop your limbs through despair." i. e. "Do not give way to despair." शिथिलय—(Denominative from शिथिल "Slack, loose") "To slacken."

II. 19, हृदयं स्ववशम् "Her free heart," "Her heart of which she was mistress." The Gods were the masters of her body. But of her heart, she herself was the mistress. न्यस्तम् "Was left as it were" (with me). The King fancies that the sighs of Urvashi were due to the passage of her heart from below her breasts to himself.

II. 19. 3. इमां वेलाम् "By this time". ग्रहीतव्यं भविष्यति= गृहीत भवेत् ।

II. 19. 8. गतम् उर्वश्याः मार्गेण "Has gone to heaven along with her", "Has gone the way of Urvashi".

II. 19. 9. वैधेयः "A fool or blockhead" मूर्खवैधेयबालिशाः। इति अमरः । सर्वत्र प्रमादी "Bungles everywhere."

ततः प्रविशति etc. The following scene in which Queen औशीनरी and her attendant are shown to be in quest of Pururavas and in which the Queen happening to come by an irrefutable evidence of the King's infidelity, exposes him at last and then leaves the stage in indignation has a close parallel in मालविकाग्निमित्र Act III.

II. 19. 18. अन्यथा "Falsely", "Incorrectly", "Have I ever before falsely informed Your Majesty?"

II. 19. 21. विश्रब्धामन्त्रितानि "Confidential talks"

II. 19. 26. इतोमुखम् "Hitherwards", "in this direction".

II. 19. 29. परिवर्तनविभाविताक्षरम् "Which as it turns round and round reveals some letters upon it". कथम् । वाच्यताम् । "How? shall I read it?"

II. 19. 33. अनुवाचय "Read to yourself". अविरुद्ध "Unobjectionable; not unfit for a lady's ears".

II. 19. 37. कौलीनम "Scandal".

II. 19. 42. 43. अनेन एव उपायनेन i. e. "Taking this very letter of Urvashi as a present to him".

II. 20. The King believes that the breeze has carried away the भूर्जपत्र and so addresses it. संभृतं पौष्पं रजः "The accumulated pollen of flowers ". मिथ्या = वृथा. " For no purpose, uselessly, in vain ". आनीते हि etc. Construe : हि (यतः) अञ्जनां प्रति आलक्षितप्रार्थनः भवान् एवंविधैः मनोविनोदनफलैः धारितं कामार्तं जनं आनीते। अंजनां प्रति आलक्षितप्रार्थनः भवान् " You who are known to have courted or made love to Anjana." Anjana was the mother of Maruti and the sweet-heart of वायु (wind). एवंविधैः मनोविनोदनफलैः । " By means of such things (i. e. such memorials as a love-letter received from the other party), intended to give some diversion to the mind (मनोविनोदनं " Consolation or diversion of the mind").. The King means, that the wind (वायु) having himself experienced a romantic love for अंजना, very well knows or ought to know the importance of such love-memorials to lovers.

II. 20. 5. म्लायमानकेसरच्छविना " Having the complexion or appearance of a fading *bakula* flower. ".

II. 20. 11. दुरागतम् The Vidushaka plays upon the word स्वागतम् which literally means "Well come", and says " It is no longer a "Well come", but an "Ill come" i.e. the antithesis of a welcome, meaning that the Queen would hardly appreciate the King's welcome, but on the contrary would resent it.

II. 20. 15. This remark of the Vidushaka must be supposed to be made जनान्तिकम् (" Aside, to the King "), although none of the Mss. gives the requisite stage-direction. He does not of course desire that the Queen should hear it. And further the question of the King to which the Vidushaka gives his reply here, is asked जनान्तिकम्. लोप्त्रम् " Stolen property ". लोप्त्रंगृहीतः कुम्भीरकः " A thief caught together with the stolen property i. e.

caught red-handed". For the idea Cf. मालविकाग्निमित्र III. कर्मगृहीतेन कुम्भीलकेन संधिच्छेदनं शिक्षितोऽस्मीति वक्तव्यं भवति॥

II. 20. 16. परसमन्वेषणार्थम् "For the purpose of finding out another (Bhurja-leaf) altogether". The King admits that he was searching for a Bhurja-leaf, but says that it was not the one the Queen had brought.

II. 20. 19. सौभाग्यम् "Good fortune" viz. his having received a letter from Urvashi containing a fervent expression of her love for him.

II. 20. 21. The Vidushaka tries to explain away the conduct of the King by saying that the King is suffering from a bilious attack and is therefore acting incoherently like a madman. The bilious attack is due to the fact that the King has not had any food till a late hour (for it is midday now). The Vidushaka therefore suggests to the Queen to arrange for the dinner of the King in order to cure him of his bilious affection. पित्तापशमनसमर्थम् "Capable of quelling down the vitiated bile" (of the King).

II. 20. 23. शोभनं खलु ब्राह्मणेन आश्वासितः वयस्यः। "Very well indeed has the Brahmin come to his friend's help". She says this of course ironically.

II. 20. 25. आश्वासितः पिशाचोऽपि (भवति।) "Even a ghost is pacified or conciliated" by the offering of food. How much more then a bilious attack?

II. 20. 26. आपादयसि "You make me to be, you show me to be". We read so, instead of प्रतिपादयसि which appears rather hackneyed and less idiomatic. बलात् "Forcibly", "Falsely". The King does not approve of the excuse put forward by the Vidushaka. He wants to adhere to the plea that it was another Bhurja-leaf that he was looking for. So he chides him in this manner.

II. 21. रम्भोरु–रम्भे इव ऊरू यस्याः सा रम्भोरूः, तत्संबोधनं 'रम्भोरु'। Although the word ऊरु ends in a short उ, still when appearing as the final member of a compound, it lengthens that उ. Cf. ऊरूत्तरपदादौपम्ये। विरम संरम्भात् "Give up your anger, or wrath or rage". सेव्यो जनः etc. "Is it ever possible that the master can get angry unless his servant is in the wrong?"

II. 21. 4. मा खलु etc.. "I must not in my light heartedness be carried away by this supplication (अनुनय)." अदाक्षिण्यकृतात् पश्चात्तापात् बिभेमि "But then, I am afraid oi the heart-burning or remorse that will be caused to me later on by my *hauteur* (अदाक्षिण्य) in spurning the King's supplication." अदाक्षिण्य "Unkindness, discourteousness, loftiness of manner". Later on (Vide III. 4. 11, 13 etc.), the Queen does in fact feel the bitings of her conscience for her having treated the King's prostration with scant ceremony.

II. 21. 7. अप्रसन्ना (i) "Turbid, muddy": (ii) "Offended, angry, in a rage".

II. 21. 9. इदम् 'This' i. e. The fact that she has gone away unreconciled and angry. न अनुपपन्नम्। "Is not wrong i. e. is as it should be i. e. it is not unreasonable".

II. 22. प्रियवचनशतोऽपि "Although couched in hundreds of sweet words". रसाद् ऋते "In the absence of genuine love". हृदयं न प्रविशति "Does not appeal to their hearts". तद्विदाम् = मणिपरीक्षकाणाम्। तद्विद् "A lapidary who is expert in his craft". कृत्रिमरागयोजितः This epithet applies both to the मणि and the अनुनय. In the former case it means

" Possessed of an artificial redness i. e. not possessing a natural red colour ". In the latter case, " Accompanied only by a semblance of love (कृत्रिमप्रेम) i. e. not showing any genuine feeling of love ". तद्विदाम् could also be connected with योषिताम् " Women, who are expert in recognizing the genuineness of the supplications of their beloveds. " Cf. मालविकाग्निमित्र III.3.

उचितः प्रणयो वरं विहन्तुं बहवः खण्डनहेतवो हि दृष्टाः ।
उपचारविधिर्मनस्विनीनां न तु पूर्वाभ्यधिकोऽपि भावशून्यः ॥

II. 22. 3. अक्षिदुःखित: " With sore eyes ".

II. 22. 4. स एव " The same " i. e. as before.

प्रणिपातलंघनात् " because of her disregarding my prostration at her feet". अस्यां धैर्यमवलंबिष्ये " I shall assume an attitude of stiffness or patient indifference towards her" Cf. Katayavema " अत्र प्रणामोपाये व्यर्थेऽपि सति उपेक्षा नामोपायः प्रयुक्त इत्यनुसंधेयम् । " Or धैर्यम् may be taken in the usual sense of courage. " I shall take courage as regards her i. e. I shall no longer be afraid of her ", since she has given me an insult in spurning my prostration. Cf. मालविकाग्निमित्र III. 23. मन्ये प्रियाहृतमनाः तस्याः प्रणिपातलंघनं सेवाम् । In other words, the King wishes to use the insult given him by the Queen " As a lever to secure his own purposes".

II. 22. 8. तावत् " For some time ". अवलम्ब्य " To support, to sustain, "

II. 23. उष्णालुः " Oppressed by heat." Katayavema उष्णासहः । It is formed from the word उष्ण according to the Sutra "शीतोष्णतृप्रेभ्यस्तदसहने " इत्यालुच् । (quoted by Katayavema). The v. l. उष्णार्तः is simpler and more direct, but for that very reason, rather suspicious. उपरि निर्भिद्य " Having pierced through or forced open at the top." कर्णिकार

is, according to Mr. Pandit, the Pangara tree, which has blood-red flowers in early spring, when it is still completely shorn of its leaves. The bee is oppressed by the heat of the sun and so resorts to the कर्णिकार bud, having pierced it at the top. The singular षट्पदः does not, at first sight, appear to harmonize with the plural मुकुलानि, and hence it has given rise to the v. l. आसेरते षट्पदाः। But if we consider the line a little more closely, we begin to perceive that the plural मुकुलानि is intentionally used by the poet. One and the same bee hops from bud to bud, pierces through and rests in each bud for a while and again proceeds to another. Thus one single bee visits several buds, one single bud not sufficing to give it complete relief from the intense heat of the sun.

कारण्डवः " A kind of water-duck. "

क्रीडावेश्मनि "In the pleasure house or pleasure-pavilion".

Cf. with this description of the noon मालविकाग्निमित्र II. 12.

ACT III.

[Like the Second Act, the third Act also opens with an Introductory Scene (technically called विष्कम्भक), which is followed by the Main Scene.

INTRODUCTORY SCENE:—Hermitage of the sage Bharata.

We learn from a dialogue between two pupils of Bharata, that the drama लक्ष्मीस्वयंवर, staged by Bharata before the heavenly audience, would have proved a complete success, but for one blemish which was due to a very unfortunate slip of the tongue on the part of Urvashi, who, while acting the part of Lakshmi, said, in her absent-mindedness, that her heart was fixed upon Pururavas, when as a matter of fact she ought to have said that it was fixed upon Purushottama. Bharata thereupon pronounced a curse upon her to the effect that she would be banished from heaven. Indra, however, took pity upon Urvashi and conferred a favour upon her by allowing her to remain with Pururavas, his friend in war, until Pururavas beholds the child that she would bear him.

THE MAIN SCENE ;—The main scene really consists of four sub-scenes as shown below :—

FIRST SCENE :—THE PALACE OF THE KING.

The King enters pining for the love of Urvashi. The Chamberlain (Latavya) communicates to him the request of the Queen that the King should be kind enough to go to the terrace of the मणिहर्म्य palace, where she would meet him, and also to pass some time there, enjoying the beauty of the moon-lit night. The King grants the request, but is surprised at such a softening of the Queen's temperament and concludes that the Queen must have been stung with remorse for her discourteous behaviour towards him. The King and Vidushaka go to the मणिहर्म्य.

SECOND SCENE :—THE TERRACE OF THE मणिहर्म्य PALACE.

The King and Vidushaka pass some time in enjoying the beauty of the moon-rise. The King's thoughts, however, return again and again to the all-engrossing theme of his unfulfilled love for Urvashi, and Vidushaka again and again comforts him with hope-inspiring words.

THIRD SCENE :—In the sky.

Urvashi dressed as an Abhisarika and Chitralekha appear in the sky and move towards the terrace of मणिहर्म्य, where the King is sitting with Vidushaka.

FOURTH SCENE :—The terrace of the मणिहर्म्य palace.

Urvashi and Chitralekha get down from the sky, and, remaining concealed by their divine power, overhear the talk of the King and Vidushaka and secretly watch everything that happens.

The King describes to Vidushaka his love-lorn condition and tries to give him an idea of the intensity of his feeling for Urvashi. Urvashi is completely satisfied about the ardour and sincerity of the King's love for her and is almost on the point of revealing herself to the King, but is cruelly disappointed by the arrival of Queen औशिनरी with her attendants.

The Queen explains to the King her object in requesting his presence there at that time, *viz.* that she wants to carry out the vow of प्रियानुप्रसादन (conciliation of the beloved) which she has been observing. In connection with that vow, she worships the Moon and the King and then gives the King an assurance that thenceforward she would treat with indulgence and toleration the King's love-affairs with other women. The Queen then departs and the King once again falls into a fit of love-longing, when he is very agreeably surprised by the sudden appearance before him of Urvashi and Chitralekha.

The King seats Urvashi by his side. Chitralekha leaves for heaven, requesting the King to take care of Urvashi. The King gives expression to his sense of joy and blessedness in being united with Urvashi, and then both of them retire for rest.]

As already remarked, this act opens with an interlude (technically called, विष्कंभ or विष्कंभक, for the meaning of which term *vide*, Introduction, Technical Names p. XXV.) between two pupils of भरत. Of these one viz. गालव speaks sanskrit, while the other called पल्लव uses Prakrit (शौरसेनी). The reason for this discrimination is, that गालव is the senior disciple of भरत, while पल्लव appears to be a novice and hence not yet possessing a facile command over the Sanskrit tongue. This becomes evident when we consider that भरत, when going to heaven entrusts the management of the अग्निशरण to गालव, while, he takes पल्लव along with him as his seat-bearer (आसनं प्राहित:।) Compare in this connection उत्तररामचरित, Act IV, विष्कंभक.

III. o. 4. त्वम् आसनं प्रतिग्राहित: । "You were made to carry the seat." It seems, Bharata had taken पल्लव to heaven to carry his seat (व्याघ्रचर्म or कृष्णाजिन) wherever he went to serve as his seat-bearer, so to say. अग्निशरण= अग्निगृह or अग्निशाला *i. e.* "The place where the sacred fire is kept," "Fire-sanctuary." संरक्षण "Keeping watch over, looking to." स्थापित "Appointed." दिव्या परिषद् "The celestial audience." आराधित "Pleased, satisfied."

III. o. 10. सरस्वतीकृतकाव्यबन्धेसरस्वतीप्रथिते "Composed by सरस्वती." तेषु तेषु रसान्तरेषु तन्मया आसीत् । The subject is दिव्या परिषद् appearing in III. रसान्तरेषु—अन्ये रसा: रसान्तराणि। रसान्तरेषु thus stands for रसेषु. रस "A sentiment; the dramatic representationof a sentiment or emotion." तन्मया " Deeply absorbed in."

III. o. 12. ते वाक्यशेष: "The remaining part of your sentence." सदोषावकाश: (दोषस्य अवकाश: दोषावकाश:, तेन सहित:।) इव (भाति ।) "Appears to imply a fault," in the dramatic performance. "Seems to hint at a fault."

III. o. 14. वचनं प्रमादस्खलितम् आसीत् "(She) committed a blunder in her speech ;" "Was guilty of a slip of the tongue."

III. o. 19. लक्ष्मीभूमिका "The character or part of लक्ष्मी." वारुणी appears to be the name of some Goddess. भावाभिनिवेश "Fixed love," "Strong inclination of the heart."

III. o. 26. भवितव्यानुविधायीनि इन्द्रियाणि "The sense-organs follow, or act according to, destiny—what is destined to happen.

III. o. 37. दिव्यं स्थानम् "Heavenly or celestial residence." प्रेक्षणावसाने "At the end of the theatrical show or dramatic representation." अत्र "Here, in this matter" *i. e.* now that you have been cursed to dwell amongst mortals. त्वयि दृष्टसंतान: भवति । "Sights or beholds the child you will bear him."

III. o. 42. सदृशम् "Befitting, becoming to." पुरुषान्तरविद: "Who knows or can read the hearts (अन्तर) of others."

III. o. 45. अपराद्धा "Has been transgressed or exceeded,"

III. o. 49. The कञ्चुकिन् or chamberlain in Indian Drama is always an old Brahmin of irreproachable character in charge of the royal harem.

III, 1. कल्ये वयसि "In the prime of life," "In vigorous youth." कल्य "Healthy, vigorous, youthful." सर्व: कुटुम्बी "Every married man." कल्पते विश्रमाय "Is able to take rest." परिणतिः "Old age." सादयन्ती शरीरम् "Wasting the body, sapping the vigour of the body." सेवाकारा (supply भवति). "Assumes the form of servitude" *i. e.* "Is passed in servitude." सेवा आकारो यस्याः सा सेवारूपा, सेवामयी वा ।

For सादयन्ती शरीरम we get a variant साधयन्ती प्रतिष्ठाम् which would mean, "Effecting stability or fixity in our position." For the older the man, the better is he qualified for the post of a कञ्चुकिन्.

Katayavema reads सेवा कारापरिणतिः and explains: सेवा कारायाः परिणतिः, बन्धनगृहस्य परिणामः । Ranganatha also has the same reading and explains: कारापरिणतिः बन्धनालयरूपा, यतो वार्द्धकेऽपि मुक्तिः सुतरां नास्तीति भावः । But this reading cannot be accepted as it fails to harmonize with the purport of the stanza. For here the कञ्चुकिन् contrasts the old age of ordinary people with the old age of the class of men to which he belongs. While the old age of others brings rest to them, his old age gives him no relief So one expects to find a word meaning "old age" to appear in a prominent position in the last two lines. This scarcely happens in the case of the reading adopted by Katayavema and Ranganatha. The कञ्चुकिन् does not in fact wish to make any statement about सेवा (service), but about "old age."

III. 1. 1. सनियमया "Who is observing the rules" in connection with the vow of प्रियानुप्रसादन "Propitiating the beloved." (See III. 12. 20) मानम् उत्सृज्य "Giving up my sense of wounded pride." मान means the indignation that a woman feels towards her husband when she finds him attached to another woman (Cf. स्त्रीणामीर्ष्याकृतो मानः कोपोऽन्यासंगिनि प्रिये ।). सन्ध्याजाप्य "Evening prayers."—वृत्तान्तः "The scene or general appearance of things."

III. 2. वासयष्टि "Perching rod." उत्कीर्णा: इव "As if sculptured out." वलभय: "The topmost parts of the palace, the turrets," or according to Mr. Pandit "The slanting wooden supports or struts jutting out from the wall close above the windows and propping up the projecting eaves of the roof." Cf. गोपानसी तु वलभी छादने वक्रदारुणि। अमर:। संदिग्धपारावता: (वलभय:) "In which the doves are confounded with" the volumes of smoke issuing from burnt incense. The doves have the same ashy colour as the smoke issuing from burnt incense. शुद्धान्तवृद्धाजन: "Old matrons of the female apartments." आचारप्रयत: "Clean or holy by or intent upon, the performance of the customary acts." सपुष्पबलिषु स्थानेषु–"In places strewn over with offerings of flowers." विभजते (subject जन:) "Arrange, place, distribute."

III. 3. गतिमान्–"In motion." अपक्षलोपात्=पक्षच्छेदाभावात्, "Because of its wings being unclipt." Mountains, so we are told in the Puranas, had formerly wings and could fly at will. But when they began to harass mankind by their wanton movements, Indra was forced to deprive them of their wings. अनुतट etc. अनुतटं पुष्पिता: कर्णिकारयष्टय: यस्मिन्। कर्णिकारयष्टि means "A thin tall. Karnikara tree." The women holding lights in their hands are compared to thin, tall Karnikara trees, which are covered with bright red flowers.

III. 4. अन्तरित "Shut out". अविनोददीर्घयामा। अविनोदेन–विनोदाभावेन दीर्घा: यामा: यस्या:। "With its hours (याम-a period of time equal to three hours) tediously long for want of diversion". Cf. मेघदूत II. 28. सव्यापारामहनि न तथा पीडयेद्‌ विप्रयोग:। शंके रात्रौ गुरुतरशुचं निर्विनोदां सखीं ते॥

III. 4. 2. मणिहर्म्यपृष्ठ The terrace of मणिहर्म्य, a palace so-called. सुदर्शन: "Well visible". यावद् रोहिणीसंयोग: (supply भवति). "Until the Moon enters the asterism of Rohini."

III. 4. 5-6. देव्या: आरम्भ: "What the Queen has proposed to do, what she has set herself about."

III. 4. 12. प्रमार्ष्टुकामा "Wishes to make amends for."

III. 5. Construe : अवधूतप्रणिपाता: मनस्विन्य: पश्चात् संतप्यमानमनसोऽपि (सत्य:) दयितानुनयै: निभृतै: (= निभृतं) व्यपत्रपन्ते ॥ Mr. Pandit construes निभृतै: with दयितानुनयै:, and understands the word निभृत (which *always* means "Secret, concealed") in the sense of "Open, manifest". According to him, the idea is : "Women who have spurned the svpplications of their beloveds, although later on they might be stung with remorse, are ashamed of openly conciliating them". He says : "निभृत = नितरां भृत. भृत = filled, full. निभृत is therefore="Very full", i.e. "Complete, not half and half, and hence *open*". But such a distortion of the sense of a word to make it yield a meaning which it never has elsewhere, is, in our opinion, scarcely warrantable. We get indeed a very good sense from the stanza by taking निभृतै: as an instrumental adverb (like उच्चै:, नीचै:, शनै:, पराचै: etc.) meaning "Silently, secretly, in their hearts". "Women, though stung with bitter remorse are in their hearts ashamed of conciliating their beloved ones." For adverbs taking instrumental endings see Whitney's Grammar sec. 1112. It must however be confessed that the use of निभृतै: as an adverb in the sense of निभृतम् is unprecedented and that one is, therefore, tempted to change निभृतै: to निभृतम् ।

III. 5. 4-5. गंगातरंगसश्रीकम् "Beautiful like the waves of the Ganges", being made of crystal-steps rising one above another. सश्रीक—श्रिया सहित: सश्रीक: । We may also take the expression to mean "Beautiful with the waves of the Ganges", supposing that the मणिहर्म्य stood quite on the bank of the Ganges.

III. 5. 12. आलोकसुभग "Charming to look at".

III. 6. हरिवाहनदिङ्मुखम् = इन्द्रदिङ्मुखम् = प्राचीनमुखम् "The face of the East" because हरिवाहन "Having yellow, tawny ruddy horses" is an epithet of Indra and he is the lord guardian of the East. उदय here stands for उदयाचल "The rising mountain" i.e. the mountain in the East from behind which the Moon appears to rise. अलकसंयमनादिव "As if by the tying up of the hair or tresses". The idea is :—So long as the Moon had not risen, the face of the eastern quarter (imagined here to be a woman), was shrouded with dismal darkness. Now this darkness is fancied to be the loosely hanging tresses of the lady in the form of the East. The Moon is thought of as the lord of the East, and so long as he was away, the East like a faithful wife did not dress her hair, but allowed them to hang loosely about her face. (Cf. क्रीडां शरीरसंस्कारं समाजोत्सवदर्शनम् । हास्यं परगृहे यानं त्यजेत्प्रोषितभर्तृका ॥). With the arrival of her lord—the Moon—she tied up hair and her face brightened up.

III. 6.2, खण्डमोदकसश्रीक "Appearing like a broken मोदक." Dissolve : खण्डमोदकेन सदृशी श्री:यस्य ।. The Moon has risen some time after it has grown dark. So the orb cannot be full and complete. The विदूषक therefore compares it to a मोदक which is white in colour, and whose apex is broken off. The मोदक is spherical in size with a small suddenly tapering apex, or मोदक may mean a लाडु or a ball of sugar. राजा द्विजातीनाम् । "The Moon the Lord or King of the twice-born." Cf. अमरः—द्विजराजः शशधरो नक्षत्रेशः क्षपाकरः । We get a variant, राजा ओषधीनाम्, which also would mean "The Moon, the Lord or King of the vegetable kingdom." But in the mouth of the Vidushaka who is a Brahmin proud of his own caste, the words राजा द्विजातीनाम् have a peculiar appropriateness and so this reading is to be preferred to the other.

III. 6. 4. औदरिक "A glutton, a gourmand, an epicure, a lover of delicate fare".

III. 7. रविमाविशते सतां क्रियायै । This refers to the अमावास्या day, when, it is believed, the Moon enters into the Sun. Cf. ऐतरेय ब्राह्मणः—चन्द्रमा वा अमावास्यायाम् आदित्यमनुप्रविशति ॥ On the अमावास्या day, certain Vedic rites and sacrifices are performed by pious, religiously-minded people. So it is said here, that the Moon promotes the religious acts of pious people by his entering into the Sun on the अमावास्या day. सुधया तर्पयते सुरान् पितॄंश्च । It is a common-place of Indian mythology, that the Gods and the spirits of departed ancestors (पितरः "The Fathers") derive their sustenance from the Moon, who is supposed to be a repository of ambrosia (सुधा or अमृत). निशि मूर्छताम् "Prevailing or waxing strong at night", हरचूडानिहितात्मने । It is well-known that the crescent Moon forms the crest-ornament of Shiva.

III. 7. 2. ते पितामहेन–"By your grandfather." See I. 3. 28. and note *ad loc.* Cf. also IV. 19, and V 21. ब्राह्मणसंक्रामिताक्षरेण "Who has conveyed his message to you

(अक्षर "Letters, syllables") through a Brahmin (i.e. myself). The moon is राजा द्विजातीनाम् (III. 6. 2.) so it is in the fitness of things that he should convey his message to the King through the विदूषक, who is a Brahmin (i. e. a द्विजाति *par excellence.*). Dissolve : ब्राह्मणे संक्रामितानि अक्षराणि येन ।

III. 7. 7. Mark the skill of the poet in making the maid-servants retire from a scene where they are no longer required. दीपिकापौनरुक्त्य–" Superfluousness of lights or lamps" i. e. "The superfluous lamps."

III. 7-14. ननु दृश्यत एवं सा। "Why, it is only too apparent or manifest", "That of course is perceptible to the eye." सा refers to अवस्था–the condition of the King's health. The Vidushaka means to say, that the King does already appear so pulled down that no comments are required from him to give an idea of his state of health.

III. 7. 17. एवम् एतत् "That is true." मनसोऽभितापः "Anguish, mental agony or suffering," as contrasted with the physical suffering referred to by the Vidushaka above in ननु दृश्यत एव सा।

III. 8, विषमशिलासंकटस्खलितवेगः। विषमशिलाः एव संकटं, तेन स्खलितः वेगः यस्य। संकट (n) "An obstacle, obstruction, impediment," Or विषमशिलाभिः संकटः, अत एव स्खलितवेगः। Here संकट would be an adjective meaning "Crowded with, hemmed in, full of." विघ्नितसमागमसुखः "Thwarted in the enjoyment of the pleasure of her union or company."

III. 8. I. परिहीयमान "Drooping, wasting, languishing." The Vidushaka means that since the King appears to him just then lively and cheerful (अधिकं शोभसे) in spite of his physical and mental sufferings, the fulfilment of his desires cannot be far off. This has reference to a belief that approaching good luck produces, mysteriously enough, a sudden cheerfulness in a person, although he is for the time being plunged in great sorrow.

III. 8. 4. निमित्तं सूचयित्वा Cf. II. 8. 9. above.

III. 9. आशाजननैः वचोभिः "With hope-inspiring words", "With hopeful speech." This refers to III. 7. 15. and 8. 3. above. गुरुव्यथम् "Whose suffering is intense." आश्वासयति "Comforts, fills with hope, consoles, reassures." Cf. II. 9. above. Ranganatha thinks that the word दक्षिणः also means here " Clever. He remarks दक्षिणश्चतुरो हि दुःखितमाश्वासयति ।

III. 9. 3. प्रत्याशा means the same as आशा "Hope." अभिसारिकावेषा ; अभिसारिकाया वेषः इव वेषः यस्याः । अभिसारिका is a woman who goes to meet her lover of her own accord being impelled by her passion. Cf. मदेन मदनेनापि प्रेरिता शिथिलत्रपा । यान्तुकाभिसरेत् कान्तं सा भवेदभिसारिका ॥ Quoted by Katayavema.

III. 9. 8. नीलांशुकपरिग्रहः । नीलांशुकस्य परिग्रहः (स्वीकारः) यस्मिन् । "Consisting of a blue robe or silken garment."

III. 9. 11-12. अपि नाम अहं पुरूरवाः भवेयम् इति । "I wish, I were Pururavas", "Would that I were Pururavas".

III. 9. 16. सुभगस्य " Of that blessed one". i. e. of Pururavas.

III. 9. 17. परिवर्तितम् इव—रूपान्तरेण परिणतमिव (Katayavema) "Transformed as it were."

III. 9. 21. हृदयचोरः "The robber of my heart."

III. 9. 25. क्रीडिष्यामि तावत् "I shall trifle with her for a while." मनोरथलब्धप्रियासमागमसुखम् अनुभवन् । This expression is intended to bear two meanings. (i) "Enjoying the pleasure of the company (or union) of his beloved (some sweet-heart of his), whom he has obtained according to his wishes." मनोरथानुरूप लब्धा या प्रिया तस्याः समागमस्य सुखम्। (ii) Enjoying the pleasure of the company of his dear one (i.e. Urvashi), whom he has conjured up in his mind or by his imagination." मनोरथे, मनोरथेन वा (न तु वस्तुतः) लब्धा या प्रिया etc. Or मनोरथेन लब्धं यत् प्रियासमागमसुखम्। The first meaning provokes a passing shadow of jealousy in Urvashi's mind as already calculated by चित्रलेखा.

III. 9. 29. मुग्धे का पुनः etc. "But, child (or simpleton), why do you entertain such a strange thought about the company of the beloved' (which I have spoken of just now)?" अन्या–" Strange unworthy, unreasonable." She means to say "Why do you understand the word प्रिया to mean any other person than yourself ?"

III. 9. 31 अदक्षिणम् " Illiberal, unkind, ungenerous, lacking breadth or generosity of out-look."

III, 9. 40. अनिर्भिन्नार्थेन "Whose meaning is not clear," "Of doubtful meaning." आकम्पितम् "Is alarmed," "Is perplexed." Urvashi's mind is full of apprehension, because from the King's words it is not clear whether she herself or some other girl is the object of his longing. स्वैरालापम् "His unrestrained, unreserved utterances."

III. 9. 46. अनुपक्रम्यः- Incurable. आतकः "Malady, disease, एवमादिभिः i. e. उपायैः।

III. 10, सर्वांगीणम्। सर्वमंगं व्याप्नोतीति। "Pervading, or applied to, the whole of the body." मणियष्टयः। "Strings or necklaces of gems." अपोहितुम् to allay, to set at rest, to dispel. लघयेत्–(denominative from लघु " Light, ") " Might lesson or mitigate," तदाश्रयिणी कथा "Some talk bearing upon her."

III. 10. 1. इदानीम् Now hat all your doubts are dispelled." इतः = अस्मिन् राजनि ।

III. 10. 6. मिष्टहरिणीमांसभोजनम् । "A dinner of dainty or delicious venison (हरिणीमांस)." Katayavema and also Ranganatha read " शिखरिणीं रसालं च etc." Ranganatha explains शिखरिणी as follows : एलालवंगकर्पूरादिसुरभिद्रव्यमिश्रितं दुग्धेन सह गालितं सितासंगतं दधि शिखरिणीति उच्यते । दध्यतिरिक्तपूर्वोक्तद्रव्यमिश्रितः पक्वकदलीफलान्तःसारोऽपि तत्पदवाच्यः ॥ शिखरिणी is thus a very high-class preparation corresponding to our श्रीखंड or शिखरण, in Maharastra. रसाल = रसालफल i. e. "Mango-fruit". Of the eight Mss. collected by Mr. Pandit, two alone contain the former reading, while all the six remaining ones contain the latter. The latter reading appears evidently to have owed its origin to some late puritanic Brahmins whose religious susceptibilities were rudely shocked to find a member of their own caste showing such a zest for meat. But if we refer to शाकुन्तल Act II. we find the विदूषक in that play also taking meat. Cf. अनियतवेलं शूलमांसभूयिष्ठ आहारो भुज्यते । We therefore think that ' मिष्टहरिणीमांसभोजनम् ' was the original reading and so have adopted it in the text following Mr. Pandit. प्रार्थयमान. "Yearning for it." संकीर्तयन्—"Talking about it." आश्वसिमि । "I comfort myself," "I take cheer."

III. 10. 8. इदम् = मिष्टहरिणीमांसभोजनम् । संपद्यते "Is easily obtained."

III. 10. 11. एवम्– refers to what the King is going to say below in Stanza 11. "I think that", "I say."

III. 10. 12. असंतुष्टे । "Oh discontented one." Urvashi is not satisfied about the sincerity of the King's love for her even after his passionate declarations in stanza 10.

She wants further proof of his love, before she casts aside the veil and shows herself to the King. चित्रलेखा therefore reproaches. her by addressing her as the discontented one.

III. 10. 13 कथम् इव "What is it that you think."

III. 11. निपीडित: "Pressed," "Struck against." कृती— "Blessed, fortunate, lucky" भुवो भर:—"A burden to the earth" i. e. existing to no purpose, in vain.

III. 11. 3. गताया: । As Katayavema points out the Genitive case is used here with the sense of "Disrespect": षष्ठी चानादरे । Panini II. 3. 38. उदासीन इव " Appears to be indifferent to me ; does not notice or mark me ; does not deign to regard me."

III. 11, 6. अतित्वरिते "Oh you impatient or hasty one," अनुत्क्षिप्त " Not cast aside," तिरस्करिणी—" Magic veil of invisibility."

III. 11. 9. वाचंयम: " One who has taken the vow of silence." The अनुस्वार in this word is prescribed by Panini VI. 3. 69 वाचयंमपुरंदरौ च ।

III. 11, 11. संवृताकारम् adv. "On your guard, collected." आकार is the outward expression of the face serving as an index to the inward thoughts and feelings.

III. 11. 15. अलम् आवेगेन "No cause for anxiety", "do not be worried at all." उपवासनियमवेषा "Wearing a dress suited to the observance of a fast."

औपहारिकम्—उपहाराणां समूह: औपहारिकम् । "Materials of worship." पूजासामग्री—Ranganatha.

III. 11. 23. ननु "Why"—It is an interrogative particle meaning किं न "Is it not that etc."

III. 11. 27. स्वस्तिवाचनम् , or स्वस्त्ययनम् as Mr. Pandit has it, means "A present of sweetmeats given to a Brahmin in order to receive his good wishes and blessing." Vide Note on II. 13. 7. above शुभदर्शना—"Cheerful. pleased in her appearance."

III. 11. 30. उभयमपि घटते "Both (causes) are quite possible." मां प्रति भाति "Appears probable to me."

III. 12. मंगलमात्रभूषणा "Having only the auspicious marks (such as the कुंकुमतिलक, the मंगलसूत्र etc.) as her ornaments." लांछित "Chequered. marked with". वपुषैव प्रसन्ना दृश्यते—"Appears well-pleased towards me, even by her very person." i. e. her bodily appearance itself bears testimony to her change of heart. व्रतापदेशोज्झितगर्वप्रवृत्तिना (qualifying वपुषा) "Which has given up its haughty deportment under the pretext of a vow." A person who is observing a vow has to give up all the passions that trouble the human mind, such as anger, greed. pride, jealousy etc.

III. 12. 8. स्थाने "Deservedly," "It is but proper or in the fitness of things that etc." देवीशब्देन उपचर्यते "Is honoured or greeted by the title देवी." "Is addressed as देवी." The word देवी means both "A queen" and "A Goddess." The King uses it in the first sense; Urvashi, however, understands it in the second sense. न परिहीयते "Does not lag behind," "Is not at all inferior to," "Does not fall short of." ओजस्वितया "In regard to splendour."

III. 12. 9. असूयापराङ्मुखम् adv. "Without the least shadow of jealousy," "In a manner averse to jealousy or free from jealousy." साधु मन्त्रितम् "You have spoken well." "That is well said."

III. 12. 12. पुरस्कृत्य "With reference to," "In regard

to" with the help of मुहूर्तम् उपरोध: "A moment's obstruction or inconvenience."

III. 12. 17. स्वस्तिवाचनवान् "Accompanied by presents of sweetmeats" (given to a Brahmin to receive his blessings.)

III. 12. 20. प्रियानुप्रसादनम्। "Propitiation or conciliation of the beloved one (husband)."

III. 13. अकारणम् "Needlessly." मृणालकोमलं गात्रम् "Your person delicate or tender like a lotus-stem." ग्लपयसि "You waste (your body)." ग्लपय् is the causal form from the root ग्लै to be wasted, to languish, to wither. The form ग्लापय् is also met with. प्रसादम् etc. Construe: य उत्सुक: (सन्) तव प्रसादम् आकांक्षति स दासजनस्त्वया किं प्रसाद्यते। Cf. शाकुंतल

III. लभेत वा प्रार्थयिता न वा श्रियम्।
श्रिया दुराप: कथमीप्सितो भवेत्॥

and कुमार V. न रत्नमन्विष्यति मृग्यते हि तत्॥

III. 13. 2. इमस्सि = एतस्याम् Although the form इमस्सि is not sanctioned by Prakrit Grammarians for the feminine gender (the correct form according to them being इमीए or इमाए), still Kalidasa uses it here and elsewhere also (in मालविकाग्निमित्र), as Mr. Pandit points out. बहुमान: "Regard, respect, esteem." This remark of Urvashi shows that her mind is apprehensive that she may fail to win the King's love permanently. For although she is sure, the King has fallen desperately in love with her just now, who knows, his respect and love for the Queen may not assert themselves in the long run? Cf. III. 14. 11, below.

III. 13. 5. नागरिका: = दक्षिणा: कामिन:। "Gallants." She means to say that cunning lovers show exaggerated attention to their first mistresses or wives, while courting others. वक्षिणाः "Solicitous to please, generous, indulgent." अन्यसंक्रान्तप्रेमाणः-अन्यासु संक्रान्तं प्रेम येषाम् ।

III. 13. 8. एतावत् "So much, this much" *i. e.* "Thus." It thus refers to the quality rather than the quantity of the King's words in stanza 13 above. मन्त्रित is the causal past pass. part. meaning "Has been made to say."

III. 13. 10. सुभाषितम् "Auspicious or good words." प्रति + आचर् "To act against, to oppose." सुभाषितम् refers to the words of the Queen in III. 13. 8, where she says that her vow has already begun to bear its fruit.

III. 13. 13. मणिहर्म्यगतान् = मणिहर्म्यपृष्ठगतान् "Touching or kissing the terrace of मणिहर्म्य."

III. 13. 14. गन्ध "Scent" or "Sandal ointment."

III. 13. 18, औपहारिकमोदकान् "Sweet balls or sweets forming part of the materials of worship."

III. 13. 22. बहुफलः "Attended with immense success." उपवासः "Fast." The fast, in fact, forms only a subordinate part of the vow the Queen is observing.

III. 13. 31. साक्षीकृत्य "In the presence of." अनुप्रसादयामि "I seek to propitiate, please or win the favour of." प्रार्थयते "Wooes." प्रीतिबन्धेन "With affection or friendship." वर्तितव्यम् = अवश्यं वर्तिष्ये । "The potential partic. shows *futurity* with *certainty.*" Pandit.

III. 13. 35. किंपरम् = किंतात्पर्यम्. "Of what import." Urvashi means to say that she does not know whether the Queen is sincere and means what she says or is only reproachful and sarcastic. विश्वासविशद "At ease with confidence." विशद "Clear, calm, untroubled." *i. e.* delighted, relieved of its tension.

III. 13. 39. महानुभावया "Exalted, noble." पतिव्रतया "Dutiful, single-minded in her devotion to her husband."

III. 13. 43. छिन्नहस्तः "Foiled in his efforts to catch," "Baffled in his attempts to catch." हस्त = हस्तकौशल "Skill of hand" in catching the fish. तादृशः "To that extent, in that manner, so much." The Vidushaka means to say that the King cannot be so dear to the Queen, since she is giving him away to other ladies of her own accord.

III. 13. 48. आत्मनः सुखावसानेन "At the cost or sacrifice of my happiness (or pleasure)." निर्वृतशरीरम् "At ease or happy in his body," "Physically happy."

III. 14. कर्तुमेव वा दासम् । "Or to make me your slave." Katayavema has हर्तुमेव for कर्तुमेव । In this case the sense would be "Or to take me back, your slave."

III. 14. 3. यथानिर्दिष्टम् "As prescribed or laid down" in works dealing with vows and observances. This speech as well as that appearing below, III. 14. 7, shows the self-respect and loftiness of manner possessed by the Queen.

III. 14. 8. अलंघितपूर्वः "Never violated before." नियमः "A rule or restriction in connection with a vow."

III. 14. 11. निवर्तय "To reclaim, to turn away, to withdraw."

III. 14. 13. किं पुनः त्वया निराशया निवर्त्यते । Supply the object हृदयं from the preceding speech. "But say, why do you withdraw your heart in despair?

III. 14. 18. विश्रब्धम् "Safely, confidently, securely." स्वैरम् "Of her own accord."

III. 14. 20. अपि नाम "May it be that; shall I hope that; would that; how I wish that etc."

III. 14. 21. कृतार्था भवेत् "May be happy or blessed, or may accomplish her object."

III. 15. कान्तम् "Charming, agreeable" We have preferred this reading of Ranganatha to Mr. Pandit's कान्ता (beloved), which is rather inconveniently separated from the word उर्वशी with which it is syntactically connected as its adjective. साध्वसवसात् मन्दायमाना "Moving slowly or slackening her pace, through fear." पदात् पदम्—"Step after step, step by step." बलादानीयेत "Would be dragged towards me (by her friend)," "Would be brought or led up to me by force."

III. 15. 2. तावत् "At once, forthwith."

III. 15. 3. संज्ञापयति–"Makes a sign or beckons to," in order to acquaint him with the fact.

III. 15. 4. नारायणोरुसंभवा वरोरू: "The fair off-spring of the thigh of Narayana."

III. 15. 7. किमत्र ज्ञेयम् । "What is there to be known?" i. e. it is as plain or evident as anything can be. Mr. Pandit has किमत्राज्ञेयम् "What is there that cannot be known?" The sense of both the expressions is ultimately the same.

III. 16. अनङ्गक्लिष्टम् "Tormented, afflicted by love." The कुमुद is a species of the lotus that blooms in moonlight only—such is the convention of poets. We read चन्द्रस्यैवांशुभि: instead of चंद्रस्येवांशुभि: as Mr. Pandit does. With our reading the contrast between तपनकिरणै: and चंद्रस्य अंशुभि: becomes emphasized as it ought to be

III. 16. 3. एकासने–"On the same seat as he himself occupies." So that his body comes into contact with that of Urvashi. Cf. III. 16. 9, below (शरीरसंपर्क गतास्मि ।)

III. 16. 5. एतत् does not refer to सुखम्, but is to be connected with उपपन्नम् in the sense of "Just now."

उपपन्नम् "Attained, obtained." The King means to

say "I was not happy before I met उर्वशी but now that उर्वशी has come to me, I may say that I am really happy."

III. 16. 9. अस्य प्रणयवतीव "Like his beloved or loving wife." पुरोभागिनीम् "Officious, obtrusive, meddlesome, forward." पुरोभागिन् means "One who takes the first share or more than his proper share," hence "One who meddles in another's affairs, obtrusive, presmptuous. meddlesome."

III. 16. 11. कथम् इहव युवयोः अस्तमितः सूर्यः । Mr. Pandit translates "What, have you been here since evening?" According to him this remark of the विदूषक is called forth by Urvashi's words: हला देव्या दत्तो महाराजः । The Vidushaka thinks that Urvashi and Chitralekha must have heard the words of the Queen in III. 13. 26. and must have been there all the evening though remaining invisible all along. But we think that this is not at all a satisfactory explanation. From III. 16. 3 and 16, 7, we see that Urvashi and Pururavas were sitting quite close to each other. And we may presume even that Pururavas began to toy with Urvashi by way of fondling and caressing her and that she too returned in her own way his fondlings and caressings, cf. III. 17 below. Now this appears rather shocking to the Vidushaka and he says in his usual light-hearted vein; "I wonder, how the Sun has set to you even here i. e. even in the presence of myself and Chitralekha." "How the Sun has set to you" means "How do you openly carry on these fondlings and caressings, which ought to be done in *strict privacy, after the Sun has set*?" In the present case of course the Sun has already set. Vidushaka's point, however, is that they must not do these things openly.

III. 17. व्यापार व्रजमि । (Ranganatha explains व्यापार as

आलिंगनादि–आरम्भ) "Take loving liberties with my person." कस्यानुमते "By whose consent."

III. 17. 2. विज्ञाप्यम् "Request," "Prayer."

III. 17. 6. वसन्तानन्तरे "Following the vernal season or spring." उपचरितव्यः=सेवितव्यः, उपस्थातव्यः। उप+चर् "To wait upon, to attend upon, to worship."

III. 17. 12. अनिमिषैः नयनैः मीनाः विडम्ब्यन्ते। "Fishes are mocked with winkless eyes." It is believed that the denizens of heaven never close their eyes, even for a moment in winking.

III. 18. अनिर्देश्यसुखः। "The happiness in which is indescribable." अनिर्देश्यं = वक्तुमशक्यम्।

III. 18. 2. अकातरा भूत्वा "Banishing all fear or apprehension from your mind."

III. 18. 10. ऋद्धिः "Good fortune."

III 19. सामन्तमौलि etc. Dissolve : सामन्तानां मौलिषु ये मणयः तैः रंजितं शासनम् (आज्ञापत्रम्) एव अंकः (वैशिष्ट्यापादकं चिह्नं) यस्य। "Having the distinguishing mark viz. that the royal edicts (mandates or commands) are tinged with the gems in the coronets of the feudatory princes." i. e. are humbly borne on their heads by feudatory princes, and are implicitly obeyed. सामन्त—"A borderchief, a tributary prince," who obeys the commands of the universal soveriegn. एकातपत्रम् अवनेः प्रभुत्वम्। (Cf. एकातपत्रं जगतः प्रभुत्वम्। Raghu. II. 47.) "Sovereignty of the whole world, characterized by one single umbrella." A universal monarch alone possesses the privilege of using the आतपत्र or छत्र. कान्तम् आज्ञाकरत्वम् "Charming servitude."

III. 19. 2. नास्ति मे विभवः etc. Urvashi means to say that she ought, really speaking, to return the compliment of the King by saying something more beautiful in admiration of the King. But she cannot excel the King in this matter-so exquisitely fine is the sentiment expressed by the King.

III. 19. 3. विरुद्धसंवर्धन: "Giving rise to contraries or paradoxes."

III. 20. ते एव "Those very i. e. those that used to pain or torment me." मनोऽनुकूला: "Pleasant or agreeable to the mind." This reading appears to us better than ममानुकूला: adopted by Mr. Pandit, because it stands in clear contrast to सुखयंति गात्रम् in line l. "The rays of the Moon delight the *body*: the shafts of cupid please the *mind*." संरंभरूक्षम् रोषदारुणम्। "Harsh (as if) through anger or malice." अनुनीतम् इव-कृतसान्त्वनमिव "Is pacified or appeased as it were."

III. 20.2. चिरकारिका-"Delaying, tarrying."

III. 21. उपनतम्=अधिगतम्-"Obtained." Literally "Which comes to one's share." रसवत्तरम् "More agreeable." निर्वाणम् "Complete or supreme happiness, satisfaction, gratification." तप्त "Scorched by the heat of the Sun." Cf. मृच्छकटिक I. सुखं हि दुःखान्यनुभूय शोभते। घनांधकारेष्विव दीपदर्शनम्।

III. 21.3. वासगृहम् "Inner apartment," "Bedchamber."

III. 21.7. अभ्यर्थना-"Earnest wish," "Eager desire." शतगुणिता इव "As if it were drawn out in length or extended a hundredfold, "As long as a hundred nights." Katayavema reads शतगुणितामिव मे गता त्रियामा। and explains: एकरात्रिः शतरात्रितुल्यकालतां गता। "Attained as it were to hundred-fold-ness."

सुभ्रु Vocative sing. According to पाणिनि, the form ought to be सुभ्रूः. But Sanskrit poets often use the form सुभ्रु. Cf. भट्टिकाव्य VI. 11. कुमारसंभव V.43. मालतीमाधव III. 8; Mallinatha sets forth the pros and cons of the case in his comment on कुमारसंभव V.43.

ACT IV.

[The fourth Act opens with an Introductory Scene technically called प्रवेशक) which serves the purpose of narrating the events that have transpired since the union of Pururavas with Urvashi as described towards the conclusion of the third Act, and of introducing the reader to the main scene of the Act.

Introductory Scene:—(LOCALITY NOT INDICATED.)

The introductory scene contains a dialogue between two Apsarases, सहजन्या and चित्रलेखा—friends of Urvashi. From their conversation we learn that Urvashi and Pururavas had gone to the Gandhamadana Grove for their honey-moon. But before they had passed many days there, a strange mishap took place resulting in their separation. Pururavas once came across a beautiful Vidyadhara damsel sporting on the sands of the Mandakini, and was so fascinated by her charms, that he at once began to devour her beauty with his eyes. When Urvashi saw this, she was so enraged that she spurned all his apologies and prostrations, and, in the frenzy of her jealous rage, rushed into the charmed and forbidden Grove of Kumara and was immediately transformed into a creeper. Pururavas has gone mad with grief at her disappearance and has been searching for his lost beloved day and night, in every nook and corner of the Grove. The Apsarases hope and pray that the King be restored to his beloved before long.

The main scene of Act IV is for the most part, a soliloquy of Pururavas gone mad over the loss of Urvashi.

In the words of Prof. Ryder it is a long lyrical monologue addressed to the various creatures and objects of the forest and inspired by despairing passion. Kalidasa was perhaps the first to introduce such a lyrical melodrama in the ancient Indian Theatre. It is a song play within the drama. Later dramatists like भवभूत (मालतीमाधव, Act 9), राजशेखर (बालरामायण, Act 5), जयदेव (प्रसन्नराघव, Act 6), हनुमत् (महानाटक, Act 4), and भास्करभट्ट (उन्मत्तराघव) have tried to imitate it with some degree of success. Its pre-eminently musical character has been perhaps respnosible for the insertion of Apabhramsha stanzas and the stage-directions for their recitation. (Vide Introduction, p. XII-XIII.).

The main scene of Act IV contains very little of dramatic action. The locality appears to be somewhere in the neighbourhood of the Gandhamadana Grove. It is a rainy day in summer. The King is presented in a frenzied and woe-begone state—almost on the verge of madness and raving—addressing the various objects he comes across—animate, sensible or insensible—birds and beasts, trees and rivers, rocks and mountains, clouds and lightnings—and beseeches them to assist him in his search of Urvashi. He indulges in all sorts of speculations and fancies about the sights and sounds he comes across, but is cruelly disappointed by them one and all. At last he lights upon a very bright precious stone which is announced by an invisible voice to be the famous संगमनीय gem, which, when worn on the body, is capable of restoring a person to his lost beloved. The King holds it in his hand and embraces a creeper which is immediately changed into Urvashi. The King is overjoyed by the incident. Urvashi greets him with happiness and victory, and relates to him how she had been transformed into a creeper, and how as a creeper she had witnessed his sad plight all along. Pururavas shows her the संगमनीय gem which she wears on her head. Urvashi reminds Pururavas of their long absence from their capital and requests him to return. Pururavas agrees and both of them depart for प्रतिष्ठान in an aerial car improvised by Urvashi from out of a cloud at his request.

It should be noted by the reader that although Pururavas is represented as having gone mad, there is a certain method in his madness—a certain coherency and reasonableness about his utterances. It is much more of a poetic madness than a real one in the strict sense of the term. The King behaves like a madman only in so far as he seeks information in all seriousness about his beloved from sources which are least of all ever likely to give any such information. In all other respects he appears to be quite normal in respect of the powers and functionings of his mind and brain. A similar type of madness is to be found also in the case of the Yaksha in the Meghaduta.]

IV. o. 1. विमनस्का "Sad, uneasy at heart".

IV. o. 5. छाया "Complexion, appearance". म्लायमान is irregular, since the root म्लै is Parasmaipadi and not Atmanepadi. We should better have म्लायत्. निर्वेद "Distress, anxiety". समदुःखा भवितुमिच्छामि "I wish to participate in your sorrow".

IV. o. 10. अप्सरोवारपर्यायेण "In the course of the rotation or coming round, of the turn for the Apsarases".

वार: "The time or turn of doing anything". पर्याय: "Rotation, coming round". सूर्यस्य पादमूलोपस्थानम् = सूर्यस्य उपस्थानम्। "Reverent service of or attendance upon the feet of the Sun". We are told in the भागवत and कौर्म Puranas, that the ऋषिs, गन्धर्वs, यक्षs and Apsarases have to attend upon the Sun by rotation. The reason why चित्रलेखा feels sore anxiety and yearning for Urvashi is that she misses her very much while attending upon the Sun, alone, and further that on account of her continuous engagement for two months in the sphere of the Sun, she is prevented from paying occasional visits to Urvashi.

IV. o. 15. इमानि दिवसानि "During these days". This is accusative of time, according Panini II. 3. 4, कालाध्वनोरत्यन्तसंयोगे। प्रणिधानस्थितया "While I stood in meditation, put myself in contemplation". अत्याहितम् "A great danger, misfortune, calamity". Strictly speaking the word ought to be अत्यहितम्. The second अ seems to be lengthened on the analogy of the word विश्वामित्र (which is really equal to विश्वमित्र). उपलब्धम् "I preceived, or learnt".

IV. o. 21. किल "It would seem or appear that etc." रतिसहाय "Companion in love-sport (रति)". गन्धमादनवनम्–गन्धमादन (m.) is the name of a suburban grove of ओषधिप्रस्थ, the capital of हिमालय. Cf. कुमारसंभव VI. 46. यस्य (ओषधिप्रस्थस्य) चोपवनं बाह्यं सुगन्धिर्गन्धमादनः।

IV. o. 24. स नाम संभोग: "That indeed is an ideal enjoyment".

IV. o. 28. मन्दाकिनी "The celestial Ganges". पुलिनम् "Sandy bank". निध्याता "Was gazed at", "Was looked at intently".

IV. o. 31. दूरारूढः खलु प्रणयः असहनः । Cf. रत्नावली III. 15 प्रकृष्टस्य प्रेम्णः स्खलितमविषह्यं हि भवति ।

IV. o. 36. गुरुशापसंमूढहृदया ।"With her heart bewildered by the curse of her preceptor sage भरत." Urvashi being a nymph ought to have known by her supernatural power that the grove of कुमार that she was about to enter was forbidden to women. But on account of the curse of भरत her memory was so stupefied, that she could not know the prohibition in regard to the grove of कुमार. Cf. IV. 40. 14–25. below काननोपान्त...etc. Katayavema reads कारणान्तरनिवर्तिना, while seven of Mr. Pandit's eight Mss. read कारणान्तरपरिवर्तिना, The meaning is: "Which would cease to be (निवर्तिना) or would undergo restoration (परिवर्तिना), through some unknown cause". But if we adopt this reading, the remark of सहजन्या (अवश्यं किमपि...समागमकारणं भविष्यति ।) in IV. o. 52. becomes redundant.

IV. o. 40. अलंघनीयम् "Beyond the reach of." Cf. मालतीमाधव I. 23. सर्वंकषा भगवती भवितव्यतैव । एकपदे "All of a sudden." अनर्थः "Dire calamity, misfortune".

IV. o. 45. अहोरात्रान् । अहश्च रात्रिश्च अहोरात्रः । Acc. of Panini V. 4. 87. अहःसर्वैकदेशसंख्यातपुण्याच्च रात्रेः । निर्वृतानामपि उत्कण्ठाकारिणा मेघोदयेन । Cf. मेघदूत I. 3 मेघालोके भवति सुखिनोऽप्यन्यथावृत्ति चेतः । Also IV. 3 below.

IV. o. 52. आकृतिविशेषाः "Noble, excellent forms *i. e.* persons". आकृतीनां विशेषाः आकृतिविशेषाः । अनुग्रहनिमित्तं समागमकारणम् । The word अनुग्रहनिमित्तम् could be taken either as a तत्पुरुष or as a बहुव्रीहि compound. In the former case the sense would be: "Some cause of reunion, which would bring about the termination of the curse." In the latter case the meaning would be: "Some cause of reunion brought about by the termination of the curse" "अनुग्रह (lit. favour, kindness) is the same as उच्छाप or प्रतिशाप i. e. "The termination of a curse." The curse in this case is the विधि or समय (i. e. prohibitive condition) referred to in IV. 40. 23 below. काटयवेम reads अनुग्रहीतृकम् । उदयोन्मुख "About to rise."

IV. o. 58. आ: इति कोपे निपात: । आ: is an exclamation of anger. हन्त "Alas."

IV. 1. संनद्ध: (i) "Fully equipped" for showering down, ready to shower, (ii) fully armed or accoutred" for battle. दूराकृष्टम् (i) extending far and wide" (ii) "stretched to its utmost." न नाम "Not indeed as I imagined". पटु: "Violent, quickly descending, pelting." कनकनिकषस्निग्धा। कनकस्य निकष: कषणरेखा तद्वत् स्निग्धा । "Glistening like a Streak of gold on a touch-stone." Cf. सौदामन्या कनकनिकषस्निग्धया दर्शयोर्वीम् । मेघदूत I. 39.

IV. 1. 1. रम्भोरू: "Whose thighs are (full, round and fair) like (the inner part of) the plantain tree."

IV. 2. पिहिता = अपिहिता "Concealed, hidden." स्वर्गाय = स्वर्गं गन्तुम् । The dative acc. to Panini II .14. क्रियार्थोपपदस्य च स्थानिन: ॥ भावार्द्रम् "Dripping with affection, saturated with love." कोऽयं विधि: "What a (queer) fate is this" "What an act of fate is this!"

IV. 2. 1. परावृत्तभागधेयानाम् । परावृत्तं भागधेयं येषां or येभ्य: ते परावृत्तभागधेया: । "From whom fortune has turned its back" अनुबन्धि "Closely following upon."

IV. 3. For the construction with two चs, see Apte's Guide Sec. 273. अहोभि: भवितव्यम् "The days are sure to be" निरातपत्वरम्यै: "Pleasant on account of the passing away (diminution or lessening) of heat." काटयवेम reads निरातपर्द्धिरम्यैः । निर्गता आतपस्य ऋद्धिः सामग्री येषां तानि निरातपर्द्धीनि । तानि च तानि रम्याणिच, निरातपर्द्धिरम्याणि । तैः । "Pleasant on account of the intensity of heat having passed away," We have, however, rejected this reading because it is cumbrous as compared with निरातपत्वरम्यैः ।

IV. 3. 1. मनसः परितापवृद्धिः "The growing distress of my mind." मुनयोऽपि व्याहरन्ति etc. Cf. महाभारत V. 132. 16. कालो वा कारणं राज्ञो राजा वा कालकारणम् । इति ते संशयो मा भूद् राजा कालस्य कारणम् ॥ प्रत्यादिश् "To order back, to countermand or counter-order." अथवा etc.....supply संपद्यते after संप्रति. "My royal paraphernalia consist of or are constituted by the signs (tokens) or accompaniments of the rainy season." प्रावृषि भवानि प्रावृषेण्यानि तैः ।

IV. 4. श्रीवितानम् "A beautiful, splendid canopy." निचुलः "A kind of reed." घर्मच्छेदात्–घर्मस्य उष्णकालस्य नाशात्, गमनात्। "On account of the passing away of summer." पटु "Shrill sharp-sounding." वंदिन् m. "A bard, panegyrist, minstrel." The peacocks are well-known as being overjoyed at the advent of the rainy season, which they welcome with loud shrieking and gay dancing. धारासारोपनयनपराः—This applies to the clouds as also to the merchants (नैगमाः). (i) धारासारस्य उपनयने तत्पराः । "Bringing down showers (आसार) of rain (धारा)." (ii) धारारूपं सारं (धनम्) तस्य उपनयनं तत्पराः । "Presenting streams of wealth" (by way of the payment of taxes). We read चाम्बुवाहाः for सानुमन्तः This latter reading does not harmonize with धारासार, which means "Showers of rain." Moreover in adopting it we fail to get the conjunctive particle च, which is badly wanted to make the sense complete.

IV. 4. 1. परिच्छद "Paraphernalia, external appendages of royalty, royal insignia." व्यवसितस्य मे "As I make up my mind to search her out." सन्दीपनम् "Aggravation, intensification."

IV. 5. कन्दली is what is called कर्दळ in Marathi. The yellow variety of this plant has red lines upon the petals of its flowers. राजि "A streak or line." सलिलगर्भैः "Surcharged with water. अन्तर्बाष्प "Suffused with tears." मां स्मरयति "Makes me remember painfully; reminds me painfully of." Cf. for a similar idea रघुवंश XIII. 29.

IV. 5. 1. सूचय् "To trace out, to ascertain."

IV. 6. स्पृशेत् "If she were to touch." वनस्थली "Forest-ground," "Forest-site." पश्चान्नता "Sunk or depressed towards the heels." गुरुनितम्बतया "On account of the heaviness or stoutness of her hips." Cf. शाकुन्तल III. 7. अभ्युन्नता पुरस्ताद् अवगाढा जघनगौरवात् पश्चात्। etc. चारुपदपंक्तिः "Line of beautiful foot-prints." अलक्तकांका "Tinged with red lac (अलक्तक)." He means to say that if Urvashi were to touch the ground with her feet, it would be possible to have some trace of her. But she being a nymph—a celestial being, capable of moving unsupported in the air—there is very little possibility of her walking so close to the ground as to leave behind her foot-prints.

IV. 6. 1 उपलक्षणम् "Mark, sign, vestige."

IV. 7. Construe : इदं (यद् दृश्यते तद्) असंशयं निम्ननाभेः (तस्या उर्वश्याः) निपतद्भिः (अत एव) हृतोष्ठरागैः नयनोदबिन्दुभिः अंकितं, रुषा भिन्नगतेः च्युतं शुकोदरश्यामं स्तनांशुकं (भवति)। ओष्ठराग "Lip-rouge." निम्ननाभि "Having a deep navel." Depth of the navel is regarded by Sanskrit poets as a sign of beauty in women. रुषा भिन्नगतेः "Moving with faltering

steps through rage." श्याम "Dark-green" स्तनांशुकम् "Breast-garment" or "Breast-scarf."

IV. 7. 1. नवशाद्वलम् "A fresh green sward or lawn." इन्द्रगोप m. a kind of red insect. प्रवृत्ति "News." अवगमयितव्या= अवगन्तव्या. निर्जन "Lonely, desolate." शैलेयस्थली "Rocky soil." आसारोच्छ्वसित "Emitting or sending forth vapour on account of rain-showers," Cf. रघुवंश XIII. 20. आरूढ "Perched or mounted upon."

IV. 8. प्रबलपुरोवात "Violent frontal wind." नर्तित "Set a-dance." Mr. Pandit reads ताडित "Struck, beaten." शिखण्ड: "Crest." दूरोन्नमितन "Out-stretched; elongated" केकागर्भेण "Full of shrieking notes." कण्ठेन "With his neck etc." The Instrumental is according to Panini II. 3. 21. इत्थंभूतलक्षणे। (उपलक्षणे तृतीया।)

IV. 9. उत्कृष्टा उद्गत: कण्ठो यस्या: सा। "With a prominent." दीर्घापाङ्गा "Having far stretched eye-corners" i. e. "Having long and large eyes." सितापांग "Having white eye-corners." दृष्टिक्षमा—दृष्टे: दर्शनस्य क्षमा योग्या "Worthy of being seen." त्वया दृष्टा भवेत्। "May I hope that you have seen?" Mark the alliteration in this stanza.

IV. 10. मृदुपवनविभिन्न: "Dishevelled or ruffled by the gentle breeze" विनाश "Disappearance". काटयवेम reads मत्प्रियाविप्रणाशात्॥ घनरुचिरकलाप: "His thick and charming plumage." नि:सपत्न: "Without a rival, rivalless". केशहस्त: "Excellent hair". The words पाश, हस्त, पक्ष and कलाप when combined with केश convey the idea of excellence and abundance. रतिविगलितबन्धे "Become loose in the course of amorous sport". This corresponds to मृदुपवनविभिन्न:॥ कुसुमसनाथे "pecked with dowers". सति "If it were cresent or existing here"; i.e. "In the presence of, by the side of, in comparison with". किं करोति एष बर्हीं। "What would this peacock have to boast of then?" Cf. रघुवंश IX. 67.

IV. 10. 2. आतपान्त "The termination or close of the summer season". संधुक्षित "Inflamed". मद "Passion"

IV. 11. मदनदूतिम् "The messenger of Cupid". The impassioned notes of the cuckoo bring estranged lovers together as they cannot hold out any longer and therefore the cuckoo is called Cupid's messenger. Strictly speaking the word दूती ends in long ई. But Kalidasa uses it often with short इ, evidently *metri causa.* Cf. रघुवंश XVII. 53; XIX. 18, 23; कुमारसंभव IV. 16. मानावभंगनिपुणम् "Skilled or dexterous in breaking down or taming the pride of women". अमोघम् अस्त्रम् "Unfailing weapon." Cf, रघुवंश IX. 47 and कुमारसंभव III. 32.

IV. 11. 1. किमाह भवती etc. This is what is technically called आकाशभाषित "Speaking in the air to some one and answering his imagined questions".

IV. 12. आत्मगतम् "Existing in me", "Arising on my side", "So far as I am concerned". प्रभुता "Ascendancy, tyranny, dominion". भावस्खलितानि "Deviation from faithful love". काटयवेम remarks : नायिकान्तरदर्शनादीनि। न अपेक्षते "Does not wait for, does not stand in need of"

IV. 12. 1. कथाच्छेदकारिणी "Cutting short or interrupting our talk (conversation)".

IV. 13. सम्यग् आहु: "It is well said that". शीतलम् "Cool" i.e. not painful. आपन्न "Distressed, in misery". राजजम्बूद्रुम "The royal (i. e. best kind of) Jambu tree". अभिमुखपाकम् = प्रत्यासन्नपाकम् "About to ripen".

IV. 13. 1. एवंगतेऽपि "Even though it is so", "Nevertheless" इतो वयम्–"Hence away we (go)". प्रियाचरण-

निक्षेपशंसी "Indicating the tread of my beloved". दक्षिणेन "To my right" or "Towards the south, in the southern direction."

IV. 14. मानसोत्सुकचेतसाम् । Cf. "कालान्तरे मानसस्य हिमदुष्टत्वात्, हिमस्य च हंसानां रोगहेतुत्वात्, अन्यत्र गता हंसाः पुनर्वर्षासु मानसमेव गच्छन्तीति प्रसिद्धिः ।" मल्लिनाथ on मेघदूत I. 11.

IV. 15. पाथेयं बिसम् उत्सृज "Lay aside (for a while) the lotus-stalk–your provision for the journey". पाथेय from पथिन्–पथि साधु पाथेयम् "Good for, serviceable on, the way"; hence "Provisions for a journey". Vide Panini IV. 4. 108. तावत् "First, before doing anything else". प्रणयिक्रिया "Service to the suppliant or petitioner"; "Fulfilling the desire of the pretitioner".

IV. 16. नतभ्रूः "Having arching brows". मदखेलपदम् "Consisting of steps graceful through passion". गतम् "gait".

IV. 17. विभावितैकदेशेन etc. The person with whom only a part of the stolen property has been detected is liable to restore the whole of that property.

IV. 17. 1. चोरानुशासी "chastiser or punisher of thieves".

IV. 18. रथांगनामन् = चक्रवाक. रथांगं चक्रं तेन युक्तं नाम यस्य । "Whose name contains the word चक्र which is expressive of a limb or part of a chario ".

रथांगश्रोणिबिम्बया "Whose hips (श्रोणिबिंब) are round like a chariot-wheel". Cf. I. 11. रथी "An eminent warrior". भृतः "Filled with, overflowing with". Mark again the alliteration.

IV. 18. 1. कः कः इत्याह । The bird cries out कः, कः of its own sweet will and without intending its cries to have any meaning for the King. The King, however, understands कः कः to mean "Who are you? who are you?"

and proceeds to answer this imagined question in stanza 19. वा साम्प्रतम् "That won't do". Cf. Marathi : अशाने नाहीं तें भागणार

IV. 19. सूर्याचन्द्रमसौ etc. The genealogy of पुरूरवस् is as follows : on his father's side he was the son of बुध, who himself was the son of the Moon. On his mother's side he was the son of इळा, the daughter (originally इळ, the son) of मित्र or the Sun. Thus the Sun was his मातामह (मातुः पिता) and the Moon was his पितामह (पितुः पिता). स्वयं वृतः etc..Cf. शाकुंतल III.19. परिग्रहबहुत्वेऽपि द्वे प्रतिष्ठे कुलस्य मे। समुद्ररसना चोर्वी सखी च युवयोरियम्।

IV. 19. 1. उपालप्स्ये "I shall remonstrate with him."

IV. 20. इति च...मयि च etc. "Although..and yet." प्रवासविरहभीरुता "Timidity in regard to separation." भावः "Attitude, disposition." पराङ्मुखः "Averse to." विधुरे "Separated from my beloved." The belief is that the चक्रवाक is so very fond of its mate that it does not brook even the least separation from her. It goes on crying plaintively even though its mate is accidentally screened from its view by a lotus-leaf at night.

IV. 20. 1. भागधेयविपर्ययाणां प्रभावः "The result of the reversal of my fate." We have thought it fit to reject Mr. Pandit's reading: भागधेयानां विपर्ययेण प्रभावप्रकाशः। on account of its clumsiness.

IV. 21. रुणद्धि "Stops, holds back, prevents from going away." ससीत्कारम्। "Murmuring or hissing."

IV. 21. 1. मधुकरे प्रणयिनं करिष्ये "I shall implore or beseech the bee (lit. the honey-gatherer).

IV. 22. यदि अपास्यः "If you had drunk i. e. enjoyed.' We get a variant अवाप्स्यः "If you had obtained."

IV. 22. 1. साधयामः । "Let us go away." साधय् "To go away." नीपस्कन्धनिषण्णहस्तः "Placing or resting his trunk on a branch of the नीप tree." The नीप blossoms and bears fruit in the rainy season.

IV. 23. अचिरोद्गतपल्लवम् "Newly sprouted," "Bearing fresh shoots." आसवसुरभिरसम् "Full of juice as fragrant as honey (आसव; or liquor)." सल्लकीभंगम् "A twig or branch of the सल्लकी tree", of which elephants are believed to be very fond. अभिलषतु "May he desire (i. e. enjoy, taste)."

IV. 23. 1. आमिषम् "Meal, daily food."

IV. 24. मदकल "Ruttish, infuriated through rut." This is addressed to the elephant. युवतिशशिकला "The bright lunar digit among the stars of young women." We can also take मदकल...शशिकला as one compound word meaning: "The bright lunar digit in the midst of young women uttering sweet, gentle, inpassioned sound." यूथिका–शबलकेशी "Having her hair bedecked (शबल–chequered) with यूथिका flowers." स्थिरयौवना "Of stable, enduring, abiding youthfulness." सुखालोका Agreeable, pleasant to look at." दूरालोके स्थिता "Has she stood within your distant sight ?" i. e. have you seen her even from afar ? Mark the alliteration.

IV. 24. 1. स्निग्धमन्द्रेण "Sweet and deep." समाश्वासितः "Reassured, comforted." प्रियोपलंभशंसिना "Intimating his having come across my beloved."

IV. 25. नाग "An elephant." दानम् (i) liberality, charity. (ii) The ichor flowing down from the temples of an elephant. अव्युच्छिन्नपृथुप्रवृत्ति (i) Proceeding uninterruptedly and in abundance; (ii) flowing down uninterruptedly and in abundance or profusely. अर्थिषु (i) In regard to suppliants; (ii) in regard to the bees. वशा "A mate." सर्वं माम् अनु ते "Everything belonging to you resembles mine."

IV. 25. 4. उपत्यका-अद्रेः आसन्ना भूमिः "The precincts of a mountain." कथमन्धकारः etc... अवलोकयामि–These words do not appear in Mr. Pandit's text. But their presence is absolutely necessary, as otherwise the words हन्त etc. become quite abrupt. शतह्रदा "Lightning."

IV. 26. अल्पकुचान्तरा–अल्पं कुचयोः अन्तरं यस्याः " Having very little space between the breasts. i. e. with fully developed breasts." The variant अल्पभुजान्तरा does not give a good sense. पर्वसु संनता "Having well-rounded and fleshy joints." इदं वनान्तरम् "This forest-region." अनंगपरिग्रहम्– "Which Cupid has made his residence," "Which is the property of Cupid," and which must therefore be very beautiful. परिग्रह "Property." पृथुनितम्ब "Having extensive sides or slopes."

IV. 27. This stanza contains the question of the King, as also the reply given by the mountain in the form of an echo. In the first case it is to be read with an interrogative intonation. " The question is मया विरहिता रामा त्वया दृष्टा ? The answer is: त्वया विरहिता रामा मया दृष्टा ।

IV. 27. 1. यथाक्रमम् " Just as I said. " प्रियतरम् "Something more agreeable." गिरिनदी "Mountain torrent." तरंगवातम् आसेविष्ये "I shall enjoy the breeze passing or blowing over the waves (towards me)." नवाम्बुकलुषाम् "Turbid or muddy with its new waters."

IV.28. भ्रूभंग "Arching of the eyebrows in anger." क्षुभित "Frightened." संरंभशिथिलम् "Loosened or disordered through hurry and confusion." आविद्धम् "With uneven steps, crookedly, tortuously." बहुशः स्खलितमभिसंधाय (i) "Thinking again and again of (brooding over) my offensive conduct." (ii) "With reference to, on account of, the many interruptions (the rocks in the bed)." असहना "Unforgiving, relentless." The last line contains the conclusion proceeding from the considerations given in the first three lines. We should supply तथा "Therefore" before नदीभावेन, to correspond with यथा "Since" in line 3.

IV. 29. प्रणयभंगपराङ्मुखचेतसः "Whose mind is averse to any breach of faithful love." प्रणयभंग = भावस्खलितानि in IV. 12 above.

IV. 29. 2. समुद्राभिसारिणी (i) "Flowing towards the sea," (ii) going up to meet the sea (her lover) like an अभिसारिका." अनिर्वेदप्राप्याणि श्रेयांसि । निर्वेदप्राप्याणि न भवन्ति. "Good fortune or happiness is not be attained by sorrowing or by despendency. Cf. अनिर्वेदः श्रियो मूलम् ।. After the words सुनयना तिरोभूता, the Northern Recension has the stanza अभिनवकुसुमस्तबकित etc. which we have given in full in the Introduction, p. XII.

IV. 30. घर्मान्तशंसि "Indicating the close of the hot season." असमग्रकेसरविषमम् "Uneven owing to the filaments not being fully developed." शिखाभरणम् "Ornaments for the hair (शिखा)." The red कदम्ब blossoms in the rainy season.

IV. 31. कृष्णशारच्छविः "Having a dark, variegated complexion." कटाक्षः "Side-glance."

IV. 31.1. अवधीरयन्निव "As if disdaining to hear my suit."

IV. 32. Cf. Raghu, IX. 55. भुग्न "Turned, bent."

IV. 32.1. हंहो = आमन्त्रणे. Vocative particle.

IV. 33. सुभगं वीक्ष्यते "Looks charming or attractive."

वीक्ष्यते = दृश्यते । With our reading वीक्षते the meaning would be "Looks in a charming manner."

IV. 33. 3. शिलाभेद " The cleft of a rock."

IV. 34. प्रभालेपी " Surrounded with lustre, casting radiance." आमिषलव: " A piece of flesh." गगनमभिवृष्टम् " The sky has rained down." काटयवेम reads गहनमभिवृष्टम् " This forest-site is drenched on all sides by rain." स्तबक " Bunch, cluster." मनुजसुतम् etc. The gem sent forth its bright rays in every direction and the poet fancies that the sun is endeavouring to lift up that jewel with his hands (कर-rays).

IV. 35. अभिवासितायाम् " Perfumed or scented with मंदार flowers." अस्रोपहताम् " Soiled with tears."

IV. 36. संगमनीय इति=संगमनीयो नाम । शैलसुताचरणरागयोनि: । शैलसुताया: पार्वत्या: चरणयो: राग: योनि: उत्पत्तिकारणं यस्य । " Produced from the red lac applied to the feet of पार्वती." आवहति " Brings about, effects."

IV. 36. 2. मृगचारी मुनि: भगवान् " Some revered ascetic living the life of a deer " i. e. feeding upon grass and roaming about like a deer. काटयवेम reads मृगचर्मधारी.

IV. 37. विलग्नमध्यया " Having a slender waist." Cf. कुमारसंभव I, 39. मध्येन सा वेदिविलग्नमध्या । Ranganatha reads निमग्नमध्यया. But as निमग्न means " Sunk, depressed " and not " Slender," it cannot be applied to the waist.

IV. 37. 3. मनोरमा " Gladdener of my heart."

IV. 38. धौताधरा " Having her lower lip washed (by tears)." स्वकालविरहात् " On account of the passing away of its season or flowering-time." विश्रान्तपुष्पोद्गमा " Without flowers." विग्नमौनमवस्थिता practising or resorting to silence on account of anxiety." चण्डी "That irascible woman." अवधूय "Having slighted me."

IV. 38. 2. परिष्वङ्गप्रणयी "Desirous of an embrace, longing for an embrace."

तत्स्थाने एव i. e. the creeper vanishes and Urvashi appears in its place.

IV. 38. 5. निर्वृतम् "overjoyed, delighted" विश्वासः न अस्ति "I cannot believe it."

IV. 39. समर्थये "I think or fancy or believe." प्रियां प्रति = प्रियाविषये "In regard to, as having reference to, my beloved." अन्यथा परिवर्तते "Turns out otherwise." This refers to the various disillusionments in regard to Urvashi, that Pururavas has had in his search of her. vide IV. 1. IV.7 IV. 14 etc.–विनिद्रे "Opened." स्पर्शविभावितप्रियः–स्पर्शेन विभाविता निश्चिता प्रिया येन सः। "Who has known definitely that it is his beloved by the (peculiar) touch (of her body)."

IV. 40. तमसि "Darkness, gloom, stupor." गतासुना–गताः असवः (प्राणाः) यस्य सः, तेन। "A dead person.' चेतना "Consciousness, sentiency."

IV. 40, 1. अभ्यन्तरकरणया–अभ्यन्तराणि करणानि यस्याः सा। "Having the senses lying hidden or concealed within." Urvashi means, although her outward form was changed into a creeper, she retained her inner consciousness intact and could preceive all that the King did in her absence.

IV. 40. 7. इदं तावत्प्रसीदतु महाराजः।=इदं तावत् क्षन्तुं प्रसीदतु महाराजः। "May Your Majesty please to pardon me this" The transitive use of प्र+सीद् is remarkable indeed.

IV. 40. 9. प्रसादयितव्यः "To be implored for pardon." सबाह्यान्तःकरणः "Together with the internal and external organs." अन्तरात्मा "My inmost soul." प्रसन्नः "Is overjoyed delighted, pleased.

IV. 40. 15. शाश्वतं कुमारव्रतम् "Perpetual celibacy." कुमारव्रतम् = ब्रह्मचर्यम् ॥ गन्धमादनकच्छः "The bordering region or outskirts of the गन्धमादन grove," विधिः "Rule, restriction prohibitive order." It is the same as the देवतासमय appearing in IV. 40. 25.

IV. 40. 25. देवतासमयम् ', The rule or prohibitive condition laid down by the diety (viz. कुमार कार्तिकेय). अगृहीतानुनया "Not accepting i. e. despising your solicitations."

IV. 41. रतिखेदसुप्तम् "Fallen into sleep on account of the fatigue or exhaustion caused by amorous enjoyment." सहेथाः potential "How could you have borne" that is to say "If it were not that your separation from me was due to your metamorphosis into a creeper.'

इदं तद् "This thing here," referring to the संगमनीय jewel which he shows to Urvashi. त्वत्संगमनिमित्त मुनेः उपलभ्य = त्वत्संगमनिमित्तत्वेन मुनेः सकाशात् ज्ञात्वा । "Having learnt from the ascetic that this was the means of your union (with me)" यथाकथितम् "As related by you, as said by you." This refers to the words of Urvashi in IV. 40. 25 गौरीचरणसंभवं मणिं विना ततो न मोक्ष्यते।

IV. 41. 6. प्रकृतिस्था "Restored to my former state."

IV. 41. 7. एवमेव "In this very position of the body."

IV. 42. Construe: ललाटनिहितस्य मणेः स्फुरता रागेण विच्छुरितम् इदं ते मुखं बालातपरक्तकमलस्य श्रियम् उद्वहति । स्फुरता रागेण विच्छुरितम् "Cavered with the gleaming (literally, "vibrating, flashing.") redness. बालातप "Morning sunshine." कमल "a white lotus."

IV. 42. 3. मह्यम् असूयन्ति "Might feel jealous about

me." since I have led you away from your city for such a long time.

IV. 43. अचिरप्रभा "Lightning." विलसितैः "Flashes." सुरकार्मुकम् = सुरधनुः "Rain-bow." सुरकार्मुकम् एव अभिनवचित्राणि तैः शोभते इति । तादृशेन । विमानतां गमितेन "Transformed into a celestial car (balloon)." खेलगमने "Oh you possessed of graceful gait."

In making Pururavas request Urvashi in this manner the poet evidently wishes to impress upon the reader's mind that although Urvashi has behaved herself so long just like a mortal, she is after all a nymph—a divine being—capable of working any miracles; that in other words, she is too much of a nymph to be a woman, as Prof. Ryder remarks.

ACT V.

[Unlike the preceding three Acts, the fifth Act has no introductory scene. Nor are there any sub-scenes. The whole of the act forms one continuous scene in the King's palace.

From a brief soliloquy of विदूषक at the beginning we learn that King Pururavas has come back to his capital with his beloved Urvashi after a rather prolonged honeymoon, and that he is quite happy now all these many years in every respect, except that he has no issue. Just then a great commotion is set afoot in the palace in as much as the much-valued संगमनीय gem has been snatched off by a vulture. The vulture is still seen whirling round in the sky with the gem in its mouth.

and the King is almost on the point of shooting it down when it flies away beyond the range of sight. The King is greatly worried by the loss of the gem. At this juncture the Chamberlain brings the report that the vulture in question was found dead transfixed with an arrow, and hands over to the King the gem and the arrow. The King reads the owner's name inscribed on the arrow and is extremely surprised to find that the arrow belongs to one Ayus—son of King Pururavas and Urvashi. The King is much perplexed to know when and how Urvashi could possibly have given birth to a son without his knowledge, seeing that he has never been away from her all these many years except on the occasion of the नैमिषीय sacrifice long ago. He is also at a loss to know, why on earth Urvashi should have concealed from him the fact of her having given birth to a son as well as the son himself. Just then a Tapasi (called Satyavati), belonging to the hermitage of the sage च्यवन, is introduced along with a boy. The Tapasi tells the King that the boy accompanying her is none else but the King's son Ayus, who was responsible for shooting down the vulture. She further tells the King, how it was Urvashi herself who, for some unknown reason, had entrusted her son Ayus to her care immediately after his birth and how Ayus was brought up with paternal care and affection and educated in all the civil and military sciences and arts by the sage Chyavana. She says in continuation that on that particular day Ayus violated the discipline of the hermitage by shooting down a vulture and that therefore, the sage च्यवन, no longer wishes to retain him with himself. She has therefore come there to hand over the boy Ayus to Urvashi and wants to see her in that very connection. Urvashi is accordingly sent for and comes in a short time. She is greatly surprised and no less delighted to find her child, now grown up into a fine boy, sitting by the side of Pururavas. The King, Urvashi and Ayus greet one another. The Tapasi now explains to Urvashi the reason why she has deemed it fit to return the boy Ayus to her and then takes her leave. Urvashi then explains in detail to the King why she has so long concealed her son from him. Her only object in doing so was to prolong as much as possible the period of her stay with the King, for, as she tells him now, Indra had allowed her to stay with Pururavas only until the latter should behold the face of his son born of Urvashi. As this has happened now she must leave the King immediately and return to heaven. The King is extremely grieved at the prospect of his separation from Urvashi and makes up his mind to resign his throne to his son Ayus and retire to forest-life, though much against the latter's wish. He forthwith issues orders for the coronation of Ayus as King. Just then, however, Narada comes down from the sky with a message from Indra that Pururavas should not resign his sceptre and sword as his assistance is likely to be required in the near future by the Gods in connection with an impending war with the demons, and that further in consideration of these likely services, Indra is pleased to ordain that Urvashi might stay with Pururavas for life. Both Pururavas and Urvashi are extremely delighted to hear this message from Indra. Narada then performs, at the wish of Indra, as he says, the ceremony of installing Prince Ayus into the position of heir-apparent (युवराज). All shower their blessings upon the young prince and the play is rounded off with a prayer for compatibility and reconciliation between wealth and learning.]

V. o. 9. नन्दनवनप्रमुखेषु देवतारण्येषु. In IV. o. 22, we were told that Pururavas and Urvashi passed there honey-moon in the गन्धमादन grove. The scene of the fourth Act is the Gandhamadana grove. So one should expect to get here गन्धमादनप्रमुखेषु instead of नन्दनवनप्रमुखेषु. ससत्कारोपचाराभिः प्रकृतिभिः अनुरज्यमानः "Highly pleased with his subjects who are honouring him with respectful homage (उपचार)." प्रकृति f. plural. "The subjects of a state." तिथिविशेषः "A special day, a peculiarly sacred day." देवीभिः सह Ranganatha has the singular देव्या । उपकार्या f. "A tent." Cf. रघुवंश XVI. 73. अनुलेपनमाल्ये अग्रभागी "The first sharer in the perfumed pastes and flowers." अनुलेपन means any perfume like sandal, yellow pigment, saffron etc. reduced to the form of a thick paste. माल्य "A flower" "Flowers collectively." अनुपलेपनं च माल्यं च अनुपलेपनमाल्यम् (a समाहारद्वन्द्व compound). The विदूषक is a Brahmin and a personal friend of the King. He, therefore, rightly claims to have a share in the scents and flowers used by the King, and further, to receive it, not after the King has finished his toilet, but while he is still doing it.

V. o. 10. तालवृन्ताधारे निक्षिप्य "Having placed it upon a fan or basket made of palm-leaves" तालवृन्त (n) means a fan made of palm-leaves. दुकूलोत्तरच्छदे । "Covered with a piece of white silk" दुकूलम् उत्तरच्छदः (covering) यस्य । अभ्यन्तरविलासिनी "Dearest wife" i. e. उर्वशी. अभ्यन्तर "Intimate, dearest." मौलिरत्नयोग्य: "Fit to be worn as the jewel in the crown (मौलि)," i. e. "Which was used as the jewel in the crown." आमिषशंकिना The vulture mistook the jewel for a bit of bloody meat, because it appeared unusually red against the back-ground of the white silken cloth.

V. 0. 25. अत्याहितम् "Misfortune, mishap." "What a mishap!" परं बहुमत: "Highly prized or valued." असमाप्तनेपथ्य: । असमाप्तं नेपथ्यं प्रसाधनं यस्य । "Who has not finished his toilet," i. e. "Without finishing his toilet."

सावेगपरिजन: "With his attendants in a hurry, or in a confused state of mind, or agitated."

V. 1. आत्मनो वधम् आहर्ता "Bringing on i. e. courting his own death." It would seem from this as also from the प्रवेशक in Shakuntala Act VI, that theft of costly things was capitally punished in the days of कालिदास. विहगतस्कर: । विहग: एव तस्कर: । "The thief of a bird," "The winged thief." तदेव प्रथमं, तत्प्रथमं, स्तेयम् । "The first theft." गोप्तु: गृहे "In the house of the protector (of mankind i. e. the King)."

V. 1. 3. मुखकोटिलग्नहेमसूत्रेण-मुखकोट्यां लग्नं हेमसूत्रं यस्य । "Whose golden thread or chain is caught in the point of his beak (मुखकोटि lit. "The point of the mouth" i. e. the beak). आकाशम् आलिखन्निव "As if drawing or tracing lines in the sky." The gem, as it was being carried by the bird swiftly in the sky, cast about its red light in the form of shooting rays and so the bird appeared to draw, as it were, red lines on the surface of the sky.

V. 2. आलंबित "Held. caught." मण्डलचारशीघ्र: । मण्डलाकारेण य: चार: (संचार:) तत्र शीघ्र: । "Moving or flying rapidly in circles." Ranganatha reads "मण्डलशीघ्रचार: "

तद्रागरेखावलयं तनोति "Draws or describes a circle of the red lustre of the jewel." अलातचक्रप्रतिमम् "Resembling the circle described by a fire-brand (अलातम्) which is rapidly turned round."

धनुर्ग्राहिणी यवनी—Ionian Greek girls were employed as servants in the courts of kings in ancient India. In the Shakuntala also (Act II) we find that King Dushyanta's retinue consists of several Ionian Greek girls and in the sixth Act of the same drama we have an Ionian maiden whose duty is to carry the bow of the King wherever he goes.

V. 2. 7. दक्षिणान्तेन "In the southern direction," "Towards the south." शासनीयः "Fit to be punished," "A culprit." कुणपभोजनः "Corpse-eater, carrion-eater." कुणपः or कुणपम् "A corpse."

V. 3. प्रभापल्लवितेन (प्रभया पल्लवितः (संजातपल्लवः) प्रभापल्लवितः तेन)=प्रभया विस्तृतेन । "Increased in size by its effulgence." The idea is that the gem appeared swollen as it were on account of the rays it emitted in all directions. दिङ्मुखस्य अवतंसकम् "An ornament for (the face of) the quarter of the sky in which the bird is flying." अशोकस्तबक "A bunch or cluster of अशोक flowers," which are red in colour.

V. 3. 3. हस्तावापः "An arm-guard." It is a leather band for protecting the arm against the strokes of the bow-string.

V. 3. 4. बाणपथः "The range of an arrow, bow-shot." क्रव्यभोजनः-कुणपभोजनः in V. 2. 7. above. क्रव्यम् "Raw flesh, carrion."

V. 4. मणिविशेषः "The excellent gem." लोहितांशः "The

planet Mars." It is so called because of its reddish appearance. परुष "Thick dark." घनच्छेद "A piece or patch of a cloud." संयुक्त "Closely attached to i. e. concealed behind." मद्वचनात् "By my order, at my command," "In my name." नागरिक: "Chief police officer of the city, the Kotwal." निवासवृक्षाश्रयी "Sitting upon its perching tree." विचीयताम् "Let him be searched out."

V. 1. 7. कुत्र गत: भवत: शासनात् मोक्ष्यते "Going where can he escape from your chastisement ?" i. e. where can he go so as to escape your punishment ?

V. 5. प्रियया supply सह. संगमित: = संयोजित:

V. 5. 1. परिगतार्थं कृ "To inform a person of something," "To acquaint one with something."

V. 6. वध्य: "Doomed or condemned to death." मार्गणतां गतेन "Transformed into an arrow." प्राप्यापराधोचितम् "Having received or met with the punishment which he deserved for his crime." The word शासनम् must be supplied after अपराधोचितम । समौलिरत्न: "Together with the crest jewel,"

V. 6. 3. पेटक (m. n.) "A safe."

V. 6. 7. नामांकित: "Bearing a name upon it." वर्णविचारक्षमा "Able to decipher or recognize or make out the letters." We know from III. 1, that the कञ्चुकिन् is an old man.

V. 6. 10. अनुवाच्य "Reading to himself." सापत्यतां रूपयति This is a very strange direction. One fails to see how this piece of acting was done so as to convey to the audience an idea of the King's fatherhood !

V. 11. नियोगम् अशून्यं कृ "To go about or attend to one's business." This is a clever device to withdraw a character from the stage, when its presence is no longer necessary.

V. 6. 14. प्रहर्तुः "Of the striker."

V. 7. ऐलसूनोः पुरूरवसः पुत्रस्य । ऐल=पुरूरवस् who was the son of इला by बुध. धनुर्भृत् "An archer, bowman." प्रहर्तुः द्विषदायुषाम् "The destroyer of the lives of his enemies."

V. 7. 2. संतान (m. n.) "Progeny, offspring."

V. 7. 3. अन्यत्र नैमिषेयसत्रात् "Except on the occasion of a sacrifice in the नैमिष forest." सत्र is a sacrifice lasting from 13 to 100 days. नैमिषम् is the name of a sacred forest in which sacrifices used to be performed in ancient times and in which सौति narrated the महाभारत and the पुराणs to the holy sages. The name is thus derived यतस्तु निमिषेणेदं निहतं दानवं बलम् । अरण्येऽस्मिंस्ततस्तेन नैमिषारण्यसञ्ज्ञितम् ॥ गर्भव्यक्तिः "Sign or revelation of pregnancy." आलक्षिता "Marked, noticed." प्रसूतिः "Offspring, progeny, issue." This refers to संतानेन occurring in V. 7. 1. Pururavas means to say that in the first place he knows of only one occasion when he was separated from Urvashi, viz. when he performed a sacrifice in the नैमिष forest. How could then Urvashi have given birth to a child without his knowledge? In the second place, even supposing that Urvashi was delivered of a child just when Pururavas was staying away from her in connection with the नैमिषीयसत्र, how could he have failed to notice any decided signs of pregnancy before that?

V. 8. आविल "Dark" (मलिन). पयोधराग्रम् "Nipple." Ranganatha also records the variant "आनीलचूचुकाग्रम्", which means the same as our reading. लवलीदलपाण्डुराननच्छायम्—लवलीदलमिव पाण्डुरा आननच्छाया यस्मिन् तत् ॥ आननच्छाया "Complexion of the face." लवली is a kind of tree with pale-green and whitish leaves. तानि दिनानि "During those days." This is Accusative of time. We get a variant कतिचिद् अहानि "For a few days." अलसेक्षणम् "With dull, languid eyes." The words किं तु show that Pururavas regards these signs as only superficial and not decided or certain.

V. 8. 3. Vidushaka means to say that the Apsarases are mysterious in their ways and habits and that they cannot be judged by human standards. It is therefore wrong for the King to wonder why he could not see any definite sign of pregnancy in her.

V. 8. 6. कः देवतारहस्यानि तर्कयिष्यति । "Who can unravel the mysteries of divine beings?"

V. 8. 10. तापसी "A female ascetic."

V. 8. 18. तत्रभवान् क्षत्रियकुमारकः "The venerable prince of the warrior-class." गृध्रलक्ष्यवेधी "Which pierced its mark viz. the vulture." अर्धनाराचः "A crescent-shaped arrow" i. e. "An arrow having a semi-circular edge."

V. 9. बाष्पायते "Sheds or emits tears." This is a denominative from the word बाष्प, which means "Tears," according to पाणिनि III. 1. 16. बाष्पोष्मभ्यामुद्वमने ॥ दृष्टिः "Eye." वात्सल्यबन्धि-वात्सल्यं बध्नातीति । "Full of affection." मनसः प्रसादः (जायते) "My mind becomes calm or tranquil; becomes gratified." प्रसादः "Calmness, composure, serenity of mind."

काटयवेम reads "वहति प्रसादम् ।" for "मनसः प्रसादः" संजातवेपथुभिः "Seized with tremor." उज्झितधैर्यवृत्तिः "Giving up all patience, firmness of mind or self-control." अदयम् "In a cruel merciless manner" i. e. "forcibly or powerfully."

V. 9. 1. एवम् "Thus" i. e. "Here, in this place."

V. 9. 6. विस्तारयिता "Lengthener," "extender," "increaser." औरसः संबन्धः "Paternal relation."

V. 10. हार्दम् "Affection, love." इदम् (to be construed with हार्दम्) "Such, so great." उत्संगवर्धितानाम् "Brought up on the lap," "Grown up on the lap."

V. 10. 7. जातमात्रः "As soon as born." मम हस्ते न्यासीकृतः "Was entrusted to me, was committed to my care." जातकर्मादि विधानम् "Sacred rites such as the birth ceremony." गृहीतविद्यः "Having mastered all the learning." अभिविनीतः "Was instructed or trained in." धनुर्वेद "The science of archery."

V. 10. 10. सनाथः "Furnished or equipped or provided with a protector."

V. 10. 13. आश्रमविरुद्धम् "Contrary to (the rules or discipline of) the hermitage."

V. 10. 17. किल "As they say" for the तापसी had not actually seen it herself. गृहीतामिषः "Holding flesh in its mouth." This flesh was in fact the संगमनीय jewel as we saw above in V. 0. 26. लक्ष्यीकृतः बाणस्य "Was made the target of his arrow" i. e. was shot down with an arrow.

V. 10. 23. निर्यातय "Return, make over." हस्तन्यासम् "The thing placed in your hands i. e. entrusted to your charge."

V 10. 25. आसनम् अनुगृह्ण "To favour a seat, to oblige a seat i. e. to be pleased to take a seat."

V. 11. सर्वांगीणः "Pervading the whole of the body with a thrilling ecstasy of joy." किल, "I have heard it said." तेन "Therefore." उपगतेन "By coming near me." The past. pass. partic. उपगत is used here as a noun in the sense of "Approaching." माम् is to be construed with आह्लादयस्व ।

V. 11.4. अशंकित: "Without any fear.

V. 11. 6. The विदूषक means to say that there is no reason why his sight should frighten Ayus, since he looks neither better nor worse than a monkey (शाखामृग) with which Ayus is already familiar in the course of his forest residence.

V. 11. 16. शिखण्डक: means "The tuft of hair on the crown of the head." सत्यवतीसूचित: "Indicated by (the presence of) सत्यवती (the तापसी)."

V. 12. त्वदालोकनतत्परा "Eager or impatient to see you" or "Fixing her gaze upon you." स्नेहप्रस्रवनिर्भिन्नम् "Saturated or wetted through and through with the flow of affection," i. e. with the milk oozing from her breasts owing to her affection for her son. निर्भिन्न literally means "Broken, pierced through." स्तनांशुकम् "Breast-garment."

V. 12. 2. प्रत्युद्गच्छ "Rise up to receive."

V. 12. 5. बहुमता "Highly esteemed."

V. 12. 10. पितरम् आराधयिता "The gladdener or delighter of thy father." The genitive is prohibited by Panini II. 3. 69. न लोकाव्ययनिष्ठाखलर्थतृनाम् ।

V. 12, 11. पुत्रवत्यै "To the blessed mother of the son." There is a peculiar appropriateness in the King's addressing उर्वशी in this manner now.

V. 12. 16. कवचहर: " Of an age fit for bearing the heavy armour upon the body." Vide पाणिनि III.2.10. वयसि च । The form would be कवचहार: if age is not meant. विसर्जयितुम् used in a passive sense "To be dismissed." उपरुध्यते "Is interfered with."

V. 12. 21. अवितृष्णा = सतृष्णा "Desirous." उपरोद्धुम् "To come in your way and cause you inconvenience," "To detain you." पुनर्दर्शनाय Cf. I. 15. 15. above.

V. 12. 24. मां प्रणिपातय "Convey or present my salutations."

V. 12. 18. पूर्वस्मिन्नाश्रमे = ब्रह्मचर्ये । द्वितीयम् = गृहस्थाश्रमम् । अध्यासितुम् "To enter upon, to step into."

V. 13. यः सुप्तवान् who used to sleep. कण्डूयन "Scratching." जातकलापम् "Who has grown his plumage." मणिकण्ठक— the name of the peacock.

V. 14. पौलोमी=शची She was the daughter of the demon पुलोम. पुरन्दरः=इन्द्रः "The destroyer of the enemies' forts" पुरं शत्रूणां नगराणि दारयतीति पुरंदरः । Cf. रघुवंश III. 23.

V. 14. 1. रोदिति—"Weeps" i. e. silently and inaudibly. Hence it is that विदूषक speaks of her as अश्रुमुखी "Shedding tears, having her face suffused with tears."

V. 15. Construe: हे सुन्दरि वंशस्थितेरधिगमात् यम महति प्रमादे उपपन्ने (सति) पीनोन्नतस्तनविसर्पिभिः अस्रैः मुक्तावलीविरचनापुनरुक्तिम् आनयन्ती किं प्ररुदिता असि । वंशस्थितेः अधिगमात् "On account of the attainment of the stability of the family" वंशस्थिति means "Stability of the family," hence "What brings about or leads to the stablity of the family i. e. a son who perpetuates the family." मुक्तावलीविरचनापुनरुक्तिम् आनयन्ती "Bringing about the superfluousness or repetition of the pearl-necklace" i. e. causing another necklace by means of the continuously flowing tears and thus making the pearl necklace superfluous. Cf. III. 7. 7. above: अभिव्यक्तायां चन्द्रिकायां किं दीपिकापौनरुक्त्येन । प्ररुदिता = रोदितुम् आरब्धा "Begun to weep."

V. 15. 5. विस्मृतास्मि that is to say the समय or condition referred to in the following sentence and in V. 15. 17. below. महेन्द्रसंकीर्तनेन "By the mention of Indra's name;" this refers to V. 14, where जयन्त, शची and इन्द्र are mentioned. आयासयति "Pains or torments me."

V. 15. 7. गृहीत "Captivated, borne away."

V. 15. 18. वंशकरस्य "Of a son, the perpetuator of the family." महाराजवियोगभीरुतया–this was the real reason why Urvashi kept away her son in the आश्रम. विद्यागमनिमित्तम् this is the pretext under which she entrusted her son to the care of सत्यवती, the तापसी. अप्रकाशम् "Secretly." एतावान् "This much," "Thus far and no farther." संवास: "Residence, dwelling with."

V. 15. 24. सुखप्रत्यर्थिता "Hostility or adverseness to the happiness of human beings."

V. 16. आश्वासितस्य "Comforted, gratified." Mark the force of the particle नाम which here means "Just, no sooner than."

व्यावर्तितातपरुजः । व्यावर्तिता आतपेन (=आतपकृता) रुक् यस्य । "Whose suffering caused by the summer-heart has been removed or allayed." वैद्युतः अग्निः "Lightning-fire."

V. 16. 2. अर्थः "Good fortune" viz. सुतोपलब्धि. अनर्थानुबन्धः "Followed by a series or succession of mishaps or misfortunes." अनुबन्धः "A series or a chain or a succession." This refers to the loss of Urvashi which the विदूषक thinks, is sure to be followed by the King's retirement to the forest as a recluse. गन्तव्यम् the potential pass. partic. is used here in the sense of the Future, = तत्रभवान् गमिष्यति ।

V. 16. 6. मामपि etc. Urvashi means to say, that this is another link in the chain of misfortunes alluded to by the विदूषक in V. 16. 2. that the King is likely to misunderstand her in that he will think that Urvaṣhi left him the moment that her son was well-educated and was restored to the King, as if her selfish object was fulfilled, and as if it was no longer necessary for her to remain with him.

V. 17. सुलभवियोगा परवत्ता "Dependence or servitude in which separation from one's beloved is only too easy or natural and to be expected at any time." परवत ("Dependent") तस्य भावः परवत्ता । आयुषि न्यस्तराज्यः । "Entrusting the government of the kingdom, delivering the charge of administration, to Ayus." विचरितमृगयूथानि "Inhabited by herds of deer," "Wherein herds of deer roam about. "The King assures Urvashi in this stanza that he will not at all misunderstand or think unkindly of her as she fears he will, for he is only too painfully aware of the wrechedness of the state of servitude.

V. 17. 1. पुंगवधारितायां धुरि "To the yoke drawn by a mighty bull or steer." दम्यः "A young bullock who is unbroken to the yoke and who requires a good deal of training and experience before he can be safely harnessed to a carriage."

V. 18. गन्धद्विपः "Scent-elephant." गन्धप्रधानो द्विपः । His ichor or rut emits such a strong odour that other elephants run away at its smell, being afraid of encountering him. Cf. यस्य गन्धं समाघ्राय न तिष्ठन्ति प्रतिद्विपाः । स वै गन्धगजो नाम नृपतेर्विजयावहः ॥ शमयति "Subdues, puts down." कलभः "A young cub." वेगोदग्रम् । वेगेन उदग्रम् "Deadly or virulent by its circulation; वेगः means the circulation or taking effect of poison." स्वकार्यसहो भरः "pre-eminence which enables one to discharge one's duty or task howsoever difficult." जात्यैव "By one's very birth" जन्मनैव "Rooted in ones very blood, not in one's age." Cf. Raghuvamsha XI. तेजसां हि न वयः समीक्ष्यते। अमात्यपरिषद् "The council of ministers." संभ्रियताम् "Let preparations be made for." सं+भृ "To bring things together."

V. 18. 4. दृष्टिप्रविघातं रूपयन्ति "Show as if their eyes were dazzled."

V. 18. 5. निरभ्रे "In the cloudless sky." विद्युत्संपातः "Flash of lightning, descent of lightning."

V. 19. गोरोचनायाः निकषः गोरोचना निकषः। स इव पिङ्गः जटाकलापः यस्य। गोरोचना is a kind of bright yellow pigment derived from the urine or bile or the head of a cow. निकषः means "A touchstone." It secondarily means a streak or line on a touchstone." Cf. IV. 1 कनकनिकषस्निग्धा etc. शशिकलामलवीतसूत्रः। शशिकला इव अमलं वीतसूत्रं यस्य। वीतसूत्रम्=उपवीतम्=यज्ञोपवीतम् "The sacred thread." मुक्तागुण etc. मुक्तागुणानां ये अतिशयाः (उत्कर्षाः) तै संभृता मण्डनश्रीः यस्य। संभृत "Heightened, enhanced." मुक्तागुणातिशय "Excellent wreaths of pearls." Or अतिशय may be conntected with संभृत, "Extremely heightened or enhanced." This is to be construed with जंगमकल्पवृक्षः हेमप्ररोहः-हेममयाः प्ररोहाः यस्य। Having golden branches." जंगम "In motion." Cf गिरिरिव गतिमान् अपक्षलोपात् III. 3. With this description of the appearance of नारद Cf. शिशुपालवध I. 4-10.

अर्घ्यम् "A respectful offering consisting of water, scents, flowers etc. made to a distinguished guest on his arrival." गंधमाल्यादिसयुक्तमुदकम् अर्घ्यमुच्यते।

V. 19. 4. अर्हणा "Worship" i. e. "Materials of worship."

V. 19. 5. मध्यमलोक=मर्त्यलोक "The world of mortals."

V. 19. 6. आवर्ज्य "Letting down" scil. the materials of worship." "Offering the materials of worship."

V. 19. 9. अपि नाम एवं स्यात् "Would that it were so."

V. 19. 11. और्वशेयः=उर्वश्याः अपत्यं पुमान् according to पाणिनि IV. 1, 92- तस्यापत्यम्. । Cf. गांगेय, वैनतेय, शाकुन्तलेय etc.

V. 19. 13. विष्टर: "A seat." Cf. V, 10. 25 above.

V. 19. 18. वनगमनाय कृतबुद्धिम् "Resolved to take to the forest." अनुशास्ति "Advises."

V. 19, 21. Construe: त्रिकालदर्शिभिः मुनिभिः भावी सुरासुरसंगरः आदिष्टः। त्रिकालदर्शिभिः "Seeing i. e. able to know the past, the present and the future" भावी "About to take place in the near future." आदिष्ट "Predicted, foretold." सांयुगीनः-संयुगे साधुः "Skilled or well-versed in warfare." See Panini IV. 4. 98. and 92: तत्र साधुः। प्रतिजनादिभ्यः खञ्।. सहधर्मचारिणी "Partner in the performance of religious duties.

V. 19. 26. अपनीतम् "Removed, extracted." इव is to be construed with शल्यम् "A dart as it were" शल्य here means "the painful thought of the imminent separation."

V. 19. 27. परवान् "Dependent."

V. 20. स्वत्कार्यं कुर्यात् "Should help you." तस्य इष्टम् आचरेः "Should act up to his desire." समेधयति "Causes to blaze," "Supports with splendour." The idea here expressed is that the sun deposits his splendour in the Fire at sun-set. The Fire does the same at sun-rise with reference to the Sun. It is this mutual helpfulness of these two Deities that keeps the world going. Cf. रघुवंश IV. 1; also आदित्यो वा अस्तं यन्नग्निमनु प्रविशति। अग्निं वा आदित्यः सायं प्रविशति। Also मालविकाग्निमित्र I. 13. अतिमात्रभासुरत्वं पुष्यति भानोः परिग्रहादनलः।

संभृत: "Collected, put together." यौवराज्याभिषेक: = यौवराज्याभिषेकसामग्री । "Materials for installation as a crown-prince or heir-apparent."

V. 20. 6. भद्रपीठम् = हेमादिमय पीठम् "A stately seat for auspicious purposes."

V. 20. 8. आवर्ज्य "Pouring down or emptying the contents of the कलशs or jars containing sacred waters." The sprinkling of water (अभिषेक) forms the central and the most important part of the coronation, and it is therefore performed by नारद himself; while Rambha is directed to do the remaining minor ceremony (निर्वर्त्यतां शेषो विधि:)

V. 20. 14. कुलधुरंधर: "Pre-eminent in the family."

V. 21. अमरमुनि: "The immortal or divine sage, the godly sage." बाधन = बुध "Mercury." देव: "His Majesty." गुणै: पितु: अनुरूप: "Worthy of your father by reason of your excellences." अतिशयिनि वंशे "In your exalted family," आशिष: समाप्ता एव "All blessings are indeed already fulfilled, are already attained or realised." Cf. Raghu. V. 34.

V. 22. Construe. उन्नतानां पुरस्तात् स्थिते अस्मिन् तव पितरि, अनाकम्प्यधैर्ये स्थितिमति त्वयि च विभक्ता राजलक्ष्मी: हिमवति जलधौ च व्यस्ततोया गंगा इव इदानीम् अधिकतरं राजते । The expression उन्नतानां पुरस्तात् स्थिते applies to the mountain Himalaya as well as to the King; while स्थितिमति and अनाकम्प्यधैर्ये apply to the Prince आयुष्म् as also to the Ocean. उन्नतानां पुरस्तात् स्थिते (i) standing at the head of the exalted (ii) standing in the forefront of the lofty. स्थितिमति (i) observing स्थिति or the rules of right conduct (ii) observing i. e, not transgressing the boundary. अनाकम्प्यधैर्य (i) of unshakable courage (ii) whose calmness is imperturbable. व्यस्ततोया "Having its waters divided or distributed," Cf. Raghuvamsa V 66.

V. 22. 2. पुत्रस्य युवराजश्रिया "The glory of heir-apparentship belonging to your son."

V. 22. 5. साधारण :–" Common. " She means to say that her good fortune was their good fortune also, as the Apsarases were but her sisters. ज्येष्ठमातरम् i. e. the Queen Aushinari.

V. 23. महासेन=कुमार कार्तिकेय who was placed by Indra at the head of the heavenly forces on the occasion of the battle with the demon तारकासुर. सैनापत्ये अभिषिक्तम् " Installed as commander-in-chief " of the army of the Gods. मरुत्वता=इन्द्रेण. सेनापतेः भावः सैनापत्यम् । Vide कुमारसंभव canto XIII.

V. 23. 1. एवम् अनुगृहीतः " Being thus favoured " i. e. by sprinkling upon his head the sacred waters of the coronation ceremony.

V. 23. 2. पाकशासनः । पाकं शास्ति इति । Indra the slayer of a demon called पाक.

भरतवाक्यम्–The final benediction or epilogue at the end of a drama called भरतवाक्य in honour of भरत the founder of Indian Drama.

V. 24. परस्परविरोधिन्योः the hostility between Wealth and Learning is proverbial in Sanskrit Literature. Cf. निसर्गभिन्नास्पदमेकसंस्थमस्मिन् द्वयं श्रीश्च सरस्वती च । रघु० VI. 29. एकसंश्रयदुर्लभम् " Very hard to find in one and the same abode." संगतम् "Union."

After this the Northern Recension has the stanza सर्वस्तरतु दुर्गाणि etc. which we have given in full in the Introduction. p. XII.

Addenda et Corrigenda to the Text and Translation.

PAGE	LINE	FOR	READ
10	Stanza 6, line 2,	चछा	चक्ष्वा
13	last line	Drop the stage direction 'Exit king etc.'	
15	Stanza 10	After the word 'eclipse,' add 'and regaining its brightness.'	
20	line 3	राजर्षि	राजर्षिं
22	line 8	ऊर्वशी	उर्वसी
24	line 10	स्था स्यामि	स्थास्यामि
25	line 7	presincts	precincts
25	line 7	sparrely	sparsely
26	line 2 from bottom	रहस्व	रहस्स
32	line 10 from bottom	दिव्र	दिव्व
40	line 9	कदम्द्	कदम्ह
46	line 2 from bottom	जहं	अहं
57	line 11	Dear m	Dear me. It is
57	last line	you me told	you told me
73	line 9 from bottom	repentence	repentance
81	last line	it	her
82	line 5	ाड	ढि
91	line 7 from bottom	another	yourself
94	line 5	किंचिदपसृत्य	किंचिदुपसृत्य :
96	line 11 from bottom	वडदि	वड्ढदि
96	line 2 from bottom	उर्वशी	उर्वशीं
99	line 9	schorched	scorched
100	line 8 from bottom	पणिधाय	पणिधाण
102	line 5	देण	तेण

PAGE	LINE	FOR	READ
105	line 14	velley	volley
105	line 4 from bottom	severence	severance
106	line 4	लिर्ङे	लिङ्गे
107	line 7	lighting	lightning
107	line 17 from bottom	Add 'through	anger,' after 'them
109	line 15	exhilerated	exhilarated
110	line 9	दक्षणेन	दक्षिणेन
111	line 3 from bottom	one's	their
113	line 15	Don't do that	That will not do
115	last linc	Severence	Severance
123	line 7	after 'me,' add	fallen at her feet
127	line 5	Severence	Severance
127	line 11 from bottom	we	you
133	line 14	people	prefect
136	line 3 from bottom	स्वादेवम्	स्यादेवम्
144	line 1	वच्छ	वच्छे

मालविकाग्निमित्रम्

MĀLAVIKĀGNIMITRA

OF

KĀLIDĀSA

INTRODUCTION.

Kalidasa—the Poet.

What De Quincy says of Shakespeare meets the case of Kālidāsa far more appropriately than that of the English poet. "That he lived and that he died and that he was a little lower than the angels," this pretty nearly makes up the amount of our undisputed report of the great poet. Tradition has given us numerous legends, but they are no more than a mere farrago of absurd anachronisms. Modern research has done a good deal indeed to lift the veil from India's past, and yet an exact and authentic account of the author is yet to be given. Of the numerous theories advanced by scholars regarding his age, only two seem now to have the support of indefeasible evidence both internal and external. There is the strong testimony of the quotations in the Mahābhāṣya of Patañjali which goes to prove that Sanskrit court epic dated from before the time of the Christian Era, and the same is now amply corroborated by the recent epigraphic researches of modern scholars. This lends feasibility to the traditional legend of a king Vikrama the founder of the Saṁvat Era—57 B. C. who had at his court a circle of nine gems including Kālidāsa, Varāhamihira and Ghaṭakarpara.

It is on the other hand contended that a comparison of the inscriptions which are mostly panegyrics of kings and which employ the Gupta Era which was first used by Candragupta Vikramāditya II, with the classical poems proves that the poetical style of the inscriptions prevailing in the fourth and fifth centuries did not much differ from the style of the Kāvyas; and on the strength of this and similar epigraphic evidence it has been sought to prove that Kālidāsa must have flourished under Candragupta II who assumed the title of Vikramāditya and succeeded his father Samudragupta in 375 A. D. and made Ujjain his capital. Vincent Smith in his early history of India (p. 304, footnote) expresses the view that the earlier works of Kālidāsa were composed before 413 A. D. during the regime of Candragupta, and his later works were written under Kumāragupta I (413 A. D. to 455 A. D.) and that possibly his literary career extended even into the reign of Skandagupta (455 A. D. 480 A. D.).

This is the sum of our knowledge of the external details of the poet's life; and yet it may be asked: Are the few broad bare facts of life the only thing one should prize? Is not the poet known to us in the far richer world of his imaginative creations? He neighbours us on every side, rouses our intellect, moves our passions, and stimulates our activity. It is well said, "The magnitude of life is not as to its external displacements but as to its subjective experiences."

The impression that one gathers of the poet from his works is that of a man, deeply learned in literature and philosophy and other traditional lore of the times, and more deeply learned in the book of natare. A charming trait of his personality is his modesty which Coleridge recognises as a sure sign of great genius. He was a widely-travelled man and was a keen observer of nature. Not only did the sublime and wild aspects of nature stir his imagination, but the milder and minuter manifestations also caught his fancy, and he is very fond of describing to us how the garden-plants bend to catch the beauty of spring, or how the march of seasons affects them.

But above all he is a student of the human heart and is rarely excelled in his "delicate appreciation of its most refined and tender emotions and his familiarity with the workings and counter-workings of its conflicting feelings." Particularly he excels in depicting love "from the first suggestion in an innocent mind to the perfection of passion." All the three plays sing of love happy at the last and 'havened after tempest.'

Of his three plays, Mālavikāgnimitra was the earliest written and Śākuntala came last, while the Vikramorvaśīya belongs to his middle period. We have merely to compare the prologues of the three plays to be convinced of this; for in our play the author deems it necessary to explain away what would seem presumption in a contemporary poet to have offered his play for exhibition before the elite to the exclusion of the plays of renowned writers. There is no such diffidence in the next two plays; moreover it will be observed from a comparison of the three plays that "his ethical outlook on life was becoming progressively deeper and more spiritual." And lastly in spite of the frequent *curiosa felicitas* of his diction, we do not come across that smoothness and rounded perfection and inevitable grace that mark the mature style of the poet.

The political background of the play.

The Mālavikāgnimitra is a drama of court intrigue. King Agnimitra is a historical character of the second century before Christ; he was the son of Puṣpamitra—,

The commander-in-chief—who killed his master Bṛhadratha Maurya and established himself as a sovereign of the Maurya dominions, thus founding a dynasty known to history as that of the Śungas (183 B. C.). As the seat of empire was in Pātaliputra, and as Agnimitra's capital is Vidiśā—the modern Bhilsa–it is possible that he was appointed as regent of certain provinces during his father's lifetime. In the later years of his reign, Puṣpamitra was threatened by serious danger. Menander, the Greek king of Kabul and the Punjab wanted to emulate the exploits of Alexander and at the head of a formidable force annexed the Indus delta, the peninsula of Saurāṣtra (Kāthiawar), Mathurā and besieged Madhyamikā (Nāgari near Chitore) and Sāketam in southern Oudh, and threatened even Pātaliputra, the capital. This invasion (155-153 B. C.) was repelled by Puṣpamitra after a severe struggle and Menander was obliged to retire to his own country. The fight with the Greek cavalry force in our play seems to be an echo of the struggle with Menander from whose repulse in 153 B. C. until the bombardment of Calicut by Vascodagama in A. D. 1502, India enjoyed immunity from attack under European leadership

The war with the king of Vidarbha also seems to be a historical occurrence, in which Yajñasena was worsted by king Agnimitra, as a result of which Vidarbha was divided between two provinces, separated by the river Varadā (Wardha) which is now the boundary between Berar aud the central Provinces. Agnimitra appointed Mādhavasena to the southern and Yajñasena to the northern principality.

The poet has very skilfully utilised these historical events for the purposes of his play. In the last act we get a report of the victory won by Agnimitra's army over the king of Vidarbha; among those who came with the good news were two girls who recognized Mālavikā as the Vidarbha princess; and this served to remove all objections, if indeed there were any, to Agnimitra's marrying below his rank. Secondly the communication by Puspamitra of the victory won by Vasumitra (his grandson, and son of Agnimitra and Dhāriṇī) over the cavalry of the Yavanas who had captured the sacrificial horse let loose by Puspamitra is an event of great joy to Dhāriṇī and to the ladies of the king's household, and in the moment of her elation, the queen unites Mālavikā with her royal lover.

Analysis of the plot.

Act I. After the invocation, the manager tells his assistant how he has received from the spectators the order to act the play 'Mālavikāgnimitra' at that spring festival; and when the latter wonders how the spectators could have passed over the compositions of famous poets and done such great honour to the work of a modern, the poet Kālidāsa, the former tells him that it is all right. 'For a poem is not good because it is old; nor is every new poem to be blamed because it is new;' he then bids him make haste and help him to carry out the order of the spectators.

Then enter Kaumudikā and Bakulāvalikā and we learn from their conversation that king Agnimitra has seen in the picture-gallery a new painting of queen Dhāriṇī and her attendants. Among them is Mālavikā, who is so beautiful that the king is smitten with love, but the jealous queen takes especial care to guard the original from the sight of the king. Then enters Gaṇadāsa, the dancing-master from whom Bakulāvalikā learns that Mālavikā has proved to be an exceedingly clever and intelligent pupil; and on his asking whence such a choice attendant is secured by the queen she informs him that the queen's brother of inferior caste, Vīrasena by name, in command of a frontier fortress, sent this girl as a present to his sister.

In the main scene of the act, the king is discovered listening to a dispatch from the king of Vidarbha, who had imprisoned the king's cousin Mādhavasena together with his wife and sister and in response to Agnimitra's demand that they should be liberated, he declares that the sister had disappeared in the confusion of the capture, and that Mādhavasena would be released only if Agnimitra set at liberty his brother-in-law, the Maurya minister. This letter so angers Agnimitra that he orders his army under the command of Vīrasena to march against the king of Vidarbha.

At this point, Gautama enters and informs the king that he has devised a plan for bringing Mālavikā into the king's presence. He has set the two dancing-masters by the ears, who soon appear on the stage, each abusing the other vigorously, and claiming for himself pre-eminence in his art. It is agreed that each shall exhibit his best pupil before the king, the queen, and the learned Parivrājikā, Kauśikī. The queen raises a number of difficulties and disfavours the whole proceeding, but her jealous opposition is overborne. The sound of the drum now is heard which was a signal for them to proceed to the concert-hall of the palace where the orchestral arrangements are by now made ready.

Act II. The scene is laid in the concert-hall. The Parivrājikā, the mistress of the ceremony, directs that

Gaṇadāsa shall exhibit his pupil first; upon which Mālavikā enters in thin stage-costume and she dances and sings a song which pretty clearly expresses her own passion for the king. The king is almost transported to find that she is lovelier than the picture; the Vidūṣaka manages to detain her for a little while by pretending that he has observed a serious flaw in her performance and when she is finally permitted to depart, both she and the king are deeply in love. The hour of noon is now announced, whereupon the exhibition of the other dancing-master is postponed.

Act. III. The scene is laid in the Pramadavana garden. From the conversation of two maids we learn that although both the teachers are thoroughly acquainted with the science of dancing, yet the teaching power of Ganadāsa was ranked the higher of the two on account of the admirable qualities of his pupil, Mālavikā. The king is now desperately in love with her but in order to spare the feelings of Dhāriṇī, he makes no use of his power to behold the object of his desire. We are further informed that a favourite Aśoka tree is late to blossom, and requires, so the belief runs, to be touched by the foot of a handsome woman to be induced to burst into blossom.

After this introductory scene, the king and the Vidūṣaka enter. The former describes how desperately he is in love with Mālavikā, whereupon the Vidūṣaka his confidant asks him to possess his soul in patience because as a matter of fact he has devised an expedient for ensuring the end that he wished to attain. He then reminds the King of his promise to join Irāvatī and pass the day enjoying a ride in the swing with her in the garden. Both now enter the garden, but before Irāvatī's arrival,

Mālavikā enters, as she is commissioned by Dhāriṇī to touch the Asoka-tree with her foot and thus induce it to blossom for the queen herself is disabled to perform the ceremony, as owing to Gautama's carelessness she has had a fall from a swing and is not able to move her feet in consequence The King and his confidant now hide in a thicket. Presently Bakulāvalikā appears on the scene and while she adorns Mālavikā for the ceremony she engages her in conversation about the King. A third pair, Irāvatī somewhat flushed with wine, and her maid Nipuṇikā, now enter, and they also conceal themselves to spy upon the two girls; the two girls believe themselves to be alone, and Mālavikā talks freely of her love and Bakulāvalikā tells her how the king also is pining for her. The King now starts forward and expresses his love for Mālavikā, whereupon Irāvatī, mad with jealousy joins the group, dismisses the two girls and rudely snapping at the king and not accepting his excuses, such as they are, leaves him with words of stinging jealousy to inform Dhāriṇī of what is going forward.

Act IV. The Vidūsaka informs the king that Mālavikā and her friend with fetters on them are locked in the cellar by queen Dhāriṇī who has given orders to the door-keeper that they shall be let out only on presentations of her signet-ring bearing the seal of a serpent. He, however, has a plan in his head, which he will presently employ to release them. The king then pays a visit to the queen to inquire how she is doing, when the Vidūsaka rushes into their presence, pretending that he has been bitten by a venomous snake on the finger, and shows them the two marks of the teeth. Then imploring the king to take care of his helpless mother he awakens genuine sympathy in the queen who readily parts with her signet-ring bearing a serpent-seal, as it was required by the poison-doctor to effect a magical cure. He thus procures the freedom of Mālavikā and her friend and leading them to the summer-house brings about a meeting between the King and Mālavikā. The love-scene is again interrupted by Irāvatī; but the timely news that princess Vasulaksmī has been terribly frightened by a brown ape and would be comforted only by him, extricates the King from a very embarrassing situation indeed. The act ends with the announcement that even before five nights have elapsed from the time of the ceremony, the Asoka tree is covered all over with blossoms.

Act V. The queen has sent word to the King that she desires him to go with her to behold the beauty of the Asoka in blossoms; the maids announce that the avenging forces of the King have subdued the King of Vidarbha. The King and the Vidūsaka now proceed to the garden where they find the queen and her attendants including Mālavikā waiting for him under the Aśoka tree. At this point the chamberlain comes with a message from the minister that the present sent by the king of Vidarbha included two accomplished maidens who were till now not introduced because they represented themselves to be fatigued with the journey. They are now brought before the group gathered under the tree, and give considerable surprise to everyone by falling prostrate before Mālavikā whom they address "Our princess". They inform the King that Mālavikā was the younger sister of prince Mādhavasena and that when he came into the power of his kinsman, the king of Vidarbha, Mālavikā was secretly carried off by Sumati, the minister of the captive prince, while attendants like them were left behind. At this point, the Parivrājikā takes up the tale and declares how her brother who was the minister of Mādhavasena, had rescued her and Mālavikā from the king of Vidarbha, and had started for Agnimitra's court ; but they were set upon and overpowered by bandits; her brother was killed and she herself separated from Mālavikā who came from the power of the foresters into that of Vīrasena and was sent by him to the queen. She, for her own part, assumed the red robes and made her way to Agnimitra's court where she found Mālavikā again. She, however, forbore to speak of this, because of a prophecy that Mālavikā would have to endure for one year only the position of a slave before she obtained a husband of equal rank. Agnimitra now issues orders regarding the terms to be granted to the king of Vidarbha, half of whose territory he now assigns to Mādhavasena the brother of Mālavikā, their dominions to lie respectively north and south of the Varadā river.

Now a letter arrives from Puspamitra announcing that Vasumitra, Agnimitra's son by Dhāriṇī, who was appointed as the defender of the sacrificial horse let loose by Puspamitra, his grand-father, has won victory over a cavalry squadron of the Yavanas. Puspamitra further invited the court to be present at the sacrifice which he would now offer.

The queen Dhāriṇī, overjoyed by the news of her son's victory, now sends an attendant to the ladies of the harem with the glad news and asks her to tell Irāvatī of the promise she had made to Mālavikā when she deputed her to perform the ceremony of fertilizing the Asoka,and of her birth also.Irāvatī communicates,though somewhat ungraciously, her concurrence in the arrangement and queen Dhārinī now presents Mālavikā to the king. The play concludes with the king's expressing the hope that he may ever retain his queen's regard and that his subjects may never suffer any calamity while Agnimitra was king.

Appreciation of the plot.

The plot of the Mālavikāgnimitra is a masterpiece of clever construction, where the interest is chiefly concentrated on the central story of the king's love for the maid, and every incident is subordinated to the main theme. The element of conflict, which is of the very essence of drama is mainly external; we see how the queen almost feebly and pathetically opposes the king's attempts to secure the sight of Mālavikā; but finding that the forces ranged against her were too strong for her, she decides to go along the current and make the better of its course rather than endeavour to stem the tide at the risk of a capsize. She cleverly withdraws from the conflict, realising it was her November to the young rival's May, and hopes forlornly that her chance lies in 'playing one new favourite against another'. The irascible Irāvatī, flushed with wine and with the grapes she has gathered in Cupid's vine-yard, next comes to disturb the noon-day tryst, and succeeds for a while to veil the sky with clouds, but a clever ruse of the Vidūṣaka and the queen's serene though not yet quite frank and open acceptance of Mālavikā combine to lift the cloud and the lovers are finally united to the discomfiture of the irascible Irāvatī, who none too calmly resigns to the inevitable. The final stages of the action are cleverly managed and the anagnorisis is a clever piece of concentrated and brief narrative, where from the maids the thread is cleverly taken up by the Parivrājikā.

It will thus be seen that the plot is essentially coherent and organic; there is no bye-plot, so that our attention is focussed upon the central theme. There is further a clever selection of incidents which are presented on the stage, the remaining being relegated to the entr' acts which are brief narratives put in the form of dialogue linking up incidents of the previous act with those of the succeeding one. These scenes—the 'scenes a faire' the scenes which had to be done, which if shirked would cause dumb disappointment in the spectator if they take place behind closed doors and if they are only narrated—these scenes are chosen with a view to arouse and sustain the interest of the audience, and present to us the spectacle of the contending forces at close grapple. These are the great dramatic moments of the story ; and there are also those scenes which have been chosen from the beauty of the spectacle such as the music-hall scene where the lovely Mālavikā draped in diaphanous garments,a vision of sensuous beauty,bursts upon our sight, or the garden-scene where the clever Bakulāvalikā artfully pours love's sugared delights into the ears of the eager maiden and the romance of the lover's noon-day tryst is rendered with all the tenderness and incisive vigour the poet could command.

Characters.

King Agnimitra is commonly criticised as an unheroic hero. He is an elderly person whose 'yeasting youth' is by now expected to clear itself and 'crystal turn again', when love's little follies are laid on the shelf One has however to remember that the poet is here dealing with a historical person and is only furnishing artistic raiment to traditional material. He has given us studies of men not in life's moments of stress and strain but in its 'secluded pleasances and verdurous wooded ways.' And here is a picture of an oriental monarch, devoting his hours of gilded leisure to the pursuit of love and beauty, for benign providence has preserved his father to pursue his ambitious career of conquest and given him a son who even at that tender age has given a foretaste of his masterful and vigorous manhood. So the king has provided himself with a philosophy of tender frailty. "Women are angels wooing, things won are done, joy's soul lies in the doing." The lovely but irascible Irāvatī is passed over and the handsome Mālavikā who has "a very shower of beauty for her earthly dower" now takes her place. He believes what the English poet has said:—

"Who loves but one lassie, just rides for a fall:
The ladies, God bless them! There is safety in numbers;
Love one, love fifty, I have room for them all."

The king does, however, realise that mere lounging and larking is not enough. Witness the quick decision he takes in dealing with the king of Vidarbha, and his last prayer is quite significant. "There is not a blessing that will not be secured by his subjects, while Agnimitra is their protector."

Mālavikā. By birth, beauty and accomplishments in the fine arts, the triune of perfect starriness, Mālavikā is the most attractive of the young maidens drawn by our poet. Her love for the king is as natural as the breaking out of blossoms, and it is this devotion of an innocent and pure maiden that hallows and elevates the love-story above the sordid pruriency of a vulgar liaison. She is extremely clever and intelligent and shows considerable acuteness when she boldly tells the king how she had reason to be afraid of the queen, considering the great fear in which the king himself stood of her. In Mālavikā the poet has given us a rare vision of sensuous beauty. 'Awake for ever in a sweet unrest' that pretty correctly pictures the temper of her mind almost throughout the play.

With regard to the other female characters of the play it may be remarked that although there is very little scope for the development of character, yet every one of them is very carefully individualised. Dhāriṇī possesses dignity and forgiveness, and Irāvatī the passionate jealousy and virulence of a co-wife. The Parivrājikā is the female counterpart of the scheming Vidūṣaka and considering that Mālavikā was her princess, there is nothing vulgar in her joining the plot of the Vidūṣaka.

The liveliest character of the play is the Vidūṣaka who is not merely invested with the traditional frippery of the conventional confidant, but is a being of flesh and blood, ready-witted, quick of discernment and resourceful. He takes almost the principal part in securing Mālavikā for the king: he sets the dancing masters by the ears, cleverly detains Mālavikā after her performance, causes queen Dhāriṇī to suffer a fall from the swing; and pretending to be bitten by a snake secures the queen's signet-ring in order to liberate Mālavikā and her friend from imprisonment. He is not the conventional Vidūṣaka of the Sanskrit play who is continually to be knocked over and set on his feet again for the cheap delight of the audience; and yet much of the humour of the play comes from his witty remarks, from his off-hand manner and from the little audacities of address which he affects from time to time.

TEXT WITH TRANSLATION

॥ श्रीः ॥

मा ल वि का ग्नि मि त्र म्।

प्रथमोऽङ्कः।

एकैश्वर्ये स्थितोऽपि प्रणतबहुफले यः स्वयं कृत्तिवासाः
कान्तासंमिश्रदेहोऽप्यविषयमनसां यः पुरस्ताद्यतीनाम्।
अष्टाभिर्यस्य कृत्स्नं जगदपि तनुभिर्बिभ्रतो नाभिमानः
सन्मार्गालोकनाय व्यपनयतु स वस्तामसीं वृत्तिमीशः॥१॥

(नान्द्यन्ते।)

सूत्रधारः (नेपथ्याभिमुखमवलोक्य)—मारिष इतस्तावत्।

(प्रविश्य।)

पारिपार्श्विकः—भाव अयमस्मि।

सूत्रधारः—अभिहितोऽस्मि परिषदा कालिदासप्रथितवस्तु माल-
६ विकाग्निमित्रं नाम नाटकमस्मिन् वसन्तोत्सवे प्रयोक्तव्यमिति।
तदारभ्यतां सङ्गीतकम्।

पारिपार्श्विकः—मा तावत्। प्रथितयशसां भाससौमिल्लकवि-
९ पुत्रादीनां प्रबन्धानतिक्रम्य वर्तमानकवेः कालिदासस्य क्रियामिमां
द्रष्टुं कथं परिषदो बहुमानः।

सूत्रधारः—अये विवेकविश्रान्तमभिहितम्। पश्य,

पुराणमित्येव न साधु सर्वं
न चापि काव्यं नवमित्यवद्यम्।

Mālavikā and Agnimitra.

PROLOGUE.

May the Lord who, though enjoying absolute sovereignty from which result many blessings to his votaries, yet himself wears an elephant-hide; who although united in body with his beloved, yet excels the ascetics whose minds are free from (pleasures of) sense; in whom there is no pride, although with his eight-fold forms he sustains the universe—may he remove your state of ignorance that you may behold the right way. (1).

(At the end of the Nāndī)

The stage-manager. (*Looking at the curtain*). Ho! mārisa, just come hither.

(Entering)

Actor. Here am I, sir.

Manager. I have been asked by this assembly to stage the play Mālavikāgnimitra composed by the poet Kālidāsa, at this spring-festival. Therefore let music be begun.

Actor. Nay, not so. How do the spectators pass over the plays of poets of established repute, such as Bhāsa, Saumilla, Kaviputra and others, and do great honour to the work of Kālidāsa, a present-day poet?

Manager. You speak thoughtlessly. See

Every old poem is not good simply because it is old; nor is a poem without charm, because it is new; sound critics favour the one or the

सन्तः परीक्ष्यान्यतरद्भजन्ते
मूढः परप्रत्ययनेयबुद्धिः ॥ २ ॥

पारिपार्श्विकः—आर्यमिश्राः प्रमाणम् ।

सूत्रधारः—तेन हि त्वरतां भवान् ।

शिरसा प्रथमगृहीतामाज्ञामिच्छामि परिषदः कर्तुम् ।
देव्या इव धारिण्याः सेवादक्षः परिजनोऽयम् ॥ ३ ॥

(निष्क्रान्तौ ।)

प्रस्तावना ।

(ततः प्रविशति चेटी ।)

४ **चेटी**—आणत्तम्हि देवीए धारिणीए अइरप्पउत्तोवदेसं चलिअं णाम णट्टअं अन्दरेण कीरिसी मालविअत्ति णट्टाअरिअं अज्जगणदासं
६ पुच्छिदुं । ता जाव संगीदसालं गच्छेमि । (इति परिक्रामति ।)
[आज्ञप्तास्मि देव्या धारिण्या अचिरप्रयुक्तोपदेशं चलितं नाम नाट्यमन्तरेण कीदृशी मालविकेति नाट्याचार्यमार्यगणदासं प्रष्टुम् । तद्यावत्सङ्गीतशालां गच्छामि ।]

(ततः प्रविशत्याभरणहस्ता द्वितीया चेटी ।)

प्रथमा (द्वितीयां दृष्ट्वा)—हला कोमुदिए कुदो दे इअं धीरदा ।
१२ जं समीवेण वि मं अदिक्कमंती इदो दिट्ठिं ण देसि ।
[सखि कौमुदिके, कुतस्त इयं धीरता । यत्समीपेनापि मामतिक्रामन्तीतो दृष्टिं न ददासि ।]

१५ **द्वितीया**—अम्मो बउलावलिआ । सहि इदं देवीए सिप्पिसआसादो आणीदं णाअमुद्दासणाहं अंगुलीअअं सिणिद्धं णिज्झाअन्ती तुह उवालम्भे पडिदम्हि । [अम्मो बकुलावलिका । सखि इदं देव्याः
१८ शिल्पिसकाशादानीतं नागमुद्रासनाथमङ्गुलीयकं स्निग्धं निध्यायन्ती तवोपालम्भे पतितास्मि ।]

बकुलावलिका (विलोक्य)—ठाणे खु सज्जदि दिट्ठी । इमिणा

other, after (proper) examination ; while a blockhead is guided by another's judgment. (2)

Actor. You speak the truth, sir.

Manager. Well then, make haste.

I long to carry out the order of the spectators which I have already received with my (bowed) head, even as this attendant of queen Dhāriṇī, intent on serving her. (3)

(Exit).

End of the Prologue

(Enter a maid).

Maid. I am ordered by queen Dhāriṇī to ascertain from the noble Ganadāsa, our dancing master, what degree of proficiency Mālavikā has attained in the Calita at which she is lately taking lessons. So I will proceed to the music hall. *(Walks round).*

(Enter another maid with an ornament in her hand).

First. *(Seeing the other)* Hola, Kaumudikā, what makes you so serious that you do not see me although you pass so close to me ?

Second. Ho, Bakulāvalikā ! Friend, I was intently looking at this ring with its serpent-seal, (just) brought from the jeweller's, and so I fell under your reproof.

Bakulāvalikā. *(Observing)* It is but proper that

२१ अंगुलीअएण उब्भिण्णकिरणकेसरेण कुसुमिदो विअ दे अग्गहत्थो
पडिभादि । [स्थाने खलु सज्जति दृष्टिः । अनेनाङ्गुलीयकेनोद्भिन्न-
२४ किरणकेसरेण कुसुमित इव तेऽग्रहस्तः प्रतिभाति ।]

कौमुदिका—हला तुमं कहिं पत्थिदासि । [हला त्वं कुत्र प्रस्थितासि ।]

बकुलावलिका—देवीए वअणेण णट्टाआरिअं अज्जगणदासं पुच्छिदुं
२७ उवदेसग्गहणे कीरिसी मालविअत्ति । [देव्या वचनेन नाट्याचार्य-
मार्यगणदासं प्रष्टुमुपदेशग्रहणे कीदृशी मालविकेति ।]

कौमुदिका—हला ईरिसेण वावारेण असण्णिहिदा वि दिट्ठा कहं
३० एसा भट्टिणा । [हला ईदृशेन व्यापारेणासन्निहितापि दृष्टा कथमेषा
भर्त्रा ।]

बकुलावलिका—आम् देवीए पस्सगदो सो जणो चित्ते दिट्ठो । [आम् देव्याः पार्श्वगतः स जनश्चित्रे दृष्टः ।]

३३ **कौमुदिका**—कहं विअ । [कथमिव ।]

बकुलावलिका—सुणाहि । चित्तसालं गदा देवी पच्चग्गवण्णराअं
चित्तलेहं आलोअन्ती चिरं चिट्ठदि । तस्सिं अन्तरे उवट्ठिदो भट्टा ।
३६ [शृणु । चित्रशालां गता देवी प्रत्यग्रवर्णरागां चित्ररेखामालोकयन्ती
चिरं तिष्ठति । तस्मिन्नन्तरे उपस्थितो भर्ता ।]

कौमुदिका—तदो तदो । [ततस्ततः ।]

३९ **बकुलावलिका**—उवआराणन्दरं एक्कासणोवविट्ठेण भट्टिणा चित्त-
गदाए देवीए परिअणमज्झगदं आसण्णपरिआरिणिं देक्खिअ देवी
पुच्छिदा । [उपचारानन्तरमेकासनोपविष्टेन भर्त्रा चित्रगताया देव्याः
४२ परिजनमध्यगतामासन्नपरिचारिणीं दृष्ट्वा देवी पृष्टा ।]

कौमुदिका—किंत्ति । [किमिति ।]

बकुलावलिका—देवि अपुव्वा इअं दारिआ तुह आसण्णा
४५ लिहिदा किंणामहेअत्ति । [देवि अपूर्वेयं दारिका तवासन्ना लिखिता
किंनामधेयेति ।]

your eyes were rivetted on it. With this ring, with its filaments of rays upshooting, the palm of your hand appears to have bloomed.

Kaumudikā. Friend, where are you going ?

Bakulāvalikā. I am going by the queen's orders to the dancing-master, the noble Ganadāsa to inquire what sort of pupil Mālavikā has shown herself.

Kaumudikā. Friend, how could she have been seen by his majesty, though she was kept out of the way by such an employment. ?

Bakulāvalikā. Why, she was seen in a picture, painted by the side of the queen.

Kaumudikā. How ?

Bakulāvalikā. Listen, the queen had gone to the painting-hall and stood looking at the picture (shining) with the freshly-laid colours. And at that very moment entered his majesty.

Kaumudikā. well, what happened next ?

Bakulāvalikā. Then after the usual salutations, his majesty sat down in the same seat with the queen, and saw in the picture, among the queen's retinue, a maid ·lose to her, and asked the queen—

Kaumudika. Pray, what ?

Bakulavālikā. 'What is the name of this extraordinary girl painted close to you, my queen '?

कौमुदिका—णं आकिदिविसेसेसु आदरो पदं करेदि। तदो तदो।
४८ [नन्वाकृतिविशेषेष्वादरः पदं करोति। ततस्ततः।]

बकुलावलिका—तदो अवहीरिदवअणो भट्टा संकिदो देवीं पुणो
पुणो णिब्बन्धिदुं पउत्तो। जाव देवी ण कहेदि दाव कुमारीए वसुल-
५१ च्छीए आचक्खिदं आउत्त एसा मालविअत्ति। [ततोऽवधीरितवचनो
भर्ता शङ्कितो देवीं पुनः पुनर्निर्बन्द्धुं प्रवृत्तः। यावद्देवी न कथयति
तावत्कुमार्या वसुलक्ष्म्याख्यातमावुत्त एषा मालविकेति।]

५४ **कौमुदिका** (सस्मितम्) सरिसं खु बालभावस्स। अदो वरं कहेहि।
[सदृशं खलु बालभावस्य। अतः परं कथय।]

बकुलावलिका—किं अण्णं। सम्पदं मालविआ सविसेसं भट्टिणो
५७ दंसणपहादो रक्खीअदि।
[किमन्यत्। साम्प्रतं मालविका सविशेषं भर्तुर्दर्शनपथाद्रक्ष्यते।]

कौमुदिका—हला अणुचिट्ठ अत्तणो णिओअं। अहं वि एदं
६० अङ्गुलीअअं देवीए उवणइस्सं। [हला अनुतिष्ठात्मनो नियोगम्।
अहमप्येतदङ्गुलीयकं देव्या उपनेष्यामि।

(इति निष्क्रान्ता।)

६३ **बकुलावलिका**—(परिक्रम्यावलोक्य च।) एसो णट्टाअरिओ
अज्जगणदासो संगीदसालादो दाणिं णिक्कमइ। जाव से अत्ताणं
दंसेमि। [एष नाट्याचार्य आर्यगणदासः सङ्गीतशालात इदानीं
निष्क्रामति। यावदस्यात्मानं दर्शयामि। (इति परिक्रामति।)

(प्रविश्य) **गणदासः**—कामं खलु सर्वस्यापि कुलविद्या बहुमता।
६९ न पुनरस्माकं नाट्यं प्रति मिथ्यागौरवम्। कुतः

देवानामिदमामनन्ति मुनयः कान्तं क्रतुं चाक्षुषं
रुद्रेणेदमुमाकृतव्यतिकरे स्वाङ्गे विभक्तं द्विधा।

Kaumudikā. Surely such forms of surpassing loveliness engage one's admiration. Pray, tell me further.

Bakulāvalikā. But finding that his words were not heeded, his majesty grew suspicious and began to importune the queen. And when the queen would not reply, the princess Vasulakṣmī made answer: "Brother, this is Mālavikā."

Kaumudikā. (*smilingly*) How like a child! Tell me what happened next.

Bakulāvalikā. What else, but that now Mālavikā is particularly guarded from the sight of his majesty.

Kaumudikā. Come now, do your errand. I, on my part, will take this ring to the queen.

(*Exit.*)

Bakulāvalikā. (*Walking round and looking.*) Here is the dancing-master, the noble Gaṇadāsa, just stepping out of the music-hall. So I will show myself. (*Walks round.*)

(*Entering.*)

Gaṇadāsa. It is true that everyone regards very highly the science affected by his family; but then the importance I attach to the dramatic art is not without foundation. For

sages look upon this as a sacrifice that is
pleasing to the eyes of the gods; Rudra has
divided it into two parts in his own person which
is blended with that of Umā. Herein are to be
observed the actions of the people prompted by

त्रैगुण्योद्भवमत्र लोकचरितं नानारसं दृश्यते
नाट्यं भिन्नरुचेर्जनस्य बहुधाप्येकं समाराधनम् ॥४॥

बकुलावलिका—(उपसृत्य) अज्ज वन्दामि । [आर्य वन्दे ।]

गणदासः—भद्रे चिरं जीव ।

बकुलावलिका—अज्ज देवी पुच्छादि अवि उवदेसग्गहणे णादिकिलेसेदि वो सिस्सा मालविअत्ति । [आर्य देवी पृच्छति अप्युपदेशग्रहणे नातिक्लेशयति वः शिष्या मालविकेति ।]

गणदासः—विज्ञाप्यतां देवी परमनिपुणा मेधाविनी चेति । किं बहुना ।

यद्यत्प्रयोगविषये भाविकमुपदिश्यते मया तस्यै ।
तत्तद्विशेषकरणात्प्रत्युपदिशतीव मे बाला ॥५॥

बकुलावलिका (आत्मगतम्)—इरावदिं अदिक्कमन्तिं विअ पेक्खामि । (प्रकाशम्) किदत्था दाणिं वो सिस्सा जस्सिं गुरुअणो एव्वं तुस्सदि । [इरावतीमतिक्रामन्तीमिव पश्यामि । कृतार्थेदानीं वः शिष्या यस्यां गुरुजन एवं तुष्यति ।]

गणदासः—भद्रे तद्विधानामसुलभत्वात्पृच्छामि । कुतो देव्यास्तत्पात्रमानीतम् ।

बकुलावलिका—अत्थि देवीए वण्णावरो भादा वीरसेणो णाम । सो भट्टिणा अन्दवालदुग्गे णम्मदाऊले ठाविदो । तेण सिप्पाहिआरे इअं जोग्गा दारिअत्ति भइणीए उवाअणं पेसिदा । [अस्ति देव्या वर्णावरो भ्राता वीरसेनो नाम । स भर्त्रा अन्तपालदुर्गे नर्मदाकूले स्थापितः । तेन शिल्पाधिकार इयं योग्या दारिकेति भगिन्यै उपायनं प्रेषिता ।]

गणदासः (स्वगतम्)—आकृतिविशेषप्रत्ययादेनामनूनवस्तुकां संभावयामि । (प्रकाशम्) भद्रे मयापि यशस्विना भवितव्यम् । पश्य

the three qualities, and exhibiting various sentiments : the dramatic art is the one chief amusement of the people, albeit they have diverse tastes. (4).

Bakulavālikā. (*approaching*) Noble sir, I salute you.

Gaṇadāsa. My good girl, may you live long.

Bakulāvalikā. Noble sir, the queen inquires if Mālavikā does not cause great trouble at her lessons.

Gaṇadāsa. Say to the queen that she is very efficient and clever.

Whatever gesture in the mimetic art is taught by me to her, that the girl, as it were, teaches to me in return by improving upon it. (5)

Bakulāvalikā. (*To herself*) she seems to me to surpass Irāvatī. (*Aloud*) Your pupil may well be looked upon as a success, since her teacher is so well satisfied with her.

Gaṇadāsa. Good girl, as such people are very difficult to meet with, I ask from where did the queen secure this rare person.

Bakulāvalikā. The queen has a brother of inferior caste, Vīrasena by name. He has been placed, by his majesty in command of a fortress on the frontier of his kingdom on the banks of the Narmadā. He it was who, thinking that the girl was fit to receive instruction in the fine arts, sent her on to his sister as a present.

Gaṇadāsa. (*To himself*) Assured by her distinguished appearance I judge that she comes of a noble family. (*Aloud*) Good girl, I am sure to succeed (with her). See

पात्रविशेषे न्यस्तं गुणान्तरं व्रजति शिल्पमाधातुः ।
जलमिव समुद्रशुक्तौ मुक्ताफलतां पयोदस्य ॥६॥

बकुलावलिका—अज्ज कहिं दाणिं वो सिस्सा। [आर्य कुत्रेदानीं वः शिष्या।]

गणदासः—इदानीमेव पञ्चाङ्गाभिनयमुपदिश्य मया विश्रम्यतामित्यभिहिता दीर्घिकावलोकनगवाक्षगता प्रवातमासेवमाना तिष्ठति।

बकुलावलिका—तेण हि अणुजाणादु मं अज्जो। जाव से अज्जस्स परिदोसणिवेदणेण उच्छाहं वड्ढेमि। [तेन ह्यनुजानातु मामार्यः। यावदस्या आर्यस्य परितोषनिवेदनेनोत्साहं वर्धयामि।

गणदासः—दृश्यतां सखी। अहमपि लब्धक्षणः स्वगृहं गच्छामि।

(इति निष्क्रान्तौ।)

मिश्रविष्कम्भकः।

(ततः प्रविशत्येकान्तस्थितपरिजनो मन्त्रिणा लेखहस्तेनान्वास्यमानो राजा।)

राजा (अनुवाचितलेखममात्यमवलोक्य।)—वाहतक, किं प्रतिपद्यते वैदर्भः।

अमात्यः—देव, आत्मविनाशम्।

राजा—लिखितं निर्देशमिदानीं श्रोतुमिच्छामि।

अमात्यः—इदमिदानीमनेन प्रतिलिखितम्—"पूज्येनाहमादिष्टः 'भवतः पितृव्यपुत्रः कुमारो माधवसेनः प्रतिश्रुतसम्बन्धो ममोपान्तिकमागच्छन्नन्तरा त्वदीयेनान्तपालेनावस्कन्द्य गृहीतः। स त्वया मदपेक्षया सकलत्रसोदर्यो मोचयितव्य' इति। तन्न वो न विदितं यत्तुल्याभिजनेषु भूमिहरेषु राज्ञां प्रवृत्तिरीदृक्। अतोऽत्र मध्यस्थः पूज्यो भवितु-

The skill of a teacher imparted to a worthy pupil attains greater excellence, as the water of a cloud is turned into a pearl in a sea-shell. (6)

Bakulāvalikā. Noble sir, where is your pupil, now?

Gaṇadāsa. Only a moment ago, after instructing her in the five-fold ways of acting, I gave her permission to retire, and she is now enjoying the sweet gentle breeze from the window which commands the view of the lake.

Bakulāvalikā. Then, noble sir. give me leave to go, so that I might stimulate her zeal by informing her how well the noble teacher is satisfied with her.

Gaṇadāsa. Well, then, go and see your friend. Meanwhile, now that I have leisure I will go home. *(exeunt both).*

End of the Misraviskambhaka.

(Enter king, with his attendants standing apart and his minister, holding a letter in his hand, in attendance.)

King. (*Looking at the minister who has read the letter*) Vāhataka, what does the Vidharbha king think of doing ?

Minister. His own ruin, your majesty.

King. Well, I would like to hear the dispatch.

Minister. This is what he writes in reply. " The revered sire orders me that Prince Mādhavasena, my uncle's son, who has promised alliance with yourself was, while going to you, attacked on the way by my frontier-guards and put into prison ; and that I should, out of regard for you, release him along with his wife and sister." But you know very well that kings act in this way towards their kinsmen of a common extraction. And therefore it behoves you to remain neutral in this

२१ मर्हति। सोदर्या पुनरस्य ग्रहणविप्लवे विनष्टा। तदन्वेषणाय प्रयतिष्ये। अथावश्यमेव माधवसेनः पूज्येन मोचयितव्यः, श्रूयतामभिसन्धिः।

मौर्यसचिवं विमुञ्चति यदि पूज्यः संयतं मम श्यालम्।
मोक्ता माधवसेनं ततोऽहमपि बन्धनात्सद्यः" ॥७॥ इति।

राजा (सरोषम्)—कथं कार्यविनिमयेन मयि व्यवहरत्यनात्मज्ञः। वाहतक, प्रकृत्यमित्रः प्रतिकूलचारी च मे वैदर्भः। तद्यातव्यपक्षे
३ स्थितस्य पूर्वसङ्कल्पितमुन्मूलनाय वीरसेनप्रमुखं दण्डचक्रमाज्ञापय।

अमात्यः—यदाज्ञापयति देवः।

राजा—अथवा किं भवान् मन्यते।

६ **अमात्यः**—शास्त्रदृष्टमाह देवः। कुतः

अचिराधिष्ठितराज्यः शत्रुः प्रकृतिष्वरूढमूलत्वात्।
नवसंरोहणशिथिलस्तरुरिव सुकरः समुद्धर्तुम् ॥ ८ ॥

राजा—तेन ह्यवितथं तन्त्रकारवचनम्। इदमेव निमित्तमादाय समुद्योज्यतां सेनापतिः।

३ **अमात्यः**—तथा।

(इति निष्क्रान्तः। परिजनश्च यथाव्यापारं राजानमभितः स्थितः।)

(प्रविश्य) **विदूषकः**—आणत्तोम्हि तत्तहोदा रण्णा। गोदम चिन्तेहि
६ दाव उवाअं जह मे जदिच्छादिट्ठपडिकिदी मालविआ पच्चक्खदंसणा होदित्ति। मए वि तं तह किदं। जाव से णिवेदेमि। (इति परिक्रामति।)

आज्ञप्तोऽस्मि तत्रभवता राज्ञा। गौतम चिन्तय तावदुपायं यथा मे

matter. As to his sister, she disappeared in the confusion that ensued at the time of his capture; and I would make every effort to recover her. Now if you desire me to release Mādhavasena, then listen to (my) terms :—

if you release my brother-in-law the minister of Maurya who suffers imprisonment (at your hands) then would I instantly release Mādhavasena from confinement. (7).

King. (*Furiously*) Would the fool bargain with me by exchange of services? Well, Vāhataka, this king of Vidharbha is my natural enemy and dares to oppose me. So give orders that our army, already kept ready under the command of Vīrasena, should extirpate him, now that he stands in the position of an (open) enemy.

Minister. As your majesty commands.

King. Well, but how do you think (about it)?

Minister. What your majesty says well accords with the teaching of politics; for

an enemy who has just come to the throne and therefore has not secured the devotion of his subjects is like a freshly planted tree that has not struck its roots deep into the soil : both can with ease be extirpated (8).

King. If that is so, may the dictum of the politicians come true. With this as the cause (of hostilities) let our commander-in-chief get ready to act.

Minister. As your majesty commands. (*Exit.*)

(*The attendants stand round the king, engaged in their respective work.*)

(*Entering*)

Vidūsaka. His Majesty has ordered me : 'Gautama, do you devise means to secure me the sight of Mālavikā in person, whose likeness was just by chance

९ यदृच्छादृष्टप्रतिकृतिर्मालविका प्रत्यक्षदर्शना भवतीति। मयापि तत्तथा कृतम्। यावदस्मै निवेदयामि।]

राजा (विदूषकं दृष्ट्वा)–अयमपरः कार्यान्तरसाचिव्योऽस्मानुपस्थितः।

१२ **विदूषकः** (उपसृत्य)—वड्ढदु भवं। [वर्धतां भवान्।]

राजा (सशिरःकम्पम्)—इत आस्यताम्। (विदूषक उपविष्टः।)

राजा—वयस्य कच्चिदुपेयोपायदर्शने व्यापृतं ते प्रज्ञाचक्षुः।

१५ **विदूषकः**—पओअसिद्धिं पुच्छ। [प्रयोगसिद्धिं पृच्छ।]

राजा—कथमिव।

विदूषकः(कर्णे)—एव्वं विअ। [एवमिव।]

१८ **राजा**—साधु वयस्य निपुणमुपक्रान्तम्। इदानीं दुरधिगमसिद्धावप्यस्मिन्नारम्भे वयमाशंसामहे। कुतः

अर्थं सप्रतिबन्धं प्रभुरधिगन्तुं सहायवानेव।
दृश्यं तमसि न पश्यति दीपेन विना सचक्षुरपि ॥ ९ ॥

(नेपथ्ये)

अलमलं बहु विकत्थ्य। राज्ञः समक्षमेवावयोरधरोत्तरव्यक्तिर्भविष्यति।

३ **राजा**—सखे त्वत्सुनीतिपादपस्य कुसुममुद्भिन्नम्।

विदूषकः—फलं वि देक्खिस्ससि। [फलमपि द्रक्ष्यसि।]

(ततः प्रविशति कञ्चुकी।)

६ **कञ्चुकी**—देव अमात्यो विज्ञापयति। अनुष्ठिता प्रभोराज्ञा। एतौ पुनर्हरदत्तगणदासौ

seen by me.' And I, on my part, have done it. So I will speak to him. (*Walks about*).

King. (*Seeing Vidūṣaka*) Here comes the minister who looks to another branch of our affairs.

Vidūsaka. (*Approaching*) Prosperity attend your majesty.

King. (*Nodding his head*) Sit here.

(*Vidūṣaka takes a seat.*)

King. Well, friend, is your eye of wisdom engaged in finding out means for the attainment of the desired object ?

Vidūsaka. Rather ask about the success of the enterprise.

King. What do you mean ?

Vidūsaka. (*Whispers in his ear.*) It is thus.

King. Good, my friend. You have begun wisely. Now I feel inspired with hope for the success of this venture, albeit success in it is so difficult to attain. For

only with the help of some friend can one
attain an object which is beset with obstacles ;
no one, even though he has the use of his eyes,
can see an object in the dark without the help
of light. (9).

(*Behind the scenes.*)

Enough of bragging. In the presence of his majesty it will be decided as to which of us is inferior or superior.

King. Friend, here has bloomed a flower on the tree of your fine intrigue.

Vidūsaka. You will see the fruit also.

(*Then enter the chamberlain.*)

Chamberlain. King, the minister begs to inform you that your order is carried out. Now these two gentlemen Haradatta and Gaṇadāsa,

उभावभिनयाचार्यौ परस्परजयोद्यतौ ।
त्वां द्रष्टुमिच्छतः साक्षाद्भावाविव शरीरिणौ ॥ १० ॥

राजा—प्रवेशय तौ ।

कञ्चुकी—यदाज्ञापयति देवः । (इति निष्क्रम्य पुनस्ताभ्यां सह प्रविश्य ।) इत इतो भवन्तौ ।

हरदत्तः (राजानमवलोक्य)—अहो दुरासदो राजमहिमा । तथाहि

न च न परिचितो न चाप्यगम्य-
श्चकितमुपैमि तथापि पार्श्वमस्य ।
सलिलनिधिरिव प्रतिक्षणं मे
भवति स एव नवो नवोऽयमक्ष्णोः ॥ ११ ॥

गणदासः—महत् खलु पुरुषाकारमिदं ज्योतिः । तथा हि—

द्वारे नियुक्तपुरुषानुमतप्रवेशः
सिंहासनान्तिकचरेण सहोपसर्पन् ।
तेजोभिरस्य विनिवर्तितदृष्टिपातै-
र्वाक्यादृते पुनरिव प्रतिवारितोऽस्मि ॥ १२ ॥

कञ्चुकी—एष देवः । उपसर्पतां भवन्तौ ।

उभौ (उपसृत्य ।)—विजयतां देवः ।

राजा—स्वागतं भवद्भ्याम् । (परिजनं विलोक्य ।) आसने तावदत्रभवतोः । [उभौ परिजनोपनीतयोरासनयोरुपविष्टौ ।]

राजा—किमिदं शिष्योपदेशकाले युगपदाचार्ययोरुपस्थानम् ।

गणदासः—देव श्रूयताम् । मया तीर्थादभिनयविद्या शिक्षिता । दत्तप्रयोगश्चास्मि । देवेन देव्या च परिगृहीतः ।

both teachers of acting, each eager to gain victory over the other, desire to see you—as if they are two dramatic sentiments embodied. (10)

King. Usher them in.

Chamberlain. As the king commands. *(Goes out and then again enters with them.)* This way, gentlemen, this way.

Haradatta. *(Looking at the king)* How awe-inspiring the majesty of the king! For

not that he is not familiar to me, nor is he not accessible, and yet I am all in a flutter as I advance towards him; though the same, he seems to change every moment before my eyes, like the mighty ocean. (11)

Gaṇadāsa. This is a great luminary masquerading in human form. Thus

although the door-guards allowed my entrance and I am advancing towards him with the attendant that moves about his throne, yet without words of prohibition, I feel forbidden by his splendour that repels my gaze. (12)

Chamberlain. Here is his majesty; advance, gentlemen.

Both. *(Advancing)* Victory to his majesty.

King. You are welcome, sirs. *(Looking at the attendant)* Bring seats for the honoured gentlemen.

(Both occupy the seats brought by the attendants.)

King. How comes it, that both of you come here together, at a time when you should be instructing your pupils?

Gaṇadāsa. Listen, your majesty; I have learnt the art of acting from a noble teacher and I have given lesson in that art and your majesty and the queen have favoured me.

राजा—दृढं जाने । ततः किम् ।

गणदासः—सोऽहममुना हरदत्तेन प्रधानपुरुषसमक्षमयं न मे पादरजसापि तुल्य इत्यधिक्षिप्तः ।

हरदत्तः—देव अयमेव मयि प्रथमं परिवादकरः । अत्रभवतः किल मम च समुद्रपल्वलयोरिवान्तरमिति । तदत्रभवानिमं मां च शास्त्रे प्रयोगे च विमृशतु । देव एव नौ विशेषज्ञः प्राश्निकः ।

विदूषकः—समत्थं पडिण्णादं । [समर्थं प्रतिज्ञातम् ।]

गणदासः—प्रथमः कल्पः । अवहितो देवः श्रोतुमर्हति ।

राजा—तिष्ठतु तावत् । पक्षपातमत्र देवी मन्यते । तत्तस्याः पण्डितकौशिक्या सहितायाः समक्षमेव न्याय्यो व्यवहारः ।

विदूषकः—सुट्ठु भवं भणादि । [सुष्ठु भवान् भणति ।]

आचार्यौ—यद्देवाय रोचते ।

राजा—मौद्गल्य, अमुं प्रस्तावं निवेद्य पण्डितकौशिक्या सार्धमाहूयतां देवी ।

कञ्चुकी—यदाज्ञापयति देवः । (इति निष्क्रम्य सपरिव्राजिकया देव्या सह प्रविश्य ।) इत इतो देवी ।

देवी (परिव्राजिकां विलोक्य)—भअवदि, हरदत्तस्स गणदासस्स अ संरम्भे कहं पेक्खसि ।

[भगवति हरदत्तस्य गणदासस्य च संरम्भे कथं पश्यसि ।]

परिव्राजिका—अलं स्वपक्षावसादशङ्कया । न परिहीयते प्रतिद्वन्द्विनो गणदासः ।

देवी—जइ वि एव्वं तह वि राअपरिग्गहो से पहाणत्तणं उवहरादि ।

[यद्यप्येवं तथापि राजपरिग्रहोऽस्य प्रधानत्वमुपहरति ।]

King. That I know full well. What of that?

Ganadāsa. And yet I was grossly insulted in the presence of prominent courtiers by Haradatta with the words: 'You are not the equal of the dust on my feet.'

Haradatta. King, it was he who started abusing me saying 'Your reverence is to me what a puddle is to the ocean!' So your highness should examine us both in the theory and practice of the art; for your highness is the only discerning judge of us both.

Vidūṣaka. A fair proposal that.

Gaṇadāsa. A capital idea! Let your highness listen to us attentively.

King. Better wait. The queen may suspect partiality in the case. So it would be only just to decide the matter in her presence and in that of the learned Kauśikī.

Vidūṣaka. You speak proper.

The teachers. Just as it pleases your highness.

King. Maudgalya, speak to the queen of this matter and call her along with the learned Kauśikī.

Chamberlain. As your majesty commands. (*Goes out and then enters along with the queen and the Parivrājikā*). This way, this way, queen.

Queen. (*Looking at the Parivrajikā.*) Revered lady, what do you think of this contest between Haradatta and Gaṇadāsa?

Parivrājikā. Have no apprehensions regarding the success of your side. For Ganadāsa is not inferior to his rival.

Queen. Even if that is so, yet the king's favour gives him the advantage.

परिव्राजिका—अयि राज्ञीशब्दभाजनमात्मानमपि तावाच्चिन्तयतु भवती । पश्य

आतिमात्रभासुरत्वं पुष्यति भानोः परिग्रहादनलः ।
अधिगच्छति महिमानं चन्द्रोऽपि निशापरिगृहीतः॥१३॥

विदूषकः—अविहा अविहा उवट्ठिदा पीठमद्दिअं पण्डिदकोसिअं पुरोकदुअ देवी । [अविहा अविहा उपस्थिता पीठमर्दिकां पण्डित-
३ कौशिकीं पुरस्कृत्य देवी ।]

राजा—पश्याम्येनाम् । यैषा

मङ्गलालङ्कृता भाति कौशिक्या यतिवेषया ।
त्रयी विग्रहवत्येव सममध्यात्मविद्यया ॥ १४ ॥

परिव्राजिका (उपसृत्य)—विजयतां देवः ।

राजा—भगवति अभिवादये ।

३ **परिव्राजिका**—

महासारप्रसवयोः सदृशक्षमयोर्द्वयोः ।
धारिणीभूतधारिण्योर्भव भर्ता शरच्छतम् ॥ १५ ॥

देवी—जेदु अज्जउत्तो । [जयत्वार्यपुत्रः ।]

राजा—स्वागतं देव्यै । (परिव्राजिकां विलोक्य ।) भगवति
३ क्रियतामासनपरिग्रहः । (सर्वे यथार्हमुपविशन्ति ।)

राजा—भगवति अत्रभवतोर्हरदत्तगणदासयोः परस्परविज्ञानसङ्घर्षो जातः । तदत्र भगवत्या प्राश्निकपदमध्यासितव्यम् ।

६ **परिव्राजिका** (सस्मितम्)—अलमुपालम्भेन । पत्तने विद्यमानेऽपि ग्रामे रत्नपरीक्षा ।

Parivrājikā. Ah, bethink yourself that you have a right to the title of 'Queen.' Don't you see

that if fire attains its extreme refulgence through the Sun's favour, the Moon too acquires greatness when favoured by the night. (13)

Vidūsaka. Holla, holla, here comes the queen along with her confidant, the learned Kauśikī.

King. I see her, who

being decked with auspicious ornaments, and accompanied by Kauśikī in the garb of an ascetic, looks like the sacred triad embodied, accompanied by the science of metaphysics. (14).

Parivrājikā. (*Advancing*) Victory attend your highness.

King. Revered lady, I salute thee.

Parivrājikā.

May you be, for hundred years, the husband of queen Dhāriṇī and of the Earth,—the one who has given birth to a heroic son and is possessed of great forgiveness, and the other that yields abundant crops owing to plenty of showers and is equally forgiving. (15)

Queen. Victory to my lord !

King. Welcome, queen. (*Looking at the Parivrājikā*) Revered lady, please to take a seat.

(*All take seats in due order.*)

King. Revered lady, there is a dispute between the noble Haradatta and Gaṇadāsa as to which of them is superior in point of learning. So the revered lady should act as their judge.

Parivrājikā. (*Smiling*) Enough of your taunts. When a town is near, would you have a jewel tested in a village ?

राजा—मा मैवम् । पण्डितकौशिकी खलु भगवती । पक्षपातिनावनयोरहं च देवी च ।

आचार्यौ—सम्यगाह देवः । मध्यस्था भगवती गुणदोषौ नः परिच्छेत्तुमर्हति ।

राजा—तेन हि प्रस्तूयतां विवादः ।

परिव्राजिका—देव प्रयोगप्रधानं हि नाट्यशास्त्रम् । किमत्र वाग्व्यवहारेण ।

राजा—कथं वा देवी मन्यते ।

देवी—जइ मं पुच्छसि एदाणं विवादो एव्व ण मे रोअदि ।
[यदि मां पृच्छसि, एतयोर्विवाद एव न मे रोचते ।]

गणदासः—न मां देवी समानविद्यतः परिभवनीयमनुमन्तुमर्हति ।

विदूषकः—होदु देक्खामो उरब्भसंवादं । किं मुहा वेअणदाणेण ।
[भवतु द्रक्ष्याम उरभ्रसम्पातम् । किं मुधा वेतनदानेन ।]

देवी—णं कलहप्पिओसि । [ननु कलहप्रियोऽसि ।]

विदूषकः—मा दाव । अण्णोण्णकलहिदाणं मत्तहत्थीणं एक्कदरस्सिं अणिज्जिदे कदो उवसमो । [मा तावत् । अन्योन्यकलहितयोर्मत्तहस्तिनोरेकतरस्मिन्ननिर्जिते कुत उपशमः ।]

राजा—ननु स्वाङ्गसौष्ठवाभिनयमुभयोर्दृष्टवती भगवती ।

परिव्राजिका—अथ किम् ।

राजा—तदिदानीमतः परं किमाभ्यां प्रत्याययितव्यम् ।

परिव्राजिका—तदेव वक्तुकामास्मि ।

श्लिष्टा क्रिया कस्यचिदात्मसंस्था
सङ्क्रान्तिरन्यस्य विशेषयुक्ता ।

King. Do not say so. For the revered lady should not forget that she is the learned Kauśikī. We two, the queen and myself, are not free from bias towards them.

The teachers. His majesty speaks the truth. The revered lady being impartial deserves to gauge our merits and demerits.

King. Well then, why not start the disputation?

Parivrājikā. Your majesty, the dramatic art is pre-eminently a practical art. What use is a mere verbal disputation?

King. But what is the view of our queen?

Queen. If you ask me, I do not relish an argument itself between them.

Gaṇadāsa. The queen should not consider me as one who is likely to suffer defeat from one who is only my equal in learning.

Vidūṣaka. Well, then let us see the fight of the two rams. What is the use of giving them wages for nothing?

Queen. You are ever fond of squabbles!

Vidūṣaka. No, not that. But where can there be peace until one of two wild elephants that have been quarrelling, is completely vanquished?

King. But I believe the revered lady has witnessed the graceful acting exhibited by them in their own person.

Parivrājikā. Well, what of that?

King. What more have they to bring forward by way of proof?

Parivrājikā. That is exactly what I desire to point out.

Some exhibit acting very well in their own person; while others show greater skill in im-

यस्योभयं साधु स शिक्षकाणां
धुरि प्रतिष्ठापयितव्य एव ॥ १६ ॥

विदूषकः—सुदं भअवदीए वअणं अज्जेहिं । एसो पिण्डिदत्थो उवदेसदंसणेण णिण्णओत्ति । [श्रुतं भगवत्या वचनमार्याभ्याम् । एष पिण्डितार्थः उपदेशदर्शनेन निर्णय इति ।]

हरदत्तः—परमुचितं नः ।

गणदासः—देवि एवं स्थितम् ।

देवी—जदा उण मन्दमेहा सिस्सा उवदेसं मलिणेदि तदा आअरिअस्स दोसो णं । [यदा पुनर्मन्दमेधा शिष्योपदेशं मलिनयति तदाचार्यस्य दोषो नु ।]

राजा—देवि एवमुपपद्यते ।

गणदासः—विनेतुरद्रव्यपरिग्रहोऽपि बुद्धिलाघवं प्रकाशयति ।

देवी (स्वगतम्)—कहं दाणिं । (गणदासं विलोक्य जनान्तिकम् ।) अलं अज्जउत्तस्स उच्छाहकारणं मणोरहं पूरिअ । (प्रकाशं ।) विरम णिरत्थआदो आरम्भादो ।

[कथमिदानीम् । अलमार्यपुत्रस्योत्साहकारणं मनोरथं पूरयित्वा । विरम निरर्थकादारम्भात् ।]

विदूषकः—सुट्ठु होदी भणादि । भो गणदास सङ्गीदावदेसेण सरस्सईउवाअणमोदआइं खादमाणस्स किं दे सुलहणिग्गहेण विवादेण ।

[सुष्ठु भवती भणति । भो गणदास सङ्गीतापदेशेन सरस्वत्युपायनमोदकानि खादतः किं ते सुलभनिग्रहेण विवादेन ।]

गणदासः—सत्यमयमेवार्थो देवीवचनस्य । श्रूयतामवसरप्राप्तमिदम् ।

parting (that art) to another ; he who excels in both these qualities deserves a pre-eminent place among teachers. (16).

Vidūsaka. My noble friends have heard the revered lady. So then, this is the sum (of what she says): the decision will be given after judging of your teaching through its exhibition (in a performance).

Haradatta. That is quite proper to us.

Ganadāsa. Queen, so it comes to that.

Queen. But if a dull-witted pupil brings disgrace on the teaching, will it be accounted as the fault of the teacher ?

King. Yes, that is how it is, my queen.

Ganadāsa. But the acceptance of a bad pupil shows the dullness of the teacher's intelligence.

Queen. (*To herself*) How now ? (*Looking at Gaṇadāsa, aside*) Do not fulfil the desire of my noble lord which will only inflame his passion. (*Aloud*) Desist from these vain proceedings.

Vidūṣaka. The queen speaks well. Ho, Gaṇadāsa, why should you trouble yourself with this disputation where you will easily suffer defeat, when under the pretext of your music, you well enjoy the presents of sweets offered to Saraswatī ?

Gaṇadāsa. This is exactly what her highness means. Now listen to this which is proper to say on the occasion :—

लब्धास्पदोऽस्मीति विवादभीरो-
स्तितिक्षमाणस्य परेण निन्दाम् ।
यस्यागमः केवलजीविकैव
तं ज्ञानपण्यं वणिजं वदन्ति ॥ १७ ॥

देवी—अइरोवणीदा दे सिस्सा । ता अवरिणिट्ठिदस्स उवदेसस्स अण्णाअं पदंसणं ।

३ [अचिरोपनीता ते शिष्या । तदपरिनिष्ठितस्योपदेशस्यान्याय्यं प्रदर्शनम् ।]

गणदासः—अत एव मे निर्बन्धः ।

देवी—तेण हि दुवे वि भअवदीए उवदेसं दंसह ।

६ [तेन हि द्वावपि भगवत्या उपदेशं दर्शयतम् ।]

परिव्राजिका—देवि नैतन्न्याय्यम् । सर्वज्ञस्याप्येकाकिनो निर्णयाभ्युपगमो दोषाय ।

९ **देवी**—(आत्मगतम् ।) मुद्धे किं मं जग्गदिं वि सुत्तं विअ करेसि । (इति सासूयं परावर्तते ।)

[मुग्धे किं मां जाग्रतीमपि सुप्तामिव करोषि ।]

१२ (राजा देवीं परिव्राजिकायै दर्शयति ।)

परिव्राजिका—(विलोक्य ।)

अनिमित्तमिन्दुवदने किमत्रभवतः पराङ्मुखी भवसि ।
प्रभवन्त्योऽपि हि भर्तृषु कारणकोपाः कुटुम्बिन्यः ॥ १८ ॥

विदूषकः—णं कारणादो एव्व अत्तणो पक्खो रक्खिदव्वो त्ति । (गणदासं विलोक्य ।) दिट्ठिआ कोवव्वाएण देवीए परित्तादो भवं ।
३ सुसिक्खिदो वि सव्वो उवदेसदंसणे ण णिउणो होदि ।

[ननु कारणादेव आत्मनः पक्षो रक्षितव्य इति । दिष्ट्या कोपव्याजेन देव्या परित्रातो भवान् । सुशिक्षितोऽपि सर्व उपदेशदर्शने न निपुणो
६ भवति ।]

a man who shrinks from contest on the ground that his position is secure, and (calmly) suffers insults by others, whose learning only serves as a means of livelihood, is called a mere huckster that traffics in knowledge. (17)

Queen. Your pupil has but lately been put under your charge. It would, therefore, be unjust to exhibit knowledge which is not yet well assimilated.

Ganadāsa. That is why I insist.

Queen. Well then, show your skill to the learned Kauśikī alone.

Parivrājikā. That is hardly fair, your highness. Even an omniscient judge may deliver a wrong judgment if he delivers it alone.

Queen. (*To herself*) You simpleton, how do you take me to be asleep when I am wide awake ? (*Turns away in a pet.*)

(The king draws the attention of the Parivrājikā to the queen.)

Parivrājikā. *(Looking)* How without cause do you, O moon-faced lady, turn yourself away from the king ? For although wives may have power over their husbands, yet they require some cause before they fall out with them. (18).

Vidūsaka. Why, the cause is plain : she wants to uphold her side. (*Looking at Gaṇadāsa.*) Fortunately for you, you have been saved by her majesty, under this pretence of resentment. For although one is very learned, yet one may not possess skill in imparting knowledge.

गणदासः—देवि श्रूयताम् । एवं जनो गृह्णाति । तदिदानीं

विवादे दर्शयिष्यन्तं क्रियासङ्क्रान्तिमात्मनः ।
यदि मां नानुजानासि परित्यक्तोऽस्म्यहं त्वया ॥१९॥

(आसनादुत्तिष्ठति ।)

देवी—(स्वगतम् ।) का गई । (प्रकाशम् ।) पहवदि आअरिओ सिस्सअणस्स ।

[का गतिः । प्रभवत्याचार्यः शिष्यजनस्य ।]

गणदासः–चिरमपदे शङ्कितोऽस्मि ।(राजानमवलोक्य) अनुज्ञातं देव्या । तदाज्ञापयतु देवः । कस्मिन्नभिनेयवस्तुन्युपदेशं दर्शयिष्यामि ।

राजा—यदादिशति भगवती ।

परिव्राजिका—किमपि देव्या मनसि वर्तते । तच्छङ्कितास्मि ।

देवी—भण विस्सद्धं । णं पहविस्सं अत्तणो परिअणस्स ।

[भणं विस्रब्धम् । ननु प्रभविष्याम्यात्मनः परिजनस्य ।]

राजा—मम चेति ब्रूहि ।

देवी—भअवदि भण दाणिं । [भगवति भणेदानीम् ।]

परिव्राजिका—चतुष्पदोद्भवं छलितं दुष्प्रयोजमुदाहरन्ति । तत्रैकार्थसंश्रयमुभयोः प्रयोगं पश्यामः । तावता ज्ञायत एवात्रभवतोरुपदेशान्तरम् ।

उभौ—यदाज्ञापयति भगवती ।

विदूषकः—तेण हि दुवे वि वग्गा पेक्खाघरए सङ्गीदरअणं कदुअ अत्तहोदो दूदं पेसअन्तु । अहवा मिअङ्गसद्दो एव्व णो उट्ठावइस्सदि ।

[तेन हि द्वावपि वर्गौ प्रेक्षागृहे सङ्गीतरचनां कृत्वात्रभवतो दूतं प्रेषयताम् । अथवा मृदङ्गशब्द एव न उत्थापयिष्यति ।]

Gaṇadāsa. Please to hear me, queen. This is how people will think. So now,

> if you will not permit me, although I am willing to show my skill in teaching in this contest,
> I would understand that you have deserted me. (19)

(*Rises from his seat.*)

Queen. (*To herself*) What help! (*Aloud*) The teacher has every authority over his pupil.

Gaṇadāsa. I was filled with vain apprehensions so long. (*Looking at the king*) So the queen consents. Let the king give orders: in what particular piece of acting should I show my skill?

King. As the revered lady commands.

Parivrājikā. There is something on the queen's mind. So I am a bit doubtful.

Queen. You may speak without fear. I shall certainly have power over my servants.

King. Say also over mine too.

Queen. Revered lady, speak then.

Parivrājikā. The chalita which depends upon four verse-quadrants is accounted to be difficult to act. Let us, therefore, witness the performance of both, by one and the same piece of acting. That will show clearly the difference in the teaching of both the gentlemen.

Both. As the revered lady commands.

Vidūṣaka. Well then, let both the parties arrange all the accessories of music in the theatre and send a messenger to his highness. Or rather the sound of the drum will be a signal for us to rise.

२१ **हरदत्तः**—तथा। (इत्युत्तिष्ठति।) (गणदासो देवीं विलोकयति।)

देवी—ण खु विअअपच्चत्थिणी अहं अज्जस्स। विअई होहि।

[न खलु विजयप्रत्यर्थिन्यहमार्यस्य। विजयी भव।]

(उभौ प्रस्थितौ।)

२५ **परिव्राजिका**—इतस्तावदाचार्यौ।

उभौ—(परिवृत्य) इमौ स्वः।

२७ **परिव्राजिका**—निर्णयाधिकारे ब्रवीमि। सर्वाङ्गसौष्ठवाभि-
व्यक्तये विरलनेपथ्ययोः पात्रयोः प्रवेशोऽस्तु।

आचार्यौ—नेदमावयोरुपदेश्यम्। (इति निष्क्रान्तौ।)

३० **देवी** (राजानवमलोक्य।)—जइ राअकज्जेसु वि ईरिसी उवा-
अणिउणदा अज्जउत्तस्स तदा सोहणं हवे।

[यदि राजकार्येष्वपीदृश्युपायनिपुणतार्यपुत्रस्य तदा शोभनं भवेत्।]

३३ **राजा**—देवि

अलमन्यथा गृहीत्वा
न खलु मनस्विनि मया प्रयुक्तमिदम्।
प्रायः समानविद्याः
परस्परयशःपुरोभागाः॥ २०॥

(नेपथ्ये मृदङ्गशब्दः। सर्वे कर्णं ददति।)

परिव्राजिका—हन्त प्रवृत्तं सङ्गीतकम्। तथा ह्येषा

जीमूतस्तनितविशङ्किभिर्मयूरै-
रुद्ग्रीवैरनुरसितस्य पुष्करस्य।
निर्ह्रादिन्युपहितमध्यमस्वरोत्था
मायूरी मदयति मार्जना मनांसि॥ २१॥

राजा—देवि सामाजिका भवामः

Haradatta. Let it be. *(Rises. Gaṇadāsa looks at the queen.)*

Queen. I am indeed not against your gaining victory. May you be victorious.

(Both start to leave.)

Parivrājikā. Here, please, professors.

Both. *(turning round)* Here we are.

Parivrājikā. I speak in the capacity of a judge. Let the actors enter in thin stage-costumes in order to exhibit the graces of all their limbs.

Teachers. That need not be told us. *(Exeunt both.)*

Queen.— *(Looking to the king)* If my noble lord shows the same command of means in political affairs, it would be to much advantage.

King. Do not misjudge me; this is not my doing, proud lady. Generally persons of equal learning are envious of one another's fame (20).

(The sound of drum is heard from behind the scenes ; all listen.)

Parivrājikā. Why, they have already started music! For this

sound of the drum, dear to the peacocks and answered by them with upstretched neck as they suspect it to be the rumble of clouds, deeply resonating, and set to the middle note, delights the mind (21).

King. My queen, let us join the audience.

देवी (स्वगतम्)—अहो अविणयो अज्जउत्तस्स ।

३ [अहो अविनय आर्यपुत्रस्य ।] (सर्वे उत्तिष्ठन्ति)

विदूषकः(अपवार्य ।)—भो वयस्स धीरं गच्छ । मा तत्तहोदी धारिणी विसंवादइस्सदि ।

६ [भो वयस्य धीरं गच्छ । मा तत्रभवती धारिणी विसंवादयिष्यति ।]

राजा—

> **धैर्यावलम्बिनमपि**
> **त्वरयति मां मुरजवाद्यरागोऽयम् ।**
> **अवतरतः सिद्धिपथं**
> **शब्दः स्वमनोरथस्येव ॥ २२ ॥**

[इति निष्क्रान्ताः सर्वे ।]

इति प्रथमोऽङ्कः ।

Queen. (*To herself*) O this indecorum of my lord !

(*All rise.*)

Vidūṣaka. (*Aside*) Keep calm, my friend, lest the queen Dhāriṇī should countermand (the whole proceeding).

King.

The sound of the drum makes me impatient
in spite of my efforts to keep calm, as though it
is the voice of my own desire that is treading
down the path of fulfilment. (22)

Exeunt Omnes.

End of Act One.

द्वितीयोऽङ्कः ।

(ततः प्रविशति सङ्गीतरचनायां कृतायामासनस्थः सवयस्यो राजा धारिणी परिव्राजिका विभवतश्च परिवारः ।)

राजा—भगवति अत्रभवतोराचार्ययोः कतरस्य प्रथममुपदेशं द्रक्ष्यामः ।

परिव्राजिका—ननु समानेऽपि ज्ञानवृद्धभावे वयोवृद्धत्वाद्गणदासः पुरस्कारमर्हति ।

राजा—तेन हि मौद्गल्य एवमत्रभवतोरावेद्य स्वनियोगमशून्यं कुरु।

कञ्चुकी—यदाज्ञापयति देवः । (इति निष्क्रान्तः)

(प्रविश्य) **गणदासः**—देव शर्मिष्ठायाः कृतिर्लयमध्या चतुष्पदा। तस्याश्चतुर्थवस्तुकं प्रयोगमेकमनाः श्रोतुमर्हति देवः ।

राजा—आचार्य बहुमानादवहितोऽस्मि । (निष्क्रान्तो गणदासः ।)

राजा—(जनान्तिकम्) वयस्य

नेपथ्यगृहगतायाश्चक्षुर्दर्शनसमुत्सुकं तस्याः ।
संहर्तुमधीरतया व्यवसितमिव मे तिरस्करणीम् ॥१॥

विदूषकः—(अपवार्य ।) भो उवट्ठिदं णअणमहु । सण्णिहिदअक्खिअं अ । ता अप्पमत्तो दाणिं पेक्खदु भवं ।

[भो उपस्थितं नयनमधु । सन्निहितमक्षिकं च । तदप्रमत्त इदानीं प्रेक्षतां भवान् ।]

(ततः प्रविशत्याचार्यप्रत्यवेक्ष्यमाणाङ्गसौष्ठवा मालविका)

विदूषकः (जनान्तिकम्) पेक्खदु भवं । ण खु से पडिच्छन्दादो परिहीअदि महुरदा । [प्रेक्षतां भवान । न खल्वस्याः प्रतिच्छन्दात् परिहीयते मधुरता ।]

ACT II.

(Then, after orchestral arrangements are got ready, enter seated the king with his friend, Dhāriṇī, Parivrājikā, and the attendants according to their rank.)

King. Revered Madam, of which of the two venerable teachers shall we first witness (the skill in) teaching?

Parivrājikā. Although they are equally old in learning, yet Gaṇadāsa deserves precedence on account of his being the elder.

King. Well then, Maudgalya, do communicate this to the gentlemen and then go about your business.

Chamberlain. As the king commands. (*Exit.*)

(*Entering*)

Gaṇadāsa. King, there is Śarmiṣṭhā's composition of four parts and sung in medium time; it behoves the king to listen to the performance of one-fourth of it very attentively.

King. Well, professor, I am respectfully attentive.

(*Exit Gaṇadāsa.*)

King. (*Aside*) friend,

mine eyes, eager to behold her who is now in
the tiring-room, are as it were proceeding to
remove the curtain owing to their impatience. (1)

Vidūsaka. (*Aside*) Friend, the honey of your eyes is come, but the wasp is close by; so be vigilant and watch.

(Enter Mālavikā with the teacher contemplating the grace of her limbs).

Vidūsaka. Behold, Sir. I am sure her charms do not fall short of the picture.

९ राजा (जनान्तिकम्) —वयस्य

चित्रगतायामस्यां कान्तिविसंवादशङ्कि मे हृदयम् ।
सम्प्रति शिथिलसमाधिं मन्ये येनेयमालिखिता ॥ २ ॥

गणदासः—वत्से मुक्तसाध्वसा सत्त्वस्था भव ।

राजा (आत्मगतम्) — अहो सर्वस्थानानवद्यता रूपस्य ।

दीर्घाक्षं शरदिन्दुकान्ति वदनं बाहू नतावंसयोः
सङ्क्षिप्तं निबिडोन्नतस्तनमुरः पार्श्वे प्रमृष्टे इव ।
मध्यः पाणिमितो नितम्बि जघनं पादावरालाङ्गुली
छन्दो नर्तयितुर्यथैव मनसि श्लिष्टं तथास्याः वपुः ॥३॥

मालविका—(उपवहनं कृत्वा चतुष्पदं वस्तु गायति)

दुल्लहो पिओ तस्सिं भव हिअअ णिरासं
अम्हो अपङ्गओ मे पप्फुरइ किं वि वामओ ।
एसो सो चिरदिट्ठो कहं उवणइदव्वो
णाह मं पराहीणं तुइ गणअ सतिण्हं ॥ ४ ॥

(इति यथारसमभिनयति ।)

[दुर्लभः प्रियस्तस्मिन् भव हृदय निराशम्
३ अहो अपाङ्गको मे प्रस्फुरति किमपि वामकः ।
एष स चिरदृष्टः कथमुपनेतव्यो
नाथ मां पराधीनां त्वयि गणय सतृष्णाम् ॥]

६ विदूषकः (जनान्तिकम्)—भो वयस्स चउप्पदवत्थुअ दुवारीकदुअ तुइ उवक्खित्तो विअ अप्पा तत्तहोदीए । [भो वयस्य, चतुष्पदवस्तुकं द्वारीकृत्य त्वय्युपक्षिप्त इवात्मा तत्रभवत्या ।]

King. *(Aside)* Friend,

when I beheld her picture, I thought she would belie the loveliness of it ; but now I think that the painter who limned her likeness had not secured full concentration. (2).

Gaṇadāsa. Child, give up fear and be composed.

King. *(To himself)* How flawless in every part is her form !

Her long eyes ; her face lovely like the moon of autumn ; the arms sloping at the shoulders ; her compact bosom with the plump and swelling breasts ; her sides as if polished ; her waist measurable by the palm of the hand ; her hips expansive ; her feet with their curved toes ; her whole body thus seems framed to suit the fancy of her teacher of dancing. (3).

Mālavikā. (*After a preliminary trying of the notes she sings the musical piece of four lines.*)

The dear one is far above thee ; my heart, despair. Ah, how the corner of my left eye throbs somewhat ! How should he, seen after a long time, be approached ? My lord, helpless that I am, know me to be filled with passion for you. (4)

(She expresses the emotion through acting.)

Vidūṣaka. (*Aside*) Ah, my friend, taking occasion of this musical piece of four parts, she seems to have given herself over to you.

राजा (जनान्तिकम्)—सखे एवमावयोर्हृदयम् । अनया खलु

जनमिममनुरक्तं विद्धि नाथेति गेये
वचनमभिनयन्त्या स्वाङ्गनिर्देशपूर्वम् ।
प्रणयगतिमदृष्ट्वा धारिणीसन्निकर्षा-
दहमिव सुकुमारप्रार्थनाव्याजमुक्तः ॥ ५ ॥

(मालविका गीतान्ते निष्क्रमितुमिच्छति ।)

विदूषकः—भोदि चिट्ठ । किं वि वो विसुमरिदो कमभेदो । तं
३ दाव पुच्छिस्सम् । [भवति तिष्ठ । किमपि वो विस्मृतः क्रमभेदः । तं तावत्प्रक्ष्यामि ।]

गणदासः—वत्से स्थीयताम् । उपदेशविशुद्धा यास्यसि ।

(मालविका निवृत्य स्थिता ।)

७ **राजा** (आत्मगतम्)—अहो सर्वास्ववस्थासु चारुता शोभां पुष्यति । तथा हि ।

वामं सन्धिस्तिमितवलयं न्यस्य हस्तं नितम्बे
कृत्वा श्यामाविटपसदृशं स्रस्तमुक्तं द्वितीयम् ।
पादाङ्गुष्ठालुलितकुसुमे कुट्टिमे पातिताक्षं
नृत्तादस्याः स्थितमतितरां कान्तमृज्वायतार्धम् ॥६॥

देवी—णं गोदमवअणं वि अज्जो हिअए करेदि । [ननु गौतमवचनमप्यार्यो हृदये करोति]

३ **गणदासः**—देवि मा मैवम् । देवप्रत्ययात्सम्भाव्यते सूक्ष्मदर्शिता गौतमस्य । पश्य ।

King. *(Aside)* friend, such the state of our hearts. For

> " Know me to be devoted to you, my lord ": as she accompanied these words of the song with gestures in which she pointed to the different parts of her body, she seemed to address me under cover of the graceful plaint, as she could see no other way of showing her love for me owing to Dhāriṇī's presence. (5)

(Mālavikā makes as if she would leave at the end of the song.)

Vidūṣaka. Wait, lady. You seem to have forgotten somewhat the proper sequence. I will, therefore, ask about it.

Gaṇadāsa. Stay, child. You will leave, when your performance will have been declared to be flawless.

(Mālavikā turns round and stays.)

King. *(To himself)* How loveliness gains fresh charms under all conditions ! For

> the left hand with its bracelet resting on the wrist, placed upon her hip, and the right hand hanging loosely down like a branch of the Śyāmā creeper; the eyes cast on the pavement where the flowers are pressed by the toes of her feet—this her posture, with the upper part of the body stretched upright, is far more attractive than her dancing (posture). (6)

Queen. Now, sir, would you mind the words even of Gautama ?

Gaṇadāsa. Not so, queen. Owing to the confidence which the king reposes in him, it is possible to expect acute perception in him. See

मन्दोऽप्यमन्दतामेति संसर्गेण विपश्चितः ।
पङ्कच्छिदः फलस्येव निकषेणाविलं पयः ॥ ७ ॥

(विदूषकं विलोक्य।) शृणुमो विवक्षितमार्यस्य ।

विदूषकः (गणदासं विलोक्य ।)—सक्खिणिं दाव पुच्छ । पच्छा
३ जो मए कमभेदो लक्खिदो तं भाणिस्सं । [साक्षिणीं तावत्पृच्छ ।
पश्चाद्यो मया क्रमभेदो लक्षितः तं भणिष्यामि ।]

गणदासः—भगवति, यथादृष्टमभिधीयतां गुणो वा दोषो वा ।

६ **परिव्राजिका**—यथादर्शनं सर्वमनवद्यम् । कुतः ।

अङ्गैरन्तर्निहितवचनैः सूचितः सम्यगर्थः
पादन्यासो लयमनुगतस्तन्मयत्वं रसेषु ।
शाखायोनिर्मृदुरभिनयस्ताद्विकल्पानुवृत्तौ
भावो भावं नुदति विषयाद्रागबन्धः स एव ॥ ८ ॥

गणदासः—देवः कथं मन्यते ।

राजा—गणदास, स्वपक्षे शिथिलाभिमाना वयं संवृत्ताः ।

३ **गणदासः**—अद्य नर्तयितास्मि ।

उपदेशं विदुः शुद्धं सन्तस्तमुपदेशिनः ।
श्यामायते न युष्मासु यः काञ्चनमिवाग्निषु ॥ ९ ॥

देवी—दिट्ठिआ परिक्खआराहणेण अहिअं वड्ढइ अज्जो ।
[दिष्ट्या परीक्षकाराधनेनाधिकं वर्धत आर्यः ।]

> even a dull person becomes sharp of intelligence by association with the wise, as turbid water attains transparency by contact with the mud-removing fruit. (7)

(*Looking at the Vidūṣaka*) We should like to heaı what the gentleman wants to say.

Vidūṣaka. (*Looking at Gaṇadāsa*) Ask the judge in the first place. Afterwards will I speak of the violation of sequence which I have observed.

Gaṇadāsa. Revered lady, speak out whatever you observed, whether merits or defects.

Parivrājikā. Everything was blameless and in accordance with the rules of the art.

> The meaning was well suggested by her limbs that were eloquently expressive ; the movement of the feet was in perfect time, and she was perfectly absorbed in the (various) sentiments ; the acting was delicate—of which the instrument of expression was the branch-like hand ; and while in the successive exhibition of its various shades one fleeting emotion seemed to drive away another from the field, yet the main sentiment (of love) remained the same throughout. (8)

Gaṇadāsa. What does his majesty think ?

King. I no longer hold the same high regard for my protege.

Gaṇadāsa. Now (I feel) I am in truth a professor of dancing.

> Wise men consider that the instruction given by a teacher is pure when the same is found to be without any fault by such as you, as they consider gold to be pure when it does not get blackened in fire. (9)

Queen. I congratulate you, sır, on being so fortunate as to satisfy your judges.

गणदासः—देवीपरिग्रहश्च मे वृद्धिहेतुः । (विदूषकं विलोक्य ।) गौतम, वदेदानीं यत्ते मनसि वर्तते ।

विदूषकः—पुढमोवदेसदंसणे पुढमं बम्हणस्स पूआ कादव्वा । सा णं वो विसुमरिदा । [प्रथमोपदेशदर्शने प्रथमं ब्राह्मणस्य पूजा कर्तव्या । सा ननु वो विस्मृता ।]

परिव्राजिका—अहो प्रयोगाभ्यन्तरः प्रश्नः ।

विदूषकः—अइ पण्डितंमण्णे किं अण्णं । मोदअखण्डणे वि असमत्था तुमं किं जाणासि । पसण्णचन्दपादसरिसेहिं केसपासेहिं एदाणं भीसिआसि । [अयि पण्डितंमन्ये, किमन्यत् । मोदकखण्डनेऽप्यसमर्था त्वं किं जानासि । प्रसन्नचन्द्रपादसदृशैः केशपाशैरेतान् भीषयसे ।]

(सर्वे प्रहसिताः । मालविका च मन्दस्मितं करोति ।)

राजा (आत्मगतम्)—उपात्तसारश्चक्षुषा मे स्वविषयः । यदनेन

> **स्मयमानमायताक्ष्याः**
> **किंचिदभिव्यक्तदशनशोभि मुखम् ।**
> **असमग्रलक्ष्यकेसर-**
> **मुच्छ्वसदिव पङ्कजं दृष्टम् ॥ १० ॥**

गणदासः—महाब्राह्मण, न खलु नेपथ्यसङ्गीतकमिदम् । अन्यथा कथं त्वामर्चनीयं नार्चयिष्यामः ।

विदूषकः—मए णाम मुद्धचादएण विअ सुक्खघणगज्जिदे अन्दरिक्खे जलपाणं इच्छिदं । [मया नाम मुग्धचातकेनेव शुष्कघनगर्जितेऽन्तरिक्षे जलपानमिष्टम् ।]

परिव्राजिका—एवमेव ।

Ganadāsa. The queen's favour, too, is responsible for my good fortune. *(Looking at the Vidūṣaka)* Now, Gautama, say what you have in your mind.

Vidūṣaka. The first time that skill is exhibited a Brāhmaṇa must be honoured ; and that you have forgotten to do.

Parivrājikā. Ha ! Ha ! What a vital point in acting !

Vidūṣaka. What else, you conceited woman ! What, indeed, do you know, when you are not able to break even balls of sweets ? You merely frighten these people here by your abundant hair that are white like the clear rays of the moon.

(They all laugh; Mālavikā too gently smiles.)

King. *(To himself)* my eye has perceived the most beautiful of the objects of sight. For

> it has beheld the smiling face of the long-eyed one, lovely with the teeth but half visible, like an opening lotus with its filaments partially seen. (10)

Gaṇadāsa. Great Brāhamaṇa, this is not a musical piece in regular stage-costume. How, otherwise, could we have failed to do you honour who deserve to be honoured ?

Vidūṣaka. I, indeed, like the simple Cātaka had asked for a drink of water when the sky was filled with the rumble of a rainless cloud.

Parivrājikā. Yes, even so.

विदूषकः—भअवदि, पण्डिदपरिदोसप्पच्चआ णं मूढा जादी । जइ भअवदीए सोहणं भणिदं तदो इमं से पारितोसिअं पयच्छम्मि । (इति राज्ञो हस्तात्कटकमाकर्षति ।) [भगवति, पण्डितपरितोषप्रत्यया ननु मूढा जातिः । यदि भगवत्या शोभनं भणितं तत इदमस्यै पारितोषिकं प्रयच्छामि ।]

देवी—चिट्ठ चिट्ठ । गुणन्तरं अआणन्तो किंति तुमं आहरणं देसि । [तिष्ठ तिष्ठ । गुणान्तरमजानन्किमिति त्वमाभरणं ददासि ।]

विदूषकः—परकेरअं ति कदुअ । [परकीयमिति कृत्वा ।]

देवी (आचार्यं विलोक्य)—अज्ज गणदास, णं दंसिदोवदेसा वो सिस्सा । [आर्य गणदास, ननु दर्शितोपदेशा वः शिष्या ।]

गणदासः—वत्से प्रतिष्ठस्वेदानीम् ।(मालविका सहाचार्येण निष्क्रान्ता।)

विदूषकः (राजानं विलोक्य । जनान्तिकम् ।)—एत्तिओ मे मदिविहवो भवन्तं सेविदुम् । [एतावान्मे मतिविभवो भवन्तं सेवितुम् ।]

राजा (जनान्तिकम् ।)—अलमलं परिच्छेदेन । अद्य हि

भाग्यास्तमयमिवाक्ष्णोर्हृदयस्य महोत्सवावसानमिव ।
द्वारपिधानमिव धृतेर्मन्ये तस्यास्तिरस्करणम् ॥११॥

विदूषकः—साहु तुमं दरिद्दो आदुरो विअ वेज्जेण उवणिज्जमाणं ओसहं इच्छसि । [साधु त्वं दरिद्र आतुर इव वैद्येनोपनीयमानमौषधमिच्छसि ।]

(प्रविश्य ।) **हरदत्तः**—देव मदीयमिदानीमुपदेशमवलोकयितुं क्रियतां प्रसादः ।

राजा (आत्मगतम् ।)—अवसितो मे दर्शनार्थः । (दाक्षिण्यमवलम्ब्य । प्रकाशम् ।) हरदत्त, ननु पर्युत्सुका एव वयम् ।

Vidūṣaka. Revered lady, those who are ignorant have to depend upon the satisfaction of the learned. If you commend her, here would I give her a present. (*So saying, he draws off a bracelet from the king's hand.*)

Queen. Hold, hold. How could you bestow the ornament before you have known a different kind of merit ?

Vidūṣaka. Because it belongs to another.

Queen. *(Looking at the professor)* Noble Gaṇadāsa, your pupil has indeed exhibited her proficiency.

Gaṇadāsa. Child, you may leave now. (*Mālavikā departs with her teacher.)*

Vidūṣaka. (*Looking at the king, aside*) Thus far only can my ingenuity help you.

King. Have done with setting a limit to your power. For now

> I regard her disappearance to be like the
> obscuration of the prosperity of mine eyes, or
> like the end of the great festivity of my heart,
> or like the closing of the portals of my joy. (11)

Vidūṣaka. Ah, well ! Like a poor patient you desire the physician to procure you medicine.

(*Entering*)

Haradatta. King please now favour me by witnessing the exhibition of my skill in teaching.

King. (*To himself*) The object of my vision has vanished ; *(Courteously, aloud)* friend Haradatta, indeed, we are so eager !

हरदत्तः—अनुगृहीतोऽस्मि ।

वैतालिकः–(नेपथ्ये) विजयतां देवः । उपारूढो मध्याह्नः । तथाहि ।

पत्रच्छायासु हंसा मुकुलितनयना दीर्घिकापद्मिनीनां
सौधान्यत्यर्थतापाद्वलभिपरिचयद्वेषिपारावतानि ।
बिन्दूत्क्षेपान्पिपासुः परिपतति शिखी भ्रान्तिमद्वारियन्त्रं
सर्वैरुस्त्रैः समग्रस्त्वमिव नृपगुणैर्दीप्यते सप्तसप्तिः ॥ १२ ॥

विदूषकः—अविहा अविहा । बम्हणस्स भोअणवेला संवुत्ता । अत्तहोदो वि । उइदवेलादिक्कमे चिकिस्सआ दोसं उदाहरन्ति । हरदत्त किं दाणिं भणसि । [अविहा अविहा । ब्राह्मणस्य भोजनवेला संवृत्ता । अत्रभवतोऽपि । उचितवेलातिक्रमे चिकित्सका दोषमुदाहरन्ति । हरदत्त, किमिदानीं भणसि ।]

हरदत्तः—नास्ति मे वचनस्यान्यस्यावकाशोऽत्र ।

राजा (हरदत्तमवलोक्य ।)—तेन हि त्वदीयमुपदेशं श्वो वयं द्रक्ष्यामः । विश्राम्यतु भवान् ।

हरदत्तः—यदाज्ञापयति देवः । (इति निष्क्रान्तः ।)

देवी—णिव्वत्तेदु अज्जउत्तो मज्जणविहिं । [निर्वर्तयत्वार्यपुत्रो मज्जनविधिम् ।]

विदूषकः—होदि, विसेसेण भोअणं तुवरावेदु । [भवति, विशेषेण भोजनं त्वरयतु ।]

परिव्राजिका (उत्थाय ।)—स्वस्ति भवते ।

(इति सपरिजनया देव्या सह निष्क्रान्ता)

विदूषकः—भो ण केवलं रूवे सिप्पे वि अदुदीया मालविआ । [भोः न केवलं रूपे शिल्पेऽप्यद्वितीया मालविका ।]

Haradatta. I feel favoured.

(Behind the scenes)

A bard.

Victory to our king! It is mid-day. Thus
the swans with closed eyes nestle under the shadows of the leaves of the lotus-plants in the ponds; while the pigeons hate to be on the terrace-tops on account of the blazing heat; the peacock dashes to the revolving water-wheel desiring to lick up the splashing drops; and the sun too, endowed with all his rays, as you with kingly virtues, is shining brilliantly. (12)

Vidūṣaka. O confound it! It is time for this Brāhmaṇa to feed himself, so likewise for your majesty; and the physicians warn us that it is a grave mistake to transgress the proper time. How do you think, Haradatta?

Haradatta. There is no occasion for words other than these from me.

King. (*Looking at Haradatta*) Well, then, we shall witness your instruction to-morrow. Rest you.

Haradatta. As the king commands. (*Exit*)

Queen. Let my noble Lord finish his bath.

Vidūṣaka. You will be particularly quick in getting the meal ready.

Parivrājikā. (*Rising*) Blessings on you.

(*Leaves along with the queen and attendants.*)

Vidūṣaka. Sir, not in loveliness alone, but also in the art is she peerless.

4

राजा—वयस्य

अव्याजसुन्दरीं तां विज्ञानेन ललितेन योजयता।
परिकल्पितो विधात्रा बाणः कामस्य विषदिग्धः॥१३॥

किं बहुना, चिन्तयितव्योऽस्मि ते।

विदूषकः—भवदा वि अहं। दिढं खु विवणिकन्दू विअ उअरब्भन्दरं डज्झइ। [भवताप्यहम्। दृढं खलु विपणिकन्दुरिवोदराभ्यन्तरं दह्यते।]

राजा—एवमेव भवान् सुहृदर्थे त्वरताम्।

विदूषकः—गहिदक्खणोम्हि। किं दु मेहावलीरुद्धजोह्ला विअ पराहीणदंसणा तत्तहोदी मालविआ। भवं वि सूणोवरिअरो गिद्धो विअ आमिसलोलुओ भीरुओ अ। ता अणादुरो भविअ कज्जसिद्धिं पत्थयन्तो मे रुच्चइ। [गृहीतक्षणोऽस्मि। किं तु मेघावलीरुद्धज्योत्स्नेव पराधीनदर्शना तत्रभवती मालविका। भवानपि सूनोपरिचरो गृध्र इव आमिषलोलुपो भीरुकश्च। तस्मादनातुरो भूत्वा कार्यसिद्धिं प्रार्थयमानो मे रोचसे।]

राजा—सखे कथमनातुरो भविष्यामि। यदा

सर्वान्तःपुरवनिताव्यापारं प्रति निवृत्तहृदयस्य।
सा वामलोचना मे स्नेहस्यैकायनीभूता॥१४॥

(इति निष्क्रान्ताः सर्वे।)

इति द्वितीयोऽङ्कः।

King. Friend,

the creator now by uniting this knowledge of the fine arts to her artless charms has surely devised a shaft of love smeared with poison. (13)

What more! You have ever to be solicitous about me.

Vidūṣaka. You too about me. For the inside of me is grilling like the frying pan in the market-place.

King. Even so, do you be quick to accomplish your friend's desire.

Vidūṣaka. I undertake the venture. But like moon-light veiled by clouds the sight of the lady Mālavikā is dependent upon another; while you, like the vulture wheeling over the slaughter-house, desire the flesh yet fear to venture. I shall, therefore, much appreciate your exercising patience while you seek success in this venture.

King. Friend, how can I curb my impatience when

that sweet-eyed beauty has become the one centre of the affection of my heart which has withdrawn its interest from all the ladies of my harem ? (14).

(Exeunt Omnes.)

Here ends the Second Act.

तृतीयोऽङ्कः ।

(ततः प्रविशति परिव्राजिकायाः परिचारिका ।)

परिचारिका—आणत्तम्हि भअवदीए । उवाअणत्थं बीजपूरअं गेण्हिअ आअच्छ त्ति । ता जाव पमदवणपालिअं महुअरिअं अण्णेसामि । (परिक्रम्य अवलोक्य च ।) एसा तवणीआसोअं ओलोअन्ती चिट्ठइ । जाव णं उवसप्पे । [आज्ञप्तास्मि भगवत्या । 'उपायनार्थे बीजपूरकं गृहीत्वागच्छ' इति । तद्यावत् प्रमदवनपालिकां मधुकरिकामन्विष्यामि । एषा तपनीयाशोकमवलोकयन्ती तिष्ठति । यावदेनामुपसर्पामि ।]

(ततः प्रविशत्युद्यानपालिका ।)

परभृतिका (उपसृत्य ।)—महुअरिए अवि सुहो दे उज्जाणव्वावारो । [मधुकरिके, अपि सुखस्त उद्यानव्यापारः ।]

मधुकरिका—अम्मो परहुदिआ । सहि साअदं दे । [अम्मो परभृतिका । सखि स्वागतं ते ।]

परभृतिका—हला भअवदी आणवेदि अरित्तपाणिणा अम्हारिसजणेण तत्तहोदी देवी देक्खिदव्वा । ता बीजपूरएण सुस्सूसिदुं इच्छम्मि त्ति । [हला, भगवत्याज्ञापयति 'अरिक्तपाणिनास्मादृशजनेन तत्रभवती देवी द्रष्टव्या । तद्बीजपूरकेण शुश्रूषितुमिच्छामि' इति ।]

मधुकरिका—णं सण्णिहिदं एव्व बीजपूरअं । कहेहि दाव अण्णोण्णसङ्घरिसिदाणं णट्टाअरिआणं उवदेसं देक्खिअ कदरो भअवदीए पसंसिदो । [ननु सन्निहितमेव बीजपूरकम् । कथय तावदन्योन्यसङ्घर्षितयोर्नाट्याचार्ययोरुपदेशं दृष्ट्वा कतरो भगवत्या प्रशंसितः ।]

परभृतिका—दुवे वि किल आआमिणो पओअणिउणा अ । किंदु सिस्सागुणविसेसेण उण्णमिदो गणदासो । [द्वावपि किलागमिनौ प्रयोगनिपुणौ च । किं तु शिष्यागुणविशेषेण उन्नमितो गणदासः ।]

ACT III.

(Enter the maid-servant of the Parivrājikā).

Maid-servant. I have been ordered by the reverend lady to fetch for her a fruit of the citron for offering as a present. I will, therefore, find out Madhukarikā, the keeper of the Pramadavana garden. *(Moving about and looking).* Here she is, looking at the gold Aśoka tree; so I will go to her.

(Enter the keeper of the Garden.)

Parabhṛtikā. *(Approaching)* Madhukarikā, I hope you find your work in the garden quite pleasant.

Madhukarikā. Ah! Friend Parabhṛtikā, you are welcome.

Parabhṛtikā. Friend, the reverend lady says:— people like us ought not to approach the queen with empty hands. I, therefore, desire to make her the gift of a citron and wait upon her.

Madhukarikā. Oh, here is a citron quite at hand. But tell me which of the two professors of dancing that had quarrelled was praised by the reverend lady after she had witnessed their skill in teaching?

Parabhṛtikā. Both are, indeed, known to be very learned and skilful teachers. But Ganadāsa was adjudged the superior of the two, owing to the excellent merits of his pupil.

मधुकरिका——अह मालविआगदं कोलीणं कहं सुणीअदि। [अथ मालविकागतं कौलीनं कथं श्रूयते ।]

परभृतिका——बलिअं खु साहिलासो भट्टा तस्सिं । केवलं देवीए धारिणीए चित्तं रक्खन्तो अत्तणो पहुत्तणं ण दंसेदि । मालविआ वि इमेसु दिअहेसु अणुहूदमुत्ता विअ मालदीमाला मिलायमाणा लक्खिअदि । अदो वरं ण आणे । विसज्जेहि मं । [बलवत् खलु साभिलाषो भर्ता तस्याम् । केवलं देव्या धारिण्याश्चित्तं रक्षन्नात्मनः प्रभुत्वं न दर्शयति । मालविकाप्येषु दिवसेष्वनुभूतमुक्तेव मालतीमाला म्लायमाना लक्ष्यते । अतः परं न जाने । विसर्जय माम् ।]

मधुकरिका——एदं साहावलम्बि बीजपूरअं गेह्न । [एतच्छाखावलम्बि बीजपूरकं गृहाण ।]

परभृतिका (नाट्येन गृहीत्वा)—हला तुमं वि इदो वरं पेसलअरं साहुअणसुस्सूसाए फलं पाविदा होहि । [हला त्वमपि इतः परं पेशलतरं साधुजनशुश्रूषायाः फलं प्राप्ता भव ।]

(इति प्रस्थिता ।)

मधुकरिका——सहि समं एव्व गच्छम्ह । अहं वि इमस्स चिराअमाणकुसुमुग्गमस्स तवणीआसोअस्स दोहदणिमित्तं देवीए विण्णवेमि । [सखि सममेव गच्छावः । अहमप्यस्य चिरायमाणकुसुमोद्गमस्य तपनीयाशोकस्य दोहदनिमित्तं देव्यै विज्ञापयामि ।]

परभृतिका—जुज्जइ । अहिआरो खु तुह । [युज्यते । अधिकारः खलु तव ।] (इति निष्क्रान्ते ।)

प्रवेशकः ।

(ततः प्रविशति कामयमानावस्थो राजा विदूषकश्च ।)

राजा (आत्मानं विलोक्य)—

शरीरं क्षामं स्यादसति दयितालिङ्गनसुखे
भवेत्सास्रं चक्षुः क्षणमपि न सा दृश्यत इति ।

Madhukarikā. Well, but what is this scandal about Mālavikā ?

Parabhṛtikā. The king has conceived a strong passion for her. Only out of regard for the feelings of queen Dhārinī, he does not exercise his power. Mālavikā, too, during all these days has grown pale like a jasmine garland worn and cast away. Beyond this I know nothing. Well, allow me to go.

Madhukarikā. Take the citron that hangs on yonder bough.

Parabhṛtikā. *(Acting as if she picks up the citron)* Ah, may you get a far more glorious fruit than this for your readiness to serve the saintly lady.

(Starts to go.)

Madhukarikā. Friend, we will go together. For I want to request the queen regarding the longing of this gold Aśoka tree which is delaying to burst into blossom.

Parabhrtikā. Quite right. Indeed, it is your duty.

(Exeunt both.)

Here ends the introductory scene.

(Enter the king in a love-lorn state, and the Vidūṣaka.)

King. *(Looking at himself)*

The body may get emaciate in the absence of the pleasure of the beloved's embrace, and the eyes tearful, as they do not get even a moment's

तया सारङ्गाक्ष्या त्वमसि न कदाचिद्विरहितं
प्रसक्ते निर्वाणे हृदय परितापं वहसि किम् ॥ १ ॥

विदूषकः—अलं भवदो धीरदं उज्झिअ परिदेविदेण। दिट्ठा मए तत्तहोदीए मालविआए पिअसही बउलावलिआ। सुणाविदा अ मए जं भवदा सन्दिट्ठं। [अलं भवतो धीरतामुज्झित्वा परिदेवितेन। दृष्टा मया तत्रभवत्या मालविकायाः प्रियसखी बकुलावलिका। श्राविता च मया यद्भवता सन्दिष्टम्।]

राजा—ततः किमुक्तवती।

विदूषकः—विण्णवेहि भट्टारं। अणुगहीदम्हि इमिणा णिओएण। किं दु सा तवस्सिणी देवीए अहिअदरं रक्खिअमाणा णाअरक्खिदो विअ णिही ण सुहं समासादइदव्वा भविस्सदि। तह वि घडइस्सं ति। [विज्ञापय भर्तारम्। 'अनुगृहीतास्मि अनेन नियोगेन। किं तु सा तपस्विनी देव्या अधिकतरं रक्ष्यमाणा नागरक्षित इव निधिर्न सुखं समासादयितव्या भविष्यति। तथापि घटयिष्यामि' इति।]

राजा—भगवन् सङ्कल्पयोने, प्रतिबन्धवत्स्वपि विषयेष्वभिनिवेश्य तथा प्रहरसि यथा जनोऽयं कालान्तरक्षमो न भवति। (सविस्मयं)

क्व रुजा हृदयप्रमाथिनी क्व च ते विश्वसनीयमायुधम्।
मृदु तीक्ष्णतरं यदुच्यते तदिदं मन्मथ दृश्यते त्वयि॥२॥

विदूषकः—णं भणामि तस्सिं साहणिज्जे कज्जे किदो मए उवाओवक्खेवो। ता पज्जवत्थावेदु भवं अत्ताणं। [ननु भणामि तस्मिन् साधनीये कार्ये कृतो मयोपायोपक्षेपः। तत्पर्यवस्थापयतु भवानात्मानम्।]

राजा—अथेमं दिवसशेषमुचितव्यापारविमुखेन चेतसा क्व न खलु यापयामि।

विदूषकः—णं भवं अज्ज पुढमं वसन्दावदारसूअआइं रत्तासोअकोरआइं उवाअणं पेसिअ णववसन्दूसवावदेसेण इरावदीए

glimpse of her ; but, my heart, never art thou severed from that fawn-eyed one : how then dost thou suffer agony even when thou gettest the highest bliss ? (1)

Vidūṣaka. Do not give up fortitude and lament. I have seen Bakulāvalikā, the dear friend of the lady Mālavikā. I have also conveyed to her your message.

King. What was her reply to that ?

Vidūṣaka. 'Request the king : I feel favoured by this command. But the poor girl is being more carefully guarded by the queen like a treasure by a cobra, and, therefore, will not be obtained with ease. Still I will do my best.'

King. Oh revered God of love, although you impel me to long for an inaccessible object, yet you smite me so sorely that I am not able to brook any delay. (*Wonderingly*)

What great disparity is there between this heart-wrenching ache, and your weapon seemingly so harmless ! What is described as both soft and piercing hard—that indeed is seen in you, O love. (2)

Vidūṣaka. Well, I say, I have devised means for the (attainment) of the object desired. Do you, therefore, compose yourself.

King. Where shall I pass the rest of the day when my mind feels such aversion for my proper duties ?

Vidūṣaka. Well, you have already heard through Nipuṇikā the request of Irāvatī, who taking occasion

णिउणिआमुहेण पत्थिदो । इच्छामि अज्जउत्तेण सह डोलाहिरोहणं अणुहोदुं ति । भवदा वि से पडिण्णादं । ता पमदवणं एव्व गच्छम्ह । [ननु भवानद्य प्रथमं वसन्तावतारसूचकानि रक्ताशोककोरकाण्युपायनं प्रेष्य नववसन्तोत्सवापदेशेन इरावत्या निपुणिकामुखेन प्रार्थितः 'इच्छाम्यार्यपुत्रेण सह दोलाधिरोहणमनुभवितुम्' इति । भवताप्यस्यै प्रतिज्ञातम् । तत्प्रमदवनमेव गच्छावः ।]

राजा—न क्षममिदम् ।

विदूषकः—कहं विअ । [कथमिव ।]

राजा—वयस्य निसर्गनिपुणाः स्त्रियः । कथं मामन्यसङ्क्रान्तहृदयमुपलालयन्तमपि ते सखी न लक्षयिष्यति । अतः पश्यामि ।

> **उचितः प्रणयो वरं विहन्तुं**
> **बहवः खण्डनहेतवो हि दृष्टाः ।**
> **उपचारविधिर्मनस्विनीनां**
> **न तु पूर्वाभ्यधिकोऽपि भावशून्यः ॥ ३ ॥**

विदूषकः—णारुहदि भवं सव्वं अन्देउरपडिट्ठिदं दक्खिण्णं एक्कपदे पिट्ठदो कादुं । [नार्हति भवान् सर्वमन्तःपुरप्रतिष्ठितं दाक्षिण्यमेकपदे पृष्ठतः कर्तुम् ।]

राजा (विचिन्त्य)—तेन हि प्रमदवनमार्गमादेशय ।

विदूषकः—इदो इदो भवं । [इत इतो भवान् ।]

(उभौ परिक्रामतः ।)

विदूषकः—णं एदं पमदवणं पवणचलिदाहिं पल्लवंगुलीहिं तुअरावेदि विअ भवन्दं । ता पविसदु भवं । [नन्वेतत्प्रमदवनं पवनचलिताभिः पल्लवाङ्गुलीभिस्त्वरयतीव भवन्तम् । तत्प्रविशतु भवान् ।]

of spring's advent has first sent you as present the buds of the red Aśoka tree indicative of the arrival of that season : " I long to enjoy sitting on the swing together with my lord." You too have promised her. So we shall proceed to the Pramadavana garden.

King. That is impossible.

Vidūṣka. How do you mean ?

King. Friend, women are naturally so cunning. Do you think she will not notice—spite of all my love-caressings—that my heart is devoted to another ? Therefore, I see clearly

> that it is better to decline this request, although it is a proper one to make at this season, for I know many excuses for declining it than to go through the form of showing regard to these proud women, may be, with greater fervour than before, when one feels not even a shred of affection for them. (3)

Vidūṣaka. You ought not all of a sudden to throw aside your unfailing courtesy to the ladies of your harem.

King. (*Reflecting*) well, then, lead the way to the Pramadavana.

Vidūṣaka. This way, this way, my friend. (*Both move about.*)

Vidūṣaka. Here we come to the Pramadavana which seems to beckon you to hurry up with its fingers of leaves waving in the wind ; so please to enter.

राजा—(स्पर्शसुखं रूपयित्वा ।)—अभिजातः खलु वसन्तः। सखे
१२ पश्य

आमत्तानां श्रवणसुभगैः कूजितैः कोकिलानां
सानुक्रोशं मनसिजरुजः सह्यतां पृच्छतेव ।
अङ्गे चूतप्रसवसुरभिर्दक्षिणो मारुतो मे
सान्द्रस्पर्शः करतल इव व्यापृतो माधवेन ॥ ४ ॥

विदूषकः—एहि । पविस णिव्वुदिलाहाअ । [एहि । प्रविश निर्वृतिलाभाय ।] (उभौ प्रविशतः ।)

३ **विदूषकः**—भो वअस्स अवहाणेण दिट्ठिं देहि । एदं खु भवन्दं विलोहइदुकामाए पमदवणलच्छीए जुवइवेसलज्जत्तअं वसंदकुसुमणेवत्थं गहिदं । [भो वयस्य अवधानेन दृष्टिं देहि । एतत्खलु भवन्तं विलोभयितुकामया प्रमदवनलक्ष्म्या युवतिवेषलज्जयितृकं वसन्तकुसुमनेपथ्यं गृहीतम् ।]

राजा—ननु विस्मयादवलोकयामि ।

रक्ताशोकरुचा विशेषितगुणो बिम्बाधरालक्तकः
प्रत्याख्यातविशेषकं कुरबकं श्यामावदातारुणम् ।
आक्रान्ता तिलकक्रियापि तिलकैर्लग्नद्विरेफाञ्जनैः
सावज्ञेव मुखप्रसाधनविधौ श्रीर्माधवी योषिताम् ॥५॥

(उभौ उद्यानशोभां निरूपयतः ।)

(ततः प्रविशति पर्युत्सुका मालविका ।)

३ **मालविका**—अविण्णादहिअअं भट्टारं अहिलसन्ती अत्तणो वि दाव लज्जेमि । कुदो विहवो सिणिद्धसहिअणस्स इमं वुत्तन्तं आअक्खिदुं । ण आणे अप्पडीआरगरुअं वेणं केत्तिअं कालं
६ मअणो मं णइस्सदि । (कतिचित्पदानि गत्वा ।) कहिं णु खु पत्थिदम्हि । (विचिन्त्य) आं सन्दिट्ठम्हि देवीए जह 'मालविए गोदमचावलादो डोलापरिब्भट्ठाए सरुजा मह चलणा । तुमं दाव

King. (*Gesticulating that he feels the pleasure of touch*) How noble is spring : see friend,

by the sweet notes of the slightly intoxicated koil, he seems to be compassionately inquiring whether I can bear the torture of love; while the south breeze with its soft touch and its incense of mango-blossoms is like the palm of spring's hand stroking my limbs. (4)

Vidūṣaka. : Come, enter and repose yourself. (*Both enter.*)

Vidūṣaka. Look attentively, my friend. Surely the presiding goddess of the Pramadavana desiring to allure you has put on the garment of spring-flowers that puts to shame the dress of a young lady.

King. Indeed, I behold it and am filled with wonderment.

The gleaming red of the Aśoka excels the paint that is applied to the bimba-like lip ; the Kurabaka with its (variety of colours) dark, and bright, and red, surpasses the paintings on the forehead ; the Tilaka blossoms with the bees clinging to them like collyrium, have thoroughly grasped the art of adorning the forehead with the tilaka mark ; thus vernal beauty seems to hold up to ridicule the art of adorning the face as practised by women. (5)

(*Both of them observe the beauty of the garden. Enter Mālavikā in a state of longing.*)

Mālavikā. How I feel ashamed of myself for being in love with the king, whose heart is unknown to me

तवणीआसोअस्स दोहलं णिव्वट्टेहि। जइ सो पञ्चरत्तब्भन्दरे कुसुमं दंसेदि तदो अहं तुह (अन्तरा निश्वस्य) अहिलासपूरइत्तअं पसादं दाइस्सं ' ति । ता जाव णिओअभूमिं पुढमं गदा होमि । जाव अणुपदं मह चलणालङ्कारहत्थाए बउलावलिआए आअन्तव्वं । परिदेविस्सं दाव विस्सद्धं मुहुत्तअं। (इति परिक्रामति) [अविज्ञात-हृदयं भर्तारमभिलषन्त्यात्मनोऽपि तावल्लज्जे। कुतो विभवः स्निग्धसखी-जनस्येमं वृत्तान्तमाख्यातुम् । न जाने अप्रतीकारगुरुकां वेदनां कियन्तं कालं मदनो मां नेष्यति । कुत्र नु खलु प्रस्थितास्मि । आम् सन्दिष्टास्मि देव्या यथा ' मालविके गौतमचापलाद् दोला-परिभ्रष्टायाः सरुजौ मम चरणौ । त्वं तावत्तपनीयाशोकस्य दोहदं निर्वर्तय । यदि स पञ्चरात्राभ्यन्तरे कुसुमं दर्शयति ततोऽहं तव (अन्तरा निःश्वस्य) अभिलाषपूरयितृकं प्रसादं दास्यामि ' इति । तद्यावन्नियोगभूमिं प्रथमं गता भवामि । यावदनुपदं मम चरणा-लङ्कारहस्तया बकुलावलिकया आगन्तव्यम् । परिदेविष्ये तावद् विस्रब्धं मुहूर्तकम् ।]

विदूषकः (दृष्ट्वा)--ही ही इअं खु सीहुपाणुव्वेजिदस्स मच्छण्डिआ उवणदा । [ही ही इयं खलु शीधुपानोद्वेजितस्य मत्स्य-ण्डिका उपनता ।]

राजा—अये किमेतत् ।

विदूषकः—एसा खु णादिपज्जत्तवेसा पज्जूसुआ विअ एआइणी मालविआ अदूरे वट्टइ । [एषा खलु नातिपर्याप्तवेषा पर्युत्सुकेव एका-किनी मालविका अदूरे वर्तते ।]

राजा (सहर्षम्)—**कथं मालविका ।**

विदूषकः—अह इं । [अथ किम्]

राजा—शक्यमिदानीमात्मानमवलम्बितुम् ।

त्वदुपलभ्य समीपगतां प्रियां
हृदयमुच्छ्वसितं मम विक्लवम् ।

Where have I the courage to speak of the circumstance to my dear friend ? I do not know how long will love submit me to this irremediably severe agony. (*Moving a few steps)* Where, indeed, am I going ? (*Reflecting*) Ah, the queen has ordered me : 'Mālavikā, having had a fall from the swing owing to the heedlessness of Gautama, I am still suffering pain in my feet. Do you, therefore, perform the ceremony of fulfilling the longing of the golden Aśoka. If within five nights from this time it shows flowers,then will I (*Heaves a sigh in the middle of her speech*) bestow on you a favour which will gratify your desire.' I will, therefore, first proceed to the place where I am to perform this duty. For immediately after me will Bakulāvalikā come with the ornaments to adorn my feet. Let me then for a while freely bewail my state. (*Moves about.*)

Vidūṣaka. (*Observing*) Here is treacle offered to you who have been troubled with drinking wine.

King. Ah, what is this ?

Vidūsaka. Here is Mālavikā, not far (from us) but scantily dressed, who looks like one afflicted, and all alone.

King. (*With joy*) How ? Mālavikā ?

Vidūṣaka. Certainly.

King. Now it is possible to support my life.

When I learnt from you that my beloved was quite close (to us) my distracted heart (at once) revived like that of a thirsty traveller,

तरुच्छत्तं पथिकस्य पिपासतः
सलिलमारसितादिव सारसात् ॥ ६ ॥

अथ क तत्रभवती ।

विदूषकः—एषा णं तरुराइमज्झादो णिक्कन्ता इदो एव्व
३ परिवट्टन्ती दीसइ । [एषा ननु तरुराजिमध्यान्निष्क्रान्ता इत एव
परिवर्तमाना दृश्यते ।]

राजा—वयस्य पश्याम्येनाम्

विपुलं नितम्बबिम्बे मध्ये क्षामं समुन्नतं कुचयोः ।
अत्यायतं नयनयोर्मम जीवितमेतदायाति ॥ ७ ॥

सखे पूर्वस्मादवस्थान्तरमुपारूढा तत्रभवती । तथा हि ।

शरकाण्डपाण्डुगण्डस्थलेयमाभाति परिमिताभरणा ।
माधवपरिणतपत्रा कतिपयकुसुमेव कुन्दलता ॥८॥

विदूषकः—एसा वि भवं विअ मअणव्वाहिणा परामिट्ठा भविस्सदि।
[एषापि भवानिव मदनव्याधिना परामृष्टा भविष्यति ।]

३**राजा**—सौहार्दमेवं पश्यति ।

मालविका—अअं सो सुउमारदोहलावेक्खी अगहिदकुसुमणे-
वत्थो उक्कण्ठिदं मं अणुकरेदि असोओ । जाव से पच्छाअ-
६सीदले सिलापट्टए णिसण्णा अत्ताणं विणोदेमि । [अयं स सुकुमार-
दोहदापेक्षी अगृहीतकुसुमनेपथ्य उत्कण्ठितां मामनुकरोत्यशोकः । याव-
९दस्य प्रच्छायशीतले शिलापट्टके निषण्णात्मानं विनोदयामि ।]

विदूषकः—सुदं भवदा उक्कण्ठिदम्हित्ति तत्तहोदीए मन्तिदं ।
[श्रुतं भवता उत्कण्ठितास्मीति तत्रभवत्या मन्त्रितम् ।]

१२**राजा**—नैतावता भवन्तं प्रसन्नतर्कं मन्ये । कुतः ।

वोढा कुरबकरजसां किसलयपुटभेदशीकरानुगतः ।
अनिमित्तामुत्कण्ठामपि जनयति मलयवातोऽयम् ॥९॥

when from the cry of the Sārasa he gathers that some river surrounded by trees is near. (6)

Well, where is she?

Vidūsaka. Here she emerges from the rows of trees and seems to be turning in this very direction.

King. Well, friend, I see her.

Ample in the hips and thin in the waist, uplifted in the bosom and very broad in the eyes she, my very life, is coming. (7)

Friend, how she seems to have changed from the former state! For

scantily decked, her broad cheeks pale like the stalk of a reed, she resembles a Kunda creeper having its leaves ripened by spring and with only a few flowers. (8)

Vidūsaka. It is likely that she too like yourself is affected with love-sickness.

King. It is only friendship that sees thus.

Mālavikā. This Aśoka awaiting the fulfilment of its delicate longing, and not assuming its robe of flowers, seems to imitate me in my love-sick condition. So I will sit on the cool slab under its shade and divert myself.

Vidūṣaka. Did you hear? She said she was in a love-sick state.

King. That is not enough to assure me of the correctness of your inference.

This Malaya breeze laden with the pollen of the Kurabaka flowers, and charged with the drops of water issuing from the opening folds of the tender sprouts, produces longing in the heart without any definite cause. (9)

5

(मालविका उपविष्टा ।)

राजा—वयस्य इतस्तावदावां लतान्तरितौ भवावः ।

३ **विदूषकः**—इरावदिं विअ अदूरे समत्थेमि । [इरावतीमिवादूरे समर्थये ।]

राजा—न हि कमलिनीं दृष्ट्वा ग्राहमवेक्षते मतङ्गजः ।

६ (इति विलोकयन्स्थितः ।)

मालविका—हिअअ णिरवलम्बादो मणोरहादो विरम । किं मं आआसेसि । [हृदय निरवलम्बान्मनोरथाद्विरम । किं मामायासयसि ।]

९ (विदूषकः राजानमवेक्षते ।)

राजा (आत्मगतम्)—प्रिये पश्य वामतां स्नेहस्य ।

औत्सुक्यहेतुं विवृणोषि न त्वं
तत्त्वावबोधैकरसो न तर्कः ।
तथापि रम्भोरु करोमि लक्ष्य-
मात्मानमेषां परिदेवितानाम् ॥ १० ॥

विदूषकः—सम्पदं भवदो णिस्संसअं भविस्सदि । एसा अप्पिदमअणसन्देसा विवित्ते णं बउलावलिआ उवट्ठिदा । [सांप्रतं
३ भवतो निःसंशयं भविष्यति । एषार्पितमदनसन्देशा विविक्ते ननु बकुलावलिकोपस्थिता ।]

राजा—अपि स्मरेदस्मदभ्यर्थनाम् ।

६ **विदूषकः**—किं दाणिं एसा दासीए सुदा तुह गरुअं सन्देसं विसुमरिस्सदि । अहं वि दाव दाणिं एदं ण विसुमरेमि । [किमिदानीमेषा दास्याः सुता तव गुरुकं सन्देशं विस्मरिष्यति । अहमपि
९ तावदिदानीमेतं न विस्मरामि ।]

(प्रविश्य चरणालङ्कारहस्ता बकुलावलिका ।)

बकुलावलिका—अवि सुहं सहीए । [अपि सुखं सख्याः ।]

(*Mālavikā sits down.*)

King. Friend, come here, let us hide behind the creepers.

Vidūṣaka. I think Irāvatī, too, is not far from here.

King. But the elephant recks not of the alligator, when he sees a lotus-plant.

(*Stands gazing.*)

Mālavikā. My heart, cease from cherishing this fruitless longing. Why should you torture me ?

(*The Vidūṣaka looks at the king.*)

King. (*To himself*) Beloved, look, how perverse is love.

You do not reveal the cause of your longing
nor does conjecture invariably give the truth ;
nevertheless, fair one, I regard myself as the
theme of these lamentations. (10)

Vidūsaka. Now will be dispelled all your doubts. For is not that Bakulāvalikā to whom I gave your message of love arriving in this solitary place ?

King. I wonder if she remembers my request.

Vidūṣaka. How would that daughter of a female slave forget your weighty message now ? Why, even I remember it perfectly well at this moment.

(*Enter Bakulāvalikā with ornaments for the feet in her hand.*)

Bakulāvalikā. Is my friend happy ?

मालविका—अम्मो बउलावलिआ । सहि साअदं दे । उवविस । [अम्मो बकुलावलिका । सखि स्वागतं ते । उपविश ।]

बकुलावलिका (उपविश्य)—हला तुमं दाव दाणिं देवीए जोग्गदाए णिउत्ता । ता एक्कं दे चलणं उवणेहि । जाव सालत्तअं सणेउरं करेमि । [हला त्वं तावदिदानीं देव्या योग्यतया नियुक्ता । तदेकं ते चरणमुपनय । यावत्सालक्तकं सनूपुरं करोमि ।]

मालविका (स्वगतम्)—हिअअ अलं सुहिददाए अअं विहवो उवट्ठिदोत्ति । कहं दाणिं अत्ताणं मोचएअं । अहवा एदं एव्व मह मिच्चुमण्डणं भविस्सदि । [हृदय अलं सुखिततया अयं विभव उपस्थित इति । कथमिदानीमात्मानं मोचयेयम् । अथवा एतदेव मे मृत्युमण्डनं भविष्यति ।]

बकुलावलिका—किं विआरेसि । उस्सुआ खु एदस्स तवणीआसोअस्स कुसुमुग्गमे देवी । [किं विचारयसि । उत्सुका खल्वेतस्य तपनीयाशोकस्य कुसुमोद्गमे देवी ।]

राजा—कथमशोकदोहदनिमित्तोऽयमारम्भः ।

विदूषकः—किं णु खु ण आणासि अकालणादो देवी इमं अन्देउरणेवत्थेण ण संजोअइस्सदित्ति । [किं नु खलु न जानासि अकारणाद्देवी इमां अन्तःपुरनेपथ्येन न संयोजयिष्यतीति ।]

मालविका (पादमुपहरन्ती)—हला मरिसेहि दाणिं । [हला मर्षयेदानीम् ।]

बकुलावलिका—अइ सरीरं सि मे । (नाट्येन चरणालङ्कारमारभते।) [अयि शरीरमसि मे ।]

राजा— **चरणान्तनिवेशितां प्रियायाः**
सरसां पश्य वयस्य रागरेखाम् ।
प्रथमामिव पल्लवप्रसूतिं
हरदग्धस्य मनोभवद्रुमस्य ॥ ११ ॥

Mālavikā. Ah! Bakulāvalikā is come! Friend you are welcome. Sit down.

Bakulāvalikā. (*Sitting down*) Friend, you have indeed been appointed by the queen, owing to your fitness. So give me one of your feet ; so that I might lay on it the Alaktaka die and put the anklet on it.

Mālavikā. (*To herself*) My heart, do not be happy that greatness comes to you. How can I secure my freedom ? Or rather this will serve as the ornament to adorn me at death.

Bakulāvalikā. Why are you hesitating ? The queen indeed, is anxious that the golden Aśoka should burst into flowers.

King. So all this preparation is due to the longing of the Aśoka !

Vidūṣaka. Why ! Don't you know that the queen will not without reason make her put on the attire of the harem ?

Mālavikā. (*Bringing close her foot*) Friend, please to pardon me.

Bakulāvalikā. You are indeed as dear to me as my very body. (*She gesticulates adorning her foot.*)

King. Friend, look at this streak of wet paint laid upon her foot, which is like the first burgeoning of leaves on the tree of love consumed by Hara. (11)

विदूषकः—चलणाणुरूवो खु तत्तहोदीए अहिआरो उवक्खित्तो। [चरणानुरूपः खलु तत्रभवत्या अधिकार उपक्षिप्तः ।]

राजा—सम्यगभिहितं भवता।

नवकिसलयरागेणाग्रपादेन बाला
स्फुरितनखरुचा द्वौ हन्तुमर्हत्यनेन।
अकुसुमितमशोकं दोहदापेक्षया वा
प्रणिहितशिरसं वा कान्तमार्द्रापराधम् ॥१२॥

विदूषकः—पारइस्ससि तत्तहोदीए अवरध्दुं। [पारयिष्यसि तत्रभवत्या अपराद्धुम् ।]

राजा—प्रतिगृहीतं वचः सिद्धिदर्शिनो ब्राह्मणस्य।

(ततः प्रविशति युक्तमदा इरावती चेटी च।)

इरावती—हञ्जे णिउणिए सुणामि बहुसो मदो किल इत्थिआजणस्स विसेसमण्डणं ति। अवि सच्चो अअं लोअवादो। [हञ्जे निपुणिके शृणोमि बहुशो मदः किल स्त्रीजनस्य विशेषमण्डनमिति। अपि सत्योऽयं लोकवादः।]

निपुणिका—पुढमं लोअवादो एव्व। अज्ज उण सच्चो संवुत्तो। [प्रथमं लोकवाद एव। अद्य पुनः सत्यः संवृत्तः।]

इरावती—अल मइ सिणेहेण। कुदो दाणिं अवगदं डोलाघरं पुढमं गदो भट्टात्ति। [अलं मयि स्नेहेन। कुत इदानीमवगतं दोलागृहं प्रथमं गतो भर्तेति।]

निपुणिका—भट्टिणीए अखण्डिदादो पणआदो। [भट्टिन्या अखण्डितात्प्रणयात्।]

इरावती—अलं सेवाए। मज्झत्थदं गेण्हिअ भणाहि। [अलं सेवया। मध्यस्थतां गृहीत्वा भण।]

निपुणिका—वसन्दोवाअणलोलुवेण अज्जगोदमेण कहिदं। तुवरदु भट्टिणी। [वसन्तोपायनलोलुपेनार्यगौतमेन कथितम्। त्वरतां भट्टिनी।]

Vidūsaka. The queen indeed has laid upon her foot a duty of which it is worthy.

King. You speak well.

With the toes of her foot red-hued like young foliage; and flashing with the lustre of the nails this girl deserves to smite two objects—the Aśoka awaiting the fulfilment of its longing before it would blossom, and the lover who, having only recently given offence, stands with bowed head. (12)

Vidūsaka. You will soon be able to give some offence.

King. I accept these words of a Brahmin who prophesies success.

(*Enter Irāvatī in a state of intoxication and an attendant.*)

Irāvatī. Girl Nipunikā, I heard it often said that intoxication is a special ornament to women. Is there any truth in this popular saying ?

Nipunikā. First it was a popular saying merely- but now it has become true.

Irāvatī. Have done with this affection towards me. How did you know that my lord went first to the house in which the swing is ?

Nipunikā. From my unfailing affection for my mistress.

Irāvatī. Give up this servile attitude—speak like one independent.

Nipuṇikā. It was the noble Vasantaka, greedy to receive presents offered in the month of spring, who told me so.

इरावती—(अवस्थासदृशं परिक्रम्य ।) हञ्जे मएण मिलाअमाणं मं अज्जउत्तदंसणे हिअअं तुवरावेदि । चलणा उण मग्गे ण प्पसरन्ति । [हञ्जे मदेन म्लायमानां मामार्यपुत्रदर्शने हृदयं त्वरयति । चरणौ पुनर्मार्गे न प्रसरतः ।]

निपुणिका—णं सम्पत्तम्ह डोलाघरअं । [ननु संप्राप्ते स्वो दोलागृहम् ।]

इरावती—णिउणिए ण एत्थ अज्जउत्तो दीसइ । [निपुणिके नात्रार्यपुत्रो दृश्यते ।]

निपुणिका—ओलोएदु भट्टिणी । परिहासणिमित्तं कहिं वि गूढेण भट्टिणा होदव्वं । अम्हे वि इमं पिअङ्गुलदापरिक्खित्तं असोअसिलापट्टअं पविसम्ह । [अवलोकयतु भट्टिनी । परिहासनिमित्तं कुत्रापि गूढेन भर्त्रा भवितव्यम् । आवामपीमं प्रियङ्गुलतापारिक्षिप्तमशोकशिलापट्टकं प्रविशावः ।]

(इरावती तथा करोति ।)

निपुणिका (परिक्रम्य विलोक्य ।)—ओलोएदु भट्टिणी । चूदङ्कुरं विइण्णन्तीणं अम्हाणं पिपीलिआहिं दट्ठं । [अवलोकयतु भट्टिनी । चूताङ्कुरं विचिन्वत्योरावयोः पिपीलिकाभिर्दष्टम् ।]

इरावती—किं विअ एदं । [किमिवैतत् ।]

निपुणिका—एसा बउलावलिआ असोअपाअवच्छाआए मालविआए चलणालङ्कारं णिव्वट्टेदि । [एषा बकुलावलिका अशोकवृक्षच्छायायां मालविकायाश्चरणालङ्कारं निर्वर्तयति ।]

इरावती (शङ्कां रूपयित्वा ।)—अभूमी इअं मालविआए । किं तक्केसि । (अभूमिरियं मालविकायाः । किं तर्कयसि ।)

निपुणिका—तक्केमि डोलापरिब्भट्ठाए सलुजचलणाए असोअदोहलाहिआरे णिउत्ता मालविअत्ति । अण्णहा कहं देवी सअं

Irāvatī. (*Moving in a manner befitting her condition*) Girl, my heart hastens me that have grown languid through intoxication, to see my lord; but my feet do not move on the way.

Nipuṇikā. Well, we have come to the house where the swing is.

Irāvatī. Nipuṇikā, my lord is not to be seen here.

Nipuṇikā. Look about you, my mistress; for the king, simply to make fun, may have lain hidden. We too shall sit down on this slab of stone under the Asoka tree which is twined round with the Priyangu creeper.

(Irāvatī does as described.)

Nipuṇikā. *(Moving about and observing* Look, mistress. While searching for mango-sprouts we have been bitten by ants.

Irāvatī. What is it?

Nipuṇikā. Here is Bakulāvalikā adorning Mālavikā's foot in the shade of the Aśoka tree.

Irāvatī. (*Expressing doubt*) This is not a place where Mālavikā can have access. What do you think, then?

Nipuṇikā. I think that the queen, having had a fall from the swing and got pain in her feet, has appointed Mālavikā to perform the ceremony of fulfilling the long-

धारिदं णेउरजुअलं परिअणस्स अणुजाणिस्सदि। [तर्कयामि दोलापरिभ्रष्टया-सरुजचरणया देव्या अशोकदोहदाधिकारे नियुक्ता मालविकेति । अन्यथा कथं देवी स्वयं धारितं नूपुरयुगलं परिजनस्यानुज्ञास्यति]

इरावती—महदी खु से सम्भावणा । [महती खल्वस्याः सम्भावना ।]

निपुणिका—किं उण ण अण्णेसीअदि भट्टा । [किंपुनर्नान्विष्यते भर्ता ।]

इरावती—हंजे मे चलणा अण्णदो ण प्पवट्टन्ति । मणो वि किं वि विआरेदि । आसङ्किदस्स दाव अन्तं गमिस्सं । (मालविकां निर्वर्ण्य आत्मगतम् ।) ठाणे खु कादरं मे हिअअं । [हञ्जे मे चरणावन्यतो न प्रवर्तेते । मनोऽपि किमपि विचारयति । आशङ्कितस्य तावदन्तं गमिष्यामि । स्थाने खलु कातरं मे हृदयम् ।]

बकुलावलिका (चरणं दर्शयन्ती ।)—हला मालविए अवि रोअदि दे अअं चलणराअरेहाविण्णासो । [हला मालविके अपि रोचते तेऽयं चरणरागरेखाविन्यासः ।]

मालविका—अत्तणो चलणगदोत्ति लज्जेमि णं पसंसिदुं । कहेहि केण पसाहणकलाए अहिविणीदासि । [आत्मनश्चरणगत इति लज्जे एनं प्रशंसितुम् । कथय केन प्रसाधनकलायामभिविनीतासि ।]

बकुलावलिका—एत्थ खु भट्टिणो सिस्सम्हि । [अत्र खलु भर्तुः शिष्यास्मि ।]

विदूषकः—तुवरेहि दाणिं गुरुदक्खिणाए । [त्वरस्वेदानीं गुरुदक्षिणायै ।]

मालविका—दिट्ठिआ ण गव्विदासि । [दिष्टया न गर्वितासि ।]

बकुलावलिका—उवदेसाणुरूवे चलणे लम्भिअ दाणिं गव्विदा भविस्सं । (स्वगतम् ।) हन्त सिद्धं मे दोच्चं । (रागं विलोक्य प्रकाशम् ।) सहि एक्कस्स दे चलणस्स अवसिदो राअणिक्खेवो ।

ing of the Aśoka tree ; how, otherwise, could the queen allow a mere servant to wear the anklets worn by herself ?

Irāvatī. She has, indeed, been highly honoured.

Nipunikā. But why should we not seek the king ?

Irāvatī. Well, girl, my feet do not move from this place, and my mind too is filled with some suspicions ; I shall first get to the end of them. (*Looking at Mālavikā, to herself*) It is but proper that my heart is filled with fear.

Bakulāvalikā. *(Pointing to the foot)* friend Mālavikā, how do you like these lines of paint on your foot ?

Mālavikā. I am ashamed of praising it, as it is on my own foot. Tell me who taught you this art of decoration.

Bakulāvalikā. I am the pupil of the king in this (art).

Vidūsakā. Be quick now to receive the present due to a teacher.

Mālavikā. Happily you are free from conceit.

Bakulāvalikā. Surely I shall be full of conceit, now that I can exhibit my skill on worthy feet. (*To herself*) O joy, my mission is done. *(Looking at the paint, aloud)*

केवलं मुहमारुदो लम्भइदव्वो । अहवा पवादो एव्व अअं पदेसो । [उपदेशानुरूपे चरणे लब्ध्वा इदानीं गर्विता भविष्यामि । हन्त, सिद्धं मे दौत्यम् । सखि एकस्य ते चरणस्यावशितो रागनिक्षेपः । केवलं मुखमारुतो लम्भयितव्यः । अथवा प्रवात एवायं प्रदेशः ।]

राजा—सखे पश्य पश्य ।

आर्द्रालक्तकमस्याश्चरणं मुखमारुतेन वीजयितुम् ।
प्रतिपन्नः प्रथमतरः सम्प्रति सेवावकाशो मे ॥ १३ ॥

विदूषकः—कुदो दे अणुसओ । चिरं भवदा एदं कमेण अणुहोदव्वं । [कुतस्तेऽनुशयः । चिरं भवतैतत्क्रमेणानुभवितव्यम् ।]

बकुलावलिका—सहि अरुणसदपत्तं विअ सोहदि दे चलणं । सव्वहा भट्टिणो अङ्कपरिवट्टिणी होहि । [सखि अरुणशतपत्रमिव शोभते ते चरणम् । सर्वथा भर्तुरङ्कपरिवर्तिनी भव ।]

(इरावती निपुणिकामुखमवेक्षते ।)

राजा—ममेयमाशीः ।

मालविका—हला अवअणीअं मन्तेसि । [हला अवचनीयं मन्त्रयसे ।]

बकुलावलिका—मन्तिदव्वं एव्व मए मन्तिदं । [मन्त्रयितव्यमेव मया मन्त्रितम् ।]

मालविका—पिआ खु अहं तुह । [प्रिया खल्वहं तव ।]

बकुलावलिका—ण केवलं मह । [न केवलं मम]

मालविका—कस्स वा अण्णस्स । [कस्य वान्यस्य ।]

बकुलावलिका—गुणेसु अहिणिवेसिणो भट्टिणो वि । [गुणेष्वभिनिवेशिनो भर्तुरपि ।]

मालविका— अलिअं मन्तासि । एदं एव्व मइ णात्थि । [अलीकं मन्त्रयसे । एतदेव मयि नास्ति ।]

बकुलावलिका—सच्चं तुइ णत्थि । भट्टिणो किसेसु सुन्दरपण्डुरेसु

Friend, I have finished laying the paint on one of your feet. Only it requires to be blown upon by the mouth ; or rather there is a good breeze here.

King. Mark, my friend, mark.

Here is an admirable opportunity for me to
wait upon her by blowing upon her foot with
the breath of my mouth—her foot which has
the paint still wet upon it. (13)

Vidūṣaka. Where is the occasion for regret ? Soon you will be enjoying (this privilege) for a long time.

Bakulāvalikā. My friend, your foot looks as lovely as a red lotus. May you, by all means, sit in the king's lap.

(Irāvatī looks at Nipuṇikā's face.)

King. To me it is a blessing.

Mālavikā. Well you are chattering absurdly.

Bakulāvalikā. I have said what I ought to say.

Mālavikā. Surely you love me.

Bakulāvalikā. Not only I but—

Mālavikā. Who else ?

Bakulāvalikā. The king also who is attracted by good qualities.

Mālavikā. You don't speak the truth ; for I haven't secured the king's love.

Bakulāvalikā. You haven't indeed ! Only it is to

अङ्गेसु दीसइ । [सत्यं त्वयि नास्ति । भर्तुः कृशेषु सुन्दरपाण्डुरेष्वङ्गेषु दृश्यते ।]

निपुणिका——पुढमगणिदं विअ हदासाए उत्तरं । [प्रथमगणितमिव हताशाया उत्तरम् ।]

बकुलावलिका——अणुराओ अणुराएण परिक्खिदव्वोत्ति सुअणवअणं पमाणीकरेहि । [अनुरागोऽनुरागेण परीक्षितव्य इति सुजनवचनं प्रमाणीकुरु ।)

मालविका——किं अत्तणो छन्देण मन्तेसि । [किमात्मनश्छन्देन मन्त्रयसे ।]

बकुलावलिका——णहि णहि । भट्टिणो खु एदाइं पणअमउआइं बिम्बन्तरिदाइं अक्खराइं । [नहि नहि । भर्तुः खल्वेतानि प्रणयमृदुकानि बिम्बान्तरितान्यक्षराणि ।]

मालविका——हला देविं चिन्तिअ ण मे हिअअं विस्ससदि । [हला देवीं चिन्तयित्वा न मे हृदयं विश्वसिति !]

बकुलावलिका——मुद्धे भमरसम्बाधोत्ति वसन्तावदारसव्वस्सभूदो किं ण चूदप्पसवो ओदंसणिज्जो । [मुग्धे भ्रमरसम्बाध इति वसन्तावतारसर्वस्वभूतः किं न चूतप्रसवोऽवतंसनीयः ।]

मालविका——तुमं दाव दुज्जादे मह अच्चन्तसहाइणी होहि । [त्वं तावद् दुर्जाते ममात्यन्तसहायिनी भव ।]

बकुलावलिका——विमद्दसुरही बउलावलिआ खु अहं । [विमर्दसुरभिर्बकुलावलिका खल्वहम् ।]

राजा—साधु बकुलावलिके साधु ।

> भावज्ञानानन्तरं प्रस्तुतेन
> प्रत्याख्याने दत्तयुक्तोत्तरेण ।
> वाक्येनेयं स्थापिता स्वे निदेशे
> स्थाने प्राणाः कामिनां दूत्यधीनाः ॥ १४ ॥

be seen in the beautifully pale and thin limbs of the king.

Nipuṇikā. How the accursed wench gives her answers as if she had got them all up beforehand.

Bakulāvalikā. You must accept the words of the good people as authoritative : love is tested by love.

Mālavikā. How do you talk as suits your fancy ?

Bakulāvalikā. No, no ; these are but the words of the king echoed by me which are so sweet through love.

Mālavikā. Friend, my heart grows diffident as I think of the queen.

Bakulāvalikā. You simple girl, is the mango-shoot-spring's all in all not to be used as an ear-ornament because bees are clinging to it ?

Mālavikā. But, surely, you will help me greatly in my distress.

Bakulāvalikā. Well, am I not a Bakula garland which gives out fragrance when crushed ?

King. Good, Bakulāvalikā, good.

Surely she has held her to her purpose by her words which were spoken after ascertaining her feelings, and which effectively answered all her objections ; it is quite proper that the life of a lover is dependent on a love-messenger. (14)

इरावती—हञ्जे पेक्ख पेक्ख । कारिदा एव्व एदस्सिं बउलावलिआए पदं मालविआ । [हञ्जे पश्य पश्य । कारितैवैतस्मिन् बकुलावलिकया पदं मालविका ।]

निपुणिका—भट्टिणि णिव्विआरस्स वि ऊसुअदाजणओ उवदेसो । [भट्टिनि निर्विकारस्याप्युत्सुकताजनक उपदेशः ।]

इरावती—ठाणे सङ्किदं मे हिअअं । गहिदत्था अणन्तरं चिन्तइस्सं । [स्थाने शङ्कितं मे हृदयम् । गृहीतार्थानन्तरं चिन्तयिष्यामि ।]

बकुलावलिका—एसो दुदीओ वि समत्तपडिकम्मो दे चलणो । जाव दुवे वि सणेउरे करेमि । (नाट्येन नूपुरयुगलमामुच्य ।) हला उट्ठेहि अणुचिट्ठ देवीए असोअविआसइत्तअं णिओअं । (उभे उत्तिष्ठतः ।) [एष द्वितीयोऽपि समाप्तपरिकर्मा ते चरणः । यावद् द्वावपि सनूपुरौ करोमि । हला उत्तिष्ठ । अनुतिष्ठ देव्या अशोकविकासयितृकं नियोगम् ।]

इरावती—सुदं देवीए णिओओत्ति दाणिं । [श्रुतं देव्या नियोग इतीदानीम ।]

बकुलावलिका—एसो उवारूढराओ उवभोअक्खमो पुरदो दे दीसइ । [एष उपारूढराग उपभोगक्षमः पुरतस्ते दृश्यते।]

मालविका (सहर्षम्)—किं भट्टा । [किं भर्ता ।]

बकुलावलिका (सस्मितम्)—ण दाव भट्टा । एसो असोअसाहावलम्बी पल्लवगुच्छो । ओदंसेहि दाव णं । [न तावद्भर्ता । एषोऽशोकशाखावलम्बी पल्लवगुच्छः । अवतंसय तावदेनम ।]

विदूषकः—अवि सुदं भवदा । [अपि श्रुतं भवता ।]

राजा—सखे पर्याप्तमेतावता कामिनाम् ।

अनातुरोत्कण्ठितयोः प्रसिध्यता
समागमेनापि रतिर्न मां प्रति ।
परस्परप्राप्तिनिराशयोर्वरं
शरीरनाशोऽपि समानुरागयोः ॥ १५ ॥

Irāvatī. Mark, girl, mark. Already has she made Mālavikā aspire after him.

Nipunikā. Mistress, even a person free from passion would become restless by such teaching.

Irāvatī. I was rightly apprenhensive. After getting at the facts, I will think (what to do).

Bakulāvalikā. I have finished painting this your other foot also. So now I will put anklets on them. *(Acting loosening the pair of anklets)* Friend, rise, do the queen's bidding of causing the Aśoka to blossom. (*Both rise.*)

Irāvatī. So now we learn that it is the queen's bidding.

Bakulāvalikā. Here before you stands one flushed (of increased redness, passion) and fit to enjoy.

Mālavikā. (*With joy)* What? The king?

Bakulāvalikā. (*Smiling*) Not the king, but a spray of leaves on a bough of the Aśoka. Make an ear-ornament of it.

Vidūsaka. Did your highness hear?

King. Friend, this much is enough for lovers.

For to me there is no pleasure in the union of lovers one of whom is ardent and the other indifferent, although it may be successfully accomplished; better it is that those whose love is equal pine away through despair of securing their union. (15)

(मालविका रचितपल्लवावतंसा सलीलमशोकाय पादं प्रहिणोति ।)

राजा—वयस्य पश्य ।

> **आदाय कर्णकिसलयमस्मादियमत्र चरणमर्पयति ।**
> **उभयोः सदृशविनिमयादात्मानं वञ्चितं मन्ये ॥१६॥**

मालविका—अवि णाम अम्हाणं संभावणा सफला हवे । [अपि नाम आवयोः सम्भावना सफला भवेत् ।]

बकुलावलिका—हला णत्थि दे दोसो णिग्गुणो अअं असोओ जइ कुसुमुब्भेदमन्थरो भवे जो ईरिसं चरणसक्कारं लहेइ । [हला नास्ति ते दोषः निर्गुणोऽयमशोकः यदि कुसुमोद्भेदमन्थरो भवेद्य ईदृशं चरणसत्कारं लभते ।]

राजा—

> **अनेन तनुमध्यया मुखरनूपुराराविणा**
> **नवाम्बुरुहकोमलेन चरणेन सम्भावितः ।**
> **अशोक यदि सद्य एव कुसुमैर्न सम्पत्स्यसे**
> **वृथा वहसि दोहदं ललितकामिसाधारणम् ॥ १७ ॥**

सखे वचनावसरपूर्वं प्रवेष्टुमिच्छामि ।

विदूषकः—एहि णं परिहासइस्सं । [एह्येनां परिहासयिष्यामि ।]

(उभौ प्रवेशं कुरुतः ।)

निपुणिका—भट्टिणि भट्टा एत्थ एव्व पविसदि । [भट्टिनि भर्ता अत्रैव प्रविशति ।]

इरावती—इदं मह पुढमं चिन्तिदं हिअएण । [इदं मम प्रथमं चिन्तितं हृदयेन ।]

विदूषकः (उपसृत्य)—होदि जुत्तं णाम अत्तहोदो पिअवअस्सो असोओ अअं वामपादेण ताडिदुं । [भवति युक्तं नामात्रभवतः प्रियवयस्योऽशोकोऽयं वामपादेन ताडयितुम् ।]

उभे (ससम्भ्रमम्)—अम्मो भट्टा । [अम्मो भर्ता ।]

(Mālavikā after arranging the tender leaves into an ear-ornament gracefully raises her foot towards the Aśoka.)

King. Friend, see.

Having taken a sprig for the ear of this (Aśoka) she is presenting to it her foot. By this mutual exchange of similar gifts I feel that I have been deluded. (16)

Mālavikā. Will this honour rendered by us to the Aśoka bear fruit ?

Bakulāvalikā. Friend, it won't be your fault; for if after receiving this honour from your foot, the Aśoka is tardy in blossoming out, it would be devoid of any good qualities.

King. Honoured with her foot delicate as a fresh lotus and loud-tinkling with the jingling anklets by this slender-waisted one, O Aśoka, if you are not immediately covered with blossoms, then in vain do you cherish the delicate longing which is also cherished by sportive lovers. (17)

Friend, I desire to show myself when an opportunity for interposing a remark presents itself.

Vidūṣaka. Come I will make fun of her. (*Both enter.*)

Nipuṇikā. Mistress, here comes the king on the scene.

Irāvatī. This was what my heart had already anticipated.

Vidūṣaka. (*Approaching*) Lady, is it proper to strike with the foot this Aśoka, the dear friend of the king ?

Both. (*confusedly*) O, the king !

विदूषकः—बउलावलिए तुए गहिदत्थाए ईरिसं अविणअं करेन्ती किं सही ण णिवारिदा। [बकुलावलिके त्वया गृहीतार्थया ईदृसमविनयं कुर्वती किं सखी न निवारिता।]

(मालविका भयं रूपयति।)

निपुणिका—भट्टिणि पेक्ख किं पवुत्तं अज्जगोदमेण। [भट्टिनि पश्य किं प्रवृत्तमार्यगौतमेन।]

इरावती—कहं बम्हबन्धू अण्णहा जिविस्सदि। [कथं ब्रह्मबन्धुरन्यथा जीविष्यति।]

बकुलावलिका—अज्ज एसा देवीए णिओअं अणुचिट्ठदि। एदस्सिं अदिक्कमे परवदी इअं। पसीददु भट्टा। [आर्य एषा देव्या नियोगमनुतिष्ठति। एतस्मिन्नतिक्रमे परवतीयम्। प्रसीदतु भर्ता।] (आत्मना सममेनां प्रणिपातयति।)

राजा—यद्येवमनपराद्धासि। उत्तिष्ठ भद्रे। (हस्तेन गृहीत्वोत्थापयति।)

विदूषकः—जुज्जइ। देवी एत्थ माणइदव्वा। [युज्यते। देव्यत्र मानयितव्या।]

राजा (विहस्य)—

किसलयमृदोर्विलासिनि कठिने निहितस्य पादपस्कन्धे।
चरणस्य न ते बाधा सम्प्रति वामस्य वामोरु॥ १८॥

(मालविका लज्जां नाटयति।)

इरावती (सासूयम्)—अहो अविणीदहिअओ खु अज्जउत्तो। [अहो अविनीतहृदयः खल्वार्यपुत्रः।]

मालविका—बउलावलिए एहि। अणुट्ठिदं अत्तणो णिओअं देवीए णिवेदेम्ह। [बकुलावलिके एहि। अनुष्ठितमात्मनो नियोगं देव्यै निवेदयावः।]

बकुलावलिका—तेण हि विण्णवेहि भट्टारं विसज्जेहि त्ति। [तेन हि विज्ञापय भर्तारं विसर्जयेति।]

Vidūsaka. Bakulāvalikā, why did not you, who knew it, prevent this your friend from doing the immodest deed ?

(Mālavikā gesticulates fear.)

Nipuṇikā. Mistress, see what the noble Gautama is about.

Irāvatī. How else could that accursed Brahmin find a living ?

Bakulāvalikā. Sir, she is doing the queen's bidding; she cannot help this transgression. Let the king be compassionate. (*She makes Mālavikā bow along with herself.*)

King. If it is thus,you are innocent. Rise, good girl.

(*Takes her by the hand and raises her.*)

Vidūṣaka. That is proper ; for the queen must be respected.

King. (*Smiling*)

Fair one, full of graces, I hope you have not
hurt your foot soft as a young shoot by placing
it on the hard stem of the tree, now. (18)

(*Mālavikā gesticulates bashfulness.*)

Irāvatī. (*Angrily*) How wanton in thought is my lord.

Mālavikā. Bakulāvalikā, come,let us go and report to the queen that we have done her bidding.

Bakulāvalikā. Well, then request the king to give you leave to depart.

९ **राजा**—भद्रे यास्यसि । मम तावदुपपन्नावसरमर्थित्वं श्रूयताम् ।

बकुलावलिका—अवहिदा सुणाहि । आणवेदु भट्टा । [अवहिता शृणु । आज्ञापयतु भर्ता ।]

१२ **राजा**—

धृतिपुष्पमयमपि जनो बध्नाति न तादृशं चिरात्प्रभृति ।
स्पर्शामृतेन पूरय दोहदमस्याप्यनन्यरुचेः ॥ १९ ॥

इरावती (सहसोपसृत्य)—पूरेहि पूरेहि । असोओ कुसुमं दंसेदि ण वा । अअं उण पुप्फइ फलइ अ । [पूरय पूरय । अशोकः कुसुमं दर्शयति न वा । अयं पुनः पुष्प्यति फलति च ।]

(सर्वे इरावतीं दृष्ट्वा सम्भ्रान्ताः ।)

६ **राजा** (अपवार्य)—वयस्य का प्रतिपत्तिरत्र ।

विदूषकः—किं अण्णं । जङ्घाबलं एव्व । [किमन्यत् । जङ्घाबलमेव ।]

९ **इरावती**—बउलावलिए साहु तुए उवक्कन्तं । मालविए तुमं दाव करेहि सफलपत्थणं अज्जउत्तं । [बकुलावलिके साधु त्वयोपक्रान्तम् । मालविके त्वं तावत् कुरु सफलप्रार्थनमार्यपुत्रम् ।]

१२ **उभौ**—पसीददु भट्टिणी । का अम्हे भट्टिणो पणअपरिग्गहस्स । [प्रसीदतु भट्टिनी । के आवां भर्तुः प्रणयपरिग्रहस्य ।]

(इति निष्क्रान्ते ।)

१५ **इरावती**—अहो अविस्ससणीआ पुरिसा । मए क्खु अत्तणो वञ्चणा वाहजणगीदिरत्ताए हरिणीए विअ असङ्किदाए ण विण्णादा । [अहो अविश्वसनीयाः पुरुषाः । मया खल्वात्मनो वञ्चना व्याधजनगी-
१८ तिरक्तया हरिण्येवाशङ्कितया न विज्ञाता ।]

विदूषकः (जनान्तिकम्)—पडिओजेहि किं वि दाणिं । किं अण्णं कम्मगहिदेण कुम्भीलएण सन्धिच्छेअणं सिक्खिदोम्हित्ति
२१ वत्तव्वं होइ । [प्रतियोजय किमपीदानीम् । किमन्यत् कर्मगृहीतेन कुम्भीलकेन सन्धिच्छेदनं शिक्षितोऽस्मीति वक्तव्यं भवति ।]

King. Fair one, you will go (presently). But listen to this request which is proper to the occasion.

Bakulāvalikā. Listen attentively. Let the king command.

King.

I too have not for a long time borne the flower of happiness ; with the nectar of touch do you satisfy the longing of one who has relish left for nothing else now. (19).

Irāvatī. (*Suddenly presenting herself*) Satisfy, satisfy ; the Aśoka may or may not bear blossoms ; but this on the other hand not only flowers but also bears fruit.

(*All are confused at the sight of Irāvatī.*)

King. (*Aside*) Friend, what is the recourse now ?

Vidūsaka. What save taking to our heels ?

Irāvatī. Bakulāvalikā, you have begun well ! Mālavikā, do you fulfil my lord's longing.

Both. Be pleased, mistress. Who are we to receive such favours from the king ? (*Exeunt*)

Irāvatī. What traitors men are ! But, guileless like a deer attracted by the hunter's song, I did not realise my deception.

Vidūsaka. (*Aside*) Invent something now. What else : a burglar caught red-handed should say that he was but learning house-breaking.

राजा——सुन्दरि, न मे मालविकायां कश्चिदर्थः । मया त्वं चिरायसीति यथाकथंचिदात्मा विनोदितः ।

इरावती—विस्ससणीओ सि । मए ण विण्णादं ईरिसं विणोदवत्थुअं अज्जउत्तेण उवलद्धंति । अण्णहा मन्दभाइणीए एव्वं ण किज्जइ । [विश्वसनीयोऽसि । मया न विज्ञातमीदृशं विनोदवस्तुकमार्यपुत्रेणोपलब्धमिति । अन्यथा मन्दभागिन्या एवं न क्रियते ।]

विदूषकः——मा दाव अत्तहोदी अत्तहोदो दक्खिण्णस्स उवरोहं भणादु । समावत्तिदिट्ठेण देवीए परिअणेण संकहा वि जइ अवराहो ठाविअदि एत्थ तुमं एव्व पमाणं । [मा तावदत्रभवती अत्रभवतो दाक्षिण्यस्योपरोधं भणतु । समापत्तिदृष्टेन देव्याः परिजनेन सङ्कथापि यद्यपराधः स्थाप्यते अत्र त्वमेव प्रमाणम् ।]

इरावती——णं संकहा णाम होदु । किंति अत्ताणं आआसइस्सं । [ननु संकथा नाम भवतु । किमित्यात्मानमायासयिष्ये ।]

[रुष्टा प्रस्थिता ।]

राजा (अनुसरन्)——प्रसीदतु भवती ।

[इरावती रशनासन्दितचरणा व्रजत्येव ।]

राजा——सुन्दरि न शोभते प्रणयिजने निरपेक्षता ।

इरावती——सढ, अविस्ससणीअहिअओ सि । [शठ, अविश्वसनीयहृदयोऽसि ।]

राजा——

शठ इति मयि तावदस्तु ते
परिचयवत्यवधीरणा प्रिये ।
चरणपातितया न चण्डि तां
विसृजसि मेखलयापि याचिता ॥ २० ॥

इरावती—इअं वि हदासा तुमं एव्व अणुसरदि । [इयमपि हताशा त्वामेवानुसरति ।]

King. Darling, I care not for Mālavikā. I was just amusing myself as you were late.

Irāvatī. You are to be relied upon. I did not know that my lord had secured such a means of amusement; otherwise luckless that I am, I would not have acted thus.

Vidūsaka. Let not my lady by her words repel his civilities. For if mere conversation with the queen's attendant met by chance is put down as an offence, then you should direct (what is proper and improper.)

Irāvatī. Be it mere conversation! Why should I worry myself? *(Starts to go in anger.)*

King. *(following)* Be pleased my lady—

(Irāvatī moves, although her feet are entangled by the girdle.)

King. Fair one, it is not good to be indifferent to a lover.

Irāvatī. Traitor, you are wholly unreliable.

King.

With the word, traitor, you may show your
usual scorn of me; but why not give it up, Oh
angry one, although besought by your girdle
that has fallen at your feet? (20)

Irāvatī. How this accursed one also sides with you?

(इति रशनामादाय राजानं ताडयितुमिच्छति ।)

राजा--वयस्य एषा हि

बाष्पासारा हेमकाञ्चीगुणेन
श्रोणीबिम्बादव्यपेक्षाच्युतेन ।
चण्डी चण्डं हन्तुमभ्युद्यता मां
विद्युद्दाम्ना मेघराजीव विन्ध्यम् ॥ २१ ॥

इरावती--किं मां भूओ वि अवरद्धं करेसि । [किं मां भूयोऽप्यपराद्धां करोषि ।] (इति रशनां हस्तेनावलम्बते ।)

राजा--

अपराधिनि मयि दण्डं संहरसि किमुद्यतं कुटिलकेशि ।
वर्धयसि विलसितं त्वं दासजनायात्र कुप्यसि च ॥ २२ ॥

(आत्मगतम्) नूनमिदानीमनुज्ञातम् । (इति पादयोः पतति ।)

इरावती--ण क्खु इमे मालविआए चलणा जे दे फरिसदोहलं पूरइस्संति । [न खल्विमौ मालविकायाश्चरणौ यौ ते स्पर्शदोहदं पूरयिष्यतः ।] (इति सचेटी निष्क्रान्ता ।)

विदूषकः—उट्ठेहि । किदप्पसादो सि । [उत्तिष्ठ । कृतप्रसादोऽसि ।]

राजा (उत्थाय इरावतीमपश्यन् ।)—कथं गतैव प्रिया ।

विदूषकः—वयस्स देवेहिं इमस्स अविणअस्स अपसारिदा णिअंतणा । दात्र सिग्घदरं अवक्कमाम जाव अङ्गारओ रासिं विअ सा अणुवक्कं ण करेइ । [वयस्य देवैरस्याविनयस्यापसारिता नियन्त्रणा । तावच्छीघ्रतरमपक्रमावः यावदङ्गारको राशिमिव सा अनुवक्रं न करोति ।]

राजा—अहो मनसिजवैषम्यम् ।

मन्ये प्रियाहृतमनास्तस्याः प्रणिपातलङ्घनं सेवाम् ।
एवं प्रणयवती सा मयि शक्यमुपेक्षितुं कुपिता ॥ २३ ॥

(इति परिक्रम्य निष्क्रान्ताः सर्वे)

इति तृतीयोऽङ्कः ॥

(Takes the girdle and desires to strike the king.)

King. Friend,

This angry lady, shedding streams of tears, is ready to strike me cruelly, with the cord of her golden girdle slipped accidently from her ample hips, as the row of clouds, full of showers of water, strikes the Vindhya mountain with the streak of lightning. (21)

Irāvatī. Why drive me to offend you a second time?

(Catches hold of the girdle.)

King. Why withdraw the scourge uplifted against my guilty self, O curly-haired one? While (thus) you add to your charms, you are still angry with your slave here. (22)

(To himself) Surely I shall find favour now. *(Falls prostrate at her feet.)*

Irāvatī. Surely these are not Mālavikā's feet to fulfil your longing to be touched by them !

(Withdraws along with her maid.)

Vidūsaka. Rise, you have found favour.

King. *(Rising and not seeing Irāvatī)* How, my darling is really gone ?

Vidūsaka. The gods have, indeed, removed the constraint in these your improper relations with Mālavikā. Let us speedily depart before she comes back again, like (angry) Mars retrogressing to his mansion in the Zodiac.

King. How perverse is love !

With the mind attracted by the loved one, I consider it a favour that she has slighted my prostration. Yet I should not neglect her, although she is so very angry with me, as she is so much attached to me. (23)

(All walk about and exeunt.)

Here ends the third Act.

चतुर्थाऽङ्कः ।

(ततः प्रविशति पर्युत्सुको राजा प्रतीहारी च ।)

राजा (आत्मगतम् ।)—

तामाश्रित्य श्रुतिपथगतामास्थया लब्धमूलः
सम्प्राप्तायां नयनविषयं रूढरागप्रवालः ।
हस्तस्पर्शैर्मुकुलित इव व्यक्तरोमोद्गमत्वात्
कुर्यात्क्लान्तं मनसिजतरुर्मां रसज्ञं फलस्य ॥ १ ॥

(प्रकाशम्) सखे गौतम ।

प्रतीहारी—जेदु भट्टा । असण्णिहिदो गोदमो । [जयतु भर्ता । असन्निहितो गौतमः ।]

राजा (आत्मगतम्)—आः, मालविकावृत्तान्तज्ञानाय प्रेषितः ।

विदूषकः—(प्रविश्य) जेदु भवं । [जयतु भवान् ।]

राजा—जयसेने जानीहि तावत् क्व देवी धारिणी कथं वा सरुजचरणत्वाद्दिनोद्यत इति ।

प्रतीहारी—जं देवो आणवेदि । [यद्देव आज्ञापयति ।] (इति निष्क्राता ।)

राजा—गौतम को वृत्तान्तस्तत्रभवत्यास्ते सख्याः ।

विदूषकः—जो बिडालगहिदाए परहुदिआए । [यो बिडालगृहीतायाः परभृतिकायाः ।]

राजा (सविषादम्)—कथमिव ।

विदूषकः—सा खु तवस्सिणी ताए पिङ्गलच्छीए सारभण्डभूमिगेहे मिच्चुमुहे विअ णिक्खित्ता । [सा खलु तपास्विनी तया पिङ्गलाक्ष्या सारभाण्डभूमिगृहे मृत्युमुख इव निक्षिप्ता ।]

राजा—ननु मत्सम्पर्कमुपलभ्य ।

ACT IV.

(Enter king in a love-sick state and a door-keeper.)

King. (*To himself*)

The tree of love which had for its object the lady about whom I had heard, struck its root when I felt interested in her; and when I saw her it put forth the shoot of passion; when I touched her hands it blossomed as my hair stood visibly erect through delight; may that same tree of love make me, weary that I am, taste the flavour of its fruit. (1).

(*Aloud*) Friend Gautama!

The door-keeper. Victory to the king! Gautama is not here.

King. (*To himself*) Ha! He has been sent to get news about Mālavikā.

(*Entering*)

Vidūṣaka. Victory to your honour!

King. Jayasenā, go and just ascertain where queen Dhāriṇī is, and how does she beguile herself, now that she has pain in her feet.

Door-keeper. As the king commands. (*Exit*).

King. Gautama, how is the lady—your friend?

Vidūṣaka. Very much like a cuckoo seized by a cat.

King. *(despondently)* How is that?

Vidūṣaka. The poor lady has been flung into the cellar where all precious things are stored up, as if into the jaws of death by that fiery-eyed one.

King. Was it because of her meeting me?

विदूषकः—अह इं। [अथ किम्।]

राजा—गौतम क एवं विमुखोऽस्माकं येन चण्डीकृता देवी।

विदूषकः—सुणादु भवं। परिव्वाजिआ मे कहेदि। हिओ किल तत्तहोदी इरावदी रुजाविहत्थचलणं देविं सुहपुच्छिआ आअदा। [श्रृणोतु भवान्। परिव्राजिका मे कथयति। ह्यः किल तत्रभवती इरावती रुजाविहस्तचरणां देवीं सुखपृच्छिका आगता।]

राजा—ततस्ततः।

विदूषकः—तदो देवीए सा पुच्छिदा किं उण लक्खिदो वल्लहजणोत्ति। तदो ताए उत्तं कुदो वा दे उवआरो। जं दे परिअणस्स वल्लहत्तणं जाणन्ती वि पुच्छसित्ति। [ततो देव्या सा पृष्टा किं पुनर्लक्षितो वल्लभजन इति। ततस्तयोक्तं कुतो वा ते उपचारः। यत्तव परिजनस्य वल्लभत्वं जानत्यपि पृच्छसीति।]

राजा—निर्भेदादृतेऽपि मालविकायामयमुपन्यासः शङ्कयति। ततस्ततः।

विदूषकः—तदो ताए अणुबन्धिज्जमाणाए भवदो अविणअं अन्तरेण परिगाहिदत्था किदा देवी। [ततस्तयानुबध्यमानया भवतोऽविनयमन्तरेण परिगृहीतार्था कृता देवी।]

राजा—अहो दीर्घरोषता तत्रभवत्याः। अतः परं कथय।

विदूषकः—किं अदो वरं। मालविआ बउलावलिआ अ णिअलवदीओ अदिट्ठसुज्जपादं पादालवासं णाअकण्णआ विअ अणुहोन्ति। [किमतःपरम्। मालविका बकुलावलिका च निगलवत्यावदृष्टसूर्यपादं पातालवासं नागकन्यके इवानुभवतः।]

राजा—कष्टं कष्टम्।

> **मधुररवा परभृतिका भ्रमरी च विबुद्धचूतसङ्गिन्यौ।**
> **कोटरमकालवृष्ट्या प्रबलपुरोवातया गमिते॥ २॥**

वयस्य, अप्यत्र कस्यचिदुपक्रमस्य गतिः स्यात्।

Vidūsaka. Exactly.

King. Gautama, who indeed hates me so that he makes the queen angry with me?

Vidūsaka. Listen, sir! The Parivrājikā tells me as a fact that yesterday the lady Irāvatī came to inquire after the health of the queen, whose feet are disabled with pain.

King. What then?

Vidūsaka. Then the queen asked her "Have you seen the loved person lately?", whereupon she replied; "why this formality when knowing as you do the way he loves (me) your servant, you ask such a question?"

King. This mode of speech must have made the queen suspect Mālavikā even when it is so vague.

Vidūsaka. And when the queen importuned her, she informed the queen of your misdemeanour.

King. How unforgiving is that Lady! Tell me what happened next?

Vidūṣaka. What happened next! Mālavikā and Bakulāvalikā are now in fetters, and are now enjoying residence in the underworld where not a ray of the sun penetrates, like two snake-maidens.

King. Alas! alas!

The sweet-voiced cuckoo and the bee clinging to the opened mango-blossom have been driven to seek a hollow by an unseasonable shower preceded by a strong gale (2).

My friend, can there be an opening here for any stratagem?

विदूषकः—कहं भविस्सदि । जं सारभण्डे वावुदा माहविआ देवीए सन्दिट्ठा । मह अङ्गुलीअअमुद्दं अदेक्खिअ ण मोत्तव्वा तुए इअं हदासा मालविआ बउलावलिआ अ त्ति । [कथं भविष्यति । यत्सारभाण्डे व्यापृता माधविका देव्या सन्दिष्टा । ममाङ्गुलीयकमुद्रामदृष्ट्वा न मोक्तव्या त्वयेयं हताशा मालविका बकुलावलिका चेति ।]

राजा (निश्वस्य सपरामर्शम् ।)—सखे किमत्र कर्तव्यम् ।

विदूषकः (विचिन्त्य)—अत्थि एत्थ उवाओ । [अस्त्यत्रोपायः ।]

राजा—क इव ।

विदूषकः (सदृष्टिक्षेपम्)—को वि अदिट्ठो सुणादि । कण्णे दे कहेमि । (उपश्लिष्य कर्णे ।) एव्वं विअ । [कोऽप्यदृष्टः शृणोति । कर्णे ते कथयामि । एवमिव ।]

राजा—साधु प्रयुज्यतां सिद्धये ।

प्रतीहारी—(प्रविश्य) देव पवादसअणे देवी णिसण्णा रत्तचन्दणधारिणा परिअणहत्थगदेण चलणेण भअवदीए कहाहिं विणोदीअमणा चिट्ठदि । [देव प्रवातशयने देवी निषण्णा रक्तचन्दनधारिणा परिजनहस्तगतेन चरणेन भगवत्या कथाभिर्विनोद्यमाना तिष्ठति ।]

राजा —अस्मत्प्रवेशयोग्योऽयमवसरः ।

विदूषकः—ता गच्छदु भवं । अहं वि देविं पेक्खिदुं अरित्तपाणी भविस्सं । [तस्मात् गच्छतु भवान् । अहमपि देवीं द्रष्टुमरिक्तपाणिर्भविष्यामि ।]

राजा—जयसेनायास्तावत्संवेद्य गच्छ ।

विदूषकः—तह । (कर्णे) भोदि एव्वं विअ । (इति निष्क्रान्तः।) [तथा । भवति एवमिव ।]

राजा—जयसेने तेन हि प्रवातशयनमार्गमादेशय ।

प्रतीहारी—इदो इदो देवो । [इत इतो देवः ।]

(ततः प्रविशति शयनस्था देवी परिव्राजिका विभवतश्च परिवारः ।)

Vidūsaka. How can there be ? For the queen has commanded Mādhavikā in charge of the treasure-house: you will not set free Mālavikā and Bakulāvalikā unless you see the seal of my ring.

King. *(Sighing and musing.)* Friend, what shall we do in the matter ?

Vidūsaka. *(Reflecting.)* Yes, there is a remedy for this.

King. What is it ?

Vidūsaka. *(Glancing around .)* Somebody might overhear; so I will whisper it in your ear. *(Draws near and whispers in his ear.)* It is thus.

King. Excellent! Put it in execution and may it succeed.

(Entering)

A door-keeper. King, the queen is reclining on a couch in a breezy place, her foot smeared with the red sandal resting in the hand of her attendant; and she is being regaled with stories by the reverend lady.

King. This is a proper occasion for me to enter.

Vidūsaka. Well, then, you go. I too will provide myself with some present and see the queen.

King. Speak to Jayasenā and then go.

Vidūsaka. All right. (*Whispers in her ear* .) Lady, it is thus.

(*Exit*)

King. Jayasenā, lead the way to where the queen reclines on a couch in the open air.

Door-keeper. This way, this way, king.

(Then enter the queen reclining on a bed, the Parivrājikā and the attendants at a respectful distance.)

देवी—भअवदि अदिरमणीअं कहावत्थु । तदो तदो । [भगवति अतिरमणीयं कथावस्तु । ततस्ततः ।]

परिव्राजिका (सदृष्टिक्षेपम्)—अतः परं पुनः कथयिष्यामि । तत्रभवानीश्वरः सम्प्राप्तः ।

देवी—अम्मो भट्टा । (अभ्युत्थातुमिच्छति ।) [अम्मो भर्ता ।]

राजा—अलमलमुपचारयन्त्रणया ।

अनुचितनूपुरविरहं नार्हसि तपनीयपीठिकालम्बम् ।
चरणं रुजापरीतं कलभाषिणि मां च पीडयितुम् ॥ ३ ॥

देवी—जेदु अज्जउत्तो । [जयत्वार्यपुत्रः ।]

परिव्राजिका—विजयतां देवः ।

राजा (परिव्राजिकां प्रणम्योपविश्य ।) देवि अपि सह्या ते वेदना ।

देवी—अत्थि मे विसेसो । [अस्ति मे विशेषः ।]

(ततः प्रविशति यज्ञोपवीतबद्धाङ्गुष्ठः सम्भ्रान्तो विदूषकः ।)

विदूषकः—परित्ताअदु परित्ताअदु । सप्पेण मिच्चुणा दट्ठोम्हि । [परित्रायतां परित्रायताम् । सर्पेण मृत्युना दष्टोऽस्मि ।]

(सर्वे विषण्णाः ।)

राजा—कष्टं कष्टम् । क्व भवान् परिभ्रान्तः ।

विदूषकः—देविं पेक्खिस्सं ति आआरपुप्फग्गहणकालणादो पमदवणं गदोम्हि । [देवीं द्रक्षाभीत्याचारपुष्पग्रहणकारणात्प्रमदवनं गतोऽस्मि ।]

देवी—हद्धि हद्धि । णं अहं एव्व बम्हणस्स जीविअसंसअणिमित्त जादा । [हा धिक् हा धिक् । नन्वहमेव ब्राह्मणस्य जीवितसंशयनिमित्तं जाता ।]

विदूषकः—तहिं असोअत्थवअस्स कालणादो पसारिदे मे हत्थे कोडरणिग्गदेण सप्परूवेण कालेण दट्ठोम्हि । णं एदाइं दुवे दन्तपदाइं । [तत्राशोकस्तबककारणात्प्रसारिते मे हस्ते कोटर-

Queen. Revered lady, the plot of the story is so interesting. What next?

Parivrājikā. (*Looking about her*) I shall tell you further on some other occasion. Here comes the king.

Queen. Ah! my lord! (*Desires to rise.*)

King. Do not worry yourself with the distressing formality.

Sweet-voiced one, it is not proper to trouble
your aching foot, unused to the severance from
anklets, and resting on the golden foot-stool,
and cause me much pain. (3)

Queen. Victory to my noble lord!

Parivrājikā. Victory attend the king!

King. (*Bowing to the Parivrājikā and taking his seat*) My queen, I hope you find the pain bearable?

Queen. I feel better now.

(*Then Enter Vidūṣaka in a hurry, his thumb tied up by the sacred thread.*)

Vidūṣaka. Help, help! I am bitten by death in the form of a serpent.

(*All are distressed.*)

King. Alas! alas! where were you wandering?

Vidūṣaka. As I wanted to see the queen, I went to the Pramadavana garden to collect flowers for the customary offering.

Queen. O fie! fie! That I should have been the cause of putting his life in danger!

Vidūṣaka. As I stretched forth my hand to get at the cluster of Aśoka flowers, I was bitten by death in

निर्गतेन सर्परूपिणा कालेन दष्टोऽस्मि । नन्वेते द्वे दन्तपदे ।] (इति दर्शयति ।)

परिव्राजिका—तेन हि दंशच्छेदः पूर्वकर्मेति श्रूयते । स तावदस्य क्रियताम् ।

छेदो दंशस्य दाहो वा क्षतेर्वा रक्तमोक्षणम् ।
एतानि दष्टमात्राणामायुषः प्रतिपत्तयः ॥ ४ ॥

राजा—सम्प्रति विषवैद्यानां कर्म । जयसेने क्षिप्रमाहूयतां ध्रुवसिद्धिः ।

प्रतीहारी—जं देवो आणवेदि । [यद्देव आज्ञापयति ।] (इति निष्क्रान्ता ।)

विदूषकः—अहो पावेण मिच्चुणा गहीदोम्हि । [अहो पापेन मृत्युना गृहीतोऽस्मि ।]

राजा—मा कातरो भूः । अविषोऽपि कदाचिद्दंशो भवेत् ।

विदूषकः—कहं ण भाइस्सं । सिमसिमाअन्ति मे अङ्गाइं । [कथं न भेष्यामि । सिमसिमायन्ति मे अङ्गानि ।] (इति विषवेगं रूपयति ।)

देवी—ही ही असुहं दंसिदं विआरेण । हला अवलम्बह णं । [ही ही अशुभं दर्शितं विकारेण । हला अवलम्बध्वमेनम् ।]

(परिजनः ससम्भ्रममवलम्बते ।)

विदूषकः (राजानमवलोक्य ।) —भो भवदो बालवअस्सोम्हि । ता अविआरेण वुद्धाए मे जणणीए जोअक्खेमं वहेहि । [भो भवतो बालवयस्योऽस्मि । तदविचारेण वृद्धाया मे जनन्या योगक्षेमं वह ।]

राजा—मा भैषीः । अचिरात्त्वां विषवैद्यश्चिकित्सते । स्थिरो भव ।

जयसेना—(प्रविश्य) देव धुवसिद्धी विण्णवेदि । इह एव्व आणीअदु गोदमोत्ति । [देव ध्रुवसिद्धिर्विज्ञापयति । इहैवानीयतां गौतम इति ।]

the form of a serpent issuing out of its hollow—why, here are the two marks of its fangs. (*Shows them.*)

Parivrājikā. Then, indeed. they say that the first thing to be done, is the excision of the bitten part. Let that be done to him.

> Excision of the bitten part, or the burning of it, or letting off blood from the wound, these are the remedies to save the lives of persons just when they are bitten. (4)

King. Now it is the work of a doctor who specialises in the treatment of poison. Jayasenā, quickly fetch Dhruvasiddhi.

Door-keeper. As my lord commands. (*Exit*)

Vidūsaka. Ah! How accursed death has seized me!

King. Don't lose heart. May be, the bite is without poison.

Vidūsaka. How can I help being afraid? How all my limbs are tingling with pain! (*Gesticulates the working of poison.*)

Queen. Alas! alas! the bite shows itself to be fatal. Help him, ho!

(*The attendants hurriedly support him.*)

Vidūsaka. (*Looking at the king*) I have been your friend since childhood. You will therefore have no hesitation in looking after the welfare of my old mother.

King. Do not be afraid. The poison-doctor will speedily cure you. Be composed.

(*Entering*)

Jayasenā. Your majesty, Dhruvasiddhi requests that Gautama should be removed to his place.

राजा—तेन हि वर्षवरपरिगृहीतमेनं तत्रभवतः सकाशं प्रापय ।

जयसेना—तह । [तथा ।]

विदूषकः (देवीं विलोक्य)—भोदि जीवेअं वा ण वा । जं मए अत्तभवन्तं सेवन्तेण दे अवरद्धं तं मरिसेहि । [भवति जीवेयं वा न वा । यन्मया अत्रभवन्तं सेवमानेन तेऽपराद्धं तन्मर्षय ।]

देवी—दीहाऊ होहि । [दीर्घायुर्भव ।]

(निष्क्रान्तो विदूषकः प्रतीहारी च ।)

राजा—प्रकृतिभीरुस्तपस्वी । ध्रुवसिद्धेरपि यथार्थनाम्नः सिद्धिं मन्ये ।

जयसेना—(प्रविश्य) जेदु भट्टा । धुवसिद्धी विण्णवेदि । उअकुम्भविहाणे सप्पमुद्दिअं किं वि कप्पइदव्वं । ता अण्णेसीअदु त्ति । [जयतु भर्ता । ध्रुवसिद्धिर्विज्ञापयति । उदकुम्भविधाने सर्पमुद्रितं किमपि कल्पयितव्यम् । तदन्विष्यतामिति ।]

देवी—इदं सप्पमुद्दिअं अंगुलीअअं । पच्छा मह एव्व हत्थे देहि णं । [इदं सर्पमुद्रितमङ्गुलीयकम् । पश्चान्ममैव हस्ते देह्येतत् ।]

(इति प्रयच्छति । जयसेना नाट्येन गृह्णाति ।)

राजा—जयसेने कर्मसिद्धावाशु प्रतिपत्तिमानय ।

जयसेना—जं देवो आणवेदि । [यद्देव आज्ञापयति ।] (इति निष्क्रान्ता ।)

परिव्राजिका—देव यथा मे हृदयमाचष्टे तथा निर्विषो गौतमः ।

राजा—भूयादेवम् ।

जयसेना—(प्रविश्य) देव णिउत्तविसवेओ अज्जगोदमो मुहुत्तेण पइदित्थो संवुत्तो । [देव निवृत्तविषवेग आर्यगौतमो मुहूर्तेन प्रकृतिस्थः संवृत्तः ।]

देवी—दिट्ठिआ वअणीआदो मुत्तम्हि । [दिष्ट्या वचनीयान्मुक्तास्मि ।]

King. Well, then, take him into his presence borne by the eunuchs of the harem.

Jayasenā. As your majesty orders.

Vidūsaka. (*Looking at the queen*) Queen, I may or may not live ; I beg (therefore) to be forgiven whatever offence I may have given you while serving the king.

Queen. May you live on to a good old age.

(*Exeunt Vidūṣaka and door-keeper.*)

King. The poor fellow is nervous by nature. I hope Dhruvasiddhi-rightly named the infallible one-will succeed.

(*Entering*)

Jayasenā. Victory to the king! Dhruvasiddhi requests that something bearing a serpent-seal should be found out for putting on the water-pitcher. Do, therefore, make a search.

Queen. Here is a ring with a serpent-seal. Later on give it back to me only. (*Offers it, Jayasenā makes as if she takes it.*)

King. Jayasenā, quickly bring word that success has been attained.

Jayasenā. As the king commands. (*Exit*)

Parivrājikā. King, as my heart tells me, Gautama is cured of poison.

King. I hope so.

(Entering) Jayasenā—My lord, cured of the effect of poison, the noble Gautama after a while became quite his usual self.

Queen. Happily I am free from blame.

जयसेना—एसो उण अमच्चो वाहदओ विण्णवेदि। राअकज्जं बहु मन्तिदव्वं। ता दंसणेण अणुग्गहं इच्छामित्ति। [एष पुनरमात्यो वाहतको विज्ञापयति। राजकार्यं बहु मन्त्रयितव्यम्। तद्दर्शनेनानुग्रहमिच्छामीति।]

देवी— गच्छदु अज्जउत्तो कज्जसिद्धीए। [गच्छत्वार्यपुत्रः कार्यसिद्धये।]

राजा (उत्थाय)—देवि आतपाक्रान्तोऽयमुद्देशः। शीतक्रिया चास्य प्रशस्ता। तदन्यत्र नीयतां शयनीयम्।

देवी—बालिआ अज्जउत्तवअणं अणुचिट्ठह। [बालिकाः आर्यपुत्रवचनमनुतिष्ठत।]

परिजनः—तह। [तथा]

(इति निष्क्रान्ता देवी परिव्राजिका परिजनश्च।)

राजा—जयसेने गूढपथेन मां प्रमदवनं प्रापय।

जयसेना—इदो इदो देवो। [इत इतो देवः।]

राजा (परिक्रम्य)—जयसेने ननु समाप्तकृत्यो गौतमः।

जयसेना—अह इं। [अथ किम्।]

राजा—

इष्टाधिगमनिमित्तं प्रयोगमेकान्तसाधुमपि मत्वा।
सन्दिग्धमेव सिद्धौ कातरमाशङ्कते चेतः॥ ५॥

विदूषकः—(प्रविश्य) जेदु भवं। सिद्धाइं मे सव्वमङ्गलकम्माइं। [जयतु भवान्। सिद्धानि मे सर्वमङ्गलकर्माणि।]

राजा—जयसेने त्वमपि नियोगमशून्यं कुरु।

जयसेना—जं देवो आणवेदि। [यद्देव आज्ञापयति]

(इति निष्क्रान्ता।)

राजा—वयस्य क्षुद्रा माधविका। न खलु किंचिद्विचारितमनया।

Jayasenā. The minister Vāhataka now requests : I have to discuss a good many affairs of the state, and so I seek to be favoured with an audience.

Queen. May my lord leave and attain success in his undertakings.

King. *(Rising)* My queen, this place is exposed to the sun, while this requires a cooling remedy; so let the bed be removed to a different place.

Queen. Girls, carry out the command of my lord.

Servants. As you bid.

(Exeunt queen, Parivrājikā and retinue.)

King. Jayasenā, take me to the Pramadavana by the secret way.

Jayasena. This way, this way, king.

King. (*moving about*) Jayasenā I hope Gautama has finished his work.

Jayasenā. Just so.

King. Although I think the devise to be decisively the best for the accomplishment of my purpose, yet my timid heart feels dubious about its attainment. (5)

(Entering)

Vidūsaka. Victory to your highness. Success attends all our auspicious undertakings.

King. Jayasenā, you too attend to your duty.

Jayasenā. As the king commands.

(Exit).

King. Friend, Mādhavikā is such a dullard ; did not she hesitate a bit ?

विदूषकः——देवीए अंगुलीअअमुद्दिअं पेक्खिअ कहं विआरेदि ।
[देव्या अङ्गुलीयकमुद्रिकां दृष्ट्वा कथं विचारयति ।]

राजा——न खलु मुद्रामधिकृत्य ब्रवीमि । तयोर्बद्धयोः किंनिमित्तोऽयं मोक्षः । किं वा देव्याः परिजनमतिक्रम्य भवान्सन्दिष्टः । इत्येवमनया प्रष्टव्यम् ।

विदूषकः——णं पुच्छिदोम्हि । पच्चुप्पण्णबुद्धिणा मए कहिदम् ।
[ननु पृष्टोऽस्मि । प्रत्युत्पन्नबुद्धिना मया कथितम् ।]

राजा——कथ्यताम् ।

विदूषकः——भणिदं मए । देव्वचिन्तएहिं विण्णाविदो राआ । सोवसग्गं वो णक्खत्तं । सव्वबन्धमोक्खो करीअदुत्ति । [भणितं मया । दैवचिन्तकैर्विज्ञापितो राजा । सोपसर्गं वो नक्षत्रम् । सर्वबन्धमोक्षः क्रियतामिति ।]

राजा (सहर्षम्) ——ततस्ततः ।

विदूषकः——तं सुणिअ देवीए इरावदीए चित्तं रक्खन्तीए राआ किल मोएदित्ति तुमं एव्व णं मोएहित्ति अहं सन्दिट्ठोम्हित्ति । तदो जुज्जइत्ति ताए सम्पादिदो अत्थो । [तच्छ्रुत्वा देव्या इरावत्याश्चित्तं रक्षन्त्या राजा किल मोचयतीति त्वमेवैनां मोचयेत्यहं सन्दिष्टोऽस्मि इति । ततो युज्यत इति तया सम्पादितोऽर्थः ।]

राजा (विदूषकं परिष्वज्य)——सखे प्रियोऽहं तव ।

न हि बुद्धिगुणेनैव सुहृदामर्थदर्शनम् ।
कार्यसिद्धिपथः सूक्ष्मः स्नेहेनाप्युपलभ्यते ॥ ६ ॥

विदूषकः——तुवरदु भवं । समुद्दघरए पिअसहीसहिअं मालविअं ठाविअ भवन्तं पच्चुग्गदोम्हि । [त्वरतां भवान् । समुद्रगृहके प्रियसखीसहितां मालविकां स्थापयित्वा भवन्तं प्रत्युद्गतोऽस्मि ।]

राजा——अहमेनां सम्भावयामि । गच्छाग्रतः ।

Vidūsaka. How could she hesitate at sight of the Queen's ring ?

King. I do not talk of the ring. But she should certainly have asked as to why these prisoners were to be liberated; and why to the exclusion of all her attendants, the queen commissioned you to bring the message.

Vidūsaka. Indeed, she asked me; and I immediately with a ready wit told her.

King. Tell me.

Vidūsaka. I said—the astrologers told the king that the constellation presiding over the king's fortunes was possessed of a malignant influence. Therefore let all prisoners be set free.

King. What then ?

Vidūsaka. On hearing that, the queen with a view to spare the feelings of Irāvatī ordered me to release them and give out that the king wanted them set at liberty; she granted my request, saying that it was quite all right.

King. *(Embracing the Vidūṣaka)* Friend, you, indeed, love me.

> For not only by force of intellect does one see how to promote a friend's interest; love too points out the narrow path to success in one's undertaking. (6)

Vidūsaka. Let your highness make haste. I have put Mālavikā and her dear friend in the Ocean-pavilion and have come to meet you.

King. Well, I will honour her. Do you go ahead.

विदूषकः—एदु भवं। (परिक्रम्य) एदं समुद्दघरअं। [एतु भवान्। इदं समुद्रगृहम्।]

राजा (साशङ्कम्) —वयस्य एषा कुसुमापचयव्यग्रहस्ता सख्यास्ते इरावत्याः परिचारिका चन्द्रिका समागच्छति। इतस्तावदावां भित्तिनिगूढौ भवावः।

विदूषकः—अहो कुम्भीलएहिं कामुएहिं अ पलिहलणिज्जा खु चन्दिआ। [अहो कुम्भीलकैः कामुकैश्च परिहरणीया चन्द्रिका।]

(उभौ यथोक्तं कुरुतः।)

राजा—गौतम कथं नु ते सखी मां प्रतिपालयति। एह्येनां गवाक्षमाश्रित्यावलोकयावः।

विदूषकः—तह। तथा। (इति विलोकयन्तौ स्थितौ।)

(ततः प्रविशति मालविका बकुलावलिका च।)

बकुलावलिका—हला पणम भट्टारं। [हला प्रणम भर्तारम्।]

राजा—मन्ये प्रतिकृतिं मे दर्शयतीति।

मालविका (सहर्षम्) णमो दे (द्वारमवलोक्य सविषादम्) कहिं भट्टा। हला विप्पलम्भेसि मं। [नमस्ते। कुत्र भर्ता। हला। विप्रलम्भयसि माम्।]

राजा—सखे हर्षविषादाभ्यामत्रभवत्याः प्रीतोऽस्मि।

सूर्योदये भवति या सूर्यास्तमये च पुण्डरीकस्य।
वदनेन सुवदनायास्ते समवस्थे क्षणादूढे ॥ ७ ॥

बकुलावलिका—णं एसो चित्तगदो भट्टा। [नन्वेष चित्रगतो भर्ता।]

उभे (प्रणिपत्य) जेदु भट्टा। [जयतु भर्ता।]

मालविका—हला तदा अहं सम्मुहट्ठिदा भट्टिणो रूवस्स तह ण वितिण्हम्हि जह अज्ज मए विभाविदो चित्तगदो भट्टा। [हला

Vidūṣaka. Come, your highness. (*moving about*) Here is the Ocean-pavilion.

King. (*Apprehensively*) Friend, here comes Candrikā, the maid of your friend Irāvatī, her hands engaged in gathering flowers. Let us, therefore, hide ourselves behind this wall here.

Vidūṣaka. Ah, thieves and lovers have to avoid the moon-light.

(*Both do what was said.*)

King. Gautama how must your friend be awaiting me? Come, let us watch her from the window.

Vidūṣaka. Well.

(*They stand looking in.*)

(*Enter Mālavikā and Bakulāvalikā.*)

Bakulāvalikā. Come, friend, salute the king.

King. I think she is showing her my likeness.

Mālavikā. (*With joy*) I salute you. (*Looking at the door, with disappointment*) Where is the king? Friend, you deceive me.

King. Friend I feel delighted at the lady's joy and disappointment both.

For in a moment the face of the lovely faced one has assumed the two appearances of the lotus—that which it wears at sun-rise and that other which it wears at sunset. (7)

Bakulāvalikā. Well, I say, here is the king in the picture.

Both (*Saluting*) Victory to the king!

Mālavikā. Friend, at that time when I stood face to face with the king, I was not so well satisfied with

तदाहं सम्मुखस्थिता भर्तू रूपस्य तथा न वितृष्णास्मि यथाद्य मय विभाविताश्चित्रगतो भर्ता ।]

विदूषकः—सुदं भवदा । अत्तहोदीए जह दिट्ठो चित्ते ण तह दिट्ठो भवं ति मंतिदं । मुहा दाणिं मञ्जूसा विअ रअणभण्डं जोव्वणगव्वं वहेसि । [श्रुतं भवता । अत्रभवत्या यथा दृष्टश्चित्रे न तथा दृष्टो भवानिति मन्त्रितम् । मुधेदानीं मञ्जूषेव रत्नभाण्डं यौवनगर्वं वहसि ।]

राजा—सखे कुतूहलवानपि निसर्गशालीनः स्त्रीजनः । पश्य—

> **कात्स्न्र्येन निर्वर्णयितुं च रूप-**
> **मिच्छन्ति तत्पूर्वसमागतानाम् ।**
> **न च प्रियेष्वायतलोचनानां**
> **समग्रपातीनि विलोचनानि ॥ ८ ॥**

मालविका—हला का एसा ईसिपरिवत्तिदवअणा भट्टिणा सिणिद्धाए दिट्ठीए णिज्झाईअदि । [हला कैषा ईषत्परिवर्तितवदना भर्त्रा स्निग्धया दृष्ट्या निध्यायते ।]

बकुलावलिका—णं इअं भट्टिणो पासगदा इरावदी । [नन्वियं भर्तुः पार्श्वगतेरावती ।]

मालविका—हला भट्टा अदक्खिणो विअ पडिभादि । जो सव्वं देवीजणं उज्झिअ एक्काए मुहे बद्धलक्खो । [हला भर्ता अदक्षिण इव प्रतिभाति । यः सर्वं देवीजनमुज्झित्वा एकस्या मुखे बद्धलक्ष्यः ।]

बकुलावलिका (आत्मगतम्)—चित्तगदं भट्टारं परमत्थं गेह्णिअ असूअदि इअं । होदु कीलिस्सं दाव एदाए । (प्रकाशम्) हला भट्टिणो वल्लहा एसा । [चित्रगतं भर्तारं परमार्थं गृहीत्वाऽसूयतीयम् । भवतु क्रीडिष्यामि तावदेतया । हला भर्तुर्वल्लभैषा ।]

मालविका—तदो किं दाणिं अत्ताणं आआसेमि । [ततः किमिदानींमात्मानमायासयामि ।] (इति सासूयं परावर्तते ।)

his beauty as at the present moment with looking at him in the picture.

Vidūṣaka. Has your honour heard? The lady says you did not look as you do here in the picture. Vainly do you bear the pride of youth as a casket a store of gems.

King. Friend, women, though filled with curiosity, are yet by nature so bashful. Observe,

they do desire to study completely the features
of those whom they meet for the first time and
yet the long-eyed ones will not allow their eyes
to fall full upon the beloved persons. (8)

Mālavikā. Friend, who is this with her slightly averted face whom the king is regarding with an affectionate gaze?

Bakulāvalikā. Surely this is Irāvatī at his side.

Mālavikā. Friend, the king seems to me to be somewhat rude, that he should neglect all his queens and fix his glance on her face alone.

Bakulāvalikā. (To *herself)* She takes the king's picture for the king himself and exhibits jealousy towards it. Well, then, let me chaff her a bit. (*Aloud*) friend, she is beloved of the king.

Mālavikā. If that be so, why should I trouble myself in vain? (*Turns away pettishly*).

१५ **राजा**—पश्य सख्या मुखम् ।

भ्रूभङ्गभिन्नतिलकं स्फुरिताधरोष्ठं
सासूयमाननमितः परिवर्तयन्त्या ।
कान्तापराधकुपितेष्वनया विनेतुः
सन्दर्शितेव ललिताभिनयस्य शिक्षा ॥९॥

विदूषकः—अणुणअसज्जो दाणिं होहि । [अनुनयसज्ज इदानीं भव ।]

३ **मालविका**—अज्जगोदमो वि एत्थ एव्व सेवदि णं । [आर्यगौतमोऽप्यत्रैव सेवत एनम् ।] (पुनः स्थानान्तराभिमुखी भवितुमिच्छति)

बकुलावलिका—(मालविकां रुध्द्वा)–ण खु कुविदा दाणिं तुमं । [न खलु कुपितेदानीं त्वम् ।]

मालविका—जइ मं चिरं कुविदं मण्णसि एसो पच्चाणीअदि कोवो । [यदि मा चिरं कुपितां मन्यसे एष प्रत्यानीयते कोपः ।]

९. **राजा** (उपसृत्य)—

कुप्यसि कुवलयनयने चित्रार्पितचेष्टया किमेवमयि ।
ननु तव साक्षादयमहनन्यसाधारणो दासः ॥ १० ॥

बकुलावलिका—जेदु भट्टा । [जयतु भर्ता ।]

मालविका (आत्मगतम्) कहं चित्तगदो भट्टा मए असूइदो । [कथं चित्रगतो भर्ता मयासूयितः ।] (सव्रीडवदना अञ्जलिं करोति । राजा मदनकातर्यं रूपयति ।)

विदूषकः—किं भवं उदासीणो विअ । [किं भवानुदासीन इव ।]

६ **राजा**—अविश्वसनीयत्वात्सख्यास्ते ।

विदूषकः—मा दाव । अत्तहोदी तुह अविस्ससणीआ । [मा तावत् । अत्रभवती तवाविश्वसनीया ।]

King. Observe the face of your friend.

As in anger she turned her face away from the (picture) so that the tilaka mark on the forehead was blurred, by the knitting of the brows, and the lower lip was made to quiver, she seemed to exhibit the graceful expression taught her by her teacher as being appropriate in the fits of anger caused by the faults of a lover. (9)

Vidūsaka. Prepare yourself now to propitiate her.

Mālavikā. And the noble Gautama too is waiting upon her in this place. (*She again desires to turn away in another direction.*)

Bakulāvalikā. (*Preventing Mūlavikā*) Surely you are not angry now.

Mālavikā. If you desire me to be angry for long, here I recall my anger.

King. (*Advancing*)

Oh Lotus-eyed one, why should you be angry thus at an action represented in the picture? Do I not here stand in my own person, a slave devoted to you alone? (10)

Bakulāvalikā. Victory to the king!

Mālavikā. (*To herself*) What? Did I get angry with the king in the picture?

(*With an apologetic expression, she folds her hands together.*)

(*The king acts as if he is distracted with love.*)

Vidūsaka. Why do you appear to be so apathetic?

King. Because your friend is so unreliable.

Vidūsaka. How! Do you distrust the lady?

९ **राजा**—श्रूयताम् ।

पथि नयनयोः स्थित्वा स्वप्ने तिरोभवति क्षणात्
सरति सहसा बाह्वोर्मध्यं गताप्यबला सती ।
मनसिजरुजा क्लिष्टस्यैवं समागममायया
कथमिव सखे विश्रब्धं स्यादिमां प्रति मे मनः ॥११॥

बकुलावलिका—सहि बहुसो किल तुए विप्पलद्धो भट्टा । ता दाव अत्ता विस्ससणिज्जो करीअदु । [सखि बहुशः किल त्वया
३ विप्रलब्धो भर्ता । तत्तावदात्मा विश्वसनीयः क्रियताम्]

मालविका—सहि मम उण मन्दभाइणीए सिविणअसमाअमो वि भट्टिणो दुल्लहो आसि । [सखि मम पुनर्मन्दभागिन्याः स्वप्नसमा-
६ गमोऽपि भर्तुर्दुर्लभ आसीत् ।]

बकुलावलिका—भट्टा देउ से उत्तरं । [भर्ता ददात्वस्या उत्तरम् ।]

९**राजा**—

उत्तरेण किमात्मैव पञ्चबाणाग्निसाक्षिकम् ।
तव सख्यै मया दत्तो न सेव्यः सेविता रहः ॥ १२ ॥

बकुलावलिका—अणुगहिदम्हि । [अनुगृहीतास्मि ।]

विदूषकः (परिक्रम्य ससम्भ्रमम् ।)—बउलावलिए एसो बालासो-
३ अरुक्खस्स पल्लवाइं हरिणो लङ्घिदुं आअच्छदि । एहि णिवारेम णं । [बकुलावलिके एष बालाशोकवृक्षस्य पल्लवानि हरिणो लङ्घितुमागच्छति । एहि निवारयाव एनम् ।]

६ **बकुलावलिका**—तह । [तथा ।] (इति प्रस्थिता ।)

राजा—एवमस्मद्रक्षणे वयस्येनावहितेन भवितव्यम् ।

विदूषकः—एदं वि गोदमो णं सन्दिस्सीअदि । [एतदपि गौतमो
९ ननु सन्दिश्यते ।]

King. Listen: your friend appears before me in a dream, and yet in a moment she vanishes from my sight; and though clasped between my arms, she suddenly slips away from them, (frail) woman though she be, how can my mind repose any trust in her while I am afflicted by the anguish of love caused by a delusive union? (II)

Bakulāvalikā. Friend, often has the king been deceived; so now prove yourself to be a person worthy of trust.

Mālavikā. But, my friend, unluckly that I am, I find union with the king even in a dream so hard to obtain.

Bakulāvalikā. King, please now to give her answer.

King.

What is the use of making any answer? For in the very presence of the fire of love have I given myself over to your friend. I am not her master, but her servant in secret. (12)

Bakulāvalikā. I am beholden to you for this answer.

Vidūṣaka. *(Walking round)* Bakulāvalikā, here is a deer, cropping the shoots of the young Aśoka tree; let us drive it off.

Bakulāvalikā. Very well. *(Starts off.)*

King. Friend, even thus must you be on the look-out at this moment when we deserve to be guarded.

Vidūṣaka. Does Gautama require to be instructed thus?

बकुलावलिका—अज्ज गोदमो अहं अप्पआसे चिट्ठामि। तुमं दुवाररक्खओ होहि। [आर्य गौतम अहमप्रकाशे तिष्ठामि। त्वं
१२ द्वाररक्षको भव।]

विदूषकः—जुज्जइ। [युज्यते!] (निष्क्रान्ता बकुलावलिका।)

विदूषकः (परिक्रम्यावलोक्य च।)—इदं दाव फलिहत्थलं। आ-
१५सीणो होमि। (तथा कृत्वा।) अहो सुहप्फरिसदा सिलाविसेसस्स। [इदं तावत्स्फटिकस्थलम्। आसीनो भवामि। अहो सुखस्पर्शता शिलाविश्लेषस्य।] (निद्रायते)

(मालविका ससाध्वसा तिष्ठति।)

२०**राजा**—

विसृज सुन्दरि सङ्गमसाध्वसं
तव चिरात्प्रभृति प्रणयोन्मुखे।
परिगृहाण गते सहकारतां
त्वमतिमुक्तलताचरितं मयि॥ १३॥

मालविका—देवीए भएण अत्तणो वि पिअं कादु ण पारेमि। [देव्या भयेनात्मनोऽपि प्रियं कर्तुं न पारयामि।]

३**राजा**—अयि न भेतव्यं न भेतव्यम्।

मालविका—जो ण भाएदि सो मए भट्टिणीदंसणे दिट्ठसमवत्थो भट्टा णं। [यो न बिभेति स मया भट्टिनीदर्शने दृष्टसमवस्थो
६ भर्ता ननु।]

राजा—

दाक्षिण्यं नाम बिम्बोष्ठि बैम्बिकानां कुलव्रतम्।
तन्मे दीर्घाक्षि ये प्राणास्ते त्वदाशानिबन्धनाः॥ १४॥

तदयमनुगृह्यतां चिरानुरक्तो जनः। (इति संश्लेषमभिनयति। मालविका नाट्येन परिहरति।)

Bakulāvalikā. *(Walking about)* Noble Gautama, I shall remain hidden from sight, and you will guard the entrance.

Vidūṣaka. That is quite proper. *(Exit Bakulāvalikā.)*

Vidūṣaka. In the meanwhile I shall lean against this crystal column. *(Doing as he says.)* How pleasant the feel of this delicious stone! *(Falls asleep.)*

(Mālavikā is overcome with fear.)

King. Give up, Oh sweet one, this fear of union, and now that I, who have for long been devoted to you, have become like the Mango-tree, do you assume the part of the Atimukta creeper towards me. (13)

Mālavikā. For fear of the queen, I cannot do what even my heart approves.

King. Well, you need have no fear.

Mālavikā. I have witnessed the courage of the king, who is now so fearless, in the presence of the queen.

King. Politeness indeed, Oh Bimba-lipped one, is the family tradition of the descendants of Bimbaka; nevertheless what life I possess depends entirely on the hope of thy favour. (14)

So favour me who am for long enamoured of thee. *(Goes close to her ; Mālavikā averts him.)*

[3]**राजा** (आत्मगतम्)—रमणीयः खलु नवाङ्गनानां मदनविषयावतारः। एषा हि।

हस्तं कम्पवती रुणद्धि रशनाव्यापारलोलाङ्गुलिं
हस्तौ स्वौ नयति स्तनावरणतामालिङ्ग्यमाना बलात्।
पातुं पक्ष्मलचक्षुरुन्नमयतः साचीकरोत्याननं
व्याजेनाप्यभिलाषपूरणसुखं निर्वर्तयत्येव मे ॥ १५ ॥

(ततः प्रविशति इरावती निपुणिका च।)

इरावती—हञ्जे निउणिए सच्चं तुए संदिट्ठं चन्दिआए समुद्दघरआलिन्दए अज्जगोदमो एआई दिट्ठोत्ति। [हञ्जे निपुणिके सत्यं त्वया सन्दिष्टं चन्द्रिकया समुद्रगृहालिन्दे आर्यगौतम एकाकी दृष्ट इति।]

निपुणिका—अण्णहा कहं भट्टिणीए विण्णएमि। [अन्यथा कथं भट्टिन्यै विज्ञापयामि।]

इरावती—तेण हि तहिं एव्व गच्छम्ह। संसआदो मुत्तं भट्टिणो पिअवअस्सं पेक्खिदुं अ। [तेन हि तत्रैव गच्छावः। संशयान्मुक्तं भर्तुः प्रियवयस्यं प्रेक्षितुं च।]

निपुणिका—सविसेसं विअ भट्टिणीए वअणं। [सविशेषमिव भट्टिन्या वचनम्।]

इरावती—आम्। चित्तगदं भट्टारं पसादेदुं। [आम्। चित्रगतं भर्तारं प्रसादयितुम्।]

निपुणिका—अह दाणिं भट्टा एव्व किं ण पच्चणुणीअदि। [अथेदानीं भर्तैव किं न प्रत्यनुनीयते।]

इरावती—मुद्धे जारिसो चित्तगदो भट्टा ण तारिसो एव्व। अण्णसङ्कन्तहिअओ अज्जउत्तो। केवलं उवआरादिक्कमं पमज्जिदुं अम्हाणं अअं आरम्भो। [मुग्धे यादृशश्चित्रगतो भर्ता न तादृश एव। अन्यसङ्क्रान्तहृदय आर्यपुत्रः। केवलमुपचारातिक्रमं प्रमार्ष्टुमस्माकमयमारम्भः।]

King. (*To himself*) How sweet the stepping of young women into the province of love; for

she moves about her hand, and stops my
Trembling, she stops my hand with its fingers moving about the girdle, she covers her breasts with her hands as perforce I embrace her; she turns aside her face with its eyes possessed of long eyelashes, as I try to raise it that I may sip it: thus does she grant me the happiness of enjoying the fulfilment of my desire even under a pretext. (15)

(Then enter Irāvatī and Nipuṇikā.)

Irāvatī. Nipuṇikā, my girl, did Candrikā really tell you that she saw the noble Gautama alone on the terrace of the ocean-pavilion?

Nipuṇikā. How otherwise should I have ventured to tell your highness so?

Irāvatī. Let us then proceed there that we might inquire after the health of the dear friend of my husband rescued from imminent peril—

Nipuṇikā. Your highness seems to have something further to say.

Irāvatī. And also to beg of my husband in the picture to forgive me.

Nipuṇikā. But how even now you don't endeavour to gain him over?

Irāvtī. Silly girl, my husband is no longer what he appears to be in the picture. He has transferred the devotion of his heart to another woman. My present purpose is therefore to atone for my transgression of the proper decorum.

निपुणिका—इदो इदो भट्टिणी। [इत इतो भट्टिनी।]

(उभे परिक्रामतः।)

चेटी (प्रविश्य)—जेदु भट्टिणी। देवी भणादि। ण मे एसो मच्छरस्स कालो। केवलं तुह खु बहुमाणं वड्ढेदुं वअस्सिआए सह णिअलबन्धणे किदा मालविआ। जइ अणुमण्णेसि अज्जउत्तं वि तुह किदे विण्णविस्सं। जं तुह इच्छिदं तं भणाहित्ति। [जयतु भट्टिनी। देवी भणति—न मे एष मत्सरस्य कालः। केवलं तव खलु बहुमानं वर्धयितुं वयस्यया सह निगलबन्धने कृता मालविका। यद्यनुमन्यसे आर्यपुत्रमपि तव कृते विज्ञापयिष्यामि। यत्तवेष्टं तद्भण इति।]

इरावती—णाअरिए, विण्णवेहि देविं। का वअं भट्टिणिं णिओएदुं। परिअणणिग्गहेण मइ दंसिदो सिणेहो। कस्स वा अण्णस्स पसादेण अअं जणो वड्ढदित्ति। [नागरिके, विज्ञापय देवीम्। का वयं भट्टिनीं नियोजयितुम्। परिजननिग्रहेण मयि दर्शितः स्नेहः। कस्य वान्यस्य प्रसादेनायं जनो वर्धत इति।]

चेटी—तह। [तथा।] (इति निष्क्रान्ता।)

निपुणिका (परिक्रम्यावलोक्य च।)—भट्टिणी एसो दुवारुच्छङ्गे समुद्दघरस्स विवणिगदो विअ वुसहो अज्जगोदमो आसीणो एव्व णिद्दाअदि। [भट्टिनी एष द्वारोत्सङ्गे समुद्रगृहस्य विपणिगत इव वृषभ आर्यगौतम आसीन एव निद्रायते।]

इरावती—अच्चाहिदं। ण क्खु सावसेसविसविआरो भवे। [अत्याहितम्। न खलु सावशेषविषविकारो भवेत्।]

निपुणिका—पसण्णमुहो दीसइ। अवि अ धुवसिद्धिणा चिइच्छिदो। ता से असङ्कणिज्जं पावं। [प्रसन्नमुखो दृश्यते। अपि च ध्रुवसिद्धिना चिकित्सितः। तदस्य अशङ्कनीयं पापम्।]

Nipuṇikā. This way, your highness, this way.

(Both walk round.)

(Entering)

A female servant. Victory to your highness ! The queen says " My time of showing jealousy is past and therefore only with a view to increase the great respect (in which you are held) that I put in fetters Mālavikā and her friend; if you give me leave, I will request my husband on your behalf Let me therefore know your wish. "

Irāvatī. Nāgarikā, tell the queen : who am I that I should commission the queen to do my bidding ? She has shown great favour to me by punishing her servants; indeed what other person has shown me such favours ?

Servant. I will do so. *(Exit)*

Nipuṇikā. *(Walking round and looking)* Your highness, here is the noble Gautama sleeping even in a sitting posture on the threshold of the ocean-pavilion like an ox in the market-place.

Irāvatī. What a pity ! Surely it cannot be that the effects of the poison still remain.

Nipuṇikā. The expression of his face is serene. Besides Dhruvasiddhi has ministered to him. Therefore we need not be afraid that his life is in peril.

विदूषकः (उत्स्वप्नायते ।)—होदि मालविए ।

[भवति मालविके ।]

४८ **निपुणिका**—सुदं भट्टिणीए । कस्स वि एसो अत्तणीणो हदासो
किदवो । सव्वकालं इदो एव्व सोत्थिवाअणमोदएहिं कुक्खिं पूरिअ
सम्पदं मालविअं उस्सिविणावेदि । [श्रुतं भट्टिन्या । कस्याप्येष
५१ आत्मनीनो हताशः कितवः । सर्वकालमित एव स्वस्तिवाचनमोदकैः
कुक्षिं पूरयित्वा साम्प्रतं मालविकां उत्स्वप्नायते ।]

विदूषकः—इरावदिं अदिक्कामन्ती होहि । [इरावतीमति-
५४ क्रामन्ती भव ।]

निपुणिका—सुदं एदं अच्चाहिदं । भुअङ्गभीरुअं बम्हबन्धुं
इमिणा भुअङ्गकुडिलेण दण्डकट्ठेण थम्भन्तरिदा भविअ भीसअम्हि ।
५७ [श्रुतमेतदत्याहितम् । भुजङ्गभीरुकं ब्रह्मबन्धुमनेन भुजङ्गकुटिलेन
दण्डकाष्ठेन स्तम्भान्तरिता भूत्वा भीषयिष्ये ।]

इरावती—एसो अरुहदि किदवो सप्पदंसस्स । [एषोऽर्हति
६० कितवः सर्पदंशस्य ।]

(निपुणिका विदूषकस्योपरि दण्डकाष्ठं पातयति ।)

विदूषकः— (सहसा प्रतिबुध्य ।) अविहा अविहा । भो दव्वी-
६३ अरो मे उवरि पडिदो । [अविहा अविहा । भो दर्वीकरो मे उपरि
पतितः ।]

राजा (सहसोपसृत्य ।)—सखे न भेतव्यं न भेतव्यम् ।

६६ **मालविका**—(अनुसृत्य) भट्टा मा दाव सहसा णिक्कम । सप्पोत्ति
भणादि । [भर्तः मा तावत्सहसा निष्काम । सर्प इति भणति ।]

इरावती—हद्धि हद्धि भट्टा इदो एव्व धावइ । [हा धिक् हा धिक्
६९ भर्ता इत एव धावति ।]

विदूषकः (सप्रहासम्) —कहं दण्डकट्ठं एदं । अहं उण जाणे जं
मए केदईकण्टएहिं दंसं करिअ सप्पस्स विअ दंसो किदो तं फलिदंति ।

Vidūsaka. (*Talks in his sleep*) Lady Mālavikā—

Nipuṇikā. Did your highness hear ? What sire begot this accursed rogue I wander ! This accursed wretch, constantly filling his belly with complimentary sweetmeats given here, is now talking in his sleep about Mālavikā !

Vidūṣaka. May you supplant Irāvatī.

Nipuṇikā. Heard this piece of ill luck ? I will hide behind the pillar and with this stick of mine, which is crooked like a snake, frighten this vile Brahmin who is afraid of serpents.

Irāvatī. Surely the traitor deserves some misfortune.

(*Nipuṇikā hurls her stick at the body of the Vidūṣaka.*)

Vidūṣaka. *(Suddenly waking up)* Woe is me! Friend, a serpent has fallen upon me.

King. *(Rushing out immediately)* Do not be afraid, my friend, do not be afraid.

Mālavikā. *(following)* Husband, do not rush out all of a sudden ; he says there is a snake there.

Irāvatī. Alas ! alas ! my lord is running in this very direction.

Vidūsaka. *(Laughing aloud)* How now ? This is a mere stick. But I think this is the just reward for the blame I had the presumption to cast upon a serpent by imitating its bite with Ketakī thorns.

७२ [कथं दण्डकाष्ठमेतत्। अहं पुनर्जाने यन्मया केतकीकण्टकाभ्यां दंशं कृत्वा सर्पस्येव दंशः कृतः तत्फलितमिति।]

(ततः प्रविशति पटाक्षेपेण बकुलावलिका।)

७८ **बकुलावलिका**—मा दाव भट्टा पविसदु। इह कुडिलगई सप्पो विअ दीसइ। [मा तावत् भर्ता प्रविशतु। इह कुटिलगतिः सर्प इव दृश्यते।]

८१ **इरावती** (राजानं सहसोपसृत्य)—अवि णिव्विग्घमणोरहो दिवासङ्केदो मिहुणस्स। [अपि निर्विघ्नमनोरथो दिवासङ्केतो मिथुनस्य।]

(सर्वे इरावतीं दृष्ट्वा सम्भ्रान्ताः।)

८४ **राजा**—प्रिये अपूर्वोऽयमुपचारः।

इरावती—बउलावलिए दिट्ठिआ दोच्चहिआरविसआ संपुण्णा दे पडिण्णा। [बकुलावलिके दिष्टया दूत्यधिकारविषया सम्पूर्णा ते प्रतिज्ञा।]

८७ **बकुलावलिका**—पसीददु भट्टिणी। किं णु खु दद्दुरा वाहरन्तित्ति देवो पुढविं विसुमरेदि। किं मए किदंति देवो पुच्छिदव्वो [प्रसीदतु भट्टिनी। किं नु खलु दर्दुरा व्याहरन्तीति देवः पृथिवीं विस्मरति।

९० किं मया कृतमिति देवः प्रष्टव्यः।]

विदूषकः—मा दाव। होदीए दंसणमेत्तेणं अत्तभवं पणिवादलङ्घणं विसुमरिदो। होदी उण अज्ज वि पसादं ण गेह्णादि। [मा तावत्।

९३ भवत्या दर्शनमात्रेणात्रभवान् प्रणिपातलङ्घनं विस्मृतः। भवती पुनः अद्यापि प्रसादं न गृह्णाति।]

इरावती—कुविदा वि दाणिं किं करिस्सं। [कुपितापीदानीं किं

९६ करिष्यामि।]

राजा—अस्थाने कोप इत्येतदनुपपन्नं त्वयि। तथा हि—

कदा मुखं वरतनु कारणादृते
तवागतं क्षणमपि कोपपात्रताम्।

(Then enter Bākulavalikā with a hurried toss of the curtain.)

Bakulāvalikā. Do not enter, Oh king; for it seems it is a serpent going in a zigzag course.

Irāvatī. *(concealing herself behind the pillar and advancing towards the king)* Did the couple find their mid-day meeting yield them the desire of their heart without any obstruction?

(All are confused at sight of Irāvatī.)

King. Darling, this is indeed a novel form of greeting.

Irāvatī. Bakulāvalikā, I congratulate you upon your making good the promise of acting as a go-between.

Bakulāvalikā. Let your highness have compassion on me; for does Indra cease to shower rain on the divine earth because the frogs croak? You may ask the king as to what I have done.

Vidūṣaka. Please, don't go on in this way. For merely on beholding you his honour forgot your repudiation of his humble prostration; but you would not be friendly with him even now.

Irāvatī. What can I do now even though I am angry?

King. It is not proper for you to be angry without cause. For

fair one, when did your face exhibit anger without cause? Would the night have the orb

अपर्वणि ग्रहकलुषेन्दुमण्डला
विभावरी कथय कथं भविष्यति ॥ १६ ॥

इरावती—अट्ठाणेत्ति सुट्ठु वाहरिदं अज्जउत्तेण। अण्णसङ्कन्तेसु अम्हाणं भाअहेएसु जइ उण कुप्पेअं अहं हस्सा हविस्सम्। [अस्थान इति सुष्ठु व्याहृतमार्यपुत्रेण। अन्यसङ्क्रान्तेष्वस्माकं भागधेयेषु यदि पुनः कुप्येयम् ततोऽहं हास्या भवेयम्]

राजा—त्वमन्यथा कल्पयसि। अहं पुनः सत्यमेवात्र कोपस्थानं न पश्यामि। कुतः

नार्हति कृतापराधोऽप्युत्सवदिवसेषु परिजनो दण्डम्।
इति मोचिते मयैते प्रणिपतितुं मामुपगते च ॥ १७ ॥

इरावती—णिउणिए गच्छ देविं विण्णवेहि। दिट्ठं देवीए पक्खवाइत्तणं अज्ज त्ति। [निपुणिके गच्छ देवीं विज्ञापय। दृष्टं देव्याः पक्षपातित्वमद्येति।]

निपुणिका—तह। [तथा।] (इति निष्क्रान्ता।)

विदूषकः(आत्मगतम्)—अहो अणत्थो संवुत्तो। बन्धणब्भट्ठो घरकवोदआ बिडालिआलोए पडिदो। [अहो अनर्थः संवृत्तः। बन्धनभ्रष्टो गृहकपोतको बिडालिकालोके पतितः।]

निपुणिका—(प्रविश्य) भट्टिणि जदिच्छादिट्ठाए माधविआए आचक्खिदं। एवं खु एदं णिव्वुत्तं। (इति कर्णे कथयति।) [भट्टिनि यदृच्छादृष्टया माधविकयाख्यातम्—एवं खल्वेतन्निर्वृत्तमिति।]

इरावती (आत्मगतम्)—उववण्णं सव्वं। बम्हबन्धुणा उब्भिण्णो दुप्पओओ। (विदूषकं विलोक्य प्रकाशम्।) इअं इमस्स कामतन्तसइवस्स णीदी। [उपपन्नं सर्वम्। ब्रह्मबन्धुनोद्भिन्नो दुष्प्रयोगः। इयमस्य कामतन्त्रसचिवस्य नीतिः।]

विदूषकः—होदि जइ णीदीए एक्कं वि अक्खरं पढेअं तदो णं

of the moon obscured by Rāhu except on the full-moon day? (16)

Irāvatī. 'Not proper'—that is a proper expression used by my husband. For now that my good fortune has passed on to another, I should only be making myself ridiculous if I were to get angry again.

King. You take it differently; but I, on my part, really do not see any cause for anger.

For it was in obedience to the precept that on festive days attendants ought not to be punished even when they have committed an offence, that I let them free and now they come to pay me their respects. (17).

Irāvatī. Nipuṇikā, go and inform the queen that I have to-day witnessed her partiality.

Nipuṇikā. Very well. (*Exit.*)

Vidūṣaka. (*To himself*) Alas! a calamity has befallen: the house-pigeon has escaped from confinement (only) to come within sight of the cat.

(*Entering*)

Nipuṇikā. (*Aside*) Queen, Mādhavikā whom I happened to meet informed me that it happened thus.

(*Whispers in her ear.*)

Irāvatī. (*To herself*) I have it now. Surely this must be an intrigue of that scoundrelly Brahmin's planning. (*Looking at the Vidūṣaka.*) This is the policy of this minister versed in the treatises on love.

गाअत्तिं वि विसुमरेअं। [भवति यदि नीत्यां एकमप्यक्षरं पठेयं ततो ननु गायत्रीमपि विस्मरेयम् ।]

राजा (स्वगतम्)—कथं नु खलु सङ्कटादस्मादात्मानं मोचयिष्यामि ।

(प्रविश्य) **जयसेना** (सावेगम्)–देव कुमारी वसुलच्छी कन्दुअं अणुधावन्ती पिङ्गलवाणरेण बलिअं उत्तासिदा अङ्कणिसण्णा देवीए पवादकिसलअं विअ वेवमाणा दाणिं वि पकिदिं ण पडिवज्जइ। [देव कुमारी वसुलक्ष्मीः कन्दुकमनुधावन्ती पिङ्गलवानरेण बलवदुत्त्रासिताङ्कनिषण्णा देव्याः प्रवातकिसलयमिव वेपमाना इदानीमपि प्रकृतिं न प्रतिपद्यते ।]

राजा—कष्टम् कष्टम् । कातरो बालभावः ।

इरावती (सावेगम्)—तुवरदु तुवरदु अज्जउत्तो णं समासासइदुं। मा दाव से सन्तासजणिओ विआरो वड्ढदु । [त्वरतां त्वरतामार्यपुत्र एनां समाश्वासयितुम् । मा तावदस्याः सन्त्रासजनितो विकारो वर्धताम् ।]

राजा—अहमेनां सञ्ज्ञापयामि। (सत्वरं परिक्रामति ।)

विदूषकः (आत्मगतम्)—साहु रे पिङ्गलवाणर साहु । सुट्ठु परित्तादो तुए सङ्कडादो सपक्खो । [साधु रे पिङ्गलवानर साधु। सुष्ठु परित्रातस्त्वया सङ्कटात् सपक्षः ।]

(निष्क्रान्तः सवयस्यो राजा इरावती निपुणिका चेटा च।)

मालविका—हला देविं चिन्तिअ वेवदि मे हिअअं । ण जाणे अदो वरं किं अणुहोदव्वं हविस्सदित्ति । [हला देवीं चिन्तयित्वा वेपते मे हृदयम् । न जाने अतः परं किमनुभवितव्यं भविष्यतीति ।]

(नेपथ्ये)

अच्छरिअं अच्छरिअं । अपुण्णे एव्व पञ्चरत्ते दोहलस्स मुउलेहिं सण्णद्धो तवणीआसोओ । जाव देवीए णिवेदेमि । [आश्चर्यमाश्च-

Vidūṣaka. Lady, if I were to read but one syllable of policy, I shall forget the Gāyatrī.

King. (*To himself*) How on earth may I get out of this sad pickle!

(*Entering*)

Jayasenā. *(Excitedly)* King,princess Vasulakṣmī while running after her ball was terribly frightened by the ape Pingalaka; and now although reclining in the lap of the queen is trembling like a spray in the breeze and does not regain consciousness in the least.

King. Alas! How very timid are children!

Irāvatī. (*In consternation*) Let my husband hasten to console her. Let not the illness produced by the fright be aggravated.

King. I will soon bring her to consciousness. (*Moves about quickly.*)

Vidūsaka. Bravo! Pingala ape, bravo! You have indeed saved your side.

(*Exeunt king, the Vidūṣaka, Irāvatī and the female door-keeper.*)

Mālavikā. Friend, I am all in a flutter as I think of the queen. I do not know what I shall have to endure next.

(Behind the scenes.)

A Marvel! A Marvel! Even before five nights have passed from the time of the Dohada ceremony, the

र्यम् । अपूर्ण एव पञ्चरात्रे दोहदस्य मुकुलैः सन्नद्धस्तपनीयाशोकः । यावद्देव्यै निवेदयामि ।]

(उभे श्रुत्वा प्रहृष्टे भवतः ।)

बकुलावलिका—समस्ससदु पिअसही । सच्चपडिण्णा देवी । [समाश्वसितु प्रियसखी । सत्यप्रतिज्ञा देवी ।]

मालविका—तेण हि पमदवणपालिआए पिट्ठदो होम्ह । [तेन हि प्रमदवनपालिकायाः पृष्ठतो भवावः ।]

बकुलावलिका—तहा । [तथा ।]

(इति निष्क्रान्ताः सर्वे ।)

॥ इति चतुर्थोऽङ्कः ॥

golden Aśoka tree is covered over with buds. So I will inform the queen.

(Both are delighted on hearing this.)

Bakulāvalikā. Cheer up, my friend, the queen will be true to her word.

Mālavikā. Well then, let us follow the keeper of the pleasure-garden close at her heels.

Bakulāvalikā. All right. *(Exeunt.)*

Here ends the Fourth Act.

पञ्चमोऽङ्कः ।

(ततः प्रविशत्युद्यानपालिका ।)

उद्यानपालिका—उवक्खित्तो मए किदसक्कारविहिणो तवणीआसोअस्स वेदिआबन्धो । जाव अणुचिट्ठिदणिओअं अत्ताणं देवीए णिवेदेमि । (परिक्रम्य) अहो देव्वस्स अणुकम्पणिज्जा मालविआ । जं तस्सिं तह चण्डीकिदा देवी इमिणा असोअकुसुमउत्तंतेण पसादसुमुही भविस्सदि । कहिं णु खु देवी भवे । (विलोक्य) अम्मो एसो देवीए परिजणब्भंतरो किं वि जदुमुद्दालंछिदं चीवरबन्धं करे गेह्णिअ चउस्सालादो कुज्जो सारसओ णिक्कमदि । पुच्छिस्सं दाव णं । [उपक्षिप्तो मया कृतसत्कारविधेस्तपनीयाशोकस्य वेदिकाबन्धः । यावदनुष्ठितनियोगमात्मानं देव्यै निवेदयामि । अहो दैवस्यानुकम्पनीया मालविका । यत् तस्यां तथा चण्डीकृता देवी अनेनाशोककुसुमवृत्तान्तेन प्रसादसुमुखी भविष्यति । कुत्र नु खलु देवी भवेत् । अम्मो एष देव्याः परिजनाभ्यन्तरः किमपि जतुमुद्रालाञ्छितं चीवरबन्धं करे गृहीत्वा चतुःशालात् कुब्जः सारसको निष्क्रामति । प्रक्ष्यामि तावदेनम् ।]

(ततः प्रविशति यथानिर्दिष्टः कुब्जः ।)

उद्यानपालिका—(उपसृत्य)—सारसअ कहिं पत्थिदोसि । [सारसक कुत्र प्रस्थितोऽसि ।]

सारसकः—महुअरिए वेअपारआणं बम्हणाणं णिच्चदक्खिणा दादव्वा । ता अज्जपुरोहिदस्स हत्थं पावइस्सं । [मधुकरिके वेदपारगाणां ब्राह्मणानां नित्यदक्षिणा दातव्या । तदार्यपुरोहितस्य हस्तं प्रापयिष्यामि ।]

मधुकरिका—किंणिमित्तं । [किंनिमित्तम् ।]

सारसकः—जदप्पहुदि सुदं सेणावइणा जण्णतुरअरक्खणे णिउत्तो भट्टिदारओ वसुमित्तो त्ति तदापहुदि तस्स आउसो णिमित्तं अट्ठा-

ACT V.

(*Enter the female keeper of the garden.*)

The keeper. I have got constructed an alter round the gold Aśoka-tree which has been duly honoured. So I will inform the queen that I have executed her order. (*Moving about.*) Ah ! Fate should really take pity on Mālavikā, so that although the queen is highly incensed against her, yet she might be inclined to favour her on account of this incident of the Aśoka putting forth flowers. Where is the queen ? (*Observing*) Ah ! the hunchback Sārasaka, one of the servants of the queen, is just issuing out of the quadrangle with a cloth-covered box sealed with a lac seal. I will ask him.

(*Enter the hunch-back as described.*)

The keeper. (*Approaching*) Sārasaka, where are you going ?

Sārasaka. Madhukarikā, the Brahmins versed in the sacred lore are to be given their daily dole. So I will put (it) into the hands of the revered priest.

Madhukarikā. What for ?

Sārasaka. Ever since the queen learnt that prince Vasumitra was appointed by the general to guard the sacrificial horse, she has been bestowing on those who

दससुवण्णप्पमाणं दक्खिणं देवी दक्खिणीएहिं पडिग्गाहेदि । [यदाप्रभृति श्रुतं सेनापतिना यज्ञतुरगरक्षणे नियुक्तो भर्तृदारको वसुमित्र इति तदाप्रभृति तस्यायुषो निमित्तमष्टादशसुवर्णप्रमाणां दक्षिणां देवी दक्षिणीयैः प्रतिग्राहयति ।]

मधुकरिका—जुज्जइ । अह कहिं देवी । किं वा अणुचिट्ठदि । [युज्यते । अथ कुत्र देवी । किं वानुतिष्ठति ।]

सारसकः—मङ्गलघरए आसणत्था विअब्भविसआदो भादुणा वीरसेणेण पेसिदं लिपिअरेहिं वाचीअमाणं लेहं सुणादि । [मङ्गलगृहे आसनस्था विदर्भविषयात् भ्रात्रा वीरसेनेन प्रेषितं लिपिकारैर्वाच्यमानं लेखं शृणोति ।]

मधुकरिका—को उण विअब्भराअवुत्तन्तो । [कः पुनर्विदर्भराजवृत्तान्तः ।]

सारसकः—वसीकिदो किल वीरसेणप्पमुहेहिं भट्टिणो विअअदण्डेहिं विअब्भणाहो । मोइदो अ से दाआदो माहवसेणो । तेण महासाराइं रअणवाहणाइं सिप्पआरिआभूइट्ठं परिअणं अ उवाअणीकरिअ भट्टिणो सआसं पेसिदो दूदो सुवो किल भट्टारं पेक्खिस्सदि । [वशीकृतः किल वीरसेनप्रमुखैर्भर्तुर्विजयदण्डैर्विदर्भनाथः । मोचितश्चास्य दायादो माधवसेनः । तेन महासाराणि रत्नवाहनानि शिल्पदारिकाभूयिष्ठं परिजनं चोपायनीकृत्य भर्तुः सकाशं प्रेषितो दूतः श्वः किल भर्तारं द्रक्ष्यति ।]

मधुकरिका—गच्छ अणुचिट्ठ अत्तणो णिओअं । अहं वि देविं पेक्खिस्सं । [गच्छ अनुतिष्ठ आत्मनो नियोगम् । अहमपि देवीं द्रक्ष्यामि ।]

(इति निष्क्रान्तौ ।)

प्रवेशकः ।

(ततः प्रविशति प्रतीहारी ।)

प्रतीहारी—आणत्तम्हि देवीए असोअसक्कारव्वावुदाए-त्तिणत्तेहि

are worthy of the dole, eighteen golden pieces in order to secure him (long) life.

Madhukarikā. That is as it should be. Where is the queen? How is she engaged?

Sārasaka. Sitting in the holy house, she is listening to a letter sent by her brother Vīrasena from the country of the Vidarbhas, read out to her by the scribes.

Madhukarikā. What could be the news from the king of the Vidarbhas?

Sārasaka. It is reported that the victorious army of our king led by Vīrasena and others has subjugated the king of the Vidarbhas, and his relative Mādhavasena is set free. He has sent many presents of very valuable jewelled vehicles, and some attendants, mostly maidens accomplished in the arts; and has dispatched a messenger who is to see his majesty tomorrow.

Madhukarikā. Go, attend to your business; I for my part will see the queen.

(Exeunt.)

Here ends the introductory scene.

(Enter the female door-keeper.)

Door-keeper—the queen who is engaged in doing honour to the Aśoka tree has given me this order: tell my lord I desire to witness for myself in the company of my lord the Asoka tree in its glory of flowers. So I

अज्जउत्तं । इच्छामि अज्जउत्तेण सह असोअरुक्खस्स पसूणलच्छिं
५४पच्चक्खीकरेदुंत्ति । ता जाव धम्मासणगदं देवं पडिवालेमि ।
[आज्ञप्तास्मि देव्या अशोकसत्कारव्यापृतया—विज्ञापयाम्यार्यपुत्रम् । इच्छाम्यार्यपुत्रेण सहाशोकवृक्षस्य प्रसूनलक्ष्मीं प्रत्यक्षीकर्तुम्' इति । तद्यावद्धर्मासनगतं देवं प्रतिपालयामि ।]

(इति परिक्रामति ।)

(नेपथ्ये) **वैतालिकौ**—दिष्ट्या दण्डेनैदारिशिरःसु वर्तते देवः ।

प्रथमः—परभृतकलव्याहारेषु त्वमात्तरतिर्मधुं
नयसि विदिशातीरोद्यानेष्वनङ्ग इवाङ्गवान् ।
विजयकरिणामालानाङ्गैरुपोढबलस्य ते
वरद वरदारोधोवृक्षैः सहावनतो रिपुः ॥ १॥

द्वितीयः—विरचितपदं वीरप्रीत्या सुरोपम सूरिभि-
श्चरितमुभयोर्मध्येकृत्य स्थितं क्रथकैशिकान् ।
तव हृतवतो दण्डानीकैर्विदर्भपतेः श्रियं
परिघगुरुभिर्दोर्भिः शौरेः प्रसह्य च रुक्मिणीम् ॥२॥

प्रतीहारी—एसो जअसद्दसूइदप्पत्थाणो भट्टा इदो एव्व आअच्छदि। अहंवि दाव इमस्स पमुहादो किंवि ओसरिअ एदं मुहालिन्दतोरणं
३समस्सिदा होमि । [एष जयशब्दसूचितप्रस्थानो भर्ता इत एवागच्छति । अहमपि तावदस्य प्रमुखात्किमप्यपसृत्य एतन्मुखालिन्दतोरणं समाश्रिता भवामि ।] (एकान्ते स्थिता ।)

६ (ततः प्रविशति सवयस्यो राजा ।)

राजा—

कान्तां विचिन्त्य सुलभेतरसम्प्रयोगां
श्रुत्वा विदर्भपतिमानमितं बलैश्च ।
धाराभिरातप इवाभिहतं सरोजं
दुःखायते च हृदयं सुखमश्नुते च ॥ ३ ॥

will now await the king who has been occupying the judgment-seat.

(Moves about.)

(Behind the scenes.)

Two Bards—Hail to our king who by the mere strength of his army tramples the heads of his enemies.

First Bard—In the gardens on the banks of the Vidiśā, vocal with the sweet warblings of the cuckoo, delighted, you spend the spring like the god of love assuming a body; while your power ever waxing, O giver of boons, the enemies have been bent down together with the trees on the banks of the Varadā, which are used as the tying posts for your victorious elephants.(1)

Second bard—O god-like (king), the acts of these two, sung in verse by the wise out of their love for heroes, have been well known all over the Kratha-kaiśikas—of you who by means of your forces took away the glory of the king of the Vidarbhas, and of Śrikrsna who by his arms as puissant as iron has forcibly carried away Rukmiṇī. (2)

Door-keeper. The king is coming here, his setting forth being announced by the shouts of victory; I will now step aside from his direct path and stand under the arch of the main terrace. *(Stands aside.)*

(Enter king with his companion.)

King. As I think how difficult it is to secure my beloved and as I hear of the subjugation of the king of the Vidarbhas by my forces, my heart feels both happy and sad, like a lotus in the sun when it is struck by the streams (of a rain shower.) (3)

विदूषकः—जह अहं पेक्खामि तह एकन्तसुहिदो भवं भाविस्सदि। [यथाहं पश्यामि तथैकान्तसुखितो भवान् भविष्यति।]

राजा—कथमिव।

विदूषकः—अज्ज किल देवीए धारिणीए पण्डिदकोसिई भणिदा। भअवदि जइ तुमं पसाहणगव्वं वहेसि ता दंसेहि मालविआए सरीरे वेदब्भं विवाहणेवत्थं ति। ताए वि सविसेसालंकिदा मालविआ। तत्तहोदी कदाचि पूरेइ भवदो मणोरहं। [अद्य खलु देव्या धारिण्या पण्डितकौशिकी भणिता। 'भगवति यदि त्वं प्रसाधनगर्वं वहसि तद्दर्शय मालविकायाः शरीरे वैदर्भं विवाहनेपथ्यम्' इति। तयापि सविशेषालङ्कृता मालविका। तत्रभवती कदाचित् पूरयति भवतो मनोरथम्।]

राजा—सखे मदपेक्षानुवृत्त्या निवृत्तेर्ष्याया धारिण्याः पूर्वचरितैः सम्भाव्यमेतत्।

प्रतीहारी (उपगम्य)—जेदु भट्टा। देवी विण्णवेदि—तवणीआसोअस्स कुसुमसोहादंसणेण मह आरम्भो सफलीकरीअदु त्ति। [जयतु भर्ता। देवी विज्ञापयति—'तपनीयाशोकस्य कुसुमशोभादर्शनेन ममारम्भः सफलीक्रियताम्' इति।]

राजा—ननु तत्रैव देवी।

प्रतीहारी—अह इं। जहारुहसम्माणसुहिदं अन्देउरं विसज्जिअ मालविआपुरोएण अत्तणो परिअणेण सह देवं पडिवालेदि। [अथ किम्। यथार्हसम्मानसुखितं अन्तःपुरं विसृज्य मालविकापुरोगेणात्मनः परिजनेन सह देवं प्रतिपालयति।]

राजा (सहर्षम्। विदूषकं विलोक्य।)—जयसेने गच्छाग्रतः।

प्रतीहारी—इदो इदो देवो। [इत इतो देवः।]

(सर्वे परिक्रामन्ति।)

विदूषकः (विलोक्य)—भो वअस्स किंचि परिवुत्तजोव्वणो विअ

Vidūṣaka. As I see it, you will surely be blessed with perfect happiness.

King. How do you mean ?

Vidūṣaka. To day queen Dhāriṇī said to the learned Kausikī : Revered lady, if you pride yourself upon your skill in decorating, then put on Mālavikā's person the wedding-attire used by the people of the Vidarbha country ; and she too got Mālavikā splendidly decked. It is, therefore, likely that her highness grants you your desire.

King. Friend, this is quite possible, to judge from the former actions of Dhāriṇī who has always followed my inclinations and has been utterly free from jealousy.

Door-keeper. *(Approaching)* Victory to the king! The queen makes this request : please to make my undertaking fruitful by coming to witness the beauty of the gold Aśoka-tree in flowers.

King. Surely the queen is there, is she not ?

Door-keeper. Yes. After dismissing the ladies of the harem who are pleased by being honoured according to their deserts, she is waiting for my lord with her own attendants headed by Mālavikā.

King. *(Joyfully looking at the Vidūṣaka)* Jayasenā, do you go ahead

Door-keeper. This way, this way, king.

(All move about.)

Vidūṣaka. *(Observing)* My friend, in this Pramada-

वसन्तो पमदवणे लक्खीअदि । [भो वयस्य किंचित्परिवृत्तयौवन इव वसन्तः प्रमदवने लक्ष्यते ।]

राजा—यथाह भवान् ।

अग्रे विकीर्णकुरवकफलजालविभिद्यमानसहकारम् ।
परिणामाभिमुखमृतोरुत्सुकयति यौवनं चेतः ॥ ४ ॥

विदूषकः (परिक्रम्य)—अहो अअं सो दिण्णणेवत्थो विअ कुसुमत्थवएहिं तवणीआसोओ । ओलोएदु भवं । [अहो अयं स दत्तनेपथ्य इव कुसुमस्तबकैस्तपनीयाशोकः अवलोकयतु भवान् ।]

राजा—स्थाने खल्वयं प्रसवमन्थरोऽभूत् । यदयमिदानीमनन्यसाधारणां शोभां उद्वहति । पश्य

सर्वाशोकतरूणां प्रथमं सूचितवसन्तविभवानाम् ।
निर्वृत्तदोहदेऽस्मिन्सङ्क्रान्तानीव कुसुमानि ॥ ५ ॥

विदूषकः—भो वीसद्धो होहि । अम्हेसु सण्णिहिदेसु वि धारिणी पस्सपरिवट्टिणिं मालविअं अणुमण्णेदि । [भो विश्रब्धो भव । अस्मासु सन्निहितेष्वपि धारिणी पार्श्वपरिवर्तिनीं मालविकामनुमन्यते ।]

राजा (सहर्षम्)—पश्य सखे

मामियमभ्युत्तिष्ठति देवी विनयादुपस्थिता प्रियया ।
विस्मृतहस्तकमलया नरेन्द्रलक्ष्म्या वसुमतीव ॥ ६ ॥

(ततः प्रविशति देवी मालविका परिव्राजिका विभवतश्च परिवारः ।)

मालविका (आत्मगतम्)—जाणामि णिमित्तं कोदुआलङ्कारस्स । तह वि भिसिणीपत्तगदं सलिलं विअ वेवइ मे हिअअं । दक्खिणेदरं वि णअणं बहुसो फुरइ । [जानामि निमित्तं कौतुकालङ्कारस्य । तथापि बिसिनीपत्रगतं सलिलमिव वेपते मे हृदयम् । दक्षिणेतरदपि नयनं बहुशः स्फुरति ।]

vana–garden here, spring seems to be somewhat past his youth.

King. It is even as you say.

Here before (us) the youth of spring now attaining its ripeness, with the Kurabakà flowers scattered, and the mango tree bursting with fruit, fills the mind with longing. (4)

Vidūṣaka. *(Moving about)* O, this gold Aśoka-tree appears to be attired in a vesture of clustering flowers. Look, your highness.

King. It was quite proper that it was tardy to blossom. For now it stands matchless in its loveliness. See,

it appears as if the flowers of all other Aśoka-trees that first exhibited the wealth of spring, have been transferred to this tree, now that its longing is fulfilled. (5)

Vidūṣaka. Be quite at ease; for even when we are near, Dhāriṇī allows Mālavikā to attend her.

King. (*With joy*) See, my friend,

the queen rises to greet me respectfully, attended by my beloved, like the Earth waited upon by royal Glory who has forgotten to hold a flower in her hand. (6)

(Then enter The queen, Mālavikā, Parivrājikā and the attendants at a respectful distance.)

Mālavikā. *(To herself)* I know the reason of this nuptial attire ; and yet, how my heart quivers like water on a lotus-leaf ! And my left eye, too, is throbbing frequently.

विदूषकः—भो वअस्स किं वि वेवाहिअणेवत्थेण सविसेसं खु सोहदि तत्तहोदी मालविआ। [भो वयस्य किमपि वैवाहिकनेपथ्येन
९ सविशेषं खलु शोभते तत्रभवती मालविका।]

राजा—पश्याम्याभरणालङ्कृतामेनाम्। यैषा

अनतिलम्बिदुकूलनिवासिनी
लघुभिराभरणैः प्रतिभाति मे।
उडुगणैरुदयोन्मुखचन्द्रिका
गतहिमैरिव चैत्रविभावरी ॥ ७ ॥

धारिणी—(उपेत्य) जेदु अज्जउत्तो। [जयत्वार्यपुत्रः।]

विदूषकः—वड्ढदु होदी। [वर्धतां भवती।]

३ **परिव्राजिका**—विजयतां देवः।

राजा—भगवति अभिवादये।

परिव्राजिका—अभिमतसिद्धिरस्तु।

६**धारिणी** (सस्मितम्)—अज्जउत्त, एसो दे अम्हेहिं तरुणीअणसहाअस्स असोओ सङ्केदघरअं सङ्कप्पिदो। [आर्यपुत्र, एष तेऽस्माभिस्तरुणीजनसहायस्याशोकः सङ्केतगृहं सङ्कल्पितः।]

९**विदूषकः**—भो आराहिओसि। [भो आराधितोऽसि।]

राजा—(सव्रीडमशोकमभितः परिक्रामन्।)

नायं देव्या भाजनत्वं न मेयः
सत्काराणामीदृशानामशोकः।
यः सावज्ञो माधवश्रीनियोगे
पुष्पैः शंसत्यादरं यत्प्रयत्ने ॥ ८ ॥

विदूषकः—भो विस्सद्धो भविअ इमं जोव्वणवदिं पेक्ख। [भो विश्रब्धो भूत्वेमां यौवनवतीं पश्य।]

३**धारिणी**—कं। [काम्।]

Vidūṣaka. My friend, the lady Mālavikā looks so lovely in that nuptial dress.

King. I see her decked in those ornaments–she who

wearing a short silk dress and with scanty ornaments, appears to me like a night in the month of Caitra when moonlight is imminent, with the clusters of stars free from mists. (7)

Dhāriṇī. (*advancing*) Victory to my lord!

Vidūṣaka. May your highness be prosperous!

Parivrājikā. May the king be victorious!

King. Revered lady, I salute thee!

Parivrājikā. May you attain the object you desire!

Dhāriṇī. (*Smiling*) my noble lord, here have we turned this Aśoka-tree into a trysting bower for you to enjoy the company of young ladies.

Vidūsaka. Come, friend, a great favour has been conferred upon you.

King. (*Bashfully walking round the Aśoka-tree.*)

This Aśoka-tree really deserves to be made the recipient of such favours inasmuch as it disregarded the command of the goddess of vernal beauty and evinced its respect for your exertions by bursting into flowers. (8)

Vidūsaka. Come, be confident, and look at this blooming young—

Dhāriṇī. Whom do you mean?

विदूषकः—तवणीआसोअस्स कुसुमसोहं । [तपनीयाशोकस्य कुसुमशोभाम् ।]

(सर्वे उपविशन्ति ।)

राजा (मालविकां विलोक्यात्मगतम् ।)—कष्टं खलु ममाद्य सान्निधिविप्रयोगः ।

अहं रथाङ्गनामेव प्रिया सहचरीव मे ।
अननुज्ञातसम्पर्का धारिणी रजनीव नौ ॥ ९ ॥

(ततः प्रविशति कञ्चुकी ।)

कञ्चुकी—जयतु देवः । अमात्यो विज्ञापयति 'तस्मिन्विदर्भराजोपायने द्वे शिल्पदारिके मार्गपरिश्रमादलसशरीरे इति कृत्वा न प्रवेशिते । सम्प्रति देवोपस्थानयोग्ये । तत्राज्ञां देवो दातुमर्हति' इति ।

राजा—प्रवेशय ते ।

कञ्चुकी—यदाज्ञापयति देवः । (इति निष्क्रम्य ताभ्यां सह पुनः प्रविश्य ।) इत इतो भवत्यौ ।

प्रथमा (जनान्तिकम्)—हला रअणिए, अपुव्वं वि एदं राउअलं पविसन्तीए पसीददि मे अब्भन्तरगदो अप्पा । [हला रजनिके अपूर्वमप्येतद्राजकुलं प्रविशन्त्याः प्रसीदति ममाभ्यन्तरगत आत्मा ।]

द्वितीया—जोसिणिए मह वि एव्वं । अत्थि खु लोअवाओ । आआमि सुहं वा दुक्खं वा हिअअं समत्थीकरेदित्ति । [ज्योत्स्निके ममाप्येवम् । अस्ति खलु लोकवादः । आगामि सुखं वा दुःखं वा हृदयं समर्थीकरोतीति ।]

प्रथमा—सो दाणिं सच्चो होदु । [स इदानीं सत्यो भवतु ।]

कञ्चुकी—एष देव्या सह देवस्तिष्ठति । उपसर्पतां भवत्यौ ।

Vidūsaka. Beauty of the flowers of the golden Aśoka.

(All sit down.)

King. *(Looking at Mālavikā, to himself)* Alas! I am at the present moment separated though near.

I am like the Cakravāka bird, and my beloved like his mate. while Dhāriṇī who does not permit our union, is like the night. (9)

(Then enter a chamberlain.)

Chamberlain. Victory to the king. The minister says that in that present sent by the king of Vidarbha were included two accomplished maidens who, as they were fatigued with the journey, were not then presented. Now they are in a fit state to appear before the king. Let the king, therefore, direct in regard to this matter.

King. Introduce them.

Chamberlain. As the king commands. (*He goes out and then reappears along with them.*) This way, this way, ladies.

First. *(Aside)* Ah, Rajanikā, although I am stepping into this palace quite unknown to me before, yet my inner self is filled with delight.

Second. Jyotsnikā ! I have exactly the same feeling. You know indeed the well known proverb : the state of the heart foretells approaching happiness or misery.

First. May it come true on the present occasion.

Chamberlain. Here are the king and the queen; may you advance, ladies.

(उभे उपसर्पतः । मालविका परिव्राजिका च चेट्यौ दृष्ट्वा परस्परमवलोकयतः ।)

उभे (प्रणिपत्य)—जेदु भट्टा । जेदु भट्टिणी । [जयतु भर्ता । जयतु भट्टिनी ।]

राजा—निषीदतम् ।

(उभे उपविष्टे ।)

राजा—कस्यां कलायामभियोगो भवत्योः ।

उभे—भट्टा सङ्गीदए अब्भंतरम्ह । [भर्तः सङ्गीते अभ्यन्तरे स्वः ।]

राजा—देवि गृह्यतामनयोरन्यतरा ।

देवी—मालविए इदो पेक्ख । कदरा दे सङ्गीदसहाइणी रुच्चइ । [मालविके इतः पश्य । कतरा ते सङ्गीतसहायिनी रोचते ।]

उभे—(मालविकां विलोक्य)—अम्मो भट्टिदारिआ । जेदु भट्टिदारिआ । [अम्मो भर्तृदारिका । जयतु भर्तृदारिका ।]

(तया सह बाष्पं विसृजतः ।)

(सर्वे सविस्मयमालोकयन्ति ।)

राजा—के भवत्यौ । का वेयम् ।

प्रथमा—देव इअं अम्हाणं भट्टिदारिआ । [देव इयमस्माकं भर्तृदारिका ।]

राजा—कथमिव ।

उभे—सुणादु भट्टा । जो सो भट्टिणा विअअदण्डेहिं विअब्भणाहं वसीकरिअ बन्धणादो मोइदो कुमारो माहवसेणो णाम तस्स इअं कणीअसी भइणी मालविआ णाम । [शृणोतु भर्ता । योऽसौ भर्त्रा विजयदण्डैर्विदर्भनाथं वशीकृत्य बन्धनान्मोचितः कुमारो माधवसेनो नाम तस्येयं कनीयसी भगिनी मालविका नाम ।]

धारिणी—कहं राअदारिआ इअं । चन्दणं खु मए पादुआपरि-

(Both advance, Mālavikā and the Parivrājikā exchange glances on seeing these two attendants.)

Both. *(Prostrating themselves)* Victory to the king! Victory to the queen!

King. Sit down.

(Both sit down.)

King. Ladies, which art have you practised?

Both. We are well versed in music, your majesty.

King. Queen, take one of these ladies.

Queen. Look here, Mālavikā. Which would you like to have to accompany you in singing?

Both. *(Seeing Mālavikā)* Ah! The princess! *(Prostrating before her)* Victory to our princess! *(They weep with her.)*

(All look on in bewilderment.)

King. Who are you, ladies? And who is this?

First. King, this is our princess.

King. What do you mean?

Both. Listen, king! This is Mālavikā the younger sister of prince Mādhavasena who was rescued from prison by you by conquering the king of Vidarbha with your victorious army.

Dhāriṇī. She is a princess! How have I been de-

होएण दूसिदं । [कथं राजदारिकेयम् । चन्दनं खलु मया पादुकापरिभोगेण दूषितम् ।]

राजा—अथात्रभवती कथमित्थंभूता ।

मालविका (निःश्वस्यात्मगतम् ।)—विहिणो णिओएण । [विधेर्नियोगेन ।]

द्वितीया—सुणादु भट्टा । दाआदवसं गदे अम्हाणं भट्टिदारए माहवसेणे तस्स अमच्चेण अज्जसुमदिणा अम्हारिसं परिअणं उज्झिअ गूढं अवणीदा एसा । [शृणोतु भर्ता । दायादवशं गतेऽस्माकं भर्तृदारके माधवसेने तस्यामात्येनार्यसुमतिना अस्मादृशं परिजनं उज्झित्वा गूढमपनीतैषा ।]

राजा—श्रुतपूर्वं मयैतावत् । ततस्ततः ।

उभे—एत्तिअं एव्व आणीमो । अदो वरं ण आणीमो । [एतावदेव जानीवः । अतः परं न जानीवः ।]

परिव्राजिका—अतः परमहं मन्दभागिनी कथयिष्यामि ।

उभे—भट्टिदारिए अज्जकोसिईए विअ सरसञ्जोओ पडिभादि । [भर्तृदारिके आर्यकौशिक्या इव स्वरसंयोगः प्रतिभाति ।]

मालविका—अह इं । [अथ किम् ।]

उभे—जदिवेसधारिणी अज्जकोसिई दुक्खेण विभावीअदि । भअवदि वन्दामो । [यतिवेषधारिणी आर्यकौशिकी दुःखेन विभाव्यते । भगवति वन्दावहे ।]

परिव्राजिका—स्वस्ति भवतीभ्याम् ।

राजा—कथमाप्तवर्गोऽयं भवत्याः ।

परिव्राजिका—एवमेतत् ।

विदूषकः—तेण हि कहेदु दाणिं भअवदी अत्तहोदीए उत्तन्तसेसं । [तेन हि कथयत्विदानीं भगवती अत्रभवत्या वृत्तान्तशेषम् ।]

परिव्राजिका (सवैक्लव्यम्)—श्रूयतां तावत् । माधवसेनसचिवं

filing sandalwood by using it as a slipper!

King. Well, then, how was this lady reduced to this state?

Mālavikā. *(Sighing, to herself)* By the decree of fate.

Second Maiden. Listen, your majesty. When our prince Mādhavasena was captured by his kinsmen, his minister, the noble Sumati, secretly carried her away, leaving behind attendants like us.

King. I have heard this before. What happened next?

Both. This is all we know. We do not know what happened afterwards.

Parivrājikā. I will now relate, wretched woman that I am, what happened next.

Both. Princess, we seem to hear the voice of the noble Kauśikī.

Mālavikā. Surely.

Both. It is difficult to recognize the noble Kauśikī in the garb of an ascetic. Revered lady, we salute you.

Parivrājikā. Blessings on you!

King. What, are these your kinsfolk?

Parivrājikā. Yes, it is so.

Vidūsaka. Please, revered lady, relate to us the rest of her story.

Parivrājikā. *(Painfully)* Listen then. Know that

६९सुमतिं ममाग्रजमवरुद्ध ।

राजा—उपलब्धम् । ततस्ततः ।

परिव्राजिका—स इमां तथागतभ्रातृकां मया सार्धमपवाह्य भव-
७२त्सम्बन्धाकाङ्क्षया पथिकसार्थं विदिशागामिनमनुप्रविष्टः ।

राजा—ततस्ततः ।

परिव्राजिका—ततश्च

तूणीरपट्टपरिणद्धभुजान्तराल-
मापार्ष्णिलम्बिशिखिबर्हकलापधारि ।
कोदण्डपाणि निनदत्प्रतिरोधकाना-
मापातदुष्प्रसहमाविरभूदनीकम् ॥ १० ॥

(मालविका भयं रूपयति ।)

विदूषकः—भोदि मा भआहि । अदिक्कन्तं खु भअवदी कहेदि ।
२ [भवति मा भैषीः । अतिक्रान्तं खलु भगवती कथयति ।]

राजा—ततस्ततः ।

परिव्राजिका—ततो मुहूर्तं बद्धयुद्धास्ते पराङ्मुखीकृताः सार्थवाह-
६योद्धारः तस्करैः ।

राजा—भगवति अतः परमिदानीं कष्टं श्रोतव्यम् ।

परिव्राजिका—ततः स मत्सोदर्यः

इमां परीप्सुर्दुर्जातेः पराभिभवकातराम् ।
भर्तृप्रियः प्रियैर्भर्तुरानृण्यमसुभिर्गतः ॥ ११ ॥

प्रथमा—हा हदो सुमदी । [हा हतः सुमतिः ।]

द्वितीया—अदो खु भट्टिदारिआए एआरिसी समवत्था संवुत्ता ।
३ [अतः खलु भर्तृदारिकाया एतादृशी समवस्था संवृत्ता ।]

(परिव्राजिका बाष्पं विकिरति ।)

Mādhavasena's minister, Sumati, is my elder brother.

King. We understand ; pray, go on.

Parivrājikā. He carried off along with myself, this lady whose brothor was reduced to such a state, and desiring to marry her to your majesty joined a caravan that was going to the Vidiśā country.

King. What next ?

Parivrājikā. And then

there appeared a host of yelling bandits, armed with bows, whose breasts were crossed by the quiver-straps, and who wore tufts of peacock-tails hanging down to their heels, and whose on-slaught was so irresistible. (10)

(Mālavikā gesticulates fright.)

Vidūsaka. Lady, do not be afraid; for the revered lady is relating something that is past.

King. What happened next ?

Parivrājikā. Then the warriors employed by the leader of the caravan joined battle for a moment with the robbers, but were soon put to flight.

King. Revered lady, the sequel to this, which we have now to hear, must be painful.

Parivrājikā. Then my brother

endeavouring to save from the ruffians this lady who was afraid of violence at their hands —my brother who loved his king so well—paid with his dear life his debt to his king. (11)

First maiden. Alas ! Sumati is killed !

Second maiden. That is how our princess is reduced to this state.

(The Parivrājikā sheds tears.)

राजा—भगवति तनुभृतामीदृशी लोकयात्रा । न शोच्यस्तत्रभवान् सफलीकृतभर्तृपिण्डः । ततः ।

परिव्राजिका—ततो मोहं गताहं यावत्संज्ञामुपलभे तावदियं दुर्लभदर्शना संवृत्ता ।

राजा—महत् खलु कृच्छ्रमनुभूतं भगवत्या ।

परिव्राजिका—ततो भ्रातुः शरीरमग्निसात्कृत्वा पुनर्नवीकृतवैधव्य-दुःखया मया त्वदीयं देशमवतीर्य इमे काषाये गृहीते ।

राजा—युक्तम् । सज्जनस्यैष पन्थाः । ततस्ततः ।

परिव्राजिका—सेयमाटविकेभ्यो वीरसेनं वीरसेनाद्देवीं गता देवीगृहे लब्धप्रवेशया मया पुनर्दृष्टेत्येतदवसानं कथायाः ।

मालविका (आत्मगतम्)—किं णु खु संपदं भट्टा भणादि । [किं नु खलु साम्प्रतं भर्ता भणति ।]

राजा—अहो परिभवोपहारिणो विनिपाताः । कुतः ।

प्रेष्यभावेन नामेयं देवीशब्दक्षमा सती ।
स्नानीयवस्त्रक्रियया पत्रोर्णं वोपयुज्यते ॥ १२ ॥

धारिणी—भअवदि तुए अहिजणवदिं मालविअं अणाचक्खन्तीए असम्पदं किदं । [भगवति त्वयाभिजनवतीं मालविकामनाचक्षाणया असाम्प्रतं कृतम् ।]

परिव्राजिका—शान्तं पापं शान्तं पापम् । कारणेनैव खलु मया नैभृत्यमवलम्बितम् ।

धारिणी—किं विअ कारणं । [किमिव कारणम् ।]

राजा—यदि वक्तव्यं कथ्यताम् ।

King. Revered lady, that is the lot of mortals. You must not lament for your noble brother who showed he had not eaten his master's salt in vain. Well, what next?

Parivrājikā. Then I fainted, and by the time I had recovered myself this lady was nowhere to be seen.

King. The revered lady has indeed passed through a severe calamity.

Parivrājikā. Then I burned the body of my brother, and with the sorrow of my widowhood renewed I came to your country and assumed these two red garments.

King. Quite proper; this is the way of life that pious men adopt. What happened next?

Parivrājikā. This lady came from the power of the foresters into that of Vīrasena, who sent her on to the queen; and so was again seen by me when I obtained admission into the queen's palace. This is the end of my story.

Mālavikā. *(To herself)* I wonder what the King will say now.

King. Alas! How indignities are heaped on those that suffer calamities. For

this lady having a right to the title of queen
has been treated by us as a slave, as a silken
garment is used for the purposes of a bathing-
cloth. (12)

Dhārinī. Revered lady, you did wrong in not telling me that Mālavikā was of noble birth.

Parivrājikā. Heaven forbid! I had indeed a very good reason for adopting secrecy.

Dhārinī. What is the reason like?

King. If it is proper to tell, then do tell us.

परिव्राजिका—श्रूयताम् । इयं पितरि जीवति केनापि देवयात्रागतेन सिद्धादेशेन साधुना मत्समक्षमादिष्टा । 'संवत्सरमात्रं प्रेष्यभावमनुभूय ततः सदृशभर्तृगामिनी भविष्यति' इति । तमेनमवश्यंभाविनमादेशमस्यास्त्वत्पादशुश्रूषया परिणमन्तमवेक्ष्य कालप्रतीक्षया मया साधु कृतमिति पश्यामि ।

राजा—युक्तोपेक्षा ।

कञ्चुकी (प्रविश्य)—देव कथान्तरेणान्तरितमिदममात्यो विज्ञापयति । 'विदर्भगतमनुष्ठेयमवधारितमस्माभिः । देवस्य तावदभिप्रायं श्रोतुमिच्छामि' इति ।

राजा—मौद्गल्य तत्रभवतोर्भ्रात्रोर्यज्ञसेनमाधवसेनयोर्द्वैराज्यमवस्थापयितुकामोऽस्मि ।

तौ पृथग्वरदाकूले शिष्टामुत्तरदक्षिणे ।
नक्तंदिवं विभज्योभौ शीतोष्णकिरणाविव ॥ १३ ॥

कञ्चुकी—देव एवममात्यपरिषदे विज्ञापयामि ।

(राजा अङ्गुल्यानुमन्यते । निष्क्रान्तः कञ्चुकी ।)

प्रथमा (जनान्तिकम्)—भट्टिदारिए दिट्ठिआ भट्टिदारओ अद्धरज्जे पदिट्ठं गमिस्सदि । [भर्तृदारिके दिष्ट्या भर्तृदारकोऽर्धराज्ये प्रतिष्ठां गमिष्यति ।]

मालविका—एत्तिअं दाव बहुमन्तव्वं जं जीवितसंसआदो मुत्तो । [एतावत्तावद्बहु मन्तव्यं यज्जीवितसंशयान्मुक्तः ।]

कञ्चुकी (प्रविश्य)—विजयतां देवः । अमात्यो विज्ञापयति । अहो कल्याणी देवस्य बुद्धिः । मन्त्रिपरिषदोऽप्येवमेव दर्शनम् । कुतः

द्विधा विभक्तां श्रियमुद्वहन्तौ
धुरं रथाश्वाविव सङ्ग्रहीतुः ।
तौ स्थास्यतस्ते नृपती निदेशे
परस्परावग्रहनिर्विकारौ ॥ १४ ॥

Parivrājikā. Listen. This lady, while her father was still living, was told in my presence by an infallible and saintly seer, at a fair held in honour of a deity, that she would have to endure the position of a slave for just a year, and would then get a husband of equal rank. Seeing that the inevitable prophecy was being fulfilled by her continuing to serve your feet, I waited for the appointed time and I think I acted rightly.

King. It was quite proper to wait patiently.

(Entering) A chamberlain. King, the minister sends the following message which I could not deliver before, as another matter had cropped up in the meanwhile: we have considered what ought to be done with reference to Vidarbha. But I would like to know the view of the king.

King. Maudgalya, I wish to appoint the two brothers Yajnasena and Mādhavasena as joint rulers:

> let them rule separately the north and south banks of the Varadā like the Sun and the Moon that divide between them and rule the night and day. (13)

Chamberlain. King, I will communicate this your view to the council of ministers.

(The King shows his assent by a movement of his finger. Exit Chamberlain.)

First maiden. *(aside)* fortunately the prince will be established in half of the Kingdom.

Mālavikā. Even this I ought to consider as a great thing that he has been rescued from peril of his life.

(*Entering*) The chamberlain. Victory to the King! The minister says 'How auspicious the King's view! The council of ministers too hold the same view ; for

> bearing up their fortune divided between them, like the horses of a chariot the yoke put upon them by the charioteer, these two kings will be ruled by you, not being distracted by mutual conflict. (14)

राजा—तेन हि मन्त्रिपरिषदं ब्रूहि । सेनापतये वीरसेनाय लिख्यतामेवं क्रियतामिति ।

कञ्चुकी—यदाज्ञापयति देवः । (इति निष्क्रम्य सप्राभृतकं लेखं गृहीत्वा पुनः प्रविश्य ।) अनुष्ठिता प्रभोराज्ञा । अयं पुनरिदानीं देवस्य सेनापतेः पुष्पमित्रस्य सकाशात्सप्राभृतको लेखः प्राप्तः । प्रत्यक्षीकरोत्विनं देवः ।

(राजा सहसोत्थाय प्राभृतकं सोपचारं परिगृह्य शिरसि कृत्वा परिजनायार्पयति । लेखं च नाट्येन उद्वेष्टयति ।)

धारिणी—अम्महे तदोमुहं एव्व मे हिअअं । सुणिस्सं दाव गुरुअणकुसलाणन्तरं पुत्तस्स वसुमित्तस्स उत्तन्तं । अदिभारे खु सेणावइणा णिउत्तो मे पुत्तओ [अम्महे ततोमुखमेव मे हृदयम् । श्रोष्यामि तावद् गुरुजनकुशलानन्तरं पुत्रस्य वसुमित्रस्य वृत्तान्तम् । अतिभारे खलु सेनापतिना नियुक्तो मे पुत्रकः ।]

राजा—(उपविश्य वाचयति ।) स्वस्ति । यज्ञशरणात्सेनापतिः पुष्पमित्रो वैदिशस्थं पुत्रमायुष्मन्तमग्निमित्रं स्नेहात्परिष्वज्यानुदर्शयति । विदितमस्तु । योऽसौ राजसूययज्ञदीक्षितेन मया राजपुत्रशतपरिवृतं गोप्तारं वसुमित्रमादिश्य संवत्सरोपावर्तनीयो निरर्गलस्तुरगो विसृष्टः स सिन्धोर्दक्षिणे रोधसि चरन्नश्वानीकेन यवनानां प्रार्थितः । तत उभयोः सेनयोर्महानासीत्सम्मर्दः ।

(धारिणी विषादं रूपयति ।)

राजा—कथमीदृशं संवृत्तम् । (शेषं पुनर्वाचयति ।)

ततः परान्पराजित्य वसुमित्रेण धन्विना ।
प्रसह्य ह्रियमाणो मे वाजिराजो निवर्तितः ॥ १५ ॥

King. Tell the council then that written orders to the effect should be sent to Vīrasena, the commander-in-chief.

Chamberlain. As the king commands. *(Goes out and re-enters with a letter accompanied by a present)* The king's order is carried out. But this letter along with a present has arrived from the commander-in-chief, king Puṣpamitra ; let the king look at it.

(The king rises quickly, puts the present respectfully upon his head and then hands it to the attendants ; he then makes as if he opens the letter.)

Dhāriṇī. Ha, how my heart is eager to learn the contents of the letter ! I would learn, after the news of the health of my father-in-law, how my son Vasumitra has been doing. Surely the commander has put a very heavy duty on my son.

King. *(Sits down and reads)* May fortune attend thee! From the sacrificial enclosure, the commander-in-chief Puṣpamitra sends this mesage to his long-lived son Agnimitra who is in the Vidiśā country, affectionately embracing him : be it known to thee : I, having been consecrated for the Rājasūya sacrifice, let loose a horse, free from all restraint, which was to be brought back at the end of a year, and appointed Vasumitra as its defender, girt round by a hundred princes ; the same horse while wandering on the right bank of the Indus, was claimed by a cavalry squadron of the Yavanas. Thereafter ensued a fierce struggle between the two armies.

(Dhāriṇī wears an expression of despondency.)

King. How could it be so ? *(Reads the rest of the letter.)*

> And then Vasumitra, the mighty bowman, having repulsed his foemen, brought back my excellent horse which was being forcibly carried off by them. (15)

धारिणी——इमिणा दाणिं अस्ससइ मे हिअअं। [अनेनेदानी-माश्वसिति मे हृदयम्।]

३**राजा** (लेखशेषं वाचयति।) सोऽहमिदानीमंशुमतेव सगरः पौत्रेण प्रत्याहृताश्वो यक्ष्ये। तदिदानीमकालहीनं विगतरोषचेतसा भवता वधूजनेन सह यज्ञसेवनायागन्तव्यमिति।

६**राजा**——अनुगृहीतोऽस्मि।

परिव्राजिका——दिष्ट्या पुत्रविजयेन दम्पती वर्धेते। (देवीं विलोक्य।)

भर्त्रासि वीरपत्नीनां श्लाघ्यायां स्थापिता धुरि।
वीरसूरिति शब्दोऽयं तनयात्त्वामुपस्थितः॥ १६॥

विदूषकः——होदि परितुट्ठोम्हि पिदरं अणुगदो वच्छोत्ति। [भवति परितुष्टोऽस्मि पितरमनुगतो वत्स इति।]

३**राजा**——मौद्गल्य कलभेन खलु यूथपतिरनुकृतः।

कञ्चुकी——

नैतावता वीरविजृम्भितेन
चित्तस्य नो विस्मयमादधाति।
यस्याप्रधृष्यः प्रभवस्त्वमुर्वे-
र्वन्हेरपां दग्धुरिवोरुजन्मा॥ १७॥

राजा——मौद्गल्य यज्ञसेनश्यालमुररीकृत्य मुच्यन्तां सर्वे बन्धनस्थाः।

कञ्चुकी——यदाज्ञापयति देवः। [इति निष्क्रान्तः]

३**धारिणी**——जअसेणे गच्छ इरावदीपमुहाणं अन्देउराणं पुत्तस्स विअअउत्तन्तं णिवेदेहि। [जयसेने गच्छ इरावतीप्रमुखानामन्तः-पुराणां पुत्रस्य विजयवृत्तान्तं निवेदय।]

६**प्रतीहारी**——तह। [तथा।] (इति प्रस्थिता।)

धारिणी——एहि दाव। [एहि तावत्।]

प्रतीहारी——(प्रतिनिवृत्य) इअम्हि [इयमस्मि।]

Dhāriṇī. Now, that relieves my heart.

King. (*Reads the rest of the letter.*) So that now I will offer a sacrifice, having had my horse brought back to me by my grandson, even as Anśumat brought back the horse to Sagara. So, now, dismissing anger from your mind, you must forthwith come with my daughter-in-law to witness the sacrifice.

King. I am indeed favoured.

Parivrājikā. I congratulate the couple on the victory of their son. (*Looking at the queen*)

By your husband you have been established
in the commendable position of the foremost of
the wives of heroes; but it is your son that gives
you the title of the mother of heroes. (16)

Vidūsaka. Your highness, I am well pleased that the son takes after his father.

King. Maudgalya, indeed, the young elephant has imitated the leader of the herd.

Chamberlain.

Not even by such great display of valour does
he produce astonishment in our minds, whose
irresistible and lofty source you are as (the sage)
Aurva is of the fire that consumes water. (17)

King. Maudgalyā, let all prisoners including the brother-in-law of Yajnasena, be set at liberty.

Chamberlain. As the king commands. *(Exit)*

Dhāriṇī. Jayasenā, go and give the news of my son's victory to Irāvatī and other ladies of the harem.

Door-keeper. As the queen orders. (*She sets off*)

Dhāriṇī. Come here a moment.

Door-keeper. (*Turning back*) Here I am

धारिणी––(जनान्तिकम्) जं मए असोअदोहलणिओए पडिण्णादं मालविआए एतं से अहिअणं अ णिवेदिअ मह वअणेण इरावदिं अणुणेहि। तुए हं सच्चादो ण परिब्भंसइदव्वात्ति । [यन्मयाशोकदोहदनियोगे प्रतिज्ञातं मालविकायै तदस्या अभिजनं च निवेद्य मम वचनेनेरावतीमनुनय––त्वयाहं सत्यान्न परिभ्रंशयितव्येति ।]

प्रतीहारी––जं भट्टिणी आणवेदि । (इति निष्क्रम्य पुनः प्रविश्य।) भट्टिणि पुत्तविअएण अविभत्तपरितोसाणं अन्देउराणं आभरणाणं रअणमञ्जूसम्हि संवुत्ता । [यद्भट्टिन्याज्ञापयति । भट्टिनि पुत्रविजयेनाविभक्तपारितोषाणामन्तःपुराणामाभरणानां रत्नमञ्जूषास्मि संवृत्ता।]

धारिणी––किं एत्थ अच्छरिअं। णं साहारणो ताणं मह अ एसो अब्भुदओ । [किमत्राश्चर्यम् । ननु साधारणस्तासां मम चैषोऽभ्युदयः।]

प्रतीहारी (जनान्तिकम्)––भट्टिणि इरावदी विण्णवेदि । सारस खु देवीए पहवंतीए तुह वअणं पुढमसङ्कप्पिदं ण जुज्जइ अण्णहा कादुं [भट्टिनि इरावती विज्ञापयति । सदृशं खलु देव्याः प्रभवन्त्यास्तव वचनं प्रथमसङ्कल्पितं न युज्यतेऽन्यथाकर्तुमिति ।]

धारिणी––भअवई तुए अणुण्णादा इच्छामि अज्जसुमदिणा पुढमसंभाविदं अज्जउत्तस्स मालविअं पडिवादेदुं । [भगवति त्वयानुज्ञाता इच्छाम्यार्यसुमतिना प्रथमसंभावितामार्यपुत्रस्य मालविकां प्रतिपादयितुम् ।]

परिव्राजिका––इदानीमपि त्वमेवास्याः प्रभवसि ।

धारिणी––(मालविकां हस्ते गृहीत्वा ।) अज्जउत्तो इइं पिअणिवेदणाणुरूवं पारितोसिअं पाडिच्छदु । [आर्यपुत्र इदं प्रियनिवेदनानुरूपं पारितोषिकं प्रतीच्छतु ।]

(राजा सव्रीडं जोषमास्ते ।)

धारिणी––(सस्मितम्) किं ओहीरेदि मं अज्जउत्तो । [किमवधीरयति मामार्यपुत्रः ।]

Dhāriṇī. *(Aside)* Tell Irāvatī from me what promise I made to Mālavikā at the time I appointed her to perform the ceremony of fulfilling the longing of the Aśoka, and tell her also of her noble birth, and entreat her that she should not cause me to deviate from truth.

Door-keeper. As the queen commands. (*Going out and again returning*) Queen, look, I have indeed become a jewelled casket to hold the ornaments (presented to me) by the ladies of the harem who have been uniformly gratified at the triumph of your son.

Dhāriṇī. What is there to astonish us in this ? For this triumph is as much theirs as mine.

Door-keeper. (*Aside)* Queen, Irāvatī says ; quite befitting is the promise which,all powerful that you are, you have already made and it should not be changed.

Dhāriṇī. Revered lady, with your consent I desire to bestow Mālavikā on my husband, for whom she was originally destined by the noble Sumati.

Parivrājikā. Now, too, you have full power over her.

Dhāriṇī. (*Taking hold of Mālavikā's hand.*) Let my husband accept this present as a fitting reward for the good news he has brought me.

(The king remains silent and abashed.)

Dhāriṇī. (*Smilingly*) Would my husband now repulse me ?

विदूषकः——होदि एसो लोअव्ववहारो सव्वो वि णववरो लज्जादुरो होदित्ति [भवति एष लोकव्यवहारः सर्वोऽपि नववरो लज्जातुरो भवतीति ।]

(राजा विदूषकमवेक्षते ।)

विदूषकः—अहवा देवीए किददेवीसद्दं मालविअं अत्तभवं पडिगहीदुं इच्छदि [अथवा देव्या कृतदेवीशब्दां मालविकामत्रभवान् प्रतिग्रहीतुमिच्छति ।]

धारिणी—एदाए राअदारिआए अहिअणेण एव्व दिण्णो देवीसद्दो । किं पुणरुत्तेण । [एतस्या राजदारिकाया अभिजनेनैव दत्तोऽस्यै देवीशब्दः । किं पुनरुक्तेन ।]

परिव्राजिका——मा मैवम् ।

अप्याकरसमुत्पन्ना मणिजातिरसंस्कृता ।
जातरूपेण कल्याणि न हि संयोगमर्हति ॥ १८ ॥

धारिणी——मरिसेदु भअवदी । अब्भुदअकहाए जं मए ण लक्खिदं । जअसेणे गच्छ । तुमं दाव कोसेअपत्तोण्णं से सिग्घं उवहर । [मर्षयतु भगवती । अभ्युदयकथया यन्मया न लक्षितम् । जयसेने गच्छ । त्वं तावत्कौशेयपत्रोर्णमस्यै शीघ्रमुपहर ।]

प्रतीहारी——जं भट्टिणी आणवेदि । (इति निष्क्रम्य पत्रोर्णं गृहीत्वा पुनः प्रविश्य ।) देवि एदं । [यद्भट्टिन्याज्ञापयति । देवि एतत् ।]

धारिणी——(मालविकामवगुण्ठ्य) दाणिं अज्जउत्तो पडिच्छदु । [इदानीमार्यपुत्रः प्रतीच्छतु ।]

राजा—देवि त्वच्छासनादप्रत्युत्तरा वयम् ।

परिव्राजिका——हन्त प्रतिगृहीता ।

विदूषकः—अहो देवीए अणुऊलदा । [अहो देव्या अनुकूलता ।]

(धारिणी परिजनमवलोकयति ।)

परिजनः (मालविकामुपेत्य)—जेदु भट्टिणी । [जयतु भट्टिनी ।]

Vidūsaka. Lady, it is commonly observed that every new bridegroom is overcome with bashfulness.

(*The king looks at the Vidūṣaka.*)

Vidūṣaka. Or perhaps his highness would accept her after the queen will have honoured her with the title of Queen.

Dhāriṇī. Her very royal birth itself entitles her to that honour. Where is the use of repetition ?

Parivrājikā. Nay, not so.

Even though sprung from a mine, yet a jewel,
O noble lady, is not worthy of union with gold
until it is polished. (18)

Dhāriṇī. Pardon me, revered lady, that I should have forgotten, owing to the news of the victory ; go, Jayasenā, and bring her quick a silken veil.

Door-keeper. As the queen commands. (*She goes out and returns with a silken veil.*) Here it is, queen.

Dhāriṇī. (*Investing Mālavikā with the veil.*) Let my husband now receive her.

King. Queen, your order leaves me no reply to make.

Parivrājikā. O joy ! She is accepted.

Vidūsaka. Dear me, how very gracious is the queen.

(*Dhāriṇī looks at her attendants.*)

Attendants. (*Advancing towards Mālavikā.*) Victory to the queen !

(धारिणी परिव्राजिकां निर्वर्णयति ।)

परिव्राजिका——नैतच्चित्रं त्वयि । कुतः ।

प्रतिपक्षेणापि पतिं सेवन्ते भर्तृवत्सलाः साध्व्यः ।
अन्यसरितां शतानि हि समुद्रगाः प्रापयन्त्यब्धिम् ॥१९॥

निपुणिका (प्रविश्य)——जेदु भट्टा । इरावदी विण्णवेदि जहा हि उवआरादिक्कमेण किदावराहाए ण मए भट्टिणो अणुऊलं आअरिदं । सम्पदं पुण्णमणोरहेण भट्टिणा अहं वि पसादमेत्तेण वि सम्भावइदव्वति । [जयतु भर्ता । इरावती विज्ञापयति । यथा हि उपचारातिक्रमेण कृतापराधया न मया भर्तुरनुकूलमाचरितम् । साम्प्रतं पूर्णमनोरथेन भर्त्रा अहमपि प्रसादमात्रेण संभावयितव्या इति]

धारिणी——णिउणिए अवस्सं ताए सन्देसं सेविदुं अज्जउत्तो जाणिस्सदि । [निपुणिके अवश्यं तस्याः सन्देशं सेवितुमार्यपुत्रो ज्ञास्यति ।]

निपुणिका——जं देवी आणवेदि । [यद्देव्याज्ञापयति ।] (इति निष्क्रान्ता ।)

परिव्राजिका——देव अहममुना भवत्संबन्धेन चरितार्थं माधवसेनं सभाजयितुमिच्छामि यदि मे तव प्रसादः ।

धारिणी——भअवदि ण जुत्तं अम्हे परिच्चत्तुं । [भगवति न युक्तमस्मान् परित्यक्तुम् ।]

राजा——भगवति मदीयेषु लेखेषु तत्रभवते त्वामुद्दिश्य सभाजनाक्षराणि पातयिष्यामि ।

परिव्राजिका——युवयोः स्नेहेन परवानयं जनः ।

धारिणी——आणवेदु अज्जउत्तो किं भूओ वि पिअं अणुचिट्ठामि । [आज्ञापयत्वार्यपुत्रः किं भूयोऽपि प्रियमनुतिष्ठामि ।]

राजा——किमतः परमपि प्रियमस्ति । तथापीदमस्तु ।

(Dhāriṇī looks towards the Parivrājikā.)

Parivrājikā. That is not sur· rising in you; for good women, who. are devoted to their husbands, serve them even by making rivals to themselves, as rivers take hundreds of streams along with them to the sea. (19)

(Entering)

Nipunikā. Victory to the King ! Irāvatī makes the following request: I ha·e offended my lord by failing to show him courtesy and acted contrary to his wishes. But now that my lord has obtained his wish, he should honour me only by showing me his favour.

Dhāriṇī. Nipuṇikā, my husband will surely see his way to grant her request.

Nipuṇikā. As the queen commands. (*Exit.*)

Parivrājikā. King, I now desire to pay my respects to Mādhavasena, who has obtained his object by becoming your relation, if you favour me.

Dhāriṇī. Revered lady, it is not proper for you to leave us.

King. Revered lady, I will send in my letters to him your complimentary messages.

Parivrājikā. Your kindness makes me your dependent.

Dhāriṇī. Let my husband command what further service I can render him.

King. What could be dearer than this? But let this also be mine—

(भरतवाक्यम् ।)

त्वं मे प्रसादसुमुखी भव चण्डि नित्य-
मेतावदेव मृगये प्रतिपक्षहेतोः ।
आशास्यमीतिविगमप्रभृति प्रजानां
सम्पत्स्यते न खलु गोप्तरि नाग्निमित्रे ॥ २० ॥

[इति निष्क्रान्ताः सर्वे ।]

॥ इति पञ्चमोऽङ्कः ॥

———

(Benediction)

Do thou, Oh angry one, ever look upon me with a propitious countenance; so much do I desire in the interest of thy rival. For as long as Agnimitra is the protector, there will not be a blessing such as the removal of any calamity, which my subjects will not secure. (20)

(Exeunt Omnes)

Here Ends the Fifth Act.

NOTES

ACT I.

From the Nāṭyaśastra we learn that before the commencement of a drama, an elaborate series of preliminaries (पूर्वरङ्ग) had to be performed, consisting chiefly of the प्रत्याहार which would announce the beginning of the performance, the अवतरण when the musicians enter and take their places, the आरम्भ when the chorus try their voices, and the आश्रवण when the musicians try their instruments, and so on up to Nāndī. All these preliminaries are performed by the सूत्रधार who then leaves the stage, and his place is immediately taken by another similar person called स्थापक who introduces the play to the audience. This elaborate practice was, however, given up later on, and we find that the सूत्रधार alone performed both the functions of the preliminaries and of the prologue. (Vide विश्वनाथ's साहित्यदर्पण.). Cf. पूर्वरङ्गं विधायादौ सूत्रधारे विनिर्गते। प्रविश्य तद्वदपरः काव्यमास्थापयेन्नटः। सूचयेद्वस्तु बीजं वा मुखं पात्रमथापि वा॥ दश. III २--३..

I. 1. In this benedictory verse, god Śiva is first praised in terms of apparent contradiction, and then is invoked to favour the audience with the inward vision of spiritual knowledge, which would remove all darkness of ignorance and make them see the Right Path clearly. He is, for instance, the Lord of this universe, established in absolute supremacy, and yet what he wears is just an elephant-hide! Lesser beings than Him, enjoying inferior glory of kingship are seen to be strutting about in fine robes and splendid costumes and thus offer a great contrast to this wearer of elephant-skin, the supreme Lord of this Universe. He stands foremost of all sages who have removed their minds from all sense-pleasures and therefore would avoid all contact with women and yet in Him we find woman forming the counter-part, the complement of his body! He is manifested in this world in eight forms with which He supports the Universe; for this however, He feels within Him not the slightest tinge of vanity! The only explanation for this contradiction is that He is not to be judged by the existing standards with which we judge men, since He is far too divine and spiritual to be weighed in human balance.

एकैश्वर्ये...बहुफले–Fixed or established in absolute (एक) supermacy, calculated to yield a great many rewards or blessings to the devotees (प्रणत). ऐश्वर्य or supremacy is endowed by the possession of eight-fold supernatural powers, known as Siddhis. They are :—अणिमा लघिमा प्राप्तिः प्राकाम्यं महिमा तथा । ईशित्वं च वशित्वं च तथा कामावसायिता ॥ (1) अणिमा, the power of assuming a minute form of the size of an atom, (2) लघिमा, the power of reducing the weight of the body to the minimum, (3) प्राप्तिः the power of getting everything, (4) प्राकाम्यं, irresistible strength of will, (5) महिमा, the power of magnifying the body, (6) ईशित्वं Lordship, Majesty, (7) वशित्वं, power of curbing the senses, and (8) कामावसायिता–power of satisfying one's desires. प्रणत...फले–प्रणतानां (भक्तानां) बहूनि फलानि यस्मात्-तास्मिन्°फले ऐश्वर्ये ।. कृत्तिवासाः–कृत्तिः (the skin, hide) वासः यस्य सः–Having the elephant-skin as his garment, god Śiva is frequently represented as being fond of wearing an elephant-skin. Cf. नृत्तारम्भे हर पशुपतेरार्द्रनागाजिनेच्छाम् । मे॰ I. 38. Also, वधूदुकूलं कलहंसलक्षणं गजाजिनं शोणितबिन्दुवर्षि च । and विभूषणोद्भासि पिनद्धभोगि वा गजाजिनालंबि दुकूलधारि वा ॥ कुमा॰ V, 67, 78. There is another reading एकश्वर्यस्थितोऽपि प्रणतबहुफलः, which too is not bad. It would mean, 'established in i. e. possessed of *one* sovereignty and yet conferring *many* blessings etc.' the contrast being in एकैश्वर्य and बहुफल.

कान्ता...देहः–कान्तया संमिश्रः देहः यस्य सः । He who has his beloved viz. Pārvatī blended within his body. God Śiva is often represented in his form of अर्धनारी-नटेश्वर, wherein his better half is not put off from his body, but forms a literally fitting complement of it ! य अविषयः...यतीनाम्. Thus he stands in ascetic excellence far ahead (पुरस्तात) of all these Yogins or sages who have completely detached their minds from all objects of the senses.

अविषयमनसाम्––न विद्यन्ते विषयाः शब्दादयो येषां तानि अविषयाणि मनांसि येषां—whose minds are dissociated from the sense-objects. The reading परस्तात् is also good. It means 'beyond, higher than.' अष्टाभि...नाभिमानः-The eight forms of god Śiva through which he manifests himself for supporting this universe are-earth, water, fire, air, ether, the sun, the moon and the sacrificer. They are referred to in the Nāndī of Śākuntalam, या सृष्टिः स्रष्टुराद्या etc. Also कुमा० VI. 26 विदितं वो यथा स्वार्था न मे काश्चित् प्रवृत्तयः । ननु मूर्तिभिरष्टाभिरित्थंभूतोऽस्मि सूचितः ॥ where Śiva himself speaks of his eight forms solely intended for the weal of the world. He has, therefore, the epithet of अष्टमूर्ति. Even with such a big task which he achieves, He has not the slightest feeling of pride (अभिमान), feeling which is too commonly met with among men who would accomplish comparatively trivial and insignificant purposes. सन्मार्गा...मीशः-May that Lord (ईश) remove your mental outlook of utter ignorance or illusion with the light of wisdom, and enable you to see the right path (सन्मार्ग) of liberation. तामसीं वृत्तिं = तमःसंबन्धिनीं वृत्तिम् । तमस् according to the सांख्य philosophy, is one of the three Guṇas viz. सत्त्व, रजस् and तमस्. सत्त्व is explained as virtue, purity, goodness; रजस् is explained as dust, mist, passion or movement; and तमस् means darkness or ignorance and is of endless variety, such as disgust, misery, sloth, drowsiness, intoxication, etc. A state of mind in which तमस् preponderates is therefore opposed to virtue, purity and knowledge, and hence it must be done away with, before true vision dawns in the mind.

I. 1. 1. नान्द्यन्ते. 'At the end of the Nāndī or benediction.' The verse, explained above, constitutes the

Nāndī, which is defined thus आशीर्नमस्क्रियारूपः श्लोकः काव्यार्थसूचकः i. e 'a verse or verses of the form of a salutation or a benediction and suggestive of the story of the drama.' It is called नांदी because by the praise which it contains it is a source of delight to the gods. Cf. नन्दन्ति देवता यस्यां तस्मान्नान्दीति कीर्तिता। Its another characteristic of suggesting the story of the drama has led commentators into ingenious attempts to find out fantastic allusions to the main elements or incidents of the drama. Our commentator काटयवेम also suggests that epithets like प्रणतबहुफल, एकैश्वर्य etc. refer to a king, while the expression कान्तासंमिश्रदेह may allude to the long cherished union with the object of his love, and the word मार्ग in सन्मार्गालोकनाय points to a particular kind of acting. Cf. अत्र प्रणतबहुफलैकैश्वर्यस्थित्या कान्तासंमिश्रणेन जगद्धरणेन ईश्वर इत्यनेन च लोकोत्तरः कश्चिद् राजाऽस्मिन् नाटके वर्ण्यत इति सूच्यते। सन्मार्गालोकनाय इत्यनेन अत्र कश्चिद् मार्गाभिनयः प्रतिपाद्यत इति सूच्यते। मार्गो नाम नाट्यविशेषः।

सूत्रधारः—The principal stage-manager who arranges the cast of characters, instructs them in their different rules, and is thus responsible for the successful performance of the drama "The threads of which he holds in his hands, as it were." According to मातृगुप्ताचार्य. he must have the following accomplishments:—

चतुरातोद्यनिष्णातोऽनेकभाषासमावृतः। नानाभाषणतत्त्वज्ञो नीतिशास्त्रार्थतत्त्ववित्॥ नानागतिप्रचारज्ञो रसभावविशारदः। नाट्यप्रयोगनिपुणो नानाशिल्पकलान्वितः॥ छन्दोविधानतत्त्वज्ञः सर्वशास्त्रविचक्षणः। तत्तद्गीतानुगलयकलातालावधारणः॥ अवधानप्रयोक्ता च योक्तॄणामुपदेशकः। एवंगुणगणोपेतः सूत्रधारोऽभिधीयते॥

I. 1. 2. मारिषः—A principal actor in the drama, the same as पारिपार्श्विक who serves as an assistant to the सूत्रधार, and therefore addresses him as भाव i. e. sir, your honour. Ordinarily it means " A learned or venerable man." नेपथ्याभिमुखम् Towards the curtain. The word नेपथ्य is used in a variety of meanings. It means (1) Dress or costume, particularly that of an actor, and is used in this sense in our drama Cf. विरलनेपथ्ययोः पात्रयोः प्रवेशोऽस्तु । Act I. (2) The tiring room where the actors dress themselves, (which is always behind the curtain) Cf. यदि नेपथ्यविधानमवसितमितस्तावदागम्यताम् । शा० I.

I. 1. 5. परिषद्–An assembly, the audience. कालिदास ...वस्तु (नाटकं) कालिदासेन ग्रथितं वस्तु यस्य तद्–whose story has been woven into the plot (of this drama) by Kālidāsa. The word वस्तु means the story or the subject-matter of the play. मालविकाग्निमित्रम्–मालविकाग्निमित्रौ अधिकृत्य कृतं नाटकम् । A drama composed with reference to मालविका (the heroine) and अग्निमित्र (the hero); compare the expression मालतीमाधवम्.

वसन्तोत्सवः–The festivities that hailed the advent of spring were formerly celebrated on the full-moon day of the month of Caitra. They were marked with great hilarity and boisterousness, men and women equally taking part in these celebrations. For these descriptions see रत्नावली Act I. On such occasions, dramatic performances were also exhibited in competitive tests, and merit was rewarded by means of prizes. These festivities now take place on the full-moon day of the month of Phālguna, and are identified with Holi celebrations. सङ्गीतकम्–Music; triple symphony, singing being accompanied by instrumental music and dancing. Cf नृत्तं गीतं तथा वाद्यं त्रयं संगीतकं स्मृतम् ।

I. 1. 8. प्रथित etc. The पारिपार्श्विक strikes a discordant note of difference, when he says that compared to the work of famous writers like भास, सौमिल्ल and कविपुत्र, the work of a modern playwright will not catch the people's imagination. People generally have a tendency to praise things of the past, while deprecating the present ones. A budding writer, therefore, of the present age, not yet known to the people by his writings, has few chances of securing the people's approval in face of the works of the well-known dramatists of the past. About सौमिल्ल and कविपुत्र we have very little information. Regarding भास, however, there has been lately a keen controversy as to whether he should be looked upon as the author of those thirteen plays published in Trivandrum Series by T. Ganapati Shastri.

I. 1. 9. वर्तमानकवि–A living poet; a poet belonging to the present age. क्रिया–work, composition, writing. Cf. शृणुत मनोभिरवहितैः क्रियामिमां कालिदासस्य । विक्र० I. 2. विवेकविश्रान्तम्–Thoughtless, unreasonable, literally–' from which reason has retired.' विवेकः विश्रान्तः यस्मिन् कर्मणि ।

I. 2. The Sūtradhāra repudiates the पारिपार्श्विक's suggestion that the audience may not favour the work of कालिदास, because he happens to be their contemporary. The people assembled here are all good critics and know how to judge of the merits of the play, after a thorough examination of its features, good or bad. They will thus, independently and with a clear, unbiased mind, examine this work, and in it they will not be swayed away by the convictions of others. In their eyes, therefore, just as age is no favourable feature of a work, similarly its modernity also is no demerit or a disqualification. Cf. तं सन्तः श्रोतुमर्हन्ति सदसद्व्यक्तिहेतवः । etc. रघु० I. 10. अवद्यम्-Fit to be condemned, censurable पर...बुद्धिः-परस्य प्रत्ययेन नेया बुद्धिर्यस्य-whose judgment is guided by the convictions of others.

I. 2. 1. आर्यमिश्राः-Respected or revered sir. मिश्र is an honorific suffix, always used in the plural. It is addressed to the सूत्रधार and not to the audience as suggested by some. पारिपार्श्विक here accepts the authoritative judgment of his superior, in a matter that had made him anxious regarding the success of the play they were going to enact.

I. 3. The सूत्रधार asks him to expedite and make a beginning for the drama, because he is very much eager to execute the order of the spectators, received by him already with a bowed head (शिरसा). And he compares his eagerness to that of the queen's maid-servant, who appears to be so keen on doing her service (सेवादक्ष) and is coming thither. Very cleverly has the poet linked up the prologue with the interlude of the main action, having introduced the character that comes on the scene immediately.

Here ends the प्रस्तावना or the Prologue called also आमुख. which generally consists of an introductory dialogue between the सूत्रधार and नटी or one of the actors. After giving an account of the author and his qualifications. it introduces the incidents of the drama. Cf. सूत्रधारो नटीं ब्रूते मार्षं वाथ विदूषकम् । स्वकार्यं प्रस्तुताक्षेपि चित्रोक्त्या यत्तदामुखम् । प्रस्तावना वा ॥. दश० III 8. Also नटी विदूषको वापि पारिपार्श्वक एव वा । सूत्रधारेण सहिताः संलापं यत्र कुर्वते ॥ चित्रैर्वाक्यैः स्वकार्योत्थैः प्रस्तुताक्षेपिभिर्मिथः । आमुखं तत्तु विज्ञेयं नाम्ना प्रस्तावनापि वा ॥ Of the प्रस्तावना, there are three varieties, according to दशरूपक (or five according to साहित्यदर्पण) of which प्रयोगातिशय or Particular Presentation is one in which a character is introduced by a remark of the stage-manager. एषोऽयमित्युपक्षेपात् सूत्रधारप्रयोगतः । पात्रप्रवेशो यत्रैष प्रयोगातिशयो मतः ॥ ३ ॥ Thus the प्रस्तावना of our drama also is of the प्रयोगातिशय type.

Next is a विष्कंभक or an interlude in which we have a conversation first between the two maids of queen Dhāriṇī and then between one of them and गणदास, the teacher of dancing. It tells us that a certain beautiful girl by name मालविका was sent as a present to the queen धारिणी by her brother वीरसेन; that she was given in the charge of the teacher गणदास for being trained in the art of dancing; that by chance she was observed in a picture by the king who was greatly impressed by her charms; and that hence the jealous queen is scrupulously guarding her from the king's observation. Incidentally it refers to a ring with the seal of a serpent engraved on it, which plays an important part in Act IV.

I. 3. 7. अचिर,..चालितं. The चालित dance in which instruction was given recently. The Prakrit पउत्त can also be translated in Sanskrit by the word प्रवृत्त,and then the expression अचिरप्रवृत्तोपदेश would mean 'lessons in which had commenced recently.' चालित, read also as छलित in some editions, is a variety of dancing in which the dancer, while acting the part of another, gives expression thereby to her own sentiments. Cf. तदेतच्चालितं नाम साक्षाद् यदभिनीयते। व्यपादिश्य परावृत्तं स्वाभिप्रायप्रकाशकम् ॥ अन्तरेण-About, with regard to ; it always governs the Accusative. कीदृशी मालविका-how मालविका fares ; how far मालविका has progressed. संगीतशाला. The concert-hall.

I. 3. 13. कुतस्ते...धीरता-' Why this seriousness or gravity ', धीरता means a serious mood of mind when the person is lost to all sense of what is passing around. Cf. भो वयस्य, धीरं गच्छ। मा तत्रभवती धारिणी विसंवादयिष्यति। and also धैर्यावलंबिनमपि त्वरयति मां मुरजवाद्यरागोऽयम्। I. 22. हृदय, मोत्ताम्य। आर्यपुत्रस्य वचनमवधार्य धीरं तावद् भव। शा० V.

I. 3. 18. शिल्पिन्-A goldsmith, an artisan. नागमुद्रासनाथं-Possessed of a serpent-seal. The word सनाथ originally meaning " with a lord or protector " retains only the sense of ' with '. त्वयोपगतया लतासनाथ इवायं केसरवृक्षकः प्रतिभाति। शा० I. स्निग्धं निध्यायन्ती-Observing closely or intently. तवोपालम्भे पतितास्मि. I fell under your reproof; I exposed myself to a taunt from you.

I. 3. 22. स्थाने-" It is but proper ". सज्जति दृष्टिः-The eyes get fixed or rivetted. उद्भिन्न...केसरेण. The ring with its up-shooting rays appearing like filaments. कुसुमितः- कुसुमं संजातमस्य - Full of blossoms ; flowered ; the derivative is obtained by the addition of the termination इतच् in the sense of तदस्य संजातम् । अग्रहस्तः–हस्तस्याग्रम् or अग्रश्चासौ हस्तश्च । The extremity or the hand ; the palm. The idea of the sentence is that the rays which have shot forth from the ring, and which appear like the filaments of a blossom, have made it appear that the palm of the hand has flowered as it were.

I. 3. 30. ईदृशेन...तापि–Even when she was kept away by such an engagement. If in the queen's attendance, it would have been easy for the king to see her. She was, however removed from the queen by her present employment as a student of dancing in the charge of गणदास, and yet the king sees her ! The reading किल instead of कथम् is certainly preferable. दृष्टा किलैषा भर्त्रा–' It is rumoured that she was observed by the king etc.' Then the reply with the particle of assent, आम् 'yes' fits in very well. I. 3. 31. पार्श्वगतः–By the side. स जनः 'That person,' refers to मालविका. I. 3. 36. चित्रशाला—A picture-hall. प्रत्यग्र...चित्ररेखा–The drawing of the picture shining with freshly-laid lours. The word रेखा means ' sketch or drawing .' Cf तथापि तस्या लावण्यं रेखया किञ्चिदन्वितम् । शा० VI. 14. I. 3. 41. उपचार–The customary obeisance or homage. Cf. गुरुपरितापानि न ते गात्राण्युपचारमर्हन्ति । शा० III. 18. आसन्नपरिचारिणी–standing close (to her).

I. 3. 45. अपूर्वा–Extraordinary, uncommon V. L. अपूर्वरूपा–' of uncommon charms' is certainly better. I.

3. 48. आकृतिविशेष-A distinguished form ; a form possessed of extraordinary loveliness. आदरः पदं करोति-Respect finds access, enters. I. 3. 51. अवधीरितवचनः—Whose words were ignored or connived at. शङ्कितः—Suspicious. निर्बन्धुम्-To importune, to ask again and again. Cf. निर्बन्धपृष्टः स जगाद सर्वं स्तुवन्ति पौराश्चरितं त्वदीयम् । रघु॰ XIV. 32. आवुत्तः-A sister's husband ; brother-in-law. आवुत्तो भगिनीपतिः । अमर॰ I.3.55. सदृशं बालभावस्य-Quite proper or suited to her child-like nature. वसुलक्ष्मी, a mere child, was not expected to know why her jealous sister, Queen धारिणी, was refusing to reply to the King's question. I. 3. 58. सविशेषम्-With special effort. दर्शन...रक्ष्यते-she is being safely kept away from the king's sight who has already taken a fancy for her, merely by observing her picture. The Queen is, therefore, guarding her from his sight to avoid further complications. I. 3. 60. नियोग-Errand. task. I. 3. 68. कामम्-Granted, admitting. सर्वस्य...बहुमता-Every one thinks highly of the lore (कुलविद्या) which he has inherited. The profession of the family is always highly valued, and one would always have nothing but praise for it in preference to all others. In ancient days in India, trades and professions were handed down amongst families from one generation to another, and no body, therefore, even thought of giving up his legacy for which he had all respect and feelings of sanctity.

I. 3. 69. न पुन...गौरवम्. Gaṇadāsa says that he, too, has a high regard for the art of dancing and dramaturgy, not merely because it happens to be his hereditary lore, but because of its intrinsic value and utility. His respect and admiration for this science is not false and undeserving, but is fully justified by the high merits of the science.

I. 4. The verse describes the merits of Nāṭya, its divine association and its great utility as the highest form of recreation for diverse people. देवानां...चाक्षुषम् Construe–मुनय इदं (नाट्यं) देवानां कान्तं चाक्षुषं क्रतुमामनन्ति । Wise men look upon the Nāṭya as a sacrifice which is pleasing to the eyes of the gods. Every human activity should have, besides its secular purpose, a religious purpose also. All sciences and lores have been associated with the final spiritual goal of man, knowledge thereof being conducive to it. Similarly, this science of dancing and histrionics has also a religious element in it. It is a form of worship of the Gods, a veritable sacrifice, more charming and delightful to their eyes than a real sacrifice where the sight of poor innocent animals being butchered is certainly disgusting. चाक्षुषं–चक्षुरनुभाव्यम्–Visual, optical, to be experienced by the eye. कान्त–Delightful, pleasing. Mr. Pandit observes that "the epithets कान्त and चाक्षुष 'lovely and agreeable for the eye to see' doubtless are intended to imply that the क्रतु proper was neither कान्त nor चाक्षुष, and refer us to a time when animal sacrifice had come to be regarded with disfavour, as being horrid and disagreeable to the eye; a time, that is to say, when Buddhistic ideas of the Vedic sacrifice predominated." The idea of looking upon नाट्य

as a form of sacrifice has its origin in the belief that this science has been evolved out of the essential portions of the four Vedas, which teach sacrifice. Cf. अत्र नाटयस्य क्रतुत्वनिरूपणं चतुर्वेदसारनाटयवेदविहितकर्मत्वादिति मन्तव्यम्। तस्य चतुर्वेदसारत्वं भारतीये प्रतिपादितम् । सर्वशास्त्रार्थसंपन्नं सर्वशिल्पप्रदर्शनम् । नाटय-संज्ञामिमं वेदं सेतिहासं करोम्यहम् ॥ एवं संकल्प्य भगवान् सर्वान् वेदाननुस्मरन् । नाटयवेदं ततश्चक्रे चतुर्वेदाङ्गसंभवम् ॥ जग्राह पाठ्यमृग्वेदात् साम्नः संगीतमेव च । यजुर्वेदादभिनयं रसानाथर्वणादपि ॥ वेदोपवेदसंबद्धो नाटयवेदो महात्मना । एवं भगवता सृष्टो ब्रह्मणा ललितात्मना ॥ रुद्रेणेद...द्विधा. This line speaks of the sacred association of नाटय with god Śiva, the primordial dancer. The dual manifestation of the God, with the male part combined with the female one (already referred to in I. 1) represents the two-fold aspect of dancing viz. लास्य 'the graceful dancing' and ताण्डव 'the rough and violent form of dancing' of which God Śiva is very much fond. He has thus divided नाटय into two parts in his own person which is blended with that of Umā or Pārvatī. उमा...व्यतिकरे (स्वाङ्गे) उमया कृतः व्यतिकरः संबन्धः यस्य तास्मिन्–His own body which is united with that of Pārvatī. The word व्यतिकर means 'Union'. Cf. उद्दण्डताण्डवमुदञ्चितलास्यलीलां । कर्तुं स्वयं युगपदेव समुत्सुकात्मा । यः कामिनीकलितकम्रतरार्धकायः । सोऽयं विभाति विभुरादिनटः पुराणः ॥ from संगीतविद्याविनोद. त्रैगुण्यो...दृश्यते–People behave, actuated by various motives and sentiments, good or bad, sinful or otherwise. All these tendencies of the mind are a result of the three-fold division of the Sattva, Rajas and Tamas, elements or portions of which enter into the mental and physical constitution of man and shape his thought, action and speech. Life is thus varied, on account of these various feelings and passions prompting man to act. नानारसम्–characterised by various sentiments. रसs are nine, including शान्त. शृङ्गारहास्यकरुणरौद्रवीरभयानकाः। बीभत्साद्भुतसंज्ञौ चेत्यष्टौ नाट्ये रसाः स्मृताः। निर्वेदः स्थायिभावोऽस्ति शान्तोऽपि नवमो रसः॥

नाट्यं...समाराधनम्. Yet even in this diversity of life and difference of tastes which people betray, the Nāṭya or the dramatic representation is found invariably to be the one form of recreation in which all people take delight and find pleasure. Drama is a picture of life and therefore all people of diverse tastes find this as a highly delightful entertainment which appeals to their heart. भिन्नरुचि–भिन्ना रुचिर्यस्य–Possessed of different tastes. Cf. नासौ न काम्यो न च वेद सम्यग् द्रष्टुं न सा भिन्नरुचिर्हि लोकः। रघु० VI. 30.

I. 4. 5. नातिक्लेशयति. Does not trouble you much. A dull pupil is always a source of great worry and trouble to the teacher who is required to explain a lot before the lesson he teaches penetrates his brain.

I. 4. 6. परमनिपुणा. Highly efficient or skilful. The skill is manifested in the practical aspect of dancing, the theory of which is first taught and then the pupil is required to exhibit the theoretical lessons in actual dancing, where graceful and perfect movement would count for efficiency. मेधाविनी. Intelligent; quick to understand; clever. किं बहुना. Why say more? In short.

I. 5. भाविकं. A graceful movement or gesture, calculated to express a certain feeling or sentiment (भाव)

He means to say "In acting (प्रयोगविषये) whatever movement, which brings out the sentiment within, I teach to her, she does it to perfection ; nay, she improves upon it ; and thus it appears that she teaches me in return as to how best it should be done. My lessons fall far short of the actual exhibition on her part, and I feel that I learn much from her in that art." विशेषकरणात–By improving upon (the lesson taught to her). I. 5. 3 अतिक्रामन्ती–Surpassing, excelling. इरावती is one of the wives of king अग्निमित्र. She was also taking lessons in dancing from the teacher. कृतार्था–Successful; one who has accomplished her object. Teacher's satisfaction is an index of the high success of the pupil. I. 5. 6 तद्विधा...त्वान्–Since persons of this sort (तद्विध) are difficult to meet with or hard to secure. तद्विधानाम्–सा विधा प्रकारः यासां–ताः तद्विधाः तासाम् । पात्रम्–A worthy person, a gem. cf. पात्रविशेषन्यस्तं गुणान्तरं व्रजति शिल्पमाधातुः । I. 6. I. 5. 11. वर्णावरः–वर्णेन अवरः–Inferior in caste ; born of a mother inferior in caste viz. वैश्य or शूद्र. अन्तपालदुर्ग–A fortress guarding the frontier of the kingdom. V. L. अन्तपालदुर्गस्थापितः–Appointed ; kept in command. Some Mss. read मंदाकिनीतीरे in the place of नर्मदाकूले. We cannot accept that reading, however, as मंदाकिनी i. e. the river Ganges was far away from the विदर्भ country which lay close to अग्निमित्र's territory. I. 5. 12 शिल्पाधिकारे योग्या–Fit to receive instruction in fine arts. शिल्प means a fine art or accomplishment. They are 64 in number and include the arts of music, dancing and acting. उपायनं प्रेषिता–was sent as a gift or present.

I. 5. 14. आकृति...प्रत्ययात्. Being convinced of the fact that she has an excellent form, I imagine that she has elements in her which are not at all inferior–(अनून) i. e She comes of a high stock or family, the blood of nobility is in her. वस्तु literally means 'element, or stuff.' This is a common idea with Sanskrit poets. Cf. न तादृशा आकृतिविशेषा गुणविरोधिनो भवन्ति । शा॰ IV. यदुच्यते पार्वति पापवृत्तये न रूपमित्यव्यभिचारि तद्वचः । कुमा॰ V. 36. यत्राकृतिस्तत्र गुणा वसन्ति । a सुभाषित. भिद्येत वा सद्वृत्तमीदृशस्य निर्माणस्य । उत्तर॰ IV. न ह्याकृतिः सुसदृशं विजहाति रूपम् । मृच्छ॰ IX. The reading आकृतिविनयप्रत्ययात् 'Judged by her fair exterior and modesty' is also good. I. 6. Construe आधातुः शिल्पं पात्रविशेषे न्यस्तं समुद्रशुक्तौ पयोदस्य जलं मुक्ताफलतामिव गुणान्तरं व्रजति । The teacher's (आधातुः) skill imparted to a worthier pupil attains greater excellence (गुणान्तरम्). A good pupil would always show to a greater advantage the teaching of his master, which would thus shine brighter than it did before. It is like the drop of water from a cloud falling in a sea-shell in the ocean and transforming itself into a lustrous pearl. It is a belief that the water-drops of a shower getting into sea–shells during the स्वाति नक्षत्र turn into pearls. Cf. स्वात्यां सागरशुक्तिमध्यपतितं सन्मौक्तिकं जायते । नीति॰. I. 6. 3. पञ्चाङ्गाभिनय The five-fold acting. The commentator अभिराम notes the five varieties of acting which are:–नृत्त, केवार, धर्मर, वागड and गीत. Some take it to mean 'the five-limb movement' or acting in which the five parts of the body viz, the mind, eye, eye-brow, hands and feet, are employed. दीर्घिका...गवाक्षगता–sitting at the window, commanding the view of the tank.

दीर्घिका–An artificial tank or lake. गवाक्ष–A round air-hole or window, looking like a bull's eye. (गोरक्षीव). प्रवातमासेवमाना–Enjoying the fresh air or the breeze. लब्धक्षणः–लब्धः क्षणः येन सः–Having got leisure. क्षण means ' leisure'. The Marathi word सण meaning ' a holiday ' comes from this word.

विष्कम्भकः–It is an explanatory scene, so called from its concisely expressing (√ वि + स्कम्भ्) into a short space those subordinate parts of the plot, not enacted before the audience, but a knowledge of which is quite essential to the comprehending of the action in the remainder of the play. Cf. वृत्तवर्तिष्यमाणानां कथांशानां निदर्शकः। संक्षिप्तार्थस्तु विष्कम्भो मध्यपात्रप्रयोजितः ॥ दश॰ I. 116. It is thus a monologue performed by one person, or a dialogue performed by two or more, of the same or different classes, according as it is शुद्ध or संकीर्ण. Cf. एकानेकंकृतः शुद्धः संकीर्णो नीचमध्यमैः ॥ or मध्येन मध्यमाभ्यां वा पात्राभ्यां संप्रयोजितः। शुद्धः स्यात् स तु संकीर्णो नीचमध्यमकल्पितः ॥ Thus we see that only the middling characters can enact a विष्कम्भक, and again it may be soliloquy by one character, as in प्रियदार्शिका, or a dialogue by two or three, as in विक्रमोर्वशीय or in our drama. It may occur at the beginning of any of the acts, even the first, just after the प्रस्तावना. Cf. आदौ विष्कम्भकं कुर्यादङ्कं वा कार्ययुक्तितः। अपेक्षितं परित्यज्य नीरसं वस्तुविस्तरम्। यदा संदर्शयेच्छेषं कुर्याद्विष्कम्भकं तदा ॥ दश॰ III. 28–29.

The main scene of the Act opens now, with the king discussing with his minister वाहतक the political situation created by the letter of his neighbour, the king of the country of विदर्भ. Relations between अग्निमित्र and this king had latterly become very strained. अग्निमित्र had already put in prison the brother-in-law of this king. Prince माधवसेन, the cousin of the king of विदर्भ had promised a matrimonial alliance with अग्निमित्र, by offering his own sister to him in marriage, and it was for this purpose that he was going over to अग्निमित्र with his wife and sister. He was however seized on the way by the frontier-guard, and in the scuffle that ensued, the sister of माधवसेन, the proposed bride of अग्निमित्र, was lost. अग्निमित्र, therefore, demanded the release of his friend and ally माधवसेन, along with his wife and sister. To this demand of his, the king of विदर्भ has sent the present reply, in which he first asks him not to interfere with his private affairs since माधवसेन was his uncle's son. If, however, taking his side अग्निमित्र would demand his release, then he would meet his wishes on one condition viz. that अग्निमित्र on his part must set free his brother-in-law, the minister of मौर्य, who has been kept in prison by him. This has greatly upset अग्निमित्र, who, as we see, dispatches his forces under the command of the general वीरसेन against the विदर्भ king, and we hear of the result of this campaign in the last act of the drama.

I. 6. 11. एकान्त...परिजनः-With his attendants standing in a corner or at a distance. I. 6. 12. प्रतिपद्यते-Proposes to do ; says in reply. अग्निमित्र had demanded in his former letter the release of माधवसेन. The letter which the minister वाहतक had in his hand was a reply to his letter. He, therefore, wants to know what the विदर्भ king intends to do, in order to meet his demand. वैदर्भः-Lit. belonging to विदर्भ; the king of the विदर्भ country, the same as modern Berar. I. 6. 14. आत्मविनाशम्-His own ruin. He means to say that his reply is so offensive that it would provoke अग्निमित्र to declare war against him and in that case nothing short of destruction would be his lot. निर्देश-The specific reply; the dispatch actually committed to writing. I. 6. 17. भवतः...मोचयितव्यः-This is a portion of अग्निमित्र's letter, reproduced for the purpose of giving a definite reply to the demand contained in it. पितृव्यपुत्रः Uncle's son, cousin. प्रातिश्रुतसंबन्धः-प्रतिश्रुतः संबन्धः येन सः-who has promised an alliance. अवस्कन्द्य गृहीतः—Having been attacked, he was captured or taken prisoner. मदपेक्षया-Out of regard for me i. e. अग्निमित्र; if you care for my friendly relations with you. सकलत्रसोदर्यः-कलत्रेण सोदर्यया च सहितः-Along with his wife and sister. सोदर्या-समानं उदरं यस्याः सा-Born from the same womb, sister.

I. 6. 19. न वो न विदितं-Not that it is not know to you; you know it full well. Two negatives give an affirmative sense. द्वौ नञौ प्रकृतार्थं गमयतः । तुल्याभिजनेषु...रीदृक्-Towards relatives of a common extraction, who are therefore likely to put forth their claim for the kingdom, this is the way how kings behave. The विदर्भ king is trying to justify his action of seizing and imprisoning his cousin माधवसेन, who by this relationship was likely to prove a menace to his own position and authority. If, therefore, he has captured him and put him in prison, there is nothing wrong about it. In fact, this is how kings are seen to behave towards their relations, who wanted to thereaten their kingship. The reading तुल्याभिजनेषु भूमेरिव: राज्ञां प्रवृत्तिः is accepted by Mr. Pandit who understands it to mean the 'conduct of kings towards kings who belong to the same family should be like that of the earth i. e. one of perfect impartiality." What is meant possibly is since both अग्निमित्र and the विदर्भ king enjoy an equal status as kings (तुल्याभिजन), अग्निमित्र should not try to heckle him and bring him to book for certain things which he i. e. the विदर्भ king has done in his own interest. Like the earth tolerant of everything, a king ought to be patient and impartial. He should stand aloof and should not try to meddle with the other king's affairs. I. 6. 20 अतोऽत्र... इति–' Therefore, you i. e. अग्निमित्र should remain neutral in this affair between me and माधवसेन.' It is a dispute between two brothers, and an outsider like अग्निमित्र should not interfere. The विदर्भ king censures mildly the conduct of अग्निमित्र in taking the side of माधवसेन as against him. मध्यस्थ:–Indifferent, neutral. मध्ये तिष्ठति सः । ग्रहणविप्लव. The confusion at the time of the capture. अथा...आभिसंधि:–' Now if you must secure the freedom of माधवसेन, then hear my condition.' माधवसेन would be released by me, only on one condition of mine i. e. of the विदर्भ king. Note the sense of the particle अथ ' If '. अभिसंधि:—condition ; terms.

I. 7. The verse sets forth the terms of the विदर्भ king. ' The release of माधवसेन is dependent upon the release of my brother-in-law, the minister of the मौर्य king.' मौर्यसचिव–According to some it is a proper name If that is not correct and he was the minister of the मौर्य king of पाटलिपुत्र, it seems probable that he was imprisoned by अग्निमित्र to prevent him from exciting the people to rebel against his (अग्निमित्र's) father पुष्यमित्र, who had murdered the last of the Maurvas, बृहद्रथ, and usurped his throne in his son's favour. The imprisonment of माधवसेन, the intended brother-in-law of अग्निमित्र, by his cousin the king of विदर्भ, was only a retaliation for his brother-in-law's imprisonment by अग्निमित्र.: संयत–Imprisoned. श्याल:—A brother-in-law; cf. the word साला. मोक्ता–First Future 1st per. sing. 'I shall release.' I. 7. 1. कार्यविनिमयः—Exchange of services. अनात्मज्ञः—आत्मानं न जानात्यसौ–One who knows not one's own self, i. e. a fool. प्रकृत्यमित्रः--A natural enemy. By the very disposition of his territory which is adjacent to me, he is my natural enemy. Cf. राजा आत्मद्रव्यप्रकृतिसंपन्नो नयस्याधिष्ठानं विजिगीषुः । तस्य समन्ततो मण्डलीभूता भूम्यन्तरा अरिप्रकृतिः। ......भूम्यनन्तरं प्रकृत्यमित्रः तुल्याभिजनस्सहजः । कौ० अ० VI. 2. A prince, according to Kauṭilya, is a विजिगीषु, and must always cherish the ambition of becoming a supreme monarch. The first king to subdue would be his neighbour, and that king, therefore, by the very situation of his kingdom is a source of trouble and hence an enemy to the विजिगीषु. प्रतिकूलचारी–Behaving in opposition to me. यातव्यपक्षे स्थित–Standing in the position of an enemy who deserves to be attacked (यातव्य). Ordinarily, though a neighbour, and therefore likely to be a danger to अग्नि-

मित्र, he need not have been attacked. But now, since relations of hostility have developed by reason of his having gone against him (प्रतिकूलचारी), he i. e. वैदर्भ king must be assailed and subjugated. पूर्वसंकल्पितं वीरसेनप्रमुखं दण्डचक्रम्. The forces or an army headed i. e. commanded by वीरसेन, already kept in readiness. उन्मूलनाय– For the purpose of uprooting or extirpating him. I. 7. 6. शास्त्रदृष्टमाह–The minister says what the king has proposed is strictly in conformity with what the science of politics teaches. Treatises like the कौटिलीय अर्थशास्त्र were in the curriculum of princes.

I. 8. The minister explains further what the political science would lay down on this point. It says definitely that an enemy newly installed on the throne does not enjoy the confidence of his subjects and is there unstable like a tree newly planted ; and hence he could be easily uprooted. अचि...राज्यः–अचिरं अधिष्ठितं राज्यं येन सः– who has newly acquired the kingdom. प्रकृति...त्वात्. By reason of his not being firmly established among the subjects (प्रकृति) ; with reference to the tree, it would mean ' Not having struck deep root in the soil (प्रकृति)'. नव...शिथिलः तरुः––A tree that is unstable or loose, having been freshly planted. समुद्धर्तुं सुकरः--Very easy to uproot.

I. 8. 1. तन्त्रकार–The writers on the science of politics. The sentence अवितथं...वचनम् should be taken in the imperative sense, or the sense of the future, supplying भविष्यति as the predicate, which the commentator काटयवेम

does. समुद्योज्यताम्-Let (the general) be made ready to act. I. 8. 4. यथाव्यापारम्-In accordance with the service which they were rendering to the king.

विदूषक-A jester, fun-making, merry fellow, who enjoys the intimacy of the king, because of his constant attendance on him to keep him lively with his jokes. Very often, we find, however, that besides this function, he greatly helps the king in his love-intrigues, by devising methods to bring about the union of the lovers, as is the case in our drama, or in रत्नावली and प्रियदर्शिका. He comes now to inform the king of his success in a plan to give the king an opportunity to see मालविका. I. 8. 6 यदृच्छा...कृतिः--यदृच्छया दृष्टा प्रतिकृतिर्यस्याः सा-whose portrait was seen accidentally (यदृच्छया). I. 8. 11 अपरः कार्यान्तरसचिवः--Another counsellor helping in a different branch of affairs viz. those of love, (while वाहतक was an advisor in politics). In the third Act he is called कामतन्त्रसाचिव. The title नर्मसाचिव also 'a minister of fun' is very often given to विदूषक. I. 8. 14 उपेय...दर्शने-उपेयस्य-साध्यस्य मालविकासाक्षाद्दर्शनस्य-उपायदर्शने-साधनज्ञाने In visualising a remedy to bring about the desired object viz. the sight of मालविका. प्रज्ञाचक्षुः—The eye of wisdom or imagination. कच्चित्-Note the use of the particle which means ' I hope'. I. 8. 15 प्रयोगसिद्धिं पृच्छ. What of merely thinking ? I have progressed much further.''Rather ask me about the success of the enterprise. " I. 8. 17 कर्णे-विदूषक was too shrewd to speak of his plans openly. The audience thus are left in the dark about it, though their curiosity in th matter is very soon satisfied.

I. 8. 18 निपुणमुपक्रान्तम्-you have commenced cleverly. दुर...रम्भे-In this venture where success is so difficult to attain. दुरधिगमा सिद्धिर्यस्मिन् स आरम्भः । आशंसामहे. We hope for (success). Cf. मनोरथाय नाशंसे किं बाहो स्पन्दसे वृथा । शा० VII.

I. 9. With all the resources at his disposal, a man, howsoever powerful, cannot dispense with the help of a friend in the attainment of an object that is beset with difficulties (सप्रतिबन्ध). He is like a lamp in darkness when one cannot see an object, though endowed with eyes, unless the light of the lamp helps him. The figure of speech is दृष्टान्त, complete in all details. अल... विकथ्य-The particle अलम् meaning 'enough' is always used with a gerund or a noun in the instrumental case. वि+कत्थ्-To brag, boast-अधरोत्तरव्यक्तिः-A decision as to who is inferior (अधर) and who is superior (उत्तर).

I. 9. 3 त्वत्सुनीति...भिन्नम्-The tree of your fine intrigue has put forth a blossom. The two teachers quarrelling clearly show that your plan has succeeded. फलमपि...द्रक्ष्यसि. This blossom is a precursor of the fruit which also you will soon see. The reward will be the sight of मालविका, which the king will soon get as a result of this quarrel.

I. 10. परस्पर...यतौ-Striving to gain victory over the other. There is another reading परस्परजयैषिणौ-Desiring to get victory etc. साक्षाद्...शरीरिणौ. The two dramatic sentiments, as it were, in bodily form (शरीरिणौ). They were teachers of acting in which the inner sentiment is fully brought out. The poet means that here they represent the two sentiments, as it were, in bodily form. I. 10, 4. दुरासदो राजमहिमा–The king's greatness or majesty fills one with awe which makes it difficult for one to approch him.

I. 11. हरदत्त explains his feelings at the sight of the king. He feels a flutter of excitement in his heart as he approaches the king even though he is familiar with him, and the king is always accessible to him. Every moment, the king changes as it were and appears new to his eyes, like the restless ocean which is never the same at any moment. नच...गम्यः–construe:—न परिचितः इति न, अगम्य इति न Not that I am not acquainted or familiar with him i.e. I am familiar with him, nor that he is unapproachable i. e. he is approachable. Instead of अगम्य, Some read अरम्य. चकितं–Tremblingly, with a flutter of fear in the heart. सलिल...मक्ष्णोः––The ocean changes its aspect every moment, without losing its freshness and grandeur ; the same is the case with this king who, too, maintains his dignified majesty and charm, even though he appears to be changing every moment. An object of beauty is thus defined by माघ–क्षणे क्षणे यन्नवतामुपैति तदेव रूपं रमणीयतायाः । Cf. तां तामवस्थां प्रतिपद्यमानं स्थितं दश व्याप्य दिशो महिम्ना। विष्णोरिवास्यानवधारणीयमीदृक्तया रूपमियत्तया वा ॥ रघु० XIII. 5. भीमकान्तैर्नृपगुणैः स बभूवोपजीविनाम् । अधृष्यश्चाभिगम्यश्च यादोरत्नैरिवार्णवः ॥ रघु० I. 16. महत् पुरुषाकारं ज्योतिः––This great lustre in human form. The king is all splendour that has assumed a human form. Cf. तेजसः सपदि राशिरुत्थितः प्रादुरास किल वाहिनीमुखे । यः प्रमृज्य नयनानि सैनिकैर्लक्षणीयपुरुषाकृतिश्चिरात् ॥ रघु० XI. 63.

I. 12. गणदास says that by the flood of majestic splendour he feels he has been pushed back as it were, even though he is trying to approach the king in the company of his attendant, after having been duly admitted into his presence by the door-keepers. °प्रवेशः-नियुक्तैः पुरुषैः अनुमतः प्रवेशः यस्य सः-whose entrance was permitted by men appointed at the door. सिंहा...चरः-सिंहासनस्य अन्तिके चरत्यसौ-An attendant moving about near the throne. विनि...दृष्टिपातैः-which repel the gaze; which dazzle the eyes. वाक्यादृते-even though no verbal order forbidding to enter was given out; without any words of prohibition. I. 12. 3. The king himself orders the seats for the two teachers. This only shows the high regard that he has for them. युगपत्-At one and the same time; simultaneous. I. 12. 6. तीर्थः-A sacred preceptor; a venerable teacher. दत्तप्रयोगश्चास्मि-And I have also given practical lessons in the art of dancing. परिगृहीतः-Favoured, patronised. I. 12. 9. सोऽहम्-I, possessed of such qualifications viz. a pupil of no ordinary teacher, having good experience of teaching the theory and the art, and in addition enjoying the patronage of Your Majesty. प्रधानपुरुष-Prominent courtiers, principal personalities. आधिक्षिप्तः-was insulted. मयि परिवादकरः-began abusing me. परिवाद means 'censure, abuse.' पल्वल-a puddle. विमृशतु-should examine. विशेषज्ञः प्राश्निकः-A discerning judge; a critical examiner who would understand the difference in merit of the two. I. 12. 14. समर्थं प्रतिज्ञातम्-very well suggested; a fair proposal that. I. 12. 15. प्रथमः कल्पः-A capital idea; an excellent (प्रथम) alternative. Cf. उदारः कल्पः । शा० V. I. 12. 16. पक्षपात–Partiality, favouritism. If the king alone would decide and if it happens that the decision is given in favour of हरदत्त, the king's man, the Queen favouring गणदास would naturally suspect it to be a case of partiality. न्याय्यो व्यवहारः–The conduct of the examination would be just and fair. न्याय्यः न्यायादनपेतः Not deviating from justice. I. 12. 20. प्रस्ताव–the present dispute; the matter under dispute. I. 12. 22. परिव्राजिका–A female ascetic. I. 12. 24. संरम्भ–struggle, contest. कथं प्रेक्षसे–what do you anticipate to be the result ? Who will win ? I. 12. 27. स्वप... कया– स्वपक्षस्यावसादः—तस्य शङ्का ।. Apprehension or fear about the defeat of your side or party. अवसाद literally means 'sinking, dropping down, losing.' न परिहीयते प्रतिद्वान्द्विनः–is not inferior to his opponent. Cf. ओजस्वितया न परिहीयते शच्याः । विक्रमो० III. I. 12. 30. ०राज...हरति–The fact that he is patronised by the king brings him into prominence or gives him a great advantage or superiority (प्रधानत्व). I. 12. 31. राज्ञी...भवती–just remember that you too are the recipient (भाजन) of the title of 'the Queen." If the king's patronage brings हरदत्त to the forefront, गणदास also will not be lagging behind, since he has been favoured by you, the Queen.

I. 13. If the fire receiving the lustre from the sun, exhibits the greatest refulgence at night, the moon too acquires greatness, being favoured by the night. हरदत्त favoured by the King is compared to अनल being nourished with his lustre by the sun while गणदास, patronised by the

Queen, resembles the moon as favoured by the night. If therefore the moon is eqally brilliant as the fire, there is no reason to fear गणदास will suffer in the contest. It is a belief that the sun reposes his lustre in the fire at the end of the day. Cf. दिनान्ते निहितं तेजः सवित्रेव हुताशनः । रघु० iv. 1. Commenting upon this, मल्लिनाथ observes, 'सौरं तेजः सायमग्निं संक्रमते'। 'आदित्यो वा अस्तं यन्नग्निमनुप्रविशति' 'अग्निं वा आदित्यः सायं प्रविशति' इत्यादि श्रुतिः प्रमाणम् ।. I. 13. 2. अविहा or better still अविधा is an interjection meaning 'help, help,' used in calling for help in danger. पीठमर्दिका– 'A lady who assists the heroine in securing her lover'. पीठमर्द refers to the man who assists the hero in his love-affairs. Cf. पीठमर्दो नाम कामपुरुषार्थसहायो नायकसमीपवर्ती पुरुषः । Com. of अभिराम. We shall see how greatly this परिव्राजिका like कामन्दकी in the मालतीमाधव was instrumental in brining about the union of the king and मालविका. An ascetic woman, she is greatly cultured and wise, speaking the Sanskrit language. दशरूप assigns a definite place to such woman as a companion or a help-mate of the heroine, styling her as लिङ्गिनी, and the qualifications she should have are:— शास्त्रेषु निष्ठा सहजश्च बोधः प्रागल्भ्यमभ्यस्तगुणा च वाणी । कालानुरोधः प्रतिभानवत्त्वमेते गुणाः कामदुघाः क्रियासु ॥

I. 14. The Queen wearing auspicious ornaments and accompanied by the ascetic कौशिकी appears like the triad or the collection of the three Vedas embodied, coupled with the spiritual lore. मङ्गलालंकृता–मङ्गलं शोभनं यथा तथा अलंकृता. "Decorated with such dress and ornaments as she must wear as the wife of a living husband; Cf.

सितांशुका मङ्गलमात्रभूषणा." विक्रमो॰ III.12 (S.P. Pandit). त्रयी–The three Vedas are ऋग्वेद, यजुर्वेद and सामवेद. अध्यात्मविद्या–The Upanişadic lore or teaching. The knowledge of आत्मन् or ब्रह्मन् i. e. the Supreme soul. विग्रहवती Possessed of a bodily form (विग्रह).

I. 15, The परिव्राजिका gives the king a blessing. May he be lord for hundred years, of the Queen धारिणी and of भूतधारिणी i. e. the earth, the supporter of the creation. Two epithets are used to describe both the Queen and the Earth. महासारप्रसव - 1 The Queen who has given birth to a heroic son; महासारः (lit. of great strength, powerful) प्रसवः संतानो यस्याः सा । . 2 The earth yielding abundant crops (प्रसव) owing to plenty of showers (आसार). सदृशक्षमा– Possessed of equal forgiveness or patience. As Pandit observes "The epithets are intended to flatter the Queen, and the blessing that the king may have none but Dhārinī and the Earth for his consorts is doubtless meant to remove from Dhārṇī's mind the remotest suspicion that she (the Parivrājikā) was or was going to be an abettor of the king's intrigue." It might as well be taken as a hint to the Queen to be broad-minded and forgive the momentary breaches of the marital bond on the part of the king ! For a similar idea Cf. परिग्रहबहुत्वेऽपि द्वे प्रतिष्ठे कुलस्य मे समुद्रवसना चोर्वी सखी च युवयोरियम् ॥. शा॰ III. 16. I. 15. 4. पर...संघर्षः–A conflict between the two teachers as to which of them has superior knowledge (विज्ञान). प्राश्निकपदम्–The position of a judge or an examiner. I. 15.

6. उपालम्भः-a taunt. पत्तने...परीक्षा-" The town being near, would you have a jewel tested in a village ? " She means that when the king, so well-versed in all arts, is available, it is foolish to ask her, an ignorant lady, to be the judge. The king represents the town, while she represents the village Cf. ता पिअवअस्सस्स देवीए पुरदो पढिस्सम् । जदो ण कत्थूरिआ कुग्गामे वणे वा विक्किणीअदि, ण सुवण्ण कसवट्टिअं विणा सिलापट्टए कसीअदि। कर्पूर॰ I. I. 15.9. मध्यस्था-Impartial, disinterested. गुणदोषौ परिच्छेत्तुम्-To measure or gauge our merit and demerit. I. 15. 12 विवादः--Dispute, discussion. The king proposes forthwith a theoretical discussion to test the knowledge of the teachers. He knew full well what the plan was, and yet he says this to avoid rousing any suspicion in the mind of the queen. I. 15. 13. प्रयोग...शास्त्रम . The dramatic science is preeminently a practical science. A theoretical discussion, therefore, will not do. वाग्व्यवहार-A verbal disputation ; a wrangling in words. I. 15. 17. यदि मां etc. This clearly shows that the queen has begun to smell the plot. I. 15. 18. न मां...मर्हति. " The queen should be pleased not to allow me to suffer defeat from one who is only my equal in learning. हरदत्त is in no way superior to me, and yet if I am not given a chance by the queen to prove my merit, हरदत्त who is at best my equal in learning (समानविद्य) would certainly assume airs of superiority and insult me. The queen should therefore allow me to enter into the contest." The reading 'न मां अभिनयाविद्यातः परिभवनीयं मन्तुमर्हसि' is given by Mr. Pandit who interprets it thus:-

'I pray you not to think that I may be beaten in the art of dancing.' I. 15. 19. उरभ्रसंपात-A fight of two rams. The विदूषक likens their contest to a ram-fight which must be staged by them, if they want to deserve the wages they get! I. 15. 21. कलहप्रियः—कलहः प्रियः यस्य सः One who likes quarrels, fond of squabbles. I. 15. 23. विदूषक protests against the queen's allegation saying in spite of his efforts to the contrary the two teachers will fight to a finish. The instance he gives is that of an elephant-fight which would never stop until one of the two is thoroughly vanquished. अन्योन्यकलहित. Quarrelling with each other. कलहित-कलहः संजातः अस्य सः कलहितः । उपशमः- Silence, peace. I. 15. 24. स्वाङ्ग...नय-The graceful acting exhibited in their own person. I.15.27. तदि...प्रत्याययितव्यम्- 'What more should they exhibit to convince us of their merit?' 'What further have these (teachers) to satisfy us about?' Notice again the attitude of the king who shows as if he is so solicitious to cut short the whole dispute now, without any further tests, what the परिव्राजिका has seen of their acting being taken as sufficient exhibition of their art. 'In reality, of course, the king only pretends to be indifferent and makes the परिव्राजिका say what is necessary to judge between the two disputants.' I. 15. 28. वक्तुकामा-वक्तुं कामो यस्याः सा. Desiring to speak out. I. 16. The परिव्राजिका explains why she cannot rest satisfied with the performance of the two teachers alone, but she must see how their pupils also acquit themselves before she decides in the matter. श्लिष्टा...संस्था The individual performance of some in the dramatic art is very well done. i. e. some excel as actors when they act personally, but are not able to teach others how to act well. श्लिष्टा. Done properly. Some read शिष्टा–' Excellent '. क्रिया–Acting, performance. आत्मसंस्था–आत्मनि संस्था यस्याः सा–Restricted to one's own self individual, personal. संक्रान्ति...युक्ता–while others distinguish themselves in transferring their art to their pupils. Some show superior skill in imparting (संक्रान्ति) that skill to another. यस्यो...एव. He certainly is the best teacher who combines in himself both the merits viz. personal acting and imparting it to his pupil. He deserves to be placed at the head (धुरि) of all teachers. धुरि lit. at the yoke. 'Just as the most powerful bull (पुंगव) is chosen from a herd of bulls to be put to the yoke i. e. chosen for the place of honour, so such a teacher should be put in front of or given the first place among all teachers.' I. 16. 3. पिण्डितार्थः–-The sum and substance, the essence. I. 16. 6. मन्दमेधा–Dull-witted. मलिनयति–Discredits or brings disgrace. I. 16. 9 देवि...यते. The king shows as if he agrees with the queen's objection. I.16.10. विनेतु...यंति. Gaṇadāsa, on the other hand, answers the queen's objection. No doubt, a bad pupil discredits the teacher for no fault of his. But can he not make a proper choice of his material? Acceptance of such a pupil of inferior stuff betrays a want or dullness of the teacher's intelligence. अद्रव्यं–A bad material, an inferior stuff i. e. a bad pupil. बुद्धिलाघवम् Inferiority of intelligence. The sentence is interpreted by some in another way. " The improvement (परिग्रह)

of a dull pupil shows the superior talent (लाघवं=कौशल्य) of the teacher (विनेतुः), " The word परिग्रह cannot, however, be taken in the sense of 'Improvement.' What गणदास means is that there is no harm in judging the merits of the teachers by the performance of their pupils. If the pupil selected happens to be inferior, that should reflect on the teacher, since he could have acted wisely in making a selection.

I. 16. 14 कथमिदानीम्-" what to do now?". The queen is chafing inwardly to find that all her attempts to frustrate the plot of विदूषक are being foiled by her own protege गणदास. उत्साहकारणं मनोरथं-The king's desire to see मालविका, if fulfilled, will only inflame his passion, or will encourage him for further endeavour. विरम... रम्भात्-Stop this vain effort. It is useless to proceed in the matter and arrange a demonstration in acting. To the teacher, it does no good, since his position is not going to be harmed in any way.

I. 16. 19. विदूषक tries to provoke him further, when he saw the Queen was dissuading him. संगीतापदेशेन-Under the pretext of music. सर......मोदकानि-The sweet balls offered as presents to the Goddess of Learning (by the inmates of the harem). सुलभनिग्रह. Where defeat is easy. निग्रह-Defeat, vanquishing; in Nyāya philosophy, it means 'a flaw in argument or a fault in syllogism by which a disputant is put down in argument.' विदूषक sarcastically says to him that गणदास should do well not to carry the dispute further, as the Queen has suggested. It would only endanger his present comfortable position, where now he can at least enjoy the delicious presents of his pupils. As the chances of his defeat are greater, he would then lose everything! I. 16. 21. अवसरप्राप्तम्-which the occasion demands.

I. 17. गणदास is greatly provoked at the sordid picture which विदूषक has drawn of him, and he, therefore, strongly protests against his insinuations. लब्धा... निन्दाम्-of a man whoputs up with insults, shrinking from a contest for fear of losing the position which he has secured. लब्धास्पदः-लब्धं आस्पदं येन सः-one who has obtained a position. तितिक्षमाण-suffering, tolerating. यस्या... वदन्ति-The knowledge of such a man wanting in the dignity of learning serves only as a means of livelihood to him. He demeans himself and his knowledge which he prostitutes for the sake of eking out the bare means of subsistence. He is thus a huckster, a trafficker in knowledge, a Bania dealing in the commodity of learning—a position which, गणदास says, he can never tolerate. I. 17. 3. अचिरोपनीता-Lately initiated, recently given over to you for instruction. The Queen turns to another objection now. The pupil is raw, having been very lately put under his charge, and has had no time to assimiliate the instruction properly. It is therefore unfair and unjust (अन्याय्य) to ask गणदास to give a demonstration. (प्रदर्शन). I. 17. 4. अत...निर्बन्धः-And that is exactly the reason why I insist on having a practical demonstration. The fact that the pupil is new is a point in my favour, and hence my insistence (निर्बन्धः). I. 17. 6. The Queen releases her final shaft. 'Well then, let the परिव्राजिका alone view the exhibition of both. The other audience is not needed." This completely upsets the plan of the विदूषक and the king who feel that everything is lost now. परिव्राजिका,however, comes to the rescue and saves the situation. I. 17. 8. नेत...दोषाय–' It is unfair to throw the whole responsibility of decision on me alone. I admit I am a judge, but I must have some one to consult before taking any definite decision. Even an omniscient judge (सर्वज्ञ) may give a wrong judgment, if he does it alone and unaided.' I.17.11. किं...करोषि–'Why do you take me to be asleep, when I am wide awake to all that is passing round.' The Queen feels thoroughly vanquished in her attempt to stop the exhibition. Even her own people have gone against her, and this naturally irritates her. सासूयम्–in anger, in a pet.

1. 18. पराङ्मुखी–पराग् मुखं यस्याः––whose face is turned away. प्रभ...विन्यः––wives no doubt have a full sway over their husbands ; yet for getting angry with them, there must be some reason or justification for it. कारणकोपाः–– कारणेन कोपो यासां ताः. परिव्राजिका mildly censures the queen's peevish attitude towards the king for which she says she i. e. the Queen has no reason whatsoever. Women rule their husbands, but there must be some sense in their moods and attitudes. I.18. 4. दिष्ट्या Fortunately, luckily. कोपव्याजेन under the pretext of resentment. विदूषक takes

this opportunity to provoke Gaṇadāsa still more. Her apparently unjustified anger is a cloak under which, he says, she wants to save him the ignominy of defeat शुचि...भवति. Not every learned man is good or skilful in imparting his knowledge. I. 18. 7. एवं गृह्णाति. This is how people understand or rather misunderstand. They think, for instance, that I am an incapable teacher and am being shielded by the Queen against inpending and certain defeat, by hook or crook!

I. 19. गणदास is greatly enraged at the attitude of the Queen and dealares that if he is not allowed to give a practical demonstration of what he has taught, he would take it that the Qneen has given him up once for all. क्रियासंक्रान्तिः-Skill in imparting the instruction in acting. परित्यक्तः--Deserted, abandoned, given up. I. 19. 1. गति :—Course. alternative. The Queen has to yield at last and give her consent to the exhibition. I. 19. 4. अपदे शंकितोऽस्मि. I had entertained doubts when there was no scope for them (अपदे). कस्मिन् अभिनेयवस्तुनि-In what particular piece of acting. I. 19. 7. यदा...वती. Note how the king refuses to give any suggestion, though he has much to say in the matter. He is thus in a position to say to the Queen later on 'न खलु मनस्विनि मया प्रयुक्त' मिदम् । किमपि...स्मि with a shrug of the shoulders, परिव्राजिका. also hesitates to make any suggestion. 'There is som thing hanging heavy on the Queen's mind, which hase made me afraid.' I. 19. 10. विस्रब्धम्. Freely, confidently. प्रभ...जनस्य I shall certainly have power over my servants, who are at my disposal and will act as you order. I. 19. 11. मम चेति ब्रूहि Note the coaxing or the flattering tone of the king. ' You have power over me as well. ' It would also mean ' you have power over my servants also. I. I9. 13. चतु...हरन्ति. The छालित (the same as चांलित) depending upon four verse quadrants or lines, is declared to be a very difficult piece to act (दुष्प्रयोज). एकार्थसंश्रयं (प्रयोगं) – The demonstration of one and the same piece of acting. I. 19. 20. वर्गौ The two parties or sides (representing the two teachers). संगीतरचना– Arrangement of all the accessories of music. उत्थापयिष्यति Will make us start to go (to the Concert hall). I. 19. 22. विजयप्रत्यार्थिनी – Opposed to his success. She tries to explain her position as one who opposed the exhibition right from the beginning. Her opposition was not prompted by her desire to see गणदास defeated. There were other motives which, of course, she cannot explain. I. 19. 27. निर्ण...ब्रवीमि. I speak in the capacity or the authority of one who has been called upon to give a judgment. सर्वा...क्तये- For the purpose of revealing to the view (आभिव्यक्ति) the graces of all the limbs. विरलनेपथ्ययोः–विरलं नेपथ्यं ययोः। Wearing thin stage–costumes. Note the shrewd romantic suggstion of the Parivrājikā, who by this wants to enable the king to observe मालविका at the height of her physical charms, so that at the very first sight he may be enamoured of her. I. 19. 32. The Queen levels a taunt at the king, before leaving the place. If he would show such resourcefulness (उपायनिपुणता) or genius in political affairs, as he has betrayed in his love-intrigues, he would certainly achieve wonders.

I. 20. अन्यथा गृहीत्वा-misunderstanding. मनस्विनी A proud lady प्रायः...भागाः—Generally men of equal learning are envious of one anothers fame. Colleagues are jealous of each other. पर...पुरोभागाः-परस्परस्य यशसि-यशोविषये पुरोभागो येषाम्। पुरोभाग-Envy, jealousy, fault-finding (दोषैकदृष्टि) I. 20. 2. हन्त-A particle implying joy or surprise.

I. 21. Construe जीमूत.......भिः उद्ग्रीवैर्मयूरैः अनुरसितस्य पुष्करस्य निर्ह्रादिनी उप...त्था मायूरी मार्जना मनांसि मदयति।. The sound of the drum, resembling the rumble of clouds has attracted the peacocks who look up with upstretched necks and reply the sound with their own notes. Thus reverberating,the sound gladdens the mind. जीमूत...किभिः-जीमूतानां स्तनितं विशङ्कन्ते ते-तैः जीमू...भिः। The peacocks who suspected it to be the thundering (स्तनित) of clouds. The peacocks are greatly delighted and begin to dance and cry at the appearance of the thundering watery clouds in the sky Cf. शुक्लापाङ्गैः सजलनयनैः स्वागतीकृत्य केकाः। प्रत्युद्यातः कथमिव भवान् गन्तुमाशु व्यवस्येत् ॥ मे० I. 22. धौतापाङ्गं हरशशिरुचा पावकेस्तं मयूरं । पश्चादद्रिग्रहणगुरुभिर्गर्जितैर्नर्तयेथाः ॥ मे० I. 44. जीमूतः-जीवनस्य-उदकस्य-मूतः-बन्धः। watery cloud. उद्ग्रीवाः-with upturned necks उद्गता ग्रीवा येषाम् ते. Cf, मनोभिरामाः शृण्वन्तो रथनेमिस्वनोन्मुखैः। षड्जसंवादिनीः केका द्विधा भिन्नाः शिखण्डिभिः॥ रघु० I. 39. अनुरसितस्य पुष्करस्य-The drum which received in reply or was answered by the notes of peacocks. निर्ह्रादिनी-Reverberating, echoing, resounding. Cf. निर्ह्रादी ते मुरज इव चेत् कन्दरेषु ध्वनिः स्यात्। मे० I. 58. उप...स्वरोत्था-उप-

हितः संयोजितः मध्यमस्वरः मध्यमसंचितस्वरः तस्मादुत्तिष्ठति उदेति-इति तथा । Arising out of i. e. beginning with the middle tone, set to the middle note. The reading उपचितमध्यमस्वरोत्था would mean 'in which the middle has gained in intensity etc.' मायूरी मार्जना-मार्जना means the sound of the drum, and this particular high pitched sound, harmonising with the middle note is dear to the peacocks, for which reason it is called मायूरी. मदयति-Delights, maddens. Note the alliteration of the sound म in the last line. I. 21. 1. सामाजिकाः-members of the audience. I. 21. 3. अविनयः-Indecorum, immodesty. The queen did note how impatient and restless the king was to go to the theatre; and he had the audacity to hasten his wife also to the place where he was expecting to see the object of his love! I. 21. 6. विदूषकः has noted that the queen is watching the king's excitement. Therefore he cautions him to be more patient. धीरं गच्छ-Go with patience, 'put on a grave mood and walk slowly.' विसंवादयिष्यति-will countermand the whole show; will thwart the plans. Mr. Pandit takes it in a different way; 'Lest the queen धारिणी should find you inconsistent with yourself i. e. lest she should discover by your impatience to go to the संगीतशाला, that the innocence you have claimed with regard to the origin of the dispute and the indifference you have shown as to the result of the contest of the two masters of dancing and music was merely assumed and that an intrigue lay at the bottom of the affair."

I. 22. The king says that howsoever he might try

to be calm, the sound of the drum hastens me on, as if it is the sound of my desire (Lit. the rattle of the mind-chariot) descending on the path of fulfilment. धैर्यविलम्बी-Observing patience or a calm attitude. सिद्धिपथः-सिद्धेः पन्थाः-The path of fruition or fulfilment.

ACT II.

The second Act is a continuation of the First, or as it is technically called, an अङ्कावतार, hinted by persons at the end of the preceding Act, and therefore we have the same characters here and no interludes. Cf. एष उत्तराङ्कस्य पूर्वाङ्कानुसंगतत्वाद् अङ्कावतारः प्रवेशकविष्कम्भकादिशून्यः । प्रथमाङ्के विदू०--तेन हीत्यारभ्य 'अह वा मिअंगसद्दो ज्जेव उट्ठावइस्सदीत्युपक्रमे मृदङ्गशब्दश्रवणानन्तरं सर्वाण्येव पात्राणि प्रथमाङ्कप्रक्रान्तानि । पात्रसंक्रान्तदर्शनं द्वितीयाङ्कादावारम्भः।...Marginal note in a Ms, cited by Pandit. कतरस्य—of which of the two. कतर is used while referring to one of the two, and कतम, one of many. Cf. न चैतद् विद्मः कतरन्नो गरीयः । यद् वा जयेम यदि वा नो जयेयुः । भग० II. 6. II. 0. 5. ज्ञानवृद्ध-Old in knowledge, advanced in learning, as opposed to वयोवृद्ध meaning advanced in age. पुरस्कार-Preference, precedence. II.0. 7. स्वनियोगं...कुरु.Occupy your place of duty (नियोग) vacated by you, fill in your post left vacant.

II. 0. 9. शर्मिष्ठायाः कृतिः—The composition of शर्मिष्ठा, the daughter of वृषपर्वन् and the wife of king ययाति who loved her deeply. Cf. ययातेरिव शर्मिष्ठा भर्तुर्बहुमता भव । पुत्रं त्वमपि

सम्राजं सेव पूरुमवाप्नुहि ॥ शा० IV. 6. लयमध्या-लयेन तालकालेन मध्या मध्यलययुक्ता-Having or to be sung in medium time. लय means 'Time in music'; तालान्तरालवर्ती यः कालोऽसौ लय ईरितः । It is of three kinds, द्रुत, मध्य and विलंबित. Cf. पादन्यासो लयमनुगतः । मा० II. 8. The medium time is selected for love-songs. Cf. अत्र शृङ्गाररसत्वात् लयमध्येत्युक्तम् । तथा चोक्तं भारतीये-शृङ्गारहास्ययोर्मध्यलयः । चतुष्पदा Having four parts, चत्वारि पदानि यस्याः सा । तस्याश्चतुर्थवस्तुकं प्रयोगं-Performance or representation with reference to the fourth theme (वस्तु) or stanza. चतुर्थस्य तुर्यस्य वस्तुनः प्रबन्धस्य प्रयोगं । " We must suppose that the poem (of शर्मिष्ठा) consisted of four stanzas, each embodying a separate theme (वस्तु)"-Pandit. एकमनाः-With a concentrated mind, attentively.

II. 1. The king tells how very eager he feels to have a sight of मालविका. The curtain, still hanging, separates her who is inside the green room (नेपथ्यगृह). His eager eyes have, however, stepped forth, as it were, in their impatience to brush aside this curtain. तिरस्करिणी-The curtain, the screen. व्यवसितम्-Is busy, has set out. II. 1. 3. नयनमधु-The honey of the eyes. The delicious sight of मालविका is as sweet as honey. Cf. इयममृतवर्तिर्नयनयोः । उत्तर० I. 38, सन्निहिता मक्षिका यस्य तद्-with the wasp hovering near (the honey). The wasp or the bee is none other than Queen धारिणी, who is guarding मालविका, as the bee would, the honey in the bee-hive. अप्रमत्तः watchful, vigilant.

II. 1. 5. आचार्य...सौष्ठवा-आचार्येण प्रत्यवेक्ष्यमाणं अङ्गानां सौष्ठवं यस्याःसा-Whose grace of the limbs was being minutely observed by the teacher. He was anxious for the success of his pupil and therefore he wants to see everything flawless. The word सौष्ठव means 'The elegance of the body. The proportionate and graceful development of the various parts of the body.' Cf. सौष्ठवं नाम अङ्गानां शोभनः अवस्थानविशेष. । यथोक्तम्–अनुच्चनीचचलतां अङ्गानां समपादताम् । कटिकूर्परशीर्षांसकण्ठानां समरूपताम् । रम्यां प्रतीकविश्रान्तिमुरसश्च समुन्नतिम् । अभ्यासोपहितां प्राहुः सौष्ठवं नृत्यवेदिनः ॥ Com. II. 1. 7. न......मधुरता Her loveliness, I am sure, does not fall short of the picture. The king had seen her portrait. विदूषक reminds him of it and says that the king will surely not feel disappointed while observing her in person now. Very often pictures inprove the appearance which in reality is not so good. Such is not the case, however, with मालविका.

II. 2. In his praise of the beauty of मालविका, the king, however, goes to the other extreme. It is the painting that falls short of her real charms. He started with doubts first, regarding her form, which he thought would fail to come up to the mark of the picture, being possibly overdrawn. But now he feels doubtful about the painter's skill, who, possibly, was distracted and hence could not secure enough concentration to do full justice to her. चित्र...हृदयम्–So long as मालविका was to me what I had observed of her only in the picture, I had a misgiving in my heart that her pictured loveliness would fail to have a real existence, i. e. would not be in consonance (विसंवाद) with what she actually is. संप्रति-

किशिता. Now I must change my opinion; and I feel that the painter who has drawn her was greatly distracted in his concentration (शिथिलसमाधि). For a similar idea Cf. यद्यत् साधु न चित्रे स्यात् क्रियते तत्तदन्यथा । तथापि तस्या लावण्यं रेखया किंचिदन्वितम् ॥ शा० VI. 14. II. 2.1. मुक्तसाध्वसा (भव) Leave off all nervousness (साध्वस). सत्त्वस्था. composed, in (your) natural element. (सत्त्वं). II. 2. 2. सर्वस्थानानवद्यता– flawlessness or perfection in every part or limb (स्थान). Pandit reads सर्वावस्थासु अनवद्यता which means "Faultlessness in all conditions." This reading cannot be accepted, as the king refers here to the perfect beauty of the various parts of her body, and not to the different conditions. The next verse makes it clear.

II. 3. दीर्घाक्षं (वदनं)-दीर्घे अक्षिणी यस्य तत् - Having long eyes. शरदिन्दुकान्ति-शरदिन्दोः कान्तिरिव कांतिर्यस्य तत्- Possessed of the loveliness (कान्ति) of the autumnal moon, which regains her lustre, being freed from obscuring clouds. अंसयोः नतौ बाहू- Arms sloping at the shoulders, bent or curved at the shoulders. संक्षिप्तं उरः- Compact bosom. निबिडोन्नतस्तनं (उरः)-निबिडौ उन्नतौ च स्तनौ यस्मिन्-Having thick (निबिड), swelling (उन्नत) breasts. पार्श्वे प्रमृष्टे इव- The two sides as if polished, lit. 'as if they were planed off' like boards that are thinned off by the plane and rendered smooth. मध्यः पाणिमितः-–The waist was so thin and small that it was measurable (मित), or could be encompassed, by the palm of the hand. Cf. मज्झे मज्झं तिवलिवलिअं डिम्भमुट्ठीअ गेज्झं । कर्पूर० I. 30. मध्येन सा वेदिविलग्नमध्या वलित्रयं चारु बभार बाला । कुमार० I. 39. नितम्बि (जघनं)- नितम्बा-

तिस्रयुक्तं ।· अरालाङ्गुली–अराला आकुञ्चिता अङ्गुलयःययोः तौ (पादौ)– with curved toes. छन्दो...वपुः– Her body is so framed that it would suit any form of dancing which the dancing teacher may fancy that she should perform. छन्दः–Will, fancy. श्लिष्टं–संगतं–conforming, suited. Cf. ।श्लिष्टा क्रिया कस्यचिदात्मसंस्था । I. 16. For the description of the beauty of मालविका's form, Cf. अङ्गं लावण्णुण्णं सवणपरिसरे लोअणा हारतारा । वच्छं थोरत्थणिल्लं तिवलिवलइअं मुट्ठिगेज्झं अ मज्झम् । चक्काआरो निअम्बो तरुणिमसमए किं णु अण्णेण कज्जं । पंचेहिं जेव्व बाला मअणजअमहावेजअन्तीअ होन्ति । कर्पूर० III. 19. उपवहनं—A preliminary humming of notes of the required melody. The other reading उपगानं, explained by the commentator as रागलप्ति, means the same thing.

II. 4. A maiden's love for her lover whom she has not yet won is the predominant sentiment of the song. She gives expression to her feelings of despair, hope, anxiety and helplessness, in succession. In the first line, for instance, there is the mood or feeling of despair (निर्वेद) on account of the fact that she realises her lover to be beyond her reach. All at once the corner of her left eye (अपाङ्ग) has begun to throb. Well, the twitching of the left eye in the case of woman is a very good indication of a prospective meeting of the lover. In the second line, therefore, there is the feeling of joy mingled with surprise (हर्षविस्मय). " But then meeting after such a long time, how should he be approached and wooed ? " The difficulty of the situation creates a feeling of anxiety, which is expressed in the third line. The anxiety deepens, as no way out of the difficulty is to be found. A feeling of helplessness (दैन्य) comes over, and the last line gives expression to this sentiment. Thus we find, though the dominating sentiment of the song is love, it gives expression to these various subordinate feelings. Cf. अत्र चतुष्पद्यां क्रमेण पादचतुष्टये निर्वेदः हर्षविस्मयः चिन्ता दैन्यं चेति भावास्तत्तदनुभावैर्मुखरागादिभिः सम्यक् प्रदर्शिता इत्यनुसंधेयम् ।

II. 4. 1. यथारसमभिनयति-Brings out the emotion through acting. As the two stage directions, one viz. उपवहनं कृत्वा चतुष्पदं वस्तु गायति, preceding the love-song and another viz. यथारसमाभिनयति show, मालविका sings the song first and then begins dancing and acting, so as to reveal the emotion of the song. The form of dancing is छलित or चलित in which, while acting the part of another, the dancer gives expression thereby to her own sentiments. परिव्राजिका, the sister of माधवसेन's minister, knew that मालविका was promised in marriage to king अग्निमित्र, and also knew further that she i. e. मालविका loves the king. She has, therefore, selected this particular song of शर्मिष्ठा, that it may serve as an appropriate medium to express her own feelings for the king. The sentiment of the song is, as the Com. says, अयोग-विप्रलंभशृङ्गारः । i. e. love in separation of a maiden who has not yet secured her lover. Cf. अत्र रसस्तु अयोगाविप्रलम्भशृङ्गारः । अप्राप्तिर्विप्रलम्भः स्याद् यूनोर्जाताभिलाषयोः ।...तत्र-संप्राप्तेः प्रागभावो यस्तमयोगं प्रचक्षते ॥ II. 4. 8. द्वारीकृत्य-Making it a medium. (त्वयि) आत्मा उपक्षिप्तः-She has as it wer surrendered herself to you. II. 4. 3. एव-

मावयोर्हृदयम्–Such is the present condition of our hearts ; that is how in our hearts we feel for each other.

II. 5. Construe :—'इमं जनं अनुरक्तं विद्धि' इति गेये वचनं स्वाङ्ग......पूर्वकं अभिनयन्त्या (मालविकया) धारिणीसंनिकर्षात् प्रणयगतिमदृष्ट्वा सुकु......व्याजं अहं उक्त इव । इमं जनं—This person. मालविका refers to herself in the third person Cf. अयं जनः कस्य हस्ते समर्पितः। शा० IV. स्वाङ्गनिर्देशपूर्वम्—To be taken as an adverbial compound with अभिनयन्त्या–Acting this expression of the song with proper gestures, pointing to (निर्देश) her own body–हस्तादिभिः प्रकाशयन्त्या । प्रणय...र्षात्–Finding no other way by which to express her love for me, as the Queen धारिणी was present in person. The presence of धारिणी deprived her of all direct ways of expressing her feelings for me, and, therefore, she had recourse to this indirect and suggestive method of revealing her love. सुकुमारप्रार्थनाव्याजम्–सुकुमारा चासौ प्रार्थना च तस्याः व्याजः यस्मिन् कर्मणि तथा (अहं उक्त इव)–An adverbial compound. She addressed me, as it were, under cover of this gentle plaint or request. The song incorporates a soft request of a maiden to her lover to succour her, helpless as she finds herself to be. This lover of the poem is a different person than the king. The king says that मालविका also finds herself in the same predicament and it appeared that she was pouring her own heart, and that her touching appeal was addressed to me and not to the lover of the poem. The word सुकुमार is taken by some in the sense of 'a youth,' meaning thereby "under the pretext of addressing the youthful lover of the poem." II. 5. 3. विदूषक is trying to detain मालविका, as she was going away after finishing her part. क्रमभेदः-The proper sequence of things to be done. II. 5. 5. उपदेशविशुद्धा-flawless as regard the performance. II. 5. 7. Ganadāsa has asked her to stay back, as she was going away. She turns round instantaneously and there stands in a very charming posture, which elicits this remark of appreciation from the king. सर्वा...पुष्यति-Beauty, under all conditions, develops fresh charms. In every posture, the beauty and loveliness of the form is always seen at an advantage. Cf. अहो सर्वास्ववस्थासु रमणीयत्वमाकृतिविशेषाणाम्। शा० VI. किमिव हि मधुराणां मण्डनं नाकृतीनाम् ॥ शा० I.

II. 6. The king describes her standing pose in all the details of the charm. The attractive features that he notes are—(i) The erect upper portion of the body, (ii) The position of the left hand on the hip, while the right is hanging down loosely, and (iii) the eyes cast down in bashfulness at the toe of her foot that is pressing the flowers on the pavement. सन्धि...वलयं (हस्तं) सन्धौ मणिबन्धे स्तिमितः निश्चलः वलयः कङ्कणं यस्य सः। The hand the bracelets of which are motionless or resting on the wrist. कृत्वा—द्वितीयम्-Making the other i. e. the right hand, which resembles (in tenderness) a branch of a श्यामा creeper, hang down loosely (स्रस्तमुक्तम्). The body of a beautiful woman is often likened to a creeper, the hands resembling the delicate branches and tender sprouts the lips. Cf. श्यामास्वङ्गं etc. मे० II. 37. also अधरः

किसलयरागः कोमलविटपानुकारिणौ बाहू ॥ शा० I. 21. स्रस्तमुक्तम्-स्रस्तं शिथिलं यथा भवति तथा मुक्तम्. Hanging down loosely. Some take it to mean " from which the pearls have gone." ! पादा...कुट्टिमे-the pavement inlaid with jewels, the flowers on which were being pressed (आलुलित) by the toe of the foot. The right part of the body was relaxed, and she was standing with her eyes cast down, in the natural bashfulness of a girl who would not stare at the audience, all the time trying to play with the flowers scattered on the pavement, with the toe of her right foot. पातिताक्षं स्थितं-the standing posture in which the eyes were cast down. The fourth line should be construed thus :—अस्याः ऋज्वायतार्धं स्थितं नृत्ताद् अतितरां कान्तम्। स्थितम्-the standing posture. A Past Passive Participle is used as a noun, according to Panini's Sutra, नपुंसके भावे क्तः । ऋज्वायतार्धम्-in which the upper part of the body (आयतार्धम्-Lit. the long half) is straight or erect. A full view of the body could be had only when she was standing erect, which she could not do during the movements of dancing. अतितरां कान्तम् Is more charming or attractive. II. 6. 1. A sort of a tussle is going on between the Queen and the विदूषक. He wants to detain her on the stage as long as possible, while the Queen would like her to go at once. Hence she remarks to गणदास, that she is surprised to find that the words of a fool like Gautama are taken so seriously by him. II. 6. 3. देवप्रत्ययात्-owing to the confidence which the king has in him. The king's confidence is certainly not misplaced. सूक्ष्मदर्शिता-A subtle insight, acute perception.

II. 7. अमन्दतां एति-Leaves off the dullness of intellect, becomes sharp of intellingence. विपाश्चेत्-A wise man. The simile is that of a mud-removing (पंकाच्छिद्) fruit of the कतक tree, which frees the turbid (आविल) water of its mud by contact with its powder or paste (निकष) and secures transparency for it. We should understand निकष to mean 'power or paste of the कतक fruit.' Similarly, argues गणदास, even a fool like विदूषक may have gained in wisdom by his association with the wise king. विवाक्षितं-वक्तुमिष्टम्—What is intended to be spoken. II. 7. 1. साक्षिणी-The witness, a judge, used with reference to परिव्राजिका. He means that the judge should give her opinion first, and then he will point out the flaw noted by him. II. 7. 5. यथादृष्टम्—just as you have observed. An outspoken plain criticism, whether with reference to the flaw or the merit is solicited. II. 7. 6. यथादर्शनम्-In accordance with the rules of the art. The reading यथाशास्त्रम् means the same thing.

II. 8. The परिव्राजिका explains how the exhibition of मालविका fully conforms to the standards of dancing. अङ्गै...वचनैः-by the various parts of her body which had words concealed in them, i. e. which are eloquently expressive. The ideas of the song were very well brought out in acting by means of the silent movements of the various parts of the body, which thus suppressed the actual words of the song within. Cf.

अन्तर्निहितानि अभ्यन्तरस्थापितानि वचनानि पदानि यैस्तैरङ्गैः हस्तादिभिः। अत्र अभ्यासपाटवादङ्गानां स्वत एवान्तर्निहितवचनत्वमुत्प्रेक्षितमिति मन्तव्यम्। लयमनुगतः-Conformed to the time of the song. In perfect time were the movements of the feet. तन्मयत्वं रसेषु-She could be perfectly one with the sentiments of the song, like despair, joy, surprise, etc. She could be perfectly absorbed in these sentiments. शाखा...नयः—The acting was soft and delicate (मृदु), in which the branch-like hand (शाखा) was used as the instrument of expression. शाखायोनिः-शाखा योनिः प्रभवः यस्य सः-Proceeding from the branch-like hand (शाखा). The graceful movements of the hand resemble the movements of a branch of a creeper. Some interpret शाखा to mean 'a measure of the hands in the dance.' Cf. शाखा नाम नृत्तहस्तानां मानप्रचारः। यथोक्तम्-शाखा तु नृत्तहस्तानां या मात्रा चित्रवर्तिने ॥ तद्विकल्पानुवृत्तौ-In the successive exhibition of the different shades in acting. तस्य आभिनयस्य विकल्पः भेदः तस्य अनुवृत्तिः अनुसृतिः। भावो... विषयात्-One emotion seemed to drive away another from the field (विषयात्). What she means is this: Various emotions pertaining to the one sentiment of love had to be acted by her ; at one time, there was despair, and just the next moment there was joy mixed with surprise. That gave place to anxiety, which was followed by despondency or a feeling of helplessness. While acting in a variety of ways to suit these emotions, she could successfully create the proper atmosphere of these varied emotions, which followed one another in quick succession, like the scenes in a movie. Cf. भावः अभिनीयमानः निर्वेदादिः विषयात् आश्रयात्। प्रकृतात् स्थायिन इत्यर्थः। भावं पूर्वाभिनीतं

संचारिणं नुदति अपाकरोति । नुदति-Drives away, dispels. Cf. मन्दं मन्दं नुदति पवनश्चानुकूलो यथा त्वाम् । मे॰ I. 10. रागबन्धः स एव-Yet the main sentiment of love remained the same throughout. The various emotions exhibited were but the resultants of love, and therefore this basic sentiment also was fully revealed in acting.

II. 8. 2. स्वपक्षे शिथिलाभिमानाः-Losing the same high regard for my side ; feeling diffident regarding the success of my side. II. 8. 3. अद्य नर्तयितास्मि-To-day, after this success in the performance which has elicited such conpliments from the judge, I feel I deserve the position of a professor in the art of dancing.

II. 9. न श्यामायते-A denominative from the adj. श्याम-Which does not turn black, which maintains its flawless quality. Gold is tested in fire and it turns black, if it is impure. Similarly the instruction of the teacher must stand the scrutiny of the judge, and is declared good only when found flawless by him Cf. तं सन्तः श्रोतुमर्हन्ति सदसद्व्यक्तिहेतवः । हेम्नः संलक्ष्यते ह्यग्नौ विशुद्धिः श्यामिकापि वा ॥ रघु॰ I. 10, आपरितोषाद्विदुषां न साधु मन्ये प्रयोगविज्ञानम् । शा॰ I. 2. II. 9. 2. दिष्टया वर्धते भवान्—I congratulate you upon ; lit. you propser with the good luck of etc,. Cf. दिष्टया धर्मपत्नीसमागमेन पुत्रमुखदर्शनेन च वर्धते भवान् । शा॰ VII. परीक्षकाराधनेन-having pleased the judges or having satisfied them. II. 9. 3. वृद्धिहेतुः-The cause of good fortune i. e. success. II. 9. 6. प्रथमोपदेशदर्शनं-At the time of the first exhibition of the instruction. He means that the beginning of every function of some consequence must be attended with the worship of a Brahmin, and the same should have been done here. II. 9. 8. अहो प्रयोगाभ्यन्तरः प्रश्नः-"Oh ! what a relevant question ! what a vital point in acting is being referred to ! " She means that his question is quite irrelevant and beside the point, having nothing to do with the present matter in hand viz. the exhibition given. II.9.9. पण्डितंमन्या-One who thinks oneself to be a wise person, a conceited woman. पंडितं आत्मानं मन्यते सा । प्रसन्न...केशपाशैः-With your abundant hair shining white like the clear (प्रसन्न) rays of the moon. पाश after a word signifying 'hair' means 'abundance, mass, quantity.' भीषयसे-Frighten. II. 9. 14. मन्दस्मितम्-a gentle smile. दशरूप mentions six varities of हास, viz. स्मित, हसित, विहसित, उपहसित, अपहसित and अतिहसित, and among these, the first two are to be noted with reference to the उत्तम characters. The मन्दस्मित, in which the teeth are slightly visible, would accordingly correspond to the हसित variety. Cf. स्मितमिह विकासिनयनं किंचिल्लक्ष्यद्विजं तु हसितं स्यात् । मधुरस्वरं विहसितं सशिरःकम्पमिदमुपहसितम् ॥ अपहसितम् सास्राक्षं विक्षिप्ताङ्गं भवत्यतिहसितम् । द्वे द्वे हसिते चैषां ज्येष्ठे मध्येऽधमे क्रमशः ॥ दश० IV. 76-77. II. 9. 15. उपा...विषयः-My eye has perceived its object possessed of the essence of glory or loveliness (उपात्तसार). उपात्त is a Past Passive Participle from उप+आ+दा, meaning 'Has taken out, is possessed of.' The object of the eye is रूप. Here is an object, the lovely smiling face of मालविका, however, which has the greatest charm about it. Cf. अनवाप्तचक्षुःफलोऽसि । येन त्वया दर्शनीयं न दृष्टम् । शा० II.

II. 10 The king compares the smiling face of मालविका, with its teeth half visible, to an opening lotus whose filaments are partially seen. स्मयमानं-A Present Part. of √स्मि I. A. किंचिदभिव्यक्तदशनशोभि-With the charm of teeth(दशन) slightly revealed. Cf. आलक्ष्यदन्तमुकुलाननिमित्तहासैः । शा० VII. 17. उच्छ्वसत्-Blooming, opening. असमग्रलक्ष्यकेसरं (पंकजं)-असमग्रं असंपूर्णं लक्ष्याः केसराः यस्य तत् । with its filaments not completely visible. The filaments correspond to her small teeth in the simile.

II. 10. 1. महाब्राह्मण-A great Brahmin, said ironically. Cf. भो महाब्राह्मण, काममेतदभिनन्दनीयम् । शा० V. नेपथ्यसङ्गीतकम्- A musical or dramatic performance in regular stage-costume, done in public. This however being a private affair, it was not necessary to observe the preliminary worship of some deity and Brahmins. II. 10. 3. मया....मिष्टम्-Like the foolish चातक bird, I expected a drink of water from the sky resounding with the rumble of rainless clouds. I thought, such a function commencing, I would be given an offering of sweet things ; it proved to be, however, a vain hope of a silly चातक bird who foolishly expects to get a few drops of water to drink from dry clouds. Cf. अरण्ये मया रुदितमासीत् । शा० II. The चातक bird imagined to be living on rain-drops, is often alluded to by the Poets. Cf. स्वस्त्यस्तु ते निर्गलिताम्बुगर्भं शरद्घनं नार्दति चातकोऽपि ॥ रघु० V. 17. रे रे चातक सावधानमनसा मित्र क्षणं श्रूयताम् । अम्भोदा बहवो हि सन्ति गगने सर्वेऽपि नैतादृशाः ॥ केचिद् वृष्टिभिरार्द्रयन्ति वसुधां गर्जन्ति केचिद् वृथा । यं यं पश्यसि तस्य तस्य पुरतो मा ब्रूहि दीनं वचः ॥ भर्तृ० I. II. 10. 9.

पण्डितपरितोष-प्रत्यया-Depending for their decision on the satisfaction of the learned. विदूषक says that he is incapable of pronouncing any judgment regarding the merits of this teacher or the other one. He depends in this matter on what the learned persons like the परिव्राजिका say, and would then form his own opinion accordingly; Cf. मूढः परप्रत्ययनेयबुद्धिः । I. 1. कटकं-A bracelet. शोभन भणितं-You said it was good, you commended her. II. 10. 3. गुणान्तरमजानन्-When you do not know the merits of the other teacher i. e. हरदत्त ; Without knowing how the pupil of हरदत्त has acquitted herself. The expression गुणान्तरम् may also mean 'The excellence of skill or merit, Cf. पात्रविशेषन्यस्तं गुणान्तरं व्रजति शिल्पमाधातुः । I. 6. Then the sentence would mean 'When you are unable to appreciate the excellence of skill in acting, why should you offer this reward, which is best given by really worthy men.' The Queen does not like the idea of the king's bracelet going into the hands of मालविका as a gift, which, though outwardly a reward, is clearly intended to be the lover's token of his love for the girl. II.10.14. परकीयमिति कृत्वा-A nice retort to the queen. 'Why, where is the harm, says he ; after all, he is not to lose anything. He takes the credit for having given as a reward what belongs to others Cf. the Marathi saying 'हलवायाच्या घरावर तुळशीपत्र.' II 10. 16. ननु... शिष्या-She suggests to गणदास to send away his pupil now that she has finished exhibiting her parts. विदूषक's raillery with the obvious intention of detaining मालविका was becoming intolerable to her and hence this hint of hers to गणदास. II. 10. 19. एता...सेवितुम्-I have exhausted my power of ingenuity now ; only thus far can my ingenuity help you : I can think of no other way to detain her any longer. II. 10. 20. अलमलं परिच्छेदेन-Do not set any limit to your genius. If you mean, you can still help me to achieve my object. Note the flattering tone of the king.

II. 11. The king explains how sad he feels, when मालविका has disappeared from view. तिरस्करणम्-disappearance, vanishing from sight. भाग्या...,अक्ष्णोः-I feel as if the sun of the good luck of my eyes has set. हृद...मिव-The heart's great festivity of joy has come to a close (अवसानं). द्वार...धृतेः-The door of pleasure (धृति) has been closed as it were. धृति also means 'Fortitude, courage,' 'The portals of fortitude have closed as it were.' II.11. 2. आतुरः-troubled with illness or disease. विदूषक means that the king is like a poor patient who has no money to pay to the physician, and yet expects him to bring the medicine for him. The king would not take any trouble himself, afraid of the risks. He wants विदूषक to arrange everything for him with a view to secure मालविका II. 11. 6. अवसिता दर्शनार्थः-when मालविका has been seen, the purpose of the exhibition is finished. दाक्षिण्यम्-outward politeness without any sincerity. Cf. दाक्षिण्येन ददाति वाचमुचितामन्तःपुरेभ्यो यदा। शा॰ VI. 5. II. 12.9. वैतालिकः-A bard, a minstrel. It is his profession to praise the king, and also to announce the hour of the day, in apt verses. उपारूढः-Developed, grown. मध्याह्नः-मध्यमहः-the mid-day.

II. 12. He describes how the mid-day heat of the sun affects the various birds. पत्रच्छायासु–in the shade of lotus-leaves. मुकुलितनयनाः हंसाः–the swans have half-closed their eyes; lit. with their eyes in the form of a bud(मुकुल). सौधम्–a great palace, a big mansion. वलभि...वतानि (सौधानि) –वलभिपरिचयस्य द्वेषिणः पारावताः येषु–तानि। The pigeons have come to hate flocking together (परिचय) on the terrace-tops (वलभि). The pigeons flocking on the roofs or terraces of the houses is a common sight. Cf. तां कस्यांचिद् भवनवलभौ सुप्तपारावतायाम् । नीत्वा रात्रिं चिरविलसनात् खिन्नविद्युत्कलत्रः ॥ मे॰ I. 38. परिचयः–' Accumulating, flocking.' It also means ' Acquaintance, contact or association;' in that case it would mean ' Hating their contact with the roofs.' बिन्दूत्क्षेपान् पिपासुः शिखी–the peacock desires licking (पिपासुः) the splashing water-drops. परिपतति– flies to, dashes to. भ्रान्तिमद् वारियन्त्रम्–A revolving water-wheel, known in Marathi by the word रहाटगाडगें. उस्रैः– by the rays. सप्तसप्तिः–a god having seven horses, i. e. the sun. दीप्यते–blazes, shines brilliantly. त्वमिव नृपगुणैः– Just as you (i. e. the king) shine with the kingly virtues. II. 12. 4. उचितवेलातिक्रमे–if the proper time of taking food is transgressed or allowed to go. चिकित्सकः– A physician. हरदत्त...भणसि–What have you to say to this? Would you like the king to miss his lunch-time, which would be so bad for his health?' विदूषक thus suggests to him not to insist on his show being exhibited just then. II. 12. 6. नास्ति...त्र–There is no scope left for me to make any other proposal. I have got to bow down to what विदूषकं says.' . II. 12. 11. मज्जनविधि-The act of bathing, the usual or customary bath. II. 12. 17. न केवलं...विका-As in her personal charm, so in her skill (शिल्प) in dancing, she has no second. अद्वितीया-Matchless, peerless, unrivalled.

II. 13. The king means to say that मालविका is already so beautiful that by her personal charms alone she can strike the heart of one with feelings of love. Now the additional accomplishment of this graceful art has lent her greater power,and she is a deadlier shaft in the hands of Cupid who has steeped it in poison as it were to make it more dreadful. अव्याजसुन्दरी-Artlessly beautiful, naturally charming without any artifical make-up. तां ललितेन विज्ञानेन योजयता-Uniting her with i.e. endowing her with the knowledge of the fine arts. परिकल्पितः-Made ready, devised, prepared. कामस्य बाणः-The shaft of Cupid. A beautiful woman is looked upon, by Sanskrit poets, as a shaft or weapon of the god of love. The verse is a good example of the निदर्शनालंकार.

II. 13. 1. चिन्तयितव्योऽस्मि ते-You have to pay serious thought to my condition. Love has made him its victim and therefore his malady has to be carefully attended to by him. II. 13. 3. विपणिकन्दुः-A cauldron or a frying pan in the market place (विपणि). II. 13. 5. एवमेव...त्वरताम्-Make haste in the cause of your friend, in the same way as you would be doing to pacify your hunger. II. 13. 9. गृहीतक्षणोऽस्मि-I have pledged my word; I have undertaken the venture. 'The phrase has origin in a formula, used in connection with the श्राद्ध ceremony. A Brahmin is duly invited to attend the ceremony, and he uses this expression, when he accepts the invitation गृहीत्वामुकसंज्ञस्यामुकगोत्रस्य चामुके । श्राद्धे तु वैश्वदेवार्थं करणीयः क्षणस्त्वया ॥ इत्येवं श्राद्धकृद् ब्रूयात् तं प्राप्नोतु भवानिति । स वदेत् प्राप्नवानी-तीतरस्तं प्रति द्विजः ॥ Cited by Pandit from शौनक॰ 16.—'The person who addresses in the words of the formula (the श्राद्धकृत्) is said *to give* the क्षण and the Brahmin to whom it is addressed, to *take* the क्षण, in the language of ignorant priests. Hence, because the word क्षण is so often used in the formula, so it has come, in the common parlance of Brahmanas, who subsist mostly upon occasional dinners at Śrāddhas, and to which class our विदूषक belonged, to signify 'an engagement at a Śrāddha, which, when once begun, must be carried out, on pain of incurring sin.' It may be observed that Vidūṣaka's way of expressing his obligation to accomplish what he has undertaken is perfectly in keeping with his character. क्षण घेणें is still used in Marathi in the sense of 'pledging one's self for the performance of a thing'—Pandit. मेघा...ज्योत्स्नेव-मेघावल्या रुद्धा चासौ ज्योत्स्ना च। Like moonlight obstructed or veiled by the clouds. सूनोपरिचरः-Hovering over the slaughter-house (सूना). आमिषलोलुपः—Greedy of the flesh (आमिष). Like the vulture, you too eagerly want to snatch the object of your love but, are afraid of धारिणी. अनातुरः-Patient, calm, unexcited. तस्मात् ...रोचसे-He means, there are hundred and one difficulties in the way of success for which you have to wait patiently. I would very much like you to exercise patience while you eagerly solicit success in this venture Note the wise counsel of विदूषक to the king.

II. 14. Construe :–सर्वा...हृदयस्य मे वामलोचना सा स्नेहस्यैकायनीभूता । सर्वा...हृदयस्य मम–Of me who have lost all heart in the activities of the ladies of my harem. Thinking of मालविका alone, I have ceased to feel any interest in the harem. वामलोचना—Possessed of lovely (वाम) eyes. स्नेहस्यैकायनीभूता-She has become the sole centre of my affection. एकायनीभूता is a च्वि form (अभूततद्भावे च्विः।). एकायनं One abode, the sole resort.

ACT III.

III. 0. 1. परिचारिका–A female attendant. III. 0. 6. बीजपूरकं–The fruit of citron, known as महाळुंग in Marathi. प्रमदवनपालिका--The female keeper of the प्रमदवन garden. Her name is मधुकरिका, lit. meaning 'a female bee,' while that of परिव्राजिका's attendant is परभृतिका meaning literally 'a cuckoo.' The same names have been given to the two female attendents in the शाकुंतल, where at the beginning of the Sixth Act they are carrying on a lively dialogue in the garden of दुष्यन्त. तपनीयाशोक:–The golden अशोक tree, so called because of its bright yellow blossoms. III. 0. 11. अपि...व्यापार:–The particle अपि, thus used at the beginning of a sentence introduces a question. 'Are you having a happy time while doing your work in the garden'? III. 0. 16. अरिक्तपाणिना–'Without empty hands.' परिव्राजिका

means that she must have some present to offer when she would visit the queen. She cannot do so empty-handed. We have a meeting between the queen and परिव्राजिका in Act IV, but it may not be the same referred to here. Shall we suppose that परिव्राजिका made it a point to see the queen as frequently as she could, with a view to see how the wind was blowing and also to remove the suspicions, if any would be entertained by the queen as regards her hand in the quarrel between the two teachers? शुश्रूषितुम्-To wait upon, to serve, III. 0. 21. अन्योन्यसंघार्षित-संघर्षित-Mutually quarrelling, disputing with each other. संघर्ष: संजात: अस्य ।. One who has a dispute. Compare a similar expression, अन्योन्यकलहितयो: in Act I. Cf. also अत्रभवतो: परस्परविज्ञानसंघर्षो जातः । Act I. III. 0. 24. आगमिनौ-Possessed of theoretical knowledge (आगम). किंतु ...गणदास:-' But then गणदास has the palm or is adjudged to be the superior of the two, because of the excellent merits (गुणविशेष) of his pupil. मालविका, the pupil of गणदास, showed superior skill to that of the pupil of हरदत्त, and hence गणदास is ranked higher (उन्नमित). This means that the king kept up his promise of witnessing the performance of हरदत्त's pupil next day, and only afterwards was the decision given in favour of गणदास. III. 0. 26. कौलीनं—कुले जातं-Lit. belonging to a family, or arising from a group of people ; a scandal, gossip. Cf. कौलीनभीतेन गृहान्निरस्ता न तेन वैदेहसुता मनस्त: । रघु० XIV. 84. कथं श्रूयते-' How is that (scandal) to be heard ; What is that ? ' III. 0. 30. बलवत् साभिलाष:-greatly enamoured, strongly or deeply attached. Cf. बलवदपि शिक्षितानामात्मन्यप्रत्ययं चेत: । शा०

I. 2. चित्तं रक्षन्--Having regard for the feelings of the queen ; out of consideration for her feelings. आत्मन: प्रभुत्वं न दर्शयति–He does not exhibit the strength of his power or authority (प्रभुत्वं). She means that the king, being so deeply attached to मालविका, could easily have got hold of her through his kingly authority. He does nothing of the kind, however, because he would not like to wound the queen's feelings, who would certainly take such things to heart. अनुभूतमुक्तेव......म्लायमाना–Fading or pale like jasmine wreath, worn (अनुभूत) and cast away (मुक्त). अनुभूतमुक्ता–आदौ अनुभूता पश्चान्मुक्ता–Enjoyed first and then thrown away. She means that मालविका also seems to have been affected by a reciprocal feeling of love, as a result of which she has lost the fresh lustre of her face latterly.

III. 0. 34. शाखावलम्बि–शाखामवलम्बते तत। Hanging on the branch. पेशलतरं–Softer, more tender than this citron fruit. मधुकरिका has been of much service to परिव्राजिका, in securing for her the required present. This service will not go unrewarded. The present of a hard fruit will yield to her a softer reward in the near future. What does she refer to ? Some happy prospect of the king's or the queen's favour ? Or was she to be lucky like मालविका in winning the king's love ? The expression त्वमपि 'you too' favours the latter suggestion. III. 0. 42. चिराय... दोहदनिमित्तं–Regarding the longing (दोहद) of this gold अशोक tree which is delaying (चिरायमाण:) to put forth its blossoms. Sanskrit poets curiously imagine in their romantic fancy that the trees have various cravings or longings like those of a pregnant woman, and only when they are satisfied, they would burst into blossom. We have a beautiful verse which mentions the different cravings of the various trees. स्त्रीणां स्पर्शात् प्रियङ्गुर्विकसति बकुलः शीधुगण्डूषसेकात् । पादाघातादशोकः तिलककुरबकौ वीक्षणालिङ्गनाभ्याम् ॥ मन्दारो नर्मवाक्यात् पटुमृदुहसनाच्चम्पको वक्त्रवातात् । चूतो गीतान्नमेरुर्विकसति च पुरो नर्तनात् कर्णिकारः ॥ According to these conventions, the अशोक tree, when it withholds its flowers, is believed to desire that a young and beautiful woman should be decorated with ornaments, dressed beautifully and should then kick it with her foot which should itself be nicely decorated. This ceremony is called the दोहदपूरण or gratifying the desire of the Aśoka.

प्रवेशकः-This is an explanatory scene serving the same purpose as the विष्कम्भक, only with this difference that the characters taking part in this scene are exclusively of the inferior class speaking the Prakrits. It must come between two Acts; and thus unlike the विष्कंभक, its existence in the first Act is not possible. Cf. तद्वदेवानुदात्तोक्त्या नीचपात्रप्रयोजितः । प्रवेशोऽङ्कद्वयस्यान्तः शेषार्थस्योपसूचकः॥

The Pravesaka tells us, among other things, that the king is now deeply in love with मालविका who too responds to his feelings in a similar way, and that he will not use his authority to gain his ends, out of respect for the queen's feelings, which thus makes him depend soley on the efforts of विदूषक and his friends. The craving of the Aśoka tree, on par with that of the king is also significantly referred to, as it gives an opportunity to मालविका to satisfiy both. This information is necessary for the audience to follow the action of the main scene which commences now.

III. 0. 47. कामयमानावस्थः-कामयमानस्य इव अवस्था यस्य सः। In the condition of a love-lorn person ; in a love-sick state. III. 1. Constant thinking of the object of his love; viz. मालविका and the acute pangs caused thereby constitute the theme of this beautiful verse. He cannot understand, says he, why his heart, which has its highest bliss i. e. मालविका enshrined within, should suffer so much torment! One suffers for want of the object which one cherishes. The body gets thin, not having obtained the pleasure of her embraces. The eyes may be in tears, because deprived of her sight. But the heart, which has stored within itself the precious treasure of love viz. मालविका, from whom it is never separated—that this heart should suffer great agony is something which is very very strange! क्षामं-Thin, emaciated Cf. मध्ये क्षामा etc. मे० II. सास्रं-अस्रैः सहितं—full of tears. सारङ्गाक्षी-सारङ्गस्य इव अक्षिणी यस्याः सा-Having eyes like those of an antelope (सारंग); gazelle-eyed. प्रसक्ते निर्वाणे-when the highest bliss is so closely connected or associated (with the heart). प्रसक्त-closely adhering to, closely connected. निर्वाणं supreme bliss, highest felicity. Cf. अये लब्धं नेत्रनिर्वाणम्। शा० III. It is also a philosophical term meaning 'absolute extinction or annihilation of individual or worldy existence' and refers to the final state of liberation or the मोक्ष according to the Buddhist philosophy. The fourth line gives us the notion of apparent contradiction or विरोध. निर्वाण has also the sense of 'the means of extinguishing fire etc.' 'When the heart is equipped with the means of extinguishing the fire within, why should it bear this torment of scorching agony?'. III. 1. 4. परिदेवितं-Lamentation, bewailing. श्राविता-was made to listen, informed. भवता संदिष्टम्-Your massage. Apparently the king has tried through विदूषक to take बकुलावलिका, the queen's maid, into confidence, and he wants her to speak the message of his love to मालविका. III. 1. 10. अनुगृहीताऽस्मि ...नियोगेन-I feel favoured by this mission entrusted to me. The mission is that of a messenger of love or a go-between. तपस्विनी-The poor pitiable girl, having the sense of the Marathi expression 'गरीब बिचारी or गरीब बापडी.' तपस्वी करुणापात्रम् । हला० नागरक्षित इव निधिः-Like a valuable treasure guarded by a cobra sitting on it. न सुखं...भविष्यति will not be easily secured, cannot be easily obtained. घटयिष्यामि-I shall try to unite or bring about a union. Cf. इत्थं नारीर्घटयितुमलं कामिभिः । शिशु० IX. 87. तप्तेन तप्तमयसा घटनाय योग्यम् ॥ विक्र० II. 16. It has also the sense of 'accomplishing an object or effecting a purpose.' Cf. तटस्थः स्वानर्थान् घटयति च मौनं च भजते । मालती० I. 14. III. 1. 13. संकल्पयोनिः-Born of fancy or thought; whose source (योनि) is thought. It is an epithet of the god of Love; Cf. epithets मनोभव, मनसिज, etc. प्रतिबन्धवत्सु विषयेषु अभिनिवेश्य-Having made one attached towards objects that are fraught with difficulties (प्रतिबन्ध). जनोऽयम्-This person i. e. I. The king refers to himself in the third person. कालान्तरक्षमो न भवति-Is unable to brook any delay; cannot bear any delay

(कालान्तर). Cf. दूरगतमन्मथा अक्षमेयं कालहरणस्य । शा॰ III. The king means that it was the god of love who impelled him to love an inaccessible object like मालविका, and now tortures him so much that he cannot brook any delay in the attainment of his object.

III. 2. The king wonders at the disparity that exists between the tender weapon like the flower and the acute heart-rending agony which it produces. हृदयप्रमाथिनी रुजा–हृदयं प्रमथ्नाति सा–A heart-wrenching agony. विश्वसनीयमायुधम्–A weapon like the flower which is seemingly harmless, which rouses no suspicion as being harmful or dangerous. The god of love has five arrows with which to strike the lovers, and they are:—अरविन्दमशोकं च चूतं च नवमल्लिका । नीलोत्पलं च पञ्चैते पञ्चबाणस्य सायकाः ॥ उन्मादनस्तापनश्च शोषणः स्तम्भनस्तथा । संमोहनश्च कामस्य पञ्चबाणाः प्रकीर्तिताः ॥. The two particles क्व and क्व bring out a great incongruity or disparity between two objects. The king says, for instance, 'Look at these two objects, Cupid's weapons viz. flowers, and the agonising torture they effect. What a great incongruity or inconsistency exists between the two! There should be some proportion between a cause and its effect. Here there is none. The effect is absolutely disproportionate to the cause.' Cf. भगवन् कुसुमायुध, त्वया चन्द्रमसा च विश्वसनीयाभ्यां प्रतिसन्धीयते कामिजनसार्थः । कुतः । तव कुसुमशरत्वं शीतरश्मित्वमिन्दो–। द्वयमिदमयथार्थं दृश्यते मद्विधेषु ॥ विसृजति हिमगर्भैरग्निमिन्दुर्मयूखै–। स्त्वमपि कुसुमबाणान् वज्रसारीकरोषि ॥ and further कुतस्ते कुसुमायुधस्य सतत्तैक्ष्ण्यमेतत् । शा॰ III. 2. मृदु तीक्ष्णतरम्–" A delicate thing is often most piercing. मन्मथः-Cupid, the god of love-मनो मथ्नाति सः । तदि... त्वयि-In you is illustrated the saying that a tender thing is often the sharpest. III. 2. 3. उपायोपक्षेप:-उपायस्य उपक्षेपः-Devising of the remedy or means. पर्यवस्थापयतु-Compose yourself; be at ease. III. 2. 5. उचितव्यापारविमुखेन चेतसा-with a mind disinclined or averse to the proper duties. क्व दिवसशेषं यापयामि-Where should I pass the rest of the day? √यापय्-The causal of या 'to go.' Cf. क्व नु खलु... श्रमक्लान्तमात्मानं विनोदयामि । शा० III. वसन्ता...कोरकानि-The buds (कोरक) of the red Asoka tree, indicative of the arrival or advent (अवतार) of spring. दोलाधिरोहणं-Sitting on the swing. III. 2. 17. निसर्गनिपुणाः-Instinctively shrewd or clever. Cf. स्त्रीणामाशिक्षितपटुत्वममानुषीषु संदृश्यते किमुत याः प्रतिबोधवत्यः । शा० V, 22. स्त्रियो हि नाम खल्वेता निसर्गादेव पण्डिताः । मृच्छ० IV.19. अन्यसंक्रान्तहृदयम्-अन्यस्यां संक्रान्तं हृदयं यस्य whose heart is transferred to another (woman). उपलालयन्तम्-Fondling, coaxing, caressing. कथं...न लक्षयिष्यमि-'How will she not detect?' The king says that his heart is already given over to मालविका, and it will be therefore very difficult for him to conceal his love when in the company of इरावती. In spite of all his fondling and caresses इरावती, with her instinctive shrewdness of a woman, will easily see through and discover his love for another woman. Cf. अन्यसंक्रान्तप्रेमाणो नागरिका अधिकं दक्षिणा भवन्ति। विक्र०III. अन्यसंक्रान्त-हृदयोऽपि प्रथमसंभावनामपेक्षते अतिशिथिलसौहार्द इदानीमेषः । शा० VI.

III. 3. The king says that all these considerations to refuse her proper request by giving various plausible excuses would be far better than allow himself to be caught in a compromising situation where he will have to pretend,to keep up an appearance of an ardent lover, even though at heart he has not the slightest attachment for her. उचितः प्रणयः. विहन्तुं वरम्–It is better to decline (विहन्तुं) the request (प्रणय) which is quite proper for this occasion. खण्डनहेतवः दृष्टाः–Many excuses to refuse (खण्डन) the request are seen i. e. are known to me. He means that any number of plausible excuses, such as urgent calls of state affairs, can be invented for the purpose of saying 'No' to the queen इरावती. उपचार...शून्यः– But a formal behaviour of courtesy with these clever women, even though full of greater ardour or fervour (पूर्वाभ्यधिकः) will certainly be found out to be lacking in the sincere feeling of love, (भावशून्य) and therefore it will not do for the present occasion when it is far better to refuse her request. Cf. प्रियवचनशतोऽपि योषितां दायिजनानुनयो रसादृते । प्रविशति हृदयं न तद्विदां मणिरिव कृत्रिमरागयोजितः ॥ विक्र० II. 22. मनस्विनीनां–objective genitive. अन्तःपुरप्रातिष्ठितं दाक्षिण्यं–Your courtesy which is a constant or unfailing feature in your behaviour towards ladies of the harem. एकपदे–All of a sudden. पृष्ठतः कर्तुम्–to keep it back, to throw away. He means that the king was never rude to the ladies who were always sure of his courteous, chivalrous behaviour. It will not do for him, therefore, to shake off his courtesy all at once and disappoint the ladies in their legitimate demands. III. 3. 9. नन्वे... भवन्तम्–The idea underlined is that of a man beckoning a friend of his to come near quickly, with the fingers of his hand. Cf. एष वातेरितपल्लवाङ्गुलीभिस्त्वरयतीव मां केसरवृक्षकः ।

शा० I. III. 3. 11. अभिजात:-Noble, high-born, nobly sympathising. ' On the meaning of this, compare also the followiug of भर्तृहरि quoted in the कुवलयानन्द:-प्रदानं प्रच्छन्नं गृहमुपगते संभ्रमविधिः । निरुत्सेको लक्ष्म्यामनभिभवगन्धाः परकथाः ॥ प्रियं कृत्वा मौनं सदसि कथनं नाप्युपकृतेः । श्रुतेऽत्यन्तासक्तिः पुरुषमभिजातं कथयति ॥'—Pandit.

III. 4. The king says that like a noble person the Spring who feels so much for him in his present suffering, first inquires of him in gentle soft words, as one would do an ailing friend, as to how far his malady is bearable; and then strokes him gently by way of encouragement. The words of the Spring are the sweet notes of cuckoos who have found their voice at the advent of Spring, while the fragrant southern breeze represents the stroking of his hand. Construe the verse thus :--आमत्तानां कोकिलानां श्रवणसुभगैः कूजितैः मनसिजरुजः सह्यतां सानुक्रोशं पृच्छता इव माधवेन चूत...सुरभिः सांद्रस्पर्शः दक्षिणो मारुत; (दक्षिणः) करतल इव अङ्गे व्यापृतः । श्रवणसुभगैः कूजितैः-The warbling (कूजित) of cuckoos agreeable or charming (सुभग) to the ear. Cf. तच्छ्रुत्वा ते श्रवणसुभगं गर्जितं मानसोत्काः । मे० I 11. सानुक्रोशम्-Compassionately. मनसिरुजः सह्यतां-The endurable nature of love's malady (रुज्). दक्षिणमारुत-The southern breeze coming from the Malaya mountain which teems with the sandal-wood forests. Such breezes are looked upon as one of the charming features of spring. Cf. कुबेरगुप्तां दिशमुष्णरश्मौ गन्तुं प्रवृत्ते समयं विलङ्घ्य । दिग्दक्षिणा गन्धवहं मुखेन व्यलीकनिश्वासमिवोत्ससर्ज । कु० III. 25. ते एहिं मलआणिला विरहिणीणीसाससंपक्किणो । जादा झत्ति सिसुत्तणे वि बहला

तम्बरुण्णपुण्णा इव ॥ कर्पूर० I. 20. The word दक्षिण has a double meaning, referring to करतल as well, in the sense of 'The palm of the right hand.' चूतप्रसवसुरभि–Fragrant with mango blossoms. सान्द्रस्पर्शः–सान्द्रः स्पर्शः यस्य सः–The word, सान्द्र means 'close, intimate'; it also means 'soft, pleasing': both the senses will do well here. व्यापृतः–Applied, used for the purpose of stroking. माधवेन–वसन्तेन.–By the Spring. III. 4. 2. निर्वृतिलाभाय. For getting happiness or pleasure. All the Mss. read णिव्वुदिलाहाअ, which apparently seems to be a direct Prakrit translation of the Sanskrit form निर्वृतिलाभाय. We should, however, expect a genitive form °लाहस्स for the Sanskrit Dative, since the Prakrit has lost the dative case.

III. विलोभयितुकामया—With a desire to tempt you. III. 5. The Vernal Beauty (माधवी श्री) is imagined to be a lovely lady who has put on the various face-decorations supplied to her by the spring, and in that she surpasses the other women. A lady's toilet consists of the red lac-dye which she applies to her lips, the various paintings to be drawn on the forehead, cheeks and the bosom, and the reddish-black mark on the forehead in saffron mixed with musk (कस्तुरी). The Vernal Beauty has all these supplied to her by the spring, and she appears to be looking down upon this art of adorning the face, as practised usually by women. विशेषितगुणः ...लक्तकः—the red lac-dye (अलक्तक), applied to the lower lip red like the बिंब fruit seems to have been surpassed (विशेषित). The red colour of the lips is often compared to that of the ripe बिंब fruit. Cf. तन्वी श्यामा शिखरिदशना पक्वबिम्बाधरोष्ठी । मे० II. प्रत्या...रुणम्-The कुरबक blossoms exhibit a variety of colours, dark, bright (अवदात) and red. They thus throw into the back-ground (प्रत्याख्यात) the charm of the creeper-like painting on the face or the cheeks. The word विशेषक or more often पत्रविशेषक refers to these creeperlike paintings on the face or the cheeks. Cf. हिमव्यपायाद्विशदाधराणामापाण्डुरीभूतमुखच्छवीनाम् । स्वेदोद्गमः किंपुरुषाङ्गनानां चक्रे पदं पत्रविशेषकेषु ॥ कुमा० III. 33. For the idea of the कुरबक blossoms serving as such paintings on the face of vernal beauty, Compare, विरचिता मधुनोपवनश्रियामभिनवा इव पत्रविशेषकाः । मधुलिहां मधुदानविशारदाः कुरबका रवकारणतां ययुः ॥ रघु० IX. 29. छम......नैः तिलकः— By the blossoms of the तिलक tree, with the bees (द्विरेफ) clinging to them like collyrium (अंजन). तिलकक्रियापि आक्रान्ता–The decoration of the saffron mark on the forehead is superseded or excelled. Cf. लग्नद्विरेफाञ्जनभक्तिचित्रं मुखे मधुश्रीस्तिलकं निवेश्य । रागेण बालारुणकोमलेन चूतप्रवालोष्ठमलंचकार ॥ कुमा० III. 30. Also अलिभिरञ्जनबिन्दुमनोहरैः कुसुमपङ्क्तिनिपातिभिरङ्कितः । न खलु शोभयति स्म वनस्थलीं न तिलकस्तिलकः प्रमदामिव ॥ रघु० IX. 41. सावज्ञेम...योषिताम्-The vernal beauty ridicules as it were (सावज्ञा) the art of adorning (प्रसाधन) the face as practised ordinarily by women (योषितां). III. 5. 2. पर्युत्सुका–In a state of anxious longing, in an excited or agitated condition. Cf. पर्युत्सुका कथयसि प्रियदर्शनां तां । विक्र०II. 16. अपि संप्रति देहि दर्शनं स्मर पर्युत्सुक एष माधवः । कुमा० IV. 28. III. 5. 14. विभवः–Power, courage. She means that she is denied the relief that she will have, if she will commuicate the whole thing to her affectionate friends. Cf.

स्निग्धजनसंविभक्तं दुःखं सह्यवेदनं भवति । शा० III. III. 5. 15. अप्रतीकारगुरुका वेदना–' The agony which is severe because it has no remedy (प्रतीकार); for it is next to impossible that I shall ever secure the king's love.' कुत्र...प्रस्थितास्मि–मालविका is so much engrossed in her thoughts of love, that she has forgotten where she was to go. गौतमचापलात्–Through the mischief of Gautama i. e. विदूषक. Perhaps it was a part of his plans to see that the Queen sustains a fall from the swing, which he might have specially contrived. This gives an opportunity to मालविका to serve as a substitute for the Queen in fulfilling the cravings of Aśoka, and thereby get a chance to meet the king. Note how very deep-laid are the plans of विदूषक with a view to help the king in his love-affairs! III. 5. 20. अन्तरा निःश्वस्य–A sigh in the middle of her speech and just before what she is going to say gives a diferent construction to the whole sentence. It is tantamount to an expression of doubt as regards the queen's promise, which मालविका thinks, she will never be able to fulfil. " The Queen said to me, that if I succeed in getting the Aśoka to blossom within five nights, she will gratify me by giving me what I cherish most in my heart! And what else is that but the king's love? Will the Queen ever gratify me on that score! It is impossible. The Queen's promise, therefore, is all vain and can never be fulfilled by her." A series of such thoughts is suggested by this stage-direction, which thus lends a beautiful touch to the whole situation. अनुपदम्–Immediately after me पदस्य पश्चात् । चरणालंकारहस्तया-With the ornaments of the feet, such as red lac-dye, anklets, costume and other ornaments of the body. III. 5.25.शीधुपानोद्वेजितस्य मत्स्याण्डिका--Sugar for one who has become helpless under the intoxicating influence of wine (शीधु). ' मत्स्यण्डिका is a kind of fine sugar, so called because it is soft and yellowish-white like sand and is composed of globules like the eggs of fish (मत्स्याण्ड) '. The use of sugar is noted as an antidote against intoxication by liquor. Cf मद्यं पीत्वा यदि वा तत्क्षणमवलेढि शर्करां सघृताम् । मदयति न जातु मद्यं मनागपि प्रथितवीर्यमपि ॥ योगरत्न, cited by Pandit. विदूषक means ' the sight of मालविका will now certainly serve as a cure to your love-malady, under whose influence you have far gone.' III. 5.29. नातिपर्याप्तवेषा-Insufficiently or scantily dressed. नातिपर्याप्तः वेषः यस्याः सा।

III. 6. उच्छ्वसितम्-Revived, taken in a fresh breath, was refreshed. विक्लवं-Afflicted, distressed. तरुगूतं... सारसात्-The king compares himself to a thirsty (विपासतः) traveller, who is anxiously looking out for water, and feels revived as it were, when he hears the cry of the cranes which indicates the existence of water some where in the grove of trees. आरसित-Crying.

III. 8. मम जीवितमेतद्-Pointing to मालविका, the king says that his very life embodied in her is coming towards him. नितंबबिम्ब-The word बिम्ब means any round or disc-like surface ; the whole word would mean, therefore, ' Round hips. ' Cf. चक्काआरे रमणफळहे को वि कंचीमरट्टो । जिस्सा

तिस्सा उणवि भणिमो भूसणं दूसणं अ ॥ कर्पू० II. 23. समुन्नतं-swelling, uplifted. अत्यायतं-stretched far, very broad. III. 7. 8. अवस्थान्तरमुपारूढा-She has developed a change in her condition. She has grown pale and wears a few ornaments; thus she looks like a Kunda creeper in spring with all its leaves ripened and a few blossoms left.

शर......स्थला-शरकाण्ड इव पाण्डु गण्डस्थलं यस्याः सा-whose broad cheeks(गण्डस्थलं) are pale like stalk of a reed(शर).परिमिताभरणा-with measured i. e. few ornaments. माधवपरिणतपत्रा-माधवेन-वसन्तेन परिणतानि पत्राणि यस्याः सा-whose leaves are ripened (परिणत) by spring. The ripened leaves correspond to the pale cheeks and the blossoms to the ornaments. Cf. छबिः पाण्डुरा। पत्राणामिव शोषणेन मरुता स्पृष्टा लता माधवी। शा० III. 10. III. 8. 3. सौहार्द-Friendship, The king means that the विदूषक infers her condition to be due to love-sickness, on account of his great attachment for him. A friend looks at every thing with a favourable eye and tries to put a construction suited to his own interest, even in the absence of proper evidence for it. Cf. सर्वः कान्तमात्मीयं पश्यति। शा० II. III. 8. 6. अयं......अशोकः-The Aśoka imitates मालविका in her love-sick condition. Both of them have their delicate longings to be fulfilled and both have not put on the flowery robes (नेपथ्य). प्रच्छायशीतले-rendered cool by the thick shade (प्रच्छाय). Cf. तेन ह्यस्यां प्रच्छायशीतलायां सप्तपर्णवेदिकायां मुहूर्तमुपविश्य परिश्रमविनोदं करोत्वार्यः। शा० I. III. 8. 12. नैता......मन्ये-with this much i. e. simply because she said that she too feels a longing in her heart (उत्कण्ठिता), I cannot assure myself with the thought that your conjecture that she is love-sick is correct. प्रसन्नतर्कः-प्रसन्नः तर्कः यस्य सः-Whose inference is clear or accurate.

III. 6. Vague longings are produced in the heart by the fragrant cool breezes in spring. वोढा-a noun of agency from √वह्, by the addition of the termination तृच्; 'One that carries along.' किस.........नुगतः-किसलयपुटभेदेभ्यः निर्गतैः सीकरैः अनुगतः। Accompanied by the particles of water issuing from the opening folds of the tender sprouts. अनिमि॰त्तामुत्कण्ठां-Causeless, vague longing. III. 9. 1. लतान्तरितौ-लताभिः अन्तरितौ-Screened or concealed by the creepers. III. 9. 5. ग्राह-A shark, crocodile, The king means that he would risk any thing for the sight of मालविका and if he sees her, he would not care for anybody. We shall, however, see later how this proves to be an idle boast of the king, who is at great pains to conciliate इरावती. III. 9. 8. निरवलम्बात्-Vain, fruitless, the basic object of which is beyond reach. III. 9. 9. विदूषक looks at the king, meaning to say "Look! here is additional evidence for what I conjucture. Don't you feel convinced?" III. 9. 10. स्नेहस्य वामतां-The perversity of love, which never runs a smooth logical straight-forward course.

III. 10. The king tries to bring out the perversity of love. "Here is मालविका in a state of anxious longing, but she has not spoken of the object of her love, for whom she is pining so much. विदूषक has put forth a conjecture with reference to me-a conjecture which does not always arrive at the truth. Very often we see how inferences go wrong. And yet in spite of all this, I am flattering myself with the thought that I am the object of her love and these lamentations are with reference to me and none else. Thus is love perverse, in that reason or no reason, the person clings obstinately to the object of his love and tries to feed himself with baseless conjectures even." For similar idea Cf. एवमात्माभिप्रायसंभावितेष्टजनचित्तवृत्तिः प्रार्थयिता विडम्ब्यते... । सर्वं तत्किल मत्परायणमहो कामी स्वतां पश्यति ॥ शा० II. तत्वावबोधैकरसः तत्वावबोधे एकरसः यस्य सः-whose chief or essential feature is the ascertainment of the truth. Too much reliance cannot be placed on inference which often is not accurate. रम्भोरु-रम्भा means a plantain tree; the expression means 'a beautiful lady having shapely round and tapering thighs like the interior stem of the plantain tree.' Cf. यास्यत्यूरुः सरसकदलीस्तम्भगौरश्चलत्वम् ॥ मे० II. लक्ष्यम्-Target, object, theme. III. 10. 3. अर्पितमदनसंदेशा-अर्पितः मदनसंदेशः यस्याः सा । To whom the message of love is given or entrusted for being communicated to मालविका. III. 10. 8. दास्याः सुता-The daughter of a slave; a term of abuse. III 10. 16. त्वं...योग्यतया नियुक्ता-You have been appointed by your fitness (योग्यतया). Mr. Pandit interprets it in an different way thus:—" You are now invested with an equality with the Queen (देव्याः योग्यतया); you are now made an equal of धारिणी; or you have been appointed to do a work fit to be done by a queen." III. 10. 20. हृदय...सुखिततया-Do not feel happy, do not flatter yourself with the happy position etc. She means that she cannot forget that she is after all a slave. The present glory is but momentary and, who knows, may serve as the last. मृत्युमण्डनं-The funeral decoration. Married women who die before their husbands or even virgins are decorated before their body is removed to the funeral pyre. She means that the unrequited love will surely cause her death, aud in that case no additional decoration will be necessary for her! III. 10. 30. हला मर्षयेदानीम्-Now pardon me To all appearances मालविका was a maid-servant and therefore on an equal footing with बकुलावलिका. She has no right to claim such services from her and therefore asks her forgiveness for this impropriety on her part.

III, 11. सरसां रागरेखाम्-The wet streak of the paint. प्रथमा...द्रुमस्य-The tree of love was consumed to ashes by God Śiva. It has however revived now, and the lines of the paint appear to be the first sprouts of that tree. मदन or the God of love was burnt by the wrath of Śivā, when he first tried to infuse in his mind feelings of love for पार्वती. The third canto of कुमारसंभव gives a beautiful description of this incident. III. 11. 2. अधिकारः (उपक्षिप्तः) The duty has been assigned. V. L. अलंकारः (उपाक्षिप्तः)-which would mean 'quite a fitting decoration (of the paint and anklets) has been laid on the foot of this lady (तत्रभवत्याः) i. e. मालविका.'

III. 12. The king observes, in his romantic fervour, that she deserves to kick two things with such a beautiful foot—the Asoka tree and her lover who has given her a fresh offence. अग्रपाद-like अपरस्त, it would mean 'the fore-part i. e. the toes of the foot.' स्फुरितकलकला

with a flashing lustre of the nails. प्रणिहितशिरसम्-with a bowed head, with his head placed at the feet of his mistress. आर्द्रापराधम्-whose offence is wet i. e. fresh or recent. The offence generally consists of infidelity on his part, as he is observed turning his eyes on to another girl; and the punishment meted out to him is a straight kick from his beloved, which he accepts ungrudgingly, nay, for which he seems to be longing in a way. Cf. एकः सख्यास्तव सह मया वामपादाभिलाषी । मे० II. 8. III. 12. पारयिष्यसि-You will be able (to offend her and get a kick in return). What he means is that very soon मालविका will be enlisted as his beloved with whom he will play the gallant. The sentence is read differently by some thus :—प्रहरिष्यति तत्रभवती त्वामपराद्धम् । 'Very soon she will strike you also, (after she has finished with the Aśoka).' III. 12. 3 सिद्धिदर्शिनः—One who foresees success. Cf. प्रातिगृहीतं ब्राणवचह्मनम् ॥ विक्र० II

III. 12. 4. युक्तमदा-In a state of intoxication. The introduction of इरावती in such a condition coupled with her youthful exuberance, explains her insolent behaviour with the king. III. 12. 7. शृणोमि...मण्डनम्--This youthful intoxication is a feature that lends special charm to women. Cf. नयनान्यरुणानि घूर्णयन् वचनानि स्खलयन् पदे पदे । असति त्वयि वारुणीमदः प्रमदानामधुना विडम्बना ॥ कुमा० IV.12. III,12. 10. प्रथमं...संवृत्तः-'Popular sayings or maxims very often have little truth in them. This saying, however, has become true because of you. The state of intoxication has really lent you a peculiar charm.' III. 12. 11 अलं मयि स्नेहेन-Cf.

सोहार्दमेवं पश्यति. । III. 12. 14. अखाण्डितात् प्रणयात्--Because of unfailing love (for my mistress). She means that the king loves her so much that he would never fail to keep this engagement. III. 12. 16 अलं सेवया...भण–Enough of this flattery. (सेवया Lit. servile attitude); speak with an impartial attitude (मध्यस्थता). III. 12. 19 वसन्तोपायनलोलुप-Greedy to receive the gifts of spring. III. 12. 30 परिहासनिमित्तम. To make fun of us; for the sake of joke. III. 12. 36. चूता...दंष्टम्–while searching for the king, निपुणिका has sighted मालविका being decorated by बकुलावलिका. Such a sight was most unpleasant and was very much like the biting of ants (पिपीलिका) for one who is up on the tree to find out a mango-sprout. पिपीलिका' The red ants living on trees. They are known in Konkan by the name of हुमले. The mango-tree is a very favourite abode of them. They configure its leaves into hollow globular nests for them'–Pandit. The sentence could be interpreted in a different way also. The Prakrit expression is दंसिदं which would gererally be translated by the Sanskrit word दार्शितं । the sentence would be–चूताङ्कुरं विचिन्वत्योरावयोः पिपीलिकाभिः दार्शितम् or as some Mss. read पिपीलिकादर्शनम्. It would then mean ' We see the red ants as we are in search of the mango-sprouts. The red ants are a sure indication of the existence of the mango-sprout in the vicinity, as smoke is that of fire. Similarly, since मालविका is here with बकुलावलिका, the king also must be nearby.' King's fondness for मालविका was an open scandal, being talked about by the inmates of the harem. इरावती also knows it, as she says later आशङ्कितस्य तावदन्तं गमिष्यामि ।. III. 12. 42. अभूमिरियं मालविकायाः–' A maid like मालविका cannot have access to this garden meant for the queens. This is therefore not a proper place (अभूमि) for her to be in! Cf. अभूमिरियमविनयस्य । शा० VII. We cannot however believe that even maids like मालविका were prohibited from entering into the प्रमदवन. If निपुणिका can come, why not मालविका ? In the प्रवेशक at the beginning of this Act, the maid of परिव्राजिका moves about in the garden unrestricted. A better way of interpreting this sentence would be this :– ' This is certainly not the proper role for मालविका to play. Being waited upon by बकुलावलिका who has decorated her feet and dressed her as befits a queen, मालविका is thus transcending all bounds proper to a maid-servant, and playing the part of a queen, which is highly improper tor her (अभूमि)." III. 12. 49. संभावना–Honour. Some Mss. read 'महती खलु मे संभावना ' It is a great honour done to *me* indeed ! ' said, of course, ironically. इरावती means that the queen धारिणी has shown the greatest disrespect to her in asking her maid-servant to play her role, instead of asking her, the queen's equal, to play that part. In her jealousy, The queen has shown to इरावती great disrespect. III. 12. 57. स्थाने...हृदयम्–She has observed the charming figure of मालविका and then said this sentence. ' It is but proper that my heart is filled with fear. The king certainly will desert me for the sake of such a girl.' III. 12. 60. चरण...विन्यासः–The drawing of the different lines of the red paint on the foot. III. 12. 62. आत्मन... प्रशंसितुम्. I feel so awkward to appreciate your skill, just because you have exhibited that on *my* foot. I am afraid it would appear I am praising my own foot and not your skill.

III. 12. 66. त्वरस्वे...दक्षिणायै–'Be quick now to receive your reward as a teacher. 'बकुलावलिका has made you her teacher in this art; and very soon she would gratify you, her teacher, with the nice present (दक्षिणा) of मालविका ! ' It can be interpreted in another way also, as a remark of विदूषक in answer to the ingenious invention of बकुलावालिका in representing the king to मालविका as her teacher. ' Well then, if that is the case, make haste to repay the obligation by giving him his due reward. Be quick to give your teacher his reward. " III. 12. 67. दिष्टया...–सि–' It is so good of you that you have not the slightest conceit; you are prepared to give the credit where it is due. ' This indicates her regard and love for the king. III. 12. 74. सिद्धं मे दौत्यम्– I have succeeded in my mission ! मालविका has clearly indicated how she feels for the king, and the way has been paved now for success in my enterprise as love-messenger. She is a soft soil, and I can hope to get immediate success. ' III. 12. 75. मुखमारुतो लम्भयितव्यः– It ought to be dried by blowing on it the wind from the mouth (मुखमारुत). प्रवातः–प्रकृष्ठ वातः यस्मिन् सः—Windy, having a good breeze.

III. 13. The king says that a very nice opportunity has come now to offer his first services of love to मालविका, viz. helping her foot to dry up by blowing on it the wind from the mouth, and he is sorry that he cannot avail himself of it. प्रथमतरः सेवावकाशः—An excellent (प्रथमतर) occasion for doing service. III. 13. 1. अनुशयः-Regret, remorse, grief. चिरं......वितव्यम् You need not be sorry for having lost this opportunity. You will get many such occasions in course of time. III. 13. 4. अरुणशतपत्रम् A red lotus having hundred petals. अंकपरिवर्तिनी-Rolling about on the lap. Note the clever and bold way in which बकुलावलिका works up the mind of मालविका in favour of the king. III. 13. 6. इरावती......प्रवेक्षते-इरावती looks at निपुणिका, with a feeling of surprise at such a bold blessing of बकुलावालिका, and also with a view to indicate that their suspicion proved correct. III. 13. 8. अवचनीयं मन्त्रयसे-You speak absurd things which you ought not to say (अवचनीय). Cf. युवामपेतम् । किमपि हृदये कृत्वा मन्त्रयेथे ।...... also इमामसंबद्धप्रलापिनीं प्रियंवदामार्यायै गौतम्यै निवेदयामि । शा॰I. III. 13. 12. प्रिया......तव. We can also take it as a question. 'Do you love me ? ' III. 13. 15. गुणे......भर्तुरपि-The king also loves you, drawn towards you by your merits for which he has great attraction (आभिनिवेश). III. 13. 18. एतदेव मयि नास्ति-'I havent that in me i. e. the king's love. Surely I know the king loves me not.' एतत् may also refer to merits. I have'nt that i. e. merit in me. मालविका says this to draw out बकुलावलिका who, she thinks, is expected to know more of the king, being his pupil and thus coming into closer contact with him. III.

13. 20. सत्यं.........दृश्यते-' you have'nt that indeed ! '.—this she says a bit ironically. She means ' who would believe that you have not the king's love ? It is fully betrayed by the thin and pale limbs of the king.' Cf. ननु भणितमेव कमलनालायमानैरङ्गैः विक्र० II. III. 13. 22. प्रथमगणित-Considered or thought well beforehand. हताशा-Lit. a disappointed creature. It is a term of abuse in the sense of ' Accursed, wretch,' approaching the Marathi expression 'मेली' III. 13. 25. अनु...कुरु-'And now follow the authoritative dictates of the wise in this matter—Love should be tested by love.' If you have any doubts as to what I have said about the king, you can realise that for yourself ; if you express your love to him you will soon find that your love is responded by him. III. 13. 27. आत्मनश्छन्देन-From your fancy or imagination. The king's love for me is your own invention and therefore not true. III. 13. 30. बिम्बान्तरितानि अक्षराणि—Words that are being echoed or exactly reproduced (by me). She means that what she has said in this matter is an echo of whatever the king has spoken ; it is not her invention. बकुलावलिका has thus clearly hinted that she speaks under instructions from the king whose message of love she is communicating. III. 13. 33. देवीं ...विश्वासिति-मालविका feels convinced of the king's love, but then there is the insurmountable difficulty of the Queen, which fills her heart with diffidence in any love's enterprise that she would undertake. III. 13. 35. भ्रमर...तंसनीयः-She means that the fear of the queen should not deter मालविका from loving the king. There may be some

risk, but nobody leaves off the pursuit of one's cherished object because of such threatening dangers. भ्रमरसंबाध-' The swarm of bees; or the dread of bees' अवतंसनीयः-Should be put on as an ear-ornament (अवतंस) Pot. Part. from अवतंसय्-A denom. from अवतंस; Cf. अवतंसयन्ति दयमानाः प्रमदाः शिरीषकुसुमानि। शा० I. 3. III. 38. त्वं...भव 'If any calamity befalls me in this enterprise, at least you will help me through.' मालविका has consented to respond to the king's love, and hence she appeals to her to help her in the perilous situation, if any would develop later. दुर्जातं-Peril, calamity; cf. मम सुरारिसंभवे दुर्जाते महाराज एव शरणमासीत्। विक्र० II. III. 13. 39.विमर्दसुरभि.-Fragrant when crushed (विमर्द). She puns on the word बकुलावलिका i. e. a garland of बकुल flowers which would emit greater fragrance when crushed. Similarly she says that मालविका would find her at her best when she is faced with danger or calamity.

III. 14. The king admires the skilful way in which बकुलावलिका has tried to win over मालविका to her purpose. भाव...प्रस्तुतेन वाक्येन-the words (in the message of love) which बकुलावलिका began to speak (प्रस्तुत), after having ascertained her love for the king (भावज्ञान). प्रत्याख्याने...त्तरेण (वाक्येन)-while pleading she gave proper replies to meet the objections (प्रत्याख्यान) raised by मालविका. स्वे निदेशे स्थापिता thus was मालविका brought round or won over to her (बकुलावलिका) purpose; made firm in her own purpose. स्थाने...धीनाः-It is quite proper that a lover's life is in the hands of his love messenger.

Everything depends on her and the way in which she would manage the affair. The success is assured if the pleading is done skilfully. III. 14. 2कारि...विका-मालविका has already been induced to get access in him i. e. to yearn for him, to love him. She has already been made ready to embark on love's adventure. Cf. काम इदानीं सकामो भवतु येनासत्यसन्धे जने सखी पदं कारिता । शा० IV. III. 14. 5. निर्विकारस्यापि-Even of a person who is unaffected by passion निपुणिका tries to put the whole blame on बकुलावलिका who, says he, is encouraging innocent मालविका in this affair. III. 14. 7. स्थाने...हृदयम् 'My heart was rightly apprehensive. I don't think बकुलावलिका is solely responsible, मालविका also has a hand in the matter.' She is not so innocent; She thus refuses to accept निपुणिका's reading of मालविका. गृहीतार्था-Who has ascertained all facts. III. 14. 11. समाप्तपरिकर्मा-Whose decoration (परिकर्मन्) has finished. परिकर्मन्-Decoration, toilet, dressing. यावदेनं कृताचारपरिकर्माणं प्रेक्षे । शा० II. III. 14. 1L. श्रुतं...दानीम्-'So now it turns to be the queen's bidding. मालविका is not here of her own accord, but because the Queen धारिणी has sent her on some mission.' 'इरावती has been suspecting that धारिणी herself is at the bottom of the affair, and thinks that she is now satisfied that her suspicions are correct and that she wants to know no more.'—Pandit. III. 14. 17. एष...दृश्यते-This speech is so worded that it refers both to the bunch of sprouts of the Aśoka tree as also to the king. With reference to the king, it would mean 'Here is he, greatly enamoured or flushed with passion (उपारूढराग) and fit to enjoy—(उपभोगक्षमः)

III. 14. 18. किं भर्ता–The trick of बकुलावलिका has succeeded and मालविका who understands her remark with reference to the king, clearly declares her love for the king. III. I4. 23. पर्याप्त...कामिनाम्–This is quite enough (पर्याप्तं) for lovers. A lover is amply satisfied to know that his love is returned by his beloved. The actual union may or may not take place.

III. 15. अनातुरोत्कण्ठितयोः समागमेन–By the union of the two in which one of them is very eager while the other is indifferent (अनातुर). प्रसिध्यतापि–Even if it succeeds. The king means that he would feel no pleasure (रति) in a union in which one of the lovers is panting with love while the other is utterly indifferent. पर... रागयोः-On the other hand, requited mutual love cares not for the bodily union and would not mind even if death ensues through the despair of securing such a union. It is far better to die loving each other though not actually united rather than be wedded to one who is utterly indifferent. 'अकृतार्थेऽपि मनसिजे रतिमुभयप्रार्थना कुरुते' । शा० II. 1. समानुरागयोः—Whose love is equal.

III. 16. सदृशाविनिमयात्. Because of this mutal exchange of similar gifts. The Aśoka tree has given her a *red* sprout for an ear-ornament, while she in return gave him a kick of her *red* foot. The exchange of gifts is thus of like objects. आत्मानं वंचितं मन्ये—' Both of them have thus satisfied each other, while I stand looking on. I feel I am deceived in my love for the girl.' Cf. वयं

तत्वान्वेषान्मधुकर हतास्त्वं खलु कृती । शा० I. 20. III. 16.5. निर्गुणः-dull, unappreciative, devoid of the good qualities of a gentleman. कुसुमोद्भेदमन्थरः-Slow to put forth blossoms. III. 17. मुखरं...विणा-मुखरैः नूपुरैः आरौति-तच्छीलमस्य-तेन । loudly tinkling with the noisy or jingling anklets. ललितं साधारणं दोहदम्-A craving that is in common with that of the gallant lovers, who too cherish a kick from their beloved. ललितकामी is explained by Mr. Pendit as 'a person fond of the graceful actions of young women' स्त्रीविलसित-कामी, विलसनशीलः कामी वा ।. III. 17.1. वचनावसरपूर्वम्-'Creating an opportunity for speaking.' 'I should enter after such an occasion to speak has been created.' III. 17. 6 इदं...हृदयेन'-did anticipate that in my heart, I had already suspected the king to be hovering about on account of his love for this girl.' III. 17.13. त्वया गृहीतार्थया-you who know everything. III, 17.18. कथं...जीविष्यति-'How otherwise should this wretched Brahmin live? It is thus that he makes his living by pampering to the king's tastes and providing him with what he wants'. ब्रह्मबंधुः-A contemptuous term for a Brahmin; an unworthy Brahmin. Cf. the Marathi word भटुरगा. III. 17. 22. एन...यम् She has not acted independently on his own initiative in this transgression; she depends on another viz. the queen who has ordered her to do this. परवती—Depending on another. जाने तपसो वीर्यं सा बाला परवतीति मे विदितम् । शा० III. 1. भगवन् परवानयं जनः प्रतिकूलाचरितं क्षमस्व मे । रघु० VII. 81.

III. 18. Construe-विलासिनि वामोरु, किसलयमृदोः ते वामस्य

चरणस्य कठिने पादस्कन्धे निहितस्य संप्रति बाधा न? विलासिनी full of graces, charming, sportive. वामोरु-Oh one possessed of lovely thighs. III. 18. 3. अहो...पुत्रः-'How immodest is my lord!' The king's appearance on the scene, his raising her by her hands, and then such a question were too much for इरावती who saw in it nothing but his indecent flirting with the girl. There is another good reading नवनीतहृदयः 'Possessed of a heart as soft as butter;' in her caustic sarcasm she means, 'What a soft heart my lord has! It melts like butter at the sight of a tender foot kicking the hard stem of a tree, while totally forgetting the engagement he has given to me'! III. 18, 9. उपपन्नावसरं अर्थित्वम्-My request whose occasion has come.

III. 19. The king means that in his case also, as in that of the Aśoka, the flower of happiness has not bloomed. He too has a craving viz. the nectar of touch. Will she satisfy this longing, since he has no desire left for anything else now? धृतिपुष्पम्-The flower of pleasure or happiness. न बध्नाति-has not borne. चिरात् प्रभृति-for a long time. अनन्यरुचेः-न विद्यते अन्यस्मिन्-अन्यस्यां वा-रुचिः यस्य सः तस्य-Having a liking for nothing else or for no other woman. III. 19. 4. अयं...फलति च-He i. e. the king will not only flower but will also bear fruit. In the case of the Aśoka there is a doubt as to whether it will put forth even flowers. But if the king is satisfied by you in his craving, he will bear both the flowers and the fruit. As Pandit observes, this is certainly a coarse allusion to the fact that मालविका would bear children to the King and thus reap a greater advantage. ' The coarseness of the allusion is in keeping with the condition of इरावती, who is under the influence of wine.' III. 19. 7. जङ्घाबल-The strength of the legs ; taking to the heels. We must try the strength of our legs and vanish. III.19.10.साधु...न्तम्-' You are carrying on very well ;' she says this, of course, sarcastically,, as one would say in Marathi, वा! फार छान चालवलंय! III. 19. 13. के...हस्य-' Insignificant maids that we are, who are we to receive such a favour of love from the king ?' III.19.17. मया...विज्ञाता-I did not realise the deception (वंचना) that was being practised on me,being all the time unsuspicious (अशंकितया) like the deer charmed (रक्तया) by the hunter's song. The deer is believed to be very much fond of the hunter's whistle or music, with which he beguiles the innocent creature into a trap. Cf. व्याधानुसारचकिता हरिणीव यासि । मृच्छ० I. Cf. also the सुभाषितः-यस्य चाप्रियमन्विच्छेत् तस्य कुर्यात् सदा प्रियम् । व्याधा मृगवधं कर्तुं सम्यग्गायन्ति सुस्वरम् । Similarly, says इरावती, that she was being deceived by the king with false promises of love and engagements, while out here he was carrying on his flirtation with another girl. III. 19. 21. प्रतियोजय-Devise, plan. कर्म......भवति - If a thief is caught in the very act of thieving (कर्मगृहीतेन), the only plausible defence that he can submit is that he was there learning the art of cutting or digging holes in the wall (सन्धिच्छेदन). Cf. लोप्त्रेण गृहीतस्य

कुम्भीलकस्यास्ति वा प्रतिवचनम् । विक्र० III. विदूषक means, you have been caught now in the very act of flirting with मालविका, and you have therefore to give some sort of defence that will absolve you from the guilt of infidelity and prove you to be innocent. Like the thief who, caught red-handed, would say that he was only taking an academical interest in the art without any personal motive of actually committing the robbery, can you not also say that you have no personal interest in मालविका whom you chanced to meet and therefore tried to pass away your time in some light-hearted conversation with her ? III. 19. 23. अर्थः-Interest. आत्मा विनोदितः-I diverted or amused myself. III. 19. 27. विश्वसनीयोऽसि-'I should cartainly believe you ;' she says this of course, ironically. ईदृशं विनोदवस्तुकं-Such a means of amusement viz. मालविका. The repetition of विनोद is for the purpose of giving a sarcastic retort to the king's expression विनोदितः. अन्यथा...क्रियते-Had I known that you had such a nice means of amusing yourself, I would certainly not have done thus, unfortunate that I am : I would never have interrupted your amusement.' III. 19. 31. मा...भणतु-'Do not say anything that would repel his courtesy.' विदूषक means, 'The king is all along behaving with you with the utmost politeness. Remarks like these, however, will only provoke him unnecessarily and would drive off all courtesy from his mind.' उपरोधं-उपरोधकारकं वचनं-words calculated to put a stop to the considerations of courtesy. समा......प्रमाणम्-Mere matter-of-fact talk with the Queen's servant met accidentally can not be looked upon as a serious offence. Is it so? I ask you as the best judge in the matter?' संकथा talk, conversation. III. 19. 38. रशनासंदितचरणा-with her feet fettered or entangled (संदित) by the girdle (रशना). It had dropped down from her waist in her angry excited condition that caused hurried movements. III. 19 39. निरपेक्षता-utter disregard, indifference. III. 19. 40. शठः—A rogue, a cunning lover who affects his love for one lady while secretly loving another-गूढविप्रियकरः ।.

III. 20. परिचयवत्यवधीरणा-It could be interpreted in two different ways; (i) परिचयवती अवधीरणा-'The usual scorn.' The king says that he has often met with such treatment of utter disregard from her; it is not a new thing to him or to her. (ii) परिचयवति अवधीरणा-Disregard shown to a person who has been too familiar. 'Familiarily breeds contempt.' It is nothing unusual, therefore, if she behaves thus towards one who stands too intimately related to her. Such is not, however, the case of the girdle, which is prostrate at her feet for the first time. चरण etc. construe—चरणपतितया मेखलयापि याचिता, हे चण्डि, तां (अवधीरणां) न विसृजसि-The girdle is at your feet, pleading for mercy on my behalf. With a male companion, you could be rude; but not so with your female companion, the girdle (मेखला Fem.). Still, Oh angry one, you do not leave off your scornful attitude. चण्डी-A hot-tempered lady. Cf. चण्डी मामवधूय पादपतितं जातानुतापा यथा । It is also read by some as चाण्डितां-'Angry attitude,' to be construed with विसृजसि. III.20. 1. इय...सरति-'This wretched girldle also sides with you.' It too appeared to be working for the king, since it would not allow इरावती to leave the place quickly, but wanted to detain her with the king.

III. 21. इरावती in tears, striking the king with the golden girdle is compared to a row of showering clouds smiting the विन्ध्य peak with lightning. वाष्पासारा to be taken with both इरावती and मेघराजि ; आसार means 'a shower.' अव्यपेक्षाच्युतेन—dropping down unexpectedly or accidentally, चण्डं हन्तुं अभ्युद्यता-Prepared to strike me hard or cruelly (चण्डं). मेघराजि-Row of clouds. III. 21. 1. भूयोऽपि-Again, for a second time. Already before she had raised the girdle to strike him; See the stage-direction इति रशनामादाय राजानं ताडयितुमिच्छति । This was the second time.

III. 22. उद्यतं दण्डं किं संहरासि-Why should you take back (संहरासि) the whip (viz, girdle) raised against me ? वर्धयासि विलसितं-You increase your charms. इरावती, flushed red with anger, and ready to strike the king with the girdle, was a fascinating sight for the king. III. 22. 1. नून...तम्-' This will be now permitted. 'She would not now object to my falling prostrate at her feet, which form of conciliation, she will receive with favour, in her present mood.' III. 22. 4. स्पर्शदोहदं पूरयिष्यतः-which will fulfil your craving for the touch. It is a sarcastic reference to what the king had demanded of मालविका-'स्पर्शामृतेन पूरय दोहदमस्याप्यनन्यरुचेः । III. 19. III. 22. 5. उत्तिष्ठ कृतप्रसादोऽसि-विदूषक says jokingly. 'The favour has been shown to you,' that is she has made her exit, and thus removed the source of disturbance! III. 22. 10. देवै... नियंत्रणा-इरावती served as a great check in his affair with मालविका. Somehow she has departed, and it is therefore a matter for rejoicing. The gods have shown us a great favour in removing this great obstacle in the way of your improper relations (अविनयस्य) with मालविका. Mr. Pandit reads differently thus-दिष्ट्या अस्याविनयस्य अप्रसादिता गता. "It is good that इरावती has erred by going away unreconciled and has thereby furnished the king with an excuse for paying his court to मालविका; if she had not done so, it would have been so very difficult to disregard a loving and unoffending wife as इरावती." Pandit. This also is a good interpretation. Even though the king's motto is-न हि कमलिनीं दृष्ट्वा ग्राहमवेक्षते मतंगजः, he can now pursue the object of his love without feeling the qualms of conscience regarding इरावती, as in her case he had done everything he could reasonably do to reconcile her. She has spurned his prostration and thus lost some moral advantage in her favour, and weakened her case. A feeling of repentence comes over then, and the woman tries to conciliate her lord Cf. अवधूतप्रणिपाताः पश्चात् संतप्यमानमनसोऽपि। निभृतैर्व्यपत्रपन्ते दयितानुनयैर्मनस्विन्यः॥ विक्र० III. 5. For a similar remark of विदूषक Cf. अनुकूलमत्रभवत एतत्। न खल्वक्षिदुःखितः अभिमुखे दीपशिखां सहते। विक्र० II. III. 22. 9. साव...करोति--before she comes back like the planet Mars (अंगारक) retrogressing to his mansion (राशि) in the Zodiac. 'In certain positions planets are said to look towards you and in others to turn away from you. When they have turned their back on you, they are said to be unfavourable, and when they are looking towards you, they are favourable. Mars is the only exception, because when it returns and looks you in the face, it is unfavourable. In the present instance, इरावती who has gone unreconciled and and turned her back upon the king is more favourable to the king's paying his attentions to मालविका, than she would be if she were to return and be reconciled, as that would make it difficult to disregard her.' III. 22. 13. मनसिजवैषम्यम्–The perversity or inconsistency of love.

III. 23. The king means that in his present condition of the mind which has been solely captured by मालविका, इरावती's spurning of his prostration is a definite service rendered to him by her; for even though she loves him, she has departed in anger. He can therefore safely ignore her for the time being. प्रणिपातलङ्घनं–The slighting of the prostration. एवं etc. Construe–मयि प्रणयवती (अपि) एवं कुपिता सा उपेक्षितुं शक्यम् ।. 'It is possible to connive at or neglect her though full of love for me, since she is in such an angry mood.' Cf. किं तु प्राणिपातलंघनादहमस्यां धैर्यमवलम्बिष्ये । विक्र० II. The perversity of love lies in the fact that he feels like ignoring the one who loves him ardently while the one towards whom he is drawn is away at a distance and almost inaccessible to him. The translation has been given with the following reading—एवं प्रणयवती सा नहि शक्यमुपेक्षितुं कुपिता ।

ACT IV.

IV. 1. The king enters in a love-sick state all the time thinking of मालविका and brooding over the possibility of his being able to taste the pleasures of love in his union with her. His love he compares to a tree which first strikes the root, then puts forth a shoot, then blossoms and lastly yields the delicious fruit. Similarly the feeling of love for मालविका was rooted in his heart when he first heard of her and felt interested in her. When he saw her, love appeared to have put forth the shoot of passion. The touch of her hands sent a thrill of horripilation through his body, a veritable blossoming, as it were, of this feeling. Will he be lucky now in tasting the joys of love, as one would the delicious flavour of the fruit? श्रुतिपथगतां तामाश्रित्य- 'Resorting to her who came to my ears i. e when I merely heard of her, as the tree gets planted in the soil.' मालविका represents the soil. श्रुतिपथगतां तां भूमिं वृक्ष इव ।. आस्था-Interest, attachment. रूढरागप्रवाल:-रूढः राग एव प्रवालः यस्य सः. The tree whose sprout of passion was put forth. मुकुलितः–मुकुलानि संजातानि अस्य-with the buds produced on the tree; for a similar idea in this line, Cf. स्पृष्टः सरोमविक्रियमङ्कुरितं मनसिजेनेव ॥ विक्र० I. 11. व्यक्त...त्वात् With the horripilation (i. e. the hair standing on their ends) becoming manifest (at the touch). कुर्या...फलस्य- Construe–मनसिजतरुः क्लान्तं मां फलस्य रसज्ञं कुर्यात् किम् ! 'I feel now weary (क्लान्त) at heart; will this tree of love enable me to taste the flavour of its fruit? रसज्ञः–रसं

जानात्यसौ—Who knows i. e. tastes the flavour. Some read कान्तं for क्लान्तं, meaning 'a lover.'

IV. 1. 6. सरुजचरणत्वात्–Because of her aching feet. IV. 1. 11. यो...काया–मालविका fares now as does a cuckoo seized by a cat, which means she is now ruined once for all. IV. 1. 16. पिङ्गलाक्षी–The queen having eyes, which turn to reddish-brown colour under the influence of wrath. सारभाण्डभूमिगृहे–In an under-ground cellar where all precious valuables or treasures (सारभाण्ड) are stored. It is a veritable death-trap for her. IV. 1. 17. मत्संपर्कम्–My contact; meeting me. IV. 1. 10. विमुखः अस्माकम् Averse to us, opposed or ill-disposed towards us. IV. 1. 23. विहस्त–Lit. Handless, i. e. disabled, incapacited, made powerless. Cf. रामापरित्राणविहस्तयोधं सेनानिवेशं तुमुलं चकार। रघु० V. 49. सुखपृच्छिका–सुखं पृच्छतीति–Inquiring after health. IV. 1. 28. किं...जन इति–'Have you lately seen the loved person i. e. the king'? Mr. Pandit who has the same reading, interprets it thus, 'Why have I not seen the beloved one i. e. you, इरावती ?' The Commentator काटयवेम reads differently–किं नु नावलोकितो वल्लभजनः । VI. 1. 29. कुतो...पृच्छसीति–' Why this formal questioning, when you know full well, how far your servant i. e. myself enjoys the king's love'? She means that धारिणी ought to know that the king does no more care for इरावती; her question therefore proceeds from mere formality and possibly smacks of some sarcasm also. Another way in which it is interpreted, "Why this formal courtesy, knowing full well that the title of the 'beloved one' belongs now to your servant i. e. मालविका ?" Mr. Pandit reads-मदो वा उपचारो वा । यत्ते पारिजनस्य वल्लभत्वं जानत्यपि पृच्छसीति—' This is either an affront (मदः lit. arrogance) or an empty form, since you ask the question, knowing that the belovedness belongs to your maid-servant.' IV. 1. 30. निर्भेदाद् ऋते-Without distinct or direct mention. ' without a giving out (निस्) of the name of मालविका.' उपन्यासः-Suggestion, reference. Cf. पावकः खलु एष वचनोपन्यासः । शा० V. IV. 1. 33. अनुबध्यमाना-Being importuned or asked again and again, being pressed. भवतो...कृता-The Queen was made acquainted i. e. informed about (अन्तरेण) your indiscretion (अविनय). IV. 1. 35. दीर्घरोषता—Long-continued, persistent anger. IV. 1. 39. निगलवत्यौ-chained in fetters. अदृष्ट...भवतः-They are enjoying their residence in the nether world where the sun's rays (पाद) are not visible, as if they were two snake-maidens (नागकन्यके). The पाताल or nether world is supposed to be inhabited by the नागs or snakes whose maidens are belived to be very beautiful.

IV. 2. विबुद्धचूतसाङ्गिन्यै-Clinging to the full-bloomed (विबुद्ध) mango-blossom. प्रबलपुरोवातया अकालवृष्ट्या-By an untimely shower preceded by (पुरस्) a strong gale. पुरोवात is understood by some to mean 'the front or the opposing wind.' कोटरं गमिते-are driven to the hollow of a tree (कोटरं) बकुलावालिका, the love-messenger, is compared to a cuckoo whom the Sanskrit poets style as Cupid's messenger; Cf. त्वां कामिनो मदनदूतिमुदाहरन्ति । वि० IV. 11; and मालविका is made to resemble the female bee. The king represents the mango tree while the hollow is the cellar. Thus the metaphor is complete.

IV. 2. 1. उपक्रमस्य गतिः-Scope for some plan or stratgem IV. 2. 5. मम.....मोक्तव्या-Prof. Tawney remarks on this, ' It is clear that the head queen exercised in some departments an amount of authority that would have de lighted the soul of Mr. J. S. Mill. ' IV. 2. 12. कर्णे ते कथयामि-A similar devise as in the I Act is introduced here, and the plan speaks highly of the inventive brain of the विदूषक. IV. 2. 16. रक्तचन्दनधारिणा-smeared with the red sandal paste. This application was to serve as an embrocation to the foot. The other reading रक्तचन्दनवारिणा is interpreted as ' an oil of red sandal wood.' IV. 2.22. जयसेना...गच्छ-the king asks विदूषक to take his female attendant जयसेना also into confidence. She has observed the विदूषक whispering some secret in the king's ears and hence this precaution. Her assistance was also necessary for putting into practice the dodge for bringing the Queen's ring to liberate मालविका and her friend बकुलावलिका. IV. 2. 33. उपचारयन्त्रणा-the restraint imposed by the conventional formality; the worry of the etiquette.

IV. 3. अनुचितनूपुरविरहं (चरणं)-अनुचितः नूपुरैः विरहः यस्य-The foot whose separation of the anklets is unusual, unaccustomed to leave off the anklets, which were removed because of the paining foot. कलभाषिणि-Talking in a sweet voice; Cf. मां वा नयाशु कलभाषिणि यत्र कान्ता । विक्र० IV. 11. IV. 3. 4. अस्ति मे विशेषः-There is a definite change for the better. The same expression occurs in शा० III. IV. 3 5. यज्ञोपवीतबद्धाङ्गुष्ठः-with his thumb tied up by the sacred thread. यज्ञोपवीतं-the sacred thread worn over the left shoulder and under the right arm ; originally it was the ceremony of investiture with the sacred thread. the विदूषक resorts to this first aid with a view apparently to stop the circulation of the poison of the snake by which he pretends to be bitten. संभ्रान्तः-Excited, agitated. IV. 3. 11. आचा...णात्-for the purpose of collecting flowers for a customary offering. Such an offering is given to the deities or to great persons when one visits them. Cf. अवाकिरन् बाललताः प्रसूनैराचारलाजैरिव पौरकन्याः । रघु० II. 10. विदूषक had already provided for his pretence when he said just before that he would find some present for the Queen whom he was visiting shortly Cf. अहमपि देवीं द्रष्टुमरिक्तपाणिर्भविष्यामि ।. He refers to it again in this sentence (देवीं द्रक्ष्यामि) with a view to make out that he has risked his life for the Queen who in a way is thus responsible for this disaster. IV. 3 13. जीवितसंशयनिमित्तं-The cause of danger (संशय) to his life. IV. 3. 19 द्वे दन्तपदे-The two marks of its fangs. These were in reality the pricks purposely caused by means of the pointed tips of the केतक plant. Observe how cleverly the विदूषक has arranged for the whole make-up.

IV. 4. दंशच्छेदः-Excision of the bitten part, amputation. क्षतेः रक्तमोक्षणम्-Bleeding the wound, taking off the blood from the wound (क्षतिः). दष्टमात्राणां-Immediately after they are bitten. आयुषः प्रतिपत्तयः-Remedies

(प्रतिपत्ति) to save the life. Cf. प्रतिकारविधानमायुषः सति शेषे हि फलाय अल्पते। रघु० VIII. The remedies have been suggested by परिव्राजिका, because as Mr. Pandit says, धारिणी should not suspect her. For we can suppose that the विदूषक must have settled his plan in consultation with the परिव्राजिका, before she went to the Queen and he came over to see the king. Her presence with the Queen was necessary, as in the first Act, for the purpose of removing any suspicion of her hand in the matter and also to help विदूषक in inducing the Queen to part with her ring. 'It is also intended to give her a character for learning and knowledge of medicine.' The remedies referred to here are found mentioned in the medicine manuals of authors like वाग्भट and others. The वैद्यचंद्रोदय mentions the following in this connection—आदौ तु स्रावयेद् रक्तं छित्वा शस्त्रेण दंशतः। बहिर्वेगीकृते रक्ते विषं तस्माद्विनश्यति ॥. IV. 4. 8. सिमसिमायन्ति—Tingle with pain. This is an onomatopoetic or imitative verb, expressive of a tremulous and aching sensation, probably convulsive. The corresponding Marathi form शिवशिवतात comes from this Prakrit word. IV.4.11. अशुभं...विकारेण. The trouble (of the snake-bit) has taken a bad turn, seems to prove fatal. योगक्षेमं वह–Look after the welfare. योग means 'a fresh acquision of things not obtained already'; while क्षेम is 'the preservation of what has been acquired.' योगश्च क्षेमश्च योगक्षेमम्। Cf. तेषां नित्याभियुक्तानां योगक्षेमं वहाम्यहम्। भग० IX. 22. The Prakrit word अविआरेण may be translated into Sanskrit in two ways:-(i) अविचारेण–' without hesitation' or (ii) अविकारेण–Without any change (in behaviour). IV. 4. 17. चिकित्सते— treats you, cures you. IV. 4. 19. ध्रुव......गौतमः—It is necessary that विदूषक must leave to effect the release of मालविका and बकुलावलिका from the prison. Having, therefore, arranged the plan, either he or the परिव्राजिका must have spoken about it to the king's physician before coming to the garden. IV. 4. 21. वर्षवर–a eunuch, an attendant in the women's apartments. वर्षधर or वर्षधर्ष also means the same thing. IV. 4. 28. यथार्थनाम्नः of one whose name is significant or true to its sense. The name ध्रुवसिद्धि of the surgeon meant 'one who gets a sure success, an infallible doctor.' IV. 4. 32. उद......कल्पयितव्यम्-For performing the magic rite of उदकुम्भविधान, something bearing a serpent-seal (सर्पमुद्रितं) has to be utilised. The उदकुंभविधान rite has been mentioned in works like the भैरवतंत्र as a magic remedy against serpent-bites. A jar is filled with water and certain Mantras are repeated. The enchanted water is then sprinkled over the part bitten by a snake, repeating the same Mantras again. It is assured that the poison of the deadliest serpent is thus counteracted. The reading उदकुंभपिधाने means 'for the purposing of covering the jar.'

IV. 4. 37. कर्मसिद्धौ–When the treatment has proved successful ; कर्म refers to the treatment of the doctor; Cf. संप्रति विषवैद्यानां कर्म ।, प्रतिपत्तिः–' News,information. The same sentence occurs in मुद्रा० IV. Cf. also कियच्चिरेणार्यपुत्रः प्रतिपत्तिं दास्यतीति । शा० VI. It may also be taken as a hint to

जयसेना to tell the king when the plot has succeeded and मालविका has been released. IV. 4. 40 यथा...निर्विषो गौतमः— The परिव्राजिका puts on an air of one who is thoroughly ignorant of the plot and makes this remark which bears these different interpretations. (i) 'As my heart tells me, गौतम is by now cured of the poison, or (ii) गौतम has been bitten by a non-poisonous snake.' To the king she suggests 'the snake-bite is a hoax and गौतम is simply pretending the effects of poison of which he has nothing.' IV. 4. 43. प्रकृतिस्थः–प्रकृतौ तिष्ठति सः-came back to the normal, his usual self or his natural condition. IV. 4. 45. वचनीयात्-From the censure or blame of having been indirectly responsible for the death of the poor Brahmin! IV. 4. 49. एष...विज्ञापयति–This is again another falsehood invented to enable the king to leave धारिणी immediately without rousing her suspicion. Note how the innocent soft-hearted Queen is being successfully duped by a pack of scoundrels around her ! IV. 4. 52. आतपाक्रान्तः–Full of the sun's heat. शीत...प्रशस्ता–A cooling remedy (शीतक्रिया) is to be preferred for this i.e. for your aching foot. The king affects a deep concern for the Queen that she may be lulled into an unsuspicious mental slumber.

IV. 5. एकान्तसाधु–Absolutely good. सन्दिग्धं–doubtful. diffident P, P. of √सम् + दिह्. The king feels doubtful whether विदूषक would succeed in releasing मालविका. IV.5. 1. सर्वमङ्गलकर्माणि–' All auspicious ceremonies, ' referring humorously to the very undertakings like the release of मालविका and the bringing about of another meeting between the two. IV. 5. 6. क्षुद्रा–Insignificant, worthless, dull-headed. IV. 5. 13. प्रत्युत्पन्नबुद्धिः–Ready-witted; also प्रत्युत्पन्नमतिः।. IV. 5. 17. दैवचिन्तकः–An astrologer. दैवं चिन्तयति सः।. सोपसर्गम्–Calculated to give trouble, having a malignant influence. सर्व...क्रियताम्–All prisoners are to be let off for the purpose of appeasing the evil star. IV. 5. 22. तच्छुत्वा...स्मीति–It was at the instance of इरावती that the two girls were imprisoned. Now, says, विदूषक to माधविका, if the Queen taking advantage of this opportunity of wholesale release, would liberate मालविका and बकुलावलिका also, इरावती would feel greatly displeased. The Queen therefore does not want to take that odium on herself, but wants to represent that the king gave direct orders for their release, and hence she i. e. धारिणी has dispatched me to to the prison-house with this ring.' चित्तं रक्षन्त्या–With a view to spare the feelings of इरावती and keep her pleased.

IV. 6. Mere intelligence is not enough. It must have an element of deep love for the friend, to goad it on and invent the subtle means of ensuring success in a friend's undertaking. The king means that because विदूषक loves him so much, therefore he is able to work thus in a subtle matter to accomplish his purpose. अर्थदर्शनम्—Visualising of the means to promote a friend's interest. सूक्ष्मः कार्यसिद्धिपथः–The subtle or the narrow path leading to succes in an undertaking. IV. 6. 2. समुद्रगृहकं–A summer-house built in the midst of water; an ocean-pavilion; so called from some ponds of water being attached to it, what we might call in Marathi जलमंदिर. IV. 6. 7. कुसु...हस्ता–with her hands busy in gathering flowers. IV.6.11. विदूषक puns on the name चंद्रिका of the attendant. 'Yes, we must avoid this maid-servant चंद्रिका. The moon-light (चंद्रिका) has to be avoided by thieves and lovers who have to work unseen.' IV. 6. 16. ते सखी–The king always refers to मालविका, while speaking to विदूषक, as 'Your friend.' Cf. जाने सख्यास्तव मयि मनः संभृतस्नेहं...। मे॰ II. 27. IV. 6. 20. प्रणम भर्तारम्–In the समुद्रगृहक was a picture of the king and his many wives. The king was portrayed as gazing at the face of इरावती, as will be clear from the later remarks. बकुला॰ refers to the picture; but she is purposely vague in order that she may enjoy herself a little at her friend's expense. IV. 6. 24. विप्रलंभयासि मां–you deceive me. मालविका did not notice the picture first and thought that the king had arrived. Hence her joy followed by disappointment when she could not see him at the door.

IV. 7. The पुण्डरीक or the white day-lotus blooms at sun-rise and closes its petals at sun-set. The face of मालविका also beamed with joy to hear that the king had come, but wore immediately a sad look of disappointment when she did not find him there. समवस्थे क्षणात् ऊढे–Within one moment she presented both the conditions of the lotus. IV. 7. 6. तदाहं...भर्ता–She means 'that when she met the king for the first time near the Aśoka tree, she could not satisfy herself by having a full look of him; various reasons like maidenly bashfulness, excitement of the occasion and the sudden interruption of इरावती deprived her of the pleasure of observing the king to her heart's content. But in this place she could see him in the picture uninterrupted and she feels now fully satisfied. Mr. Pandit completes the first sentence after अद्य, and reads the next sentence विभावितश्चित्रगतदर्शनो भर्ता as a separate one. न वितृष्णास्मि. My thirst for his sight was not quenched; I did not feel satisfied. IV. 7. 11. मञ्जूषा–A casket, a treasure-box. विदूषक purposely puts a different construction on this sentence to ridicule the king and remarks, ' See what मालविका says. In vain do you think yourself handsome. You did not appear to her half so charming while bodily present as you do in the picture. And yet you are proud of your personal charms which are not at all striking on the exterior. It is the pride of a casket or a box which contains the charming jewels inside, while the exterior of it is all dull and unimpressive.' IV. 7. 13. निसर्गशालीनः–modest or bashful by nature (निसर्ग). Cf. निसर्गादेवाप्रगल्भस्तपस्विकन्याजनः । शा० II. The word शालीन is generally explained as शालाप्रवेशमर्हतीति—one who is fit to enter an apartment of a house i. e. well-behaved, shy.

IV. 8. The particles च...च mean ' though...yet.' कार्त्स्न्येन...समागतानाम्. Although women desire to observe in full or completely (कार्त्स्न्येन) the features of their (lovers) whom they meet for the very first time (तत्पूर्व-

समागतानाम्-तदेव पूर्वं यस्मिन् कर्मणि यथा तथा समागतानां). न च...विलोचनानि-yet broad as their eyes are, they do not fall fully (न समग्रपातीनि) on their lovers. Their eyes are not directed full in the face but are half-averted or cast down through shyness. There is विरोधाभास between आयतलोचनानां and न समग्रपातीनि. Cf. अभिमुखे मयि संहृतमीक्षणम् । शा० II. 11. also विवृण्वती शैलसुतापि भावमङ्गैः स्फुरद्बालकदम्बकल्पैः । साचीकृता चारुतरेण तस्थौ मुखेन पर्यस्तविलोचनेन ॥ कुमा० III. 68. IV. 8. बद्धलक्ष्यः-बद्धं लक्ष्यं येन सः-who has fixed his gaze on the face. मालविका, while observing the picture minutely, gradually transformed herself into the atmosphere and the scene of the picture and has begun to think that the king with his many wives was actually present. In the picture, of course, the king would be constantly looking at इरावती. In an atmosphere of reality, however, she thought it rather strange of the king and hence her remark. We have such a devise in the शाकुंतल also, where in the VI Act the king forgets that he is observing a picture of शकुंतला and begins addressing her and the bee hovering about her. IV. 8. 11. परमार्थे-In reality, as present actually and not in a picture. क्रीडिष्यामि एतया-I'll make fun of her.

IV. 9. भ्रूभङ्गाभिन्नतिलकं (आननं)—भ्रूभङ्गैः भिन्नः तिलकः यस्मिन्-The face on which the saffron mark on the forehead was broken i. e. disfigured by the knitting of eyebrows. स्फुरिताधरोष्ठं (आननं) The face the lower lip of which was throbbing in anger. The two expressions may be taken as adverbial phrases going with परावर्तयन्त्या. कान्ता etc. Construe :—कान्ता...कुपितेषु ललिताभिनयस्य विनेतुः शिक्षा अनया संदर्शितेव । She gave an exhibition, as it were, of her teacher's lesson in graceful acting appropriate in fits of anger caused by the faults of a lover. IV. 9. 1. अनुनयः-Conciliation, propitiation. He means that the king as her lover, should step forth now to conciliate her. IV. 9. 4. आर्ये...एनम्-The king has two sources of distraction One is इरावती whom she can hope to supercede and the other, this विदूषक who rarely left the king alone. She feels jealousy even for विदूषक and hence she turns in another direction pettishly. अत्रैव i. e. near the king. IV. 9. 8. प्रत्यानीयते i. e. त्यज्यते-Is left off, abandoned.

IV. 9. चित्रार्पितचेष्टया. at an action (चेष्टा) shown in a picture. किमेवमयि should be split up as किं एवं अयि. If we split it up as किं एव मयि, then the verbal form of √कुप्, which generally governs the dative, will have to be construed with the locative. अनन्यसाधारणः-Not claimed by any one else, not common (साधारण) to others, devoted to none else. IV. 10. 4. कातर्य-Nervousness, distraction. IV. 10. 5. उदासीनः-Indifferent, apathetic, unconcerned. IV. 10. 8. अत्र...नीया-To be taken as a question. Pandit reads-अत्रभवत्यामयं तवाविश्वासः ?

IV. 11. The king explains why he has lost all faith in मालविका who plays hide and seek with him in a dream and therefore he is not sure whether he has really got her, she being so deceptive. तिरोभवति-vanishes from sight, disappears. Some read स्थित्वा स्थित्वा

in place of स्थित्वा स्वप्ने. 'Having come repeatedly.' Our reading is better. सरति–Slips away, darts off. अबला सती Though she is a weak woman. He means that मालविका a frail creature though clasped between my powerful arms slips away suddenly. मनसिज etc. Construe– मनसिजरुजा क्लिष्टस्य मे मनः एवं समागममायया इमां प्रति विश्रब्धं कथमिव स्यात् ? I am already afflicted by the pang of love; and in such a condition she plays with me with such a delusive union. How can I, therefore, repose any trust in her? समागममायया can also be taken with क्लिष्टस्य. IV. 11. 5. मम...आसीत्–She means, 'My condition is even worse and therefore more pitiable. The king is lucky enough to have at least a dream. To me, however, even the sleep is denied and therefore there is no consolation of meeting him even in a dream' Cf. प्रजागरात् खिलीभूतस्तस्याः स्वप्ने समागमः। बाष्पस्तु न ददात्येनां द्रष्टुं चित्रगतामपि॥ शा० VI. 22.

IV. 12. बकुलावलिका has asked her to give a reply. The king says 'why should I give a reply? I give my own self to her, and for this ceremony the fire of love stands as the witness.' In a marriage ceremony, the bride is given to the bride-groom in the presence of the sacred fire. In this, the fire of love represents this divinity. न सेव्यः सेविता रहः–'No longer am I her master. I am her humble servant who would offer her this service of love in secret.' It is a clear hint to the विदूषक and बकुलावलिका to clear off! Cf. अद्यप्रभृत्यवनताङ्गि तवास्मि दासः। कुमा० V. 86. IV. 12. 4. पल्लवानि लंघितुं–To browse upon or to crop the tender sprouts. This is a pretext to go away with बकुलावलिका, leaving the king alone with मालविका. For a similar devise which प्रियंवदा uses with a view to go away with अनसूया leaving दुष्यंत and शकुंतला to-gether, Cf. अनसूये यथैष इतोदत्तदृष्टिरुत्सुको मृगपोतको मातरमन्विष्यति। एहि संयोजयाव एनम्। शा० III. IV. 12. 7. एवम्-Even thus i. e. as you are watchful about the Aśoka tree, in the same way should you guard us. IV. 12. 8. Cf. नेदमावयोरुपदेश्यम्। I. IV. 12. 11. अप्रकाशे-In the dark, hidden from sight. IV. 12. 16. स्फटिकस्थलम्. Crystal pavement. IV. 12. 18. ससाध्वसा-Full of nervousness.

IV. 13. तव...प्रणयोन्मुखे-may either be taken with संगमसाध्वसं विसृज or with सहकारतां गते मयि. 'Leave off your nervousness of union with me who have been so eagerly yearning for your love'; For the second interpretation, see the translation. अतिमुक्तलताचरितं गृहाण-Assume the part or the behaviour of the अतिमुक्त creeper towards me who have become a mango-tree (सहकार). He asks her to embrace him closely. The अतिमुक्तलता is seen to coil itself or grasp with its tendrils the mango-tree on which it is propped up. The plant is identified with what is known in Marathi by the name of कुसरी or कस्तुरीमोगरा. For such tender associations between the mango-tree and the अतिमुक्तलता, Cf. मिथुनं परिकल्पितं त्वया सहकारः फलिनी च नन्विमौ। रघु० VIII. 6. 1. क इदानीं सहकारमन्तरेणातिमुक्तलतां पल्लवितां सहते। शा० III. IV.13.2. आत्मनोऽपि प्रियं-'Such a thing viz. embracing, which I would like so much.' It may also refer to her love for the king which her heart approves. IV. 13. 6. यो न...ननु-She means, it does not lie in the mouth of the king to tell her not to be afraid of the Queen. Just recently she had witnessed a scene in which she saw how confused and frightened the king was when इरावती surprised them. (Cf. सर्वे इरावतीं दृष्ट्वा संभ्रान्ताः) If, therefore, the king would be bold enough to accept in मालविका his beloved before the Queen, she too would have no fear in acting in response to his love. It is indeed a very nice thrust which मालविका boldly levels at the king.

IV. 14. The king explains that it was not fear of इरावती but traditional courtesy of lovers that dictated him in such a behaviour with her. He should not, therefore, be misunderstood. He loves her alone to the exclusion of all. His very life now depended on her. बैम्बिकानां-of the descendants of बिम्बक, a name of one of the forefathers of अग्निमित्र. कुलव्रतम्-A family vow or tradition of behaving with uniform politeness with ladies. 'A कुलव्रत is a family custom inherited from generation to generation and has to be observed by every member of a family even when divided.' (Pandit). त्वदाशानिबन्धनाः-तव आशा निबन्धनं येषाम्. Sustained entirely by the tie of hope of thy favour or love. IV. 14. 15. न... तारः-Descent of young women (नवाङ्गनानां) into the field or the province (विषय) of love; their first step into the atmosphere of love.

IV. 15. कम्पवती-Trembling through nervousness. रश...गुलिं हस्तं रुणद्धि-She obstructs my hand as its fingers move about to loosen the girdle (रशनाव्यापार). Cf. नाभिदेशनिहितः सकम्पया शंकरस्य रुरुधे तया करः । कुमा० VIII. 4. पातुं etc. construe- पक्ष्मलचक्षुराननं पातुं उन्नमयतः मम साचीकरोति-she averts or turns aside (साचीकरोति) her face as I raise to sip it-her face having long eye-lashes (पक्ष्मल). For a similar idea Cf. मुहुरंगुलिसंवृत्ताधरोष्ठं प्रतिषेधाक्षरविक्लवाभिरामम् । मुखमंसविवर्ति पक्ष्मलाक्ष्याः कथमप्युन्नमितं न चुम्बितं तु ॥ शा० III. 25. साचीकरोति-Makes crooked, turns or bends aside. Cf. साचीकृता चारुतरेण तस्थौ मुखेन पर्यस्तविलोचनेन । कुमा० III. 68. व्याजेनापि-Even under the pretext of refusing to satisfy my desire. He means that मालविका showed as if she was refusing to grant me my desire of embracing her; and yet with all her show of resistence, she has gratified me. Cf. चुम्बनेष्वधरदानवर्जितं खिन्नहस्तमदयोपगूहनम् । क्लिष्टमन्मथमपि प्रियं प्रभोर्दुर्लभप्रातिकृतं वधूरतम् ॥ कुमा० VIII. 8.

IV. 15. 4. अलिन्दः-A terrace before a house-door. While on guard on the crystal pavement, चंद्रिका seems to have observed विदूषक. She reported the matter to निपुणिका who in her turn lost no time in carrying the news to her mistress इरावती ! A similar expression occurs in विक्र० II. हंजे निपुणिके, सत्यं त्वया भणितमिदं लताग्रहं प्रविशन्नार्यमाणवकसहाय आर्यपुत्रो दृष्ट इति । IV. 15.10. सविशेषम्-with something more important (विशेषं) that remains to be told. The reading सावशेषं is better. Cf. वयस्य, तिष्ठ । शृणु सावशेषं मे वचः॥शा० II. After speaking out संश...प्रेक्षितुं च-इरावती stopped in hesitation, although ordinarily she should have continued further. Hence this remark. Instead of प्रेक्षितुं Mr. Pandit reads पुच्छिदुं i. e. प्रष्टुम्-' To inquire of the king's friend about his health etc.' IV. 15. 16. अये...नीयते–Why go to the *picture* to ask for forgiveness ? Why not approach the *king* himself when he is at hand ?

IV. 15. 19. The translation in our edition was given with the following variant reading of this sentence—यादृशश्चित्रगतो भर्ता तादृश एव अन्यसंक्रान्तहृदय आर्यपुत्रः– A husband drawn in a picture is the same as a husband who has transfersred his love to another. Here is he transferred to the picture and there transferred in mind to the woman. There is no difference between the two. Hence I select the picture. This is of course said in bitter sarcasm. Our reading of the text is however better. यादृश...आर्यपुत्रः–She means ' The picture will make it clear that when it was drawn, the king deeply loved me. He is there looking at *me* in the presence of all his wives. He has not remained the same (न तादृश) now. He loves another viz. मालविका. If I go to him now, it would be like approaching a different person and not *my* lord. Hence I select the picture. ' केवल...आरम्भः–' And I am doing it. i. e. approaching the picture to ask for forgiveness, because I spurned his prostration and I feel it was a transgression or violation (अतिक्रम) on my part of the proper decorum that should be observed by a wife towards her husband. This apology is therefore meant to wipe out or atone for (प्रमार्ष्टुं) the sin and thus satisfy my conscience. I know I do not stand to gain anything thereby.' Cf. ऐ न जानामि...भवतो व्रतव्यपदेशेन मुक्तरोषा प्रणिपातलंघनं प्रमाष्टुकामेति ।

विक्र० III. IV. 15. 28. तव बहुमानं वर्धयितुं-' With a view to increase that great regard in which I hold you.' धारिणी means that for herself she has no jealousy left in her mind. That time has already gone. She imprisoned मालविका apparently to spare the feelings of इरावती, or out of regard for her as her co-wife. She knows the king pretty well and therefore it is useless to thwart his wishes, however unreasonable they may be. यथ... प्रिष्यामि-I would also intercede and request the king on your behalf if you allow. I have come to know, to my grief, of the recent happenings which have brought about an estrangement between you and the king. If you therefore permit me, I would speak to the king and request him to be reconciled with you.' IV. 15.40. विपाणिगत इव वृषभः-Like a bull in the market-place (विपाणि). The bull here referred to is the पोळ or वळु, let loose as a part of funeral obsequies. He is held sacred, feeds fat on the grain offered to him in religious charity and has the fullest liberty everywhere. He is usually found squatting lazily near some shop and dozes away without any fear of being disturbed. 'Even the Cattle Trespass Acts do not trouble him, because the people willingly put up with him. It does not seem that much change has come over the institution of these bulls since the days of कालिदास '-Pandit. IV. 15. 41. अत्याहितं-महाभीतिः-A disaster, calamity. IV. 15. 45. पापं-Evil, danger to life. IV. 15. 46. भवति मालविके -विदूषक is raving by instalments. He has said this, and falls into sound sleep again. During this interval

निपुणिका has her observation. Again he blurts out इरावती मातिक्रामन्ती भव. IV. 15.51. कस्या...कितवः-whose son (आत्मनीनः) is this accursed rogue? By what ungrateful sire was he begotten? The translation is given with the following reading :—कस्यैष आत्मानियोगसंपादने विश्वसनीयो हताशः। सर्व...उत्स्वप्रायते-The ingratitude of the विदूषक is fully betrayed in that he feeds himself on the sweet presents of इरावती and constantly thinks of promoting the interest of her rival मालविका even in his dreams. IV. 15.63. दर्वीकरः-A snake. दर्वी means the expanded hood of a snake. IV. 15. 72. अहं...फलितमिति-The two tooth-marks which विदूषक showed to the Queen as those of a serpent were really the pricks of the केतकी thorns. विदूषक says, 'At that time I managed to obtain these marks from the केतकी thorns and falsely represented them as the marks of the serpent's fangs. It was in a way a mockery of the snake. Observing this stick, therefore, I thought that my action of ridiculing a serpent has turned upon me and has given me the punishment I deserved(फलितम्). विदूषक refers to 'the common notion that a person who falsely pretends an evil is visited by the fates with a reality of it in retribution.' IV. 15. 73. पटाक्षेपेण-Tossing aside the curtain. When a character has to enter the stage in the hurry of excitement without previously indicating its entrance, this is the devise used. IV. 15. 79. इह...दृश्यते-बकुलावालिका has scented the arrival of इरावती on the scene, and hence this veiled hint. IV. 15. 82. दिवासंकेतः-The mid-day engagement or meeting (संकेत). IV. 15. 84. अपूर्व उपचारः-An extraordinary form of greeting. IV. 15. 86. दूत्याधिकारविषया प्रातिज्ञा- your promise (given to the king) in your capacity as a go-between. IV. 15. 89. किं तु...विस्मरति-' Does the god of rain forget the earth because frogs croak ?' She tries to flatter इरावती by comparing her to the earth, while the attempts of मालविका and बकुलावलिका to win over the king are compared to the croaking of frogs. When the rainy season is eminent, the frogs begin croaking, and thereby appealing to the god of rain as it were to send them a few showers. Now the god of rain may do so to satisfy their thirst and stop their croaking, but that can never take his mind off the earth whom he has to gratify by his fertilising showers. Similarly मालविका may try to divert the king's attention towards her by her language of love and she may succeed in it for some time. But these attempts of insignificant frog-like creatures like मालविका can never make the king forgetful of his chief love viz. इरावती, dignified and honourable as she is like the earth. The sentence can be interpreted in another way also. ' Frogs like इरावती may croak and squeal in thier pettish jealousy; will the king, however, forget his present chief beloved मालविका ? ' बकुला० says thus, being touched to the quick by the ironical congratulations of इरावती on her success in the mission of a go-between, smarting, as she was, under the recent insult of imprisonment. There is another reading- किं नु...देवः पृथिवीं वर्षितुं स्मरति-Does the god remember to send his showers on the earth, *because* the frogs crook ? He does this of his own accord, without being reminded by the frogs Similarly he loves मालविका out of a spontaneous impulse of his heart, not because बकुलावालिका urges him by her suggestions. Some further read...वर्षितुं विरमति–Does Indra cease to send his showers on the earth, because frogs croak ? Will the king stop loving मालविका, because every time इरावती makes a scene by way of protesting against his love for मालविका ? IV. 15. 94. प्रसादं न गृह्णाति–you do not assume your loving friendly nature, you are not reconciled. IV. 16. अपर्वाणि–When it is not the full-moon day. पर्वन् is the day of the full moon and the new moon. Here the eclipse of the moon is referred to and therefore the full moon day is meant, as the moon's eclipse is to be had only on that day. ग्रहकलुषेन्दुमण्डला–With the moon's orb obscured or clouded by the ग्रह i. e. the planet राहु who is supposed to bring about the eclipse by swallowing the moon for that period. The full-moon justifies an eclipse; so also there should be some justification for इरावती's anger. For a similar expression Cf. वद प्रदोषे स्फुटचन्द्रतारका विभावरी यद्यरुणाय कल्पते। कुमा० V. 44. IV. 16. 4. ततो......भवेयम्–'Then I should be an object of laughter or a butt of ridicule.' इरावती purposely misinterpretes the king's expression अस्थाने कोपः and means that when she is no longer being loved by the king, she has really no reason to be angry with *him* for loving another. She has lost all claim over him and therefore her anger would only be laughed at, instead of mending matters. IV 16. 5. अन्यथा कल्पयसि–you take it differently, you misunderstand. The presence of मालविका with me here is being misconstrued by you.

IV. 17. The king tries to account for मालविका's coming over to समुद्रगृह and meeting him. उत्सवदिवसेषु-On festive days. IV. 17. 2. दृष्टं...मयेति-' The Queen's partiality for me has been witnessed to-day.' She means ' the queen always professed an amount of love for me i. e. इरावती; very recently she said that she imprisoned मालविका for my sake. (तव खलु बहुमानं बर्धयितुं etc.). So long, however, there was no evidence for it and I am glad to say that to-day I got a very convincing proof of her love for me.' She says this in a bitter ironical manner. Some interpret it thus ' the Queen's partiality i. e. love for the king is visualised to-day. The girls were imprisoned apparently for my sake, but here they are released for the sake of the king for whom she is more solicitous.' The first interpretation is to be preferred, as it is in keeping with the sarcastic manner of her remarks, which she has maintained all along. IV. 17. 7. बन्धन...पतित: ' The house-pigeon let loose from the cage is sighted by a cat. मालविका successfully released from her confinement is immediately seen by इरावती.' It may also refer to the Queen धारिणी-' इरावती has sent the whole report of this meeting to the queen, who will surely deal with मालविका very severely now.' Some understand it as a reference to the king. 'The house-pigeon viz. the king has somehow extricated himself from the clutches of इरावती angered by him. On hearing of this report, however, the Queen धारिणी also will be enraged and the king has now to save his face with her.' The reading चिल्लायाः मुखे पतितः would mean fallen into the beak of a kite.' IV. 17. 10. यदृच्छादृष्टया-Met by chance. seen accidently. Cf. समापत्तिदृष्टेन. IV. 17. 13. उद्भिन्नः दुष्प्रयोगः-The intrigue has been evolved or planned. कामतंत्रसचिवः-A minister well-versed in the science or the manuals on love IV. 17. 17. भवति...विस्मरेयम्-'If I were to read but a single syllable of policy (नीति), I shall forget the गायत्री.' गायत्री is a sacred verse of a Rgvedic hymn in praise of the Sun. and is incorporated in the Sandhyā prayer of a Brahmin. The verse is as follows :—तत्सवितुर्वरेण्यं भर्गो देवस्य धीमहि । धियो यो नः प्रचोदयात्॥ R. V. III. 62. 10. विदूषक swears an oath that he has not conned a single syllable from the treatises of love and as such knows nothing of its policy; if what he says is false, he incurs the sin of forgetting the गायत्री, the sacred treasure of a Brahmin. Another way in which it has been interpreted by some is :-' I am such a block-head and so short of memory, that it is with great difficulty that I have learnt by heart the गायत्री verse; now if I were to put an additional strain on my memory by trying to learn a single syllable of other works like the manuals on love, I am afraid I shall forget the गायत्री and therefore lose my Brahmin-hood" IV. 17. 25. बलवदुत्रासिता-Terribly frightened. प्रवातकिसलयमिव वेपमाना-Trembling like a tender sprout in a gust of wind. पिङ्गलवानरः-A brown monkey or the monkey of the name of पिङ्गल. IV. 17.35. सपक्षः-' your friend, your caste-fellow.' विदूषक, for his mischievous characteristics is not only regarded by others as belonging to the fraternity of animals, chiefly monkeys, but even he himself does so in keeping with his character as a buffoon. Cf. किमिति शाङ्क्ष्यते । आश्रमवासपरिचित एव शाखामृगः । विक्र० II. IV. 17. 43. पञ्चरात्रम्-पञ्चानां रात्रीणां समाहारः-A period of five nights. सन्नद्धः-Equipped with, covered with, pervaded with. (व्याप्तः). IV. 17. 47. सत्यप्रतिज्ञा देवी-The queen will be true to her promise of fulfilling her desires, if the Asoka would blossom within five nights.

ACT V.

V. 0. 9. वेदिकाबन्धः उपाक्षिप्तः-An altar or a dias covered with a roof round the Aśoka tree has been laid i. e. created (उपक्षिप्तः). The सत्कारविधि or the honour done to the Aśoka refers to the kicking by मालविका. The tree very soon put forth blossoms and when it was reported to धारिणी, she gave orders for erecting this altar. V. 0. 10. अहो देवस्य...भविष्यति-We should interpret the sentence thus :—' Oh ! After all it was Fate which took pity upon her. The other opposing forces were all rallied round her, but she could at last provoke feelings of compassion in her Fate which favoured her by getting the Aśoka to blossom. And now the queen, though so much enraged, will be certainly disposed fa to vour her. प्रसादसुमुखी-with a benign pleasing face inclined to show favour. परिजनाभ्यन्तरः-One of the servants. जतुमुद्रालांछितं चीवरबन्धम्-A package in some cloth (चीवर) marked i. e. sealed (लांछितं) with a lac (जतु) seal. V. L. चीरमंजूषा-A leather-box. चतुःशालं-A quadrangle enclosed by four buildings. कुब्जः सारसकः-A hunch-back servant by name सारसक. Generally the servants selected for the harem were dwarfs (वामनs), eunuchs (वर्षवरs), hunch-backs, or foresters (किरातs) under the command of an old chamberlain (कंचुकिन्)! V. 0. 20. वेदपारगाणां-To (the Brahmins) well-versed in the Vedic lore. The reading विद्यापारायणं अनुतिष्ठतां-would mean ' who are performing the अनुष्ठान or the religious rite, consisting of the recital of vedic hymns for a certain number of times within a fixed period for the purpose of averting a calamity or danger. V. 0. 27. सेनापतिना-By the सेनापति i. e. पुष्पमित्र, the father of अग्निमित्र. ' He still retained his title of सेनापति of the मौर्य kings, the last of whom he had deposed, and usurping whose throne, he had put his own son अग्निमित्र on it. This is analogous to the title of पेशवा by the late rulers of the Deccan, who instead of being the Peshavas or the ministers of the descendants of Shivaji, were in reality their masters.' यज्ञतुरगः-The sacrificial horse let loose without restraint. He was permitted to roam about freely in all countries, followed by a strong escort of the king who desires to establish his supremacy over all kings. A king in whose territory the horse enters has either to submit or to give a fight with a view to try his strength. After the world-wide tour the अश्वमेध sacrifice is performed. For the description of such a horse, see उत्तररामचरित, Act IV दक्षिणीयै: प्रतिग्राहयति-Makes the Brahmins, who are worthy of such gifts, receive the dole (दक्षिणा). V. 0. 34. मङ्गलगृहं-An apartment or a part of the palace for sacred purposes, where possibly the gods were worshipped ; like the modern देवगृह. लिपिकार:—A clerk, a scribe or a writer. V. 0. 43. महासाराणि रत्नवाहनानि-Very valuable jewelled vehicles. The word रत्नवाहन is taken by some to mean 'A vessel of gems,' while Prof. Tawney translates the word as 'waggon-loads of jewels.' शिल्पदारिकाभूयिष्ठं (परिजनं)-servants mostly consisting (भूयिष्ठ) of maidens accomplished in the arts. Cf. अभिरूपभूयिष्ठा परिषदियम् । शा० I. The compound should be solved as शिल्पदारिकाः भूयिष्ठाः or भूयिष्ठं यस्मिन् ।.

Here ends the Praveśaka which is introduced to inform the audience of the great victory won by वीरसेन over the विदर्भ king,as a consequence of which माधवसेन is set free. Out of gratitude he sends, among many presents, accomplished maids, and we are told that a sacrificial horse is let loose under the escort of prince वसुमित्र, the son of धारिणी.-V. 0. 57 धर्मासनं-The judgment seat. V. 0. 59. दण्डेनैव-By force, by the strength of the army. Among four political expedients (viz. साम Peaceful negotiation, दान gift, भेद split and दण्ड Force), the last one alone is being utilised.

V. 1. The verse means while the king is enjoying tbe spring in his gardens on the banks of विदिशा i. e. in his own capital, his armies have vanquished the king of विदर्भ on the banks of वरदा. पर...वान्-construe-पर...रेषु विदिशा...नेषु आत्तरतिः त्वं अङ्गवान् (अपि) अनङ्ग इव नयसि। आत्तरतिः-आत्ता गृहीता रतिः प्रीतिः येन-You who take delight (in the gardens); the king is compared to अनङ्ग or Cupid, the body-less, so called because god Śiva burnt his body to ashes. The word आत्तरति can be taken with (अंगवान्) अनङ्ग also, in which case it would mean 'who had taken with him his wife रति, having himself assumed a body (अंगवान्). परभृत...व्याहारेषु-(उद्यानेषु) परभृतानां कोकिलानां कलः व्याहारः येषु-Vocal with the sweet (कलं) warbling of cuckoos. Some construe it with आत्तरतिः-The king finding pleasure in the utterance (व्याहार) of the dependents i. e. bards. विदिशा.-'The river Vidiśā is in Malwa and Professor Wilson identifies it with the Bess, a small stream that joins the Betwa where the modern Bhilsa (supposed to be the same as the ancient city of the name of विदिशा) is situated.'—Pandit. उपोढ-बलस्य ते-'of you whose army (बल) is powerful.' आलानाङ्गैः-(वृक्षैः) The trees which serve as the tying posts (आलान) for the victorious elephants. The word आलान means a post to which an elephant is tied' Cf. आलाने गृह्यते हस्ती-। मृच्छ० III. It also means 'a chain or a rope and in this sense, the reading आलानाङ्कैः 'having marks of chains' would be better. It should be noted that in ancient warfare, a squadron of elephants constituted an essential part of the fighting forces. वरद-वरान् ददात्यसौ-' Oh giver of boons.' वर...वृक्षैः सहावनतो रिपुः-It is a good illustration of the figure of speech सहोक्ति. The heads of enemies were humbled or bent down along with the tops of trees by your victorious elephants. वरदा is the modern Wurda, a tributary of गोदावरी. V. 2. Construe :--हे सुरोपम, क्रथकैशिकान् मध्येकृत्य स्थितं उभयोः चरितं सूरिभिः वीरप्रीत्या विरचितपदं (आस्ति) । दण्डानीकैः विदर्भपतेः श्रियं हृतवतः तव । परिघगुरुभिः दोर्भिः प्रसह्य रुक्मिणीं (हृतवतः) शौरेः च । The bard says, ' that the poets sing of the glorious achievements of these two heroes over the Vidarbhas ; formerly it was श्रीकृष्ण who forcibly carried away रुक्मिणी, the daughter of the विदर्भ king भीमक, and now it is you who have snatched the Vidarbha king's glory. सूरिभिः चरितं विरचितपदम्-The poets have celebrated or sung the exploits in verse. विरचितानि पदानि-पद्यानि-यस्मिन् तत् । Mr. Pandit observes ' It appears that in the time of कालिदास, there were extant, written by learned scholars, memoirs (चरितs) of king अग्निमित्र, in which his victory over the Vidarbhas was celebrated. These memoirs would appear to be other and older than the accounts found in the Purānas, because सूरि is a modest term,and is not applied to the authors of the Purānas which pretend to have been composed by the Rishi Vyāsa.' सुरोपम-God-like. क्रथकैशिकान् मध्येकृत्य -Putting the क्रथकैशिकs in the middle, while on both the sides were the two heroes श्रीकृष्ण and अग्निमित्र, i. e. the क्रथकैशिकs were the common enemy of both over whom victorv was obtained; and even in songs the common or the middle factor was the क्रथकैशिकs for the exploits of both श्रीकृष्ण and अग्निमित्र. क्रथकैशिकs are the same as विदर्भs. दण्डानीकः-By means of your armies (अनीकं). परिघगुरुभिः दोर्भिः-With arms as powerful and long as an iron bar of a gate (परिघ). Cf. एकः कृत्स्नां नगरपरिघप्रांशुबाहुर्भुनक्ति । शा० II. 15.

प्रसह्य-हठात् or बलात्-Forcibly. शौरि is an epithet of कृष्ण who was the grand-son of the यादव king शूर by name. The story of the kidnapping of रुक्मिणी is well-known. She was first betrothed to शिशुपाल against her will. She however, loved कृष्ण and secretly sent him a message requesting him to carry her away. कृष्ण successfully took her away just on the wedding day, after a severe fight with her brother रुक्मि and the forces of शिशुपाल. V. 2. 4. मुखालिन्दतोरणं-The arch (तोरण) of the main (मुख) terrace.

V. 3. सुलभेतरसंप्रयोगां- सुलभेतरः संप्रयोगः यस्याः-Whose union is not easy (सुलभेतर-other than easy) to secure. दुःखायते-Feels grieved or sorry, Denom. of दुःख. The king says that the joy he feels at the news of his victory is not unalloyed, but is mingled with a feeling of sadness at the thought that मालविका appears to be still unattainable. His heart, full of such contrary feelings, he compares to a lotus in the hot sun being sprinkled with cooling showers. सुखमश्नुते-Enjoys happiness. च-च has the sense of simultaneous action of two things. V. 3. 2. एकान्तसुखितः-Absolutely or perfectly happy without the slightest distress on account of मालविका. V. 3. 9. वैदर्भविवाहनेपथ्यम्-The wedding-dress which it is customary for the women in the विदर्भ country to wear. Perhaps it is a speciality of the विदर्भ people. तत्रभवती......मनोरथम्-विदूषक means, ' it is not with any idle curiosity that मालविका is thus attired in the wedding-costume. The queen intends possibly to celebrate your marriage with मालविका.'

V. 3. 22. मद......मेतत्-What you say is not impossible judging from her former actions (पूर्वचरितैः), since she is known to adapt herself or conform to my expectations which she has never thwarted. The queen did not object to my marriage with इरावती, on a former occasion. She is thus free from jealousy (निवृत्तेर्ष्या), and is always willing to surrender and subordinate her wishes to mine. मदपेक्षानुवृत्त्या-मदपेक्षाणां अनुवृत्तिः-तया or as a बहुव्रीहि compound मदपेक्षायाः अनुवृत्तिः यस्याः सा-तस्याः। The word may thus be looked upon as Instr. Sing or Gen. Sing. V. 3. 21. मालविकापुरोगेण परिजनेन-With her retinue of which मालविका is the foremost (पुरोगा-पुरो गच्छति सा.). It is not without any suggestion that this detail is mentioned by the प्रतीहारी who knows full well the king's maid and knows also that the king is sure to hasten to the place on hearing this.

V. 4. अग्रे In front of us, on the outer side of the tree. विकीर्ण...सहकारं (यौवनं)—विकीर्णानि कुरबकानि, फलजालैश्च विभिद्यमानाः सहकाराः यस्मिन्-In which the कुरबक flowers were scattered (in front of us), and the mango-trees were bursting with the net-work of fruit. There too are the indications of the advanced state (परिणाम) of spring. The reading फलजालविभुज्यमान...would mean, bending under the load of fruit etc.' चेत उत्सुकयति-Fills the mind with eagerness, at the thought that the spring coming to a close,the days of enjoyment will be very soon over. V. 4.5. यद...उद्वहति-Unlike others, Aśoka was late in blossoming and therefore now when all others have lost the glory of their blossoms, this Aṣoka with its Dohada satisfied, has burst into an uncommon or extraordinary splendour of its blossoms.

V. 5. सूचितवसन्तविभवानां--The other Aśoka trees which exhibited the wealth or glory of spring. Some read मुकुलानि 'buds' instead of कुसुमानि. V. 5. 2. विश्रब्धो ...मन्यते--विदूषक means that the present behaviour of धारिणी who allows मालविका to be with her even though the king is approaching, offers a contrast to her behaviour on earlier occasions when she made a special effort to keep her out of his sight. Does it not indicate that धारिणी has reconciled herself to your love of मालविका and would no longer put any obstacle in the way of your winning मालविका ?

V. 6. The Queen is imagined to be the earth (वसुमती) while मालविका by her side is compared to लक्ष्मी The Goddess of wealth bereft of a lotus in her hand. Laxmi is always represented as having her seat on a lotus and also a lotus in her hand. The poet fancies, however, that on this occasion it appears as if she has forgotten to equip herself with it (विस्मृतहस्तकमलया). There is another reading विनयादनूत्थिता प्रियया. 'My beloved who rose immediately after the Queen'. This reading is also good, and it cannot be argued that this action of मालविका is contrary to her position as a maid. Possibly धारिणी saw the king coming first and when she rose from her seat, मालविका noticed the king and she also immediately left her seat. For विस्मृत some read विस्तृत meaning 'with an expanded lotus in her hand.' This reading would require मालविका also to have a lotus. For this association of a lotus with लक्ष्मी, Cf. छायामण्डललक्ष्येण तमदृश्य[1] किल स्वयम्। पद्मा पद्मातपत्रेण भेजे साम्राज्यदीक्षितम् ॥ रघु० IV 5.

V. 4. जानामि निमित्तं etc. I know the reason of this festive decoration (कौतुकालंकार). The निमित्त was, of course, the festive occasion that was being celebrated by the queen, because the Aśoka had put forth blossoms. It cannot be, as some imagine, the prospective marriage of मालविका with the king. The Queen will never willingly consent to it, unless forced to do so. She argues, therefore, that the reason is such as has nothing to do with me personally. And yet (तथापि) my heart flutters and my left (दक्षिणेतरत्) eye twitches often, a good omen indicating the fruition of my desire viz. union with my lord. Throbbing of the left eye is considered a good sign, suggestive of a prospective union with the person loved. The opposite is the case with men.

V. 7. अन...सिनी–Wearing a silk garment (दुकूल) not hanging too far (अनतिलंबि). लघुभिः आभरणैः—with a few ornaments. लघुभिः should also be construed with उडुगणैः 'with a few clusters of stars.' उदयोन्मुखचन्द्रिका–उदयोन्मुखा चंद्रिका यस्याः सा–(चैत्रविभावरी)–The Caitra night with the moon-light imminent. The first quarter of the night is indicated. गतहिमैः–free from the (enveloping) mist. The ornaments correspond to the stars while the light which the rising moon spreads beforehand beautifully represents the pale-coloured silk dress. V. 7. 5. अभिमतसिद्धिरस्तु– Note the blessing of परिव्राजिका who thereby hints at the prospective union of the two lovers. V.7.8. संकेतगृहं काल्पितः –This tree is fixed as a trysting bower or a rendezvous where lovers should meet by appointment. It is the very tree which was the scene of the first meeting of the king and मालविका. The Queen knows this and therefore she clearly indicates thereby that far from resenting the king's latest adventure, she is in a mood to favour their union and thus reconcile herself with the king. V. 7. 9. आराधितोऽसि–'You have been propitiated or won over. The Queen is trying to make amends and win your favour.'

V. 8. नायं etc. Construe—अयं अशोकः ईदृशानां सत्काराणां भाजनत्वं न नेयः (इति) न। (अपि तु नेयः एव). This अशोक tree *must* be made the recipient of such honours of favours, like the construction of the altar etc. माधवश्रीनियोगे सावज्ञः– Who treated with contempt the injunction of the goddess of vernal beauty (माधवश्री), i. e. who did not flower at a time when spring demanded it, but waited for your efforts in the matter. The king means that since the tree showed so much regard for you by putting forth biossoms when *you* favoured him, he deserves to be honoured by you. V. 8. 1. विश्रब्धो etc. A similar devise like the one used by बकुलावलिका (III. 14. 16) is used here by विदूषक, who uses vague language so that this remark may refer to मालविका as also अशोकशोभा. And when confronted by धारिणी as to whom he means, he replies with his ready wit that he referred to अशोकशोभा ! V. 8. 6, संनिधिविप्रयोगः-Separation in the very presence of the person whom you love. Though the beloved is near, the presence of other people makes it difficult to take any liberty of even touch or talk with her, and therefore for all practical purposes, it amounts to separation. Compare the varieties of वियोग in the drama भावबंधन of of the Marathi dramatist Gadkari.

V. 9. रथाङ्गनामा-रथाङ्गस्य चक्रस्य नाम यस्य सः-The चक्रवाक bird who is named after a part of the chariot i. e. the wheel. The convention about this bird with Sanskrit poets is that the male is separated from its mate at sunset to be reunited when the day begins. The distance between the two may not be more than that of a leaf. It imagines however, that it is far away and cries piteously for the whole night. Their love for each other is proverbial. Kālidāsa has used this convention so often in his works. Cf. रथांगनाम्नोरिव भावबन्धनं बभूव यत्प्रेम परस्पराश्रयम् । रघु० III. 24. चक्रवाकवधूः, आमंत्रयस्व सहचरम् । उपस्थिता रजनी । शा० III. निनाय सात्यंतहिमोत्किरानिलाः सहस्यरात्रीरुदवासतत्पराः । परस्पराक्रंदिनि चक्रवाकयोः पुरोवियुक्ते मिथुने कृपावती ॥ कुमा० V. 26. रथांगनामन् वियुतो रथांगश्रोणिबिंबया । अयं त्वां पृच्छति रथी मनोरथशतैर्वृतः॥ विक्र० IV. Similarly here the queen धारिणी, who represents the night has practically brought about a separation of these two lovers though they are very near each other, since she would not permit their mutual contact (अननुज्ञातसंपर्का) V. 9. 3. मार्ग...शरीरे-With their persons languid (अलस) owing to the fatigue of the journey. V. 9. 11. प्रसीदति...आत्मा–My inner self feels delighted.

V. 9. 14. आगामि...करोति–The approaching happiness or misery strengthens the heart accordingly. The heart gets fortified beforehand to receive the shock of calamity or joy. समर्थीकरोति–Strengthens, is fortified, having for its subject सुखं वा दु:खं वा. It can also be taken in another way 'the heart indicates or foretells the coming happiness or misery.' समर्थीकरोति however has not the sense of indicating and hence the first interpretation is to be preferred. Here it is an agreeable indication and therefore some delightful event is to happen. V.9.24. अभियोगः–Application, special study, proficiency. V. 9. 25 अभ्यन्तरे–well-versed, proficient. Cf. अनभ्यन्तरे आवां मदनगतस्य वृत्तान्तस्य । शा० III. V. 9. 43. चन्दनं...दूषितं–She means that मालविका, a Princess, was treated by her as an ordinary maid. A sandal wood which ought to be better used for sacred purposes, was defiled (दूषितं) by her, being used (परिभोग) as a slipper (पादुका). V. 9. 58. स्वरसंयोगः–Voice, lit. a combination of sounds. V. 9. 61. दुःखेन विभाव्यते–Is recognised with difficulty (दुःखेन). V. 9. 71. तथागतभ्रातृकां–तथागतः भ्राता यस्याः सा–whose brother माधवसेन was reduced to such a plight viz. imprisonment at the hands of the विदर्भ king. पथिकसार्थ–A group of travellers, a caravan. V. 10. The main sentence is–प्रतिरोधकानां अनीकं आविरभूत्, while the other compounds go to qualify अनीकं. तूणीर...रालं–तूणीरपट्टैः परिणद्धानि भुजान्तरालानि यस्मिन्–whose chests (lit. the intervening space between two arms) were encircled with the quiver-straps (तूणीरपट्ट). आ...धारि आपार्ष्णि लंबिनं शिखिनां बर्हकलापं धारयति तत्-wearing tufts of peacock feathers (शिखिबर्ह), reaching down up to the heels कोदण्डपाणि-कोदण्डा पाणिषु यस्मिन्-with bows held in hands, armed with bows. निनदत्-Shouting, yelling, प्रतिरोधकानां अनीकं a host of highway-man or bandits आपातदुष्प्रसहम्-आपातः (attack, our laught) दुष्प्रसहः (Irresistible, hard to stand or endure) यस्य. V. 10. 1. मालविका भयं रूपयति-मालविका, in her timidity of heart, feels as if the incident of which the memory is fresh,is happening at this very time and hence her fright which she gesticulates. Compare a similar situation in the उत्तररामचरित, where in the first Act, सीता also is filled with fear as she observes the various pictures in the Picture-gallery. V. 10. 5. पराङ्मुखीकृताः-Were turned back or routed.

V. 11. दुर्जातेः परीप्सुः-Desirous of rescuing her from the ruffians or barbarians. दुर्जातिः-A wicked tribe. V. L. दुर्जाते-'In this disaster.' असुभिः आनृण्यं गतः-Paid back the debt with his life, i. e. was killed in the scuffle. V. 11. 5. ईदृशी लोकयात्रा Such is the lot, lit. the way of life, of those who have a body or mortals (तनुभृतां) Cf. मरणं प्रकृतिः शरीरिणां । रघु० VIII. 87. सफलीकृतभर्तृपिण्डः-Who made the food (पिंड) he had eaten of his master yield a fruit, i. e. who proved true to the salt he had eaten. V. 11. 7. संज्ञा-consciousness. V. 11. 9. कृच्छ्रं-Distress,misery V. 11. 10. पुनर्नवीकृतवैधव्यदुःखया-Whose sorrow of widowhood (वैधव्य) was revived. The death of my brother renewed my grief for the loss of my husband, which so long I had managed to suppress, but which now revived with greater intensity, as I felt forlorn. काषाये गृहीते-I took to these yellowish-brown garments i. e. I renounced the world and turned an ascetic woman. It may not necessarily refer to the Buddhist order of nuns. Even Brahmanic Sanyāsins used to wear these coloured garments. Cf. नाहं काषायं वृत्तिहेतोः प्रपन्नः। स्वप्न० when यौगंधरायण taking to these robes is certainly not a Buddhist monk. We may, therefore, look upon परिव्राजिका, not as a Buddhist nun, but an ascetic woman of the Brahmanic order. V. 11. 13. आटविकः-A forest-dweller; a derivative noun from अटवि. अवसानं-End V. 11. 15. किं...भणति-" The force of 'now' is that मालविका is afraid lest the king should refuse to marry her, because she was without protection during the time that she passed from the wild men to Virasena, and from the latter to the Queen "—Pandit. A similar situation we get in the शाकुंतल as well. The message of काश्यप has been given and शाङ्गंधर requests the king to accept शकुंतला his legal wife. At this शकुंतला remarks to herself. ' किं नु खल्वार्यपुत्रो भणति । शा० V. V. 11. 17 परिभवोपहारिणः विनिपाताः-calamities (विनिपात) which bring on indignities or humiliation (परिभव).

V. 12. प्रेष्यभाव-The position of a servant who could be ordered about (प्रेष्य). स्नानीयवस्त्रक्रियया उपयुज्यते-is used to serve as a bath-towel. पत्रोर्णम्-wove-silk, a silken garment. No man of some sense would use a silken cloth as a bathing towel. Similarly a Princess, worth the title of a queen (देवीशब्दक्षमा) should not have been treated as a maid servant. V. 12. 3. असांप्रतं-अयोग्यं--improper V. 12. 5.नैभृत्यं-Abstract noun from निभृत-Secrecy. V. 12. 8. देवयात्रागतेन-who had come in the course of an idol-procession. देवयात्रा--A procession in honour of a deity going from place to place, just like the आषाढी यात्रा going from Alandi to Pandharpur. V. L. लोकयात्रागतेन 'who had come down to the state of a mortal.' सिद्धादेशेन-whose prophecy (आदेश) was infallible. तमेनं......पश्यामि-When I saw that the sure prophecy was proving true, (परिणमन्तं) as she was here serving at your feet as a maid, I thought I had better bide the (कालप्रतीक्षा) time and I think I did well acting accordingly. V. 12. 13. उपेक्षा-waiting. Some take it to mean 'Respect for prophecy.' V.12.14. कथांतरेणांतरितं-Put off or side-tracked by another episode or matter. The stage-direction प्रविश्य appears to be unnecessary, as the chamberlian was all along on the stage. V.12. 17.द्वैराज्यं-Doube rule,joint kingship.

V. 13. शिष्टाम्-Let the two brothers rule. Inperative II Dual of √शास्. 'to govern.' V. 13. 1. अमात्यपरिषद्-The council of ministers the cabinet. V.13.9. कल्याणी बुद्धिः Benevolent, generous mind. दर्शनम्-View, opinion. V. V. 14. संग्रहीतुः-of the charioteer ; it should be construed with ते,'of you.then controller or chastiser.' The two brothers यज्ञसेन and माधवसेन,with no one to put them up, were fighting. Now under your control,they will be peaceful.परस्परावग्रहनिर्विकारौ-unaffected or undistracted (निर्विकारौ) by mutual squabbles. V. 14. 5. सप्राभृतकः-Accompanied with a present (प्राभृत). उद्वेष्टयति-loosens, opens. V. 14. 11. ततो-

मुखम्—Turned in that directions. अतिभारे–In a great burden, in a heavy responsibility. V. L. अधिकारे 'in a responsible post.' V. 14. 14. स्वस्ति–A letter in Sanskrit always begins with this word. यज्ञशरणात्–From the sacrificial compound, noting the place whence the letter was dispatched. राजसूयदीक्षितेन–Consecrated for the राजसूज sacrifice. It is a great sacrifice performed by a universal monarch (in which the tributary princes also took part), generally at the time of his coronation as a mark of his undisputed sovereignty. दीक्षित–दीक्षा संजाता अस्य–Who has performed the consecration ceremony for making himself fit for performing the sacrifice. संवत्सरोपावर्तनयिः-which was to be brought back after a year. निरर्गलः-without restrain or check. रोधसि–On the bank. अश्वानीकेन प्रार्थितः-was claimed i. e. seized by the cavalry. संमर्दः-struggle, conflict. V. 15.3. अंशुमतेव सगरः-Like सगर whose horse was brought back by अंशुमान्. The horse of king Sagara was carried away by इंद्र to the nether world, where the sixty thousand sons of सगर traced him in the territory of कपिल. They attacked the sage who enraged burnt them all to ashes. The horse was later brought back by his grandson अंशुमान्. While भगीरथ brought the heavenly गङ्गा to the earth and thence to the पाताल to purify his ancestors. अकालहीनं- Without any delay or loss of time. विगतरोषचेतसा- With a mind free from anger. Various views have been given about the causes that laid to the strained relations between the father and the son. Mr. Pandit conjectures that 'अग्निमित्र had disapproved of his father having sent out the boy वसुमित्र as champion of the courser.' This is not probable, however, as the क्षत्रिय kings instead of resenting did always exult in such adventures. "The real ground for anger seems to be due to the religious opinions of the two. अग्निमित्र was indulgent towards the Buddhists while पुष्यमित्र tried to uproot it out of India."

V. 16. परिव्राजिका says that by her marriage with अग्निमित्र, the queen धारिणी has already been the foremost वीरपत्नी; and now by such a valiant son, she is to get the title of a वीरमाता. वीरसू:-वीरं सुते सा-Onewho gives birth to a hero. V. 16. 3. कलभ-A young elephant. Some rightly put this sentence in the mouth of परिव्राजिका; the king could not have referred to himself in a such boastful Language. यूथपतिः-The leader of a herd of elephants.

V. 17. वीर-विजृंभितेन-By such an unfolding of valour, such heroic display. यस्य त्वमप्रधृष्यः उच्चैः प्रभवः-Whose source i. e. father (प्रभवः) you are, unassailable (अप्रधृष्यः) and lofty (उच्चैः--उन्नतः). The कंचुकिन् means 'with you as his father, it is no wonder that he has displayed such heroism. What else is to be expected?' अपां दग्धुः वह्नेः ऊरुजन्मा--Like the thigh-born sage Aurva who is the generator of the subterranean fire that consumes the oceanic waters. The legend about the sage और्व is as follows :—The कार्तवीर्यs or the sons of कृतवीर्य destroyed all the descen dants of भृगु, for the purpose of appropriating their rich treasures, and they even went to the length of killing children in the womb of their mothers. One of the women concealed her embryo in her thigh, and the son who was thus born came therefore to be called और्व (Thigh-born). To have his revenge, he produced a fire-flame which blinded all the कार्तवीर्यs and proved a great menace to the whole world. He was therefore, induced to cast the flame into the ocean, where it lies hidden with the face of a mare (hence called वडवानल). It is believed to be responsible for keeping the ocean within its fixed limits, the additional annual supply of water being consumed by this fire. V. 17. 1. उररीकृत्य–Including (the brother-in-law of यज्ञसेन, the same as मौर्यसचिव referred to in Act I.). V. 17. 11. मम वचनेन... व्येति–' Entreat her on my behalf that I should not be forced to fail in keeping my promise.' The Queen had given her word of honour to मालविका, before she was asked to fulfil the longing of Aśoka. The time has now come when she must gratify मालविकाs desire of uniting her in marriage with the king. And in that, no objection should be raised on the score of her low birth because it has been amply proved now that मालविका is a Princess. इरावती therefore is to be requested not to oppose the queen in fulfilling her promise given to मालविका–viz. अभिलाषपूरयितृकं प्रसादं ते दास्यामि ।. V. 17. 17. अविभक्तपरितोषाणां–whose joy is undivided i. e. equal to your joy. रत्नमंजूषा संवृत्ता–She means that she has received so many ornaments as presents from the ladies for having told them the glad news, that she has become a veritable casket or box of jewels. V. 17. 22. सदृशं...मिति इरावती means that was highly worthy of the Queen to have given such a promise before; she is all powerful, being the chief Queen; and now, therefore, it should not be retracted. Note that she first gets a formal consent of इरावती before proceeding to celebrate the union of the two lovers. Mr. Pandit observes, ' Irāvatī's message is not altogether cordial. She is a little bitter as shown by प्रभवन्त्या (which is equivalent to : ' what is the use of consulting me ? You are so powerful that you will do what you wish ') and प्रथमसंकाल्पितं (which means : 'what is the use of asking me now ? You have already arranged it '.) V. 17. 26. प्रथमसंभावितां-Already destined before. V. 11. 30. प्रियनिवेदनानुरूपं पारितोषिकं-A reward highly befitting the good news regarding वसुमित्र's victory. No other prize would be so fitting as this मालविका. V.17. 32. जोषमास्ते-sits silent (जोषं). V. 17. 33. किं...पुत्रः-The Queen knew full well that the king will never refuse such a reward. Jokingly, therefore, she asks him this question. अवधीरयति-Despises, ignores. V. 17. 36. लोकव्यवहारः-a common custom of the world. V. 17. 40. कृतदेवीशब्दां-who has been honoured by the title of Queen. He would not like her to be treated as an ordinary wife, but on equal footing with the Queen धारिणी not only by reason of his marriage with her but by her high birth as well. Kings possibly had two classes of wives ; one class recruited from lower grades of society, inferior to the king in rank and nobility of birth, while the other class was recruited from royal families.

V. 18. आकरसमनुत्पन्ना-Sprung from a mine (आकरः). असंस्कृता-unpolished. जातरूपं-gold. परिव्राजिका means that मालविका though born in a royal family must first be dubbed a queen before she is married to the king. मालविका represents a jewel while the king is the gold. V. 18. 4. कौशेयपत्रोर्ण-A silken veil. ' धारिणी means that in the joy of the news she forgot to dress मालविका as a princess, to honour her with a महावस्त्र as a princess ought to be. V. 18. 9. त्वच्छास...वयम्-The king shows as if he is reluctantly accepting मालविका, simply because such are his Queen's orders. V. 18. 10. हन्त-A particle expressive of joy. She is delighted that the ambition so long cherished has been fulfilled, and her attempts have borne fruit. V. I9. 12. धारिणी looks up towards the servants indicating to them that they should now greet their new queen with a customary salutation. V. 19. 14. When the formal greeting is offered to मालविका, धारिणी looks at परिव्राजिका to see what view she takes of her action.

V. 19. प्रतिपक्षणोपि-Even by creating a rival for themselves. She means, in their deep love for their husbands, they are prepared for any sacrifice ; even at the risk of having a rival for them, they would willingly consent to a marriage of their husband to another woman, simply out of consideration for the pleasure and happiness of their lord. The case of the big rivers which carry along with them many smaller rivers illustrates the point very well. समुद्रगा–समुद्रं गच्छति सा–A river. V. 19. 6. प्रसादमात्रेण–Only reconciliation and pardon. इरावती means that the provocation given by her should now be forgotten by the king since he has secured what he desired most, and that he should at least show her a favourable disposition devoid of any ill-feeling, although all expectation of love is at an end now. V. 19 8. अवश्यं...ज्ञास्यति–He will certainly see his way (ज्ञास्यति) to conform to her request. The reading अनुज्ञास्यति would mean 'will grant her request.' V. I9. 12. चरितार्थम्–कृतार्थ–चरितः अर्थः यस्य सः–Who has accomplished his purpose; Cf. –वत्से, चरितार्थासि । शा० VII. सभाजयितुं– To pay my respects Cf. स्नेहात् सभाजयितुमेत्य दिनान्यमूनि । नीत्वोत्सवेन जनको ऽद्य गतो विदेहान् ॥ उत्तर० I.; also ऋषयो देवं सभाजयितुमागताः । शा० V. सभाजनाक्षराणि–Complementary words. He means that परिव्राजिका need not personally go to congratulate him; her compliments will be conveyed to माधवसेन by the king in his own letters. भरतवाक्यम्–The verse in a drama, a sort of benediction, said to be in honour of भरत, the founder of the dramatic science. The remark तथापीदमस्तु भरतवाक्यम् generally occurs at the end of every play.

V. 20. त्वं...हेतोः–The king means, 'Angry as you are, you should always be disposed to favour me by reconciliation. In the interest of your rival, this is what I beg of you.' The request looks raher strange. The king would not like to impose any restrictions on himself in matters of love; his wife, however, should have a conciliating attitude always, though there might be fits of anger and jealousy. She should always look with a favourable eye on his amorous activities in which he would have no restraint! ईतिविगमप्रभृति आशास्यं-A blessing such as the removal of national calamities (ईतिs); they are, excessive rain, drought, locusts, rats' birds and foreign raids. गोप्तरि अग्निमित्रे न खलु न संपत्स्यते-So long as king अग्निमित्र is their protector, these blessings will surely be secured for the subjects.

This भरतवाक्य should really have been pronounced by an actor as an actor and not as king अग्निमित्र. Here, however, the king speaks it. According to the commentator काटयवेम only the last two lines of the verse constitutes the भरतवाक्य. Cf. इतः परं (i. e. after the first two lines) भरतवाक्यम् ।...सत्यत्र नाटकान्ते भरतेन सर्वकालसाधारण्येनाशंसावचने कर्तव्ये अत्र प्रजानां आशास्यासिद्धिं प्रति गोप्तुरग्निमित्रस्य कथनं तत्कालराजोपलक्षणामिति मन्तव्यम् ॥

APPENDIX A.

श्लोकसूची.

APPENDIX B—METRICAL TABLE

Number of Syllables	Name of the Metre	Where employed	Total	Measure.
8	अनुष्टुप्	I. 10, 14, 15, 19; II. 7, 9; IV. 4, 6, 12, 14; V. 9, 11, 12, 13, 15, 16, 18.	17	पञ्चमं लघु सर्वत्र सप्तमं द्विचतुर्थयोः । गुरु षष्ठं च पादानां चतुर्णां स्यादनुष्टुभि ॥
11	इन्द्रवज्रा	V. 17.	1	स्यादिन्द्रवज्रा यदि तौ जगौ गः ।
"	उपजाति	I. 2, 16, 17; III. 10; IV. 8; V. 14.	6	स्यादिन्द्रवज्रा यदि तौ जगौ गः । उपेन्द्रवज्रा प्रथमे लघौ सा । } इत्यनयोरुपजातिः ।
"	शालिनी	III. 14, 21; V. 8.	3	मात्तौ गौ चेच्छालिनी वेदलोकैः ।
12	द्रुतविलम्बित	III. 6; IV. 13; V. 7.	3	द्रुतविलम्बितमाह नभौ भरौ ।
"	वंशस्थ	III. 15.	1	जतौ तु वंशस्थमुदीरितं जरौ ।
13	प्रहर्षिणी	I. 21.	1	त्र्याशाभिर्मनजरगाः प्रहर्षिणीयम् ।
"	रुचिरा	IV. 16.	1	जभौ सजौ गिति रुचिरा चतुर्ग्रहैः ।
14	वसन्ततिलका	I. 12; IV. 9; V. 3, 10, 20.	5	उक्ता वसन्ततिलका तभजा जगौ गः ।
15	मालिनी	II. 5; III. 12	2	ननमयययुतेयं मालिनी भोगिलोकैः ।

17	पृथ्वी	III. 17.	1	जसौ जसयला वसुग्रहयतिश्च पृथ्वी गुरुः ।
,,	मन्दाक्रान्ता	II. 6, 8 ; III. 4 ; IV. 1.	4	मन्दाक्रान्ताम्बुधिरसनगैर्मो भनौ तौ गयुग्मम् ।
,,	शिखरिणी	III. 1.	1	रसै रुद्रैश्छिन्ना यमनसभला गः शिखरिणी ।
,,	हरिणी	IV. 11 ; V. 1, 2.	3	नसमरसला गः षड्वेदैर्हयैर्हरिणी मता ।
19	शार्दूलविक्रीडित	I. 4 ; II. 3 , III. 5 ; IV. 15.	4	सूर्याश्वैर्यदि मः सजौ सततगाः शार्दूलविक्रीडितम् ।
21	स्रग्धरा	I. 1 ; II. 12.	2	म्रभ्नैर्यानां त्रयेण त्रिमुनियतियुता स्रग्धरा कीर्तितेयम् ।
10/11	वैतालीय (वियोगिनी)	III. 2.	1	विषमे ससजा गुरुः समे सभरा लोऽथ गुरुर्वियोगिनी ।
11/12	अपरवक्त्र	III. 20.	1	अयुजि ननरला गुरुः समे तदपरवक्त्रमिदं नजौ जरौ ।
,,	औपच्छन्दसिक	III. 3, 11.	2	पर्यन्ते यौ तथैव (वैतालीये इव) शेषमौपच्छन्दसिकं सुधीभिरुक्तम् ।
12/13	पुष्पिताग्रा	I. 11.	1	अयुजि नयुगरेफतो यकारो युजि तु नजौ जरगाश्च पुष्पिताग्रा।
	आर्या	I. 3, 5, 6, 7, 8, 9, 13, 18, 20, 22 ; II. 1, 2, 10, 11, 13, 14 ; III. 7, 8, 9 ; 13, 16, 18, 19, 22, 23 ; IV. 2, 3, 5, 7, 10, 17 ; V. 4, 5, 6, 19.	35	यस्याः प्रथमे पादे द्वादश मात्रास्तथा तृतीयेऽपि । अष्टादश द्वितीये चतुर्थके पञ्चदश सार्या ॥